MW00759722

ABSOLUTE JAVA™

5th Edition

Walter Savitch

University of California, San Diego

Contributor

Kenrick Mock

University of Alaska Anchorage

PEARSON

Boston Columbus Indianapolis New York San Francisco Upper Saddle River
Amsterdam Cape Town Dubai London Madrid Milan Munich Paris Montréal Toronto
Delhi Mexico City São Paulo Sydney Hong Kong Seoul Singapore Taipei Tokyo

Vice President and Editorial Director, ECS: Marcia Horton
Editor in Chief: Michael Hirsch
Executive Editor: Matt Goldstein
Editorial Assistant: Emma Snider
Vice President Marketing: Patrice Jones
Marketing Manager: Yez Alayan
Marketing Coordinator: Kathryn Ferranti
Vice President and Director of Production: Vince O'Brien
Managing Editor: Jeff Holcomb
Senior Production Project Manager: Marilyn Lloyd
Manufacturing Manager: Nick Skilitis
Operations Specialist: Lisa McDowell
Text Designer: Joyce Cosentino Wells
Cover Designer: Anthony Gemmellaro
Cover Image: B0NGR1 Alamy
Media Editor: Dan Sandin
Text Permissions—assessment: Dana Weightman
Text Permissions—clearance: Jenn Kennett/Creative Compliance
Full-Service Vendor: GEX Publishing Services
Project Management: GEX Publishing Services
Printer/Binder: Edwards Brothers
Cover Printer: Lehigh-Phoenix Color

This book was composed in InDesign. Basal font is Adobe Garamond 10/12. Display font is Optima LT Std.

Credits and acknowledgments borrowed from other sources and reproduced, with permission, in this textbook appear on the appropriate page within text.

CIP data available upon request

10 9 8 7 6 5 4 3 2 1

PEARSON

ISBN 10: 0-13-283031-0
ISBN 13: 978-0-13-283031-7

Preface

This book is designed to serve as a textbook and reference for programming in the Java language. Although it does include programming techniques, it is organized around the features of the Java language rather than any particular curriculum of programming techniques. The main audience I had in mind when writing this book was undergraduate students who have not had extensive programming experience with the Java language. As such, it would be a suitable Java text or reference for either a first programming course or a later computer science course that uses Java. This book is designed to accommodate a wide range of users. The introductory chapters are written at a level that is accessible to beginners, while the boxed sections of those chapters serve to quickly introduce more experienced programmers to basic Java syntax. Later chapters are still designed to be accessible, but are written at a level suitable for students who have progressed to these more advanced topics.

CHANGES IN THIS EDITION

This fifth edition presents the same programming philosophy as the fourth edition. For instructors, you can teach the same course, presenting the same topics in the same order with no changes in the material covered or the chapters assigned. The changes to this edition consist almost exclusively of supplementary material added to the chapters of the previous edition, namely:

- Updates have been made for language changes in Java 7, such as allowing strings in switch statements.
- Twenty-five new programming projects have been added. By request, some of these are longer and less prescriptive projects to give the student more practice designing programming solutions.
- 15 new video notes have been created for a total of 46 video notes. These videos cover specific topics and offer solutions to the programming projects; they have been added to the book's website. The solutions walk students through the process of problem solving and coding to reinforce key programming concepts. An icon appears in the margin of the book when a video is available regarding the corresponding topic in the text.
- Chapter 2 now describes how to use the Scanner class to read from a text file so data-based programming projects can be explored prior to detailed coverage of File I/O in Chapter 10.
- A brief introduction to the Random class has been added to Chapter 3.
- Chapter 9 on exception handling begins with a new introduction of try/catch for handling input mismatch exceptions before discussing how to throw custom exceptions.
- A recursive algorithm to search the file system has been added to Chapter 11.
- Material on race conditions and thread synchronization has been added to Chapter 19.
- Ten new self-test exercises have been added along with the new material.

NO NONSTANDARD SOFTWARE

Only classes in the standard Java libraries are used. No nonstandard software is used anywhere in the book.

JAVA COVERAGE

All programs have been tested with Java 7. Oracle is not proposing any changes to future versions of Java that would affect the approach in this book.

OBJECT-ORIENTED PROGRAMMING

This book gives extensive coverage of encapsulation, inheritance, and polymorphism as realized in the Java language. The chapters on Swing GUIs provide coverage of and extensive practice with event driven programming. A chapter on UML and patterns gives additional coverage of OOP-related material.

FLEXIBILITY IN TOPIC ORDERING

This book allows instructors wide latitude in reordering the material. This is important if a book is to serve as a reference. It is also in keeping with my philosophy of writing books that accommodate themselves to an instructor's style rather than tying the instructor to an author's personal preference of topic ordering. With this in mind, each chapter has a prerequisite section at the beginning; this section explains what material must be covered before doing each section of the chapter. Starred sections, which are explained next, further add to flexibility.

STARRED SECTIONS

Each chapter has a number of starred (★) sections, which can be considered optional. These sections contain material that beginners might find difficult and that can be omitted or delayed without hurting the continuity of the text. It is hoped that eventually the reader would return and cover this material. For more advanced students, the starred sections should not be viewed as optional.

ACCESSIBLE TO STUDENTS

It is not enough for a book to present the right topics in the right order. It is not even enough for it to be clear and correct when read by an instructor or other expert. The material needs to be presented in a way that is accessible to the person who does not yet know the content. Like my other textbooks that have proven to be very popular, this book was written to be friendly and accessible to the student.

SUMMARY BOXES

Each major point is summarized in a short boxed section. These boxed sections are spread throughout each chapter. They serve as summaries of the material, as a quick reference source, and as a way to quickly learn the Java syntax for features the reader knows about in general but for which he or she needs to know the Java particulars.

SELF-TEST EXERCISES

Each chapter contains numerous Self-Test Exercises at strategic points in the chapter. Complete answers for all the Self-Test Exercises are given at the end of each chapter.

VIDEO NOTES

VideoNote

VideoNotes are step-by-step videos that guide readers through the solution to an end-of-chapter problem or further illuminate a concept presented in the text. Icons in the text indicate where a VideoNote enhances a topic. Fully navigable problems allow for self-paced instruction. VideoNotes are located at www.pearsonhighered.com/savitch.

OTHER FEATURES

Pitfall sections, programming tip sections, and examples of complete programs with sample I/O are given throughout each chapter. Each chapter ends with a summary section and a collection of programming projects suitable to assign to students.

ONLINE PRACTICE AND ASSESSMENT WITH MyProgrammingLab

MyProgrammingLab™

MyProgrammingLab helps students fully grasp the logic, semantics, and syntax of programming. Through practice exercises and immediate, personalized feedback, MyProgrammingLab improves the programming competence of beginning students who often struggle with the basic concepts and paradigms of popular high-level programming languages.

A self-study and homework tool, a MyProgrammingLab course consists of hundreds of small practice problems organized around the structure of this textbook. For students, the system automatically detects errors in the logic and syntax of their code submissions and offers targeted hints that enable students to figure out what went wrong—and why. For instructors, a comprehensive gradebook tracks correct and incorrect answers and stores the code inputted by students for review.

MyProgrammingLab is offered to users of this book in partnership with Turing's Craft, the makers of the CodeLab interactive programming exercise system. For a full demonstration, to see feedback from instructors and students, or to get started using MyProgrammingLab in your course, visit www.myprogramminglab.com.

SUPPORT MATERIAL

The following support materials are available to all users of this book at www.pearsonhighered.com/cssupport:

- Source code from the book

The following resources are available to qualified instructors only at www.pearsonhighered.com/irc. Please contact your local sales representative for access information:

- Instructor's Manual with Solutions
- PowerPoint® slides

Integrated Development Environment Resource Kits

Professors who adopt this text can order it for students with a kit containing seven popular Java IDEs (the most recent JDK from Oracle, Eclipse, NetBeans, jGRASP, DrJava, BlueJ, and TextPad). The kit also includes access to a website containing written and video tutorials for getting started in each IDE. For ordering information, please contact your campus Pearson Education representative or visit www.pearsonhighered.com.

ACKNOWLEDGMENTS

Numerous individuals have contributed invaluable help and support in making this book happen: My former editor, Susan Hartman at Addison-Wesley, first conceived of the idea for this book and worked with me on the first editions; My current editor, Matt Goldstein, provided support and inspiration for getting subsequent editions reviewed, revised, and out the door; Chelsea Kharakozova, Marilyn Lloyd, Yez Alayan, and the other fine people at Pearson also provided valuable assistance and encouragement. Thanks also to GEX Publishing Services for their expert work in producing the final typeset book.

The following reviewers provided corrections and suggestions for this book. Their contributions were a great help. I thank them all. In alphabetical order they are:

Jim Adams	Chandler-Gilbert Community College
Gerald W. Adkins	Georgia College & State University
Dr. Bay Arinze	Drexel University
Prof. Richard G. Baldwin	Austin Community College
Kevin Bierre	Rochester Institute of Technology
Jon Bjornstad	Gavilan College
Janet Brown-Sederberg	Massasoit Community College
Tom Brown	Texas A&M University, Commerce
Charlotte Busch	Texas A&M University, Corpus Christi
Stephen Chandler	NW Shoals Community College
KY Daisy Fan	Cornell University
Adrienne Decker	University of Buffalo
Brian Downs	Century College
Keith Frikken	Miami University
Ahmad Ghafarian	North Georgia College & State University
Arthur Geis	College of DuPage
Massoud Ghyam	University of Southern California
Susan G. Glenn	Gordon College
Nigel Gwee	Louisiana State University
Judy Hankins	Middle Tennessee State University
May Hou	Norfolk State University

Sterling Hough	NHTI
Chris Howard	DeVry University
Eliot Jacobson	University of California, Santa Barbara
Balaji Janamanchi	Texas Tech University
Suresh Kalathur	Boston University
Edwin Kay	Lehigh University
Dr. Clifford R. Kettemborough	IT Consultant and Professor
Frank Levey	Manatee Community College
Xia Lin	Drexel University
Mark M. Meysenburg	Doane College
Sridhar P. Nerur	The University of Texas at Arlington
Hoang M. Nguyen	Deanza College
Rick Ord	University of California, San Diego
Prof. Bryson R. Payne	North Georgia College & State University
David Primeaux	Virginia Commonwealth University
Neil Rhodes	University of California, San Diego
W. Brent Seales	University of Kentucky
Lili Shashaani	Duquesne University
Riyaz Sikora	The University of Texas at Arlington
Jeff Six	University of Delaware
Donald J Smith	Community College of Allegheny County
Tom Smith	Skidmore College
Xueqing (Clare) Tang	Governors State University
Ronald F. Taylor	Wright State University
Thomas VanDrunen	Wheaton College
Shon Vick	University of Maryland, Baltimore County
Natalie S. Wear	University of South Florida
Dale Welch	University of West Florida
David A. Wheeler	
Wook-Sung Yoo	Gannon University

Special thanks goes to Kenrick Mock (University of Alaska Anchorage) who executed the updating of this edition. He once again had the difficult job of satisfying me, the editor, and himself. I thank him for a truly excellent job.

Walter Savitch

LOCATION OF VIDEONOTES IN THE TEXT

VideoNote

www.pearsonhighered.com/savitch

Chapter 16	Solution to Programming Project 16.3, page 937 Solution to Programming Project 16.5, page 938
Chapter 17	GUI Layout Using an IDE, page 969 Solution to Programming Project 17.1, page 1013
Chapter 18	Walkthrough of a Simple Drawing Program, page 1042 Solution to Programming Project 18.7, page 1077
Chapter 19	Walkthrough of a Program with Race Conditions, page 1094 Solution to Programming Project 19.3, page 1135 Solution to Programming Project 19.11, page 1136
Chapter 20	No video notes (Chapter on website)

Brief Contents

Contents

Chapter 4 Defining Classes I 173

Getting Started 1

1 Getting Started

She starts—she moves—she seems to feel
The thrill of life along her keel.

HENRY WADSWORTH LONGFELLOW, *The Building of the Ship*

Introduction

This chapter introduces you to the Java language and gives you enough details to allow you to write simple programs involving expressions, assignments, and console output. The details about assignments and expressions are similar to that of most other high-level languages. Every language has its own way of handling strings and console output, so even the experienced programmer should look at that material. Even if you are already an experienced programmer in some language other than Java, you should read at least the subsection entitled "A Sample Java Application Program" in Section 1.1 and preferably all of Section 1.2. You should also read all of Section 1.3 (on strings) and at least skim Section 1.4 to find out about Java defined constants and comments.

Prerequisites

This book is self-contained and requires no preparation other than some simple high school algebra.

1.1 Introduction to Java

Eliminating the middle man is not necessarily a good idea.

Found in my old economics class notes.

In this section, we give you an overview of the Java programming language.

Origins of the Java Language ★

Java is well-known as a programming language for Internet applications. However, this book, and many other books and programmers, consider Java a general-purpose programming language that is suitable for most any application, whether it involves the Internet or not. The first version of Java was neither of these things, but it evolved into both.

In 1991, James Gosling led a team at Sun Microsystems that developed the first version of Java (which was not yet called *Java*). This first version of the language was designed for programming home appliances, such as washing machines and television sets. Although that may not be a very glamorous application area, it is no easy task to design such a language. Home appliances are controlled by a wide variety of computer processors (chips). The language that Gosling was designing needed to work on all these different processors. Moreover, a home appliance is typically an inexpensive item, so the manufacturer would be unwilling to invest large amounts of money into developing complicated compilers. (A *compiler* translates a program into a language the processor can understand.) To simplify the tasks of writing compilers (translation programs) for each class of appliances, the team used a two-step translation process. The programs are first translated into an **intermediate language** that is the same for all appliances (or all computers), and then a small, easy-to-write—and hence, inexpensive—program translates this intermediate language into the machine language for a particular appliance or computer. This intermediate language is called **Java byte-code**, or simply, **byte-code**. Since there is only one intermediate language, the hardest step of the two-step translation from program to intermediate language to machine language is the same for all appliances (or all computers); hence, most of the cost of translating to multiple machine languages was saved. The language for programming appliances never caught on with appliance manufacturers, but the Java language into which it evolved has become a widely used programming language. Today, Java is owned by Oracle Corporation, which purchased Sun Microsystems in 2010.

intermediate language

byte-code

code

Why call it *byte-code*? The word **code** is commonly used to mean a program or part of a program. A byte is a small unit of storage (eight bits to be precise). Computer-readable information is typically organized into bytes. So the term *byte-code* suggests a program that is readable by a computer as opposed to a person.

In 1994, Patrick Naughton and Jonathan Payne at Sun Microsystems developed a Web browser that could run (Java) programs over the Internet, which has evolved into the browser known as HotJava. This was the start of Java's connection to the Internet. In the fall of 1995, Netscape Incorporated made its Web browser capable of running Java programs. Other companies followed suit and have developed software that accommodates Java programs.

Objects and Methods

OOP

Java is an **object-oriented programming (OOP)** language. What is OOP? The world around us is made up of objects, such as people, automobiles, buildings, streets, adding machines, papers, and so forth. Each of these objects has the ability to perform certain actions, and each of these actions has some effect on some of the other objects in the world. OOP is a programming methodology that views a program as similarly consisting of objects that interact with each other by means of actions.

object

method

class

Object-oriented programming has its own specialized terminology. The objects are called, appropriately enough, **objects**. The actions that an object can take are called **methods**. Objects of the same kind are said to have the same *type* or, more often, are said to be in the same **class**. For example, in an airport simulation program, all the

> **Why Is the Language Named "Java"?**
>
> The current custom is to name programming languages according to the whims of their designers. Java is no exception. There are conflicting explanations of the origin of the name "Java." Despite these differing stories, one thing is clear: The word "Java" does not refer to any property or serious history of the Java language. One believable story about where the name came from is that it was thought of when, after a fruitless meeting trying to come up with a new name for the language, the development team went out for coffee. Hence, the inspiration for the name "Java."

simulated airplanes might belong to the same class, probably called the `Airplane` class. All objects within a class have the same methods. Thus, in a simulation program, all airplanes have the same methods (or possible actions), such as taking off, flying to a specific location, landing, and so forth. However, all simulated airplanes are not identical. They can have different characteristics, which are indicated in the program by associating different data (that is, some different information) with each particular airplane object. For example, the data associated with an airplane object might be two numbers for its speed and altitude.

If you have used some other programming language, it might help to explain Java terminology in terms of the vocabulary used in other languages. Things that are called *procedures*, *methods*, *functions*, or *subprograms* in other languages are all called *methods* in Java. In Java, all methods (and for that matter, any programming constructs whatsoever) are part of a *class*. As we will see, a Java **application program** is a class with a method named `main`; when you run the Java program, the run-time system automatically invokes the method named `main` (that is, it automatically initiates the `main` action). An application program is a "regular" Java program, and, as we are about to see, there is another kind of Java program known as an *applet*. Other Java terminology is pretty much the same as the terminology in most other programming languages and, in any case, will be explained when each concept is introduced.

application program

Applets ★

applet

application

There are two kinds of Java programs, **applets** and **applications**. An application, or application program, is just a regular program. Although the name *applet* may sound like it has something to do with apples, it really means a *little Java application*, not a little apple. Applets and applications are almost identical. The difference is that applications are meant to be run on your computer like any other program, whereas an **applet** is meant to be run from a Web browser, and so can be sent to another location on the Internet and run there. Applets always use a windowing interface, but not all programs with a windowing interface are applets, as you will see in Chapters 16–18.

applet viewer

Although applets were designed to be run from a Web browser, they can also be run with a program known as an **applet viewer**. The applet viewer is really meant as a debugging aid and not as the final environment to allow users to run applets. Nonetheless, applets are now often run as stand-alone programs using an applet viewer.[1] We find this to be a somewhat unfortunate accident of history. Java has multiple libraries of software for designing windowing interfaces that run without a connection to a browser. We prefer to use these libraries, rather than applets, to write windowing programs that will not be run from a Web browser. In this book, we show you how to do windowing interfaces as applets and as programs with no connection to a Web browser. In fact, the two approaches have a large overlap of both techniques and the Java libraries that they use. Once you know how to design and write either applets or applications, it is easy to learn to write the other of these two kinds of programs.

An applet always has a windowing interface. An application program may have a windowing interface or use simple console I/O. So as not to detract from the code being studied, most of our example programs, particularly early in this book, use simple console I/O (that is, simple text I/O).

A Sample Java Application Program

Display 1.1 contains a simple Java program and the screen displays produced when it is run. A Java program is really a class definition (whatever that is) with a method named `main`. When the program is run, the method named `main` is invoked; that is, the action specified by `main` is carried out. The body of the method `main` is enclosed in braces, { }, so that when the program is run, the statements in the braces are executed. (If you are not even vaguely familiar with the words *class* and *method*, they will be explained. Read on.)

The following line says that this program is a class called `FirstProgram`:

```
public class FirstProgram
{
```

The next two lines, shown below, begin the definition of the `main` method:

```
public static void main(String[] args)
{
```

The details of exactly what a Java class is and what words such as `public`, `static`, `void`, and so forth mean will be explained in the next few chapters. Until then, think of these opening lines, repeated below, as being a rather wordy way of saying "Begin the program named `FirstProgram`."

```
public class FirstProgram
{
    public static void main(String[] args)
    {
```

[1]An applet viewer does indeed use a browser to run an applet, but the look and feel is that of a stand-alone program with no interaction with a browser.

Display 1.1 A Sample Java Program

```
public class FirstProgram
{
   public static void main(String[] args)
   {
      System.out.println("Hello reader.");
      System.out.println("Welcome to Java.");

      System.out.println("Let's demonstrate a simple calculation.");
      int answer;
      answer = 2 + 2;
      System.out.println("2 plus 2 is " + answer);
   }
}
```

Name of class (program)

The `main` *method*

Sample Dialogue

```
Hello reader.
Welcome to Java.
Let's demonstrate a simple calculation.
2 plus 2 is 4
```

The next two lines, shown in what follows, are the first actions the program performs:

println

```
System.out.println("Hello reader.");
System.out.println("Welcome to Java.");
```

Each of these lines begins with `System.out.println`. Each one causes the quoted string given within the parentheses to be output to the screen. For example, consider

```
System.out.println("Hello reader.");
```

This causes the line

```
Hello reader.
```

to be written to the screen. The output produced by the next line that begins with `System.out.println` will go on the following line. Thus, these two lines cause the following output:

```
Hello reader.
Welcome to Java.
```

System.out.println

These lines that begin with `System.out.println` are a way of saying "output what is shown in parentheses," and the details of why the instruction is written this way need not concern us yet. However, we can tell you a little about what is going on here.

As stated earlier, Java programs work by having things called *objects* perform actions. The actions performed by an object are called *methods*. `System.out` is an object used for sending output to the screen; `println` is the method (that is, the action) that this object performs. The action is to send what is in parentheses to the screen. When an object performs an action using a method, it is called **invoking** (or **calling**) the method. In a Java program, you write such a method invocation by writing the object followed by a **dot** (period), followed by the method name, and some parentheses that may or may not have something inside them. The thing (or things) inside the parentheses is called an **argument(s)**, which provides information needed by the method to carry out its action. In each of these two lines and the similar line that follows them, the method is `println`. The method `println` writes something to the screen, and the argument (a string in quotes) tells it what it should write.

invoking

dot

argument

Invoking a method is also sometimes called **sending a message** to the object. With this view, a message is sent to the object (by invoking a method) and in response, the object performs some action (namely the action taken by the method invoked). We seldom use the terminology *sending a message*, but it is standard terminology used by some programmers and authors.

sending a message

Variable declarations in Java are similar to what they are in other programming languages. The following line from Display 1.1 declares the variable `answer`:

variable `int`

```
int answer;
```

The type `int` is one of the Java types for integers (whole numbers). So, this line says that `answer` is a variable that can hold a single integer (whole number).

The following line is the only real computing done by this first program:

equal sign

```
answer = 2 + 2;
```

assignment operator

In Java, the equal sign is used as the **assignment operator**, which is an instruction to set the value of the variable on the left-hand side of the equal sign. In the preceding program line, the equal sign does not mean that `answer` *is equal to* `2 + 2`. Instead, the equal sign is an instruction to the computer to *make* `answer` *equal to* `2 + 2`.

The last program action is

```
System.out.println("2 plus 2 is " + answer);
```

This is an output statement of the same kind as we discussed earlier, but there is something new in it. Note that the string `"2 plus 2 is "` is followed by a plus sign and the variable `answer`. In this case, the plus sign is an operator to concatenate (connect) two strings. However, the variable `answer` is not a string. If one of the two operands to `+` is a string, Java will convert the other operand, such as the value of `answer`, to a string. In this program, `answer` has the value `4`, so `answer` is converted to the string `"4"` and then concatenated to the string `"2 plus 2 is "`, so the output statement under discussion is equivalent to

```
System.out.println("2 plus 2 is 4");
```

The remainder of this first program consists of two closing braces. The first closing brace ends the definition of the method `main`. The last closing brace ends the definition of the class named `FirstProgram`.

MyProgrammingLab™

Self-Test Exercises

1. If the following statement were used in a Java program, it would cause something to be written to the screen. What would it cause to be written to the screen?

```
System.out.println("Java is not a drink.");
```

2. Give a statement or statements that can be used in a Java program to write the following to the screen:

```
I like Java.
You like tea.
```

3. Write a complete Java program that uses `System.out.println` to output the following to the screen when run:

```
Hello World!
```

Note that you do not need to fully understand all the details of the program in order to write the program. You can simply follow the model of the program in Display 1.1.

Byte-Code and the Java Virtual Machine

high-level, low-level, and machine languages

Most modern programming languages are designed to be (relatively) easy for people to write and to understand. These languages are called **high-level languages**. The language that the computer can directly understand is called **machine language**. Machine language or any language similar to machine language is called a **low-level language**. A program written in a high-level language, such as Java, must be translated into a program in machine language before the program can be run. The program that does the translating (or at least most of the translating) is called a **compiler** and the translation process is called **compiling**.

compiler

Compiler

A **compiler** is a program that translates a high-level-language program, such as a Java program, into an equivalent low-level-language program.

One disadvantage of most programming languages is that the compiler translates the high-level-language program directly into the machine language for your computer. Since different computers have different machine languages, this means you need a different compiler for each type of computer. Java, however, uses a slightly different and much more versatile approach to compiling.

While some versions of Java do translate your program into machine language for your particular computer, the original Java compiler and most compilers today do not. Instead, the Java compiler translates your Java program into a language called **byte-code**. Byte-code is not the machine language for any particular computer; it is the machine language for a fictitious computer called the **Java Virtual Machine (JVM)**. The Java Virtual Machine is very similar to all typical computers. Thus, it is easy to translate a program written in byte-code into a program in the machine language for any particular computer. The term *JVM* is also used to refer to the software that implements the fictitious computer. There are two ways the JVM can do this translation: through an **interpreter** and through a **Just-In-Time (JIT)** compiler.

byte-code

Java Virtual Machine (JVM)

Interpreter

Just-In-Time (JIT)

An interpreter combines the translation of the byte-code and the execution of the corresponding machine language instructions. The interpreter works by translating an instruction of byte-code into instructions expressed in your computer's machine language and then executing those instructions on your computer. It does this one byte-code instruction at a time. Thus, an interpreter translates and executes the instructions in the byte-code one after the other, rather than translating the entire byte-code program at once.

Modern implementations of the JVM use a JIT compiler, which uses a combination of interpretation and compilation. The JIT compiler reads the byte-code in chunks and compiles entire chunks to native machine language instructions as needed. The compiled machine language instructions are remembered—i.e., cached—for future use, so the chunk needs to be compiled only once. This model generally runs programs faster than the interpreted model, which always has to translate the next byte-code instruction to machine code instructions.

To run a Java program, first use the compiler to translate the Java program into byte-code. Then, use the JVM for your computer to translate byte-code instructions to machine language and to run the machine language instructions.

It sounds as though Java byte-code just adds an extra step in the process. Why not write compilers that translate directly from Java to the machine language for your particular computer? This is what is done for most other programming languages. However, Java byte-code makes your Java program very portable. After you compile your Java program into byte-code, you can use that byte-code on any computer. When you run your program on another type of computer, you do not need to recompile it. This means that you can send your byte-code over the Internet to another computer and have it easily run on that computer. This is one of the reasons Java is good for Internet applications. This model is also more secure. If a Java program behaves badly, it only does so within the context of the JVM instead of behaving badly directly on your native machine. Of course, every kind of computer must have its own program to implement the Java Virtual Machine.

Byte-Code

The Java compiler translates your Java program into a language called **byte-code**, which is the machine language for a fictitious computer. It is easy to translate this byte-code into the machine language of any particular computer. Each type of computer will have its own software to implement the Java Virtual Machine that translates and executes byte-code instructions.

When compiling and running a Java program, you are usually not even aware of the fact that your program is translated into byte-code and not directly translated into machine language code. You normally give two commands: one to compile your program (into byte-code) and one to run your program. The **run command** executes the Java Virtual Machine on the byte-code.

run command

When you use a compiler, the terminology can get a bit confusing, because both the input to the compiler program and the output from the compiler program are also programs. Everything in sight is some kind of program. To make sure it is clear which program we mean, we call the input program (which in our case will be a Java program) the **source program**, or **source code**, and call the translated low-level-language program that the compiler produces the **object program**, or **object code**. The word **code** just means a program or a part of a program.

source code

object code

code

Class Loader ★

A Java program is divided into smaller parts called *classes*, and normally each class definition is in a separate file and is compiled separately. In order to run your program, the byte-code for these various classes needs to be connected together. The connecting is done by a program known as the **class loader**. It is typically done automatically, so you normally need not be concerned with it. (In other programming languages, the program corresponding to the Java class loader is called a *linker*.)

Compiling a Java Program or Class

VideoNote
Compiling a Java Program

As we noted in the previous subsection, a Java program is divided into classes. Before you can run a Java program, you must compile these classes.

Before you can compile a Java program, each class definition used in the program (and written by you, the programmer) should be in a separate file. Moreover, the name of the file should be the same as the name of the class, except that the file name has `.java` added to the end. The program in Display 1.1 is a class called `FirstProgram`, so it should be in a file named `FirstProgram.java`. This program has only one class, but a more typical Java program would consist of several classes.

`.java` files

If you are using an IDE (Integrated Development Environment), there will be a simple command to compile your Java program from the editor. You will have to check your local documentation to see exactly what this command is, but it is bound to be very simple. (In the TextPad environment, the command is Compile Java on the Tools menu.)

If you want or need to compile your Java program or class with a one-line command given to the operating system, it is easy to do. We will describe the commands for the Java system distributed by Oracle (usually called "the SDK" or "the JDK") in the following paragraphs.

Suppose you want to compile a class named `FirstProgram`. It will be in a file named `FirstProgram.java`. To compile it, simply give the following command:

`javac`

```
javac FirstProgram.java
```

You should be in the same directory (folder) as the file `FirstProgram.java` when you give this `javac` command. To compile any Java class, whether it is a full program or not, the command is `javac` followed by the name of the file containing the class.

`.class` files

When you compile a Java class, the resulting byte-code for that class is placed in a file of the same name, except that the ending is changed from `.java` to `.class`. So, when you compile a class named `FirstProgram` in the file `FirstProgram.java`, the resulting byte-code is stored in a file named `FirstProgram.class`.

Running a Java Program

A Java program can consist of a number of different classes, each in a different file. When you run a Java application program, only run the class that you think of as the program; that is, the class that contains a `main` method. Look for the following line, which starts the `main` method:

```
public static void main(String[] args)
```

The critical words to look for are `public static void main`. The remaining portion of the line might be spelled slightly different in some cases.

If you are using an IDE, you will have a menu command that can be used to run a Java program. You will have to check your local documentation to see exactly what this command is. (In the TextPad environment, the command is Run Java Application on the Tools menu.)

If you want or need to run your Java program with a one-line command given to the operating system, then (in most cases) you can run a Java program by giving the command `java` followed by the name of the class containing the `main` method. For example, for the program in Display 1.1, you would give the following one-line command:

```
java FirstProgram
```

Note that when you run a program, you use the class name, such as `FirstProgram`, without any `.java` or `.class` ending.

When you run a Java program, you are actually running the Java byte-code interpreter on the compiled version of your program. When you run your program, the system will automatically load in any classes you need and run the byte-code interpreter on those classes as well.

We have been assuming that the Java compiler and related software are already set up for you. We are also assuming that all the files are in one directory. (Directories are also called *folders*.) If you need to set up the Java compiler and system software, consult the manuals that came with the software. If you wish to spread your class definitions across multiple directories, that is not difficult, but we will not concern ourselves with that detail until later.

Syntax and Semantics

The description of a programming language, or any other kind of language, can be thought of as having two parts, called the *syntax* and *semantics* of the language.

The **syntax** tells what arrangement of words and punctuation is legal in the language. The syntax is often called the language's *grammar rules*. For Java, the syntax describes what arrangements of words and punctuation are allowed in a class or program definition.

The **semantics** of a language describes the meaning of things written while following the syntax rules of the language. For a Java program, the syntax describes how you write a program and the semantics describes what happens when you run the program.

When writing a program in Java, you are always using both the syntax and the semantics of the Java language.

TIP: Error Messages

bug

debugging

A mistake in a program is called a **bug**. For this reason, the process of eliminating mistakes in your program is called **debugging**. There are three commonly recognized types of bugs or errors, which are known as *syntax errors*, *run-time errors*, and *logic errors*. Let's consider them in order.

syntax error

A **syntax error** is a grammatical mistake in your program; that is, a mistake in the allowed arrangement of words and punctuations. If you violate one of these rules—for example, by omitting a required punctuation—it is a syntax error. The compiler will catch syntax errors and output an error message telling you that it has found the error, where it thinks the error is, and what it thinks the error is. If the compiler says you have a syntax error, you undoubtedly do. However, the compiler could be incorrect about where and what the error is.

run-time error

An error that is not detected until your program is run is called a **run-time error**. If the computer detects a run-time error when your program is run, then it will output an error message. The error message may not be easy to understand, but at least it lets you know that something is wrong.

logic error

A mistake in the underlying algorithm for your program is called a **logic error**. If your program has only logic errors, it will compile and run without any error message. You have written a valid Java program, but you have not written a program that does what you want. The program runs and gives output, but the output is incorrect. For example, if you were to mistakenly use the multiplication sign in place of the addition sign, it would be a logic error. Logic errors are the hardest kind of error to locate, because the computer does not give you any error messages. ■

MyProgrammingLab™

Self-Test Exercises

4. What is a compiler?

5. What is a source program?

6. What is an object program?

7. What do you call a program that runs Java byte-code instructions?

8. Suppose you define a class named `NiceClass` in a file. What name should the file have?

9. Suppose you compile the class `NiceClass`. What will be the name of the file with the resulting byte-code?

1.2 Expressions and Assignment Statements

Once a person has understood the way variables are used in programming, he has understood the quintessence of programming.

E. W. DIJKSTRA, *Notes on Structured Programming*

Variables, expressions, and assignments in Java are similar to their counterparts in most other general purpose languages. In this section, we describe the details.

Identifiers

identifier

The name of a variable (or other item you might define in a program) is called an **identifier**. A Java identifier must not start with a digit and all the characters must be letters, digits, or the underscore (_) symbol. (The symbol $ is also allowed, but it is reserved for special purposes only, so you should not typically use $ in your Java identifiers.) For example, the following are all valid identifiers:

```
x x1 x_1 _abc ABC123z7 sum RATE count data2 bigBonus
```

All of the preceding names are legal and would be accepted by the compiler, but the first five are poor choices for identifiers, since they are not descriptive of the identifier's use. None of the following are legal identifiers and all would be rejected by the compiler:

```
12  3X  %change  data-1  myfirst.java  PROG.CLASS
```

The first two are not allowed because they start with a digit. The remaining four are not identifiers because they contain symbols other than letters, digits, and the underscore symbol.

case-sensitive

Java is a **case-sensitive** language; that is, it distinguishes between upper- and lowercase letters in the spelling of identifiers. Hence, the following are three distinct identifiers and could be used to name three distinct variables:

```
rate  RATE  Rate
```

However, it is usually not a good idea to use two such variants in the same program, because that might be confusing. Although it is not required by Java, variables are usually spelled with their first letter in lowercase. The convention that has become universal in Java programming is to spell variable names with a mix of upper- and lowercase letters (and digits), to always start a variable name with a lowercase letter, and to indicate "word" boundaries with an uppercase letter, as illustrated by the following variable names:

```
topSpeed  bankRate1  bankRate2  timeOfArrival
```

A Java identifier can theoretically be of any length, and the compiler will accept even unreasonably long identifiers.

Names (Identifiers)

The name of something in a Java program, such as a variable, class, method, or object name, must not start with a digit and may only contain letters, digits (0 through 9), and the underscore character (_). Upper- and lowercase letters are considered to be different characters. (The symbol $ is also allowed, but it is reserved for special purposes only, so you should not typically use $ in a Java name.)

Names in a program are called **identifiers**.

Although it is not required by the Java language, the common practice, and the one followed in this book, is to start the names of classes with uppercase letters and to start the names of variables, objects, and methods with lowercase letters. These names are usually spelled using only letters and digits.

keyword

There is a special class of identifiers, called **keywords** or **reserved words**, that have a predefined meaning in Java and that you cannot use as names for variables or anything else. In the code displays of this book, keywords are shown in a different color, as illustrated by the keyword `public`. A complete list of keywords is given in Appendix 1.

Some predefined words, such as `System` and `println`, are not keywords. These predefined words are not part of the core Java language and you are allowed to redefine them. Although these words are not keywords, they are defined in libraries required by the Java language standard. Needless to say, using a predefined identifier for anything other than its standard meaning can be confusing and dangerous, and thus should be avoided. The safest and easiest practice is to treat all predefined identifiers as if they are keywords.

Variables

declare

Every variable in a Java program must be declared before it is used. When you **declare** a variable, you are telling the compiler—and, ultimately, the computer—what kind of data you will be storing in the variable. For example, the following are two declarations that might occur in a Java program:

```
int numberOfBeans;
double oneWeight, totalWeight;
```

floating-point number

The first declares the variable `numberOfBeans` so that it can hold a value of type `int`; that is, a whole number. The name `int` is an abbreviation for "integer." The type `int` is the default type for whole numbers. The second definition declares `oneWeight` and `totalWeight` to be variables of type `double`, which is the default type for numbers with a decimal point (known as **floating-point numbers**). As illustrated here, when there is more than one variable in a declaration, the variables are separated by commas. Also, note that each declaration ends with a semicolon.

Every variable must be declared before it is used. A variable may be declared anyplace, so long as it is declared before it is used. Of course, variables should always be declared in a location that makes the program easier to read. Typically, variables are declared either just before they are used or at the start of a block (indicated by an opening brace {). Any legal identifier, other than a keyword, may be used for a variable name.

Variable Declarations

In Java, a variable must be declared before it is used. Variables are declared as described here.

SYNTAX

Type Variable_1, Variable_2,. . .;

EXAMPLES

```
int count, numberOfDragons, numberOfTrolls;
char answer;
double speed, distance;
```

Syntactic Variables

Remember that when you see something such as *Type*, *Variable_1*, or *Variable_2*, these words do not literally appear in your Java code. They are **syntactic variables**, which means they are replaced by something of the category that they describe. For example, *Type* can be replaced by `int`, `double`, `char`, or any other type name. *Variable_1* and *Variable_2* can each be replaced by any variable name.

primitive types

Java has basic types for characters, different kinds of integers, and different kinds of floating-point numbers (numbers with a decimal point), as well as a type for the values `true` and `false`. These basic types are known as **primitive types**. Display 1.2 shows all of Java's primitive types. The preferred type for integers is `int`. The type `char` is the type for single characters and can store common Unicode characters. The preferred type for floating-point numbers is `double`. The type `boolean` has the two values `true` and `false`. (Unlike some other programming languages, the Java values `true` and `false` are not integers and will not be automatically converted to integers.) Objects of the predefined class `String` represent strings of characters. `String` is not a primitive type, but is often considered a basic type along with the primitive types. The class `String` is discussed later in this chapter.

Assignment Statements

assignment statement

assignment operator

The most direct way to change the value of a variable is to use an **assignment statement**. In Java, the equal sign is used as the **assignment operator**. An assignment statement always consists of a variable on the left-hand side of the assignment operator (the equal sign) and an expression on the right-hand side. An assignment statement ends with a semicolon. The expression on the right-hand side of the equal sign may be a variable, a number, or a more complicated expression made up of variables, numbers,

Display 1.2 Primitive Types

TYPE NAME	KIND OF VALUE	MEMORY USED	SIZE RANGE
`boolean`	`true` or `false`	1 byte	Not applicable
`char`	Single character (Unicode)	2 bytes	Common Unicode characters
`byte`	Integer	1 byte	−128 to 127
`short`	Integer	2 bytes	−32768 to 32767
`int`	Integer	4 bytes	−2147483648 to 2147483647
`long`	Integer	8 bytes	−9223372036854775808 to 9223372036854775807
`float`	Floating-point number	4 bytes	$\pm 3.40282347 \times 10^{+38}$ to $\pm 1.40239846 \times 10^{-45}$
`double`	Floating-point number	8 bytes	$\pm 1.76769313486231570 \times 10^{+308}$ to $\pm 4.94065645841246544 \times 10^{-324}$

operators, and method invocations. An assignment statement instructs the computer to evaluate (that is, to compute the value of) the expression on the right-hand side of the equal sign and to set the value of the variable on the left-hand side equal to the value of that expression. The following are examples of Java assignment statements:

```
totalWeight = oneWeight * numberOfBeans;
temperature = 98.6;
count = count + 2;
```

The first assignment statement sets the value of `totalWeight` equal to the number in the variable `oneWeight` multiplied by the number in `numberOfBeans`. (Multiplication is expressed using the asterisk `*` in Java.) The second assignment statement sets the value of `temperature` to `98.6`. The third assignment statement increases the value of the variable `count` by `2`.

Note that a variable may occur on both sides of the assignment operator (both sides of the equal sign). The assigned statement

```
count = count + 2;
```

sets the new value of `count` equal to the old value of `count` plus `2`.

When used with variables of a class type, the assignment operator requires a bit more explanation, which we will give in Chapter 4.

Assignment Statements with Primitive Types

An assignment statement with a variable of a primitive type on the left-hand side of the equal sign causes the following actions: First, the expression on the right-hand side of the equal sign is evaluated, and then the variable on the left-hand side of the equal sign is set equal to this value.

SYNTAX

Variable = Expression;

EXAMPLE

```
distance = rate * time;
count = count + 2;
```

An assigned statement may be used as an expression that evaluates to a value. When used this way, the variable on the left-hand side of the equal sign is changed as we have described, and the new value of the variable is also the value of the assignment expression. For example,

```
number = 3;
```

both changes the value of `number` to `3` and evaluates to the value `3`. This allows you to chain assignment statements. The following changes the values of both the variables, `number1` and `number2`, to `3`:

```
number2 = (number1 = 3);
```

The assignment operator automatically is executed right to left if there are no parentheses, so this is normally written in the following equivalent way:

```
number2 = number1 = 3;
```

TIP: Initialize Variables

uninitialized variable

A variable that has been declared but that has not yet been given a value by some means, such as an assignment statement, is said to be **uninitialized**. In some instances, an uninitialized variable may be given some default value, but this is not true in all cases. Moreover, it makes your program clearer to explicitly give the variable a value, even if you are simply reassigning it the default value. (The exact details on default values have been known to change and should not be counted on.)[2]

One easy way to ensure that you do not have an uninitialized variable is to initialize it within the declaration. Simply combine the declaration and an assignment statement, as in the following examples:

```
int count = 0;
double speed = 65.5;
char grade = 'A';
int initialCount = 50, finalCount;
```

Note that you can initialize some variables and not initialize others in a declaration.

Sometimes the compiler may say that you have failed to initialize a variable. In most cases, this will indeed have occurred. Occasionally, the compiler is mistaken. However, the compiler will not compile your program until you convince it that the variable in question is initialized. To make the compiler happy, initialize the variable when it is declared, even if the variable will be given a different value before the variable is used for anything. In such cases, you cannot argue with the compiler. ■

[2]The official rules are that the variables we are now using, which we will later call *local variables*, are not automatically initialized. Later in this book, we will introduce variables called *static variables* and *instance variables*, which are automatically initialized. However, we urge you to never rely on automatic initialization.

Initializing a Variable in a Declaration

You can combine the declaration of a variable with an assignment statement that gives the variable a value.

SYNTAX

Type Variable_1 = , *Variable_2* = *Expression__2*, ...;

Some of the variables may have no equal sign and no expression, as in the first example.

EXAMPLE

```
int numberReceived = 0, lastNumber, numberOfStations = 5;
double speed = 98.9, distance = speed * 10;
char initial = 'J';
```

More Assignment Statements ★

There is a shorthand notation that combines the assignment operator (=) and an arithmetic operator so that a given variable can have its value changed by adding, subtracting, multiplying, or dividing by a specified value. The general form is

Variable Op = Expression

which is equivalent to

Variable = Variable Op (Expression)

The *Expression* can be another variable, a constant, or a more complicated arithmetic expression. The *Op* can be any of +, −, *, /, or %, as well as some operators we have not yet discussed—the operator % has also not yet been discussed but is explained later in this chapter. (A full list of values for *Op* can be seen at the bottom of the precedence table in Appendix 2.) Below are examples:

EXAMPLE:	EQUIVALENT TO:
`count += 2;`	`count = count + 2;`
`total -= discount;`	`total = total - discount;`
`bonus *= 2;`	`bonus = bonus * 2;`
`time /= rushFactor;`	`time = time / rushFactor;`
`change %= 100;`	`change = change % 100;`
`amount *= count1 + count2;`	`amount = amount * (count1 + count2);`

MyProgrammingLab™

Self-Test Exercises

10. Which of the following may be used as variable names in Java?

```
rate1, 1stPlayer, myprogram.java, long,
TimeLimit, numberOfWindows
```

11. Can a Java program have two different variables named `number` and `Number`?

12. Give the declaration for two variables called `feet` and `inches`. Both variables are of type `int` and both are to be initialized to zero in the declaration.

13. Give the declaration for two variables called `count` and `distance`. `count` is of type `int` and is initialized to zero. `distance` is of type `double` and is initialized to `1.5`.

14. Write a Java assignment statement that will set the value of the variable `distance` to the value of the variable `time` multiplied by `80`. All variables are of type `int`.

15. Write a Java assignment statement that will set the value of the variable `interest` to the value of the variable `balance` multiplied by the value of the variable `rate`. The variables are of type `double`.

16. What is the output produced by the following lines of program code?

```
char a, b;
a = 'b';
System.out.println(a);
b = 'c';
System.out.println(b);
a = b;
System.out.println(a);
```

Assignment Compatibility

As a general rule, you cannot store a value of one type in a variable of another type. For example, the compiler will object to the following:

```
int intVariable;
intVariable = 2.99;
```

The problem is a type mismatch. The constant `2.99` is of type `double` and the variable `intVariable` is of type `int`.

assigning `int` values to `double` variables

There are some special cases where it is permitted to assign a value of one type to a variable of another type. It is acceptable to assign a value of an integer type, such as `int`, to a variable of a floating-point type, such as the type `double`. For example, the following is both legal and acceptable style:

```
double doubleVariable;
doubleVariable = 2;
```

The preceding will set the value of the variable named `doubleVariable` equal to `2.0`.

Similarly, assignments of integer type variables to floating-point type variables are also allowed. For example, the following is permitted:

```
int intVariable;
intVariable = 42;
double doubleVariable;
doubleVariable = intVariable;
```

More generally, you can assign a value of any type in the following list to a variable of any type that appears further down in the list:

```
byte —> short —> int —> long —> float —> double
```

For example, you can assign a value of type `int` to a variable of type `long`, `float`, or `double` (or of course to a variable of type `int`), but you cannot assign a value of type `int` to a variable of type `byte` or `short`. Note that this is not an arbitrary ordering of the types. As you move down the list from left to right, the range of allowed values for the types becomes larger.

You can assign a value of type `char` to a variable of type `int` or to any of the numeric types that follow `int` in our list of types (but not to those that precede `int`). However, in most cases it is not wise to assign a character to an `int` variable, because the result could be confusing.[3]

If you want to assign a value of type `double` to a variable of type `int`, then you must change the type of the value by using a *type cast*, as explained in the subsection later in this chapter entitled "Type Casting."

integers and booleans

In many languages other than Java, you can assign integers to variables of type `boolean` and assign `boolean` values to integer variables. You cannot do that in Java. In Java, the `boolean` values `true` and `false` are not integers nor will they be automatically converted to integers. (In fact, it is not even legal to do an explicit type cast from the type `boolean` to the type `int` or vice versa. Explicit type casts are discussed later in this chapter in the subsection "Type Casting.")

Constants

constants

literals

Constants or **literals** are names for one specific value. For example, `2` and `3.1459` are two constants. We prefer the name *constants* because it contrasts nicely with the word *variables*. Constants do not change value; variables can change their values.

---

[3]Readers who have used certain other languages, such as C or C++, may be surprised to learn that you cannot assign a value of type `char` to a variable of type `byte`. This is because Java uses the Unicode character set rather than the ASCII character set, and so Java reserves two bytes of memory for each value of type `char`, but naturally only reserves one byte of memory for values of type `byte`. This is one of the few cases where you might notice that Java uses the Unicode character set. Indeed, if you convert from an `int` to a `char` or vice versa, you can expect to get the usual correspondence of ASCII numbers and characters. It is also true that you cannot assign a value of type `char` to a variable of type `short`, even though they both use two bytes of memory.

> **Assignment Compatibilities**
>
> You can assign a value of any type on the following list to a variable of any type that appears further down on the list:
>
> `byte -> short -> int -> long -> float -> double`
>
> In particular, note that you can assign a value of any integer type to a variable of any floating-point type. You can also assign a value of type `char` to a variable of type `int` or of any type that followers `int` in the above list.

Integer constants are written in the way you are used to writing numbers. Constants of type `int` (or any other integer type) must not contain a decimal point. Constants of floating-point types (`float` and `double`) may be written in either of two forms. The simple form for floating-point constants is like the everyday way of writing decimal fractions. When written in this form, a floating-point constant must contain a decimal point. No number constant (neither integer nor floating point) in Java may contain a comma.

e notation

A more complicated notation for floating-point constants, such as constants of type `double`, is called **scientific notation** or **floating-point notation** and is particularly handy for writing very large numbers and very small fractions. For instance,

3.67×10^5, which is the same as `367000.0`,

is best expressed in Java by the constant `3.67e5`. The number

5.89×10^{-4}, which is the same as `0.000589`,

is best expressed in Java by the constant `5.89e-4`. The `e` stands for *exponent* and means "multiply by 10 to the power that follows." The `e` may be either upper- or lowercase.

Think of the number after the `e` as telling you the direction and number of digits to move the decimal point. For example, to change `3.49e4` to a numeral without an `e`, move the decimal point `4` places to the right to obtain `34900.0`, which is another way of writing the same number. If the number after the `e` is negative, move the decimal point the indicated number of spaces to the left, inserting extra zeros if need be. So, `3.49e-2` is the same as `0.0349`.

The number before the `e` may contain a decimal point, although that is not required. However, the exponent after the `e` definitely must *not* contain a decimal point.

Constants of type `char` are expressed by placing the character in single quotes, as illustrated in what follows:

```
char symbol = 'Z';
```

Note that the left and right single quote symbols are the same symbol.

> **What Is Doubled?**
>
> How did the floating-point type `double` get its name? Is there another type for floating-point numbers called "single" that is half as big? Something like that is true. There is a type that uses half as much storage, namely the type `float`. Many programming languages traditionally used two types for floating-point numbers. One type used less storage and was very imprecise (that is, it did not allow very many significant digits). The second type used *double* the amount of storage and so could be much more precise; it also allowed numbers that were larger (although programmers tend to care more about precision than about size). The kind of numbers that used twice as much storage were called *double precision* numbers; those that used less storage were called *single precision*. Following this tradition, the type that (more or less) corresponds to this double precision type in Java was named `double` in Java. The type that corresponds to single precision in Java was called `float`.
>
> (Actually, the type name `double` was inherited from C++, but this explanation applies to why the type was named `double` in C++, and so ultimately it is the explanation of why the type is called `double` in Java.)

Constants for strings of characters are given in double quotes, as illustrated by the following line taken from Display 1.1:

```
System.out.println("Welcome to Java.");
```

quotes

Be sure to notice that string constants are placed inside of double quotes, while constants of type `char` are placed inside of single quotes. The two kinds of quotes mean different things. In particular, `'A'` and `"A"` mean different things. `'A'` is a value of type `char` and can be stored in a variable of type `char`. `"A"` is a string of characters. The fact that the string happens to contain only one character does *not* make the string `"A"` a value of type `char`. Also notice that, for both strings and characters, the left and right quotes are the same. We will have more to say about strings later in this chapter.

The type `boolean` has two constants, `true` and `false`. These two constants may be assigned to a variable of type `boolean` or used anyplace else an expression of type `boolean` is allowed. They must be spelled with all lowercase letters.

Arithmetic Operators and Expressions

As in most other languages, Java allows you to form expressions using variables, constants, and the arithmetic operators: `+` (addition), `-` (subtraction), `*` (multiplication), `/` (division), and `%` (modulo, remainder). These expressions can be used anyplace it is legal to use a value of the type produced by the expression.

mixing types

All of the arithmetic operators can be used with numbers of type `int`, numbers of type `double`, and even with one number of each type. However, the type of the value produced and the exact value of the result depend on the types of the numbers being combined. If both operands (that is, both numbers) are of type `int`, then the result of combining them with an arithmetic operator is of type `int`. If one, or both, of the operands is of type `double`, then the result is of type `double`. For example, if the variables `baseAmount` and `increase` are both of type `int`, then the number produced by the following expression is of type `int`:

```
baseAmount + increase
```

However, if one, or both, of the two variables is of type `double`, then the result is of type `double`. This is also true if you replace the operator `+` with any of the operators `-`, `*`, `/`, or `%`.

More generally, you can combine any of the arithmetic types in expressions. If all the types are integer types, the result will be the integer type. If at least one of the subexpressions is of a floating-point type, the result will be a floating-point type.

Knowing whether the value produced is of an integer type or a floating-point type is typically all that you need to know. However, if you need to know the exact type of the value produced by an arithmetic expression, it can be determined as follows: The type of the value produced is one of the types used in the expression. Of all the types used in the expression, it is, with rare exceptions, the last type (reading left to right) on the following list:

```
byte -> short -> int -> long -> float -> double
```

Here are the rare exceptions: Of all the types used in the expression, if the last type (reading left to right) is `byte` or `short`, then the type of the value produced is `int`. In other words, an expression never evaluates to either of the types `byte` or `short`. These exceptions have to do with an implementation detail that need not concern us, especially since we almost never use the types `byte` and `short` in this book.

Note that this sequence of types is the same sequence of types we saw when discussing assignment compatibility. As you go from left to right, the types increase in the range of values they allow.[4]

Parentheses and Precedence Rules ★

If you want to specify exactly what subexpressions are combined with each operator, you can fully parenthesize an expression. For example,

```
((base + (rate * hours))/(2 + rate))
```

If you omit some parentheses in an arithmetic expression, Java will, in effect, put in parentheses for you. When adding parentheses, Java follows rules called **precedence rules**

[4]Although we discourage the practice, you can use values and variables of type `char` in arithmetic expressions using operators such as `+`. If you do so, the `char` values and variables will contribute to the expression as if they were of type `int`.

that determine how the operators, such as + and *, are enclosed in parentheses. These precedence rules are similar to rules used in algebra. For example,

```
base + rate * hours
```

is evaluated by Java as if it were parenthesized as follows:

```
base + (rate * hours)
```

So, the multiplication will be done before the addition.

Except in some standard cases, such as a string of additions or a simple multiplication embedded inside an addition, it is usually best to include the parentheses, even if the intended groupings are the ones dictated by the precedence rules. The parentheses make the expression easier to read and less prone to programmer error.

A partial list of precedence rules is given in Display 1.3. A complete set of Java precedence rules is given in Appendix 2. Operators that are listed higher on the list are said to have **higher precedence**. When the computer is deciding which of two adjacent operations to group with parentheses, it groups the operation of higher precedence and its apparent arguments before the operation of lower precedence. Some operators have equal precedence, in which case the order of operations is determined by **associativity rules**. A brief summary of associativity rules is that binary operators of equal precedence are grouped in left-to-right order.[5] Unary operators of equal precedence are grouped in right-to-left order. So, for example,

```
base + rate + hours
```

is interpreted by Java to be the same as

```
(base + rate) + hours
```

And, for example,

```
+-+rate
```

is interpreted by Java to be the same as

```
+(-(+rate))
```

For now you can think of the explicit parentheses put in by the programmer and the implicit parentheses determined by precedence and associativity rules as determining the order in which operations are performed. For example, in

```
base + (rate * hours)
```

the multiplication is performed first and the addition is performed second.

[5]There is one exception to this rule. A string of assignment operators, such as `n1 = n2 = n3;`, is performed right to left, as we noted earlier in this chapter.

Display 1.3 Precedence Rules

Highest Precedence

First: the unary operators: `+`, `-`, `++`, `--`, and `!`

Second: the binary arithmetic operators: `*`, `/`, and `%`

Third: the binary arithmetic operators: `+` and `-`

Lowest Precedence

The actual situation is a bit more complicated than what we have described for evaluating expressions, but we will not encounter any of these complications in this chapter. A complete discussion of evaluating expressions using precedence and associativity rules will be given in Chapter 3.

Integer and Floating-Point Division

integer division

When used with one or both operands of type `double`, the division operator, `/`, behaves as you might expect. However, when used with two operands of type `int`, the division operator yields the integer part resulting from division. In other words, integer division discards the part after the decimal point. So, `10/3` is `3` (not `3.3333`...), `5/2` is `2` (not `2.5`), and `11/3` is `3` (not `3.6666`...). Notice that the number *is not rounded*; the part after the decimal point is discarded no matter how large it is.

the `%` operator

The operator `%` can be used with operands of type `int` to recover the information lost when you use `/` to do division with numbers of type `int`. When used with values of type `int`, the two operators `/` and `%` yield the two numbers produced when you perform the long division algorithm you learned in grade school. For example, `14` divided by `3` is `4` with a remainder of `2`. The `/` operation yields the number of times one number "goes into" another (often called the *quotient*). The `%` operation gives the remainder. For example, the statements

```
System.out.println("14 divided by 3 is " + (14 / 3));
System.out.println("with a remainder of " + (14 % 3));
```

yield the following output:

```
14 divided by 3 is 4
with a remainder of 2
```

The `%` operator can be used to count by 2s, 3s, or any other number. For example, if you want to do something to every other integer, you need to know if the integer is even or odd. Then, you can do it to every even integer (or alternatively every odd integer). An integer `n` is even if `n % 2` is equal to `0` and the integer is odd if `n % 2` is equal to `1`. Similarly, to do something to every third integer, your program might step through all integers `n` but only do the action when `n % 3` is equal to `0`.

PITFALL: Round-Off Errors in Floating-Point Numbers

For all practical purposes, floating-point numbers are only approximate quantities. For example, in formal mathematics, the floating-point number `1.0/3.0` is equal to

```
0.3333333...
```

where the three dots indicate that the `3`s go on forever. The computer stores numbers in a format somewhat like this decimal representation, but it has room for only a limited number of digits. If it can store only 10 digits after the decimal, then `1.0/3.0` is stored as

```
0.3333333333
```

with only 10 threes. Thus, `1.0/3.0` is stored as a number that is slightly smaller than one-third. In other words, the value stored as `1.0/3.0` is only approximately equal to one-third.

In reality, the computer stores numbers in binary notation, rather than in base 10 notation, but the principles and the consequences are the same. Some floating-point numbers lose accuracy when they are stored in the computer.

Floating-point numbers (such as numbers of type `double`) and integers (such as numbers of type `int`) are stored differently. Floating-point numbers are, in effect, stored as approximate quantities. Integers are stored as exact quantities. This difference sometimes can be subtle. For example, the numbers `42` and `42.0` are different in Java. The whole number `42` is of type `int` and is an exact quantity. The number `42.0` is of type `double` because it contains a fractional part (even though the fraction is `0`), and so `42.0` is stored with only limited accuracy.

As a result of this limited accuracy, arithmetic done on floating-point numbers only gives approximate results. Moreover, one can easily get results on floating-point numbers that are very far from the true result you would obtain if the numbers could have unlimited accuracy (unlimited number of digits after the decimal point). For example, if a banking program used numbers of type `double` to represent amounts of money and did not do sophisticated manipulations to preserve accuracy, it would quickly bring the bank to ruin since the computed amounts of money would frequently be very incorrect. Dealing with these inaccuracies in floating-point numbers is part of the field of Numerical Analysis, a topic we will not discuss in this book. But, there is an easy way to obtain accuracy when dealing with amounts of money: Use integers instead of floating-point numbers (perhaps one integer for the dollar amount and another integer for the cents amount). ■

Although the `%` operator is primarily used with integers, it can also be used with two floating-point numbers, such as two values of type `double`. However, we will not discuss nor use `%` with floating-point numbers.

PITFALL: Division with Whole Numbers

When you use the division operator / on two integers, the result is an integer. This can be a problem if you expect a fraction. Moreover, the problem can easily go unnoticed, resulting in a program that looks fine but is producing incorrect output without you even being aware of the problem. For example, suppose you are a landscape architect who charges $5,000 per mile to landscape a highway, and suppose you know the length in feet of the highway you are working on. The price you charge can easily be calculated by the following Java statement:

```
totalPrice = 5000 * (feet / 5280.0);
```

This works because there are 5,280 feet in a mile. If the stretch of highway you are landscaping is 15,000 feet long, this formula will tell you that the total price is

```
5000 * (15000 / 5280.0)
```

Your Java program obtains the final value as follows: `15000/5280.0` is computed as `2.84`. Then, the program multiplies `5000` by `2.84` to produce the value `14200.00`. With the aid of your Java program, you know that you should charge $14,200 for the project.

Now suppose the variable `feet` is of type `int`, and you forget to put in the decimal point and the zero, so that the assignment statement in your program reads as follows:

```
totalPrice = 5000 * (feet / 5280);
```

It still looks fine, but will cause serious problems. If you use this second form of the assignment statement, you are dividing two values of type `int`, so the result of the division `feet/5280` is `15000/5280`, which is the `int` value `2` (instead of the value `2.84`, which you think you are getting). So the value assigned to `totalPrice` is `5000*2`, or `10000.00`. If you forget the decimal point, you will charge $10,000. However, as we have already seen, the correct value is $14,200. A missing decimal point has cost you $4,200. Note that this will be true whether the type of `totalPrice` is `int` or `double`; the damage is done before the value is assigned to `totalPrice`. ■

MyProgrammingLab™

Self-Test Exercises

17. Convert each of the following mathematical formulas to a Java expression:

$$3x \qquad 3x+y \qquad \frac{x+y}{7} \qquad \frac{3x+y}{z+2}$$

18. What is the output of the following program lines?

```
double number = (1/3) * 3;
System.out.println("(1/3) * 3 is equal to " + number);
```

MyProgrammingLab™

Self-Test Exercises (continued)

19. What is the output produced by the following lines of program code?

```
int quotient, remainder;
quotient = 7 / 3;
remainder = 7 % 3;
System.out.println("quotient = " + quotient);
System.out.println("remainder = " + remainder);
```

20. What is the output produced by the following code?

```
int result = 11;
result /= 2;
System.out.println("result is " + result);
```

21. Given the following fragment that purports to convert from degrees Celsius to degrees Fahrenheit, answer the following questions:

```
double celsius = 20;
double fahrenheit;
fahrenheit = (9 / 5) * celsius + 32.0;
```

   a. What value is assigned to `fahrenheit`?

   b. Explain what is actually happening, and what the programmer likely wanted.

   c. Rewrite the code as the programmer intended.

Type Casting

A type cast takes a value of one type and produces a value of another type that is Java's best guess of an equivalent value. We will motivate type casts with a simple division example.

Consider the expression `9/2`. In Java, this expression evaluates to `4`, because when both operands are of an integer type, Java performs integer division. In some situations, you might want the answer to be the `double` value `4.5`. You can get a result of `4.5` by using the "equivalent" floating-point value `2.0` in place of the integer value `2`, as in the expression `9/2.0`, which evaluates to `4.5`. But, what if the `9` and the `2` are the values of variables of type `int` named `n` and `m`. Then, `n/m` yields `4`. If you want floating-point division in this case, you must do a type cast from `int` to `double` (or another floating-point type), such as in the following:

```
double ans = n/(double)m;
```

The expression

```
(double)m
```

is a type cast. The expression takes an `int` (in this example, the value of `m`) and evaluates to an "equivalent" value of type `double`. So, if the value of `m` is `2`, the expression `(double)m` evaluates to the `double` value `2.0`.

Note that `(double)m` does not change the value of the variable `m`. If `m` has the value `2` before this expression is evaluated, then `m` still has the value `2` after the expression is evaluated.

You may use other type names in place of `double` to obtain a type cast to another type. We said this produces an "equivalent" value of the target type. The word "equivalent" is in quotes because there is no clear notion of equivalent that applies between any two types. In the case of a type cast from an integer type to a floating-point type, the effect is to add a decimal point and a zero. A type cast in the other direction, from a floating-point type to an integer type, simply deletes the decimal point and all digits after the decimal point. Note that when type casting from a floating-point type to an integer type, the number is truncated, not rounded: `(int)2.9` is `2`; it is not `3`.

As we noted earlier, you can always assign a value of an integer type to a variable of a floating-point type, as in the following:

```
double d = 5;
```

In such cases Java performs an automatic type cast, converting the `5` to `5.0` and placing `5.0` in the variable `d`. You cannot store the `5` as the value of `d` without a type cast, but sometimes Java does the type cast for you. Such an automatic type cast is sometimes called a **type coercion**.

type coercion

By contrast, you cannot place a `double` value in an `int` variable without an explicit type cast. The following is illegal:

```
int i = 5.5; //Illegal
```

Instead, you must add an explicit type cast, like so:

```
int i = (int)5.5;
```

Increment and Decrement Operators

The **increment operator** `++` adds one to the value of a variable. The **decrement operator** `--` subtracts one from the value of a variable. They are usually used with variables of type `int`, but they can be used with any numeric type. If `n` is a variable of a numeric type, then `n++` increases the value of `n` by one and `n--` decreases the value of `n` by one. So, `n++` and `n--` (when followed by a semicolon) are executable statements. For example, the statements

```
int n = 1, m = 7;
n++;
System.out.println("The value of n is changed to " + n);
m--;
System.out.println("The value of m is changed to " + m);
```

yield the following output:

```
The value of n is changed to 2
The value of m is changed to 6
```

An expression such as `n++` also evaluates to a number as well as changing the value of the variable `n`, so `n++` can be used in an arithmetic expression such as the following:

```
2*(n++)
```

The expression `n++` changes the value of `n` by adding one to it, but it evaluates to the value `n` had *before* it was increased. For example, consider the following code:

```
int n = 2;
int valueProduced = 2*(n++);
System.out.println(valueProduced);
System.out.println(n);
```

This code produces the following output:

```
4
3
```

Notice the expression `2*(n++)`. When Java evaluates this expression, it uses the value that `number` has *before* it is incremented, not the value that it has after it is incremented. Thus, the value produced by the expression `n++` is `2`, even though the increment operator changes the value of `n` to `3`. This may seem strange, but sometimes it is just what you want. And, as you are about to see, if you want an expression that behaves differently, you can have it.

The expression `++n` also increments the value of the variable `n` by one, but it evaluates to the value `n` has after it is increased. For example, consider the following code:

```
int n = 2;
int valueProduced = 2*(++n);
System.out.println(valueProduced);
System.out.println(n);
```

This code is the same as the previous piece of code except that the `++` is before the variable, so this code will produce the following output:

```
6
3
```

v++ versus ++v

Notice that the two increment operators `n++` and `++n` have the exact same effect on a variable `n`: They both increase the value of `n` by one. But the two expressions evaluate to different values. Remember, if the `++` is *before* the variable, then the incrementing is done *before* the value is returned; if the `++` is *after* the variable, then the incrementing is done *after* the value is returned.

decrement operator

Everything we said about the increment operator applies to the decrement operator as well, except that the value of the variable is decreased by one rather than increased by one. For example, consider the following code:

```
int n = 8;
int valueProduced = n--;
System.out.println(valueProduced);
System.out.println(n);
```

This produces the following output:

```
8
7
```

On the other hand, the code

```
int n = 8;
int valueProduced = --n;
System.out.println(valueProduced);
System.out.println(n);
```

produces the following output:

```
7
7
```

Both `n--` and `--n` change the value of `n` by subtracting one, but they evaluate to different values. `n--` evaluates to the value `n` had before it was decremented; on the other hand, `--n` evaluates to the value `n` has after it is decremented.

You cannot apply the increment and decrement operators to anything other than a single variable. Expressions such as `(x + y)++`, `--(x + y)`, `5++`, and so forth are all illegal in Java.

The use of the increment and decrement operators can be confusing when used inside of more complicated expressions, and so, we prefer to not use increment or decrement operators inside of expressions, but to only use them as simple statements, such as the following:

```
n++;
```

MyProgrammingLab™

Self-Test Exercises

22. What is the output produced by the following lines of program code?

```
int n = (int)3.9;
System.out.println("n == " + n);
```

MyProgrammingLab™

Self-Test Exercises (continued)

23. What is the output produced by the following lines of program code?

```
int n = 3;
n++;
System.out.println("n == " + n);
n--;
System.out.println("n == " + n);
```

1.3 The Class String

Words, words, mere words, no matter from the heart.

WILLIAM SHAKESPEARE, *Troilus and Cressida*

String

There is no primitive type for strings in Java. However, there is a class called String that can be used to store and process strings of characters. This section introduces the class String.

String Constants and Variables

You have already seen constants of type String. The quoted string

```
"Hello reader."
```

which appears in the following statement from Display 1.1, is a string constant:

```
System.out.println("Hello reader.");
```

A quoted string is a value of type String, although it is normally called an *object* of type String rather than a value of type String. An object of type String is a sequence of characters treated as a single item. A variable of type String can name one of these string objects.

For example, the following declares blessing to be the name for a String variable:

```
String blessing;
```

The following assignment statement sets the value of blessing so that blessing serves as another name for the String object "Live long and prosper.":

```
blessing = "Live long and prosper.";
```

The declaration and assignment can be combined into a single statement, as follows:

```
String blessing = "Live long and prosper.";
```

You can write the object named by the `String` variable `blessing` to the screen as follows:

```
System.out.println(blessing);
```

which produces the screen output

```
Live long and prosper.
```

> **The `String` Class**
>
> The class `String` is a predefined class that is automatically made available to you when you are programming in Java. Objects of type `String` are strings of characters that are written within double quotes. For example, the following declares the variable `motto` to be of type `String` and makes `motto` a name for the `String` object `"We aim to please."`.
>
> ```
> String motto = "We aim to please.";
> ```

Concatenation of Strings

+ operator

concatenation

When you use the **+ operator** on two strings, the result is the string obtained by connecting the two strings to get a longer string. This is called **concatenation**. So, when it is used with strings, the + is sometimes called the **concatenation operator**. For example, consider the following:

```
String noun = "Strings";
String sentence;
sentence = noun + "are cool.";
System.out.println(sentence);
```

This will set the variable `sentence` to `"Stringsare cool."` and will output the following to the screen:

```
Stringsare cool.
```

Note that no spaces are added when you concatenate two strings. If you want `sentence` set to `"Strings are cool."`, then you should change the assignment statement to add the extra space. For example, the following will add the desired space:

```
sentence = noun + " are cool.";
```

We added a space before the word `"are"`.

You can concatenate any number of `Strings` using the + operator. Moreover, you can use the + operator to concatenate a `String` to almost any other type of item. The result is always a `String`. In most situations, Java will convert an item of any type to

Using the + Sign with Strings

If you connect two strings with the + operator, the result is the concatenation (pasting) of the two strings.

EXAMPLE

```
String name = "Chiana";
String farewell = "Good bye " + name;
System.out.println(farewell);
```

This sets `farewell` to the string `"Good bye Chiana"`. So, it outputs the following to the screen:

```
Good bye Chiana
```

Note that we added a space at the end of `"Good bye "`.

a string when you connect it to a string with the + operator. For numbers, it does the obvious thing. For example,

```
String solution = "The answer is " + 42;
```

will set the `String` variable `solution` to `"The answer is 42"`. Java converts the integer constant `42` to the string `"42"` and then concatenates the two strings `"The answer is "` and `"42"` to obtain the longer string `"The answer is 42"`.

Notice that a number or other value is converted to a string object only when it is connected to a string with a plus sign. If it is connected to another number with a plus sign, it is not converted to a string. For example,

```
System.out.println("100" + 42);
```

outputs

```
10042
```

but

```
System.out.println(100 + 42);
```

outputs

```
142
```

Classes

Classes are central to Java and you will soon be defining and using your own classes. The class `String` gives us an opportunity to introduce some of the notation and

class **object** **method**

terminology used for classes. A class is the name for a type whose values are objects. Objects are entities that store data and can take actions. For example, objects of the class `String` store data consisting of strings of characters, such as `"Hello"`. The actions that an object can take are called methods. Most of the methods for the class `String` return some value—that is, produce some value. For example, the method `length()` returns the number of characters in a `String` object. So, `"Hello".length()` returns the integer `5`, which can be stored in an `int` variable as follows:

```
int n = "Hello".length();
```

As indicated by the example `"Hello".length()`, a method is called into action by writing a name for the object followed by a dot followed by the method name with parentheses. When you call a method into action, you are (or your code is) said to invoke the method or call the method, and the object before the dot is known as the **calling object**.

method call or method invocation

calling object

Although you can call a method with a constant object, as in `"Hello".length()`, it is more common to use a variable as the calling object, as illustrated by the following:

```
String greeting = "Hello";
int n = greeting.length();
```

Information needed for the method invocation is given in the parentheses. In some cases, such as the method `length`, no information is needed (other than the data in the calling object) and the parentheses are empty. In other cases, which we see soon, there is some information that must be provided inside the parentheses. The information in parentheses is known as an **argument** (or arguments).

argument

sending a message

Invoking a method is also sometimes called **sending a message** to the object. With this view, a message is sent to the object (by invoking a method) and in response the object performs some action. For example, in response to the message

```
greeting.length()
```

the object `greeting` answers with the value `5`.

All objects within a class have the same methods, but each object can have different data. For example, the two `String` objects `"Hello"` and `"Good-Bye"` have different data—that is, different strings of characters. However, they have the same methods. Thus, because we know that the `String` object `"Hello"` has the method `length()`, we know that the `String` object `"Good-Bye"` must also have the method `length()`.

You now have seen two kinds of types in Java: primitive types and class types. The main difference you have seen between these two kinds of types is that classes have methods and primitive types do not. We will later see more differences between classes and primitive types. A smaller difference between primitive types and class types is that all the primitive types are spelled using only lowercase letters but, by convention, class types are spelled with their first letter in uppercase, as in `String`.

Classes, Objects, and Methods

A Java program works by having things called **objects** perform actions. The actions are known as **methods** and typically involve data contained in the object. All objects of the same kind are said to be of the same class. So, a **class** is a category of objects. When the object performs the action of a given method, it is called **invoking** the method (or **calling** the method). Information provided to the method in parentheses is called the **argument** (or arguments).

For example, in Display 1.1, `System.out` is an object, `println` is a method, and the following is an invocation of the method by this object using the argument `"Hello reader."`:

```
System.out.println("Hello reader.");
```

String Methods

The class `String` has a number of useful methods that can be used for string-processing applications. A sample of these `String` methods is presented in Display 1.4. Some of the notation and terminology used in Display 1.4 is described in the box entitled "Returned Value." A more complete list of String methods is given in Appendix 5.

Returned Value

An expression such as `numberOfGirls + numberOfBoys` produces a value. If `numberOfGirls` has the value `2` and `numberOfBoys` has the value `10`, then the number produced is `12`. The number `12` is the result of evaluating the expression.

Some method invocations are simple kinds of expression, and any such method invocation evaluates to some value. If a method invocation produces a value, we say that the method *returns* the value. For example, suppose your program executes

```
String greeting = "Hello!";
```

After that, if you evaluate `greeting.length()`, the value returned will be `6`. So the following code outputs the integer `6`:

```
String greeting = "Hello!";
System.out.println(greeting.length());
```

A method can return different values depending on what happens in your program. However, each method can return values of only one type. For example, the method `length` of the class `String` always returns an `int` value. In Display 1.4, the type given before the method name is the type of the values returned by that method. Since `length` always returns an `int` value, the entry for `length` begins

```
int length()
```

As with any method, a `String` method is called (invoked) by writing a `String` object, a dot, the name of the method, and finally a pair of parentheses that enclose any arguments to the method. Let's look at some examples.

`length` As we've already noted, the method `length` can be used to find out the number of characters in a string. You can use a call to the method `length` anywhere that you can use a value of type `int`. For example, all of the following are legal Java statements:

```
String greeting = "Hello";
int count = greeting.length();
System.out.println("Length is " + greeting.length());
```

Display 1.4 **Some Methods in the Class `String`** (part 1 of 4)

`int length()`

Returns the length of the calling object (which is a string) as a value of type `int`.

EXAMPLE

After program executes `String greeting = "Hello!";`
`greeting.length()` returns `6`.

`boolean equals(`*Other_String*`)`

Returns `true` if the calling object string and the *Other_String* are equal. Otherwise, returns `false`.

EXAMPLE

After program executes `String greeting = "Hello";`
`greeting.equals("Hello")` returns `true`
`greeting.equals("Good-Bye")` returns `false`
`greeting.equals("hello")` returns `false`

Note that case matters. `"Hello"` and `"hello"` are not equal because one starts with an uppercase letter and the other starts with a lowercase letter.

`boolean equalsIgnoreCase(`*Other_String*`)`

Returns `true` if the calling object string and the *Other_String* are equal, considering upper- and lowercase versions of a letter to be the same. Otherwise, returns `false`.

EXAMPLE

After program executes `String name = "mary!";`
`greeting.equalsIgnoreCase("Mary!")` returns `true`

Display 1.4 Some Methods in the Class `String` (part 2 of 4)

`String toLowerCase( )`

Returns a string with the same characters as the calling object string, but with all letter characters converted to lowercase.

EXAMPLE

After program executes `String greeting = "Hi Mary!";`
`greeting.toLowerCase()` returns `"hi mary!"`.

`String toUpperCase( )`

Returns a string with the same characters as the calling object string, but with all letter characters converted to uppercase.

EXAMPLE

After program executes `String greeting = "Hi Mary!";`
`greeting.toUpperCase()` returns `"HI MARY!"`.

`String trim( )`

Returns a string with the same characters as the calling object string, but with leading and trailing white space removed. White space characters are the characters that print as white space on paper, such as the blank (space) character, the tab character, and the new-line character `'\n'`.

EXAMPLE

After program executes `String pause = " Hmm ";`
`pause.trim()` returns `"Hmm"`.

`char charAt`(*Position*)

Returns the character in the calling object string at the *Position*. Positions are counted 0, 1, 2, etc.

EXAMPLE

After program executes `String greeting = "Hello!";`
`greeting.charAt(0)` returns `'H'`, and
`greeting.charAt(1)` returns `'e'`.

`String substring`(*Start*)

Returns the substring of the calling object string starting from *Start* through to the end of the calling object. Positions are counted 0, 1, 2, etc. Be sure to notice that the character at position *Start* is included in the value returned.

EXAMPLE

After program executes `String sample = "AbcdefG";`
`sample.substring(2)` returns `"cdefG"`.

(continued)

Display 1.4 **Some Methods in the Class `String`** (part 3 of 4)

`String substring(`*Start*, *End*`)`

Returns the substring of the calling object string starting from position *Start* through, but not including, position *End* of the calling object. Positions are counted 0, 1, 2, etc. Be sure to notice that the character at position *Start* is included in the value returned, but the character at position *End* is not included.

EXAMPLE

After program executes `String sample = "AbcdefG";`
`sample.substring(2, 5)` returns `"cde"`.

`int indexOf(`*A_String*`)`

Returns the index (position) of the first occurrence of the string *A_String* in the calling object string. Positions are counted 0, 1, 2, etc. Returns `-1` if *A_String* is not found.

EXAMPLE

After program executes `String greeting = "Hi Mary!";`
`greeting.indexOf("Mary")` returns `3`, and
`greeting.indexOf("Sally")` returns `-1`.

`int indexOf(`*A_String*, *Start*`)`

Returns the index (position) of the first occurrence of the string *A_String* in the calling object string that occurs at or after position *Start*. Positions are counted 0, 1, 2, etc. Returns `-1` if *A_String* is not found.

EXAMPLE

After program executes `String name = "Mary, Mary quite contrary";`
`name.indexOf("Mary", 1)` returns `6`.
The same value is returned if `1` is replaced by any number up to and including `6`.
`name.indexOf("Mary", 0)` returns `0`.
`name.indexOf("Mary", 8)` returns `-1`.

`int lastIndexOf(`*A_String*`)`

Returns the index (position) of the last occurrence of the string *A_String* in the calling object string. Positions are counted 0, 1, 2, etc. Returns `-1`, if *A_String* is not found.

EXAMPLE

After program executes `String name = "Mary, Mary, Mary quite so";`
`greeting.indexOf("Mary")` returns `0`, and
`name.lastIndexOf("Mary")` returns `12`.

Display 1.4 Some Methods in the Class **String** (part 4 of 4)

`int compareTo(A_String)`

Compares the calling object string and the string argument to see which comes first in the lexicographic ordering. Lexicographic order is the same as alphabetical order but with the characters ordered as in Appendix 3. Note that in Appendix 3, all the uppercase letters are in regular alphabetical order and all the lowercase letters are in alphabetical order, but all the uppercase letters precede all the lowercase letters. So, lexicographic ordering is the same as alphabetical ordering provided both strings are either all uppercase letters or both strings are all lowercase letters. If the calling string is first, it returns a negative value. If the two strings are equal, it returns zero. If the argument is first, it returns a positive number.

EXAMPLE

After program executes `String entry = "adventure";`
`entry.compareTo("zoo")` returns a negative number,
`entry.compareTo("adventure")` returns `0`, and
`entry.compareTo("above")` returns a positive number.

`int compareToIgnoreCase(A_String)`

Compares the calling object string and the string argument to see which comes first in the lexicographic ordering, treating upper- and lowercase letters as being the same. (To be precise, all uppercase letters are treated as if they were their lowercase versions in doing the comparison.) Thus, if both strings consist entirely of letters, the comparison is for ordinary alphabetical order. If the calling string is first, it returns a negative value. If the two strings are equal ignoring case, it returns zero. If the argument is first, it returns a positive number.

EXAMPLE

After program executes `String entry = "adventure";`
`entry.compareToIgnoreCase("Zoo")` returns a negative number,
`entry.compareToIgnoreCase("Adventure")` returns `0`, and
`"Zoo".compareToIgnoreCase(entry)` returns a positive number.

position

Some methods for the class `String` depend on counting **positions** in the string. Positions are counted starting with 0, not with 1. So, in the string `"Surf time"`, `'S'` is in position `0`, `'u'` is in position `1`, and so forth. A position is usually referred to as an **index**. So, it would be preferable to say: `'S'` is at index `0`, `'u'` is at index `1`, and so on.

index

The method `indexOf` can be used to find the index of a substring of the calling objects. For example, consider

```
String phrase = "Java is fun.";
```

After this declaration, the invocation `phrase.indexOf("is")` will return `5` because the `'i'` of `"is"` is at index `5`. (Remember, the first index is `0`, not `1`.) This is illustrated in Display 1.5.

Display 1.5 String Indexes

The 12 characters in the string `"Java is fun."` have indexes `0` through `11`.

0	1	2	3	4	5	6	7	8	9	10	11
J	a	v	a		i	s		f	u	n	.

Notice that the blanks and the period count as characters in the string.

Escape Sequences

**backslash **

escape sequence

A backslash, \, preceding a character tells the compiler that the character following the \ does not have its usual meaning. Such a sequence is called an **escape sequence** or an **escape character**. The sequence is typed in as two characters with no space between the symbols. Several escape sequences are defined in Java.

If you want to put a backslash, \, or a quote symbol, `"`, into a string constant, you must escape the ability of the `"` to terminate a string constant by using `\"`, or the ability of the \ to escape, by using `\\`. The `\\` tells the compiler you mean a real backslash, \, not an escape sequence, and `\"` means a quote character, not the end of a string constant. A list of escape sequences is given in Display 1.6.

It is important to note that each escape sequence is a single character, even though it is spelled with two symbols. So, the string `"Say \"Hi\"!"` contains 9 characters (`'S'`, `'a'`, `'y'`, the blank character, `'\"'`, `'H'`, `'i'`, `'\"'`, and `'!'`), not 11 characters.

Including a backslash in a quoted string is a little tricky. For example, the string `"abc\def"` is likely to produce the error message "Invalid escape character." To include a backslash in a string, you need to use two backslashes. The string `"abc\\def"`, if output to the screen, would produce

```
abc\def
```

Display 1.6 Escape Sequences

```
\" Double quote.
\' Single quote.
\\ Backslash.
\n New line. Go to the beginning of the next line.
\r Carriage return. Go to the beginning of the current line.
\t Tab. White space up to the next tab stop.
```

The escape sequence \n indicates the start of a new line. For example, the statement

```
System.out.println("To be or\nNot to be.");
```

will write the following to the screen:

```
To be or
Not to be.
```

You do not need to use the escape sequence \' to include a single quote inside a quoted string. For example, "Time's up!" is a valid quoted string. However, you do need \' if you want to indicate the constant for the single-quote character, as in

```
char singleQuote = '\'';
```

String Processing

immutable object

In Java, an object of type String is an **immutable object**, meaning that the characters in the String object cannot be changed. This will eventually prove to be important to us, but at this stage of our exploration of Java, it is a misleading statement. To see that an object of type String cannot be changed, note that none of the methods in Display 1.4 changes the value of the String calling object. There are more String methods than those shown in Display 1.4, but none of them lets you write statements that say things such as "Change the fifth character in the calling object string to 'x'." This was done intentionally to make the implementation of the String class more efficient and for other reasons that we will discuss later in this book. There is another string class, called StringBuffer, that has methods for altering its string object. We will not discuss the class StringBuffer in this text, but a table explaining many of the methods of the class StringBuffer is included in Appendix 5.

Although there is no method that allows you to change the value of a String object, such as "Hello", you can still write programs that change the value of a String variable, which is probably all you want anyway. To perform the change, simply use an assignment statement, as in the following example:

```
String name = "Soprano";
name = "Anthony " + name;
```

The assignment statement in the second line changes the value of the name variable so that the string it names changes from "Soprano" to "Anthony Soprano". Display 1.7 contains a demonstration of some simple string processing.

The Unicode Character Set ★

ASCII

Until recently, most programming languages used the ASCII character set, which is given in Appendix 3. The **ASCII** character set is simply a list of all the characters normally used on an English-language keyboard plus a few special characters. In this list, each character has been assigned a number so that characters can be stored by storing the corresponding number. Java (and now many other programming languages) uses the Unicode character set. The **Unicode** character set includes the

Unicode

Display 1.7 Using the `String` Class

```
public class StringProcessingDemo
{
    public static void main(String[] args)
    {
        String sentence = "I hate text processing!";
        int position = sentence.indexOf("hate");
        String ending =
                sentence.substring(position + "hate".length());

        System.out.println("01234567890123456789012");
        System.out.println(sentence);
        System.out.println("The word \"hate\" starts at index "
                                                  + position);
        sentence = sentence.substring(0, position) + "adore"
                                                  + ending;
        System.out.println("The changed string is:");
        System.out.println(sentence);
    }
}
```

You could just use `4` here, but if you had a `String` variable instead of `"hate"`, you would have to use `length` as shown.

Sample Dialogue

```
01234567890123456789012
I hate text processing!
The word "hate" starts at index 2
The changed string is:
I adore text processing!
```

ASCII character set plus many of the characters used in languages with a different alphabet from English. This is not likely to be a big issue if you are using an English-language keyboard. Normally, you can just program as if Java were using the ASCII character set. The ASCII character set is a subset of the Unicode character set, and the subset you are likely to use. Thus, Appendix 3, which lists the ASCII character set, in fact lists the subset of the Unicode character set that we will use in this book. The advantage of the Unicode character set is that it makes it possible to easily handle languages other than English. For example, it is legal to spell a Java identifier using the letters of the Greek alphabet (although you may want a Greek-language keyboard and monitor to do this). The disadvantage of the Unicode character set is that it sometimes requires more computer memory to store each character than it would if Java used only the ASCII character set.

MyProgrammingLab™

Self-Test Exercises

24. What is the output produced by the following?

```
String verbPhrase = "is money";
System.out.println("Time" + verbPhrase);
```

25. What is the output produced by the following?

```
String test = "abcdefg";
System.out.println(test.length());
System.out.println(test.charAt(1));
```

26. What is the output produced by the following?

```
String test = "abcdefg";
System.out.println(test.substring(3));
```

27. What is the output produced by the following?

```
System.out.println("abc\ndef");
```

28. What is the output produced by the following?

```
System.out.println("abc\\ndef");
```

29. What is the output produced by the following?

```
String test = "Hello Tony";
test = test.toUpperCase();
System.out.println(test);
```

30. What is the output of the following two lines of Java code?

```
System.out.println("2 + 2 = " + (2 + 2));
System.out.println("2 + 2 = " + 2 + 2);
```

31. Suppose `sam` is an object of a class named `Person` and suppose `increaseAge` is a method for the class `Person` that takes one argument that is an integer. How do you write an invocation of the method `increaseAge` using `sam` as the calling object and using the argument `10`? The method `increaseAge` will change the data in `sam` so that it simulates `sam` aging by 10 years.

32. The following code is supposed to output the string in lowercase letters but it has an error. What is wrong?

```
String test = "WHY ARE YOU SHOUTING?";
test.toLowerCase();
System.out.println(test);
```

1.4 Program Style

In matters of grave importance,
style, not sincerity, is the vital thing.

OSCAR WILDE, *The Importance of Being Earnest*

Java programming style is similar to that used in other languages. The goal is to make your code easy to read and easy to modify. This section gives some basic points on good programming style in general and some information on the conventions normally followed by Java programmers.

Naming Constants

There are two problems with numbers in a computer program. The first is that they carry no mnemonic value. For example, when the number `10` is encountered in a program, it gives no hint of its significance. If the program is a banking program, it might be the number of branch offices or the number of teller windows at the main office. To understand the program, you need to know the significance of each constant. The second problem is that when a program needs to have some numbers changed, the changing tends to introduce errors. Suppose that `10` occurs 12 times in a banking program. Four of the times it represents the number of branch offices, and eight of the times it represents the number of teller windows at the main office. When the bank opens a new branch and the program needs to be updated, there is a good chance that some of the `10`s that should be changed to `11` will not be, or some that should not be changed will be. The way to avoid these problems is to name each number and use the name instead of the number within your program. For example, a banking program might have two constants with the names `BRANCH_COUNT` and `WINDOW_COUNT`. Both of these numbers might have a value of `10`, but when the bank opens a new branch, all you need to do to update the program is to change the definition of `BRANCH_COUNT`.

One way to name a number is to initialize a variable to that number value, as in the following example:

```
int BRANCH_COUNT = 10;
int WINDOW_COUNT = 10;
```

There is, however, one problem with this method of naming number constants: You might inadvertently change the value of one of these variables. Java provides a way of marking an initialized variable so that it cannot be changed. The syntax is

```
public static final Type Variable = Constant;
```

For example, the names `BRANCH_COUNT` and `WINDOW_COUNT` can be given values that cannot be changed by your code as follows:

```
public static final int BRANCH_COUNT = 10;
public static final int WINDOW_COUNT = 10;
```

Constants defined this way must be placed outside of the `main` method and, when we start having more methods, outside of any other methods. This is illustrated in Display 1.8. When we start writing programs and classes with multiple methods, you will see that the defined constants can be used in all the methods of a class. However, if a constant is only going to be used inside a single method, then it can be defined inside the method without the keyword `public`.

Display 1.8 Comments and a Named Constant

```
/**
 Program to show interest on a sample account balance.
 Author: Jane Q. Programmer.
 E-mail Address: janeq@somemachine.etc.etc.
 Last Changed: September 21, 2004.
*/
public class ShowInterest
{
    public static final double INTEREST_RATE = 2.5;

    public static void main(String[] args)
    {
        double balance = 100;
        double interest; //as a percent

        interest = balance * (INTEREST_RATE / 100.0);
        System.out.println("On a balance of $" + balance);
        System.out.println("you will earn interest of $"
                                            + interest);
        System.out.println("All in just one short year.");
    }

}
```

Although it would not be as clear, it is legal to place the definition of `INTEREST_RATE` here instead. (arrow points to line 22, between the closing brace of `main` and the closing brace of the class)

Sample Dialogue

```
On a balance of $100.0
you will earn interest of $2.5
All in just one short year.
```

We will fully explain the modifiers `public static final` later in this book, but we can now explain most of what they mean. The part

```
int BRANCH_COUNT = 10;
```

simply declares `BRANCH_COUNT` as a variable and initializes it to `10`. The words that precede this modify the variable `BRANCH_COUNT` in various ways. The word `public` says there are no restrictions on where you can use the name `BRANCH_COUNT`. The word static will have to wait until Chapter 5 for an explanation, but be sure to include it.The word `final` means that the value `10` is the *final* value assignment to `BRANCH_COUNT`, or, to phrase it another way, that the program is not allowed to change the value of `BRANCH_COUNT`.

Naming Constants

The syntax for defining a name for a constant outside of a method, such as a name for a number, is as follows:

SYNTAX

`public static final` *Type Variable = Constant*;

EXAMPLE

```
public static final int MAX_SPEED = 65;
public static final double MIN_SIZE = 0.5;
public static final String GREETING = "Hello friend!";
public static final char GOAL = 'A';
```

Although it is not required, it is the normal practice of programmers to spell named constants using all uppercase letters with the underscore symbol used to separate "words."

Java Spelling Conventions

In Java, as in all programming languages, identifiers for variables, methods, and other items should always be meaningful names that are suggestive of the identifiers' meanings. Although it is not required by the Java language, the common practice of Java programmers is to start the names of classes with uppercase letters and to start the names of variables, objects, and methods with lowercase letters. Defined constants are normally spelled with all uppercase letters and underscore symbols for "punctuation," as we did in the previous subsection, "Naming Constants."

For example, `String`, `FirstProgram`, and `JOptionPane` are classes, although we have not yet discussed the last one. The identifiers `println`, `balance`, and `readLine` should each be either a variable, an object, or a method.

Since blanks are not allowed in Java identifiers, "word" boundaries are indicated by an uppercase letter, as in `numberOfPods`. Since defined constants are spelled with all uppercase letters, the underscore symbol is used for "word" boundaries, as in `MAX_SPEED`.

The identifier `System.out` seems to violate this convention, since it names an object but yet begins with an uppercase letter. It does not violate the convention, but the explanation hinges on a topic we have not yet covered. `System` is the name of a class. Within the class named `System`, there is a definition of an object named `out`. So, the identifier `System.out` is used to indicate the object `out` (starting with a lowercase letter for an object) that is defined in the class `System` (starting with an uppercase letter for a class). This sort of dot notation will be explained later in the book.

There is one Java convention that people new to Java often find strange. Java programmers normally do not use abbreviations in identifiers, but rather spell things out in full. A Java programmer would not use `numStars`. He or she would use `numberOfStars`. A Java programmer would not use `FirstProg`. He or she would use `FirstProgram`. This can produce long identifiers and sometimes exceedingly long identifiers. For example, the names of two standard Java classes are `BufferedReader` and `ArrayIndexOutOfBoundsException`. The first will be used in the next chapter and the second will be used later in this book. These long names cause you to do more typing and program lines quickly become too long. However, there is a very good reason for using these long names: There is seldom any confusion on how the identifiers are spelled. With abbreviations, you often cannot recall how the identifier was abbreviated. Was it `BufReader` or `BuffReader` or `BufferedR` or `BR` or something else? Because all the words are spelled out, you know it must be `BufferedReader`. Once they get used to using these long names, most programmers learn to prefer them.

Comments

//comments

There are two ways to insert **comments** in a Java program. In Java, the symbols `//` are used to indicate the start of a comment. All of the text between the `//` and the end of the line is a comment. The compiler simply ignores anything that follows `//` on a line. If you want a comment that covers more than one line, place a `//` on each line of the comment. The symbols `//` are two slashes (without a space between them). Comments indicated with `//` are often called **line comments**.

line comments

/*comments*/

There is another way to insert comments in a Java program. Anything between the symbol pair `/*` and the symbol pair `*/` is considered a comment and is ignored by the compiler. Unlike the `//` comments, which require an additional `//` on each line, the `/*` to `*/` comments can span several lines like so:

```
/*This is a multi-line comment.
Note that there is no comment symbol
of any kind on the second line.*/
```

block comments

Comments of the `/*  */` type are often called **block comments**. These block comments may be inserted anywhere in a program that a space or line break is allowed. However, they should not be inserted anywhere except where they do not distract from the layout of the program. Usually comments are only placed at the ends of lines or on separate lines by themselves.

Java comes with a program called `javadoc` that will automatically extract documentation from the classes you define. The workings of the `javadoc` program dictate when you normally use each kind of comment.

The `javadoc` program will extract a `/*  */` comment in certain situations, but it will not extract a `//` comment. We will say more about `javadoc` and comments after we discuss defining classes. In the meantime, you may notice the following conventions in our code:

We use line comments (that is, the // kind) for comments meant only for the code writer or for a programmer who modifies the code and not for any other programmer who merely uses the code.

For comments that would become part of the documentation for users of our code, we use block comments (that is, the `/* */` kind). The `javadoc` program allows you to indicate whether or not a block comment is eligible to be extracted for documentation. If the opening `/*` has an extra asterisk, as in `/**`, then the comment is eligible to be extracted. If there is only one asterisk, `javadoc` will not extract the comment. For this reason, our block comments invariably open with `/**`.

when to comment

It is difficult to say just how many comments a program should contain. The only correct answer is "just enough," which of course conveys little to the novice programmer. It will take some experience to get a feel for when it is best to include a comment. Whenever something is important and not obvious, it merits a comment. However, providing too many comments is as bad as providing too few. A program that has a comment on each line is so buried in comments that the structure of the program is hidden in a sea of obvious observations. Comments such as the following contribute nothing to understanding and should not appear in a program:

```
interest = balance * rate; //Computes the interest.
```

self-documenting

A well-written program is called **self-documenting**, which means that the structure of the program is clear from the choice of identifier names and the indenting pattern. A completely self-documenting program would need none of these // comments that are only for the programmer who reads or modifies the code. That may be an ideal that is not always realizable, but if your code is full of // comments and you follow our convention on when to use them, then either you simply have too many comments or your code is poorly designed.

A very simple example of the two kinds of comments is given in Display 1.8.

Indenting

We will say more about indenting as we introduce more Java. However, the general rule is easy to understand and follow. When one structure is nested inside another structure, the inside structure is indented one more level. For example, in our programs, the `main` method is indented one level, and the statements inside the main method are indented two levels. We prefer to use four spaces for each level of indenting because more than four spaces eats up too much line length. It is possible to get by with indenting only two or three spaces for each level so long as you are consistent. One space for a level of indenting is not enough to be clearly visible.

MyProgrammingLab™

Self-Test Exercises

33. What are the two kinds of comments in Java?

34. What is the output produced by the following Java code?

```
/**
  Code for Exercise.
*/
System.out.println("Hello");
//System.out.print("Mr. or Ms. ");
System.out.println("Student");
```

35. What is the normal spelling convention for named constants?

36. Write a line of Java code that will give the name `ANSWER` to the `int` value `42`. In other words, make `ANSWER` a named constant for `42`.

Chapter Summary

- Compiling a Java class or program produces *byte-code*, which is the machine language for a fictitious computer. When you run the byte-code, a program called an *interpreter* translates and executes the byte-code instructions on your computer one instruction at a time.
- A variable can be used to hold values, such as numbers. The type of the variable must match the type of the value stored in the variable. All variables must be declared before they are used.
- The equal sign, `=`, is used as the *assignment operator* in Java. An *assignment statement* is an instruction to change the value of a variable.
- Each variable should be initialized before the program uses its value.
- Parentheses in arithmetic expressions indicate which arguments are given to an operator. When parentheses are omitted, Java adds implicit parentheses using *precedence rules* and *associativity rules*.
- You can have variables and constants of type `String`. `String` is a class type, not a *primitive type*.
- You can use the plus sign to concatenate two strings.
- There are methods in the class `String` that can be used for string processing.
- Variables (and all other items in a program) should be given names that indicate how they are used.
- You should define names for number constants in a program and use these names rather than writing out the numbers within your program.
- Programs should be self-documenting to the extent possible. However, you should also insert comments to explain any unclear points.

Answers to Self-Test Exercises

1. `Java is not a drink.`

2.
```
System.out.println("I like Java.");
System.out.println("You like tea.");
```

3.
```
public class HelloWorld
{
    public static void main(String[] args)
    {
      System.out.println("Hello World!");
    }
}
```

4. A compiler translates a program written in a programming language such as Java into a program in a low-level language. When you compile a Java program, the compiler translates your Java program into a program expressed in Java byte-code.

5. The program that is input to a compiler is called the *source program.*

6. The translated program that is produced by a compiler is called the *object program* or *object code.*

7. A program that runs Java byte-code instructions is called an *interpreter.* It is also often called the *Java Virtual Machine (JVM).*

8. `NiceClass.java`

9. `NiceClass.class`

10. `1stPlayer` may not be used because it starts with a digit; `myprogram.java` may not be used because it contains an illegal symbol, the dot; `long` may not be used because it is a keyword. All the others may be used as variable names. However, `TimeLimit`, while legal, violates the style rule that all variable names begin with a lowercase letter.

11. Yes, a Java program can have two different variables named `number` and `Number`. However, it would not be good style to do so.

12. `int feet = 0, inches = 0;`

13.
```
int count = 0;
double distance = 1.5;
```

14. `distance = time * 80;`

15. `interest = balance * rate;`

16.
```
b
c
c
```

17. `3*x`
`3*x + y`
`(x + y)/7` Note that `x + y/7` is not correct.
`(3*x + y)/(z + 2)`

18. `(1/3) * 3 is equal to 0.0`

Since `1` and `3` are of type `int`, the `/` operator performs integer division, which discards the remainder, so the value of `1/3` is `0`, not `0.3333 . . .` . This makes the value of the entire expression `0 * 3`, which of course is `0`.

19. `quotient = 2`
`remainder = 1`

20. `result is 5`

21. a. `52.0`

b. `9/5` has `int` value `1`; because the numerator and denominator are both of type `int`, integer division is done; the fractional part is discarded. The programmer probably wanted floating-point division, which does not discard the part after the decimal point.

c. `fahrenheit = (9.0/5) * celsius + 32.0;`
or
`fahrenheit = 1.8 * celsius + 32.0;`

22. `n = = 3`

23. `n = = 4`
`n = = 3`

24. `Time is money`

25. `7`
`b`

26. `defg`

27. `abc`
`def`

28. `abc\ndef`

29. `HELLO TONY`

30. The output is

```
2 + 2 = 4
2 + 2 = 22
```

In the expression `"2 + 2 = " + (2 + 2)`, the integers `2` and `2` in `(2 + 2)` are added to obtain the integer `4`. When `4` is connected to the string `"2 + 2"` with a plus sign, the integer `4` is converted to the string `"4"` and the result is the string `"2 + 2 = 4"`. However `"2 + 2 = " + 2 + 2` is interpreted by Java to mean

```
("2 + 2 = " + 2) + 2
```

The first integer `2` is changed to the string `"2"` because it is being combined with the string `"2 + 2"`. The result is the string `"2 + 2 = 2"`. The last integer `2` is combined with the string `"2 + 2 = 2"`. So, the last `2` is converted to the string `"2"`. So the final result is

```
"2 + 2 = 2" + "2"
```

which is `"2 + 2 = 22"`.

31. `sam.increaseAge(10);`

32. The method `toLowerCase` doesn't change the string `test`. To change it, we must set test equal to the string returned by `toLowerCase`:

```
test = test.toLowerCase();
```

33. The two kinds of comments are `//` comments and `/* */` comments. Everything following a `//` on the same line is a comment. Everything between a `/*` and a matching `*/` is a comment.

34.
```
Hello
Student
```

35. The normal spelling convention is to spell named constants using all uppercase letters with the underscore symbol used to separate words.

36. `public static final int ANSWER = 42;`

MyProgrammingLab™

Programming Projects

Visit www.myprogramminglab.com to complete select exercises online and get instant feedback.

1. One way to measure the amount of energy that is expended during exercise is to use metabolic equivalents (MET). Here are some METS for various activities:

Running 6 MPH:	10 METS
Basketball:	8 METS
Sleeping:	1 MET

The number of calories burned per minute may be estimated using the following formula:

$$\text{Calories/Minute} = 0.0175 \times \text{MET} \times \text{Weight in kilograms}$$

Write a program that calculates and outputs the total number of calories burned for a 150-pound person who runs 6 MPH for 30 minutes, plays basketball for 30 minutes, and then sleeps for 6 hours. One kilogram is equal to 2.2 pounds.

2. The video game machines at your local arcade output coupons according to how well you play the game. You can redeem 10 coupons for a candy bar or 3 coupons for a gumball. You prefer candy bars to gumballs. Write a program that defines a

variable initially assigned to the number of coupons you win. Next, the program should output how many candy bars and gumballs you can get if you spend all of your coupons on candy bars first, and any remaining coupons on gumballs.

3. Write a program that starts with the string variable `first` set to your first name and the string variable `last` set to your last name. Both names should be all lowercase. Your program should then create a new string that contains your full name in pig latin with the first letter capitalized for the first and last name. Use only the pig latin rule of moving the first letter to the end of the word and adding "ay." Output the pig latin name to the screen. Use the `substring` and `toUpperCase` methods to construct the new name.

   For example, given

   ```
   first = "walt";
   last = "savitch";
   ```

   the program should create a new string with the text "Altway Avitchsay" and print it.

4. A government research lab has concluded that an artificial sweetener commonly used in diet soda pop will cause death in laboratory mice. A friend of yours is desperate to lose weight but cannot give up soda pop. Your friend wants to know how much diet soda pop it is possible to drink without dying as a result. Write a program to supply the answer. The program has no input but does have defined constants for the following items: the amount of artificial sweetener needed to kill a mouse, the weight of the mouse, the starting weight of the dieter, and the desired weight of the dieter. To ensure the safety of your friend, be sure the program uses the weight at which the dieter will stop dieting, rather than the dieter's current weight, to calculate how much soda pop the dieter can safely drink. You may use any reasonable values for these defined constants. Assume that diet soda contains 1/10th of 1% artificial sweetener. Use another named constant for this fraction. You may want to express the percent as the `double` value `0.001`. (If your program turns out not to use a defined constant, you may remove that defined constant from your program.)

5. Write a program that starts with a line of text and then outputs that line of text with the first occurrence of `"hate"` changed to `"love"`. For example, a possible sample output might be

   ```
   The line of text to be changed is:
   I hate you.
   I have rephrased that line to read:
   I love you.
   ```

   You can assume that the word `"hate"` occurs in the input. If the word `"hate"` occurs more than once in the line, your program will replace only the first occurrence of `"hate"`. Since we will not discuss input until Chapter 2, use a defined constant for the string to be changed. To make your program work for another string, you should only need to change the definition of this defined constant.

6. Bicyclists can calculate their speed if the gear size and cadence is known. *Gear size* refers to the effective diameter of the wheel. Gear size multiplied by pi (3.14) gives the distance travelled with one turn of the pedals. *Cadence* refers to the number of pedal revolutions per minute (rpm). The speed in miles per hour is calculated by the following:

$$\text{Speed (mph)} =$$
$$\text{Gear Size (inches)} \times \pi \times \frac{1\text{(ft)}}{12\text{ (inches)}} \times \frac{1\text{(mile)}}{5280\text{ (ft)}} \times \text{Cadence (rpm)} \times \frac{60\text{ (minutes)}}{\text{(hour)}}$$

This is a program that calculates the speed for a gear size of 100 inches and a cadence of 90 rpm. This would be considered a high cadence and a maximum gear size for a typical bicycle. In writing your program, don't forget that the expression 1/12 will result in 0, because both 1 and 12 are integers, and when the integer division is performed, the fractional part is discarded.

VideoNote
Solution to Programming Project 1.7

7. Write a program that outputs the number of hours, minutes, and seconds that corresponds to 50,391 total seconds. The output should be 13 hours, 59 minutes, and 51 seconds. Test your program with a different number of total seconds to ensure that it works for other cases.

8. The following program will compile and run, but it uses poor programming style. Modify the program so that it uses the spelling conventions, constant naming conventions, and formatting style recommended in this book.

```
public class messy {
public static void main(String[] args)
{
double TIME; double PACE;
System.out.println("This program calculates your pace given a time
and distance traveled.");
TIME = 35.5; /* 35 minutes and 30 seconds */
PACE = TIME / distance;
System.out.println("Your pace is " + PACE + " miles per hour.");
}
public static final double distance = 6.21;
}
```

9. A simple rule to estimate your ideal body weight is to allow 110 pounds for the first 5 feet of height and 5 pounds for each additional inch. Write a program with a variable for the height of a person in feet and another variable for the additional inches. Assume the person is at least 5 feet tall. For example, a person that is 6 feet and 3 inches tall would be represented with a variable that stores the number 6 and another variable that stores the number 3. Based on these values, calculate and output the ideal body weight.

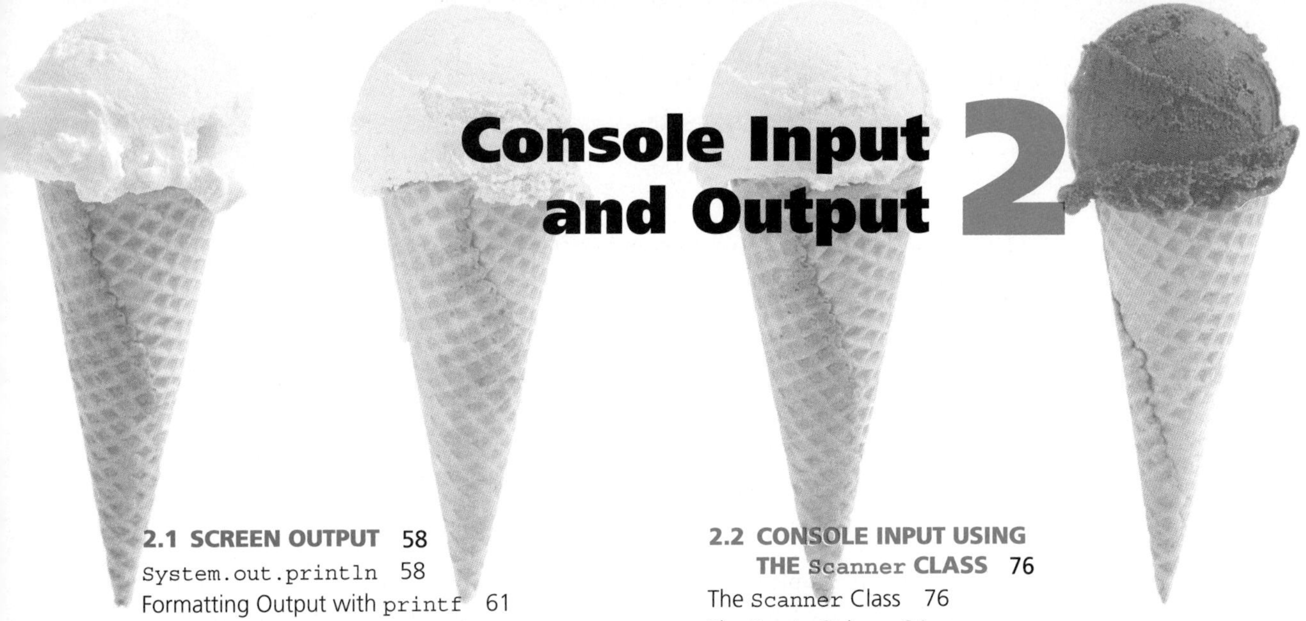

Console Input and Output 2

2 Console Input and Output

Don't imagine you know what a computer terminal is. A computer terminal is not some clunky old television with a typewriter in front of it. It is an interface where the mind and the body can connect with the universe and move bits of it about.

DOUGLAS ADAMS, *Mostly Harmless*
(the fifth volume in The Hitchhiker's Trilogy*)*

Introduction

console I/O

This chapter covers simple output to the screen and input from the keyboard, often called **console I/O**. We have already used console output, but this chapter covers it in more detail. In particular, this chapter shows you how to format numerical output so that you control such detail as the number of digits shown after the decimal point. This chapter also covers the `Scanner` class, which was introduced in version 5.0 of Java and can be used for console input.

Prerequisites

This chapter uses material from Chapter 1.

2.1 Screen Output

Let me tell the world.

WILLIAM SHAKESPEARE, *Henry IV*

In this section, we review `System.out.println` and present some material on formatting numeric output. As part of that material, we give a brief introduction to *packages* and *import statements*. Packages are Java libraries of classes. Import statements make classes from a package available to your program.

System.out.println

System.out println

We have already been using `System.out.println` for screen output. In Display 1.7, we used statements such as the following to send output to the display screen:

```
System.out.println("The changed string is:");
System.out.println(sentence);
```

`System.out` is an object that is part of the Java language, and `println` is a method invoked by that object. It may seem strange to spell an object name with a dot in it, but that need not concern us for now.

When you use `System.out.println` for output, the data to be output is given as an argument in parentheses, and the statement ends with a semicolon. Things you can output are strings of text in double quotes, such as `"The changed string is:"`; `String` variables such as `sentence`; variables of other types such as variables of type `int`; numbers such as `5` or `7.3`; and almost any other object or value. If you want to output more than one thing, simply place an addition sign between the things you want to output. For example,

```
System.out.println("Answer is = " + 42
                   + " Accuracy is = " + precision);
```

If the value of `precision` is `0.01`, the output will be

```
Answer is = 42 Accuracy is = 0.01
```

Notice the space at the start of `" Accuracy is = "`. No space is added automatically.

The `+` operator used here is the concatenation operator that we discussed earlier. So the above output statement converts the number `42` to the string `"42"` and then forms the following string using concatenation:

```
"Answer is = 42 Accuracy is = 0.01"
```

`System.out.println` then outputs this longer string.

Every invocation of `println` ends a line of output. For example, consider the following statements:

```
System.out.println("A wet bird");
System.out.println("never flies at night.");
```

These two statements cause the following output to appear on the screen:

```
A wet bird
never flies at night.
```

`print` versus `println`

If you want the output from two or more output statements to place all their output on a single line, then use `print` instead of `println`. For example, consider the following statements:

```
System.out.print("A ");
System.out.print("wet ");
System.out.println("bird");
System.out.println("never flies at night.");
```

`println` Output

You can output one line to the screen using `System.out.println`. The items that are output can be quoted strings, variables, numbers, or almost any object you can define in Java. To output more than one item, place a plus sign between the items.

SYNTAX

```
System.out.println(Item_1 + Item_2 + ... + Last_Item);
```

EXAMPLE

```
System.out.println("Welcome to Java.");
System.out.println("Elapsed time = " + time + " seconds");
```

They produce the same output as our previous example:

```
A wet bird
never flies at night.
```

Notice that a new line is not started until you use `println`, rather than `print`. Also notice that the new line starts *after* outputting the items specified in the `println`. This is the only difference between `print` and `println`.

`println` versus `print`

The only difference between `System.out.println` and `System.out.print` is that with `println`, the *next* output goes on a *new line*, whereas with `print`, the next output is placed on the *same line*.

EXAMPLE

```
System.out.print("Tom ");
System.out.print("Dick ");
System.out.println("and ");
System.out.print("Harry ");
```

This produces the following output:

```
Tom Dick and
Harry
```

(The output would look the same whether the last line reads `print` or `println`.)

Another way to describe the difference between `print` and `println` is to note that

```
System.out.println(SomeThing);
```

is equivalent to

```
System.out.print(SomeThing + "\n");
```

MyProgrammingLab™

Self-Test Exercises

1. What output is produced by the following lines?

```
String s = "Hello" + "Joe";
System.out.println(s);
```

2. Write Java statements that will cause the following to be written to the screen:

```
One two buckle your shoe.
Three four shut the door.
```

3. What is the difference between `System.out.println` and `System.out.print`?

4. What is the output produced by the following lines?

```
System.out.println(2 + " " + 2);
System.out.println(2 + 2);
```

TIP: Different Approaches to Formatting Output

If you have a variable of type `double` that stores some amount of money, you would like your programs to output the amount in a nice format. However, if you just use `System.out.println`, you are likely to get output that looks like the following:

```
Your cost, including tax, is $19.98327634144
```

You would like the output to look like this:

```
Your cost, including tax, is $19.98
```

To obtain this nicer form of output, you need some formatting tools.

In this chapter, we will present three approaches to formatting numeric (and other) output. We will discuss the method `printf` and the two formatting classes `NumberFormat` and `DecimalFormat`. The `printf` method is often the simplest way to format output. However, `printf` uses an older methodology and so some authorities prefer to use `NumberFormat`, `DecimalFormat`, or similar formatting classes because these classes use a programming methodology that is perhaps more in the spirit of modern (object-oriented) programming. We will let you (or your instructor if you are in a class) decide which methodology to use. After this chapter, this book seldom uses any of these formatting details. ■

Formatting Output with `printf`

`System.out.printf`

Starting with version 5.0, Java includes a method named `printf` that can be used to give output in a specific format. This method is used the same way as the method `print` but allows you to add formatting instructions that specify such things as the number of digits to include after a decimal point. For example, consider the following:

```
double price = 19.8;
System.out.print("$");
System.out.printf("%6.2f", price);
System.out.println(" each");
```

This code outputs the following line:

```
$ 19.80 each
```

The line

```
System.out.printf("%6.2f", price);
```

outputs the string `" 19.80"` (one blank followed by `19.80`), which is the value of the variable `price` written in the format `%6.2f`. In these simple examples, the first argument to `printf` is a string known as the **format specifier**, and the second argument is the number or other value to be output in that format. Let's explain this first sample format specifier.

format specifier

field width

The format specifier `%6.2f` says to output a floating-point number in a **field** (number of spaces) of width `6` (room for six characters) and to show exactly two digits after the decimal point. So, `19.8` is expressed as `"19.80"` in a field of width 6. Because `"19.80"` has only `five` characters, a blank character is added to obtain the six-character string `" 19.80"`. Any extra blank space is added to the front (left-hand end) of the value output. That explains the `6.2` in the format specifier `%6.2f`. The `f` means the output is a floating-point number, that is, a number with a decimal point. We will have more to say about the character `%` shortly, but among other things, it indicates that a format specification (in this case, `6.2f`) follows.

Before we go on, let's note a few details about the method `printf`. Note that the first argument is a string that gives a format specifier. Also, note that `printf`, like `print`, does not advance the output to the next line. The method `printf` is like `print`, not like `println`, in this regard.

The first argument to `printf` can include text as well as a format specifier. For example, consider the following variant on our example:

```
double price = 19.8;
System.out.printf("$%6.2f each", price);
System.out.println();
```

This code also outputs the following line:

```
$ 19.80 each
```

The text before and after the format specifier `%6.2f` is output along with the formatted number. The character `%` signals the end of text to output and the start of the

conversion character

format specifier. The end of a format specifier is indicated by a **conversion character** (`f` in our example).

Other possible format specifiers are described in Display 2.1. (A more complete list of specifiers is given in Appendix 4.) The conversion character specifies the type of value that is output in the specified format. Note that the first number specifies the total number of spaces used to output the value. If that number is larger than the number of spaces needed for the output, extra blanks are added to the beginning of the value output. If that number is smaller than the number of spaces needed for the output, enough extra space is added to allow the value to be output; no matter what field width is specified, `printf` uses enough space to fit in the entire value output. Both of the numbers in a format specifier such as `%6.2f` are optional. You may omit either or both numbers, in which case Java chooses an appropriate default value or values (for example, `%6f` and `%.2f`). Note that the dot goes with the second number. You can use a format specifier that is just a `%` followed by a conversion character, such as `%f` or `%g`, in which case Java decides on the format details for you. For example, the format specifier `%f` is equivalent to `%.6f`, meaning six spaces after the decimal point and no extra space around the output.

`e` and `g`

The `e` and `g` format specifiers are partially explained in Display 2.1. We still need to explain the meaning of the number after the decimal point in `e` and `g` format specifiers, such as `%8.3e` and `%8.3g`. The first number, `8` in the examples, is the total field width for the value output. The second number (the number after the decimal point) specifies the number of digits after the decimal point of the output. So the numbers, such as `8.3`, have the same meaning in the `f`, `e`, and `g` formats.

Display 2.1 Format Specifiers for `System.out.printf`

CONVERSION CHARACTER	TYPE OF OUTPUT	EXAMPLES
d	Decimal (ordinary) integer	`%5d` `%d`
f	Fixed-point (everyday notation) floating point	`%6.2f` `%f`
e	E-notation floating point	`%8.3e` `%e`
g	General floating point (Java decides whether to use E-notation or not)	`%8.3g` `%g`
s	String	`%12s` `%s`
c	Character	`%2c` `%c`

s and c

The s and c formats, for strings and characters, may include one number that specifies the field width for outputting the value, such as %15s and %2c. If no number is given, the value is output with no leading or trailing blank space.

right justified

left justified

When the value output does not fill the field width specified, blanks are added in front of the value output. The output is then said to be **right justified**. If you add a hyphen after the %, any extra blank space is placed after the value output, and the output is said to be **left justified**. For example, the lines

```
double value = 12.123;
System.out.printf("Start%8.2fEnd", value);
System.out.println();
System.out.printf("Start%-8.2fEnd", value);
System.out.println();
```

produce the following output. The first line has three spaces before the 12.12 and the second has three spaces after the 12.12.

```
Start   12.12End
Start12.12   End
```

more arguments

format string

So far we have used printf to output only one value. However, printf can output any number of values. The first argument always is a string known as the **format string**, which can be followed with any number of additional arguments, each of which is a value to output. The format string should include one format specifier, such as %6.2f or %s, for each value output, and they should be in the same order as the values to be output. For example,

```
double price = 19.8;
String name = "magic apple";
System.out.printf("$%6.2f for each %s.", price, name);
System.out.println();
System.out.println("Wow");
```

This code outputs the following:

```
$ 19.80 for each magic apple.
Wow
```

new lines

Note that the format string may contain text as well as format specifiers, and this text is output along with the values of the other arguments to printf.

You can include line breaks in a format string. For example, the following two lines

```
System.out.printf("$%6.2f for each %s.", price, name);
System.out.println();
```

can be replaced by the single line below, which uses the escape sequence \n:

```
System.out.printf("$%6.2f for each %s.\n", price, name);
```

%n

Although it is legal to use the escape sequence `\n` to indicate a line break in a format string, it is preferable to use `%n`. Exactly what happens when a `\n` is output can be system dependent, whereas `%n` should always mean a simple new line on any system. So our last line of code would be a little more robust if rewritten using `%n` as follows:

```
System.out.printf("$%6.2f for each %s.%n", price, name);
```

Many of the details we have discussed about `printf` are illustrated in the program given in Display 2.2.

TIP: Formatting Monetary Amounts with `printf`

A good format specifier for outputting an amount of money stored as a value of type `double` (or other floating-point value) is `%.2f`. It says to include exactly two digits after the decimal point and to use the smallest field width that the value will fit into. For example,

```
double price = 19.99;
System.out.printf("The price is $%.2f each.", price);
```

produces the following output:

```
The price is $19.99 each.
```

Display 2.2 **The `printf` Method** (part 1 of 2)

```
public class PrintfDemo
{
    public static void main(String[] args)
    {
        String aString = "abc";

        System.out.println("String output:");
        System.out.println("START1234567890");
        System.out.printf("START%sEND %n", aString);
        System.out.printf("START%4sEND %n", aString);
        System.out.printf("START%2sEND %n", aString);
        System.out.println();

        char oneCharacter = 'Z';

        System.out.println("Character output:");
        System.out.println("START1234567890");
        System.out.printf("START%cEND %n", oneCharacter);
        System.out.printf("START%4cEND %n", oneCharacter);
        System.out.println();
```

(continued)

Display 2.2 The `printf` Method (part 2 of 2)

```
        double d = 12345.123456789;

        System.out.println("Floating-point output:");
        System.out.println("START1234567890");
        System.out.printf("START%fEND %n", d);
        System.out.printf("START%.4fEND %n", d);
        System.out.printf("START%.2fEND %n", d);
        System.out.printf("START%12.4fEND %n", d);
        System.out.printf("START%eEND %n", d);
        System.out.printf("START%12.5eEND %n", d);
    }
}
```

Sample Dialogue

```
String output:
START1234567890
STARTabcEND
START abcEND
STARTabcEND

Character output:
START1234567890
STARTZEND
START   ZEND

Floating-point output:
START1234567890
START12345.123457END
START12345.1235END
START12345.12END
START  12345.1235END
START1.234512e+04END
START 1.23451e+04END
```

The value is always output. If the specified field width is too small, extra space is taken.

Note that the output is rounded, not truncated, when digits are discarded.

TIP: Legacy Code

legacy code

Some code is so expensive to replace, it is used even if it is "old fashioned" or otherwise less than ideal. This sort of code is called **legacy code**. One approach to legacy code is to translate it into a more modern language. The Java method `printf` is essentially the same as a function[1] in the C language that is also named `printf`. This was done intentionally so that it would be easier to translate C code into Java code. ■

[1] Methods are called *functions* in the C and C++ languages.

> **System.out.printf**
>
> System.out.printf is used for formatted screen output. System.out.printf can have any number of arguments. The first argument is always a format string for the remaining arguments. All the arguments except the first are values to be output to the screen, and these values are output in the formats specified by the format string. The format string can contain text as well as format specifiers, and this text is output along with the values.

MyProgrammingLab™

Self-Test Exercises

5. What output is produced by the following code?

```
String aString = "Jelly beans";

System.out.println("START1234567890");
System.out.printf("START%sEND %n", aString);
System.out.printf("START%4sEND %n", aString);
System.out.printf("START%13sEND %n", aString);
System.out.println();
```

6. What output is produced by the following code? For each output line, describe whether the line begins or ends with a blank or blanks.

```
String aString = "Jelly beans";
double d = 123.1234567890;

System.out.println("START1234567890");
System.out.printf("START%sEND %n %9.4f %n", aString, d);
```

7. Write a Java statement to output the value in variable `d` of type `double` to the screen. The output should be in `e`-notation with three digits after the decimal point. The output should be in a field of width 15.

Money Formats Using `NumberFormat` ★

NumberFormat

Using the class `NumberFormat`, you can tell Java to use the appropriate format when outputting amounts of money. The technique is illustrated in Display 2.3. Let's look at the code in the `main` method that does the formatting. First consider the following:

```
NumberFormat moneyFormatter =
                    NumberFormat.getCurrencyInstance();
```

The method invocation `NumberFormat.getCurrencyInstance()` produces an object of the class `NumberFormat` and names the object `moneyFormatter`. You can use any

Display 2.3 **Currency Format** (part 1 of 2)

```
import java.text.NumberFormat;
import java.util.Locale;

public class CurrencyFormatDemo
{
    public static void main(String[] args)
    {
        System.out.println("Without formatting:");

        System.out.println(19.8);
        System.out.println(19.81111);
        System.out.println(19.89999);
        System.out.println(19);
        System.out.println();

        System.out.println("Default location:");
        NumberFormat moneyFormatter =
                            NumberFormat.getCurrencyInstance();

        System.out.println(moneyFormatter.format(19.8));
        System.out.println(moneyFormatter.format(19.81111));
        System.out.println(moneyFormatter.format(19.89999));
        System.out.println(moneyFormatter.format(19));
        System.out.println();

        System.out.println("US as location:");
        NumberFormat moneyFormatter2 =
                            NumberFormat.getCurrencyInstance(Locale.US);

        System.out.println(moneyFormatter2.format(19.8));
        System.out.println(moneyFormatter2.format(19.81111));
        System.out.println(moneyFormatter2.format(19.89999));
        System.out.println(moneyFormatter2.format(19));
    }

}
```

If you use only the default location, you do not need to import `Locale`.

Notice that this number is rounded to 19.90.

valid identifier (other than a keyword) in place of `moneyFormatter`. This object `moneyFormatter` has a method named `format` that takes a floating-point number as an argument and returns a `String` value representing that number in the local currency (the default currency). For example, the following invocation

```
moneyFormatter.format(19.8)
```

Display 2.3 **Currency Format** (part 2 of 2)

Sample Dialogue

```
Without formatting:
19.8
19.81111
19.89999
19

Default location:
$19.80
$19.81
$19.90
$19.00

US as location:
$19.80
$19.81
$19.90
$19.00
```

This assumes that the system is set to use U.S. as the default location. If you are not in the U.S., you will probably get the format for your local currency.

This should give you the format for U.S. currency no matter what country has been set as the default location.

returns the `String` value `"$19.80"`, assuming the default currency is the U.S. dollar. In Display 2.3, this method invocation occurs inside a `System.out.println` statement, but it is legal anyplace a `String` value is legal. For example, the following would be legal:

```
String moneyString = moneyFormatter.format(19.8);
```

In order to make the class `NumberFormat` available to your code, you must include the following near the start of the file with your program:

```
import java.text.NumberFormat;
```

This is illustrated in Display 2.3.

The method invocation `NumberFormat.getCurrencyInstance()` produces an object that formats numbers according to the default location. In Display 2.3, we are assuming the default location is the United States, and so the numbers are output as U.S. dollars. On other systems, the default should be set to the local currency. If you wish, you can specify the location, and hence the local currency, by giving an argument to `NumberFormat.getCurrencyInstance`. For example, in Display 2.3, we used the constant `Locale.US` to specify that the location is the United States. The relevant line from Display 2.3 is repeated in what follows:

```
NumberFormat moneyFormatter2 =
                NumberFormat.getCurrencyInstance(Locale.US);
```

Some constants for other countries (and hence other currencies) are given in Display 2.4. However, unless your screen is capable of displaying the currency symbol for the country whose constant you use, the output might not be as desired.

These location constants are objects of the class `Locale`. In order to make the class `Locale` and these constants available to your code, you must include the following near the start of the file with your program:

```
import java.util.Locale;
```

If you do not use any of these location constants and use only the default location, you do not need this `import` statement.

The notation `Locale.US` may seem a bit strange, but it follows a convention that is frequently used in Java code. The constant is named `US`, but we want specifically that constant named `US` that is defined in the class `Locale`. So we use `Locale.US`. The notation `Locale.US` means the constant `US` as defined in the class `Locale`.

Importing Packages and Classes

package

Libraries in Java are called **packages**. A package is simply a collection of classes that has been given a name and stored in such a way as to make it easily accessible to your Java programs. Java has a large number of standard packages that automatically come with Java. Two such packages are named `java.text` and `java.util`. In Display 2.3, we used the class `NumberFormat`, which is a member of the package `java.text`. In order to use `NumberFormat`, you must import the class, which we did as follows:

java.text

```
import java.text.NumberFormat;
```

Display 2.4 Locale Constants for Currencies of Different Countries

Locale.CANADA	Canada (for currency, the format is the same as U.S.)
Locale.CHINA	China
Locale.FRANCE	France
Locale.GERMANY	Germany
Locale.ITALY	Italy
Localo.JAPAN	Japan
Locale.KOREA	Korea
Locale.TAIWAN	Taiwan
Locale.UK	United Kingdom (English pound)
Locale.US	United States

> **Outputting Amounts of Money**
>
> Using the class `NumberFormat`, you can output an amount of money correctly formatted. The procedure to do so is described here.
>
> Place the following near the start of the file containing your program:
>
> ```
> import java.text.NumberFormat;
> ```
>
> In your program code, create an object of the class `NumberFormat` as follows:
>
> ```
> NumberFormat formatterObject =
>                  NumberFormat.getCurrencyInstance();
> ```
>
> When outputting numbers for amounts of money, change the number to a value of type `String` using the method `FormatterObject.format`, as illustrated in the following:
>
> ```
> double moneyAmount = 9.99;
> System.out.println(formatterObject.format(moneyAmount));
> ```
>
> The string produced by invocations such as `formatterObject.format(moneyAmount)` adds the dollar sign and ensures that there are exactly two digits after the decimal point. (This is assuming the U.S. dollar is the default currency.)
>
> The numbers formatted in this way may be of type `double`, `int`, or `long`. You may use any (nonkeyword) identifier in place of `formatterObject`. A complete example is given in Display 2.3.
>
> The above always outputs the money amount in the default currency, which is typically the local currency. You can specify the country whose currency you want. See the text for details.

import statement

This kind of statement is called an **import statement**. In this example, the import statement tells Java to look in the package `java.text` to find the definition of the class `NumberFormat`.

If you want to import all the classes in the `java.text` package, use the following:

```
import java.text.*;
```

Then you can use any class in the `java.text` package.

You don't lose any efficiency in importing the entire package instead of importing only the classes you use. However, many programmers find that it is an aid to documentation if they import only the classes they use, which is what we will do in this book.

`java.util`

In Display 2.3, we also used the class `Locale`, which is in the `java.util` package. So we also included the following import statement:

```
import java.util.Locale;
```

java.lang

One package requires no import statement. The package `java.lang` contains classes that are fundamental to Java programming. These classes are so basic that the package is always imported automatically. Any class in `java.lang` does not need an import statement to make it available to your code. So, when we say that a class is in the package `java.lang`, you can simply use that class in your program without needing any import statement. For example, the class `String` is in the `java.lang` package, so you can use it without any import statement.

More material on packages is covered in Chapter 5.

MyProgrammingLab™

Self-Test Exercises

8. What output is produced by the following code? (Assume a proper `import` statement has been given.)

```
NumberFormat exerciseFormatter =
                 NumberFormat.getCurrencyInstance(Locale.US);
double d1 = 1.2345, d2 = 15.67890;
System.out.println(exerciseFormatter.format(d1));
System.out.println(exerciseFormatter.format(d2));
```

9. Suppose the class `Robot` is a part of the standard Java libraries and is in the package named `java.awt`. What `import` statement do you need to make the class `Robot` available to your program or other class?

The `DecimalFormat` Class ★

`System.out.println` will let you output numbers but has no facilities to format the numbers. If you want to output a number in a specific format, such as having a specified number of digits after the decimal point, then you must convert the number to a string that shows the number in the desired format and then use `System.out.println` to output the string. Earlier in this chapter, we saw one way to accomplish this for amounts of money. The class `DecimalFormat` provides a versatile facility to format numbers in a variety of ways.

The class `DecimalFormat` is in the Java package named `java.text`. So you must add the following (or something similar) to the beginning of the file with your program or other class that uses the class `DecimalFormat`:

import

```
import java.text.DecimalFormat;
```

An object of the class `DecimalFormat` has a number of different methods that can be used to produce numeral strings in various formats. In this subsection, we discuss one of these methods, which is named `format`. The general approach to using the `format` method is discussed in the following pages.

patterns

Create an object of the class `DecimalFormat`, using a `String` *Pattern* as follows:

```
DecimalFormat Variable_Name = new DecimalFormat(Pattern);
```

For example,

```
DecimalFormat formattingObject = new DecimalFormat("000.000");
```

The method `format` of the class `DecimalFormat` can then be used to convert a floating-point number, such as one of type `double`, to a corresponding numeral `String` following the *Pattern* used to create the `DecimalFormat` object. Specifically, an invocation of `format` takes the form

Decimal_Format_Object.`format`(*Double_Expression*)

which returns a `String` value for a string representation of the value of *Double_Expression*. *Double_Expression* can be any expression, such as a variable or sum of variables, that evaluates to a value of type `double`.

For example, consider the following code:

```
DecimalFormat formattingObject = new DecimalFormat("000.0000");
String numeral = formattingObject.format(12.3456789);
System.out.println(numeral);
```

This produces the following output:

```
012.3457
```

Of course, you can use an invocation of `format`, such as `formattingObject.format(12.3456789)`, directly in `System.out.println`. So, the following code produces the same output:

```
System.out.println(formattingObject.format(12.3456789));
```

The format of the string produced is determined by the *Pattern* string that was used as the argument to the constructor that created the object of the class `DecimalFormat`. For example, the pattern `"000.0000"` means that there will be three digits before the decimal point and four digits after the decimal point. Note that the result is rounded when the number of digits is less than the number of digits available in the number being formatted. If the format pattern is not consistent with the value of the number, such as a pattern that asks for two digits before the decimal point for a number such as `123.456`, then the format rules are violated so that no digits are lost.

A pattern can specify the exact number of digits before and after the decimal, or it can specify minimum numbers of digits. The character `'0'` is used to represent a required digit, and the character `'#'` is used to indicate an optional digit. For example, the pattern `"#0.0##"` indicates one or two digits before the decimal point and one, two, or three digits after the decimal point. The optional digit `'#'` is shown if it is a nonzero digit and is not shown if it is a zero digit. The `'#'` optional digits should go where zero placeholders would appear in a numeral string; in other words, any `'#'` optional digits precede the zero digits `'0'` before the decimal point in the pattern, and any '#' optional digits follow the zero digits '0' after the decimal point in the pattern. Use "#0.0##"; do not use "0#.0##" or "#0.##0".

For example, consider the following code:

```
DecimalFormat formattingObject = new DecimalFormat("#0.0##");
System.out.println(formattingObject.format(12.3456789));
System.out.println(formattingObject.format(1.23456789));
```

This produces the following output:

```
12.346
1.235
```

percentages

The character '%' placed at the end of a pattern indicates that the number is to be expressed as a percentage. The '%' causes the number to be multiplied by 100 and appends a percent sign, '%'. Examples of this and other formatting patterns are given in Display 2.5.

E-notation

E-notation is specified by including an 'E' in the pattern string. For example, the pattern '00.###E0" approximates specifying two digits before the decimal point, three or fewer digits after the decimal point, and at least one digit after the 'E', as in 12.346E1. As you can see by the examples of E-notation in Display 2.5, the exact details of which E-notation string is produced can be a bit more involved than our explanation so far. Here are a couple more details:

The number of digits indicated after the 'E' is the minimum number of digits used for the exponent. As many more digits as are needed will be used.

mantissa

The **mantissa** is the decimal number before the 'E'. The minimum number of significant digits in the mantissa (that is, the sum of the number of digits before and after the decimal point) is the *minimum* of the number of digits indicated before the decimal point plus the *maximum* of the number of digits indicated after the decimal point. For example, 12345 formatted with "##0.##E0" is "12.3E3".

To get a feel for how E-notation patterns work, it would pay to play with a few cases. In any event, do not count on a very precisely specified number of significant digits.

DecimalFormat Class

Objects of the class DecimalFormat are used to produce strings of a specified format from numbers. As such, these objects can be used to format numeric output. The object is associated with a pattern when it is created using new. The object can then be used with the method format to create strings that satisfy the format. See Display 2.5 for examples of the DecimalFormat class in use.

Display 2.5 The `DecimalFormat` Class (part 1 of 2)

```java
import java.text.DecimalFormat;

public class DecimalFormatDemo
{
    public static void main(String[] args)
    {
        DecimalFormat pattern00dot000 = new DecimalFormat("00.000");
        DecimalFormat pattern0dot00 = new DecimalFormat("0.00");

        double d = 12.3456789;
        System.out.println("Pattern 00.000");
        System.out.println(pattern00dot000.format(d));
        System.out.println("Pattern 0.00");
        System.out.println(pattern0dot00.format(d));

        double money = 19.8;
        System.out.println("Pattern 0.00");
        System.out.println("$" + pattern0dot00.format(money));

        DecimalFormat percent = new DecimalFormat("0.00%");

        System.out.println("Pattern 0.00%");
        System.out.println(percent.format(0.308));

        DecimalFormat eNotation1 =
            new DecimalFormat("#0.###E0"); //1 or 2 digits before point
        DecimalFormat eNotation2 =
            new DecimalFormat("00.###E0"); //2 digits before point

        System.out.println("Pattern #0.###E0");
        System.out.println(eNotation1.format(123.456));
        System.out.println("Pattern 00.###E0");
        System.out.println(eNotation2.format(123.456));

        double smallNumber = 0.0000123456;
        System.out.println("Pattern #0.###E0");
        System.out.println(eNotation1.format(smallNumber));
        System.out.println("Pattern 00.###E0");
        System.out.println(eNotation2.format(smallNumber));
    }
}
```

(continued)

Display 2.5 The `DecimalFormat` Class (part 2 of 2)

Sample Dialogue

```
Pattern 00.000
12.346
Pattern 0.00
12.35
Pattern 0.00
$19.80
Pattern 0.00%
30.80%
Pattern #0.###E0
1.2346E2
Pattern 00.###E0
12.346E1
Pattern #0.###E0
12.346E-6
Pattern 00.###E0
12.346E-6
```

The number is always given, even if this requires violating the format pattern.

2.2 Console Input Using the `Scanner` Class

Let the world tell me.

FRANK SHAKESPEARE, *Franky I*

Starting with version 5.0, Java includes a class for doing simple keyboard input. In this section, we show you how to do keyboard input using this class, which is named `Scanner`.

The `Scanner` Class

Display 2.6 contains a simple program that uses the `Scanner` class to read two `int` values typed in on the keyboard. The numbers entered on the keyboard are shown in **bold**. Let's go over the `Scanner`-related details line by line. The following line, which should be placed near the start of the file, tells Java where to find the definition of the `Scanner` class:

import

```
import java.util.Scanner;
```

This line says the `Scanner` class is in the `java.util` package; `util` is short for *utility*, but in Java code, you always use the abbreviated spelling `util`. A package is simply a library of classes. This import statement makes the `Scanner` class available to your program.

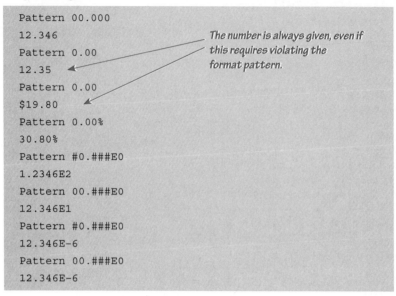

Display 2.6 **Keyboard Input Demonstration**

```
import java.util.Scanner;

public class ScannerDemo
{
    public static void main(String[] args)
    {
        Scanner keyboard = new Scanner(System.in);

        System.out.println("Enter the number of pods followed by");
        System.out.println("the number of peas in a pod:");
        int numberOfPods = keyboard.nextInt();
        int peasPerPod = keyboard.nextInt();

        int totalNumberOfPeas = numberOfPods*peasPerPod;

        System.out.print(numberOfPods + " pods and ");
        System.out.println(peasPerPod + " peas per pod.");
        System.out.println("The total number of peas = "
                                              + totalNumberOfPeas);
    }
}
```

Makes the `Scanner` class available to your program.

Creates an object of the class `Scanner` and names the object `keyboard`.

Each reads one `int` from the keyboard

Sample Dialogue 1

```
Enter the number of pods followed by
the number of peas in a pod:
22 10
22 pods and 10 peas per pod.
The total number of peas = 220
```

The numbers that are input must be separated by whitespace, such as one or more blanks.

Sample Dialogue 2

```
Enter the number of pods followed by
the number of peas in a pod:
22
10
22 pods and 10 peas per pod.
The total number of peas = 220
```

A line break is also considered whitespace and can be used to separate the numbers typed in at the keyboard.

The following line creates an object of the class `Scanner` and names the object `keyboard`:

```
Scanner keyboard = new Scanner(System.in);
```

After this line appears, you can use methods of the `Scanner` class with the object `keyboard` to read data that the user types on the keyboard. For example, the method

nextInt

`nextInt` reads one `int` value typed on the keyboard. So, the following line from Display 2.6 reads one value of type `int` and makes that the value of the variable `numberOfPods`:

```
int numberOfPods = keyboard.nextInt();
```

In Display 2.6, two such statements each read one `int` value that the user types in at the keyboard:

```
int numberOfPods = keyboard.nextInt();
int peasPerPod = keyboard.nextInt();
```

whitespace

The numbers typed in must be separated by **whitespace**, such as one or more spaces, a line break, or other whitespace. Whitespace is any string of characters, such as blank spaces, tabs, and line breaks, that prints as whitespace when written on (white) paper.

We often use the identifier `keyboard` for our `Scanner` object because the object is being used for keyboard input. However, you may use other names. If you instead want your object of the class `Scanner` to be named `scannerObject`, you would use the following:

```
Scanner scannerObject = new Scanner(System.in);
```

To read a single `int` value from the keyboard and save it in the `int` variable `n1`, you would then use the following:

```
n1 = scannerObject.nextInt();
```

This is illustrated in the program in Display 2.7.

The program in Display 2.7 also illustrates some of the other `Scanner` methods for

nextDouble

reading values from the keyboard. The method `nextDouble` works in exactly the same way as `nextInt`, except that it reads a value of type `double`. The following example is from Display 2.7:

```
double d1, d2;
d1 = scannerObject.nextDouble();
d2 = scannerObject.nextDouble();
System.out.println("You entered " + d1 + " and " + d2);
```

Display 2.7 **Another Keyboard Input Demonstration** (part 1 of 2)

```
import java.util.Scanner;

public class ScannerDemo2
{
    public static void main(String[] args)
    {
       int n1, n2;
       Scanner scannerObject = new Scanner(System.in);

       System.out.println("Enter two whole numbers");
       System.out.println("separated by one or more spaces:");

       n1 = scannerObject.nextInt();
       n2 = scannerObject.nextInt();
       System.out.println("You entered " + n1 + " and " + n2);

       System.out.println("Next enter two numbers.");
       System.out.println("Decimal points are allowed.");

       double d1, d2;
       d1 = scannerObject.nextDouble();
       d2 = scannerObject.nextDouble();
       System.out.println("You entered " + d1 + " and " + d2);

       System.out.println("Next enter two words:");

       String word1 = scannerObject.next();
       String word2 = scannerObject.next();
       System.out.println("You entered \"" +
                              word1 + "\" and \"" + word2 + "\"");

       String junk = scannerObject.nextLine(); //To get rid of '\n'

       System.out.println("Next enter a line of text:");
       String line = scannerObject.nextLine();
       System.out.println("You entered: \"" + line + "\"");
    }
}
```

Creates an object of the class **`Scanner`** *and names the object* **`scannerObject`**.

Reads one **`int`** *from the keyboard.*

Reads one **`double`** *from the keyboard.*

Reads one word from the keyboard.

(continued)

Display 2.7 **Another Keyboard Input Demonstration** (part 2 of 2)

Sample Dialogue

```
Enter two whole numbers
separated by one or more spaces:
  42   43
You entered 42 and 43
Next enter two numbers.
A decimal point is OK.
 9.99  57
You entered 9.99 and 57.0
Next enter two words:
jelly beans
You entered "jelly" and "beans"
Next enter a line of text:
Java flavored jelly beans are my favorite.
You entered "Java flavored jelly beans are my favorite."
```

The method `next` reads in a word, as illustrated by the following lines from Display 2.7:

```
String word1 = scannerObject.next();
String word2 = scannerObject.next();
```

If the input line is

```
jelly beans
```

then this will assign `w1` the string `"jelly"` and `w2` the string `"beans"`.

word

For the method `next`, a **word** is any string of nonwhitespace characters delimited by whitespace characters such as blanks or the beginning or ending of a line.

If you want to read in an entire line, you would use the method `nextLine`. For example,

```
String line = scannerObject.nextLine();
```

reads in one line of input and places the string that is read into the variable `line`.

The end of an input line is indicated by the escape sequence `'\n'`. This `'\n'` character is what you input when you press the Enter (Return) key on the keyboard. On the screen, it is indicated by the ending of one line and the beginning of the next line. When `nextLine` reads a line of text, it reads this `'\n'` character, so the next reading of input begins on the next line. However, the `'\n'` does not become part of the string value returned. So, in the previous code, the string named by the variable `line` does not end with the `'\n'` character.

These and other methods for reading in values from the keyboard are given in Display 2.8.

Display 2.8 Methods of the **`Scanner`** Class (part 1 of 2)

The `Scanner` class can be used to obtain input from files as well as from the keyboard. However, here we are assuming it is being used only for input from the keyboard.

To set things up for keyboard input, you need the following at the beginning of the file with the keyboard input code:

```
import java.util.Scanner;
```

You also need the following before the first keyboard input statement:

`Scanner` *Scanner_Object_Name* = `new Scanner(System.in);`

The *`Scanner_Object_Name`* can then be used with the following methods to read and return various types of data typed on the keyboard.

Values to be read should be separated by whitespace characters, such as blanks and/or new lines. When reading values, these whitespace characters are skipped. (It is possible to change the separators from whitespace to something else, but whitespace is the default and is what we will use.)

Scanner_Object_Name`.nextInt()`

Returns the next value of type `int` that is typed on the keyboard.

Scanner_Object_Name`.nextLong()`

Returns the next value of type `long` that is typed on the keyboard.

Scanner_Object_Name`.nextByte()`

Returns the next value of type `byte` that is typed on the keyboard.

Scanner_Object_Name`.nextShort()`

Returns the next value of type `short` that is typed on the keyboard.

Scanner_Object_Name `.nextDouble()`

Returns the next value of type `double` that is typed on the keyboard.

Scanner_Object_Name `.nextFloat()`

Returns the next value of type `float` that is typed on the keyboard.

Scanner_Object_Name `.next()`

Returns the `String` value consisting of the next keyboard characters up to, but not including, the first delimiter character. The default delimiters are whitespace characters.

(continued)

Display 2.8 Methods of the Scanner Class (part 2 of 2)

Scanner_Object_Name `.nextBoolean()`

Returns the next value of type `boolean` that is typed on the keyboard. The values of `true` and `false` are entered as the strings `"true"` and `"false"`. Any combination of upper- and/or lowercase letters is allowed in spelling `"true"` and `"false"`.

Scanner_Object_Name `.nextLine()`

Reads the rest of the current keyboard input line and returns the characters read as a value of type `String`. Note that the line terminator '\n' is read and discarded; it is not included in the string returned.

Scanner_Object_Name `.useDelimiter(`*New_Delimiter*`);`

Changes the delimiter for keyboard input with *Scanner_Object_Name*. The *New_Delimiter* is a value of type `String`. After this statement is executed, *New_Delimiter* is the only delimiter that separates words or numbers. See the subsection "Other Input Delimiters", later in this chapter, for details.

Keyboard Input Using the `Scanner` Class

You can use an object of the class `Scanner` to read input from the keyboard. To make the `Scanner` class available for use in your code, you should include the following at the start of the file that contains your program (or other code that does keyboard input):

```
import java.util.Scanner;
```

Before you do any keyboard input, you must create an object of the class `Scanner` as follows:

```
Scanner Object_Name = new Scanner(System.in);
```

where *Object_Name* is any (nonkeyword) Java identifier. For example,

```
Scanner keyboard = new Scanner(System.in);
```

The methods `nextInt`, `nextDouble`, and `next` read a value of type `int`, a value of type `double`, and a word, respectively. The method `nextLine` reads the remainder of the current input line including the terminating `'\n'`. However, the `'\n'` is not included in the string value returned. Other input methods are given in Display 2.8.

SYNTAX

```
Int_Variable = Object_Name.nextInt()
Double_Variable = Object_Name.nextDouble();
String_Variable = Object_Name.next();
String_Variable = Object_Name.nextLine();
```

EXAMPLE

```
int number;
number = keyboard.nextInt();
double cost;
cost = keyboard.nextDouble();
String word;
word = keyboard.next();
String line;
line = keyboard.nextLine();
```

PITFALL: Dealing with the Line Terminator, '\n'

The method `nextLine` of the class `Scanner` reads the *remainder* of a line of text *starting wherever the last keyboard reading left off.* For example, suppose you create an object of the class `Scanner` as follows:

```
Scanner keyboard = new Scanner(System.in);
```

Suppose you continue with the following code:

VideoNote
Pitfalls Involving `nextLine()`

```
int n = keyboard.nextInt();
String s1 = keyboard.nextLine();
String s2 = keyboard.nextLine();
```

Now, assume that the input typed on the keyboard is the following:

```
2 heads are
better than
1 head.
```

This sets the value of the variable `n` to `2`, that of the variable `s1` to `"heads are"`, and that of the variable `s2` to `"better than"`.

So far there are no problems, but suppose the input were instead as follows:

```
2
heads are better than
1 head.
```

You might expect the value of `n` to be set to `2`, the value of the variable `s1` to `"heads are better than"`, and that of the variable `s2` to `"1 head."` But that is not what happens.

What actually happens is that the value of the variable `n` is set to `2`, that of the variable `s1` is set to the empty string, and that of the variable `s2` to `"heads are better than"`. The method `nextInt` reads the `2` but does not read the end-of-line character `'\n'`. So the first `nextLine` invocation reads the rest of the line that contains the `2`.

(continued)

PITFALL: (continued)

There is nothing more on that line (except for `'\n'`), so `nextLine` returns the empty string. The second invocation of `nextLine` begins on the next line and reads `"heads are better than"`.

When combining different methods for reading from the keyboard, you sometimes have to include an extra invocation of `nextLine` to get rid of the end of a line (to get rid of a `'\n'`). This is illustrated in Display 2.7. ■

The Empty String

empty string

A string can have any number of characters. For example, `"Hello"` has five characters. There is a string with zero characters, which is called the **empty string**. The empty string is written with a pair of double quotes, with nothing in between the quotes, like so: `""`. The empty string is encountered more often than you might think. If your code is executing the `nextLine` method to read a line of text, and the user types nothing on the line other than pressing the Enter (Return) key, then the `nextLine` method reads the empty string.

TIP: Prompt for Input

Always prompt the user when your program needs the user to input some data, as in the following example:

```
System.out.println("Enter the number of pods followed by");
System.out.println("the number of peas in a pod:");
```
■

TIP: Echo Input

echo input

You should normally **echo input**. That is, you should write to the screen all input that your program receives from the keyboard. This way, the user can check that the input has been entered correctly. For example, the following two statements from the program in Display 2.9 echo the values that were read for the number of pods and the number of peas per pod:

```
System.out.print(numberOfPods + " pods and ");
System.out.println(peasPerPod + " peas per pod.");
```

It might seem that there is no need to echo input, because the user's input is automatically displayed on the screen as the user enters it. Why bother to write it to the screen a second time? The input might be incorrect even though it looks correct. For example, the user might type a comma instead of a decimal point or the letter O in place of a zero. Echoing the input can expose such problems. ■

Display 2.9 **Self-Service Checkout Line**

```
import java.util.Scanner;

public class SelfService
{
    public static void main(String[] args)
    {
        Scanner keyboard = new Scanner(System.in);

        System.out.println("Enter number of items purchased");
        System.out.println("followed by the cost of one item.");
        System.out.println("Do not use a dollar sign.");

        int count = keyboard.nextInt();
        double price = keyboard.nextDouble();
        double total = count*price;

        System.out.printf("%d items at $%.2f each.%n", count, price);
        System.out.printf("Total amount due $%.2f.%n", total);

        System.out.println("Please take your merchandise.");
        System.out.printf("Place $%.2f in an envelope %n", total);
        System.out.println("and slide it under the office door.");
        System.out.println("Thank you for using the self-service line.");
    }
}
```

The dot after `%.2f` is a period in the text, not part of the format specifier.

Sample Dialogue

```
Enter number of items purchased
followed by the cost of one item.
Do not use a dollar sign.
  10   19.99
10 items at $19.99 each.
Total amount due $199.90.
Please take your merchandise.
Place $199.90 in an envelope
and slide it under the office door.
Thank you for using the self-service line.
```

MyProgrammingLab™

Self-Test Exercises

10. Write an import statement that makes the `Scanner` class available to your program or other class.

11. Write a line of code that creates a `Scanner` object named `frank` to be used for obtaining keyboard input.

12. Write a line of code that uses the object `frank` from the previous exercise to read in a word from the keyboard and store the word in the `String` variable named `w`.

13. Write a complete Java program that reads in a line of keyboard input containing two values of type `int` (separated by one or more spaces) and outputs the two numbers as well as the sum of the two numbers.

14. Write a complete Java program that reads in a line of text containing exactly three words (separated by any kind or amount of whitespace) and outputs the line with spacing corrected; that is, the output has no space before the first word and exactly one space between each pair of adjacent words.

15. Something could go wrong with the following code. Identify and fix the problem.

```
Scanner keyboard = new Scanner(System.in);
System.out.println("Enter your age.");
int age = keyboard.nextInt();
System.out.println("Enter your name.");
String name = keyboard.nextLine();
System.out.println(name + ",you are " + age + " years old.");
```

EXAMPLE: Self-Service Checkout

Display 2.9 contains a first draft of a program to use in the self-service line of a hardware store. It still needs some more details and even some more hardware for accepting payment. However, it does illustrate the use of the `Scanner` class for keyboard input and the `printf` method for formatted output.

Note that in `printf`, we used the format specifier `%.2f` for amounts of money. This specifies a floating-point number with exactly two digits after the decimal point, but gives no field width. Because no field width is given, the number output is placed in the fewest number of spaces that still allows the full value to be shown.

Other Input Delimiters

When using the `Scanner` class for keyboard input, you can change the delimiters that separate keyboard input to almost any combination of characters, but the details are a bit involved. In this book, we will describe only one simple kind of delimiter change. We will tell you how to change the delimiters from whitespace to one specific delimiter string.

For example, suppose you create a `Scanner` object as follows:

```
Scanner keyboard2 = new Scanner(System.in);
```

You can change the delimiter for the object `keyboard2` to `"##"` as follows:

```
keyboard2.useDelimiter("##");
```

After this invocation of the `useDelimiter` method, `"##"` will be the only input delimiter for the input object `keyboard2`. Note that whitespace will no longer be a delimiter for keyboard input done with `keyboard2`. For example, suppose the user enters the following keyboard input:

```
one two##three##
```

The following code would read the two strings `"one  two"` and `"three"` and make them the values of the variables `word1` and `word2`:

```
String word1, word2;
word1 = keyboard2.next();
word2 = keyboard2.next();
```

This is illustrated in Display 2.10. Note that you can have two different objects of the class `Scanner` with different delimiters in the same program.

Note that no whitespace characters, not even line breaks, serve as an input delimiter for `keyboard2` once this change is made to `keyboard2`.

MyProgrammingLab™

Self-Test Exercises

16. Suppose your code creates an object of the class `Scanner` named `keyboard` (as described in this chapter). Write code to change the delimiter for `keyboard` to a comma followed by a blank.

17. Continue with the object `keyboard` from Self-Test Exercise 16. Consider the following input:

```
one,two three, four, five
```

What values will the following code assign to the variables `word1` and `word2`?

```
String word1 = keyboard.next();
String word2 = keyboard.next();
```

Display 2.10 **Changing the Input Delimiter**

```java
import java.util.Scanner;

public class DelimiterDemo
{
    public static void main(String[] args)
    {
        Scanner keyboard1 = new Scanner(System.in);
        Scanner keyboard2 = new Scanner(System.in);
        keyboard2.useDelimiter("##");
        //Delimiter for keyboard1 is whitespace.
        //Delimiter for keyboard2 is ##.

        String word1, word2;
        System.out.println("Enter a line of text:");
        word1 = keyboard1.next();
        word2 = keyboard1.next();
        System.out.println("For keyboard1 the two words read are:");
        System.out.println(word1);
        System.out.println(word2);
        String junk = keyboard1.nextLine(); //To get rid of rest of line.

        System.out.println("Reenter the same line of text:");
        word1 = keyboard2.next();
        word2 = keyboard2.next();
        System.out.println("For keyboard2 the two words read are:");
        System.out.println(word1);
        System.out.println(word2);
    }
}
```

Sample Dialogue

```
Enter a line of text:
one two##three##
For keyboard1 the two words read are:
one
two##three##
Reenter the same line of text:
one two##three##
For keyboard2 the two words read are:
one two
three
```

2.3 Introduction to File Input

You shall see them on a beautiful quarto page, where a neat rivulet of text shall meander through a meadow of margin.

RICHARD BRINSLEY SHERIDAN, *The School for Scandal*

The `Scanner` class can also be used to read data from a text file. To do this, we must create a `Scanner` object and link it to the file on the disk. Once this is done, the program can read from the `Scanner` object in the same exact way that we read from the console, except the input will come from the file instead of typed from the keyboard. Details about reading and writing from files are not discussed until Chapter 10 and require an understanding of programming concepts we have not yet covered. However, we can provide just enough here so that your programs can read from text files. This will allow you to work on problems with real-world data that would otherwise be too much work to type into your program every time it is run.

The `Scanner` Class for Text File Input

To read from a text file, we need to import the classes `FileInputStream` and `FileNotFoundException` in addition to the `Scanner` class:

```
import java.io.FileInputStream;
import java.io.FileNotFoundException;
```

The `FileInputStream` class handles the connection between a Java program and a file on the disk. The `FileNotFoundException` class is used if a program attempts to open a file that doesn't exist.

To open the file, we create an object of type `Scanner` and then connect it with a `FileInputStream` object associated with the file. We have to handle the scenario where we try to open a file that doesn't exist. One way to do this is with a `try/catch` block. This is discussed more thoroughly in Chapter 9, but the basic format to open a file looks like this:

```
Scanner fileIn = null;  // initializes fileIn to empty
try
{
  // Attempt to open the file
  fileIn = new Scanner(new FileInputStream("PathToFile"));
}
catch (FileNotFoundException e)
{
  // If the file could not be found, this code is executed
  // and then the program exits
```

```
    System.out.println("File not found.");
    System.exit(0);
}
...  Code continues here
```

This code will create a `Scanner` variable named `fileIn` and initialize it to an empty (`null`) object. Next, Java will run the code inside the `try` block. If the file is not found, then control jumps directly to the `catch` block. In our example, we print out an error message and make the program exit immediately with the statement `System.exit(0)`.

If the file is found, then the `catch` block is skipped entirely and the program continues to execute whatever code comes after the catch. At this point, we can use `fileIn` exactly the same way we used a `Scanner` object connected to the console, except input will be provided from the file, not the keyboard.

For example, we can use `fileIn.nextInt()` to read an integer from the file, `fileIn.nextDouble()` to read a double from the file, `fileIn.next()` to read a string token from the file, or `fileIn.nextLine()` to read an entire line from the text file. Java begins reading from the beginning of the file and proceeds toward the end as data is read.

Unlike reading from the console, we might want to know if we have reached the end of the file. We can use `fileIn.hasNextLine()` to determine if there is data to read. When we are done with the file, we can close it with `fileIn.close()`, which will release any resources that have been allocated by Java in association with the file.

A complete example is shown in Displays 2.11 and 2.12. Display 2.11 shows the contents of a text file named `player.txt`. This file can be created by any program that saves in the plain text format. As an example, let's say that the file contains information about the last player to play a game. The first line of the file contains the high score of the player, 100510, and the second line contains the name of the player, Gordon Freeman. The program in Display 2.12 reads in this information and displays it. It reads in the high score using `nextInt()` and then reads in the name using `nextLine()`. Note that we have to use an additional `nextLine()` after the `nextInt()` to deal with the newline character for the exact same reason discussed earlier in this chapter in the Pitfall in Section 2.2 titled Dealing with the Line Terminator, '\n'.

Display 2.11 Sample Text File, **`player.txt`**, to Store a Player's High Score and Name

```
100510
Gordon Freeman
```

Display 2.12 **Program to Read the Text File in Display 2.11**

```
import java.util.Scanner;
import java.io.FileInputStream;
import java.io.FileNotFoundException;

public class TextFileDemo
{
  public static void main(String[] args)
  {
    Scanner fileIn = null;  // Initializes fileIn to empty
    try
    {
      // Attempt to open the file
      fileIn = new Scanner(
          new FileInputStream("player.txt"));
    }
    catch (FileNotFoundException e)
    {
      // This block executed if the file is not found
      // and then the program exits
      System.out.println("File not found.");
      System.exit(0);
    }

    // If the program gets here then
    // the file was opened successfully
    int highscore;
    String name;

    System.out.println("Text left to read? " +
        fileIn.hasNextLine());
    highscore = fileIn.nextInt();
    fileIn.nextLine(); // Read newline left from nextInt()
    name = fileIn.nextLine();

    System.out.println("Name: " + name);
    System.out.println("High score: " + highscore);
    System.out.println("Text left to read? " +
        fileIn.hasNextLine());
    fileIn.close();
  }
}
```

try and catch is explained in more detail in Chapter 9.

The file `player.txt` should be in the same directory as the Java program. You can also supply a full pathname to the file.

This line is explained earlier in this chapter in the Pitfall section "Dealing with the Line Terminator `'\n'`"

Sample Dialogue

```
Text left to read? true
Name: Gordon Freeman
High score: 100510
Text left to read? False
```

MyProgrammingLab™

Self-Test Exercises

18. What would the program in Display 2.12 output if there is no file named `player.txt` in the same directory as the Java program?

19. What is missing from the following code, which attempts to open a file and read an integer?

```
import java.util.Scanner;
import java.io.FileInputStream;
import java.io.FileNotFoundException;

public class ReadInteger
{
    public static void main(String[] args)
    {
        Scanner fileIn = new Scanner(
          new FileInputStream("datafile.txt"));
        int num = fileIn.nextInt();
        System.out.println(num);
    }
}
```

Chapter Summary

- You can use `System.out.println` for simple console output.
- You can use `System.out.printf` for formatted console output.
- You can use `NumberFormat.getCurrencyInstance()` to produce an object that can convert numbers to strings that show the number as a correctly formatted currency amount, for example, by adding a dollar sign and having exactly two digits after the decimal point.
- You can use the class `DecimalFormat` to output numbers using almost any format you desire.
- You can use an object of the class `Scanner` for reading keyboard input.
- You can use an object of the class `Scanner` for reading input from a text file.

Answers to Self-Test Exercises

1. `HelloJoe`

2.
```
System.out.println("One two buckle your shoe.");
System.out.println("Three four shut the door.");
```

3. `System.out.println` ends a line of input, so the next output goes on the next line. With `System.out.print`, the next output goes on the same line.

4. 2 2

```
4
```

Note that

```
2 + " " + 2
```

contains a string, namely `" "`. So, Java knows it is supposed to produce a string. On the other hand, `2 + 2` contains only integers. So Java thinks `+` denotes addition in this second case and produces the value `4` to be output.

5.
```
START1234567890
STARTJelly beansEND
STARTJelly beansEND
START  Jelly beansEND
```

6. The last two of the following lines end with a blank. The last line begins with two blanks, one that follows `%n` in the format string and one because the field width is `9` but the number to be output fills only eight spaces.

```
START1234567890
STARTJelly beansEND
  123.1235
```

7. `System.out.printf("%15.3e", d);`

8.
```
$1.23
$15.68
```

9. Either

```
import java.awt.Robot;
```

or

```
import java.awt.*;
```

10. `import java.util.Scanner;`

11. `Scanner frank = new Scanner(System.in);`

12. `w = frank.next();`

13.
```
import java.util.Scanner;
public class Exercise
{
   public static void main(String[] args)
   {
      Scanner keyboard = new Scanner(System.in);

      System.out.println("Enter two numbers.");
      int n1 = keyboard.nextInt();
      int n2 = keyboard.nextInt();

      int sum = n1 + n2;

      System.out.println(n1 + " plus " + n2 + " is " + sum);
   }
}
```

14.
```
import java.util.Scanner;

public class Exercise2
{
   public static void main(String[] args)
   {
      Scanner keyboard = new Scanner(System.in);

      System.out.println("Enter a line with three words:");
      String w1 = keyboard.next();
      String w2 = keyboard.next();
      String w3 = keyboard.next();
      System.out.println(w1 + " " + w2 + " " + w3);
   }
}
```

15. The newline character is left in the input buffer after the `nextInt()` call and should be removed prior to calling `nextLine()`. This can be fixed by adding another `nextLine()` call:

```
Scanner keyboard = new Scanner(System.in);
System.out.println("Enter your age.");
int age = keyboard.nextInt();
keyboard.nextLine();
System.out.println("Enter your name.");
String name = keyboard.nextLine();
System.out.println(name+", you are "+age+" years old.");
```

16. `keyboard.useDelimiter(", ");`

17. `w1` is assigned `"one,two three"`; `w2` is assigned `"four"`.

18. The program will output `"File not found."` and exit.

19. The statement that attempts to open the file must be inside a try/catch block, as follows:

```
try
{
   Scanner fileIn = new Scanner(
     new FileInputStream("datafile.txt"));
   int num = fileIn.nextInt();
   System.out.println(num);
}
catch (FileNotFoundException e)
{
     System.out.println("File not found.");
}
```

Alternately, the line `throws FileNotFoundException` could be added to the end of the definition of the main method, but this approach is not recommended because the exception will simply be handed off to the JVM and it will halt the program.

MyProgrammingLab™ Programming Projects

Visit www.myprogramminglab.com to complete select exercises online and get instant feedback.

1. The Babylonian algorithm to compute the square root of a positive number *n* is as follows:
   1. Make a `guess` at the answer (you can pick *n*/2 as your initial guess).
   2. Compute `r = n / guess`
   3. Set `guess = (guess +r)/ 2`
   4. Go back to step 2 for as many iterations as necessary. The more you repeat steps 2 and 3, the closer `guess` will become to the square root of `n`.

   Write a program that inputs a double for `n`, iterates through the Babylonian algorithm five times, and outputs the answer as a `double` to two decimal places. Your answer will be most accurate for small values of `n`.
2. (This is a version with input of an exercise from Chapter 1.) Write a program that inputs two string variables, `first` and `last`, which the user should enter with his or her name. First, convert both strings to all lowercase. Your program should then create a new string that contains the full name in pig latin with the first letter capitalized for the first and last name. Use only the pig latin rule of moving the first letter to the end of the word and adding "ay." Output the pig latin name to the screen. Use the `substring` and `toUpperCase` methods to construct the new name.

   For example, if the user inputs "Walt" for the first name and "Savitch" for the last name, then the program should create a new string with the text "Altway Avitchsay" and print it.
3. Write a program that reads in two integers typed on the keyboard and outputs their sum, difference, and product.
4. An automobile is used for commuting purposes. Write a program that takes as input the distance of the commute in miles, the automobile's fuel consumption rate in miles per gallon, and the price of a gallon of gas. The program should then output the cost of the commute.
5. The straight-line method for computing the yearly depreciation in value *D* for an item is given by the following formula:

$$D = \frac{P - S}{Y}$$

   where *P* is the purchase price, *S* is the salvage value, and *Y* is the number of years the item is used. Write a program that takes as input the purchase price of an item, the expected number of years of service, and the expected salvage value. The program should then output the yearly depreciation for the item.

6. (This is a better version of an exercise from Chapter 1.) A government research lab has concluded that an artificial sweetener commonly used in diet soda pop causes death in laboratory mice. A friend of yours is desperate to lose weight but cannot give up soda pop. Your friend wants to know how much diet soda pop it is possible to drink without dying as a result. Write a program to supply the answer. The input to the program is the amount of artificial sweetener needed to kill a mouse, the weight of the mouse, and the desired weight of the dieter. Assume that diet soda contains 1/10th of 1% artificial sweetener. Use a named constant for this fraction. You may want to express the percent as the `double` value `0.001`.

7. Write a program that determines the change to be dispensed from a vending machine. An item in the machine can cost between 25 cents and 1 dollar, in 5-cent increments (25, 30, 35, . . . 90, 95, or 100), and the machine accepts only a single dollar bill to pay for the item. For example, a possible sample dialog might be the following:

```
Enter price of item
(from 25 cents to a dollar, in 5-cent increments):
45

You bought an item for 45 cents and gave me a dollar,
so your change is
2 quarters,
0 dimes, and
1 nickels.
```

8. Write a program that reads in a line of text and then outputs that line of text first in all uppercase letters and then in all lowercase letters.

9. (This is a better version of an exercise from Chapter 1.) Write a program that reads in a line of text and then outputs that line of text with the first occurrence of `"hate"` changed to `"love"`. For example, a possible sample dialog might be the following:

```
Enter a line of text.
I hate you.
I have rephrased that line to read:
I love you.
```

You can assume that the word `"hate"` occurs in the input. If the word `"hate"` occurs more than once in the line, your program should replace only the first occurrence of `"hate"`.

10. Write a program that inputs the name, quantity, and price of three items. The name may contain spaces. Output a bill with a tax rate of 6.25%. All prices should be output to two decimal places. The bill should be formatted in columns with 30 characters for the name, 10 characters for the quantity, 10 characters for the price, and 10 characters for the total. Sample input and output is shown as follows:

```
Input name of item 1:
lollipops
```

```
Input quantity of item 1:
10
Input price of item 1:
0.50
Input name of item 2:
diet soda
Input quantity of item 2:
3
Input price of item 2:
1.25

Input name of item 3:
chocolate bar
Input quantity of item 3:
20
Input price of item 3:
0.75

Your bill:

Item                 Quantity     Price       Total
lollipops            10           0.50        5.00
diet soda            3            1.25        3.75
chocolate bar        20           0.75        15.00

Subtotal                                      23.75
6.25% sales tax                                1.48
Total                                         25.23
```

VideoNote
Solution to Programming Project 2.11

11. Write a program that calculates the total grade for three classroom exercises as a percentage. Use the `DecimalFormat` class to output the value as a percent. The scores should be summarized in a table. Input the assignment information in this order: name of assignment (may include spaces), points earned (integer), and total points possible (integer). The percentage is the sum of the total points earned divided by the total points possible. Sample input and output is shown as follows:

```
Name of exercise 1:
Group Project
Score received for exercise 1:
10
Total points possible for exercise 1:
10

Name of exercise 2:
Homework
Score received for exercise 2:
7
Total points possible for exercise 2:
12
```

```
Name of exercise 3:
Presentation
Score received for exercise 3:
5
Total points possible for exercise 3:
8
Exercise            Score           Total Possible
Group Project       10              10
Homework            7               12
Presentation        5               8
Total               22              30
Your total is 22 out of 30, or 73.33%.
```

VideoNote
Solution to Programming Project 2.12

12. (This is a variant of an exercise from Chapter 1.) Create a text file that contains the text `"I hate programming!"` Write a program that reads in this line of text from the file and then the text with the first occurrence of `"hate"` changed to `"love"`. In this case, the program would output `"I love programming!"` Your program should work with any line of text that contains the word `"hate"`, not just the example given in this problem. If the word `"hate"` occurs more than once in the line, your program should replace only the first occurrence of `"hate"`.

13. (This is an extension of an exercise from Chapter 1.) A simple rule to estimate your ideal body weight is to allow 110 pounds for the first 5 feet of height and 5 pounds for each additional inch. Create the following text in a text file. It contains the names and heights in feet and inches of Tom Atto (6'3"), Eaton Wright (5'5"), and Cary Oki (5'11"):

```
Tom Atto
6
3
Eaton Wright
5
5
Cary Oki
5
11
```

Write a program that reads the data in the file and outputs the full name and ideal body weight for each person. In the next chapter, you will learn about loops, which allow for a more efficient way to solve this problem.

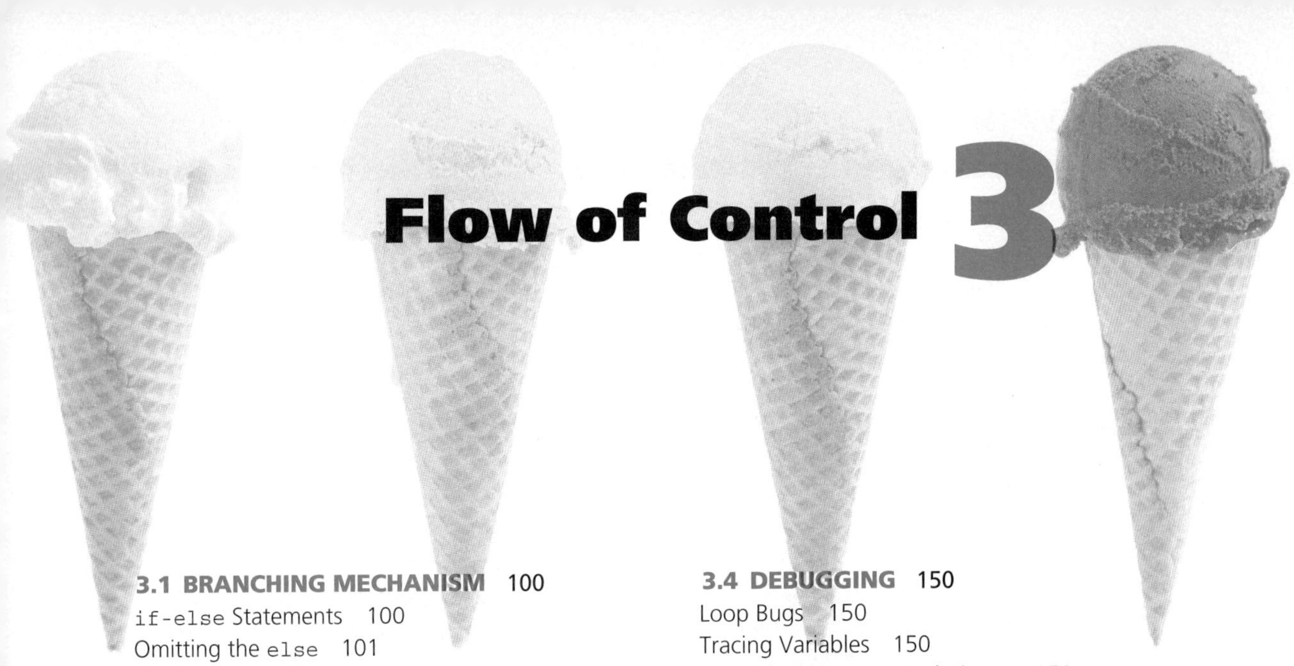

Flow of Control 3

3 Flow of Control

If you think we're wax-works," he said, "you ought to pay, you know. Wax-works weren't made to be looked at for nothing. Nohow!" "Contrariwise," added the one marked "DEE," "if you think we're alive, you ought to speak."

LEWIS CARROLL, *Through the Looking-Glass*

Introduction

As in most programming languages, Java handles flow of control with branching and looping statements. Java branching and looping statements are the same as in the C and C++ languages and are very similar to those in other programming languages. (However, the Boolean expressions that control Java branches and loops are a bit different in Java from what they are in C and C++.)

Most branching and looping statements are controlled by Boolean expressions. A Boolean expression is any expression that is either true or false. In Java, the primitive type `boolean` has only the two values, `true` and `false`, and Boolean expressions evaluate to one of these two values. Before we discuss Boolean expressions and the type `boolean`, we will introduce the Java branching statements using only Boolean expressions whose meaning is intuitively obvious. This will serve to motivate our discussion of Boolean expressions.

Prerequisites

This chapter uses material from Chapters 1 and 2.

3.1 Branching Mechanism

When you come to a fork in the road, take it.

Attributed to Yogi Berra

`if-else` Statements

An `if-else` statement chooses between two alternative statements based on the value of a Boolean expression. For example, suppose you want to design a program to compute a week's salary for an hourly employee. Assume the firm pays an overtime rate of one-and-one-half times the regular rate for all hours after the first 40 hours worked. When the employee works 40 or more hours, the pay is then equal to

```
rate*40 + 1.5*rate*(hours - 40)
```

However, if the employee works less than 40 hours, the correct pay formula is simply

```
rate*hours
```

The following `if-else` statement computes the correct pay for an employee whether the employee works less than 40 hours or works 40 or more hours:

```
if (hours > 40)
    grossPay = rate*40 + 1.5*rate*(hours - 40);
else
    grossPay = rate*hours;
```

The syntax for an `if-else` statement is given in the box entitled "`if-else` Statement." If the Boolean expression in parentheses (after the `if`) evaluates to `true`, then the statement before the `else` is executed. If the Boolean expression evaluates to `false`, then the statement after the `else` is executed.

Remember that when you use a Boolean expression in an `if-else` statement, the Boolean expression must be enclosed in **parentheses**.

parentheses

Notice that an `if-else` statement has smaller statements embedded in it. Most of the statement forms in Java allow you to make larger statements out of smaller ones by combining the smaller statements in certain ways.

Omitting the `else`

Sometimes you want one of the two alternatives in an `if-else` statement to do nothing at all. In Java, this can be accomplished by omitting the `else` part. These sorts of statements are referred to as **`if` statements** to distinguish them from `if-else` statements. For example, the first of the following two statements is an `if` statement:

`if` statement

```
if (sales > minimum)
    salary = salary + bonus;
System.out.println("salary = $" + salary);
```

If the value of `sales` is greater than the value of `minimum`, the assignment statement is executed and then the following `System.out.println` statement is executed. On the other hand, if the value of `sales` is less than or equal to `minimum`, then the embedded assignment statement is not executed, so the `if` statement causes no change (that is, no bonus is added to the base salary), and the program proceeds directly to the `System.out.println` statement.

Compound Statements

if-else with multiple statements

compound statement

You will often want the branches of an `if-else` statement to execute more than one statement each. To accomplish this, enclose the statements for each branch between a pair of braces, { and }. A list of statements enclosed in a pair of braces is called a **compound statement**. A compound statement is treated as a single statement by Java and may be used anywhere that a single statement may be used. Thus, the "Multiple Statement Alternatives" version described in the box entitled "`if-else` Statement" is really just a special case of the "simple" case with one statement in each branch.

`if-else` Statement

The `if-else` statement chooses between two alternative actions based on the value of a `Boolean_Expression`; that is, an expression that is either `true` or `false`, such as `balance < 0`.

SYNTAX

```
if (Boolean_Expression)
    Yes_Statement
else
    No_Statement
```

Be sure to note that the `Boolean_Expression` *must be enclosed in parentheses.*

If *Boolean_Expression* is `true`, then *Yes_Statement* is executed. If *Boolean_Expression* is `false`, then *No_Statement* is executed.

EXAMPLE

```
if (time < limit)
     System.out.println("You made it.");
else
     System.out.println("You missed the deadline.");
```

Omitting the `else` Part

You may omit the `else` part to obtain what is often called an **`if` statement**.

SYNTAX

```
if (Boolean_Expression)
    Action_Statement
```

If *Boolean_Expression* is true, then *Action_Statement* is executed; otherwise, nothing happens and the program goes on to the next statement.

EXAMPLE

```
if (weight > ideal)
    calorieAllotment = calorieAllotment - 500;
```

Multiple Statement Alternatives

In an `if-else` statement, you can have one or both alternatives contain several statements. To accomplish this, group the statements using braces, as in the following example:

```
if (myScore > yourScore)
{
      System.out.println("I win!");
      wager = wager + 100;
}
else
{
      System.out.println("I wish these were golf scores.");
      wager = 0;
}
```

TIP: Placing of Braces

There are two commonly used ways of indenting and placing braces in `if-else` statements. They are illustrated as follows:

```
if (myScore > yourScore)
{
    System.out.println("I win!");
    wager = wager + 100;
}
else
{
    System.out.println("I wish these were golf scores.");
    wager = 0;
}
```

and

```
if (myScore > yourScore) {
    System.out.println("I win!");
    wager = wager + 100;
} else {
    System.out.println("I wish these were golf scores.");
    wager = 0;
}
```

The only difference is the placement of braces. The first form is called the *Allman style*, named after programmer Eric Allman. We find the Allman style easier to read and so we prefer it in this book. The second form is called the *Kernighan & Ritchie* or *K&R style*, named after Dennis Ritchie (the designer of C) and Brian Kernighan (author of the first C tutorial). The K&R style saves lines, so some programmers prefer it or some minor variant of it.

Be sure to note the indenting pattern in these examples. ■

Nested Statements

As you have seen, `if-else` statements and `if` statements contain smaller statements within them. Thus far, we have used compound statements and simple statements, such as assignment statements, as these smaller substatements, but there are other possibilities. In fact, any statement at all can be used as a subpart of an `if-else` statement or other statement that has one or more statements within it.

indenting

When nesting statements, you normally indent each level of nested substatements, although there are some special situations (such as a multiway `if-else` statement) where this rule is not followed.

MyProgrammingLab™

Self-Test Exercises

1. Write an `if-else` statement that outputs the word `"High"` if the value of the variable `score` is greater than 100 and outputs `"Low"` if the value of `score` is at most 100. The variable `score` is of type `int`.

2. Suppose `savings` and `expenses` are variables of type `double` that have been given values. Write an `if-else` statement that outputs the word `"Solvent"`, decreases the value of `savings` by the value of `expenses`, and sets the value of `expenses` to zero, provided that savings is larger than `expenses`. If, however, savings is less than or equal to expenses, the `if-else` statement should simply output the word `"Bankrupt"` without changing the value of any variables.

3. Suppose `number` is a variable of type `int`. Write an `if-else` statement that outputs the word `"Positive"` if the value of the variable `number` is greater than 0 and outputs the words "`Not positive`" if the value of `number` is less than or equal to 0.

4. Suppose `salary` and `deductions` are variables of type `double` that have been given values. Write an `if-else` statement that outputs the word `"Crazy"` if `salary` is less than `deductions`; otherwise, it should output `"OK"` and set the variable `net` equal to `salary` minus `deductions`.

Multiway `if-else` Statement

multiway `if-else` statement

The **multiway `if-else` statement** is not really a different kind of Java statement. It is simply an ordinary `if-else` statement nested inside `if-else` statements, but it is thought of as a different kind of statement and is indented differently from other nested statements so as to reflect this thinking.

The syntax for a multiway `if-else` statement and a simple example are given in the box entitled "Multiway `if-else` Statement." Note that the Boolean expressions are aligned with one another, and their corresponding actions are also aligned with one another. This makes it easy to see the correspondence between Boolean expressions and actions. The Boolean expressions are evaluated in order until a `true` Boolean expression is found. At that point, the evaluation of Boolean expressions stops, and the action corresponding to the first `true` Boolean expression is executed. The final `else` is optional. If there is a final `else` and all the Boolean expressions are `false`, the final action is executed. If there is no final `else` and all the Boolean expressions are `false`, then no action is taken. An example of a multiway `if-else` statement is given in the following Programming Example.

Multiway `if-else` Statement

SYNTAX

```
if (Boolean_Expression_1)
     Statement_1
else if (Boolean_Expression_2)
     Statement_2
          .
          .
          .
else if (Boolean_Expression_n)
     Statement_n
else
     Statement_For_All_Other_Possibilities
```

EXAMPLE

```
if (numberOfPeople < 50)
   System.out.println("Less than 50 people");
else if (numberOfPeople < 100)
   System.out.println("At least 50 and less than 100 people");
else if (numberOfPeople < 200)
   System.out.println("At least 100 and less than 200 people");
else
   System.out.println("At least 200 people");
```

The Boolean expressions are checked in order until the first `true` Boolean expression is encountered, and then the corresponding statement is executed. If none of the Boolean expressions is `true`, then the *Statement_For_All_Other_Possibilities* is executed.

EXAMPLE: State Income Tax

Display 3.1 contains a program that uses a multiway `if-else` statement to compute state income tax. This state computes tax according to the following rate schedule:

1. No tax is paid on the first $15,000 of net income.
2. A tax of 5% is assessed on each dollar of net income from $15,001 to $30,000.
3. A tax of 10% is assessed on each dollar of net income over $30,000.

(continued)

EXAMPLE: (continued)

The program uses a multiway `if-else` statement with one action for each of the above three cases. The condition for the second case is actually more complicated than it needs to be. The computer will not get to the second condition unless it has already tried the first condition and found it to be `false`. Thus, you know that whenever the computer tries the second condition, it knows that `netIncome` is greater than `15000`. Hence, you can replace the line

```
else if ((netIncome > 15000) && (netIncome <= 30000))
```

with the following, and the program will perform exactly the same:

```
else if (netIncome <= 30000)
```

MyProgrammingLab™

Self-Test Exercises

5. What output will be produced by the following code?

```
int extra = 2;
if (extra < 0)
    System.out.println("small");
else if (extra == 0)
    System.out.println("medium");
else
    System.out.println("large");
```

6. What would be the output in Exercise 5 if the assignment were changed to the following?

```
int extra = -37;
```

7. What would be the output in Exercise 5 if the assignment were changed to the following?

```
int extra = 0;
```

8. Write a multiway `if-else` statement that classifies the value of an `int` variable `n` into one of the following categories and writes out an appropriate message:

```
n < 0 or 0 ≤ n < 100 or n ≥ 100
```

Hint: Remember that the Boolean expressions are checked in order.

Display 3.1 Tax Program

```
import java.util.Scanner;

public class IncomeTax
{
    public static void main(String[] args)
    {
        Scanner keyboard = new Scanner(System.in);
        double netIncome, tax, fivePercentTax, tenPercentTax;

        System.out.println("Enter net income.\n"
                        + "Do not include a dollar sign or any commas.");
        netIncome = keyboard.nextDouble( );

        if (netIncome <= 15000)
            tax = 0;
        else if ((netIncome > 15000) && (netIncome <= 30000))
            //tax = 5% of amount over $15,000
            tax = (0.05*(netIncome - 15000));
        else //netIncome > $30,000
        {
            //fivePercentTax = 5% of income from $15,000 to $30,000.
            fivePercentTax = 0.05*15000;
            //tenPercentTax = 10% of income over $30,000.
            tenPercentTax = 0.10*(netIncome - 30000);
            tax = (fivePercentTax + tenPercentTax);
        }

        System.out.printf("Tax due = $%.2f", tax);
    }
}
```

Sample Dialogue

```
Enter net income.
Do not include a dollar sign or any commas.
40000
Tax due = $1750.00
```

The `switch` Statement

`switch` statement

The **`switch` statement** is the only other kind of Java statement that implements multiway branches. The syntax for a `switch` statement and a simple example are shown in the box entitled "The `switch` Statement."

controlling expression

case labels

When a `switch` statement is executed, one of a number of different branches is executed. The choice of which branch to execute is determined by a **controlling expression** given in parentheses after the keyword `switch`. Following this are a number of occurrences of the reserved word `case` followed by a constant and a colon. These constants are called **case labels**. The controlling expression for a `switch` statement must be one of the types `char`, `int`, `short`, `byte`, or `String`.[1] The `String` data type is allowed only in Java 7 or higher. The case labels must all be of the same type as the controlling expression. No case label can occur more than once, because that would be an ambiguous instruction. There may also be a section labeled `default:`, which is usually last.

When the `switch` statement is executed, the controlling expression is evaluated and the computer looks at the case labels. If it finds a case label that equals the value of the controlling expression, it executes the code for that case label.

`break` statement

The `switch` statement ends when either a `break` statement is executed or the end of the `switch` statement is reached. A **`break` statement** consists of the keyword `break` followed by a semicolon. When the computer executes the statements after a case label, it continues until it reaches a `break` statement. When the computer encounters a `break` statement, the `switch` statement ends. If you omit the `break` statements, then after executing the code for one case, the computer will go on to execute the code for the next case.

Note that you can have two case labels for the same section of code, as in the following portion of a `switch` statement:

```
case 'A':
case 'a':
    System.out.println("Excellent. You need not take the final.");
    break;
```

Because the first case has no `break` statement (in fact, no statements at all), the effect is the same as having two labels for one case, but Java syntax requires one keyword case for each label, such as `'A'` and `'a'`.

`default`

If no case label has a constant that matches the value of the controlling expression, then the statements following the **`default`** label are executed. You need not have a `default` section. If there is no `default` section and no match is found for the value of the controlling expression, then nothing happens when the `switch` statement is executed. However, it is safest to always have a `default` section. If you think your case labels list all possible outcomes, you can put an error message in the `default` section.

The default case need not be the last case in a `switch` statement, but making it the last case, as we have always done, makes the code clearer.

A sample `switch` statement is shown in Display 3.2. Notice that the case labels do not need to be listed in order and do not need to span a complete interval.

[1] As we will learn in Chapter 6, the type may also be an enumerated type.

The `switch` Statement

SYNTAX

```
switch (Controlling_Expression)
{
    case Case_Label_1:
         Statement_Sequence_1
         break;
    case Case_Label_2:
           Statement_Sequence_2
         break;
                .
                .
                .
    case Case_Label_n:
            Statement_Sequence_n
            break;
    default:
            Default_Statement_Sequence
            break;
}
```

Each Case_Label is a constant of the same type as the Controlling_Expression. The Controlling_Expression must be of type **char, int, short, byte,** *or* **string.**

A **break** *may be omitted. If there is no* **break**, *execution just continues to the next case.*

The **default** *case is optional.*

EXAMPLE

```
int vehicleClass;
double toll;
      .
      .
      .
switch (vehicleClass)
{
   case 1:
       System.out.println("Passenger car.");
       toll = 0.50;
       break;
   case 2:
       System.out.println("Bus.");
       toll = 1.50;
       break;
   case 3:
       System.out.println("Truck.");
       toll = 2.00;
       break;
   default:
       System.out.println("Unknown vehicle class!");
       break;
}
```

Display 3.2 **A switch Statement** (part 1 of 2)

```
import java.util.Scanner;

public class SwitchDemo
{
    public static void main(String[] args)
    {
        Scanner keyboard = new Scanner(System.in);

        System.out.println("Enter number of ice cream flavors:");
        int numberOfFlavors = keyboard.nextInt( );

        switch (numberOfFlavors)
        {
           case 32:
               System.out.println("Nice selection.");
               break;
           case 1:
               System.out.println("I bet it's vanilla.");
               break;
           case 2:
           case 3:
           case 4:
               System.out.println(numberOfFlavors + "flavors");
               System.out.println("is acceptable.");
               break;
           default:
               System.out.println("I didn't plan for");
               System.out.println(numberOfFlavors + " flavors.");
               break;
        }
    }
}
```

Controlling expression

Case labels

break *statement*

Sample Dialogue 1

```
Enter number of ice cream flavors:
1
I bet it's vanilla.
```

Sample Dialogue 2

```
Enter number of ice cream flavors:
32
Nice selection.
```

Display 3.2 **A switch Statement** (part 2 of 2)

Sample Dialogue 3

```
Enter number of ice cream flavors:
3
3 flavors
is acceptable.
```

Sample Dialogue 4

```
Enter number of ice cream flavors:
9
I didn't plan for
9 flavors.
```

PITFALL: Forgetting a break in a switch Statement

If you forget a `break` in a `switch` statement, the compiler does not issue an error message. You will have written a syntactically correct `switch` statement, but it will not do what you intended it to do. Notice the annotation in the example in the box entitled "The `switch` Statement."

The last case in a `switch` statement does not need a `break`, but it is a good idea to include it nonetheless. That way, if a new case is added after the last case, you will not forget to add a `break` (because it is already there). This advice about `break` statements also applies to the default case when it is last. It is best to place the default case last, but that is not required by the Java language, so there is always a possibility of somebody adding a case after the default case. ■

MyProgrammingLab™

Self-Test Exercises

9. What is the output produced by the following code?

```
char letter = 'B';
switch (letter)
{
    case 'A':
    case 'a':
        System.out.println("Some kind of A.");
    case 'B':
    case 'b':
        System.out.println("Some kind of B.");
        break;
    default:
        System.out.println("Something else.");
        break;
}
```

(continued)

MyProgrammingLab™

Self-Test Exercises (continued)

10. What is the output produced by the following code?

```
int key = 1;
switch (key + 1)
{
    case 1:
         System.out.println("Apples");
         break;
    case 2:
         System.out.println("Oranges");
         break;
    case 3:
         System.out.println("Peaches");
    case 4:
         System.out.println("Plums");
         break;
    default:
         System.out.println("Fruitless");
}
```

11. What would be the output in Exercise 10 if the first line were changed to the following?

```
int key = 3;
```

12. What would be the output in Exercise 10 if the first line were changed to the following?

```
int key = 5;
```

The Conditional Operator ★

conditional operator

ternary operator

arithmetic `if`

You can embed a branch inside of an expression by using a ternary operator known as the **conditional operator** (also called the **ternary operator** or **arithmetic `if`**). Its use is reminiscent of an older programming style, and we do not advise using it. It is included here for the sake of completeness (and in case you disagree with our programming style).

The conditional operator is a notational variant on certain forms of the `if-else` statement. The following example illustrates the conditional operator. Consider the following `if-else` statement:

```
if (n1 > n2)
    max = n1;
else
    max = n2;
```

This can be expressed using the *conditional operator* as follows:

```
max = (n1 > n2) ? n1 : n2;
```

The expression on the right-hand side of the assignment statement is the conditional operator expression:

```
(n1 > n2) ? n1 : n2
```

The `?` and `:` together form a ternary operator known as the conditional operator. A conditional operator expression starts with a Boolean expression followed by a `?` and then followed by two expressions separated with a colon. If the Boolean expression is `true`, then the value of the first of the two expressions is returned as the value of the entire expression; otherwise, the value of the second of the two expressions is returned as the value of the entire expression.

3.2 Boolean Expressions

"Contrariwise," continued Tweedledee, "if it was so, it might be; and if it were so, it would be; but as it isn't, it ain't. That's logic."

LEWIS CARROLL, *Through the Looking-Glass*

Boolean expression

Now that we have motivated Boolean expressions by using them in `if-else` statements, we will discuss them and the type `boolean` in more detail. A **Boolean expression** is simply an expression that is either `true` or `false`. The name *Boolean* is derived from George Boole, a 19th-century English logician and mathematician whose work was related to these kinds of expressions.

Simple Boolean Expressions

We have already been using simple Boolean expressions in `if-else` statements. The simplest Boolean expressions are comparisons of two expressions, such as

```
time < limit
```

and

```
balance <= 0
```

A Boolean expression does not need to be enclosed in parentheses to qualify as a Boolean expression, although it does need to be enclosed in parentheses when it is used in an `if-else` statement.

Display 3.3 shows the various Java comparison operators you can use to compare two expressions.

PITFALL: Using = in Place of ==

Because the equal sign, =, is used for assignment in Java, something else is needed to indicate equality. In Java, equality is indicated with two equal signs with no space between them, as in

```
if (yourScore == myScore)
    System.out.println("A tie.");
```

Fortunately, if you do use = in place of ==, Java will probably give you a compiler error message. (The only case that does not give an error message is when the expression in parentheses happens to form a correct assignment to a `boolean` variable.) ■

Display 3.3 **Java Comparison Operators**

MATH NOTATION	NAME	JAVA NOTATION	JAVA EXAMPLES
=	Equal to	`==`	`x + 7 == 2*y` `answer == 'y'`
≠	Not equal to	`!=`	`score != 0` `answer != 'y'`
>	Greater than	`>`	`time > limit`
≥	Greater than or equal to	`>=`	`age >= 21`
<	Less than	`<`	`pressure < max`
≤	Less than or equal to	`<=`	`time <=limit`

The Methods `equals` and `equalsIgnoreCase`

When testing strings for equality, do not use ==. Instead, use either `equals` or `equalsIgnoreCase`.

SYNTAX

String.`equals`(*Other_String*)
String.`equalsIgnoreCase`(*Other_String*)

EXAMPLE

```
String s1;
   .
   .
   .
```

```
if ( s1.equals("Hello") )
    System.out.println("The string is Hello.");
else
    System.out.println("The string is not Hello.");
```

PITFALL: Using == with Strings

Although `==` correctly tests two values of a primitive type, such as two numbers, to see whether they are equal, it has a different meaning when applied to objects, such as objects of the class `String`.[2] Recall that an object is something whose type is a class, such as a string. All strings are in the class `String` (that is, are of type `String`), so `==` applied to two strings does not test to see whether the strings are equal. Instead, it tests whether two strings refer to the same object. We will discuss references in Chapter 15. To test two strings (or any two objects) to see if they have equal values, you should use the method `equals` rather than `==`. For example, suppose `s1` and `s2` are `String` variables that have been given values, and consider the statement

```
if (s1.equals(s2))
    System.out.println("They are equal strings.");
else
    System.out.println("They are not equal strings.");
```

If `s1` and `s2` name strings that contain the same characters in the same order, then the output will be

```
They are equal strings.
```

The notation may seem a bit awkward at first, because it is not symmetric between the two things being tested for equality. The two expressions

```
s1.equals(s2)
s2.equals(s1)
```

are equivalent.

The method `equalsIgnoreCase` behaves similarly to `equals`, except that with `equalsIgnoreCase`, the upper- and lowercase versions of the same letter are considered the same. For example, `"Hello"` and `"hello"` are not equal because their first characters, `'H'` and `'h'`, are different characters. But they would be considered equal by the method `equalsIgnoreCase`. For example, the following will output `Equal ignoring case.`:

```
if ("Hello".equalsIgnoreCase("hello"))
    System.out.println("Equal ignoring case.");
```

(continued)

[2] When applied to two strings (or any two objects), `==` tests to see if they are stored in the same memory location, but we will not discuss that until Chapter 4. For now, we need only note that `==` does something other than test for the equality of two strings.

PITFALL: (continued)

Notice that it is perfectly legal to use a quoted string with a `String` method, as in the preceding use of `equalsIgnoreCase`. A quoted string is an object of type `String` and has all the methods that any other object of type `String` has.

For the kinds of applications we are looking at in this chapter, you could also use == to test for equality of objects of type `String`, and it would deliver the correct answer. However, there are situations in which == does not correctly test strings for equality, so you should get in the habit of using equals rather than == to test strings. ■

Lexicographic and Alphabetical Order

lexicographic ordering

The method `compareTo` tests two strings to determine their lexicographic order. **Lexicographic ordering** is similar to alphabetic ordering and is sometimes, but not always, the same as alphabetic ordering. The easiest way to think about lexicographic ordering is to think of it as being the same as alphabetic ordering *but with the alphabet ordered differently*. Specifically, in lexicographic ordering, the letters and other characters are ordered as in the ASCII ordering, which is shown in Appendix 3.

compareTo

If `s1` and `s2` are two variables of type `String` that have been given `String` values, then

```
s1.compareTo(s2)
```

returns a negative number if `s1` comes before `s2` in lexicographic ordering, returns zero if the two strings are equal, and returns a positive number if `s2` comes before `s1`. Thus,

```
s1.compareTo(s2) < 0
```

returns true if `s1` comes before `s2` in lexicographic order and returns false otherwise. For example, the following will produce correct output:

```
if (s1.compareTo(s2) < 0)
    System.out.println(
        s1 + " precedes " + s2 + " in lexicographic ordering");
else if (s1.compareTo(s2) < 0)
    System.out.println(
        s1 + " follows " + s2 + " in lexicographic ordering");
else //s1.compareTo(s2) == 0
    System.out.println(s1 + " equals " + s2);
```

If you look at the ordering of characters in Appendix 3, you will see that *all* uppercase letters come before *all* lowercase letters. For example, `'Z'` comes before `'a'` in lexicographic order. So when comparing two strings consisting of a mix of lower- and uppercase letters, lexicographic and alphabetic ordering are not the same. However, as shown in Appendix 3, all the lowercase letters are in alphabetic order. So for any two strings of all lowercase letters, lexicographic order is the same as ordinary alphabetic order. Similarly, in the ordering of Appendix 3, all the uppercase letters are in alphabetic order. So for any two strings of all uppercase letters, lexicographic order is the same as ordinary alphabetic order. Thus, if you treat all uppercase letters as if they were lowercase, then lexicographic ordering becomes the same as alphabetic ordering. This is exactly what the method compareToIgnoreCase does. Thus, the following produces correct output:

compareTo IgnoreCase

```
if (s1.compareToIgnoreCase(s2) < 0)
    System.out.println(
        s1 + " precedes " + s2 + " in ALPHABETIC ordering");
else if (s1.compareToIgnoreCase(s2) > 0)
    System.out.println(
        s1 + " follows " + s2 + " in ALPHABETIC ordering");
else //s1.compareToIgnoreCase(s2) == 0
    System.out.println(s1 + " equals " + s2 + " IGNORING CASE");
```

The above code will compile and produce results no matter what characters are in the strings s1 and s2. However, alphabetic order and the output make sense only if the two strings consist entirely of letters.

The program in Display 3.4 illustrates some of the string comparisons we have just discussed.

MyProgrammingLab™

Self-Test Exercises

13. Suppose n1 and n2 are two int variables that have been given values. Write a Boolean expression that returns true if the value of n1 is greater than or equal to the value of n2; otherwise, it should return false.

14. Suppose n1 and n2 are two int variables that have been given values. Write an if-else statement that outputs "n1" if n1 is greater than or equal to n2, and that outputs "n2" otherwise.

15. Suppose variable1 and variable2 are two variables that have been given values. How do you test whether they are equal when the variables are of type int? How do you test whether they are equal when the variables are of type String?

16. Assume that nextWord is a String variable that has been given a String value consisting entirely of letters. Write some Java code that outputs the message "First half of the alphabet", provided nextWord precedes "N" in alphabetic ordering. If nextWord does not precede "N" in alphabetic ordering, the code should output "Second half of the alphabet". (Note that "N" uses double quotes to produce a String value, as opposed to using single quotes to produce a char value.)

Display 3.4 Comparing Strings

```
public class StringComparisonDemo
{
    public static void main(String[] args)
    {
        String s1 = "Java isn't just for breakfast.";
        String s2 = "JAVA isn't just for breakfast.";

        if (s1.equals(s2))
            System.out.println("The two lines are equal.");
        else
            System.out.println("The two lines are not equal.");
        if (s2.equals(s1))
            System.out.println("The two lines are equal.");
        else
            System.out.println("The two lines are not equal.");
        if (s1.equalsIgnoreCase(s2))
            System.out.println(
            "But the lines are equal, ignoring case.");
        else
            System.out.println(
            "Lines are not equal, even ignoring case.");

        String s3 = "A cup of java is a joy forever.";
        if (s3.compareToIgnoreCase(s1) < 0)
        {
            System.out.println("\"" + s3 + "\"");
            System.out.println("precedes");
            System.out.println("\"" + s1 + "\"");
            System.out.println("in alphabetic ordering");
        }
        else
            System.out.println("s3 does not precede s1.");
    }
}
```

Sample Dialogue

```
The two lines are not equal.
The two lines are not equal.
But the lines are equal, ignoring case.
"A cup of java is a joy forever."
precedes
"Java isn't just for breakfast."
in alphabetic ordering
```

Building Boolean Expressions

&& means "and"

You can combine two Boolean expressions using the "and" operator, which is spelled `&&` in Java. For example, the following Boolean expression is `true` provided `number` is greater than 2 and `number` is less than 7:

```
(number > 2) && (number < 7)
```

When two Boolean expressions are connected using `&&`, the entire expression is `true`, provided both of the smaller Boolean expressions are `true`; otherwise, the entire expression is `false`.

> ### The "and" Operator &&
>
> You can form a more elaborate Boolean expression by combining two simpler Boolean expressions using the "and" operator **&&**
>
> **SYNTAX (FOR A BOOLEAN EXPRESSION USING &&)**
>
> (*Boolean_Exp_1*) && (*Boolean_Exp_2*)
>
> **EXAMPLE (WITHIN AN `if-else` STATEMENT)**
>
> ```
> if ( (score > 0) && (score < 10) )
>     System.out.println("score is between 0 and 10.");
> else
>     System.out.println("score is not between 0 and 10.");
> ```
>
> If the value of `score` is greater than 0 and the value of `score` is also less than 10, then the first `System.out.println` statement is executed; otherwise, the second `System.out.println` statement is executed.

|| means "or"

You can also combine two Boolean expressions using the "or" operator, which is spelled `||` in Java. For example, the following is `true` provided `count` is less than 3 or `count` is greater than 12:

```
(count < 3) || (count > 12)
```

When two Boolean expressions are connected using `||`, the entire expression is `true`, provided that one or both of the smaller Boolean expressions are `true`; otherwise, the entire expression is `false`.

You can negate any Boolean expression using the `!` operator. If you want to negate a Boolean expression, place the expression in parentheses and place the `!` operator in front of it. For example, `! (savings < debt)` means "savings is not less than debt." The `!` operator can usually be avoided. For example,

```
!(savings < debt)
```

is equivalent to `savings >= debt`. In some cases, you can safely omit the parentheses, but the parentheses never do any harm. The exact details on omitting parentheses are given later in this chapter in the subsection entitled "Precedence and Associativity Rules."

The "or" Operator ||

You can form a more elaborate Boolean expression by combining two simpler Boolean expressions using the "or" operator ||.

SYNTAX (FOR A BOOLEAN EXPRESSION USING ||)

(*Boolean_Exp_1*) || (*Boolean_Exp_2*)

EXAMPLE (WITHIN AN `if-else` STATEMENT)

```
if ((salary > expenses) || (savings > expenses))
    System.out.println("Solvent");
else
    System.out.println("Bankrupt");
```

If `salary` is greater than `expenses` or `savings` is greater than `expenses` (or both), then the first `System.out.println` statement is executed; otherwise, the second `System.out.println` statement is executed.

PITFALL: Strings of Inequalities

Do not use a string of inequalities such as `min < result < max`. If you do, your program will produce a compiler error message. Instead, you must use two inequalities connected with an `&&`, as follows:

```
(min < result) && (result < max)
```

MyProgrammingLab™

Self-Test Exercises

17. Write an `if-else` statement that outputs the word "Passed" provided the value of the variable `exam` is greater than or equal to 60 and also the value of the variable `programsDone` is greater than or equal to 10. Otherwise, the `if-else` statement should output the word "Failed". The variables `exam` and `programsDone` are both of type `int`.

18. Write an `if-else` statement that outputs the word "Emergency" provided the value of the variable `pressure` is greater than 100 or the value of the variable `temperature` is greater than or equal to 212. Otherwise, the `if-else` statement should output the word "OK". The variables `pressure` and `temperature` are both of type `int`.

Evaluating Boolean Expressions

Boolean expressions are used to control branch and loop statements. However, a Boolean expression has an independent identity apart from any branch statement or loop statement you might use it in. A Boolean expression returns either `true` or `false`.

A variable of type `boolean` can store the values `true` and `false`. Thus, you can set a variable of type `boolean` equal to a Boolean expression. For example,

```
boolean madeIt = (time < limit) && (limit < max);
```

A Boolean expression can be evaluated in the same way that an arithmetic expression is evaluated. The only difference is that an arithmetic expression uses operations such as `+`, `*`, and `/` and produces a number as the final result, whereas a Boolean expression uses relational operations such as `==` and `<` and Boolean operations such as `&&`, `||`, and `!`, and produces one of the two values `true` and `false` as the final result.

First, let's review evaluating an arithmetic expression. The same technique will work in the same way to evaluate Boolean expressions. Consider the following arithmetic expression:

```
(number + 1) * (number + 3)
```

Assume that the variable `number` has the value 2. To evaluate this arithmetic expression, you evaluate the two sums to obtain the numbers 3 and 5, and then you combine these two numbers 3 and 5 using the `*` operator to obtain 15 as the final value. Notice that in performing this evaluation, you do not multiply the expressions `(number + 1)` and `(number + 3)`. Instead, you multiply the values of these expressions. You use 3; you do not use `(number + 1)`. You use 5; you do not use `(number + 3)`.

The computer evaluates Boolean expressions the same way. Subexpressions are evaluated to obtain values, each of which is either `true` or `false`. In particular, `==`, `!=`, `<`, `<=`, and so forth operate on pairs of any primitive type to produce a Boolean value of `true` or `false`. These individual values of `true` or `false` are then combined according to the rules in the **truth tables** shown in Display 3.5. For example, consider the Boolean expression

truth tables

```
!( ( count < 3) || (count > 7) )
```

which might be the controlling expression for an `if-else` statement. Suppose the value of `count` is 8. In this case, `(count < 3)` evaluates to `false` and `(count > 7)` evaluates to `true`, so the preceding Boolean expression is equivalent to

```
!(false || true)
```

Consulting the tables for `||` (which is labeled "OR"), the computer sees that the expression inside the parentheses evaluates to `true`. Thus, the computer sees that the entire expression is equivalent to

```
!(true)
```

Consulting the tables again, the computer sees that `!(true)` evaluates to `false`, and so it concludes that `false` is the value of the original Boolean expression.

The `boolean` Values Are `true` and `false`

`true` and `false` are predefined constants of type `boolean`. (They must be written in lowercase.) In Java, a Boolean expression evaluates to the `boolean` value `true` when it is satisfied, and it evaluates to the `boolean` value `false` when it is not satisfied.

Display 3.5 Truth Tables

AND		
Exp_1	*Exp_2*	*Exp_1 && Exp_2*
true	true	true
true	false	false
false	true	false
false	false	false

OR		
Exp_1	*Exp_2*	*Exp_1 || Exp_2*
true	true	true
true	false	true
false	true	true
false	false	false

NOT	
Exp	*!(Exp)*
true	false
false	true

boolean variables in assignments

A `boolean` variable—that is, one of type `boolean`—can be given the value of a Boolean expression by using an assignment statement, in the same way that you use an assignment statement to set the value of an `int` variable or any other type of variable. For example, the following sets the value of the `boolean` variable `isPositive` to `false`:

```
int number = -5;
boolean isPositive;
isPositive = (number > 0);
```

If you prefer, you can combine the last two lines as follows:

```
boolean isPositive = (number > 0);
```

The parentheses are not needed, but they do make it a bit easier to read.

Once a `boolean` variable has a value, you can use the `boolean` variable just as you would use any other Boolean expression. For example, the following code

```
boolean isPositive = (number > 0);
if (isPositive)
    System.out.println("The number is positive.");
else
    System.out.println("The number is negative or zero.");
```

is equivalent to

```
if (number > 0)
    System.out.println("The number is positive.");
else
    System.out.println("The number is negative or zero.");
```

Of course, this is just a toy example. It is unlikely that anybody would use the first of the preceding two examples, but you might use something like it if the value of `number`, and therefore the value of the Boolean expression, might change. For example, the following code could (by some stretch of the imagination) be part of a program to evaluate lottery tickets:

```
boolean isPositive = (number > 0);
while (number > 0);
{
    System.out.println("Wow!");
    number = number - 1000;
}
if (isPositive)
    System.out.println("Your number is positive.");
else
    System.out.println("Sorry, number is not positive.");
System.out.println("Only positive numbers can win.");
```

`true` and `false` Are Not Numbers

Many programming languages traditionally use `1` and `0` for `true` and `false`. The latest versions of most languages have changed things so that now most languages have a type such as `boolean` with values for `true` and `false`. However, even in these newer language versions, values of type `boolean` are automatically converted to integers and vice versa when context requires it. In particular, C++ automatically makes such conversions.

In Java, the values `true` and `false` are not numbers, nor can they be type cast to any numeric type. Similarly, values of type `int` cannot be type cast to `boolean` values.

TIP: Naming Boolean Variables

Name a `boolean` variable with a statement that will be `true` when the value of the `boolean` variable is `true`, such as `isPositive`, `pressureOK`, and so forth. That way you can easily understand the meaning of the `boolean` variable when it is used in an `if-else` statement or other control statement. Avoid names that do not unambiguously describe the meaning of the variable's value. Do not use names such as `numberSign`, `pressureStatus`, and so forth. ■

Short-Circuit and Complete Evaluation

Java takes an occasional shortcut when evaluating a Boolean expression. Notice that in many cases, you need to evaluate only the first of two or more subexpressions in a Boolean expression. For example, consider the following:

```
(savings >= 0) && (dependents > 1)
```

If `savings` is negative, then `(savings >= 0)` is `false`, and, as you can see in the tables in Display 3.5, when one subexpression in an `&&` expression is `false`, then the whole expression is `false`, no matter whether the other expression is `true` or `false`. Thus, if we know that the first expression is `false`, there is no need to evaluate the second expression. A similar thing happens with `||` expressions. If the first of two expressions joined with the `||` operator is `true`, then you know the entire expression is `true`, whether the second expression is `true` or `false`. In some situations, the Java language can and does use these facts to save itself the trouble of evaluating the second subexpression in a logical expression connected with an `&&` or an `||`. Java first evaluates the leftmost of the two expressions joined by an `&&` or an `||`. If that gives it enough information to determine the final value of the expression (independent of the value of the second expression), then Java does not bother to evaluate the second expression. This method of evaluation is called **short-circuit evaluation** or **lazy evaluation**.

short-circuit evaluation

lazy evaluation

Now let's look at an example using `&&` that illustrates the advantage of short-circuit evaluation, and let's give the Boolean expression some context by placing it in an `if` statement:

```
if ( (kids != 0) && ((pieces/kids) >= 2) )
    System.out.println("Each child may have two pieces!");
```

If the value of `kids` is not zero, this statement involves no subtleties. However, suppose the value of `kids` is zero and consider how short-circuit evaluation handles this case. The expression `(kids != 0)` evaluates to `false`, so there would be no need to evaluate the second expression. Using short-circuit evaluation, Java says that the entire expression is `false`, without bothering to evaluate the second expression. This prevents a run-time error, since evaluating the second expression would involve dividing by zero.

complete evaluation

Java also allows you to ask for **complete evaluation**. In complete evaluation, when two expressions are joined by an "and" or an "or," both subexpressions are always evaluated, and then the truth tables are used to obtain the value of the final expression. To obtain complete evaluation in Java, you use `&` rather than `&&` for "and" and use `|` in place of `||` for "or."

In most situations, short-circuit evaluation and complete evaluation give the same result, but, as you have just seen, there are times when short-circuit evaluation can avoid a run-time error. There are also some situations in which complete evaluation is preferred, but we will not use those techniques in this book. We will always use `&&` and `||` to obtain short-circuit evaluation.

Precedence and Associativity Rules

precedence rules

associativity rules

Boolean expressions (and arithmetic expressions) need not be fully parenthesized. If you omit parentheses, Java follows **precedence rules** and **associativity rules** in place of the missing parentheses. One easy way to think of the process is to think of the computer adding parentheses according to these precedence and associativity rules. Some of the Java precedence and associativity rules are given in Display 3.6. (A complete set of precedence and associativity rules is given in Appendix 2.) The computer uses precedence rules to decide where to insert parentheses, but the precedence rules do not differentiate between two operators at the same precedence level, in which case the computer uses the associativity rules to "break the tie."

higher precedence

If one operator occurs higher on the list than another in the precedence table (Display 3.6), the higher one is said to have **higher precedence**. If one operator has higher precedence than another, the operator of higher precedence is grouped with its operands (its arguments) before the operator of lower precedence. For example, if the computer is faced with the expression

```
balance * rate + bonus
```

it notices that `*` has a higher precedence than `+`, so it first groups `*` and its operands, as follows:

```
(balance * rate) + bonus
```

Next, it groups `+` with its operands to obtain the fully parenthesized expression

```
((balance * rate) + bonus)
```

Sometimes two operators have the same precedence, in which case the parentheses are added using the associativity rules. To illustrate this, let's consider another example:

```
bonus + balance * rate / correctionFactor - penalty
```

The operators `*` and `/` have higher precedence than either `+` or `-`, so `*` and `/` are grouped first. But `*` and `/` have equal precedence, so the computer consults the associativity rule for `*` and `/`, which says they associate from left to right. This means that the `*`, which is the leftmost of `*` and `/`, is grouped first. So the computer interprets the expression as

```
bonus + (balance * rate) / correctionFactor - penalty
```

which in turn is interpreted as

```
bonus + ((balance * rate) / correctionFactor) - penalty
```

because `/` has higher precedence than either `+` or `-`.

This expression is still not fully parenthesized, however. The computer still must choose to group `+` first or `-` first. According to Display 3.6, `+` and `-` have equal precedence.

Display 3.6 **Precedence and Associativity Rules**

Highest Precedence ↓ *Lowest Precedence*

<table>
<tr><th>PRECEDENCE</th><th>ASSOCIATIVITY</th></tr>
<tr><td>From highest at top to lowest at bottom. Operators in the same group have equal precedence.</td><td></td></tr>
<tr><td>Dot operator, array indexing, and method invocation., [ ], ( )</td><td>Left to right</td></tr>
<tr><td>++ (postfix, as in x++), -- (postfix)</td><td>Right to left</td></tr>
<tr><td>The unary operators: +, -, ++ (prefix, as in ++x), -- (prefix), and !</td><td>Right to left</td></tr>
<tr><td>Type casts (Type)</td><td>Right to left</td></tr>
<tr><td>The binary operators *, /, %</td><td>Left to right</td></tr>
<tr><td>The binary operators +, -</td><td>Left to right</td></tr>
<tr><td>The binary operators <, >, <=, >=</td><td>Left to right</td></tr>
<tr><td>The binary operators ==, ! =</td><td>Left to right</td></tr>
<tr><td>The binary operator &</td><td>Left to right</td></tr>
<tr><td>The binary operator |</td><td>Left to right</td></tr>
<tr><td>The binary operator &&</td><td>Left to right</td></tr>
<tr><td>The binary operator ||</td><td>Left to right</td></tr>
<tr><td>The ternary operator (conditional operator) ?:</td><td>Right to left</td></tr>
<tr><td>The assignment operators =, *=, /=, %=, +=, -=, & =, |=</td><td>Right to left</td></tr>
</table>

So the computer must use the associativity rules, which say that + and - are associated left to right. So, it interprets the expression as

```
(bonus + ((balance * rate) / correctionFactor)) - penalty
```

which in turn is interpreted as the following fully parenthesized expression:

```
((bonus + ((balance * rate) / correctionFactor)) - penalty)
```

As you can see from studying the table in Display 3.6, most binary operators associate from left to right. But the assignment operators associate from right to left. So the expression

```
number1 = number2 = number3
```

means

```
number1 = (number2 = number3)
```

which in turn is interpreted as the following fully parenthesized expression:

```
(number1 = (number2 = number3))
```

However, this fully parenthesized expression may not look like it means anything until we explain a bit more about the assignment operator.

Although we do not advocate using the assignment operator `=` as part of a complex expression, it is an operator that returns a value, just as `+` and `*` do. When an assignment operator `=` is used in an expression, it changes the value of the variable on the left-hand side of the assignment operator and also returns a value—namely, the new value of the variable on the left-hand side of the expression. So `(number2 = number3)` sets `number2` equal to the value of `number3` and returns the value of `number3`. Thus,

```
number1 = number2 = number3
```

which is equivalent to

```
(number1 = (number2 = number3))
```

sets both `number2` and `number1` equal to the value of `number3`. It is best to not use assignment statements inside of expressions, although simple chains of assignment operators such as the following are clear and acceptable:

```
number1 = number2 = number3;
```

Although we discourage using expressions that combine the assignment operator and other operators in complicated ways, let's try to parenthesize one just for practice. Consider the following:

```
number1 = number2 = number3 + 7 * factor
```

The operator of highest precedence is `*`, and the operator of next-highest precedence is `+`, so this expression is equivalent to

```
number1 = number2 = (number3 + (7 * factor))
```

which leaves only the assignment operators to group. They associate right to left, so the fully parenthesized equivalent version of our expression is

```
(number1 = (number2 = (number3 + (7 * factor))))
```

(Note that there is no case where two operators have equal precedence but one associates from left to right while the other associates from right to left. That must be true or else there would be cases with conflicting instructions for inserting parentheses.)

binding

The association of operands with operators is called **binding**. For example, when parentheses determine which two expressions (two operands) are being added by a particular + sign, that is called binding the two operands to the + sign. A fully parenthesized expression accomplishes binding for all the operators in an expression.

These examples should make it clear that it can be risky to depend too heavily on the precedence and associativity rules. It is best to include most parentheses and to omit parentheses only in situations where the intended meaning is very obvious, such as a simple combination of * and +, or a simple chain of &&'s or a simple chain of ||'s. The following examples have some omitted parentheses, but their meaning should be clear:

```
rate * time + lead
(time < limit) && (yourScore > theirScore) && (yourScore > 0)
(expenses < income) || (expenses < savings) || (creditRating > 0)
```

Notice that the precedence rules include both arithmetic operators such as + and * as well as Boolean operators such as && and ||. This is because many expressions combine arithmetic and Boolean operations, as in the following simple example:

```
(number + 1) > 2 || (number + 5) < -3
```

If you check the precedence rules given in Display 3.6, you will see that this expression is equivalent to

```
(((number + 1) > 2) || ((number + 5) < (-3)))
```

because > and < have higher precedence than ||. In fact, you could omit all the parentheses in the above expression and it would have the same meaning (but would be less clear).

It might seem that once an expression is fully parenthesized, the meaning of the expression is then determined. It would seem that to evaluate the expression, you (or the computer) simply evaluate the inner expressions before the outer ones. So, in

```
((number + 1) > 2) || ((number + 5) < (-3))
```

first the expressions (number + 1), (number + 5), and (-3) are evaluated (in any order), then the > and < are evaluated, and then the || is applied. That happens to work in this simple case. In this case, it does not matter which of (number + 1), (number + 5), and (-3) is evaluated first, but in certain other expressions it will be necessary to specify which subexpression is evaluated first. The rules for evaluating a fully parenthesized expression are (and indeed must be) more complicated than just evaluating inner expressions before outer expressions.

For an expression with no side effects, the rule of performing inner parenthesized expressions before outer ones is all you need. That rule will get you through most simple expressions, but for expressions with side effects, you need to learn the rest of the story, which is what we will do next.

side effects

The complications come from the fact that some expressions have *side effects*. When we say an expression has **side effects**, we mean that in addition to returning a value, the expression also changes something, such as the value of a variable. Expressions with the assignment operator have side effects; `pay = bonus`, for example, changes the value of `pay`. Increment and decrement operators have side effects; `++n` changes the value of `n`. In expressions that include operators with side effects, you need more rules.

For example, consider

```
((result = (++n)) + (other = (2*(++n))))
```

The parentheses seem to say that you or the computer should first evaluate the two increment operators, `++n` and `++n`, but the parentheses do not say which of the two `++n's` to do first. If `n` has the value 2 and we evaluate the leftmost `++n` first, then the variable `result` is set to 3 and the variable `other` is set to 8 (and the entire expression evaluates to 11). But if we evaluate the rightmost `++n` first, then `other` is set to 6 and `result` is set to 4 (and the entire expression evaluates to 10). We need a rule to determine the order of evaluation when we have a tie such as this. However, rather than simply adding a rule to break such ties, Java instead takes a completely different approach.

To evaluate an expression, Java uses the following three rules:

1. Java first does binding; that is, it first fully parenthesizes the expression using precedence and associativity rules, just as we have outlined.
2. Then it simply evaluates expressions left to right.
3. If an operator is waiting for its two (or one or three) operands to be evaluated, then that operator is evaluated as soon as its operands have been evaluated.

We will first do an example with no side effects and then an example of an expression with side effects. First, the simple example; consider the expression

```
6 + 7 * n - 12
```

and assume the value of `n` is 2. Using the precedence and associativity rules, we add parentheses one pair at a time as follows:

```
6 + (7 * n) - 12
```

then

```
(6 + (7 * n)) - 12
```

and finally the fully parenthesized version

```
((6 + (7 * n)) - 12)
```

Next, we evaluate subexpressions left to right. (6 evaluates to 6 and 7 evaluates to 7, but that is so obvious we will not make a big deal of it.) The variable n evaluates to 2. (Remember, we assumed the value of n was 2.) So, we can rewrite the expression as

```
((6 + (7 * 2)) - 12)
```

The * is the only operator that has both of its operands evaluated, so it evaluates to 14 to produce

```
((6 + 14) - 12)
```

Now + has both of its operands evaluated, so (6 + 14) evaluates to 20 to yield

```
(20 - 12)
```

which in turn evaluates to 8. So 8 is the value for the entire expression.

This may seem like more work than it should be, but remember, the computer is following an algorithm and proceeds step by step; it does not get inspired to make simplifying assumptions.

Next, let's consider an expression with side effects. In fact, let's consider the one we fully parenthesized earlier. Consider the following fully parenthesized expression and assume the value of n is 2:

```
((result = (++n)) + (other = (2*(++n))))
```

Subexpressions are evaluated left to right. So, `result` is evaluated first. When used with the assignment operator =, a variable simply evaluates to itself. So, `result` is evaluated and waiting. Next, ++n is evaluated, and it returns the value 3. The expression is now known to be equivalent to

```
((result = 3) + (other = (2*(++n))))
```

Now the assignment operator = has its two operands evaluated, so `(result = 3)` is evaluated. Evaluating `(result = 3)` sets the value of `result` equal to 3 and returns the value 3. Thus, the expression is now known to be equivalent to

```
(3 + (other = (2*(++n))))
```

(and the side effect of setting `result` equal to 3 has happened). Proceeding left to right, the next thing to evaluate is the variable `other`, which simply evaluates to itself, so you need not rewrite anything.

Proceeding left to right, the next subexpression that can be evaluated is n, which evaluates to 3. (Remember, n has already been incremented once, so n now has the value 3.) Then ++ has its only argument evaluated, so it is ready to be evaluated. The evaluation of (++n) has the side effect of setting n equal to 4 and evaluates to 4. So, the entire expression is equivalent to

```
(3 + (other = (2*4)))
```

The only subexpression that has its operands evaluated is (2*4), so it is evaluated to 8 to produce

```
(3 + (other = 8))
```

Now the assignment operator = has both of its operands evaluated, so it evaluates to 8 and has the side effect of setting `other` equal to 8. Thus, we know the value of the expression is

```
(3 + 8)
```

which evaluates to 11. So, the entire expression evaluates to 11 (and has the side effects of setting `result` equal to 3, setting `n` equal to 4, and setting other equal to 8). These rules also allow for method invocations in expressions. For example, in

```
(++n > 0) && (s.length( ) > n)
```

the variable `n` is incremented before `n` is compared to `s. length( )`. When we start defining and using more methods, you will see less-contrived examples of expressions that include method invocations.

All of these rules for evaluating expressions are summarized in the box entitled "Rules for Evaluating Expressions."

Rules for Evaluating Expressions

Expressions are evaluated as follows:

1. Binding: Determine the equivalent fully parenthesized expression using the precedence and associativity rules.
2. Proceeding left to right, evaluate whatever subexpressions you can evaluate. (These subexpressions will be operands or method arguments. For example, in simple cases they may be numeric constants or variables.)
3. Evaluate each outer operation (and method invocation) as soon as all of its operands (all its arguments) have been evaluated.

MyProgrammingLab™

Self-Test Exercises

19. Determine the value, `true` or `false`, of each of the following Boolean expressions, assuming that the value of the variable `count` is 0 and the value of the variable `limit` is 10. (Give your answer as one of the values `true` or `false`.)

    a. `(count == 0) && (limit < 20)`

    b. `count == 0 && limit < 20`

    c. `(limit > 20) || (count < 5)`

(continued)

MyProgrammingLab™

Self-Test Exercises (continued)

d. `!(count == 12)`

e. `(count == 1) && (x < y)`

f. `(count < 10) || (x < y)`

g. `!( ((count < 10) || (x < y)) && (count >= 0) )`

h. `((limit/count) > 7) || (limit < 20)`

i. `(limit < 20) || ((limit/count) > 7)`

j. `((limit/count) > 7) && (limit < 0)`

k. `(limit < 0) && ((limit/count) > 7)`

20. Does the following sequence produce a division by zero?

```
int j = -1;
if ((j > 0) && (1/(j+1) > 10))
   System.out.println(i);
```

21. Convert the following expression to an equivalent fully parenthesized expression:

```
bonus + day * rate / correctionFactor * newGuy - penalty
```

3.3 Loops

"Few tasks are more like the torture of Sisyphus than housework, with its endless repetition: the clean becomes soiled, the soiled is made clean, over and over, day after day."

SIMONE DE BEAUVOIR

body of the loop

iteration

Looping mechanisms in Java are similar to those in other high-level languages. The three Java loop statements are the `while` statement, the `do-while` statement, and the `for` statement. The same terminology is used with Java as with other languages. The code that is repeated in a loop is called the **body of the loop**. Each repetition of the loop body is called an **iteration** of the loop.

`while` Statement and `do-while` Statement

`while` and `do-while` compared

The syntax for the `while` statement and its variant, the `do-while` statement, is given later in this chapter in the box entitled "Syntax for `while` and `do-while` Statements." In both cases, the multistatement body is a special case of the loop with a single-statement body. The multistatement body is a single compound statement. Examples of `while` and `do-while` statements are given in Display 3.7.

The important difference between the `while` and `do-while` loops involves when the controlling Boolean expression is checked. With a `while` statement, the Boolean expression is checked *before* the loop body is executed. If the Boolean expression evaluates to `false`, then the body is not executed at all. With a `do-while` statement, the body of

Display 3.7 **Demonstration of `while` Loops and `do-while` Loops** (part 1 of 2)

```
public class WhileDemo
{
    public static void main(String[] args)
    {
        int countDown;

        System.out.println("First while loop:");
        countDown = 3;
        while (countDown > 0)
        {
            System.out.println("Hello");
            countDown = countDown - 1;
        }

        System.out.println("Second while loop:");
        countDown = 0;
        while (countDown > 0)
        {
            System.out.println("Hello");
            countDown = countDown - 1;
        }

        System.out.println("First do-while loop:");
        countDown = 3;
        do
        {
            System.out.println("Hello");
            countDown = countDown - 1;
        } while (countDown > 0);

        System.out.println("Second do-while loop:");
        countDown = 0;
        do
        {
            System.out.println("Hello");
            countDown = countDown - 1;
        } while (countDown > 0);
    }
}
```

(continued)

Display 3.7 **Demonstration of `while` Loops and `do-while` Loops** (part 2 of 2)

Sample Dialogue

```
First while loop:
Hello
Hello
Hello
Second while loop:
First do-while loop:
Hello
Hello
Hello
Second do-while loop:
Hello
```

A `while` loop can iterate its body zero times.

A `do-while` loop always iterates its body at least one time.

the loop is executed first and the Boolean expression is checked *after* the loop body is executed. Thus, the `do-while` statement always executes the loop body at least once. After this start-up, the `while` loop and the `do-while` loop behave the same way. After each iteration of the loop body, the Boolean expression is again checked, and if it is `true`, the loop is iterated again. If it has changed from `true` to `false`, then the loop statement ends.

executing the body zero times

The first thing that happens when a `while` loop is executed is that the controlling Boolean expression is evaluated. If the Boolean expression evaluates to `false` at that point, the body of the loop is never executed. It might seem pointless to execute the body of a loop zero times, but that is sometimes the desired action. For example, a `while` loop is often used to sum a list of numbers, but the list could be empty. To be more specific, a checkbook-balancing program might use a `while` loop to sum the values of all the checks you have written in a month, but you might take a month's vacation and write no checks at all. In that case, there are zero numbers to sum, so the loop is iterated zero times.

Algorithms and Pseudocode

algorithm

Dealing with the syntax rules of a programming language is not the hard part of solving a problem with a computer program. The hard part is coming up with the underlying method of solution. This method of solution is called an algorithm. An **algorithm** is a set of precise instructions that leads to a solution. Some approximately equivalent words to *algorithm* are *recipe*, *method*, *directions*, *procedure*, and *routine*.

pseudocode

An algorithm is normally written in a mixture of a programming language (in our case, Java) and English (or other human language). This mixture of programming language and human language is known as **pseudocode**. Using pseudocode frees you from worrying about fine details of Java syntax so that you can concentrate on the method of solution. Underlying the program in Display 3.8 is an algorithm that can be expressed as the following pseudocode:

Syntax for `while` and `do-while` Statements

A `while` STATEMENT WITH A SINGLE-STATEMENT BODY

```
while (Boolean_Expression)
    Statement
```

A `while` STATEMENT WITH A MULTISTATEMENT BODY

```
while (Boolean_Expression)
{
    Statement_1
    Statement_2
      .
      .
      .
    Statement_Last
}
```

A `do-while` STATEMENT WITH A SINGLE-STATEMENT BODY

```
do
    Statement
while (Boolean Expression);
```

A `do-while` STATEMENT WITH A MULTISTATEMENT BODY

Do not forget the final semicolon.

```
do
{
    Statement_1
    Statement_2
      .
      .
      .
    Statement_Last
} while (Boolean_Expression);
```

```
Give the user instructions.
count = 0;
sum = 0;
Read a number and store it in a variable named next.
while (next >= 0)
{
    sum = sum + next;
    count++;
    Read a number and store it in next.
}
The average is sum/count provided count is not zero.
Output the results.
```

Display 3.8 Averaging a List of Scores

```
import java.util.Scanner;
public class Averager
{
    public static void main(String[] args)
    {
        Scanner keyboard = new Scanner(System.in);
        System.out.println("Enter a list of nonnegative scores.");
        System.out.println("Mark the end with a negative number.");
        System.out.println("I will compute their average.");

        double next, sum = 0;
        int count = 0;

        next = keyboard.nextDouble( );
        while (next >= 0)
        {
            sum = sum + next;
            count++;
            next = keyboard.nextDouble( );
        }

        if (count == 0)
            System.out.println("No scores entered.");
        else
        {
            double average = sum/count;
            System.out.println(count + " scores read.");
            System.out.println("The average is " + average);
        }
    }
}
```

Sample Dialogue

```
Enter a list of nonnegative scores.
Mark the end with a negative number.
I will compute their average.
87.5 0 89 99.9 -1
4 scores read.
The average is 69.1.
```

Note that when using pseudocode, we do not necessarily declare variables or worry about the fine syntax details of Java. The only rule is that the pseudocode must be precise and clear enough for a good programmer to convert the pseudocode to syntactically correct Java code.

As you will see, significant programs are written not as a single algorithm, but as a set of interacting algorithms; however, each of these algorithms is normally designed in pseudocode unless the algorithm is exceedingly simple.

EXAMPLE: Averaging a List of Scores

Display 3.8 shows a program that reads in a list of scores and computes their average. It illustrates a number of techniques that are commonly used with loops.

sentinel values

The scores are all nonnegative. This allows the program to use a negative number as an end marker. Note that the negative number is not one of the numbers being averaged in. This sort of end marker is known as a **sentinel value**. A sentinel value need not be a negative number, but it must be some value that cannot occur as a "real" input value. For example, if the input list were a list of even integers, then you could use an odd integer as a sentinel value.

To get the loop to end properly, we want the Boolean expression

```
next >= 0
```

checked before adding in the number read. This way we avoid adding in the sentinel value. So, we want the loop body to end with

```
next = keyboard.nextDouble( );
```

To make things work out, this in turn requires that we also place this line before the loop. A loop often needs some preliminary statements to set things up before the loop is executed.

MyProgrammingLab™

Self-Test Exercises

22. What is the output produced by the following?

```
int n = 10;
while (n > 0)
{
    System.out.println(n);
    n = n - 3;
}
```

23. What output would be produced in Exercise 22 if the > sign were replaced with < ?

(continued)

MyProgrammingLab™

Self-Test Exercises (continued)

24. What is the output produced by the following?

```
int n = 10;
do
{
    System.out.println(n);
    n = n - 3;
} while (n > 0);
```

25. What output would be produced in Exercise 24 if the > sign were replaced with < ?

26. What is the output produced by the following?

```
int n = -42;
do
{
    System.out.println(n);
    n = n - 3;
} while (n > 0);
```

27. What is the most important difference between a `while` statement and a `do-while` statement?

The `for` Statement

`for` statement

The third and final loop statement in Java is the **`for` statement**. The `for` statement is most commonly used to step through some integer variable in equal increments. The `for` statement is, however, a completely general looping mechanism that can do anything that a `while` loop can do.

For example, the following `for` statement sums the integers 1 through 10:

```
sum = 0;
for (n = 1; n <= 10; n++)
    sum = sum + n;
```

A `for` statement begins with the keyword `for` followed by three expressions in parentheses that tell the computer what to do with the controlling variable(s). The beginning of a `for` statement looks like the following:

```
for (Initialization; Boolean_Expression; Update)
```

The first expression tells how the variable, variables, or other things are initialized, the second expression gives a Boolean expression that is used to check for when the loop should end, and the last expression tells how the loop control variable or variables are updated after each iteration of the loop body. The loop body is a single statement (typically a compound statement) that follows the heading we just described.

The three expressions at the start of a `for` statement are separated by two, and only two, semicolons. Do not succumb to the temptation to place a semicolon after the third expression. (The technical explanation is that these three things are expressions, not statements, and so do not require a semicolon at the end.)

A `for` statement often uses a single `int` variable to control loop iteration and loop ending. However, the three expressions at the start of a `for` statement may be any Java expressions and therefore may involve more (or even fewer) than one variable, and the variables can be of any type.

The semantics of the `for` statement are given in Display 3.9. The syntax for a `for` statement is given in Display 3.10. Display 3.10 also explains how the `for` statement can be viewed as a notational variant of the `while` loop.

The `for` Statement

SYNTAX

```
for (Initialization; Boolean_Expression; Update)
        Body
```

The *Body* may be any Java statement—either a simple statement or, more likely, a compound statement consisting of a list of statements enclosed in braces, {}. Notice that the three things in parentheses are separated by two, not three, semicolons.

You are allowed to use any Java expression for the *Initializing* and the *Update* expressions. Therefore, you may use more, or fewer, than one variable in the expressions; moreover, the variables may be of any type.

EXAMPLE

```
int next, sum = 0;
for (next = 0; next <= 10; next++)
{
    sum = sum + next;
    System.out.println("sum up to " + next + " is " + sum);
}
```

A variable can be declared in the heading of a `for` statement at the same time that it is initialized. For example,

```
for (int n = 1; n < 10; n++)
     System.out.println(n);
```

There are some subtleties to worry about when you declare a variable in the heading of a `for` statement. These subtleties are discussed in Chapter 4 in the Programming Tip subsection entitled "Declaring Variables in a `for` Statement." It might be wise to avoid such subtle declarations within a `for` statement until you reach Chapter 4, but we mention it here for reference value.

Display 3.9 Semantics of the `for` Statement

```
for (Initialization; Boolean_Expression; Update)
        Body
```

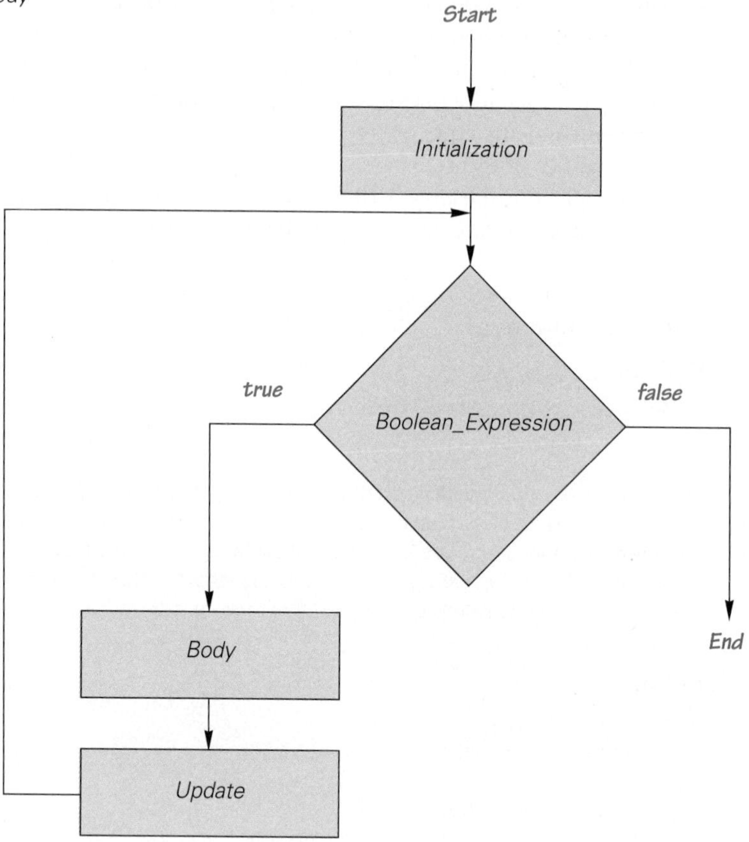

Display 3.10 `for` Statement Syntax and Alternate Semantics (part 1 of 2)

`for` Statement Syntax

```
for (Initialization; Boolean_Expression; Update)
        Body
```

EXAMPLE

```
for (number = 100; number >= 0; number--)
     System.out.println(number + " bottles of beer on the shelf.");
```

Display 3.10 `for` Statement Syntax and Alternate Semantics (part 2 of 2)

Equivalent `while` Loop Syntax

```
Initialization;
while (Boolean_Expression)
{
     Body;
     Update;
}
```

EQUIVALENT EXAMPLE

```
number = 100;
while (number >= 0)
{
     System.out.println(number + " bottles of beer on the shelf.");
     number--;
}
```

Sample Dialogue

```
100 bottles of beer on the shelf.
99 bottles of beer on the shelf.
                .
                .
                .
0 bottles of beer on the shelf.
```

The Comma in `for` Statements

A `for` loop can contain multiple initialization actions. Simply separate the actions with commas, as in the following:

```
for (term = 1, sum = 0; term <= 10; term++)
    sum = sum + term;
```

This `for` loop has two initializing actions. The variable `term` is initialized to 1, and the variable `sum` is also initialized to 0. Note that you use a comma, not a semicolon, to separate the initialization actions.

You can also use commas to place multiple update actions in a `for` loop. This can lead to a situation in which the `for` loop has an empty body but still does something useful. For example, the previous `for` loop can be rewritten to the following equivalent version:

```
for (term = 1, sum = 0; term <= 10; sum = sum + term, term++)
    //Empty body;
```

This, in effect, makes the loop body part of the update action. We find that it makes for a more readable style if you use the update action only for variables that control the loop, as in the previous version of this `for` loop. We do not advocate using `for` loops with no body, but if you do so, annotate it with a comment such as we did in the preceding `for` loop. As indicated in the upcoming Pitfall, "Extra Semicolon in a `for` Statement," a `for` loop with no body can also occur as the result of a programmer error.

The comma used in a `for` statement, as we just illustrated, is quite limited in how it can be used. You can use it with assignment statements and with incremented and decremented variables (such as `term++` or `term--`), but not with just any arbitrary statements. In particular, both declaring variables and using the comma in `for` statements can be troublesome. For example, the following is illegal:

```
for (int term = 1, double sum = 0; term <= 10; term++)
    sum = sum + term;
```

Even the following is illegal:

```
double sum;
for (int term = 1, sum = 0; term <= 10; term++)
    sum = sum + term;
```

Java will interpret

```
int term = 1, sum = 0;
```

as declaring both `term` and `sum` to be `int` variables and complain that `sum` is already declared.

If you do not declare `sum` anyplace else (and it is acceptable to make `sum` an `int` variable instead of a `double` variable), then the following, although we discourage it, is legal:

```
for (int term = 1, sum = 0; term <= 10; term++)
    sum = sum + term;
```

The first part in parentheses (up to the semicolon) declares both `term` and `sum` to be `int` variables and initializes both of them.

It is best to simply avoid these possibly confusing examples. When using the comma in a `for` statement, it is safest to simply declare all variables outside the `for` statement. If you declare all variables outside the `for` loop, the rules are no longer complicated.

A `for` loop can have only one Boolean expression to test for ending the `for` loop. However, you can perform multiple tests by connecting the tests using `&&` or `||` operators to form one larger Boolean expression.

(C, C++, and some other programming languages have a general-purpose comma operator. Readers who have programmed in one of these languages need to be warned that, in Java, there is no comma operator. In Java, the comma is a separator, not an operator, and its use is very restricted compared with the comma operator in C and C++.)

TIP: Repeat *N* Times Loops

The simplest way to produce a loop that repeats the loop body a predetermined number of times is with a `for` statement. For example, the following is a loop that repeats its loop body three times:

```
for (int count = 1; count <= 3; count++)
    System.out.println("Hip, Hip, Hurray");
```

The body of a `for` statement need not make any reference to a loop control variable, such as the variable `count`. ■

PITFALL: Extra Semicolon in a `for` Statement

You normally do not place a semicolon after the closing parenthesis at the beginning of a `for` loop. To see what can happen, consider the following `for` loop:

```
for (int count = 1; count <= 10; count++); <-------- Problem semicolon.
    System.out.println("Hello");
```

If you did not notice the extra semicolon, you might expect this `for` loop to write `Hello` to the screen 10 times. If you do notice the semicolon, you might expect the compiler to issue an error message. Neither of those things happens. If you embed this `for` loop in a complete program, the compiler will not complain. If you run the program, only one `Hello` will be output instead of 10 Hellos. What is happening? To answer that question, we need a little background.

One way to create a statement in Java is to put a semicolon after something. If you put a semicolon after `number++`, you change the expression

```
number++
```

into the statement

```
number++;
```

empty statement

null statement

If you place a semicolon after nothing, you still create a statement. Thus, the semicolon by itself is a statement, which is called the **empty statement** or the **null statement**. The empty statement performs no action, but still is a statement. Therefore, the following is a complete and legitimate `for` loop, whose body is the empty statement:

```
for (int count = 1; count <= 10; count++);
```

(continued)

PITFALL: (continued)

This `for` loop is indeed iterated 10 times, but since the body is the empty statement, nothing happens when the body is iterated. This loop does nothing, and it does nothing 10 times! After completing this `for` loop, the computer goes on to execute the following, which writes `Hello` to the screen one time:

```
System.out.println("Hello");
```

This same sort of problem can arise with a `while` loop. Be careful to not place a semicolon after the closing parenthesis that encloses the Boolean expression at the start of a `while` loop. A `do-while` loop has just the opposite problem. You must remember to always end a `do-while` loop with a semicolon. ■

PITFALL: Infinite Loops

A `while` loop, `do-while` loop, or `for` loop does not terminate as long as the controlling Boolean expression evaluates to `true`. This Boolean expression normally contains a variable that will be changed by the loop body, and usually the value of this variable eventually is changed in a way that makes the Boolean expression false and therefore terminates the loop. However, if you make a mistake and write your program so that the Boolean expression is always true, then the loop will run forever.

infinite loop

A loop that runs forever is called an **infinite loop**.

Unfortunately, examples of infinite loops are not hard to come by. First, let's describe a loop that *does* terminate. The following Java code writes out the positive even numbers less than 12. That is, it outputs the numbers 2, 4, 6, 8, and 10, one per line, and then the loop ends.

```
number = 2;
while (number != 12)
{
    System.out.println(number);
    number = number + 2;
}
```

The value of `number` is increased by 2 on each loop iteration until it reaches 12. At that point, the Boolean expression after the word `while` is no longer true, so the loop ends.

Now suppose you want to write out the odd numbers less than 12, rather than the even numbers. You might mistakenly think that all you need to do is change the initializing statement to

```
number = 1;
```

But this mistake will create an infinite loop. Because the value of `number` goes from 11 to 13, the value of `number` is never equal to 12, so the loop never terminates.

PITFALL: (continued)

This sort of problem is common when loops are terminated by checking a numeric quantity using `==` or `!=`. When dealing with numbers, it is always safer to test for passing a value. For example, the following will work fine as the first line of our `while` loop:

```
while (number < 12)
```

With this change, `number` can be initialized to any number and the loop will still terminate.

There is one subtlety about infinite loops that you need to keep in mind. A loop might terminate for some input values but be an infinite loop for other values. Just because you tested your loop for some program input values and found that the loop ended does not mean that it will not be an infinite loop for some other input values.

A program that is in an infinite loop might run forever unless some external force stops it, so it is a good idea to learn how to force a program to terminate. The method for forcing a program to stop varies from operating system to operating system. The keystrokes Control-C will terminate a program on many operating systems. (To type Control-C, hold down the Control key while pressing the C key.)

In simple programs, an infinite loop is almost always an error. However, some programs are intentionally written to run forever, such as the main outer loop in an airline reservation program that just keeps asking for more reservations until you shut down the computer (or otherwise terminate the program in an atypical way). ■

Nested Loops

nested loops

VideoNote **Nested Loop Example**

It is perfectly legal to nest one loop statement inside another loop statement. For example, the following nests one `for` loop inside another `for` loop:

```
int rowNum, columnNum;
for (rowNum = 1; rowNum <= 3; rowNum++)
{
    for (columnNum = 1; columnNum <= 2; columnNum++)
       System.out.print(" row " + rowNum + " column " + columnNum);
    System.out.println( );
}
```

This produces the following output:

```
row 1 column 1 row 1 column 2
row 2 column 1 row 2 column 2
row 3 column 1 row 3 column 2
```

For each iteration of the outer loop, the inner loop is iterated from beginning to end and then one `println` statement is executed to end the line.

(It is best to avoid nested loops by placing the inner loop inside a method definition and placing a method invocation inside the outer loop. Method definitions are covered in Chapters 4 and 5.)

MyProgrammingLab™

Self-Test Exercises

28. What is the output of the following?

```
for (int count = 1; count < 5; count++)
     System.out.print((2 * count) + " ");
```

29. What is the output of the following?

```
for (int n = 10; n > 0; n = n - 2)
     System.out.println("Hello " + n);
```

30. What is the output of the following?

```
for (double sample = 2; sample > 0; sample = sample - 0.5)
    System.out.print(sample + " ");
```

31. Rewrite the following `for` statement as a `while` loop (and possibly some additional statements):

```
int n;
for (n = 10; n > 0; n = n - 2)
    System.out.println("Hello " + n);
```

32. What is the output of the following loop? Identify the connection between the value of `n` and the value of the variable `log`.

```
int n = 1024;
int log = 0;
for (int i = 1; i < n; i = i * 2)
   log++;
System.out.println(n + " " + log);
```

33. What is the output of the following loop? Comment on the code. (This is not the same as the previous exercise.)

```
int n = 1024;
int log = 0;
for (int i = 1; i < n; i = i * 2);
   log++;
System.out.println(n + " " + log);
```

34. Predict the output of the following nested loops:

```
int n, m;
for (n = 1; n <= 10; n++)
    for (m = 10; m >= 1; m--)
        System.out.println(n + " times " + m
                                    + " = " + n*m);
```

MyProgrammingLab™

Self-Test Exercises (continued)

35. For each of the following situations, tell which type of loop (`while`, `do-while`, or `for`) would work best:

    a. Summing a series, such as `1/2 + 1/3 + 1/4 + 1/5 + . . . 1/10.`

    b. Reading in the list of exam scores for one student.

    c. Reading in the number of days of sick leave taken by employees in a department.

36. What is the output of the following?

```
int number = 10;
while (number > 0)
{
    System.out.println(number);
    number = number + 3;
}
```

37. What is the output of the following?

```
int n, limit = 10;
for (n = 1; n < limit; n++)
{
    System.out.println("n == " + n);
    System.out.println("limit == " + limit);
   limit = n + 2;
}
```

38. What is the output produced by the following?

```
int number = 10;
while (number > 0)
{
    number = number - 2;
    if (number == 4)
        break;
    System.out.println(number);
}
System.out.println("The end.");
```

39. What is the output produced by the following?

```
int number = 10;
while (number > 0)
{
    number = number - 2;
    if (number == 4)
        continue;
    System.out.println(number);
}
System.out.println("The end.");
```

The `break` and `continue` Statements ★

In previous subsections, we described the basic flow of control for the `while`, `do-while`, and `for` loops. This is how the loops should normally be used and they are usually are. However, you can alter the flow of control in two additional ways: You can insert either a `break` statement or insert a `continue` statement. The `break` statement ends the loop. The `continue` statement ends the current iteration of the loop body. The `break` and `continue` statements can be used with any of the Java loop statements.

`break` statement

We described the `break` statement earlier in this chapter when we discussed the `switch` statement. The **`break` statement** consists of the keyword `break` followed by a semicolon. When executed, the `break` statement ends the nearest enclosing `switch` or loop statement.

`continue` statement

The **`continue` statement** consists of the keyword `continue` followed by a semicolon. When executed, the `continue` statement ends the current loop body iteration of the nearest enclosing loop statement.

One point that you should note when using the `continue` statement in a `for` loop is that the `continue` statement transfers control to the update expression. Thus, any loop control variable will be updated immediately after the `continue` statement is executed.

Note that a `break` statement completely ends the loop. In contrast, a `continue` statement merely ends one loop iteration, and the next iteration (if any) continues the loop.

You never absolutely need a `break` or `continue` statement. Any code that uses a `break` or `continue` statement can be rewritten to do the same thing without a `break` or `continue` statement. The `continue` statement can be particularly tricky and can make your code hard to read. It may be best to avoid the `continue` statement completely or at least use it only on very rare occasions. The use of the `break` and `continue` statements in loops is controversial, with many experts saying they should never be used. You will need to make your own decision on whether you will use either or both of these statements.

You can nest one loop statement inside another loop statement. When doing so, remember that any `break` or `continue` statement applies to the innermost loop statement containing the `break` or `continue` statement. If there is a `switch` statement inside a loop, any `break` statement applies to the innermost loop or `switch` statement.

There is a type of `break` statement that, when used in nested loops, can end any containing loop, not just the innermost loop. If you label an enclosing loop statement with an *Identifier*, then the following version of the `break` statement will exit the labeled loop, even if it is not the innermost enclosing loop:

```
break Identifier;
```

label

To **label** a loop statement, simply precede it with an *Identifier* and a colon. The following is an outline of some sample code that uses a labeled `break` statement:

```
outerLoop:
do
```

```
{
      ...
      while (next >= 0)
      {
        next = keyboard.nextInt( );
        if (next < -100)
            break outerLoop;
        ...
      }
        ...
      answer = ...
} while (answer.equalsIgnoreCase("yes"));
```

The identifier `outerLoop` labels the outer loop, which is a `do` loop. If the number read into the variable `next` is negative but not less than –100, then the inner `while` loop ends normally. If, however, the number read is less than –100, then the labeled `break` statement is executed, and that ends the enclosing `do` loop.

You can actually label any statement, not just loop statements and `switch` statements. A labeled `break` will always end the enclosing statement with the matching label, no matter what kind of statement is labeled.

The labeled `break` can be handy when you have a `switch` statement in the body of a loop and you want a `break` statement that ends the loop rather than just ending the `switch` statement.

The `exit` Statement

The `break` statement ends a loop (or `switch` statement) but does not end the program. The following statement immediately ends the program:

```
System.exit(0);
```

`System` is a predefined Java class that is automatically provided by Java, and `exit` is a method in the class `System`. The method `exit` ends the program as soon as it is invoked. In the programs that we will write, the integer argument 0 can be any integer, but by tradition we use 0, because 0 is used to indicate a normal ending of the program.

The following is a bit of code that uses the `exit` statement:

```
System.out.println("Enter a negative number:");
int negNumber = keyboard.nextInt( );
if (negNumber >= 0)
{
    System.out.println(negNumber + " is not a negative number.");
    System.out.println("Program aborting.");
    System.exit(0);
}
```

There are more examples of the use of `System.exit` in Chapter 4.

3.4 Debugging

A man who has committed a mistake and doesn't correct it is committing another mistake.

CONFUCIUS

Loop Bugs

There is a pattern to the kinds of mistakes you are most likely to make when programming with loops. Moreover, there are some standard techniques you can use to locate and fix bugs in your loops.

The two most common kinds of loop errors are unintended infinite loops and *off-by-one* errors. We have already discussed infinite loops, but we still need to consider off-by-one errors.

off-by-one error

If your loop has an **off-by-one error**, that means the loop repeats the loop body one too many or one too few times. These sorts of errors can result from carelessness in designing a controlling Boolean expression. For example, if you use less-than when you should use less-than-or-equal, this can easily make your loop iterate the body the wrong number of times.

Use of `==` to test for equality in the controlling Boolean expression of a loop can often lead to an off-by-one error or an infinite loop. This sort of equality testing can work satisfactorily for integers and characters, but is not reliable for floating-point numbers. This is because the floating-point numbers are approximate quantities, and `==` tests for exact equality. The result of such a test is unpredictable. When comparing floating-point numbers, always use something involving less-than or greater-than, such as `<=`; do not use `==` or `!=`. Using `==` or `!=` to test floating-point numbers can produce an off-by-one error or an unintended infinite loop or even some other type of error. Even when using integer variables, it is best to avoid using `==` and `!=` and to instead use something involving less-than or greater-than.

Off-by-one errors can easily go unnoticed. If a loop is iterated one too many times or one too few times, the results might still look reasonable but be off by enough to cause trouble later on. Always make a specific check for off-by-one errors by comparing your loop results to results you know to be true by some other means, such as a pencil-and-paper calculation.

Tracing Variables

tracing variables

One good way to discover errors in a loop or any kind of code is to trace some key variables. **Tracing variables** means watching the variables change value while the program is running. Most programs do not output each variable's value every time the variable changes, but being able to see all of these variable changes can help you to debug your program.

Many IDEs (Integrated Development Environments) have a built-in utility that lets you easily trace variables without making any changes to your program. These debugging systems vary from one IDE to another. If you have such a debugging facility, it is worth learning how to use it.

If you do not want to use such a debugging facility, you can trace variables by inserting some temporary output statements in your program. For example, the following code compiles but still contains an error:

```
int n = 10;
int sum = 10;
while (n > 1)
{
   sum = sum + n;
   n--;
}
System.out.println("The sum of the integers 1 to 10 is " + sum);
```

To find out what is wrong, you can trace the variables n and sum by inserting output statements as follows:

```
int n = 10;
int sum = 10;
while (n > 1)
{
   System.out.println("At the beginning of the loop: n = " + n);
   //trace
   System.out.println("At the beginning of the loop: sum = " + sum);
   //trace
   sum = sum + n;
   n--;
   System.out.println("At the end of the loop: n = " + n); //trace
   System.out.println("At the end of the loop: sum = " + sum);
   //trace
}
System.out.println("The sum of the integers 1 to 10 is " + sum);
```

The first four lines of the execution are as follows:

```
At the beginning of the loop: n = 10
At the beginning of the loop: sum = 10
At the end of the loop: n = 9
At the end of the loop: sum = 20
```

We can immediately see that something is wrong. The variable sum has been set to 20. Since it was initialized to 10, it is set to 10 + 10, which is incorrect if we want to sum the numbers from 1 to 10. There are several ways to correct the problem. One solution is given as the answer to Self-Test Exercise 40.

General Debugging Techniques

Tracing errors can sometimes be a difficult and time-consuming task. It is not uncommon to spend more time debugging a piece of code than it took to write the code in the first place. If you are having difficulties finding the source of your errors, then there are some general debugging techniques to consider.

Examine the system as a whole and do not assume that the bug occurs in one particular place. If the program is giving incorrect output values, then you should examine the source code, different test cases using a range of input and output values, and the logic behind the algorithm itself. For example, consider the tax program in Display 3.1. If the wrong tax is displayed, you might spend a lot of time trying to find an error in the code that calculates the tax. However, the error might simply be that the input values were different from those you were expecting, leading to an apparently incorrect program output. For example, in German the decimal point and comma are reversed from the English usage. Thus, an income of 25,000.50 becomes 25.000,50. A German programmer might make this type of error if the code was written assuming input in the English format. Although this scenario might seem like a stretch, consider the $125 million Mars Climate Orbiter launched by NASA in 1998. In 1999, it was lost approaching the planet because one team used metric units while another used English units to control the spacecraft's thrusters.

Determining the precise cause and location of a bug is one of the first steps in fixing the error. Examine the input and output behavior for different test cases to try to localize the error. A related technique is to trace variables to show what code the program is executing and what values are contained in key variables. You might also focus on code that has recently changed or code that has had errors before. Finally, you can also try removing code. If you comment out blocks of code and the error still remains, then the culprit is in the uncommented code. The process can be repeated until the location of the error can be pinpointed. The `/*` and `*/` notation is particularly useful to comment out large blocks of code. After the error has been fixed, it is easy to remove the comments and reactivate the code.

The first mistakes you should look for are common errors that are easy to make. These are described throughout this textbook in the Pitfall sections. Examples of common errors include off-by-one errors, comparing floating-point types with `==`, adding extra semicolons that terminate a loop early, or using `==` to compare strings for equality.

Some novice programmers may become frustrated if they cannot find the bug and may resort to guessing. This technique involves changing the code without really understanding the effect of the change but hoping that it will fix the error. Avoid such slipshod hackery at all costs! Sometimes this method will work for the first few simple programs that you write. However, it will almost certainly fail for larger programs and will most likely introduce new errors to the program. Make sure that you understand the logical impact a change to the code will make before committing the modification.

Finally, if allowed by your instructor, you could show the program to someone else. A fresh set of eyes can sometimes quickly pinpoint an error that you have been missing. Taking a break and returning to the problem a few hours later or the next day can also sometimes help in discovering an error.

EXAMPLE: Debugging an Input Validation Loop

VideoNote Debugging Walkthrough

Let's illustrate both good and bad debugging techniques with an example. Suppose our program is presenting a menu where the user can select 'A' or 'B'. The purpose of the following code is to validate user input from the keyboard and to make the user type a choice again if something other than 'A' or 'B' is entered. To be more user-friendly, the program should allow users to make their selections in either upper- or lowercase.

EXAMPLE: (continued)

```
String s = "";
char c = ' ';
Scanner keyboard = new Scanner(System.in);

do
{
  System.out.println("Enter 'A' for option A " +
    "or 'B' for option B.");
  s = keyboard.next( );
  s.toLowerCase( );
  c = s.substring(0,1);
}
while ((c != 'a') || (c != 'b'));
```

This program generates a syntax error when compiled:

```
c = s.substring(0,1); : incompatible types
found : java.lang.String
required: char
```

The intent was to extract the first character from the string entered by the user and check to see whether it is `'a'` or `'b'`. The `substring(0,1)` call returns a `String` containing the first character of `s`, but `c` is of type `char` and the types need to match on both sides of the assignment. If we employ the "guessing" debugging technique, then we might make the types match by changing the data type of `c` to `String`. Such a change will "fix" this error, but it will cause new errors because the rest of the code treats `c` like a `char`. As a result, we have added even more errors! Before making any change, consider the larger context and what the effect of the change will be. In this case, the simplest and best fix is to use

```
c = s.charAt(0)
```

to retrieve the first character from `s` instead of retrieving a substring.

At this point, we have corrected the syntax error and our program will compile, but it will still not run correctly. A sample execution is shown as follows:

```
Enter 'A' for option A or 'B' for option B.
C
Enter 'A' for option A or 'B' for option B.
B
Enter 'A' for option A or 'B' for option B.
A
Enter 'A' for option A or 'B' for option B.
(Control-C)
```

The program is stuck in an infinite loop even when we type in a valid choice. The only way to stop it is to break out of the program (in the sample output this is done by hitting Control-C, but you may have to use a different method depending on your computing environment).

(continued)

EXAMPLE: (continued)

At this point, we could employ tracing to try to locate the source of the error. Here is the code with output statements inserted:

```
do
{
    System.out.println("Enter 'A' for option A " +
      "or 'B' for option B.");
    s = keyboard.next( );
    System.out.println("String s = " + s);
    s.toLowerCase( );
    System.out.println("Lowercase s = " + s);
    c = s.charAt(0);
    System.out.println("c = " + c);
}
while ((c != 'a') || (c != 'b'));
```

Sample output is as follows:

```
Enter 'A' for option A or 'B' for option B.
A
String s = A
Lowercase s = A
c = A
Enter 'A' for option A or 'B' for option B.
```

The `println` statements make it clear what is wrong—the string `s` does not change to lowercase. A review of the `toLowerCase( )` documentation reveals that this method does not change the calling string, but instead returns a new string converted to lowercase. The calling string remains unchanged. To fix the error, we can assign the lowercase string back to the original string with

```
s = s.toLowerCase( );
```

However, we are not done yet. Even after fixing the lowercase error, the program is still stuck in an infinite loop, even when we enter `'A'` or `'B'`. A novice programmer might "patch" the program like so to exit the loop:

```
do
{
    System.out.println("Enter 'A' for option A " +
      "or 'B' for option B.");
    s = keyboard.next( );
    s = s.toLowerCase( );
    c = s.charAt(0);
    if ( c == 'a')
     break;
    if (c == 'b')
     break;
}
```

EXAMPLE: (continued)

```
while ((c != 'a') || (c != 'b'));
```

This forces the loop to exit if `'a'` or `'b'` is entered, and it will make the program work. Unfortunately, the result is a coding atrocity that should be avoided at all costs. This "quick fix" does not address the root cause of the error—only the symptoms. Moreover, such patches usually will not work for new cases. This particular fix also results in inconsistent code because the expression `((c! = 'a') || (c! = 'b'))` becomes meaningless when we already handle the `'a'` and `'b'` with the `if` and `break` statements.

To really find the bug, we can turn again to tracing, this time focusing on the Boolean values that control the `do-while` loop:

```
do
{
   System.out.println("Enter 'A' for option A " +
     "or 'B' for option B.");
   s = keyboard.next( );
   s = s.toLowerCase( );
   c = s.charAt(0);
   System.out.println("c != 'a' is " + (c!= 'a'));
   System.out.println("c != 'b' is " + (c!= 'b'));
   System.out.println("(c != 'a') || (c != 'b')) is "
        + ((c != 'a') || (c != 'b')));
}
while ((c != 'a') || (c != 'b'));
```

The sample output is now as follows:

```
Enter 'A' for option A or 'B' for option B.
A
c != 'a' is false
c != 'b' is true
(c != 'a') || (c != 'b')) is true
```

Since `c` equals `'a'`, the statement `(c != 'a')` evaluates to `false` and the statement `(c !='b')` evaluates to `true`. When combined, `(false || true)` is `true`, which makes the loop repeat. In spoken English, it sounds like "c not equal to `'a'`" or "c not equal to `'b'`" is a correct condition to repeat the loop. After all, if the character typed in is not `'a'` or the character typed in is not `'b'`, then the user should be prompted to try again. Logically however, if `(c != 'a')` is `false` (i.e., the character is `'a'`), then `(c != 'b')` must be true. A character cannot make both expressions `false`, so the final Boolean condition will always be `true`. The solution is to replace the "or" with an "and" so that the loop repeats only if `(c != 'a') && (c != 'b'))`. This makes the loop repeat as long as the input character is not `'a'` and it is not `'b'`.

(continued)

EXAMPLE: (continued)

An even better solution is to declare a `boolean` variable to control the `do-while` loop. Inside the body of the loop, we can set this variable to `false` when the loop should exit. This technique has the benefit of making the code logic easier to follow, especially if we pick a meaningful name for the variable. In the following example, it is easy to see that the loop repeats if `invalidKey` is `true`:

```
boolean invalidKey;
do
{
   System.out.println("Enter 'A' for option A " +
     "or 'B' for option B.");
   s = keyboard.next( );
   s = s.toLowerCase( );
   c = s.charAt(0);
   if (c == 'a')
    invalidKey = false;
   else if (c == 'b')
    invalidKey = false;
   else
    invalidKey = true;
}
while (invalidKey);
```

Preventive Coding

The best way to make debugging easier is to make no mistakes in the first place. Although this is unrealistic for programs of any complexity, there are some techniques we can use to eliminate or reduce the number of bugs in a program.

incremental development

Incremental development is the technique of writing a small amount of code and testing it before moving on and writing more code. The test may require some new code, or a "test harness," that will not be part of your final program but exercises your code in some way to see if it is working. This technique makes debugging easier because if the test fails, then the error is likely in the small section of the new code that was just written.

When an error is made, be sure to learn from your mistake so you do not make it again in the future. Did the mistake occur because of sloppy programming? Was there some aspect of the program's design that you did not understand or left off before writing the code? Was there something you could have done to find the error more quickly or prevent it from happening at all? Are there other errors in your program similar to the one you just fixed? A critical review of your coding and debugging techniques should become a learning experience so you do not repeat your mistakes.

code review

Finally, show your code to other programmers. Another developer might be able to immediately spot an error in your code and eliminate a lengthy debugging process. Many software development organizations have a formal process called **code review** that involves the inspection of code by other programmers. Such reviews have the additional benefit that programmers end up sharing coding techniques and learning best practices in the process of reviewing each other's code. A related technique is called **pair programming**, in which two programmers work together at the same computer. The programmers take turns, one typing while the other watches and looks for errors and thinks about the task at hand.

pair programming

Assertion Checks ★

assertion

An **assertion** is a sentence that says (asserts) something about the state of your program. An assertion must be a sentence that is either true or false and should be true if there are no mistakes in your program. You can place assertions in your code by making them comments. For example, all the comments in the following code are assertions:

```
int n = 0;
int sum = 0;
//n == 0 and sum == 0
while (n < 100)
{
    n++;
    sum = sum + n;
     //sum == 1 + 2 + 3 + ... + n
}
//sum == 1 + 2 + 3 + ... + 100
```

Note that each of these assertions can be either true or false, depending on the values of n and sum, and they all should be true if the program is performing correctly.

Java has a special statement to check whether an assertion is true. An assertion check statement has the following form:

assert

```
assert Boolean_Expression;
```

If you run your program in the proper way, the assertion check behaves as follows: If the *Boolean_Expression* evaluates to `true`, nothing happens, but if the *Boolean_Expression* evaluates to `false`, the program ends and outputs an error message saying that an assertion failed.

For example, the previously displayed code can be written as follows, with the first comment replaced by an assertion check:

```
int n = 0;
int sum = 0;
assert (n == 0) && (sum == 0);
while (n < 100)
{
    n++;
    sum = sum + n;
     //sum == 1 + 2 + 3 + ... + n
}
//sum == 1 + 2 + 3 + ... + 100
```

Note that we translated only one of the three comments into an assertion check. Not all assertion comments lend themselves to becoming assertion checks. For example, there is no simple way to convert the other two comments into Boolean expressions. Doing so would not be impossible, but you would need to use code that would itself be more complicated than what you would be checking.

assertion check

Assertion Checking

An **assertion check** is a Java statement consisting of the keyword `assert` followed by a Boolean expression and a semicolon. If assertion checking is turned on and the Boolean expression in the assertion check evaluates to `false` when the assertion check is executed, the program will end and output a suitable error message. If assertion checking is not turned on, the assertion check is treated as a comment.

SYNTAX

`assert` *Boolean_Expression*`;`

EXAMPLE

```
assert (n == 0) && (sum == 0);
```

You can turn assertion checking on and off. When debugging code, you can turn assertion checking on so that a failed assertion will produce an error message. Once your code is debugged, you can turn assertion checking off and your code will run more efficiently.

A program or other class containing assertions is compiled in the usual way. After all classes used in a program are compiled, you can run the program with assertion checking either turned on or turned off.

If you compile your classes from the command line, you would compile a class with assertion in the usual way:

```
javac YourProgram.java
```

You can then run your program with assertion checking turned on or off. The normal way of running a program has assertion checking turned off. To run your program with assertion checking turned on, use the following command:

```
java -enableassertions YourProgram
```

If you are using an IDE, check the documentation for your IDE to see how to handle assertion checking. If you do not find an entry for "assertion checking," which is likely, check to see how you set run options. (With TextPad, you can set things up for assertion checking as follows: On the Configure menu, choose Preferences, and then choose the

Run Java Application command and set the "Prompt for parameters" option for it.[3] After you set this preference, when you run a program, a window will appear in which you can enter options for the `java run` command—for example, `-enableassertions`.)

MyProgrammingLab™

Self-Test Exercises

40. Fix the bug in the code in the earlier subsection "Tracing Variables."

41. Add some suitable output statements to the following code so that all variables are traced:

```
int n, sum = 0;
for (n = 1; n < 10; n++)
    sum = sum + n;
System.out.println("1 + 2 + ...+ 9 + 10 == " + sum);
```

42. What is the bug in the following code? What do you call this kind of loop bug?

```
int n, sum = 0;
for (n = 1; n < 10; n++)
    sum = sum + n;
System.out.println("1 + 2 + ...+ 9 + 10 == " + sum);
```

43. Write an assertion check that checks to see that the value of the variable `time` is less than or equal to the value of the variable `limit`. Both variables are of type `int`.

3.5 Random Number Generation ★

The generation of random numbers is too important to be left to chance.

ROBERT COVEYOU

random numbers

pseudorandom

Games and simulation programs often require the computer to generate random numbers. For example, a card game might need a way to randomly shuffle the cards in the deck or to roll a pair of dice. In this section, we briefly discuss two ways to generate random numbers in Java. Although we generally use the term **random**, Java really generates **pseudorandom** numbers. That is, Java can generate a sequence of numbers that looks random but this sequence of numbers is initialized by a "seed" value. If the same seed value is used to initialize the random number generator, then the exact same sequence of numbers will be generated.

[3] If you are running applets, you also need to select the "Prompt for parameters" option for the Run Java Applet command on the Tools submenu.

The `Random` Object

Java includes an object called `Random` that can be used to generate many different types of random numbers. In this section, we discuss only how to generate random integers and doubles from a uniform distribution (this is when every number that could possibly be generated has an equally likely chance to appear) but the `Random` class supports other distributions.

To use the `Random` class, we first have to import it just like we imported the `Scanner` class:

```
import java.util.Random;
```

Next, we have to create an object of type `Random` that can generate the random numbers for us. This follows the same pattern as creating a `Scanner` object to read from the keyboard.

```
Random randomGenerator = new Random();
```

Similarly, just as you created only one `Scanner` object to read in all of your keyboard inputs, in general you should create only one `Random` object to generate all of your random numbers. In particular, older versions of Java used the computer's clock to seed the random number generator. This meant that two `Random` objects created within the same millisecond would generate the same sequence of numbers. Newer versions of Java do not have this limitation, but normally only one instance of a `Random` object is needed.

To generate a random integer in the range of all possible integers, use

```
int r = randomGenerator.nextInt();
```

To generate a random integer in the range from 0 to n-1, use

```
int r = randomGenerator.nextInt(n);
```

If you want a random number in a different range, then you can scale the number by adding an offset. For example, to generate a random number that is 4, 5, or 6, use

```
int r = randomGenerator.nextInt(3) + 4;
```

This generates a number that is 0, 1, or 2 and then adds 4 to get a number that is 4, 5, or 6.

To generate a random `double`, use

```
double r = randomGenerator.nextDouble();
```

This returns a number that is greater than or equal to 0.0 but less than 1.0. Display 3.11 demonstrates flipping a virtual coin five times by generating five random numbers that are either 0 or 1, where 0 corresponds to tails and 1 corresponds to heads.

Display 3.11 Comparing Strings

```
import java.util.Random;
public class CoinFlipDemo
{
    public static void main(String[] args)
    {
        Random randomGenerator = new Random();
        int counter = 1;

        while (counter <= 5)
        {
            System.out.print("Flip number " + counter + ": ");
            int coinFlip = randomGenerator.nextInt(2);
            if (coinFlip == 1)
                System.out.println("Heads");
            else
                System.out.println("Tails");
            counter++;
        }
    }
}
```

Sample Dialogue (output will vary)

```
Flip number 1: Heads
Flip number 2: Tails
Flip number 3: Heads
Flip number 4: Heads
Flip number 5: Tails
```

The `Math.random()` Method

Java also includes a method to generate random doubles without requiring the user to create an instance of the `Random` class. The method `Math.random()` returns a random double that is greater than or equal to 0.0 but less than 1.0. In fact, when this method is called for the first time, Java internally creates an instance of the `Random` class and invokes the `nextDouble()` method. This can be convenient if you do not want to create your own `Random` object.

Often the range between 0.0 and 1.0 is not what is desired, so it becomes necessary to scale the range by multiplying and translating the value by addition. Commonly, an `int` is desired, which requires a typecast. For example, if you need an `int` in the range from 1 to 6, the following code could be used:

```
int num = (int)(Math.random() * 6) + 1;
```

MyProgrammingLab™

Self-Test Exercises

44. What numbers could be generated by `randomGenerator.nextInt(5) + 10;` where `randomGenerator` is an object of type `Random`?
45. What numbers could be generated by `randomGenerator.nextDouble() * 3 + 1;` where `randomGenerator` is an object of type `Random`?
46. Use the method `Math.random()` to generate a random `double` that is greater than or equal to 10.0 but less than 20.0.

Chapter Summary

- The Java branching statements are the `if-else` statement and the `switch` *statement*.
- A `switch` statement is a multiway branching statement. You can also form multiway branching statements by nesting `if-else` statements to form a multiway `if-else` statement.
- *Boolean expressions* are evaluated similar to the way arithmetic expressions are evaluated. The value of a Boolean expression can be saved in a variable of type `boolean`.
- The Java loop statements are the `while`, `do-while`, and `for` statements.
- A `do-while` statement always iterates its loop body at least one time. Both a `while` statement and a `for` *statement* might iterate its loop body zero times.
- A `for` loop can be used to obtain the equivalent of the instruction "repeat the loop body *n* times."
- Tracing variables is a good method for debugging loops.
- An *assertion* check can be added to your Java code so that if the assertion is false, your program halts with an error message.
- The object `Random` can be used to generate *pseudorandom* integers or doubles.

Answers to Self-Test Exercises

1.
```
if (score > 100)
    System.out.println("High")
else
    System.out.println("Low");
```

2.
```
if (savings > expenses)
{
    System.out.println("Solvent");
    savings = savings - expenses;
    expenses = 0;}
else
{
    System.out.println("Bankrupt");
}
```

3.
```
if (number > 0)
    System.out.println("Positive");
else
    System.out.println("Not positive");
```

4.
```
if (salary < deductions)
{
    System.out.println("Crazy");
}
else
{
    System.out.println("OK");
    net = salary - deductions;
}
```

5. `large`
6. `small`
7. `medium`
8.
```
if (n < 0)
    System.out.println(n + " is less than zero.");
else if(n < 100)
    System.out.println(
              n + " is between 0 and 99 (inclusive).");
else
    System.out.println(n + " is 100 or larger.");
```

9. `Some kind of B.`
10. `Oranges`
11. `Plums`
12. `Fruitless`
13. `n1 >= n2`
14.
```
if (n1 >= n2)
    System.out.println("n1");
else
    System.out.println("n2");
```

15. When the variables are of type `int`, you test for equality using `==`, as follows:

```
variable1 == variable2
```

When the variables are of type `String`, you test for equality using the method `equals`, as follows:

```
variable1.equals(variable2)
```

In some cases, you might want to use `equalsIgnoreCase` instead of `equals`.

16.
```
if (nextWord.compareToIgnoreCase("N") < 0)
    System.out.println("First half of the alphabet");
else
    System.out.println("Second half of the alphabet");
```

17.
```
if ( (exam >= 60) && (programsDone >= 10) )
    System.out.println("Passed");
else
    System.out.println("Failed");
```

18.
```
if ( (pressure > 100) || (temperature >= 212) )
    System.out.println("Emergency");
else
    System.out.println("OK");
```

19. a. `true`.

b. `true`. Note that expressions a and b mean exactly the same thing. Because the operators `==` and `<` have higher precedence than `&&`, you do not need to include the parentheses. The parentheses do, however, make it easier to read. Most people find the expression in option a easier to read than the expression in option b, even though they mean the same thing.

c. `true`.

d. `true`.

e. `false`. Because the value of the first subexpression, `(count == 1)`, is `false`, you know that the entire expression is `false` without bothering to evaluate the second subexpression. Thus, it does not matter what the values of `x` and `y` are. This is called *short-circuit evaluation*, which is what Java does.

f. `true`. Since the value of the first subexpression, `(count < 10)`, is `true`, you know that the entire expression is `true` without bothering to evaluate the second subexpression. Thus, it does not matter what the values of `x` and `y` are. This is called *short-circuit evaluation*, which is what Java does.

g. `false`. Notice that the expression in g includes the expression in option f as a subexpression. This subexpression is evaluated using short-circuit evaluation as we described for option f. The entire expression in g is equivalent to

```
!( (true || (x < y)) && true )
```

which in turn is equivalent to `!( true && true )`, and that is equivalent to `!(true)`, which is equivalent to the final value of `false`.

h. This expression produces an error when it is evaluated because the first subexpression, `((limit/count) > 7)`, involves a division by zero.

i. `true`. Since the value of the first subexpression, `(limit < 20)`, is `true`, you know that the entire expression is `true` without bothering to evaluate the second subexpression. Thus, the second subexpression, `((limit/count) > 7)`, is never evaluated, so the fact that it involves a division by zero is never noticed by the computer. This is *short-circuit evaluation*, which is what Java does.

j. This expression produces an error when it is evaluated because the first subexpression, `((limit/count) > 7)`, involves a division by zero.

k. `false`. Since the value of the first subexpression, `(limit < 0)`, is `false`, you know that the entire expression is `false` without bothering to evaluate the second subexpression. Thus, the second subexpression, `((limit/count) > 7)`, is never evaluated, so the fact that it involves a division by zero is never noticed by the computer. This is *short-circuit evaluation*, which is what Java does.

20. No. Since `(j > 0)` is `false` and Java uses short-circuit evaluation for `&&`, the expression `(1/(j+1) > 10)` is never evaluated.

21. `((bonus + (((day * rate) / correctionFactor) * newGuy)) - penalty)`

22.
```
10
7
4
1
```

23. There will be no output. Because `n > 0` is `false`, the loop body is executed zero times.

24.
```
10
7
4
1
```

25. `10`

A `do-while` loop always executes its body at least one time.

26. –42

A `do-while` loop always executes its body at least one time.

27. With a `do-while` statement, the loop body is always executed at least once. With a `while` statement, there can be conditions under which the loop body is not executed at all.

28. `2 4 6 8`

29.
```
Hello 10
Hello 8
Hello 6
Hello 4
Hello 2
```

30. `2.0 1.5 1.0 0.5`

31.
```
n = 10;
while (n > 0)
{
    System.out.println("Hello " + n);
    n = n - 2;
}
```

32. The output is `1024 10`. The second number is the log to the base 2 of the first number. (If the first number is not a power of 2, then only an approximation to the log base 2 is produced.)

33. The output is `1024 1`. The semicolon after the first line of the `for` loop is probably a pitfall error.

34. The output is too long to reproduce here. The pattern is as follows:
```
1 times 10 = 10
1 times 9 = 9
    .
    .
    .
1 times 1 = 1
2 times 10 = 20
2 times 9 = 18
    .
    .
    .
2 times 1 = 2
3 times 10 = 30
    .
    .
    .
```

35. a. A `for` loop

    b. and c. Both require a `while` loop because the input list might be empty. (A for loop also might work, but a `do-while` loop definitely would not work.)

36. This is an infinite loop. The first few lines of output are
```
10
12
16
19
21
```

37. This is an infinite loop. The first few lines of output are
```
n == 1
limit == 10;
n == 2
limit == 3
n == 3
```

```
limit == 4
n == 4
limit == 5
```

38.
```
8
6
The end.
```

39.
```
8
6
2
0
The end.
```

40. If you look at the trace, you will see that after one iteration, the value of `sum` is 20. But the value should be 10 + 9, or 19. This should lead you to think that the variable `n` is not decremented at the correct time. Indeed, the bug is that the two statements

```
sum = sum + n;
n-- ;
```

should be reversed to

```
n-- ;
sum = sum + n;
```

41.
```
int n, sum = 0;
for (n = 1; n < 10; n++)
{
   System.out.println("n == " + n + " sum == " + sum);
       //Above line is a trace.
   sum = sum + n;
}
System.out.println("After loop");//trace
System.out.println("n == " + n + " sum == " + sum);//trace
System.out.println("1 + 2 + ...+ 9 + 10 == " + sum);
```

If you study the output of this trace, you will see that 10 is never added in. This is a bug in the loop.

42. This is the code you traced in the previous exercise. If you study the output of this trace, you will see that 10 is never added in. This is an off-by-one error.

43. `assert (time <= limit);`

44. 10, 11, 12, 13 or 14

45. A double that is greater than or equal to 1 but less than 4.

46. `double d = Math.random() * 10 + 10;`

MyProgrammingLab™

Programming Projects

Visit www.myprogramminglab.com to complete select exercises online and get instant feedback.

1. (This is a version of Programming Project 2.1 from Chapter 2.) The Babylonian algorithm to compute the square root of a positive number `n` is as follows:
   1. Make a guess at the answer (you can pick `n/2` as your initial guess).
   2. Compute `r = n / guess`.
   3. Set `guess = (guess +r) / 2`.
   4. Go back to step 2 until the last two `guess` values are within 1% of each other.

   Write a program that inputs a double for `n`, iterates through the Babylonian algorithm until the `guess` is within 1% of the previous `guess`, and outputs the answer as a `double` to two decimal places. Your answer should be accurate even for large values of `n`.

2. In the game of craps, a pass line bet proceeds as follows: Two six-sided dice are rolled; the first roll of the dice in a craps round is called the "come out roll." A come out roll of 7 or 11 automatically wins, and a come out roll of 2, 3, or 12 automatically loses. If 4, 5, 6, 8, 9, or 10 is rolled on the come out roll, that number becomes "the point." The player keeps rolling the dice until either 7 or the point is rolled. If the point is rolled first, then the player wins the bet. If a 7 is rolled first, then the player loses.

   Write a program that simulates a game of craps using these rules without human input. Instead of asking for a wager, the program should calculate whether the player would win or lose. The program should simulate rolling the two dice and calculate the sum. Add a loop so that the program plays 10,000 games. Add counters that count how many times the player wins, and how many times the player loses. At the end of the 10,000 games, compute the probability of winning [i.e., `Wins / (Wins + Losses)`] and output this value. Over the long run, who is going to win the most games, you or the house?

3. One way to estimate the adult height of a child is to use the following formula, which uses the height of the parents:

   $$H_{\text{male\_child}} = ((H_{\text{mother}} \times 13/12) + H_{\text{father}})/2$$
   $$H_{\text{female\_child}} = ((H_{\text{father}} \times 12/13) + H_{\text{mother}})/2$$

   All heights are in inches. Write a program that takes as input the gender of the child, the height of the mother in inches, and the height of the father in inches, and outputs the estimated adult height of the child in inches. The program should allow the user to enter a new set of values and output the predicted height until the user decides to exit. The user should be able to input the heights in feet and inches, and the program should output the estimated height of the child in feet and inches. Use the `int` data type to store the heights.

4. It is difficult to make a budget that spans several years, because prices are not stable. If your company needs 200 pencils per year, you cannot simply use this year's price as the cost of pencils two years from now. Because of inflation, the cost is likely to be higher than it is today. Write a program to gauge the expected cost of an item in a specified number of years. The program asks for the cost of the item, the number of years from now that the item will be purchased, and the rate of inflation. The program then outputs the estimated cost of the item after the specified period. Have the user enter the inflation rate as a percentage, such as 5.6 (percent). Your program should then convert the percent to a fraction, such as 0.056, and should use a loop to estimate the price adjusted for inflation.

5. You have just purchased a stereo system that cost $1,000 on the following credit plan: no down payment, an interest rate of 18% per year (and hence 1.5% per month), and monthly payments of $50. The monthly payment of $50 is used to pay the interest, and whatever is left is used to pay part of the remaining debt. Hence, the first month you pay 1.5% of $1,000 in interest. That is $15 in interest. So, the remaining $35 is deducted from your debt, which leaves you with a debt of $965.00. The next month, you pay interest of 1.5% of $965.00, which is $14.48. Hence, you can deduct $35.52 (which is $50 – $14.48) from the amount you owe. Write a program that tells you how many months it will take you to pay off the loan, as well as the total amount of interest paid over the life of the loan. Use a loop to calculate the amount of interest and the size of the debt after each month. (Your final program need not output the monthly amount of interest paid and remaining debt, but you may want to write a preliminary version of the program that does output these values.) Use a variable to count the number of loop iterations and hence, the number of months until the debt is zero. You may want to use other variables as well. The last payment may be less than $50 if the debt is small, but do not forget the interest. If you owe $50, your monthly payment of $50 will not pay off your debt, although it will come close. One month's interest on $50 is only 75 cents.

6. The Fibonacci numbers F_n are defined as follows: F_0 is 1, F_1 is 1, and

$$F_{i+2} = F_i + F_{i+1}$$

$i = 0, 1, 2, \ldots$. In other words, each number is the sum of the previous two numbers. The first few Fibonacci numbers are 1, 1, 2, 3, 5, and 8. One place where these numbers occur is as certain population growth rates. If a population has no deaths, then the series shows the size of the population after each time period. It takes an organism two time periods to mature to reproducing age, and then the organism reproduces once every time period. The formula applies most straightforwardly to asexual reproduction at a rate of one offspring per time period. In any event, the green crud population grows at this rate and has a time period of five days. Hence, if a green crud population starts out as 10 pounds of crud, then in 5 days, there is still 10 pounds of crud; in 10 days, there is 20 pounds of crud; in 15 days, 30 pounds; in 20 days, 50 pounds; and so forth. Write a program that takes both the initial size of a green crud population (in pounds) and a number of days as input and outputs the number of pounds of green crud after that many days. Assume that the population size is the same for four days and then increases every fifth day. Your program should allow the user to repeat this calculation as often as desired.

7. The value e^x can be approximated by the following sum:

   $1 + x + x^2/2! + x^3/3! + \ldots + x^n/n!$

   Write a program that takes a value x as input and outputs this sum for n taken to be each of the values 1 to 10, 50, and 100. Your program should repeat the calculation for new values of x until the user says she or he is through. The expression $n!$ is called the *factorial* of n and is defined as

   $n! = 1 * 2 * 3 * \ldots * n$

   Use variables of type `double` to store the factorials (or arrange your calculation to avoid any direct calculation of factorials); otherwise, you are likely to produce integer overflow, that is, integers larger than Java allows.

8. In cryptarithmetic puzzles, mathematical equations are written using letters. Each letter can be a digit from 0 to 9, but no two letters can be the same. Here is a sample problem:

   ```
   SEND + MORE = MONEY
   ```

   A solution to the puzzle is S = 9, R = 8, O = 0, M = 1, Y = 2, E = 5, N = 6, D = 7. Write a program that finds a solution to the cryptarithmetic puzzle of the following:

   ```
   TOO + TOO + TOO + TOO = GOOD
   ```

   The simplest technique is to use a nested loop for each unique letter (in this case T, O, G, D). The loops would systematically assign the digits from 0 to 9 to each letter. For example, it might first try T = 0, O = 0, G = 0, D = 0, then T = 0, O = 0, G = 0, D = 1, then T = 0, O = 0, G = 0, D = 2, etc., up to T = 9, O = 9, G = 9, D = 9. In the loop body, test that each variable is unique and that the equation is satisfied. Output the values for the letters that satisfy the equation.

VideoNote
Solution to Programming Project 3.9

9. Write a program that calculates the total grade for N classroom exercises as a percentage. Use the `DecimalFormat` class to output the value as a percent. The user should input the value for N followed by each of the N scores and totals. Calculate the overall percentage (sum of the total points earned divided by the total points possible) and output it using the `DecimalFormat` class. Sample input and output is shown below.

   ```
   How many exercises to input?
   3

   Score received for exercise 1:
   10
   Total points possible for exercise 1:
   10

   Score received for exercise 2:
   7
   Total points possible for exercise 2:
   12

   Score received for exercise 3:
   5
   ```

```
Total points possible for exercise 3:
8
Your total is 22 out of 30, or 73.33%.
```

10. The game of Pig is a simple two-player dice game in which the first player to reach 100 or more points wins. Players take turns. On each turn, a player rolls a six-sided die:
    - If the player rolls a 1, then the player gets no new points and it becomes the other player's turn.
    - If the player rolls 2 through 6, then he or she can either
      - ROLL AGAIN or
      - HOLD. At this point, the sum of all rolls is added to the player's score and it becomes the other player's turn.

    Write a program that plays the game of Pig, where one player is a human and the other is the computer. When it is the human's turn, the program should show the score of both players and the previous roll. Allow the human to input "r" to roll again or "h" to hold.

    The computer program should play according to the following rule:

    - Keep rolling when it is the computer's turn until it has accumulated 20 or more points, then hold. If the computer wins or rolls a 1, then the turn ends immediately.

    Allow the human to roll first.

11. You have three identical prizes to give away and a pool of 30 finalists. The finalists are assigned numbers from 1 to 30. Write a program to randomly select the numbers of three finalists to receive a prize. Make sure not to pick the same number twice. For example, picking finalists 3, 15, 29 would be valid but picking 3, 3, 31 would be invalid because finalist number 3 is listed twice and 31 is not a valid finalist number.

12. Redo or do for the first time Programming Project 2.13 from Chapter 2 but this time use a loop to read the names from the file. Your program should also handle an arbitrary number of entries in the file instead of handling only three entries. To do this, your program must check to see if there is still data left to read (i.e., it has reached the end of the file). The appropriate methods to read from a file are described in Section 2.3.

VideoNote
Solution to Programming Project 3.13

13. The file `words.txt` on the book's website contains 87,314 words from the English language. Write a program that reads through this file and finds the longest word that is a palindrome.

14. The file `words.txt` on the book's website contains 87,314 words from the English language. Write a program that reads through this file and finds the word that has the most consecutive vowels. For example, the word "bedouin" has three consecutive vowels.

15. This problem is based on a "Nifty Assignment" by Steve Wolfman (http://nifty.stanford.edu/2006/wolfman-pretid). Consider lists of numbers from real-life data sources; for example, a list containing the number of students enrolled in different course sections, the number of comments posted for different Facebook status updates, the number of books in different library holdings, the number of votes per precinct, etc. It might seem like the leading digit of each number in the list could be 1–9 with an equally likely probability. However, Benford's Law states that the leading digit is 1 about 30% of the time and drops with larger digits. The leading digit is 9 only about 5% of the time.

    Write a program that tests Benford's Law. Collect a list of at least 100 numbers from some real-life data source and enter them into a text file. Your program should loop through the list of numbers and count how many times 1 is the first digit, 2 is the first digit, etc. For each digit, output the percentage it appears as the first digit.

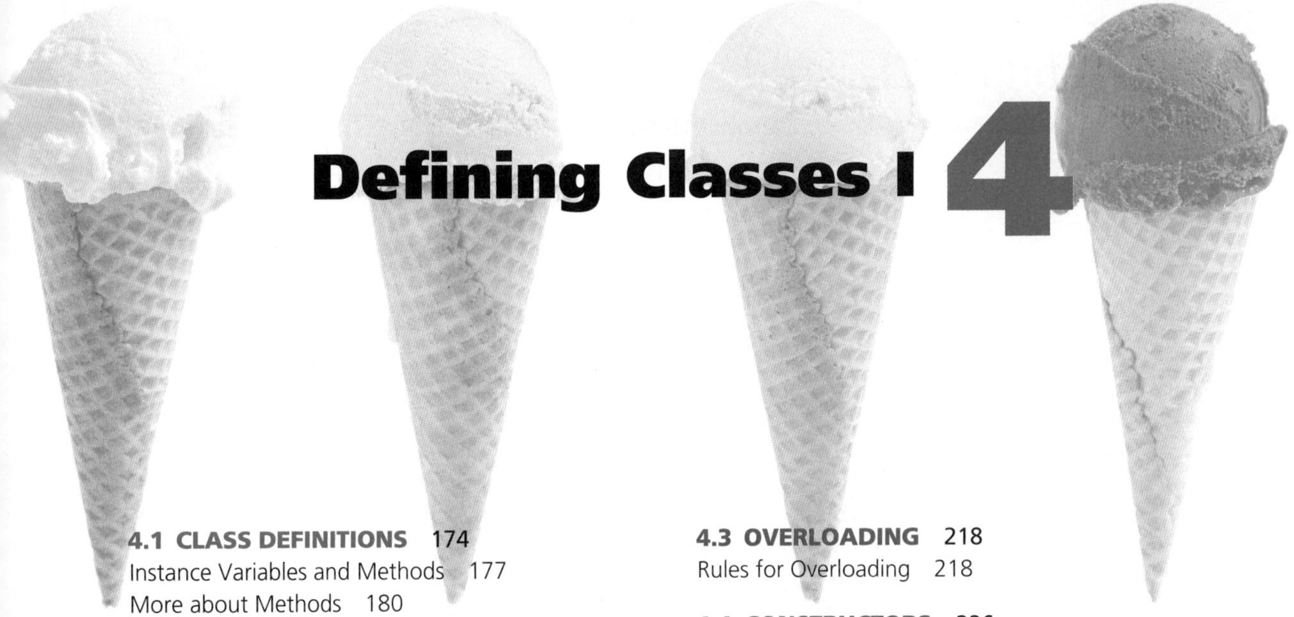

Defining Classes I 4

4 Defining Classes I

The loftier the building,
the deeper must the
foundation be laid.

THOMAS KEMPIS

Introduction

Classes are the single most important language feature that facilitates object-oriented programming (OOP), the dominant programming methodology in use today. You have already been using predefined classes. `String` and `Scanner` are two of the classes we have used. An object is a value of a class type and is referred to as an *instance of the class*. An object differs from a value of a primitive type in that it has methods (actions) as well as data. For example, `"Hello"` is an object of the class `String`. It has the characters in the string as its data and also has a number of methods, such as `length`. You already know how to use classes, objects, and methods. This chapter tells you how to define classes and their methods.

Prerequisites

This chapter uses material from Chapters 1, 2, and 3. This chapter requires a basic understanding of the Java programming language, including the ability to write simple programs using expressions, assignments, and console I/O. You should be able to output numbers, as well as have an understanding of how the `Scanner` class can be used in console I/O. You should also know how to manage the flow of control using branching and looping statements, as well as understand how to use Boolean expressions.

4.1 Class Definitions

"The Time has come," the Walrus said,
"to talk of many things:
of shoes and ships and sealing wax
of cabbages and kings."

LEWIS CARROLL, *Through the Looking-Glass*

A Java program consists of objects from various classes interacting with one another. Before we go into the details of how you define classes, let's review some of the terminology used with classes. Among other things, a class is a type and you can declare variables of a class type. A value of a class type is called an **object**. An object has both data and actions. The actions are called **methods**. Each object can have different data,

object

method

but all objects of a class have the same types of data and all objects in a class have the same methods. An object is usually referred to as an object of the class or as an **instance** **instance of the class** rather than as a value of the class, but it is a value of the class type. To make this abstract discussion come alive, we need a sample definition.

> **A Class Is a Type**
>
> If A is a class, then the phrases "bla is of type A," "bla is an instance of the class A," and "bla is an object of the class A" all mean the same thing.

Display 4.1 contains a definition for a class named `DateFirstTry` and a program that demonstrates using the class. Objects of this class represent dates such as December 31, 2012 and July 4, 1776. This class is unrealistically simple, but it will serve to introduce you to the syntax for a class definition. Each object of this class has three pieces of data: a string for the month name, an integer for the day of the month, and another integer for the year. The objects have only one method, which is named `writeOutput`. Both the data items and the methods are sometimes called **members** of the object, because they belong to the object. The data items are also sometimes called **fields**. We will call the data items **instance variables** and use the term *method* instead of *member*.

member

field

instance variable

The following three lines from the start of the class definition define three instance variables (three data members):

```
public String month;
public int day;
public int year; //a four digit number.
```

The word `public` simply means that there are no restrictions on how these instance variables are used. Each of these lines declares one instance variable name. You can think of an object of the class as a complex item with instance variables inside of it. So, an instance variable can be thought of as a smaller variable inside each object of the class. In this case, the instance variables are called `month`, `day`, and `year`.

An object of a class is typically named by a variable of the class type. For example, the program `DateFirstTryDemo` in Display 4.1 declares the two variables `date1` and `date2` to be of type `DateFirstTry`, as follows:

```
DateFirstTry date1, date2;
```

This gives us variables of the class `DateFirstTry`, but so far there are no objects of the class. Objects are class values that are named by the variables. To obtain an object, you must use the `new` operator to create a "new" object. For example, the following creates an object of the class `DateFirstTry` and names it with the variable `date1`:

new

```
date1 = new DateFirstTry();
```

Display 4.1 A Simple Class

This class definition goes in a file named **`DateFirstTry.java`**.

```
public class DateFirstTry
{
    public String month;
    public int day;
    public int year; //a four digit number.

    public void writeOutput()
    {
        System.out.println(month + " " + day + ", " + year);
    }
}
```

Later in this chapter, we will see that these three **`public`** *modifiers should be replaced with* **`private`**.

This class definition (program) goes in a file named **`DateFirstTryDemo.java`**.

```
public class DateFirstTryDemo
{
   public static void main(String[] args)
   {
         DateFirstTry date1, date2;
         date1 = new DateFirstTry();
         date2 = new DateFirstTry();
         date1.month = "December";
         date1.day = 31;
         date1.year = 2012;
         System.out.println("date1:");
         date1.writeOutput();

         date2.month = "July";
         date2.day = 4;
         date2.year = 1776;
         System.out.println("date2:");
         date2.writeOutput();
   }
}
```

Sample Dialogue

```
date1:
December 31, 2012
date2:
July 4, 1776
```

We will discuss this kind of statement in more detail later in this chapter when we discuss something called a *constructor*. For now simply note that

```
Class_Variable = new Class_Name( );
```

creates a new object of the specified class and associates it with the class variable.[1] Because the class variable now names an object of the class, we will often refer to the class variable as an object of the class. (This is really the same usage as when we refer to an `int` variable `n` as "the integer `n`," even though the integer is, strictly speaking, not `n` but the value of `n`.)

Unlike what we did in Display 4.1, the declaration of a class variable and the creation of the object are more typically combined into one statement, as follows:

```
DateFirstTry date1 = new DateFirstTry();
```

The `new` Operator

The `new` operator is used to create an object of a class and associate the object with a variable that names it.

SYNTAX

Class_Variable = `new` *Class_Name*( );

EXAMPLE

```
DateFirstTry date;
date = new DateFirstTry();
```

which is usually written in the following equivalent form:

```
DateFirstTry date = new DateFirstTry();
```

Instance Variables and Methods

We will illustrate the details about instance variables using the class and program in Display 4.1. Each object of the class `DateFirstTry` has three instance variables, which can be named by giving the object name followed by a dot and the name of the instance variable. For example, the object `date1` in the program `DateFirstTryDemo` has the following three instance variables:

```
date1.month
date1.day
date1.year
```

Similarly, if you replace `date1` with `date2`, you obtain the three instance variables for the object `date2`. Note that `date1` and `date2` together have a total of six instance variables. The instance variables `date1.month` and `date2.month`, for example, are two different (instance) variables.

[1] For many, the word "new" suggests a memory allocation. As we will see, the `new` operator does indeed produce a memory allocation.

The instance variables in Display 4.1 can be used just like any other variables. For example, `date1.month` can be used just like any other variable of type `String`. The instance variables `date1.day` and `date1.year` can be used just like any other variables of type `int`. Thus, although the following is not in the spirit of the class definition, it is legal and would compile:

```
date1.month = "Hello friend.";
```

More likely assignments to instance variables are given in the program `DateFirstTryDemo`.

The class `DateFirstTry` has only one method, which is named `writeOutput`. We reproduce the definition of the method here:

```
public void writeOutput()  <------------ Heading
{                                                          Body
    System.out.println(month + " " + day + ", " + year);
}
```

All method definitions belong to some class, and all method definitions are given inside the definition of the class to which they belong. A method definition is divided into two parts, a **heading** and a **method body**, as illustrated by the annotation on the method definition. The word `void` means this is a method for performing an action as opposed to producing a value. We will say more about method definitions later in this chapter (including some indication of why the word `void` was chosen to indicate an action). You have already been using methods from predefined classes. The way you invoke a method from a class definition you write is the same as the way you do it for a predefined class. For example, the following from the program `DateFirstTryDemo` is an invocation of the method `writeOutput` with `date1` as the calling object:

heading

method body

```
date1.writeOutput();
```

This invocation is equivalent to execution of the method body. So, this invocation is equivalent to

```
System.out.println(month + " " + day + ", " + year);
```

However, we need to say more about exactly how this is equivalent. If you simply replace the method invocation with this `System.out.println` statement, you will get a compiler error message. Note that within the definition for the method `writeOutput`, the names of the instance variables are used without any calling object. This is because the method will be invoked with different calling objects at different times. When an instance variable is used in a method definition, it is understood to be the instance variable of the calling object. So in the program `DateFirstTryDemo`,

```
date1.writeOutput();
```

Class Definition

The following shows the form of a class definition that is most commonly used; however, it is legal to intermix the method definitions and the instance variable declarations.

SYNTAX

```
public class Class_Name
{
    Instance_Variable_Declaration_1
    Instance_Variable_Declaration_2
        . . .
    Instance_Variable_Declaration_Last

    Method_Definition_1
    Method_Definition_2
        . . .
    Method_Definition_Last
}
```

EXAMPLES

See Displays 4.1 and 4.2.

is equivalent to

```
System.out.println(date1.month + " " + date1.day
                               + ", " + date1.year);
```

Similarly,

```
date2.writeOutput();
```

is equivalent to

```
System.out.println(date2.month + " " + date2.day
                               + ", " + date2.year);
```

File Names and Locations

Remember that a file must be named the same as the class it contains with an added `.java` at the end. For example, a class named `MyClass` must be in a file named `MyClass.java`.

We will eventually see other ways to arrange files, but at this point, your program and all the classes it uses should be in the same directory (same folder).

MyProgrammingLab™

Self-Test Exercises

1. Write a method called makeItNewYears that could be added to the class DateFirstTry in Display 4.1. The method makeItNewYears has no parameters and sets the month instance variable to "January" and the day instance variable to 1. It does not change the year instance variable.

2. Write a method called yellIfNewYear that could be added to the class DateFirstTry in Display 4.1. The method yellIfNewYear has no parameters and outputs the string "Hurrah!" provided the month instance variable has the value "January" and the day instance variable has the value 1. Otherwise, it outputs the string "Not New Year's Day."

More about Methods

As we noted for predefined methods, methods of the classes you define are of two kinds: methods that return (compute) some value and methods that perform an action other than returning a value. For example, the method println of the object System.out is an example of a method that performs an action other than returning a value; in this case, the action is to write something to the screen. The method nextInt of the class Scanner, introduced in Chapter 2, is a method that returns a value; in this case, the value returned is a number typed in by the user. A method that performs some action other than returning a value is called a void method. This same distinction between void methods and methods that return a value applies to methods in the classes you define. The two kinds of methods require slight differences in how they are defined.

Both kinds of methods have a method heading and a method body, which are similar but not identical for the two kinds of methods. The method heading for a void method is of the form

```
public void Method_Name(Parameter_List)
```

The method heading for a method that returns a value is

```
public Type_Returned Method_Name (Parameter_List)
```

Later in the chapter, we will see that public may sometimes be replaced by a more restricted modifier and that it is possible to add additional modifiers, but these templates will do right now. For now, our examples will have an empty *Parameter_List*.

If a method returns a value, then it can return different values in different situations, but all values returned must be of the same type, which is specified as the type returned. For example, if a method has the heading

```
public double myMethod()
```

then the method always returns a value of type `double`, and the heading

```
public String yourMethod()
```

indicates a method that always returns a value of type `String`.

The following is a `void` method heading:

```
public void ourMethod()
```

Notice that when the method returns no value at all, we use the keyword `void` in place of a type. If you think of `void` as meaning "no returned type," the word `void` begins to make sense.

invocation

An **invocation** of a method that returns a value can be used as an expression anyplace that a value of the *Type_Returned* can be used. For example, suppose `anObject` is an object of a class with methods having our sample heading; in this case, the following are legal:

```
double d = anObject.myMethod();
String aStringVariable = anObject.yourMethod();
```

A `void` method does not return a value, but simply performs an action, so an invocation of a `void` method is a statement. A `void` method is invoked as in the following example:

```
anObject.ourMethod();
```

Note the ending semicolon.

So far, we have avoided the topic of parameter lists by only giving examples with empty parameter lists, but note that parentheses are required even for an empty parameter list. Parameter lists are discussed later in this chapter.

body

The **body** of a `void` method definition is simply a list of declarations and statements enclosed in a pair of braces, {}. For example, the following is a complete `void` method definition:

```
public void ourMethod()
{
    System.out.println("Hello");
    System.out.println("from our method.");
}
```

The body of a method that returns a value is the same as the body of a `void` method but with one additional requirement. The body of a method that returns a value must contain at least one `return` statement. A **`return` statement** is of the form

`return` statement

```
return Expression;
```

where *Expression* can be any expression that evaluates to something of the *Type_Returned* that is listed in the method heading. For example, the following is a complete definition of a method that returns a value:

```
public String yourMethod()
{
    Scanner keyboard = new Scanner(System.in);
    System.out.println("Enter a line of text");
    String result = keyboard.nextLine();
    return result + " was entered.";
}
```

Notice that a method that returns a value can do other things besides returning a value, but style rules dictate that whatever else it does should be related to the value returned.

A `return` statement always ends a method invocation. Once the `return` statement is executed, the method ends, and any remaining statements in the method definition are not executed.

`return` in a `void` method

If you want to end a `void` method before it runs out of statements, you can use a `return` statement without any expression, as follows:

```
return;
```

A `void` method need not have any `return` statements, but you can place a `return` statement in a `void` method if there are situations that require the method to end before all the code is executed.

Method Definitions

There are two kinds of methods: methods that return a value and methods, known as `void` methods, that perform some action other than returning a value.

Definition of a Method That Returns a Value

SYNTAX

```
public Type_Returned Method_Name(Parameter_List)
{
    <List of statements, at least one of which
            must contain a return statement.>
}
```

If there are no *Parameters*, then the parentheses are empty.

EXAMPLE

```
public int getDay()
{
    return day;
}
```

void Method Definition

SYNTAX

```
public void Method_Name(Parameter_List)
{
   <List of statements>
}
```

If there are no *Parameters*, then the parentheses are empty.

EXAMPLE

```
public void writeOutput( )
{
    System.out.println(month + " " + day + ", " + year);
}
```

All method definitions are inside of some class definition. See Display 4.2 to see these example method definitions in the context of a class.

When an instance variable name is used in a method definition, it refers to an instance variable of the calling object.

return Statements

The definition of a method that returns a value must have one or more `return` statements. A `return` statement specifies the value returned by the method and ends the method invocation.

SYNTAX

```
return Expression;
```

EXAMPLE

```
public int getYear( )
{
    return year;
}
```

A `void` method definition need not have a `return` statement. However, a `return` statement can be used in a `void` method to cause the method to immediately end. The form for a `return` statement in a `void` method is

```
return;
```

Although it may seem that we have lost sight of the fact, all these method definitions must be inside of some class definition. Java does not have any stand-alone methods that are not in any class. Display 4.2 rewrites the class given in Display 4.1 but this time we have added a more diverse set of methods. Display 4.3 contains a sample program that illustrates how the methods of the class in Display 4.2 are used.

TIP: Any Method Can Be Used as a `void` Method

A method that returns a value can also perform some action besides returning a value. If you want that action, but do not need the returned value, you can invoke the method as if it were a `void` method and the returned value will simply be discarded. For example, the following contains two invocations of the method `nextLine()`, which returns a value of type `String`. Both are legal.

```
Scanner keyboard = new Scanner(System.in);
    . . .
String inputString = keyboard.nextLine();
    . . .
System.out.println("Press Enter to continue with program.");
keyboard.nextLine(); //Reads a line and discards it. ■
```

Display 4.2 **A Class with More Methods** (part 1 of 2)

```
import java.util.Scanner;

public class DateSecondTry
{
    private String month;
    private int day;
    private int year; //a four digit number.

    public void writeOutput()
    {
        System.out.println(month + " " + day + ", " + year);
    }

    public void readInput()
    {
        Scanner keyboard = new Scanner(System.in);
        System.out.println("Enter month, day, and year.");
        System.out.println("Do not use a comma.");
        month = keyboard.next();
        day = keyboard.nextInt();
        year = keyboard.nextInt();
    }
```

The significance of the modifier `private` is discussed in the subsection "`public` and `private` Modifiers" in Section 4.2 a bit later in this chapter.

Display 4.2 A Class with More Methods (part 2 of 2)

```
    public int getDay()
    {
        return day;
    }
    public int getYear()
    {
        return year;
    }

    public int getMonth()
    {
        if (month.equalsIgnoreCase("January"))
            return 1;
        else if (month.equalsIgnoreCase("February"))
            return 2;
        else if (month.equalsIgnoreCase("March"))
            return 3;
        else if (month.equalsIgnoreCase("April"))
            return 4;
        else if (month.equalsIgnoreCase("May"))
            return 5;
        else if (month.equals("June"))
            return 6;
        else if (month.equalsIgnoreCase("July"))
            return 7;
        else if (month.equalsIgnoreCase("August"))
            return 8;
        else if (month.equalsIgnoreCase("September"))
            return 9;
        else if (month.equalsIgnoreCase("October"))
            return 10;
        else if (month.equalsIgnoreCase("November"))
            return 11;
        else if (month.equalsIgnoreCase("December"))
            return 12;
        else
        {
            System.out.println("Fatal Error");
            System.exit(0);
            return 0; //Needed to keep the compiler happy
        }
    }
}
```

MyProgrammingLab™

Self-Test Exercises

3. Write a method called `getNextYear` that could be added to the class `DateSecondTry` in Display 4.2. The method `getNextYear` returns an `int` value equal to the value of the `year` instance variable plus one.

Display 4.3 Using the Class in Display 4.2

```
public class DemoOfDateSecondTry
{
    public static void main(String[] args)
    {
        DateSecondTry date = new DateSecondTry();
        date.readInput();

        int dayNumber = date.getDay();
        System.out.println("That is the " + dayNumber
                            + "th day of the month.");
    }
}
```

An invocation of a `void` method is a statement.

An invocation of a method that returns a value is an expression that can be used anyplace that a value of the type returned by the method can be used.

Sample Dialogue

```
Enter month, day, and year.
Do not use a comma.
July 4 1776
That is the 4th day of the month.
```

Local Variables

Look at the definition of the method `readInput()` given in Display 4.2. That method definition includes the declaration of a variable called `keyboard`. A variable declared within a method is called a **local variable**. It is called *local* because its meaning is local to—that is, confined to—the method definition. If you have two methods and each of them declares a variable of the same name—for example, if both were named `keyboard`—they would be two different variables that just happen to have the same name. Any change that is made to the variable named `keyboard` within one method would have no effect upon the variable named `keyboard` in the other method.

local variable

As we noted in Chapter 1, the `main` part of a program is itself a method. All variables declared in `main` are variables local to the method `main`. If a variable declared in `main` happens to have the same name as a variable declared in some other method, they are two different variables that just happen to have the same name. Thus, all the variables we have seen so far are either local variables or instance variables. There is only one more kind of variable in Java, which is known as a *static variable*. Static variables will be discussed in Chapter 5.

> **Local Variable**
>
> A variable declared within a method definition is called a **local variable**. If two methods each have a local variable of the same name, they are two different variables that just happen to have the same name.

> **Global Variables**
>
> Thus far, we have discussed two kinds of variables: instance variables, whose meaning is confined to an object of a class, and local variables, whose meaning is confined to a method definition. Some other programming languages have another kind of variable called a **global variable**, whose meaning is confined only to the program. Java does not have these global variables.

Blocks

block

compound statement

The terms **block** and **compound statement** mean the same thing—namely, a set of Java statements enclosed in braces, {}. However, programmers tend to use the two terms in different contexts. When you declare a variable within a compound statement, the compound statement is usually called a *block*.

> **Blocks**
>
> A **block** is another name for a compound statement—that is, a list of statements enclosed in braces. However, programmers tend to use the two terms in different contexts. When you declare a variable within a compound statement, the compound statement is usually called a *block*. The variables declared in a block are local to the block, so these variables disappear when the execution of the block is completed. However, even though the variables are local to the block, their names cannot be used for anything else within the same method definition.

If you declare a variable within a block, that variable is local to the block. This means that when the block ends, all variables declared within the block disappear. In many programming languages, you can even use that variable's name to name some other variable outside the block. However, *in Java, you cannot have two variables with the same name inside a single method definition*. Local variables within blocks can sometimes create problems in Java. It is sometimes easier to declare the variables outside the block. If you declare a variable outside a block, you can use it both inside and outside the block, and it will have the same meaning in both locations.

TIP: Declaring Variables in a `for` Statement

You can declare a variable (or variables) within the initialization portion of a `for` statement, as in the following:

```
int sum = 0;
for (int n = 1; n < 10; n++)
    sum = sum + n;
```

If you declare `n` in this way, the variable `n` will be *local to the* `for` *loop*. This means that `n` cannot be used outside the `for` loop. For example, the following use of `n` in the `System.out.println` statement is illegal:

```
for (int n = 1; n < 10; n++)
    sum = sum + n;
System.out.println(n); //Illegal
```

Declaring variables inside a `for` loop can sometimes be more of a nuisance than a helpful feature. We tend to avoid declaring variables inside a `for` loop except for very simple cases that have no potential for confusion. ■

MyProgrammingLab™

Self-Test Exercises

4. Write a method called `happyGreeting` that could be added to the class `DateSecondTry` in Display 4.2. The method `happyGreeting` writes the string `"Happy Days!"` to the screen a number of times equal to the value of the instance variable `day`. For example, if the value of `day` is `3`, then it should write the following to the screen:

```
Happy Days!
Happy Days!
Happy Days!
```

Use a local variable.

Parameters of a Primitive Type

parameter

All the method definitions we have seen thus far had no parameters, which was indicated by an empty set of parentheses in the method heading. A **parameter** is like a blank that is filled in with a particular value when the method is invoked. (What we are calling *parameters* are also called *formal parameters*.) The value that is plugged in for

argument

the parameter is called an **argument**.[2] We have already used arguments with predefined methods. For example, the string `"Hello"` is the argument to the method `println` in the following method invocation:

```
System.out.println("Hello");
```

Display 4.4 contains the definition of a method named `setDate` that has the three parameters `newMonth`, `newDay`, and `newYear`. It also contains the definition of a method named `monthString` that has one parameter of type `int`.

Arguments are given in parentheses at the end of the method invocation. For example, in the following call from Display 4.4, the integers `6` and `17` and the variable `year` are the arguments plugged in for `newMonth`, `newDay`, and `newYear`, respectively:

```
date.setDate(6, 17, year);
```

When you have a method invocation such as the preceding, the argument (such as `6`) is plugged in for the corresponding formal parameter (such as `newMonth`) *everywhere that the parameter occurs in the method definition*. After all the arguments have been plugged in for their corresponding parameters, the code in the body of the method definition is executed.

The following invocation of the method `monthString` occurs within the definition of the method `setDate` in Display 4.4:

```
month = monthString(newMonth);
```

The argument is `newMonth`, which is plugged in for the parameter `monthNumber` in the definition of the method `monthString`.

Note that each of the formal parameters must be preceded by a type name, even if there is more than one parameter of the same type. Corresponding arguments must match the type of their corresponding formal parameter, although in some simple cases, an automatic type cast might be performed by Java. For example, if you plug in an argument of type `int` for a parameter of type `double`, Java automatically type casts the `int` value to a value of type `double`. The following list shows the type casts that Java automatically performs for you. An argument in a method invocation that is of any of these types is automatically type cast to any of the types that appear to its right, if that is needed to match a formal parameter.[3]

```
byte -> short -> int -> long -> float -> double
```

---

[2] Some programmers use the term *actual parameters* for what we are calling *arguments*.

[3] An argument of type `char` is also converted to a matching number type, if the formal parameter is of type `int` or any type to the right of `int` in our list of types.

Display 4.4 **Methods with Parameters** (part 1 of 2)

```
import java.util.Scanner;

public class DateThirdTry
{
    private String month;
    private int day;
    private int year; //a four digit number.

    public void setDate(int newMonth, int newDay, int newYear)
    {
        month = monthString(newMonth);
        day = newDay;
        year = newYear;
    }

    public String monthString(int monthNumber)
    {
        switch (monthNumber)
        {
        case 1:
            return "January";
        case 2:
            return "February";
        case 3:
            return "March";
        case 4:
            return "April";
        case 5:
            return "May";
        case 6:
            return "June";
        case 7:
            return "July";
        case 8:
            return "August";
        case 9:
            return "September";
        case 10:
            return "October";
        case 11:
            return "November";
        case 12:
            return "December";
```

The significance of the modifier `private` *is discussed later in the subsection "*`public` *and* `private` *Modifiers" in Section 4.2.*

The method `setDate` *has an* `int` *parameter for the month, even though the month instance variable is of type* `String`*. The method* `setDate` *converts the month* `int` *value to a string with a call to the method* `monthString`*.*

This is the file `DateThirdTry.java`*.*

Display 4.4 Methods with Parameters (part 2 of 2)

```
            default:
                System.out.println("Fatal Error");
                System.exit(0);
                return "Error"; //to keep the compiler happy
            }
        }
        <The rest of the method definitions are identical to the ones given in Display 4.2>.
}
```

This is the file `DateThirdTry.java`.

```
public class DateThirdTryDemo
{
   public static void main(String[]args)
   {
        DateThirdTry date = new DateThirdTry();
        int year = 1882;
        date.setDate(6, 17, year);
        date.writeOutput();
    }
}
```

This is the file `DateThirdTryDemo.java`.

The variable `year` *is NOT plugged in for the parameter* `newYear` *in the definition of the method* `setDate`. *Only the value of* `year`, *namely* `1882`, *is plugged in for the parameter* `newYear`.

Sample Dialogue

```
June 17, 1882
```

Note that this is exactly the same as the automatic type casting we discussed in Chapter 1 for storing values of one type in a variable of another type. The more general rule is that you can use a value of any of the listed types anywhere that Java expects a value of a type further down on the list.

Note that the correspondence of the parameters and arguments is determined by their order in the lists in parentheses. In a method invocation, there must be exactly the same number of arguments in parentheses as there are formal parameters in the method definition heading. The first argument in the method invocation is plugged in for the first parameter in the method definition heading, the second argument in the method invocation is plugged in for the second parameter in the heading of the method definition, and so forth. This is diagrammed in Display 4.5.

Display 4.5 Correspondence between Formal Parameters and Arguments

```
Public class DateThirdTry
{
    private String month;
    private int day;
    private int year; //a four digit number.
    public void setDate(int newMonth, int newDay, int newYear)
    {
        month = monthString(newMonth);
        day = newDay;
        year = newYear;
    }
    . . .
```

This is in the file **DateThirdTry.java.**

Only the value of **year**, *Namely* **1882**, *is plugged in for the parameter* **newYear.**

```
public class DateThirdTryDemo
{
   public static void main(String[] args)
   {
       DateThirdTry date = new DateThirdTry();
       int year = 1882;
       date.setDate(6, 17, year);
       date.writeOutput();
   }
}
```

This is in the file **DateThirdTryDemo.java.** *This is the file for a program that uses the class* **DateThirdTry.**

The arrows show which argument is plugged in for which formal parameter.

Parameters of a Primitive Type

Parameters are given in parentheses after the method name in the heading of a method definition. A parameter of a primitive type, such as `int`, `double`, or `char`, is a local variable. When the method is invoked, the parameter is initialized to the value of the corresponding argument in the method invocation. This mechanism is known as the **call-by-value** parameter mechanism. The argument in a method invocation can be a literal constant, such as 2 or `'A'`; a variable; or any expression that yields a value of the appropriate type. This is the only kind of parameter that Java has for parameters of a primitive type. (Parameters of a class type are discussed in Chapter 5.)

> **`main` Is a `void` Method**
>
> The `main` part of a program is a `void` method, as indicated by its heading:
>
> ```
> public static void main(String[] args)
> ```
>
> The word `static` will be explained in Chapter 5. The identifier `args` is a parameter of type `String[]`, which is the type for an array of strings. Arrays are discussed in Chapter 6, and you need not be concerned about them until then. In the examples in this book, we never use the parameter `args`. Because `args` is a parameter, you may replace it with any other nonkeyword identifier and your program will have the same meaning. Aside from possibly changing the name of the parameter `args`, the heading of the `main` method must be exactly as shown above. Although we will not be using the parameter `args`, we will tell you how to use it in Chapter 6.
>
> A program in Java is just a class that has a `main` method. When you give a command to run a Java program, the run-time system invokes the method `main`.

It is important to note that only the value of the argument is used in this substitution process. If an argument in a method invocation is a variable (such as `year` in Display 4.4), it is the value of the variable that is plugged in for its corresponding parameter; it is not the variable name that is plugged in. For example, in Display 4.4, the value of the variable `year` (that is, `1882`) is plugged in for the parameter `newYear`. The variable `year` is not plugged into the body of the method `setDate`. Because only the value of the argument is used, this method of plugging in arguments for formal parameters is known as the **call-by-value** mechanism. In Java, this is the only method of substitution that is used with parameters of a primitive type, such as `int`, `double`, and `char`. As you will eventually see, this is, strictly speaking, also the only method of substitution that is used with parameters of a class type. However, there are other differences that make parameters of a class type appear to use a different substitution mechanism. For now, we are concerned only with parameters and arguments of primitive types, such as `int`, `double`, and `char`. (Although the type `String` is a class type, you will not go wrong if you consider it to behave like a primitive type when an argument of type `String` is plugged in for its corresponding parameter. However, for most class types, you need to think a bit differently about how arguments are plugged in for parameters. We discuss parameters of a class type in Chapter 5.)

call-by-value

parameters as local variables

In most cases, you can think of a parameter as a kind of blank, or placeholder, that is filled in by the value of its corresponding argument in the method invocation. However, parameters are more than just blanks; a parameter is actually a local variable. When the method is invoked, the value of an argument is computed, and the corresponding parameter, which is a local variable, is initialized to this value. Occasionally, it is useful to use a parameter as a local variable. An example of a parameter used as a local variable is given in Display 4.6. In that display, notice the parameter `minutesWorked` in the method `computeFee`. The value of `minutesWorked` is changed within the body of the method definition. This is allowed because a parameter is a local variable.

Display 4.6 **A Formal Parameter Used as a Local Variable** (part 1 of 2)

This is the file `Bill.java`.

```
import java.util.Scanner;

public class Bill
{
    public static final double RATE = 150.00; //Dollars per quarter hour

    private int hours;
    private int minutes;
    private double fee;

    public void inputTimeWorked()
    {
        System.out.println("Enter number of full hours worked");
        System.out.println("followed by number of minutes:");
        Scanner keyboard = new Scanner(System.in);
        hours = keyboard.nextInt();
        minutes = keyboard.nextInt();
    }

    private double computeFee(int hoursWorked, int minutesWorked)
    {
        minutesWorked = hoursWorked*60 + minutesWorked;
        int quarterHours = minutesWorked/15;
            //Any remaining fraction of a quarter hour is not
            //charged for.
        return quarterHours*RATE;
    }

    public void updateFee()
    {
        fee = computeFee(hours, minutes);
    }

    public void outputBill()
    {
        System.out.println("Time worked: ");
        System.out.println(hours + " hours and " + minutes +
                           " minutes");
        System.out.println("Rate: $" + RATE + " per quarter hour.");
        System.out.println("Amount due: $" + fee);
    }
}
```

`computeFee` *uses the parameter* `minutesWorked` *as a local variable.*

Although `minutes` *is plugged in for* `minutesWorked` *and* `minutesWorked` *is changed, the value of* `minutes` *is not changed.*

Display 4.6 A Formal Parameter Used as a Local Variable (part 2 of 2)

```
public class BillingDialog
{
    public static void main(String[] args)
    {
        System.out.println("Welcome to the law offices of");
        System.out.println("Dewey, Cheatham, and Howe.");
        Bill yourBill = new Bill();
        yourBill.inputTimeWorked();
        yourBill.updateFee();
        yourBill.outputBill();
        System.out.println("We have placed a lien on your house.");
        System.out.println("It has been our pleasure to serve you.");
    }
}
```

This is the file `BillingDialog.java.`

Sample Dialogue

```
Welcome to the law offices of
Dewey, Cheatham, and Howe.
Enter number of full hours worked
followed by number of minutes:
3 48
Time worked:
2 hours and 48 minutes
Rate: $150.0 per quarter hour.
Amount due: $2250.0
We have placed a lien on your house.
It has been our pleasure to serve you.
```

PITFALL: Use of the Terms "Parameter" and "Argument"

The use of the terms *parameter* and *argument* that we follow in this book is consistent with common usage, but people also often use the terms *parameter* and *argument* interchangeably. When you see these terms, you must determine their exact meaning from context. Many people use the term *parameter* for both what we call *parameters* and what we call *arguments*. Other people use the term *argument* both for what we call *parameters* and what we call *arguments*. Do not expect consistency in how people use these two terms.

formal parameters

actual parameter

The term **formal parameter** is often used for what we describe as a *parameter*. We will sometimes use this term for emphasis. The term **actual parameter** is often used for what we call an *argument*. We do not use this term in this book, but you will encounter it in other books. ■

MyProgrammingLab™

Self-Test Exercises

5. Write a method called `fractionDone` that could be added to the class `DateThirdTry` in Display 4.4. The method `fractionDone` has a parameter `targetDay` of type `int` (for a day of the month) and returns a value of type double. The value returned is the value of the `day` instance variable divided by the `int` parameter `targetDay`. (So it returns the fraction of the time passed so far this month where the goal is reaching the `targetDay`.) Use floating-point division, not integer division. To get floating-point division, copy the value of the `day` instance variable into a local variable of type `double` and use this local variable in place of the day instance variable in the division. (You may assume the parameter `targetDay` is a valid day of the month that is greater than the value of the `day` instance variable.)

6. Write a method called `advanceYear` that could be added to the class `DateThirdTry` in Display 4.4. The method `advanceYear` has one parameter of type `int`. The method `advanceYear` increases the value of the `year` instance variable by the amount of this one parameter.

7. Suppose we redefine the method `setDate` in Display 4.4 to the following:

```
public void setDate(int newMonth, int newDay,int newYear)
{
    month = monthString(newMonth);
    day = newDay;
    year = newYear;
    System.out.println("Date changed to "
                  + newMonth + " " + newDay + ", " + newYear);
}
```

Indicate all instances of `newMonth` that have their value changed to `6` in the following invocation (also from Display 4.4):

```
date.setDate(6, 17, year);
```

8. Is the following a legal method definition that could be added to the class `DateThirdTry` in Display 4.4?

```
public void multiWriteOutput(int count)
{
    while (count > 0)
    {
        writeOutput();
        count--;
    }
}
```

9. Consider the definition of the method `monthString` in Display 4.4. Why are there no `break` statements in the `switch` statement?

Simple Cases with Class Parameters

Methods can have parameters of a class type. Parameters of a class type are more subtle and more powerful than parameters of a primitive type. We will discuss parameters of class types in detail in Chapter 5. In the meantime, we will occasionally use a class type parameter in very simple situations. For these cases, you do not need to know any details about class type parameters except that, in some sense or other, the class argument is plugged in for the class parameter.

The `this` Parameter

As we noted earlier, if `today` is of type `DateSecondTry` (see Display 4.2), then

```
today.writeOutput();
```

is equivalent to

```
System.out.println(today.month + " " + today.day
                                      + ", " + today.year);
```

This is because, although the definition of `writeOutput` reads

```
public void writeOutput()
{
    System.out.println(month + " " + day + ", " + year);
}
```

it really means

```
public void writeOutput()
{
    System.out.println(<the calling object>.month + " "
        + <the calling object>.day + ", " + <the calling object>.year);
}
```

The instance variables are understood to have <the calling object>. in front of them. Sometimes it is handy, and on rare occasions even necessary, to have an explicit name for the calling object. Inside a Java method definition, you can use the keyword `this` as a name for the calling object. So, the following is a valid Java method definition that is equivalent to the one we are discussing:

```
public void writeOutput()
{
    System.out.println(this.month + " " + this.day
                                      + ", " + this.year);
}
```

The definition of `writeOutput` in Display 4.2 could be replaced by this completely equivalent version. Moreover, this version is in some sense the true version. The version without the `this` and a dot in front of each instance variable is just an abbreviation for this version. However, the abbreviation of omitting the `this` is used frequently.

`this` parameter

The keyword `this` is known as the **`this` parameter**. The `this` parameter is a kind of hidden parameter. It does not appear on the parameter list of a method, but is still a parameter. When a method is invoked, the calling object is automatically plugged in for `this`.

> **The `this` Parameter**
>
> Within a method definition, you can use the keyword `this` as a name for the calling object. If an instance variable or another method in the class is used without any calling object, then `this` is understood to be the calling object.

There is one common situation that requires the use of the `this` parameter. You often want to have the parameters in a method such as `setDate` be the same as the instance variables. A first, although incorrect, try at doing this is the following rewriting of the method `setDate` from Display 4.4:

```
public void setDate(int month, int day, int year) //Not correct
{
    month = monthString(month);
    day = day;
    year = year;
}
```

This rewritten version does not do what we want. When you declare a local variable in a method definition, then within the method definition, that name always refers to the local variable. A parameter is a local variable, so this rule applies to parameters. Consider the following assignment statement in our rewritten method definition:

```
day = day;
```

mask a variable

Both the identifiers `day` refer to the parameter `day`. The identifier `day` does not refer to the instance variable `day`. All occurrences of the identifier `day` refer to the parameter `day`. This is often described by saying the parameter `day` **masks** or hides the instance variable `day`. Similar remarks apply to the parameters `month` and `year`.

This rewritten method definition of the method `setDate` will produce a compiler error message because the following attempts to assign a `String` value to the `int` variable (the parameter) `month`:

```
month = monthString(month);
```

However, in many situations, this sort of rewriting will produce a method definition that will compile but that will not do what it is supposed to do.

To correctly rewrite the method `setDate`, we need some way to say "the instance variable `month`" as opposed to the parameter `month`. The way to say "the instance variable `month`" is `this.month`. Similar remarks apply to the other two parameters. So, the correct rewriting of the method `setDate` is as follows:

```
public void setDate(int month, int day, int year)
{
    this.month = monthString(month);
    this.day = day;
    this.year = year;
}
```

This version is completely equivalent to the version in Display 4.4.

Self-Test Exercises

10. The method `writeOutput` in Display 4.2 uses the instance variables `month`, `day`, and `year`, but gives no object name for these instance variables. Every instance variable must belong to some object. To what object or objects do these instance variables in the definition of `writeOutput` belong?
11. Rewrite the definitions of the methods `getDay` and `getYear` in Display 4.2 using the `this` parameter.
12. Rewrite the method `getMonth` in Display 4.2 using the `this` parameter.

Methods That Return a Boolean Value

There is nothing special about methods that return a value of type `boolean`. The type `boolean` is a primitive type, just like the types `int` and `double`. A method that returns a value of type `boolean` must have a `return` statement of the form

```
return Boolean_Expression;
```

So, an invocation of a method that returns a value of type `boolean` returns either `true` or `false`. It thus makes sense to use an invocation of such a method to control an `if-else` statement, to control a `while` loop, or to control anyplace else that a Boolean expression is allowed. Although there is nothing new here, people who have not used `boolean` valued methods before sometimes find them to be uncomfortable. So we will go through one small example.

The following is a method definition that could be added to the class `DateThirdTry` in Display 4.4:

```
public boolean isBetween(int lowYear, int highYear)
{
    return ( (year > lowYear) && (year < highYear) );
}
```

Consider the following lines of code:

```
DateThirdTry date = new DateThirdTry();
date.setDate(1, 2, 3001);
if (date.isBetween(2000, 4000))
    System.out.println(
          "The date is between the years 2000 and 4000");
else
    System.out.println(
          "The date is not between the years 2000 and 4000");
```

The expression `date.isBetween(2000, 4000)` is an invocation of a method that returns a `boolean` value—that is, returns one of the two values `true` and `false`. So, it makes perfectly good sense to use it as the controlling Boolean expression in an `if-else` statement. The expression `year` in the definition of `isBetween` really means `this.year`, and `this` stands for the calling object. In `date.isBetween(2000, 4000)` the calling object is `date`. So, this returns the value

```
(date.year > lowYear) && (date.year < highYear)
```

But, `2000` and `4000` are plugged in for the parameters `lowYear` and `highYear`, respectively. So, this expression is equivalent to

```
(date.year > 2000) && (date.year < 4000)
```

Thus, the `if-else` statement is equivalent to[4]

```
if ((date.year > 2000) && (date.year < 4000))
    System.out.println(
                 "The date is between the years 2000 and 4000.");
else
    System.out.println(
               "The date is not between the years 2000 and 4000.");
```

Thus, the output produced is

```
The date is between the years 2000 and 4000.
```

Another example of a `boolean` valued method, which we will, in fact, add to our date class, follows:

```
public boolean precedes(DateFourthTry otherDate)
{
    return ( (year < otherDate.year) ||
```

[4] Later in this chapter, we will see that because `year` is marked `private`, it is not legal to write `date.year` in a program, but the meaning of such an expression is clear even if you cannot include it in a program.

```
        (year == otherDate.year && getMonth() < otherDate.getMonth())
        ||
        (year == otherDate.year && month.equals(otherDate.month)
                                     && day < otherDate.day) );
}
```

The version of our date class with this method is given in Display 4.7. The other new methods in that class will be discussed shortly in the subsection entitled "The Methods `equals` and `toString`." Right now, let's discuss this new method named `precedes`.

An invocation of the method `precedes` has the following form, where `date1` and `date2` are two objects of our date class:

```
date1.precedes(date2)
```

This is a Boolean expression that returns `true` if `date1` comes before `date2`. Because it is a Boolean expression, it can be used anyplace a Boolean expression is allowed, such as to control an `if-else` or `while` statement. For example,

```
if (date1.precedes(date2))
    System.out.println("date1 comes before date2.");
else
    System.out.println("date2 comes before or is equal to date1.");
```

Display 4.7 **A Class with Methods `equals` and `toString`** (part 1 of 2)

```
import java.util.Scanner;

public class DateFourthTry
{
    private String month;
    private int day;
    private int year; //a four digit number.

    public String toString()
    {
        return (month + " " + day + ", " + year);
    }

    public void writeOutput()
    {
        System.out.println(month + " " + day + ", " + year);
    }

    public boolean equals(DateFourthTry otherDate)
    {
        return ( (month.equals(otherDate.month))
                 && (day == otherDate.day) && (year == otherDate.year) );
    }
```

This is the method `equals` *in the class* `DateFourthTry`.

This is the method `equals` *in the class* `String`.

(continued)

Display 4.7 A Class with Methods **equals** and **toString** (part 2 of 2)

```
    public boolean precedes(DateFourthTry otherDate)
    {
        return ( (year < otherDate.year) ||
           (year == otherDate.year && getMonth() <
              otherDate.getMonth()) ||
           (year == otherDate.year && month.equals(otherDate.month)
                                       && day < otherDate.day) );
    }
```

<The rest of the method definitions are identical to the ones in `DateThirdTry` *in Display 4.4.>*

```
}
```

The `return` statement in the definition of the method `precedes` may look intimidating, but it is really straightforward. It says that `date1.precedes(date2)` returns `true`, provided one of the following three conditions is satisfied:

```
date1.year < date2.year
date1.year equals date2.year and date1.month comes before
date2.month date1 and date2 have the same year and month and
            date1.day < date2.day.
```

If you give it a bit of thought, you will realize that `date1` precedes `date2` in time precisely when one of these three conditions is satisfied.

The Methods equals and toString

Java expects certain methods to be in all, or almost all, classes. This is because some of the standard Java libraries have software that assumes such methods are defined. Two of these methods are `equals` and `toString`. Therefore, you should include such methods and be certain to spell their names exactly as we have done. Use `equals`, not `same` or `areEqual`. Do not even use `equal` without the `s`. Similar remarks apply to the `toString` method. After we have developed more material, we will explain this in more detail. In particular, we will then explain how to give a better method definition for `equals`. For now, just get in the habit of including these methods.

equals

The method `equals` is a `boolean` valued method to compare two objects of the class to see if they satisfy the intuitive notion of "being equal." So, the heading should be

```
public boolean equals(Class_Name Parameter_Name)
```

Display 4.7 contains definitions of the methods `equals` and `toString` that we might add to our date class, which is now named `DateFourthTry`. The heading of that `equals` method is

```
public boolean equals(DateFourthTry otherDate)
```

When you use the method `equals` to compare two objects of the class `DateFourthTry`, one object is the calling object and the other object is the argument, like so:

```
date1.equals(date2)
```

or equivalently,

```
date2.equals(date1)
```

Because the method `equals` returns a value of type `boolean`, you can use an invocation of `equals` as the Boolean expression in an `if-else` statement, as shown in Display 4.8. Similarly, you can also use it anyplace else that a Boolean expression is allowed.

There is no absolute notion of "equality" that you must follow in your definition of `equals`. You can define the method `equals` any way you wish, but to be useful, it should reflect some notion of "equality" that is useful for the software you are

Display 4.8 Using the Methods `equals` and `toString`

```
public class EqualsAndToStringDemo
{
    public static void main(String[] args)
    {
        DateFourthTry date1 = new DateFourthTry(),
                      date2 = new DateFourthTry();
        date1.setDate(6, 17, 1882);
        date2.setDate(6, 17, 1882);

        if (date1.equals(date2))
            System.out.println(date1 + " equals " + date2);
        else
            System.out.println(date1 + " does not equal " + date2);

        date1.setDate(7, 28, 1750);

        if (date1.precedes(date2))
            System.out.println(date1 + " comes before " + date2);
        else
            System.out.println(date2 + " comes before or is equal to "
                                     + date1);
    }
}
```

These are equivalent to `date1.toString()`.

These are equivalent to `date2.toString()`.

Sample Dialogue

```
June 17, 1882 equals June 17, 1882
July 28, 1750 comes before June 17, 1882
```

designing. A common way to define `equals` for simple classes of the kind we are looking at now is to say `equals` returns `true` if each instance variable of one object equals the corresponding instance variable of the other object. This is how we defined `equals` in Display 4.7.

If the definition of `equals` in Display 4.7 seems less than clear, it may help to rewrite it as follows using the `this` parameter:

```
public boolean equals(DateFourthTry otherDate)
{
    return ( ((this.month).equals(otherDate.month))
      && (this.day == otherDate.day) && (this.year ==
      otherDate.year) );
}
```

So, if `date1` and `date2` are objects of the class `DateFourthTry`, then `date1.equals (date2)` returns `true` provided the three instance variables in `date1` have values that are equal to the three instance variables in `date2`.

Also, note that the method in the definition of `equals` that is used to compare months is not the `equals` for the class `DateFourthTry` but the `equals` for the class `String`. You know this because the calling object, which is `this.month`, is of type `String`.

Remember that we use the `equals` method of the class `String` because == does not work correctly for comparing `String` values. This was discussed in the Pitfall section of Chapter 3 entitled "Using == with Strings.")

In Chapter 7, you will see that there are reasons to make the definition of the `equals` method a bit more involved. But the spirit of what an `equals` method should be is very much like what we are now doing, and it is the best we can do with what we know so far.

toString

The method `toString` should be defined so that it returns a `String` value that represents the data in the object. One nice thing about the method `toString` is that it makes it easy to output an object to the screen. If `date` is of type `DateFourthTry`, then you can output the date to the screen as follows:

```
System.out.println(date.toString());
```

println used with objects

In fact, `System.out.println` was written so that it automatically invokes `toString()` if you do not include it. So, the object `date` can also be output by the following simpler and equivalent statement:

```
System.out.println(date);
```

This means that the method `writeOutput` in Display 4.7 is superfluous and could safely be omitted from the class definition.

If you look at Display 4.8, you will see that `toString` is also called automatically when the object is connected to some other string with a +, as in

```
System.out.println(date1 + " equals " + date2);
```

+ used with objects

In this case, it is really the plus operator that causes the automatic invocation of `toString()`. So, the following is also legal:

```
String s = date1 + " equals " + date2;
```

The preceding is equivalent to

```
String s = date1.toString() + " equals " + date2.toString();
```

Recursive Methods

recursive method

Java does allow **recursive method** definitions. Recursive methods are covered in Chapter 11. If you do not know what recursive methods are, do not be concerned until you reach that chapter. If you want to read about these methods early, you can read Sections 11.1 and 11.2 of Chapter 11 after you complete Chapter 5.

The Methods `equals` and `toString`

Usually, your class definitions should contain an `equals` method and a `toString` method. An `equals` method compares the calling object to another object and should return `true` when the two objects are intuitively equal. When comparing objects of a class type, you normally use the method `equals` not `==`.

The `toString` method should return a string representation of the data in the calling object. If a class has a `toString` method, you can use an object of the class as an argument to the methods `System.out.println` and `System.out.print`.

See Display 4.7 for an example of a class with `equals` and `toString` methods.

TIP: Testing Methods

driver program

Each method should be tested in a program in which it is the only untested program. If you test methods this way, then when you find an error, you will know which method contains the error. A program that does nothing but test a method is called a **driver program**.

bottom-up testing

If one method contains an invocation of another method in the same class, this can complicate the testing task. One way to test a method is to first test all the methods invoked by that method and then test the method itself. This is called **bottom-up testing**.

(continued)

TIP: (continued)

stub

It is sometimes impossible or inconvenient to test a method without using some other method that has not yet been written or has not yet been tested. In this case, you can use a simplified version of the missing or untested method. These simplified methods are called **stubs**. These stubs will not necessarily perform the correct calculation, but they will deliver values that suffice for testing, and they are simple enough that you can have confidence in their performance. For example, the following is a possible stub:

```
/**
 Computes the probability of rain based on temperature, barometric
 pressure, and relative humidity. Returns the probability as a
 fraction between 0 and 1.
*/
public double rainChance(double temperature,
                              double pressure,double humidity)
{
    return 0.5; //Not correct but good enough for a stub.
}
```

■

The Fundamental Rule for Testing Methods

Every method should be tested in a program in which every other method in the testing program has already been fully tested and debugged.

MyProgrammingLab™

Self-Test Exercises

13. In the definition of `precedes` in Display 4.7, we used

```
month.equals(otherDate.month)
```

to test whether two months are equal; but we used

```
getMonth() < otherDate.getMonth()
```

to test whether one month comes before another. Why did we use `month` in one case and `getMonth` in another case?

14. What is the fundamental rule for testing methods?

4.2 Information Hiding and Encapsulation

We all know—the Times *knows—but we pretend we don't.*

VIRGINIA WOOLF, *Monday or Tuesday*

information hiding

Information hiding means that you separate the description of how to use a class from the implementation details, such as how the class methods are defined. You do this so that a programmer who uses the class does not need to know the implementation details of the class definition. The programmer who uses the class can consider the implementation details as hidden, since he or she does not need to look at them. Information hiding is a way of avoiding information overloading. It keeps the information needed by a programmer using the class within reasonable bounds. Another term for information hiding is **abstraction**. The use of the term *abstraction* for information hiding makes sense if you think about it a bit. When you abstract something, you are discarding some of the details.

abstraction

encapsulation

Encapsulation means grouping software into a unit in such a way that it is easy to use because there is a well-defined simple interface. So, encapsulation and information hiding are two sides of the same coin.

Java has a way of officially hiding details of a class definition. To hide details, mark them as `private`, a concept we discuss next.

VideoNote
Information Hiding Example

Encapsulation

Encapsulation means that the data and the actions are combined into a single item (in our case, a class object) and that the details of the implementation are hidden. The terms *information hiding* and *encapsulation* deal with the same general principle: If a class is well designed, a programmer who uses a class need not know all the details of the implementation of the class but need only know a much simpler description of how to use the class.

API

The term **API** stands for *application programming interface*. The API for a class is a description of how to use the class. If your class is well designed, using the encapsulation techniques we discuss in this book, then a programmer who uses your class need only read the API and need not look at the details of your code for the class definition.

ADT

The term **ADT** is short for *abstract data type*. An ADT is a data type that is written using good information hiding techniques.

`public` and `private` Modifiers

public

private

Compare the instance variables in Displays 4.1 and 4.2. In Display 4.1, each instance variable is prefaced with the modifier `public`. In Display 4.2, each instance variable is prefaced with the modifier `private`. The modifier `public` means that there are no restrictions on where the instance variable can be used. The modifier `private` means that the instance variable cannot be accessed by name outside of the class definition.

For example, the following would produce a compiler error message if used in a program:

```
DateSecondTry date = new DateSecondTry();
date.month = "January";
date.day = 1;
date.year = 2006;
```

In fact, any one of the three assignments would be enough to trigger a compiler error. This is because, as shown in Display 4.2, each of the instance variables `month`, `day`, and `year` is labeled `private`.

If, on the other hand, we had used the class `DateFirstTry` from Display 4.1 instead of the class `DateSecondTry` in the preceding code, the code would be legal and would compile and run with no error messages. This is because, in the definition of `DateFirstTry` (Display 4.1), each of the instance variables `month`, `day`, and `year` is labeled `public`.

It is considered good programming practice to make all instance variables private. As we will explain a little later in this chapter, this is intended to simplify the task of any programmer using the class. But before we say anything about how, on balance, this simplifies the job of a programmer who uses the class, let's see how it complicates the job of a programmer who uses the class.

Once you label an instance variable as `private`, there is then no way to change its value (nor to reference the instance variable in any other way) except by using one of the methods belonging to the class. Note that even when an instance variable is private, you can still access it through methods of the class. For the class `DateSecondTry`, you can change the values of the instance variables with the method `readInput`, and you can obtain the values of the instance variables with the methods whose names start with `get`. So, the qualifier `private` does not make it impossible to access the instance variables. It just makes it illegal to use their names, which can be a minor nuisance.

The modifiers `public` and `private` before a method definition have a similar meaning. If the method is labeled `public`, there are no restrictions on its usage. If the method is labeled `private`, the method can only be used in the definition of another method of the same class.

Any instance variable can be labeled either `public` or `private`. Any method can be `public` or `private`. However, normal good programming practices require that *all* instance variables be private and that typically, most methods be public. Normally, a method is private only if it is being used solely as a helping method in the definition of other methods.

EXAMPLE: Yet Another Date Class

Display 4.9 contains another, much improved, definition of a class for a date. Note that all instance variables are private and that two methods are private. We made the methods `dateOK` and `monthString` private because they are just helping methods used in the definitions of other methods. A user of the class `DateFifthTry` would not (in fact, cannot) use either of the methods `dateOK` or `monthString`. This is all hidden information that need not concern a programmer using the class. The method `monthString` was public in previous versions of our date classes because we had not yet discussed the `private` modifier. It is now marked `private` because it is just a helping method.

Note that the class `DateFifthTry` uses the method `dateOK` to make sure that any changes to instance variables make sense. Because the methods of the class `DateFifthTry` use the method `dateOK` to check for impossible dates, you cannot use any methods, such as `readInput` or `setDate`, to set the instance variables so that they represent an impossible date such as January 63, 2005. If you try to do so, your program would end with an error message. (To make our definition of the method `dateOK` simple, we did not check for certain impossible dates, such as February 31, but it would be easy to exclude these dates as well.)

The methods `dateOK` and `equals` each return a value of type `boolean`. That means they return a value that is either `true` or `false` and so can be used as the Boolean expression in an `if-else` statement, `while` statement, or other loop statement. This is illustrated by the following, which is taken from the definition of the method `setDate` in Display 4.9:

```
if (dateOK(month, day, year))
{
    this.month = monthString(month);
    this.day = day;
    this.year = year;
}
else
{
    System.out.println("Fatal Error");
    System.exit(0);
}
```

Note that, although all the instance variables are private, a programmer using the class can still change or access the value of an instance variable using the methods that start with `set` or `get`. This is discussed more fully in the next subsection, "Accessor and Mutator Methods."

(continued)

EXAMPLE: (continued)

Note that there is a difference between what we might call the *inside view* and the *outside view* of the class `DateFifthTry`. A date such as July 4, 1776, is represented inside the class object as the string value `"July"` and the two `int` values `4` and `1776`. But if a programmer using the same class object asks for the date using `getMonth`, `getDay`, and `getYear`, he or she will get the three `int` values `7`, `4`, and `1776`. From inside the class, a month is a string value, but from outside the class, a month is an integer. The description of the data in a class object need not be a simple direct description of the instance variables. (To further emphasize the fact that the month has an inside view as a string but an outside view as a number, we have written the method `readInput` for the class `DateFifthTry` so that the user enters the month as an integer rather than a string.)

Note that the method definitions in a class need not be given in any particular order. In particular, it is perfectly acceptable to give the definition the method `dateOK` after the definitions of methods that use `dateOK`. Indeed, any ordering of the method definitions is acceptable. Use whatever order seems to make the class easiest to read. (Those who come to Java from certain other programming languages should note that there is no kind of forward reference needed when a method is used before it is defined.)

MyProgrammingLab™

Self-Test Exercises

15. Following the style guidelines given in this book, when should an instance variable be marked `private`?
16. Following the style guidelines given in this book, when should a method be marked `private`?

Accessor and Mutator Methods

You should always make all instance variables in a class private. However, you may sometimes need to do something with the data in a class object. The special-purpose methods, such as `toString`, `equals`, and any input methods, will allow you to do many things with the data in an object. But sooner or later you will want to do something with the data for which there are no special-purpose methods. How can you do anything new with the data in an object? The answer is that you can do anything that you might reasonably want (and that the class design specifications consider to be legitimate), provided you equip your classes with suitable *accessor* and *mutator* methods. These are methods that allow you to access and change the data in an object, usually in a very general way. **Accessor methods** allow you to obtain the data. In Display 4.9, the methods `getMonth`, `getDay`, and `getYear` are accessor methods. The

accessor methods

accessor methods need not literally return the values of each instance variable, but they must return something equivalent to those values. For example, the method `getMonth` returns the number of the month, even though the month is stored in a `String` instance variable. Although it is not required by the Java language, it is a generally accepted good programming practice to spell the names of accessor methods starting with `get`.

mutator methods

Mutator methods allow you to change the data in a class object. In Display 4.9, the methods whose names begin with the word `set` are mutator methods. It is a generally accepted good programming practice to use names that begin with the word `set` for mutator methods. Your class definitions will typically provide a complete set of public accessor methods and at least some public mutator methods. There are, however, important classes, such as the class `String`, that have no public mutator methods.

At first glance, it may seem as if accessor and mutator methods defeat the purpose of making instance variables private, but if you look carefully at the mutator methods in Display 4.9, you will see that the mutator and accessor methods are not equivalent to making the instance variables public. Notice the mutator methods, that is, the ones that begin with `set`. They all test for an illegal date and end the program with an error message if there is an attempt to set the instance variables to any illegal values. If the variables were public, you could set the data to values that do not make sense for a date, such as January 42, 1930. With mutator methods, you can control and filter changes to the data. (As it is, you can still set the data to values that do not represent a real date, such as February 31, but as we already noted, it would be easy to exclude these dates as well. We did not exclude these dates to keep the example simple. See Self-Test Exercise 19 for a more complete date check method.)

Display 4.9 **Yet Another Date Class** (part 1 of 4)

```
import java.util.Scanner;

public class DateFifthTry
{
    private String month;
    private int day;
    private int year; //a four digit number.

    public void writeOutput()
    {
        System.out.println(month + " " + day + ", " + year);
    }

    public void readInput()
    {
```

Note that this version of `readInput` has the user enter the month as an integer rather than as a string. In this class, a month is an integer to the user, but is a string inside the class.

(continued)

Display 4.9 **Yet Another Date Class** (part 2 of 4)

```
        boolean tryAgain = true;
        Scanner keyboard = new Scanner(System.in);
        while (tryAgain)
        {
            System.out.println("Enter month, day, and year");
            System.out.println("as three integers:");
            System.out.println("do not use commas or other punctuations.");
            int monthInput = keyboard.nextInt();
            int dayInput = keyboard.nextInt();
            int yearInput = keyboard.nextInt();
            if (dateOK(monthInput, dayInput, yearInput))
            {
                setDate(monthInput, dayInput, yearInput);
                tryAgain = false;
            }
            else
                System.out.println("Illegal date. Reenter input.");
        }
    }

    public void setDate(int month, int day, int year)
    {
        if (dateOK(month, day, year))
        {
            this.month = monthString(month);
            this.day = day;
            this.year = year;
        }
        else
        {
            System.out.println("Fatal Error");
            System.exit(0);
        }
    }

    public void setMonth(int monthNumber)
    {
        if ((monthNumber <= 0) || (monthNumber > 12))
        {
            System.out.println("Fatal Error");
            System.exit(0);
        }
        else
            month = monthString(monthNumber);
    }
```

Note that this version of **readInput** *checks to see that the input is reasonable.*

Display 4.9 **Yet Another Date Class** (part 3 of 4)

```
    public void setDay(int day)
    {
        if ((day <= 0) || (day > 31))
        {
            System.out.println("Fatal Error");
            System.exit(0);
        }
        else
            this.day = day;
    }

    public void setYear(int year)
    {
        if ( (year < 1000) || (year > 9999) )
        {
            System.out.println("Fatal Error");
            System.exit(0);
        }
        else
            this.year = year;
    }

    public boolean equals(DateFifthTry otherDate)
    {
        return ( (month.equalsIgnoreCase(otherDate.month))
                  && (day == otherDate.day) && (year ==
                  otherDate.year) );
    }
```

Within the definition of `DateFifthTry`*, you can directly access private instance variables of any object of type* `DateFifthTry`.

```
    public boolean precedes(DateFifthTry otherDate)
    {
        return ( (year < otherDate.year) ||
           (year == otherDate.year && getMonth() <
           otherDate.getMonth()) ||
           (year == otherDate.year && month.equals(otherDate.month)
                                    && day < otherDate.day) );
    }
```

Within the definition of `DateFifthTry`*, you can directly access private instance variables of any object of type* `DateFifthTry`.

<*The definitions of the following methods are the same as in Displays 4.2 and 4.7:* `getMonth`, `getDay`, `getYear`, *and* `toString`.>

```
    private boolean dateOK(int monthInt, int dayInt, int yearInt)
    {
```

(continued)

Display 4.9 Yet Another Date Class (part 4 of 4)

```
        return ( (monthInt >= 1) && (monthInt <= 12) &&
                 (dayInt >= 1) && (dayInt <= 31) &&
                 (yearInt >= 1000) && (yearInt <= 9999) );
    }

    private String monthString(int monthNumber)
    {
        switch (monthNumber)
        {
        case 1:
            return "January";
        case 2:
            return "February";
        case 3:
            return "March";
        case 4:
            return "April";
        case 5:
            return "May";
        case 6:
            return "June";
        case 7:
            return "July";
        case 8:
            return "August";
        case 9:
            return "September";
        case 10:
            return "October";
        case 11:
            return "November";
        case 12:
            return "December";
        default:
            System.out.println("Fatal Error");
            System.exit(0);
            return "Error"; //to keep the compiler happy
        }
    }
}
```

The way that a well-designed class definition uses private instance variables and public accessor and mutator methods to implement the principle of encapsulation is diagrammed in Display 4.10.

Display 4.10 Encapsulation

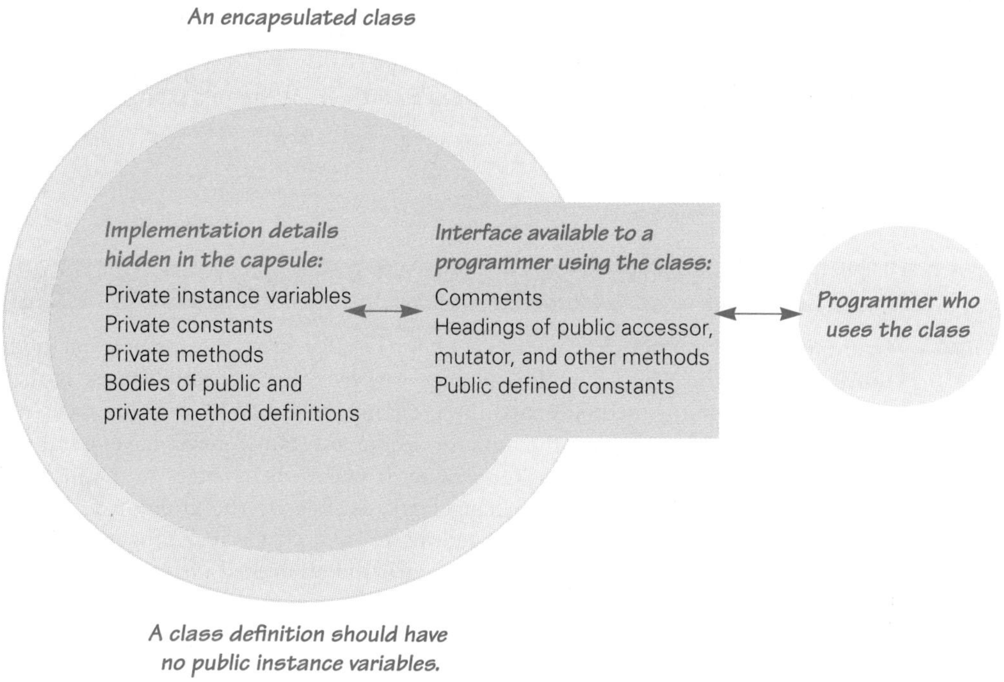

TIP: A Class Has Access to Private Members of All Objects of the Class

Consider the definition of the method `equals` for the class `DateFifthTry`, given in Display 4.9 and repeated as follows:

```
public boolean equals(DateFifthTry otherDate)
{
    return ( (month.equalsIgnoreCase(otherDate.month))
            && (day == otherDate.day) &&
            (year == otherDate.year) );
}
```

You might object that `otherDate.month`, `otherDate.day`, and `otherDate.year` are illegal because `month`, `day`, and `year` are private instance variables of some object other than the calling object. Normally, that objection would be correct. However, the object `otherDate` is of the same type as the class being defined, so this is legal. In the definition of a class, you can access private members of any object of the class, not just private members of the calling object.

(continued)

TIP: (continued)

Similar remarks apply to the method `precedes` in the same class. In one place in the definition of `precedes`, we used `otherDate.getMonth()` rather than `otherDate.month` only because we wanted the month as an integer instead of a string. We did, in fact, use `otherDate.month` elsewhere in the definition of `precedes`. ■

TIP: Mutator Methods Can Return a Boolean Value ★

In the definition of the class `DateFifthTry` (Display 4.9), the mutator methods tested to see if the new values for instance variables were sensible values. If they were not, the mutator method ended the program and issued an error message. An alternative approach is to have the mutator do the test, but to never have it end the program. Instead, it returns a `boolean` value. It makes the changes to the instance variables and returns `true` if the changes are sensible. If the attempted changes are not sensible, the mutator method returns `false`. That way a programmer can program in an alternative action to be taken if the attempted changes to instance variables do not make sense.

For example, an alternative definition of the method `setMonth` of the class `DateFifthTry` (Display 4.9) is the following:

```
public boolean setMonth(int monthNumber)
{
    if ((monthNumber <= 0) || (monthNumber > 12))
        return false;
    else
    {
        month = monthString(monthNumber);
        return true;
    }
}
```

A sample use of this `boolean` valued version of `setMonth` could be the following:

```
DateFifthTry date = new DateFifthTry();
...
System.out.println("Enter month as a number:");
int number = keyboard.nextInt();
while (!date.setMonth(number))
{
    System.out.println("Not a legal month number. Try again.");
    System.out.println("Enter month as a number:");
    number = keyboard.nextInt();
}
```

■

Preconditions and Postconditions

precondition

postcondition

One good way to write a method comment is to break it down into two kinds of information, called the *precondition* and the *postcondition*. The **precondition** states what is assumed to be true when the method is called. The method should not be used and cannot be expected to perform correctly unless the precondition holds. The **postcondition** describes the effect of the method call; that is, the postcondition tells what will be true after the method is executed in a situation in which the precondition holds. For a method that returns a value, the postcondition describes the value returned by the method.

The following is an example of a method heading from Display 4.9 with a precondition and postcondition added:

```
/**
Precondition: All instance variables of the calling object have
values.
Postcondition: The data in the calling object has been written to
the screen.
*/
public void writeOutput()
```

You do not need to know the definition of the method `writeOutput` to use this method. All that you need to know to use this method is given by the precondition and postcondition. (The importance of this is more dramatic when the definition of the method is longer than that of `writeOutput`.)

When the only postcondition is a description of the value returned, programmers usually omit the word `Postcondition`, as in the following example:

```
/**
Precondition: All instance variables of the calling object have
values.
Returns a string describing the data in the calling object.
*/
public String toString()
```

Some programmers choose not to use the words *precondition* and *postcondition* in their method comments. However, whether you use the words or not, you should always think in terms of precondition and postcondition when designing a method and when deciding what to include in the method comment.

MyProgrammingLab™

Self-Test Exercises

17. List all the accessor methods in the class `DateFifthTry` in Display 4.9.

18. List all the mutator methods in the class `DateFifthTry` in Display 4.9.

(continued)

MyProgrammingLab™

Self-Test Exercises (continued)

19. Write a better version of the method `dateOK` with three `int` parameters (Display 4.9). This version should check for the correct number of days in each month and should not just allow 31 days in any month. It will help to define another helping method named `leapYear`, which takes an `int` argument for a year and returns `true` if the year is a leap year. February has 29 days in leap years and only 28 days in other years. Use the following rule for determining if the year is a leap year: A year is a leap year if it is divisible by 4 but is not divisible by 100, or if it is divisible by 400.

4.3 Overloading

A good name is better than precious ointment.

Ecclesiastes 7:1

Two (or more) different classes can have methods with the same name. For example, many classes have a method named `toString`. It is easy to see why this is acceptable. The type of the calling object allows Java to decide which definition of the method `toString` to use. It uses the definition of `toString` given in the definition of the class for the calling object. You may be more surprised to learn that two or more methods *in the same class* can have the same method name. This is called **overloading** and is the topic of this section.

overloading

Rules for Overloading

In Display 4.11, we have added two methods named `setDate` to our date class so that there is a total of three methods named `setDate`. This is an example of overloading the method name `setDate`. On the following three lines, we display the headings of these three methods:

```
public void setDate(int month, int day,int year)
public void setDate(String month, int day,int year)
public void setDate(int year)
```

Notice that each method has a different parameter list. The first two differ in the type of their first parameter. The last one differs from the other two by having a different number of parameters.

Method signature

The name of a method and the list of parameter types in the heading of the method definition is called the **method signature**. The signatures for these three method definitions are

```
setDate(int, int, int)
setDate(String, int, int)
setDate(int)
```

Display 4.11 **Overloading Method Names** (part 1 of 2)

```
import java.util.Scanner;

public class DateSixthTry
{
   private String month;
   private int day;
   private int year; //a four digit number.

   public void setDate(int monthInt, int day, int year)
   {
      if (dateOK(monthInt, day, year))
      {
          this.month = monthString(monthInt);
          this.day = day;
          this.year = year;
      }
      else
      {
           System.out.println("Fatal Error");
           System.exit(0);
      }
   }

   public void setDate(String monthString, int day, int year)
   {
      if (dateOK(monthString, day, year))
      {
          this.month = monthString;
          this.day = day;
          this.year = year;
      }
      else
      {
          System.out.println("Fatal Error");
          System.exit(0);
      }
   }

   public void setDate(int year)
   {
       setDate(1, 1, year);
   }
```

There are three different methods named `setDate`.

Two different methods named `setDate`.

(continued)

Display 4.11 Overloading Method Names (part 2 of 2)

```
    private boolean dateOK(int monthInt, int dayInt, int yearInt)
    {
        return ( (monthInt >= 1) && (monthInt <= 12) &&
                 (dayInt >= 1) && (dayInt <= 31) &&
                 (yearInt >= 1000) && (yearInt <= 9999) );
    }

    private boolean dateOK(String monthString, int dayInt, int yearInt)
    {
        return ( monthOK(monthString) &&
                 (dayInt >= 1) && (dayInt <= 31) &&
                 (yearInt >= 1000) && (yearInt <= 9999) );
    }

    private boolean monthOK(String month)
    {
        return (month.equals("January") || month.equals("February") ||
                month.equals("March") || month.equals("April") ||
                month.equals("May") || month.equals("June") ||
                month.equals("July") || month.equals("August") ||
                month.equals("September") || month.equals("October") ||
                month.equals("November") || month.equals("December") );
    }

    public void readInput()
    {
        boolean tryAgain = true;
        Scanner keyboard = new Scanner(System.in);
        while (tryAgain)
        {
            System.out.println("Enter month, day, and year.");
              System.out.println("Do not use a comma.");
            String monthInput = keyboard.next();
            int dayInput = keyboard.nextInt();
            int yearInput = keyboard.nextInt();
            if (dateOK(monthInput, dayInput, yearInput) )
            {
                setDate(monthInput, dayInput, yearInput);
                tryAgain = false;
            }
            else
                System.out.println("Illegal date. Reenter input.");
        }
    }
  <The rest of the methods are the same as in Display 4.9, except that
          the parameter to equals and precedes is, of course, of type DateSixthTry.>
}
```

Two different methods named **dateOK**.

When you overload a method name, each of the method definitions in the class must have a different signature.

Signature

The **signature** of a method consists of the method name and the list of types for parameters that are listed in the heading of the method name.

EXAMPLE

If a method has the heading

```
public int computeSomething(int n1,double x1,
                              double x2, String name);
```

then the signature is

```
computeSomething(int, double, double,String)
```

Note that the return type is not part of the method signature.

In Display 4.11, we also overloaded the method name `dateOK` so that there are two different methods named `dateOK`. The two signatures for the two methods named `dateOK` are

```
dateOK(int, int, int)
dateOK(String, int, int)
```

Display 4.12 gives a simple example of a program using the overloaded method name `setDate`. Note that for each invocation of a method named `setDate`, only one of the definitions of `setDate` has a signature that matches the types of the arguments.

Overloading

Within one class, you can have two (or more) definitions of a single method name. This is called **overloading** the method name. When you overload a method name, any two definitions of the method name must have different signatures; that is, any two definitions of the method name either must have different numbers of parameters or some parameter position must be of differing types in the two definitions.

PITFALL: Overloading and Automatic Type Conversion

Automatic type conversion of arguments (such as converting an `int` to a `double` when the parameter is of type `double`) and overloading can sometimes interact in unfortunate ways. So, you need to know how these two things interact.

For example, consider the following method that might be added to the class `DateSixthTry` in Display 4.11:

```
public void increase(double factor)
{
    year = (int)(year + factor*year);
}
```

If you add this method to the class `DateSixthTry`, then the following presents no problems, where `date` is an object of type `DateSixthTry` that has been set to some date:

```
date.increase(2);
```

The `int` value of 2 is type cast to the `double` value `2.0`, and the value of `date.year` is changed as follows:

```
date.year = (int)(date.year + 2.0*date.year);
```

(Because `year` is private in the class `DateSixthTry`, you cannot write this in a program that uses the class `DateSixthTry`, but the meaning of this expression is clear.)

So far, so good. But now suppose we also add the following method definition to the class `DateSixthTry`:

```
public void increase(int term)
{
   year = year + term;
}
```

This is a valid overloading because the two methods named `increase` take parameters of different types. With both of these methods named `increase` added to the class, the following now behaves differently:

```
date.increase(2);
```

If Java can find an exact match of types, it uses the method definition with an exact match before it tries to do any automatic type casts. So now the displayed invocation of `date.increase` is equivalent to

```
date.year = date.year + 2;
```

However, if you meant to use an argument of `2.0` for `date.increase` and instead used 2, counting on an automatic type cast, then this is not what you want. It is best to avoid overloading where there is a potential for interacting dangerously with automatic type casting, as in the examples discussed in this Pitfall section.

PITFALL: (continued)

In some cases of overloading, a single method invocation can be resolved in two different ways, depending on how overloading and type conversion interact. Such ambiguous method invocations are not allowed in Java and will produce an error message. For example, you can overload a method named `doSomething` by giving two definitions that have the following two method headings in a `SampleClass`:

```
public class SampleClass
{
    public void doSomething(double n1, int n2)
        .
        .
        .
    public void doSomething(int n1, double n2)
        .
        .
        .
```

Such overloading is legal, but there is a problem. Suppose `aSampleObject` is an object of type `SampleClass`. An invocation such as the following will produce an error message, because Java cannot decide which overloaded definition of `doSomething` to use:

```
aSampleObject.doSomething(5, 10);
```

Java cannot decide whether it should convert the `int` value 5 to a `double` value and use the first definition of `doSomething`, or whether it should convert the `int` value 10 to a double value and use the second definition. In this situation, the Java compiler issues an error message indicating that the method invocation is ambiguous.

The following two method invocations are allowed:

```
aSampleObject.doSomething(5.0, 10);
aSampleObject.doSomething(5, 10.0);
```

However, such situations, while legal, are confusing and should be avoided. ■

Display 4.12 **Using an Overloaded Method Name** (part 1 of 2)

```
public class OverloadingDemo
{
    public static void main(String[] args)
    {
        DateSixthTry date1 = new DateSixthTry(),
                     date2 = new DateSixthTry(),
                     date3 = new DateSixthTry();
```

(continued)

Display 4.12 Using an Overloaded Method Name (part 2 of 2)

```
        date1.setDate(1, 2, 2008);
        date2.setDate("February", 2, 2008);
        date3.setDate(2008);

        System.out.println(date1);
        System.out.println(date2);
        System.out.println(date3);
    }
}
```

Sample Dialogue

```
January 2, 2008
February 2, 2008
January 1, 2008
```

Overloading and Automatic Type Conversion

Java always looks for a method signature that exactly matches the method invocation before it tries to use automatic type conversion. If Java can find a definition of a method that exactly matches the types of the arguments, it uses that definition. Only after it fails to find an exact match does Java try automatic type conversions to find a method definition that matches the (type cast) types of the method invocation.

PITFALL: You Cannot Overload Based on the Type Returned

Note that the signature of a method lists only the method name and the types of the parameters and does not include the type returned. When you overload a method name, any two methods must have different signatures. The type returned has nothing to do with the signature of a method. For example, a class could not have two method definitions with the following headings:

```
public class SampleClass2
{
    public int computeSomething(int n)
        .
        .
        .
    public double computeSomething(int n)
        .
        .
        .
```

PITFALL: (continued)

If you think about it, there is no way that Java could allow this sort of overloading. Suppose `anObject` is an object of the class `SampleClass2`. Then in the following assignment, Java could not decide which of the above two method definitions to use:

```
double answer = anObject.computeSomething(10);
```

Either a value of type `int` or a value of type `double` can legally be assigned to the variable `answer`. So, either method definition could be used. Because of such problems, Java says it is illegal to have both of these method headings in the same class. ■

You Cannot Overload Operators in Java

Many programming languages, such as C++, allow you to overload an operator, such as +, so that the operator can be used with objects of some class you define, as well as be used for such things as numbers. You cannot do this in Java. If you want to have an "addition" in your class, you must use a method name, such as add, and ordinary method syntax; you cannot define operators, such as the + operator, to work with objects of a class you define.

MyProgrammingLab™

Self-Test Exercises

20. What is the signature of each of the following method headings?

```
public void doSomething(int p1, char p2, int p3)
public void setMonth(int newMonth)
public void setMonth(String newMonth)
public int amount(int balance, double duration)
public double amount(int balance, double duration)
```

21. Consider the class `DateSixthTry` in Display 4.11. Would it be legal to add two method definitions with the following two method headings to the class `DateSixthTry`?

```
public void setMonth(int newMonth)
public void setMonth(String newMonth)
```

22. Consider the class `DateSixthTry` in Display 4.11. Would it be legal to add two method definitions with the following two method headings to the class `DateSixthTry`?

```
public void setMonth(int newMonth)
private void setMonth(int newMonth)
```

(continued)

MyProgrammingLab™ **Self-Test Exercises** (continued)

23. Consider the class `DateSixthTry` in Display 4.11. Would it be legal to add two method definitions with the following two method headings to the class `DateSixthTry`?

```
public int getMonth()
public String getMonth()
```

4.4 Constructors

Well begun is half done.

Proverb

You often want to initialize the instance variables for an object when you create the object. As you will see later in this book, there are other initializing actions you might also want to take, but initializing instance variables is the most common sort of initialization. A **constructor** is a special variety of method that is designed to perform such initialization. In this section, we tell you how to define and use constructors.

constructor

Constructor Definitions

Although you may not have realized it, you have already been using constructors every time you used the `new` operator to create an object, as in the following example:

```
DateSixthTry date1 = new DateSixthTry();
```

The expression `new DateSixthTry()` is an invocation of a constructor. A constructor is a special variety of method that, among other things, must have the same name as the class. So, the first occurrence of `DateSixthTry` in the previous code is a class name, and the second occurrence of `DateSixthTry` is the name of a constructor. If you add no constructor definitions to your class, then Java automatically creates a constructor that takes no arguments. We have been using this automatically provided constructor up until now. The automatically provided constructor creates the object but does little else. It is preferable to define your own constructors so that you can have the constructor initialize instance variables, or do whatever other initialization actions you want.

In Display 4.13, we have rewritten our date class one last time by adding five constructors. Since this is our final date class, we have included all method definitions in the display so you can see the entire class definition. (We have omitted `writeOutput` because it would be superfluous, as noted in the earlier subsection entitled "The Methods `equals` and `toString`.")

Display 4.13 **A Class with Constructors** (part 1 of 5)

This is our final definition of a class whose objects are dates.

```java
import java.util.Scanner;

public class Date
{
    private String month;
    private int day;
    private int year; //a four digit number.

    public Date()
    {
        month = "January";
        day = 1;
        year = 1000;
    }
```

No-argument constructor.

```java
    public Date(int monthInt, int day, int year)
    {
        setDate(monthInt, day, year);
    }
```

You can invoke another method inside a constructor definition.

```java
    public Date(String monthString, int day, int year)
    {
        setDate(monthString, day, year);
    }

    public Date(int year)
    {
        setDate(1, 1, year);
    }
```

A constructor usually initializes all instance variables, even if there is not a corresponding parameter.

```java
    public Date(Date aDate)
    {
        if (aDate == null) //Not a real date.
        {
            System.out.println("Fatal Error.");
            System.exit(0);
        }

        month = aDate.month;
        day = aDate.day;
        year = aDate.year;
    }
```

We will have more to say about this constructor in Chapter 5. Although you have had enough material to use this constructor, you need not worry about it until Section 5.3 of Chapter 5.

(continued)

Display 4.13 A Class with Constructors (part 2 of 5)

```
    public void setDate(int monthInt, int day, int year)
    {
        if (dateOK(monthInt, day, year))
        {
            this.month = monthString(monthInt);
            this.day = day;
            this.year = year;
        }
        else
        {
            System.out.println("Fatal Error");
            System.exit(0);
        }
    }

    public void setDate(String monthString, int day, int year)
    {
        if (dateOK(monthString, day, year))
        {
            this.month = monthString;
            this.day = day;
            this.year = year;
        }
        else
        {
            System.out.println("Fatal Error");
            System.exit(0);
        }
    }

    public void setDate(int year)
    {
        setDate(1, 1, year);
    }

    public void setYear(int year)
    {
        if ( (year < 1000) || (year > 9999) )
        {
            System.out.println("Fatal Error");
            System.exit(0);
        }
        else
            this.year = year;
    }
```

The mutator methods, whose names begin with `set`*, are used to reset the data in an object after the object has been created using* `new` *and a constructor.*

Display 4.13 **A Class with Constructors** (part 3 of 5)

```
    public void setMonth(int monthNumber)
    {
        if ((monthNumber <= 0) || (monthNumber > 12))
        {
            System.out.println("Fatal Error");
            System.exit(0);
        }
        else
            month = monthString(monthNumber);
    }

    public void setDay(int day)
    {
        if ((day <= 0) || (day > 31))
        {
            System.out.println("Fatal Error");
            System.exit(0);
        }
        else
            this.day = day;
    }

    public int getMonth()
    {
       if (month.equals("January"))
           return 1;
       else if (month.equals("February"))
           return 2;
       else if (month.equals("March"))
           return 3;
            . . .
<The omitted cases are obvious, but if need be, you can see all the cases in Display 4.2.>
            . . .
       else if (month.equals("November"))
           return 11;
       else if (month.equals("December"))
           return 12;
       else
       {
           System.out.println("Fatal Error");
           System.exit(0);
           return 0; //Needed to keep the compiler happy
       }
    }
```

(continued)

Display 4.13 **A Class with Constructors** (part 4 of 5)

```
    public int getDay()
    {
        return day;
    }
```

We have omitted the method `writeOutput` *because it would be superfluous, as noted in the subsection entitled "The Methods* `equals` *and* `toString`*."*

```
    public int getYear()
    {
        return year;
    }

    public String toString()
    {
        return (month + " " + day + ", " + year);
    }

    public boolean equals(Date otherDate)
    {
        return ( (month.equals(otherDate.month))
                  && (day == otherDate.day) && (year ==
                  otherDate.year) );
    }
```

The method `equals` *of the class* `String`.

```
    public Boolean precedes(Date otherDate)
    {
        return ( (year < otherDate.year) ||
           (year == otherDate.year && getMonth() <
           otherDate.getMonth()) ||
           (year == otherDate.year && month.equals(otherDate.month)
                                         && day < otherDate.day) );
    }

    public void readInput()
    {
        boolean tryAgain = true;
        Scanner keyboard = new Scanner(System.in);
        while (tryAgain)
        {
            System.out.println("Enter month, day, and year.");
            System.out.println("Do not use a comma.");
            String monthInput = keyboard.next();
            int dayInput = keyboard.nextInt();
            int yearInput = keyboard.nextInt();
            if (dateOK(monthInput, dayInput, yearInput) )
            {
                setDate(monthInput, dayInput, yearInput);
                tryAgain = false;
            }
```

Display 4.13 A Class with Constructors (part 5 of 5)

```
        else
            System.out.println("Illegal date. Reenter input.");
    }
}

private boolean dateOK(int monthInt, int dayInt, int yearInt)
{
    return ( (monthInt >= 1) && (monthInt <= 12) &&
             (dayInt >= 1) && (dayInt <= 31) &&
             (yearInt >= 1000) && (yearInt <= 9999) );
}

private boolean dateOK(String monthString, int dayInt, int
                                     yearInt)
{
    return ( monthOK(monthString) &&
             (dayInt >= 1) && (dayInt <= 31) &&
             (yearInt >= 1000) && (yearInt <= 9999) );
}

private boolean monthOK(String month)
{
    return (month.equals("January") || month.equals("February") ||
            month.equals("March") || month.equals("April") ||
            month.equals("May") || month.equals("June") ||
            month.equals("July") || month.equals("August") ||
            month.equals("September") ||
                month.equals("October") ||
            month.equals("November") ||
                month.equals("December") );
}

private String monthString(int monthNumber)
{
    switch (monthNumber)
    {
    case 1:
        return "January";
         . . .
```

The private methods need not be last, but that's as good a place as any.

<The omitted cases are obvious, but if need be, you can see all the cases in Display 4.9.>

```
         . . .
    default:
        System.out.println("Fatal Error");
        System.exit(0);
        return "Error"; //to keep the compiler happy
    }
}
}
```

In Display 4.13, we have used overloading to create five constructors for the class `Date`. It is normal to have more than one constructor. Because every constructor must have the same name as the class, all the constructors in a class must have the same name. So, when you define multiple constructors, you must use overloading.

Note that when you define a constructor, you do not give any return type for the constructor; you do not even use `void` in place of a return type. Also notice that constructors are normally public.

All the constructor definitions in Display 4.13 initialize all the instance variables, even if there is no parameter corresponding to that instance variable. This is normal.

In a constructor definition, you can do pretty much anything that you can do in any ordinary method definition, but normally you perform only initialization tasks such as initialization of instance variables.

constructor arguments

When you create a new object with the operator `new`, you must always include the name of a constructor after the operator `new`. This is the way you invoke a constructor. As with any method invocation, you list any arguments in parentheses after the constructor name (which is the same as the class name). For example, suppose you want to use `new` to create a new object of the class `Date` defined in Display 4.13. You might do so as follows:

```
Date birthday = new Date("December", 16, 1770);
```

This is a call to the constructor for the class `Date` that takes three arguments: one of type `String` and two of type `int`. This creates a new object to represent the date December 16, 1770, and sets the variable `birthday` so that it names this new object. Another example is the following:

```
Date newYearsDay = new Date(3000);
```

This creates a new object to represent the date January 1, 3000, and sets the variable `newYearsDay` so that it names this new object.

Constructor

A **constructor** is a variety of method that is called when an object of the class is created using `new`. Constructors are used to initialize objects. A constructor must have the same name as the class to which it belongs. Arguments for a constructor are given in parentheses after the class name, as in the following examples.

EXAMPLES

```
Date birthday = new Date("December", 16, 1770),
     theDate = new Date(2008);
```

A constructor is defined very much like any ordinary method except that it does not have a type returned and does not even include a `void` in the constructor heading. See Display 4.13 for examples of constructor definitions.

resetting object values

A constructor is called when you create a new object, such as with the operator `new`. An attempt to call a constructor in any other way, such as the following, is illegal:

```
birthday.Date("January", 27, 1756); //Illegal!
```

Because you cannot call a constructor for an object after it is created, you need some other way to change the values of the instance variables of an object. That is the purpose of the `setDate` methods and other methods that begin with `set` in Display 4.13. If `birthday` already names an object that was created with `new`, you can change the values of the instance variables as follows:

```
birthday.setDate("January", 27, 1756);
```

Although it is not required, such methods that reset instance variables normally are given names that start with `set`.

Although you cannot use a constructor to reset the instance variables of an already created object, you can do something that looks very similar. The following is legal:

```
Date birthday = new Date("December", 16, 1770);
                  .
                  .
                  .
    birthday = new Date("January", 27, 1756);
```

However, the second invocation of the constructor does not simply change the values of instance variables for the object. Instead, it discards the old object and allocates storage for a new object before setting the instance variables. So, for efficiency (and occasionally for other reasons we have not yet discussed), it is preferable to use a method such as `setDate` to change the data in the instance variables of an already created object.

Display 4.14 contains a demonstration program for the constructors defined in Display 4.13.

Display 4.14 **Use of Constructors** (part 1 of 2)

```
public class ConstructorsDemo
{
    public static void main(String[] args)
    {
        Date date1 = new Date("December", 16, 1770),
             date2 = new Date(1, 27, 1756),
             date3 = new Date(1882),
             date4 = new Date();
        System.out.println("Whose birthday is " + date1 + "?");
        System.out.println("Whose birthday is " + date2 + "?");
        System.out.println("Whose birthday is " + date3 + "?");
        System.out.println("The default date is " + date4 + ".");
    }
}
```

(continued)

Display 4.14 Use of Constructors (part 2 of 2)

Sample Dialogue

```
Whose birthday is December 16, 1770?
Whose birthday is January 27, 1756?
Whose birthday is January 1, 1882?
The default date is January 1, 1000.
```

Is a Constructor Really a Method?

There are differing opinions on whether or not a constructor should be called a *method*. Most authorities call a constructor a method but emphasize that it is a special kind of method with many properties not shared with other kinds of methods. Some authorities say a constructor is a method-like entity but not, strictly speaking, a method. All authorities agree about what a constructor is; the only disagreement is over whether or not it should be referred to as *a method*. Thus, this is not a major issue. However, whenever you hear a phrase such as "all methods," you should make sure you know whether it does or does not include constructors. To avoid confusion, we try to use the phrase "constructors and methods" when we want to include constructors.

TIP: You Can Invoke Another Method in a Constructor

It is perfectly legal to invoke another method within the definition of a constructor. For example, several of the constructors in Display 4.13 invoke a mutator method to set the values of the instance variables. This is legal because the first action taken by a constructor is to automatically create an object with instance variables. You do not write any code to create this object. Java creates it automatically when the constructor is invoked. Any method invocation in the body of the constructor definition has this object as its calling object.

You can even include an invocation of one constructor within the definition of another constructor. However, we will not discuss the syntax for doing that in this chapter. It will be covered in Chapter 7. ■

TIP: A Constructor Has a `this` Parameter

Just like the ordinary methods we discussed before we introduced constructors, every constructor has a `this` parameter. The `this` parameter can be used explicitly, but it is more often understood to be present although not written down. Whenever an instance variable of the class is used in a constructor (without an object name and a dot before it), it is understood to have an implicit `this` and dot before it. Similarly, whenever

TIP: (continued)

a method is used in a constructor and the method has no explicit calling object, the method is understood to have `this` and a dot before it; that is, it is understood to have `this` as its calling object.

As noted in the previous Programming Tip, the first action taken by a constructor is to automatically create an object with instance variables. This object is automatically plugged in for the `this` parameter. So, within the definition of a constructor, the `this` parameter refers to the object created by the constructor. ■

TIP: Include a No-Argument Constructor

no-argument costructor

A constructor that takes no arguments is called a **no-argument constructor** or **no-arg constructor**. If you define a class and include absolutely no constructors of any kind, then a no-argument constructor is automatically created. This no-argument constructor does not do much, but it does give you an object of the class type. So, if the definition of the class `MyClass` contains absolutely no constructor definitions, then the following is legal:

```
MyClass myObject = new MyClass();
```

If your class definition includes one or more constructors of any kind, then no constructor is generated automatically. So, for example, suppose you define a class called `YourClass`. If you include one or more constructors that each take one or more arguments, but you do not include a no-argument constructor in your class definition, then there is not a no-argument constructor and the following is illegal:

```
YourClass yourObject = new YourClass();
```

The problem with the above declaration is that it asks the compiler to invoke the no-argument constructor, but there is not a no-argument constructor present.

To avoid problems, you should normally include a no-argument constructor in any class you define. If you do not want the no-argument constructor to initialize any instance variables, you can simply give it an empty body when you implement it. The following constructor definition is perfectly legal. It does nothing but create an object (and, as we will see later in this chapter, set the instance variables equal to default values):

```
public MyClass()
{/*Do nothing.*/}
```

(continued)

TIP: (continued)

default constructor

A no-argument constructor is also known as a **default constructor**. However, the term *default constructor* is misleading because, as we have explained, a no-argument constructor is not always provided by default. There is now a movement to replace *default constructor* with the term *no-argument constructor*, but you will frequently encounter the former term. ■

No-Argument Constructor

A constructor with no parameters is called a **no-argument constructor**. If your class definition contains absolutely no constructor definitions, then Java will automatically create a no-argument constructor. If your class definition contains one or more constructor definitions, then Java does not automatically generate any constructor; in this case, what you define is what you get. Most of the classes you define should include a definition of a no-argument constructor.

EXAMPLE: The Final Date Class

The final version of our class for a date is given in Display 4.13. We will be using this class `Date` again in Chapter 5.

MyProgrammingLab™

Self-Test Exercises

24. If a class is named `CoolClass`, what names are allowed as names for constructors in the class `CoolClass`?

25. Suppose you have defined a class such as the following for use in a program:

```
public class YourClass
{
    private int information;
    private char moreInformation;
    public YourClass(int newInfo, char moreNewInfo)
    {
        <Details not shown.>
    }
    public YourClass()
    {
```

MyProgrammingLab™

Self-Test Exercises (continued)

```
        <Details not shown.>
    }
    public void doStuff()
    {
        <Details not shown.>
    }
}
```

Which of the following are legal in a program that uses this class?

```
YourClass anObject = new YourClass(42, 'A');
YourClass anotherObject = new YourClass(41.99, 'A');
YourClass yetAnotherObject = new YourClass();
yetAnotherObject.doStuff();
YourClass oneMoreObject;
oneMoreObject.doStuff();
oneMoreObject.YourClass(99, 'B');
```

26. What is a no-argument constructor? Does every class have a no-argument constructor? What is a default constructor?

Default Variable Initializations

Local variables are not automatically initialized in Java, so you must explicitly initialize a local variable before using it. Instance variables, on the other hand, are automatically initialized. Instance variables of type `boolean` are automatically initialized to `false`. Instance variables of other primitive types are automatically initialized to the zero of their type. Instance variables of a class type are automatically initialized to `null`, which is a kind of placeholder for an object that will be filled in later. We will discuss `null` in Chapter 5. Although instance variables are automatically initialized, we prefer to always explicitly initialize them in a constructor, even if the initializing value is the same as the default initialization. That makes the code clearer.

An Alternative Way to Initialize Instance Variables

Instance variables are normally initialized in constructors, which is where we prefer to initialize them. However, there is an alternative. You can initialize instance variables when you declare them in a class definition, as illustrated by the following:

```
public class Date
{
    private String month = "January";
    private int day = 1;
    private int year = 1000;
```

If you initialize instance variables in this way, you may or may not want to define constructors. But if you do define any constructors, it is usually best to define a no-argument constructor even if the body of the no-argument constructor is empty.

EXAMPLE: A Pet Record Class

Display 4.15 contains another example of a class definition. In this case, the objects of the class represent pet records consisting of the pet's name, age, and weight. Notice the similarities and differences between the constructors and the mutator methods (the ones whose names begin with `set`). They both set instance variables, but they are used differently. The constructors are used to create and initialize new objects of the class. However, after the object is created using a constructor and `new`, any changes to the object are performed by the mutator methods such as `set` or `setAge`. This is illustrated by the program in Display 4.16.

It would be possible to use constructors in place of the mutators, such as the method `set`. For example, the program in Display 4.16 would produce the same dialogue if you replace the line

```
usersPet.set(name, age, weight);
```

with

```
usersPet = new Pet(name, age, weight);
```

Even so, this use of constructors is a bad idea.

The following mutator method invocation simply changes the values of the instance variables of the object named by `usersPet`:

```
usersPet.set(name, age, weight);
```

However, the following use of a constructor creates a completely new object, which is a much less efficient process than just changing the values of some instance variables:

```
usersPet = new Pet(name, age, weight);
```

Display 4.15 A Class for Pet Records (part 1 of 4)

```
/**
 Class for basic pet records: name, age, and weight.
*/
public class Pet
{
    private String name;
    private int age; //in years
    private double weight; //in pounds

```

Display 4.15 A Class for Pet Records (part 2 of 4)

```
    public String toString()
    {
        return ("Name: " + name + " Age: " + age + " years"
                       + "\nWeight: " + weight + " pounds");
    }

    public Pet(String initialName,int initialAge,
                                     double initialWeight)
    {
        name = initialName;
        if ((initialAge < 0) || (initialWeight < 0))
        {
            System.out.println("Error: Negative age or weight.");
            System.exit(0);
        }
        else
        {
            age = initialAge;
            weight = initialWeight;
        }
    }

    public void set(String newName,int newAge,double newWeight)
    {
        name = newName;
        if ((newAge < 0) || (newWeight < 0))
        {
            System.out.println("Error: Negative age or weight.");
            System.exit(0);
        }
        else
        {
            age = newAge;
            weight = newWeight;
        }
    }
    public Pet(String initialName)
    {
        name = initialName;
        age = 0;
        weight = 0;
    }

    public void setName(String newName)
    {
        name = newName;
    }

```

Constructors are only called when you create an object, such as with `new`*. To change an already existing object, you use one or more methods such as these* `set` *methods.*

Constructors normally set all instance variables, even if there is not a full set of parameters.

Age and weight are unchanged.

(continued)

Display 4.15 **A Class for Pet Records** (part 3 of 4)

```
    public Pet(int initialAge)
    {
        name = "No name yet.";
        weight = 0;
        if (initialAge < 0)
        {
            System.out.println("Error: Negative age.");
            System.exit(0);
        }
        else
            age = initialAge;
    }

    public void setAge(int newAge)
    {
        if (newAge < 0)
        {
            System.out.println("Error: Negative age.");
            System.exit(0);
        }
        else
            age = newAge;
    }

    public Pet(double initialWeight)
    {
        name = "No name yet";
        age = 0;
        if (initialWeight < 0)
        {
            System.out.println("Error: Negative weight.");
            System.exit(0);
        }
        else
            weight = initialWeight;
    }
    public void setWeight(double newWeight)
    {
```

Name and weight are unchanged. (annotation pointing to `age = newAge;`)

Display 4.15 A Class for Pet Records (part 4 of 4)

```
        if (newWeight < 0)
        {
            System.out.println("Error: Negative weight.");
            System.exit(0);
        }
        else
            weight = newWeight;
    }
    public Pet()
    {
        name = "No name yet.";
        age = 0;
        weight = 0;
    }

    public String getName()
    {
        return name;
    }

    public int getAge()
    {
        return age;
    }

    public double getWeight()
    {
        return weight;
    }
}
```

Name and age are unchanged.

Display 4.16 Using Constructors and Set Methods (part 1 of 2)

```
import java.util.Scanner;
public class PetDemo
{
    public static void main(String[] args)
    {
```

(continued)

Display 4.16 Using Constructors and Set Methods (part 2 of 2)

```
        Pet usersPet = new Pet("Jane Doe");
        System.out.println("My records on your pet are incomplete.");
        System.out.println("Here is what they currently say:");
        System.out.println(usersPet);

        Scanner keyboard = new Scanner(System.in);
        System.out.println("Please enter the pet's name:");
        String name = keyboard.nextLine();
        System.out.println("Please enter the pet's age:");
        int age = keyboard.nextInt();
        System.out.println("Please enter the pet's weight:");
        double weight = keyboard.nextDouble();
        usersPet.set(name, age, weight);
        System.out.println("My records now say:");
        System.out.println(usersPet);
    }
}
```

This is equivalent to `System.out.println(usersPet.toString());`

Sample Dialogue

```
My records on your pet are incomplete.
Here is what they currently say:
Name: Jane Doe Age: 0 years
Weight: 0.0 pounds
Please enter the pet's name:
Fang Junior
Please enter the pet's age:
5
Please enter the pet's weight:
87.5
My records now say:
Name: Fang Junior Age: 5 years
Weight: 87.5 pounds
```

The `StringTokenizer` Class ✶

The `StringTokenizer` class is used to recover the words in a multiword string. It is often used when reading input. However, when we covered input in Chapter 2, we could not cover the `StringTokenizer` class because use of the `StringTokenizer` class normally involves knowledge of loops and constructors, two topics that we had not yet covered. We now have covered enough material to explain the `StringTokenizer` class.

One approach to reading keyboard input is to read an entire line of input into a variable of type String—for example, with the method nextLine of the Scanner class—and then to use the StringTokenizer class to decompose the string in the variable into words.

The class StringTokenizer is in the standard Java package (library) java.util. To tell Java where to find the class StringTokenizer, any class or program that uses the class StringTokenizer must contain the following (or something similar) at the start of the file:

import

```
import java.util.StringTokenizer;
```

Perhaps the most common use of the StringTokenizer class is to decompose a line of input. However, the StringTokenizer class can be used to decompose any string. The following example illustrates a typical way that the class StringTokenizer is used:

```
StringTokenizer wordFactory =
   new StringTokenizer("A single word can be critical.");
while(wordFactory.hasMoreTokens())
{
    System.out.println(wordFactory.nextToken());
}
```

This will produce the following output:

```
A
single
word
can
be
critical.
```

The constructor invocation

```
new StringTokenizer("A single word can be critical.")
```

produces a new object of the class StringTokenizer. The assignment statement

```
StringTokenizer wordFactory =
   new StringTokenizer("A single word can be critical.");
```

gives this StringTokenizer object the name wordFactory. You may use any string in place of "A single word can be critical." and any variable name in place of wordFactory. The StringTokenizer object created in this way can be used to produce the individual words in the string used as the argument to the StringTokenizer constructor. These individual words are called **tokens**.

tokens

`nextToken`

The method `nextToken` returns the first token (word) when it is invoked for the first time, returns the second token when it is invoked the second time, and so forth. If your code invokes `nextToken` after it has returned all the tokens in its string, then your program will halt and issue an error message.

`hasMoreTokens`

The method `hasMoreTokens` is a method that returns a value of type `boolean`; that is, it returns either `true` or `false`. Thus, an invocation of `hasMoreTokens`, such as the following

```
wordFactory.hasMoreTokens()
```

is a Boolean expression, and so it can be used to control a `while` loop. The method `hasMoreTokens` returns `true` as long as `nextToken` has not yet returned all the tokens in the string, and it returns `false` after the method `nextToken` has returned all the tokens in the string.

choosing delimeters

When the constructor for `StringTokenizer` is used with a single argument, as in the preceding example, the tokens are substrings of nonwhitespace characters, and the whitespace characters are used as the separators for the tokens. Any string of one or more whitespace characters is considered a separator. Thus, in the preceding example, the last token produced by the method `nextToken` is `"critical."` including the period. This is because the period is not a whitespace character and so is not a separator.

You can specify your own set of separator characters. When you create your own set of separator characters, you give a second argument to the constructor for `StringTokenizer`. The second argument is a string consisting of all the separator characters. Thus, if you want your separators to consist of the blank, the new-line character, the period, and the comma, you could proceed as in the following example:

```
StringTokenizer wordfactory2 =
   new StringTokenizer("Give me the word, my friend.", " \n.,");
while(wordfactory2.hasMoreTokens())
{
    System.out.println(wordfactory2.nextToken());
}
```

This will produce the output

```
Give
me
the
word
my
friend
```

Notice that the period and comma are not part of the tokens produced, because they are now token separators. Also note that the string of token separators is the second argument to the constructor.

Some of the methods for the class `StringTokenizer` are summarized in Display 4.17. A sample use of `StringTokenizer` is given in Display 4.18.

Display 4.17 Some Methods in the Class `StringTokenizer`

The class `StringTokenizer` is in the `java.util package.`

`public StringTokenizer(String theString)`

Constructor for a tokenizer that will use whitespace characters as separators when finding tokens in `theString.`

`public StringTokenizer(String theString, String delimiters)`

Constructor for a tokenizer that will use the characters in the string `delimiters` as separators when finding tokens in `theString.`

`public boolean hasMoreTokens()`

Tests whether there are more tokens available from this tokenizer's string. When used in conjunction with `nextToken`, it returns true as long as `nextToken` has not yet returned all the tokens in the string; returns `false` otherwise.

`public String nextToken()`

Returns the next token from this tokenizer's string. (Throws `NoSuchElementException` if there are no more tokens to return.)[5]

`public String nextToken(String delimiters)`

First changes the delimiter characters to those in the string `delimiters`. Then returns the next token from this tokenizer's string. After the invocation is completed, the delimiter characters are those in the string `delimiters`. (Throws `NoSuchElementException` if there are no more tokens to return. Throws `NullPointer-Exception` if `delimiters` is `null`.)[5]

`public int countTokens()`

Returns the number of tokens remaining to be returned by `nextToken`.

[5]Exceptions are covered in Chapter 9. You can ignore any reference to `NoSuchElementException` until you reach Chapter 9. We include it here for reference value only.

Display 4.18 Use of the `StringTokenizer` Class

```
import java.util.Scanner;
import java.util.StringTokenizer;
```

```
public class StringTokenizerDemo
{
    public static void main(String[] args)
    {
        Scanner keyboard = new Scanner(System.in);

        System.out.println("Enter your last name");
        System.out.println("followed by your first and middle names.");
        System.out.println("If you have no middle name,");
        System.out.println("enter \"None\".");
        String inputLine = keyboard.nextLine();

        String delimiters = ", "; //Comma and blank space
        StringTokenizer nameFactory =
            new StringTokenizer(inputLine, delimiters);

        String lastName = nameFactory.nextToken();
        String firstName = nameFactory.nextToken();
        String middleName = nameFactory.nextToken();
        if (middleName.equalsIgnoreCase("None"))
            middleName = ""; //Empty string
        System.out.println("Hello " + firstName
                            + " " + middleName + " " + lastName);
    }
}
```

Sample Dialogue

```
Enter your last name
followed by your first and middle names.
If you have no middle name,
enter None.
Savitch, Walter None
Hello Walter Savitch
```

Note that the comma is not read because it is a delimiter.

MyProgrammingLab™

Self-Test Exercises

27. What would be the last line in the dialog in Display 4.18 if the user entered the following input line instead of the one shown in Display 4.18? (The comma is omitted.)

```
Savitch Walter None
```

VideoNote
Example Using the String Tokenizer Class on a CSV File

28. What would be the last line in the dialog in Display 4.18 if the user entered the following input line instead of the one shown in Display 4.18?

```
Tom, Dick, and Harry
```

Chapter Summary

- Objects have both instance variables and methods. A class is a type whose values are objects. All objects in a class have the same methods and the same types of instance variables.
- There are two main kinds of methods: methods that return a value and `void` methods. (Some specialized methods, such as constructors, are neither `void` methods nor methods that return a value.)
- When defining a method, the `this` parameter is a name used for the calling object.
- Normally, your classes should have both an `equals` method and a `toString` method.
- If an instance variable or method is marked `private`, then it cannot be directly referenced anyplace except in the definition of a method of the same class.
- Outside of the class in which it is defined, a private instance variable can be accessed via accessor methods and changed via mutator methods.
- A variable declared in a method is said to be a *local variable*. The meaning of a local variable is confined to the method in which it is declared. The local variable goes away when a method invocation ends. The name of a local variable can be reused for something else outside of the method in which it is declared.
- A parameter is like a blank in a method definition that is filled in with an argument when the method is invoked. A parameter is actually a local variable that is initialized to the value of the corresponding argument. This is known as the *call-by-value* parameter-passing mechanism.
- If a variable is used as an argument to a method, then only the value of the variable, not the variable itself, is plugged in to the corresponding parameter.

- *Encapsulation* means that the data and the actions are combined into a single item (in our case, a class object) and that the *details of the implementation are hidden*. Making all instance variables private is part of the encapsulation process.
- A class can have two (or more) different definitions for the same method name, provided the two definitions have different numbers of parameters or some parameters of differing types. This is called *overloading* the method name.
- A constructor is a variety of method that is called when you create an object of the class using `new`. A constructor is intended to be used to perform initialization tasks such as initializing instance variables. A constructor must have the same name as the class to which it belongs.
- A constructor with no parameters is called a *no-argument constructor*. If your class definition includes no constructor definitions at all, then Java automatically provides a no-argument constructor. If your class definition contains any constructor definitions at all, then no additional constructors are provided by Java. Your class definitions should usually include a no-argument constructor.

Answers to Self-Test Exercises

1.
```
public void makeItNewYears( )
{
    month = "January";
    day = 1;
}
```

2.
```
public void yellIfNewYear( )
{
    if ( (month.equalsIgnorewCase("January")) && (day == 1) )
        System.out.println("Hurrah!");
    else
        System.out.println("Not New Year's Day.");
}
```

3.
```
public int getNextYear( )
{
    int nextYear = year + 1;
    return nextYear;
}
```

4.
```
public void happyGreeting( )
{
    int count;
    for (count = 1; count <= day; count++)
        System.out.println("Happy Days!");
}
```

5.
```
public double fractionDone (int targetDay)
{
    double doubleDay = day;
    return doubleDay/targetDay;
}
```

6.
```
public void advanceYear(int increase)
{
    year = year + increase;
}
```

7. The instances of `newMonth` that have their values changed to `6` are indicated in color as follows:

```
public void setDate(int newMonth, int newDay, int newYear)
{
    month = monthString(newMonth);
    day = newDay;
    year = newYear;
    System.out.println("Date changed to "
            + newMonth + " " + newDay + ", " + newYear);
}
```

The point being emphasized here is that all instances of `newMonth` have their values changed to 6. Technically speaking, the parameter `newMonth` is a local variable. So, there is only one local variable named `newMonth` whose value is changed to `6`, but the net effect, in this case, is the same as replacing all occurrences of `newMonth` with `6`.

8. Yes, it is legal. The point being emphasized here is that the parameter `count` is a local variable and so can have its value changed, in this case by the decrement operator.

9. Each case has a `return` statement. A `return` statement always ends the method invocation, and hence ends the execution of the `switch` statement. So, a `break` statement would be redundant.

10. They are assumed to be instance variables of the calling object.

11.
```
public int getDay()
{
    return this.day;
}
public int getYear()
{
    return this.year;
}
```

12.
```
public int getMonth()
{
    if (this.month.equals("January"))
        return 1;
    else if (this.month.equals("February"))
        return 2;
    else if (this.month.equals("March"))
        return 3;
    else if (this.month.equals("April"))
        return 4;
    else if (this.month.equals("May"))
        return 5;
    else if (this.month.equals("June"))
        return 6;
    else if (this.month.equals("July"))
        return 7;
    else if (this.month.equals("August"))
        return 8;
    else if (this.month.equals("September"))
        return 9;
    else if (this.month.equals("October"))
        return 10;
    else if (this.month.equals("November"))
        return 11;
    else if (this.month.equals("December"))
        return 12;
    else
    {
        System.out.println("Fatal Error");
        System.exit(0);
        return 0; //Needed to keep the compiler happy
    }
}
```

13. The instance variable `month` contains a string, so we used `month` with `equals`. It would have been just as good to use

    ```
    getMonth() == otherDate.getMonth()
    ```

    We used `getMonth()` with the less-than sign because it is of type `int` and so works with the less-than sign. The instance variable `month` is of type `String` and does not work with the less-than sign.

14. Every method should be tested in a program in which every other method in the testing program has already been fully tested and debugged.

15. All instance variables should be marked `private`.

16. Normally, a method is private only if it is being used solely as a helping method in the definition of other methods.

17. `getMonth`, `getDay`, and `getYear`.

18. `setDate`, `setMonth`, `setDay`, and `setYear`.

19.
```
private boolean dateOK(int monthInt, int dayInt, int yearInt)
{
    if ((yearInt < 1000) || (yearInt > 999))
        return false;

    switch (monthInt)
    {
    case 1:
        return (dayInt >= 1) && (dayInt <= 31);
    case 2:
        if (leapYear(yearInt))
            return (dayInt >= 1) && (dayInt <= 29);
        else
            return (dayInt >= 1) && (dayInt <= 28);
    case 3:
        return (dayInt >= 1) && (dayInt <= 31);
    case 4:
        return (dayInt >= 1) && (dayInt <= 30);
    case 5:
        return (dayInt >= 1) && (dayInt <= 31);
    case 6:
        return (dayInt >= 1) && (dayInt <= 30);
    case 7:
        return (dayInt >= 1) && (dayInt <= 31);
    case 8:
        return (dayInt >= 1) && (dayInt <= 31);
    case 9:
        return (dayInt >= 1) && (dayInt <= 30);
    case 10:
        return (dayInt >= 1) && (dayInt <= 31);
    case 11:
        return (dayInt >= 1) && (dayInt <= 30);
    case 12:
        return (dayInt >= 1) && (dayInt <= 31);
    default:
        return false;
    }
}
```

```
/**
Returns true if yearInt is a leap year.
*/
private boolean leapYear(int yearInt)
{
     return ((yearInt % 4 == 0) && (yearInt % 100 != 0))
              || (yearInt % 400 == 0);
}
```

20.
```
doSomething(int, char, int)
setMonth(int)
setMonth(String)
amount(int, double)
amount(int, double)
```

21. Yes, it is legal because they have different signatures. This is a valid example of overloading.

22. No, it would be illegal because they have the same signature.

23. No, it would be illegal. You cannot overload on the basis of the type of the returned value.

24. If a class is named `CoolClass`, then all constructors must be named `CoolClass`.

25.
```
YourClass anObject = new YourClass(42, 'A'); //Legal
YourClass anotherObject = new YourClass(41.99, 'A'); //Not legal
YourClass yetAnotherObject = new YourClass(); //Legal
yetAnotherObject.doStuff(); //Legal
YourClass oneMoreObject; //Legal
oneMoreObject.doStuff(); //Not legal
oneMoreObject.YourClass(99, 'B'); //Not legal
```

26. A no-argument constructor is a constructor with no parameters. If you define a class and define some constructors but do not define a no-argument constructor, then the class will have no no-argument constructor. *Default constructor* is another name for a no-argument constructor.

27. The last line would be the same. Because the blank space is a delimiter, a blank space is enough to separate the tokens.

28.
```
Hello Dick and Tom
```

The other token in the input line is just not used.

MyProgrammingLab™ Programming Projects

Visit www.myprogramminglab.com to complete select exercises online and get instant feedback.

1. Write a program that outputs the lyrics for "Ninety-nine Bottles of Beer on the Wall." Your program should print the number of bottles in English, not as a number. For example,

   Ninety-nine bottles of beer on the wall,

   Ninety-nine bottles of beer,

   Take one down, pass it around,

   Ninety-eight bottles of beer on the wall.

   ...

   One bottle of beer on the wall,

   One bottle of beer,

   Take one down, pass it around,

   Zero bottles of beer on the wall.

   Your program should not use ninety-nine output statements!

   Design your program with a class named `BeerSong` whose constructor takes an integer parameter that is the number of bottles of beer initially on the wall. If the parameter is less than zero, set the number of bottles to zero. Similarly, if the parameter is greater than 99, set the number of beer bottles to 99. Then make a public method called `printSong` that outputs all stanzas from the number of bottles of beer down to zero. Add any additional private methods you find helpful.

2. Define a class called `Fraction`. This class is used to represent a ratio of two integers. Include mutator methods that allow the user to set the numerator and the denominator. Also include a method that returns the value of numerator divided by denominator as a `double`. Include an additional method that outputs the value of the fraction reduced to lowest terms (e.g., instead of outputting 20/60, the method should output 1/3). This will require finding the greatest common divisor for the numerator and denominator, then dividing both by that number. Embed your class in a test program.

3. Define a class called `Odometer` that will be used to track fuel and mileage for an automobile. The class should have instance variables to track the miles driven and the fuel efficiency of the vehicle in miles per gallon. Include a mutator method to reset the odometer to zero miles, a mutator method to set the fuel efficiency, a mutator method that accepts miles driven for a trip and adds it to the odometer's total, and an accessor method that returns the number of gallons of gasoline that the vehicle has consumed since the odometer was last reset.

   Use your class with a test program that creates several trips with different fuel efficiencies. You should decide which variables should be public, if any.

4. Define a class called `BlogEntry` that could be used to store an entry for a Web log. The class should have instance variables to store the poster's username, text of the entry, and the date of the entry using the `Date` class from this chapter. Add a constructor that allows the user of the class to set all instance variables. Also add a method, `DisplayEntry`, that outputs all of the instance variables, and another method called `getSummary` that returns the first 10 words from the text (or the entire text if it is less than 10 words). Test your class from your main method.
5. Define a class called `Counter` whose objects count things. An object of this class records a count that is a nonnegative integer. Include methods to set the counter to 0, to increase the count by 1, and to decrease the count by 1. Be sure that no method allows the value of the counter to become negative. Include an accessor method that returns the current count value and a method that outputs the count to the screen. There should be no input method or other mutator methods. The only method that can set the counter is the one that sets it to 0. Also, include a `toString` method and an `equals` method. Write a program (or programs) to test all the methods in your class definition.
6. Write a grading program for a class with the following grading policies:
   a. There are three quizzes, each graded on the basis of 10 points.
   b. There is one midterm exam, graded on the basis of 100 points.
   c. There is one final exam, graded on the basis of 100 points.

   The final exam counts for 40% of the grade. The midterm counts for 35% of the grade. The three quizzes together count for a total of 25% of the grade. (Do not forget to convert the quiz scores to percentages before they are averaged in.)

   Any grade of 90 or more is an A, any grade of 80 or more (but less than 90) is a B, any grade of 70 or more (but less than 80) is a C, any grade of 60 or more (but less than 70) is a D, and any grade below 60 is an F. The program should read in the student's scores and output the student's record, which consists of three quiz scores and two exam scores, as well as the student's overall numeric score for the entire course and final letter grade.

   Define and use a class for the student record. The class should have instance variables for the quizzes, midterm, final, overall numeric score for the course, and final letter grade. The overall numeric score is a number in the range 0 to 100, which represents the weighted average of the student's work. The class should have methods to compute the overall numeric grade and the final letter grade. These last methods should be `void` methods that set the appropriate instance variables. Your class should have a reasonable set of accessor and mutator methods, an `equals` method, and a `toString` method, whether or not your program uses them. You may add other methods if you wish.
7. Write a `Temperature` class that has two instance variables: a temperature value (a floating-point number) and a character for the scale, either `C` for Celsius or `F` for Fahrenheit. The class should have four constructor methods: one for each instance

variable (assume zero degrees if no value is specified and Celsius if no scale is specified), one with two parameters for the two instance variables, and a no-argument constructor (set to zero degrees Celsius). Include the following: (1) two accessor methods to return the temperature—one to return the degrees Celsius, the other to return the degrees Fahrenheit—use the following formulas to write the two methods, and round to the nearest tenth of a degree:

$$\text{DegreesC} = 5(\text{degreesF} - 32)/9$$
$$\text{DegreesF} = (9(\text{degreesC})/5) + 32;$$

(2) three mutator methods: one to set the value, one to set the scale (`F` or `C`), and one to set both; (3) three comparison methods: an `equals` method to test whether two temperatures are equal, one method to test whether one temperature is greater than another, and one method to test whether one temperature is less than another (note that a Celsius temperature can be equal to a Fahrenheit temperature as indicated by the above formulas); and (4) a suitable `toString` method. Then write a driver program (or programs) that tests all the methods. Be sure to use each of the constructors, to include at least one true and one false case for each of the comparison methods, and to test at least the following temperature equalities: 0.0 degrees C = 32.0 degrees F, –40.0 degrees C = –40.0 degrees F, and 100.0 degrees C = 212.0 degrees F.

8. Redefine the class `Date` in Display 4.13 so that the instance variable for the month is of type `int` instead of type `String`. None of the method headings should change in any way. In particular, no `String` type parameters should change to `int` type parameters. You must redefine the methods to make things work out. Any program that uses the `Date` class from Display 4.13 should be able to use your `Date` class without any changes in the program. In particular, the program in Display 4.14 should work the same whether the `Date` class is defined as in Display 4.13 or is defined as you do it for this project. Write a test program (or programs) that tests each method in your class definition.

VideoNote
Solution to Programming Project 4.9

9. Define a class whose objects are records on animal species. The class should have instance variables for the species name, population, and growth rate. The growth rate is a percentage that can be positive or negative and can exceed 100%. Include a suitable collection of constructors, mutator methods, and accessor methods. Include a `toString` method and an `equals` method. Include a `boolean` valued method named `endangered` that returns `true` when the growth rate is negative and returns `false` otherwise. Write a test program (or programs) that tests each method in your class definition.

10. Your vet's office is using the `Pet` class defined in Display 4.15 and would like to include a way to calculate the dosage amount for drugs that are commonly administered for dogs and cats. Make the following modifications to the class:

    - Add an instance variable that indicates if the type of the pet is a dog or a cat.
    - Modify the constructor and the set method to include the type of pet (i.e., dog or cat).

- Add a method named `acepromazine( )` that returns as a `double` the dosage in ml for the sedative acepromazine.
- Add a method named `carprofen( )` that returns as a `double` the dosage in ml for the pain killer carprofen.

The dosage calculation is

$$\text{Dosage (ml)} = \frac{\text{Weight}}{2.2} \times \frac{\text{mg per kg}}{\text{mg per ml}}$$

Weight is in pounds.

- For acepromazine, use mg per ml = 10, and mg per kg = 0.03 for dogs and 0.002 for cats.
- For carprofen, use mg per ml = 12, and mg per kg = 0.5 for dogs and 0.25 for cats.

Modify the main method in Display 4.16 to include tests of the new methods.

11. Create a class named `Pizza` that stores information about a single pizza. It should contain the following:

- Private instance variables to store the size of the pizza (either small, medium, or large), the number of cheese toppings, the number of pepperoni toppings, and the number of ham toppings.
- Constructor(s) that set all of the instance variables.
- Public methods to get and set the instance variables.
- A public method named `calcCost( )` that returns a `double` that is the cost of the pizza.

  Pizza cost is determined by:

  Small: \$10 + \$2 per topping
  Medium: \$12 + \$2 per topping
  Large: \$14 + \$2 per topping

- A public method named `getDescription( )` that returns a String containing the pizza size, quantity of each topping, and the pizza cost as calculated by `calcCost( )`.

Write test code to create several pizzas and output their descriptions. For example, a large pizza with one cheese, one pepperoni and two ham toppings should cost a total of \$22.

12. This programming project extends Programming Project 4.11. Create a `PizzaOrder` class that allows up to three pizzas to be saved in an order. Each pizza saved should be a `Pizza` object as described in Programming Project 4.11. In addition to appropriate instance variables and constructors, add the following methods:

- `public void setNumPizzas(int numPizzas)`—sets the number of pizzas in the order. `numPizzas` must be between 1 and 3.

- `public void setPizza1(Pizza pizza1)`—sets the first pizza in the order.
- `public void setPizza2(Pizza pizza2)`—sets the second pizza in the order.
- `public void setPizza3(Pizza pizza3)`—sets the third pizza in the order.
- `public double calcTotal()`—returns the total cost of the order.

Write a `main` method to test the class. The `setPizza2` and `setPizza3` methods will be used only if there are two or three pizzas in the order, respectively. Sample code illustrating the methods is shown below. Note that first three lines are incomplete. You must complete them as part of the Programming Project.

```
Pizza pizza1 = // Code to create a large pizza, 1 cheese, 1 ham
Pizza pizza2 = // Code to create a medium pizza, 2 cheese, 2 pepperoni
PizzaOrder order = // Code to create an order
order.setNumPizzas(2); // 2 pizzas in the order
order.setPizza1(pizza1); // Set first pizza
order.setPizza2(pizza2); // Set second pizza
double total = order.calcTotal(); // Should be 18+20 = 38
```

13. Your Community Supported Agriculture (CSA) farm delivers a box of fresh fruits and vegetables to your house once a week. For this Programming Project, define the class `BoxOfProduce` that contains exactly three bundles of fruits or vegetables. You can represent the fruits or vegetables as three instance variables of type `String`. Add an appropriate constructor, accessor, and mutator methods. Also write a `toString()` method that returns as a String the complete contents of the box.

    Next, write a main method that creates a `BoxOfProduce` with three items randomly selected from this list:

    ```
    Broccoli
    Tomato
    Kiwi
    Kale
    Tomatillo
    ```

    This list should be stored in a text file that is read in by your program. For now you can assume that the list contains exactly five types of fruits or vegetables.

    Do not worry if your program randomly selects duplicate produce for the three items. Next, the main method should display the contents of the box and allow the user to substitute any one of the five possible fruits or vegetables for any of the fruits or vegetables selected for the box. After the user is done with substitutions, output the final contents of the box to be delivered. If you create additional methods to select the random items and to select valid substitutions, then your main method will be simpler to write.

14. A comma-separated values (CSV) file is a simple text format used to store a list of records. A comma is used as a delimiter to separate the fields for each record. This format is commonly used to transfer data between a spreadsheet or database. In this Programming Project, consider a store that sells five products abbreviated as A, B, C, D, and E. Customers can rate each product from 1–5, where 1 is poor and 5 is excellent. The ratings are stored in a CSV file where each row contains the customer's rating for each product. Here is a sample file with three customer ratings:

```
A,B,C,D,E

3,0,5,1,2

1,1,4,2,1

0,0,5,1,3
```

In this file format, the first line gives the products. The digit 0 indicates that a customer did not rate a product. In this case, the first customer rated A as 3, C as 5, D as 1, and E as 2. Product B was not rated. The third customer rated C as 5, D as 1, and E as 3. The third customer did not rate A or B.

Create a text file in this format with sample ratings. Then, write a program that reads in this text file and extracts each rating using the `StringTokenizer` class. Finally, the program should output the average rating for each product. Customers that did not rate a product should not be considered when computing the average rating for that product. Your program can assume there will always be exactly five products but it should work with an arbitrary number of customer ratings.

Defining Classes II 5

5 Defining Classes II

After a certain high level of technical skill is achieved, science and art tend to coalesce in esthetics, plasticity, and form. The greatest scientists are always artists as well.

ALBERT EINSTEIN, Quoted in Alice Calaprice, *The Quotable Einstein*

Introduction

This chapter is a continuation of Chapter 4. It covers the rest of the core material on defining classes. We start by discussing *static methods* and *static variables*, which are methods and variables that belong to the class as a whole and not to particular objects. We then go on to discuss how class type variables name objects of their class and how class type parameters are handled in Java.

This chapter also discusses *packages*, which are Java's way of grouping classes into libraries. We end this chapter with a discussion of `javadoc`, a program that automatically extracts documentation from classes and packages.

Prerequisites

This chapter uses material from Chapters 1 through 4.

Sections 5.3 and 5.4 are independent of each other and may be covered in any order. Section 5.3 covers some subtle points about references, and Section 5.4 covers packages and `javadoc`. The material on `javadoc` is not used in the rest of this book. The other material in Sections 5.3 and 5.4 is not heavily used in the next few chapters and can be digested as needed if the material seems difficult on first reading.

The material on packages in Section 5.4 assumes that you know about directories (which are called folders in some operating systems), that you know about path names for directories (folders), and that you know about PATH (environment) variables. These are not Java topics. They are part of your operating system, and the details depend on your particular operating system. If you can find out how to set the PATH variable on your operating system, then you will know enough about these topics to understand the material on packages in Section 5.4.

5.1 Static Methods and Static Variables

All for one, one for all, that is our device.

ALEXANDRE DUMAS, *The Three Musketeers*

Static Methods

static methods

Some methods do not require a calling object. Methods to perform simple numeric calculations are good examples. For example, a method to compute the maximum of two integers has no obvious candidate for a calling object. In Java, you can define a method so that it requires no calling object. Such methods are known as **static methods**. You define a static method in the same way as any other method, but you add the keyword `static` to the method definition heading, as in the following example:

```
public static int maximum(int n1, int n2)
{
    if (n1 > n2)
        return n1;
    else
        return n2;
}
```

Although a static method requires no calling object, it still belongs to some class, and its definition is given inside the class definition. When you invoke a static method, you normally use the class name in place of a calling object. So if the above definition of the method `maximum` were in a class named `SomeClass`, then the following is a sample invocation of `maximum`:

```
int budget = SomeClass.maximum(yourMoney, myMoney);
```

where `yourMoney` and `myMoney` are variables of type `int` that contain some values.

A sample of some static method definitions, as well as a program that uses the methods, are given in Display 5.1.

We have already been using one static method. The method `exit` in the class `System` is a static method. To end a program immediately, we have used the following invocation of the static method `exit`:

```
System.exit(0);
```

Note that with a static method, the class name serves the same purpose as a calling object. (It would be legal to create an object of the class `System` and use it to invoke the method `exit`, but that is confusing style; we usually use the class name when invoking a static method.)

Display 5.1 **Static Methods** (part 1 of 2)

```
/**
Class with static methods for circles and spheres.
*/
public class RoundStuff
{
    public static final double PI = 3.14159;

    /**
     Return the area of a circle of the given radius.
    */
    public static double area(double radius)
    {
        return (PI*radius*radius);
    }

    /**
     Return the volume of a sphere of the given radius.
    */
    public static double volume(double radius)
    {
        return ((4.0/3.0)*PI*radius*radius*radius);
    }
}
```

This is the file **RoundStuff.java.**

```
import java.util.Scanner;

public class RoundStuffDemo
{
    public static void main(String[] args)
    {
        Scanner keyboard = new Scanner(System.in);
        System.out.println("Enter radius:");
        double radius = keyboard.nextDouble();

        System.out.println("A circle of radius"
                                        + radius + "inches");
        System.out.println("has an area of " +
             RoundStuff.area(radius) + " square inches.");
        System.out.println("A sphere of radius"
                                        + radius + "inches");
        System.out.println("has an volume of " +
             RoundStuff.volume(radius) + "cubic inches.");
    }
}
```

This is the file **RoundStuffDemo.java.**

Display 5.1 **Static Methods** (part 2 of 2)

Sample Dialogue

```
Enter radius:
2
A circle of radius 2.0 inches
has an area of 12.56636 square inches.
A sphere of radius 2.0 inches
has a volume of 33.51029333333333 cubic inches.
```

Within the definition of a static method, you cannot do anything that refers to a calling object, such as accessing an instance variable. This makes perfectly good sense, because a static method can be invoked without using any calling object and so can be invoked when there are no instance variables. (Remember instance variables belong to the calling object.) The best way to think about this restriction is in terms of the `this` parameter. In a static method, you cannot use the `this` parameter, either explicitly or implicitly. For example, the name of an instance variable by itself has an implicit `this` and a dot before it. So you cannot use an instance variable in the definition of a static method.

Static Methods

A **static method** is one that can be used without a calling object. With a static method, you normally use the class name in place of a calling object.

When you define a static method, you place the keyword `static` in the heading of the definition.

Since it does not need a calling object, a static method cannot refer to an instance variable of the class, nor can it invoke a nonstatic method of the class (unless it creates a new object of the class and uses that object as the calling object). Another way to phrase it is that, in the definition of a static method, you cannot use an instance variable or method that has an implicit or explicit `this` for a calling object.

PITFALL: Invoking a Nonstatic Method Within a Static Method

If `myMethod()` is a nonstatic (that is, ordinary) method in a class, then within the definition of any method of this class, an invocation of the form

```
myMethod();
```

means

```
this.myMethod();
```

(continued)

PITFALL: (continued)

and so it is illegal within the definition of a static method. (A static method has no `this`.)

However, it is legal to invoke a static method within the definition of another static method.

There is one way that you can invoke a nonstatic method within a static method: if you create an object of the class and use that object (rather than `this`) as the calling object. For example, suppose `myMethod()` is a nonstatic method in the class `MyClass`. Then, as we already discussed, the following is illegal within the definition of a static method in the class `MyClass`:

```
myMethod();
```

However, the following is perfectly legal in a static method or any method definition:

```
MyClass anObject = new MyClass();
anObject.myMethod();
```

The method `main` is a static method, and you will often see code similar to this in the `main` method of a class. This point is discussed in the Tip "You Can Put a `main` in Any Class." ■

TIP: You Can Put a `main` in Any Class

So far, whenever we have used a class in the `main` part of a program, that `main` method was by itself in a different class definition within another file. However, sometimes it makes sense to have a `main` method within a regular class definition. The class can then be used for two purposes: It can be used to create objects in other classes, or it can be run as a program. For example, you can combine the class definition `RoundStuff` and the program `RoundStuffDemo` (both in Display 5.1) by placing the `main` method inside the definition of the class `RoundStuff`, to obtain the class definition shown in Display 5.2.

Another example of a class with a `main` added is given in Display 5.3. Note that in addition to the static method `main`, the class has another static method named `toCelsius`. The class has both static and nonstatic methods. Note that the static method `toCelsius` can be invoked without the class name or a calling object because it is in another static method (namely `main`) in the same class. However, the nonstatic method `toString` requires an explicit calling object (`temperatureObject`). Java requires that a program's `main` method be static. Thus, within a `main` method, you cannot invoke a nonstatic method of the same class (such as `toString`) unless you create an object of the class and use it as a calling object for the nonstatic method.

You do not want to place just any `main` method in a class definition that is to be used as a regular class to create objects. One handy trick is to place a small diagnostic program in a `main` method that is inside of your class definition. ■

Display 5.2 Class Definition with a `main` Added

```
import java.util.Scanner;

/**
Class with static methods for circles and spheres.
*/
public class RoundStuff2
{
    public static final double PI = 3.14159;

    /**
     Return the area of a circle of the given radius.
    */
    public static double area(double radius)
    {
       return (PI*radius*radius);
    }

    /**
    Return the volume of a sphere of the given radius.
    */
    public static double volume(double radius)
    {
           return ((4.0/3.0)*PI*radius*radius*radius);
    }

    public static void main(String[] args)
    {
        Scanner keyboard = new Scanner(System.in);
        System.out.println("Enter radius:");
        double radius = keyboard.nextDouble();

        System.out.println("A circle of radius "
                                       + radius + "inches");
        System.out.println("has an area of " +
             RoundStuff.area(radius) + " square inches.");
        System.out.println("A sphere of radius "
                                       + radius + "inches");
        System.out.println("has an volume of " +
             RoundStuff.volume(radius) + " cubic inches.");
    }
}
```

The dialogue is the same as in Display 5.1.

Display 5.3 **Another Class with a `main` Added** (part 1 of 2)

```
import java.util.Scanner;

/**
Class for a temperature (expressed in degrees Celsius).
*/
public class Temperature
{
    private double degrees; //Celsius

    public Temperature()
    {
        degrees = 0;
    }

    public Temperature (double initialDegrees)
    {
        degrees = initialDegrees;
    }

    public void setDegrees (double newDegrees)
    {
        degrees = newDegrees;
    }

    public double getDegrees()
    {
        return degrees;
    }

    public String toString()
    {
        return (degrees + "C");
    }

    public boolean equals(Temperature otherTemperature)
    {
        return (degrees == otherTemperature.degrees);
    }
    /**
     Returns number of Celsius degrees equal to
     degreesF Fahrenheit degrees.
    */
```

Note that this class has a `main` method and both static and nonstatic methods.

Display 5.3 **Another Class with a `main` Added** (part 2 of 2)

```
    public static double toCelsius(double degreesF)
    {

        return 5*(degreesF - 32)/9;
    }
    public static void main(String[] args)
    {
        double degreesF, degreesC;

        Scanner keyboard = new Scanner(System.in);
        System.out.println("Enter degrees Fahrenheit:");
        degreesF = keyboard.nextDouble();

        degreesC = toCelsius(degreesF);

        Temperature temperatureObject = new Temperature(degreesC);
        System.out.println("Equivalent Celsius temperature is"
                              + temperatureObject.toString());
    }
}
```

Because this is in the definition of the class `Temperature`*, this is equivalent to* `Temperature.toCelsius(degreesF)`.

Because `main` *is a static method,* `toString` *must have a specified calling object such as* `temperatureObject`.

Sample Dialogue

```
Enter degrees Fahrenheit:
212
Equivalent Celsius temperature is 100.0 C
```

MyProgrammingLab™

Self-Test Exercises

1. Is the following legal? The class `RoundStuff` is defined in Display 5.1.

```
RoundStuff roundObject = new RoundStuff();
System.out.println("A circle of radius 5.5 has area"
                   + roundObject.area(5.5);
```

2. In Display 5.1, we did not define any constructors for the class `RoundStuff`. Is this poor programming style?
3. Can a class contain both static and nonstatic (that is, regular) methods?
4. Can you invoke a nonstatic method within a static method?
5. Can you invoke a static method within a nonstatic method?
6. Can you reference an instance variable within a static method? Why or why not?

Static Variables

static variable

A class can have static variables as well as static methods. A **static variable** is a variable that belongs to the class as a whole and not just to one object. Each object has its own copies of the instance variables. However, with a static variable, there is only one copy of the variable, and all the objects can use this one variable. Thus, a static variable can be used by objects to communicate between the objects. One object can change the static variable, and another object can read that change. To make a variable static, you declare it like an instance variable but add the modifier `static` as follows:

```
private static int turn;
```

Or if you wish to initialize the static variable, which is typical, you might declare it as follows instead:

```
private static int turn = 0;
```

default initialization

If you do not initialize a static variable, it is automatically initialized to a default value: Static variables of type `boolean` are automatically initialized to `false`. Static variables of other primitive types are automatically initialized to the zero of their type. Static variables of a class type are automatically initialized to `null`, which is a kind of placeholder for an object that we will discuss later in this chapter. However, we prefer to explicitly initialize static variables, either as just shown or in a constructor.

Display 5.4 shows an example of a class with a static variable along with a demonstration program. Notice that the two objects, `lover1` and `lover2`, access the same static variable `turn`.

As we already noted, you cannot directly access an instance variable within the definition of a static method. However, it is perfectly legal to access a static variable within a static method, because a static variable belongs to the class as a whole. This is illustrated by the method `getTurn` in Display 5.4. When we write `turn` in the definition of the static method `getTurn`, it does not mean `this.turn`; it means `TurnTaker.turn`. If the static variable `turn` were marked `public` instead of `private`, it would even be legal to use `TurnTaker.turn` outside of the definition of the class `TurnTaker`.

Defined constants that we have already been using, such as the following, are a special kind of static variable:

```
public static final double PI = 3.14159;
```

The modifier `final` in this example means that the static variable `PI` cannot be changed. Such defined constants are normally public and can be used outside the class. This defined constant appears in the class `RoundStuff` in Display 5.1. To use this constant outside of the class `RoundStuff`, you write the constant in the form `RoundStuff.PI`.

Good programming style dictates that static variables should normally be marked `private` unless they are marked `final`, that is, unless they are defined constants. The reason is the same as the reason for making instance variables `private`.

Display 5.4 **A Static Variable** (part 1 of 2)

```
public class TurnTaker
{
    private static int turn = 0;

    private int myTurn;
    private String name;

    public TurnTaker(String theName, int theTurn)
    {
        name = theName;
        if (theTurn >= 0)
            myTurn = theTurn;
        else
        {
            System.out.println("Fatal Error.");
            System.exit(0);
        }
    }

    public TurnTaker()
    {
        name = "No name yet";
        myTurn = 0; //Indicating no turn.
    }

    public String getName()
    {
        return name;
    }

    public static int getTurn()
    {
        turn++;
        return turn;
    }

    public boolean isMyTurn()
    {
        return (turn == myTurn);
    }
}
```

This is the file **TurnTaker.java.**

You cannot access an instance variable in a static method, but you can access a static variable in a static method.

(continued)

Display 5.4 **A Static Variable** (part 2 of 2)

```
public class StaticDemo
{
    public static void main(String[] args)
    {
        TurnTaker lover1 = new TurnTaker("Romeo", 1);
        TurnTaker lover2 = new TurnTaker("Juliet", 3);
        for (int i = 1; i < 5; i++)
        {
            System.out.println("Turn = " + TurnTaker.getTurn());
            if (lover1.isMyTurn())
                System.out.println("Love from" + lover1.getName());
            if (lover2.isMyTurn())
                System.out.println("Love from" + lover2.getName());
        }
    }
}
```

This is the file `StaticDemo.java.`

Sample Dialogue

```
Turn = 1
Love from Romeo
Turn = 2
Turn = 3
Love from Juliet
Turn = 4
```

Another example of a static variable is given in Display 5.5. The static variable `numberOfInvocations` is used to keep track of how many invocations have been made by all objects of the class `StaticDemo`. The program counts all invocations of the methods defined in Display 5.4, except for the method `main`.

Display 5.5 **A Static Variable** (part 1 of 2)

```
public class InvocationCounter
{
    private static int numberOfInvocations = 0;

    public void demoMethod()
    {
        numberOfInvocations++;
        //In a real example, more code would go here.
}
```

`object1` *and* `object2` *use the same static variable* `numberOfInvocations.`

Display 5.5 **A Static Variable** (part 2 of 2)

```
    public void outPutCount()
    {
        numberOfInvocations++;
        System.out.println("Number of invocations so far = "
                                        + numberOfInvocations);
    }

    public static int numberSoFar()
    {
        numberOfInvocations++;
        return numberOfInvocations;
    }

    public static void main(String[] args)
    {
        int i;
        InvocationCounter object1 = new InvocationCounter();
        for (i= 1; i <= 5 ; i++)
        object1.demoMethod();
        object1.outPutCount();

        InvocationCounter object2 = new InvocationCounter();
        for (i= 1; i <= 5 ; i++)
        {
           object2.demoMethod();
           object2.outPutCount();
        }

        System.out.println("Totalnumber of invocations = "
                                 + numberSoFar());
    }
}
```

Outputs 6 for five invocations of `demoMethod` *and one invocation of* `outputCount`.

Sample Dialogue

```
Number of invocations so far = 6
Number of invocations so far = 8
Number of invocations so far = 10
Number of invocations so far = 12
Number of invocations so far = 14
Number of invocations so far = 16
Total number of invocations = 17
```

Static Variables

A **static variable** belongs to the class as a whole. All objects of the class can read and change the static variable. Static variables should normally be private, unless they happen to be defined constants.

SYNTAX

```
private static Type Variable_Name;
private static Type Variable_Name = Initial_Value;
public static final Type Variable_Name = Constant_Value;
```

EXAMPLES

```
private static String lastUser;
private static int turn = 0;
public static final double PI = 3.14159;
```

MyProgrammingLab™

Self-Test Exercises

7. What is the difference between a static variable and an instance variable?
8. Can you use an *instance variable* (without an object name and dot) in the definition of a *static method* of the same class? Can you use an *instance variable* (without an object name and dot) in the definition of a *nonstatic (ordinary) method* of the same class?
9. Can you use a *static variable* in the definition of a static method of the same class? Can you use a *static variable* in the definition of a *nonstatic (ordinary) method* of the same class?
10. Can you use the `this` parameter in the definition of a static method?
11. When we defined the class `Date` in Display 4.11 in Chapter 4, we had not yet discussed static methods, so we did not mark any of the methods `static`. However, some of the methods could have been marked `static` (and should have been marked `static`, if only we had known what that meant). Which of the methods can be marked `static`? (If you omit the modifier `static` when it is appropriate, then the method cannot be invoked with the class name; it must be invoked with a calling object.)
12. Following the style guidelines given in this book, when should a static variable be marked `private`?
13. What do static methods and static variables have in common? After all, they are both called *static*, so it sounds like they have something in common.

The `Math` Class

`Math` methods

The class `Math` provides a number of standard mathematical methods. The class `Math` is provided automatically and requires no `import` statement. Some of the methods in the class `Math` are described in Display 5.6. A more complete list of methods is given in Appendix 5. All of these methods are static, which means that you normally use the class name `Math` in place of a calling object.

Display 5.6 Some Methods in the Class **`Math`** (part 1 of 2)

The `Math` class is in the `java.lang` package, so it requires no `import` statement.

```
public static double pow(double base, double exponent)
```

Returns `base` to the power `exponent`.

EXAMPLE

`Math.pow(2.0,3.0)` returns `8.0`.

```
public static double abs(double argument)
public static float abs(float argument)
public static long abs(long argument)
public static int abs(int argument)
```

Returns the absolute value of the `argument`. (The method name `abs` is overloaded to produce four similar methods.)

EXAMPLE

`Math.abs(-6)` and `Math.abs(6)` both return 6. `Math.abs(-5.5)` and `Math.abs(5.5)` both return `5.5`.

```
public static double min(double n1, double n2)
public static float min(float n1, float n2)
public static long min(long n1, long n2)
public static int min(int n1, int n2)
```

Returns the minimum of the arguments `n1` and `n2`. (The method name `min` is overloaded to produce four similar methods.)

EXAMPLE

`Math.min(3, 2)` returns `2`.

```
public static double max(double n1, double n2)
public static float max(float n1, float n2)
public static long max(long n1, long n2)
public static int max(int n1, int n2)
```

Returns the maximum of the arguments `n1` and `n2`. (The method name `max` is overloaded to produce four similar methods.)

EXAMPLE

`Math.max(3, 2)` returns `3`.

(continued)

Display 5.6 Some Methods in the Class `Math` (part 2 of 2)

```
public static long round(double argument)
public static int round(float argument)
```

Rounds its `argument`.

EXAMPLE

`Math.round(3.2)` returns `3`; `Math.round(3.6)` returns `4`.

```
public static double ceil(double argument)
```

Returns the smallest whole number greater than or equal to the `argument`.

EXAMPLE

`Math.ceil(3.2)` and `Math.ceil(3.9)` both return `4.0`.

```
public static double floor(double argument)
```

Returns the largest whole number less than or equal to the `argument`.

EXAMPLE

`Math.floor(3.2)` and `Math.floor(3.9)` both return `3.0`.

```
public static double sqrt(double argument)
```

Returns the square root of its `argument`.

EXAMPLE

`Math.sqrt(4)` returns `2.0`.

```
public static double random()
```

Returns a random number greater than or equal to 0.0 and less than 1.0.

EXAMPLE

`Math.random()` returns 0.5505562535943004 (sample number; returns a pseudo-random number that is less than 1 and greater than or equal to 0).

The class `Math` has three similar methods named `round`, `floor`, and `ceil`. Some of these return a value of type `double`, but they all return a value that is intuitively a whole number that is close to the value of their arguments. The method `round` rounds a number to the nearest whole number, and (if the argument is a `double`) it returns that whole number as a value of type `long`. If you want that whole number as a value of type `int`, you must use a type cast as in the following:

```
double exact = 7.56;
int roundedValue = (int)Math.round(exact);
```

You cannot assign a `long` value to a variable of type `int`, even if it is a value such as `8`, which could just as well have been an `int`. A value such as `8` can be of type either `int` or `long` (or even of type `short` or `byte`) depending on how it was created.

floor and ceil

The methods floor and ceil are similar to, but not identical to, round. Neither one rounds, although they both yield a whole number that is close to their argument. They both return a whole number as a value of type double (not of type int or long). The method floor returns the nearest whole number that is less than or equal to its argument. So Math.floor(5.9) returns 5.0, not 6.0. Math.floor(5.2) also returns 5.0.

The method ceil returns the nearest whole number that is greater than or equal to its argument. The word ceil is short for "ceiling." Math.ceil(5.1) returns 6.0, not 5.0. Math.ceil(5.9) also returns 6.0.

If you want to store the value returned by either floor or ceil in a variable of type int, you must use a type cast as in the following example:

```
double exact = 7.56;
int lowEstimate = (int)Math.floor(exact);
int highEstimate = (int)Math.ceil(exact);
```

Math.floor(exact) returns the double value 7.0, and the variable lowEstimate receives the int value 7. Math.ceil(exact) returns the double value 8.0, and the variable highEstimate receives the int value 8.

Because values of type double are effectively approximate values, a safer way to compute the floor or ceiling as an int value is the following:

```
double exact = 7.56;
int lowEstimate = (int)Math.round(Math.floor(exact));
int highEstimate = (int)Math.round(Math.ceil(exact));
```

This way, if Math.floor(exact) returns slightly less than 7.0, the final result will still be 7 and not 6, and if Math.ceil(exact) returns slightly less than 8.0, the final result will still be 8 and not 7.

Math constants

The class Math also has the two predefined constants E and PI. The constant PI (often written π in mathematical formulas) is used in calculations involving circles, spheres, and other geometric figures based on circles. PI is approximately 3.14159. The constant E is the base of the natural logarithm system (often written *e* in mathematical formulas) and is approximately 2.72. (We do not use the predefined constant E in this text.) The constants PI and E are defined constants, as described in Chapter 1. For example, the following computes the area of a circle, given its radius:

```
area = Math.PI * radius * radius;
```

Notice that because the constants PI and E are defined in the class Math, they must have the class name Math and a dot before them. For example, in Display 5.7, we have redone the program in Display 5.2, but this time we used the constant Math.PI instead of including our own definition of PI.

Display 5.7 Using **`Math.PI`**

```
import java.util.Scanner;

/**
Class with static methods for circles and spheres.
*/
public class RoundStuff3
{

    /**
    Return the area of a circle of the given radius.
    */
    public static double area(double radius)
    {
        return (Math.PI*radius*radius);
    }

    /**
     Return the volume of a sphere of the given radius.
    */
    public static double volume(double radius)
    {
        return ((4.0/3.0)*Math.PI*radius*radius*radius);
    }

    public static void main(String[] args)
    {
        Scanner keyboard = new Scanner(System.in);
        System.out.println("Enter radius:");
        double radius = keyboard.nextDouble();

        System.out.println("A circle of radius"
                                       + radius + "inches");
        System.out.println("has an area of" +
             RoundStuff.area(radius) + "square inches.");
        System.out.println("A sphere of radius"
                                       + radius + "inches");
        System.out.println("has a volume of " +
             RoundStuff.volume(radius) + "cubic inches.");
    }
}
```

The dialogue is the same as in Display 5.1.

Finally, the class `Math` also includes a method to generate random numbers. The method `random` returns a pseudo-random number that is greater than or equal to 0.0 and less than 1.0. A pseudo-random number is a number that appears random, but is really generated by a deterministic function. See Chapter 3 for additional discussion about random number generation.

MyProgrammingLab™

Self-Test Exercises

14. What values are returned by each of the following?

```
Math.round(3.2), Math.round(3.6),
Math.floor(3.2), Math.floor(3.6),
Math.ceil(3.2), and Math.ceil(3.6).
```

15. Suppose `answer` is a variable of type `double`. Write an assignment statement to assign `Math.round(answer)` to the `int` variable `roundedAnswer`.

16. Suppose `n` is of type `int` and `m` is of type `long`. What is the type of the value returned by `Math.min(n, m)`? Is it `int` or `long`?

Wrapper Classes

Java treats the primitive types, such as `int` and `double`, differently from the class types, such as the class `String` and the programmer-defined classes. For example, later in this chapter you will see that an argument to a method is treated differently depending on whether the argument is of a primitive or class type. At times, you may find yourself in a situation where you want to use a value of a primitive type but you want or need the value to be an object of a class type. **Wrapper classes** provide a class type corresponding to each of the primitive types so that you can have an object of a class type that behaves somewhat like its corresponding value of a primitive type.

wrapper class

To convert a value of a primitive type to an "equivalent" value of a class type, you create an object of the corresponding wrapper class using the primitive type value as an argument to the wrapper class constructor. The wrapper class for the primitive type `int` is the predefined class `Integer`. If you want to convert an `int` value, such as `42`, to an object of type `Integer`, you can do so as follows:

`integer` class

```
Integer integerObject = new Integer(42);
```

The variable `integerObject` now names an object of the class `Integer` that corresponds to the `int` value `42`. (The object `integerObject` does, in fact, have the `int` value `42` stored in an instance variable of the object `integerObject`.) This process of going from a value of a primitive type to an object of its wrapper class is sometimes called **boxing**, and as you will see in the next subsection, you can let Java automatically do all the work of boxing for you.

boxing

To go in the reverse direction, from an object of type `Integer` to the corresponding `int` value, you can do the following:

```
int i = integerObject.intValue();
```

The method `intValue()` recovers the corresponding `int` value from an object of type `Integer`. This process of going from an object of a wrapper class to the corresponding value of a primitive type is sometimes called **unboxing**, and as you will see in the next subsection, you can let Java automatically do all the work of unboxing for you.

unboxing

other wrapper classes

The wrapper classes for the primitive types `byte`, `short`, `long`, `float`, `double`, and `char` are `Byte`, `Short`, `Long`, `Float`, `Double`, and `Character`, respectively. The methods for converting from the wrapper class object to the corresponding primitive type are `intValue` for the class `Integer`, as we have already seen, `byteValue` for the class `Byte`, `shortValue` for the class `Short`, `longValue` for the class `Long`, `floatValue` for the class `Float`, `doubleValue` for the class `Double`, and `charValue` for the class `Character`.

> **Wrapper Classes**
>
> Every primitive type has a corresponding wrapper class. A **wrapper class** allows you to have a class object that corresponds to a value of a primitive type. Wrapper classes also contain a number of useful predefined constants and static methods.

Automatic Boxing and Unboxing

Converting from a value of a primitive type, such as `int`, to a corresponding object of its associated wrapper class, such as `Integer`, is called **boxing**. You can think of the object as a "box" that contains the value of the primitive type. In fact, the wrapper object does contain the value of the primitive type as the value of a private instance variable. The following are examples of boxing:

```
Integer numberOfSamuri = new Integer(47);
Double price = new Double(499.99);
Character grade = new Character('A');
```

automatic boxing

Starting with version 5.0, Java will automatically do this boxing, so the previous three assignments can be written in the following equivalent, but simpler, forms:

```
Integer numberOfSamuri = 47;
Double price = 499.99;
Character grade = 'A';
```

This is an automatic type cast. What is actually done by Java is what we showed in the forms using the `new`, but it is handy to be able to write the assignments in the simpler form.

automatic unboxing

The reverse conversion from an object of a wrapper class to a value of its associated primitive type is called **unboxing**. Unboxing is also done automatically in Java (starting in version 5.0). The following are examples of automatic unboxing:

```
Integer numberOfSamuri = new Integer(47);
int n = numberOfSamuri;
Double price = new Double(499.99);
double d = price;
Character grade = new Character('A');
char c = grade;
```

Java automatically applies the appropriate accessor method (`intValue`, `doubleValue`, or `charValue` in these cases) to obtain the value of the primitive type that is assigned to the variable. So the previous examples of automatic unboxing are equivalent to the following code, which is what you had to write in older versions of Java that did not do automatic unboxing:

```
Integer numberOfSamuri = new Integer(47);
int n = numberOfSamuri.intValue();
Double price = new Double(499.99);
double d = price.doubleValue();
Character grade = new Character('A');
char c = grade.charValue();
```

Our previous examples involved either only automatic boxing or only automatic unboxing. That was done to simplify the discussion by allowing you to see each of automatic boxing and automatic unboxing in isolation. However, code can often involve a combination of automatic boxing and unboxing. For example, consider the following code, which uses both automatic boxing and automatic unboxing:

```
Double price = 19.90;
price = price + 5.12;
```

This code is equivalent to the following, which is what you had to write in older versions of Java that did not do automatic boxing and unboxing:

```
Double price = new  Double(19.90);
price = new Double(price.doubleValue() + 5.12);
```

Automatic boxing and unboxing applies to parameters as well as to the simple assignment statements we just discussed. You can plug in a value of a primitive type, such as a value of type `int`, for a parameter of the associated wrapper class, such as `Integer`. Similarly, you can plug a wrapper class argument, such as an argument of type `Integer`, for a parameter of the associated primitive type, such as `int`.

MyProgrammingLab™

Self-Test Exercises

17. Which of the following are legal?

```
Integer n = new Integer(42);
int m = 42;
n = m;
m = n;
```

If any are illegal, explain how to write a valid Java statement that does what the illegal statement is trying to do.

18. In the following, is the value of the variable `price` after the assignment statement an object of the class `Double` or a value of the primitive type `double`?

```
Double price = 1.99;
```

19. In the following, is the value of the variable `count` after the assignment statement an object of the class `Integer` or a value of the primitive type `int`?

```
int count = new Integer(12);
```

Static Methods in Wrapper Classes

The material on wrapper classes that we have seen thus far explains why they are called *wrapper classes*. However, possibly more importantly, the wrapper classes contain a number of useful constants and static methods. So, wrapper classes have two distinct personalities: one is their ability to produce class objects corresponding to values of primitive types, and the other is as a repository of useful constants and methods. It was not necessary to combine these two personalities into one kind of class. Java could have had two sets of classes, one for each personality, but the designers of the Java libraries chose to have only one set of classes for both personalities.

largest and smallest values

You can use the associated wrapper class to find the value of the **largest and smallest values** of any of the primitive number types. For example, the largest and smallest values of type `int` are

`Integer.MAX_VALUE` and `Integer.MIN_VALUE`

The largest and smallest values of type `double` are

`Double.MAX_VALUE` and `Double.MIN_VALUE`

parseDouble

Wrapper classes have static methods that can be used to convert back and forth between string representations of numbers and the corresponding number of type `int`, `double`, `long`, or `float`. For example, the static method `parseDouble` of the wrapper class `Double` converts a string to a value of type `double`. So, the code

```
Double.parseDouble("199.98")
```

returns the `double` value `199.98`. If there is any possibility that the string named by `theString` has extra leading or trailing blanks, you should instead use

```
Double.parseDouble(theString.trim())
```

The method `trim` is a method in the class `String` that trims off leading and trailing whitespace, such as blanks.

If the string is not a correctly formed numeral, then the invocation of `Double.parseDouble` will cause your program to end. The use of `trim` helps somewhat in avoiding this problem.

parseInt

Similarly, the static methods `Integer.parseInt`, `Long.parseLong`, and `Float.parseFloat` convert from string representations to numbers of the corresponding primitive types `int`, `long`, and `float`, respectively.

Each of the numeric wrapper classes also has a static method called `toString` that converts in the other direction, from a numeric value to a string representation of the numeric value. For example,

```
Double.toString(123.99)
```

returns the string value `"123.99"`.

Character

`Character`, the wrapper class for the primitive type `char`, contains a number of static methods that are useful for string processing. Some of these methods are shown in Display 5.8. A simple example of using the static method `toUpperCase` of the class `Character` is given in Display 5.9. As is typical, this program combines the string-processing methods of the class `String` with the character-processing methods in the class `Character`.

Boolean

There is also a wrapper class `Boolean` corresponding to the primitive type `boolean`. It has names for two constants of type `Boolean`: `Boolean.TRUE` and `Boolean.FALSE`, which are the `Boolean` objects corresponding to the values `true` and `false` of the primitive type `boolean`.

Display 5.8 **Some Methods in the Class Character** (part 1 of 2)

The class `Character` is in the `java.lang` package, so it requires no `import` statement.

`public static char toUpperCase(char argument)`

Returns the uppercase version of its `argument`. If the `argument` is not a letter, it is returned unchanged.

EXAMPLE

`Character.toUpperCase('a')` and `Character.toUpperCase('A')` both return `'A'`.

`public static char toLowerCase(char argument)`

Returns the lowercase version of its `argument`. If the `argument` is not a letter, it is returned unchanged.

EXAMPLE

`Character.toLowerCase('a')` and `Character.toLowerCase('A')` both return `'a'`.

(continued)

Display 5.8 **Some Methods in the Class Character** (part 2 of 2)

`public static boolean isUpperCase(char argument)`

Returns `true` if its `argument` is an uppercase letter; otherwise returns `false`.

EXAMPLE

`Character.isUpperCase('a')` returns `true`. `Character.isUpperCase('a')` and `Character.isUpperCase('%')` both return `false`.

`public static boolean isLowerCase(char argument)`

Returns `true` if its argument is a lowercase letter; otherwise returns `false`.

EXAMPLE

`Character.isLowerCase('a')` returns true. `Character.isLowerCase('A')` and `Character.isLowerCase('%')` both return `false`.

`public static boolean isWhitespace(char argument)`

Returns `true` if its `argument` is a whitespace character; otherwise returns `false`. Whitespace characters are those that print as white space, such as the space character (blank character), the tab character `('\t')`, and the line break character `('\n')`.

EXAMPLE

`Character.isWhitespace(' ')` returns `true`.
`Character.isWhitespace('A')` returns `false`.

`public static boolean isLetter(char argument)`

Returns `true` if its argument is a letter; otherwise returns `false`.

EXAMPLE

`Character.isLetter('A')` returns `true`. `Character.isLetter('%')` and `Character.isLetter ('5')` both return `false`.

`public static boolean isDigit(char argument)`

Returns `true` if its `argument` is a digit; otherwise returns `false`.

EXAMPLE

`Character.isDigit('5')` returns `true`. `Character.isDigit('A')` and `Character.isDigit('%')` both return `false`.

`public static boolean isLetterOrDigit(char argument)`

Returns `true` if its `argument` is a letter or a digit; otherwise returns `false`.

EXAMPLE

`Character.isLetterOrDigit('A')` and `Character.isLetterOrDigit('5')` both return `true`. `Character.isLetterOrDigit('&')` returns `false`.

PITFALL: A Wrapper Class Does Not Have a No-Argument Constructor

Normally, it is good programming practice to define a no-argument constructor for any class you define. However, on rare occasions, a no-argument constructor simply does not make sense. The wrapper classes discussed in the previous subsection do not have a no-argument constructor, which is reasonable if you think about it. To use the static methods in a wrapper class, you need no calling object and hence need no constructor at all. The other function of a wrapper class is to provide a class object corresponding to a value of a primitive type. For example,

```
new Integer(42)
```

creates an object of the class `Integer` that corresponds to the `int` value `42`. There is no no-argument constructor for the class `Integer`, because it makes no sense to have an object of the class `Integer` unless it corresponds to an `int` value, and if it does correspond to an `int` value, that `int` value is naturally an argument to the constructor. ■

Display 5.9 String Processing with a Method from the Class `Character` (part 1 of 2)

```
import java.util.Scanner;

/**
Illustrate the use of a static method from the class Character.
*/

public class StringProcessor
{
    public static void main (String[] args)
    {
        System.out.println("Enter a one line sentence:");
        Scanner keyboard = new Scanner(System.in);
        String sentence = keyboard.nextLine();

        sentence = sentence.toLowerCase();
        char firstCharacter = sentence.charAt(0);
        sentence = Character.toUpperCase(firstCharacter)
                        + sentence.substring(1);

        System.out.println("The revised sentence is:");
        System.out.println(sentence);
    }
}
```

(continued)

Display 5.9 String Processing with a Method from the Class **Character** (part 2 of 2)

Sample Dialogue

```
Enter a one line sentence:
is you is OR is you ain't my BABY?
The revised sentence is:
Is you is or is you ain't my baby?
```

MyProgrammingLab™

Self-Test Exercises

20. What is the output produced by the following code?

```
Character characterObject1 = new Character('a');
Character characterObject2 = new Character('A');
if (characterObject1.equals(characterObject2))
    System.out.println("Objects are equal.");
else
    System.out.println("Objects are Not equal.");
```

21. Suppose `result` is a variable of type `double` that has a value. Write a Java expression that returns a string that is the normal way of writing the value in `result`.

22. Suppose `stringForm` is a variable of type `String` that names a `String` that is the normal way of writing some `double`, such as `"41.99"`. Write a Java expression that returns the `double` value named by `stringForm`.

23. How would you do Exercise 22 if the string might contain leading and/or trailing blanks, such as `" 41.99 "`?

24. Write Java code to output the largest and smallest values of type `long` allowed in Java.

25. How do you create an object of the class `Character` that corresponds to the letter `'Z'`?

26. Does the class `Character` have a no-argument constructor?

5.2 References and Class Parameters

Do not mistake the pointing finger for the moon.

ZEN SAYING

Variables of a class type and variables of a primitive type behave quite differently in Java. Variables of a primitive type name their values in a straightforward way. For example, if `n` is an `int` variable, then `n` can contain a value of type `int`, such as `42`. If `v` is a variable of a class type, then `v` does not directly contain an object of its class. Instead, `v` names an object by containing the memory address of where the object is located in memory. In this section, we discuss how a variable of a class type names objects, and we also discuss the related topic of how method parameters of a class type behave in Java.

Variables and Memory

secondary and main memory

A computer has two forms of memory called *secondary memory* and *main memory*. The **secondary memory** is used to hold files for more or less permanent storage. The **main memory** is used by the computer when it is running a program. Values stored in a program's variables are kept in this main memory. It will help our understanding of class type variables to learn a few details about how program variables are represented in main memory. For now, assume that each variable in a program is of some primitive type, such as `int`, `double`, or `char`. Once you understand how variables of a primitive type are stored in memory, it will be easier to describe how variables of a class type behave.

byte

address

Main memory consists of a long list of numbered locations called **bytes**, each containing eight bits; that is, eight 0/1 digits. The number that identifies a byte is called its **address**. A data item, such as a number or a letter, can be stored in one of these bytes, and the address of the byte is then used to find the data item when it is needed.

memory location

variables of a primitive type

Most data types have values that require more than one byte of storage. When a data type requires more than one byte of storage, several adjacent bytes are used to hold the data item. In this case, the entire chunk of memory that holds the data item is still called a **memory location**. The address of the first of the bytes that make up this memory location is used as the address for this larger memory location. Thus, as a practical matter, you can think of the computer's main memory as a long list of memory locations of *varying sizes*. The size of each of these locations is expressed in bytes, and the address of the first byte is used as the address (name) of that memory location. Display 5.10 shows a picture of a hypothetical computer's main memory. Each primitive type variable in a program is assigned one of these memory locations, and the value of the variable is stored in this memory location.

Bytes and Addresses

Main memory is divided into numbered locations called **bytes**. The number associated with a byte is called its **address**. A group of consecutive bytes is used as the location for the value of a variable. The address of the first byte in the group is used as the address of this larger memory location.

Why Eight Bits?

A **byte** is a memory location that can hold 8 bits. What is so special about 8? Why not 10 bits? There are two reasons why 8 is special. First, 8 is a power of 2 (8 is 2^3). Since computers use bits, which have only two possible values, powers of 2 are more convenient than powers of 10. Second, it turns out that 7 bits are required to code a single character of the ASCII character set. So 8 bits (1 byte) is the smallest power of 2 that will hold a single ASCII character.

Display 5.10 Variables in Memory

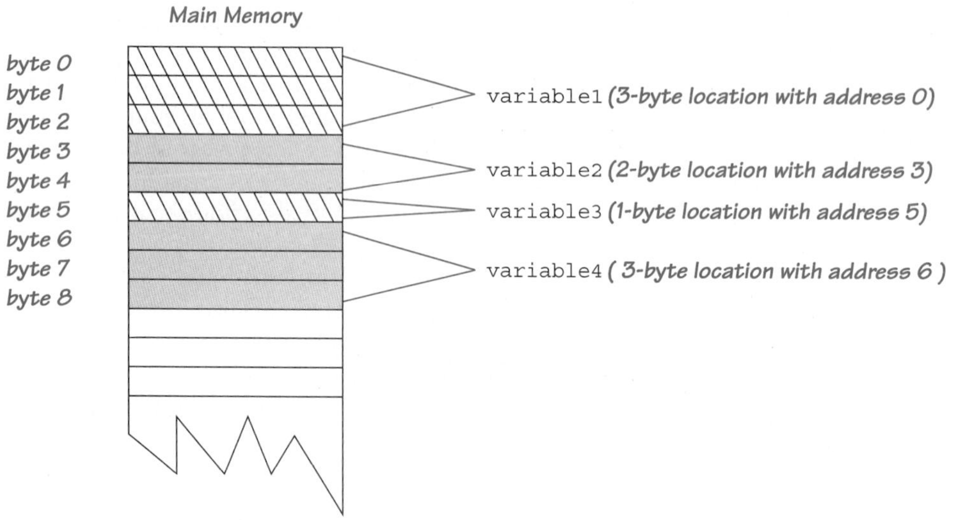

References

In order to have a simple example to help explain *references*, we will use the class `ToyClass` defined in Display 5.11.

Variables of a class type name objects of their class differently than how variables of primitive types, such as `int` or `char`, store their values. Every variable, whether of a primitive type or a class type, is implemented as a location in the computer memory. For a variable of a primitive type, the value of the variable is stored in the memory location assigned to the variable. However, a variable of a class type stores only the memory address of where an object is located. The object named by the variable is stored in some other location in memory, and the variable contains only the memory

Display 5.11 A Simple Class

```
public class ToyClass
{
    private String name;
    private int number;

    public ToyClass(String initialName, int initialNumber)
    {
        name = initialName;
        number = initialNumber;
    }

    public ToyClass()
    {
        name = "No name yet.";
        number = 0;
    }

    public void set(String newName, int newNumber)
    {
        name = newName;
        number = newNumber;
    }

    public String toString()
    {
        return (name + " " + number);
    }

    public static void changer(ToyClass aParameter)
    {
        aParameter.name = "Hot Shot";
        aParameter.number = 42;
    }

    public boolean equals(ToyClass otherObject)
    {
        return ((name.equals(otherObject.name))
                  && (number = otherObject.number) );
    }
}
```

references

address of where the object is stored. This memory address is called a **reference** (to the object).[1] This is diagrammed in Display 5.12.

Variables of a primitive type and variables of a class type are different for a reason. A value of a primitive type, such as the type `int`, always requires the same amount of memory to store one value. There is a maximum value of type `int`, so values of type `int` have a limit on their size. However, an object of a class type, such as an object of the class `String`, might be of any size. The memory location for a variable of type `String` is of a fixed size, so it cannot store an arbitrarily long string. It can, however, store the address of any string because there is a limit to the size of an address.

Because variables of a class type contain a reference (memory address), two variables may contain the same reference, and in such a situation, both variables name the same object. Any change to the object named by one of these variables will produce a change to the object named by the other variable, because they are the same object. For example, consider the following code. (The class `ToyClass` is defined in Display 5.11, but the meaning of the code should be obvious and you should not need to look up the definition.)

```
ToyClass variable1 = new ToyClass("Joe", 42);
ToyClass variable2;
variable2 = variable1; //Now both variables name the same object.
variable2.set("Josephine", 1);
System.out.println(variable1); //Invokes variable1's toString
                               //method
```

The output is

```
Josephine 1
```

The object named by `variable1` has been changed without ever using the name `variable1`. This is diagrammed in Display 5.13.

Variables of a Class Type Hold References

A variable of a primitive type stores a value of that type. However, a variable of a class type does not store an object of that class. A variable of a class type stores the reference (memory address) of where the object is located in the computer's memory. This causes some operations, such as = and ==, to behave quite differently for variables of a class type than they do for variables of a primitive type.

Reference Types

A type whose variables contain references are called **reference types**. In Java, class types are reference types, but primitive types are not reference types.

[1] Readers familiar with languages that use pointers will recognize a reference as another name for a pointer. However, Java does not use the term *pointer*, but instead uses the term *reference*. Moreover, these references are handled automatically. There are no programmer-accessible pointer (reference) operations for dereferencing or other pointer operations. The details are all handled automatically in Java.

Display 5.12 Class Type Variables Store a Reference

```
public class ToyClass
{
    private String name;
    private int number;
```

The complete definition of the class `ToyClass` *is given in Display 5.11.*

```
ToyClass sampleVariable;
```

Creates the variable `sampleVariable` *in memory but assigns it no value.*

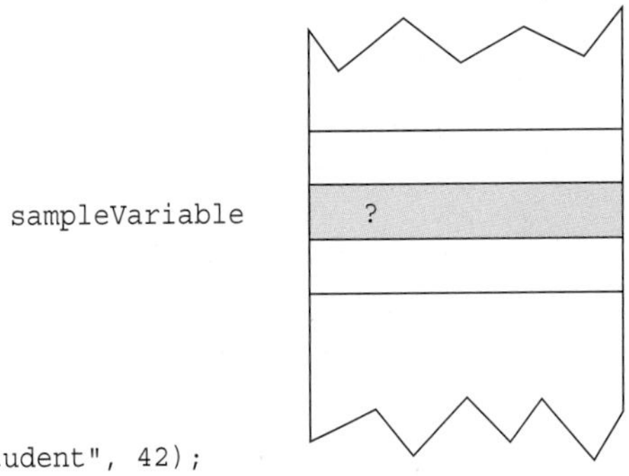


```
sampleVariable =
new ToyClass("Josephine Student", 42);
```

Creates an object, places the object someplace in memory, and then places the address of the object in the variable `sampleVariable`. *We do not know what the address of the object is, but let's assume it is* `2056`. *The exact number does not matter.*

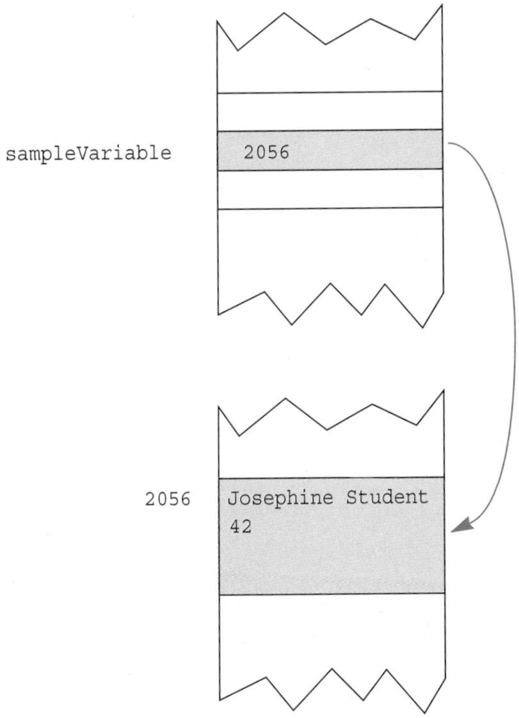

For emphasis, we made the arrow point to the memory location referenced.

Display 5.13 **Assignment Operator with Class Type Variables** (part 1 of 2)

```
ToyClass variable1 = new ToyClass("Joe", 42);
ToyClass variable2;
```

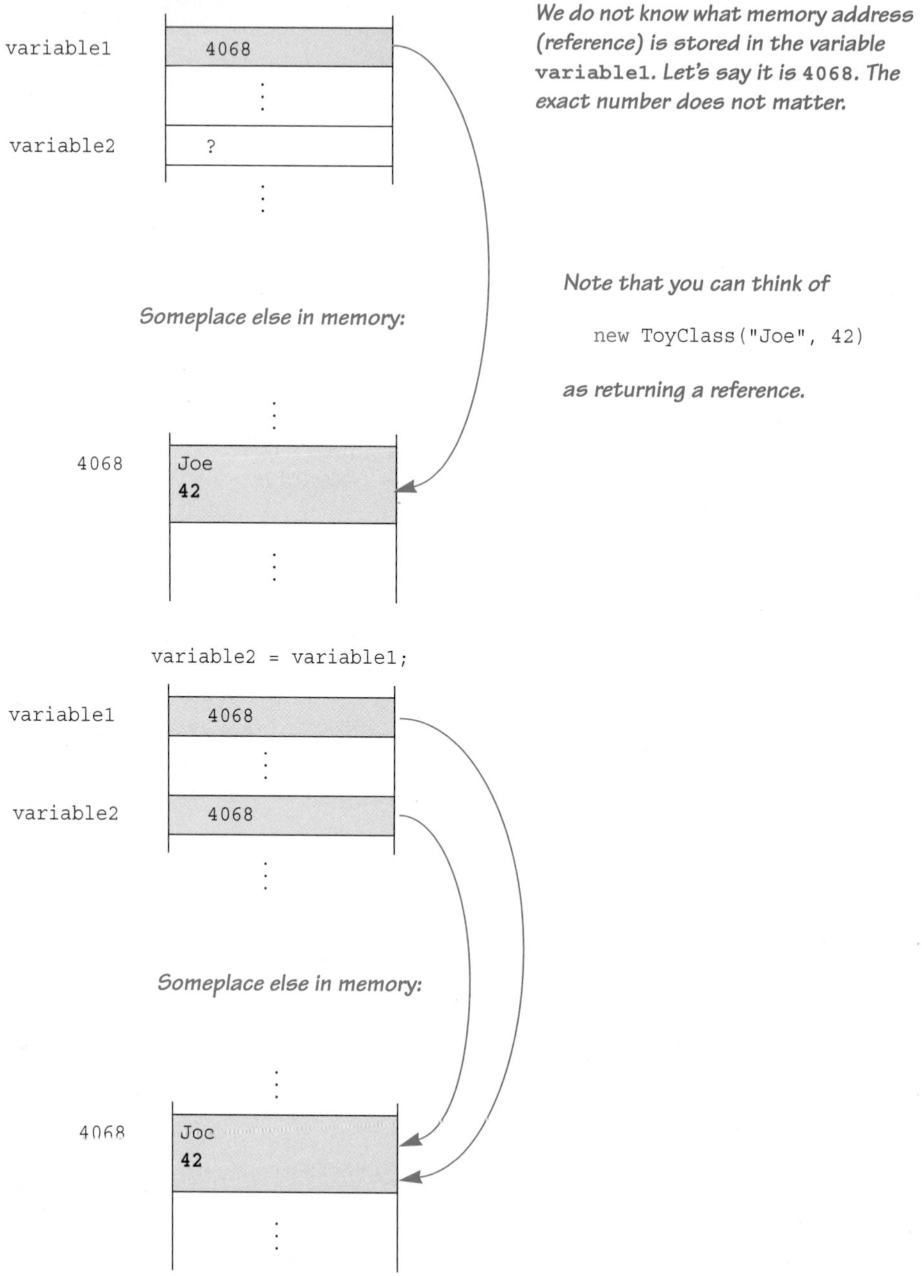
variable1
4068
variable2
?
We do not know what memory address (reference) is stored in the variable variable1. Let's say it is 4068. The exact number does not matter.
Someplace else in memory:
Note that you can think of
new ToyClass("Joe", 42)
as returning a reference.
4068
Joe
42
variable2 = variable1;
variable1
4068
variable2
4068
Someplace else in memory:
4068
Joe
42

Display 5.13 Assignment Operator with Class Type Variables (part 2 of 2)

```
variable2.set("Josephine", 1);
```

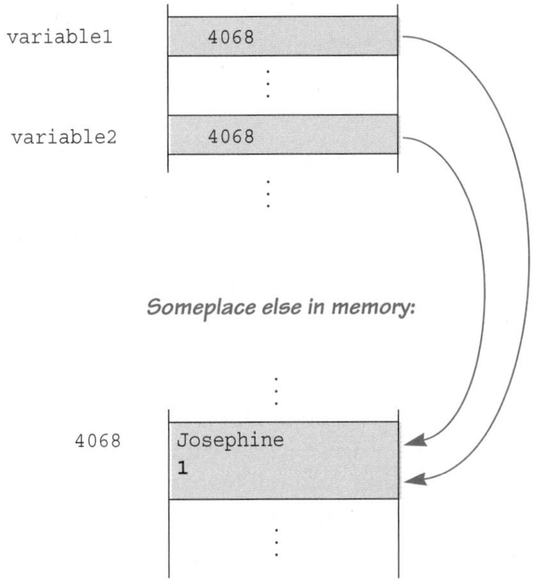

assignment with variables of a class type

Note that when you use the assignment operator with variables of a class type, you are assigning a reference (memory address), so the result of the following is to make `variable1` and `variable2` two names for the same object:

```
variable2 = variable1;
```

A variable of a class type stores a memory address, and a memory address is a number. However, a variable of a class type cannot be used like a variable of a number type, such as `int` or `double`. This is intentional. The important property of a memory address is that it identifies a memory location. The fact that the implementors used numbers, rather than letters or strings or something else, to name memory locations is an accidental property. Java prevents you from using this accidental property to stop you from doing things such as obtaining access to restricted memory or otherwise screwing up the computer.

Class Parameters

Strictly speaking, all parameters in Java are call-by-value parameters. This means that when an argument is plugged in for a parameter (of any type), the argument is evaluated and the value obtained is used to initialize the value of the parameter. (Recall that a parameter is really a local variable.) However, in the case of a parameter of a class type, the value plugged in is a reference (memory address), which makes class parameters behave quite differently from parameters of a primitive type.

Recall that the following makes `variable1` and `variable2` two names for the same object:

```
ToyClass variable1 = new ToyClass("Joe", 42);
ToyClass variable2;
variable2 = variable1;
```

So, any change made to `variable2` is, in fact, made to `variable1`. The same thing happens with parameters of a class type. The parameter is a local variable that is set equal to the value of its argument. But if its argument is a variable of a class type, this copies a reference into the parameter. So, the parameter becomes another name for the argument, and any change made to the object named by the parameter is made to the object named by the argument, because they are the same object. Thus, a method can change the instance variables of an object given as an argument. A simple program to illustrate this is given in Display 5.14. Display 5.15 contains a diagram of the computer's memory as the program in Display 5.14 is executed.

Many programming languages have a parameter passing mechanism known as *call-by-reference*. If you are familiar with call-by-reference parameters, we should note that the Java parameter passing mechanism is similar to, but is not exactly the same as, call-by-reference.

Display 5.14 Parameters of a Class Type

`ToyClass` is defined in Display 5.11.

```
public class ClassParameterDemo
{
    public static void main(String[] args)
    {
        ToyClass anObject = new ToyClass("Mr. Cellophane", 0);
        System.out.println(anObject);
        System.out.println(
                  "Now we call changer with anObject as argument.");
        ToyClass.changer(anObject);
        System.out.println(anObject);
    }
}
```

Notice that the method `changer` changed the instance variables in the object `anObject`.

Sample Dialogue

```
Mr. Cellophane 0
Now we call changer with anObject as argument.
Hot Shot 42
```

Differences Between Primitive and Class-Type Parameters

A method cannot change the value of a variable of a primitive type that is an argument to the method. On the other hand, a method can change the values of the instance variables of an argument of a class type. This is illustrated in Display 5.16.

Display 5.15 Memory Picture for Display 5.14 (part 1 of 2)

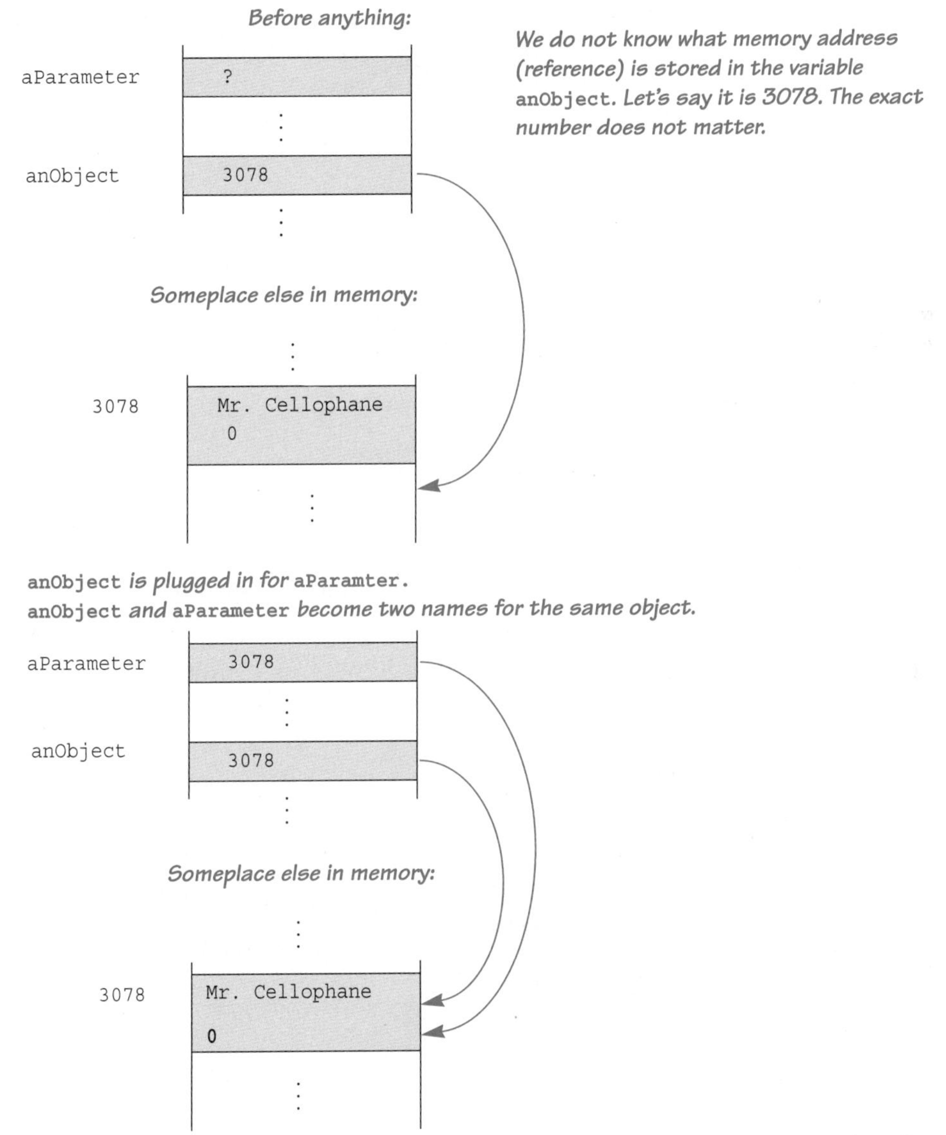
Before anything:
We do not know what memory address (reference) is stored in the variable anObject. Let's say it is 3078. The exact number does not matter.
aParameter
?
anObject
3078
Someplace else in memory:
3078
Mr. Cellophane
0
anObject is plugged in for aParamter.
anObject and aParameter become two names for the same object.
aParameter
3078
anObject
3078
Someplace else in memory:
3078
Mr. Cellophane
0

(continued)

Display 5.15 **Memory Picture for Display 5.14** (part 2 of 2)

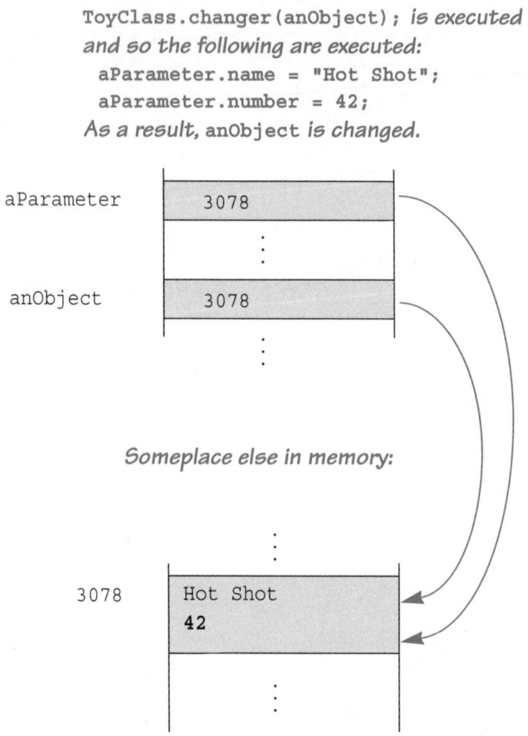
ToyClass.changer(anObject); is executed
and so the following are executed:
aParameter.name = "Hot Shot";
aParameter.number = 42;
As a result, anObject is changed.
aParameter
3078
anObject
3078
Someplace else in memory:
3078
Hot Shot
42

Display 5.16 **Comparing Parameters of a Class Type and a Primitive Type** (part 1 of 2)

```
public class ParametersDemo
{
    public static void main(String[] args)
    {
        ToyClass2 object1 = new ToyClass2(),
                  object2 = new ToyClass2();
        object1.set("Scorpius",1);
        object2.set("John Crichton", 2);
        System.out.println("Value of object2 before call to method:");
        System.out.println(object2);
        object1.makeEqual(object2);
        System.out.println("Value of object2 after call to method:");
        System.out.println(object2);

```

ToyClass2 is defined in Display 5.17.

Display 5.16 **Comparing Parameters of a Class Type and a Primitive Type** (part 2 of 2)

```
        int aNumber = 42;
        System.out.println("Value of aNumber before call to method:"
                    + aNumber);
        object1.tryToMakeEqual(aNumber);
        System.out.println("Value of aNumber after call to method:"
                    + aNumber);
    }
}
```

Sample Dialogue

```
Value of object2 before call to method:
John Crichton 2
Value of object2 after call to method:
Scorpius 1
Value of aNumber before call to method: 42
Value of aNumber after call to method: 42
```

An argument of a class type can change.

An argument of a primitive type cannot change.

PITFALL: Use of = and == with Variables of a Class Type

You have already seen that the assignment operator used with variables of a class type produces two variables that name the same object, which is very different from how assignment behaves with variables of a primitive type.

== with variables of a class type

The test for equality using == with variables of a class type also behaves in what may seem like a peculiar way. The operator == does not check that the objects have the same values for their instance variables. It merely checks for equality of memory addresses, so two objects in two different locations in memory would test as being "not equal" when compared using ==, even if their instance variables contain equivalent data. For example, consider the following code. (The class `ToyClass2` is defined in Display 5.17.)

```
ToyClass2 variable1 = new ToyClass2("Chiana", 3),
          variable2 = new ToyClass2("Chiana", 3);
if (variable1 == variable2)
    System.out.println("Equal using ==");
else
    System.out.println("Not equal using ==");
```

This code will produce the output

```
Not equal using ==
```

(continued)

PITFALL: (continued)

Even though these two variables name objects that are intuitively equal, they are stored in two different locations in the computer's memory. This is why you usually use an `equals` method to compare objects of a class type. The variables `variable1` and `variable2` would be considered "equal" if compared using the `equals` method as defined for the class `ToyClass2` (Display 5.17). ■

Display 5.17 A Toy Class to Use in Display 5.16

```
public class ToyClass2
{
    private String name;
    private int number;

    public void set(String newName, int newNumber)
    {
        name = newName;
        number = newNumber;
    }

    public String toString()
    {
        return (name + " " + number);
    }

    public void makeEqual(ToyClass2 anObject)
    {
        anObject.name = this .name;
        anObject.number = this .number;
    }

    public void tryToMakeEqual(int aNumber)
    {
        aNumber = this .number;
    }

    public boolean equals(ToyClass2 otherObject)
    {
        return ( (name.equals(otherObject.name))
                  && (number == otherObject.number) );
    }

<Other methods can be the same as in Display 5.11, although no
    other methods are needed or used in the current discussion.>
}
```

Read the text for a discussion of the problem with this method. (annotation pointing to `tryToMakeEqual`)

MyProgrammingLab™

Self-Test Exercises

27. What is a reference type? Are class types reference types? Are primitive types (such as `int`) reference types?

28. When comparing two objects of a class type to see if they are "equal" or not, should you use `==` or the method `equals`?

29. When comparing two objects of a primitive type (such as `int`) to see if they are "equal" or not, should you use `==` or the method `equals`?

30. Can a method with an argument of a class type change the values of the instance variables in the object named by the argument? For example, if the argument is of type `ToyClass` defined in Display 5.11, can the method change the `name` of its argument?

31. Suppose a method has a parameter of type `int` and the method is given an `int` variable as an argument. Could the method have been defined so that it changes the value of the variable given as an argument?

The Constant `null`

`null`

The constant `null` is a special constant that may be assigned to a variable of any class type. It is used to indicate that the variable has no "real value." If the compiler insists that you initialize a variable of a class type and there is no suitable object with which to initialize it, you can use the value `null`, as in the following example:

```
YourClass yourObject = null;
```

It is also common to use `null` in constructors to initialize instance variables of a class type when there is no obvious object to use. We will eventually see other uses for the constant `null`.

Note that `null` is not an object. It is like a reference (memory address) that does not refer to any object (does not name any memory location). So if you want to test whether a class variable contains `null`, you use `==` or `!=`; you do not use an `equals` method. For example, the following correctly tests for `null`:

```
if (yourObject == null)
    System.out.println("No real object here.");
```

`null`

`null` is a special constant that can be used to give a value to any variable of any class type. The constant `null` is not an object but a sort of placeholder for a reference to an object. Because it is like a reference (memory address), use `==` and `!=` rather than the method `equals` when you test to see whether a variable contains `null`.

PITFALL: Null Pointer Exception

If the compiler asks you to initialize a class variable, you can always initialize the variable to `null`. However, `null` is not an object, so you cannot invoke a method using a variable that is initialized to `null`. If you try, you will get an error message that says "Null Pointer Exception." For example, the following code would produce a "Null Pointer Exception" if it were included in a program:

```
ToyClass2 aVariable = null;
String representation = aVariable.toString();
```

The problem is that you are trying to invoke the method `toString()` using `null` as a calling object. But `null` is not an object; it is just a placeholder. So `null` has no methods. Because you are using `null` incorrectly, the error message reads "Null Pointer Exception." You get this error message any time a class variable has not been assigned a (reference to an) object, even if you have not assigned `null` to the variable. Any time you get a "Null Pointer Exception," look for an uninitialized class variable.

The way to correct the problem is to use `new` to create a class object, as follows:

```
ToyClass2 aVariable = new ToyClass2("Chiana", 3);
String representation = aVariable.toString();
```

■

The `new` Operator and Anonymous Objects

Consider an expression such as the following, where `ToyClass` is defined in Display 5.11:

```
ToyClass variable1 = new ToyClass("Joe", 42);
```

As illustrated in Display 5.13, the portion `new ToyClass("Joe", 42)` is an invocation of a constructor. You can think of the constructor as returning a reference to the location in memory of the object created by the constructor. If you take this view, the equal sign in this line of code is just an ordinary assignment operator.

There are times when you create an object using `new` and use the object as an argument to a method, but then never again use the object. In such cases, you need not give the object a variable name. You can instead use the expression with the `new` operator and the constructor directly as the argument. For example, suppose you want to test to see whether the object in `variable1` (in the earlier line of code) is equal to an object with the same number and with the name spelled in all uppercase letters. You can do so as follows:

```
if (variable1.equals(new ToyClass("JOE", 42)))
    System.out.println("Equal");
else
    System.out.println("Not equal");
```

This is equivalent to the following:

```
ToyClass temp = new ToyClass("JOE", 42);
if (variable1.equals(temp))
    System.out.println("Equal");
else
    System.out.println("Not equal");
```

In the second version, the object is created, and its reference is placed in the variable `temp`. Then `temp` is plugged in for the parameter in the `equals` method. But all the parameter passing mechanism does is to take the reference stored in `temp` and plug it into the parameter for `equals`. The first version simplifies the process. It creates the reference to the object and directly plugs it into the parameter in `equals`. It bypasses the variable `temp` but ends up plugging in the same reference as the argument to `equals`.

When not assigned to a variable, an expression such as

```
new ToyClass("JOE", 42)
```

anonymous object

is known as an **anonymous object**. It evaluates a reference to an object of the class. It is called *anonymous* because the object is not assigned a variable to serve as its name. We will eventually encounter situations where the use of such anonymous objects is common.

Anonymous Objects

An expression with a `new` operator and a constructor creates a new object and returns a reference to the object. If this reference is not assigned to a variable, but instead the expression with new and the constructor is used as an argument to some method, then the object produced is called an **anonymous object**.

EXAMPLE

```
if (variable1.equals(new ToyClass("JOE", 42)))
    System.out.println("Equal");
else
    System.out.println("Not equal");
```

The expression `new ToyClass("JOE", 42)` (or more exactly, the object it creates) is an example of an anonymous object.

EXAMPLE: Another Approach to Keyboard Input ★

This example uses the class `StringTokenizer`, which was covered in a starred section of Chapter 4. If you have not yet studied the `StringTokenizer` class, you may omit this example until you have done so.

The program in Display 5.18 is an example of the use of both the `StringTokenizer` class and the method `Double.parseDouble` to read multiple values of type `double` entered on a single line and separated with something other than whitespace.

(continued)

EXAMPLE: (continued)

The entire line is read as a single long string using the method `nextLine` of the `Scanner` class. The long string is decomposed into tokens using the class `StingTokenizer`. The tokens are the numbers that were input, but they are in the form of string values, not values of type `double`. Finally, the tokens are converted to values of type `double` using the method `Double.parseDouble`.

Note that the `String` variables are initialized to `null`. If you omit the nulls, the compiler will complain that the variables `string1` and `string2` might not be initialized before they are used. The compiler is incorrect but it does no good to argue with it. Including `null` as initial values for the variables `string1` and `string2` will keep the compiler happy and allow you to run the program.

Display 5.18 Use of the Method **`Double.parseDouble`** (part 1 of 2)

```
import java.util.Scanner;
import java.util.StringTokenizer;

public class InputExample
{
    public static void main(String[] args)
    {
        Scanner keyboard = new Scanner(System.in);

        System.out.println("Enter two numbers on a line.");
        System.out.println("Place a comma between the numbers.");
        System.out.println("Extra blank space is OK.");
        String inputLine = keyboard.nextLine();

        String delimiters = ", "; //Comma and blank space
        StringTokenizer numberFactory =
             new StringTokenizer(inputLine, delimiters);

        String string1 = null;
        String string2 = null;
        if (numberFactory.countTokens() >= 2)
        {
            string1 = numberFactory.nextToken();
            string2 = numberFactory.nextToken();
        }
        else
        {
            System.out.println("Fatal Error.");
            System.exit(0);
        }
```

Display 5.18 Use of the Method `Double.parseDouble` (part 2 of 2)

```
        double number1 = Double.parseDouble(string1);
        double number2 = Double.parseDouble(string2);

        System.out.print("You input ");
        System.out.println(number1 + " and " + number2);
    }
}
```

Sample Dialogue

```
Enter two numbers on a line.
Place a comma between the numbers.
Extra blank space is OK.
    41.98, 42
You input is 41.98 and 42.0
```

Self-Test Exercises

32. What is wrong with a program that starts as follows? The class `ToyClass` is defined in Display 5.11.

```
ToyClass anObject = null ;
anObject.set("Josephine", 42);
```

33. What is the type of the constant `null`?

34. Suppose `aVariable` is a variable of a class type. Which of the following correctly tests to see whether `aVariable` contains `null`?

```
aVariable.equals(null)
aVariable == null
```

35. Is the following legal in Java? The class `ToyClass` is defined in Display 5.11.

```
System.out.println(new ToyClass("Mr. Cellophane", 0));
```

TIP: Use Static Imports ★

You have already seen `import` statements, such as the following from Display 5.9:

```
import java.util.Scanner;
```

static `import` statement

There is another form of `import` statement which, while not essential, can be a convenience. These are called **static `import` statements** and are best explained with an example.

(continued)

TIP: (continued)

It would be convenient to be able to write static method invocations in the following simple form:

```
toUpperCase(firstCharacter)
```

instead of having to write the following longer version (taken from Display 5.9):

```
Character.toUpperCase(firstCharacter)
```

If you add the following static `import` statement to the start of your program, you can then write the invocation of `toUpperCase` in the desired shorter way:

```
import static java.lang.Character.toUpperCase;
```

The class `Character` is in the Java package `java.lang`. Note that you need to give the package name as well as the class name, just as you did with ordinary `import` statements, such as the above `import` statement for the class `Scanner` in the `java.util` package.

The package `java.lang` is imported automatically. So you can, for example, use the method `Character.toUpperCase` without any `import` statement of any kind. But note that there is nothing special about the package `java.lang` when it comes to static import statements. If you want to use the abbreviated form `toUpperCase`, you must give a static `import` statement.

If you use the following form of the static `import` statement, then your code can use the name of any static method in the class `Character` without the preface of `Character` and a dot.

```
import static java.lang.Character.*;
```

For example, consider the program in Display 5.9. If you replace

```
import java.util.Scanner;
```

with either

```
import java.util.Scanner;
import static java.lang.Character.toUpperCase;
```

or

```
import java.util.Scanner;
import static java.lang.Character.*;
```

then you can change the statement

```
sentence = Character.toUpperCase(firstCharacter)
                                        + sentence.substring(1);
```

to

TIP: (continued)

```
sentence = toUpperCase(firstCharacter)
                             + sentence.substring(1);
```

One word of warning: This works for static methods only. This does not in any way apply to ordinary nonstatic methods.

extra code on website

The program `StaticImportDemo.java` on the accompanying website redoes the program in Display 5.9 using a static `import` statement in this way.

You can, of course, do this with `Character` replaced by any other class, and then you can use static methods in that class without the need to preface the method name with the class name and a dot.

static `import` of constants

You can use static `import` statements for constants as well as methods. If you want to use `PI` instead of `Math.PI` in the program in Display 5.7, just include one of the following `import` statements at the beginning of the program file:

```
import static java.lang.Math.PI;
```

or

```
import static java.lang.Math.*;
```

extra code on website

The program `StaticImportDemo2.java` on the accompanying website redoes the program in Display 5.7 using a static `import` statement in this way. ■

5.3 Using and Misusing References

Loose lips sink ships.

MILITARY SLOGAN

Just as a military campaign requires constant vigilance to ensure that its plans are kept secret, so your programming requires constant vigilance to ensure that private instance variables remain truly private. As we will see, adding the `private` modifier before instance variable declarations is not always all that you need to do. There can be privacy leaks in a poorly designed class just as there can be privacy leaks in a military campaign.

The material in this section is important but more subtle and harder to digest than the material we have seen before now. If you want, you may postpone reading this section until you have had more practice defining and using classes. You do not need the material in this section to understand Section 5.4.

EXAMPLE: A Person Class

It is common to have instance variables of a class type. The class `Person` defined in Display 5.19 has two instance variables of type `Date`. So, the class `Person` has instance variables of a class type. (The class `Date` was defined in Chapter 4, Display 4.11. We have reproduced the relevant portions of the date class definition in Display 5.20.) In fact, all the instance variables for the class `Person` are of class types. An object of the class `Person` has the basic data about people that is found in such places as on tombstones and in author listings in library catalogues. It describes a person by giving the person's name, date of birth, and date of death. If the person is still alive, then the value `null` is used as the date of death. (So `null` is good.) A simple program illustrating the class `Person` is given in Display 5.21. We will discuss a few details about the class `Person` here, but most of the various methods in the class `Person` will be discussed as we cover the corresponding topic in the following subsections.

Normally, a class definition should include a no-argument constructor. However, there are cases where a no-argument constructor makes little sense. For example, the wrapper classes such as `Integer` and `Double` do not have no-argument constructors, as we explained in the Pitfall subsection "A Wrapper Class Does Not Have a No-Argument Constructor," which appeared earlier in this chapter. The class `Person` also does not have a no-argument constructor for a reason. A person may have no date of death, but a person always has a date of birth. A no-argument constructor should initialize all instance variables, but there is no suitable value to initialize the instance variable `born` unless it is provided as an argument to the constructor. In particular, it makes no sense to initialize the instance variable `born` to `null`; that would indicate that the person was never born. It makes little sense to have a person who was never born, so it makes little sense to have a no-argument constructor for the class `Person`. Note that because we defined some constructors for the class `Person` but did not define a no-argument constructor, it follows that the class `Person` does not have a no-argument constructor.

Since we are assuming that an object of the class `Person` always has a birth date (which is not `null`), the following should always be true of an object of the class `Person`:

> An object of the class `Person` has a date of birth (which is not `null`), and if the object has a date of death, then the date of death is equal to or later than the date of birth.

If you check the definition of the class `Person`, you will see that this statement is always true. It is true of every object created by a constructor, and all the other methods preserve the truth of this statement. In fact, the private method `consistent` was designed to provide a check for this property. A statement, such as the above, that is always true for every object of the class is called a **class invariant**.

Note that the definition of `equals` for the class `Person` includes an invocation of `equals` for the class `String` and an invocation of the method `equals` for the class `Date`. Java determines which `equals` method is being invoked from the type of its calling object. Because the instance variable `name` is of type `String`, the invocation `name.equals(...)` is an invocation of the method `equals` for the class `String`. Because the instance variable `born` is of type `Date`, the invocation `born.equals(...)` is an invocation of the method `equals` for the class `Date`.

Similarly, the definition of the method `toString` for the class `Person` includes invocations of the method `toString` for the class `Date`.

Display 5.19 **A Person Class** (part 1 of 5)

```
/**
 Class for a person with a name and dates for birth and death.
 Class invariant: A Person always has a date of birth, and if the Person
 has a date of death, then the date of death is equal to or later than the
 date of birth.
*/
public class Person
{
    private String name;
    private Date born;
    private Date died; //null indicates still alive.

    public Person(String initialName, Date birthDate, Date deathDate)
    {
        if (consistent(birthDate, deathDate))
        {
            name = initialName;
            born = new Date(birthDate);
            if (deathDate == null)
                died = null;
            else
                 died = new Date(deathDate);
        }
        else
        {
            System.out.println("Inconsistent dates.Aborting.");
            System.exit(0);
        }
    }

    public Person(Person original)
    {
        if (original == null )
        {
            System.out.println("Fatal error.");
            System.exit(0);
        }

        name = original.name;
        born = new Date(original.born);

        if (original.died == null)
            died = null;
        else
        died = new Date(original.died);
    }
```

The class `Date` was defined in Display 4.11 and many of the details are repeated in Display 5.20.

We will discuss `Date` and the significance of these constructor invocations later in this chapter in the subsection entitled "Copy Constructors."

Copy constructor.

(continued)

Display 5.19   A Person Class (part 2 of 5)

```
43 public void set(String newName, Date birthDate, Date deathDate)
 <Definition of this method is Self Test Exercise 4.1>

44 public String toString()
45 {
46 String diedString;
47 if (died == null)
48 diedString = ""; //Empty string
49 else
50 diedString = died.toString();

51 return (name + ", " + born + "-" + diedString);
52 }

53 public boolean equals(Person otherPerson)
54 {
55 if (otherPerson == null)
56 return false;
57 else
58 return (name.equals(otherPerson.name)
59 && born.equals(otherPerson.born)
60 && datesMatch(died, otherPerson.died));
61 }

62 /**
63 To match, date1 and date2 must either be the same date or must both be null.
64 */
65 private static boolean datesMatch(Date date1, Date date2)
66 {
67 if (date1 == null)
68 return (date2 == null);
69 else if (date2 == null) //&& date1 != null
70 return false ;
71 else //both dates are not null.
72 return (date1.equals(date2));
73 }

74 /**
75 Precondition: newDate is a consistent date of birth.
76 Postcondition: Date of birth of the calling object is newDate.
77 */
78 public void setBirthDate(Date newDate)
79 {
80 if (consistent(newDate, died))
81 born = new Date(newDate);
82 else
```

This is the toString method of the class Date.

This is equivalent to born.toString( ).

This is the equals method for the class String.

This is the equals method for the class Date.

Display 5.19   A Person Class (part 3 of 5)

```
83 {
84 System.out.println("Inconsistent dates. Aborting.");
85 System.exit(0);
86 }
87 }

88 /**
89 Precondition: newDate is a consistent date of death.
90 Postcondition: Date of death of the calling object is newDate.
91 */
92 public void setDeathDate(Date newDate)
93 {
94
95 if (!consistent(born, newDate))
96 {
97 System.out.println("Inconsistent dates. Aborting.");
98 System.exit(0);
99 }
100
101 if (newDate == null)
102 died = null;
103 else
104 died = new Date(newDate);
105 }

106 public void setName(String newName)
107 {
108 name = newName;
109 }

110 /**
111 Precondition: The date of birth has been set, and changing the year
112 part of the date of birth will give a consistent date of birth.
113 Postcondition: The year of birth is (changed to) newYear.
114 */
115 public void setBirthYear(int newYear)
116 {
117 if (born == null) //Precondition is violated.
118 {
119 System.out.println("Fatal Error. Aborting.");
120 System.exit(0);
121 }
122 born.setYear(newYear);
123 if (!consistent(born, died))
124 {
125 System.out.println("Inconsistent dates. Aborting.");
126 System.exit(0);
127 }
128 }
```

The date of death can be null. *However, there is no corresponding code in* setBirthDate *because the method* consistent *ensures that the date of* birth *is never* null.

(continued)

Display 5.19 A Person Class (part 4 of 5)

```
    /**
     Precondition: The date of death has been set, and changing the year
     part of the date of death will give a consistent date of death.
     Postcondition: The year of death is (changed to) newYear.
    */
    public void setDeathYear(int newYear)
    {
        if (died == null) //Precondition is violated
        {
             System.out.println("Fatal Error. Aborting.");
             System.exit(0);
        }
        died.setYear(newYear);
        if (!consistent(born, died))
        {
             System.out.println("Inconsistent dates. Aborting.");
             System.exit(0);
        }
    }

    public String getName()
    {
        return name;
    }

    public Date getBirthDate()
    {
        return new Date(born);
    }

    public Date getDeathDate()
    {
        if (died == null)
            return null;
        else
            return new Date(died);
    }

    /**
     To be consistent, birthDate must not be null. If there is no date of
     death (deathDate == null), that is consistent with any birthDate.
     Otherwise, the birthDate must come before or be equal to the
     deathDate.
    */
```

Display 5.19 A Person Class (part 5 of 5)

```
    private static boolean consistent(Date birthDate, Date deathDate)
    {
        if (birthDate == null)
            return false;
        else if (deathDate == null)
            return true;
        else
            return (birthDate.precedes(deathDate)
                      || birthDate.equals(deathDate));
    }
}
```

> **Class Invariant**
>
> A statement that is always true for every object of the class is called a **class invariant**. A class invariant can help to define a class in a consistent and organized way.

PITFALL: `null` Can Be an Argument to a Method

If a method has a parameter of a class type, then `null` can be used as the corresponding argument when the method is invoked. Sometimes using `null` as an argument can be the result of an error, but it can sometimes be an intentional argument. For example, the class `Person` (Display 5.19) uses `null` for a date of death to indicate that the person is still alive. So `null` is sometimes a perfectly normal argument for methods such as `consistent`. Method definitions should account for `null` as a possible argument and not assume the method always receives a true object to plug in for a class parameter.

Notice the definition of the method `equals` for the class `Person`. A test for equality has the form

```
object1.equals(object2)
```

The calling object `object1` must be a true object of the class `Person`; a calling object cannot be `null`. However, the argument `object2` can be either a true object or `null`. If the argument is `null`, then `equals` should return `false`, because a true object cannot reasonably be considered to be equal to `null`. In fact, the Java documentation specifies that when the argument to an `equals` method is `null`, the `equals` method should return `false`. Notice that our definition does return `false` when the argument is `null`. ■

Display 5.20 The Class `Date` (Partial Definition) (part 1 of 2)

This is not a complete definition of the class `Date`. The complete definition of the class `Date` is in Display 4.11, but this has the details that are important to what we are discussing in this chapter.

```
public class Date
{
    private String month;
    private int day;
    private int year; //A four digit number.

    public Date(String monthString, int day, int year)
    {
        setDate (monthString, day, year);
    }

    public Date(Date aDate)
    {
        if (aDate == null) //Not a real date.
        {
            System.out.println("Fatal Error.");
            System.exit(0);
        }

        month = aDate.month;
        day = aDate.day;
        year = aDate.year;
    }

    public void setDate(String monthString, int day, int year)
    {
        if (dateOK(monthString, day, year))
        {
            this.month = monthString;
            this.day = day;
            this.year = year;
        }
        else
        {
            System.out.println("Fatal Error");
            System.exit(0);
        }
    }
    public void setYear(int year)
    {
        if ( (year < 1000) || (year > 9999) )
        {
```

Copy constructor.

The method `dateOK` checks that the date is a legitimate date, such as not having more than 31 days.

Display 5.20 **The Class `Date` (Partial Definition)** (part 2 of 2)

```
                System.out.println("Fatal Error");
                System.exit(0);
            }
            else
                this.year = year;
        }
        public String toString()
                ...
        public boolean equals(Date otherDate)
                ....
        /**
         Returns true if the calling object date is before otherDate (in time).
        */
        public boolean precedes(Date otherDate)
                ...
        private boolean dateOK(String monthString, int dayInt, int yearInt)
                ...
}
```

The complete definition of `equals` is given later in this chapter in the answer to Self-Test Exercise 37, and is a better version than the one given in Chapter 4.

These methods have the obvious meanings. If you need to see a full definition, see Display 4.11 in Chapter 4 and Self-Test Exercise 37 later in this chapter.

MyProgrammingLab™

Self-Test Exercises

36. What is the difference between the following two pieces of code? The first piece appears in Display 5.21.

```
Person adams =
        new Person("John Adams",
             new Date("February", 15, 1947), null);
//Second piece is below:

Date theDate = new Date("February", 15, 1947);
Person adams = new Person("John Adams", theDate, null);
```

37. When we defined the class `Date` in Chapter 4 (Display 4.11), we had not yet discussed `null`. So, the definition of `equals` given there did not account for the possibility that the argument could be `null`. Rewrite the definition of `equals` for the class `Date` to account for the possibility that the argument might be `null`.

Display 5.21 Demonstrating the Class **Person**

```
public class PersonDemo
{
    public static void main(String[]args)
    {
        Person bach =
            new Person("Johann Sebastian Bach",
                 new Date("March", 21, 1685), new Date("July", 28, 1750));
        Person stravinsky =
            new Person("Igor Stravinsky",
                 new Date("June", 17, 1882), new Date("April", 6, 1971));
        Person adams =
            new Person("John Adams",
                 new Date("February", 15, 1947), null );

        System.out.println("A Short List of Composers:");
        System.out.println(bach);
        System.out.println(stravinsky);
        System.out.println(adams);

        Person bachTwin = new Person(bach);
        System.out.println("Comparing bach and bachTwin:");
        if (bachTwin == bach)
            System.out.println("Same reference for both.");
        else
            System.out.println("Distinct copies.");

        if (bachTwin.equals(bach))
            System.out.println("Same data.");
        else
            System.out.println("Not same data.");
    }
}
```

Sample Dialogue

```
A Short List of Composers:
Johann Sebastian Bach, March 21, 1685-July 28, 1750
Igor Stravinsky, June 17, 1882-April 6, 1971
John Adams, February 15, 1947-
Comparing bach and bachTwin:
Distinct copies.
Same data.
```

Copy Constructors

copy constructor

A **copy constructor** is a constructor with a single argument of the same type as the class. The copy constructor should create an object that is a separate, independent object but with the instance variables set so that it is an exact copy of the argument object.

For example, Display 5.20 reproduces the copy constructor for the class `Date` defined in Display 4.11. The copy constructor, or any other constructor, creates a new object of the class `Date`. This happens automatically and is not shown in the code for the copy constructor. The code for the copy constructor then goes on to set the instance variables to the values equal to those of its one parameter, `aDate`. But the new date created is a separate object even though it represents the same date. Consider the following code:

```
Date date1 = new Date("January", 1, 2006);
Date date2 = new Date(date1);
```

After this code is executed, both `date1` and `date2` represent the date January 1, 2006, but they are two different objects. So, if we change one of these objects, it will not change the other. For example, consider

```
date2.setDate("July", 4, 1776);
System.out.println(date1);
```

The output produced is

```
January 1, 2006
```

When we changed `date2`, we did not change `date1`. This may not be a difficult or even subtle point, but it is critically important to much of what we discuss in this section of the chapter. (See Self-Test Exercise 39 in this chapter to see the copy constructor contrasted with the assignment operator.)

Now let's consider the copy constructor for the class `Person` (Display 5.19), which is a bit more complicated. It is reproduced in what follows:

```
public Person(Person original)
{
    if (original == null)
    {
        System.out.println("Fatal error.");
        System.exit(0);
    }
    name = original.name;
    born = new Date(original.born);
    if (original.died == null)
        died = null;
    else
        died = new Date(original.died);
}
```

We want the object created to be an independent copy of `original`. That would not happen if we had used the following instead:

```
public Person(Person original) //Unsafe
{
    if (original == null )
    {
        System.out.println("Fatal error.");
        System.exit(0);
    }
    name = original.name;
    born = original.born; //Not good.
    died = original.died; //Not good.
}
```

Although this alternate definition looks innocent enough and may work fine in many situations, it does have serious problems.

Assume we had used the unsafe version of the copy constructor instead of the one in Display 5.19. The "Not good." code simply copies references from `original.born` and `original.died` to the corresponding arguments of the object being created by the constructor. So, the object created is not an independent copy of the `original` object. For example, consider the code

```
Person original =
      new Person("Natalie Dressed",
      new Date("April", 1, 1984), null);
Person copy = new Person(original);
copy.setBirthYear(1800);
System.out.println(original);
```

The output would be

```
Natalie Dressed, April 1, 1800-
```

When we changed the birth year in the object `copy`, we also changed the birth year in the object `original`. This is because we are using our unsafe version of the copy constructor. Both `original.born` and `copy.born` contain the same reference to the same `Date` object.

This all happens because we used the unsafe version of the copy constructor. Fortunately, here we use a safer version of the copy constructor that sets the `born` instance variables as follows:

```
born = new Date(original.born);
```

which is equivalent to

```
this.born = new Date(original.born);
```

This version, which we did use, makes the instance variable `this.born` an independent `Date` object that represents the same date as `original.born`. So if you change a date in the `Person` object created by the copy constructor, you will not change that date in the `original Person` object.

Note that if a class, such as `Person`, has instance variables of a class type, such as the instance variables `born` and `died`, then to define a correct copy constructor for the class `Person`, you must already have copy constructors for the class `Date` of the instance variables. The easiest way to ensure this for all your classes is to always include a copy constructor in every class you define.

Copy Constructor

A **copy constructor** is a constructor with one parameter of the same type as the class. A copy constructor should be designed so the object it creates is intuitively an exact copy of its parameter, but a completely independent copy. See Displays 5.19 and 5.20 for examples of copy constructors.

`clone`

The Java documentation says to use a method named `clone` instead of a copy constructor, and, as you will see later in this book, there are situations where the copy constructor will not work as desired and you need the `clone` method. However, we do not yet have enough background to delve into this method.(It is discussed later in this book in Chapters 8 and 13.) Despite the Java documentation, many excellent programmers prefer to sometimes use copy constructors. In this book, we will use both copy constructors and the clone method.

PITFALL: Privacy Leaks

leaking accessor methods

Consider the accessor method `getBirthDate` for the class `Person` (Display 5.19), which we reproduce in what follows:

```
public Date getBirthDate()
{
    return new Date(born);
}
```

Do not make the mistake of defining the accessor method as follows:

```
public Date getBirthDate() //Unsafe
{
    return born; //Not good
}
```

(continued)

PITFALL: (continued)

Assume we had used the unsafe version of `getBirthDate` instead of the one in Display 5.19. It would then be possible for a program that uses the class `Person` to change the private instance variable `born` to any date whatsoever and bypass the checks in constructor and mutator methods of the class `Person`. For example, consider the following code, which might appear in some program that uses the class `Person`:

```
Person citizen = new Person(
"Joe Citizen", new Date("January", 1, 1900), new Date("January", 1,
     1990));
Date dateName = citizen.getBirthDate();
dateName.setDate("April", 1, 3000);
```

privacy leak

This code changes the date of birth so it is after the date of death (an impossibility in the universe as we know it). This citizen was not born until after he or she died! This sort of situation is known as a **privacy leak**, because it allows a programmer to circumvent the `private` modifier before an instance variable such as `born`, and to change the private instance variable to anything whatsoever.

The following code would be illegal in our program:

```
citizen.born.setDate("April", 1, 3000); //Illegal
```

This is illegal because `born` is a private instance variable. However, with the unsafe version of `getBirthDate` (and we are now assuming that we did use the unsafe version), the variable `dateName` contains the same reference as `citizen.born` and so the following is legal and equivalent to the illegal statement:

```
dateName.setDate("April", 1, 3000); //Legal and equivalent to
   //illegal statement.
```

It is as if you have a friend named Robert who is also known as Bob. Some bully wants to beat up Robert, so you say "You cannot beat up Robert." The bully says "OK, I will not beat up Robert, but I will beat up Bob." Bob and Robert are two names for the same person. So, if you protect Robert but do not protect Bob, you have really accomplished nothing.

This is all if we used the unsafe version of `getBirthDate`, which simply returns the reference in the private instance variable born. Fortunately, here we use a safer version of `getBirthDate`, which has the following `return` statement:

```
return new Date(born);
```

PITFALL: (continued)

This return statement does not return the reference in the private instance variable born. Instead, it uses the copy constructor to return a reference to a new object that is an exact copy of the object named by born. If the copy is changed, that has no effect on the date whose reference is in the instance variable born. Thus, a privacy leak is avoided.

leaking mutator methods

Note that returning a reference is not the only possible source of privacy leaks. A privacy leak can also arise from an incorrectly defined constructor or mutator method. Notice the definition for the method setBirthDate in Display 5.19 and reproduced as follows:

```
public void setBirthDate(Date newDate)
{
    if (consistent(newDate, died))
        born = new Date(newDate);
    else
    {
        System.out.println("Inconsistent dates. Aborting.");
        System.exit(0);
    }
}
```

Note that the instance variable born is set to a copy of the parameter newDate. Suppose that instead of

```
born = new Date(newDate);
```

we simply use

```
born = newDate;
```

And suppose we use the following code in some program:

```
Person personObject = new Person(
  "Josephine", new Date("January", 1, 2000), null);
Date dateName = new Date("February", 2, 2002);
personObject.setBirthDate(dateName);
```

where personObject names an object of the class Person. The following will change the year part of the Date object named by the born instance variable of the object personObject and will do so without going through the checks in the mutator methods for Person:

```
dateName.setYear(1000);
```

(continued)

PITFALL: (continued)

Because `dateName` contains the same reference as the private instance variable born of the object `personObject`, changing the year part of `dateName` changes the year part of the private instance variable born of `personObject`. Not only does this bypass the consistency checks in the mutator method `setBirthDate`, but it also is a likely source of an inadvertent change to the `born` instance variable.

If we define `setBirthDate` as we did in Display 5.19 and as shown in the following, this problem does not happen. (If you do not see this, go through the code step by step and trace what happens.)

```
public void setBirthDate(Date newDate)
{
    if (consistent(newDate, died))
        born = new Date(newDate);
    . . .
```

One final word of warning: Using copy constructors in this manner is not the officially sanctioned way to make copies of an object in Java. The authorized way to is to define a method named `clone`. We will discuss `clone` methods in Chapters 8 and 13. In Chapter 8, we show you that, in some situations, there are advantages to using a `clone` method instead of a copy constructor. In Chapter 13, we describe the official way to define the `clone` method. For what we will be doing until then, a copy constructor will be a very adequate way of creating copies of an object.

clone

MyProgrammingLab™

Self Test Exercises

38. What is a copy constructor?

39. What output is produced by the following code?

```
Date date1 = new Date("January", 1, 2006);
Date date2;
date2 = date1;
date2.setDate("July", 4, 1776);
System.out.println(date1);
```

What output is produced by the following code? Only the third line is different from the previous case.

```
Date date1 = new Date("January", 1, 2006);
Date date2;
date2 = new Date(date1);
date2.setDate("July", 4, 1776);
System.out.println(date1);
```

MyProgrammingLab™

Self Test Exercises

40. What output is produced by the following code?

```
Person original =
             new Person("Natalie Dressed",
                             new Date("April", 1, 1984), null);
Person copy = new Person(original);
copy.setBirthDate(new Date("April", 1, 1800));
System.out.println(original)
```

Mutable and Immutable Classes

Contrast the accessor methods `getName` and `getBirthDate` of the class `Person` (Display 5.19). We reproduce the two methods in what follows:

```
public String getName()
{
    return name;
}


public Date getBirthDate()
{
    return new Date(born);
}
```

Notice that the method `getBirthDate` does not simply return the reference in the instance variable `born`, but instead uses the copy constructor to return a reference to a copy of the birth date object. We already explained why we do this. If we return the reference in the instance variable `born`, then we can place this reference in a variable of type `Date`, and that variable could serve as another name for the private instance variable `born`, which would allow us to violate the privacy of the instance variable `born` by changing it using a mutator method of the class `Date`. This is exactly what we discussed in the previous subsection. So why not do something similar in the method `getName`?

The method `getName` simply returns the reference in the private instance variable `name`. So, if we do the following in a program, then the variable `nameAlias` will be another name for the `String` object of the private instance variable `name`:

```
Person citizen = new Person(
"Joe Citizen", new Date("January", 1, 1900), new Date("January",
1, 1990));
String nameAlias = citizen.getName();
```

It looks as though we could use a mutator method from the class `String` to change the name referenced by `nameAlias` and so violate the privacy of the instance variable `name`. Is something wrong? Do we have to rewrite the method `getName` to use the copy constructor for the class `String`? No, everything is fine. We cannot use a mutator method with `nameAlias` because the class `String` has no mutator methods! The class `String` contains no methods that change any of the data in a `String` object.

At first, it may seem as though you can change the data in an object of the class `String`. What about the string processing we have seen, such as the following?

```
String greeting = "Hello";
greeting = greeting + "friend.";
```

Have we not changed the data in the `String` object from `"Hello"` to `"Hello friend."`? No, we have not. The expression `greeting + "friend."` does not change the object `"Hello"`; it creates a new object, so the assignment statement

```
greeting = greeting + "friend.";
```

replaces the reference to `"Hello"` with a reference to the different `String` object `"Hello friend."` The object `"Hello"` is unchanged. To see that this is true, consider the following code:

```
String greeting = "Hello";
String helloVariable = greeting;
greeting = greeting + "friend.";
System.out.println(helloVariable);
```

This produces the output `"Hello"`. If the object `"Hello"` had been changed, the output would have been `"Hello friend."`

immutable

A class that contains no methods (other than constructors) that change any of the data in an object of the class is called an **immutable class**, and objects of the class are called **immutable objects**. The class `String` is an immutable class. It is perfectly safe to return a reference to an immutable object, because the object cannot be changed in any undesirable way; in fact, it cannot be changed in any way whatsoever.

mutable

A class that contains public mutator methods or other public methods, such as input methods, that can change the data in an object of the class is called a **mutable class**, and objects of the class are called **mutable objects**. The class `Date` is an example of a mutable class; many, perhaps most, of the classes you define will be mutable classes. As we noted in the Pitfall entitled "Privacy Leaks" (but using other words): You should never write a method that returns a mutable object, but should instead use a copy constructor (or other means) to return a reference to a completely independent copy of the mutable object.

TIP: Deep Copy versus Shallow Copy

In the previous two subsections, we contrasted the following two ways of defining the method `getBirthDate` (Display 5.19):

VideoNote
Deep Copy vs. Shallow Copy Example

```
public Date getBirthDate()
{
    return new Date(born);
}
public Date getBirthDate() //Unsafe
{
    return born; //Not good
}
```

As we noted, the first definition is the better one (and the one used in Display 5.19). The first definition returns what is known as a *deep copy* of the object born. The second definition returns what is known as a *shallow copy* of the object `born`.

deep copy

A **deep copy** of an object is a copy that, with one exception, has no references in common with the original. The one exception is that references to immutable objects are allowed to be shared (because immutable objects cannot change in any way and so cannot be changed in any undesirable way). For example, the first definition of `getBirthDate` returns a deep copy of the date stored by the instance variable `born`. So, if you change the object returned by `getBirthDate`, this does not change the `Date` object named by the instance variable `born`. The reason is that we defined the copy constructor for the class `Date` to create a deep copy (Display 5.20). Normally, copy constructors and accessor methods should return a deep copy.

shallow copy

Any copy that is not a deep copy is called a **shallow copy**. For example, the second definition of `getBirthDate` returns a shallow copy of the date stored by the instance variable `born`.

We will have more to say about deep and shallow copies in later chapters. ■

Never Return a Reference to a Mutable Private Object

A class that contains mutator methods or other methods, such as input methods, that can change the data in an object of the class is called a **mutable class**, and objects of the class are called **mutable objects**. When defining accessor methods (or almost any methods), your method should not return a reference to a mutable object. Instead, use a copy constructor (or other means) to return a reference to a completely independent copy of the mutable object.

TIP: Assume Your Coworkers Are Malicious

Our discussion of privacy leaks in the previous subsections was concerned with the effect of somebody trying to defeat the privacy of an instance variable. You might object that your coworkers are nice people and would not knowingly sabotage your software. That is probably true, and we do not mean to accuse your coworkers of malicious intent. However, the same action that can be performed intentionally by a malicious enemy can also be performed inadvertently by your friends or even by you yourself. The best way to guard against such honest mistakes is to pretend that you are defending against a malicious enemy. ■

MyProgrammingLab™

Self-Test Exercises

41. Complete the definition of the method `set` for the class `Person` (Display 5.19).

42. Classify each of the following classes as either mutable or immutable: `Date` (Display 4.11), `Person` (Display 5.19), and `String`.

43. Normally, it is dangerous to return a reference to a private instance variable of class type, but it is OK if the class type is `String`. What is special about the class `String` that makes this true?

5.4 Packages and `javadoc`

... he furnished me,
From mine own library with volumes that
I prize above my dukedom.

WILLIAM SHAKESPEARE, *The Tempest*

In this section, we cover packages, which are Java libraries, and then cover the `javadoc` program, which automatically extracts documentation from packages and classes. Although these are important topics, they are not used in the rest of this book. You can study this section at any time you wish; you need not cover this section before studying any other topic in this book.

This section does not use any of the material in Section 5.3, and so can be covered before Section 5.3.

This section assumes that you know about directories (which are called folders in some operating systems), that you know about path names for directories (folders), and that you know about PATH (environment) variables. These are not Java topics. They are part of your operating system, and the details depend on your particular operating system. If you can find out how to set the PATH variable on your operating system, you will know enough about these topics to understand this section.

Packages and `import` Statements

package

A **package** is Java's way of forming a library of classes. You can make a package from a group of classes and then use the package of classes in any other class or program you write without the need to move the classes to the directory (folder) in which you are working. All you need to do is include an **`import` statement** that names the package. We have already used `import` statements with some predefined standard Java packages. For example, the following, which we have used before, makes available the class `Scanner` of the package `java.util`:

`import` statement

```
import java.util.Scanner;
```

You can make all the classes in the package available by using the following instead:

```
Import java.util.*;
```

There is no overhead cost for importing the entire package as opposed to just a few classes.

The `import` statements should be at the beginning of the file. Only blank lines, comments, and `package` statements may precede the list of `import` statements. We discuss `package` statements next.

`import` Statement

You can use a class from a package in any program or class definition by placing an **`import` statement** that names the package and the class from the package at the start of the file containing the program (or class definition). The program (or class definition) need not be in the same directory as the classes in the package.

SYNTAX

```
import Package_Name.Class;
```

EXAMPLE

```
import java.util.Scanner;
```

You can import all the classes in a package by using an asterisk in place of the class's name.

SYNTAX

```
import Package_Name.*;
```

EXAMPLE

```
import java.util.*;
```

To make a package, group all the classes together into a single directory (folder) and add the following package statement to the beginning of each class file:

```
package Package_Name;
```

This package statement should be at the beginning of the file. Only blank lines and comments may precede the package statement. If there are both import statements and package statements, any package statements come before the import statements. Aside from the addition of the package statement, class files are just as we have already described them. (It is technically only the .class files that must be in the package directory.)

The Package java.lang

The package java.lang contains classes that are fundamental to Java programming. These classes are so basic that the package is always imported automatically. Any class in java.lang does not need an import statement to make it available to your code. For example, the classes Math and String and the wrapper classes introduced earlier in this chapter are all in the package java.lang.

Package

A **package** is a collection of classes that have been grouped together into a directory and given a package name. The classes in the package are each placed in a separate file, and the file is given the same name as the class, just as we have been doing all along. Each file in the package must have the following at the beginning of the file. Only comments and blank lines may precede this package statement.

SYNTAX

```
package Package_Name;
```

EXAMPLES

```
package utilities.numericstuff;
package java.util;
```

Package Names and Directories

A package name is not an arbitrary identifier. It is a form of path name to the directory containing the classes in the package.

In order to find the directory for a package, Java needs two things: the name of the package and the value of your *CLASSPATH variable*.

CLASSPATH variable

You should already be familiar with the environment variable of your operating system that is known as the *PATH variable*. The **CLASSPATH variable** is a similar environment variable used to help locate Java packages. The value of your CLASSPATH variable tells Java where to begin its search for a package. It is not a Java variable. It is an environment variable that is part of your operating system. The value of your CLASSPATH variable is a list of directories. The exact syntax for this list varies from one operating system to another, but it should be the same syntax as that used for the (ordinary) PATH variable. When Java is looking for a package, it begins its search in the directories listed in the CLASSPATH variable.

The name of a package specifies the relative path name for the directory that contains the package classes. It is a relative path name because it assumes that you start in one of the directories listed in the value of your CLASSPATH variable. For example, suppose the following is a directory listed in your CLASSPATH variable (your operating system might use / instead of \):

```
\libraries\newlibraries
```

And suppose your package classes are in the directory

```
\libraries\newlibraries\utilities\numericstuff
```

In this case, the package *should* be named

```
utilities.numericstuff
```

and all the classes in the file must start with the package statement

```
package utilities.numericstuff;
```

The dot in the package name means essentially the same thing as the \ or /, whichever symbol your operating system uses for directory paths. The package name tells you (and Java) what subdirectories to go through to find the package classes, starting from a directory on the class path. This is depicted in Display 5.22. (If there happen to be two directories in the CLASSPATH variable that can be used, then of all the ones that can be used, Java always uses the first one listed in the CLASSPATH variable.)

Any class that uses the class in this `utilities.numericstuff` package must contain either the `import` statement

```
import utilities.numericstuff.*;
```

or an `import` statement for each class in the package that is used.

The way you set the value of your CLASSPATH variable depends on your operating system, but we can give you some suggestions that may work. The CLASSPATH variable is usually spelled as one word with all uppercase letters, as in `CLASSPATH`. You will probably have a plain old PATH variable that tells the operating system where to find the code for commands such as `javac` and other commands that you can give as single-line commands. If you can find out how to set the PATH variable, you should be able to set the CLASSPATH variable in the same way.

Display 5.22 A Package Name

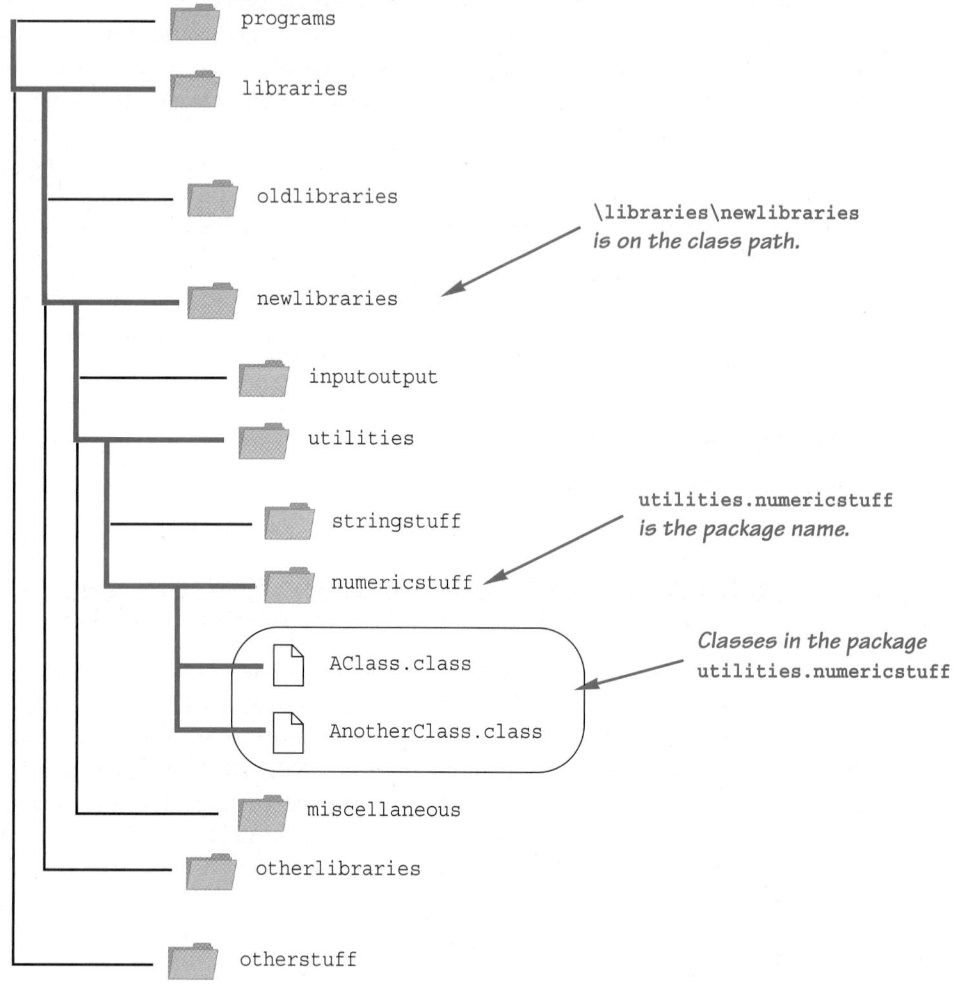

If you are on a UNIX system, you are likely to be able to set the CLASSPATH with some command similar to the following:

```
set CLASSPATH=/libraries/newlibraries;/otherstuff/specialjava;.
export CLASSPATH
```

If this does not work, you might try omitting the word `set` or replacing `set` with `setenv`. You might also try placing the list of directories in quotes. There are many versions of UNIX, all with their own minor variations. You may need to consult a local expert or check the documentation for your operating system.

If you are using a Windows machine, you can set the CLASSPATH variable by setting or creating an environment variable named CLASSPATH using the Control Panel.

In this book, we are assuming that class path directories are separated by a semicolon. That is common, but some operating systems use some other separator, such as a colon. Check your documentation if a semicolon does not work as a separator.

Package Names and the CLASSPATH Variable

A package name must be a path name for the directory that contains the classes in the package, but the package name uses dots in place of \ or / (whichever your operating system uses). When naming the package, use a relative path name that starts from any directory listed in the value of the CLASSPATH (environment) variable.

EXAMPLES

```
utilities.numericstuff
java.util
```

PITFALL: Subdirectories Are Not Automatically Imported

Suppose you have two packages, utilities.numericstuff and utilities.numericstuff.statistical. In this case, you know that utilities.numericstuff.statistical is in a subdirectory (subfolder) of the directory (folder) containing utilities.numericstuff. This leads some programmers to assume that the following import statement imports both packages:

```
import utilities.numericstuff.*;
```

This is not true. When you import an entire package, you do not import subdirectory packages.

To import all classes in both of these packages, you need

```
import utilities.numericstuff.*;

import utilities.numericstuff.statistical.*;
```

■

The Default Package

default package

All the classes in your current directory (that do not belong to some other package) belong to an unnamed package called the **default package**. As long as the current directory is on your CLASSPATH, all the classes in the default package are automatically available to your code. This is why we always assume that all the classes we defined are in the same directory. That way, we need not clutter our discussion with concern about import statements.

PITFALL: Not Including the Current Directory in Your Class Path

current directory

Your CLASSPATH variable allows you to list more than one directory. Most operating systems use the dot to indicate the current directory. The **current directory** is not any one specific directory; it is the directory in which you are currently "located." If you do not know what your current directory is, then it is probably the directory that contains the class you are writing. For example, the following value for a CLASSPATH variable lists two ordinary directories and the current directory:

```
\libraries\newlibraries;\otherstuff\specialjava;.
```

Whenever you set or change the CLASSPATH variable, be sure to include the current directory as one of the alternatives. With the above displayed CLASSPATH value, if the package is not found by starting in either of the previous two directories, Java will look in the subdirectories of the current directory. If you want Java to check the current directory before the other directories on the CLASSPATH variable, list the current directory (the dot) first, as follows:

```
.;\libraries\newlibraries;\otherstuff\specialjava
```

When looking for a package, Java tries the directories in the class path in order and uses the first one that works.

Omitting the current directory from the CLASSPATH variable can interfere with running Java programs, regardless of whether or not the programs use packages. If the current directory is omitted, then Java may not even be able to find the `.class` file for the program itself, so you may not be able to run any programs at all. Thus, if you do set the CLASSPATH variable, it is critical that you include the current directory in the CLASSPATH. No such problems will occur if you have not set the CLASSPATH variable at all; it arises only if you decide to set the CLASSPATH variable.

If you are having problems setting the CLASSPATH variable, one interim solution is to delete the CLASSPATH variable completely and to keep all the class files for one program in the same directory. This will allow you to still do some work while you seek advice on setting the CLASSPATH variable. ■

Specifying a Class Path When You Compile ★

You can specify a class path when you compile a class. To do so, add `-classpath` followed by the class path as illustrated in the following:

```
javac -classpath .;C:\lib\numeric;C:\otherstuff YourClass.java
```

In a UNIX environment, replace the semicolons with colons. This will compile `YourClass.java`, overriding any CLASSPATH setting, and use the class path given after `-classpath`. Note that the directories are separated by semicolons. If you want classes in the current directory to be available to your class, then be sure the class path includes the current directory, which is indicated by a dot.

When you run the class compiled as just shown, you should again use the `-classpath` option as follows:

```
java -classpath .;C:\libraries\numeric;C:\otherstuff YourClass
```

It is important to include the current directory on the class path when you run the program. If your program is in the default package, it will not be found unless you include the current directory. It is best to get in the habit of always including the current directory in all class paths.

Because the class path specified in compiling and running your classes is input to a program (`javac or java`) that is part of the Java environment and is not a command to the operating system, you can use either / or \ in the class path, no matter which of these two your operating system uses.

Name Clashes ★

name clash

In addition to being a way of organizing libraries, packages also provide a way to deal with *name clashes*. A **name clash** is a situation in which two classes have the same name. If different programmers writing different packages used the same name for a class, the ambiguity can be resolved by using the package name.

Suppose a package named `sallyspack` contains a class called `HighClass`, and another package named `joespack` also contains a class named `HighClass`. You can use both classes named `HighClass` in the same program by using the more complete names `sallyspack.HighClass` and `joespack.HighClass`. For example,

```
sallyspack.HighClass object1 = new sallyspack.HighClass();
joespack.HighClass object2 = new joespack.HighClass();
```

fully qualified class name

These names that include the package name, such as `sallyspack.HighClass` and `joespack.HighClass`, are called **fully qualified class names**.

If you use fully qualified class names, you do not need to import the class, since this longer class name includes the package name.

MyProgrammingLab™

Self-Test Exercises

44. Suppose you want to use the class `CoolClass` in the package `mypackages.library1` in a program you write. What do you need to do to make this class available to your program? What do you need to do to make all the classes in the package available to your program?

45. What do you need to do to make a class a member of the package named `mypackages.library1`?

46. Can a package have any name you want, or are there restrictions on what you can use for a package name? Explain any restrictions.

Introduction to `javadoc` ★

The principles of encapsulation using information hiding say that you should separate the *interface* of a class (the instructions on how to use the class) from the *implementation* (the detailed code that tells the computer how the class does its work). In some other programming languages, such as C++, you normally define a class in two files. One file contains something like the interface or API that tells a programmer all that he or she needs to know to use the class. The other file contains the implementation details that are needed for the class code to run. This system is an obvious way to separate interface from implementation, but it is not what Java does.

Java does not divide a class definition into two files. Instead, Java has the interface and implementation of a class mixed together into a single file. If this were the end of the story, Java would not do a good job of encapsulation using information hiding. However, Java has a very good way of separating the interface from the implementation of a class. Java comes with a program named `javadoc` that automatically extracts the interface from a class definition. If your class definition is correctly commented, a programmer using your class need only look at this API (documentation) produced by `javadoc`. The documentation produced by `javadoc` is identical in format to the documentation for the standard Java library classes.

`javadoc`

The result of running `javadoc` on a class is to produce an HTML file with the API (interface) documentation for the class. *HTML* is the basic language used to produce documents to view with a Web browser, so the documentation produced by `javadoc` is viewed on a Web browser. A brief introduction to HTML is given in Chapter 20. However, you need not know any HTML to run `javadoc` or to read the documentation it produces.

`javadoc` can be used to obtain documentation for a single class. However, it is primarily intended to obtain documentation for an entire package.

We will first discuss how you should comment your classes so that you can get the most value out of `javadoc`. We will then describe how you run the `javadoc` program.

Commenting Classes for `javadoc` ★

To get a more useful `javadoc` document, you must write your comments in a particular way. All the classes in this book have been commented for use with `javadoc`. However, to save space, the comments in this book are briefer than what would be ideal for `javadoc`.

The `javadoc` program extracts the heading for your class (or classes) as well as the headings for all public methods, public instance variables, public static variables, and certain comments. No method bodies and no private items are extracted when `javadoc` is run in the normal default mode.

For `javadoc` (in default mode) to extract a comment, the comment must satisfy two conditions:

1. The comment must *immediately precede* a public class definition, a public method definition, or other public item.
2. The comment must be a block comment (that is, the /* and */ style of comment), and the opening /* must contain an extra *. So the comment must be marked by /** at the beginning and */ at the end.

Unless you explicitly set an extra option to javadoc, line comments (that is, // style comments) are not extracted, and comments preceding any private items also are not extracted.

The comment that precedes a public method definition can include any general information that you would like. There is also special syntax for inserting descriptions of parameters, any value returned, and any exceptions that might be thrown. We have not yet discussed exceptions. That is done in Chapter 9, but we include mention of them here so this section will serve as a more complete reference on javadoc. You need not worry about exceptions or the details about "throws" discussed here until you reach Chapter 9.

@ tag

The special information about parameters and so forth are preceded by the @ symbol and are called **@ tags**. The following is an example of a method comment for use with javadoc:

```
/**
 Tests for equality of two objects of type Person. To be equal,
 the two objects must have the same name, same birth date, and
 same death date.

 @param otherPerson The person being compared to the calling
 object.
 @return Returns true if the calling object equals otherPerson.
*/
public boolean equals(Person otherPerson)
```

(The method equals is from the class Person defined in Display 5.19. If you need more context, look at that display.)

Note that the @ tags all come after any general comment and that each @ tag is on a line by itself. The following are some of the @ tags allowed:

@param *Parameter_Name Parameter_Description*
@return *Description_Of_Value_Returned*
@throws *Exception_Type Explanation*
@deprecated
@see *Package_Name.Class_Name*
@author *Author*
@version *Version_Information*

The @ tags should appear in the above order—first @param, then @return, then @throws, and so forth. If there are multiple parameters, they should each have their own @param and appear on a separate line. The parameters and their @param description should be listed in their left-to-right order in the parameter list. If there are multiple authors, they should each have their own @author and appear on a separate line. The author and version information is not extracted unless suitable option flags have been set, as described in the next subsection.

deprecated

If @deprecated is included in a method comment, then the documentation notes that the method is *deprecated*. A **deprecated** method is one that is being phased out. To allow for backward compatibility, the method still works, but it should not be used in new code.

If an @ tag is included for an item, javadoc extracts the explanation for that item and includes it in the documentation. You should always include a more or less complete set of @ tags in the comment for each of your methods. In this book, we omit the @ tags to save space, but we encourage you to always include them. The comments that are not part of an @ tag appear as a general comment for the method, along with the method heading.

You can also insert HTML commands in your comments so that you gain more control over javadoc, but that is not necessary and may not even be desirable. HTML commands can clutter the comments, making them harder to read when you look at the source code.

Running javadoc ★

To run javadoc on a package, all you need to do is give the following command:

```
javadoc -d Documentation_Directory Package_Name
```

It would be normal to run this command from the directory containing the classes in the package, but it can be run from any directory, provided you have correctly set the CLASSPATH environment variable. The *Documentation_Directory* is the name of the directory in which you want javadoc to place the HTML documents that it produces. For example, the following might be used to obtain documentation on the package mylibraries.numericstuff:

```
javadoc -d documentation/mypackages mylibraries.numericstuff
```

The HTML documents produced will be in the subdirectory documentation/mypackages of where this command is run. If you prefer, you may use a complete path name in place of the relative path name documentation/mypackages. If you omit the -d and *Documentation_Directory*, javadoc will create suitable directories for the documentation.

You can link to standard Java documents so that your HTML documents include live links to standard classes and methods. The syntax is as follows:

```
javadoc -link Link_To_Standard_Docs -d Documentation_Directory
Package_Name
```

Link_To_Standard_Docs is either a path to a local version of the Java documentation or the URL of the Oracle Web site with standard Java documentation. As of this writing, that URL is

```
http://download.oracle.com/javase/7/docs/api/
```

You need not run `javadoc` on an entire package. You can run `javadoc` on a single class file. For example, the following should be run from the directory containing `Date.java` and will produce documentation for the class `Date`:

```
javadoc Date.java
```

You can run `javadoc` on all classes in a directory with

```
javadoc *.java
```

You can add the `-d` and/or `-link` options to any of these commands. For example,

```
javadoc -link http://download.oracle.com/javase/7/docs/api/ -d
mydocs *.java
```

These and other options for `javadoc` are summarized in Display 5.23.

When running `javadoc`, you typically get more directories and many more HTML files than you might expect. To get a better understanding of `javadoc`, you should try running it in various settings and observe the files it produces.

Display 5.23 Options for `java.doc`

OPTIONS	DESCRIPTION
`-link`	Provides a link to another set of documentation. Normally, this is used with either a path name to a local version of the Java documentation or the URL of the Oracle Web site with standard Java documentation.
`-d`	Specifies a directory to hold the documentation generated. *Documentation_Directory* may be a relative or absolute path name.
`-author`	Includes author information (from `@author` tags). This information is omitted unless this option is set.
`-version`	Includes version information (from `@version` tags). This information is omitted unless this option is set.
`-classpath`	Overrides the CLASSPATH environment variable and makes the CLASSPATH for the execution of this invocation of `javadoc`. It does not permanently change the CLASSPATH variable.
`-private`	Includes private members as well as public members in the documentation.

Self-Test Exercises

47. When run in default mode, does `javadoc` ever extract the body of a method definition? When run in default mode, does `javadoc` ever extract anything marked private in a class definition?

48. When run in default mode, what comments does `javadoc` extract and what comments does it not extract?

Chapter Summary

- A *static method* is one that does not require a calling object, but can use the class name in place of the calling object.
- A *static variable* is similar to an instance variable except that there is only one copy of the static variable that is used by all objects of the class.
- A *wrapper class* allows you to have a class object that corresponds to a value of a primitive type. Wrapper classes also contain a number of useful predefined constants and static methods.
- A variable of a class type stores the reference (memory address) of where the object is located in the computer's memory. This causes some operations, such as `=` and `==`, to behave quite differently for variables of a class type than they do for variables of a primitive type.
- When you use the assignment operator with two variables of a class type, the two variables become two names for the same object.
- A method cannot change the value of a variable of a primitive type that is an argument to the method. On the other hand, a method can change the values of the instance variables of an argument of a class type. This is because with class parameters, it is a reference that is plugged in to the parameter.
- `null` is a special constant that can be used to give a value to any variable of any class type.
- An expression with a `new` operator and a constructor can be used as an argument to a method. Such an argument is called an *anonymous object*.
- A *copy constructor* is a constructor with one parameter of the same type as the class. A copy constructor should be designed so the object it creates is intuitively an exact copy of its parameter, but is a completely independent copy—that is, a *deep copy*.
- A class that contains mutator methods or any methods that can change the data in an object of the class is called a *mutable class*, and objects of the class are called *mutable objects*. When defining accessor methods (or almost any methods), your method should not return a reference to a mutable object. Instead, use a copy constructor (or other means) to return a reference to a deep copy of the mutable object.

- *Packages* are Java's version of class libraries.
- Java comes with a program named `javadoc` that automatically extracts the interface from all the classes in a package or from a single class definition.

Answers to Self-Test Exercises

1. Yes, it is legal, although it would be preferable style to use the class name `RoundStuff` in place of `roundObject`.
2. No, all methods in the class are static, so there is no need to create objects. If we follow our style rules, no constructors would ever be used, so there is no need for constructors.
3. Yes, a class can contain both static and nonstatic (that is, regular) methods.
4. You cannot invoke a nonstatic method within a static method (unless you create an object to serve as the calling object of the nonstatic method).
5. You can invoke a static method within a nonstatic method.
6. You cannot reference an instance variable within a static method, because a static method can be used without a calling object and hence without any instance variables.
7. Each object of a class has its own copy of each instance variable, but a single copy of each static variable is shared by all objects.
8. No, you cannot use an instance variable (without an object name and dot) in the definition of a static method of the same class. Yes, you can use an instance variable (without an object name and dot) in the definition of a nonstatic method of the same class.
9. Yes, you can use a static variable in the definition of a static method of the same class. Yes, you can use a static variable in the definition of a nonstatic method of the same class. So, you can use a static variable in any method.
10. No, you cannot use either an explicit or an implicit occurrence of the `this` parameter in the definition of a static method.
11. All methods with the following names could and should be marked `static`: `dateOK`, `monthOK`, and `monthString`.
12. All static variables should be marked `private` with the exception of one case: If the static variable is used as a named constant (that is, if it is marked `final`), then it can be marked either `public` or `private` depending on the particular situation.
13. They can both be named by using the class name and a dot, rather than an object name and a dot.

14. `3`, `4`,

    `3.0`, `3.0`,

    `4.0`, and `4.0`
15. `roundedAnswer = (int)Math.round(answer);`
16. `long`. Because one argument is of type long, the int argument is automatically type cast to `long`.
17. They are all legal.
18. An object of the class `Double`; the assignment is equivalent to

```
Double price = new Double(1.99);
```

19. A value of the primitive type `int`; the assignment is equivalent to

```
int count = (new Integer(12)).intValue();
```

20. `Objects are Not equal.`
21. `Double.toString(result)`
22. `Double.parseDouble(stringForm)`
23. `Double.parseDouble(stringForm.trim())`
24.
```
System.out.println("Largest long is" + Long.MAX_VALUE +
                   "Smallest long is" + Long.MIN_VALUE);
```
25. `Character zeeObject = new Character('Z');`
26. No, none of the wrapper classes discussed in this chapter have no-argument constructors.
27. A *reference type* is a type whose variables contain references, that is, memory addresses. Class types are reference types. Primitive types are not reference types.
28. When comparing two objects of a class type, you should use the method `equals`.
29. When comparing two objects of a primitive type, you should you use `==`.
30. Yes, a method with an argument of a class type can change the values of the instance variables in the object named by the argument.
31. No, a method cannot change the value of an `int` variable given as an argument to the method.
32. The variable `anObject` names no object, so the invocation of the `set` method is an error. One way to fix things is as follows:

```
ToyClass anObject = new ToyClass();
anObject.set("Josephine", 42);
```

33. The constant `null` can be assigned to a variable of any class type. It does not really have a type, but you can think of its type as being the type of a memory address. You can also think of `null` as being of every class type.

34. `aVariable == null`

35. It is unlikely but it is legal. This is an example of an anonymous object, as described in the text.

extra code on website

36. The only difference is that the object of type `Date` is given the name `theDate` in the second version. It makes no difference to the object `adams`.

37. The following definition of `equals` is used in the file `Date.java` in the Chapter 5 directory of the source code on the website:

```
public boolean equals(Date otherDate)
{
    if (otherDate == null)
        return false;
    else
        return ( (month.equals(otherDate.month)) &&
           (day == otherDate.day) && (year == otherDate.year) );
}
```

38. A copy constructor is a constructor with one parameter of the same type as the class. A copy constructor should be designed so that the object it creates is intuitively an exact copy of its parameter, but a completely independent copy, that is, a deep copy.

39. The first piece of code produces the output

```
July 4, 1776
```

The second piece of code produces the output

```
January 1, 2006
```

40. `Natalie Dressed, April 1, 1984-`

41.
```
public void set(String newName, Date birthDate, Date deathDate)
{
    if (consistent(birthDate, deathDate))
    {
            name = newName;
            born = new Date(birthDate);
            if (deathDate == null)
                died = null;
            else
                died = new Date(deathDate);
    }
    else
    {
        System.out.println("Inconsistent dates. Aborting.");
        System.exit(0);
    }
}
```

Note that the following is not a good definition because it could lead to a privacy leak:

```
public void set(String newName, Date birthDate, Date deathDate)
{//Not good
    name = newName;
    born = birthDate;
    died = deathDate;
}
```

42. The class `String` is an immutable class. The classes `Date` and `Person` are mutable classes.
43. The class `String` is an immutable class.
44. To make the class available to your program, you need to insert the following at the start of the file containing your class:

    ```
    import mypackages.library1.CoolClass;
    ```

    To make all the classes in the package available to your program, insert the following instead:

    ```
    import mypackages.library1.*;
    ```

45. To make a class a member of the package named `mypackages.library1`, you must insert the following at the start of the file with the class definition and place the file in the directory corresponding to the package (as described in the text):

    ```
    package mypackages.library1;
    ```

    (Only the `.class` file is required to be in the directory corresponding to the package, but it may be cleaner and easier to place both the `.java` file and the `.class` file there.)
46. A package name must be a path name for the directory that contains the classes in the package, but the package name uses dots in place of \ or / (whichever your operating system uses). When naming the package, you use a relative path name that starts from any directory named in the value of the CLASSPATH (environment) variable.
47. `javadoc` never extracts the body of a method definition, nor (when run in default mode) does `javadoc` ever extract anything marked `private` in a class definition.
48. When run in default mode, `javadoc` extracts only comments that satisfy the following two conditions:
    1. The comment must immediately precede a public class definition, a public method definition, or other public item.
    2. The comment must use the `/*` and `*/` style, and the opening `/*` must contain an extra `*`. So the comment must be marked by `/**` at the beginning and `*/` at the end. In particular, `javadoc` does not extract any `//` style comments.

MyProgrammingLab™ Programming Projects

Visit www.myprogramminglab.com to complete select exercises online and get instant feedback.

1. You operate several hot dog stands distributed throughout town. Define a class named `HotDogStand` that has an instance variable for the hot dog stand's ID number and an instance variable for how many hot dogs the stand has sold that day. Create a constructor that allows a user of the class to initialize both values.

   Also create a method named `justSold` that increments by one the number of hot dogs the stand has sold. The idea is that this method will be invoked each time the stand sells a hot dog so that you can track the total number of hot dogs sold by the stand. Add another method that returns the number of hot dogs sold.

   Finally, add a static variable that tracks the total number of hot dogs sold by all hot dog stands and a static method that returns the value in this variable.

   Write a main method to test your class with at least three hot dog stands that each sell a variety of hot dogs.

2. Define a class called `Fraction`. This class is used to represent a ratio of two integers. Include mutator methods that allow the user to set the numerator and the denominator. Also include a method that displays the fraction on the screen as a ratio (e.g., 5/9). This method does not need to reduce the fraction to lowest terms.

   Include an additional method, `equals`, that takes as input another `Fraction` and returns `true` if the two fractions are identical and `false` if they are not. This method should treat the fractions reduced to lowest terms; that is, if one fraction is 20/60 and the other is 1/3, then the method should return `true`.

   Embed your class in a test program that allows the user to create a fraction. Then the program should loop repeatedly until the user decides to quit. Inside the body of the loop, the program should allow the user to enter a target fraction into an anonymous object and learn whether the fractions are identical.

3. In the land of Puzzlevania, Aaron, Bob, and Charlie had an argument over which one of them was the greatest puzzler of all time. To end the argument once and for all, they agreed on a duel to the death. Aaron was a poor shooter and only hit his target with a probability of 1/3. Bob was a bit better and hit his target with a probability of 1/2. Charlie was an expert marksman and never missed. A hit means a kill and the person hit drops out of the duel.

   To compensate for the inequities in their marksmanship skills, the three decided that they would fire in turns, starting with Aaron, followed by Bob, and then by Charlie. The cycle would repeat until there was one man standing, and that man would be the Greatest Puzzler of All Time.

   An obvious and reasonable strategy is for each man to shoot at the most accurate shooter still alive, on the grounds that this shooter is the deadliest and has the best chance of hitting back.

Write a program to simulate the duel using this strategy. Your program should use random numbers and the probabilities given in the problem to determine whether a shooter hits the target. Create a class named `Duelist` that contains the dueler's name and shooting accuracy, a Boolean indicating whether the dueler is still alive, and a method `ShootAtTarget(Duelist target)` that sets the target to dead if the dueler hits his target (using a random number and the shooting accuracy) and does nothing otherwise.

Once you can simulate a single duel, add a loop to your program that simulates 10,000 duels. Count the number of times that each contestant wins and print the probability of winning for each contestant (e.g., for Aaron your program might output "Aaron won 3,595/10,000 duels or 35.95%").

An alternate strategy is for Aaron to intentionally miss on his first shot. Modify the program to accommodate this new strategy and output the probability of winning for each contestant. Which strategy is better for Aaron: to intentionally miss on the first shot or to try and hit the best shooter? Who has the best chance of winning, the best shooter or the worst shooter?

4. You are interested in keeping track of the team members and competition information for your school's annual entries in computer science programming competitions. Each team consists of exactly four team members. Every year your team competes in two competitions. As an initial start for your database, create a class named `Team` that has the following instance variables:

```
// Name for the team
String teamName;
// Names for each team members.
String name1, name2, name3, name4;
// Info on each competition
Competition competition1, competition2;
```

Note that there is a much better way to represent the team members and competitions using arrays; this is covered in a subsequent chapter. The class should also have a method that outputs all the names of all team members and the competition information to the console.

The `Competition` class contains variables to track the following:

String: Name of the competition, Name of the winning team, Name of the runner-up

Integer: Year of the competition

Implement the `Team` and `Competition` classes with appropriate constructor, accessor, and mutator methods. In entering data for past competitions, you note that an entry is usually very similar to the previous year's entry. To help with the data entry, create a deep copy constructor for the `Team` class. Test your copy constructor by creating a copy of an existing team object, changing the competition information for the copy, and outputting the data for the original and the copy. The original object should be unchanged if your deep copy constructor is working properly.

5. Part One: Define a class named `Money` whose objects represent amounts of U.S. money. The class should have two instance variables of type `int` for the dollars and cents in the amount of money. Include a constructor with two parameters of type `int` for the dollars and cents, one with one constructor of type `int` for an amount of dollars with zero cents, and a no-argument constructor. Include the methods `add` and `minus` for addition and subtraction of amounts of money. These methods should be static methods, should each have two parameters of type `Money`, and return a value of type `Money`. Include a reasonable set of accessor and mutator methods as well as the methods `equals` and `toString`. Write a test program for your class.

   Part Two: Add a second version of the methods for addition and subtraction. These methods should have the same names as the static version but should use a calling object and a single argument. For example, this version of the `add` method (for addition) has a calling object and one argument. So `m1.add(m2)` returns the result of adding the `Money` objects `m1` and `m2`. Note that your class should have all these methods; for example, there should be two methods named `add`.

   Alternate Part Two: Add a second version of the methods for addition and subtraction. These methods should have the same names as the static version but should use a calling object and a single argument. The methods should be `void` methods. The result should be given as the changed value of the calling object. For example, this version of the `add` method (for addition) has a calling object and one argument. Therefore,

```
m1.add(m2);
```

   changes the values of the instance variables of `m1` so they represent the result of adding `m2` to the original version of `m1`. Note that your class should have all these methods; for example, there should be two methods named `add`.

   (If you want to do both Part Two and Alternate Part Two, they must be two classes. You cannot include the methods from both Part Two and Alternate Part Two in a single class. Do you know why?)

6. Part One: Define a class for rational numbers. A rational number is a number that can be represented as the quotient of two integers. For example, 1/2, 3/4, 64/2, and so forth are all rational numbers. (By 1/2 and so forth, we mean the everyday meaning of the fraction, not the integer division this expression would produce in a Java program.) Represent rational numbers as two values of type `int`, one for the numerator and one for the denominator. Your class should have two instance variables of type `int`. Call the class `Rational`. Include a constructor with two arguments that can be used to set the instance variables of an object to any values. Also include a constructor that has only a single parameter of type `int`; call this single parameter `wholeNumber` and define the constructor so that the object will be initialized to the rational number `wholeNumber/1`. Also include a no-argument constructor that initializes an object to 0 (that is, to 0/1). Note that the numerator,

the denominator, or both may contain a minus sign. Define methods for addition, subtraction, multiplication, and division of objects of your class `Rational`. These methods should be static methods that each have two parameters of type `Rational` and return a value of type `Rational`. For example, `Rational.add(r1, r2)` will return the result of adding the two rational numbers (two objects of the class `Rational`, `r1` and `r2`). Define accessor and mutator methods as well as the methods `equals` and `toString`. You should include a method to normalize the sign of the rational number so that the denominator is positive and the numerator is either positive or negative. For example, after normalization, $4/-8$ would be represented the same as $-4/8$. Also write a test program to test your class.

Hints: Two rational numbers a/b and c/d are equal if $a*d$ equals $c*b$.

Part Two: Add a second version of the methods for addition, subtraction, multiplication, and division. These methods should have the same names as the static version but should use a calling object and a single argument. For example, this version of the `add` method (for addition) has a calling object and one argument. So `r1.add(r2)` returns the result of adding the rationals `r1` and `r2`. Note that your class should have all these methods; for example, there should be two methods named `add`.

Alternate Part Two: Add a second version of the methods for addition, subtraction, multiplication, and division. These methods should have the same names as the static version but should use a calling object and a single argument. The methods should be `void` methods. The result is given as the changed value of the calling object. For example, this version of the `add` method (for addition) has a calling object and one argument. Therefore,

```
r1.add(r2);
```

changes the values of the instance variables of `r1` so they represent the result of adding `r2` to the original version of `r1`. Note that your class should have all these methods; for example, there should be two methods named `add`.

(If you want to do both Part Two and Alternate Part Two, they must be two classes. You cannot include the methods from both Part Two and Alternate Part Two in a single class. Do you know why?)

7. Part One: Define a class for complex numbers. A complex number is a number of the form

```
a + b*i
```

For our purposes, a and b are numbers of type `double`, and i is a number that represents the quantity $\sqrt{-1}$. Represent a complex number as two values of type `double`. Name the instance variables `real` and `imaginary`. (The instance variable for the number that is multiplied by i is the one called `imaginary`.) Call the class `Complex`. Include a constructor with two parameters of type `double` that can be used to set the instance variables of an object to any values. Also include a constructor that has only a single parameter of type `double`; call this parameter `realPart` and define the constructor so that the object will be initialized to `realPart + 0*i`. Also include a no-argument constructor that initializes an object to 0 (that is, to `0 + 0*i`). Define accessor and mutator methods as well as the methods `equals` and `toString`. Define static methods for addition, subtraction, and multiplication of objects of your class `Complex`. These methods should be static and should each have two parameters of type `Complex` and return a value of type `Complex`. For example, `Complex.add(c1, c2)` will return the result of adding the two complex numbers (two objects of the class `Complex`) `c1` and `c2`. Also write a test program to test your class.

Hints: To add or subtract two complex numbers, you add or subtract the two instance variables of type `double`. The product of two complex numbers is given by the following formula:

```
(a + b *i)*(c + d *i) = (a *c - b *d) + (a *d + b *c)*i
```

Part Two: Add a second version of the methods for addition, subtraction, and multiplication. These methods should have the same names as the static version but should use a calling object and a single argument. For example, this version of the `add` method (for addition) has a calling object and one argument. So `c1.add(c2)` returns the result of adding the complex numbers `c1` and `c2`. Note that your class should have all these methods; for example, there should be two methods named `add`.

Alternate Part Two: Add a second version of the methods for addition, subtraction, and multiplication. These methods should have the same names as the static version but should use a calling object and a single argument. The methods will be `void` methods. The result is given as the changed value of the calling object. For example, this version of the `add` method (for addition) has a calling object and one argument. Therefore,

```
c1.add(c2);
```

changes the values of the instance variables of `c1` so they represent the result of adding `c2` to the original version of `c1`. Note that your class should have all these methods; for example, there should be two methods named `add`.

(If you want to do both Part Two and Alternate Part Two, they must be two classes. You cannot include the methods from both Part Two and Alternate Part Two in a single class. Do you know why?)

8. Programming Project 4.12 asked you to create a `PizzaOrder` class that stores an order consisting of up to three pizzas. Extend this class with the following methods and constructor:

- `public int getNumPizzas()`—returns the number of pizzas in the order.
- `public Pizza getPizza1()`—returns the first pizza in the order or `null` if `pizza1` is not set.
- `public Pizza getPizza2()`—returns the second pizza in the order or `null` if `pizza2` is not set.
- `public Pizza getPizza3()`—returns the third pizza in the order or `null` if `pizza3` is not set.

- A copy constructor that takes another `PizzaOrder` object and makes an independent copy of its pizzas. This might be useful if using an old order as a starting point for a new order.

Write a main method to test the new methods. Changing the pizzas in the new order should not change the pizzas in the original order. For example,

```
Pizza pizza1 = // Code to create a large pizza, 1 cheese, 1 ham
Pizza pizza2 = // Code to create a medium pizza, 2 cheese,
               // 2 pepperoni
PizzaOrder order1 = // Code to create an order
order1.setNumPizzas(2); // 2 pizzas in the order
order1.setPizza1(pizza1); // Set first pizza
order1.setPizza2(pizza2); // Set second pizza
double total = order1.calcTotal(); // Should be 18+20 = 38
PizzaOrder order2 = new PizzaOrder(order1); // Use copy
                        // constructor
order2.getPizza1().setNumCheeseToppings(3); // Change toppings
double total = order2.calcTotal(); // Should be 22 + 20 = 42
double origTotal = order1.calcTotal(); // Should still be 38
```

Note that the first three lines of code are incomplete. You must complete them as part of the Programming Project.

VideoNote
Solution to Programming Project 5.9

9. Use `javadoc` to generate HTML documentation for the code in Display 5.19. Use the `@author` and `@version` tag for the description of the entire class. Add a comment for every public method or constructor using the `@param` and `@return` tags when appropriate.

10. First, complete Programming Project 4.13 from Chapter 4.

    Modify the main method with a loop so that an arbitrary number of `BoxOfProduce` objects are created and substitutions are allowed for each box. Add a menu so the user can decide when to stop creating boxes.

    You would like to throw in a free recipe flyer for salsa verde if the box contains tomatillos. However, there are only five recipe flyers. Add a static variable to the `BoxOfProduce` class that counts the number of recipe flyers remaining and initialize it to 5. Also add an instance variable that indicates whether or not the box contains a recipe flyer and modify the `toString()` method to also output "`salsa verde recipe`" if the box contains a recipe flyer. Finally, add logic inside the class so that if the box contains at least one order of tomatillos then it automatically gets a recipe flyer until all of the recipe flyers are gone. Note that a box should only get one recipe flyer even if there are multiple orders of tomatillos.

    Test your class by creating boxes with tomatillos from your menu until all of the flyers are gone.

Arrays 6

6 Arrays

Memory is necessary for all the operations of reason.

BLAISE PASCAL, *Pensées*

Introduction

An *array* is a data structure used to process a collection of data that is all of the same type, such as a list of numbers of type `double` or a list of strings. In this chapter, we introduce you to the basics of defining and using arrays in Java.

Prerequisites

Section 6.1 requires understanding of only Chapters 1 through 3 and Section 4.1 of Chapter 4. Indeed, much less than all of Section 4.1 is needed. All you really need from Section 4.1 is to have some idea of what an object is and what an instance variable is.

The remaining sections require Chapters 1 through 5 with the exception that an understanding of Section 5.4 on packages and `javadoc` is not required.

6.1 Introduction to Arrays

It is a capital mistake to theorize before one has data.

SIR ARTHUR CONAN DOYLE, *Scandal in Bohemia* (SHERLOCK HOLMES)

Suppose we wish to write a program that reads in five test scores and performs some manipulations on these scores. For instance, the program might compute the highest test score and then output the amount by which each score falls short of the highest. The highest score is not known until all five scores are read in. Hence, all five scores must be retained in storage so that after the highest score is computed, each score can be compared to it. To retain the five scores, we will need something equivalent to five variables of type `int`. We could use five individual variables of type `int`, but keeping track of five variables is hard, and we may later want to change our program to handle 100 scores; certainly, keeping track of 100 variables is impractical. An array is the perfect solution. An **array** behaves like a list of variables with a uniform naming mechanism that can be declared in a single line of simple code. For example, the names for the five individual variables we need might be `score[0]`, `score[1]`, `score[2]`, `score[3]`, and `score[4]`. The part that does not change—in this case, `score`—is the name of the array. The part that can change is the integer in the square brackets `[]`.

array

Creating and Accessing Arrays

In Java, an array is a special kind of object, but it is often more useful to think of it as a collection of variables all of the same type. For example, an array that behaves like a collection of five variables of type `double` can be created as follows:

```
double[] score = new double[5];
```

This is like declaring the following to be five variables of type `double`:

indexed variable

```
score[0], score[1], score[2], score[3], score[4]
```

subscripted variable

element

index, subscript

length, size

The individual variables that make up the array are referred to in a variety of different ways. We will call them **indexed variables**, though they are also sometimes called **subscripted variables** or **elements** of the array. The number in square brackets is called an **index** or a **subscript**. In Java, *indices are numbered starting with* `0`, *not any number*. The number of indexed variables in an array is called the **length** or **size** of the array. When an array is created, the length of the array is given in square brackets after the array name. The indexed variables are then numbered (also using square brackets) starting with `0` and ending with the integer that is *one less than the length of the array.*

The following example:

```
double[] score = new double[5];
```

is really shorthand for the following two statements:

```
double[] score;
score = new double[5];
```

The first statement declares the variable `score` to be of the array type `double[]`. The second statement creates an array with five indexed variables of type `double` and makes the variable `score` a name for the array. You may use any expression that evaluates to a nonnegative `int` value in place of the `5` in square brackets. In particular, you can fill a variable with a value read from the keyboard and use the variable in place of the `5`. In this way, the size of the array can be determined when the program is run.

base type

An array can have indexed variables of any type, as long as they are all of the same type. This type is called the **base type** of the array. In our example, the base type of the array `score` is `double`. To declare an array with base type `int`, simply use the type name `int` instead of `double` when the array is declared and created. The base type of an array can be any type. In particular, it can be a class type.

Each of the five indexed variables of our example array `score` can be used just like any other variable of type `double`. For example, all of the following are allowed in Java:

```
score[3] = 32;
score[0] = score[3] + 10;
System.out.println(score[0]);
```

The five indexed variables of our sample array `score` are more than just five plain old variables of type `double`. That number in square brackets is part of the indexed variable's name. So, your program can compute the name of one of these variables.

> **Declaring and Creating an Array**
>
> Declare an array name and create an array in almost the same way that you create and name objects of classes. There is only a slight difference in the syntax.
>
> **SYNTAX**
>
> *Base_Type*`[]` *Array_Name* `= new` *Base_Type*`[`*Length*`];`
>
> The *Length* may be given as any expression that evaluates to a nonnegative integer. In particular, *Length* can be an `int` variable.
>
> **EXAMPLES**
>
> ```
> char[] line = new char[80];
> double[] reading = new double[300];
> Person[] specimen = new Person[100];
> ```
>
> `Person` is a class.

Instead of writing an integer constant in the square brackets, you can use any expression that evaluates to an integer that is at least `0` and at most `4`. So, the following is allowed:

```
System.out.println(score[index] + " is at position " + index);
```

where `index` is a variable of type `int` that has been given one of the values `0`, `1`, `2`, `3`, or `4`.

When we refer to these indexed variables grouped together into one collective item, we will call them an *array*. So, we can refer to the array named `score` (without using any square brackets).

The program in Display 6.1 shows an example of using our sample array `score` as five indexed variables, all of type `double`.

Note that the program can compute the name of an indexed variable by using a variable as the index, as in the following `for` loop:

```
for (index = 0; index < 5; index++)
    System.out.println(score[index] + " differs from max by "
                                      + (max - score[index]));
```

square brackets [ ]

Do not confuse the three ways to use the **square brackets `[]`** with an array name. First, the square brackets can be used to create a type name, such as the `double[]` in the following:

```
double[] score;
```

Second, the square brackets can be used with an integer value as part of the special syntax Java uses to create a new array, as in

```
score = new double[5];
```

Display 6.1 **An Array Used in a Program** (part 1 of 2)

```
import java.util.Scanner;

public class ArrayOfScores
{
    /**
     Reads in 5 scores and shows how much each
     score differs from the highest score.
    */
    public static void main(String[] args)
    {
        Scanner keyboard = new Scanner(System.in);
        double[] score = new double[5];
        int index;
        double max;

        System.out.println("Enter 5 scores:");
        score[0] = keyboard.nextDouble();
        max = score[0];
        for (index = 1; index < 5; index++)
        {
            score[index] = keyboard.nextDouble();
            if (score[index] > max)
                max = score[index];
        //max is the largest of the values score[0],..., score[index].
        }

        System.out.println("The highest score is " + max);
        System.out.println("The scores are:");
        for (index = 0; index < 5; index++)
            System.out.println(score[index] + " differs from max by "
                                        + (max - score[index]));
    }
}
```

Sample Dialogue

```
Enter 5 scores:
80  99.9  75  100  85.5
The highest score is 100
The scores are:
80.0 differs from max by 20
99.9 differs from max by 0.1
75.0 differs from max by 25
100.0 differs from max by 0.0
85.5 differs from max by 14.5
```

Due to imprecision in floating-point arithmetic, this value probably will only be a close approximation to `0.1`.

(continued)

Display 6.1 An Array Used in a Program (part 2 of 2)

A Common Way to Visualize an Array:

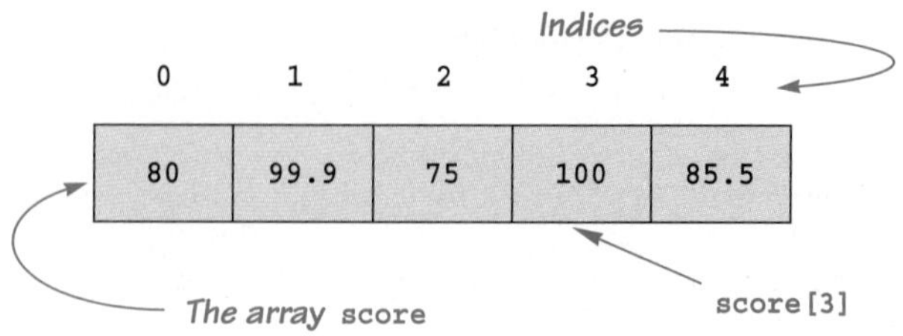

The third use of square brackets is to name an indexed variable of the array, such as `score[0]` or `score[3]`, as illustrated by the following line:

```
max = score[0];
```

As we mentioned previously, the integer inside the square brackets can be any expression that evaluates to a suitable integer, as illustrated by the following:

```
int next = 1;
score[next + 3] = 100;
System.out.println(
            "Score at position 4 is " + score[next + 3]);
```

Note that, in the preceding code, `score[next + 3]` and `score[4]` are the same indexed variable, because `next + 3` evaluates to `4`.

The `length` Instance Variable

In Java, an array is considered to be an object, and, like other objects, it might have instance variables. As it turns out, an array has only one public instance variable, which is named `length`. This instance variable is automatically set to the size of the array when the array is created. For example, if you create an array as follows,

```
double[] score = new double[5];
```

then `score.length` has a value of `5`.

The `length` instance variable can be used to make your program clearer by replacing an unnamed constant (such as `5`), whose meaning may not be obvious, with a meaningful name such as `score.length`. In Display 6.2, we rewrote the program in Display 6.1 using the `length` instance variable.

Display 6.2 The `length` Instance Variable

The sample dialogue is the same as in Display 6.1.

```
import java.util.Scanner;

public class ArrayOfScores2
{
    /**
     Reads in 5 scores and shows how much each
     Score differs from the highest score.
    */
    public static void main(String[] args)
    {
        Scanner keyboard = new Scanner(System.in);
        double[] score = new double[5];
        int index;
        double max;

        System.out.println("Enter " + score.length + " scores:");
        score[0] = keyboard.nextDouble();
        max = score[0];
        for (index = 1; index < score.length; index++)
        {
            score[index] = keyboard.nextDouble();
            if (score[index] > max)
                max = score[index];
        //max is the largest of the values score[0],..., score[index].
        }

        System.out.println("The highest score is " + max);
        System.out.println("The scores are:");
        for (index = 0; index < score.length; index++)
            System.out.println(score[index] + " differs from max by "
                                          + (max - score[index]));
    }
}
```

The `length` instance variable cannot be changed by your program (other than by creating a new array with another use of `new`).[1] For example, the following is illegal:

```
score.length = 10; //Illegal
```

[1]The technical details are as follows: The instance variable `length` is created when the array is created and is declared to be `public final int`.

TIP: Use `for` Loops with Arrays

The second `for` loop in Display 6.2 illustrates a common way to step through an entire array using a `for` loop:

```
for (index = 0; index < score.length; index++)
    System.out.println(score[index] + " differs from max by "
                                    + (max - score[index]));
```

The `for` loop is ideally suited for performing array manipulations. ■

PITFALL: Array Indices Always Start with Zero

The indices of an array always start with `0` and end with the integer that is one less than the size of the array. ■

PITFALL: Array Index Out of Bounds

The most common programming error made when using arrays is attempting to use a nonexistent array index. For example, consider the following:

```
int[] a = new int[6];
```

When using the array `a`, every index expression must evaluate to one of the integers `0` through `5`. For example, if your program contains the indexed variable `a[i]`, the `i` must evaluate to one of the six integers `0`, `1`, `2`, `3`, `4`, or `5`. If `i` evaluates to anything else, that is an error. When an index expression evaluates to some value other than those allowed by the array declaration, the index is said to be **out of bounds**. If your program attempts to use an array index that is out of bounds, then your program will end with an error message.[2] Note that this is a run-time error message, not a compiler error message.

illegal array index

out of bounds

Array indices get out of bounds most commonly at the first or last iteration of a loop that processes the array. So, it pays to carefully check all array processing loops to be certain that they begin and end with legal array indices. ■

[2]Technically speaking, an `ArrayIndexOutOfBounds` Exception is thrown. We will discuss exceptions in Chapter 9. Until you learn about handling exceptions, they will simply appear as error conditions to you.

Initializing Arrays

An array can be initialized when it is declared. When initializing the array, the values for the various indexed variables are enclosed in braces and separated with commas. The expression with the braces is placed on the right-hand side of an assignment operator. For example,

```
int [] age = {2, 12, 1};
```

The array length (size) is automatically set to the number of values in the braces. So, this initializing declaration is equivalent to the following statements:

```
int [] age = new int [3];
age[0] = 2;
age[1] = 12;
age[2] = 1;
```

You can also initialize array elements using a `for` loop. For example,

```
double[] reading = new double[100];
int index;
for (index = 0; index < reading.length; index++)
    reading[index] = 42.0;
```

automatic initialization

If you do not initialize the elements of an array, they will automatically be initialized to a default value for the base type. The default values are the usual ones. For numeric types, the default value is the zero of the type. For base type `char`, the default value is the nonprintable zeroth character `(char)0`, not the space character. For the type `boolean`, the default value is `false`. For class types, the default value is `null`. For example, if you do not initialize an array of `doubles`, each element of the array will be initialized to `0.0`.

MyProgrammingLab™

Self-Test Exercises

1. In the array declaration

   ```
   String[] word = new String[5];
   ```

   what is

   a. the array name?
   b. the base type?
   c. the length of the array?
   d. the range of values an index accessing this array can have?
   e. one of the indexed variables (or elements) of this array?

(continued)

MyProgrammingLab™

Self-Test Exercises (continued)

2. In the array

```
double[] score = new double[10];
```

what is

a. the value of `score.length`?
b. the first index of `score`?
c. the last index of `score`?

3. What is the output of the following code?

```
char[] letter = {'a', 'b', 'c'};
for (int index = 0; index < letter.length; index++)
    System.out.print(letter[index] + ", ");
```

4. What is the output of the following code?

```
double[] a = {1.1, 2.2, 3.3};
System.out.println(a[0] + " " + a[1] + " " + a[2]);
a[1] = a[2];
System.out.println(a[0] + " " + a[1] + " " + a[2]);
```

5. What is wrong with the following piece of code?

```
int[] sampleArray = new int[10];
for (int index = 1; index <= sampleArray.length; index++)
     sampleArray[index] = 3*index;
```

6. Suppose we expect the elements of the array `a` to be ordered so that

```
a[0] ≤ a [1] ≤ a [2]≤ ...
```

However, to be safe we want our program to test the array and issue a warning in case it turns out that some elements are out of order. The following code is supposed to output such a warning, but it contains a bug. What is the bug?

```
double[] a = new double[10];
    <Some code to fill the array a goes here.>
for (int index = 0; index < a.length; index++)
    if (a[index] > a[index + 1])
         System.out.println("Array elements " + index +
             " and " + (index + 1) + " are out of order.");
```

PITFALL: An Array of Characters Is Not a String

An array of characters, such as the array `a` created below, is conceptually a list of characters; therefore, it is conceptually like a string:

```
char[] a = {'A', ' ', 'B', 'i', 'g', ' ', 'H', 'i', '!'};
```

However, an array of characters, such as `a`, is not an object of the class `String`. In particular, the following is illegal in Java:

```
String s = a;
```

Similarly, you cannot normally use an array of characters, such as `a`, as an argument for a parameter of type `String`.

It is, however, easy to convert an array of characters to an object of type `String`. The class `String` has a constructor that has a single parameter of type `char[]`. So, you can obtain a `String` value corresponding to an array of characters, such as `a`, as follows:

```
String s = new String(a);
```

The object `s` will have the same sequence of characters as the array `a`. The object `s` is an independent copy; any changes made to `a` will have no effect on `s`. Note that this always uses the entire array `a`.

There is also a `String` constructor that allows you to specify a subrange of an array of characters `a`. For example,

```
String s2 = new String(a, 2, 3);
```

produces a `String` object with `3` characters from the array `a` starting at index `2`. So, if `a` is as above, then

```
System.out.println(s2);
```

outputs

```
Big
```

Although an array of characters is not an object of the class `String`, it does have some things in common with `String` objects. For example, you can output an array of characters using `println`, as follows,

```
System.out.println(a);
```

which produces the output

```
A Big Hi!
```

provided `a` is as given previously. ■

6.2 Arrays and References

A little more than kin, and less than kind.

WILLIAM SHAKESPEARE, *Hamlet*

Just like a variable of one of the class types you have seen, a variable of an array type holds a reference. In this section, we explore the consequences of this fact, including a discussion of array parameters. We will see that arrays are objects and that array types can be considered class types, but somewhat different kinds of class types than what you are used to. Arrays and the kinds of classes we have seen before this chapter are *a little more than kin, and less than kind.*

Arrays Are Objects

There are two ways to view an array: as a collection of indexed variables and as a single item whose value is a collection of values of the base type. In Section 6.1, we discussed using arrays as a collection of indexed variables. We will now discuss arrays from the second point of view.

An array can be viewed as a single item whose value is a collection of values of the base type. An array variable (as opposed to an array indexed variable) names the array as a single item. For example, the following declares a variable of an array type:

```
double[] a;
```

This variable a can and will contain a single value. The expression

```
new double[10]
```

creates an array object and stores the object in memory. The following assignment statement places a reference to (the memory address of) this array object in the variable a:

```
a = new double[10];
```

Typically, we combine all this into a single statement as follows:

```
double[] a = new double[10];
```

Notice that this is almost exactly the same as the way that we view objects of a class type. In Java, an array is considered an object. Whenever Java documentation says that something applies to objects, it means that it applies to arrays as well as objects of the class types we have seen up to now. You will eventually see examples of methods that can take arguments that may be objects of any kind. These methods will accept array objects as arguments as well as objects of an ordinary class type. Arrays are somewhat peculiar in how they relate to classes. Some authorities say array types are not classes and some say they are. But, all authorities agree that the arrays themselves are objects. Given that arrays are objects, it seems that one should view array types as classes, and we will do so. However, although an array type `double[]` is a class, the syntax for creating an array object is a bit different. To create an array, use the following syntax:

```
double[] a = new double[10];
```

You can view the expression `new double[10]` as an invocation of a constructor that uses a nonstandard syntax. (The nonstandard syntax was used to be consistent with the syntax used for arrays in older programming languages.)

As we have already seen, every array has an instance variable named `length`, which is a good example of viewing an array as an object. As with any other class type, array variables contain memory addresses, or, as they are usually called in Java, *references*. So, array types are reference types.[3]

Since an array is an object, you might be tempted to think of the indexed variables of an array, such as `a[0]`, `a[1]`, and so forth, as being instance variables of the object. This is actually a pretty good analogy, but it is not literally true. Indexed variables are not instance variables of the array. Indexed variables are a special kind of variable peculiar to arrays. The only instance variable in an array is the `length` instance variable.

An array object is a collection of items of the base type. Viewed as such, an array is an object that can be assigned with the assignment operator and plugged in for a parameter of an array type. Because an array type is a reference type, the behaviors of arrays with respect to assignment `=`, `==`, and parameter passing mechanisms are the same as what we have already described for classes. In the next few subsections, we discuss these details about arrays.

Arrays Are Objects

In Java, arrays are considered to be objects, and, although there is some disagreement on this point, you can safely view an array type as a class type.

Array Types Reference Types

A variable of an array type holds the address of where the array object is stored in memory. This memory address is called a **reference** to the array object.

---

[3]In many programming languages, such as C++, arrays are also reference types just as they are in Java. So, this detail about arrays is not peculiar to Java.

PITFALL: Arrays with a Class Base Type

The base type of an array can be of any type, including a class type. For example, suppose `Date` is a class and consider the following:

```
Date[] holidayList = new Date[20];
```

VideoNote
Arrays of Objects

This creates the 20 indexed variables (`holidayList[0]`, `holidayList[1]`, ..., `holidayList[19]`). It is important to note that this creates 20 *indexed variables* of type `Date`. This does not create 20 *objects* of type `Date`. (The index variables are automatically initialized to `null`, not to an object of the class `Date`.) Like any other variable of type `Date`, the indexed variables require an invocation of a constructor using `new` to create an object. One way to complete the initialization of the array `holidayList` is as follows:

```
Date[] holidayList = new Date[20];
for (int i = 0; i < holidayList.length; i++)
    holidayList[i] = new Date( );
```

If you omit the `for` loop (and do not do something else more or less equivalent), then when you run your code, you will undoubtedly get an error message indicating a "null pointer exception." If you do not use `new` to create an object, an indexed variable like `holidayList[i]` is just a variable that names no object and hence cannot be used as the calling object for any method. Whenever you are using an array with a class base type and you get an error message referring to a "Null Pointer Exception," it is likely that your indexed variables do not name any objects and you need to add something such as the above `for` loop. ■

Array Parameters

You can use both array indexed variables and entire arrays as arguments to methods, although they are different types of parameters. We first discuss array indexed variables as arguments to methods.

indexed variable arguments

An indexed variable can be an argument to a method in exactly the same way that any variable of the array base type can be an argument. For example, suppose a program contains the following declarations:

```
double n = 0;
double[] a = new double[10];
int i;
```

If `myMethod` takes one argument of type `double`, then the following is legal:

```
myMethod(n);
```

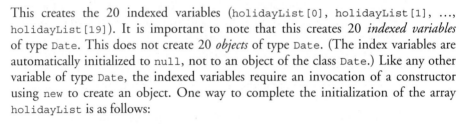

Since an indexed variable of the array `a` is also a variable of type `double`, just like `n`, the following is equally legal:

```
myMethod(a[3]);
```

There is one subtlety that does apply to indexed variables used as arguments. For example, consider the following method call:

```
myMethod(a[i]);
```

If the value of `i` is `3`, then the argument is `a[3]`. On the other hand, if the value of `i` is `0`, then this call is equivalent to the following:

```
myMethod(a[0]);
```

The indexed expression is evaluated to determine exactly which indexed variable is given as the argument.

Array Indexed Variables as Arguments

An array indexed variable can be used as an argument anyplace that a variable of the array's base type can be used. For example, suppose you have the following:

```
double[] a = new double[10];
```

Indexed variables such as `a[3]` and `a[index]` can then be used as arguments to any method that accepts a `double` as an argument.

entire array parameters

You can also define a method that has a formal parameter for an entire array so that when the method is called, the argument that is plugged in for this formal parameter is an entire array. Whenever you need to specify an array type, the type name has the form *Base_Type*`[]`, so this is how you specify a parameter type for an entire array. For example, the method `doubleArrayElements`, given in what follows, will accept any array of `double` as its single argument:

```
public class SampleClass
{
    public static void doubleArrayElements(double[] a)
    {
        int i;
        for (i = 0; i < a.length; i++)
            a[i] = a[i]*2;
    }
    < The rest of the class definition goes here.>
}
```

To illustrate this, suppose you have the following in some method definition,

```
double[] a = new double[10];
double[] b = new double[30];
```

and suppose that the elements of the arrays a and b have been given values. Both of the following are then legal method invocations:

```
SampleClass.doubleArrayElements(a);
SampleClass.doubleArrayElements(b);
```

Note that no square brackets are used when you give an entire array as an argument to a method.

An array type is a reference type just as a class type is, so, as with a class type argument, a method can change the data in an array argument. To phrase it more precisely, a method can change the values stored in the indexed variables of an array argument. This is illustrated by the preceding method `doubleArrayElements`.

length of array arguments

An array type parameter does not specify the length of the array argument that may be plugged in for the parameter. An array knows its length and stores it in the `length` instance variable. The same array parameter can be replaced with array arguments of different lengths. Note that the preceding method `doubleArrayElements` can take an array of any length as an argument.

PITFALL: Use of = and == with Arrays

assignment with arrays

Array types are reference types; that is, an array variable contains the memory address of the array it names. The assignment operator copies this memory address. For example, consider the following code:

```
double[] a = new double[10];
double[] b = new double[10];
int i;
for (i = 0; i < a.length; i++)
    a[i] = i;
b = a;
System.out.println("a[2] = " + a[2] + " b[2] = " + b[2]);
a[2] = 42;
System.out.println("a[2] = " + a[2] + " b[2] = " + b[2]);
```

This will produce the following output:

```
a[2] = 2.0 b[2] = 2.0
a[2] = 42.0 b[2] = 42.0
```

PITFALL: (continued)

The assignment statement `b = a;` copies the memory address from `a` to `b` so that the array variable `b` contains the same memory address as the array variable `a`. After the assignment statement, `a` and `b` are two different names for the same array. Thus, when we change the value of `a[2]`, we are also changing the value of `b[2]`.

Unless you want two array variables to be two names for the same array (and on rare occasions, you do want this), you should not use the assignment operator with arrays. If you want the arrays `a` and `b` in the preceding code to be different arrays with the same values in each index position, then instead of the assignment statement

```
b = a;
```

you need to use something such as the following:

```
int i;
for (i = 0; (i < a.length) && (i < b.length); i++)
    b[i] = a[i];
```

Note that the above code will not make `b` an exact copy of `a`, unless `a` and `b` have the same length.

== with arrays

The equality operator == does not test two arrays to see if they contain the same values. It tests two arrays to see if they are stored in the same location in the computer's memory. For example, consider the following code:

```
int[] c = new int[10];
int[] d = new int[10];
int i;
for (i = 0; i < c.length; i++)
    c[i] = i;
for (i = 0; i < d.length; i++)
    d[i] = i;

if (c == d)
    System.out.println("c and d are equal by ==.");
else
    System.out.println("c and d are not equal by ==.");
```

This produces the output

```
c and d are not equal by ==
```

(continued)

PITFALL: (continued)

even though `c` and `d` contain the same integers in the same indexed variables. A comparison using `==` will say they are not equal because `==` checks only the contents of the array variables `c` and `d`, which are memory addresses, and `c` and `d` contain different memory addresses.

If you want to test two arrays to see if they contain the same elements, then you can define an `equalArrays` method for the arrays, just as you defined an `equals` method for a class. Display 6.3 contains one possible definition of `equalArrays` for arrays in a small demonstration class. ■

MyProgrammingLab™

Self-Test Exercises

7. Consider the following class definition:

```
public class SomeClass
{
    public static void doSomething(int n)
    {
        <Some code goes in here.>
    }
<The rest of the definition is irrelevant to this question.>
```

Which of the following are acceptable method calls?

```
int[] a = {4, 5, 6};
int number = 2;
SomeClass.doSomething(number);
SomeClass.doSomething(a[2]);
SomeClass.doSomething(a[3]);
SomeClass.doSomething(a[number]);
SomeClass.doSomething(a);
```

8. Write a method definition for a static `void` method called `oneMore`, which has a formal parameter for an array of integers and increases the value of each array element by one. (The definition will go in a class, but you need only give the method definition.)

9. Write a method named `outOfOrder` that takes as a parameter an array of `double` and returns a value of type `int`. This method will test the array for being out of order, meaning that the array violates the condition:

```
a[0] <= a[1] <= a[2] <= ...
```

MyProgrammingLab™

Self-Test Exercises (continued)

The method returns -1 if the elements are not out of order; otherwise, it returns the index of the first element of the array that is out of order. For example, consider the following declaration:

```
double[] a = {1.2, 2.1, 3.3, 2.5, 4.5,
                7.9, 5.4, 8.7, 9.9, 1.0};
```

In the array above, a[2] and a[3] are the first pair out of order, and a[3] is the first element out of order, so the method returns 3. If the array is sorted, the method returns -1.

10. The following method definition will compile, but does not work as you might hope. What is wrong with it?

```
public static void doubleSize(int[] a)
{
    a = new int[a.length * 2];
}
```

Array Parameters and Array Arguments

An argument to a method may be an entire array. Array arguments are like objects of a class, in that the method can change the data in an array argument; that is, a method can change the values stored in the indexed variables of an array argument. A method with an array parameter is defined and invoked as illustrated by the following examples. Note that the array parameter specifies the base type of the array, but not the length of the array.

EXAMPLE (OF ARRAY PARAMETERS)

```
public class AClass
{
    public static void listChars(char[] a)
    {
        int i;
        for (i = 0; i < a.length; i++)
            System.out.println(a[i] + " ");
    }
    public static void zeroAll(int[] anArray)
    {
        int i;
        for (i = 0; i < anArray.length; i++)
            anArray[i] = 0;
    }
        ...
}
```

EXAMPLE (OF ARRAY ARGUMENTS)

```
char[] c = new char[10];
int[] a = new int[10];
int[] b = new int[20];

    <Some code to fill the arrays goes here.>

AClass.listChars(c);
AClass.zeroAll(a);
AClass.zeroAll(b);
```

Note that arrays `a` and `b` have different lengths. Also note that no square brackets are used with array arguments.

Display 6.3 **Testing Arrays for Equality** (part 1 of 2)

```
public class DifferentEquals
{
    /**
     A demonstration to see how == and an equalArrays method are different.
    */
    public static void main(String[] args)
    {
        int[] c = new int[10];
        int[] d = new int[10];


        int i;
        for (i = 0; i < c.length; i++)
            c[i] = i;
        for (i = 0; i < d.length; i++)
            d[i] = i;
        if (c == d)
            System.out.println("c and d are equal by ==.");
        else
            System.out.println("c and d are not equal by ==.");

        System.out.println("== only tests memory addresses.");

        if (equalArrays(c, d))
            System.out.println(
                    "c and d are equal by the equalArrays method.");
        else
            System.out.println(
                    "c and d are not equal by the equalArrays method.");
```

The arrays `c` and `d` contain the same integers in each index position.

Display 6.3 **Testing Arrays for Equality** (part 2 of 2)

```
            System.out.println(
                  "An equalArrays method is usually a more useful test.");
    }

    public static boolean equalArrays(int[] a, int[] b)
    {
        if (a.length != b.length)
            return false;
        else
        {
            int i = 0;
            while (i < a.length)
            {
                if (a[i] != b[i])
                    return false;
                i++;
            }
        }

        return true;
    }

}
```

Sample Dialogue

```
c and d are not equal by ==.
== only tests memory addresses.
c and d are equal by the equalArrays method.
An equalArrays method is usually a more useful test.
```

Arguments for the Method `main` ★

The heading for the `main` method of a program looks as if it has a parameter for an array of base type of `String`:

```
public static void main(String[] args)
```

The identifier `args` is in fact a parameter of type `String[]`. Because `args` is a parameter, it could be replaced by any other nonkeyword identifier. The identifier `args` is traditional, but it is perfectly legal to use some other identifier.

We have never given `main` an array argument, or any other kind of argument, when we ran any of our programs. So, what did Java use as an argument to plug in for `args`? If no argument is given when you run your program, then a default empty array of strings is automatically provided as a default argument to `main` when you run your program.

It is possible to run a Java program in a way that provides an argument to plug in for this array of `String` parameters. You do not provide it as an array. You provide any number of string arguments when you run the program, and those string arguments will automatically be made elements of the array argument that is plugged in for `args` (or whatever name you use for the parameter to `main`). This is normally done by running the program from the command line of the operating system, like so:

```
java YourProgram Do Be Do
```

This will set `args[0]` to `"Do"`, `args[1]` to `"Be"`, `args[2]` to `"Do"`, and `args.length` to `3`. These three indexed variables can be used in the method `main`, as in the following sample program:

```
public class YourProgram
{
    public static void main(String[] args)
    {
        System.out.println(args[1] + " " + args[0]
                                        + " " + args[1]);
    }
}
```

If the above program is run from the command line as follows,

```
java YourProgram Do Be Do
```

the output produced by the program will be

```
Be Do Be
```

Be sure to note that the argument to `main` is an array of *strings*. If you want numbers, you must convert the string representations of the numbers to values of a number type or types.

The Method `main` Has an Array Parameter

The heading for the `main` method of a program is as follows:

```
public static void main(String[] args)
```

The identifier `args` is a parameter for an array of base type `String`. The details are explained in the text.

Methods that Return an Array

In Java, a method may return an array. You specify the return type for a method that returns an array in the same way that you specify a type for an array parameter. For example, the following is an example of a method that returns an array:

```
public static char[] upperCaseVersion(char[] a)
{
    char[] temp = new char[a.length];
    char i;
    for (i = 0; i < a.length; i++)
        temp[i] = Character.toUpperCase(a[i]);
    return temp;
}
```

Returning an Array

A method can return an array. The details are basically the same as for a method that returns an object of a class type.

SYNTAX (FOR A TYPICAL WAY OF RETURNING AN ARRAY)

```
public static Base_Type [] Method_Name(Parameter_List)
{
    Base_Type[] temp = new Base_Type[Array_Size]
   <Some code to fill temp goes here.>
    return temp;
}
```

The method need not be static and need not be public. You do not necessarily need to use a local array variable such as `temp`.

EXAMPLE (ASSUMED TO BE IN A CLASS DEFINITION)

```
public static int [] incrementedArray(int[] a,int increment)
{
    int[] temp = new int[a.length];
    int i;
    for (i = 0; i < a.length; i++)
        temp[i] = a[i] + increment;
    return temp;
}
```

Array Type Names

Whenever you need an array type name, whether for the type of an array variable declaration, the type of an array parameter, or the type for a method that returns an array, you specify the type name in the same way.

SYNTAX

Base_Type[]

EXAMPLES

```
double[] a = new double[10];
int[] giveIntArray(char[] arrayParameter)
{ ... }
```

MyProgrammingLab™

Self-Test Exercises

11. Give the definition of a method called `halfArray` that has a single parameter for an array of base type `double` and that returns another array of base type `double` that has the same length and in which each element has been divided by `2.0`. Make it a static method. To test it, you can add it to any class or, better yet, write a class with a test program in the method `main`.

12. What is wrong with the following method definition? It is an alternate definition of the method by the same name defined in the previous subsection. It will compile.

```
public static char[] upperCaseVersion(char[] a)
{
    char i;
    for (i = 0; i < a.length; i++)
         a[i] = Character.toUpperCase(a[i]);
    return a;
}
```

6.3 Programming with Arrays

Never trust to general impressions, my boy,
but concentrate yourself upon details.

SIR ARTHUR CONAN DOYLE,
A Case of Identity (SHERLOCK HOLMES)

In this section, we discuss partially filled arrays as well as how to use arrays as class instance variables.

Partially Filled Arrays

Often the exact size needed for an array is not known when a program is written or the size may vary from one run of the program to another. One common and easy way to handle this situation is to declare the array to be of the largest size the program could possibly need. The program is then free to use as much or as little of the array as needed.

partially filled array

Partially filled arrays require some care. The program must keep track of how much of the array is used and must not reference any indexed variable that has not been given a meaningful value. The program in Display 6.4 illustrates this point. It reads in a list of golf scores and shows how much each score differs from the average. This program will work for lists as short as 1 score, as long as 10 scores, and of any length in between. The scores are stored in the array `score`, which has 10 indexed variables, but the program uses only as much of the array as it needs. The variable `numberUsed` keeps track of how many elements are stored in the array. The elements (that is, the scores) are stored in positions `score[0]` through `score[numberUsed – 1]`. The details are very similar to what they would be if `numberUsed` were `score.length` and the entire array were used. Note that the variable `numberUsed` usually must be an argument to any method that manipulates the partially filled array. For example, the methods `showDifference` and `computeAverage` use the argument `numberUsed` to ensure that only meaningful array indices are used.

Display 6.4 **Partially Filled Array** (part 1 of 3)

```
import java.util.Scanner;

public class GolfScores
{
    public static final int MAX_NUMBER_SCORES = 10;

    /**
     Shows differences between each of a list of golf scores and their
     average.
    */
    public static void main(String[] args)
    {
        double[] score = new double[MAX_NUMBER_SCORES];
        int numberUsed = 0;

        System.out.println("This program reads golf scores and shows");
        System.out.println("how much each differs from the average.");
        System.out.println("Enter golf scores:");
        numberUsed = fillArray(score);
        showDifference(score, numberUsed);
    }
```

Contrary to normal practice, this allows fractional scores, such as 71.5. However, this makes it a better example for our purposes. (Anyway, when I play golf, losing a ball is only half a stroke penalty. Try it sometime.)

(continued)

Display 6.4 **Partially Filled Array** (part 2 of 3)

```
    /**
     Reads values into the array a. Returns the number of values placed
     in the array a.
    */
    public static int fillArray(double[] a)
    {
        System.out.println("Enter up to " + a.length
                             + " nonnegative numbers.");
        System.out.println("Mark the end of the list with a negative
        number.");
        Scanner keyboard = new Scanner(System.in);

        double next;
        int index = 0;
        next = keyboard.nextDouble();
        while ((next >= 0) && (index < a.length))
        {
            a[index] = next;
            index++;
            next = keyboard.nextDouble();
           //index is the number of array indexed variables used so far.
        }
        //index is the total number of array indexed variables used.
        if (next >= 0)
             System.out.println("Could only read in "
                              + a.length + " input values.");

        return index;
    }

    /**
     Precondition: numberUsed <= a.length.
                   a[0] through a[numberUsed-1] have values.
     Returns the average of numbers a[0] through a[numberUsed-1].
    */
    public static double computeAverage(double[] a, int numberUsed)
    {
        double total = 0;
        for (int index = 0; index < numberUsed; index++)
            total = total + a[index];
        if (numberUsed > 0)
        {
            return (total/numberUsed);
        }
        else
        {
            System.out.println("ERROR: Trying to average 0 numbers.");
            System.out.println("computeAverage returns 0.");
            return 0;
        }
    }
```

The value of `index` is the number of values stored in the array.

Display 6.4 **Partially Filled Array** (part 3 of 3)

```
    /**
     Precondition: numberUsed <= a.length.
                   The first numberUsed indexed variables of a have values.
     Postcondition: Gives screen output showing how much each of the first
     numberUsed elements of the array a differ from their average.
    */
    public static void showDifference(double[] a, int numberUsed)
    {
        double average = computeAverage(a, numberUsed);
        System.out.println("Average of the " + numberUsed
                                          + " scores = " + average);
        System.out.println("The scores are:");
        for (int index = 0; index < numberUsed; index++)
        System.out.println(a[index] + " differs from average by "
                                 + (a[index] - average));
    }
}
```

Sample Dialogue

```
This program reads golf scores and shows
how much each differs from the average.
Enter golf scores:
Enter up to 10 nonnegative numbers.
Mark the end of the list with a negative number.
69 74 68 -1
Average of the 3 scores = 70.3333
The scores are:
69.0 differs from average by -1.33333
74.0 differs from average by 3.66667
68.0 differs from average by -2.33333
```

MyProgrammingLab™

Self-Test Exercises

13. Complete the definition of the following method that could be added to the class `GolfScores` in Display 6.4:

```
/**
 Precondition: numberUsed <= argumentArray.length;
 the first numberUsed indexed variables of argumentArray
 have values.
 Returns an array of length numberUsed whose ith element
 is argumentArray[i] - adjustment.
*/
public static double[] differenceArray(
 double[] argumentArray, int numberUsed, double adjustment)
```

(continued)

MyProgrammingLab™

Self-Test Exercises (continued)

14. Rewrite the class `GolfScores` from Display 6.4 using the method `differenceArray` from Self-Test Exercise 13.

15. Rewrite the class `GolfScores` from Display 6.4 making the array of scores a static variable. Also, make the `int` variable `numberUsed` a static variable. Start with Display 6.4, not with the answer to Self-Test Exercise 14. *Hint:* All, or at least most, methods will have no parameters.

EXAMPLE: A Class for Partially Filled Arrays

If you are going to use some array in a disciplined way, such as using the array as a partially filled array, then it is often best to create a class that has the array as an instance variable and to have the constructors and methods of the class provide the needed operations as methods. For example, in Display 6.5, we wrote a class for a partially filled array of doubles. In Display 6.6, we wrote the program in Display 6.4 using this class.

In Display 6.6, we wrote the code to be exactly analogous to that of Display 6.4 so that you could see how one program mirrors the other. However, this resulted in occasionally recomputing a value several times. For example, the method `computeAverage` contains the following expression three times:

```
a.getNumberOfElements( )
```

Because the `PartiallyFilledArray a` is not changed in this method, these each return the same value. Some programmers advocate computing this value once only and saving the value in a variable. These programmers would use something such as the following for the definition of `computeAverage` rather than what we used in Display 6.6. The variable `numberOfElementsIna` is used to save a value so it need not be recomputed.

```
public static double computeAverage(PartiallyFilledArray a)
{
    double total = 0;
    double numberOfElementsIna = a.getNumberOfElements();
    for (int index = 0; index < numberOfElementsIna; index++)
        total = total + a.getElement(index);
    if (numberOfElementsIna > 0)
    {
        return (total/numberOfElementsIna);
    }
    else
    {
```

EXAMPLE: (continued)

```
            System.out.println(
                        "ERROR: Trying to average 0 numbers.");
            System.out.println("computeAverage returns 0.");
            return 0;
        }
    }
```

This is not likely to produce a noticeable difference in the efficiency of the program in Display 6.6, but if the number of elements in the `PartiallyFilledArray` were large so that the for loop would be executed many times, it might make a difference in a situation where efficiency is critical.

Display 6.5 **Partially Filled Array Class** (part 1 of 4)

```
/**
 Class for a partially filled array of doubles. The class enforces the
 following invariant: All elements are at the beginning of the array in
 locations 0, 1, 2, and so forth up to a highest index with no gaps.
*/
public class PartiallyFilledArray
{
    private int maxNumberElements; //Same as a.length
    private double[] a;
    private int numberUsed; //Number of indices currently in use

    /**
     Sets the maximum number of allowable elements to 10.
    */
    PartiallyFilledArray()
    {
        maxNumberElements = 10;
        a = new double[maxNumberElements];
        numberUsed = 0;
    }

    /**
     Precondition arraySize > 0.
    */
    PartiallyFilledArray(int arraySize)
    {
        if (arraySize <= 0)
        {
            System.out.println("Error Array size zero or negative.");
            System.exit(0);
        }
```

(continued)

Display 6.5 **Partially Filled Array Class** (part 2 of 4)

```
        maxNumberElements = arraySize;
        a = new double[maxNumberElements];
        numberUsed = 0;
    }
    PartiallyFilledArray(PartiallyFilledArray original)
    {
        if (original == null)
        {
            System.out.println("Fatal Error: aborting program.");
            System.exit(0);
        }
        maxNumberElements =
                 original.maxNumberElements;
        numberUsed = original.numberUsed;
        a = new double[maxNumberElements];
        for (int i = 0; i < numberUsed; i++)
            a[i] = original.a[i];
    }
```

Note that the instance variable **a** *is a copy of* **original.a**. *The following would not be correct:* **a = original.a;**. *This point is discussed later in this chapter in the subsection entitled "Privacy Leaks with Array Instance variables."*

```
    /**
     Adds newElement to the first unused array position.
    */
    public void add(double newElement)
    {
        if (numberUsed >= a.length)
        {
            System.out.println("Error: Adding to a full array.");
            System.exit(0);
        }
        else
        {
            a[numberUsed] = newElement;
            numberUsed++;
        }
    }

    public double getElement(int index)
    {
        if (index < 0 || index >= numberUsed)
        {
            System.out.println("Error:Illegal or unused index.");
            System.exit(0);
        }
        return a[index];
    }
```

Display 6.5 **Partially Filled Array Class** (part 3 of 4)

```
    /**
     index must be an index in use or the first unused index.
    */
    public void resetElement(int index, double newValue)
    {
        if (index < 0 || index >= maxNumberElements)
        {
            System.out.println("Error:Illegal index.");
            System.exit(0);
        }
        else if (index > numberUsed)
        {
            System.out.println(
                      "Error: Changing an index that is too large.");
            System.exit(0);
        }
        else
            a[index] = newValue;
    }

    public void deleteLast()
    {
        if (empty())
        {
            System.out.println("Error:Deleting from an empty array.");
            System.exit(0);
        }
        else
            numberUsed--;
    }
    /**
     Deletes the element in position index. Moves down all elements with
     indices higher than the deleted element.
    */
    public void delete(int index)
    {
        if (index < 0 || index >= numberUsed)
        {
            System.out.println("Error:Illegal or unused index.");
            System.exit(0);
        }

        for (int i = index; i < numberUsed; i++)
            a[i] = a[i + 1];
        numberUsed--;
    }
```

(continued)

Display 6.5 **Partially Filled Array Class** (part 4 of 4)

```
    public boolean empty()
    {
        return (numberUsed == 0);
    }

    public boolean full()
    {
        return (numberUsed == maxNumberElements);
    }

    public int getMaxCapacity()
    {
        return maxNumberElements;
    }

    public int getNumberOfElements()
    {
        return numberUsed;
    }
}
```

TIP: Accessor Methods Need Not Simply Return Instance Variables

Note that in the class `PartiallyFilledArray` in Display 6.5, there is no accessor method that returns a copy of the entire instance variable `a`. The reason this was not done is that, when the class is used as intended, a user of the class `PartiallyFilledArray` would have no need for the entire array `a`. That is an implementation detail. The other methods that start with `get` allow a programmer using the class to obtain all the data that he or she needs. ■

The "for-each" Loop ★

As you have already seen, you can use a `for` loop to cycle through all the elements in an array. For example,

```
double[] a = new double[10];
<Some code to fill the array a>
for (int i = 0; i < a.length; i++)
    System.out.println(a[i]);
```

The standard Java libraries contain definitions of a number of so-called *collection classes*. A collection class is a class whose objects store a collection of values. You cannot cycle

Display 6.6 **Display 6.4 Redone Using the Class `PartiallyFilledArray`** (part 1 of 2)

Sample dialog is the same as in Display 6.4.

```
import java.util.Scanner;

/**
 Demonstrates Using the class PartiallyFilledArray,
*/
public class GolfScoresVersion2
{

    public static final int MAX_NUMBER_SCORES = 10;

    /**
     Shows the differences between each of a list of golf scores and
     their average.
    */
    public static void main(String[] args)
    {
        PartiallyFilledArray score =
                         new PartiallyFilledArray(MAX_NUMBER_SCORES);

        System.out.println("This program reads golf scores and shows");
        System.out.println("how much each differs from the average.");

        System.out.println("Enter golf scores:");
        fillArray(score);
        showDifference(score);
    }
    /**
     Reads values into the PartiallyFilledArray a.
    */
    public static void fillArray(PartiallyFilledArray a)
    {
        System.out.println("Enter up to " + a.getMaxCapacity()
                              + " nonnegative numbers, one per line.");
        System.out.println("Mark the end of the list with a negative
        number");
        Scanner keyboard = new Scanner(System.in);

        double next = keyboard.nextDouble();
        while ((next >= 0) && (!a.full()))
        {
            a.add(next);
            next = keyboard.nextDouble();
        }
        if (next >= 0)
             System.out.println("Could only read in "
                                 + a.getMaxCapacity() + " input values.");
     }
```

(continued)

Display 6.6 **Display 6.4 Redone Using the Class `PartiallyFilledArray`** (part 2 of 2)

```
    /**
     Returns the average of numbers in the PartiallyFilledArray a.
    */
    public static double computeAverage(PartiallyFilledArray a)
    {
        double total = 0;
        for (int index = 0; index < a.getNumberOfElements(); index++)
            total = total + a.getElement(index);

        if (a.getNumberOfElements() > 0)
        {
            return (total/a.getNumberOfElements());
        }
        else
        {
            System.out.println("ERROR: Trying to average 0 numbers.");
            System.out.println("computeAverage returns 0.");
            return 0;
        }
    }

    /**
     Gives screen output showing how much each of the
     elements in the PartiallyFilledArray a differ from the average.
    */
    public static void showDifference(PartiallyFilledArray a)
    {
        double average = computeAverage(a);
        System.out.println("Average of the " + a.getNumberOfElements()
                                    + " scores = " + average);
        System.out.println("The scores are:");
        for (int index = 0; index < a.getNumberOfElements(); index++)
            System.out.println(a.getElement(index)
                                    + "differs from average by"
                                    + (a.getElement(index)- average));
    }

}
```

through all the elements of a collection object with this kind of `for` loop, because these collection classes normally do not have indices associated with their elements, as an array does.[4] However, starting with version 5.0, Java has added a new kind of `for` loop that can cycle through all the elements in a collection even though there are no indices

[4]You can construct a similar for loop using something called an *iterator* in place of the array index but we will not go into that until later in this book.

for the elements (as there are with an array). This new kind of `for` loop is called a

for-each loop

for-each loop or **enhanced for loop**. We will discuss these for-each loops in detail when we cover collections (Chapter 16). However, these new for-each loops can be used with arrays as well as with objects of these collection classes. In this subsection, we tell you how to use for-each loops with arrays in case you want to get started using them. However, we do not use the for-each loop in this book until we discuss collection classes in Chapter 16.

The following code ends with a for-each loop that is equivalent to the regular `for` loop that we gave at the start of this subsection:

```
double[] a = new double[10];
<Some code to fill the array a>
for (double element : a)
    System.out.println(element);
```

You can read the line beginning with `for` as "for each `element` in `a`, do the following." Note that the variable, `element`, has the same type as the elements in the array. The variable, like `element`, must be declared in the for-each loop as we have done. If you attempt to declare `element` before the for-each loop, you will get a compiler error message.

The general syntax for a for-each loop statement used with an array is

```
for (Array_Base_Type Variable : Array_Name)
    Statement
```

Be sure to notice that you use a colon (not a semicolon) after the *Variable*. You may use any legal variable name for the *Variable*; you do not have to use `element`. Although it is not required, the *Statement* typically contains the *Variable*. When the for-each loop is executed, the *Statement* is executed once for each element of the array. More specifically, for each `element` of the array, the *Variable* is set to the array element and then the *Statement* is executed.

The for-each loop can make your code a lot cleaner and a lot less error prone. If you are not using the indexed variable in a `for` loop for anything other than as a way to cycle through all the array elements, then a for-each loop is preferable. For example,

```
for (double element : a)
    sum += element;
```

is preferable to

```
for (int i = 0; i < a.length; i++)
    sum += a[i];
```

The two loops do the same thing, but the second one mentions an index `i` that is not used for anything other than enumerating the array elements. Also, the syntax for the for-each loop is simpler than that of the regular `for` loop.

On the other hand, you should leave the following `for` loop as is and not attempt to convert it to a for-each loop:

```
for (int i = 0; i < a.length; i++)
    a[i]= 2*i;
```

Because this `for` loop uses the index `i` in the body of the `for` loop and uses it in an essential way, it does not make sense to convert this `for` loop to a for-each loop.

For-Each Loop for Arrays

SYNTAX

```
for (Array_Base_Type Variable : Array_Name)
    Statement
```

EXAMPLES

```
for (double element : a)
    sum += element;
```

The array a has base type `double`. This for-each loop sets each element of the array a to `0.0`.

A good way to read the first line of the example is "For each `element` in a, do the following."

Methods with a Variable Number of Parameters ★

Because of overloading, you can have a method named `max` that returns the largest of two `int` values and have another method named `max` that takes three `int` arguments and returns the largest of the three. If you decide you need a method that returns the largest of four `int` values, you can define a version of the method `max` that takes four arguments. However, with this approach, there is no way to cover all cases of computing the maximum of some number of `int` values. Covering all cases in this way would require an infinite number of definitions for the method name `max`, and no programmer has enough time to write an infinite number of definitions. What we would like is a single method definition for a method named `max` that can take any number of `int` arguments. Starting with version 5.0, Java lets you define methods that take any number of arguments. For example, the following is the definition of a method named `max` that takes any number of `int` arguments and returns the largest of its arguments:

```
public static int max(int... arg)
{
    if (arg.length == 0)
    {
       System.out.println("Fatal Error: "+
          "maximum of zero values.");
       System.exit(0);
    }
```

```
        int largest = arg[0];
        for (int i = 1; i < arg.length; i++)
            if (arg[i] > largest)
                largest = arg[i];
        return largest;
    }
```

This method max works by taking its int arguments and placing them in an array named arg whose base type is int. For example, suppose this definition of the method max is in a class named UtilityClass, and consider the following method call:

```
int highestScore = UtilityClass.max(3, 2, 5, 1);
```

The array arg is automatically declared and initialized as follows:

```
int[] arg = {3, 2, 5, 1};
```

So, `arg[0] == 3`, `arg[1] == 2`, `arg[2] == 5`, and `arg[3] == 1`. After this, the code in the body of the method definition is executed. Display 6.7 shows a sample program that uses this method max.

Note that a method (such as max) that takes any number of arguments is basically a method that takes an array as an argument, except that the job of placing values in the

Display 6.7 Method with a Variable Number of Parameters (part 1 of 2)

```
public class UtilityClass
{
    /**
     Returns the largest of any number of int values.
    */
    public static int max(int... arg)
    {
        if (arg.length == 0)
        {
            System.out.println("Fatal Error: maximum of zero values.");
            System.exit(0);
        }

        int largest = arg[0];
        for (int i = 1; i < arg.length; i++)
            if (arg[i] > largest)
              largest = arg[i];
        return largest;
    }
}
```

This is the file `UtilityClass.java`

(continued)

Display 6.7 **Method with a Variable Number of Parameters** (part 2 of 2)

This is the file `VariableParameterDemo.java`

```
import java.util.Scanner;

public class VariableParameterDemo
{
    public static void main(String[] args)
    {
        System.out.println("Enter scores for Tom, Dick, and Harriet:");
        Scanner keyboard = new Scanner(System.in);
        int tomsScore = keyboard.nextInt();
        int dicksScore = keyboard.nextInt();
        int harrietsScore = keyboard.nextInt();

        int highestScore = UtilityClass.max(tomsScore, dicksScore,
                                            harrietsScore);

        System.out.println("Highest score = " + highestScore);
    }
}
```

Sample Dialogue

```
Enter scores for Tom, Dick, and Harriet:
55 100 99
Highest score = 100
```

array is done automatically for the programmer. The values for the array are given as arguments, and Java automatically creates an array and places the arguments in the array.

vararg specification

ellipsis

A parameter specification that specifies any number of parameters, such as `int... arg`, is called a **vararg specification**. (It would make more sense to call it a *varparameter* specification, but the word *vararg* is too well entrenched, so we will go along with common usage.) The three dots in a vararg specification are called an **ellipsis**. Note that the ellipsis is part of the Java syntax and not an abbreviation used in this book. You type in the three dots.

You can have only one variable parameter specification, such as `int... arg`, in a method definition. However, you may also have any number of ordinary parameters, in which case the vararg specification must be the last item on the parameter list. This is illustrated in Display 6.8, which we discuss in the next subsection.

In Chapter 2, you saw one example of a method that accepts a variable number of arguments, namely the method `System.out.printf`. However, we could not tell you how to define such methods yourself until we covered the basics about arrays.

Method with a Variable Number of Parameters

A method with a variable number of parameters has a vararg specification as the last item on its parameter list. A vararg specification has the following form:

Type... *Array_Name*

Some examples of vararg specifications are

```
int... arg
double... a
String... unwanted
```

Displays 6.7 and 6.8 show two of these vararg specifications in complete method definitions.

In any invocation of a method with a vararg specification, you handle arguments corresponding to regular parameters in the usual way. Following the arguments for regular parameters, you can have any number of arguments of the type given in the vararg specification. These arguments are automatically placed in an array, and the array can be used in the method definition. A full description of the details is given in this chapter.

MyProgrammingLab™

Self-Test Exercises

16. Redo the definition of the method `max` in Display 6.7 using a for-each loop in place of the regular `for` loop.

17. What would be the dialogue in Display 6.8 if we omit the following line from the program?

```
sentence = Utility2.censor(sentence, " ,"); //Deletes extra commas
```

EXAMPLE: A String Processing Example ★

This example uses material from the earlier starred subsection "Methods with a Variable Number of Parameters." If you have not read that subsection, you should skip this example.

Display 6.8 contains a utility class with the string processing method named `censor` and an example of a program that uses that method. The method `censor` takes a single `String` parameter followed by any number of additional parameters of type `String`. The first parameter will be a sentence or other string that may contain substrings you want to delete. The method returns its first parameter with all occurrences of the remaining string parameters removed.

(continued)

EXAMPLE: (continued)

Note that the method censor has one regular parameter followed by a specification for any number of additional string parameters. In this case, all parameters are of type String. However, that first regular parameter (or parameters) in a method heading can be of any type (or types); they need not match the type of the vararg specification. We just happen to want the type String here.

Because the first parameter is of type String and the vararg specification in this case says the remaining arguments are of type String, you might wonder why we did not omit the first String parameter sentence, have only a vararg specification, and then use unwanted[0] to serve the same role as sentence. If we did so, then the method censor could be called with no arguments at all. A vararg specification allows any number of arguments, including the possibility of zero arguments. However, we want to insist that the method censor have at least one argument, and the parameter sentence ensures that censor will always have at least one argument.

Privacy Leaks with Array Instance Variables

In Chapter 5, we explained why it is a compromise of privacy for a class to have an accessor (or other method) that returns a reference to a private mutable object. As we noted there, an accessor method should instead return a reference to a *deep copy* of the private object. (See the Pitfall subsection of Chapter 5 entitled "Privacy Leaks.") At the time, we had in mind returning the contents of a private instance variable of a class type. However, the lesson applies equally well to private instance variables of an array type.

For example, suppose that you decide that you want an accessor method for the array instance variable in the class PartiallyFilledArray in Display 6.5. You might be tempted to define the accessor method as follows:

```
public double[] getInsideArray( ) // Problematic version
{
    return a;
}
```

As indicated in the comment, this definition has a problem, which is this accessor method allows a programmer to change the array object named by the private instance variable a in ways that bypass the checks built into the mutator methods of the class PartiallyFilledArray. To see why this is true, *suppose we added this definition of the method* getInsideArray *to the class* PartiallyFilledArray, and then consider the following code:

```
PartiallyFilledArray leakyArray =
                    new PartiallyFilledArray(10);
double[] arrayName = leakyArray.getInsideArray( );
```

The variable arrayName and the private instance variable a now contain the same reference, so both arrayName and the private instance variable a name the same array. Using arrayName as a name for the array named by the private instance variable a, we

Display 6.8 **String Processing Method with a Variable Number of Parameters** (part 1 of 2)

Both methods use the parameter sentence as a local variable. If this puzzles you, review the material on parameters in Chapters 4 and 5, particularly Display 4.5 in Chapter 4.

```java
public class Utility2
{
    /**
     Returns the first argument with all occurrences of other arguments deleted;
    */
    public static String censor(String sentence, String... unwanted)
   {
        for (int i = 0; i < unwanted.length; i++)
            sentence = deleteOne(sentence, unwanted[i]);
        return sentence;
    }

    /**
     Returns sentence with all occurrences of oneUnwanted removed.
    */
    private static String deleteOne(String sentence, String oneUnwanted)
    {
        String ending;
        int position = sentence.indexOf(oneUnwanted);
        while (position >= 0) //While word was found in sentence
        {
            ending = sentence.substring(position + oneUnwanted.length());
            sentence = sentence.substring(0, position) + ending;
            position = sentence.indexOf(oneUnwanted);
        }
        return sentence;
    }
}
```

If you have trouble following this string processing, review the subsection entitled "String Processing" in Chapter 1.

This is the file **`Utility2.java`**.

This is the file **`StringProcessingDemo.java`**.

```java
import java.util.Scanner;

public class StringProcessingDemo
{

    public static void main(String[] args)
    {
        System.out.println("What did you eat for dinner?");
        Scanner keyboard = new Scanner(System.in);
        String sentence = keyboard.nextLine();
        sentence = Utility2.censor(sentence,
                           "candy", "french fries", "salt", "beer");
        sentence = Utility2.censor(sentence, " ,"); //Deletes extra commas
        System.out.println("You would be healthier if you could answer:");
        System.out.println(sentence);
    }
}
```

(continued)

Display 6.8 **String Processing Method with a Variable Number of Parameters** (part 2 of 2)

Sample Dialogue

```
What did you eat for dinner?
I ate salt cod, broccoli, french fries, salt peanuts, and apples.
You would be healthier if you could answer:
I ate cod, broccoli, peanuts, and apples.
```

can now fill the indexed variables of `a` in any order and need not fill the array starting at the first element. This violates the spirit of the `private` modifier for the array instance variable `a`. For this reason, the accessor method `getInsideArray` should return a deep copy of the array named by the private instance variable `a`. A safe definition of `getInsideArray` is the following:

```
public double[] getInsideArray( ) // Good version
{
    //Recall that maxNumberElements == a.length.
    double[] temp = new double[maxNumberElements];
    for (int i = 0; i < maxNumberElements; i++)
        temp[i] = a[i];
    return temp;
}
```

If a private instance variable is an array type that has a class as its base type, then you need to be sure to make copies of the class objects in the array when you make a copy of the array. This is illustrated by the toy class in Display 6.9.

Display 6.9 also includes a copy constructor. As illustrated in that display, the copy constructor should make a completely independent copy of the array instance variable (that is, a deep copy) in the same way that the accessor method does. This same point is also illustrated by the copy constructor in Display 6.5.

Display 6.9 **Accessor Method for an Array Instance Variable** (part 1 of 2)

```
/**
 Demonstrates the correct way to define an accessor
 method to a private array of class objects.
*/
public class ToyExample
{
    private Date[] a;
```

The class `Date` is defined in Display 4.11, but you do not need to know the details of the definition to understand the point of this example.

Display 6.9 Accessor Method for an Array Instance Variable (part 2 of 2)

```
    public ToyExample(int arraySize)
    {
        a = new Date[arraySize];
        for (int i = 0; i < arraySize; i++)
            a[i] = new Date();
    }

    public ToyExample(ToyExample object)          <- Copy constructor for ToyExample.
    {
        int lengthOfArrays = object.a.length;
        this.a = new Date[lengthOfArrays];
        for (int i = 0; i < lengthOfArrays; i++)
            this.a[i] = new Date(object.a[i]);   <- Copy constructor for Date.
    }

    public Date[] getDateArray()                  <- Accessor method.
    {
        Date[] temp = new Date[a.length];
        for (int i = 0; i < a.length; i++)
            temp[i] = new Date(a[i]);             <- Copy constructor for Date.
        return temp;
    }

    <There presumably are other methods that are not shown,
                          but they are irrelevant to the point at hand.>

}
```

MyProgrammingLab™

Self-Test Exercises

18. Define a method named `removeAll` that can be added to the class `PartiallyFilledArray`. This method has no parameters. When invoked, the method `removeAll` deletes all the elements in its calling object.

19. Define a method named `increaseCapacity` that can be added to the class `PartiallyFilledArray` in Display 6.5. The method has one `int` parameter named `newCapacity` that increases the capacity of the `PartiallyFilledArray` so that it can hold up to `newCapacity` numbers. If `newCapacity` is less than or equal to `maxNumberOfElements`, then the method does nothing. If `newCapacity` is greater than `maxNumberOfElements`, then `maxNumberElements` is set equal to `newCapacity` and a new array of length `newCapacity` is created for the array instance variable `a`. The old values of the array instance variable are copied to the newly created array.

EXAMPLE: Sorting an Array

In this example, we define a method called `sort` that will sort a partially filled array of numbers so that they are ordered from smallest to largest.

The procedure `sort` has one array parameter, `a`. The array `a` will be partially filled, so there is an additional formal parameter called `numberUsed`, which tells how many array positions are used. Thus, the heading for the method `sort` will be

```
public static void sort(double[] a, int numberUsed)
```

The method `sort` rearranges the elements in array `a` so that after the method call is completed, the elements are sorted as follows:

```
a[0] ≤ a[1] ≤ a[2] ≤ ... ≤ a[numberUsed - 1]
```

The algorithm we use to do the sorting is called **selection sort**. It is one of the easiest of the sorting algorithms to understand.

One way to design an algorithm is to rely on the definition of the problem. In this case, the problem is to sort an array `a` from smallest to largest. That means rearranging the values so that `a[0]` is the smallest, `a[1]` the next smallest, and so forth. That definition yields an outline for the selection sort algorithm:

```
for (int index = 0; index < numberUsed; index++)
    Place the indexth smallest element in a[index]
```

There are many ways to realize this general approach. The details could be developed by using two arrays and copying the elements from one array to the other in sorted order, but using one array should be both adequate and economical. Therefore, the method `sort` uses only the one array containing the values to be sorted. The method `sort` rearranges the values in the array `a` by interchanging pairs of values. Let us go through a concrete example so that you can see how the algorithm works.

Consider the array shown in Display 6.10. The selection sort algorithm will place the smallest value in `a[0]`. The smallest value is the value in `a[4]`. So the algorithm interchanges the values of `a[0]` and `a[4]`. The algorithm then looks for the next smallest element. The value in `a[0]` is now the smallest element, so the next smallest element is the smallest of the remaining elements `a[1]`, `a[2]`, `a[3]`,..., `a[9]`. In the example in Display 6.10, the next smallest element is in `a[6]`, so the algorithm interchanges the values of `a[1]` and `a[6]`. This positioning of the second smallest element is illustrated in the fourth and fifth array pictures in Display 6.10. The algorithm then positions the third smallest element, and so forth. As the sorting proceeds, the beginning array elements are set equal to the correct sorted values. The sorted portion of the array grows by adding elements one after the other from the elements in the unsorted end of the array. Notice that the algorithm need not do anything with the value in the last indexed variable, `a[9]`, because once the other elements are positioned correctly, `a[9]` must also have the correct value. After all, the correct value for `a[9]` is the smallest value left to be moved, and the only value left to be moved is the value that is already in `a[9]`.

EXAMPLE: (continued)

The definition of the method `sort`, included in a class, is given in Display 6.11. `sort` uses the method `indexOfSmallest` to find the index of the smallest element in the unsorted end of the array, and then it does an interchange to move this next smallest element down into the sorted part of the array.

The method `interchange`, shown in Display 6.11, is used to interchange the values of indexed variables. For example, the following call will interchange the values of `a[0]` and `a[4]`:

```
interchange(0, 4, a);
```

A sample use of the `sort` method is given in Display 6.12.

Display 6.10 Selection Sort

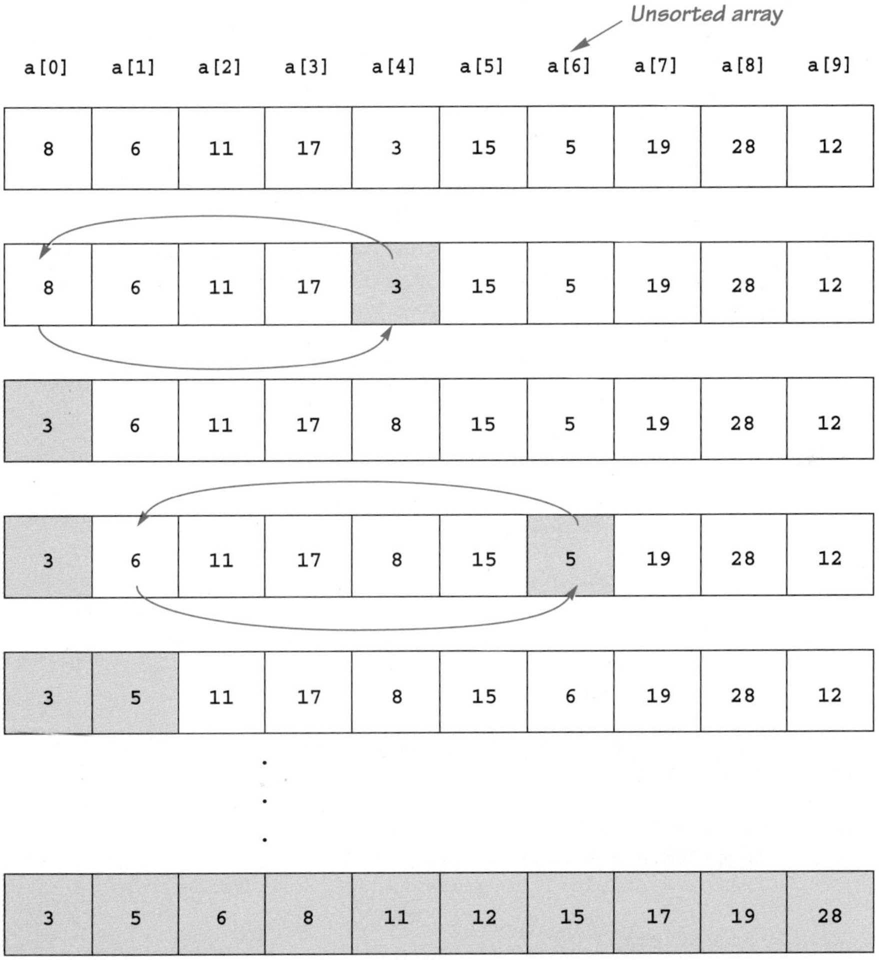

MyProgrammingLab™

Self-Test Exercises

20. How would you need to change the method `sort` in Display 6.11 so that it can sort an array of values of type `double` into decreasing order, instead of increasing order?

21. If an array of `int` values has a value that occurs twice (such as `b[0] == 42` and `b[7] == 42`) and you sort the array using the method `SelectionSort.sort`, will there be one or two copies of the repeated value after the array is sorted?

Display 6.11 Selection Sort Class (part 1 of 2)

```
public class SelectionSort
{
    /**
     Precondition: numberUsed <= a.length;
                   The first numberUsed indexed variables have values.
     Action: Sorts a so that a[0] <= a[1] <= ... <= a[numberUsed - 1].
    */
    public static void sort(double[] a, int numberUsed)
    {
        int index, indexOfNextSmallest;
        for (index = 0; index < numberUsed - 1; index++)
        {//Place the correct value in a[index]:
           indexOfNextSmallest = indexOfSmallest(index, a, numberUsed);
           interchange(index,indexOfNextSmallest, a);
           //a[0] <= a[1] <= ...<= a[index] and these are the smallest
           //of the original array elements. The remaining positions
           //contain the rest of the original array elements.
        }
    }

    /**
     Returns the index of the smallest value among
     a[startIndex], a[startIndex+1], ... a[numberUsed - 1]
    */
    private static int indexOfSmallest(int startIndex,
                                       double[] a, int numberUsed)
    {
        double min = a[startIndex];
        int indexOfMin = startIndex;
        int index;
        for (index = startIndex + 1; index < numberUsed; index++)
          if (a[index] < min)
          {
              min = a[index];
              indexOfMin = index;
              //min is smallest of a[startIndex] through a[index]
          }
        return indexOfMin;
    }
```

Display 6.11 **Selection Sort Class** (part 2 of 2)

```
    /**
     Precondition: i and j are legal indices for the array a.
     Postcondition: Values of a[i] and a[j] have been interchanged.
    */
    private static void interchange(int i, int j, double[] a)
    {
        double temp;
        temp = a[i];
        a[i] = a[j];
        a[j] = temp; //original value of a[i]
    }
}
```

Display 6.12 **Demonstration of the SelectionSort Class**

```
public class SelectionSortDemo
{
    public static void main(String[] args)
    {
        double[] b = {7.7, 5.5, 11, 3, 16, 4.4, 20, 14, 13, 42};

        System.out.println("Array contents before sorting:");
        int i;
        for (i = 0; i < b.length; i++)
            System.out.print(b[i] + " ");
        System.out.println();

        SelectionSort.sort(b, b.length);

        System.out.println("Sorted array values:");
        for (i = 0; i < b.length; i++)
          System.out.print(b[i] + " ");
        System.out.println();
    }
}
```

Sample Dialogue

```
Array contents before sorting:
7.7 5.5 11.0 3.0 16.0 4.4 20.0 14.0 13.0 42.0
Sorted array values:
3.0 4.4 5.5 7.7 11.0 13.0 14.0 16.0 20.0 42.0
```

Enumerated Types ★

enumerated type

Sometimes you need a simple type consisting of a short list of named values. For example, the values might be clothing sizes, the days of the week, or some other brief list. Starting with version 5.0, Java allows you to have such an **enumerated type**. For example, the following is an enumerated type for the days of a five-day work week:

```
enum WorkDay {MONDAY, TUESDAY, WEDNESDAY, THURSDAY, FRIDAY};
```

A value of an enumerated type is a kind of named constant and so, by convention, is spelled with all uppercase letters. So, we used, for example, `MONDAY`, not `Monday`, in the above definition of the enumerated type `WorkDay`. Using `Monday` would have been legal, but poor style.

As with any other type, you can have variables of an enumerated type; for example,

```
WorkDay meetingDay, availableDay;
```

A variable of an enumerated type can have a value that must be either one of the values listed in the definition of the type or else the special value `null`, which serves as a placeholder indicating that the variable has no "real" value. For example, you can set the value of a variable of an enumerated type with an assignment statement, as follows:

```
meetingDay = WorkDay.THURSDAY;
```

Note that when you write the value of an enumerated type, you need to preface the name of the value, such as `THURSDAY`, with the name of the type. For example, you use `WorkDay.THURSDAY`, not `THURSDAY`.

As with any other type, you can combine the declaration of a variable with the assignment of a value to the variable, as in

```
WorkDay meetingDay = WorkDay.THURSDAY;
```

A program that demonstrates the syntax for using enumerated types is given in Display 6.13. Be sure to notice that we placed the definition of the enumerated type outside of the `main` method in the same place that you would give named constants.

Display 6.13 **An Enumerated Type** (part 1 of 2)

```
public class EnumDemo
{
    enum WorkDay {MONDAY, TUESDAY, WEDNESDAY, THURSDAY, FRIDAY};

    public static void main(String[] args)
    {
        WorkDay startDay = WorkDay.MONDAY;
        WorkDay endDay = WorkDay.FRIDAY;
```

Display 6.13 **An Enumerated Type** (part 2 of 2)

```
        System.out.println("Work starts on " + startDay);
        System.out.println("Work ends on " + endDay);
    }
}
```

Sample Dialogue

```
Work starts on MONDAY
Work ends on FRIDAY
```

Enumerated Type

An **enumerated type** is a type for which you give all the values of the type in a typically short list. A value of an enumerated type is a kind of named constant and so, by convention, is spelled with all uppercase letters.

SYNTAX

`enum` *Type_Name* {*FIRST_VALUE*, *SECOND_VALUE*, ..., *LAST_VALUE*};

Starting with version 5.0, `enum` is a keyword in Java.

EXAMPLE

```
enum Flavor {VANILLA, CHOCOLATE, STRAWBERRY};
```

The definition of an enumerated type is normally placed outside of all methods in the same place that you give named constants. The location for an enumerated type definition is illustrated in Display 6.13. (The definition can be placed in other locations, but we will not need to place them anywhere else.)

You can output the value of a variable of an enumerated type using `println`. For example,

```
System.out.println(WorkDay.THURSDAY);
```

will produce the following screen output:

```
THURSDAY
```

Note that the type name `WorkDay` is not output. Other examples of outputting an enumerated type value are given in Display 6.13.

The values of an enumerated type, such as `WorkDay.THURSDAY`, are not `String` values. In fact, you should not care what kind of values they are. How they are implemented is not relevant to being able to use the values of an enumerated type. All you really need to know is that, for example, `WorkDay.THURSDAY` and `WorkDay.FRIDAY` are different values and will test as being different if you compare them with `==`.

Although values of an enumerated type are not `String` values, they are used for tasks that could be done by `String` values; however, enumerated types work better than `String` values for some tasks. You could use a `String` variable in place of a variable of an enumerated type. For example, you could use

```
String meetingDay = "THURSDAY";
```

instead of

```
WorkDay meetingDay = WorkDay.THURSDAY;
```

However, using a `String` variable allows for the possibility of setting the variable equal to a nonsense value, such as `"SUNDAY"` or `"GaGa"` for a work day, and to do so without the computer issuing any warning statement. With an enumerated type, you know the only possible values for a variable of that type are the values given in the enumerated type definition; if you try to give the variable a different value, you will get an error message.

An enumerated type is actually a class, and its values are objects of the class. Some methods that are automatically provided with every enumerated type are given in Display 6.14.

Display 6.14 **Some Methods Included with Every Enumerated Type** (part 1 of 2)

`public boolean equals(`*Any_Value_Of_An_Enumerated_Type*`)`

Returns `true` if its argument is the same value as the calling value. While it is perfectly legal to use `equals`, it is easier and more common to use `==`.

EXAMPLE

For enumerated types, `(`*Value1*`.equals(`*Value2*`))` is equivalent to `(`*Value1* `==` *Value2*`)`.

`public String toString( )`

Returns the calling value as a string. This is often invoked automatically. For example, this method is invoked automatically when you output a value of the enumerated type using `System.out.println` or when you concatenate a value of the enumerated type to a string. See Display 6.15 for an example of this automatic invocation.

EXAMPLE

`WorkDay.MONDAY.toString( )` returns `"MONDAY"`. The enumerated type `WorkDay` is defined in Display 6.13.

Display 6.14 Some Methods Included with Every Enumerated Type (part 2 of 2)

`public int ordinal( )`

Returns the position of the calling value in the list of enumerated type values. The first position is 0.

EXAMPLE

`WorkDay.MONDAY.ordinal( )` returns `0`, `WorkDay.TUESDAY.ordinal( )` returns `1`, and so forth. The enumerated type `WorkDay` is defined in Display 6.13.

`public int compareTo(`*Any_Value_Of_The_Enumerated_Type*`)`

Returns a negative value if the calling object precedes the argument in the list of values, returns `0` if the calling object equals the argument, and returns a positive value if the argument precedes the calling object.

EXAMPLE

`WorkDay.TUESDAY.compareTo(WorkDay.THURSDAY)` returns a negative value. The type `WorkDay` is defined in Display 6.13.

`public` *EnumeratedType* `[] values( )`

Returns an array whose elements are the values of the enumerated type in the order in which they are listed in the definition of the enumerated type.

EXAMPLE

See Display 6.15.

`public static` *EnumeratedType* `valueOf(String name)`

Returns the enumerated type value with the specified name. The string name must be an exact match.

EXAMPLE

`WorkDay.valueOf("THURSDAY")` returns `WorkDay.THURSDAY`. The type `WorkDay` is defined in Display 6.13.

When comparing two variables (or constants) of an enumerated type, you can use the `equals` method, but it is more common to instead use the `==` operator. For example,

```
if (meetingDay == availableDay)
    System.out.println("Meeting will be on schedule.");
if (meetingDay == WorkDay.THURSDAY)
    System.out.println("Long weekend!");
```

With enumerated types, the `equals` method and the `==` operator are equivalent, but the `==` operator has nicer syntax.

To get the full potential from an enumerated type, you need some way to cycle through all its values. The static method `values( )` provides you with that ability. This method returns an array whose elements are the values of the enumerated type, and is provided automatically for every enumerated type. Display 6.15 gives a simple example of using the method `values( )` to cycle through all the values in an enumerated type. (This is one situation where it is much cleaner to use a for-each loop instead of an ordinary `for` loop. If you have read the starred section on the for-each loop, be sure to do Self-Test Exercise 22, which redoes Display 6.15 using a for-each loop.)

The `values` Method

Every enumerated type has a static method named `values( )`, which returns an array whose elements are the values of the enumerated type in the order in which they are listed in the definition of the enumerated type. The base type for the array returned is the enumerated type. See Display 6.15 for an example.

Display 6.15 The Method **`values`** (part 1 of 2)

```
import java.util.Scanner;

public class EnumValuesDemo
{
    enum WorkDay {MONDAY, TUESDAY, WEDNESDAY, THURSDAY, FRIDAY};

    public static void main(String[] args)
    {
        WorkDay[] day = WorkDay.values();

        Scanner keyboard = new Scanner(System.in);
        double hours = 0, sum = 0;

        for (int i = 0; i < day.length; i++)
        {
            System.out.println("Enter hours worked for " + day[i]);
            hours = keyboard.nextDouble();
             sum = sum + hours;
        }

        System.out.println("Total hours work = " + sum);
    }
}
```

This is equivalent to `day[i].toString()`.

Display 6.15 **The Method values** (part 2 of 2)

Sample Dialogue

```
Enter hours worked for MONDAY
8
Enter hours worked for TUESDAY
8
Enter hours worked for WEDNESDAY
8
Enter hours worked for THURSDAY
8
Enter hours worked for FRIDAY
7.5
Total hours worked = 39.5
```

TIP: Enumerated Types in `switch` Statements ★

You can use an enumerated type to control a `switch` statement. In other words, the type of the controlling expression in a `switch` statement can be an enumerated type. This is illustrated in Display 6.16. Note that the case labels must be unqualified names; use `VANILLA`, not `Flavor.VANILLA`.

This program uses the static method `valueOf` to convert an input string to a value of the enumerated type. For example,

```
Flavor.valueOf("STRAWBERRY")
```

returns `Flavor.STRAWBERRY`. Note that the program changes the input to all uppercase letters before giving it as an argument to the method `valueOf`. The method `valueOf` requires an exact match. An invocation of `Flavor.valueOf("Vanilla")` will end your program with an error message;[5] you must use `"VANILLA"` to match the exact spelling (including upper- versus lowercase) of the value in `Flavor`.

At this point, you may wonder what the difference is between `STRAWBERRY` and `Flavor.STRAWBERRY` and how to tell which one to use in a given situation. The value of the enumerated type is `STRAWBERRY`. We write `Flavor.STRAWBERRY` to say we mean `STRAWBERRY` as defined in `Flavor`, as opposed to `STRAWBERRY` as defined in some other type, such as

```
enum Berry {STRAWBERRY. BLUEBERRY, RASPBERRY};
```

(continued)

[5]After you cover exceptions in Chapter 9, you will be able to cope with answers such as `PISTACHIO` that do not correspond to any value of type `Flavor`. An invocation of `Flavor.valueOf("PISTACHIO")` will throw an *IlllegalArgumentException*, something explained in Chapter 9. Until then, your program will simply give an error message when `valueOf` cannot cope with its argument.

TIP: (continued)

A single program with both type definitions (`Flavor` and `Berry`) could use both `Flavor.STRAWBERRY` and `Berry.STRAWBERRY`.

So, when can you use `STRAWBERRY` instead of `Flavor.STRAWBERRY`? The approximate answer is when there is enough context for the compiler to know `STRAWBERRY` means `STRAWBERRY` as defined in the type `Flavor`. For example, in a `switch` statement, if the type of the controlling expression is `Flavor`, then `STRAWBERRY` can only mean `Flavor.STRAWBERRY`. This rule will help in remembering when to use `STRAWBERRY` and when to use `Flavor.STRAWBERRY`. But, sometimes you may simply have to check a reference or try the two possibilities out and see which one (or ones) the compiler accepts. ■

Display 6.16 **Enumerated Type in a `switch` Statement** (part 1 of 2)

```
import java.util.Scanner;

public class EnumSwitchDemo
{
    enum Flavor {VANILLA, CHOCOLATE, STRAWBERRY};

    public static void main(String[] args)
    {
        Flavor favorite = null;
        Scanner keyboard = new Scanner(System.in);

        System.out.println("What is your favorite flavor?");
        String answer = keyboard.next();
        answer = answer.toUpperCase();
        favorite = Flavor.valueOf(answer);

        switch (favorite)
        {
            case VANILLA:
                System.out.println("Classic");
                break;
            case CHOCOLATE:
                System.out.println("Rich");
                break;
            default:
                System.out.println("I bet you said STRAWBERRY.");
                break;
        }
    }
}
```

The case labels must have just the name of the value without the type name and dot.

Display 6.16 Enumerated Type in a `switch` Statement (part 2 of 2)

Sample Dialogue

```
What is your favorite flavor?
Vanilla
Classic
```

Sample Dialogue

```
What is your favorite flavor?
STRAWBERRY
I bet you said STRAWBERRY.
```

Sample Dialogue

```
What is your favorite flavor?
PISTACHIO
```

This input causes the program to end and issue an error message.

MyProgrammingLab™

Self-Test Exercise

22. Rewrite the program in Display 6.15 using a for-each loop.

6.4 Multidimensional Arrays

Two indices are better than one.

ANONYMOUS

Java allows you to declare arrays with more than one index. In this section, we describe these multidimensional arrays.

Multidimensional Array Basics

array declarations

It is sometimes useful to have an array with more than one index, and this is allowed in Java. The following creates an array of characters called `page`. The array `page` has two indices, the first index ranging from `0` to `29` and the second from `0` to `99`.

```
char[][] page = new char[30][100];
```

This is equivalent to the following two steps:

```
char[][] page;
page = new char[30][100];
```

indexed variables

The **indexed variables** for this array each have two indices. For example, `page[0][0]`, `page[15][32]`, and `page[29][99]` are three of the indexed variables for this array. Note that each index must be enclosed in its own set of square brackets. As was true of the one-dimensional arrays we have already seen, each indexed variable for a multidimensional array is a variable of the base type—in this case, the type `char`.

An array may have any number of indices, but perhaps the most common number is two. A two-dimensional array can be visualized as a two-dimensional display with the first index giving the row and the second index giving the column. For example, the array indexed variables of the two-dimensional array `a`, declared and created as

```
char[][] a = new char[5][12];
```

can be visualized as follows:

```
a[0][0], a[0][1], a[0][2], ..., a[0][11]
a[1][0], a[1][1], a[1][2], ..., a[1][11]
a[2][0], a[2][1], a[2][2], ..., a[2][11]
a[3][0], a[3][1], a[3][2], ..., a[3][11]
a[4][0], a[4][1], a[4][2], ..., a[4][11]
```

You might use the array `a` to store all the characters on a (very small) page of text that has 5 lines (numbered 0 through 4) and 12 characters on each line (numbered 0 through 11).

Declaring and Creating a Multidimensional Array

You declare a multidimensional array variable and create a multidimensional array object in basically the same way that you create and name a one-dimensional array. You simply use as many square brackets as there are indices.

SYNTAX

Base_Type [] . . . [] *Variable_Name* = new *Base_Type* [*Length_1*]...[*Length_n*];

EXAMPLES

```
char[][] a = new char[5][12];
char[][] page = new char[30][100];
double[][] table = new double[100][10];
int[][][] figure = new int[10][20][30];
Person[][] entry = new Person[10][10];
```

`Person` is a class.

a multidimensional array is an array of arrays

In Java, a two-dimensional array, such as `a`, is actually an array of arrays. The above array `a` is actually a one-dimensional array of size `5`, whose base type is a one-dimensional array of characters of size `12`. This is diagrammed in Display 6.17. As shown in that display, the array variable `a` contains a reference to a one-dimensional array of length `5` with a base type of `char[]`; that is, the base type of `a` is the type for an entire one-dimensional array of characters. Each indexed variable `a[0]`, `a[1]`, and so forth contains a reference to a one-dimensional array of characters.

Display 6.17 Two-Dimensional Array as an Array of Arrays

```
char[][] a = new char[5][12];
```

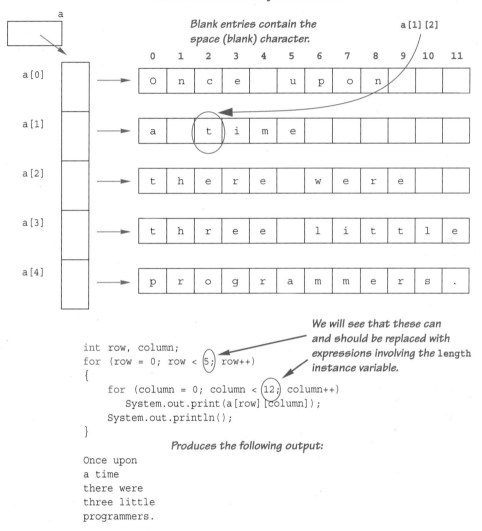

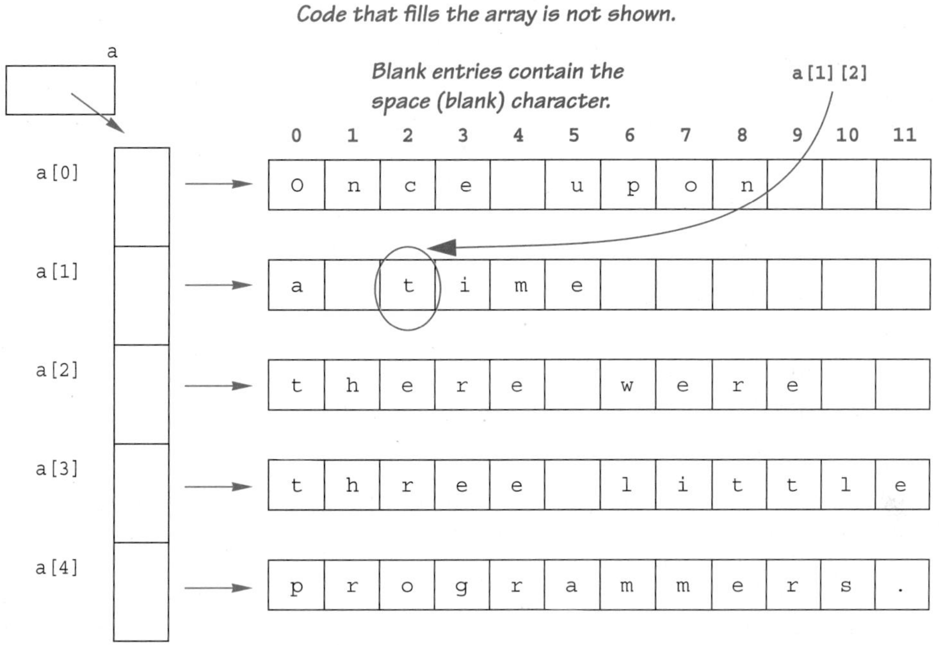

We will see that these can and should be replaced with expressions involving the `length` *instance variable.*

```
int row, column;
for (row = 0; row < 5; row++)
{
    for (column = 0; column < 12; column++)
       System.out.print(a[row][column]);
    System.out.println();
}
```

Produces the following output:

```
Once upon
a time
there were
three little
programmers.
```

A three-dimensional array is an array of arrays of arrays, and so forth for higher dimensions.

Normally, the fact that a two-dimensional array is an array of arrays need not concern you, and you can usually act as if the array a is actually an array with two indices (rather than an array of arrays, which is harder to keep track of). There are, however, some situations where a two-dimensional array looks very much like an array of arrays. For example, you will see that when using the instance variable `length`, you must think of a two-dimensional array as an array of arrays.

Using the `length` Instance Variable

Suppose you want to fill all the elements in the following two-dimensional array with `'Z'`:

```
char[][] page = new char[30][100];
```

You can use a nested `for` loop such as the following:

```
int row, column;
for (row = 0; row < page.length; row++)
   for (column = 0; column < page[row].length; column++)
     page[row][column] = 'Z';
```

Let's analyze this nested `for` loop in a bit more detail. The array `page` is actually a one-dimensional array of length `30`, and each of the 30 indexed variables `page[0]` through `page[29]` is a one-dimensional array with base type `char` and with a length of `100`. That is why the first `for` loop is terminated using `page.length`. For a two-dimensional array such as `page`, the value of `length` is the number of first indices or, equivalently, the number of rows—in this case, `30`. Now let's consider the inside `for` loop.

The 0th row in the two-dimensional array `page` is the one-dimensional array `page[0]`, and it has `page[0].length` entries. More generally, `page[row]` is a one-dimensional array of `chars`, and it has `page[row].length` entries. This is why the inner for loop is terminated using `page[row].length`. Of course, in this case, `page[0].length`, `page[1].length`, and so forth through to `page[29].length` are all equal and all equal to `100`. (If you read the optional section entitled "Ragged Arrays," which follows this section, you will see that these need not all be equal.)

MyProgrammingLab™

Self-Test Exercise

23. What is the output produced by the following code?

```
int[][] myArray = new int[4][4];
int index1, index2;
for (index1 = 0; index1 < myArray.length; index1++)
    for (index2 = 0;
              index2 < myArray[index1].length; index2++)
        myArray[index1][index2] = index2;
for (index1 = 0; index1 < myArray.length; index1++)
{
    for (index2 = 0;
              index2 < myArray[index1].length; index2++)
        System.out.print(myArray[index1][index2] + " ");
    System.out.println();
}
```

Ragged Arrays ★

ragged arrays

Most programmers typically create a two-dimensional array with the same number of entries for each row. However, it is possible for different rows to have a different numbers of columns. These sorts of arrays are called **ragged arrays**.

To help explain the details, let's start with an ordinary, nonragged two-dimensional array, created as follows:

```
double[][] a = new double[3][5];
```

This is equivalent to the following:

```
double[][] a;
a = new double[3][];
a[0] = new double[5];
a[1] = new double[5];
a[2] = new double[5];
```

The line

```
a = new double[3][];
```

makes `a` the name of an array with room for three entries, each of which can be an array of `doubles` that can be of any length. The next three lines each create an array of `doubles` of length `5` to be named by `a[0]`, `a[1]`, and `a[2]`. The net result is a two-dimensional array of base type `double` with three rows and five columns.

If you want, you can make each of `a[0]`, `a[1]`, and `a[2]` a different length. The following code makes a ragged array `b` in which each row has a different length:

```
double[][] b;
b = new double[3][];
b[0] = new double[5];
b[1] = new double[10];
b[2] = new double[4];
```

There are situations in which you can profitably use ragged arrays, but most applications do not require them. However, if you understand ragged arrays, you will have a better understanding of how all multidimensional arrays work in Java.

Multidimensional Array Parameters and Returned Values

array arguments

Methods may have multidimensional array parameters and may have a multidimensional array type as the type for the value returned. The situation is similar to that of the one-dimensional case, except that you use more square brackets when specifying the type name. For example, the following method will display a two-dimensional array in the usual way as rows and columns:[6]

```
public static void showMatrix(int[][] a)
{
    int row, column;
    for (row = 0; row < a.length; row++)
    {
        for (column = 0; column < a[row].length; column++)
            System.out.print(a[row][column] + " ");
        System.out.println();
    }
}
```

returning an array

If you want to return a multidimensional array, you use the same kind of type specification as you use for a multidimensional array parameter. For example, the following method returns a two-dimensional array with base type `double`:

```
/**
 Precondition: Each dimension of a is at least the value of size.
 The array returned is the same as the size-by-size upper upper-
 left corner of the array a.
*/
public static double[][] corner(double[][] a,int size)
{
    double[][] temp = new double[size][size];
    int row, column;
    for (row = 0; row < size; row++)
        for (column = 0; column < size; column++)
            temp[row][column] = a[row][column];
   return temp;
}
```

EXAMPLE: A Grade Book Class

Display 6.18 contains a class for grade records in a class whose only recorded scores are quiz scores. An object of this class has three array instance variables. One is a two-dimensional array named `grade` that records the grade of each student on each quiz. For example, the score that student number `4` received on quiz number `1` is recorded in `grade[3][0]`. Because the student numbers and quiz numbers start with `1` and the array indices start with `0`, we subtract one from the student number or quiz number to obtain the corresponding array index.

[6]It is worth noting that this method works fine for ragged arrays.

EXAMPLE: (continued)

All the raw data is in the array `grade`, but two other arrays hold computed data. The array `studentAverage` is used to record the average quiz score for each of the students. For example, the program sets `studentAverage[0]` equal to the average of the quiz scores received by student `1`, `studentAverage[1]` equal to the average of the quiz scores received by student `2`, and so forth. The array `quizAverage` is used to record the average score for each quiz. For example, the program sets `quizAverage[0]` equal to the average of all the student scores for quiz `1`, `quizAverage[1]` records the average score for quiz `2`, and so forth. Display 6.19 illustrates the relationship between the arrays `grade`, `studentAverage`, and `quizAverage`. In that display, we have shown some sample data for the array `grade`. The data in `grade`, in turn, determines the values that are stored in `studentAverage` and in `quizAverage`. Display 6.19 also shows these computed values for `studentAverage` and `quizAverage`. The two arrays `studentAverage` and `quizAverage` are created and filled by the constructor that creates the `GradeBook` object. (The constructors do this by calling private helping methods.)

The no-argument constructor for the class `GradeBook` obtains the data for the array instance variable `grade` via a dialog with the user. Although this is not my favorite way to define a no-argument constructor, some programmers like it and you should see an example of it. Another alternative would be to have a no-argument constructor that essentially does nothing and then have an input method that sets all the instance variables, including creating the array objects.

A very simple demonstration program along with the dialog it produces is given in Display 6.20.

Display 6.18 **A Grade Book Class** (part 1 of 4)

```
import java.util.Scanner;

public class GradeBook
{

    private int numberOfStudents; // Same as studentAverage.length.
    private int numberOfQuizzes; // Same as quizAverage.length.

    private int[][] grade; //numberOfStudents rows and numberOfQuizzes
                           //columns.
    private double[] studentAverage;
    private double[] quizAverage;

    public GradeBook(int[][] a)
    {
        if (a.length == 0 || a[0].length == 0)
        {
            System.out.println("Empty grade records. Aborting.");
            System.exit(0);
        }
```

(continued)

Display 6.18 A Grade Book Class (part 2 of 4)

```
        numberOfStudents = a.length;
        numberOfQuizzes = a[0].length;
        fillGrade(a);
        fillStudentAverage();
        fillQuizAverage();
    }

    public GradeBook(GradeBook book)
    {
        numberOfStudents = book.numberOfStudents;
        numberOfQuizzes = book.numberOfQuizzes;
        fillGrade(book.grade);
        fillStudentAverage();
        fillQuizAverage();
    }

    public GradeBook()
    {
        Scanner keyboard = new Scanner(System.in);

        System.out.println("Enter number of students:");
        numberOfStudents = keyboard.nextInt();

        System.out.println("Enter number of quizzes:");
        numberOfQuizzes = keyboard.nextInt();

        grade = new int[numberOfStudents][numberOfQuizzes];
        for (int studentNumber = 1;
                    studentNumber <= numberOfStudents; studentNumber++)
          for (int quizNumber = 1;
                        quizNumber <= numberOfQuizzes; quizNumber++)
          {
              System.out.println("Enter score for student number "
                                           + studentNumber);
              System.out.println("on quiz number " + quizNumber);
              grade[studentNumber - 1][quizNumber - 1] =
                                               keyboard.nextInt();
          }

        fillStudentAverage();
        fillQuizAverage();
    }

    private void fillGrade(int[][] a)
    {
        grade = new int[numberOfStudents][numberOfQuizzes];
       for (int studentNumber = 1;
                     studentNumber <= numberOfStudents; studentNumber++)
       {
```

This class should have more accessor and mutator methods, but we have omitted them to save space. See Self-Test Exercises 24 through 27.

Display 6.18 **A Grade Book Class** (part 3 of 4)

```
            for (int quizNumber = 1;
                           quizNumber <= numberOfQuizzes; quizNumber++)
                grade[studentNumber][quizNumber] =
                                        a[studentNumber][quizNumber];
        }
    }

    /**
      Fills the array studentAverage using the data from the array grade.
    */
    private void fillStudentAverage()
    {
        studentAverage = new double[numberOfStudents];

        for (int studentNumber = 1;
                         studentNumber<=numberOfStudents;studentNumber++)
        {//Process one studentNumber:
            double sum = 0;
            for (int quizNumber = 1;
                           quizNumber <= numberOfQuizzes; quizNumber++)
                sum = sum + grade[studentNumber - 1][quizNumber - 1];
            //sum contains the sum of the quiz scores for student number
            //studentNumber.
            studentAverage[studentNumber - 1] = sum/numberOfQuizzes;
            //Average for student studentNumber is
            //studentAverage[studentNumber - 1]
         }
    }
    /**
      Fills the array quizAverage using the data from the array grade.
    */
    private void fillQuizAverage()
    {
        quizAverage = new double[numberOfQuizzes];

        for (int quizNumber = 1; quizNumber <= numberOfQuizzes; quizNumber++)
        {//Process one quiz (for all students):
            double sum = 0;
            for (int studentNumber = 1;
                            studentNumber <= numberOfStudents;
                            studentNumber++)
                sum = sum + grade[studentNumber - 1][quizNumber - 1];
        //sum contains the sum of all student scores on quiz number
        //quizNumber.
            quizAverage[quizNumber - 1] = sum/numberOfStudents;
        //Average for quiz quizNumber is the value of
        //quizAverage[quizNumber - 1]
        }
    }
```

(continued)

Display 6.18 **A Grade Book Class** (part 4 of 4)

```
    public void display()
    {
        for (int studentNumber = 1;
                    studentNumber <= numberOfStudents; studentNumber++)

        {//Display for one studentNumber:
            System.out.print("Student " + studentNumber + " Quizzes: ");
            for (int quizNumber = 1;
                              quizNumber <= numberOfQuizzes; quizNumber++)
              System.out.print(grade[studentNumber - 1][quizNumber - 1] +
              " ");
            System.out.println(" Ave = " +
                              studentAverage[studentNumber - 1] );
        }

        System.out.println("Quiz averages: ");
        for (int quizNumber = 1; quizNumber <= numberOfQuizzes;
                                  quizNumber++)
           System.out.print("Quiz " + quizNumber
                           + " Ave = " + quizAverage[quizNumber - 1] +
                           " ");
        System.out.println();
    }
```

Display 6.19 The Two-Dimensional Array grade

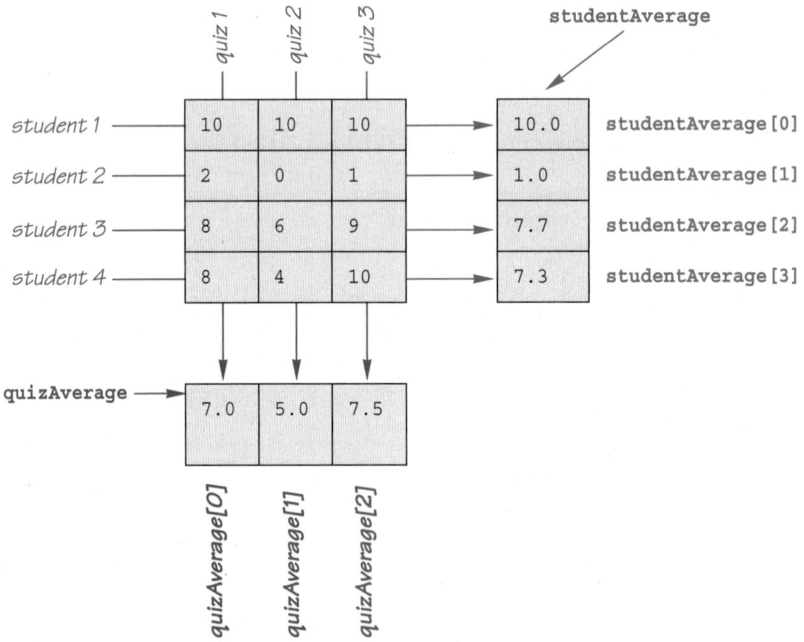

Display 6.20 **Demonstration of the Class GradeBook**

```
public class GradeBookDemo
{
    public static void main(String[] args)
    {
        GradeBook book = new GradeBook();
        book.display();
    }
}
```

Sample Dialogue

```
Enter number of students:
4
Enter number of quizzes:
3
Enter score for student number 1
on quiz number 1
10
Enter score for student number 1
on quiz number 2
10

   <The rest of the input dialog is omitted to save space.>

Student 1 Quizzes: 10 10 10 Ave = 10.0
Student 2 Quizzes: 2 0 1 Ave = 1.0
Student 3 Quizzes: 8 6 9 Ave = 7.66666666667
Student 4 Quizzes: 8 4 10 Ave = 7.33333333333
Quiz averages:
Quiz 1 Ave = 7.0 Quiz 2 Ave = 5.0 Quiz 3 Ave = 7.5
```

MyProgrammingLab™

Self-Test Exercises

24. Write a method definition for a method with the following heading. The method is to be added to the class `GradeBook` in Display 6.18.

```
/**
 Returns the grade that student numbered studentNumber received
 on quiz number quizNumber.
*/
public int getGrade(int studentNumber,int quizNumber)
```

(continued)

MyProgrammingLab™

Self-Test Exercises (continued)

25. Write a method definition for a method with the following heading. The method is to be added to the class `GradeBook` in Display 6.18.

```
/**
 Changes the grade for student number studentNumber on quiz
 number quizNumber to newGrade.
*/
public void changeGrade(int studentNumber,
                        int quizNumber, int newGrade))
```

26. Write a method definition for a method with the following heading. The method is to be added to the class `GradeBook` in Display 6.18.

```
/**
 Returns an array with the average quiz score for each student.
*/
public double[] getStudentAverages( )
```

27. Write a method definition for a method with the following heading. The method is to be added to the class `GradeBook` in Display 6.18.

```
/**
 Returns an array with the average score for each quiz.
*/
public double[] getQuizAverages( )
```

Chapter Summary

- An *array* can be used to store and manipulate a collection of data that is all of the same type.
- The *indexed variables* of an array can be used just like any other variables of the *base type* of the array.
- Arrays are objects that are created with `new` just like the class objects we discussed before this chapter (although there is a slight difference in the syntax used).
- A `for` loop is a good way to step through the elements of an array and perform some program action on each indexed variable.
- The most common programming error made when using arrays is to attempt to access a nonexistent array index. Always check the first and last iterations of a loop that manipulates an array to make sure it does not use an index that is illegally small or illegally large.

- The indexed variables of an array can be used as an argument to be plugged in for a parameter of the array's base type.
- A method can have parameters of an array type. When the method is invoked, an entire array is plugged in for the array parameter.
- A method may return an array as the value returned by the method.
- When using a *partially filled array*, your program needs an additional variable of type `int` to keep track of how much of the array is being used.
- An instance variable of a class can be of an array type.
- If you need an array with more than one index, you can use a multidimensional array, which is actually an array of arrays.

Answers to Self-Test Exercises

1. a. `word`

   b. `String`

   c. `5`

   d. `0` through `4` inclusive

   e. Any of the following would be correct:
   `word[0], word[1], word[2], word[3], word[4]`

2. a. `10`

   b. `0`

   c. `9`

3. `a, b, c,`

4.
```
1.1 2.2 3.3
1.1 3.3 3.3
```

5. The `for` loop uses indices `1` through `sampleArray.length`, but the correct indices are `0` through `sampleArray.length – 1`. The last index, `sampleArray.length`, is out of bounds. What was probably intended is the following:

```
int[] sampleArray = new int[10];
for (int index = 0; index < sampleArray.length; index++)
    sampleArray[index] = 3*index;
```

6. The last value of `index` is `a.length – 1`, which is the last index of the array. However, when `index` has the value `a.length – 1`, `a[index + 1]` has an index that is out of bounds because `index + 1` is one more than the largest array index. The `for` loop ending condition should instead be `index < a.length – 1`.

7.
```
SomeClass.doSomething(number); //Legal.
SomeClass.doSomething(a[2]); //Legal.
SomeClass.doSomething(a[3]); //Illegal. Index out of bounds.
SomeClass.doSomething(a[number]); //Legal.
SomeClass.doSomething(a); //Illegal.
```

8.
```
public static void oneMore(int[] a)
{
    for (int i = 0; i < a.length; i++)
        a[i] = a[i] + 1;
}
```

9.
```
public static int outOfOrder(double[]a)
{
    for (int index = 0; index < a.length - 1; index++)
    if (a[index] > a[index + 1])
          return (index + 1);
    return - 1;
}
```

10. This method is legal but pointless. When invoked, it has no effect on its argument. The parameter `a` is a local variable that contains a reference. The reference does indeed get changed so it refers to an array of double the size of the argument, but that reference goes away when the method ends. A method can change the values of the indexed variables of its argument, but it cannot change the reference in the array variable used as an argument.

11.
```
public static double[] halfArray(double[] a)
{
    double[] temp = new double[a.length];
    for (int i = 0; i < a.length; i++)
        temp[i] = a[i]/2.0;
    return temp;
}
```

12. The method will compile and run. The array returned has the correct values for its elements. However, the method will change the values of its array argument. If you want to change the values in the array argument, a `void` method would make more sense. If you want to return an array, you should probably return a new array (as in the version in the previous subsection), not return a changed version of the argument array.

13.
```
/**
 Precondition: numberUsed <= argumentArray.length;
 the first numberUsed indexed variables of argumentArray
 have values.
 Returns an array of length numberUsed whose ith element
 is argumentArray[i] - adjustment.
*/
```

```
public static double[] differenceArray(
 double[] argumentArray, int numberUsed, double adjustment)
{
    double[] temp = new double[numberUsed];
    for (int i = 0; i < numberUsed; i++)
        temp[i] = argumentArray[i] - adjustment;
    return temp;
}
```

14. The only changes are to add the method `differenceArray` and to rewrite the method `showDifference` as follows (the complete class definition is in the file `GolfScoresExercise.java` on the accompanying website):

extra code on website

```
public static void showDifference(double[] a,
                                           int numberUsed)
{
    double average = computeAverage(a, numberUsed);
    System.out.println("Average of the " + numberUsed
                                 + " scores = " + average);
    double[] difference =
                   differenceArray(a, numberUsed, average);
    System.out.println("The scores are:");
    for (int index = 0; index < numberUsed; index++)
          System.out.println(a[index] +
                               " differs from average by "
                                         + difference[index]);
}
```

15. The main differences are to remove parameters, replace the array name `a` by `score`, and make the method `fillArray` a `void` method. This code is in the file `GolfScoresStaticExercise.java` on the accompanying website.

extra code on website

```
import java.util.Scanner;

public class GolfScoresStaticExercise
{
    public static final int MAX_NUMBER_SCORES = 10;
    private static double[] score =
                       new double[MAX_NUMBER_SCORES];
    private static int numberUsed = 0;

    /**
     Shows differences between each of a list of golf scores
     and their average.
    */
    public static void main(String[] args)
    {
```

```
        System.out.println(
                  "This program reads golf scores and shows");
        System.out.println(
                  "how much each differs from the average.");

        System.out.println("Enter golf scores:");
        fillArray( );
        showDifference( );
    }

    /**
     Reads values into the array score.
    */
    public static void fillArray( )
    {
        System.out.println("Enter up to " + score.length
                       + " nonnegative numbers:");
        System.out.println(
           "Mark the end of the list with a negative number.");
        Scanner keyboard = new Scanner(System.in);

        double next;
        int index = 0;
        next = keyboard.nextDouble( );
        while ((next >= 0) && (index < score.length))
        {
            score[index] = next;
            index++;
            next = keyboard.nextDouble( );
            //index is the number of
            //array indexed variables used so far.
        }
        //index is the total number of array indexed variables used.

        if (next >= 0)
             System.out.println("Could only read in "
                            + score.length + " input values.");

        numberUsed = index;
    }

    /**
     Precondition: numberUsed <= score.length.
                   score[0] through score[numberUsed-1] have values.
     Returns the average of numbers ascore[0] through
     score[numberUsed-1].
    */
```

```
public static double computeAverage( )
{
    double total = 0;
    for (int index = 0; index < numberUsed; index++)
        total = total + score[index];
    if (numberUsed > 0)
    {
        return (total/numberUsed);
    }
    else
    {
        System.out.println(
                "ERROR: Trying to average 0 numbers.");
        System.out.println("computeAverage returns 0.");
        return 0;
    }
}

   /**
    Precondition: numberUsed <= score.length.
    The first numberUsed indexed variables of score have values.
    Postcondition: Gives screen output showing how much each of the
    first numberUsed elements of the array a differ from the average.
   */
   public static void showDifference( )
   {
       double average = computeAverage( );
       System.out.println("Average of the " + numberUsed
                                        + " scores = " + average);
       System.out.println("The scores are:");
       for (int index = 0; index < numberUsed; index++)
       System.out.println(score[index] +
                                     " differs from average by "
                                   + (score[index] - average));
   }
}
```

16.
```
public static int max(int... arg)
    {
        if (arg.length == 0)
        {
        System.out.println(
                  "Fatal Error: maximum of zero values.");
        System.exit(0);
        }
```

```
    int largest = Integer.MIN_VALUE;
    for (int element : arg)
        if (element > largest)
            largest = element;
    return largest;
}
```

17. The last line would change to the following:

```
I ate cod, broccoli, , peanuts, and apples.
```

18.
```
public void removeAll( )
{
     numberUsed = 0;
}
```

19.
```
public void increaseCapacity(int newCapacity)
{
    if (newCapacity > numberUsed)
    {
        maxNumberElements = newCapacity;
        double[] temp = new double[newCapacity];
        for (int i = 0; i < a.length; i++)
            temp[i] = a[i];
        a = temp;
    }//else do nothing.
}
```

20. All you need to do to make your code work for sorting into decreasing order is to replace the with in the following line of the definition of `indexOfSmallest`:

```
if (a[index] < min)
```

However, to make your code easy to read, you should also rename the method `indexOfSmallest` to `indexOfLargest`, rename the variable `min` to `max`, and rename the variable `indexOfMin` to `indexOfMax`. You should rewrite some of the comments to reflect these changes as well.

extra code on website

21. If an array has a value that occurs more than once and you sort the array using the method `SelectionSort.sort`, then there will be as many copies of the repeated value after the array is sorted as there originally were in the array.

22. We give two slightly different versions. Both versions are on the accompanying website.

```
import java.util.Scanner;

public class ForEachEnumDemo
{
    enum WorkDay {MONDAY, TUESDAY, WEDNESDAY, THURSDAY,FRIDAY};

    public static void main(String[] args)
    {
        WorkDay[] day = WorkDay.values( );
```

```
        Scanner keyboard = new Scanner(System.in);
        double hours = 0, sum = 0;

        for (WorkDay oneDay : day)
        {
             System.out.println("Enter hours worked for " +
             oneDay);
             hours = keyboard.nextDouble();
             sum = sum + hours;
        }

        System.out.println("Total hours work = " + sum);
    }
}

import java.util.Scanner;

public class ForEachEnumDemo2
{
    enum WorkDay {MONDAY, TUESDAY, WEDNESDAY, THURSDAY, FRIDAY};
    public static void main(String[] args)
    {
        Scanner keyboard = new Scanner(System.in);
        double hours = 0, sum = 0;

        for (WorkDay oneDay : WorkDay.values())
        {
            System.out.println("Enter hours worked for " + oneDay);
            hours = keyboard.nextDouble();
            sum = sum + hours;
        }

        System.out.println("Total hours work = " + sum);
    }
}
```

23.
```
0 1 2 3
0 1 2 3
0 1 2 3
0 1 2 3
```

24. If the array indices are out of bounds, then Java will halt the program with an error message, so no other checks on the parameters are needed.

```
/**
 Returns the grade that student number studentNumber received on
 quiz number quizNumber.
*/
public int getGrade(int studentNumber, int quizNumber)
{
    return grade[studentNumber][quizNumber];
}
```

25. If the array indices are out of bounds, then Java will halt the program with an error message, so no other checks on the parameters are needed.

```
/**
Changes the grade for student number studentNumber on quiz number
quizNumber to newGrade.
*/
public void changeGrade(int studentNumber,
                    int quizNumber, int newGrade)
{
    grade[studentNumber][quizNumber] = newGrade;
}
```

26.
```
/**
 Returns an array with the average quiz score for each student.
*/
public double[] getStudentAverages( )
{
    int arraySize = studentAverage.length;
    double[] temp = new double[arraySize];
    for (int i = 0; i < arraySize; i++)
        temp[i] = studentAverage[i];
    return temp;
}
```

27.
```
/**
 Returns an array with the average score for each quiz.
*/
public double[] getQuizAverages( )
{
    int arraySize = quizAverage.length;
    double[] temp = new double[arraySize];
    for (int i = 0; i < arraySize; i++)
        temp[i] = quizAverage[i];
    return temp;
}
```

MyProgrammingLab™

Programming Projects

Visit www.myprogramminglab.com to complete select exercises online and get instant feedback.

1. In the sport of diving, seven judges award a score between 0 and 10, where each score may be a floating-point value. The highest and lowest scores are thrown out and the remaining scores are added together. The sum is then multiplied by the degree of difficulty for that dive. The degree of difficulty ranges from 1.2 to 3.8 points. The total is then multiplied by 0.6 to determine the diver's score.

Write a computer program that inputs a degree of difficulty and seven judges' scores and outputs the overall score for that dive. The program should ensure that all inputs are within the allowable data ranges.

2. A common memory matching game played by young children is to start with a deck of cards that contain identical pairs. For example, given six cards in the deck, two might be labeled 1, two labeled 2, and two labeled 3. The cards are shuffled and placed face down on the table. A player then selects two cards that are face down, turns them face up, and if the cards match, they are left face up. If the two cards do not match, they are returned to their original face down position. The game continues until all cards are face up.

   Write a program that plays the memory matching game. Use 16 cards that are laid out in a 4 × 4 square and are labeled with pairs of numbers from 1 to 8. Your program should allow the player to specify the cards that he or she would like to select through a coordinate system.

   For example, in the following layout,

```
      1  2  3  4
   ---------------
1  |  8  *  *  *
2  |  *  *  *  *
3  |  *  8  *  *
4  |  *  *  *  *
```

   all of the face down cards are indicated by *. The pairs of 8 that are face up are at coordinates (1,1) and (2,3). To hide the cards that have been temporarily placed face up, output a large number of newlines to force the old board off the screen.

   Hint: Use a 2D array for the arrangement of cards and another 2D array that indicates if a card is face up or face down. Or, a more elegant solution is to create a single 2D array where each element is an object that stores both the card's value and face. Write a function that "shuffles" the cards in the array by repeatedly selecting two cards at random and swapping them.

3. Write a program that reads in the average monthly rainfall for a city for each month of the year and then reads in the actual monthly rainfall for each of the previous 12 months. The program should then print out a nicely formatted table showing the rainfall for each of the previous 12 months as well as how much above or below average the rainfall was for each month. The average monthly rainfall is given for the months January, February, and so forth, in order. To obtain the actual rainfall for the previous 12 months, the program should first ask what the current month is and then ask for the rainfall figures for the previous 12 months. The output should correctly label the months. There are a variety of ways to deal with the month names. One straightforward method is to code the months as integers and then do a conversion to a string for the month name before doing the output. A large

`switch` statement is acceptable in an output method. The month input can be handled in any manner you wish so long as it is relatively easy and pleasant for the user. Include a loop that allows the user to repeat this entire calculation until the user requests that the program end.

4. Write a static method called `deleteRepeats` that has a partially filled array of characters as a formal parameter and that deletes all repeated letters from the array. Because a partially filled array requires two arguments, the method should actually have two formal parameters: an array parameter and a formal parameter of type `int` that gives the number of array positions used. When a letter is deleted, the remaining letters are moved one position to fill in the gap. This creates empty positions at the end of the array so that less of the array is used. Because the formal parameter is a partially filled array, a second formal parameter of type `int` should tell how many array positions are filled. This second formal parameter cannot be changed by a Java method, so have the method return the new value for this parameter. For example, consider the following code:

```
char a[10];
a[0] = 'a';
a[1] = 'b';
a[2] = 'a';
a[3] = 'c';
int size = 4;
size = deleteRepeats(a, size);
```

After this code is executed, the value of `a[0]` is `'a'`, the value of `a[1]` is `'b'`, the value of `a[2]` is `'c'`, and the value of `size` is `3`. (The value of `a[3]` is no longer of any concern, because the partially filled array no longer uses this indexed variable.) You may assume that the partially filled array contains only lowercase letters. Write a suitable test program for your method.

5. The standard deviation of a list of numbers is a measure of how much the numbers deviate from the average. If the standard deviation is small, the numbers are clustered close to the average. If the standard deviation is large, the numbers are scattered far from the average. The standard deviation of a list of numbers n_1, n_2, n_3, and so forth is defined as the square root of the average of the following numbers:

$(n_1 - a)^2$, $(n_2 - a)^2$, $(n_3 - a)^2$, and so forth.

The number a is the average of the numbers n_1, n_2, n_3, and so forth.

Define a static method that takes a partially filled array of numbers as its argument and returns the standard deviation of the numbers in the partially filled array. Because a partially filled array requires two arguments, the method should actually have two formal parameters, an array parameter and a formal parameter of type `int` that gives the number of array positions used. The numbers in the array should be of type `double`. Write a suitable test program for your method.

6. Write a program that reads numbers from the keyboard into an array of type `int[]`. You may assume that there will be 50 or fewer entries in the array. Your program allows any number of numbers to be entered, up to 50. The output is to be a two-column list. The first column is a list of the distinct array elements; the second column is the count of the number of occurrences of each element. The list should be sorted on entries in the first column, largest to smallest.

   For the array

   ```
   -12 3 -12 4 1 1 -12 1 -1 1 2 3 4 2 3 -12
   ```

   the output should be

   ```
     N   Count
     4   2
     3   3
     2   2
     1   4
    -1   1
   -12   4
   ```

7. An array can be used to store large integers one digit at a time.

   For example, the integer `1234` could be stored in the array `a` by setting `a[0]` to `1`, `a[1]` to `2`, `a[2]` to `3`, and `a[3]` to `4`. However, for this exercise you might find it more useful to store the digits backward; that is, place `4` in `a[0]`, `3` in `a[1]`, `2` in `a[2]`, and `1` in `a[3]`. In this exercise, write a program that reads in 2 positive integers that are 20 or fewer digits in length and then outputs the sum of the 2 numbers. Your program will read the digits as values of type `char` so that the number `1234` is read as the four characters `'1'`, `'2'`, `'3'`, and `'4'`. After they are read into the program, the characters are changed to values of type `int`. The digits should be read into a partially filled array; you might find it useful to reverse the order of the elements in the array after the array is filled with data from the keyboard. (Whether or not you reverse the order of the elements in the array is up to you. It can be done either way, and each way has its advantages and disadvantages.) Your program should perform the addition by implementing the usual paper-and-pencil addition algorithm. The result of the addition should be stored in an array of size 20, and the result should then be written to the screen. If the result of the addition is an integer with more than the maximum number of digits (that is, more than 20 digits), then your program should issue a message saying that it has encountered "integer overflow." You should be able to change the maximum length of the integers by changing only one named constant. Include a loop that allows the user to continue to do more additions until the user says the program should end.

VideoNote
Solution to Programming Project 6.8

8. Design a class called `BubbleSort` that is similar to the class `SelectionSort` given in Display 6.11. The class `BubbleSort` will be used in the same way as the class `SelectionSort`, but it will use the bubble sort algorithm.

   The bubble sort algorithm checks all adjacent pairs of elements in the array from the beginning to the end and interchanges any two elements that are out of order. This process is repeated until the array is sorted. The algorithm is as follows:

   Bubble Sort Algorithm to Sort an Array `a`

   Repeat the following until the array `a` is sorted:

```
for (index = 0; index < a.length - 1; index++)
     if (a[index] > a[index + 1])
        Interchange the values of a[index] and a[index + 1].
```

   The bubble sort algorithm is good for sorting an array that is "almost sorted." It is not competitive with other sorting methods for most other situations.

9. Enhance the definition of the class `PartiallyFilledArray` (Display 6.5) in the following way: When the user attempts to add one additional element and there is no room in the array instance variable `a`, the user is allowed to add the element. The object creates a second array that is twice the size of the array `a`, copies values from the array `a` to the user's new array, makes this array (or more precisely its reference) the new value of a, and then adds the element to this new larger array `a`. Hence, this new class should have no limit (other than the physical size of the computer) to how many numbers it can hold. The instance variable `maxNumberOfElements` remains and the method `getMaxCapacity` is unchanged, but these now refer to the currently allocated memory and not to an absolute upper bound. Write a suitable test program.

10. Write a program that will allow two users to play tic-tac-toe. The program should ask for moves alternately from player X and player O. The program displays the game positions as follows:

```
1  2  3

4  5  6

7  8  9
```

   The players enter their moves by entering the position number they wish to mark. After each move, the program displays the changed board. A sample board configuration is

```
X  X  O

4  5  6

O  8  9
```

11. Write a program to assign passengers seats in an airplane. Assume a small airplane with seat numberings as follows:

```
1 A B C D
2 A B C D
3 A B C D
4 A B C D
5 A B C D
6 A B C D
7 A B C D
```

The program should display the seat pattern, with an `'X'` marking the seats already assigned. For example, after seats 1A, 2B, and 4C are taken, the display should look like the following:

```
1 X B C D
2 A X C D
3 A B C D
4 A B X D
5 A B C D
6 A B C D
7 A B C D
```

After displaying the seats available, the program should prompt for the seat desired, the user can type in a seat, and then the display of available seats should be updated. This continues until all seats are filled or until the user signals that the program should end. If the user types in a seat that is already assigned, the program should say that that seat is occupied and ask for another choice.

12. Write a program that plays a simple trivia game. The game should have five questions. Each question has a corresponding answer and point value between 1 and 3 based on the difficulty of the question. Implement the game using three arrays. An array of type `String` should be used for the questions. Another array of type `String` should be used to store the answers. An array of type `int` should be used for the point values. All three arrays should be declared to be of size 5.

The index into the three arrays can be used to tie the question, answer, and point value together. For example, the item at index 0 for each array would correspond to question 1, answer 1, and the point value for question 1. The item at index 1 for each array would correspond to question 2, answer 2, and the point value for question 2, and so forth. Manually hardcode the five questions, answers, and point values into your program using trivia of your choice.

Your program should ask the player each question one at a time and allow the player to enter an answer. If the player's answer matches thc actual answer, the player wins the number of points for that question. If the player's answer is incorrect, the player wins no points for the question. Your program should show the correct answer if the player is incorrect. After the player has answered all five questions, the game is over, and your program should display the player's total score.

13. Modify Programming Project 6.12 to use a single array instead of three arrays. This can be accomplished by creating a `Trivia` object that encapsulates the question, answer, and point value for a particular trivia question. Next, create a single array of five `Trivia` objects instead of three separate arrays for the question, answer, and point values. This change will make your game more scalable if there were ever additional properties to add to a `Trivia` object (you would not need to add another array for each property). Although the program has internally changed to a single array of objects, the execution of the program should be identical to before.

14. Traditional password entry schemes are susceptible to "shoulder surfing" in which an attacker watches an unsuspecting user enter his or her password or PIN number and uses it later to gain access to the account. One way to combat this problem is with a randomized challenge-response system. In these systems, the user enters different information every time based on a secret in response to a randomly generated challenge. Consider the following scheme in which the password consists of a five-digit PIN number (00000 to 99999). Each digit is assigned a random number that is 1, 2, or 3. The user enters the random numbers that correspond to their PIN instead of their actual PIN numbers.

    For example, consider an actual PIN number of 12345. To authenticate it, the user would be presented with a screen such as the following:

    ```
    PIN: 0 1 2 3 4 5 6 7 8 9
    NUM: 3 2 3 1 1 3 2 2 1 3
    ```

    The user would enter 23113 instead of 12345. This does not divulge the password even if an attacker intercepts the entry because 23113 could correspond to other PIN numbers, such as 69440 or 70439. The next time the user logs in, a different sequence of random numbers would be generated, such as the following:

    ```
    PIN: 0 1 2 3 4 5 6 7 8 9
    NUM: 1 1 2 3 1 2 2 3 3 3
    ```

    Your program should simulate the authentication process. Store an actual PIN number in your program. The program should use an array to assign random numbers to the digits from 0 to 9. Output the random digits to the screen, input the response from the user, and output whether or not the user's response correctly matches the PIN number.

VideoNote
Solution to Programming Project 6.15

15. Programming Project 4.12 asked you to create a `PizzaOrder` class that stores an order consisting of up to three pizzas. Modify the class to store the pizzas using an array. This will allow the class to include an arbitrary number of pizzas in the order instead of a maximum of three. The `setNumPizzas` method can be used to create an array of the appropriate size. The array structure allows you to eliminate the methods `setPizza1`, `setPizza2`, and `setPizza3` and replace them with a single method, `setPizza(int index, Pizza newPizza)`. Include appropriate tests to determine if the new `PizzaOrder` class is working correctly.

16. Programming Project 3.15 asked you to explore Benford's Law. An easier way to write the program is to use an array to store the digit counts. That is, `count[0]` might store the number of times 0 is the first digit (if that is possible in your data set), `count[1]` might store the number of times 1 is the first digit, and so forth. Redo Programming Project 3.15 using arrays.

    Write a program that tests Benford's Law. Collect a list of at least 100 numbers from some real-life data source and enter them into a text file. Your program should use an array to store the digit counts. That is, `count[0]` might store the number of times 0 is the first digit (if that is possible in your data set), `count[1]` might store the number of times 1 is the first digit, and so forth. For each digit, output the percentage it appears as the first digit.

17. Programming Project 4.14 asked you to read in a CSV file of product ratings. The file was limited to exactly five products. Redo Programming Project 4.14, except calculate the name of each product and how many products are in the file based on the header line. Then read the CSV file and translate the data into a 2D array that stores all of the ratings. Finally, output the average rating for each product.

18. Programming Project 4.13 asked you to create a `BoxOfProduce` class representing a box of produce to deliver from a CSA farm. The box contained exactly three items. Modify the class so it uses an array of type `String` to represent the items in the box. You can still start with three random items to place in the box, but your menu should be modified to allow the user to add additional items and still substitute one item for another. You will likely need to modify the constructor of the `BoxOfProduce` class and also add new methods.

19. Some word games require the player to find words that can be formed using the letters of another word. For example, given the word *SWIMMING*, other words that can be formed using the letters include *SWIM*, *WIN*, *WING*, *SING*, *MIMING*, etc. Write a program that lets the user enter a word and then output all the words contained in the file `words.txt` that can be formed from the letters of the entered word. One algorithm to do this is to compare the letter histograms for each word. Create an array that counts up the number of each letter in the entered word (e.g., one S, one W, two I, two M, etc.) and then creates a similar array for the current word read from the file. The two arrays can be compared to see if the word from the file could be created out of the letters from the entered word.

Inheritance 7

7 Inheritance

Like mother, like daughter.

COMMON SAYING

Introduction

Object-oriented programming (OOP) is a popular and powerful programming philosophy. One of the main techniques of OOP is known as *inheritance*. **Inheritance** means that a very general form of a class can be defined and compiled. Later, more specialized versions of that class may be defined by starting with the already defined class and adding more specialized instance variables and methods. The specialized classes are said to *inherit* the methods and instance variables of the previously defined general class. In this chapter, we cover inheritance in general and more specifically how it is realized in Java.

Prerequisites

This chapter does not use any material on arrays from Chapter 6. It does require Chapters 1 through 5 with the exception that most of the chapter does not require Section 5.4 on packages and `javadoc`. In this chapter, the subsection "Protected and Package Access" is the only section that requires any knowledge from Section 5.4, and it requires only the material on packages, and not the material on `javadoc`. If you omit the subsection "Protected and Package Access," you will not suffer any loss of continuity in reading this chapter.

7.1 Inheritance Basics

If there is anything that we wish to change in the child, we should first examine it and see whether it is not something that could better be changed in ourselves.

CARL GUSTAV JUNG, *the integration of the personality*

Inheritance is the process by which a new class—known as a *derived class*—is created from another class, called the *base class*. A derived class automatically has all the instance variables and all the methods that the base class has, and can have additional methods and/or additional instance variables.

Derived Classes

Suppose we are designing a record-keeping program that has records for salaried employees and hourly employees. There is a natural hierarchy for grouping these classes. These are all classes of people who share the property of being employees.

Employees who are paid an hourly wage are one subset of employees. Another subset consists of salaried employees who are paid a fixed wage each month. Although the program may not need any type corresponding to the set of all employees, thinking in terms of the more general concept of employees can be useful. For example, all employees have a name and a hire date (when they started working for the company), and the methods for setting and changing names and hire dates will be the same for salaried and hourly employees. The classes for hourly employees and salaried employees may be further subdivided as diagrammed in Display 7.1.

Within Java, you can define a class called `Employee` that includes all employees (salaried or hourly), and then use this class to define classes for hourly employees and salaried employees. You can then, in turn, use classes such as `HourlyEmployee` to define classes such as `PartTimeHourlyEmployee`, and so forth.

Display 7.2 shows our definition for the class `Employee`. This class is a pretty ordinary class. What is interesting about this class is how we use it to create a class for hourly employees and a class for salaried employees. It is legal to create an object of the class `Employee`, but our reason for defining the class `Employee` is so that we can define derived classes for different kinds of employees.

Display 7.1 A Class Hierarchy

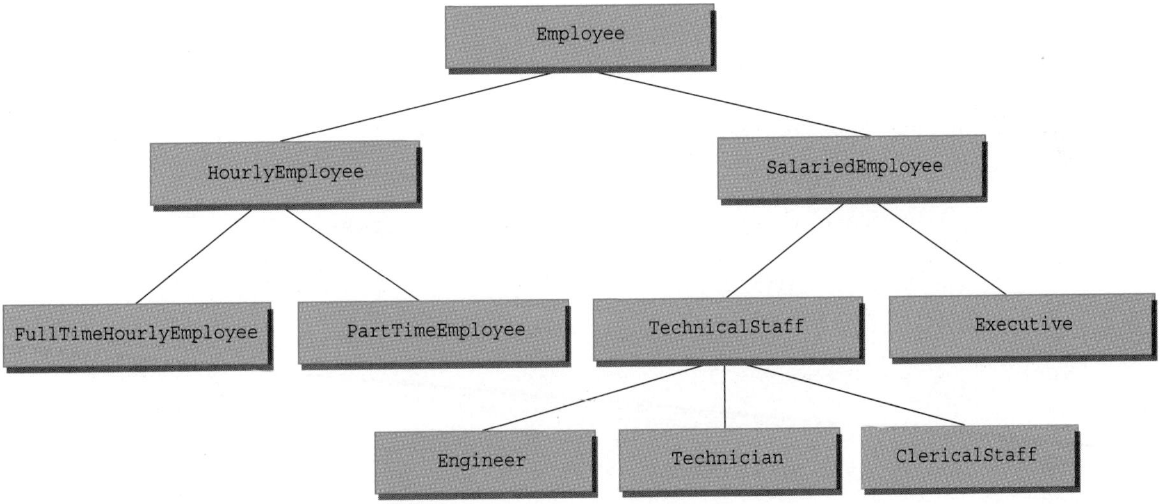

Display 7.2 The Base Class Employee (part 1 of 2)

```
/**
Class Invariant: All objects have a name string and hire date.
A name string of "No name" indicates no real name specified yet.
A hire date of January 1, 1000 indicates no real hire date specified yet.
*/
public class Employee
{
    private String name;
    private Date hireDate;
    public Employee()
    {
        name = "No name";
        hireDate = new Date("January", 1, 1000); //Just a placeholder.
    }

    /**
    Precondition: Neither theName nor theDate is null.
    */
    public Employee(String theName, Date theDate)
    {
        if (theName == null || theDate == null)
        {
            System.out.println("Fatal Error creating employee.");
            System.exit(0);
        }
        name = theName;
        hireDate = new Date(theDate);
    }

    public Employee(Employee originalObject)
    {
        name = originalObject.name;
        hireDate = new Date(originalObject.hireDate);
    }

    public String getName()
    {
        return name;
    }

    public Date getHireDate()
    {
        return new Date(hireDate);
    }
```

The class `Date` is defined in Display 4.13.

Display 7.2 **The Base Class Employee** (part 2 of 2)

```
    /**
     Precondition newName is not null.
    */
    public void setName(String newName)
    {
        if (newName == null)
        {
            System.out.println("Fatal Error setting employee name.");
            System.exit(0);
        }
        else
            name = newName;
    }

    /**
    Precondition newDate is not null.
    */
    public void setHireDate(Date newDate)
    {
        if (newDate == null)
        {
            System.out.println("Fatal Error setting employee hire " +
            "date.");
            System.exit(0);
        }
        else
            hireDate = new Date(newDate);
    }


    public String toString()
    {
        return (name + " " + hireDate.toString());
    }

    public boolean equals(Employee otherEmployee)
    {
        return (name.equals(otherEmployee.name)
                      && hireDate.equals(otherEmployee.hireDate));
    }
}
```

Display 7.3 contains the definition of a class for hourly employees. An hourly employee is an employee, so we define the class `HourlyEmployee` to be a *derived* class of the class `Employee`. A **derived class** is a class defined by adding instance variables and methods to an existing class. The existing class that the derived class is built upon is called the **base class**. In our example, `Employee` is the base class and `HourlyEmployee` is the derived class. As you can see in Display 7.3, the way we indicate that `HourlyEmployee` is a derived class of `Employee` is by including the phrase `extends Employee` on the first line of the class definition, like so:

derived class

base class

`extends`

```
public class HourlyEmployee extends Employee
```

subclass and superclass

A derived class is also called a **subclass**, in which case the base class is usually called a **superclass**. However, we prefer to use the terms *derived class* and *base class*.

When you define a derived class, you give only the added instance variables and the added methods. For example, the class `HourlyEmployee` has all the instance variables and all the methods of the class `Employee`, but you do not mention them in the definition of `HourlyEmployee`. Every object of the class `HourlyEmployee` has instance variables called `name` and `hireDate`, but you do not specify the instance variable `name` or the instance variable `hireDate` in the definition of the class `HourlyEmployee`. The class `HourlyEmployee` (or any other derived class) is said to **inherit** the instance variables and methods of the base class that it extends. For this reason, the topic of derived classes is called **inheritance**.

inheritance

Just as it inherits the instance variables of the class `Employee`, the class `HourlyEmployee` inherits all the methods from the class `Employee`. So, the class `HourlyEmployee` inherits the methods `getName`, `getHireDate`, `setName`, and `setHireDate`, from the class `Employee`.

For example, suppose you create a new object of the class `HourlyEmployee` as follows:

```
HourlyEmployee joe = new HourlyEmployee();
```

Then, the name of the object `joe` can be changed using the method `setName`, which the class `HourlyEmployee` inherited from the class `Employee`. The inherited method `setName` is used just like any other method; for example,

```
joe.setName("Josephine");
```

A small demonstration of this is given in Display 7.4.

VideoNote
Inheritance Walkthrough

Display 7.5 contains the definition of the class `SalariedEmployee`, which is also derived from the class `Employee`. The class `SalariedEmployee` inherits all the instance variables and methods of the class `Employee`. Inheritance allows you to reuse code, such as the code in the class `Employee`, without needing to literally copy the code into the definitions of the derived classes, such as `HourlyEmployee` and `SalariedEmployee`.

Display 7.3 The Derived Class **HourlyEmployee** (part 1 of 3)

```
/**
 Class Invariant: All objects have a name string, hire date, nonnegative
 wage rate, and nonnegative number of hours worked. A name string of
 "No name" indicates no real name specified yet. A hire date of
 January 1, 1000 indicates no real hire date specified yet.
*/
public class HourlyEmployee extends Employee
{
    private double wageRate;
    private double hours; //for the month
```

It will take the rest of Section 7.1 to explain this class definition.

```
    public HourlyEmployee()
    {
        super();
        wageRate = 0;
        hours = 0;
    }
```

If this line is omitted, Java will still invoke the no-argument constructor for the base class.

```
    /**
     Precondition: Neither theName nor theDate is null;
     theWageRate and theHours are nonnegative.
    */
    public HourlyEmployee(String theName, Date theDate,
                          double theWageRate, double theHours)
    {
        super(theName, theDate);
        if ((theWageRate >= 0) && (theHours >= 0))
        {
            wageRate = theWageRate;
            hours = theHours;
        }
        else
        {
            System.out.println(
                 "Fatal Error: creating an illegal hourly employee.");
            System.exit(0);
        }
    }

    public HourlyEmployee(HourlyEmployee originalObject)
    {
        super (originalObject);
```

An object of the class **HourlyEmployee** *is also an instance of the class* **Employee**.

(continued)

Display 7.3 The Derived Class **HourlyEmployee** (part 2 of 3)

```
            wageRate = originalObject.wageRate;
            hours = originalObject.hours;
        }
        public double getRate()
        {
            return wageRate;
        }
        public double getHours()
        {
            return hours;
        }

        /**
         Returns the pay for the month.
        */
        public double getPay()
        {
            return wageRate*hours;
        }

        /**
         Precondition: hoursWorked is nonnegative.
        */
        public void setHours(double hoursWorked)
        {
              if (hoursWorked >= 0)
                  hours = hoursWorked;
              else
              {
                  System.out.println("Fatal Error: Negative hours worked.");
                  System.exit(0);
              }
        }

        /**
         precondition: newWageRate is nonnegative.
        */
        public void setRate(double newWageRate)
        {
              if (newWageRate >= 0)
                  wageRate = newWageRate;
              else
              {
                  System.out.println("Fatal Error: Negative wage rate.");
                  System.exit(0);
```

Display 7.3 The Derived Class **HourlyEmployee** (part 3 of 3)

```
        }
    }
```

The method `toString` is overridden so it is different in the derived class `HourlyEmployee` than it is in the base class `Employee`.

```
    public String toString()
    {
        return (getName() + " " + getHireDate().toString()
                + "\n$" + wageRate + " per hour for " + hours + " hours");
    }

    public boolean equals(HourlyEmployee other)
    {
       return (getName().equals(other.getName())
                && getHireDate().equals(other.getHireDate())
                && wageRate == other.wageRate
                && hours == other.hours);
    }
}
```

We will show you a better way to define `equals` in the subsection "The Right Way to Define equals."

Derived Class (Subclass)

Define a **derived class** by starting with another already defined class and adding (or changing) methods, instance variables, and static variables. The class you start with is called the **base class**. The derived class inherits all the public methods, all the public and private instance variables, and all the public and private static variables from the base class, and it can add more instance variables, more static variables, and more methods. So, of the things we have seen thus far, the only members not inherited are private methods. (As discussed in the subsection "Overriding a Method Definition," the derived class definition can also change the definition of an inherited method.) A derived class is also called a **subclass**, in which case the base class is usually called a **superclass**.

SYNTAX

```
public class Derived_Class_Name extends Base_Class_Name
{
        Declarations_of_Added_Static_Variables
        Declarations_of_Added_Instance_Variables
        Definitions_of_Added__And_Overridden_Methods
}
```

EXAMPLE

See Displays 7.3 and 7.5.

Display 7.4 **Inheritance Demonstration**

The methods `getName` *and* `setName` *are inherited from the base class* `Employee`.

```
public class InheritanceDemo
{
    public static void main(String[] args)
    {
        HourlyEmployee joe = new HourlyEmployee("Joe Worker",
                                    new Date("January", 1, 2004),
                                        50.50, 160);

        System.out.println("joe's longer name is " +
           joe.getName());

        System.out.println("Changing joe's name to Josephine.");
        joe.setName("Josephine");

        System.out.println("joe's record is as follows:");
        System.out.println(joe);
    }
}
```

Sample Dialogue

```
joe's longer name is Joe Worker
Changing joe's name to Josephine.
joe's record is as follows:
Josephine January 1, 2004
$50.5 per hour for 160 hours
```

Inherited Members

A derived class automatically has all the instance variables, all the static variables, and all the public methods of the base class. These members from the base class are said to be **inherited**. These inherited methods and inherited instance and static variables are, with one exception, not mentioned in the definition of the derived class, but they are automatically members of the derived class. The one exception is as follows: As explained in the subsection "Overriding a Method Definition," you can give a definition for an inherited method in the definition of the derived class; this will redefine the meaning of the method for the derived class.

Display 7.5 The Derived Class `SalariedEmployee` (part 1 of 2)

```
1 /**
2 Class Invariant: All objects have a name string, hire date,
3 and nonnegative salary. A name string of "No name" indicates
4 no real name specified yet. A hire date of January 1, 1000 indicates
5 no real hire date specified yet.
6 */
7 public class SalariedEmployee extends Employee
8 {
9 private double salary; //annual

10 public SalariedEmployee()
11 {
12 super();
13 salary = 0;
14 }

15 /**
16 Precondition: Neither theName nor theDate are null;
17 theSalary is nonnegative.
18 */
19 public SalariedEmployee(String theName, Date theDate, double theSalary)
20 {
21 super(theName, theDate);
22 if (theSalary >= 0)
23 salary = theSalary;
24 else
25 {
26 System.out.println("Fatal Error: Negative salary.");
27 System.exit(0);
28 }
29 }

30 public SalariedEmployee(SalariedEmployee originalObject)
31 {
32 super(originalObject);
33 salary = originalObject.salary;
34 }

35 public double getSalary()
36 {
37 return salary;
38 }
```

It will take the rest of Section 7.1 to fully explain this class definition.

If this line is omitted, Java will still invoke the no-argument constructor for the base class.

An object of the class `SalariedEmployee` is also an object of the class `Employee`.

(continued)

Display 7.5 **The Derived Class `SalariedEmployee`** (part 2 of 2)

```
    /**
     Returns the pay for the month.
    */
    public double getPay()
    {
        return salary/12;
    }

    /**
     Precondition: newSalary is nonnegative.
    */
    public void setSalary(double newSalary)
    {
          if (newSalary >= 0)
              salary = newSalary;
          else
          {
              System.out.println("Fatal Error: Negative salary.");
              System.exit(0);
          }
    }

    public String toString()
    {
        return (getName() + " " + getHireDate().toString()
                                     + "\n$" + salary + " per year");
    }

    public boolean equals(SalariedEmployee other)
    {
        return (getName().equals(other.getName())
                && getHireDate().equals(other.getHireDate())
                && salary == other.salary);
    }
}
```

We will show you a better way to define `equals` in the subsection "The Right Way to Define equals."

parent class

child class

ancestor class

descendent class

Parent and Child Classes

A base class is often called the **parent class**. A derived class is then called a **child class**. This analogy is often carried one step further. A class that is a parent of a parent of a parent of another class (or some other number of "parent of" iterations) is often called an **ancestor class**. If class A is an ancestor of class B, then class B is often called a **descendent** of class A.

Overriding a Method Definition

overriding

The definition of an inherited method can be changed in the definition of a derived class so that it has a meaning in the derived class that is different from what it is in the base class. This is called **overriding** the definition of the inherited method. For example, the methods `toString` and `equals` are overridden (redefined) in the definition of the derived class `HourlyEmployee`. They are also overridden in the class `SalariedEmployee`. To override a method definition, simply give the new definition of the method in the class definition, just as you would with a method that is added in the derived class.

> **Overriding a Method Definition**
>
> A derived class inherits methods that belong to the base class. However, if a derived class requires a different definition for an inherited method, the method may be redefined in the derived class. This is called **overriding** the method definition.

> **The `final` Modifier**
>
> If you add the modifier `final` to the definition of a method, it indicates that the method may not be redefined in a derived class. If you add the modifier `final` to the definition of a class, it indicates that the class may not be used as a base class to derive other classes. We will say more about the `final` modifier in Chapter 8.

Changing the Return Type of an Overridden Method

In a derived class, you can override (change) the definition of a method from the base class. As a general rule, when overriding a method definition, you may *not* change the type returned by the method, and you may not change a `void` method to a method that returns a value, nor a method that returns a value to a `void` method. The one exception to this rule is if the returned type is a class type, then you may change the returned type to that of any descendent class of the returned type. For example, if a function returns the type `Employee` (Display 7.2), when you override the function definition in a derived class, you may change the returned type to `HourlyEmployee` (Display 7.3), `SalariedEmployee` (Display 7.5), or any other descendent class of the class `Employee`. This sort of changed return type is known as a **covariant return type** and is new in Java version 5.0; it was not allowed in earlier versions of Java. Earlier versions of Java allowed absolutely no changes to the returned type. We will give complete examples of changing the returned type of an overridden method in Chapter 8. Here we will just outline an example.

covariant return type

For example, suppose one class definition includes the following details:

```
public class BaseClass
{
      . . .
    public Employee getSomeone(int someKey)
      . . .
```

In this case, the following details would be allowed in a derived class:

```
public class DerivedClass extends BaseClass
{
      . . .
    public HourlyEmployee getSomeone(int someKey)
      . . .
```

When the method definition for `getSomeone` is overridden in `DerivedClass`, the returned type is changed from `Employee` to `HourlyEmployee`.

It is worth noting that when you change the returned type of an overridden method in this way, such as from `Employee` to `HourlyEmployee`, you are not really changing the returned type so much as placing additional restrictions on it. Every `HourlyEmployee` is an `Employee` with some additional properties that, while they are properties of every `HourlyEmployee`, are not properties of every `Employee`. Any code that was written for a method of the base class and that assumed the value returned by the method is `Employee` will be legal for an overridden version of the method that returns an `HourlyEmployee`. This is true because every `HourlyEmployee` is an `Employee`.

Changing the Access Permission of an Overridden Method

You can change the access permission of an overridden method from `private` in the base class to `public` in the derived class (or in any other way that makes access permissions more permissive). For example, if the following is a method heading in a base case,

```
private void doSomething()
```

then you can use the following heading when overriding the method definition in a derived class:

```
public void doSomething()
```

Note that you cannot change permissions to make them more restricted in the derived class. You can change `private` to `public`, but you cannot change `public` to `private`.

This makes sense, because you want code written for the base class method to work for the derived class method. You can use a public method anyplace that you can use a private method, but it is not true that you can use a private method anyplace that you can use a public method.

PITFALL: Overriding versus Overloading

Do not confuse *overriding* (that is, redefining) a method definition in a derived class with *overloading* a method name. When you override a method definition, the new method definition given in the derived class has the exact same number and types of parameters. On the other hand, if the method in the derived class were to have a different number of parameters or a parameter of a different type from the method in the base class, then the derived class would have both methods. That would be overloading. For example, suppose we add the following method to the definition of the class `HourlyEmployee` (Display 7.3):

```
public void setName(String firstName, String lastName)
{
   if ( (firstName == null) || (lastName == null) )
   {
      System.out.println("Fatal Error setting employee name.");
      System.exit(0);
   }
   else
      name = firstName + " " + lastName;
}
```

The class `HourlyEmployee` would then have this two-argument method `setName`, and it would also inherit the following one-argument method `setName` from the base class `Employee`:

```
public void setName(String newName)
{
   if (newName == null)
   {
      System.out.println("Fatal Error setting employee name.");
      System.exit(0);
   }
   else
      name = newName;
}
```

The class `HourlyEmployee` would have two methods named `setName`. This would be *overloading* the method name `setName`.

(continued)

PITFALL: (continued)

On the other hand, both the class `Employee` and the class `HourlyEmployee` define a method with the following method heading:

```
public String toString()
```

In this case, the class `HourlyEmployee` has only one method named `toString()`, but the definition of the method `toString()` in the class `HourlyEmployee` is different from the definition of `toString()` in the class `Employee`; the method `toString()` has been *overridden* (that is, redefined).

If you get overriding and overloading confused, you do have one consolation. They are both legal. ■

The `super` Constructor

You can invoke a constructor of the base class within the definition of a derived class constructor. A constructor for a derived class uses a constructor from the base class in a special way. A constructor for the base class normally initializes all the data inherited from the base class. So a constructor for a derived class begins with an invocation of a constructor for the base class. The details are described next.

There is a special syntax for invoking the base class constructor that is illustrated by the constructor definitions for the class `HourlyEmployee` given in Display 7.3. In what follows, we have reproduced the beginning of one of the constructor definitions for the class `HourlyEmployee` taken from that display:

```
public HourlyEmployee(String theName, Date theDate,
                      double theWageRate, double theHours)
{
    super(theName, theDate);
    if ((theWageRate >= 0) && (theHours >= 0))
    {
        wageRate = theWageRate;
        hours = theHours;
    }
    else
    . . .
```

The line

super

```
super(theName, theDate);
```

is a call to a constructor for the base class, which in this case is a call to a constructor for the class `Employee`.

MyProgrammingLab™

Self-Test Exercises

1. Suppose the class named `DiscountSale` is a derived class of a class called `Sale`. Suppose the class `Sale` has instance variables named `price` and `numberOfItems`. Will an object of the class `DiscountSale` also have instance variables named `price` and `numberOfItems`?

2. Suppose the class named `DiscountSale` is a derived class of a class called `Sale`, and suppose the class `Sale` has public methods named `getTotal` and `getTax`. Will an object of the class `DiscountSale` have methods named `getTotal` and `getTax`? If so, do these methods have to perform the exact same actions in the class `DiscountSale` as in the class `Sale`?

3. Suppose the class named `DiscountSale` is a derived class of a class called `Sale`, and suppose the class `Sale` has a method with the following heading and no other methods named `getTax`, as follows:

   ```
   public double getTax()
   ```

   And suppose the definition of the class `DiscountSale` has a method definition with the following heading and no other method definitions for methods named `getTax`, as follows:

   ```
   public double getTax(double rate)
   ```

   How many methods named `getTax` will the class `DiscountSale` have and what are their headings?

4. The class `HourlyEmployee` (Display 7.3) has methods named `getName` and `getRate` (among others). Why does the definition of the class `HourlyEmployee` contain a definition of the method `getRate` but no definition of the method `getName`?

There are some restrictions on how you can use the base class constructor call `super`. You cannot use an instance variable as an argument to `super`. Also, the call to the base class constructor (`super`) must always be the first action taken in a constructor definition. You cannot use it later in the definition of a constructor.

Notice that you use the keyword `super` to call the constructor of the base class. You do not use the name of the constructor; you do *not* use

```
Employee(theName, theDate); //ILLEGAL
```

If a constructor definition for a derived class does not include an invocation of a constructor for the base class, then the no-argument constructor of the base class is invoked automatically as the first action of the derived class constructor. So, the following definition of the no-argument constructor for the class `HourlyEmployee` (with `super` omitted) is equivalent to the version we gave in Display 7.3:

```
public HourlyEmployee()
{
    wageRate = 0;
    hours = 0;
}
```

A derived class object has all the instance variables of the base class. These inherited instance variables should be initialized, and the base class constructor is the most convenient place to initialize these inherited instance variables. That is why you should always include a call to one of the base class constructors when you define a constructor for a derived class. As already noted, if you do not include a call to a base class constructor (using `super`), then the no-argument constructor of the base class is called automatically. (If there is no no-argument constructor for the base class, that is an error condition.)

Call to a Base Class Constructor

Within the definition of a constructor for a class, you can use `super` as a name for a constructor of the base class. Any invocation of `super` must be the first action taken by the constructor.

EXAMPLE

```
public SalariedEmployee(SalariedEmployee originalObject)
{
    super(originalObject); //Invocation of base class
                           //constructor.
    salary = originalObject.salary;
}
```

The `this` Constructor

`this`

When defining a constructor, it is sometimes convenient to be able to call one of the other constructors in the same class. You can use the keyword `this` as a method name to invoke a constructor in the same class. This use of `this` is similar to the use of `super`, but with `this`, the call is to a constructor of the same class, not to a constructor for the base class. For example, consider the following alternate, and equivalent, definition of the no-argument constructor for the class `HourlyEmployee` (from Display 7.3):

```
public HourlyEmployee()
{
    this("No name", new Date("January", 1, 1000), 0, 0);
}
```

The line with `this` is an invocation of the constructor with the following heading:

```
public HourlyEmployee(String theName, Date theDate,
                      double theWageRate, double theHours)
```

The restrictions on how you can use the base class constructor call `super` also apply to the `this` constructor. You cannot use an instance variable as an argument to `this`. Also, any call to the constructor `this` must always be the first action taken in a constructor definition. Thus, a constructor definition cannot contain both an invocation of `super` and an invocation of `this`. If you want to include both a call to `super` and a call to `this`, use a call with `this`, and have the constructor that is called with `this` have `super` as its first action.

Call to Another Constructor in the Same Class

Within the definition of a constructor for a class, you can use `this` as a name for another constructor in the same class. Any invocation of `this` must be the first action taken by the constructor.

EXAMPLE

```
public HourlyEmployee()
{
    this("No name", new Date("January", 1, 1000), 0,0);
}
```

TIP: An Object of a Derived Class Has More than One Type

An object of a derived class has the type of the derived class. It also has the type of the base class, and more generally, it has the type of every one of its ancestor classes. For example, consider the following copy constructor definition from the class `HourlyEmployee` (Display 7.3):

```
public HourlyEmployee(HourlyEmployee originalObject)
{
    super(originalObject);
    wageRate = originalObject.wageRate;
    hours = originalObject.hours;
}
```

(continued)

TIP: (continued)

The line

```
super(originalObject);
```

is an invocation of a constructor for the base class `Employee`. The class `Employee` has no constructor with a parameter of type `HourlyEmployee`, but `originalObject` is of type `HourlyEmployee`. Fortunately, every object of type `HourlyEmployee` is also of type `Employee`. So, this invocation of `super` is an invocation of the copy constructor for the class `Employee`.

The fact that every object is not only of its own type but is also of the type of its ancestor classes simply reflects what happens in the everyday world. An hourly employee is an employee as well as an hourly employee. This sometimes is referred to as the **"is a" relationship**: For example, an `HourlyEmployee` is an `Employee`.

"is a" relationship

Display 7.6 contains a program demonstrating that an `HourlyEmployee` and a `SalariedEmployee` are also `Employee` objects. The method `showEmployee` requires an argument of type `Employee`. The objects `joe` and `sam` are of type `Employee` because they are instances of classes derived from the class `Employee` and so are suitable arguments for `showEmployee`. ■

An Object of a Derived Class Has More than One Type

An object of a derived class has the type of the derived class, and it also has the type of the base class. More generally, a derived class has the type of every one of its ancestor classes. So, you can assign an object of a derived class to a variable of any ancestor type (but not the other way around). You can plug in a derived class object for a parameter of any of its ancestor types. More generally, you can use a derived class object anyplace you can use an object of any of its ancestor types.

Display 7.6 An Object Belongs to Multiple Classes

```
public class IsADemo
{
    public static void main(String[] args)
    {
        SalariedEmployee joe = new SalariedEmployee("Josephine",
                                new Date("January", 1, 2004), 100000);
        HourlyEmployee sam = new HourlyEmployee("Sam",
                                new Date("February", 1, 2003), 50.50, 40);

        System.out.println("joe's longer name is " + joe.getName());
        System.out.println("showEmployee(joe) invoked:");
        showEmployee(joe);

        System.out.println("showEmployee(sam) invoked:");
        showEmployee(sam);

    }

    public static void showEmployee(Employee employeeObject)
    {
            System.out.println(employeeObject.getName());
            System.out.println(employeeObject.getHireDate());
    }
}
```

A **SalariedEmployee** *is an* **Employee**.

An **HourlyEmployee** *is an* **Employee**.

Sample Dialogue

```
joe's longer name is Josephine
showEmployee(joe) invoked:
Josephine
January 1, 2004
showEmployee(sam) invoked:
Sam
February 1, 2003
```

PITFALL: The Terms *Subclass* and *Superclass*

subclass and superclass

Many programmers and authors use the term *subclass* for a derived class and use *superclass* for its base class (or any of its ancestor classes). This is logical. For example, the collection of all hourly employees in the world is a subclass of all employees. Similarly, the collection of all objects of type `HourlyEmployee` is a subcollection of the collection of all objects of the class `Employee`. As you add more instance variables and methods, you restrict the number of objects that can satisfy the class definition. Despite this logic, people often reverse the terms *subclass* and *superclass*. Remember that these terms refer to the collections of objects of the derived class and the base class and not to the number of instance variables or methods. A derived class is a *subclass* (not a *superclass*) of its base class. Another way to remember which is a superclass is to recall that the `super` constructor invocation is an invocation of the base class and so the base class is the *superclass*. ■

MyProgrammingLab™

Self-Test Exercises

5. Is the following program legal? The relevant classes are defined in Displays 7.2, 7.3, and 7.5.

```
public class EmployeeDemo
{
    public static void main(String[] args)
    {
        HourlyEmployee joe =
             new HourlyEmployee("Joe Young",
                 new Date("February", 1, 2004), 10.50, 40);
        SalariedEmployee boss =
             new SalariedEmployee("Mr. Big Shot",
                 new Date("January", 1, 1999), 100000);
        printName(joe);
        printName(boss);
    }
    public void printName(Employee object)
    {
        System.out.println(object.getName());
    }
}
```

6. Give a definition for a class `TitledEmployee` that is a derived class of the base class `SalariedEmployee` given in Display 7.5. The class `TitledEmployee` has one additional instance variable of type `String` called `title`. It also has two additional methods: `getTitle`, which takes no arguments and returns a `String`, and `setTitle`, which is a `void` method that takes one argument of type `String`. It also overrides (redefines) the method definition for `getName`, so that the string returned includes the title as well as the name of the employee.

EXAMPLE: An Enhanced `StringTokenizer` Class ★

Inheritance allows you to reuse all the code written for a base class in a derived class, and it lets you reuse it without copying it or even seeing the code in the base class. This means that, among other things, if one of the standard Java library classes does not have all the methods you want it to have, you can, in most cases, define a derived class that has the desired additional methods. In this subsection, we give a simple example of this process. This example requires that you have already covered the basics about arrays given in Section 6.1 of Chapter 6. It also requires you to have read the starred section on the `StringTokenizer` class in Chapter 4. If you have not covered this material, you will have to skip this example until you cover it.

The `StringTokenizer` class allows you to generate all the tokens in a string one time, but sometimes you want to cycle through the tokens a second or third time. There are lots of ways to accomplish this. For example, you can use the `StringTokenizer` constructor two (or more) times to create two (or more) `StringTokenizer` objects. However, it would be cleaner and more efficient if you could do it with just one `StringTokenizer` object. Display 7.7 shows a derived class of the `StringTokenizer` class that allows you to cycle through the tokens in a string any number of times. This class is called `EnhancedStringTokenizer`. The class `EnhancedStringTokenizer` behaves exactly the same as the `StringTokenizer` class, except that the class `EnhancedStringTokenizer` has one additional method named `tokensSoFar`. This method has no parameters and returns an array of strings containing all the tokens that have so far been returned by the methods named `nextToken`. After an object of the class `EnhancedStringTokenizer` has gone through all the tokens with the methods `nextToken`, it can invoke the method `tokensSoFar` to produce an array containing all the tokens. This array can be used to cycle through the tokens any number of additional times. A simple example of this is given in the program in Display 7.8.

The class `EnhancedStringTokenizer` has methods, such as `countTokens`, that it inherits unchanged from the class `StringTokenizer`. The class `EnhancedString Tokenizer` also has two methods—namely, the two methods named `nextToken`—whose definitions are overridden. From the outside, the methods named `nextToken` of the class `EnhancedStringTokenizer` behave exactly the same as the methods named `nextToken` in the class `StringTokenizer`. However, each of the two methods named `nextToken` of the class `EnhancedStringTokenizer` also save the tokens in an array instance variable, `a`, so that an array of tokens can be returned by the method `tokensSoFar`. The method `tokensSoFar` is the only completely new method in the derived class `EnhancedStringTokenizer`.

(continued)

EXAMPLE: (continued)

Notice that the definitions of the methods named `nextToken` in the class `EnhancedStringTokenizer` each include an invocation of `super.nextToken`, which is the version of the corresponding method `nextToken` in the base class `StringTokenizer`. Each overridden version of the method `nextToken` uses the method `super.nextToken` to produce the token it returns, but before returning the token, it stores the token in the array instance variable `a`. The instance variable `count` contains a count of the number of tokens stored in the array instance variable `a`.[1]

Display 7.7 **Enhanced `StringTokenizer`** (part 1 of 2)

```
import java.util.StringTokenizer;

public class EnhancedStringTokenizer extends StringTokenizer
{
    private String[] a;
    private int count;

    public EnhancedStringTokenizer(String theString)
    {
        super (theString);
        a = new String[countTokens()];
        count = 0;
    }

    public EnhancedStringTokenizer(String theString, String delimiters)
    {
        super (theString, delimiters);
        a = new String[countTokens()];
        count = 0;
    }

    /**
     Returns the same value as the same method in the StringTokenizer
     class, but it also stores data for the method tokensSoFar to use.
    */
    public String nextToken()
    {
```

The method `countTokens` is inherited and is not overridden. (points to `a = new String[countTokens()];`)

This method `nextToken` has its definition overridden. (points to `public String nextToken()`)

[1] The class `StringTokenizer` also has a method named `nextElement` with a return type of `Object`. This method should also be overridden. We have not yet even mentioned this method because we have not yet discussed the class `Object`. For now, you can simply pretend `StringTokenizer` has no such method `nextElement`. We will discuss this point in Self-Test Exercise 23 later in this chapter after we introduce the class `Object`.

Display 7.7 Enhanced **StringTokenizer** (part 2 of 2)

```
        String token = super.nextToken();
        a[count] = token;
        count++;
        return token;
    }

    /**
     Returns the same value as the same method in the StringTokenizer
     class, and changes the delimiter set in the same way as does the
     same method in the StringTokenizer class, but it also stores data
     for the method tokensSoFar to use.
    */
    public String nextToken(String delimiters)
    {
        String token = super.nextToken(delimiters);
        a[count] = token;
        count++;
        return token;
    }
     /**
     Returns an array of all tokens produced so far. Array returned
     has length equal to the number of tokens produced so far.
    */
    public String[] tokensSoFar()
    {
        String[] arrayToReturn = new String[count];
        for (int i = 0; i < count; i++)
            arrayToReturn[i] = a[i];
        return arrayToReturn;
    }
}
```

`super.nextTokens` *is the version of* `nextToken` *defined in the base class* `StringTokenizer`*. This is explained more fully in Section 7.3.*

This method `nextToken` *also has its definition overridden.*

`super.nextTokens` *is the version of* `nextToken` *defined in the base class* `StringTokenizer`*.*

`tokensSoFar` *is a new method.*

Display 7.8 Use of the **EnhancedStringTokenizer** Class (part 1 of 2)

```
import java.util.Scanner;

public class EnhancedStringTokenizerDemo
{
    public static void main(String[] args)
    {
        Scanner keyboard = new Scanner(System.in);

        System.out.println("Enter a sentence:");
        String sentence = keyboard.nextLine();
```

(continued)

Display 7.8 Use of the **EnhancedStringTokenizer** Class (part 2 of 2)

```
        EnhancedStringTokenizer wordFactory =
             new EnhancedStringTokenizer(sentence);
        System.out.println("Your sentence with extra blanks deleted:");
        while (wordFactory.hasMoreTokens())
            System.out.print(wordFactory.nextToken() + " ");
        System.out.println();
      //All tokens have been dispensed.

      System.out.println("Sentence with each word on a separate line:");
      String[] token = wordFactory.tokensSoFar();
      for (int i = 0; i < token.length; i++)
          System.out.println(token[i]);
   }
}
```

Sample Dialogue

```
Enter a sentence:
    I    love    you,   madly.
Your sentence with extra blanks deleted:
I love you, madly.
Sentence with each word on a separate line:
I
love
you,
madly.
```

7.2 Encapsulation and Inheritance

Ignorance is bliss.

PROVERB

This section is a continuation of Section 7.1 and uses the same example classes we used there. In this section, we consider how the information-hiding facilities of Java, primarily the `private` modifier, interact with inheritance.

PITFALL: Use of Private Instance Variables from the Base Class

An object of the class `HourlyEmployee` (Display 7.3) inherits, among other things, an instance variable called `name` from the class `Employee` (Display 7.2). For example, the following would set the value of the instance variable `name` of the `HourlyEmployee` object `joe` to `"Josephine"`:

```
joe.setName("Josephine");
```

But you must be a bit careful about how you manipulate inherited instance variables such as `name`. The instance variable `name` of the class `HourlyEmployee` was inherited from the class `Employee`, but the instance variable `name` is a private instance variable in the definition of the class `Employee`. That means that `name` can only be accessed by name within the definition of a method in the class `Employee`. An instance variable (or method) that is private in a base class is not accessible *by name* in the definition of a method in *any other class, not even in a method definition of a derived class.*

For example, notice the following method definition taken from the definition of the class `HourlyEmployee` in Display 7.3:

```
public String toString()
{
    return (getName() + " " + getHireDate().toString()
      + "\n$" + wageRate + " per hour for " + hours + " hours");
}
```

You might wonder why we needed to use the methods `getName` and `getHireDate`. You might be tempted to rewrite the method definition as follows:

```
public String toString() //Illegal version
{
    return (name + " " + hireDate.toString()
     + "\n$" + wageRate + " per hour for " + hours + " hours");
}
```

As the comment indicates, this will not work. The instance variables `name` and `hireDate` are private instance variables in the class `Employee`, and although a derived class such as `HourlyEmployee` inherits these instance variables, it cannot access them directly. You must instead use some public methods to access the instance variable `name` or `hireDate`, as we did in Display 7.3.

In the definition of a derived class, you cannot mention a private inherited instance variable by name. You must instead use public accessor and mutator methods (such as `getName` and `setName`) that were defined in the base class.

The fact that a private instance variable of a base class cannot be accessed in the definition of a method of a derived class often seems wrong to people. After all, if you are an hourly employee and you want to change your name, nobody says, "Sorry, `name` is a private instance variable of the class `Employee`." If you are an hourly employee, you

(continued)

PITFALL: (continued)

are also an employee. In Java, this is also true; an object of the class `HourlyEmployee` is also an object of the class `Employee`. However, the laws on the use of private instance variables and methods must be as we described, or else they would be compromised. If private instance variables of a class were accessible in method definitions of a derived class, then anytime you want to access a private instance variable, you could simply create a derived class and access it in a method of that class, which would mean that all private instance variables would be accessible to anybody who wants to put in a little extra effort. This scenario illustrates the problem, but the big problem is unintentional errors, not intentional subversion. If private instance variables of a class were accessible in method definitions of a derived class, then the instance variables might be changed by mistake or in inappropriate ways. (Remember, accessor and mutator methods can guard against inappropriate changes to instance variables.)

We will discuss one possible way to get around this restriction on private instance variables of the base class in the upcoming subsection entitled "Protected and Package Access." ■

MyProgrammingLab™

Self-Test Exercises

7. Would the following be legal for the definition of a method to add to the class `Employee` (Display 7.2)? (Remember, the question is whether it is legal, not whether it is sensible.)

```
public void crazyMethod()
{
    Employee object = new Employee("Joe",
                                   new Date("January", 1, 2005));
    System.out.println("Hello " + object.name);
}
```

   Would it be legal to add this `crazyMethod` to the class `HourlyEmployee`?

8. Suppose you change the modifier before the instance variable `name` from `private` to `public` in the class `Employee`. Would it then be legal to add the method `crazyMethod` (from Self-Test Exercise 7) to the class `HourlyEmployee`?

PITFALL: Private Methods Are Effectively Not Inherited

As we noted in the Pitfall section, "Use of Private Instance Variables from the Base Class," an instance variable (or method) that is private in a base class is not directly accessible outside of the definition of the base class, *not even in a method definition for a derived class*. The private methods of the base class are just like private variables in terms of not being directly available. But in the case of methods, the restriction

PITFALL: (continued)

is more dramatic. A private variable can be accessed indirectly via an accessor or mutator method. A private method is simply not available. It is just as if the private method were not inherited. (In one sense, private methods in the base class may be indirectly available in the derived class. If a private method is used in the definition of a public method of the base class, then that public method can be invoked in the derived class, or any other class, so the private method can be indirectly invoked.)

This should not be a problem. Private methods should just be used as helping methods, so their use should be limited to the class in which they are defined. If you want a method to be used as a helping method in a number of inherited classes, then it is not *just* a helping method, and you should make the method public. ■

Protected and Package Access

As you have seen, you cannot access (by name) a private instance variable or private method of the base class within the definition of a derived class. There are two classifications of instance variables and methods that allow them to be accessed by name in a derived class. The two classifications are *protected access*, which always gives access, and *package access*, which gives access if the derived class is in the same package as the base class.

If a method or instance variable is modified by `protected` (rather than `public` or `private`), then it can be accessed by name inside its own class definition, it can be accessed by name inside any class derived from it, and it can also be accessed by name in the definition of any class in the same package (even if the class in the same package is not derived from it). However, the `protected` method or instance variable cannot be accessed by name in any other classes. Thus, if an instance variable is marked `protected` in the class `Parent` and the class `Child` is derived from the class `Parent`, then the instance variable can be accessed by name inside any method definition in the class `Child`. However, in a class that is not in the same package as `Parent` and is not derived from `Parent`, it is as if the `protected` instance variable were `private`.

For example, consider the class `HourlyEmployee` that was derived from the base class `Employee`. We were required to use accessor and mutator methods to manipulate the inherited instance variables in the definition of `HourlyEmployee`. Consider the definition of the `toString` method of the class `HourlyEmployee`, which we repeat here:

```
public String toString()
{
    return (getName() + " " + getHireDate().toString()
      + "\n$" + wageRate + " per hour for " + hours + " hours");
}
```

If the private instance variables `name` and `hireDate` had been marked `protected` in the class `Employee`, the definition of `toString` in the derived class `HourlyEmployee` could be simplified to the following:

```
public String toString() //Legal if instance variables in
                         // Employee are marked protected
{
    return (name + " " + hireDate.toString()
     + "\n$" + wageRate + " per hour for " + hours + " hours");
}
```

> **The `protected` Modifier**
>
> If a method or instance variable is modified by `protected` (rather than `public` or `private`), then it can be accessed by name inside its own class definition, by name inside any class derived from it, and by name in the definition of any class in the same package.

The `protected` modifier provides very weak protection compared to the `private` modifier, because it allows direct access to any programmer who is willing to go through the bother of defining a suitable derived class. Many programming authorities discourage the use of the `protected` modifier. Instance variables should normally not be marked `protected`. On rare occasions, you may want to have a method marked `protected`. If you want an access intermediate between `public` and `private`, then the access described in the next paragraph is often a preferable alternative to `protected`.

You may have noticed that if you forget to place one of the modifiers `public`, `private`, or `protected` before an instance variable or method definition, then your class definition will still compile. If you do not place any of these modifiers before an instance variable or method definition, then the instance variable or method can be accessed by name inside the definition of any class in the same package, but not outside of the package. This is called **package access**, **default access**, or **friendly access**. Use package access in situations where you have a package of cooperating classes that act as a single encapsulated unit. Note that package access is more restricted than `protected`, and that package access gives more control to the programmer defining the classes. If you control the package directory (folder), then you control who is allowed package access.

The diagram in Display 7.9 may help you to understand who has access to members with public, private, protected, and package access. The diagram tells who can directly access, by name, variables that have public, private, protected, and package access. The same access rules apply to methods that have public, private, protected, and package access.

Display 7.9 **Access Modifiers**

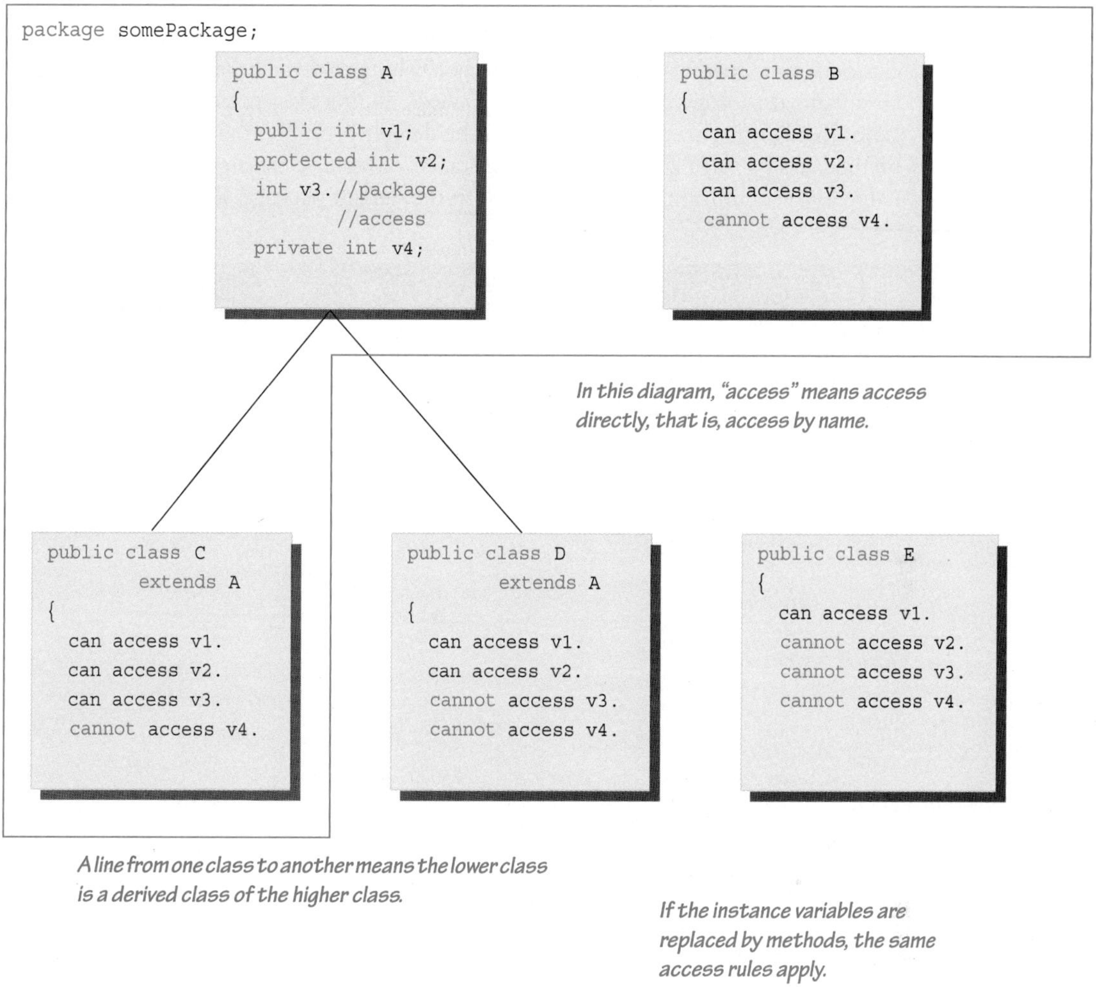
package somePackage;
public class A
{
public int v1;
protected int v2;
int v3. //package
//access
private int v4;
public class B
{
can access v1.
can access v2.
can access v3.
cannot access v4.
In this diagram, "access" means access directly, that is, access by name.
public class C
extends A
{
can access v1.
can access v2.
can access v3.
cannot access v4.
public class D
extends A
{
can access v1.
can access v2.
cannot access v3.
cannot access v4.
public class E
{
can access v1.
cannot access v2.
cannot access v3.
cannot access v4.
A line from one class to another means the lower class is a derived class of the higher class.
If the instance variables are replaced by methods, the same access rules apply.

Package Access

If you do not place any of the modifiers `public`, `private`, or `protected` before an instance variable or method definition, then the instance variable or method is said to have **package access**. Package access is also known as **default access** and as **friendly access**. If an instance variable or method has package access, it can be accessed by name inside the definition of any class in the same package, but not outside of the package.

PITFALL: Forgetting about the Default Package

When considering package access, do not forget the default package. Recall that all the classes in your current directory (that do not belong to some other package) belong to an unnamed package called the *default package*. So, if a class in your current directory is not in any other package, then it is in the default package. If an instance variable or method has package access, then that instance variable or method can be accessed by name in the definition of any other class in the default package. ■

PITFALL: A Restriction on Protected Access ★

The situation described in this pitfall does not occur often, but when it does, it can be very puzzling if you do not understand what is going on.

Suppose class `D` is derived from class `B`, the instance variable `n` has protected access in class `B`, and the classes `D` and `B` are in different packages, so the class definitions begin as follows:

```
package one;

public class B
{
    protected int n;
    ...
}

package two;

import one.B;

public class D extends B
{
    ...
}
```

Then the following is a legitimate method that can appear in the definition of class `D`:

```
public void demo()
{
    n = 42; //n is inherited from B.
}
```

PITFALL: (continued)

The following is also a legitimate method definition for the derived class `D`:

```
public void demo2()
{
    D object = new D();
    object.n = 42; //n is inherited from B.
}
```

However, the following is not allowed as a method of `D`:

```
public void demo3()
{
    B object = new B();
    object.n = 42;//Error
}
```

The compiler will give an error message saying that `n` is protected in `B`.

Similar remarks apply to protected methods.

A class can access its own classes' inherited variables and methods that are marked protected in the base class, but cannot directly access any such instance variables or methods of an object of the base class (or of any other derived class of the base class). In the above example, `n` is an instance variable of the base class `B` and an instance variable of the derived class `D`. `D` can access `n` whenever `n` is used as an instance variable of `D`, but `D` cannot access `n` when `n` is used as an instance variable of `B`.

If the classes `B` and `D` are in the same package, you will not get the error message because, in Java, protected access implies package access. In particular, if the classes `B` and `D` are both in the default package, you will not get the error message. ■

MyProgrammingLab™

Self-Test Exercises

9. Suppose you change the modifier before the instance variable `name` from `private` to `protected` in the class `Employee` (Display 7.2). Would it then be legal to add the method `crazyMethod` (from Self-Test Exercise 7) to the class `HourlyEmployee` (Display 7.3)?

10. Which is more restricted, protected access or package access?

(continued)

MyProgrammingLab™

Self-Test Exercises (continued)

11. Suppose class D is derived from class B, the method doStuff() has protected access in class B, and the classes D and B are in different packages, so the class definitions begin as follows:

```
package one;
public class B
{
    protected void doStuff()
    {
     ...
}

package two;
import one.B;
public class D extends B
{
     ...
}
```

Is the following a legitimate method that can appear in the definition of the class D?

```
public void demo()
{
    doStuff();//doStuff is inherited from B.
}
```

12. Suppose B and D are as described in Self-Test Exercise 11. Is the following a legitimate method that can appear in the definition of the class D?

```
public void demo2()
{
    D object = new D();
    object.doStuff();//doStuff is inherited from B.
}
```

13. Suppose B and D are as described in Self-Test Exercise 11. Is the following a legitimate method that can appear in the definition of the class D?

```
public void demo3()
{
    B object = new B();
    object.doStuff();
}
```

7.3 Programming with Inheritance

The devil is in the details.

COMMON SAYING

In the previous section, we described the basic idea and details of derived classes. In this section, we continue that discussion and go on to cover some more subtle points about derived classes. In the process, we also discuss the class `Object`, which is an ancestor class of all Java classes, and we describe a better way to define an `equals` method.

TIP: Static Variables Are Inherited

Static variables in a base class are inherited by any derived classes. The modifiers `public`, `private`, and `protected`, and package access have the same meaning for static variables as they do for instance variables. ■

TIP: "is a" versus "has a"

"is a" relationship

Early in this chapter, we defined a derived class called `HourlyEmployee` using the class `Employee` as the base class. In such a case, an object of the derived class `HourlyEmployee` is also an instance of the class `Employee`, or, stated more simply, an `HourlyEmployee` *is an* `Employee`. This is an example of the **"is a" relationship** between classes. It is one way to make a more complex class out of a simpler class.

"has a" relationship

composition

Another way to make a more complex class out of a simpler class is known as the **"has a" relationship**. For example, the class `Employee` defined earlier has an instance variable of the class type `Date`. We express this relationship by saying an `Employee` "has a" `Date`. Using the "has a" relationship to build a class (such as building the class `Employee` by using `Date` as an instance variable) is often called **composition**.

Because the class `HourlyEmployee` inherits the instance variable of type `Date` from the class `Employee`, it is also correct to say an `HourlyEmployee` "has a" `Date`. Thus, an `HourlyEmployee` *is an* `Employee` and *has a* `Date`. ■

Access to a Redefined Base Method

`super` relationship

Suppose you redefine a method so that it has a different definition in the derived class from what it has in the base class. The definition that was given in the base class is not completely lost to the derived class objects. However, if you want to invoke the version of the method given in the base class with an object in the derived class, you need some way to say, "use the definition of this method as given in the base class (even though I am an object of the derived class)." The way you say this is to use the keyword `super` as if it were a calling object.

For example, the method `toString` of the class `HourlyEmployee` (Display 7.3) is defined as follows:

```
public String toString() //in the derived class HourlyEmployee
{
    return (getName() + " " + getHireDate().toString()
     + "\n$" + wageRate + " per hour for " + hours + " hours");
}
```

This overrides the following definition of `toString()` that was given in the definition of the base class `Employee`:

```
public String toString() //in the base class Employee
{
    return (name + " " + hireDate.toString());
}
```

We can use the version of the method `toString()` defined in the base class `Employee` to simplify the definition of the method `toString()` in the derived class `HourlyEmployee`. The following is an equivalent way to define `toString()` in the derived class `HourlyEmployee`:

```
public String toString() //in the derived class HourlyEmployee
{
   return (super.toString()
      + "\n$" + wageRate + " per hour for " + hours + " hours");
}
```

The expression `super.toString()` is an invocation of the method `toString()` using the definition of `toString()` given in the base class `Employee`.

You can only use `super` in this way within the definition of a method in a derived class. Outside of the definition of the derived class, you cannot invoke an overridden method of the base class using an object of the derived class.

Invoking the Old Version of an Overridden Method?

Within the definition of a method of a derived class, you can invoke the base class version of an overridden method of the base class by prefacing the method name with `super` and a dot. Outside of the derived class definition, there is no way to invoke the base class version of an overridden method using an object of the derived class.

EXAMPLE

```
public String toString()
{
   return (super.toString()
       + "\n$" + wageRate + " per hour for " + hours + " hours");
}
```

PITFALL: You Cannot Use Multiple `super`s

As we already noted, within the definition of a method of a derived class, you can call an overridden method of the base class by prefacing the method name with `super` and a dot. However, you cannot repeat the use of `super` to invoke a method from some ancestor class other than a direct parent. For example, suppose that the class `Employee` were derived from the class `Person`, and the class `HourlyEmployee` is derived from the class `Employee`. You might think that you can invoke a method of the class `Person` within the definition of the class `HourlyEmployee`, by using `super.super`, as in

```
super.super.toString() //ILLEGAL!
```

However, as the comment indicates, it is illegal to have such multiple `super`s in Java. ■

MyProgrammingLab™

Self-Test Exercises

14. Redefine the `toString` method of the class `SalariedEmployee` (Display 7.5) so that it uses `super.toString()`. This new definition of `toString` will be equivalent to the one given in Display 7.5.

15. Redefine the `equals` method for the class `HourlyEmployee` (Display 7.3) using `super.equals` to invoke the `equals` method of the base class `Employee`.

16. Is the following program legal? The relevant classes are defined in Displays 7.2 and 7.3.

```
public class EmployeeDemo
{
    public static void main(String[] args)
    {
        HourlyEmployee joe =
             new HourlyEmployee("Joe Young",
                     new Date("Feb", 1, 2004), 10.50, 40);
        String nameNDate = joe.super.toString();
        System.out.println(nameNDate);
    }
}
```

(continued)

MyProgrammingLab™

Self-Test Exercises (continued)

17. Suppose you add the following defined constant to the class `Employee` (Display 7.2):

```
public static final int STANDARD_HOURS = 160; //per month
```

Would it then be legal to add the following method to the class `HourlyEmployee` (Display 7.3)?

```
public void setHoursToStandard()
{
    hours = STANDARD_HOURS;
}
```

The Class `Object`

Java has a class that is an ancestor of every class. In Java, every class is a derived class of a derived class of . . . (for some number of iterations of "a derived class of") of the class `Object`. So, every object of every class is of type `Object`, as well as being of the type of its class (and also of the types of all its ancestor classes). Even classes that you define yourself are descendent classes of the class `Object`. If you do not make your class a derived class of some class, then Java will automatically make it a derived class of the class `Object`.

`Object` class

The class `Object` allows you to write Java code for methods with a parameter of type `Object` that can be replaced by an object of any class whatsoever. You will eventually encounter library methods that accept an argument of type `Object` and hence can be used with an argument that is an object of absolutely any class.

> **The Class `Object`**
>
> In Java, every class is a descendent of the class `Object`. So, every object of every class is of type `Object`, as well as being of the type of its class.

The class `Object` is in the package `java.lang`, which is always imported automatically. So, you do not need any `import` statement to make the class `Object` available to your code.

The class `Object` does have some methods that every Java class inherits. For example, every object inherits the methods `equals` and `toString` from some ancestor class, which either is the class `Object` or a class that itself inherited the methods ultimately from the class `Object`. However, the inherited methods `equals` and `toString` will not work correctly for (almost) any class you define. You need to override the inherited method definitions with new, more appropriate definitions.

`toString`

It is important to include definitions of the methods `toString` and `equals` in the classes you define, because some Java library classes assume your class has such methods. There are no subtleties involved in defining (actually redefining or overriding) the method `toString`. We have seen good examples of the method `toString` in many of our class definitions. The definition of the overridden method `equals` does have some subtleties; we discuss them in the next subsection.

`equals`

clone Another method inherited from the class `Object` is the method `clone`, which is intended to return a copy of the calling object. We discuss the method `clone` in Chapters 8 and 13.

The Right Way to Define `equals`

Earlier we said that the class `Object` has an `equals` method, and that when you define a class with an `equals` method, you should override the definition of the method `equals` given in the class `Object`. However, we did not, strictly speaking, follow our own advice. The heading for the method `equals` in our definition of the class `Employee` (Display 7.2) is as follows:

```
public boolean equals(Employee otherEmployee)
```

On the other hand, the heading for the method `equals` in the class `Object` is as follows:

```
public boolean equals(Object otherObject)
```

The two `equals` methods have different parameter types, so we have not overridden the definition of `equals` We have merely overloaded the method `equals`. The class `Employee` has both of these methods named `equals`.

In most situations, this will not matter. However, there are situations in which it does. Some library methods assume your class's definition of `equals` has the following heading, the same as in the class `Object`:

```
public boolean equals(Object otherObject)
```

We need to change the type of the parameter for the `equals` method in the class `Employee` from type `Employee` to type `Object`. A first try might produce the following:

```
public boolean equals(Object otherObject)
{
    Employee otherEmployee = (Employee)otherObject;
    return (name.equals(otherEmployee.name)
             && hireDate.equals(otherEmployee.hireDate));
}
```

We needed to type cast the parameter `otherObject` from type `Object` to type `Employee`. If we omit the type cast and simply proceed with `otherObject`, the compiler will give an error message when it sees the following:

```
otherObject.name
```

The class `Object` does not have an instance variable named `name`.

This first try at an improved `equals` method does override the definition of `equals` given in the class `Object` and will work well in many cases. However, it still has a shortcoming.

Our definition of `equals` now allows an argument that can be any kind of object whatsoever. What happens if the method `equals` is used with an argument that is not an `Employee`? A run-time error will occur when the type cast to `Employee` is executed.

We need to make our definition work for any kind of object. If the object is not an `Employee`, we simply return `false`. The calling object is an `Employee`, so if the argument is not an `Employee`, they should not be considered equal. But how can we tell whether the parameter is or is not of type `Employee`?

Every object inherits the method `getClass()` from the class `Object`. The method `getClass()` is marked `final` in the class `Object`, so it cannot be overridden. For any object `o`, `o.getClass()` returns a representation of the class used to create `o`. For example, after the following is executed,

```
o = new Employee();
```

`o.getClass()` returns a representation `Employee`.

We will not describe the details of this representation except to say that two such representations should be compared with `==` or `!=` if you want to know if two representations are the same. Thus,

```
if (object1.getClass() == object2.getClass())
    System.out.println("Same class.");
else
    System.out.println("Not the same class.");
```

will output `"Same class."` if `object1` and `object2` were created with the same class when they were created using `new`, and output `"Not the same class."` otherwise.

Our final version of the method `equals` is shown in Display 7.10. Note that we have also taken care of one more possible case. The predefined constant `null` can be plugged in for a parameter of type `Object`. The Java documentation says that an `equals` method should return `false` when comparing an object and the value `null`. So that is what we have done.

extra code on website

On the accompanying website, the subdirectory `improvedEquals` (of the directory for this chapter) has a definition of the class `Employee` that includes this definition of `equals`.

Display 7.10 A Better **`equals`** Method for the Class **`Employee`**

```
public boolean equals(Object otherObject)
{
    if (otherObject == null)
        return false;
    else if (getClass() != otherObject.getClass())
        return false;
    else
    {
        Employee otherEmployee = (Employee)otherObject;
        return (name.equals(otherEmployee.name)
          && hireDate.equals(otherEmployee.hireDate));
    }
}
```

TIP: getClass versus instanceof ★

Many authors suggest that in the definition of `equals` for a class such as `Employee`, given in Display 7.10, you should not use

```
else if (getClass() != otherObject.getClass())
     return false;
```

but should instead use

```
else if (!(otherObject instanceof Employee))
     return false;
```

What is the difference and which should you use? At first glance, it seems like you should use `instanceof` in the definition of `equals`. The `instanceof` operator checks to see if an object is of the type given as its second argument. The syntax is

instanceof

Object `instanceof` *Class_Name*

which returns `true` if *Object* is of type *Class_Name*; otherwise it returns `false`. So, the following will return `true` if `otherObject` is of type `Employee`:

```
(otherObject instanceof Employee)
```

Suppose that (contrary to what we really did) we instead used `instanceof` in our definition of `equals` for the class `Employee` and also used `instanceof` in our definition for the class `HourlyEmployee`, so that the definition of `equals` for `HourlyEmployee` is as follows:

```
public boolean equals(Object otherObject)
//This is NOT the right way to define equals.
{
    if (otherObject == null)
        return false;
    else if (!(otherObject instanceof HourlyEmployee))
        return false;
    else
    {
        HourlyEmployee otherHourlyEmployee =
                              (HourlyEmployee)otherObject;
         return (super.equals(otherHourlyEmployee)
               && (wageRate == otherHourlyEmployee.wageRate)
               && (hours == otherHourlyEmployee.hours));
    }
}
```

(continued)

TIP: (continued)

Assuming that the equals method for both Employee and HourlyEmployee are defined using instanceof (as previously mentioned), consider the following situation:

```
Employee e =
      new Employee("Joe Worker", new Date("January", 1, 2004));
HourlyEmployee hourlyE = new HourlyEmployee("Joe Worker",
                        new Date("January", 1, 2004), 50.50, 160);
```

Then, with the definition of equals that uses instanceof, we get that

```
e.equals(hourlyE)
```

returns true, because hourlyE is an Employee with the same name and hire date as e. So far, it sounds reasonable.

However, since we are assuming that we also used instanceof in the definition of equals for the class HourlyEmployee, we also get that

```
hourlyE.equals(e)
```

returns false because e instanceof HourlyEmployee returns false. (e is an Employee but e is not an HourlyEmployee.)

So, if we define equals in both classes using instanceof, then e equals hourlyE, but hourlyE does not equal e. That is no way for equals to behave.

Since instanceof does not yield a suitable definition of equals, you should instead use getClass() as we did in Display 7.10. If we use getClass() in a similar way in the definition of equals for the class HourlyEmployee (see Self-Test Exercise 19), then

```
e.equals(hourlyE)
```

and

```
hourlyE.equals(e)
```

both return false. ■

instanceof and getClass() ★

Both the instanceof operator and the getClass() method can be used to check the class of an object. The instanceof operator simply tests an object for type. The getClass() method, used in a test with == or !=, tests if two objects were created with the same class. The details follow.

THE instanceof OPERATOR

The instanceof operator checks if an object is of the type given as its second argument. The syntax is

```
Object instanceof Class_Name
```

which returns true if *Object* is of type *Class_Name*; otherwise it returns false. So, the following will return true if otherObject is of type Employee:

```
(otherObject instanceof Employee)
```

Note that this means it returns true if otherObject is of the type of any descendent class of Employee, because in that case otherObject is also of type Employee.

THE getClass() METHOD

Every object inherits the method getClass() from the class Object. The method getClass() is marked final in the class Object, so it cannot be overridden. For any object of any class,

```
object.getClass()
```

returns a representation of the class that was used with new to create object. Any two such representations can be compared with == or != to determine whether or not they represent the same class. Thus,

```
if (object1.getClass() == object2.getClass())
    System.out.println("Same class.");
else
    System.out.println("Not the same class.");
```

will output Same class if object1 and object2 were created with the same class when they were created using new, and output Not same class otherwise.

(continued)

EXAMPLE

Suppose that `HourlyEmployee` is a derived class of `Employee` and that `employeeObject` and `hourlyEmployeeObject` are created as follows:

```
Employee employeeObject = new Employee();
HourlyEmployee hourlyEmployeeObject = new HourlyEmployee();
```

Then,

```
employeeObject.getClass() == hourlyEmployeeObject.getClass()
```

returns `false`.

```
employeeObject instanceof Employee
```

returns `true`.

```
hourlyEmployeeObject instanceof Employee
```

returns `true`.

```
employeeObject instanceof HourlyEmployee
```

returns `false`.

```
hourlyEmployeeObject instanceof HourlyEmployee
```

returns `true`.

MyProgrammingLab™

Self-Test Exercises

18. Redefine the method `equals` given in Display 7.10 using `instanceof` instead of `getClass()`. Give the complete definition. Remember, we do not want you to define `equals` this way in your class definitions; this is just an exercise.

19. Redefine the `equals` method of the class `HourlyEmployee` (Display 7.3) so that it has a parameter of type `Object` and follows the other guidelines we gave for an `equals` method. Assume the definition of the method `equals` for the class `Employee` has been changed to be as in Display 7.10. (Remember, you should use `getClass()`, not `instanceof`.)

MyProgrammingLab™

Self-Test Exercises (continued)

20. Redefine the equals method of the class SalariedEmployee (Display 7.5) so that it has a parameter of type Object and follows the other guidelines we gave for an equals method. Assume the definition of the method equals for the class Employee has been changed to be as in Display 7.10. (Remember, you should use getClass(), not instanceof.)

21. Redefine the equals method of the class Date(Display 4.13) so that it has a parameter of type Object and follows the other guidelines we gave for an equals method. (Remember, you should use getClass(), not instanceof.)

22. What is the output produced by the following program? (The classes Employee and HourlyEmployee were defined in this chapter.)

```
public class Test
{
    public static void main(String[] args)
    {
        Employee object1 = new Employee();
        Employee object2 = new HourlyEmployee();

        if (object1.getClass( ) == object2.getClass( ))
            System.out.println("Same class.");
        else
            System.out.println("Not the same class.");
    }
}
```

23. (This exercise requires that you have covered the starred subsection "An Enhanced StringTokenizer Class *," earlier in this chapter.)

    Although we did not discuss it when we covered the class StringTokenizer, the class StringTokenizer has a method with the following heading:

```
public Object nextElement()
```

    The method nextElement() returns the same string as the method nextToken(), but nextElement() returns it as something of type Object, as opposed to type String. Give a suitable definition of nextElement to add to the definition of EnhancedStringTokenizer. This definition will override the definition of nextElement in the class StringTokenizer. (*Hint*: the definition is just like the definition of nextToken except for fixing the type of the string returned.)

Chapter Summary

- *Inheritance* provides a tool for code reuse by deriving one class from another. The *derived class* automatically inherits the features of the old (base) class and may add features as well.
- A derived class object inherits the instance variables, static variables, and public methods of the *base class*, and may add additional instance variables, static variables, and methods.
- An object of a derived class has the type of the derived class, and it also has the type of the base class, and more generally, has the type of every one of its *ancestor classes*.
- If an instance variable is marked `private` in a base class, then it cannot be accessed by name in a derived class.
- Private methods are effectively not inherited.
- A method may be redefined in a derived class so that it performs differently from how it performs in the base class. This is called *overriding* the method definition. The definition for an overridden method is given in the class definition of the derived class, in the same way as the definitions of any added methods.
- A constructor of a base class can be used in the definition of a constructor for a derived class. The keyword `super` is used as the name for a constructor of the base class.
- A constructor definition can use the keyword `this`, as if it were a method name, to invoke a constructor of the same class.
- If a constructor does not contain an invocation of either `super` or `this`, then Java automatically inserts an invocation of `super()` as the first action in the body of the constructor definition.
- A `protected` instance variable or method in the base class can be accessed by name in the definition of a method of a derived class and in the definition of any method in the same package.
- If an instance variable or method has none of the modifiers `public`, `private`, or `protected`, then it is said to have *package access*. An instance variable or method with package access can be accessed by name in the definition of any method in the same package.
- The class `Object` is an ancestor class of every class in Java.
- The `equals` method for a class should have `Object` as the type of its one parameter.

Answers to Self-Test Exercises

1. Yes, it will have the instance variables. A derived class has all the instance variables that the base class has and can add more instance variables besides.
2. Yes, it will have the methods. A derived class has all the public methods that the base class has and can also add more methods. If the derived class does not override (redefine) a method definition, then it performs exactly the same action in the derived class as it does in the base class. However, the base class can contain an overriding definition of (a new definition of) a method, and the new definition will replace the old definition (provided it has the same number and types of parameters).
3. The class `DiscountSale` will have two methods named `getTax` and will have the following two headings. This is an example of overloading.

```
public double getTax()
public double getTax(double rate)
```

4. The method `getName` is inherited from the class `Employee` and so needs no definition. The method `getRate` is a new method added in the class `HourlyEmployee` and so needs to be defined.
5. Yes. You can plug in an object of a derived class for a parameter of the base class type. An `HourlyEmployee` is an `Employee`. A `SalariedEmployee` is an `Employee`.
6.
```
public class TitledEmployee extends SalariedEmployee
{
    private String title;

    public TitledEmployee()
    {
        super ("no name", newDate("January," 1, 1000), 0);
        title = "No title";
    }

    public TitledEmployee(String theName, String theTitle,
                          Date theDate, double theSalary)
    {
        super (theName, theDate, theSalary);
        title = theTitle;
    }

    public String getTitle()
    {
        return title;
    }
```

```
    public void setTitle(String theTitle)
    {
        title = theTitle;
    }

    public String getName()
    {
        return (title + super.getName());
    }
}
```

7. It would be legal to add `crazyMethod` to the class `Employee`. It would not be legal to add `crazyMethod` to the class `HourlyEmployee` because, although the class `HourlyEmployee` has an instance variable `name`, `name` is private in the base class `Employee` and so cannot be accessed by name in `HourlyEmployee`.
8. Yes, it would be legal as long as `name` is marked `public` in the base class `Employee`.
9. Yes, it would be legal as long as `name` is marked `protected` in the base class `Employee`.
10. Package access is more restricted. Anything allowed by package access is also allowed by protected access, but protected access allows even more.
11. Yes, it is legitimate.
12. Yes, it is legitimate.
13. No, it is not legitimate. The compiler will give an error message saying `doStuff()` is protected in `B`.
14.
```
public String toString()
{
        return (super.toString()
                        + "\n$" + salary + " per year");
}
```
15.
```
public boolean equals(HourlyEmployee other)
{
    return (super.equals(other)
                && wageRate == other.wageRate
                && hours == other.hours);
}
```
A better definition of `equals` for the class `HourlyEmployee` is given in Display 7.10.
16. It is not legal. You cannot use `super` in this way. `super.toString()` as used here refers to `toString()` in the class `Employee` and can only be used in definitions of classes derived from `Employee`. Moreover, you cannot have a calling object, such as `joe`, before `super`, so this is even illegal if you add `extends Employee` to the first line of the class definition.

17. Yes, all static variables are inherited. Because a defined constant is a form of static variable, it is inherited. So, the class `HourlyEmployee` inherits the constant `STANDARD_HOURS` from the class `Employee`.

18.
```
public boolean equals(Object otherObject)
//This is NOT the right way to define equals.
{
    if (otherObject == null)
        return false;
    else if (!(otherObject instanceof Employee))
        return false;
    else
    {
        Employee otherEmployee = (Employee)otherObject;
        return (name.equals(otherEmployee.name)
           && hireDate.equals(otherEmployee.hireDate));
    }
}
```

extra code on website

19. A version of the `HourlyEmployee` class with this definition of `equals` is in the subdirectory `improvedEquals` of the `ch07` directory on the accompanying website.

```
public boolean equals(Object otherObject)
{
    if (otherObject == null)
        return false;
    else if (getClass() != otherObject.getClass())
        return false;
    else
    {
        HourlyEmployee otherHourlyEmployee =
                              (HourlyEmployee)otherObject;
        return (super.equals(otherHourlyEmployee)
              && (wageRate == otherHourlyEmployee.wageRate)
              && (hours == otherHourlyEmployee.hours));
    }
}
```

extra code on website

20. A version of the `SalariedEmployee` class with this definition of `equals` is in the subdirectory `improvedEquals` of the `ch07` directory on the accompanying website.

```
public boolean equals(Object otherObject)
{
    if (otherObject == null)
        return false;
    else if (getClass() != otherObject.getClass())
        return false;
    else
    {
```

```
            SalariedEmployee otherSalariedEmployee =
                                (SalariedEmployee)otherObject;
            return (super.equals(otherSalariedEmployee)
                  && (salary == otherSalariedEmployee.salary));
        }
    }
```

extra code on website

21. A version of the `Date` class with this definition of `equals` is in the subdirectory `improvedEquals` of the `ch07` directory on the accompanying website.

```
public boolean equals(Object otherObject)
{
    if (otherObject == null)
      return false;
    else if (getClass() != otherObject.getClass())
       return false;
    else
    {
          Date otherDate =
                        (Date)otherObject;
          return ( month.equals(otherDate.month)
                   && (day == otherDate.day)
                   && (year == otherDate.year) );
    }
}
```

22. `Not the same class.`

extra code on website

23. The following is included in the definition of `EnhancedStringTokenizer` on the accompanying website.

```
public Object nextElement()
{
    String token = super.nextToken();
    a[count] = token;
    count++;
    return (Object)token;
}
```

MyProgrammingLab™

Programming Projects

Visit www.myprogramminglab.com to complete select exercises online and get instant feedback.

1. Define a class named `Payment` that contains an instance variable of type `double` that stores the amount of the payment and appropriate accessor and mutator methods. Also create a method named `paymentDetails` that outputs an English sentence to describe the amount of the payment.

Next, define a class named `CashPayment` that is derived from `Payment`. This class should redefine the `paymentDetails` method to indicate that the payment is in cash. Include appropriate constructor(s).

Define a class named `CreditCardPayment` that is derived from `Payment`. This class should contain instance variables for the name on the card, expiration date, and credit card number. Include appropriate constructor(s). Finally, redefine the `paymentDetails` method to include all credit card information in the printout.

Create a `main` method that creates at least two `CashPayment` and two `CreditCardPayment` objects with different values and calls `paymentDetails` for each.

2. Define a class named `Document` that contains an instance variable of type `String` named `text` that stores any textual content for the document. Create a method named `toString` that returns the `text` field and also include a method to set this value.

   Next, define a class for `Email` that is derived from `Document` and includes instance variables for the `sender`, `recipient`, and `title` of an email message. Implement appropriate accessor and mutator methods. The body of the email message should be stored in the inherited variable `text`. Redefine the `toString` method to concatenate all text fields.

   Similarly, define a class for `File` that is derived from `Document` and includes a instance variable for the `pathname`. The textual contents of the file should be stored in the inherited variable `text`. Redefine the `toString` method to concatenate all text fields.

   Finally, create several sample objects of type `Email` and `File` in your `main` method. Test your objects by passing them to the following subroutine that returns true if the object contains the specified keyword in the text property.

```
public static boolean ContainsKeyword(Document docObject,
                                      String keyword)
{
        if (docObject.toString().indexOf(keyword,0) >= 0)
           return true;
        return false;
}
```

VideoNote
Solution to Programming Project 7.3

3. The following is some code designed by J. Hacker for a video game. There is an `Alien` class to represent a monster and an `AlienPack` class that represents a band of aliens and how much damage they can inflict:

```
class Alien
{
     public static final int SNAKE_ALIEN = 0;
     public static final int OGRE_ALIEN = 1;
     public static final int MARSHMALLOW_MAN_ALIEN = 2;

     public int type; // Stores one of the three above types
     public int health; // 0=dead, 100=full strength
     public String name;
```

```
        public Alien (int type,int health, String name)
        {
            this.type = type;
            this.health = health;
            this.name = name;
        }
    }
    public class AlienPack
    {
        private Alien[] aliens;

        public AlienPack (int numAliens)
        {
            aliens = new Alien[numAliens];
        }
        public void addAlien(Alien newAlien, int index)
        {
            aliens[index] = newAlien;
        }
        public Alien[] getAliens()
        {
            return aliens;
        }
    public int calculateDamage()
    {
        int damage = 0;
        for (int i=0; i < aliens.length; i++)
        {
            if (aliens[i].type==Alien.SNAKE_ALIEN)
            {
                damage +=10;// Snake does 10 damage
            }
            else if (aliens[i].type==Alien.OGRE_ALIEN)
            {
                damage +=6;// Ogre does 6 damage
            }
            else if (aliens[i].type==
            Alien.MARSHMALLOW_MAN_ALIEN)
            {
                damage +=1;
            // Marshmallow Man does 1 damage
            }
        }
        return damage;
      }
    }
```

The code is not very object oriented and does not support information hiding in the `Alien` class. Rewrite the code so that inheritance is used to represent the different types of aliens instead of the "type" parameter. This should result in deletion of the "type" parameter. Also rewrite the `Alien` class to hide the instance variables and create a `getDamage` method for each derived class that returns the amount of damage the alien inflicts. Finally, rewrite the `calculateDamage` method to use `getDamage` and write a `main` method that tests the code.

4. Define a class called `Administrator`, which is a derived class of the class `SalariedEmployee` in Display 7.5 You are to supply the following additional instance variables and methods:

   - An instance variable of type `String` that contains the administrator's title (such as `"Director"` or `"Vice President"`).
   - An instance variable of type `String` that contains the administrator's area of responsibility (such as `"Production"`, `"Accounting"`, or `"Personnel"`).
   - An instance variable of type `String` that contains the name of this administrator's immediate supervisor.
   - Suitable constructors, and suitable accessor and mutator methods.
   - A method for reading in an administrator's data from the keyboard.

   Override the definitions for the methods `equals` and `toString` so they are appropriate to the class `Administrator`.

   Also, write a suitable test program.

5. Give the definition of a class named `Doctor` whose objects are records for a clinic's doctors. This class will be a derived class of the class `SalariedEmployee` given in Display 7.5. A `Doctor` record has the doctor's specialty (such as `"Pediatrician"`, `"Obstetrician"`, `"General Practitioner"`, and so forth; so use the type `String`) and office visit fee (use type `double`). Be sure your class has a reasonable complement of constructors, accessor, and mutator methods, and suitably defined `equals` and `toString` methods. Write a program to test all your methods.

VideoNote
Solution to Programming Project 7.5

6. Create a class called `Vehicle` that has the manufacturer's name (type `String`), number of cylinders in the engine (type `int`), and owner (type `Person` given next). Then, create a class called `Truck` that is derived from `Vehicle` and has the following additional properties: the load capacity in tons (type `double` since it may contain a fractional part) and towing capacity in pounds (type `int`). Be sure your class has a reasonable complement of constructors, accessor and mutator methods, and suitably defined `equals` and `toString` methods. Write a program to test all your methods.

   The definition of the class `Person` follows. Completing the definitions of the methods is part of this programming project.

```
public class Person
{
    private String name;
```

```
    public Person()
    {...}
    public Person(String theName)
    {...}
    public Person(Person theObject)
    {...}
    public String getName()
    {...}
    public void setName(String theName)
    {...}
    public String toString()
    {...}
    public boolean equals(Object other)
    {...}
}
```

7. Give the definition of two classes, `Patient` and `Billing`, whose objects are records for a clinic. `Patient` will be derived from the class `Person` given in Programming Project 7.6. A `Patient` record has the patient's name (inherited from the class `Person`) and primary physician of type `Doctor` defined in Programming Project 7.5 A `Billing` object will contain a `Patient` object, a `Doctor` object, and an amount due of type `double`. Be sure your classes have a reasonable complement of constructors, accessor, and mutator methods, and suitably defined `equals` and `toString` methods. First write a driver program to test all your methods, then write a test program that creates at least two patients, at least two doctors, and at least two `Billing` records, and then prints out the total income from the `Billing` records.
8. Programming Project 4.10 required adding an instance variable to the `Pet` class defined in Display 4.15 to indicate if the pet is a dog or cat. A better organization is to define `Pet` as a superclass of the `Dog` and `Cat` classes. This organization eliminates the need for an instance variable to indicate the type of the pet. Do or redo Programming Project 4.10 with inheritance. The `acepromazine()` and `carprofen()` methods should be defined in the `Pet` class to simply return 0. Override both methods in the `Dog` and `Cat` classes to calculate the correct dosage. Write a main method with appropriate tests to exercise the changes.

9. Programming Project 6.18 asked you to use an array of Strings to store the fruits and vegetables shipped in a `BoxOfProduce` object for a CSA farm.

   Modify your solution further by creating a `Produce` class. This class should have an instance variable of type `String` for the name, appropriate constructors, and a public `toString()` method. Then create a `Fruit` and a `Vegetable` class that are derived from `Produce`. These classes should have constructors that take the name as a `String` and invoke the appropriate constructor from the base class to set the name.

   Next, modify the text file of produce so it indicates whether each item is a fruit or a vegetable. Here is one possible organization, although you can use others:

```
Broccoli,Vegetable
Tomato,Fruit
Kiwi,Fruit
Kale,Vegetable
Tomatillo,Fruit
```

   Finally, modify the `BoxOfProduce` class so it creates an array of type `Produce` instead of type `String`. The class should read the produce from the text file and create instances of either `Fruit` or `Vegetable`, with the appropriate name, in the array. After a box is finished, loop through the contents of the array and output how many fruit and how many vegetables are in the box. The rest of the program should behave the same as the solution to Programming Project 6.18.

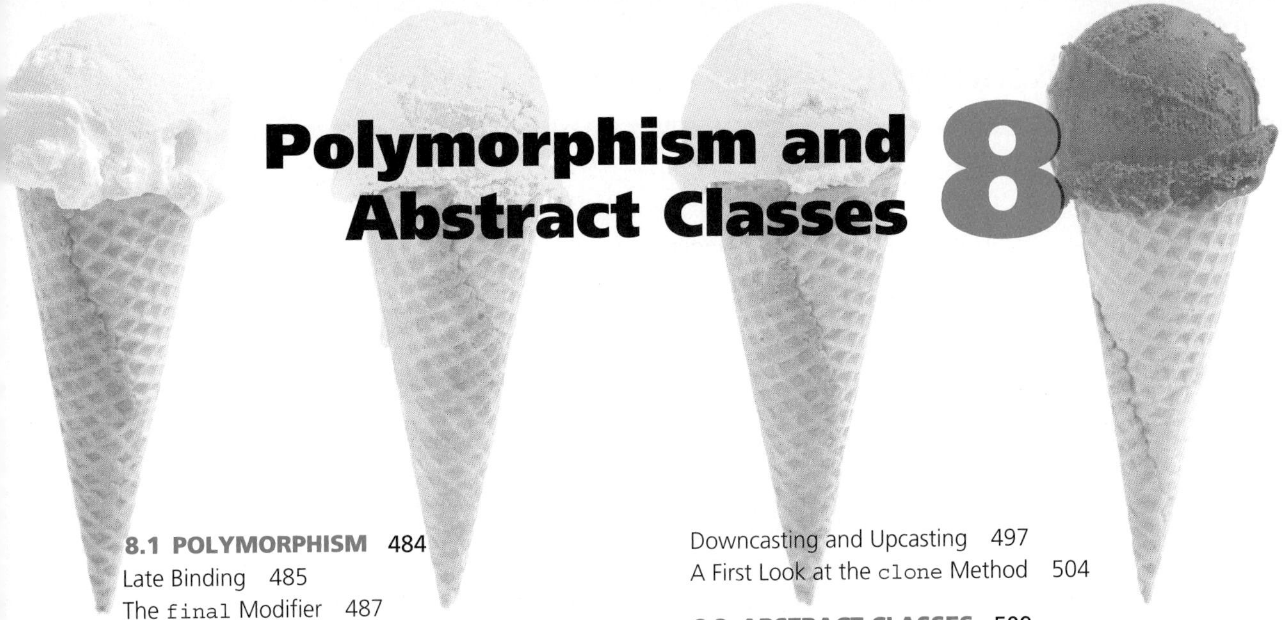

8 Polymorphism and Abstract Classes

8 Polymorphism and Abstract Classes

Don't make any commitments until you have to.

ANONYMOUS

Introduction

The three main programming mechanisms that constitute object-oriented programming (OOP) are encapsulation, inheritance, and polymorphism. We have already covered the first two. In this chapter, we discuss polymorphism. *Polymorphism* refers to the ability to associate many meanings to one method name by means of a special mechanism known as *late binding* or *dynamic binding*.

This chapter also covers *abstract classes*, which are classes in which some methods are not fully defined. Abstract classes are designed to be used only as base classes for defining new classes. You cannot create instances of (objects of) an abstract class; you can only create instances of its descendent classes.

Both polymorphism and abstract classes deal with code in which a method is used before it is defined. Although this may sound paradoxical, it all works out smoothly in Java.

Prerequisites

This chapter requires Chapters 1 through 5 and Chapter 7, with the exception that Section 5.4 on packages and `javadoc` is not required. This chapter does not use any material on arrays from Chapter 6.

Sections 8.1 on polymorphism and 8.2 on abstract classes are independent of each other, and you may cover Section 8.2 before Section 8.1 if you wish.

8.1 Polymorphism

I did it my way.

FRANK SINATRA

Inheritance allows you to define a base class and to define software for the base class. That software can then be used not only for objects of the base class but also for objects of any class derived from the base class. *Polymorphism* allows you to make changes in the method definition for the derived classes and to have those changes apply to the software written *in the base class*. This all happens automatically in Java, but it is important to understand the process. To understand polymorphism, we need a concrete example. The next subsection begins with such an example.

Late Binding

Suppose you are designing software for a graphics package that has classes for several kinds of figures, such as rectangles, circles, ovals, and so forth. Each figure might be an object of a different class. For example, the `Rectangle` class might have instance variables for a height, width, and center point, while the `Circle` class might have instance variables for a center point and a radius. In a well-designed programming project, all of these classes would be descendents of a single parent class called, for example, `Figure`. Now, suppose you want a method to draw a figure on the screen. To draw a circle, you need different instructions from those you need to draw a rectangle. So, each class needs to have a different method to draw its kind of figure. However, because the methods belong to the classes, they can all be called `draw`. If `r` is a `Rectangle` object and `c` is a `Circle` object, then `r.draw()` and `c.draw()` can be methods implemented with different code. All this is not new, but next we are going to expand on this.

Now, the parent class `Figure` may have methods that apply to all figures. For example, it might have a method called `center` that moves a figure to the center of the screen by erasing it and then redrawing it in the center of the screen. The method `center` of the class `Figure` might use the method `draw` to redraw the figure in the center of the screen. When you think of using the inherited method `center` with figures of the classes `Rectangle` and `Circle`, you begin to see that there are complications here.

To make the point clear and more dramatic, let's suppose the class `Figure` is already written and in use and at some later time you add a class for a brand-new kind of figure—say, the class `Triangle`. Now `Triangle` can be a derived class of the class `Figure`, so the method `center` will be inherited from the class `Figure` and thus should apply to (and perform correctly for!) all `Triangles`. But there is a complication. The method `center` uses `draw`, and the method `draw` is different for each type of figure. But, the method `center` is defined in the class `Figure`, which means the method `center` was compiled before we wrote the code for the method `draw` of the class `Triangle`. When we invoke the method `center` with an object of the class `Triangle`, we want the code for the method `center` to use a method that was not even defined when we compiled the method `center`—namely, the method `draw` for the class `Triangle`. Can this be made to happen in Java? Yes, it can, and moreover, it happens automatically. You need not do anything special when you define either the base class `Figure` or the derived class `Triangle`.

late binding

The situation we discussed for the method `center` in the derived class `Triangle` works out as we want because Java uses a mechanism known as **late binding** or **dynamic binding**. Let's see how late binding works in this case involving figure classes.

dynamic binding

binding

early binding

Binding refers to the process of associating a method definition with a method invocation. If the method definition is associated with the method invocation when the code is compiled, that is called **early binding**. If the method invocation is associated with the method invocation when the method is invoked (at run time), that is called **late binding** or **dynamic binding**. Java uses late binding for all methods except for a few cases discussed later in this chapter. Let's see how late binding works in the case of our method `center`.

Recall that the method `center` was defined in the class `Figure` and that the definition of the method `center` included an invocation of the method `draw`. If, contrary to fact, Java used early binding, then when the code for the method `center` compiles, the invocation of the method `draw` would be bound to the currently available definition of `draw`, which is the one given in the definition of `Figure`. If early binding were used, the method `center` would behave exactly the same for all derived classes of the class `Figure` as it does for objects created using the class `Figure`. But, fortunately, Java uses late binding, so when `center` is invoked by an object of the class `Triangle`, the invocation of `draw` (inside the method `center`) is not bound to a definition of draw until the invocation actually takes place. At this point in time, the run-time system knows the calling object is an instance of the class `Triangle` and so uses the definition of `draw` given in the definition of the class `Triangle` (even if the invocation of `draw` is inside the definition of the method `center`). So, the method `center` behaves differently for an object of the class `Triangle` than it would for an object that is just a plain old `Figure`. With late binding, as in Java, things automatically work out the way you normally want them to.

VideoNote
Late Binding Example

Note that in order for late binding to work, each object must somehow know which definition of each method applies to that object. So, when an object is created in a system using late binding, the description of the object must include (either directly or indirectly) a description of where the appropriate definition of each method is located. This additional overhead is the penalty you pay for the convenience of late binding.

Late Binding

With **late binding**, the definition of a method is not bound to an invocation of the method until run time—in fact, not until the time at which the particular invocation takes place. Java uses late binding (for all methods except those discussed in the Pitfall section entitled "No Late Binding for Static Methods").

polymorphism

The terms **polymorphism** and *late binding* are essentially just different words for the same concept. The term *polymorphism* refers to the processes of assigning multiple meanings to the same method name using late binding.

Polymorphism

Polymorphism refers to the ability to associate many meanings to one method name by means of the late binding mechanism. Thus, polymorphism and late binding are really the same topic.

The `final` Modifier

final

You can mark a method to indicate that it cannot be overridden with a new definition in a derived class. Do this by adding the **`final`** modifier to the method heading, as in the following sample heading:

```
public final void someMethod()
{
        .
        .
        .
```

An entire class can be declared final, in which case you cannot use it as a base class to derive any other class from it. The syntax for declaring a class to be final is illustrated in what follows:

```
public final class SomeClass
{
        .
        .
        .
```

If a method is marked as `final`, it means the compiler can use early binding with that particular method, which enables the compiler to be more efficient. However, the added efficiency is normally not great, and we suggest not using the `final` modifier solely for reasons of efficiency. (Also, it can sometimes aid security to mark certain methods as `final`.)

You can view the `final` modifier as a way of turning off late binding for a method (or an entire class). Of course, it does more than just turn off late binding—it turns off the ability to redefine the method in any descendent class.

The `final` Modifier

If you add the modifier `final` to the definition of a method, it indicates that the method may not be redefined in a derived class. If you add the modifier `final` to the definition of a class, it indicates that the class may not be used as a base class to derive other classes.

EXAMPLE: Sales Records

Suppose you are designing a record-keeping program for an automobile parts store. You want to make the program versatile, but you are not sure you can account for all possible situations. For example, you want to keep track of sales, but you cannot anticipate all types of sales. At first, there will only be regular sales to retail customers who go to the store to buy one particular part. However, later you may want to add sales with discounts or mail order sales with a shipping charge. All of these sales will be for an item with a basic price and ultimately will produce some bill. For a simple sale, the bill is just the basic price, but if you later add discounts, then some kinds of bills will also depend on the size of the discount. Now your program needs to compute daily gross sales, which intuitively should just be the sum of all the individual sales bills. You may also want to calculate the largest and smallest sales of the day or the average sale for the day. All of these can be calculated from the individual bills, but many of the methods for computing the bills will not be added until later, when you decide what types of sales you will be dealing with. Because Java uses late binding, you can write a program to total all bills, even though you will not determine the code for some of the bills until later. (For simplicity in this first example, we assume that each sale is for just one item, although we could—but will not here—account for sales of multiple items.)

Display 8.1 contains the definition for a class named `Sale`. All types of sales will be derived classes of the class `Sale`. The class `Sale` corresponds to simple sales of a single item with no added discounts and no added charges. Note that the methods `lessThan` and `equalDeals` both include invocations of the method `bill`. We can later define derived classes of the class `Sale` and define their versions of the method `bill`, and the definitions of the methods `lessThan` and `equalDeals` (which we gave with the class `Sale`) will use the version of the method `bill` that corresponds to the object of the derived class.

For example, Display 8.2 shows the derived class `DiscountSale`. Notice that this class requires a different definition for its version of the method `bill`. Now the methods `lessThan` and `equalDeals`, which use the method `bill`, are inherited from the base class `Sale`. But, when the methods `lessThan` and `equalDeals` are used with an object of the class `DiscountSale`, they will use the version of the method definition for `bill` that was given with the class `DiscountSale`. This is indeed a pretty fancy trick for Java to pull off. Consider the method call `d1.lessThan(d2)` for objects `d1` and `d2` of the class `DiscountSale`. The definition of the method `lessThan` (even for an object of the class `DiscountSale`) is given in the definition of the base class `Sale`, which was compiled before we ever even thought of the class `DiscountSale`. Yet, in the method call `d1.lessThan(d2)`, the line that calls the method `bill` knows enough to use the definition of the method `bill` given for the class `DiscountSale`. This all works out because Java uses late binding.

Display 8.3 gives a sample program that illustrates how the late binding of the method `bill` and the methods that use `bill` work in a complete program.

Display 8.1 The Base Class `Sale` (part 1 of 3)

```
/**
Class for a simple sale of one item with no tax, discount, or other
adjustments.
Class invariant: The price is always nonnegative; the name is a nonempty
string.
*/
public class Sale
{
    private String name; //A nonempty string
    private double price; //nonnegative

    public Sale()
    {
        name = "No name yet";
        price = 0;
    }

    /**
     Precondition: theName is a nonempty string; thePrice is nonnegative.
    */
    public Sale(String theName, double thePrice)
    {
        setName(theName);
        setPrice(thePrice);
    }

    public Sale(Sale originalObject)
    {
      if (originalObject == null)
      {
          System.out.println("Error: null Sale object.");
          System.exit(0);
      }
      //else
      name = originalObject.name;
      price = originalObject.price;
    }

    public static void announcement()
    {
        System.out.println("This is the Sale class.");
    }

    public double getPrice()
    {
        return price;
    }
```

(continued)

Display 8.1 The Base Class `Sale` (part 2 of 3)

```
    /**
      Precondition: newPrice is nonnegative.
     */
    public void setPrice(double newPrice)
    {
        if (newPrice >= 0)
            price = newPrice;
        else
        {
            System.out.println("Error: Negative price.");
            System.exit(0);
        }
    }

    public String getName()
    {
        return name;
    }

    /**
      Precondition: newName is a nonempty string.
     */
    public void setName(String newName)
    {
        if (newName != null && newName != "")
            name = newName;
        else
        {
            System.out.println("Error: Improper name value.");
            System.exit(0);
        }
    }

    public String toString()
    {
        return (name + " Price and total cost = $" + price);
    }

    public double bill()
    {
        return price;
    }
```

Display 8.1 The Base Class `Sale` (part 3 of 3)

```
    /*
     Returns true if the names are the same and the bill for the calling
     object is equal to the bill for otherSale; otherwise returns false.
     Also returns false if otherObject is null.
    */
    public boolean equalDeals(Sale otherSale)
    {
        if (otherSale == null)
            return false;
        else
            return (name.equals(otherSale.name)
                && bill() == otherSale.bill());
    }

    /*
     Returns true if the bill for the calling object is less
     than the bill for otherSale; otherwise returns false.
    */
    public boolean lessThan (Sale otherSale)
    {
        if (otherSale == null)
        {
            System.out.println("Error: null Sale object.");
            System.exit(0);
        }
        //else
        return (bill() < otherSale.bill());
    }

    public boolean equals(Object otherObject)
    {
        if (otherObject == null)
            return false;
        else if (getClass() != otherObject.getClass())
            return false;
        else
        {
          Sale otherSale = (Sale)otherObject;
          return (name.equals(otherSale.name)
            && (price == otherSale.price));
        }
    }
}
```

When invoked, these methods will use the definition of the method `bill` that is appropriate for each of the objects.

Display 8.2 **The Derived Class `DiscountSale`** (part 1 of 2)

```
/**
 Class for a sale of one item with discount expressed as a percent of
 the price, but no other adjustments.
 Class invariant: The price is always nonnegative; the name is a
 nonempty string; the discount is always nonnegative.
*/
public class DiscountSale extends Sale
{
    private double discount; //A percent of the price. Cannot be
                             //negative.
    public DiscountSale()
    {
        super();
        discount = 0;
    }

    /**
     Precondition: theName is a nonempty string; thePrice is
     nonnegative; theDiscount is expressed as a percent of the price
     and is nonnegative.
    */
    public DiscountSale(String theName,
                        double thePrice, double theDiscount)
    {
        super (theName, thePrice);
        setDiscount(theDiscount);
    }

    public DiscountSale(DiscountSale originalObject)
    {
        super (originalObject);
        discount = originalObject.discount;
    }

    public static void announcement()
    {
        System.out.println("This is the DiscountSale class.");
    }

    public double bill()
    {
        double fraction = discount/100;
        return (1 - fraction)*getPrice();
    }
```

The meaning would be unchanged if this line were omitted. (annotation pointing to `super();`)

Display 8.2 The Derived Class `DiscountSale` (part 2 of 2)

```
    public double getDiscount()
    {
        return discount;
    }

    /**
     Precondition: Discount is nonnegative.
    */
    public void setDiscount(double newDiscount)
    {
        if (newDiscount >= 0)
            discount = newDiscount;
        else
        {
            System.out.println("Error: Negative discount.");
            System.exit(0);
        }
    }

    public String toString()
    {
        return (getName() + " Price = $" + getPrice()
                + " Discount = " + discount + "%\n"
                + " Total cost = $" + bill());
    }

    public boolean equals(Object otherObject)
```

The rest of the definition of `equals` is located in Self-Test Exercise 4.

```
}
```

Display 8.3 Late Binding Demonstration

```
/**
 Demonstrates late binding.
*/
public class LateBindingDemo
{
    public static void main(String[] args)
    {
        Sale simple = new Sale("floor mat", 10.00);
           //One item at $10.00.
        DiscountSale discount = new DiscountSale("floor mat", 11.00,
           10); //One item at $11.00 with a 10% discount.
        System.out.println(simple);
        System.out.println(discount);

        if (discount.lessThan(simple))
            System.out.println("Discounted item is cheaper.");
        else
            System.out.println("Discounted item is not cheaper.");

        Sale regularPrice = new Sale("cup holder", 9.90);
           //One item at $9.90.
        DiscountSale specialPrice = new DiscountSale("cup holder",
           11.00,10);
           //One item at $11.00 with a 10% discount.
        System.out.println(regularPrice);
        System.out.println(specialPrice);

        if (specialPrice.equalDeals(regularPrice))
            System.out.println("Deals are equal.");
        else
            System.out.println("Deals are not equal.");
    }
}
```

The method `lessThan` uses different definitions for `discount.bill()` and `simple.bill()`.

The method `equalDeals` uses different definitions for `specialPrice.bill()` and `regularPrice.bill()`.

The `equalDeals` method says that two items are equal provided they have the same name and the same bill (same total cost). It does not matter how the bill (the total cost) is calculated.

Sample Dialogue

```
floor mat Price and total cost = $10.0
floor mat Price = $11.0 Discount = 10.0%
   Total cost = $9.9
Discounted item is cheaper.
cup holder Price and total cost = $9.9
cup holder Price = $11.0 Discount = 10.0%
   Total cost = $9.9
Deals are equal
```

MyProgrammingLab™

Self-Test Exercises

1. Explain the difference between the terms *late binding* and *polymorphism*.
2. Suppose you modify the definitions of the class `Sale` (Display 8.1) by adding the modifier `final` to the definition of the method `bill`. How would that change the output of the program in Display 8.3?
3. Would it be legal to add the following method definition to the class `DiscountSale`?

```
public static boolean isAGoodBuy(Sale theSale)
{
    return (theSale.getDiscount() > 20);
}
```

4. Complete the definition of the method `equals` for the class `DiscountSale` (Display 8.2).

Late Binding with `toString`

In the subsection "The Methods `equals` and `toString`" in Chapter 4, we noted that if you include an appropriate `toString` method in the definition of a class, then you can output an object of the class using `System.out.println`. For example, the following works because `Sale` has a suitable `toString` method:

```
Sale aSale = new Sale("tire gauge", 9.95);
System.out.println(aSale);
```

This produces the following screen output:

```
tire gauge Price and total cost = $9.95
```

This happens because Java uses late binding. We explain this here.

The method invocation `System.out.println(aSale)` is an invocation of the method `println` with the calling object `System.out`. One definition of the method `println` has a single argument of type `Object`. The definition is equivalent to the following:

```
public void println(Object theObject)
{
    System.out.println(theObject.toString());
}
```

(The invocation of the method `println` inside the braces is a different, overloaded definition of the method `println`. That invocation inside the braces uses a method `println` that has a parameter of type `String`, not a parameter of type `Object`.)

This definition of `println` was given before the class `Sale` was defined. Yet in the invocation

```
System.out.println(aSale);
```

with an argument `aSale` of type `Sale` (and hence also of type `Object`), it is the definition of `toString` in the class `Sale` that is used, not the definition of `toString` in the class `Object`. Late binding is what makes this work.

PITFALL: No Late Binding for Static Methods

Java does not use late binding with private methods, methods marked `final`, or static methods. With private methods and `final` methods, this is not an issue because dynamic binding would serve no purpose anyway. However, with static methods it can make a difference when the static method is invoked using a calling object. Such cases arise more often than you might think.

static binding

When Java (or any language) does not use late binding, it uses **static binding**. With static binding, the decision of which definition of a method to use with a calling object is made at compile time based on the type of the variable naming the object.

Display 8.4 illustrates the effect of static binding on a static method with a calling object. Note that the static method `announcement()` in the class `Sale` has its definition overridden in the derived class `DiscountSale`. However, when an object of type `DiscountSale` is named by a variable of type `Sale`, it is the definition `announcement()` in the class `Sale` that is used, not the definition of `announcement` in the class `DiscountSale`.

"So, what's the big deal?" you may ask. A static method is normally called with a class name and not a calling object. It may look that way, but there are cases where a static method has a calling object in an inconspicuous way. If you invoke a static method within the definition of a nonstatic method but without any class name or calling object, then the calling object is an implicit `this`, which is a calling object. For example, suppose you add the following method to the class `Sale`:

```
public void showAdvertisement()
{
    announcement();
    System.out.println(toString( ));
}
```

Suppose further that the method `showAdvertisement` is not overridden in the class `DiscountSale`, then the method `showAdvertisement` is inherited unchanged from `Sale`.

PITFALL: (continued)

Now consider the following code:

```
Sale s = new Sale("floor mat", 10.00);
DiscountSale discount = new DiscountSale("floor mat", 11.00,10);
s.showAdertisement();
discount.showAdertisement();
```

You might expect the following output:

```
This is the Sale class.
floor mat Price and total cost = $10.0
This is the DiscountSale class.
floor mat Price = $11.0 Discount = 10.0%
Total cost = $9.9
```

However, because the definition used for the static method `announcement`, inside of `showAdvertisement`, is determined at compile time (based on the type of the variable holding the calling object), the output actually is the following, where the change is shown in blue:

```
This is the Sale class.
floor mat Price and total cost = $10.0
This is the Sale class.
floor mat Price = $11.0 Discount = 10.0%
Total cost = $9.9
```

Java uses late binding with the nonstatic method `toString` but static binding with the static method `announcement`. ■

Downcasting and Upcasting

The following is perfectly legal (given the class definitions in Displays 8.1 and 8.2):

```
Sale saleVariable;
DiscountSale discountVariable =
                new DiscountSale("paint", 15, 10);
saleVariable = discountVariable;
System.out.println(saleVariable.toString());
```

An object of a derived class (in this case, the derived class `DiscountSale`) also has the type of its base class (in this case, `Sale`) and so can be assigned to a variable of the base class type. Now let's consider the invocation of the method `toString()` on the last line of the preceding code.

Display 8.4 No Late Binding with Static Methods ★

```
/**
 Demonstrates that static methods use static binding.
*/
public class StaticMethodsDemo
{
    public static void main(String[] args)
    {
        Sale.announcement();
        DiscountSale.announcement();
        System.out.println(
            "That showed that you can override a static method " +
            "definition.");

            Sale s = new Sale();
            DiscountSale discount = new DiscountSale();
            s.announcement();
            discount.announcement();
            System.out.println("No surprises so far, but wait.");

            Sale discount2 = discount;
            System.out.println(
                "discount2 is a DiscountSale object in a Sale variable.");
            System.out.println("Which definition of announcement() will " +
               "it use?");
            discount2.announcement();
            System.out.println(
                "It used the Sale version of announcement()!");
    }
}
```

Java uses static binding with static methods so the choice of which definition of a static method to use is determined by the type of the variable, not by the object.

`discount` and `discount2` name the same object, but one is a variable of type `Sale` and one is a variable of type `DiscountSale`.

Sample Dialogue

```
This is the Sale class.
This is the DiscountSale class.
That showed that you can override a static method definition.
This is the Sale class.
This is the DiscountSale class.
No surprises so far, but wait.
discount2 is a DiscountSale object in a Sale variable.
Which definition of announcement() will it use?
This is the Sale class.
It used the Sale version of announcement()!
```

If Java had used late binding with static methods, then this would have been the other announcement.

Because Java uses late binding, the invocation

```
saleVariable.toString()
```

uses the definition of the method `toString` given in the class `DiscountSale`. So the output is

```
paint Price = $15.0 Discount = 10.0%
   Total cost = $13.5
```

Because of late binding, the meaning of the method `toString` is determined by the object, not by the type of the variable `saleVariable`.

You may well respond, "Who cares? Why would I ever want to assign an object of type `DiscountSale` to a variable of type `Sale`?"[1] You make such assignments more often than you might think, but you tend to not notice them because they happen behind the scenes. Recall that a parameter is really a local variable, so every time you use an argument of type `DiscountSale` for a parameter of type `Sale`, you are assigning an object of type `DiscountSale` to a variable of type `Sale`. For example, consider the following invocation taken from the definition of the copy constructor for `DiscountSale` (Display 8.2):

```
super(originalObject);
```

In this invocation, `originalObject` is of type `DiscountSale`, but `super` is the copy constructor for the base class `Sale`. Therefore, `super` has a parameter of type `Sale`, which is a local variable of type `Sale` that is set equal to the argument `originalObject` of type `DiscountSale`.

Note that the type of the variable naming an object determines which method names can be used in an invocation with that calling object. (Self-Test Exercise 3 may help you to understand this point.) However, the object itself always determines the meaning of a method invocation performed by an object; this is what we mean by *late binding*.

> **An Object Knows the Definitions of Its Methods**
>
> The type of a class variable determines which method names can be used with the variable, but the object named by the variable determines which definition of the method name is used. A special case of this rule is the following: The type of a class parameter determines which method names can be used with the parameter, but the argument determines which definition of the method name is used.

[1]It is actually the references to the object that are assigned, not the objects themselves, but that subtlety is not relevant to what we are discussing here, and the language is already complicated enough.

upcasting

Assigning an object of a derived class to a variable of a base class (or any ancestor class) is often called **upcasting** because it is like a type cast to the type of the base class. In the normal way of writing inheritance diagrams, base classes are drawn above derived classes.[2]

downcasting

When you do a type cast from a base case to a derived class (or from any ancestor class to any descendent class), it is called a **downcast**. Upcasting is pretty straightforward; there are no funny cases to worry about, and in Java things always work out the way you want them to. Downcasting is more troublesome. First of all, downcasting does not always make sense. For example, the downcast

```
Sale saleVariable = new Sale("paint", 15);
DiscountSale discountVariable;
discountVariable = (DiscountSale)saleVariable;//Error
```

does not make sense because the object named by `saleVariable` has no instance variable named `discount` and so cannot be an object of type `DiscountSale`. Every `DiscountSale` is a `Sale`, but not every `Sale` is a `DiscountSale`, as indicated by this example. It is your responsibility to use downcasting only in situations where it makes sense.

It is instructive to note that

```
discountVariable = (DiscountSale)saleVariable;
```

produces a run-time error but will compile with no error. However, the following, which is also illegal, produces a compile-time error:

```
discountVariable = saleVariable;
```

Java catches these downcasting errors as soon as it can, which may be at compile time or at run time, depending on the case.

Although downcasting can be dangerous, it is sometimes necessary. For example, we inevitably use downcasting when we define an `equals` method for a class. For example, note the following line from the definition of `equals` in the class `Sale` (Display 8.1):

```
Sale otherSale = (Sale)otherObject;
```

This is a downcast from the type `Object` to the type `Sale`. Without this downcast, the instance variables `name` and `price` in the `return` statement, reproduced as follows, would be illegal, because the class `Object` has no such instance variables:

```
return (name.equals(otherSale.name)
        && (price == otherSale.price));
```

---

[2] We prefer to think of an object of the derived class as actually having the type of its base class as well as its own type. So this is not, strictly speaking, a type cast, but it does no harm to follow standard usage and call it a type cast in this case.

PITFALL: Downcasting

It is the responsibility of the programmer to use downcasting only in situations where it makes sense. The compiler makes no checks to see if downcasting is reasonable. However, if you use downcasting in a situation in which it does not make sense, you will usually get a run-time error message. ■

TIP: Checking to See Whether Downcasting Is Legitimate ★

You can use the `instanceof` operator to test whether or not downcasting is sensible. Downcasting to a specific type is reasonable if the object being cast is an instance of that type, which is exactly what the `instanceof` operator tests for.

instanceof

The `instanceof` operator checks whether an object is of the type given as its second argument. The syntax is

```
Object instanceof Class_Name
```

which returns `true` if *`Object`* is of type *`Class_Name`*; otherwise it returns `false`. So, the following will return `true` if `someObject` is of type `DiscountSale`:

```
someObject instanceof DiscountSale
```

Note that because every object of every descendent class of `DiscountSale` is also of type `DiscountSale`, this expression will return `true` if `someObject` is an instance of any descendent class of `DiscountSale`.

So, if you want to type cast to `DiscountSale`, then you can make the casts safer as follows:

```
DiscountSale ds = new DiscountSale();
if (someObject instanceof DiscountSale)
{
    ds = (DiscountSale)someObject;
    System.out.println("ds was changed to " + someObject);
}
else
    System.out.println("ds was not changed.");
```

`someObject` might be, for example, a variable of type `Sale` or of type `Object`. ■

MyProgrammingLab™

Self-Test Exercises

5. Consider the following code, which is identical to the code discussed earlier in the opening of the subsection, "Downcasting and Upcasting," except that we added the type cast shown in color:

```
Sale saleVariable;
DiscountSale discountVariable =
               new DiscountSale("paint", 15, 10);
saleVariable = (Sale)discountVariable;
System.out.println(saleVariable.toString());
```

We saw that without the type cast, the definition of the `toString` method used is the one given in the definition of the class `DiscountSale`. With this added type cast, will the definition of the `toString` method used still be the one given in `DiscountSale` or will it be the one given in the definition of `Sale`?

6. Would it be legal to add the following method definition to the class `DiscountSale`?

What about adding it to the class `Sale`?

```
public static void showDiscount(Sale object)
{
    System.out.println("Discount = "
                        + object.getDiscount());
}
```

7. ★ What output is produced by the following code?

```
Sale someObject = new DiscountSale("map", 5, 0);
DiscountSale ds = new DiscountSale();
if (someObject instanceof DiscountSale)
{
    ds = (DiscountSale)someObject;
    System.out.println("ds was changed to " + someObject);
}
else
    System.out.println("ds was not changed.");
```

MyProgrammingLab™

Self-Test Exercises (continued)

8. ★ What output is produced by the following code?

```
Sale someObject = new Sale("map", 5);
DiscountSale ds = new DiscountSale();
if (someObject instanceof DiscountSale)
{
    ds = (DiscountSale)someObject;
    System.out.println("ds was changed to " + someObject);
}
else
    System.out.println("ds was not changed.");
```

9. ★ Suppose we removed the qualifier `static` from the method `announcement()` in both `Sale` (Display 8.1) and `DiscountSale` (Display 8.2). What would be the output produced by the following code (which is similar to the end of Display 8.4)?

```
Sale s = new Sale( );
DiscountSale discount = new DiscountSale( );
s.announcement( );
discount.announcement( );
System.out.println("No surprises so far, but wait.");

Sale discount2 = discount;
System.out.println(
   "discount2 is a DiscountSale object in a Sale variable.");
System.out.println(
     "Which definition of announcement( ) will it use?");
discount2.announcement( );
System.out.println(
       "Did it use the Sale version of announcement()?");
```

A First Look at the `clone` Method

clone

Every object inherits a method named `clone` from the class `Object`. The method `clone` has no parameters and is supposed to return a copy of the calling object. However, the inherited version of `clone` was not designed to be used as is. Instead, you are expected to override the definition of `clone` with a version appropriate for the class you are defining. The officially sanctioned way to define the method `clone` turns out to be a bit complicated and requires material we do not cover until Chapter 13, so we will describe how to do so in that chapter. In this section, we will describe a simple way to define `clone` that will work in most situations and will allow us to discuss how polymorphism interacts with the `clone` method. If you are in a hurry to see the officially sanctioned way to define `clone`, you can read Chapter 13 immediately after this section (Section 8.1) with no loss of continuity in your reading.

The method `clone` has no parameters and should return a copy of the calling object. The returned object should have identical data to that of the calling object, but it normally should be a different object (an identical twin or "a clone"). You usually want the `clone` method to return the same kind of copy as what we have been defining for copy constructors, which is what is known as a *deep copy*. (You many want to review the subsection entitled "Copy Constructors" in Chapter 5.)

A `clone` method serves very much the same purpose as a copy constructor but, as you will see in the Pitfall titled "Limitations of Copy Constructors" there are situations where a `clone` method works as you want, whereas a copy constructor does not perform as desired.

As with other methods inherited from the class `Object`, the method `clone` needs to be redefined (overridden) before it performs properly. The heading for the method `clone` in the class `Object` is as follows:

```
protected Object clone()
```

If a class has a copy constructor, you can define the `clone` method for that class by using the copy constructor to create the copy returned by the `clone` method. For example, consider the class `Sale` defined in Display 8.1. The following definition of the `clone` method can be added to the definition of `Sale` given in Display 8.1:

```
public Sale clone()
{
    return new Sale(this);
}
```

Using a copy constructor is not the officially sanctioned way to define a `clone` method, and in fact, the Java documentation says you should not define it this way. However, it does work correctly, and some authorities say it is acceptable. In Chapter 13, we will discuss the official way of defining the method `clone` when we introduce the `Cloneable` interface.

Note that, as we defined the method `clone` for the class `Sale`, the method `clone` has `Sale` as its return type and is given `public` rather than `protected` access. Despite these changes in the method heading, this definition overrides the method `clone` inherited from the class `Object`. As we noted in Chapter 7, a change to a more permissive access, such as from `protected` to `public`, is always allowed when overriding a method definition. Changing the return type from `Object` to `Sale` is allowed because `Sale` (and every other class, for that matter) is a descendent class of the class `Object`. This is an example of a covariant return type, as discussed in the subsection of Chapter 7 entitled "Changing the Return Type of an Overridden Method."

The `clone` method for the `DiscountSale` class can be defined similarly:

```
public DiscountSale clone()
{
    return new DiscountSale(this);
}
```

extra code on website

The definitions of the classes `Sale` and `DiscountSale` on the website that accompanies this book each include the method `clone` defined as we just described.

PITFALL: Sometimes the `clone` Method Return Type Is `Object`

Prior to version 5.0, Java did not allow covariant return types, and so did not allow any changes whatsoever in the return type of an overridden method. In those earlier versions of Java, the `clone` method for all classes had `Object` as its return type. This is because the `clone` method for a class overrides the `clone` method of the class `Object`, and the `clone` method of the class `Object` has a return type of `Object`. If you encounter a `clone` method for a class that was designed and coded before version 5.0 of Java, the `clone` method will have a return type of `Object`. When using such older `clone` methods, you will need to use a type cast on the value returned by `clone`.

For example, suppose the class `OldClass` was defined before Java 5.0. If `original` is an object of the class `OldClass`, then the following will produce a compiler error message:

```
OldClass copy = original.clone();
```

The problem is that `original.clone()` returns a value of type `Object`, while the variable `copy` is of type `OldClass`. To correct the situation, you must add a type cast as follows:

```
OldClass copy = (OldClass)original.clone();
```

(continued)

PITFALL: (continued)

You may encounter this problem even with classes defined after Java version 5.0. In Java version 5.0 and later, it is perfectly legal to use `Object` as a return type for a `clone` method (even if that is not the preferred return type). When in doubt, it causes no harm to include the type cast. For example, the following is legal for the `clone` method of the class `Sale` defined in the previous section:

```
Sale copySale = originalSale.clone();
```

However, adding the following type cast produces no problems:

```
Sale copySale = (Sale)originalSale.clone();
```

When in doubt about the `clone` method of a class, include the type cast. ■

PITFALL: Limitations of Copy Constructors ★

Copy constructors work well in most simple cases. However, there are situations where they do not—indeed, cannot—do their job. That is why Java favors using the method `clone` in place of using a copy constructor. Here is a simple example of where the copy constructor does not do its job, but the `clone` method does.

For this discussion, assume that the classes `Sale` and `DiscountSale` each have a `clone` method added. The definitions of these `clone` methods are given in the previous subsection.

Suppose you have a method with the following heading (the methods `Sale` and `DiscountSale` were defined in Displays 8.1 and 8.2):

```
/**
 Supposedly returns a safe copy of a. That is, if b is the array
 returned, then b[i] is supposedly an independent copy of a[i].
*/
public static Sale[] badCopy(Sale[] a)
{
    Sale[] b = new Sale[a.length];
    for (int i = 0; i < a.length; i++)
        b[i] = new Sale(a[i]);//Problem here!
    return b;
}
```

Now if your array `a` contains objects from derived classes of `Sale`, such as objects of type `DiscountSale`, then `badCopy(a)` will not return a true copy of `a`. Every element of the array `badCopy(a)` will be a plain old `Sale`, because the `Sale` copy constructor produces only plain old `Sale` objects; no element in `badCopy(a)` will be an instance of the class `DiscountSale`.

PITFALL: (continued)

If we instead use the method `clone`, things work out as they should; the following is the correct way to define our copy method:

```
public static Sale[] goodCopy(Sale[] a)
{
    Sale[] b = new Sale[a.length];
    for (int i = 0; i < a.length; i++)
        b[i] = a[i].clone();
    return b;
}
```

Because of late binding (polymorphism), `a[i].clone()` always means the correct version of the `clone` method. If `a[i]` is an object created with a constructor of the class `DiscountSale`, `a[i].clone()` will invoke the definition of `clone()` given in the definition of the class `DiscountSale`. If `a[i]` is an object created with a constructor of the class `Sale`, `a[i].clone()` will invoke the definition of `clone()` given in the definition of the class `Sale`. This is illustrated in Display 8.5.

This may seem like a sleight of hand. After all, in the classes `Sale` and `DiscountSale`, we defined the method `clone` in terms of copy constructors. We reproduce the definitions of `clone` from the class `Sale` and `DiscountSale` as follows:

```
//For Sale class
public Sale clone()
{
    return new Sale(this);
}
//For DiscountSale class
public DiscountSale clone()
{
    return new DiscountSale(this);
}
```

So, why is using the method `clone` any different than using a copy constructor? The difference is simply that the method creating the copy of an element `a[i]` has the same name `clone` in all the classes, and polymorphism works with method names. The copy constructors named `Sale` and `DiscountSale` have different names, and polymorphism has nothing to do with methods of different names.

We will have more to say about the clone method in Chapter 13 when we discuss the `Cloneable` interface. ■

Display 8.5 Copy Constructor Versus `clone` Method (part 1 of 2)

This program assumes that a `clone` *method has been added to the class* `Sale` *and to the class* `DiscountSale`*.*

```
/**
 Demonstrates where the clone method works,
 but copy constructors do not.
*/
public class CopyingDemo
{
    public static void main(String[] args)
    {
        Sale[] a = new Sale[2];
        a[0] = new Sale("atomic coffee mug", 130.00);
        a[1] = new DiscountSale("invisible paint", 5.00, 10);
        int i;

        Sale[] b = badCopy(a);

        System.out.println("With copy constructors:");
        for (i = 0; i < a.length; i++)
        {
            System.out.println("a[" + i + "] = " + a[i]);
            System.out.println("b[" + i + "] = " + b[i]);
            System.out.println();
        }
        System.out.println();

        b = goodCopy(a);

        System.out.println("With clone method:");
        for (i = 0; i < a.length; i++)
        {
            System.out.println("a[" + i + "] = " + a[i]);
            System.out.println("b[" + i + "] = " + b[i]);
            System.out.println();
        }

    }

    /**
     Supposedly returns a safe copy of a. That is, if b is the
     array returned, then b[i] is supposedly an independent copy of a[i].
    */

    public static Sale[] badCopy(Sale[] a)
    {
        Sale[] b = new Sale[a.length];
        for (int i = 0; i < a.length; i++)
            b[i] = new Sale(a[i]);//Problem here!
        return b;
    }

```

Display 8.5 Copy Constructor Versus `clone` Method (part 2 of 2)

```
        /**
         Returns a safe copy of a. That is, if b is the
         array returned, then b[i] is an independent copy of a[i].
        */
        public static Sale[] goodCopy(Sale[] a)
        {
            Sale[] b = new Sale[a.length];
            for (int i = 0; i < a.length; i++)
                b[i] = a[i].clone( );
            return b;
        }
    }
```

Sample Dialogue

```
With copy constructors:
a[0] = atomic coffee mug Price and total cost = $130.0
b[0] = atomic coffee mug Price and total cost = $130.0

a[1] = invisible paint Price = $5.0 Discount 10.0%
   Total cost = $4.5
b[1] = invisible paint Price and total cost = $5.0

With clone method:
a[0] = atomic coffee mug Price and total cost = $130.0
b[0] = atomic coffee mug Price and total cost = $130.0

a[1] = invisible paint Price = $5.0 Discount 10.0%
   Total cost = $4.5
b[1] = invisible paint Price = $5.0 Discount 10.0%
   Total cost = $4.5
```

The copy constructor lost the discount.

The `clone` method did not lose the discount.

8.2 Abstract Classes

It is for us, the living, rather to be dedicated here to the unfinished work which they who fought here have thus far so nobly advanced.

ABRAHAM LINCOLN, *Gettysburg address*

An abstract class is a class that has some methods without complete definitions. You cannot create an object using an abstract class constructor, but you can use an abstract class as a base class to define a derived class.

Abstract Classes

In Chapter 7, we defined a class named `Employee` and two of its derived classes, `HourlyEmployee` and `SalariedEmployee`. Display 8.6 repeats the details of these class definitions, which we will use in this discussion.

Suppose that when we define the class `Employee`, we know that we are going to frequently compare employees to see if they have the same pay. We might add the following method to the class `Employee`:

```
public boolean samePay(Employee other)
{
    return (this.getPay() == other.getPay());
}
```

There is, however, one problem with adding the method `samePay` to the class `Employee`: The method `samePay` includes an invocation of the method `getPay`, and the class `Employee` has no `getPay` method. Moreover, there is no reasonable definition we might give for a `getPay` method so that we could add it to the class `Employee`. The only instance variables in the class `Employee` give an employee's name and hire date, but give no information about pay. To see how we should proceed, let's compare objects of the class `Employee` to employees in the real world.

Every real-world employee does have some pay because every real-world employee is either an hourly employee or a salaried employee, and the two derived classes `HourlyEmployee` and `SalariedEmployee` each have a `getPay` method. The problem is that we do not know how to define the `getPay` method until we know if the employee is an hourly or salaried. We would like to postpone the definition of the `getPay` method and give it only in each derived class of the `Employee` class. We would like to simply add a note to the `Employee` class that says: "There will be a method `getPay` for each `Employee` but we do not yet know how it is defined." Java lets us do exactly what we want. The official Java equivalent of our promissory note about the method `getPay` is to make `getPay` an **abstract method**. An abstract method has a heading just like an ordinary method, but no method body. The syntax rules of Java require the modifier `abstract` and require a semicolon in place of the missing method body, as illustrated by the following:

abstract method

```
public abstract double getPay();
```

Display 8.6 **Employee** Class and Its Derived Classes (part 1 of 2)

These show the details needed for the current discussion. You should not need to review the entire class definitions from Chapter 7. Complete definitions of all these classes are given in the subdirectory for this chapter on the website that comes with this text.

```
public class Employee
{
    private String name;
    private Date hireDate;
```

The class `Date` is defined in Display 4.13, but the details are not important to the current discussion. There is no need to review the definition of the class `Date`.

```
    public Employee()
```

The body of the constructor is given in Display 7.2 should initialize the instance variables, but the details are not needed for this discussion.

```
    public boolean equals(Object otherObject)
```

The body of the method equals is the same as in Display 7.10, but the details of the definition are not important to the current discussion.

All other constructor and other method definitions are exactly the same as in Display 7.2.

The class `Employee` has no method named `getPay`.

```
}
```

```
public class SalariedEmployee extends Employee
{
    private double salary; //annual

    /**
     Returns the pay for the month.
    */
    public double getPay()
    {
        return salary / 12;
    }

    public boolean equals(Object otherObject)
```

The rest of the definition of equals is the same as in the answer to Self-Test Exercise 20 of Chapter 7, but the details of the definition are not important to the current discussion.

All constructor and other method definitions are exactly the same as in Display 7.5.

```
}
```

(continued)

Display 8.6 **Employee** Class and Its Derived Classes (part 2 of 2)

```
public class HourlyEmployee extends Employee
{
    private double wageRate;
    private double hours; //for the month

    /**
     Returns the pay for the month.
    */
    public double getPay()
    {
        return wageRate * hours;
    }

    public boolean equals(Object otherObject)
    {
        if (otherObject == null)
            return false;
        else if (getClass() != otherObject.getClass( ))
            return false;
        else
        {
            HourlyEmployee otherHourlyEmployee =
                                   (HourlyEmployee)otherObject;
            return (super.equals(otherHourlyEmployee)
                 && (wageRate == otherHourlyEmployee.wageRate)
                 && (hours == otherHourlyEmployee.hours));
        }
    }
```

All constructor and other method definitions are exactly the same as in Display 7.3.

```
}
```

If we add this abstract method `getPay` to the class `Employee`, then we are free to add the method `samePay` to the class `Employee`.

abstract cannot be private

An abstract method can be thought of as the interface part of a method with the implementation details omitted. Because a private method is normally only a helping method and so not part of the interface for a programmer using the class, it follows that it does not make sense to have a private abstract method. Java enforces this reasoning. In Java, an abstract method cannot be private. Normally an abstract method is public but protected, and package (default) access is allowed.

An abstract method serves a purpose, even though it is not given a full definition. It serves as a placeholder for a method that must be defined in all (nonabstract) derived classes. Note that in Display 8.7, the method `samePay` includes invocations of the method `getPay`. If the abstract method `getPay` were omitted, this invocation of `getPay` would be illegal.

> ### Abstract Method
>
> An **abstract method** serves as a placeholder for a method that will be fully defined in a descendent class. An abstract method has a complete method heading with the addition of the modifier `abstract`. It has no method body but does end with a semicolon in place of a method body. An abstract method cannot be private.
>
> **EXAMPLES**
>
> ```
> public abstract double getPay();
> public abstract void doSomething(int count);
> ```

abstract class

A class that has at least one abstract method is called an **abstract class** and, in Java, must have the modifier `abstract` added to the class heading. The redefined, now abstract, class `Employee` is shown in Display 8.7.

An abstract class can have any number of abstract methods. In addition, it can have, and typically does have, other regular (fully defined) methods. If a derived class of an abstract class does not give full definitions to all the abstract methods, or if the derived class adds an abstract method, then the derived class is also an abstract class and must include the modifier `abstract` in its heading.

concrete class

In contrast with the term *abstract class*, a class with no abstract methods is called a **concrete class**.

Display 8.7 **`Employee`** Class as an Abstract Class (part 1 of 2)

```
/**
 Class Invariant: All objects have a name string and hire date.
 A name string of "No name" indicates no real name specified yet.
 A hire date of January 1, 1000 indicates no real hire date specified
 yet.
*/
public abstract class Employee
{
    private String name;
    private Date hireDate;

    public abstract double getPay();

    public Employee()
    {
         name = "No name";
         hireDate = new Date("January", 1, 1000);
                  //Just a placeholder.
    }

    public boolean samePay(Employee other)
    {
        if (other == null)
```

The class `Date` is defined in Display 4.13, but the details are not relevant to the current discussion of abstract methods and classes. There is no need to review the definition of the class `Date`.

(continued)

Display 8.7 `Employee` Class as an Abstract Class (part 2 of 2)

```
        {
            System.out.println("Error: null Employee object.");
            System.exit(0);
        }
        //else
        return (this.getPay() == other.getPay());
    }
```

All other constructor and other method definitions are exactly the same as in Display 7.2. In particular, they are not abstract methods.

```
}
```

Abstract Class

An **abstract class** is a class with one or more abstract methods. An abstract class must have the modifier `abstract` included in the class heading, as illustrated by the example.

EXAMPLE

```
public abstract class Employee
{
    private String name;
    private Date hireDate;

    public abstract double getPay();
         ...
```

PITFALL: You Cannot Create Instances of an Abstract Class

You cannot use an abstract class constructor to create an object of the abstract class. You can only create objects of the derived classes of the abstract class. For example, with the class `Employee` defined as in Display 8.7, the following would be illegal:

```
Employee joe = new Employee(); //Illegal because
                               //Employee is an abstract class.
```

But, this is no problem. The object `joe` could not correspond to any real-world employee. Any real-world employee is either hourly or a salaried. In the real world, one cannot be just an employee. One must be either an hourly employee or a salaried employee. Still, it is useful to discuss employees in general. In particular, we can compare employees to see if they have the same pay, even though the way of calculating the pay might be different for the two employees. ■

TIP: An Abstract Class Is a Type

You cannot create an object of an abstract class (unless it is actually an object of some concrete descendent class). Nonetheless, it makes perfectly good sense to have a parameter of an abstract class type such as `Employee` (as defined in Display 8.7). Then, an object of any of the descendent classes of `Employee` can be plugged in for the parameter. It even makes sense to have a variable of an abstract class type such as `Employee`, although it can only name objects of its concrete descendent classes. ■

An Abstract Class Is a Type

You can have a parameter of an abstract class type such as the abstract class `Employee` defined in Display 8.7. Then, an object of any of the concrete descendent classes of `Employee` can be plugged in for the parameter. You can also have variables of an abstract class type such as `Employee`, although it can only name objects of its concrete descendent classes.

Self-Test Exercises

10. Can a method definition include an invocation of an abstract method?
11. Can you have a variable whose type is an abstract class?
12. Can you have a parameter whose type is an abstract class?
13. Is it legal to have an abstract class in which all methods are abstract?
14. The abstract class `Employee` (Display 8.7) uses the method definitions from Display 7.2. After we did Display 7.2, we later gave the following improved version of `equals`:

```
public boolean equals(Object otherObject)
{
    if (otherObject == null)
        return false;
    else if (getClass() != otherObject.getClass())
        return false;
    else
    {
        Employee otherEmployee =
                        (Employee)otherObject;
        return (name.equals(otherEmployee.name)
         && hireDate.equals(otherEmployee.hireDate));
    }
}
```

Would it be legal to replace the version of `equals` for the abstract class `Employee` with this improved version?

(continued)

MyProgrammingLab™

Self-Test Exercises (continued)

15. The abstract class `Employee` given in Display 8.7 has a constructor (in fact, it has more than one, although only one is shown in Display 8.7). But using a constructor to create an instance of an abstract class, as in the following, is illegal:

```
Employee joe = new Employee(); //Illegal
```

So why bother to have any constructors in an abstract class? Aren't they useless?

Chapter Summary

- *Late binding* (also called *dynamic binding*) means that the decision of which version of a method is appropriate is decided at run time. Java uses late binding.
- *Polymorphism* means using the process of late binding to allow different objects to use different method actions for the same method name. *Polymorphism* is essentially another word for *late binding*.
- You can assign an object of a derived class to a variable of its base class (or any ancestor class), but you cannot do the reverse.
- If you add the modifier `final` to the definition of a method, it indicates that the method may not be redefined in a derived class. If you add the modifier `final` to the definition of a class, it indicates that the class may not be used as a base class to derive other classes.
- An *abstract method* serves as a placeholder for a method that will be fully defined in a descendent class.
- An *abstract class* is a class with one or more abstract methods.
- An abstract class is designed to be used as a base class to derive other classes. You cannot create an object of an abstract class type (unless it is an object of some concrete descendent class).
- An abstract class is a type. You can have variables whose type is an abstract class and you can have parameters whose type is an abstract type.

Answers to Self-Test Exercises

1. In essence, there is no difference between the two terms. There is only a slight difference in their usage. *Late binding* refers to the mechanism used to decide which method definition to use when a method is invoked, and *polymorphism* refers to the fact that the same method name can have different meanings because of late binding.
2. There would be problems well before you wrote the program in Display 8.3. Since `final` means you cannot change the definition of the method `bill` in a derived

class, the definition of the method `DiscountSale` would not compile. If you omit the definition of the method `bill` from the class `DiscountSale`, the output would change to

```
floor mat Price and total cost = $10.0
floor mat Price = $11.0 Discount = 10.0%
   Total cost = $11.0
Discounted item is not cheaper.
cup holder Price and total cost = $9.9
cup holder Price = $11.0 Discount = 10.0%
   Total cost = $11.0
Items are not equal.
```

Note that all objects use the definition of `bill` given in the definition of `Sale`.

3. It would not be legal to add it to any class definition because the class `Sale` has no method named `getDiscount` and so the invocation

```
theSale.getDiscount()
```

is not allowed. If the type of the parameter were changed from `Sale` to `DiscountSale`, it would then be legal.

4.
```
public boolean equals(Object otherObject)
{
    if (otherObject == null)
        return false;
    else if (getClass() != otherObject.getClass())
        return false;
    else
    {
        DiscountSale otherDiscountSale =
                         (DiscountSale)otherObject;
        return (super.equals(otherDiscountSale)
            && discount == otherDiscountSale.discount);
    }
}
```

5. The definition of `toString` always depends on the object and not on any type cast. So, the definition used is the same as without the added type cast; that is, the definition of `toString` that is used is the one given in `DiscountSale`.

6. It would not be legal to add it to any class definition because the parameter is of type `Sale`, and `Sale` has no method named `getDiscount`. If the parameter type were changed to `DiscountSale`, it would then be legal to add it to any class definition.

7.
```
ds was changed to map Price $ 5.0 discount 0.0%
Total cost $5.0
```

8.
```
ds was not changed.
```

9. The output would be the following (the main change from Display 8.4 is shown in blue):

```
This is the Sale class.
This is the DiscountSale class.
No surprises so far, but wait.
discount2 is a DiscountSale object in a Sale variable.
Which definition of announcement() will it use?
This is the DiscountSale class.
Did it use the Sale version of announcement()?
```

10. Yes. See Display 8.7.
11. Yes, you can have a variable whose type is an abstract class.
12. Yes, you can have a parameter whose type is an abstract class.
13. Yes, it is legal to have an abstract class in which all methods are abstract.
14. Yes, it would be legal to replace the version of `equals` for the abstract class `Employee` with this improved version. In fact, the version of `Employee` on the accompanying website does use the improved version of `equals`.
15. No, you can still use constructors to hold code that might be useful in derived classes. The constructors in the derived classes can—in fact, must—include invocations of constructors in the base (abstract) class. (Recall the use of `super` as a name for the base class constructor.)

MyProgrammingLab™

Programming Projects

Visit www.myprogramminglab.com to complete select exercises online and get instant feedback.

VideoNote **Solution to Programming Project 8.1**

1. In Programming Project 7.3 from Chapter 7, the `Alien` class was rewritten to use inheritance. The rewritten `Alien` class should be made `abstract` because there will never be a need to create an instance of it, only its derived classes. Change this to an abstract class and also make the `getDamage` method an abstract method. Test the class from your `main` method to ensure that it still operates as expected.
2. Create a class named `Movie` that can be used with your video rental business. The `Movie` class should track the Motion Picture Association of America (MPAA) rating (e.g., Rated G, PG-13, R), ID Number, and movie title with appropriate accessor and mutator methods. Also create an `equals()` method that overrides `Object`'s `equals()` method, where two movies are equal if their ID number is identical. Next, create three additional classes named `Action`, `Comedy`, and `Drama` that are derived from `Movie`. Finally, create an overridden method named `calcLateFees` that takes as input the number of days a movie is late and returns the late fee for that movie. The default late fee is $2/day. Action movies have a late fee of $3/day, comedies are $2.50/day, and dramas are $2/day. Test your classes from a `main` method.
3. Extend the previous problem with a `Rental` class. This class should store a `Movie` that is rented, an integer representing the ID of the customer that rented the movie, and an integer indicating how many days late the movie is. Add a method

that calculates the late fees for the rental. In your `main` method, create an array of type `Rental` filled with sample data of all types of movies. Then, create a method named `lateFeesOwed` that iterates through the array and returns the total amount of late fees that are outstanding.

4. The goal for this programming project is to create a simple 2D predator–prey simulation. In this simulation, the prey is ants, and the predators are doodlebugs. These critters live in a world composed of a 20 × 20 grid of cells. Only one critter may occupy a cell at a time. The grid is enclosed, so a critter is not allowed to move off the edges of the grid. Time is simulated in time steps. Each critter performs some action every time step.

   The ants behave according to the following model:

   - Move. Every time step, randomly try to move up, down, left, or right. If the cell in the selected direction is occupied or would move the ant off the grid, then the ant stays in the current cell.
   - Breed. If an ant survives for three time steps, then at the end of the third time step (i.e., after moving), the ant will breed. This is simulated by creating a new ant in an adjacent (up, down, left, or right) cell that is empty. If there is no empty cell available, no breeding occurs. Once an offspring is produced, the ant cannot produce an offspring until three more time steps have elapsed.

   The doodlebugs behave according to the following model:

   - Move. Every time step, if there is an adjacent cell (up, down, left, or right) occupied by an ant, then the doodlebug will move to that cell and eat the ant. Otherwise, the doodlebug moves according to the same rules as the ant. Note that a doodlebug cannot eat other doodlebugs.
   - Breed. If a doodlebug survives for eight time steps, then at the end of the time step, it will spawn off a new doodlebug in the same manner as the ant.
   - Starve. If a doodlebug has not eaten an ant within the last three time steps, then at the end of the third time step, it will starve and die. The doodlebug should then be removed from the grid of cells.

   During one turn, all the doodlebugs should move before the ants.

   Write a program to implement this simulation and draw the world using ASCII characters of "o" for an ant and "X" for a doodlebug. Create a class named `Organism` that encapsulates basic data common to both ants and doodlebugs.

   This class should have an overridden method named `move` that is defined in the derived classes of `Ant` and `Doodlebug`. You may need additional data structures to keep track of which critters have moved.

   Initialize the world with 5 doodlebugs and 100 ants. After each time step, prompt the user to press Enter to move to the next time step. You should see a cyclical pattern between the population of predators and prey, although random perturbations may lead to the elimination of one or both species.

5. Consider a graphics system that has classes for various figures—say, rectangles, boxes, triangles, circles, and so on. For example, a rectangle might have data

members' height, width, and center point, while a box and circle might have only a center point and an edge length or radius, respectively. In a well-designed system, these would be derived from a common class, `Figure`. You are to implement such a system.

The class `Figure` is the base class. You should add only `Rectangle` and `Triangle` classes derived from `Figure`. Each class has stubs for methods `erase` and `draw`. Each of these methods outputs a message telling the name of the class and what method has been called. Because these are just stubs, they do nothing more than output this message. The method `center` calls the `erase` and `draw` methods to erase and redraw the figure at the center. Because you have only stubs for `erase` and `draw`, center will not do any "centering" but will call the methods `erase` and `draw`, which will allow you to see which versions of `draw` and `center` it calls. Also, add an output message in the method `center` that announces that `center` is being called. The methods should take no arguments. Also, define a demonstration program for your classes.

For a real example, you would have to replace the definition of each of these methods with code to do the actual drawing. You will be asked to do this in Programming Project 8.6.

6. Flesh out Programming Project 8.5. Give new definitions for the various constructors and methods `center`, `draw`, and `erase` of the class `Figure`; `draw` and `erase` of the class `Triangle`; and `draw` and `erase` of the class `Rectangle`. Use character graphics; that is, the various `draw` methods will place regular keyboard characters on the screen in the desired shape. Use the character `'*'` for all the character graphics. That way, the `draw` methods actually draw figures on the screen by placing the character `'*'` at suitable locations on the screen. For the `erase` methods, you can simply clear the screen (by outputting blank lines or by doing something more sophisticated). There are a lot of details in this project and you will have to decide on some of them on your own.

7. Define a class named `MultiItemSale` that represents a sale of multiple items of type `Sale` given in Display 8.1 (or of the types of any of its descendent classes). The class `MultiItemSale` will have an instance variable whose type is `Sale[]`, which will be used as a partially filled array. There will also be another instance variable of type `int` that keeps track of how much of this array is currently used. The exact details on methods and other instance variables, if any, are up to you. Use this class in a program that obtains information for items of type `Sale` and of type `DiscountSale` (Display 8.2) and that computes the total bill for the list of items sold.

8. Programming Project 7.8 required rewriting the solution to Programming Project 4.10 with inheritance. Redo or do Programming Project 7.8, but instead define the `Pet` class as an abstract class. The `acepromazine()` and `carprofen()` methods should be defined as abstract methods.

   In your main method, define an array of type `Pet` and add two instances of cats and two instances of dogs to the array. Iterate through the array and output how much carprofen and acepromazine each pet would require.

VideoNote
Solution to Programming Project 8.9

9. The following is a short snippet of code that simulates rolling a 6-sided dice 100 times. There is an equal chance of rolling any digit from 1 to 6.

```
public static void printDiceRolls(Random randGenerator)
{
    for (int i = 0; i < 100; i++)
    {
        System.out.println(randGenerator.nextInt(6) + 1);
    }
}

public static void main(String[] args)
{
    Random randGenerator = new Random();
    printDiceRolls(randGenerator);
}
```

Create your own class, `LoadedDice`, that is derived from `Random`. The constructor for `LoadedDice` needs to only invoke `Random`'s constructor. Override the `public int nextInt(int num)` method so that with a 50% chance, your new method always returns the largest number possible (i.e., `num` – 1), and with a 50% chance, it returns what `Random`'s `nextInt` method would return.

Test your class by replacing the main method with the following:

```
    LoadedDice myDice = new LoadedDice();
    printDiceRolls(myDice);
```

You do not need to change the `printDiceRolls` method even though it takes a parameter of type `Random`. Polymorphism tells Java to invoke `LoadedDice`'s `nextInt()` method instead of `Random`'s `nextInt()` method.

Exception Handling 9

9 Exception Handling

It's the exception that proves the rule.

COMMON SAYING

Introduction

One way to divide the task of designing and coding a method is to code two main cases separately: the case where nothing unusual happens and the case where exceptional things happen. Once you have the program working for the case where things always go smoothly, you can then code the second case where notable things can happen. In Java, there is a way to mirror this approach in your code. Write your code more or less as if nothing very unusual happens. After that, use the Java exception handling facilities to add code for those unusual cases.

The most important use of exceptions is to deal with methods that have some special case that is handled differently depending on how the method is used. For example, if there is a division by zero in the method, then it may turn out that for some invocations of the method, the program should end, but for other invocations of the method, something else should happen. Such a method can be defined to throw an exception if the special case occurs; that exception will permit the special case to be handled outside of the method. This allows the special case to be handled differently for different invocations of the method.

throw exception

handle exception

In Java, exception handling proceeds as follows: Either some library software or your code provides a mechanism that signals when something unusual happens. This is called **throwing an exception**. At another place in your program, you place the code that deals with the exceptional case. This is called **handling the exception**. This method of programming makes for cleaner code. Of course, we still need to explain the details of how you do this in Java.

Prerequisites

Almost this entire chapter uses only material from Chapters 1 through 5 and Chapter 7. The only exception is the subsection "`ArrayIndexOutOfBoundsException`," which also uses material from Chapter 6. However, that subsection may be omitted if you have not yet covered Chapter 6. Chapter 8 is not needed for this chapter.

9.1 Exception Handling Basics

Well the program works for most cases. I didn't know it had to work for that case.

COMPUTER SCIENCE STUDENT, *appealing a grade*

Exception handling is meant to be used sparingly and in some situations that are more involved than what is reasonable to include in an introductory example. So, in some cases, we will teach you the exception handling details of Java by means of simple examples that would not normally use exception handling. This makes a lot of sense for learning about the exception handling details of Java, but do not forget that these examples are toy examples and, in practice, you would not use exception handling for anything this simple.

`try-catch` Mechanism

The basic way of handling exceptions in Java consists of the `try-throw-catch` trio. At this point, we will start with only `try` and `catch`. The general setup consists of a `try` block followed by one or more `catch` blocks. First let's describe what a try block is. A **`try` block** has the following syntax:

`try` block

```
try
{
    Some_Code_That_May_Throw_An_Exception
}
```

This `try` block contains the code for the basic algorithm that tells what to do when everything goes smoothly. It is called a `try` block because it "tries" to execute the case where all goes well.

Now, an exception can be "thrown" as a way of indicating that something unusual happened. For example, if our code tries to divide by zero, then an `ArithmeticException` object is thrown. In most of this chapter, our own code will throw the exception, but initially we will have existing Java classes do the throwing.

As the name suggests, when something is "thrown," something goes from one place to another place. In Java, what goes from one place to another is the flow of control as well as the exception object that is thrown. When an exception is thrown, the code in the surrounding `try` block stops executing and (normally) another portion of code, known as a **`catch` block**, begins execution. The `catch` block has a parameter, and the exception object thrown is plugged in for this `catch` block parameter. This executing of the `catch` block is called **catching the exception** or **handling the exception**. When an exception is thrown, it should ultimately be handled by (caught by) some `catch` block. The appropriate `catch` block immediately follows the `try` block; for example,

`catch` block

handling an exception

```
catch(Exception e)
{
    String message = e.getMessage();
    System.out.println(message);
    System.exit(0);
}
```

This catch block looks very much like a method definition that has a parameter of a type Exception. By using the type Exception, this catch block will catch any possible exception that is thrown. We will see at the end of this section that we can also restrict the catch block to specific exception classes. The catch block is not a method definition, but in some ways, it is like a method. It is a separate piece of code that is executed when your code throws an exception. The catch block in the previous example will print out a message about the exception that was thrown.

So, when an exception is thrown, it is similar to a method call, but instead of calling a method, it calls the catch block and says to execute the code in the catch block. A catch block is often referred to as an **exception handler**.

exception handler

Let's focus on the identifier e in the following line from a catch block:

```
catch (Exception e)
```

catch block parameter

That identifier e in the catch block heading is called the catch **block parameter**. Each catch block can have at most one catch block parameter. The catch block parameter does two things:

- The catch block parameter is preceded by an exception class name that specifies what type of thrown exception object the catch block can catch. If the class name is Exception, then the block can catch any exception.
- The catch block parameter gives you a name for the thrown object that is caught, so you can write code in the catch block that does things with the thrown object that is caught.

Although the identifier e is often used for the catch block parameter, this is not required. You may use any nonkeyword identifier for the catch block parameter just as you can for a method parameter.

catch Block Parameter

The catch block parameter is an identifier in the heading of a catch block that serves as a placeholder for an exception that might be thrown. When a suitable exception is thrown in the preceding try block, that exception is plugged in for the catch block parameter. The identifier e is often used for catch block parameters, but this is not required. You can use any legal (nonkeyword) identifier for a catch block parameter.

SYNTAX

```
catch (Exception_Class_Name Catch_Block_Parameter)
{
    Code to be performed if an exception of the named exception class is thrown in
    the try block.
}
```

You may use any legal identifier for the *Catch_Block_Parameter*.

EXAMPLE

In the following, e is the catch block parameter.

```
catch(Exception e)
{
    System.out.println(e.getMessage());
    System.out.println("Aborting program.");
    System.exit(0);
}
```

Let's consider two possible cases of what can happen when a try block is executed: (1) no exception is thrown in the try block, and (2) an exception is thrown in the try block and caught in the catch block. (Later in the Tip, "What Happens if an Exception Is Never Caught?," we will describe a third case where the catch block does not catch the exception.)

- If no exception is thrown, the code in the try block is executed to the end of the try block, the catch block is skipped, and execution continues with the code placed after the catch block.
- If an exception is thrown in the try block, the rest of the code in the try block is skipped and (in simple cases) control is transferred to a following catch block. The thrown object is plugged in for the catch block parameter, and the code in the catch block is executed. And then (provided the catch block code does not end the program or do something else to end the catch block code prematurely), the code that follows that catch block is executed.

Exception Handling with the `Scanner` Class

As a concrete example, consider a program that reads an `int` value from the keyboard using the `nextInt` method of the `Scanner` class. You have probably noticed that the program will end with an error message if the user enters something other than a well-formed `int` value. That is true as far as it goes, but the full detail is that if the user enters something other than a well-formed `int` value, an exception of type `InputMismatchException` will be thrown. If the exception is not caught, your program ends with an error message. However, you can catch the exception, and in the `catch` block, give code for some alternative action, such as asking the user to reenter the input. You are not required to account for an `InputMismatchException` by catching it in a `catch` block or declaring it in a `throws` clause (this is because `InputMismatchException` is a descendent class of `RuntimeException`). However, you are allowed to catch an `InputMismatchException` in a `catch` block, which can sometimes be useful.

`InputMismatchException` is in the standard Java package `java.util`, so if your program mentions `InputMismatchException`, then it needs an import statement, such as the following:

```
import java.util.InputMismatchException;
```

Display 9.1 contains an example of how you might usefully catch an `InputMismatchException`. This program gets an input `int` value from the keyboard and then does nothing with it other than echo the input value. However, you can use code such as this to require robust input for any program that uses keyboard input. The Tip "Exception Control Loops" explains the general technique we used for the loop in Display 9.1.

TIP: Exception Controlled Loops

Sometimes when an exception is thrown, such as an `InputMismatchException` for an ill-formed input, you want your code to simply repeat some code so that the user can get things right on a second or subsequent try. One way to set up your code to repeat a loop every time a particular exception is thrown is as follows:

```
boolean done = false;

while (!done)
{
    try
    {
        Code that may throw an exception in the class Exception_Class.
        done = true; //Will end the loop.
        <Possibly more code.>
    }
    catch(Exception_Class e)
    {
        <Some code.>
    }
}
```

Note that if an exception is thrown in the first piece of code in the `try` block, then the `try` block ends before the line that sets `done` to `true` is executed, so the loop body is repeated. If no exception is thrown, then `done` is set to `true` and the loop body is not repeated.

Display 9.1 contains an example of such a loop. Minor variations on this outline can accommodate a range of different situations for which you want to repeat code on throwing an exception. ■

Display 9.1 **An Exception Controlled Loop**

```
import java.util.Scanner;
import java.util.InputMismatchException;

public class InputMismatchExceptionDemo
{
    public static void main(String[] args)
    {
        Scanner keyboard = new Scanner(System.in);
        int number = 0; //to keep compiler happy
        boolean done = false;

        while (! done)
        {
            try
            {
              System.out.println("Enter a whole number:");
              number = keyboard.nextInt();
              done = true;
            }
            catch(InputMismatchException e)
            {
              keyboard.nextLine();
              System.out.println("Not a correctly written whole
              number.");
              System.out.println("Try again.");
            }
        }

        System.out.println("You entered " + number);
    }
}
```

If `nextInt` *throws an exception, the* `try` *block ends and the* `Boolean` *variable* `done` *is not set to* `true`.

Sample Dialogue

```
Enter a whole number:
forty two
Not a correctly written whole number.
Try again.
Enter a whole number:
Fortytwo
Not a correctly written whole number.
Try again.
Enter a whole number:
42
You entered 42
```

MyProgrammingLab™

Self-Test Exercises

1. How would the dialogue in Display 9.1 change if you were to omit the following line from the catch block? (Try it and see.)

```
keyboard.nextLine();
```

2. Give the definition for the following method. Use the techniques given in Display 9.1.

```
/**
 Precondition: keyboard is an object of the class Scanner that
 has been set up for keyboard input (as we have been doing
 right along). Returns: An int value entered at the keyboard.
 If the user enters an incorrectly formed input, she or he
 is prompted to reenter the value,
*/
public static int getInt(Scanner keyboard)
```

Throwing Exceptions

In the previous example, an exception was thrown by the `nextInt()` method if a noninteger was entered. We did not write the method that threw the exception; we were responsible only for catching and handling any exceptions. For many programs, this pattern is all that is necessary.

However, it is also possible for your own code to throw the exception. To do this, use a `throw` statement inside the `try` block in the format

```
throw new Exception(String_describing_the_exception);
```

The following is an example of a `try` block with `throw` statements included (copied from Display 9.3, which computes pairs of men and women for a dance studio):

```
try
{
    if (men == 0 && women == 0)
        throw new Exception("Lesson is canceled. No students.");
    else if (men == 0)
        throw new Exception("Lesson is canceled. No men.");
    else if (women == 0)
        throw new Exception("Lesson is canceled. No women.");
    // women >= 0 && men >= 0
    if (women >= men)
        System.out.println("Each man must dance with " +
                                   women/(double)men + "women.");
    else
        System.out.println("Each woman must dance with " +
                                   men/(double)women + " men.");
}
```

throw statement

This `try` block contains the following three `throw` statements:

```
throw new Exception("Lesson is canceled. No students.");
throw new Exception("Lesson is canceled. No men.");
throw new Exception("Lesson is canceled. No women.");
```

throwing an exception

The value thrown is an argument to the `throw` operator and is always an object of some exception class. The execution of a `throw` statement is called *throwing an exception.*

`throw` Statement

SYNTAX

throw new *Exception_Class_Name (Possibly_Some_Arguments);*

When the `throw` statement is executed, the execution of the surrounding `try` block is stopped and (normally) control is transferred to a `catch` block. The code in the `catch` block is executed next. See the box entitled "`try-throw-catch`" later in this chapter for more details.

EXAMPLE

```
throw new Exception("Division by zero.");
```

The `getMessage` Method

Every exception has a `String` instance variable that contains some message, which typically identifies the reason for the exception. For example, if the exception is thrown as follows,

throw new Exception(*String_Argument*);

then the string given as an argument to the constructor `Exception` is used as the value of this `String` instance variable. If the object is called `e`, then the method call `e.getMessage()` returns this string.

EXAMPLE

Suppose the following `throw` statement is executed in a `try` block:

```
throw new Exception("Input must be positive.");
```

And suppose the following is a `catch` block immediately following the `try` block:

```
catch (Exception e)
{
    System.out.println(e.getMessage());
    System.out.println("Program aborted.");
    System.exit(0);
}
```

In this case, the method call `e.getMessage()` returns the string
`"Input must be positive."`

EXAMPLE: A Toy Example of Exception Handling

Display 9.2 contains a simple program that might, by some stretch of the imagination, be used at a dance studio. This program does not use exception handling, and you would not normally use exception handling for anything this simple. The setting for use of the program is a dance lesson. The program simply checks to see if there are more men than women or more women than men and then announces how many partners each man or woman will have. The exceptional case is when there are no men or no women or both. In that exceptional case, the dance lesson is canceled.

In Display 9.3, we rewrote the program using exception handling. The nonexceptional cases go inside the `try` block, and the `try` block checks for the exceptional cases. The exceptional cases are not handled in the `try` block, but if detected, they are signaled by throwing an exception. The following three lines taken from inside the multiway `if-else` statement are the code for throwing the exception:

```
throw new Exception("Lesson is canceled. No students.");
throw new Exception("Lesson is canceled. No men.");
throw new Exception("Lesson is canceled. No women.");
```

If the program does not encounter an exceptional case, then none of these statements that throw an exception is executed. In that case, we need not even know what happens when an exception is thrown. If no exception is thrown, then the code in the section labeled "`catch` block" is skipped and the program proceeds to the last statement, which happens to output `"Begin the lesson."` Now, let's see what happens in an exceptional case.

If the number of men or the number of women is zero (or both), that is an exceptional case in this program and results in an exception being **thrown**. To make things concrete, let's say that the number of men is zero, but the number of women is not zero. In that case, the following statement is executed, which is how Java throws an exception:

```
throw new Exception("Lesson is canceled. No men.");
```

Let's analyze this statement. The following is the invocation of a constructor for the class `Exception`, which is the standard Java package `java.lang`.

```
new Exception("Lesson is canceled. No men.");
```

The created `Exception` object is not assigned to a variable, but rather is used as an (anonymous) argument to the `throw` operator. (Anonymous arguments were discussed in Chapter 5.) The keyword `throw` is an operator with syntax similar to the

EXAMPLE: (continued)

unary + or unary - operators. To make it look more like an operator, you can write it with parentheses around the argument, as follows:

```
throw (new Exception("Lesson is canceled. No men."));
```

Although it is perfectly legal and sensible to include these extra parentheses, nobody includes them.

To understand this process of throwing, you need to know two things: What is this `Exception` class? And what does the `throw` operator do with the `Exception` object? The class `Exception` is another class from the standard Java package `java.lang`. As you have already seen, the class `Exception` has a constructor that takes a single `String` argument. The `Exception` object created stores this `String` argument (in a private instance variable). As you will see, this `String` argument can later be retrieved from the `Exception` object.

The `throw` operator causes a change in the flow of control and delivers the `Exception` object to a suitable place, as we are about to explain. When the `throw` operator is executed, the `try` block ends immediately and control passes to the following `catch` block. (If it helps, you can draw an analogy between the execution of the `throw` operator in a `try` block and the execution of a `break` statement in a loop or `switch` statement.) When control is transferred to the `catch` block, the `Exception` object that is thrown is plugged in for the `catch` block parameter `e`. So, the expression `e.getMessage()` returns the string `"Lesson is canceled. No men."` The method `getMessage()` of the class `Exception` is an accessor method that retrieves the `String` in the private instance variable of the `Exception` object—that is, the `String` used as an argument to the `Exception` constructor.

To see if you get the basic idea of how this exception throwing mechanism works, study the Sample Dialogues in Displays 9.2 and 9.3. The next few sections explain this mechanism in more detail.

Display 9.2 **Handling a Special Case without Exception Handling** (part 1 of 3)

```
import java.util.Scanner;

public class DanceLesson
{
    public static void main(String[] args)
    {
        Scanner keyboard = new Scanner(System.in);

        System.out.println("Enter number of male dancers:");
        int men = keyboard.nextInt();

        System.out.println("Enter number of female dancers: ");
        int women = keyboard.nextInt();
```

(continued)

Display 9.2 **Handling a Special Case without Exception Handling** (part 2 of 3)

```
        if (men == 0 && women == 0)
        {
            System.out.println("Lesson is canceled. No students.");
            System.exit(0);
        }
        else if (men == 0)
        {
           System.out.println("Lesson is canceled. No men.");
           System.exit(0);
        }
        else if (women == 0)
        {
           System.out.println("Lesson is canceled. No women.");
           System.exit(0);
        }

        // women >= 0 && men >= 0
        if (women >= men)
           System.out.println("Each man must dance with " +
                                    women/(double)men + " women.");
        else
           System.out.println("Each woman must dance with " +
                                    men/(double)women + " men.");
        System.out.println("Begin the lesson.");
    }
}
```

Sample Dialogue 1

```
Enter number of male dancers:
4
Enter number of female dancers:
6
Each man must dance with 1.5 women.
Begin the lesson.
```

Sample Dialogue 2

```
Enter number of male dancers:
0
Enter number of female dancers:
0
Lesson is canceled. No students.
```

Display 9.2 **Handling a Special Case without Exception Handling** (part 3 of 3)

Sample Dialogue 3

```
Enter number of male dancers:
0
Enter number of female dancers:
5
Lesson is canceled. No men.
```

Sample Dialogue 4

```
Enter number of male dancers:
4
Enter number of female dancers:
0
Lesson is canceled. No women.
```

Display 9.3 **Same Thing Using Exception Handling** (part 1 of 3)

```
import java.util.Scanner;

public class DanceLesson2
{
    public static void main(String[] args)
    {
        Scanner keyboard = new Scanner(System.in);

        System.out.println("Enter number of male dancers:");
        int men = keyboard.nextInt();
        System.out.println("Enter number of female dancers:");
        int women = keyboard.nextInt();
```

This is just a toy example to learn Java syntax. Do not take it as an example of good typical use of exception handling.

(continued)

Display 9.3 **Same Thing Using Exception Handling** (part 2 of 3)

```
        try
        {
            if (men == 0 && women == 0)
                throw new Exception("Lesson is canceled. No students.");
            else if (men == 0)
                throw new Exception("Lesson is canceled. No men.");
            else if (women == 0)
                throw new Exception("Lesson is canceled. No women.");

            // women >= 0 && men >= 0
            if (women >= men)
                System.out.println("Each man must dance with " +
                                        women/(double)men + " women.");
            else
                System.out.println("Each woman must dance with " +
                                        men/(double)women + " men.");
        }
        catch(Exception e)
        {
            String message = e.getMessage();
            System.out.println(message);
            System.exit(0);
        }

        System.out.println("Begin the lesson.");
    }

}
```

try *block* (lines `try { … }`)

catch *block* (lines `catch(Exception e) { … }`)

Sample Dialogue 1

```
Enter number of male dancers:
4
Enter number of female dancers:
6
Each man must dance with 1.5 women.
Begin the lesson.
```

Sample Dialogue 2

```
Enter number of male dancers:
0
Enter number of female dancers:
0
Lesson is canceled. No students.
```

Note that this dialogue and the dialogues that follow do not say **"Begin the lesson"**.

Display 9.3 Same Thing Using Exception Handling (part 3 of 3)

Sample Dialogue 3

```
Enter number of male dancers:
0
Enter number of female dancers:
5
Lesson is canceled. No men.
```

Sample Dialogue 4

```
Enter number of male dancers:
4
Enter number of female dancers:
0
Lesson is canceled. No women.
```

Exception Classes

There are more exception classes than just the single class `Exception`. There are more exception classes in the standard Java libraries and you can define your own. All the exception classes in the Java libraries have—and the exception classes you define should have—the following properties:

- There is a constructor that takes a single argument of type `String`.
- The class has an accessor method `getMessage()` that can recover the string given as an argument to the constructor when the exception object was created.

`try-throw-catch`

When used together, the `try`, `throw`, and `catch` statements are the basic mechanism for throwing and catching exceptions. The `throw` statement throws the exception. The `catch` block catches the exception. The `throw` statement is normally included in a `try` block. When the exception is thrown, the `try` block ends and then the code in the `catch` block is executed. After the `catch` block is completed, the code after the `catch` block(s) is executed (provided the `catch` block has not ended the program or performed some other special action).

If no exception is thrown in the `try` block, then after the `try` block is completed, program execution continues with the code after the `catch` block(s). (In other words, if no exception is thrown, the `catch` block(s) are ignored.)

(continued)

SYNTAX

```
try
{
    Some_Statements
    <Either a throw statement or
                a method invocation that might throw an exception
                or other statement that might throw an exception.>
    Some_More_Statements
}
catch (Exception_Class_Name Catch_Block_Parameter)
{
    <Code to be performed if an exception of the named exception
                                class is thrown in the try block.>
}
```

You may use any legal identifier for the *Catch_Block_Parameter*; a common choice is `e`. The code in the `catch` block may refer to the *Catch_Block_Parameter*. If there is an explicit `throw` statement, it is usually embedded in an `if` statement or an `if-else` statement. There may be any number of `throw` statements and/or any number of method invocations that may throw exceptions. Each `catch` block can list only one exception, but there can be more than one `catch` block.

EXAMPLE

See Display 9.3.

Exception Classes from Standard Packages

Numerous predefined exception classes are included in the standard packages that come with Java. The names of predefined exceptions are designed to be self-explanatory. Some sample predefined exceptions are

```
IOException
NoSuchMethodException
FileNotFoundException
```

`Exception`

The predefined exception class `Exception` is the root class for all exceptions. Every exception class is a descendent of the class `Exception` (that is, it is derived directly from the class `Exception` or from a class that is derived from the class `Exception`, or it arises from some longer chain of derivations ultimately starting with the class `Exception`). You can use the class `Exception` itself, just as we did in Display 9.3, but you are even more likely to use it to define a derived class of the class `Exception`. The class `Exception` is in the `java.lang` package and so requires no import statement.

> **The Class `Exception`**
>
> Every exception class is a descendent class of the class `Exception`. You can use the class `Exception` itself in a class or program, but you are even more likely to use it to define a derived class of the class `Exception`. The class `Exception` is in the `java.lang` package and so requires no import statement.

MyProgrammingLab™

Self-Test Exercises

3. What output is produced by the following code?

```
int waitTime = 46;

try
{
    System.out.println("Try block entered.");
    if (waitTime > 30)
        throw new Exception("Over 30.");
    else if (waitTime < 30)
        throw new Exception("Under 30.");
    else
        System.out.println("No exception.");
    System.out.println("Leaving try block.");
}
catch(Exception thrownObject)
{
    System.out.println(thrownObject.getMessage());
}
System.out.println("After catch block");
```

4. Suppose that in Self-Test Exercise 3, the line

```
int waitTime = 46;
```

is changed to

```
int waitTime = 12;
```

How would this affect the output?

5. In the code given in Self-Test Exercise 3, what are the `throw` statements?

6. What happens when a `throw` statement is executed? This is a general question. Explain what happens in general, not simply what happens in the code in Exercise 1 or some other sample code.

7. In the code given in Self-Test Exercise 3, what is the `try` block?

(continued)

MyProgrammingLab™

Self-Test Exercises (continued)

8. In the code given in Self-Test Exercise 3, what is the `catch` block?

9. In the code given in Self-Test Exercise 3, what is the `catch` block parameter?

10. Is the following legal?

```
Exception exceptionObject =
                      new Exception("Oops!");
```

11. Is the following legal?

```
Exception exceptionObject =
                      new Exception("Oops!");
throw exceptionObject;
```

Defining Exception Classes

A `throw` statement can throw an exception object of any exception class. A common thing to do is to define an exception class whose objects can carry the precise kinds of information you want thrown to the `catch` block. An even more important reason for defining a specialized exception class is so that you can have a different type to identify each possible kind of exceptional situation.

Every exception class you define must be a derived class of some already defined exception class. An exception class can be a derived class of any exception class in the standard Java libraries or of any exception class that you have already successfully defined. Our examples will be derived classes of the class `Exception`.

constructors

When defining an exception class, the constructors are the most important members. Often there are no other members, other than those inherited from the base class. For example, in Display 9.4, we have defined an exception class called `DivisionByZeroException` whose only members are a no-argument constructor and a constructor with one `String` parameter. In most cases, these two constructors are all the exception class definition contains. However, the class does inherit all the methods of the class `Exception`.[1] In particular, the class `DivisionByZeroException` inherits the method `getMessage`, which returns a string message. In the no-argument constructor, this string message is set with the following, which is the first line in the no-argument constructor definition:

```
super("Division by Zero!");
```

This is a call to a constructor of the base class `Exception`. As we have already noted, when you pass a string to the constructor for the class `Exception`, it sets the value

[1]Some programmers would prefer to derive the `DivisionByZeroException` class from the predefined class `ArithmeticException`, but that would make it a kind of exception that you are not required to catch in your code, so you would lose the help of the compiler in keeping track of uncaught exceptions. For more details, see the subsection "Exceptions to the Catch or Declare Rule" later in this chapter. If this footnote does not make sense to you, you can safely ignore it.

of a `String` instance variable that can later be recovered with a call to `getMessage`. The method `getMessage` is an ordinary accessor method of the class `Exception`. The class `DivisionByZeroException` inherits this `String` instance variable as well as the accessor method `getMessage`.

For example, in Display 9.5, we give a sample program that uses this exception class. The exception is thrown using the no-argument constructor, as follows:

```
throw new DivisionByZeroException();
```

Display 9.4 **A Programmer-Defined Exception Class**

```
public class DivisionByZeroException extends Exception
{
    public DivisionByZeroException()
    {
        super("Division by Zero!");
    }

    public DivisionByZeroException(String message)
    {
        super(message);
    }
}
```

You can do more in an exception constructor, but this form is common.

`super` is an invocation of the constructor for the base class `Exception`.

Display 9.5 **Using a Programmer-Defined Exception Class** (part 1 of 3)

```
import java.util.Scanner;

public class DivisionDemoFirstVersion
{

    public static void main(String[] args)
    {
        try
        {
            Scanner keyboard = new Scanner(System.in);

            System.out.println("Enter numerator:");
            int numerator = keyboard.nextInt();
            System.out.println("Enter denominator:");
            int denominator = keyboard.nextInt();
```

We will present an improved version of this program later in this chapter in Display 9.10.

(continued)

Display 9.5 Using a Programmer-Defined Exception Class (part 2 of 3)

```
            if (denominator == 0)
                throw new DivisionByZeroException();

            double quotient = numerator/(double)denominator;
            System.out.println(numerator + "/"
                                     + denominator
                                     + " = " + quotient);
        }
        catch (DivisionByZeroException e)
        {
            System.out.println(e.getMessage());
            secondChance();
        }

        System.out.println("End of program.");
    }

    public static void secondChance()
    {
        Scanner keyboard = new Scanner(System.in);
        System.out.println("Try again:");
        System.out.println("Enter numerator:");
        int numerator = keyboard.nextInt();
        System.out.println("Enter denominator:");
        System.out.println("Be sure the denominator is not zero.");
        int denominator = keyboard.nextInt();

        if (denominator == 0)
        {
            System.out.println("I cannot do division by zero.");
            System.out.println("Aborting program.");
            System.exit(0);
        }

        double quotient = ((double)numerator)/denominator;
        System.out.println(numerator + "/"
                                     + denominator
                                     + " = " + quotient);
    }
}
```

Sometimes it is better to handle an exceptional case without throwing an exception.

Display 9.5 Using a Programmer-Defined Exception Class (part 3 of 3)

Sample Dialogue 1

```
Enter numerator:
11
Enter denominator:
5
11/5 = 2.2
End of program.
```

Sample Dialogue 2

```
Enter numerator:
11
Enter denominator:
0
Division by Zero!
Try again.
Enter numerator:
11
Enter denominator:
Be sure the denominator is not zero.
5
11/5 = 2.2
End of program.
```

Sample Dialogue 3

```
Enter numerator:
11
Enter denominator:
0
Division by Zero!
Try again.
Enter numerator:
11
Enter denominator:
Be sure the denominator is not zero.
0
I cannot do division by zero.
Aborting program.
```

This exception is caught in the `catch` block shown in Display 9.5. Consider the following line from that `catch` block:

```
System.out.println(e.getMessage());
```

This line produces the following output to the screen in Sample Dialogues 2 and 3 (in Display 9.5):

```
Division by Zero!
```

The definition of the class `DivisionByZeroException` in Display 9.4 has a second constructor with one parameter of type `String`. This constructor allows you to choose any message you like when you throw an exception. If the `throw` statement in Display 9.5 had instead used the string argument

```
throw new DivisionByZeroException(
                        "Oops. Shouldn't divide by zero.");
```

then in Sample Dialogues 2 and 3, the statement

```
System.out.println(e.getMessage());
```

would have produced the following output to the screen:

```
Oops. Shouldn't divide by zero.
```

Notice that in Display 9.5, the `try` block is the normal part of the program. If all goes routinely, that is the only code that will be executed, and the dialogue will be like the one shown in Sample Dialogue 1. In the exceptional case, when the user enters a zero for a denominator, the exception is thrown and then is caught in the `catch` block. The `catch` block outputs the message of the exception and then calls the method `secondChance`. The method `secondChance` gives the user a second chance to enter the input correctly and then carries out the calculation. If the user tries a second time to divide by zero, the method ends the program. The method `secondChance` is there only for this exceptional case. So, we have separated the code for the exceptional case of a division by zero into a separate method, where it will not clutter the code for the normal case.

TIP: Preserve `getMessage`

For all predefined exception classes, `getMessage` will return the string that is passed as an argument to the constructor (or will return a default string if no argument is used with the constructor). For example, if the exception is thrown as follows,

```
throw new Exception("Wow, this is exceptional!");
```

then "Wow, this is exceptional!" is used as the value of the `String` instance variable of the object created. If the object is called `e`, the method invocation `e.getMessage()` returns "Wow, this is exceptional!" You want to preserve this behavior in the exception classes you define.

TIP: (continued)

For example, suppose you are defining an exception class named `NegativeNumberException`. Be sure to include a constructor with a string parameter that begins with a call to `super`, as illustrated by the following constructor:

```
public NegativeNumberException(String message)
{
    super (message);
}
```

The call to `super` is a call to a constructor of the base class. If the base class constructor handles the message correctly, then so will a class defined in this way.

You should also include a no-argument constructor in each exception class. This no-argument constructor should set a default value to be retrieved by `getMessage`. The constructor should begin with a call to `super`, as illustrated by the following constructor:

```
public NegativeNumberException()
{
    super("Negative Number Exception!");
}
```

If `getMessage` works as we described for the base class, then this sort of no-argument constructor will work correctly for the new exception class being defined. A full definition of the class `NegativeNumberException` is given in Display 9.9. ■

Exception Object Characteristics

The two most important things about an exception object are its type (the exception class) and a message that it carries in an instance variable of type `String`. This string can be recovered with the accessor method `getMessage`. This string allows your code to send a message along with an exception object, so that the `catch` block can use the message.

Programmer-Defined Exception Classes

You may define your own exception classes, but every such class must be a derived class of an already existing exception class (either from one of the standard Java libraries or programmer defined).

GUIDELINES

- If you have no compelling reason to use any other class as the base class, use the class `Exception` as the base class.
- You should define two (or more) constructors, as described later in this list.

(continued)

- Your exception class inherits the method `getMessage`. Normally, you do not need to add any other methods, but it is legal to do so.
- You should start each constructor definition with a call to the constructor of the base class, such as the following:

```
super("Sample Exception thrown!");
```

- You should include a no-argument constructor, in which case the call to `super` should have a string argument that indicates what kind of exception it is. This string can then be recovered by using the `getMessage` method.
- You should also include a constructor that takes a single string argument. In this case, the string should be an argument in a call to `super`. That way, the string can be recovered with a call to `getMessage`.

EXAMPLE

```
public class SampleException extends Exception
{
    public SampleException()
    {
        super("Sample Exception thrown!");
    }

    public SampleException(String message)
    {
        super(message);
    }
}
```

extra code on website

The class `SampleException` is on the website that comes with this text.

TIP: An Exception Class Can Carry a Message of Any Type

It is possible to define your exception classes so they have constructors that take arguments of other types that are stored in instance variables. In such cases, you would define accessor methods for the value stored in the instance variable. For example, if that is desired, you can have an exception class that carries an `int` as a message. In that case, you would need a new accessor method name, perhaps `getBadNumber()`. An example of one such exception class is given in Display 9.6. Display 9.7 is a demonstration of how to use the accessor method `getBadNumber()`. This is just a toy program, but it does illustrate the details of how an exception object can carry a numeric message. ■

Display 9.6 An Exception Class with an `int` Message (part 1 of 2)

```
public class BadNumberException extends Exception
{
    private int badNumber;
    public BadNumberException(int number)
    {
```

Display 9.6 An Exception Class with an `int` Message (part 2 of 2)

```
        super ("BadNumberException");
        badNumber = number;
    }
    public BadNumberException()
    {
        super ("BadNumberException");
    }
    public BadNumberException(String message)
    {
        super (message);
    }
    public int getBadNumber()
    {
        return badNumber;
    }
}
```

Display 9.7 Demonstration of How to Use `BadNumberException` (part 1 of 2)

```
import java.util.Scanner;
public class BadNumberExceptionDemo
{
    public static void main(String[] args)
    {
        try
        {
            Scanner keyboard = new Scanner(System.in);
            System.out.println("Enter one of the numbers 42 and 24:");
            int inputNumber = keyboard.nextInt();
            if ((inputNumber != 42) && (inputNumber != 24))
                throw new BadNumberException(inputNumber);
            System.out.println("Thank you for entering " + inputNumber);
        }
        catch(BadNumberException e)
        {
            System.out.println(e.getBadNumber() +
                                         " is not what I asked for.");
        }
        System.out.println("End of program.");
    }
}
```

(continued)

Display 9.7 Demonstration of How to Use **BadNumberException** (part 2 of 2)

Sample Dialogue 1

```
Enter one of the numbers 42 and 24:
42
Thank you for entering 42
End of program.
```

Sample Dialogue 2

```
Enter one of the numbers 42 and 24:
44
44 is not what I asked for.
End of program.
```

MyProgrammingLab™

Self-Test Exercises

12. Define an exception class called `PowerFailureException`. The class should have a constructor with no parameters. If an exception is thrown with this zero-argument constructor, `getMessage` should return `"Power Failure!"` The class should also have a constructor with a single parameter of type `String`. If an exception is thrown with this constructor, then `getMessage` returns the value that was used as an argument to the constructor.

13. Define an exception class called `TooMuchStuffException`. The class should have a constructor with no parameters. If an exception is thrown with this zero-argument constructor, `getMessage` should return `"Too much stuff!"` The class should also have a constructor with a single parameter of type `String`. If an exception is thrown with this constructor, then `getMessage` returns the value that was used as an argument to the constructor.

14. Suppose the exception class `ExerciseException` is defined as follows:

```
public class ExerciseException extends Exception
{
    public ExerciseException()
    {
        super("Exercise Exception thrown!");
        System.out.println("Exception thrown.");
    }

    public ExerciseException(String message)
    {
        super(message);
        System.out.println(
          "ExerciseException invoked with an argument.");
    }
}
```

MyProgrammingLab™

Self-Test Exercises (continued)

What output would be produced by the following code (which is just an exercise and not likely to occur in a program)?

```
ExerciseException e =
               new ExerciseException("Do Be Do");
System.out.println(e.getMessage());
```

extra code on website

The class `ExerciseException` is on the website that comes with this text.

15. Suppose the exception class `TestException` is defined as follows:

```
public class TestException extends Exception
{
    public TestException()
    {
        super("Test Exception thrown!");
        System.out.println(
                   "Test exception thrown!!");
    }

    public TestException(String message)
    {
        super(message);
        System.out.println(
         "Test exception thrown with an argument!");
    }

    public void testMethod()
    {
        System.out.println("Message is " + getMessage());
    }
}
```

What output would be produced by the following code (which is just an exercise and not likely to occur in a program)?

```
TestException exceptionObject = new TestException();
System.out.println(exceptionObject.getMessage());
exceptionObject.testMethod();
```

extra code on website

The class `TestException` is on the website that comes with this text.

16. Suppose the exception class `MyException` is defined as follows:

```
public class MyException extends Exception
{
    public MyException()
    {
        super("My Exception thrown!");
    }
```

(continued)

MyProgrammingLab™

Self-Test Exercises (continued)

```
    public MyException(String message)
    {
        super("MyException: " + message);
    }
}
```

What output would be produced by the following code (which is just an exercise and not likely to occur in a program)?

```
int number;
try
{
    System.out.println("try block entered:");
    number = 42;
    if (number > 0)
        throw new MyException("Hi Mom!");
    System.out.println("Leaving try block.");
}

catch(MyException exceptionObject)
{
    System.out.println(exceptionObject.getMessage());
}
System.out.println("End of example.");
```

extra code on website

The class `MyException` is on the website that comes with this text.

17. Suppose that in Self-Test Exercise 16, the `catch` block were changed to the following. (The type `MyException` is replaced with `Exception`.) How would this affect the output?

```
catch(Exception exceptionObject)
{
    System.out.println(exceptionObject.getMessage());
}
```

18. Suppose that in Self-Test Exercise 16, the line

```
number = 42;
```

were changed to

```
number = -58;
```

How would this affect the output?

MyProgrammingLab™

Self-Test Exercises (continued)

19. Although an exception class normally carries only a string message, you can define exception classes to carry a message of any type. For example, objects of the following type can also carry a `double` "message" (as well as a string message):

```
public class DoubleException extends Exception
{
    private double doubleMessage;

    public DoubleException()
    {
        super("DoubleException thrown!");
    }

    public DoubleException(String message)
    {
        super(message);
    }

    public DoubleException(double number)
    {
        super("DoubleException thrown!");
        doubleMessage = number;
    }

    public double getNumber()
    {
        return doubleMessage;
    }
}
```

What output would be produced by the following code (which is just an exercise and not likely to occur in a program)?

```
DoubleException e =
                new DoubleException(41.9);

System.out.println(e.getNumber());
System.out.println(e.getMessage());
```

extra code on website

The class `DoubleException` is on the website that comes with this text.

20. There is an exception class named `IOException` that is defined in the standard Java libraries. Can you define an exception class as a derived class of the predefined class `IOException`, or must a defined exception class be derived from the class `Exception`?

Multiple `catch` Blocks

A `try` block can potentially throw any number of exception values, and they can be of differing types. In any one execution of the `try` block, at most one exception will be thrown (since a `throw` statement ends the execution of the `try` block), but different types of exception values can be thrown on different occasions when the `try` block is executed. Each `catch` block can only catch values of the exception class type given in the `catch` block heading. However, you can catch exception values of differing types by placing more than one `catch` block after a `try` block. For example, the program in Display 9.8 has two `catch` blocks after its `try` block. The class `NegativeNumberException`, which is used in that program, is given in Display 9.9.

Display 9.8 **Catching Multiple Exceptions** (part 1 of 2)

```
import java.util.Scanner;

public class MoreCatchBlocksDemo
{
    public static void main(String[] args)
    {
        Scanner keyboard = new Scanner(System.in);

        try
        {
            System.out.println("How many pencils do you have?");
            int pencils = keyboard.nextInt();

            if (pencils < 0)
                throw new NegativeNumberException("pencils");

            System.out.println("How many erasers do you have?");
            int erasers = keyboard.nextInt();
            double pencilsPerEraser;

            if (erasers < 0)
                throw new NegativeNumberException("erasers");
            else if (erasers != 0)
                pencilsPerEraser = pencils/(double)erasers;
            else
                throw new DivisionByZeroException();

            System.out.println("Each eraser must last through "
                + pencilsPerEraser + " pencils.");
        }
        catch(NegativeNumberException e)
        {
            System.out.println("Cannot have a negative number of "
                + e.getMessage());
        }
        catch(DivisionByZeroException e)
        {
            System.out.println("Do not make any mistakes.");
```

Display 9.8 **Catching Multiple Exceptions** (part 2 of 2)

```
        }

        System.out.println("End of program.");
    }
}
```

Sample Dialogue 1

```
How many pencils do you have?
5
How many erasers do you have?
2
Each eraser must last through 2.5 pencils
End of program.
```

Sample Dialogue 2

```
How many pencils do you have?
-2
Cannot have a negative number of pencils
End of program.
```

Sample Dialogue 3

```
How many pencils do you have?
5
How many erasers do you have?
0
Do not make any mistakes.
End of program.
```

PITFALL: Catch the More Specific Exception First

When catching multiple exceptions, the order of the `catch` blocks can be important. When an exception is thrown in a `try` block, the `catch` blocks are examined in order, and the first one that matches the type of the exception thrown is the one that is executed. Thus, the following ordering of `catch` blocks would not be good:

```
catch (Exception e)
{
        .
        .
        .
}
```

(continued)

PITFALL: (continued)

```
catch(NegativeNumberException e)
{
        .
        .
        .
}
```

The second `catch` *block can never be reached.*

With this ordering, the `catch` block for `NegativeNumberException` would never be used, because all exceptions are caught by the first `catch` block. Fortunately, the compiler will warn you about this. The correct ordering is to reverse the `catch` blocks so that the more specific exception comes before its parent exception class, as shown in the following:

```
catch(NegativeNumberException e)
{
        .
        .
        .
}
catch(Exception e)
{
        .
        .
        .
}
```

Display 9.9 The Class **`NegativeNumberException`**

```
public class NegativeNumberException extends Exception
{
    public NegativeNumberException()
    {
        super("Negative Number Exception!");
    }
    public NegativeNumberException(String message)
    {
        super(message);
    }
}
```

MyProgrammingLab™

Self-Test Exercises

21. What output will be produced by the following code? (The definition of the class `NegativeNumberException` is given in Display 9.9.)

```
int n;
try
{
    n = 42;
    if (n > 0)
        throw new Exception();
    else if (n < 0)
        throw new NegativeNumberException();
    else
        System.out.println("Bingo!");
}
catch(NegativeNumberException e)
{
    System.out.println("First catch.");
}
catch(Exception e)
{
    System.out.println("Second catch.");
}
System.out.println("End of exercise.");
```

22. Suppose that in Self-Test Exercise 21, the line

```
n = 42;
```

is changed to

```
n = -42;
```

How would this affect the output?

23. Suppose that in Self-Test Exercise 21, the line

```
n = 42;
```

is changed to

```
n = 0;
```

How would this affect the output?

9.2 Throwing Exceptions in Methods

The buck stops here.

HARRY S TRUMAN (sign on Truman's desk while he was president)

So far, our examples of exception handling have been toy examples. We have not yet shown any examples of a program that makes good and realistic use of exception handling. However, now you know enough about exception handling to discuss more realistic uses of it. This section explains the single most important exception handling technique, namely throwing an exception in a method and catching it outside the method.

Throwing an Exception in a Method

Sometimes it makes sense to throw an exception in a method but not catch it in the method. For example, you might have a method with code that throws an exception if there is an attempt to divide by zero, but you may not want to catch the exception in that method. Perhaps some programs that use that method should simply end if the exception is thrown, and other programs that use the method should do something else. So, you would not know what to do with the exception if you caught it inside the method. In such cases, it makes sense to not catch the exception in the method definition, but instead to have any program (or other code) that uses the method place the method invocation in a `try` block and catch the exception in a `catch` block that follows that `try` block.

Look at the program in Display 9.10. It has a `try` block, but there is no `throw` statement visible in the `try` block. The statement that does the throwing in that program is

```
if (bottom == 0)
    throw new DivisionByZeroException();
```

This statement is not visible in the `try` block. However, it is in the `try` block in terms of program execution, because it is in the definition of the method `safeDivide`, and there is an invocation of `safeDivide` in the `try` block.

The meaning of `throws DivisionByZero` in the heading of `safeDivide` is discussed in the next subsection.

Display 9.10 Use of a **throws** Clause (part 1 of 2)

```
import java.util.Scanner;

public class DivisionDemoSecondVersion
{
    public static void main(String[] args)
    {
        Scanner keyboard = new Scanner(System.in);

        try
        {
            System.out.println("Enter numerator:");
            int numerator = keyboard.nextInt();
            System.out.println("Enter denominator:");
            int denominator = keyboard.nextInt();
            double quotient = safeDivide(numerator, denominator);
            System.out.println(numerator + "/"
                                      + denominator
                                      + " = " + quotient);
        }
        catch (DivisionByZeroException e)
        {
            System.out.println(e.getMessage());
            secondChance();
        }

        System.out.println("End of program.");
    }


    public static double safeDivide(int top, int bottom)
                            throws DivisionByZeroException
    {
        if (bottom == 0)
            throw new DivisionByZeroException();

        return top/(double)bottom;
    }
```

(continued)

Display 9.10 Use of a `throws` Clause (part 2 of 2)

```
    public static void secondChance()
    {
        Scanner keyboard = new Scanner(System.in);

        try
        {
            System.out.println("Enter numerator:");
            int numerator = keyboard.nextInt();
            System.out.println("Enter denominator:");
            int denominator = keyboard.nextInt();

            double quotient = safeDivide(numerator, denominator);
            System.out.println(numerator + "/"
                                           + denominator
                                           + " = " + quotient);
        }
        catch(DivisionByZeroException e)
        {
            System.out.println("I cannot do division by zero.");
            System.out.println("Aborting program.");
            System.exit(0);
        }
    }
}
```

The input/output dialogues are identical to those for the program in Display 9.5.

Declaring Exceptions in a `throws` Clause

`throws` clause

declaring an exception

If a method does not catch an exception, then (in most cases) it must at least warn programmers that any invocation of the method might possibly throw an exception. This warning is called a *throws clause*, and including an exception class in a `throws` clause is called **declaring the exception**. For example, a method that might possibly throw a `DivisionByZeroException` and that does not catch the exception would have a heading similar to the following:

```
public void sampleMethod() throws DivisionByZeroException
```

`throws` clause

The part `throws DivisionByZeroException` is a **`throws` clause** stating that an invocation of the method `sampleMethod` might throw a `DivisionByZeroException`.

If there is more than one possible exception that can be thrown in the method definition, then the exception types are separated by commas, as illustrated in what follows:

```
public void sampleMethod()
                throws DivisionByZeroException, SomeOtherException
```

Most "ordinary" exceptions that might be thrown when a method is invoked must be accounted for in one of two ways:

- The possible exception can be caught in a `catch` block within the method definition.
- The possible exception can be declared at the start of the method definition by placing the exception class name in a `throws` clause (and letting whoever uses the method worry about how to handle the exception).

Catch or Declare Rule

This is often called the **Catch or Declare Rule**. In any one method, you can mix the two alternatives, catching some exceptions and declaring others in a `throws` clause.

You already know about the first technique, handling exceptions in a `catch` block. The second technique is a form of shifting responsibility ("passing the buck"). For example, suppose `yourMethod` has a `throws` clause as follows:

```
public void yourMethod() throws DivisionByZeroException
```

In this case, `yourMethod` is absolved of the responsibility of catching any exceptions of type `DivisionByZeroException` that might occur when `yourMethod` is executed. If, however, there is another method (`myMethod`) that includes an invocation of `yourMethod`, then `myMethod` must handle the exception. When you add a `throws` clause to `yourMethod`, you are saying to `myMethod`, "If you invoke `yourMethod`, you must handle any `DivisionByZeroException` that is thrown." In effect, `yourMethod` has passed the responsibility for any exceptions of type `DivisionByZeroException` from itself to any method that calls it.

Of course, if `yourMethod` passes responsibility to `myMethod` by including `DivisionByZeroException` in a `throws` clause, then `myMethod` may also pass the responsibility to whoever calls it by including the same `throws` clause in its definition. But in a well-written program, every exception that is thrown should eventually be caught by a `catch` block in some method that does not just declare the exception class in a `throws` clause.

`throws` Clause

If you define a method that might throw exceptions of some particular class, then normally either your method definition must include a `catch` block that will catch the exception or you must declare (that is, list) the exception class within a `throws` clause, as described in what follows.

SYNTAX (COVERS MOST COMMON CASES)

`public` *Type_Or_void Method*(*Parameter_List*) `throws` *List_Of_Exceptions*
Body_Of_Method

EXAMPLE

```
public void yourMethod(int n) throws MyException, YourException
{
        .
        .
        .
}
```

When an exception is thrown in a method but not caught in that method, that immediately ends the method invocation.

Be sure to note that the `throws` clause for a method is for exceptions that "get outside" the method. If they do not get outside the method, they do not belong in the `throws` clause. If they get outside the method, they belong in the `throws` clause no matter where they originate. If an exception is thrown in a `try` block that is inside a method definition and is caught in a `catch` block inside the method definition, then its exception class need not be listed in the `throws` clause. If a method definition includes an invocation of another method and that other method can throw an exception that is not caught, then the exception class of that exception should be placed in the `throws` clause.

Throwing an Exception Can End a Method

If a method throws an exception, and the exception is not caught inside the method, then the method invocation ends immediately after the exception is thrown.

In Display 9.10, we have rewritten the program from Display 9.5 so that the exception is thrown in the method `safeDivide`. The method `main` includes a call to the method `safeDivide` and puts the call in a `try` block. Because the method `safeDivide` can throw a `DivisionByZeroException` that is not caught in the method `safeDivide`, we need to declare this in a `throws` clause at the start of the definition of `safeDivide`. If we set up our program in this way, the case in which nothing goes wrong is completely isolated and easy to read. It is not even cluttered by `try` blocks and `catch` blocks.

Catch or Declare Rule

Most "ordinary" exceptions that might be thrown when a method is invoked must be accounted for in one of two ways:

- The possible exception can be caught in a `catch` block within the method definition.
- The possible exception can be declared at the start of the method definition by placing the exception class name in a `throws` clause (and letting whoever uses the method worry about how to handle the exception).

This is known as the **Catch or Declare Rule**. In any one method, you can mix the two alternatives, catching some exceptions and declaring others in a `throws` clause.

If you use a class that is subject to the Catch or Declare Rule and you do not follow the rule, you will get a compiler error message. The box entitled "Checked and Unchecked Exceptions" explains exactly which exception classes are subject to the Catch or Declare Rule.

The next subsection, entitled "Exceptions to the Catch or Declare Rule," explains exactly which exception classes are subject to the Catch or Declare Rule. However, the compiler will ensure that you follow the Catch or Declare Rule when it is required. So if you do not know whether a class is subject to the Catch or Declare Rule, you can rely on the compiler to tell you. If you use a class that is subject to the Catch or Declare Rule and you do not follow the rule, you will get a compiler error message.

Exceptions to the Catch or Declare Rule

As we already noted, in most "ordinary" cases, an exception must either be caught in a `catch` block or declared in a `throws` clause. This is the Catch or Declare Rule, but there are exceptions to this rule. There are some classes whose exceptions you do not need to account for in this way (although you can catch them in a `catch` block if you want to). These are typically exceptions that result from errors of some sort. They usually indicate that your code should be fixed, not that you need to add a `catch` block. They are often thrown by methods in standard library classes, but it would be legal to throw one of these exceptions in the code you write.

Exceptions that are descendents of the class `RuntimeException` do not need to be accounted for in a `catch` block or `throws` clause. Another category of classes called `Error` classes behave like exception classes in that they can be thrown and caught in a `catch` block. However, you are not required to account for `Error` objects in a `catch` block or `throws` clause. The situation is diagrammed as a class hierarchy in Display 9.11. All the classes shown in blue follow the Catch or Declare Rule, which says that if their objects are thrown, then they must either be caught in a `catch` block or declared in a `throws` clause. All the classes shown in yellow are exempt from the Catch or Declare Rule.

Display 9.11 Hierarchy of **`Throwable`** Objects

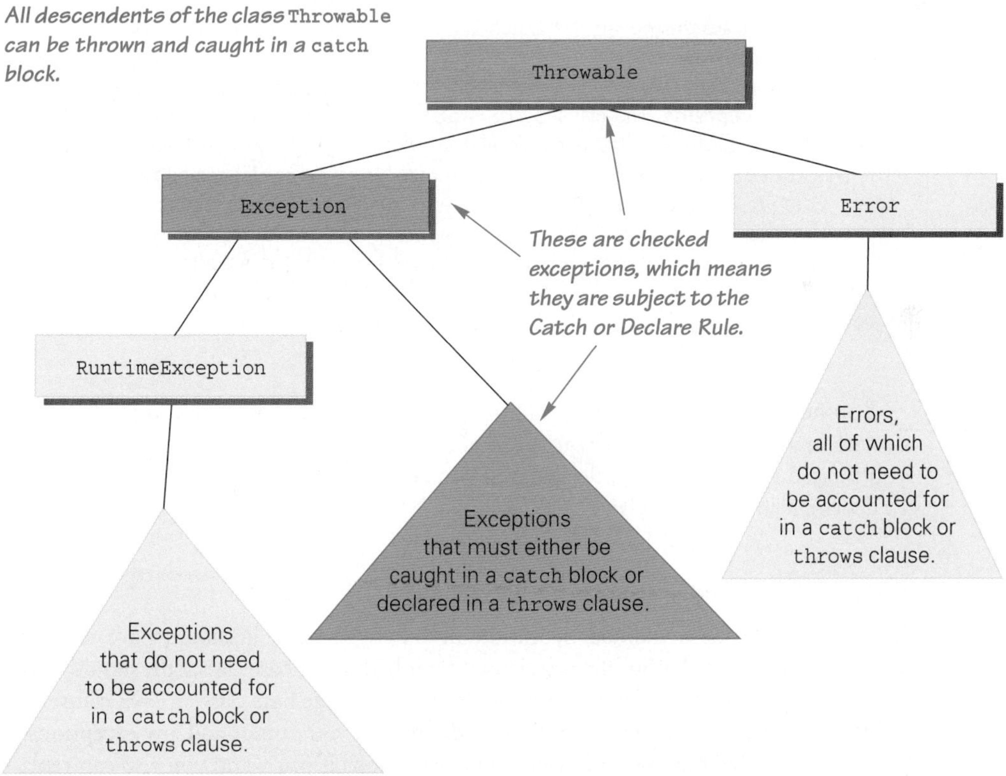
All descendents of the class Throwable can be thrown and caught in a catch block.
Throwable
Exception
Error
These are checked exceptions, which means they are subject to the Catch or Declare Rule.
RuntimeException
Exceptions that do not need to be accounted for in a catch block or throws clause.
Exceptions that must either be caught in a catch block or declared in a throws clause.
Errors, all of which do not need to be accounted for in a catch block or throws clause.

What Happens if an Exception Is Never Caught?

If every method up to and including the `main` method simply includes a `throws` clause for a particular class of exceptions, then it may turn out that an exception of that class is thrown but never caught. In such cases, when an exception is thrown but never caught, then for the kinds of programs we have seen so far, the program ends with an error message giving the name of the exception class. (In Chapter 17 we will discuss programs with windowing interfaces that are known as *GUI programs*. For GUI programs, if an exception is thrown but never caught, then nothing happens, but if your code does not somehow account for the thrown exception, then the user may be left in an unexplained situation.)

In a well-written program, every exception that is thrown should eventually be caught by a `catch` block in some method.

checked and unchecked exceptions

Exception classes that follow the Catch or Declare Rule are often called **checked exceptions**. Exceptions that are exempt from the Catch or Declare Rule are often called **unchecked exceptions**.

Checked and Unchecked Exceptions

Exceptions that are subject to the Catch or Declare Rule are called **checked exceptions** because the compiler *checks* to see if they are accounted for with a `catch` block or `throws` clause. Exceptions that are *not* subject to the Catch or Declare Rule are called **unchecked exceptions.** The classes `Throwable`, `Exception`, and all descendents of the class `Exception` are checked exceptions. All other exceptions are unchecked exceptions. The class `Error` and all its descendent classes are called **error classes** and are *not* subject to the Catch or Declare Rule. Although they are technically not exceptions, you can safely consider these error classes to be unchecked exceptions. (Strictly speaking, the class `Throwable` is neither an exception nor an error class, but it is seldom used and can be treated as a checked exception if it is used.)

You need not worry too much about which exceptions you do and do not need to declare in a `throws` clause. If you fail to account for some exception that Java requires you to account for, the compiler will tell you about it, and you can then either catch it or declare it in a `throws` clause.

`throws` Clause in Derived Classes

When you override a method definition in a derived class, it should have the same exception classes listed in its `throws` clause that it had in the base class, or it should have a `throws` clause whose exceptions are a subset of those in the base class `throws` clause. Put another way, when you override a method definition, you cannot add any exceptions to the `throws` clause (but you can delete some exceptions if you want; you also can replace an exception class by any descendent exception class). This makes sense, because an object of the derived class might be used anyplace an object of the base class can be used, so an overridden method must fit into any code written for an object of the base class.

When to Use Exceptions

So far, most of our examples of exception handling have been unrealistically simple. A better guideline for how you should use exceptions is to separate throwing an exception and catching the exception into separate methods. In most cases, you should include any `throw` statement within a method definition, list the exception class in a `throws` clause for that method, and place the `try` and `catch` blocks in *a different method.* In outline form, the technique is as follows:

```
public void yourMethod()throws YourException
{
        ...
    throw new YourException(<Maybe an argument.>);
        ...
}
```

Then, when `yourMethod` is used by some `otherMethod`, the `otherMethod` must account for the exception. For example,

```
public void otherMethod()
{
        ...
    try
    {
            ...
        yourMethod();
            ...
    }
    catch(YourException e)
    {
        <Handle exception.>
    }
        ...
}
```

Even this kind of use of a `throw` statement should be reserved for cases where it is unavoidable. *If you can easily handle a problem in some other way, do not throw an exception. Reserve* `throw` *statements for situations in which the way the exceptional condition is handled depends on how and where the method is used.* If the way that the exceptional condition is handled depends on how and where the method is invoked, then the best thing to do is to let the programmer who invokes the method handle the exception. In all other situations, it is preferable to avoid throwing exceptions. Let's outline a sample scenario of this kind of situation.

Suppose you are writing a library of methods to deal with patient monitoring systems for hospitals. One method might compute the patient's average daily temperature by accessing the patient's record in some file and dividing the sum of the temperatures by the number of times the temperature was taken. Now suppose these methods are used for creating different systems to be used in different situations. What should happen if the patient's temperature was never taken and so the averaging would involve a division by zero? In an intensive care unit, this would indicate something is very wrong. So for this system, when this potential division by zero would occur, an emergency message should be sent out. However, for a system that is to be used in a less urgent setting, such as outpatient care or even in some noncritical wards, it might have no significance, and so a simple note in the patient's record would suffice. In this scenario, the method for doing the averaging of the temperatures should throw an exception when this division by zero occurs, list the exception in the `throws` clause, and let each system handle the exception case in the way that is appropriate to that system.

When to Throw an Exception

Exceptions should be reserved for situations where a method has an exceptional case and individual invocations of the method would handle the exceptional case differently. In this situation, you would throw an exception in the method definition and not catch the exception in the method, but list it in the `throws` clause for the method. This way the programmers who invoke the method can handle the exception differently in different situations.

Event-Driven Programming ★

event-driven programming

firing an event

Exception handling is our first example of a programming methodology known as **event-driven programming**. With event-driven programming, objects are defined so that they send **events**, which are themselves objects, to other objects that handle the events. Sending the event is called **firing the event**. In exception handing, the event objects are the exception objects. They are fired (thrown) by an object when the object invokes a method that throws the exception. An exception event is sent to a `catch` block, where it is handled. Of course, a `catch` block is not exactly an object, but the idea is the same. Also, our programs have mixed event-driven programming (exception handling) with more traditional programming techniques.When we study how you construct windowing systems using the Swing libraries (Chapter 17), you will see examples of programming where the dominant technique is event-driven programming.

MyProgrammingLab™

Self-Test Exercises

24. What is the output produced by the following program?

```
public class Exercise
{
    public static void main(String[] args)
    {
        try
```

MyProgrammingLab™

Self-Test Exercises (continued)

```
        {
            System.out.println("Trying");
            sampleMethod(98.6);
            System.out.println("Trying after call.");
        }
        catch(Exception e)
        {
            System.out.println("Catching.");
        }

        System.out.println("End program.");
    }

    public static void sampleMethod(double test)
                                       throws Exception
    {
         System.out.println("Starting sampleMethod.");
         if (test < 100)
                throw new Exception();
    }
}
```

extra code on website

The class `Exercise` is on the website that comes with this text.

25. Suppose that in Self-Test Exercise 22, the line

```
sampleMethod(98.6);
```

in the `try` block is changed to

```
sampleMethod(212);
```

How would this affect the output?

26. Correct the following method definition by adding a suitable `throws` clause:

```
public static void doStuff(int n)
{
    if (n < 0)
        throw new Exception("Negative number.");
}
```

27. What happens if an exception is thrown inside a method invocation, but the exception is not caught inside the method?

28. Suppose there is an invocation of method A inside of method B, and an invocation of method B inside of method C. When method C is invoked, this leads to an invocation of method B, and that in turn leads to an invocation of method A. Now, suppose that method A throws an exception but does not catch it within A. Where might the exception be caught? In B? In C? Outside of C?

9.3 More Programming Techniques for Exception Handling

Only use this in exceptional circumstances.

WARREN PEACE, *The Lieutenant's Tool*

In this section, we present a number of the finer points about programming with exception handling in Java.

PITFALL: Nested try-catch Blocks

You can place a try block and its following catch blocks inside a larger try block or inside a larger catch block. On rare occasions this may be useful, but it is almost always better to place the inner try catch blocks inside a method definition and place an invocation of the method in the outer try or catch block (or maybe just eliminate one or more try blocks completely).

If you place a try block and its following catch blocks inside a larger catch block, you will need to use different names for the catch block parameters in the inner and outer blocks. This has to do with how Java handles nested blocks of any kind. Remember, try blocks and catch blocks are blocks.

If you place a try block and its following catch blocks inside a larger try block, and an exception is thrown in the inner try block but is not caught in the inner catch blocks, then the exception is thrown to the outer try block for processing and might be caught in one of its catch blocks. ■

The finally Block ★

The finally block contains code to be executed whether or not an exception is thrown in a try block. The finally block, if used, is placed after a try block and its following catch blocks. The general syntax is as follows:

```
try
{
   ...
}
catch(ExceptionClass1 e)
{
   ...
}
.
.
.
```

```
catch(ExceptionClassLast e)
{
    . . .
}
finally
{
   < Code to be executed whether or not an exception is thrown or caught.>
}
```

Now, suppose that the try-catch-finally blocks are inside a method definition. (After all, every set of try-catch-finally blocks is inside of some method, even if it is only the method main.) There are three possibilities when the code in the try-catch-finally blocks is run:

- The try block runs to the end and no exception is thrown. In this case, the finally block is executed after the try block.
- An exception is thrown in the try block and is caught in one of the catch blocks positioned after the try block. In this case, the finally block is executed after the catch block is executed.
- An exception is thrown in the try block and there is no matching catch block in the method to catch the exception. In this case, the method invocation ends and the exception object is thrown to the enclosing method. However, the finally block is executed before the method ends. Note that you cannot account for this last case simply by placing code after the catch blocks.

MyProgrammingLab™

Self-Test Exercises

29. Can you have a try block and corresponding catch blocks inside another larger try block?

30. Can you have a try block and corresponding catch blocks inside another larger catch block?

31. What is the output produced by the following program? What would the output be if the argument to exerciseMethod were -42 instead of 42? (The class NegativeNumberException is defined in Display 9.8, but you need not review that definition to do this exercise.)

```
public class FinallyDemo
{
    public static void main(String[] args)
    {
        try
        {
            exerciseMethod(42);
        }
```

(continued)

MyProgrammingLab™

Self-Test Exercises (continued)

```
            catch(Exception e)
            {
                System.out.println("Caught in main.");
            }
        }
        public static void exerciseMethod(int n) throws Exception
        {
            try
            {
                if (n > 0)
                    throw new Exception();
                else if (n < 0)
                    throw new NegativeNumberException();
                else
                    System.out.println("No Exception.");
                System.out.println("Still in sampleMethod.");
            }
            catch(NegativeNumberException e)
            {
                System.out.println("Caught in sampleMethod.");
            }
            finally
            {
                System.out.println("In finally block.");
            }
            System.out.println("After finally block.");
        }
    }
```

extra code on website

The class `FinallyDemo` is on the website that comes with this text.

Rethrowing an Exception ★

A `catch` block can contain code that throws an exception. In rare cases, you may find it useful to catch an exception and then, depending on the string produced by `getMessage` or depending on something else, decide to throw the same or a different exception for handling further up the chain of exception handling blocks.

The `AssertionError` Class ★

When we discussed the `assert` operator and assertion checking in Chapter 3, we said that if your program contains an assertion check and the assertion check fails, your program will end with an error message. This statement is more or less true, but it is incomplete. What happens is that an object of the class `AssertionError` is thrown. If it is not caught in a `catch` block, your program ends with an error message. However, if you wish, you can catch it in a `catch` block, although that is not a very common thing to do. The `AssertionError` class is in the `java.lang` package and so requires no import statement.

As the name suggests, the class `AssertionError` is derived from the class `Error`, so you are not required to either catch it in a `catch` block or declare it in a `throws` clause.

`ArrayIndexOutOfBoundsException`

Read Section 6.1 of Chapter 6, which covers array basics, before reading this short subsection. If you have not yet covered some of Chapter 6, omit this section and return to it at a later time.

If your program attempts to use an array index that is out of bounds, an `ArrayIndexOutOfBoundsException` is thrown and your program ends, unless the exception is caught in a `catch` block. `ArrayIndexOutOfBoundsException` is a descendent of the class `RuntimeException` and so need not be caught or accounted for in a `throws` clause. This sort of exception normally indicates that there is something wrong with your code and means that you need to fix your code, not catch an exception. Thus, an `ArrayIndexOutOfBoundsException` normally functions more like a run-time error message than a regular exception.

`ArrayIndexOutOfBoundsException` is in the standard Java package `java.lang` and so requires no import statement should you decide to use it by name.

Chapter Summary

- Exception handling allows you to design and code the normal case for your program separately from the code that handles exceptional situations.
- An exception can be thrown in a `try` *block*. Alternatively, an exception can be thrown in a method definition that does not include a `try` block (or does not include a `catch` block to catch that type of exception). In this case, an invocation of the method can be placed in a `try` block.
- An exception is caught in a `catch` *block*.
- A `try` block must be followed by at least one `catch` block and can be followed by more than one `catch` block. If there are multiple `catch` blocks, always list the `catch` block for a more specific exception class before the `catch` block for a more general exception class.
- The best use of exceptions is to throw an exception in a method (but not catch it in the method)—but to do this only when the way the exception is handled will vary from one invocation of the method to another. There is seldom any other situation that can profitably benefit from throwing an exception.
- If an exception is thrown in a method but not caught in that method, then if the exception is not a descendent of the class `RuntimeException` (and is not a descendent of the class `Error`), the exception type must be listed in the `throws` clause for that method.

Answers to Self-Test Exercises

1. Assuming the first item input is not a correctly formed `int` value, the program will go into an infinite loop after reading the first item input. The screen will continually output a prompt for an input number. The problem is that unless the new-line symbol `'\n'` is read, the program will continue to try to read on the first input line and so continually reads in the empty string.

2. The following is the method definition embedded in a test program. This program would give the same dialogue as the one in Display 9.1. The program is included on the website that accompanies this book.

extra code on website

```
import java.util.Scanner;
import java.util.InputMismatchException;
public class getIntDemo
{
    /**
    Precondition: keyboard is an object of the class Scanner that
    has been set up for keyboard input (as we have been doing right
    along).
    Returns: An int value entered at the keyboard.
    If the user enters an incorrectly formed input, she or he
    is prompted to reenter the value,
    */
    public static int getInt(Scanner keyboard)
    {
        int number = 0; //to keep compiler happy
        boolean done = false;

        while (! done)
        {
          try
          {
               System.out.println("Enter a whole number:");
               number = keyboard.nextInt();
               done = true;
          }
          catch(InputMismatchException e)
          {
               keyboard.nextLine();
               System.out.println(
                      "Not a correctly written whole number.");
               System.out.println("Try again.");
          }
        }
        return number;
    }
```

```
    public static void main(String[] args)
    {
        Scanner keyboardArg = new Scanner(System.in);
        int number = getInt(keyboardArg);
        System.out.println("You entered " + number);
    }
}
```

3. ```
   Try block entered.
   Over 30.
   After catch block
   ```

4. The output would then be

   ```
   Try block entered.
   Under 30.
   After catch block
   ```

5. There are two `throw` statements:

   ```
   throw new Exception("Over 30.");
   throw new Exception("Under 30.");
   ```

6. When a `throw` statement is executed, it is the end of the enclosing `try` block. No other statements in the `try` block are executed, and control passes to the following `catch` block(s). When we say that control passes to the following `catch` block, we mean that the exception object that is thrown is plugged in for the `catch` block parameter and the code in the `catch` block is executed.

7. ```
   try
   {
      System.out.println("Try block entered.");
      if (waitTime > 30)
          throw new Exception("Over 30.");
      else if (waitTime < 30)
          throw new Exception("Under 30.");
      else
          System.out.println("No exception.");
      System.out.println("Leaving try block.");
   }
   ```

8. ```
   catch(Exception thrownObject)
   {
       System.out.println(thrownObject.getMessage());
   }
   ```

9. `thrownObject`

10. Yes, it is legal.

11. Yes, it is legal.

12. ```
    public class PowerFailureException extends Exception
    ```

```
{
   public PowerFailureException()
   {
       super("Power Failure!");
   }
   public PowerFailureException(String message)
   {
       super(message);
   }
}
```

13.
```
public class TooMuchStuffException extends Exception
{
    public TooMuchStuffException()
    {
        super("Too much stuff!");
    }
    public TooMuchStuffException(String message)
    {
        super(message);
    }
}
```

14.
```
ExerciseException invoked with an argument.
Do Be Do
```

15.
```
Test exception thrown!!
Test Exception thrown!
Message is Test Exception thrown!
```

16.
```
try block entered:
MyException: Hi Mom!
End of example.
```

17. The output would be the same.

18. The output would then be
```
try block entered:
Leaving try block.
End of example.
```

19.
```
41.9
DoubleException thrown!
```

20. Yes, you can define an exception class as a derived class of the class `IOException`.

21.
```
Second catch.
End of exercise.
```

22. The output would then be

```
First catch.
End of exercise.
```

23. The output would then be

```
Bingo!
End of exercise.
```

24.
```
Trying
Starting sampleMethod.
Catching.
End program.
```

25. The output would then be

```
Trying
Starting sampleMethod.
Trying after call.
End program.
```

26.
```
public static void doStuff(int n) throws Exception
{
    if (n < 0)
        throw new Exception("Negative number.");
}
```

27. If a method throws an exception and the exception is not caught inside the method, then the method invocation ends immediately after the exception is thrown. If the method invocation is inside a `try` block, then the exception is thrown to a matching `catch` block, if there is one. If there is no `catch` block matching the exception, then the method invocation ends as soon as that exception is thrown.

28. It might be caught in method B. If it is not caught in method B, it might be caught in method C. If it is not caught in method C, it might be caught outside of method C.

29. Yes, you can have a `try` block and corresponding `catch` blocks inside another larger `try` block.

30. Yes, you can have a `try` block and corresponding `catch` blocks inside another larger `catch` block.

31.
```
In finally block.
Caught in main.
```

If the argument to `sampleMethod` is `-42` instead of `42`, the output would be

```
Caught in sampleMethod.
In finally block.
After finally block.
```

MyProgrammingLab™

Programming Projects

Visit www.myprogramminglab.com to complete select exercises online and get instant feedback.

VideoNote
Solution to Programming Project 9.1

1. Write a program that calculates the average of *N* integers. The program should prompt the user to enter the value for *N* and then afterward must enter all *N* numbers. If the user enters a nonpositive value for *N*, then an exception should be thrown (and caught) with the message "*N* must be positive." If there is any exception as the user is entering the *N* numbers, an error message should be displayed, and the user prompted to enter the number again.

2. Here is a snippet of code that inputs two integers and divides them:

```
Scanner scan = new Scanner(System.in);
int n1, n2;
double r;

n1 = scan.nextInt();
n2 = scan.nextInt();
r = (double) n1 / n2;
```

   Place this code into a `try-catch` block with multiple catches so that different error messages are printed if we attempt to divide by zero or if the user enters textual data instead of integers (`java.util.InputMismatchException`). If either of these conditions occurs, then the program should loop back and let the user enter new data.

3. Modify the previous exercise so that the snippet of code is placed inside a method. The method should be named `ReturnRatio`, read the input from the keyboard, and throw different exceptions if there is a division by zero or an input mismatch between text and an integer. Create your own exception class for the case of division by zero. Invoke `ReturnRatio` from your `main` method and catch the exceptions in `main`. The `main` method should invoke the `ReturnRatio` method again if any exception occurs.

4. (This is a version of an exercise from Chapter 5.) Programming Project 5.2 from Chapter 5 asked you to create a class named `Fraction`. This class is used to represent a ratio of two integers. It should include mutator functions that allow the user to set the numerator and the denominator along with a method that displays the fraction on the screen as a ratio (e.g., 5/9). Modify the class so that it throws the exception `DenominatorIsZeroException` if the denominator is set to zero. Do not forget to account for the constructors! You will have to create the `DenominatorIsZeroException` class and it should be derived from `Exception`.

   Write a `main` method that tests the new `Fraction` class, attempts to set the denominator to zero, and catches the `DenominatorIsZeroException` exception.

5. Write a program that converts dates from numerical month/day/year format to normal "month day, year" format (for example, 12/25/2000 corresponds to December 25, 2000). You will define three exception classes, one called `MonthException`, another called `DayException`, and a third called `YearException`. If the user enters

anything other than a legal month number (integers from `1` to `12`), your program will throw and catch a `MonthException` and ask the user to reenter the month. Similarly, if the user enters anything other than a valid day number (integers from `1` to either `28`, `29`, `30`, or `31`, depending on the month and year), then your program will throw and catch a `DayException` and ask the user to reenter the day. If the user enters a year that is not in the range 1000 to 3000 (inclusive), then your program will throw and catch a `YearException` and ask the user to reenter the year. (There is nothing very special about the numbers 1000 and 3000 other than giving a good range of likely dates.) See Self-Test Exercise 19 in Chapter 4 for details on leap years.

6. Write a program that can serve as a simple calculator. This calculator keeps track of a single number (of type `double`) that is called `result` and that starts out as 0.0. Each cycle allows the user to repeatedly add, subtract, multiply, or divide by a second number. The result of one of these operations becomes the new value of `result`. The calculation ends when the user enters the letter R for "result" (either in upper- or lowercase). The user is allowed to do another calculation from the beginning as often as desired.

   The input format is shown in the following sample dialogue. If the user enters any operator symbol other than `+`, `–`, `*`, or `/`, then an `UnknownOperatorException` is thrown and the user is asked to reenter that line of input. Defining the class `UnknownOperatorException` is part of this project.

```
Calculator is on.
result = 0.0
+5
result + 5.0 = 5.0
new result = 5.0
* 2.2
result * 2.2 = 11.0
updated result = 11.0
% 10
% is an unknown operation.
Reenter, your last line:
* 0.1
result * 0.1 = 1.1
updated result = 1.1
r
Final result = 1.1
Again? (y/n)
yes
result = 0.0
+10
result + 10.0 = 10.0
new result = 10.0
/2
result / 2.0 = 5.0
```

```
updated result = 5.0
r
Final result = 5.0
Again? (y/n)
N
End of Program
```

VideoNote **Solution to Programming Project 9.7**

7. A method that returns a special error code is usually better accomplished throwing an exception instead. The following class maintains an account balance.

```
class Account
{
      private double balance;
      public Account()
      {
            balance = 0;
      }
      public Account(double initialDeposit)
      {
            balance = initialDeposit;
      }
      public double getBalance()
      {
            return balance;
      }
      // returns new balance or -1 if error
      public double deposit(double amount)
      {
            if (amount > 0)
                 balance += amount;
            else
                 return -1;// Code indicating error
            return balance;
      }
      // returns new balance or -1 if invalid amount
      public double withdraw(double amount)
      {
            if ((amount > balance) || (amount < 0))
                 return -1;
            else
                 balance -= amount;
            return balance;
      }
}
```

Rewrite the class so that it throws appropriate exceptions instead of returning –1 as an error code. Write test code that attempts to withdraw and deposit invalid amounts and catches the exceptions that are thrown.

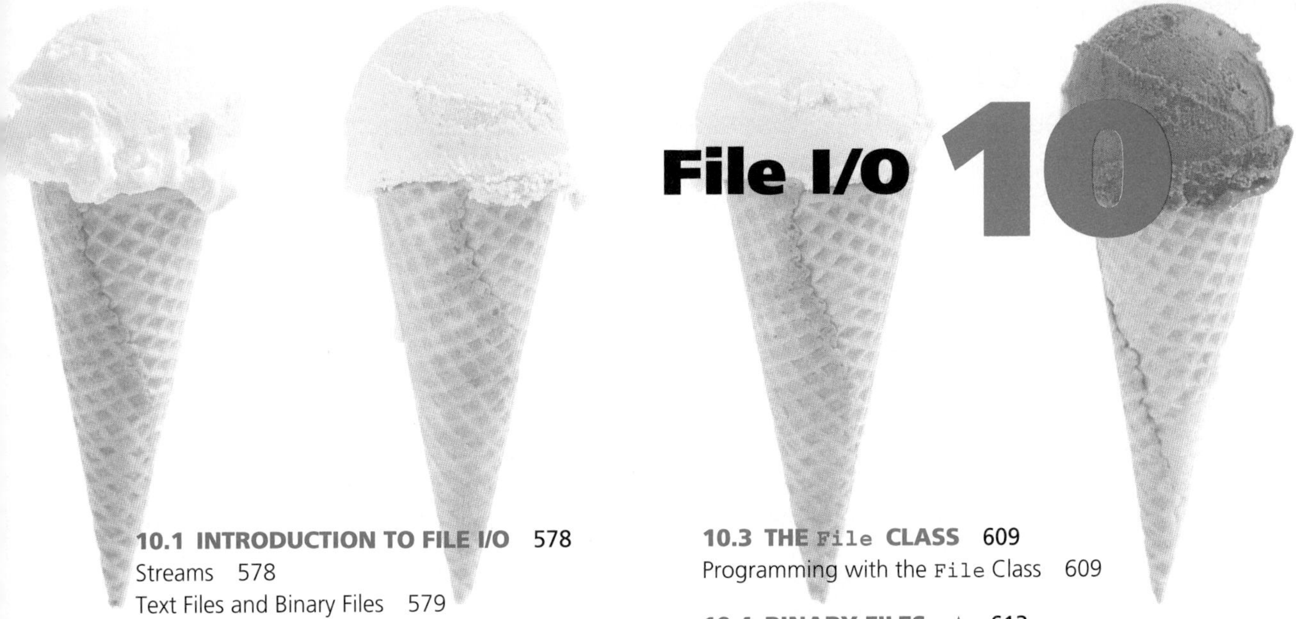

File I/O 10

10 File I/O

As a leaf is carried by a stream, whether the stream ends in a lake or in the sea, so too is the output of your program carried by a stream, not knowing if the stream goes to the screen or to a file.

WASHROOM WALL OF A COMPUTER SCIENCE DEPARTMENT (1995)

Introduction

In this chapter, we explain how you can write your programs to take input from a file and send output to a file. This chapter covers the most common ways of doing file I/O in Java. However, it is not an exhaustive study of Java I/O classes. The Java I/O class library contains bewilderingly many classes and an exhaustive treatment of all of them would be a book by itself.

Prerequisites

You need only some of Chapter 9 on exception handling to read this chapter. You do not need Chapters 6, 7, or 8 on arrays, inheritance, and polymorphism, except in the final subsection, which covers writing and reading of arrays to binary files. If you have not yet covered some basic material on one-dimensional arrays, you can, of course, simply omit this last subsection.

You may postpone all or part of this chapter if you wish. Nothing in the rest of this book requires any of this chapter.

10.1 Introduction to File I/O

Good Heavens! For more than forty years I have been speaking prose without knowing it.

MOLIÈRE, *LE Bourgeois Gentilhomme*

In this section, we go over some basic concepts about file I/O before we go into any Java details.

Streams

stream
input stream
output stream

A **stream** is an object that allows for the flow of data between your program and some I/O device or some file. If the flow is into your program, the stream is called an **input stream**. If the flow is out of your program, the stream is called an **output stream**. If the input stream flows from the keyboard, then your program will take input from the keyboard. If the input stream flows from a file, then your program will take its input from that file. Similarly, an output stream can go to the screen or to a file.

`System.out`

`System.in`

Although you may not realize it, you have already been using streams in your programs when you have output something to the screen. `System.out` (used in `System.out.println`) is an output stream connected to the screen. `System.in` is an input stream connected to the keyboard. You used `System.in` in expressions such as the following:

```
Scanner keyboard = new Scanner(System.in);
```

These two streams are automatically available to your program. You can define other streams that come from or go to files. Once you have defined them, you can use them in your program in ways that are similar to how you use `System.out` and `System.in`.

> **Streams**
>
> A **stream** is a flow of data. If the data flows *into your program*, then the stream is called an **input stream**. If the data flows *out of your program*, the stream is called an **output stream**.
>
> Streams are used for both console I/O, which you have been using already, and file I/O.

Text Files and Binary Files

text file

ASCII file

binary file

Text files are files that appear to contain sequences of characters when viewed in a text editor or read by a program. For example, the files that contain your Java programs are text files. **Text files** are sometimes also called **ASCII files** because they contain data encoded using a scheme known as ASCII coding. Files whose contents must be handled as sequences of binary digits are called **binary files**.

Although it is not technically correct, you can safely think of a text file as containing a sequence of characters, and think of a binary file as containing a sequence of binary digits. Another way to distinguish between binary files and text files is to note that text files are designed to be read by human beings, whereas binary files are designed to be read only by programs.

One advantage of text files is that they are usually the same on all computers, so you can move your text files from one computer to another with few or no problems. The implementation of binary files usually differs from one computer to another, so your binary data files ordinarily must be read only on the same type of computer, and with the same programming language, as the computer that created that file.

The benefit of binary files is that they are more efficient to process than text files. Unlike other programming languages, Java also gives its binary files some of the advantages of text files. In particular, Java binary files are platform independent; that is, with Java, you can move your binary files from one type of computer to another and your Java programs will still be able to read the binary files. This combines the portability of text files with the efficiency of binary files.

The one big asset of text files is that you can read and write to them using a text editor. With binary files, all the reading and writing must normally be done by a program.

> **Text Files versus Binary Files**
>
> Files that you write and read using an editor are called **text files**. **Binary files** represent data in a way that is not convenient to read with a text editor, but that can be written to and read from a program very efficiently.

MyProgrammingLab™

Self-Test Exercises

1. A stream is a flow of data. From where and to where does the data flow in an input stream? From where and to where does the data flow in an output stream?

2. What is the difference between a binary file and a text file?

10.2 Text Files

Polonius: What do you read, my lord?
Hamlet: Words, words, words.

WILLIAM SHAKESPEARE, *Hamlet*

In this section, we describe the most common ways to do text file I/O in Java.

Writing to a Text File

PrintWriter

The class `PrintWriter` is the preferred stream class for writing to a text file. An object of the class `PrintWriter` has the methods `print` and `println`, which are like the methods `System.out.print` and `System.out.println` that you can use for screen output. However, with an object of the class `PrintWriter`, the output goes to a text file. Display 10.1 contains a simple program that uses `PrintWriter` to send output to a text file. Let's look at the details of that program.

java.io

All the file I/O–related classes we introduce in this chapter are in the package `java.io`, so all our program files begin with import statements similar to the ones in Display 10.1.

The program in Display 10.1 creates a text file named `stuff.txt` that a person can read using an editor, or that another Java program can read. The program creates an object of the class `PrintWriter` as follows:

```
outputStream =
        new PrintWriter(new FileOutputStream("stuff.txt"));
```

opening a file

The variable `outputStream` is of type `PrintWriter` and is declared outside the `try` block. The preceding two lines of code connect the stream named `outputStream` to the file named `stuff.txt`. This is called **opening the file**. When you connect a file to a stream in this way, your program always starts with an empty file. If the file `stuff.txt` already exists, the old contents of `stuff.txt` will be lost. If the file `stuff.txt` does not exist, then a new, empty file named `stuff.txt` will be created.

We want to associate the output stream `outputStream` with the file named `stuff.txt`. However, the class `PrintWriter` has no constructor that takes a file name as its argument. So we use the class `FileOutputStream` to create a stream that can be used as an argument to a `PrintWriter` constructor. The expression

`FileOutputStream`

```
new FileOutputStream("stuff.txt")
```

takes a file name as an argument and creates an anonymous object of the class `FileOutputStream`, which is then used as an argument to a constructor for the class `PrintWriter` as follows:

```
new PrintWriter(new FileOutputStream("stuff.txt"))
```

file name

This produces an object of the class `PrintWriter` that is connected to the file `stuff.txt`. Note that the name of the file, in this case, `stuff.txt`, is given as a `String` value and so is given in quotes.

reading the file name

If you want to read the file name from the keyboard, you could read the name to a variable of type `String` and use the `String` variable as the argument to the `FileOutputStream` constructor.

`FileNotFoundException`

When you open a text file in the way just discussed, a `FileNotFoundException` can be thrown, and any such possible exception should be caught in a `catch` block. (Actually, it is the `FileOutputStream` constructor that might throw the `FileNotFoundException`, but the net effect is the same.)

Notice that the `try` block in Display 10.1 encloses only the opening of the file. That is the only place that an exception might be thrown. Also note that the variable `outputStream` is declared outside of the `try` block—this is so that this variable can be used outside of the `try` block. Remember, anything declared in a block (even in a `try` block) is local to the block.

Display 10.1 Sending Output to a Text File (part 1 of 2)

```
import java.io.PrintWriter;
import java.io.FileOutputStream;
import java.io.FileNotFoundException;

public class TextFileOutputDemo
{
    public static void main(String[] args)
    {
        PrintWriter outputStream = null;
        try
        {
            outputStream =
                 new PrintWriter(new FileOutputStream("stuff.txt"));
        }
        catch (FileNotFoundException e)
```

(continued)

Display 10.1 **Sending Output to a Text File** (part 2 of 2)

```
        {
            System.out.println("Error opening the file stuff.txt.");
            System.exit(0);
        }

        System.out.println("Writing to file.");

        outputStream.println("The quick brown fox");
        outputStream.println("jumps over the lazy dog.");

        outputStream.close();

        System.out.println("End of program.");
    }
}
```

Sample Dialogue

```
Writing to file.
End of program.
```

FILE `stuff.txt` (after the program is run.)

```
The quick brown fox
jumps over the lazy dog.
```

You can read this file using a text editor.

Opening a Text File for Writing Output

You create a stream of the class `PrintWriter` and connect it to a text file for writing as follows.

SYNTAX

```
PrintWriter Output_Stream_Name;
Output_Stream_Name =
        new PrintWriter(new FileOutputStream(File_Name));
```

EXAMPLE

```
PrintWriter outputStream = null;
outputStream =
        new PrintWriter(new FileOutputStream("stuff.txt"));
```

After this, you can use the methods `println` and `print` to write to the file.

When used in this way, the `FileOutputStream` constructor, and thus the `PrintWriter` constructor invocation, can throw a `FileNotFoundException`, which is a kind of `IOException`.

File Names

The rules for how you spell file names depend on your operating system, not on Java. When you give a file name to a Java constructor for a stream, you are not giving the constructor a Java identifier. You are giving the constructor a string corresponding to the file name. A suffix, such as `.txt` in `stuff.txt`, has no special meaning to a Java program. We are using the suffix `.txt` to indicate a text file, but that is just a common convention. You can use any file names that are allowed by your operating system.

A File Has Two Names

Every input file and every output file used by your program has two names: (1) the real file name that is used by the operating system and (2) the name of the stream that is connected to the file.

The stream name serves as a temporary name for the file and is the name that is primarily used within your program. After you connect the file to the stream, your program always refers to the file by using the stream name.

We said that when you open a text file for writing output to the file, the constructor might throw a `FileNotFoundException`. But in this situation you want to create a new file for output, so why would you care that the file was not found? The answer is simply that the exception is poorly named. A `FileNotFoundException` does not mean that the file was not found. In this case, it actually means that the file could not be created. A `FileNotFoundException` is thrown if it is impossible to create the file—for example, because the file name is already used for a directory (folder) name.

`IOException`

When dealing with file I/O, there are many situations in which your code might throw an exception of some class, such as `FileNotFoundException`. Many of these various exception classes are descended classes of the class `IOException`. The class `IOException` is the root class for various exception classes having to do with input and output.

A `FileNotFoundException` is a kind of `IOException`, so a `catch` block for an `IOException` would also work and would look more sensible. However, it is best to catch the most specific exception that you can, because that can give more information.

`println` As illustrated in Display 10.1, the method `println` of the class `PrintWriter` works the same for writing to a text file as the method `System.out.println` works
`print` for writing to the screen. The class `PrintWriter` also has the methods `print` and

printf — printf, which behave just like System.out.print and System.out.printf except that the output goes to a text file. Display 10.2 describes some of the methods in the class PrintWriter.

Display 10.2 Some Methods of the Class **PrintWriter** (part 1 of 2)

PrintWriter and FileOutputStream are in the java.io package.

```
public PrintWriter(OutputStream streamObject)
```

This is the only constructor you are likely to need. There is no constructor that accepts a file name as an argument. If you want to create a stream using a file name, use

new PrintWriter(new FileOutputStream(*File_Name*))

When the constructor is used in this way, a blank file is created. If there already is a file named *File_Name*, then the old contents of the file are lost. If you want instead to append new text to the end of the old file contents, use

new PrintWriter(new FileOutputStream(*File_Name*, true))

(For an explanation of the argument true, read the later subsection "Appending to a Text File.")

When used in either of these ways, the FileOutputStream constructor, and so the PrintWriter constructor invocation, can throw a FileNotFoundException, which is a kind of IOException.

If you want to create a stream using an object of the class File, you can use a File object in place of the *File_Name*. (The File class will be covered later in Section 10.3. We discuss it here so that you will have a more complete reference in this display, but you can ignore the reference to the class File until after you have read that section.)

public void println(*Argument*)

The *Argument* can be a string, character, integer, floating-point number, boolean value, or any combination of these, connected with + signs. The *Argument* can also be any object, although it will not work as desired unless the object has a properly defined toString() method. The *Argument* is output to the file connected to the stream. After the *Argument* has been output, the line ends, and so the next output is sent to the next line.

public void print(*Argument*)

This is the same as println, except that this method does not end the line, so the next output will be on the same line.

public PrintWriter printf(*Argument*)

This is the same as System.out.printf, except that this method sends output to a text file rather than to the screen. It returns the calling object. However, we have always used printf as a void method.

Display 10.2 Some Methods of the Class `PrintWriter` (part 2 of 2)

```
public void close()
```

Closes the stream's connection to a file. The following method calls `flush` before closing the file:

```
public void flush()
```

Flushes the output stream. This forces an actual physical write to the file of any data that has been buffered and not yet physically written to the file. Normally, you should not need to invoke `flush`.

When your program is finished writing to a file, it should **close** the stream connected to that file. In Display 10.1, the stream connected to the file `stuff.txt` is closed with the statement

```
outputStream.close();
```

The class `PrintWriter`, and every other class for file output or file input streams, has a method named `close`. When this method is invoked, the system releases any resources used to connect the stream to the file and does any other housekeeping that is needed. If your program does not close a file before the program ends, Java will close it for you when the program ends, but it is safest to close the file with an explicit call to `close`.

buffered

buffer

Output streams connected to files are often **buffered**, which means that, rather than physically writing every instance of output data as soon as possible, the data is saved in a temporary location, known as a **buffer**; when enough data is accumulated in this temporary location, it is physically written to the file. This can add to efficiency, since physical writes to a file can be slow. The method `flush` causes a physical write to the file of any buffered data. The method `close` includes an invocation of the method `flush`.

Closing a File

When your program is finished writing to a file or reading from a file, it should close the stream connected to that file by invoking the method named `close`.

SYNTAX

Stream_Object`.close();`

EXAMPLE

```
outputStream.close();
inputStream.close();
```

It may seem like there is no reason to use the method `close` to close a file. If your program ends normally but without closing a file, the system will automatically close it for you. So why should you bother to close files with an explicit call to the method `close`? There are at least two reasons. First, if your program ends abnormally, then

Java may not be able to close the file for you. This could damage the file. In particular, if it is an output file, any buffered output will not have been physically written to the file. So, the file will be incomplete. The sooner you close a file, the less likely it is that this will happen. Second, if your program writes to a file and later reads from the same file, it must close the file after it is through writing to the file and then reopen the file for reading. (Java does have a class that allows a file to be opened for both reading and writing, which we will discuss later in Section 10.5.)

PITFALL: A `try` Block Is a Block

Notice that in Display 10.1, we declare the variable `outputStream` outside of the `try` block. If you were to move that declaration inside the `try` block, you would get a compiler error message. Let's see why.

Suppose you replace

```
PrintWriter outputStream = null;
try
{
    outputStream =
       new PrintWriter(new FileOutputStream("stuff.txt"));
}
```

in Display 10.1 with the following:

```
try
{
     PrintWriter outputStream =
        new PrintWriter(new FileOutputStream("stuff.txt"));
}
```

This replacement looks innocent enough, but it makes the variable `outputStream` a local variable for the `try` block, which would mean that you could not use `outputStream` outside of the `try` block. If you make this change and `try` to compile the changed program, you will get an error message saying that `outputStream`, when used outside the `try` block, is an undefined identifier. ■

PITFALL: Overwriting an Output File

When you connect a stream to a text file for writing to the text file, as illustrated by what follows, you always produce an empty file:

```
outputStream =
        new PrintWriter(new FileOutputStream("stuff.txt"));
```

If there is no file named `stuff.txt`, this will create an empty file named `stuff.txt`. If a file named `stuff.txt` already exists, then this will eliminate that file and create a new, empty file named `stuff.txt`. So if there is a file named `stuff.txt` before this file opening, then all the data in that file will be lost. The later section

PITFALL: (continued)

"The File Class" tells you how to test to see whether a file already exists so that you can avoid accidentally overwriting a file. The following subsection, "Appending to a Text File," shows you how to add data to a text file without losing the data that is already in the file. ■

Appending to a Text File

appending

When you open a text file for writing in the way we did it in Display 10.1, and a file with the given name already exists, the old contents are lost. However, sometimes you instead want to add the program output to the end of the file. This is called **appending to a file**. If you want to append program output to the file `stuff.txt`, connect the file to the stream `outputStream` in the following manner:

```
outputStream =
   new PrintWriter(new FileOutputStream("stuff.txt", true ));
```

If the file `stuff.txt` does not already exist, Java will create an empty file of that name and append the output to the end of this empty file. So if there is no file named `stuff.txt`, the effect of opening the file is the same as in Display 10.1. However, if the file `stuff.txt` already exists, then the old contents will remain, and the program's output will be placed after the old contents of the file.

When appending to a text file in this way, you would still use the same `try` and `catch` blocks as in Display 10.1.

That second argument of `true` deserves a bit of explanation. Why did the designers use `true` to signal appending? Why not something such as the string `"append"`? The reason is that this version of the constructor for the class `FileOutputStream` was designed to also allow you to use a Boolean variable (or expression) to decide whether you append to an existing file or create a new file. For example, the following might be used:

```
System.out.println(
             "Enter A for append or N for a new file:");
char answer;
<Use your favorite way to read a single character into the variable answer.>
boolean append = (answer == 'A' || answer == 'a');
outputStream = new PrintWriter(
  new FileOutputStream("stuff.txt", append));
```

From this point on, your program writes to the file in exactly the same way that the program in Display 10.1 does. If the user answers with upper- or lowercase A, then any input will be added after the old file contents. If the user answers with upper- or lowercase N (or with anything other than an A), then any old contents of the file are lost.

TIP: `toString` Helps with Text File Output

In Chapter 4, we noted that if a class has a suitable `toString()` method and `anObject` is an object of that class, then `anObject` can be used as an argument to `System.out.println`, which will produce sensible output.[1] The same thing applies to the methods `println` and `print` of the class `PrintWriter`. Both `println` and `print` of the class `PrintWriter` can take any object as an argument and will produce reasonable output so long as the object has a sensible `toString()` method. ■

Opening a Text File for Appending

To create an object of the class **`PrintWriter`** and connect it to a text file for appending to the end of the text already in the file, proceed as follows.

SYNTAX

```
Output_Stream_Name =
    new PrintWriter(
        new FileOutputStream(File_Name, True_Boolean_Expression));
```

EXAMPLE

```
PrintWriter outputStream;
outputStream =
   new PrintWriter(new FileOutputStream("stuff.txt", true));
```

After this statement, you can use the methods `println` and `print` to write to the file, and the new text will be written after the old text in the file.

(If you want to create a stream using an object of the class `File`, you can use a `File` object in place of the *File_Name*. The `File` class is discussed later in the section entitled "The `File` Class.")

When used in this way, the `FileOutputStream` constructor, and so the `PrintWriter` constructor invocation, can throw a `FileNotFoundException`, which is a kind of `IOException`.

MyProgrammingLab™

Self-Test Exercises

3. What kind of exception might be thrown by the following, and what would it indicate if this exception is thrown?

```
PrintWriter outputStream =
     new PrintWriter(new FileOutputStream("stuff.txt"));
```

[1]There is a more detailed discussion of this in Chapter 8, but you need not read Chapter 8 to use this fact.

MyProgrammingLab™

Self-Test Exercises (continued)

4. Does the class `PrintWriter` have a constructor that accepts a string (for a file name) as an argument, so that the following code would be legal?

```
PrintWriter outputStream =
     new PrintWriter("stuff.txt");
```

5. Write some code that will create a stream named `outStream` that is a member of the class `PrintWriter`, and that connects this stream to a text file named `sam` so that your program can send output to the file. Do this so that the file `sam` always starts out empty. So, if there already is a file named `sam`, the old contents of `sam` are lost.

6. As in Self-Test Exercise 5, write some code that will create a stream named `outStream` that is a member of the class `PrintWriter`, and that connects this stream to a text file named `sam` so that your program can send output to the file. This time, however, do it in such a way that, if the file `sam` already exists, the old contents of `sam` will not be lost and the program output will be written after the old contents of the file.

7. The class `Person` was defined in Display 5.19 of Chapter 5. Suppose `mary` is an object of the class `Person`, which has a `toString` method defined, and suppose `outputStream` is connected to a text file as in Display 10.1. Will the following send sensible output to the file connected to `outputStream`?

```
outputStream.println(mary);
```

Reading from a Text File

VideoNote
Reading a Text File

The two most common stream classes used for reading from a text file are the `Scanner` class and the `BufferedReader` class. We will discuss both of these approaches to reading from a text file. The `Scanner` class offers a richer group of methods for reading from a text file and is our preferred class to use when reading from a text file. However, the `BufferedReader` class is also widely used and is a reasonable choice. You, or your instructor, will need to decide which class you will use.

Reading a Text File Using `Scanner`

The same `Scanner` class that we used for reading from the keyboard can also be used for reading from a text file. To do so, replace the argument `System.in` (in the `Scanner` constructor) with a suitable stream that is connected to the text file. This is a good illustration of the notion of a *stream*. The class `Scanner` does not care if its stream argument comes from the keyboard or from a text file.

The use of `Scanner` for reading from a text file is illustrated in Display 10.3, which contains a program that reads three numbers and a line of text from a text file named `morestuff.txt` and writes them back to the screen. The file `morestuff.txt` is a text file that a person could have created with a text editor or that a Java program could have created using `PrintWriter`.

opening a file

The program opens the `Scanner` stream and connects it to the text file `morestuff.txt` as follows:

```
Scanner inputStream = null;
    ...
inputStream = new Scanner(new FileInputStream("stuff.txt"));
```

The class `Scanner`, like the class `PrintWriter`, has no constructor that takes a file name as its argument, so we need to use another class—in this case, the class `FileInputStream`—to convert the file name to an object that can be a suitable argument to the `Scanner` constructor.

Note that the methods `nextInt` and `nextLine` read from the text files in exactly the same way as they read from the keyboard. The other `Scanner` methods for reading input (given in Display 2.6 and repeated in Display 10.6) also behave the same when reading from a text file as they do when used to read from the keyboard.

Opening a Text File for Reading with `Scanner`

Create a stream of the class `Scanner` and connect it to a text file for reading as follows:

SYNTAX

```
Scanner Stream_Object =
            new Scanner(new FileInputStream(File_Name));
```

EXAMPLE

```
Scanner inputStream =
        new Scanner(new FileInputStream("morestuff.txt"));
```

After this statement, you can use the methods `nextInt`, `nextDouble`, `nextLine`, and so forth to read from the named text files just as you have used these methods to read from the keyboard.

When used in this way, the `FileInputStream` constructor, and hence the `Scanner` constructor invocation, can throw a `FileNotFoundException`, which is a kind of `IOException`.

`FileNotFoundException`

If your program attempts to open a file for reading and there is no such file, then a `FileNotFoundException` is thrown. As you saw earlier in this chapter, a `FileNotFoundException` is also thrown in some other situations. A `FileNotFoundException` is a kind of `IOException`.

Display 10.3 **Reading Input from a Text File Using `Scanner`** (part 1 of 2)

```
import java.util.Scanner;
import java.io.FileInputStream;
import java.io.FileNotFoundException;

public class TextFileScannerDemo
{
    public static void main(String[] args)
    {
        System.out.println("I will read three numbers and a line");
        System.out.println("of text from the file morestuff.txt.");

        Scanner inputStream = null;

        try
        {
            inputStream =
               new Scanner(new FileInputStream("morestuff.txt"));
        }
        catch (FileNotFoundException e)
        {
            System.out.println("File morestuff.txt was not found");
            System.out.println("or could not be opened.");
            System.exit(0);
        }
        int n1 = inputStream.nextInt( );
        int n2 = inputStream.nextInt( );
        int n3 = inputStream.nextInt( );

        inputStream.nextLine(); //To go to the next line

        String line = inputStream.nextLine();

        System.out.println("The three numbers read from the file are:");
        System.out.println(n1 + ", " + n2 + ", and " + n3);

        System.out.println("The line read from the file is:");
        System.out.println(line);

        inputStream.close( );
    }
}
```

FILE `morestuff.txt`

```
1 2
3 4
Eat my shorts.
```

This file could have been made with a text editor or by another Java program.

(continued)

Display 10.3 Reading Input from a Text File Using `Scanner` (part 2 of 2)

Screen Output

```
I will read three numbers and a line
of text from the file morestuff.txt.
The three numbers read from the file are:
1, 2, and 3
The line read from the file is:
Eat my shorts.
```

Testing for the End of a Text File with `Scanner`

When using the class `Scanner`, if your program tries to read beyond the end of the file with any of the input methods, such as `nextInt` or `nextLine`, then the method throws an exception. If all goes well and there are no problems, such as using `nextInt` when the input is not a correctly formed `int`, then the exception thrown will be `NoSuchElementException`. This throwing of a `NoSuchElementException` can be used to signal the end of input. However, there is a more robust way of testing for the end of input from a text file. Each of the input methods (such as `nextInt` and `nextLine`) has a corresponding method (such `hasNextInt` and `hasNextLine`) that checks to see if there is any more well-formed input of the appropriate type. The nice thing about these methods is that they report when there is not a suitable next token for any reason; they do not check only for the end of a file. For example, `hasNextInt` returns `false` if there is no more file input of any kind or if the next token is not a well-formed `int` value. It returns `true` if there is a well-formed `int` as the next token.

A sample program that illustrates the use of `hasNextLine` to test for the end of input is given in Display 10.4. A sample program that illustrates the use of `hasNextInt` to test for the end of input is given in Display 10.5. A summary of some of the methods in the `Scanner` class is given in Display 10.6.

Checking for the End of a Text File with `Scanner`

You can check for the end of input with methods such as `hasNextInt`, `hasNextLine`, and so forth.

Display 10.4 Checking for the End of a Text File with **hasNextLine** (part 1 of 2)

```
import java.util.Scanner;
import java.io.FileInputStream;
import java.io.FileNotFoundException;
import java.io.PrintWriter;
import java.io.FileOutputStream;

public class HasNextLineDemo
{
    public static void main(String[] args)
    {
        Scanner inputStream = null;
        PrintWriter outputStream = null;

        try
        {
          inputStream =
               new Scanner(new FileInputStream("original.txt"));
          outputStream = new PrintWriter(
                      new FileOutputStream("numbered.txt"));
        }
        catch(FileNotFoundException e)
        {
           System.out.println("Problem opening files.");
           System.exit(0);
        }

        String line = null;
        int count = 0;
        while (inputStream.hasNextLine( ))
        {
            line = inputStream.nextLine( );
            count++;
            outputStream.println(count + " " + line);
        }

        inputStream.close( );
        outputStream.close( );
    }
}
```

```
File original.txt

 Little Miss Muffet
 sat on a tuffet
 eating her curves away.
 Along came a spider
 who sat down beside her
 and said "Will you marry me?"
```

(continued)

Display 10.4 Checking for the End of a Text File with **hasNextLine** (part 2 of 2)

File numbered.txt (after the program is run)

```
1 Little Miss Muffet
2 sat on a tuffet
3 eating her curves away.
4 Along came a spider
5 who sat down beside her
6 and said "Will you marry me?"
```

Display 10.5 Checking for the End of a Text File with **hasNextInt**

```java
import java.util.Scanner;
import java.io.FileInputStream;
import java.io.FileNotFoundException;

public class HasNextIntDemo
{
    public static void main(String[] args)
    {
        Scanner inputStream = null;

        try
        {
           inputStream =
              new Scanner(new FileInputStream("data.txt"));
        }
        catch(FileNotFoundException e)
        {
           System.out.println("File data.txt was not found");
           System.out.println("or could not be opened.");
           System.exit(0);
        }

        int next, sum = 0;
        while (inputStream.hasNextInt( ))
        {
            next = inputStream.nextInt( );
            sum = sum + next;
        }

        inputStream.close( );

        System.out.println("The sum of the numbers is " + sum);
    }
}
```

File data.txt

```
1 2
3 4 hi 5
```

Reading ends when either the end of the file is reached or a token that is not an `int` is reached. So, the 5 is never read.

Screen Output

```
The sum of the numbers is 10
```

Display 10.6 **Methods in the Class `Scanner`** (part 1 of 4)

`Scanner` is in the `java.util` package.

```
public Scanner(InputStream streamObject)
```

There is no constructor that accepts a file name as an argument. If you want to create a stream using a file name, you can use

```
new Scanner(new FileInputStream(File_Name))
```

When used in this way, the `FileInputStream` constructor, and thus the `Scanner` constructor invocation, can throw a `FileNotFoundException`, which is a kind of `IOException`.

To create a stream connected to the keyboard, use

```
new Scanner(System.in)
```

```
public Scanner(File fileObject)
```

The `File` class will be covered in the section entitled "The `File` Class," later in this chapter. We discuss it here so that you will have a more complete reference in this display, but you can ignore this entry until after you have read that section.

If you want to create a stream using a file name, you can use

```
new Scanner(new File(File_Name))
```

```
public int nextInt()
```

Returns the next token as an `int`, provided the next token is a well-formed string representation of an `int`.

Throws a `NoSuchElementException` if there are no more tokens.

Throws an `InputMismatchException` if the next token is not a well-formed string representation of an `int`.

Throws an `IllegalStateException` if the `Scanner` stream is closed.

```
public boolean hasNextInt()
```

Returns `true` if the next token is a well-formed string representation of an `int`; otherwise returns `false`.

Throws an `IllegalStateException` if the `Scanner` stream is closed.

```
public long nextLong()
```

Returns the next token as a `long`, provided the next token is a well-formed string representation of a `long`.

Throws a `NoSuchElementException` if there are no more tokens.

Throws an `InputMismatchException` if the next token is not a well-formed string representation of a `long`.

Throws an `IllegalStateException` if the `Scanner` stream is closed.

(continued)

Display 10.6 **Methods in the Class `Scanner`** (part 2 of 4)

```
public boolean hasNextLong()
```

Returns `true` if the next token is a well-formed string representation of a `long`; otherwise returns `false`.

Throws an `IllegalStateException` if the `Scanner` stream is closed.

```
public byte nextByte()
```

Returns the next token as a `byte`, provided the next token is a well-formed string representation of a `byte`.

Throws a `NoSuchElementException` if there are no more tokens.

Throws an `InputMismatchException` if the next token is not a well-formed string representation of a `byte`.

Throws an `IllegalStateException` if the `Scanner` stream is closed.

```
public boolean hasNextByte()
```

Returns `true` if the next token is a well-formed string representation of a `byte`; otherwise returns `false`.

Throws an `IllegalStateException` if the `Scanner` stream is closed.

```
public short nextShort()
```

Returns the next token as a `short`, provided the next token is a well-formed string representation of a `short`.

Throws a `NoSuchElementException` if there are no more tokens.

Throws an `InputMismatchException` if the next token is not a well-formed string representation of a `short`.

Throws an `IllegalStateException` if the `Scanner` stream is closed.

```
public boolean hasNextShort()
```

Returns `true` if the next token is a well-formed string representation of a `short`; otherwise returns `false`.

Throws an `IllegalStateException` if the `Scanner` stream is closed.

```
public double nextDouble()
```

Returns the next token as a `double`, provided the next token is a well-formed string representation of a `double`.

Throws a `NoSuchElementException` if there are no more tokens.

Throws an `InputMismatchException` if the next token is not a well-formed string representation of a `double`.

Throws an `IllegalStateException` if the `Scanner` stream is closed.

Display 10.6 **Methods in the Class `Scanner`** (part 3 of 4)

```
public boolean hasNextDouble()
```

Returns `true` if the next token is a well-formed string representation of a `double`; otherwise returns false.

Throws an `IllegalStateException` if the `Scanner` stream is closed.

```
public float nextFloat()
```

Returns the next token as a `float`, provided the next token is a well-formed string representation of a `float`.

Throws a `NoSuchElementException` if there are no more tokens.

Throws an `InputMismatchException` if the next token is not a well-formed string representation of a `float`.

Throws an `IllegalStateException` if the `Scanner` stream is closed.

```
public boolean hasNextFloat()
```

Returns `true` if the next token is a well-formed string representation of a `float`; otherwise returns `false`.

Throws an `IllegalStateException` if the `Scanner` stream is closed.

```
public String next()
```

Returns the next token.

Throws a `NoSuchElementException` if there are no more tokens.

Throws an `IllegalStateException` if the `Scanner` stream is closed.

```
public boolean hasNext()
```

Returns `true` if there is another token. May wait for a next token to enter the stream.

Throws an `IllegalStateException` if the `Scanner` stream is closed.

```
public boolean nextBoolean()
```

Returns the next token as a `boolean` value, provided the next token is a well-formed string representation of a `boolean`.

Throws a `NoSuchElementException` if there are no more tokens.

Throws an `InputMismatchException` if the next token is not a well-formed string representation of a `boolean` value.

Throws an `IllegalStateException` if the `Scanner` stream is closed.

```
public boolean hasNextBoolean()
```

Returns `true` if the next token is a well-formed string representation of a `boolean` value; otherwise returns `false`.

Throws an `IllegalStateException` if the `Scanner` stream is closed.

(continued)

Display 10.6 **Methods in the Class `Scanner`** (part 4 of 4)

```
public String nextLine()
```

Returns the rest of the current input line. Note that the line terminator `'\n'` is read and discarded; it is not included in the string returned.

Throws a `NoSuchElementException` if there are no more lines.

Throws an `IllegalStateException` if the Scanner stream is closed.

```
public boolean hasNextLine()
```

Returns `true` if there is a next line. May wait for a next line to enter the stream.

Throws an `IllegalStateException` if the `Scanner` stream is closed.

```
public Scanner useDelimiter(String newDelimiter);
```

Changes the delimiter for input so that `newDelimiter` will be the only delimiter that separates words or numbers. See the subsection "Other Input Delimiters" in Chapter 2 for the details. (You can use this method to set the delimiters to a more complex pattern than just a single string, but we are not covering that.)

Returns the calling object, but we have always used it as a `void` method.

Unchecked Exceptions

The exception classes `NoSuchElementException`, `InputMismatchException`, and `IllegalStateException` are all unchecked exceptions, which means that an exception of any of these classes is not required to be caught or declared in a `throws` clause.

MyProgrammingLab™

Self-Test Exercises

8. Write some code that will create a stream named `fileIn` that is a member of the class `Scanner`. It should connect the stream to a text file named `sally` so that your program can read input from the text file `sally`.

9. Might the method `nextInt` in the class `Scanner` throw an exception? If so, what type of exception?

10. If the method `hasNextInt` returns `false`, does that mean that reading has reached the end of the file?

MyProgrammingLab™

Self-Test Exercises (continued)

11. Might the following throw an exception that needs to be caught or declared in a `throws` clause?

```
Scanner inputStream =
        new Scanner(new FileInputStream("morestuff.txt"));
```

(The stream `inputStream` would be used to read from the text file `morestuff.txt`.)

Reading a Text File Using `BufferedReader`

`BufferedReader`

Until the `Scanner` class was introduced with version 5.0 of Java, the class `BufferedReader` was the preferred stream class to use for reading from a text file. It is still a commonly used class for reading from a text file. The use of `BufferedReader` is illustrated in Display 10.7, which contains a program that reads two lines from a text file named `morestuff2.txt` and writes them back to the screen. The file `morestuff2.txt` is a text file that a person could have created with a text editor or that a Java program could have created using `PrintWriter`.

opening a file

The program opens the text file `morestuff2.txt` as follows:

```
BufferedReader inputStream =
        new BufferedReader(new FileReader("morestuff2.txt"));
```

The class `BufferedReader`, like the classes `PrintWriter` and `Scanner`, has no constructor that takes a file name as its argument, so we need to use another class—in this case, the class `FileReader`—to convert the file name to an object that can be an argument to `BufferedReader`.

`readLine`

An object of the class `BufferedReader` that is connected to a text file, as in Display 10.7, has a method named `readLine` that is like the method `nextLine` of the `Scanner` class. This use of `readLine` to read from a text file is illustrated in Display 10.7.

Display 10.8 describes some of the methods in the class `BufferedReader`. Notice that there are only two methods for reading from a text file, `readLine` and `read`. We have already discussed `readLine`.

Display 10.7 Reading Input from a Text File Using **`BufferedReader`** (part 1 of 2)

```
import java.io.BufferedReader;
import java.io.FileReader;
import java.io.FileNotFoundException;
import java.io.IOException;

public class TextFileInputDemo
{
    public static void main(String[] args)
    {
```

(continued)

Display 10.7 Reading Input from a Text File Using **BufferedReader** (part 2 of 2)

```
        try
        {
            BufferedReader inputStream =
               new BufferedReader(new FileReader("morestuff2.txt"));

            String line = inputStream.readLine();
            System.out.println(
                            "The first line read from the file is:");
            System.out.println(line);

            line = inputStream.readLine();
            System.out.println(
                            "The second line read from the file is:");
            System.out.println(line);
            inputStream.close();
        }
        catch(FileNotFoundException e)
        {
            System.out.println("File morestuff2.txt was not found");
            System.out.println("or could not be opened.");
        }
        catch(IOException e)
        {
            System.out.println("Error reading from morestuff2.txt.");
        }
    }
}
```

FILE morestuff2.txt

```
1 2 3
Jack jump over
the candle stick.
```

This file could have been made with a text editor or by another Java program.

Screen Output

```
The first line read from the file is:
1 2 3
The second line read from the file is:
Jack jump over
```

Opening a Text File for Reading with `BufferedReader`

Create a stream of the class `BufferedReader` and connect it to a text file for reading as follows:

SYNTAX

```
BufferedReader Stream_Object =
            new BufferedReader(new FileReader(File_Name));
```

EXAMPLE

```
BufferedReader inputStream =
        new BufferedReader(new FileReader("morestuff2.txt"));
```

After this statement, you can use the methods `readLine` and `read` to read from the file.

When used in this way, the `FileReader` constructor, and hence the `BufferedReader` constructor invocation, can throw a `FileNotFoundException`, which is a kind of `IOException`.

Display 10.8 Some Methods of the Class `BufferedReader` (part 1 of 2)

`BufferedReader` and `FileReader` are in the `java.io` package.

```
public BufferedReader(Reader readerObject)
```

This is the only constructor you are likely to need. There is no constructor that accepts a file name as an argument. If you want to create a stream using a file name, use

```
new BufferedReader(new FileReader(File_Name))
```

When used in this way, the `FileReader` constructor, and thus the `BufferedReader` constructor invocation, can throw a `FileNotFoundException`, which is a kind of `IOException`.

The `File` class will be covered later in the section entitled "The `File` Class." We discuss it here so that you will have a more complete reference in this display, but you can ignore the following reference to the class `File` until after you have read that section.

If you want to create a stream using an object of the class `File`, use

```
new BufferedReader(new FileReader(File_Object))
```

When used in this way, the `FileReader` constructor, and thus the `BufferedReader` constructor invocation, can throw a `FileNotFoundException`, which is a kind of `IOException`.

```
public String readLine() throws IOException
```

Reads a line of input from the input stream and returns that line. If the read goes beyond the end of the file, `null` is returned. (Note that an `EOFException` is not thrown at the end of a file. The end of a file is signaled by returning `null`.)

(continued)

Display 10.8 Some Methods of the Class `BufferedReader` (part 2 of 2)

```
public int read()throws IOException
```

Reads a single character from the input stream and returns that character as an `int` value. If the read goes beyond the end of the file, then `-1` is returned. Note that the value is returned as an `int`. To obtain a `char`, you must perform a type cast on the value returned. The end of a file is signaled by returning `-1`. (All of the "real" characters return a positive integer.)

```
public long skip(long n) throws IOException
```

Skips n characters.

```
public void close()throws IOException
```

Closes the stream's connection to a file.

`read` method

The method `read` reads a single character. But note that `read` returns a value of type `int` that corresponds to the character read; it does not return the character itself. Thus, to get the character, you must use a type cast, as in

```
char next = (char)(inputStream.read());
```

If `inputStream` is in the class `BufferedReader` and is connected to a text file, this will set `next` equal to the first character in the file that has not yet been read.

Notice that the program in Display 10.7 catches two kinds of exceptions, `FileNotFoundException` and `IOException`. An attempt to open the file may throw a `FileNotFoundException`, and any of the invocations of `inputStream.readLine()` may throw an `IOException`. Because `FileNotFoundException` is a kind of `IOException`, you could use only the `catch` block for `IOException`. However, if you were to do this, then you would get less information if an exception were thrown. If you use only one `catch` block and an exception is thrown, you will not know if the problem occurred when opening the file or when reading from the file after it was opened.

MyProgrammingLab™

Self-Test Exercises

12. Write some code that will create a stream named `fileIn` that is a member of the class `BufferedReader` and that connects the stream to a text file named `joe` so that your program can read input from the text file `joe`.

13. What is the type of a value returned by the method `readLine` in the class `BufferedReader`? What is the type of a value returned by the method `read` in the class `BufferedReader`?

14. Might the methods `read` and `readLine` in the class `BufferedReader` throw an exception? If so, what type of exception?

MyProgrammingLab™

Self-Test Exercises (continued)

15. One difference between the `try` blocks in Display 10.1 and Display 10.7 is that the `try` block in Display 10.1 encloses only the opening of the file, while the `try` block in Display 10.7 encloses most of the action in the program. Why is the `try` block in Display 10.7 larger than the one in Display 10.1?

16. Might the following throw an exception that needs to be caught or declared in a `throws` clause?

```
BufferedReader inputStream =
    new BufferedReader(new FileReader("morestuff2.txt"));
```

(The stream `inputStream` would be used to read from the text file `morestuff2.txt`.)

TIP: Reading Numbers with `BufferedReader`

Unlike the `Scanner` class, the class `BufferedReader` has no methods to read a number from a text file. You must write your code to read the number as a string and convert the string to a value of a numeric type, such as `int` or `double`. To read a single number on a line by itself, read it using the method `readLine`, and then use `Integer.parseInt`, `Double.parseDouble`, or some similar method to convert the string read to a number. If there are multiple numbers on a single line, read the line using `readLine` and then use the `StringTokenizer` class to decompose the string into tokens. Next, use `Integer.parseInt` or a similar method to convert each token to a number.

`Integer.parseInt`, `Double.parseDouble`, and similar methods that convert strings to numbers are explained in Chapter 5 in the subsection entitled "Wrapper Classes." The `StringTokenizer` class is discussed in Chapter 4 in the starred subsection entitled "The `StringTokenizer` Class". ■

Testing for the End of a Text File with `BufferedReader`

When using the class `BufferedReader`, if your program tries to read beyond the end of the file with either of the methods `readLine` or `read`, then the method returns a special value to signal that the end of the file has been reached. When `readLine` tries to read beyond the end of a file, it returns the value `null`. Thus, your program can test for the end of the file by testing to see if `readLine` returns `null`. This technique is illustrated in Display 10.9. When the method `read` tries to read beyond the end of a file, it returns the value `-1`. Because the `int` value corresponding to each ordinary character is positive, this can be used to test for the end of a file.

> **Checking for the End of a Text File with `BufferedReader`**
>
> The method `readLine` of the class `BufferedReader` returns `null` when it tries to read beyond the end of a text file. The method `read` of the class `BufferedReader` returns `-1` when it tries to read beyond the end of a text file.

Display 10.9 Checking for the End of a Text File with **`BufferedReader`** (part 1 of 2)

```
import java.io.BufferedReader;
import java.io.FileReader;
import java.io.PrintWriter;
import java.io.FileOutputStream;
import java.io.FileNotFoundException;
import java.io.IOException;

/**
 Makes numbered.txt the same as original.txt, but with each line numbered.
*/
public class TextEOFDemo
{
   public static void main(String[] args)
   {
      try
      {
         BufferedReader inputStream =
               new BufferedReader(new FileReader("original.txt"));
         PrintWriter outputStream =
               new PrintWriter(new FileOutputStream("numbered.txt"));

         int count = 0;
         String line = inputStream.readLine();
         while (line != null)
         {
            count++;
            outputStream.println(count + " " + line);
            line = inputStream.readLine();
         }
         inputStream.close();
         outputStream.close();
      }
      catch(FileNotFoundException e)
      {
         System.out.println("Problem opening files.");
      }
      catch(IOException e)
      {
         System.out.println("Error reading from original.txt.");
      }
   }
}
```

Display 10.9 Checking for the End of a Text File with `BufferedReader` (part 2 of 2)

FILE `original.txt`

```
Little Miss Muffet
sat on a tuffet
eating her curves away.
Along came a spider
who sat down beside her
and said "Will you marry me?"
```

FILE `numbered.txt` (after the program is run)

```
1 Little Miss Muffet
2 sat on a tuffet
3 eating her curves away.
4 Along came a spider
5 who sat down beside her
6 and said "Will you marry me?"
```

If your version of `numbered.txt` *has numbered blank lines after line* 6*, that means you had blank lines at the end of* `original.txt`.

MyProgrammingLab™

Self-Test Exercises

17. Does the class `BufferedReader` have a method to read an `int` value from a text file?

18. What happens when the method `readLine` in the class `BufferedReader` attempts to read beyond the end of a file? How can you use this to test for the end of a file?

19. What is the type of the value returned by the method `read` in the class `BufferedReader`?

20. What happens when the method `read` in the class `BufferedReader` attempts to read beyond the end of a file? How can you use this to test for the end of a file?

21. Does the program in Display 10.9 work correctly if `original.txt` is an empty file?

Path Names

When giving a file name as an argument to a constructor for opening a file in any of the ways we have discussed, you may use a simple file name, in which case it is assumed that the file is in the same directory (folder) as the one in which the program is run. You can also use a full or relative path name.

path names

A **path name** not only gives the name of the file, but also tells what directory (folder) the file is in. A **full path name**, as the name suggests, gives a complete path name, starting from the root directory. A **relative path name** gives the path to the file, starting with the directory that your program is in. The way that you specify path names depends on your particular operating system.

A typical UNIX path name is

```
/user/sallyz/data/data.txt
```

To create a `BufferedReader` input stream connected to this file, use

```
BufferedReader inputStream =
           new BufferedReader(
               new FileReader("/user/sallyz/data/data.txt"));
```

Windows uses \ instead of / in path names. A typical Windows path name is

```
C:\dataFiles\goodData\data.txt
```

To create a `BufferedReader` input stream connected to this file, use

```
BufferedReader inputStream =
    new BufferedReader(
        new FileReader("C:\\dataFiles\\goodData\\data.txt"));
```

using \, \\, or /

Note that you need to use \\ in place of \, since otherwise Java will interpret a backslash paired with a character, such as `\d`, as an escape character. Although you must worry about using a backslash (\) in a quoted string, this problem does not occur with path names read in from the keyboard.

One way to avoid these escape character problems altogether is to always use UNIX conventions when writing path names. A Java program will accept a path name written in either Windows or UNIX format, even if it is run on a computer with an operating system that does not match the syntax. Thus, an alternate way to create a `BufferedReader` input stream connected to the Windows file

```
C:\dataFiles\goodData\data.txt
```

is the following:

```
BufferedReader inputStream =
      new BufferedReader(
         new FileReader("C:/dataFiles/goodData/data.txt"));
```

Nested Constructor Invocations

Expressions with two constructors, such as the following, are common when dealing with Java's library of I/O classes:

```
new BufferedReader(new FileReader("original.txt"))
```

This is a manifestation of the general approach to how Java I/O libraries work. Each I/O class serves one or a small number of functions. To obtain full functionality, you normally need to combine two (or more) class constructors. For example, in the previous code, the object `new FileReader("original.txt")` establishes a connection with the file `original.txt` but provides only very primitive methods for input. The constructor for `BufferedReader` takes this file reader object and adds a richer collection of input methods. In these cases, the inner object, such as `new FileReader("original.txt")`, is transformed into an instance variable of the outer object, such as `BufferedReader`.

MyProgrammingLab™

Self-Test Exercises

22. Of the classes `PrintWriter`, `Scanner`, `BufferedReader`, `FileReader`, and `FileOutputStream`, which have a constructor that accepts a file name as an argument so that the stream created by the constructor invocation is connected to the named file?

23. Is the following legal?

```
FileReader readerObject =
           new FileReader("myFile.txt");
BufferedReader inputStream =
           new BufferedReader(readerObject);
```

`System.in`, `System.out`, and `System.err`

The streams `System.in`, `System.out`, and `System.err` are three streams that are automatically available to your Java code. You have already been using `System.in` and `System.out`. `System.err` is just like `System.out`, except that it has a different name. For example, both of the following statements will send the string `"Hello"` to the screen so the screen receives two lines, each containing `"Hello"`:

```
System.out.println("Hello");
System.err.println("Hello");
```

The output stream `System.out` is intended to be used for normal output from code that is not in trouble. `System.err` is meant to be used for error messages.

redirecting output

Having two different standard output streams can be handy when you redirect output. For example, you can redirect the regular output to one file and redirect the error messages to a different file. Java allows you to redirect any of these three standard streams to or from a file (or other I/O device). This is done with the static methods `setIn`, `setOut`, and `setErr` of the class `System`.

For example, suppose your code connects the output stream `errStream` (of a type to be specified later) to a text file. You can then redirect the stream `System.err` to this text file as follows:

```
System.setErr(errStream);
```

If the following appears later in your code,

```
System.out.println("Hello from System.out.");
System.err.println("Hello from System.err.");
```

then `"Hello from System.out."` will be written to the screen, but `"Hello from System.err."` will be written to the file connected to the output stream `errStream`. A simple program illustrating this is given in Display 10.10.

Note that the arguments to the redirecting methods must be of the types shown in the following headings, and that these are classes we do not discuss in this book:

```
public static void setIn(InputStream inStream)
public static void setOut(PrintStream outStream)
public static void setErr(PrintStream outStream)
```

None of the input or output streams we constructed in our previous programs are of a type suitable to be an argument to any of these redirection methods. Space constraints keep us from giving any more details on the stream classes that are suitable for producing arguments for these redirection methods. However, you can use Display 10.10 as a model to allow you to redirect either `System.err` or `System.out` to a text file of your choice.

MyProgrammingLab™

Self-Test Exercises

24. Suppose you want the program in Display 10.10 to send an error message to the screen and regular (`System.out`) output to the file `errormessages.txt`. (This is the reverse of what the program in Display 10.10 does.) How would you change the program in Display 10.10?

25. Suppose you want the program in Display 10.10 to send all output (both `System.out` and `System.err`) to the file `errormessages.txt`. How would you change the program in Display 10.10?

Display 10.10 **Redirecting Error Messages** (part 1 of 2)

```
import java.io.PrintStream;
import java.io.FileOutputStream;
import java.io.FileNotFoundException;

public class RedirectionDemo
{
   public static void main(String[] args)
   {
       PrintStream errStream = null;
       try
       {
           errStream =
                new PrintStream(
                       new FileOutputStream("errormessages.txt"));
       }
       catch(FileNotFoundException e)
       {
          System.out.println(
                  "Error opening file with FileOutputStream.");
          System.exit(0);
       }
```

Note the stream classes used.

Display 10.10 Redirecting Error Messages (part 2 of 2)

```
        System.setErr(errStream);

        System.err.println("Hello from System.err.");
        System.out.println("Hello from System.out.");
        System.err.println("Hello again from System.err.");

        errStream.close();
    }
}
```

None of `System.in`, `System.out`, *or* `System.err` *needs to be closed, but the streams you create should be explicitly closed.*

FILE errormessages.txt

```
Hello from System.err.
Hello again from System.err.
```

Screen Output

```
Hello from System.out.
```

10.3 The `File` Class

The scars of others should teach us caution.

SAINT JEROME

In this section, we describe the class `File`, which is not really an I/O stream class but is often used in conjunction with file I/O. The class `File` is so important to file I/O programming that it was even placed in the `java.io` package.

Programming with the `File` Class

The `File` class contains methods that allow you to check various properties of a file, such as whether there is a file with a specified name, whether the file can be written to, and so forth. Display 10.11 gives a sample program that uses the class `File` with text files. (The class `File` works the same with binary files as it does with text files.)

abstract name

Note that the `File` class constructor takes a name, known as the **abstract name**, as an (string) argument. So the `File` class really checks properties of names. For example, the method `exists` tests whether there is a file with the abstract name. Moreover, the abstract name may be a potential directory (folder) name. For example, the method `isDirectory` tests whether the abstract name is the name of a directory (folder). The abstract name may be either a relative path name (which includes the case of a simple file name) or a full path name.

Display 10.12 lists some of the methods in the class `File`.

The `File` Class

The `File` class is like a wrapper class for file names. The constructor for the class `File` takes a string as an argument and produces an object that can be thought of as the file with that name. You can use the `File` object and methods of the class `File` to answer questions, such as the following: Does the file exist? Does your program have permission to read the file? Does your program have permission to write to the file? Display 10.14 has a summary of some of the methods for the class `File`.

EXAMPLE

```
File fileObject = new File("data.txt");
if ( ! fileObject.canRead())
    System.out.println("File data.txt is not readable.");
```

Display 10.11 Using the `File` Class (part 1 of 2)

```
import java.util.Scanner;
import java.io.File;
import java.io.PrintWriter;
import java.io.FileOutputStream;
import java.io.FileNotFoundException;
public class FileClassDemo
{
    public static void main(String[] args)
    {
        Scanner keyboard = new Scanner(System.in);
        String line = null;
        String fileName = null;

        System.out.println("I will store a line of text for you.");
        System.out.println("Enter the line of text:");
        line = keyboard.nextLine();
        System.out.println("Enter a file name to hold the line:");
        fileName = keyboard.nextLine();
        File fileObject = new File(fileName);

        while (fileObject.exists())
        {
           System.out.println("There already is a file named "
                                            + fileName);
           System.out.println("Enter a different file name:");
           fileName = keyboard.nextLine();
           fileObject = new File(fileName);
        }
```

Display 10.11 Using the **File** Class (part 2 of 2)

```
        PrintWriter outputStream = null;
        try
        {
            outputStream =
                new PrintWriter(new FileOutputStream(fileName));
        }
        catch(FileNotFoundException e)
        {
            System.out.println("Error opening the file " + fileName);
            System.exit(0);
        }

        System.out.println("Writing \"" + line + "\"");
        System.out.println("to the file" + fileName);
        outputStream.println(line);

        outputStream.close();
        System.out.println("Writing completed.");
    }
}
```

If you wish, you can use **fileObject** *instead of* **fileName** *as the argument to* **FileOutputStream**.

Sample Dialogue

The dialogue assumes that there already is a file named **myLine.txt** *but that there is no file named* **mySaying.txt**.

```
I will store a line of text for you.
Enter the line of text:
May the hair on your toes grow long and curly.
Enter a file name to hold the line:
myLine.txt
There already is a file named myLine.txt
Enter a different file name:
mySaying.txt
Writing "May the hair on your toes grow long and curly."
to the file mySaying.txt
Writing completed.
```

Display 10.12 Some Methods in the Class **File** (part 1 of 3)

`File` is in the `java.io` package.

`public File(String File_Name)`

A constructor. *File_Name* can be either a full or a relative path name (which includes the case of a simple file name). *File_Name* is referred to as the **abstract path name**.

`public boolean exists()`

Tests whether there is a file with the abstract path name.

(continued)

Display 10.12 Some Methods in the Class `File` (part 2 of 3)

`public boolean canRead()`

Tests whether the program can read from the file. Returns `true` if the file named by the abstract path name exists and is readable by the program; otherwise returns `false`.

`public boolean setReadOnly()`

Sets the file represented by the abstract path name to be read only. Returns `true` if successful; otherwise returns `false`.

`public boolean canWrite()`

Tests whether the program can write to the file. Returns `true` if the file named by the abstract path name exists and is writable by the program; otherwise returns `false`.

`public boolean delete()`

Tries to delete the file or directory named by the abstract path name. A directory must be empty to be removed. Returns `true` if it was able to delete the file or directory. Returns `false` if it was unable to delete the file or directory.

`public boolean createNewFile() throws IOException`

Creates a new empty file named by the abstract path name, provided that a file of that name does not already exist. Returns `true` if successful, and returns `false` otherwise.

`public String getName()`

Returns the last name in the abstract path name (that is, the simple file name). Returns the empty string if the abstract path name is the empty string.

`public String getPath()`

Returns the abstract path name as a `String` value.

`public boolean renameTo(File` *New_Name*`)`

Renames the file represented by the abstract path name to *New_Name*. Returns `true` if successful; otherwise returns `false`. *New_Name* can be a relative or absolute path name. This may require moving the file. Whether or not the file can be moved is system dependent.

`public boolean isFile()`

Returns `true` if a file exists that is named by the abstract path name and the file is a normal file; otherwise returns `false`. The meaning of *normal* is system dependent. Any file created by a Java program is guaranteed to be normal.

`public boolean isDirectory()`

Returns `true` if a directory (folder) exists that is named by the abstract path name; otherwise returns `false`.

`public boolean mkdir()`

Makes a directory named by the abstract path name. Will not create parent directories. See `mkdirs`, which follows. Returns `true` if successful; otherwise returns `false`.

Display 10.12 Some Methods in the Class `File` (part 3 of 3)

```
public boolean mkdirs()
```

Makes a directory named by the abstract path name. Will create any necessary but nonexistent parent directories. Returns `true` if successful; otherwise returns `false`. Note that if it fails, then some of the parent directories may have been created.

```
public long length()
```

Returns the length in bytes of the file named by the abstract path name. If the file does not exist or the abstract path name designates a directory, then the value returned is not specified and may be anything.

MyProgrammingLab™

Self-Test Exercises

26. Write a complete (although simple) Java program that tests whether or not the directory (folder) containing the program also contains a file named `Sally.txt`. The program has no input, and the only output tells whether or not there is a file named `Sally.txt`.

27. Write a complete Java program that asks the user for a file name, tests whether the file exists, and, if the file exists, asks the user whether or not it should be deleted. It then either deletes or does not delete the file as the user requests.

10.4 Binary Files ★

A little more than kin, and less than kind.

WILLIAM SHAKESPEARE, *Hamlet*

Binary files store data in the same format that is used in the computer's memory to store the values of variables. For example, a value of type `int` is stored as the same sequence of bytes (same sequence of zeros and ones) whether it is stored in an `int` variable in memory or in a binary file. So, no conversion of any kind needs to be performed when you store or retrieve a value in a binary file. This is why binary files can be handled more efficiently than text files.

Java binary files are unlike binary files in other programming languages in that they are portable. A binary file created by a Java program can be moved from one computer to another and still be read by a Java program—but only by a Java program. They cannot normally be read with a text editor or with a program written in any programming language other than Java.

The preferred stream classes for processing binary files are `ObjectInputStream` and `ObjectOutputStream`. Each has methods to read or write data one byte at a time. These streams can also automatically convert numbers and characters to bytes that can be stored in a binary file. They allow your program to be written as if the data placed in the file, or read from the file, is not just bytes but also strings or items of any of Java's primitive data types, such as `int`, `char`, and `double`, or even objects of classes you define. If you do not need to access your files using an editor, then the easiest and most efficient way to read data from and write data to files is to use binary files in the way we describe here.

We conclude this section with a discussion of how you can use `ObjectOutputStream` and `ObjectInputStream` to write and later read objects of any class you define. This will let you store objects of the classes you define in binary files and later read them back, all with the same convenience and efficiency that you get when storing strings and primitive type data in binary files.

Writing Simple Data to a Binary File

The class `ObjectOutputStream` is the preferred stream class for writing to a binary file.[2] An object of the class `ObjectOutputStream` has methods to write strings and values of any of the primitive types to a binary file. Display 10.13 shows a sample program that writes values of type `int` to a binary file. Display 10.14 describes the methods used for writing data of other types to a binary file.

Display 10.13 **Writing to a Binary File** (part 1 of 2)

```
import java.io.ObjectOutputStream;
import java.io.FileOutputStream;
import java.io.IOException;

public class BinaryOutputDemo
{
   public static void main(String[] args)
   {
      try
      {
         ObjectOutputStream outputStream =
             new ObjectOutputStream(
             new FileOutputStream("numbers.dat"));

         int i;
         for (i = 0; i < 5; i++)
             outputStream.writeInt(i);

         System.out.println("Numbers written to the file numbers.dat.");
         outputStream.close();
      }
```

[2] `DataOutputStream` is also widely used and behaves exactly as we describe for `ObjectOutputStream` in this section. However, the techniques given in the subsections "Binary I/O of Objects" and "Array Objects in Binary Files" work only for `ObjectOutputStream`; they do not work for `DataOutputStream`.

Display 10.13 **Writing to a Binary File** (part 2 of 2)

```
        catch (IOException e)
        {
            System.out.println("Problem with file output.");
        }
    }
}
```

File Representation (after program is run)

```
0
1
2
3
4
```

This is a binary file. It really contains representations of each number as bytes—that is, zeros and ones—and is read as bytes. You cannot read this file with your text editor.

Display 10.14 **Some Methods in the Class `ObjectOutputStream`** (part 1 of 2)

`ObjectOutputStream` and `FileOutputStream` are in the `java.io package.`

```
public ObjectOutputStream(OutputStream streamObject)
```

There is no constructor that takes a file name as an argument. If you want to create a stream using a file name, use

`new ObjectOutputStream(new FileOutputStream(`*File_Name*`))`

This creates a blank file. If there already is a file named *File_Name*, then the old contents of the file are lost.

If you want to create a stream using an object of the class `File`, use

`new ObjectOutputStream(new FileOutputStream(`*File_Object*`))`

The constructor for `FileOutputStream` may throw a `FileNotFoundException`, which is a kind of `IOException`. If the `FileOutputStream` constructor succeeds, then the constructor for `ObjectOutputStream` may throw a different `IOException`.

```
public void writeInt(int n) throws IOException
```

Writes the `int` value `n` to the output stream.

```
public void writeShort(short n) throws IOException
```

Writes the `short` value `n` to the output stream.

```
public void writeLong(long n) throws IOException
```

Writes the `long` value `n` to the output stream.

```
public void writeDouble(double x) throws IOException
```

Writes the `double` value `x` to the output stream.

(continued)

Display 10.14 Some Methods in the Class `ObjectOutputStream` (part 2 of 2)

```
public void writeFloat(float x) throws IOException
```

Writes the `float` value `x` to the output stream.

```
public void writeChar(int n) throws IOException
```

Writes the `char` value `n` to the output stream. Note that it expects its argument to be an `int` value. However, if you simply use the `char` value, then Java will automatically type cast it to an `int` value. The following are equivalent:

```
outputStream.writeChar((int)'A');
```

and

```
outputStream.writeChar('A');
```

```
public void writeUTF(String aString) throws IOException
```

Writes the `String` value `aString` to the output stream. `UTF` refers to a particular method of encoding the string. To read the string back from the file, you should use the method `readUTF` of the class `ObjectInputStream`.

```
public void writeObject(Object anObject) throws IOException
```

Writes its argument to the output stream. The object argument should be an object of a serializable class, a concept discussed later in the section titled "The `Serializable` Interface." Throws various `IOExceptions`.

```
public void close()throws IOException
```

Closes the stream's connection to a file. This method calls `flush` before closing the file.

```
public void flush()throws IOException
```

Flushes the output stream. This forces an actual physical write to the file of any data that has been buffered and not yet physically written to the file. Normally, you should not need to invoke `flush`.

Notice that almost all the code in the sample program in Display 10.13 is in a `try` block. Any part of the code that does binary file I/O in the ways we are describing can throw an `IOException`.

The output stream for writing to the binary file `numbers.dat` is created and named with the following:

```
ObjectOutputStream outputStream =
 new ObjectOutputStream(new
 FileOutputStream("numbers.dat"));
```

opening a file

As with text files, this is called **opening the file**. If the file `numbers.dat` does not already exist, this statement will create an empty file named `numbers.dat`. If the file `numbers.dat` already exists, this statement will erase the contents of the file so that the file starts out empty. The situation is basically the same as what you learned for text files, except that we are using a different class.

As is typical of Java I/O classes, the constructor for the class `ObjectOutputStream` takes another I/O class object as an argument—in this case, an anonymous argument of the class `FileOutputStream`.

Opening a Binary File for Output

You create a stream of the class `ObjectOutputStream` and connect it to a binary file as follows:

SYNTAX

```
ObjectOutputStream Output_Stream_Name =
    new ObjectOutputStream(new FileOutputStream(File_Name));
```

The constructor for `FileOutputStream` may throw a `FileNotFoundException`, which is a kind of `IOException`. If the `FileOutputStream` constructor succeeds, then the constructor for `ObjectOutputStream` may throw a different `IOException`. A single `catch` block for `IOException` would cover all cases.

EXAMPLES

```
ObjectOutputStream myOutputStream =
           new ObjectOutputStream(new
           FileOutputStream("mydata.dat"));
```

After opening the file, you can use the methods of the class `ObjectOutputStream` (Display 10.14) to write to the file.

The class `ObjectOutputStream` does not have a method named `println`, as we had with text file output and screen output. However, as shown in Display 10.13, an object of the class `ObjectOutputStream` does have a method named `writeInt` that can write a single `int` value to a file, and it also has the other output methods described in Display 10.14.

writeInt

In Display 10.13, we made it look as though the numbers in the file `numbers.dat` were written one per line in a human-readable form. That is not what happens, however. There are no lines or other separators between the numbers. Instead, the numbers are written in the file one immediately after the other, and they are encoded as a sequence of bytes in the same way that the numbers would be encoded in the computer's main memory. These coded `int` values cannot be read using your editor. Realistically, they can be read only by another Java program.

You can use a stream from the class `ObjectOutputStream` to output values of any primitive type and also to write data of the type `String`. Each primitive data type has a corresponding write method in the class `ObjectOutputStream`. We have already mentioned the write methods for outputting `int` values. The methods for the other primitive types are completely analogous to `writeInt`. For example, the following would write a `double` value, a `boolean` value, and a `char` value to the binary file connected to the `ObjectOutputStream` object `outputStream`:

```
outputStream.writeDouble(9.99);
outputStream.writeBoolean(false);
outputStream.writeChar((int)'A');
```

writeChar

The method `writeChar` has one possibly surprising property: It expects its argument to be of type `int`. So if you start with a value of type `char`, the `char` value can be type cast to an `int` before it is given to the method `writeChar`. For example, to output the contents of a `char` variable named `symbol`, you can use

```
outputStream.writeChar((int)symbol);
```

In actual fact, you do not need to write in the type cast to an `int`, because Java automatically performs a type cast from a `char` value to an `int` value for you. So, the following is equivalent to the previous invocation of `writeChar`:

```
outputStream.writeChar(symbol);
```

writeUTF for strings

To output a value of type `String`, use the method `writeUTF`. For example, if `outputStream` is a stream of type `ObjectOutputStream`, the following will write the string `"Hello friend."` to the file connected to that stream:

```
outputStream.writeUTF("Hello friend.");
```

You may write output of different types to the same file. So, you may write a combination of, for example, `int`, `double`, and `String` values. However, mixing types in a file does require special care to make it possible to read them back out of the file. To read them back, you need to know the order in which the various types appear in the file, because, as you will see, a program that reads from the file will use a different method to read data of each different type.

closing a binary file

Note that, as illustrated in Display 10.13 and as you will see shortly, you close a binary output or input stream in the same way that you close a stream connected to a text file.

UTF and `writeUTF`

Recall that Java uses the Unicode character set, which is a set of characters that includes many characters used in languages whose character sets are different from English. Readers of this book are undoubtedly using editors and operating systems that use the ASCII character set, which is the character set normally used for English and for our Java programs. The ASCII character set is a subset of the Unicode character set, so the Unicode character set has a lot of characters you probably do not need. There is a standard way of encoding all the Unicode characters, but for English-speaking countries, it is not a very efficient coding scheme. The UTF coding scheme is an alternative scheme that still codes all Unicode characters, but that favors the ASCII character set. The UTF coding method gives short, efficient codes for the ASCII characters. The price is that it gives long, inefficient codes to the other Unicode characters. However, because you probably do not use the other Unicode characters, this is a very favorable trade-off. The method `writeUTF` uses the UTF coding method to write strings to a binary file.

The method `writeInt` writes integers into a file using the same number of bytes—that is, the same number of zeros and ones—to store any integer. Similarly, the method `writeLong` uses the same number of bytes to store each value of type `long`. (But the methods `writeInt` and `writeLong` use a different number of bytes from each other.) The situation is the same for all the other write methods that write primitive types to binary files. However, the method `writeUTF` uses differing numbers of bytes to store different strings in a file. Longer strings require more bytes than shorter strings. This can present a problem to Java, because there are no separators between data items in a binary file. The way that Java manages to make this work is by writing some extra information at the start of each string. This extra information tells how many bytes are used to write the string, so `readUTF` knows how many bytes to read and convert. (The method `readUTF` will be discussed a little later in this chapter, but, as you may have already guessed, it reads a `String` value that was written using the UTF coding method.)

The situation with `writeUTF` is even a little more complicated than what we discussed in the previous paragraph. Notice that we said that the information at the start of the string code in the file tells how many *bytes* to read, *not how many characters are in the string*. These two figures are not the same. With the UTF way of encoding, different characters are encoded in different numbers of bytes. However, all the ASCII characters are stored in just one byte, and you are undoubtedly using only ASCII characters, so this difference is more theoretical than real to you now.

Reading Simple Data from a Binary File

The stream class `ObjectInputStream` is used to read from a file that has been written to using `ObjectOutputStream`. Display 10.15 gives some of the most commonly used methods for this class. If you compare that table with the methods for `ObjectOutputStream` given in Display 10.14, you will see that each output method in `ObjectOutputStream` has a corresponding input method in `ObjectInputStream`. For example, if you write an integer to a file using the method `writeInt` of `ObjectOutputStream`, then you can read that integer back with the method `readInt` of `ObjectInputStream`. If you write a number to a file using the method `writeDouble` of `ObjectOutputStream`, then you can read that number back with the method `readDouble` of `ObjectInputStream`, and so forth. Display 10.16 gives an example of using `readInt` in this way.

MyProgrammingLab™

Self-Test Exercises

28. How do you open the binary file `bindata.dat` so that it is connected to an output stream of type `ObjectOutputStream` that is named `outputThisWay`?

29. Give two statements that will write the values of the two `double` variables `v1` and `v2` to the file `bindata.dat`. Use the stream `outputThisWay` that you created as the answer to Self-Test Exercise 28.

30. Give a statement that will write the string value `"Hello"` to the file `bindata.dat`. Use the stream `outputThisWay` that you created as the answer to Self-Test Exercise 28.

31. Give a statement that will close the stream `outputThisWay` created as the answer to Self-Test Exercise 28.

The input stream for reading from the binary file `numbers.dat` is opened as follows:

```
ObjectInputStream inputStream =
          new ObjectInputStream(new
          FileInputStream("numbers.dat"));
```

Note that this is identical to how we opened a file using `ObjectOutputStream` in Display 10.13, except that here we have used the classes `ObjectInputStream` and `FileInputStream` instead of `ObjectOutputStream` and `FileOutputStream`.

Opening a Binary File for Reading

Create a stream of the class `ObjectInputStream` and connect it to a binary file as follows:

SYNTAX

```
ObjectInputStream Input_Stream_Name =
      new ObjectInputStream(new FileInputStream(File_Name));
```

The constructor for `FileInputStream` may throw a `FileNotFoundException`, which is a kind of `IOException`. If the `FileInputStream` constructor succeeds, then the constructor for `ObjectInputStream` may throw a different `IOException`.

EXAMPLES

```
ObjectInputStream inputFile =
      new ObjectInputStream(new
      FileInputStream("somefile.dat"));
```

After this, you can use the methods in Display 10.15 to read from the file.

Display 10.15 Some Methods in the Class `ObjectInputStream` (part 1 of 3)

The classes `ObjectInputStream` and `FileInputStream` are in the `java.io` package.

```
public ObjectInputStream(InputStream streamObject)
```

There is no constructor that takes a file name as an argument. If you want to create a stream using a file name, use

```
new ObjectInputStream(new FileInputStream(File_Name))
```

Alternatively, you can use an object of the class `File` in place of the *File_Name*, as follows:

```
new ObjectInputStream(new FileInputStream(File_Object))
```

The constructor for `FileInputStream` may throw a `FileNotFoundException`, which is a kind of `IOException`. If the `FileInputStream` constructor succeeds, then the constructor for `ObjectInputStream` may throw a different `IOException`.

Display 10.15 Some Methods in the Class `ObjectInputStream` (part 2 of 3)

```
public int readInt() throws IOException
```

Reads an `int` value from the input stream and returns that `int` value. If `readInt` tries to read a value from the file and that value was not written using the method `writeInt` of the class `ObjectOutputStream` (or written in some equivalent way), then problems will occur. If an attempt is made to read beyond the end of the file, an `EOFException` is thrown.

```
public int readShort() throws IOException
```

Reads a `short` value from the input stream and returns that `short` value. If `readShort` tries to read a value from the file and that value was not written using the method `writeShort` of the class `ObjectOutputStream` (or written in some equivalent way), then problems will occur. If an attempt is made to read beyond the end of the file, an `EOFException` is thrown.

```
public long readLong() throws IOException
```

Reads a `long` value from the input stream and returns that `long` value. If `readLong` tries to read a value from the file and that value was not written using the method `writeLong` of the class `ObjectOutputStream` (or written in some equivalent way), then problems will occur. If an attempt is made to read beyond the end of the file, an `EOFException` is thrown.

```
public double readDouble() throws IOException
```

Reads a `double` value from the input stream and returns that `double` value. If `readDouble` tries to read a value from the file and that value was not written using the method `writeDouble` of the class `ObjectOutputStream` (or written in some equivalent way), then problems will occur. If an attempt is made to read beyond the end of the file, an `EOFException` is thrown.

```
public float readFloat() throws IOException
```

Reads a `float` value from the input stream and returns that `float` value. If `readFloat` tries to read a value from the file and that value was not written using the method `writeFloat` of the class `ObjectOutputStream` (or written in some equivalent way), then problems will occur. If an attempt is made to read beyond the end of the file, an `EOFException` is thrown.

```
public char readChar() throws IOException
```

Reads a `char` value from the input stream and returns that `char` value. If `readChar` tries to read a value from the file and that value was not written using the method `writeChar` of the class `ObjectOutputStream` (or written in some equivalent way), then problems will occur. If an attempt is made to read beyond the end of the file, an `EOFException` is thrown.

```
public boolean readBoolean() throws IOException
```

Reads a `boolean` value from the input stream and returns that `boolean` value. If `readBoolean` tries to read a value from the file and that value was not written using the method `writeBoolean` of the class `ObjectOutputStream` (or written in some equivalent way), then problems will occur. If an attempt is made to read beyond the end of the file, an `EOFException` is thrown.

(continued)

Display 10.15 Some Methods in the Class `ObjectInputStream` (part 3 of 3)

```
public String readUTF()throws IOException
```

Reads a `String` value from the input stream and returns that `String` value. If `readUTF` tries to read a value from the file and that value was not written using the method `writeUTF` of the class `ObjectOutputStream` (or written in some equivalent way), then problems will occur. If an attempt is made to read beyond the end of the file, an `EOFException` is thrown.

```
Object readObject() throws ClassNotFoundException, IOException
```

Reads an object from the input stream. The object read should have been written using `writeObject` of the class `ObjectOutputStream`. Throws a `ClassNotFoundException` if a serialized object cannot be found. If an attempt is made to read beyond the end of the file, an `EOFException` is thrown. May throw various other `IOExceptions`.

```
public int skipBytes(int n) throws IOException
```

Skips `n` bytes.

```
public void close()throws IOException
```

Closes the stream's connection to a file.

reading multiple types

`ObjectInputStream` allows you to read input values of different types from the same file. So, you may read a combination of, for example, `int` values, `double` values, and `String` values. However, if the next data item in the file is not of the type expected by the reading method, the result is likely to be a mess. For example, if your program writes an integer using `writeInt`, then any program that reads that integer should read it using `readInt`. If you instead use `readLong` or `readDouble`, your program will misbehave.

closing a binary file

Note that, as illustrated in Display 10.16, you close a binary input stream in the same way that you close all the other I/O streams we have seen.

MyProgrammingLab™

Self-Test Exercises

32. Write code to open the binary file named `someStuff` and connect it to an `ObjectInputStream` object named `inputThing` so it is ready for reading.
33. Give a statement that will read a number of type `double` from the file `someStuff` and place the value in a variable named `number`. Use the stream `inputThing` that you created in Self-Test Exercise 32. (Assume the first thing written to the file was written using the method `writeDouble` of the class `ObjectOutputStream` and assume `number` is of type `double`.)
34. Give a statement that will close the stream `inputThing` created in Self-Test Exercise 32.
35. Can one program write a number to a file using `writeInt` and then have another program read that number using `readLong`? Can a program read that number using `readDouble`?
36. Can you use `readUTF` to read a string from a text file?

Display 10.16 Reading from a Binary File

```
import java.io.ObjectInputStream;
import java.io.FileInputStream;
import java.io.IOException;
import java.io.FileNotFoundException;

public class BinaryInputDemo
{
  public static void main(String[] args)
  {
     try
     {
         ObjectInputStream inputStream =
           new ObjectInputStream(new FileInputStream("numbers.dat"));

         System.out.println("Reading the file numbers.dat.");
         int n1 = inputStream.readInt();
         int n2 = inputStream.readInt();

         System.out.println("Numbers read from file:");
         System.out.println(n1);
         System.out.println(n2);
         inputStream.close();
     }
     catch(FileNotFoundException e)
     {
         System.out.println("Cannot find file numbers.dat.");
     }
     catch(IOException e)
     {
         System.out.println("Problems with input from numbers.dat.");
     }
     System.out.println("End of program.");
  }
}
```

Sample Dialogue

```
Reading the file numbers.dat.
Numbers read from file:
0
1
End of program.
```

Assumes the program in Display 10.13 was run to create the file `numbers.dat`.

Checking for the End of a Binary File

EOF-Exception

All of the ObjectInputStream methods that read from a binary file will throw an EOFException when they try to read beyond the end of a file. So, your code can test for the end of a binary file by catching an EOFException as illustrated in Display 10.17.

In Display 10.17, the reading is placed in an "infinite loop" through the use of true as the Boolean expression in the while loop. The loop is not really infinite, because when the end of the file is reached, an exception is thrown, and that ends the entire try block and passes control to the catch block.

> **EOFException**
>
> If your program is reading from a binary file using any of the methods listed in Display 10.15 for the class ObjectInputStream, and your program attempts to read beyond the end of the file, then an EOFException is thrown. This can be used to end a loop that reads all the data in a file.
>
> The class EOFException is a derived class of the class IOException. So, every exception of type EOFException is also of type IOException.

Display 10.17 Using **EOFException** (part 1 of 2)

```
import java.io.ObjectInputStream;
import java.io.FileInputStream;
import java.io.EOFException;
import java.io.IOException;
import java.io.FileNotFoundException;

public class EOFDemo
{
    public static void main(String[] args)
    {
        try
        {
            ObjectInputStream inputStream =
              new ObjectInputStream(new FileInputStream("numbers.dat"));
            int number;
            System.out.println("Reading numbers in numbers.dat");
            try
            {
                while (true)
                {
                    number = inputStream.readInt( );
                    System.out.println(number);
                }
            }
```

Display 10.17 Using `EOFException` (part 2 of 2)

```
            catch(EOFException e)
            {
                System.out.println("No more numbers in the file.");
            }
            inputStream.close();
        }
        catch(FileNotFoundException e)
        {
            System.out.println("Cannot find file numbers.dat.");
        }
        catch(IOException e)
        {
            System.out.println("Problem with input from file
            numbers.dat.");
        }
    }
}
```

Sample Dialogue

```
Reading numbers in numbers.dat
0
1
2
3
4
No more numbers in the file.
```

Assumes the program in Display 10.13 was run to create the file `numbers.dat`.

PITFALL: Checking for the End of a File in the Wrong Way

Different file-reading methods check for the end of a file in different ways. If you test for the end of a file in the wrong way, one of two things will probably happen: Your program will either go into an unintended infinite loop, or it will terminate abnormally.

For the classes discussed in this book , the following rules apply: If your program is reading from a binary file, then an `EOFException` will be thrown when the reading goes beyond the end of the file. If your program is reading from a text file, then no `EOFException` will be thrown when reading goes beyond the end of the file. ■

MyProgrammingLab™

Self-Test Exercises

37. When opening a binary file for output in the ways discussed in this chapter, might an exception be thrown? What kind of exception? When opening a binary file for input in the ways discussed in this chapter, might an exception be thrown? What kind of exception?

38. Suppose a binary file contains three numbers written to the file with the method `writeDouble` of the class `ObjectOutputStream`. Suppose further that your program reads all three numbers with three invocations of the method `readDouble` of the class `ObjectInputStream`. When will an `EOFException` be thrown? Right after reading the third number? When your program tries to read a fourth number? Some other time?

39. The following appears in the program in Display 10.17:

```
try
{
   while (true)
   {
      number = inputStream.readInt();
      System.out.println(number);
   }
}
catch(EOFException e)
{
     System.out.println("No more numbers in the file.");
}
```

Why isn't this an infinite loop?

Binary I/O of Objects

You can output objects of classes you define as easily as you output `int` values using `writeInt`, and you can later read the objects back into your program as easily as you read `int` values with the method `readInt`. For you to be able to do this, the class of objects that your code is writing and reading must implement the `Serializable` interface.

`Serializable` interface

We will discuss interfaces in general in Chapter 13. However, the `Serializable` interface is particularly easy to use and requires no knowledge of interfaces. All you need to do to make a class implement the `Serializable` interface is add the two words `implements Serializable` to the heading of the class definition, as in the following example:

```
public class Person implements Serializable
{
```

The `Serializable` interface is in the same `java.io` package that contains all the I/O classes we have discussed in this chapter. For example, in Display 10.18, we define a toy class named `SomeClass` that implements the `Serializable` interface. We will explain the effect of the `Serializable` interface a bit later in this chapter, but first let's see how you do binary file I/O with a serializable class, such as this class `SomeClass` in Display 10.18.

Display 10.19 illustrates how class objects can be written to and read from a binary file. To write an object of a class such as `SomeClass` to a binary file, simply use the method `writeObject` of the class `ObjectOutputStream`. You use `writeObject` in the same way that you use the other methods of the class `ObjectOutputStream`, such as `writeInt`, but you use an object as the argument.

writeObject

If an object is written to a file with `writeObject`, then it can be read back out of the file with `readObject` of the stream class `ObjectInputStream`, as also illustrated in Display 10.19. The method `readObject` returns its value as an object of type `Object`. If you want to use the values retuned by `readObject` as an object of a class such as `SomeClass`, you must do a type cast, as shown in Display 10.19.

readObject

The `Serializable` Interface

serializable

A class that implements the `Serializable` interface is said to be a **serializable** class. To use objects of a class with `writeObject` and `readObject`, that class must be serializable. But to make the class serializable, we change nothing in the class. All we do is add the phrase `implements Serializable`. This phrase tells the run-time system that it is OK to treat objects of the class in a particular way when doing file I/O. If a class is

Display 10.18 A Serializable Class

```java
import java.io.Serializable;

public class SomeClass implements Serializable
{
    private int number;
    private char letter;

    public SomeClass()
    {
        number = 0;
        letter = 'A';
    }

    public SomeClass(int theNumber, char theLetter)
    {
        number = theNumber;
        letter = theLetter;
    }
    public String toString()
    {
        return "Number = " + number
                           + " Letter = " + letter;
    }
}
```

Display 10.19 **Binary File I/O of Objects** (part 1 of 2)

```
import java.io.ObjectOutputStream;
import java.io.FileOutputStream;
import java.io.ObjectInputStream;
import java.io.FileInputStream;
import java.io.IOException;
import java.io.FileNotFoundException;

/**
 Demonstrates binary file I/O of serializable class objects.
*/
public class ObjectIODemo
{
   public static void main(String[] args)
   {
       try
       {
           ObjectOutputStream outputStream =
              new ObjectOutputStream(new FileOutputStream("datafile"));

           SomeClass oneObject = new SomeClass(1, 'A');
           SomeClass anotherObject = new SomeClass(42, 'Z');

           outputStream.writeObject(oneObject);
           outputStream.writeObject(anotherObject);

           outputStream.close();

           System.out.println("Data sent to file.");
       }
       catch(IOException e)
       {
          System.out.println("Problem with file output.");
       }

       System.out.println(
               "Now let's reopen the file and display the data.");
       try
       {
           ObjectInputStream inputStream =
             new ObjectInputStream(new FileInputStream("datafile"));

          SomeClass readOne = (SomeClass)inputStream.readObject( );
          SomeClass readTwo = (SomeClass)inputStream.readObject( );

          System.out.println("The following were read from the file:");
          System.out.println(readOne);
          System.out.println(readTwo);
       }
       catch(FileNotFoundException e)
       {
           System.out.println("Cannot find datafile.");
       }
```

Notice the type casts.

Display 10.19 **Binary File I/O of Objects** (part 2 of 2)

```
        catch(ClassNotFoundException e)
        {
            System.out.println("Problems with file input.");
        }
        catch(IOException e)
        {
            System.out.println("Problems with file input.");
        }
            System.out.println("End of program.");
    }
}
```

Sample Dialogue

```
Data sent to file.
Now let's reopen the file and display the data.
The following were read from the file:
Number = 1 Letter = A
Number = 42 Letter = Z
End of program.
```

serializable, Java assigns a serial number to each object of the class that it writes to a stream of type `ObjectOutputStream`. If the same object is written to the stream more than once, then after the first time, Java writes only the serial number for the object and not a full description of the object's data. This makes file I/O more efficient and makes the files smaller. When read back out with a stream of type `ObjectInputStream`, duplicate serial numbers are returned as references to the same object. Note that this means that if two variables contain references to the same object and you write the objects to the file and later read them from the file, then the two objects that are read will again be references to the same object. So nothing in the structure of your object data is lost when you write the objects to the file and later read them back.

class instance variables

When a serializable class has instance variables of a class type, then the classes for the instance variables must also be serializable, and so on for all levels of **class instance variables** within classes. So, a class is not serializable unless the classes for all instance variables are also serializable.

Why aren't all classes made serializable? For security reasons. The serial number system makes it easier for programmers to get access to the object data written to secondary storage. Also, for some classes, it may not make sense to write objects to secondary storage, because they would be meaningless when read out again later. For example, if the object contains system-dependent data, the data may be meaningless when later read out.

PITFALL: Mixing Class Types in the Same File

The best way to write and read objects using `ObjectOutputStream` and `ObjectInputStream` is to store only data of one class type in any one file. If you store objects of multiple class types or even objects of only one class type mixed in with primitive type data, it has been our experience that the system can get confused and you could lose data. ■

Array Objects in Binary Files

An array is an object and hence a suitable argument for `writeObject`. An entire array can be saved to a binary file using `writeObject` and later read using `readObject`. When doing so, if the array has a base type that is a class, then the class must be serializable. This means that if you store all your data for one serializable class in a single array, then you can output all your data to a binary file with one invocation of `writeObject`.

This way of storing an array in a binary file is illustrated in Display 10.20. Note that the base class type, `SomeClass`, is serializable. Also, notice the type cast that uses the array type `SomeClass[]`. Because `readObject` returns its value as an object of type `Object`, it must be type cast to the correct array type.

MyProgrammingLab™

Self-Test Exercises

40. How do you make a class implement the `Serializable` interface?

41. What import statement do you need to be able to use the `Serializable` interface?

42. What is the return type for the method `readObject` of the class `ObjectInputStream`?

43. Is an array of type `Object`?

Display 10.20 **File I/O of an Array Object** (part 1 of 3)

```
import java.io.ObjectOutputStream;
import java.io.FileOutputStream;
import java.io.ObjectInputStream;
import java.io.FileInputStream;
import java.io.IOException;
import java.io.FileNotFoundException;

public class ArrayIODemo
{

    public static void main(String[] args)
```

Display 10.20 **File I/O of an Array Object** (part 2 of 3)

```
    {
        SomeClass[] a = new SomeClass[2];
        a[0] = new SomeClass(1, 'A');
        a[1] = new SomeClass(2, 'B');

        try
        {
            ObjectOutputStream outputStream =
                new ObjectOutputStream(new FileOutputStream("arrayfile"));
            outputStream.writeObject(a);
            outputStream.close( );
        }
        catch(IOException e)
        {
            System.out.println("Error writing to file.");
            System.exit(0);
        }

         System.out.println(
                 "Array written to file arrayfile.");

        System.out.println(
              "Now let's reopen the file and display the array.");

        SomeClass[] b = null ;

        try
        {
            ObjectInputStream inputStream =
                new ObjectInputStream(new FileInputStream("arrayfile"));
            b = (SomeClass[])inputStream.readObject();
            inputStream.close();
        }
        catch(FileNotFoundException e)
        {
           System.out.println("Cannot find file arrayfile.");
           System.exit(0);
        }
        catch(ClassNotFoundException e)
        {
            System.out.println("Problems with file input.");
            System.exit(0);
        }
        catch(IOException e)
        {
            System.out.println("Problems with file input.");
            System.exit(0);
        }
        System.out.println(
              "The following array elements were read from the file:");
        int i;
```

Notice the type cast.

(continued)

Display 10.20 File I/O of an Array Object (part 3 of 3)

```
            for (i = 0; i < b.length; i++)
               System.out.println(b[i]);
          System.out.println("End of program.");
        }
  }
```

Sample Dialogue

```
Array written to file arrayfile.
Now let's reopen the file and display the array.
The following array elements were read from the file:
Number = 1 Letter = A
Number = 2 Letter = B
End of program.
```

10.5 Random Access to Binary Files ★

Anytime, anywhere.

Common response to a challenge for a confrontation

The streams for sequential access to files, which we discussed in the previous sections of this chapter, are the ones most often used for file access in Java. However, some applications that require very rapid access to records in very large databases require some sort of random access to particular parts of a file. Such applications might best be done with specialized database software. But perhaps you are given the job of writing such a package in Java, or perhaps you are just curious about how such things are done in Java. Java does provide for random access to files so that your program can both read from and write to random locations in a file. In this section, we will describe simple uses of random access to files.

Reading and Writing to the Same File

If you want random access to both read and write to a file in Java, use the stream class `RandomAccessFile`, which is in the `java.io` package like all other file I/O classes.

file pointer

A random access file consists of a sequence of numbered bytes. There is a kind of marker called the **file pointer** that is always positioned at one of these bytes. All reads and writes take place starting at the location of the file pointer. You can move the file pointer to a new location with the method `seek`.

Although a random access file is byte oriented, there are methods to allow for reading or writing values of the primitive types and of string values to a random access file. In fact, these are the same methods as those we already used for sequential access files, as previously discussed. A `RandomAccessFile` stream has methods `writeInt`, `writeDouble`, `writeUTF`, and so forth, as well as methods `readInt`, `readDouble`,

Display 10.21 Some Methods of the Class `RandomAccessFile` (part 1 of 3)

The class `RandomAccessFile` is in the `java.io` package.

```
public RandomAccessFile(String fileName, String mode)

public RandomAccessFile(File fileObject, String mode)
```

Opens the file, does not delete data already in the file, but does position the file pointer at the first (zeroth) location.

The mode must be one of the following:

`"r"` Open for reading only.
`"rw"` Open for reading and writing.
`"rws"` Same as `"rw"`, and also requires that every update to the file's content or metadata be written synchronously to the underlying storage device.
`"rwd"` Same as `"rw"`, and also requires that every update to the file's content be written synchronously to the underlying storage device.
`"rws"` and `"rwd"` are not covered in this book text.

```
public long getFilePointer() throws IOException
```

Returns the current location of the file pointer. Locations are numbered starting with 0.

```
public void seek(long location) throws IOException
```

Moves the file pointer to the specified `location`.

```
public long length() throws IOException
```

Returns the length of the file.

```
public void setLength(long newLength) throws IOException
```

Sets the length of this file.

If the present length of the file as returned by the `length` method is greater than the `newLength` argument, then the file will be truncated. In this case, if the file pointer location as returned by the `getFilePointer` method is greater than `newLength`, then after this method returns, the file pointer location will be equal to `newLength`.

If the present `length` of the file as returned by the `length` method is smaller than `newLength`, then the file will be extended. In this case, the contents of the extended portion of the file are not defined.

```
public void close() throws IOException
```

Closes the stream's connection to a file.

```
public void write(int b) throws IOException
```

Writes the specified byte to the file.

```
public void write(byte [] a) throws IOException
```

Writes `a.length` bytes from the specified byte array to the file.

(continued)

Display 10.21 Some Methods of the Class `RandomAccessFile` (part 2 of 3)

```
public final void writeByte(byte b) throws IOException
```

Writes the `byte` b to the file.

```
public final void writeShort(short n) throws IOException
```

Writes the `short` n to the file.

```
public final void writeInt(int n) throws IOException
```

Writes the `int` n to the file.

```
public final void writeLong(long n) throws IOException
```

Writes the `long` n to the file.

```
public final void writeDouble(double d) throws IOException
```

Writes the `double` d to the file.

```
public final void writeFloat(float f) throws IOException
```

Writes the `float` f to the file.

```
public final void writeChar(char c) throws IOException
```

Writes the `char` c to the file.

```
public final void writeBoolean(boolean b) throws IOException
```

Writes the `boolean` b to the file.

```
public final void writeUTF(String s) throws IOException
```

Writes the `String` s to the file.

```
public int read()throws IOException
```

Reads a byte of data from the file and returns it as an integer in the range 0 to 255.

```
public int read(byte [] a) throws IOException
```

Reads `a.length` bytes of data from the file into the array of bytes `a`. Returns the number of bytes read or -1 if the end of the file is encountered.

```
public final byte readByte()throws IOException
```

Reads a `byte` value from the file and returns that value. If an attempt is made to read beyond the end of the file, an `EOFException` is thrown.

```
public final short readShort()throws IOException
```

Reads a `short` value from the file and returns that value. If an attempt is made to read beyond the end of the file, an `EOFException` is thrown.

Display 10.21 Some Methods of the Class `RandomAccessFile` (part 3 of 3)

```
public final int readInt) throws IOException
```

Reads an `int` value from the file and returns that value. If an attempt is made to read beyond the end of the file, an `EOFException` is thrown.

```
public final long readLong()throws IOException
```

Reads a `long` value from the file and returns that value. If an attempt is made to read beyond the end of the file, an `EOFException` is thrown.

```
public final double readDouble()throws IOException
```

Reads a `double` value from the file and returns that value. If an attempt is made to read beyond the end of the file, an `EOFException` is thrown.

```
public final float readFloat()throws IOException
```

Reads a `float` value from the file and returns that value. If an attempt is made to read beyond the end of the file, an `EOFException` is thrown.

```
public final char readChar()throws IOException
```

Reads a `char` value from the file and returns that value. If an attempt is made to read beyond the end of the file, an `EOFException` is thrown.

```
public final boolean readBoolean()throws IOException
```

Reads a `boolean` value from the file and returns that value. If an attempt is made to read beyond the end of the file, an `EOFException` is thrown.

```
public final String readUTF()throws IOException
```

Reads a `String` value from the file and returns that value. If an attempt is made to read beyond the end of the file, an `EOFException` is thrown.

`readUTF`, and so on. However, the class `RandomAccessFile` does not have the methods `writeObject` or `readObject`. The most important methods of the class `RandomAccessFile` are given in Display 10.21. A demonstration program for random access files is given in Display 10.22.

opening a file

The constructor for `RandomAccessFile` takes either a string name for the file or an object of the class `File` as its first argument. The second argument must be one of the four strings `"rw"`, `"r"`, and two modes we do not discuss in this book, `"rws"` and `"rwd"`. The string `"rw"` means your code can both read and write to the file after it is open. The string `"r"` means your code can read from the file but cannot write to the file.

If the file already exists, then when it is opened, the length is not reset to `0`, but the file pointer will be positioned at the start of the file, which is what you would expect at least for `"r"`. If the length of the file is not what you want, you can change it with the method `setLength`. In particular, you can use `setLength` to empty the file.

Display 10.22 **Random Access to a File** (part 1 of 2)

```
import java.io.RandomAccessFile;
import java.io.IOException;
import java.io.FileNotFoundException;

public class RandomAccessDemo
{
   public static void main(String[] args)
   {
      try
      {
         RandomAccessFile ioStream =
            new RandomAccessFile("bytedata", "rw");

         System.out.println("Writing 3  bytes to the file bytedata.");
         ioStream.writeByte(1);
         ioStream.writeByte(2);
         ioStream.writeByte(3);
         System.out.println("The length of the file is now = "
                            + ioStream.length());
         System.out.println("The file pointer location is "
                            + ioStream.getFilePointer());

         System.out.println("Moving the file pointer to location 1.");
         ioStream.seek(1);
         byte oneByte = ioStream.readByte();
         System.out.println("The value at location 1 is " + oneByte);
         oneByte = ioStream.readByte();
         System.out.println("The value at the next location is "
                           + oneByte);

         System.out.println("Now we move the file pointer back to");
         System.out.println("location 1, and change the byte.");
         ioStream.seek(1);
         ioStream.writeByte(9);
         ioStream.seek(1);
         oneByte = ioStream.readByte();
         System.out.println("The value at location 1 is now "
                           + oneByte);

         System.out.println("Now we go to the end of the file");
         System.out.println("and write a double.");
         ioStream.seek(ioStream.length());
         ioStream.writeDouble(41.99);
         System.out.println("The length of the file is now = "
                           + ioStream.length());
```

Display 10.22 **Random Access to a File** (part 2 of 2)

```
            System.out.println("Returning to location 3,");
            System.out.println("where we wrote the double.");
            ioStream.seek(3);
            double oneDouble = ioStream.readDouble();
            System.out.println("The double value at location 3  is "
                                                  + oneDouble);

            ioStream.close();
        }
        catch(FileNotFoundException e)
        {
             System.out.println("Problem opening file.");
        }
        catch(IOException e)
        {
             System.out.println("Problems with file I/O.");
        }
        System.out.println("End of program.");
    }
}
```

The location of `readDouble` *must be a location where* `writeDouble` *wrote to the file.*

The dialog assumes the file `bytedata` *did not exist before the program was run.*

Sample Dialogue

```
Writing 3 bytes to the file bytedata.
The length of the file is now = 3
The file pointer location is 3
Moving the file pointer to location 1.
The value at location 1 is 2
The value at the next location is 3
Now we move the file pointer back to
location 1, and change the byte.
The value at location 1 is now 9
Now we go to the end of the file
and write a double.
The length of the file is now = 11
Returning to location 3,
where we wrote the double.
The double value at location 3 is 41.99
End of program.
```

Byte locations are numbered starting with zero.

Three 1-byte values and 1 `double` *value that uses 8 bytes = 11 bytes total.*

PITFALL: `RandomAccessFile` Need Not Start Empty

If a file already exists, then when it is opened with `RandomAccessFile`, the length is not reset to `0`, but the file pointer will be positioned at the start of the file. So, old data in the file is not lost and the file pointer is set for the most likely position for reading, not the most likely position for writing.

MyProgrammingLab™

Self-Test Exercises

44. If you run the program in Display 10.22 a second time, will the output be the same?

45. How can you modify the program in Display 10.22 so the file always starts out empty?

Chapter Summary

- Files that are considered to be strings of characters and that look like characters to your program and your editor are called *text files*. Files whose contents must be handled as strings of binary digits are called *binary files*.
- You can use the class `PrintWriter` to write to a text file and can use the class `Scanner` or `BufferedReader` to read from a text file.
- The class `File` can be used to check whether there is a file with a given name. It can also check whether your program is allowed to read the file and/or allowed to write to the file.
- Your program can use the class `ObjectOutputStream` to write to a binary file and can use the class `ObjectInputStream` to read from a binary file.
- Your program can use the method `writeObject` of the class `ObjectOutputStream` to write class objects to a binary file. The objects can be read back with the method `readObject` of the class `ObjectInputStream`.
- To use the method `writeObject` of the class `ObjectOutputStream` or the method `readObject` of the class `ObjectInputStream`, the class whose objects are written to a file must implement the `Serializable` interface.
- The way that you test for the end of a file depends on whether your program is reading from a text file or a binary file.
- You can use the class `RandomAccessFile` to create a stream that gives random access to the bytes in a file.

Answers to Self-Test Exercises

1. With an input stream, data flows from a file or input device to your program. With an output stream, data flows from your program to a file or output device.

2. A binary file contains data that is processed as binary data. A text file allows your program and editor to view the file as if it contained a sequence of characters. A text file can be viewed with an editor, whereas a binary file cannot.

3. A `FileNotFoundException` would be thrown if the file cannot be opened because, for example, there is already a directory (folder) named `stuff.txt`. Note that if the file does not exist but can be created, then no exception is thrown. If you answered `IOException`, you are not wrong, because a `FileNotFoundException` is an `IOException`. However, the better answer is the more specific exception class—namely, `FileNotFoundException`.

4. No. This is why we use an object of the class `FileOutputStream` as an argument. The correct way to express the code displayed in the question is as follows:

```
PrintWriter outputStream =
      new PrintWriter(new FileOutputStream("stuff.txt"));
```

5.
```
PrintWriter outputStream =
      new PrintWriter(new FileOutputStream("sam");
```

6.
```
PrintWriter outStream =
      new PrintWriter(new FileOutputStream("sam", true ));
```

7. Yes, it will send suitable output to the text file because the class `Person` has a well-defined `toString()` method.

8.
```
Scanner fileIn =
        new Scanner(new FileInputStream("sally"));
```

9. It throws a `NoSuchElementException` if there are no more tokens. It throws an `InputMismatchException` if the next token is not a well-formed string representation of an `int`. It throws an `IllegalStateException` if the `Scanner` stream is closed.

10. No. Reading may have reached the end of the file, but another possibility is that the next token may not be a well-formed string representation of an `int` value.

11. The `FileInputStream` constructor, and thus the `Scanner` constructor invocation, can throw a `FileNotFoundException`. This exception needs to be caught or declared in a `throws` clause.

12.
```
BufferedReader fileIn =
                  new BufferedReader(new FileReader("joe"));
```

13. The method `readLine` returns a value of type `String`. The method `read` reads a single *character*, but it returns it as a value of type `int`. To get the value to be of type `char`, you need to do a type cast.

14. Both `read` and `readLine` in the class `BufferedReader` might throw an `IOException`.

15. The `try` block in Display 10.7 is larger so that it includes the invocations of the method `readLine`, which might throw an `IOException`. The method `println` in Display 10.1 does not throw any exceptions that must be caught.

16. Yes.

17. No, you must read the number as a string and then convert the string to a number with `Integer.parseInt` (or in some other way).

18. When the method `readLine` tries to read beyond the end of a file, it returns the value `null`. Thus, you can test for the end of a file by testing for `null`.

19. The method `read` reads a single *character*, but it returns it as a value of type `int`. To get the value to be of type `char`, you need to do a type cast.

20. When the method `read` tries to read beyond the end of a file, it returns the value `-1`. Thus, you can test for the end of a file by testing for the value `-1`. This works because all "real" characters return a positive `int` value.

21. Yes, if `original.txt` is an empty file, then the file `numbered.txt` produced by the program will also be empty.

22. Only the classes `FileReader` and `FileOutputStream` have a constructor that accepts a file name as an argument. (Although we have not discussed it, the class `Scanner` has a constructor that takes a `String` argument, but the argument is not a file name.)

23. Yes, it is legal.

24. Replace

```
System.setErr(errStream);
```

with

```
System.setOut(errStream);
```

25. Add

```
System.setOut(errStream);
```

to get

```
System.setErr(errStream);
System.setOut(errStream);
```

26.
```
import java.io.File;
public class FileExercise
{
    public static void main(String[] args)
    {
        File fileObject =new File("Sally.txt");
```

```
            if (fileObject.exists())
                System.out.println(
                    "There is a file named Sally.txt.");
            else
                System.out.println(
                    "There is no file named Sally.txt.");
        }
    }
```

27.
```
import java.io.IOException;
import java.io.File;
import java.util.Scanner;

public class FileExercise2
{
    public static void main(String[] args)
    {
        Scanner keyboard = new Scanner(System.in);
        String fileName = null ;
        File fileObject = null ;

        try
        {
            System.out.print("Enter a file name and I will");
            System.out.println(" tell you if it exists.");
            fileName = keyboard.next();
            fileObject = new File(fileName);

            if (fileObject.exists())
            {
                System.out.println("There is a file named"
                                               + fileName);
                System.out.println("Delete the file? (y/n)");
                char answer = (char)System.in.read();

                if ((answer == 'y') || (answer == 'Y'))
                {
                    if (fileObject.delete())
                        System.out.println("File deleted.");
                    else
                        System.out.println(
                                      "Cannot delete file.");
                }
            }
            else
                System.out.println(
                               "No file named " + fileName);
        }
```

```
            catch(IOException e)
            {
                System.out.println(
                                "Error reading from keyboard.");
            }
        }
    }
```

28.
```
ObjectOutputStream outputThisWay =
                 new ObjectOutputStream(
                      new FileOutputStream("bindata.dat"));
```

29.
```
outputThisWay.writeDouble(v1);
outputThisWay.writeDouble(v2);
```

30. `outputThisWay.writeUTF("Hello");`

31. `outputThisWay.close();`

32.
```
ObjectInputStream inputThing =
                 new ObjectInputStream(
                      new FileInputStream("someStuff"));
```

33. `number = inputThing.readDouble();`

34. `inputThing.close();`

35. If a number is written to a file with `writeInt`, it should be read only with `readInt`. If you use `readLong` or `readDouble` to read the number, something will go wrong.

36. You should not use `readUTF` to read a string from a text file. You should use `readUTF` only to read a string from a binary file. Moreover, the string should have been written to that file using `writeUTF`.

37. When opening a binary file for either output or input in the ways discussed in this chapter, a `FileNotFoundException` might be thrown and other `IOExceptions` may be thrown.

38. An `EOFException` is thrown when your program tries to read the (nonexisting) fourth number.

39. It is not an infinite loop because when the end of the file is reached, an exception will be thrown, and that will end the entire `try` block.

40. You add the two words `implements Serializable` to the beginning of the class definition. You also must do this for the classes for the instance variables and so on for all levels of class instance variables within classes.

41. `import java.io.Serializable;` or `import java.io.*;`

42. The return type is `Object`, which means the returned value usually needs to be type cast.

43. Yes. That is why it is a legitimate argument for `writeObject`.

44. No. Each time the program is run, the file will get longer.

45. Add the following near the start of `main`:

```
ioStream.setLength(0);
```

MyProgrammingLab™

Programming Projects

Visit www.myprogramminglab.com to complete select exercises online and get instant feedback.

PROJECTS INVOLVING ONLY TEXT FILES

VideoNote **Solution to Programming Project 10.1**

1. The text files `boynames.txt` and `girlnames.txt`, which are included in the source code for this book text, contain a list of the 1,000 most popular boy and girl names in the United States for the year 2003 as compiled by the Social Security Administration.

   These are blank-delimited files, where the most popular name is listed first, the second most popular name is listed second, and so on, to the 1,000th most popular name, which is listed last. Each line consists of the first name followed by a blank space and then the number of registered births using that name in the year. For example, the `girlnames.txt` file begins with

   Emily 25494

   Emma 22532

   Madison 19986

   This indicates that Emily was the most popular name with 25,494 registered namings, Emma was the second most popular with 22,532, and Madison was the third most popular with 19,986.

   Write a program that reads both the girl and boy files into memory using arrays. Then, allow the user to input a name. The program should search through both arrays. If there is a match, then it should output the popularity ranking and the number of namings. The program should also indicate if there is no match.

   For example, if the user enters the name "Justice," then the program should output

   ```
   Justice is ranked 456 in popularity among girls with 655 namings.
   Justice is ranked 401 in popularity among boys with 653 namings.
   ```

   If the user enters the name "Walter," then the program should output

   ```
   Walter is not ranked among the top 1000 girl names.
   Walter is ranked 356 in popularity among boys with 775 namings.
   ```

2. Write a program that will search a text file of strings representing numbers of type `int` and will write the largest and the smallest numbers to the screen. The file contains nothing but strings representing numbers of type `int`, one per line.

3. Write a program that takes its input from a text file of strings representing numbers of type `double` and outputs the average of the numbers in the file to the screen. The file contains nothing but strings representing numbers of type `double`, one per line.

4. Write a program that takes its input from a text file of strings representing numbers of type `double`. The program outputs to the screen the average and standard deviation of the numbers in the file. The file contains nothing but strings representing numbers of type `double`, one per line. The standard deviation of a list of numbers n_1, n_2, n_3, and so forth is defined as the square root of the average of the following numbers:

   $(n_1 - a)^2$, $(n_2 - a)^2$, $(n_3 - a)^2$, and so forth.

   The number a is the average of the numbers n_1, n_2, n_3, and so forth. *Hint:* Write your program so that it first reads the entire file and computes the average of all the numbers, then closes the file, and then reopens the file and computes the standard deviation. You will find it helpful to first do Programming Project 10.3 and then modify that program in order to obtain the program for this project.

5. Write a program to edit text files for extra blanks. The program will replace any string of two or more blanks with a single blank. Your program should work as follows: Create a temporary file. Copy from the file to the temporary file but do not copy extra blanks. Copy the contents of the temporary file back into the original file. Use a method (or methods) in the class `File` to remove the temporary file. You will also want to use the class `File` for other things in your program. The temporary file should have a name that is different from all existing files so that the existing files are not affected (except for the file being edited). Your program will ask the user for the name of the file to be edited. However, it will not ask the user for the name of the temporary file but instead will generate the name within the program. You can generate the name any way that is clear and efficient. One possible way to generate the temporary file is to start with an unlikely name, such as `"TempX"`, and to append a character, such as `'X'`, until a name is found that does not name an existing file.

6. Write a program that gives and takes advice on program writing. The program starts by writing a piece of advice to the screen and asking the user to type in a different piece of advice. The program then ends. The next person to run the program receives the advice given by the person who last ran the program. The advice is kept in a text file and the content of the file changes after each run of the program. You can use your editor to enter the initial piece of advice in the file so that the first person who runs the program receives some advice. Allow the user to type in advice of any length so that it can be any number of lines long. The user is told to end his or her advice by pressing the Return key two times. Your program can then test to see that it has reached the end of the input by checking to see when it reads two consecutive occurrences of the character `'\n'`.

7. Write a class that keeps track of the top five high scores that could be used for a video game. Internally, the class should store the top scores in a data structure of your choice (the most straightforward way is to use arrays). Each entry consists of a name and a score. The data stored in memory should be synchronized with a text file for persistent storage. For example, here are the contents of a sample file where Ronaldo has the highest score and Pele has the third highest score:

```
Ronaldo
10400
Didier
9800
Pele
9750
Kaka
8400
Cristiano
8000
```

The constructor should test if the file exists. If it does not exist, then the file should be created with blank names for each of the players and a score of 0. If the file does exist, then the data from the file should be read into the class's instance variables. Along with appropriate constructors, accessors, and mutators, add the following methods:

- `void playerScore(String name, int score)`: Whenever a game is over, this method is called with the player's name and final score. If the name is one of the top five, then it should be added to the list and the lowest score should be dropped out. If the score is not in the top five, then nothing happens.
- `String[] getTopNames()`: Returns an array of the names of the top players, with the top player first, the second best player second, etc.
- `int[] getTopScores()`: Returns an array of the scores of the top players, with the highest score first, the second highest score second, etc.

Test your program with several calls to `playerScore` and print out the list of top names and scores to ensure that the correct values are stored. When the program is restarted, it should remember the top scores from the last session.

PROJECTS INVOLVING BINARY FILES

VideoNote **Solution to Programming Project 10.8**

8. Write a program that will search a binary file of numbers of type `int` and write the largest and the smallest numbers to the screen. The file contains nothing but numbers of type `int` written to the file with `writeInt`.
9. Write a program that takes its input from a binary file of numbers of type `double` and outputs the average of the numbers in the file to the screen. The file contains nothing but numbers of type `double` written to the file with `writeDouble`.
10. Write a program that takes its input from a binary file of numbers of type `double`. The file contains nothing but numbers of type `double` written to the file with `writeDouble`. The program outputs to the screen the average and standard deviation of the numbers in the file. The standard deviation of a list of numbers n_1, n_2, n_3, and so forth is defined as the square root of the average of the following numbers:

    $(n_1 - a)^2$, $(n_2 - a)^2$, $(n_3 - a)^2$, and so forth.

The number a is the average of the numbers n_1, n_2, n_3, and so forth. *Hint:* Write your program so that it first reads the entire file and computes the average of all the numbers, then closes the file, and then reopens the file and computes the standard deviation. You will find it helpful to first do Programming Project 10.8 and then modify that program in order to obtain the program for this project.

11. Change the definition of the class `Person` in Display 5.19 to be serializable. Note that this requires that you also change the class `Date`. Then write a program to maintain a binary file of records of people (records of type `Person`). Allow commands to delete a record specified by the person's name, to add a record, to retrieve and display a record, and to obtain all records of people within a specified age range. To obtain the age of a person, you need the current date. Your program will ask the user for the current date when the program begins. You can do this with random access files, but do not use random access files for this exercise. Use a file or files that record records with the method `writeObject` of the class `ObjectOutputStream`.

12. Programming Projects 6.12 and 6.13 asked you to write a program to play a simple trivia game consisting of five questions. The questions, answers, and point values were hardcoded into array(s). This programming project involves moving the trivia questions into one or more binary files instead, and then loading the trivia questions into memory when the program starts.

    First, write a program that allows an administrator to manage the questions for the trivia game. When the program is run, it should check to see if a data file exists. If the data file exists, then the trivia questions should be loaded from the data file into array(s) in memory. If the data file does not exist, start the program with no trivia questions in memory. The program should then present a menu that allows the administrator to list all trivia items (question, answer, and value) in the database, add a new trivia item, or delete an existing trivia item. Upon exiting the program, the trivia data in memory should be stored to one or more binary files using the `writeObject` method.

    Second, modify either solution to Programming Projects 6.12 or 6.13 to read in the trivia data from the binary file created by the administrator's program. Note that the game is no longer limited to five questions, since an arbitrary number of trivia items may be created by the administrator's program and stored in the binary file(s).

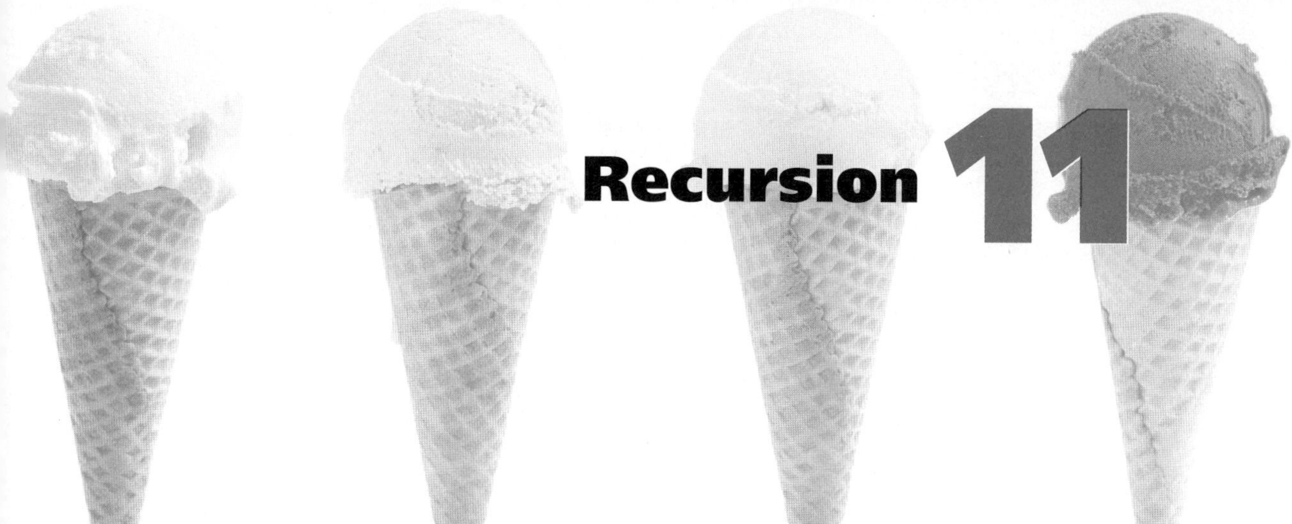

Recursion 11

11 Recursion

After a lecture on cosmology and the structure of the solar system, William James was accosted by a little old lady.

"Your theory that the sun is the center of the solar system, and the earth is a ball which rotates around it has a very convincing ring to it, Mr. James, but it's wrong. I've got a better theory," said the little old lady.

"And what is that, madam?" inquired James politely.

"That we live on a crust of earth which is on the back of a giant turtle."

Not wishing to demolish this absurd little theory by bringing to bear the masses of scientific evidence he had at his command, James decided to gently dissuade his opponent by making her see some of the inadequacies of her position.

"If your theory is correct, madam," he asked, "what does this turtle stand on?"

"You're a very clever man, Mr. James, and that's a very good question" replied the little old lady, "but I have an answer to it. And it is this: the first turtle stands on the back of a second, far larger, turtle, who stands directly under him."

"But what does this second turtle stand on?" persisted James patiently.

To this the little old lady crowed triumphantly. "It's no use, Mr. James— it's turtles all the way down."

J. R. ROSS, *Constraints on Variables in Syntax*

Introduction

recursive method

A method definition that includes a call to itself is said to be **recursive**. Like most modern programming languages, Java allows methods to be recursive; if used with a little care, this can be a useful programming technique. In this chapter, we introduce the basic techniques needed for defining successful recursive methods. There is nothing in this chapter that is truly unique to Java. If you are already familiar with recursion, you can safely skip this chapter. No new Java elements are introduced here.

Prerequisites

Except for the subsections on binary search and searching for a file, this chapter uses material only from Chapters 1–5. The subsection entitled "Binary Search" also uses the basic material on one-dimensional arrays from Chapter 6 and the Example entitled "Finding a File" uses material from the `File` class in Chapter 10.

You may postpone all or part of this chapter if you wish. Nothing in the rest of this book requires any of this chapter.

11.1 Recursive `void` Methods

I remembered too that night which is at the middle of the Thousand and One Nights when Scheherazade (through a magical oversight of the copyist) begins to relate word for word the story of the Thousand and One Nights, establishing the risk of coming once again to the night when she must repeat it, and thus to infinity.

JORGE LUIS BORGES, *The Garden of Forking Paths*

When you are writing a method to solve a task, one basic design technique is to break the task into subtasks. Sometimes it turns out that at least one of the subtasks is a smaller example of the same task. For example, if the task is to search a list for a particular value, you might divide this into the subtask of searching the first half of the list and the subtask of searching the second half of the list. The subtasks of searching the halves of the list are "smaller" versions of the original task. Whenever one subtask is a smaller version of the original task to be accomplished, you can solve the original task by using a recursive method. We begin with a simple example to illustrate this technique. (For simplicity, our examples are static methods; however, recursive methods need not be static.)

Recursion

In Java, a method definition may contain an invocation of the method being defined. In such cases, the method is said to be **recursive**.

EXAMPLE: Vertical Numbers

Display 11.1 contains a demonstration program for a recursive method named `writeVertical`, which takes one (nonnegative) `int` argument and writes that `int` to the screen with the digits going down the screen one per line. For example, the invocation

```
writeVertical(1234);
```

would produce the output

```
1
2
3
4
```

(continued)

Display 11.1 A Recursive `void` Method

```
public class RecursionDemo1
{
    public static void main(String[] args)
    {
        System.out.println("writeVertical(3):");
        writeVertical(3);

        System.out.println("writeVertical(12):");
        writeVertical(12);

        System.out.println("writeVertical(123):");
        writeVertical(123);
    }

    public static void writeVertical(int n)
    {
        if (n < 10)
        {
            System.out.println(n);
        }
        else //n is two or more digits long:
        {
            writeVertical(n / 10);
            System.out.println(n % 10);
        }
    }
}
```

Sample Dialogue

```
writeVertical(3):
3
writeVertical(12):
1
2
writeVertical(123):
1
2
3
```

EXAMPLE: (continued)

The task to be performed by `writeVertical` may be broken down into the following two subtasks:

Simple Case: If `n < 10`, then write the number `n` to the screen.

After all, if the number is only one digit long, the task is trivial.

Recursive Case: If `n >= 10`, then do two subtasks:

1. Output all the digits except the last digit.
2. Output the last digit.

For example, if the argument were `1234`, the first part would output

```
1
2
3
```

and the second part would output `4`. This decomposition of tasks into subtasks can be used to derive the method definition.

Subtask 1 is a smaller version of the original task, so we can implement this subtask with a recursive call. Subtask 2 is just the simple case we listed previously. Thus, an outline of our algorithm for the method `writeVertical` with parameter `n` is given by the following pseudocode:

```
if (n < 10)
{
    System.out.println(n);
}
else //n is two or more digits long:
{
    writeVertical(the number n with the last digit removed);
    System.out.println(the last digit of n);
}
```

Recursive subtask

If you observe the following identities, it is easy to convert this pseudocode to a complete Java method definition:

`n / 10` is the number `n` with the last digit removed.
`n % 10` is the last digit of `n`.

For example, `1234 / 10` evaluates to `123` and `1234 % 10` evaluates to `4`.

(continued)

EXAMPLE: (continued)

The following is the complete code for the method:

```
public static void writeVertical(int n)
{
    if (n < 10)
    {
        System.out.println(n);
    }
    else //n is two or more digits long:
    {
        writeVertical(n / 10);
        System.out.println(n % 10);
    }
}
```

Tracing a Recursive Call

Let's see exactly what happens when the following method call is made (as in Display 11.1):

```
writeVertical(123);
```

When this method call is executed, the computer proceeds just as it would with any method call. The argument `123` is substituted for the parameter `n`, and the body of the method is executed. After the substitution of `123` for `n`, the code to be executed is equivalent to

```
if (123 < 10)
{
    System.out.println(123);
}
else //n is two or more digits long:
{
    writeVertical(123 / 10);   <-- Computation will stop here until the recursive call returns.
    System.out.println(123 % 10);
}
```

Because `123` is not less than `10`, the `else` part is executed. However, the `else` part begins with the method call

```
writeVertical(n / 10);
```

which (because n is equal to 123) is the call

```
writeVertical(123 / 10);
```

which is equivalent to

```
writeVertical(12);
```

When execution reaches this recursive call, the current method computation is placed in suspended animation and this recursive call is executed. When this recursive call is finished, the execution of the suspended computation will return to this point and the suspended computation will continue from this point.

The recursive call

```
writeVertical(12);
```

is handled just like any other method call. The argument 12 is substituted for the parameter n, and the body of the method is executed. After substituting 12 for n, there are two computations, one suspended and one active, as follows:

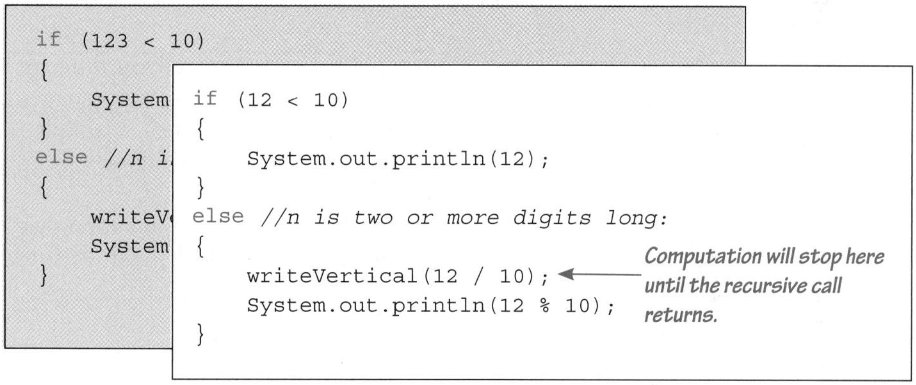
if (123 < 10)
{
System
}
else //n i
{
writeV
System
}
if (12 < 10)
{
System.out.println(12);
}
else //n is two or more digits long:
{
writeVertical(12 / 10);
System.out.println(12 % 10);
}
Computation will stop here until the recursive call returns.

Because 12 is not less than 10, the else part is executed. However, as you already saw, the else part begins with a recursive call. The argument for the recursive call is n/10, which in this case is equivalent to 12/10. So, this second computation of the method writeVertical is suspended, and the following recursive call is executed:

```
writeVertical(12 / 10);
```

which is equivalent to

```
writeVertical(1);
```

At this point, there are two suspended computations waiting to resume, and the computer begins to execute this new recursive call, which is handled just like all the previous recursive calls. The argument `1` is substituted for the parameter `n`, and the body of the method is executed. At this point, the computation looks like the following:

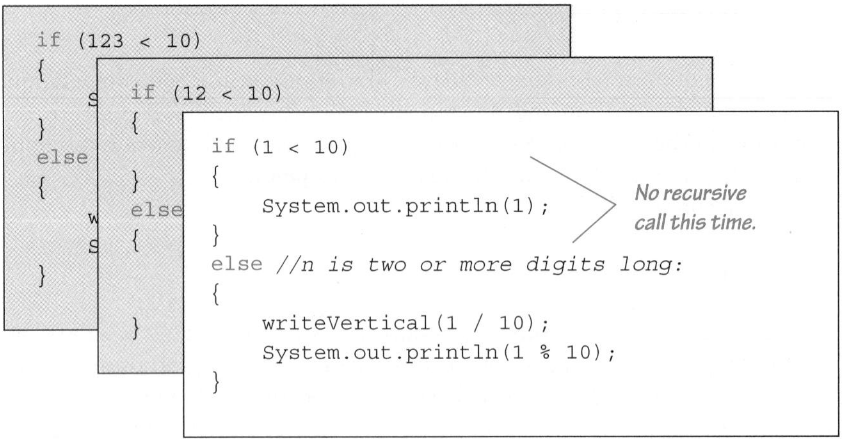
if (123 < 10)
if (12 < 10)
if (1 < 10)
{
System.out.println(1);
}
else //n is two or more digits long:
{
writeVertical(1 / 10);
System.out.println(1 % 10);
}
No recursive call this time.

output the digit 1

When the body of the method is executed this time, something different happens. Because `1` is less than `10`, the Boolean expression in the `if-else` statement is `true`, so the statement before the `else` is executed. That statement is simply an output statement that writes the argument `1` to the screen, so the call `writeVertical(1)` writes `1` to the screen and ends without any recursive call.

When the call `writeVertical(1)` ends, the suspended computation that is waiting for it to end resumes where that suspended computation left off, as shown by the following:

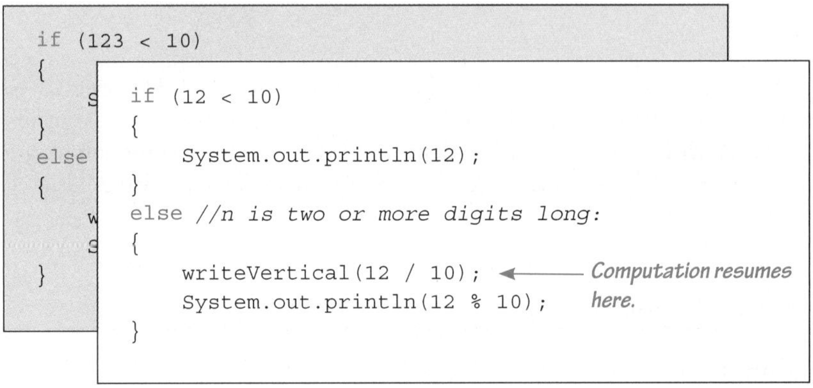
if (123 < 10)
if (12 < 10)
{
System.out.println(12);
}
else //n is two or more digits long:
{
writeVertical(12 / 10);
System.out.println(12 % 10);
}
Computation resumes here.

output the digit 2

When this suspended computation resumes, it executes an output statement that outputs the value `12 % 10`, which is `2`. That ends that computation, but there is yet another suspended computation waiting to resume. When this last suspended computation resumes, the situation is

```
if (123 < 10)
{
    System.out.println(123);
}
else //n is two or more digits long:
{
    writeVertical(123 / 10);<------   Computation resumes
    System.out.println(123 % 10);     here.
}
```

output the digit 3

When this last suspended computation resumes, it outputs the value `123 % 10`, which is `3`, and the execution of the original method call ends. And, sure enough, the digits `1`, `2`, and `3` have been written to the screen one per line, in that order.

A Closer Look at Recursion

The definition of the method `writeVertical` uses recursion. Yet, we did nothing new or different in evaluating the method call `writeVertical(123)`. We treated it just like any of the method calls we saw in previous chapters. We simply substituted the argument `123` for the parameter `n` and then executed the code in the body of the method definition. When we reached the recursive call

```
writeVertical(123 / 10)
```

we simply repeated this process one more time.

how recursion works

The computer keeps track of recursive calls in the following way. When a method is called, the computer plugs in the arguments for the parameter(s) and begins to execute the code. If it should encounter a recursive call, then it temporarily stops its computation, because it must know the result of the recursive call before it can proceed. It saves all the information it needs to continue the computation later on, and proceeds to evaluate the recursive call. When the recursive call is completed, the computer returns to finish the outer computation.

how recursion ends

The Java language places no restrictions on how recursive calls are used in method definitions. However, in order for a recursive method definition to be useful, it must be designed so that any call of the method must ultimately terminate with some piece of code that does not depend on recursion. The method may call itself, and that recursive call may call the method again. The process may be repeated any number of times. However, the process will not terminate unless eventually one of the recursive calls does not depend on recursion to return a value. The general outline of a successful recursive method definition is as follows:

- One or more cases in which the method accomplishes its task by using recursive call(s) to accomplish one or more smaller versions of the task.

base case

stopping case

- One or more cases in which the method accomplishes its task without the use of any recursive calls. These cases without any recursive calls are called **base cases** or **stopping cases**.

Often an `if-else` statement determines which of the cases will be executed. A typical scenario is for the original method call to execute a case that includes a recursive call. That recursive call may in turn execute a case that requires another recursive call. For some number of times, each recursive call produces another recursive call, but eventually one of the stopping cases should apply. *Every call of the method must eventually lead to a stopping case, or else the method call will never end because of an infinite chain of recursive calls.* (In practice, a call that includes an infinite chain of recursive calls will usually terminate abnormally rather than actually running forever.)

The most common way to ensure that a stopping case is eventually reached is to write the method so that some (positive) numeric quantity is decreased on each recursive call and to provide a stopping case for some "small" value. This is how we designed the method `writeVertical` in Display 11.1. When the method `writeVertical` is called, that call produces a recursive call with a smaller argument. This continues with each recursive call producing another recursive call until the argument is less than `10`. When the argument is less than `10`, the method call ends without producing any more recursive calls and the process works its way back to the original call and the process ends.

General Form of a Recursive Method Definition

The general outline of a successful recursive method definition is as follows:

- One or more cases that include one or more recursive calls to the method being defined. These recursive calls should solve "smaller" versions of the task performed by the method being defined.
- One or more cases that include no recursive calls. These cases without any recursive calls are called **base cases** or **stopping cases**.

PITFALL: Infinite Recursion

In the example of the method `writeVertical` discussed in the previous subsections, the series of recursive calls eventually reached a call of the method that did not involve recursion (that is, a stopping case was reached). If, on the other hand, every recursive call produces another recursive call, then a call to the method will, in theory, run forever. This is called **infinite recursion**. In practice, such a method will typically run until the computer runs out of resources and the program terminates abnormally.

Examples of infinite recursion are not hard to come by. The following is a syntactically correct Java method definition, which might result from an attempt to define an alternative version of the method `writeVertical`:

```
public static void newWriteVertical(int n)
{
        newWriteVertical(n / 10);
        System.out.println(n % 10);
}
```

If you embed this definition in a program that calls this method, the program will compile with no error messages and you can run the program. Moreover, the definition even has a certain reasonableness to it. It says that to output the argument to `newWriteVertical`, first output all but the last digit and then output the last digit. However, when called, this method will produce an infinite sequence of recursive calls. If you call `newWriteVertical(12)`, that execution will stop to execute the recursive call `newWriteVertical(12/10)`, which is equivalent to `newWriteVertical(1)`. The execution of that recursive call will, in turn, stop to execute the recursive call

```
newWriteVertical(1 / 10);
```

which is equivalent to

```
newWriteVertical(0);
```

This, in turn, will stop to execute the recursive call `newWriteVertical(0 / 10);` which is also equivalent to

```
newWriteVertical(0);
```

This will produce another recursive call to again execute the same recursive method call `newWriteVertical(0);` and so on, forever. Because the definition of `newWriteVertical` has no stopping case, the process will proceed forever (or until the computer runs out of resources). ■

MyProgrammingLab™

Self-Test Exercises

1. What is the output of the following program?

```
public class Exercise1
{
    public static void main(String[] args)
    {
        cheers(3);
    }
    public static void cheers(int n)
    {
        if (n == 1)
        {
            System.out.println("Hurray");
        }
        else
        {
            System.out.println("Hip");
            cheers(n - 1);
        }
    }
}
```

2. Write a recursive `void` method that has one parameter that is an integer and that writes to the screen the number of asterisks `'*'` given by the argument. The output should be all on one line. You can assume the argument is positive.

3. Write a recursive `void` method that has one parameter, which is a positive integer. When called, the method writes its argument to the screen backward. That is, if the argument is `1234`, it outputs the following to the screen:

```
4321
```

4. Write a recursive `void` method that takes a single (positive) `int` argument `n` and writes the integers `1, 2, ..., n` to the screen.

5. Write a recursive `void` method that takes a single (positive) `int` argument `n` and writes integers `n, n-1, ..., 3, 2, 1` to the screen. *Hint:* The solution for Self-Test Exercise 4 and this exercise vary by an exchange of as little as two lines.

Stacks for Recursion ★

stack

To keep track of recursion, and a number of other things, most computer systems use a structure called a *stack*. A **stack** is a very specialized kind of memory structure that is analogous to a stack of paper. In this analogy, there is an inexhaustible supply of extra blank sheets of paper. To place some information in the stack, it is written on one of these sheets of paper and placed on top of the stack of papers. To place more information in the stack, a clean sheet of paper is taken, the information is written on it, and this new sheet of paper is placed on top of the stack. In this straightforward way, more and more information may be placed on the stack.

Getting information out of the stack is also accomplished by a very simple procedure. The top sheet of paper can be read, and when it is no longer needed, it is thrown away. There is one complication: Only the top sheet of paper is accessible. In order to read, say, the third sheet from the top, the top two sheets must be thrown away. Because the last sheet that is put on the stack is the first sheet taken off the stack, a stack is often called a **last-in/first-out** memory structure, abbreviated as **LIFO**.

last-in/ first-out

Using a stack, the computer can easily keep track of recursion. Whenever a method is called, a new sheet of paper is taken. The method definition is copied onto this sheet of paper, and the arguments are plugged for the method parameters. Then the computer starts to execute the body of the method definition. When it encounters a recursive call, it stops the computation it is doing on that sheet in order to compute the value returned by the recursive call. But, before computing the recursive call, it saves enough information so that, when it does finally determine the value returned by the recursive call, it can continue the stopped computation. This saved information is written on a sheet of paper and placed on the stack. A new sheet of paper is used for the recursive call. The computer writes a second copy of the method definition on this new sheet of paper, plugs in the arguments for the method parameters, and starts to execute the recursive call. When it gets to a recursive call within the recursively called copy, it repeats the process of saving information on the stack and using a new sheet of paper for the new recursive call. This process is illustrated in the earlier subsection entitled "Tracing a Recursive Call." Even though we did not call it a stack at the time, the illustrations of computations placed one on top of the other illustrate the actions of the stack.

This process continues until some recursive call to the method completes its computation without producing any more recursive calls. When this happens, the computer turns its attention to the top sheet of paper on the stack. This sheet contains the partially completed computation that is waiting for the recursive computation that just ended. So, it is possible to proceed with that suspended computation. When that suspended computation ends, the computer discards that sheet of paper and the suspended computation that is below it on the stack becomes the computation on top of the stack. The computer turns its attention to the suspended computation that is now on the top of the stack, and so forth. The process continues until the computation on the bottom sheet is completed. Depending on how many recursive calls are made and how the method definition is written, the stack may grow and shrink in any fashion. Notice that the sheets in the stack can only be accessed in a last-in/first-out fashion—but, this is exactly what is needed to keep track of recursive calls. Each suspended version is waiting for the completion of the version directly above it on the stack.

stack frame

activation record

Of course, computers do not have stacks of paper. This is just an analogy. The computer uses portions of memory rather than pieces of paper. The contents of one of these portions of memory ("sheets of paper") is called a **stack frame** or **activation record**. These stack frames are handled in the last-in/first-out manner we just discussed.

(These stack frames do not contain a complete copy of the method definition, but merely reference a single copy of the method definition. However, a stack frame contains enough information to allow the computer to act as if the stack frame contains a complete copy of the method definition.)

VideoNote
Recursion and the Stack

Stack ★

A **stack** is a last-in/first-out memory structure. The first item referenced or removed from a stack is always the last item entered into the stack. Stacks are used by computers to keep track of recursion (and for other purposes).

PITFALL: Stack Overflow ★

There is always some limit to the size of the stack. If there is a long chain in which a method makes a recursive call to itself, and that call results in another recursive call, and that call produces yet another recursive call, and so forth, then each recursive call in this chain will cause another suspended computation to be placed on the stack. If this chain is too long, then the stack will attempt to grow beyond its limit. This is an error condition known as a **stack overflow**. If you receive an error message that says *stack overflow*, it is likely that some method call has produced an excessively long chain of recursive calls. One common cause of stack overflow is infinite recursion. If a method is recursing infinitely, then it will eventually try to make the stack exceed any stack size limit. ■

Recursion versus Iteration

Recursion is not absolutely necessary. In fact, some programming languages do not allow it. Any task that can be accomplished using recursion can also be done in some other way without using recursion. For example, Display 11.2 contains a nonrecursive version of the method given in Display 11.1. The nonrecursive version of a method typically uses a loop (or loops) of some sort in place of recursion. For this reason, the nonrecursive version is usually referred to as an **iterative version**. If the definition of the method `writeVertical` given in Display 11.1 is replaced by the version given in Display 11.2, then the output will be the same. As is true in this case, a recursive version of a method can sometimes be much simpler than an iterative version. The full program with the iterative version of the method is given in the file `IterativeDemo1` on the accompanying website.

iterative version

extra code on website

A recursively written method will usually run slower and use more storage than an equivalent iterative version. The computer must do extra work manipulating the stack to keep track of the recursion. However, because the system does all this for you automatically, using recursion can sometimes make your job as a programmer easier, and can sometimes produce code that is easier to understand. Additionally, there are some cases in which the compiler or JVM can convert a recursive algorithm into an iterative version for you.

Display 11.2 **Iterative Version of the Method in Display 11.1**

```
public static void writeVertical(int n)
{
    int nsTens = 1;
    int leftEndPiece = n;
    while (leftEndPiece > 9)
    {
        leftEndPiece = leftEndPiece / 10;
        nsTens = nsTens * 10;
    }
    //nsTens is a power of 10 that has the same number
    //of digits as n. For example, if n is 2345, then
    //nsTens is 1000.

    for (int powerOf10 = nsTens;
             powerOf10 > 0; powerOf10 = powerOf10 / 10)
    {
        System.out.println(n / powerOf10);
        n = n % powerOf10;
    }
}
```

MyProgrammingLab™

Self-Test Exercises

6. If your program produces an error message that says *stack overflow*, what is a likely source of the error?
7. Write an iterative version of the method `cheers` defined in Self-Test Exercise 1.
8. Write an iterative version of the method defined in Self-Test Exercise 2.
9. Write an iterative version of the method defined in Self-Test Exercise 3.
10. Trace the recursive solution you made to Self-Test Exercise 4.
11. Trace the recursive solution you made to Self-Test Exercise 5.

11.2 Recursive Methods That Return a Value

To iterate is human, to recurse divine.

ANONYMOUS

General Form for a Recursive Method That Returns a Value

The recursive methods you have seen thus far are all `void` methods, but recursion is not limited to these methods. A recursive method can return a value of any type. The technique for designing recursive methods that return a value is basically the same as what you learned for `void` methods. An outline for a successful recursive method definition that returns a value is as follows:

- One or more cases in which the value returned is computed in terms of calls to the same method (that is, using recursive calls). As is the case with `void` methods, the arguments for the recursive calls should intuitively be "smaller."
- One or more cases in which the value returned is computed without the use of any recursive calls. These cases without any recursive calls are called **base cases** or **stopping cases** (just as they were with `void` methods).

This technique is illustrated in the next Programming Example.

EXAMPLE: Another Powers Method

In Chapter 5, we introduced the static method `pow` of the class `Math`, that computes powers. For example, `Math.pow(2.0,3.0)` returns $2.0^{3.0}$, so the following sets the variable `result` equal to `8.0`:

```
double result = Math.pow(2.0, 3.0);
```

The method `pow` takes two arguments of type `double` and returns a value of type `double`. Display 11.3 contains a recursive definition for a static method that is similar to `pow`, but that works with the type `int` rather than `double`. This new method is called `power`. For example, the following will set the value of `result2` equal to `8`, because 2^3 is `8`:

```
int result2 = power(2, 3);
```

Outside the defining class, this would be written as

```
int result2 = RecursionDemo2.power(2, 3);
```

Our main reason for defining the method `power` is to have a simple example of a recursive method, but there are situations in which the method `power` would be preferable to the method `pow`. The method `pow` returns a value of type `double`, which is only an approximate quantity. The method `power` returns a value of type `int`, which is an exact quantity. In some situations, you might need the additional accuracy provided by the method `power`.

The definition of the method `power` is based on the following formula:

x^n is equal to $x^{n-1} * x$

EXAMPLE: (continued)

Translating this formula into Java says that the value returned by `power(x, n)` should be the same as the value of the expression

```
power(x, n - 1)*x
```

The definition of the method `power` given in Display 11.3 does return this value for `power(x, n)`, provided `n > 0`.

The case where `n` is equal to `0` is the stopping case. If `n` is `0`, then `power(x, n)` simply returns `1` (because x^0 is `1`).

Let's see what happens when the method `power` is called with some sample values. First, consider the simple expression:

```
power(2, 0)
```

When the method is called, the value of `x` is set equal to `2`, the value of `n` is set equal to `0`, and the code in the body of the method definition is executed. Because the value of `n` is a legal value, the `if-else` statement is executed. Because this value of `n` is not greater than `0`, the `return` statement after the `else` is used, so the method call returns `1`. Thus, the following would set the value of `result3` equal to `1`:

```
int result3 = power(2, 0);
```

Now let's look at an example that involves a recursive call. Consider the expression

```
power(2, 1)
```

When the method is called, the value of `x` is set equal to `2`, the value of `n` is set equal to `1`, and the code in the body of the method definition is executed. Because this value of `n` is greater than `0`, the following `return` statement is used to determine the value returned:

```
return ( power(x, n - 1)*x );
```

which in this case is equivalent to

```
return ( power(2, 0)*2 );
```

At this point, the computation of `power(2, 1)` is suspended, a copy of this suspended computation is placed on the stack, and the computer then starts a new method call to compute the value of `power(2, 0)`. As you have already seen, the value of `power(2, 0)` is `1`. After determining the value of `power(2, 0)`, the computer replaces the expression

(continued)

EXAMPLE: (continued)

`power(2, 0)` with its value of `1` and resumes the suspended computation. The resumed computation determines the final value for `power(2, 1)` from the above `return` statement as

```
Power(2, 0)*2 is 1*2 which is 2
```

so the final value returned for `power(2, 1)` is `2`. So, the following would set the value of `result4` equal to `2`:

```
int result4 = power(2, 1);
```

Larger numbers for the second argument will produce longer chains of recursive calls. For example, consider the statement

```
System.out.println(power(2, 3));
```

The value of `power(2, 3)` is calculated as follows:

```
power(2, 3) is power(2, 2)*2
  power(2, 2) is power(2, 1)*2
    power(2, 1) is power(2, 0)*2
      power(2, 0) is 1 (stopping case)
```

When the computer reaches the stopping case, `power(2, 0)`, there are three suspended computations. After calculating the value returned for the stopping case, it resumes the most recently suspended computations to determine the value of `power(2, 1)`. After that, the computer completes each of the other suspended computations, using each value computed as a value to plug into another suspended computation, until it reaches and completes the computation for the original call `power(2, 3)`. The details of the entire computation are illustrated in Display 11.4.

Display 11.3 **The Recursive Method `power`** (part 1 of 2)

```
public class RecursionDemo2
{
    public static void main(String[] args)
    {
        for (int n = 0; n < 4; n++)
            System.out.println("3 to the power " + n
                + " is " + power(3, n));
    }

    public static int power(int x, int n)
    {
```

Display 11.3 **The Recursive Method `power`** (part 2 of 2)

```
        if  (n < 0)
        {
            System.out.println("Illegal argument to power.");
            System.exit(0);
        }
        if  (n > 0)
            return  ( power(x, n - 1)*x );
        else  // n == 0
             return  (1);
    }
}
```

Sample Dialogue

```
3 to the power 0 is 1
3 to the power 1 is 3
3 to the power 2 is 9
3 to the power 3 is 27
```

Display 11.4 Evaluating the Recursive Method Call `power(2,3)`

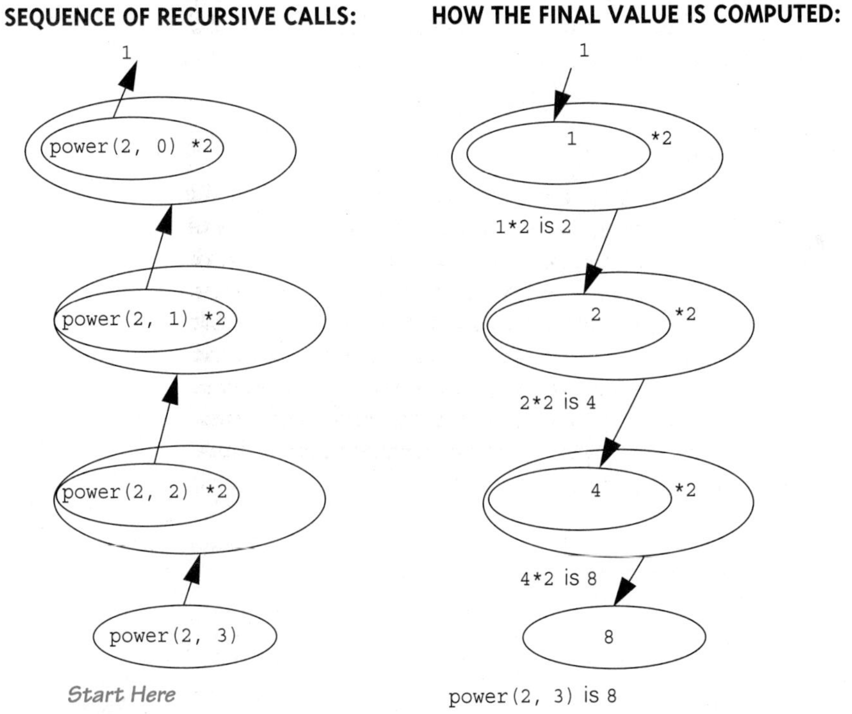

MyProgrammingLab™

Self-Test Exercises

12. What is the output of the following program?

```
public class Exercise12
{
    public static void main(String[] args)
    {
        System.out.println(mystery(3));
    }

    public static int mystery(int n)
    {
        if (n <= 1)
            return 1;
        else
            return ( mystery(n - 1) + n );
    }
}
```

13. What is the output of the following program? What well-known mathematical method is `rose`?

```
public class Exercise13
{
    public static void main(String[] args)
    {
        System.out.println(rose(4));
    }

    public static int rose(int n)
    {
        if (n <= 0)
            return 1;
        else
            return ( rose(n - 1) * n );
    }
}
```

14. Redefine the method `power` (Display 11.3) so that it also works for negative exponents. To do this, you also have to change the type of the value returned to `double`. The method heading for the redefined version of `power` is as follows:

```
/**
 Precondition: If n < 0, then x is not 0.
 Returns x to the power n.
*/
public static double power(int x, int n)
```

Hint: x^{-n} is equal to $1/(x^n)$.

11.3 Thinking Recursively

There are two kinds of people in the world, those who divide the world into two kinds of people and those who do not.

ANONYMOUS

Recursive Design Techniques

When defining and using recursive methods, you do not want to be continually aware of the stack and the suspended computations. The power of recursion comes from the fact that you can ignore that detail and let the computer do the bookkeeping for you. Consider the example of the method `power` in Display 11.3. The way to think of the definition of `power` is as follows:

`power(x, n)` returns `power(x, n - 1)*x`

Because x^n is equal to $x^{n-1}*x$, this is the correct value to return, provided that the computation will always reach a stopping case and will correctly compute the stopping case. So, after checking that the recursive part of the definition is correct, all you need to check is that the chain of recursive calls will always reach a stopping case and that the stopping case will always return the correct value. In other words, all that you need to do is check that the following three properties are satisfied:

criteria for methods that return a value

1. There is no infinite recursion. (A recursive call may lead to another recursive call, which may lead to another, and so forth, but every such chain of recursive calls eventually reaches a stopping case.)
2. Each stopping case returns the correct value for that case.
3. For the cases that involve recursion: *if* all recursive calls return the correct value, *then* the final value returned by the method is the correct value.

For example, consider the method `power` in Display 11.3:

1. **There is no infinite recursion**: The second argument to `power(x, n)` is decreased by one in each recursive call, so any chain of recursive calls must eventually reach the case `power(x, 0)`, which is the stopping case. Thus, there is no infinite recursion.
2. **Each stopping case returns the correct value for that case**: The only stopping case is `power(x, 0)`. A call of the form `power(x, 0)` always returns `1`, and the correct value for x^0 is `1`. So, the stopping case returns the correct value.
3. **For the cases that involve recursion, *if* all recursive calls return the correct value, *then* the final value returned by the method is the correct value**: The only case that involves recursion is when `n > 1`. When `n > 1`, `power(x, n)` returns

   `power(x, n - 1)*x.`

To see that this is the correct value to return, note that, *if* `power(x, n - 1)` returns the correct value, *then* `power(x, n - 1)` returns x^{n-1} and so `power(x, n)` returns

x^{n-1} `*` x, which is x^n

This is the correct value for `power(x, n)`.

That is all you need to check to be sure that the definition of `power` is correct. (The previous technique is known as *mathematical induction*, a concept that you may have heard about in a mathematics class. However, you do not need to be familiar with the term *mathematical induction* to use this technique.)

criteria for `void` methods

We gave you three criteria to use in checking the correctness of a recursive method that returns a value. Basically, the same rules can be applied to a recursive `void` method. If you show that your recursive `void` method definition satisfies the following three criteria, then you will know that your `void` method performs correctly:

1. There is no infinite recursion.
2. Each stopping case performs the correct action for that case.
3. For each of the cases that involve recursion, *if* all recursive calls perform their actions correctly, *then* the entire case performs correctly.

Binary Search ★

In this subsection, we will develop a recursive method that searches an array to find out whether it contains a specified value. For example, the array may contain a list of the numbers for credit cards that are no longer valid. A store clerk needs to search the list to see if a customer's card is valid or invalid.

The indices of the array `a` are the integers `0` through `finalIndex`. To make the task of searching the array easier, we will assume that the array is sorted. Hence, we know the following:

```
a[0] ≤ a[1] ≤ a[2] ≤ ... ≤ a[finalIndex]
```

In fact, the binary search algorithm we will use requires that the array be sorted like this.

When searching an array, you are likely to want to know both whether the value is in the array and, if it is, where it is in the array. For example, if you are searching for a credit card number, then the array index may serve as a record number. Another array indexed by these same indices may hold a phone number or other information to use for reporting the suspicious card. Hence, if the sought-after value is in the array, we will have our method return an index of where the sought-after value is located. If the value is not in the array, our method will return `-1`. (The array may contain repeats, which is why we say "an index" and not "the index.")

Now let us proceed to produce an algorithm to solve this task. It will help to visualize the problem in very concrete terms. Suppose the list of numbers is so long that it takes a book to list them all. This is in fact how invalid credit card numbers are distributed to stores that do not have access to computers. If you are a clerk and are handed a credit card, you must check to see if it is on the list and hence invalid. How would you proceed? Open the book to the middle and see if the number is there. If it is not and it is smaller than the middle number, then work backward toward the beginning of the book. If the number is larger than the middle number, you work your way toward the end of the book. This idea produces our first draft of an algorithm:

algorithm first version

```
mid = approximate midpoint between 0 and finalIndex;
if (key == a[mid])
    return mid;
else if (key < a[mid])
    search a[0] through a[mid - 1];
else if (key > a[mid])
    search a[mid + 1] through a[finalIndex];
```

Because the searchings of the shorter lists are smaller versions of the very task we are designing the algorithm to perform, this algorithm naturally lends itself to the use of recursion. The smaller lists can be searched with recursive calls to the algorithm itself.

Our pseudocode is a bit too imprecise to be easily translated into Java code. The problem has to do with the recursive calls. There are two recursive calls shown:

```
search a[0] through a[mid - 1];
          and
search a[mid + 1] through a[finalIndex];
```

more parameters

To implement these recursive calls, we need two more parameters. A recursive call specifies that a subrange of the array is to be searched. In one case, it is the elements indexed by `0` through `mid - 1`. In the other case, it is the elements indexed by `mid + 1` through `finalIndex`. The two extra parameters will specify the first and last indices of the search, so we will call them `first` and `last`. Using these parameters for the lowest and highest indices, instead of `0` and `finalIndex`, we can express the pseudocode more precisely as follows:

algorithm first refinement

```
To search a[first] through a[last] do the following:
mid = approximate midpoint between first and last;
if (key == a[mid])
    return mid;
else if (key < a[mid])
    return the result of searching a[first] through a[mid - 1];
else if (key > a[mid])
    return the result of searching a[mid + 1] through a[last];
```

To search the entire array, the algorithm would be executed with `first` set equal to `0` and `last` set equal to `finalIndex`. The recursive calls will use other values for `first` and `last`. For example, the first recursive call would set `first` equal to `0` and `last` equal to the calculated value `mid - 1`.

stopping case

As with any recursive algorithm, we must ensure that our algorithm ends rather than producing infinite recursion. If the sought-after number is found on the list, then there is no recursive call and the process terminates, but we need some way to detect when the number is not on the list. On each recursive call, the value of `first` is increased or the value of `last` is decreased. If they ever pass each other and `first` actually becomes larger than `last`, then we will know that there are no more indices left to check and that the number `key` is not in the array. If we add this test to our pseudocode, we obtain a complete solution, as shown in Display 11.5.

algorithm final version

Now we can routinely translate the pseudocode into Java code. The result is shown in Display 11.6. The method `search` is an implementation of the recursive algorithm given in Display 11.5. A diagram of how the method performs on a sample array is given in Display 11.7. Display 11.8 illustrates how the method `search` is used.

Notice that the method `search` solves a more general problem than the original task. Our goal was to design a method to search an entire array. Yet the method will let us search any interval of the array by specifying the indices `first` and `last`. This is common when designing recursive methods. Frequently, it is necessary to solve a more general problem in order to be able to express the recursive algorithm. In this case, we want only the answer in the case where `first` and `last` are set equal to `0` and `finalIndex`. However, the recursive calls will set them to values other than `0` and `finalIndex`.

Display 11.5 Pseudocode for Binary Search ★

ALGORITHM TO SEARCH **a[first]** THROUGH **a[last]**

```
/**
 Precondition:
 a[first]<= a[first + 1] <= a[first + 2] <= ... <= a[last]
*/
```

TO LOCATE THE VALUE KEY

```
if (first > last) //A stopping case
    return -1;
else
{
    mid = approximate midpoint between first and last;
    if (key == a[mid]) //A stopping case
        return mid;
    else if key < a[mid]//A case with recursion
        return the result of searching a[first] through a[mid - 1];
    else if key > a[mid] //A case with recursion
        return the result of searching a[mid + 1] through a[last];
}
```

Display 11.6 **Recursive Method for Binary Search ★**

```
public class BinarySearch
{
    /**
     Searches the array a for key. If key is not in the array segment,
     then -1 is returned. Otherwise returns an index in the segment such
     that key == a[index].
     Precondition: a[first] <= a[first + 1]<= ... <= a[last]
    */
    public static int search(int[] a, int first, int last, int key)
    {
        int result = 0; //to keep the compiler happy.

        if (first > last)
            result = -1;
        else
        {
            int mid = (first + last)/2;

            if (key == a[mid])
                result = mid;
            else if (key < a[mid])
                result = search(a, first, mid - 1, key);
            else if (key > a[mid])
                result = search(a, mid + 1, last, key);
        }
        return result;
    }
}
```

In the earlier subsection entitled "Tracing a Recursive Call," we gave three criteria that you should check to ensure that a recursive `void` method definition is correct. Let's check these three things for the method `search` given in Display 11.6:

1. **There is no infinite recursion**: On each recursive call, the value of `first` is increased or the value of `last` is decreased. If the chain of recursive calls does not end in some other way, then eventually the method will be called with `first` larger than `last`, which is a stopping case.

2. **Each stopping case performs the correct action for that case**: There are two stopping cases, when `first > last` and when `key == a[mid]`. Let's consider each case.

   If `first > last`, there are no array elements between `a[first]` and `a[last]`, so `key` is not in this segment of the array. (Nothing is in this segment of the array!) So, if `first > last`, the method `search` correctly returns `-1`, indicating that `key` is not in the specified range of the array.

   If `key == a[mid]`, the algorithm correctly sets `location` equal to `mid`. Thus, both stopping cases are correct.

Display 11.7 Execution of the Method **search** ★

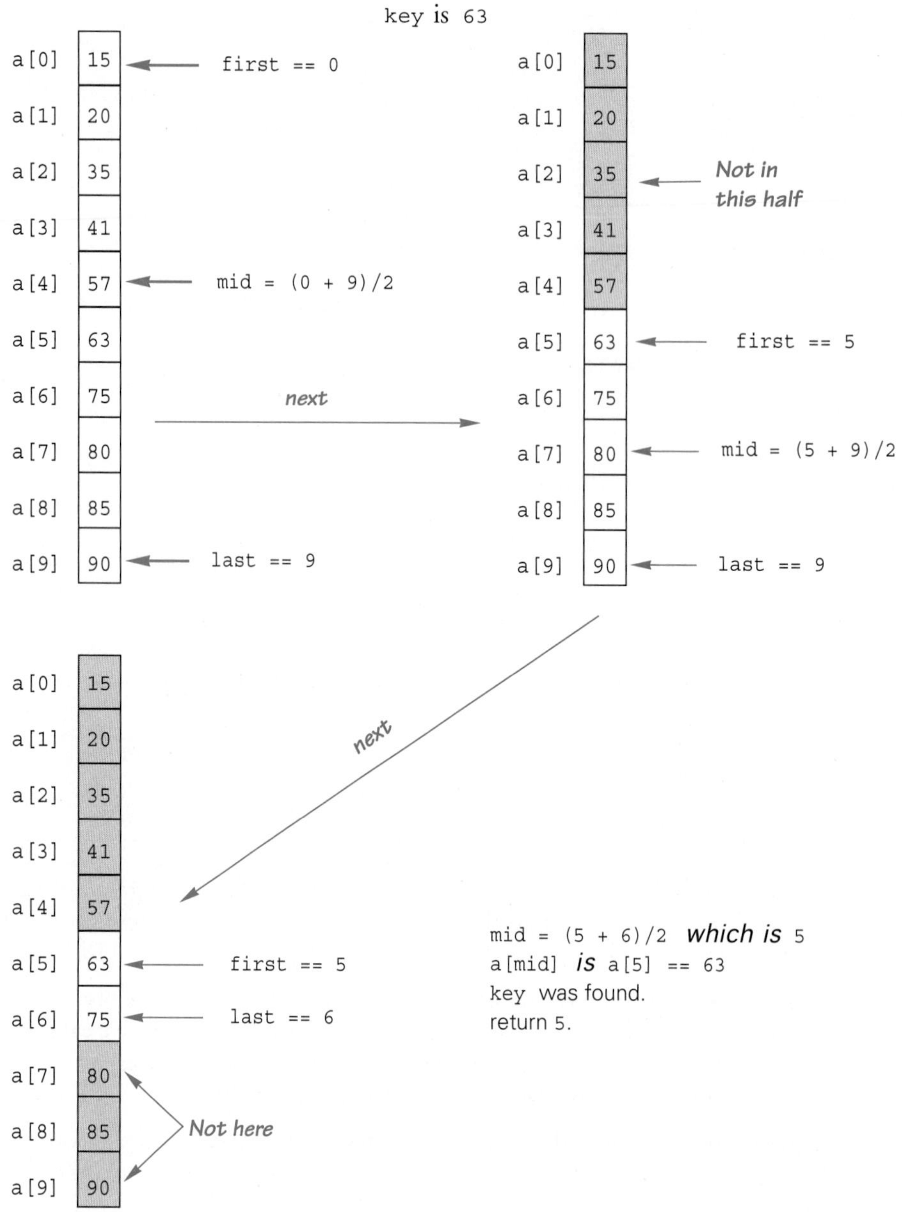

Display 11.8 Using the `search` Method ★

```
public class BinarySearchDemo
{
    public static void main(String[] args)
    {
        int[] a = {-2, 0, 2, 4, 6, 8, 10, 12, 14, 16};
        int finalIndex = 9;

        System.out.println("Array contains:");
        for (int i = 0; i < a.length; i++)
            System.out.print(a[i] + " ");
        System.out.println();
        System.out.println();

        int result;
        for (int key = -3; key < 5; key++)
        {
            result = BinarySearch.search(a, 0, finalIndex, key);
            if (result >= 0)
                System.out.println(key + " is at index " + result);
            else
                System.out.println(key + " is not in the array.");
        }
    }
}
```

Sample Dialogue

```
Array contains:
-2 0 2 4 6 8 10 12 14 16

-3 is not in the array.
-2 is at index 0
-1 is not in the array.
0 is at index 1
1 is not in the array.
2 is at index 2
3 is not in the array.
4 is at index 3
```

3. **For each of the cases that involve recursion, *if* all recursive calls perform their actions correctly, *then* the entire case performs correctly**: There are two cases in which there are recursive calls, when `key < a[mid]` and when `key > a[mid]`. We need to check each of these two cases.

   First, suppose `key < a[mid]`. In this case, because the array is sorted, we know that if `key` is anywhere in the array, then `key` is one of the elements `a[first]` through `a[mid - 1]`. Thus, the method need only search these elements, which is exactly what the recursive call

   ```
   search(a, first, mid - 1, key)
   ```

   does. So if the recursive call is correct, then the entire action is correct.

   Next, suppose `key > a[mid]`. In this case, because the array is sorted, we know that if `key` is anywhere in the array, then `key` is one of the elements `a[mid + 1]` through `a[last]`. Thus, the method need only search these elements, which is exactly what the recursive call

   ```
   search(a, mid + 1, last, key)
   ```

   does. So if the recursive call is correct, then the entire action is correct. Thus, in both cases, the method performs the correct action (assuming that the recursive calls perform the correct action).

The method `search` passes all three of our tests, so it is a good recursive method definition.

Efficiency of Binary Search ★

The binary search algorithm is extremely fast compared to an algorithm that simply tries all array elements in order. In the binary search, you eliminate about half the array from consideration right at the start. You then eliminate a quarter, then an eighth of the array, and so forth. These savings add up to a dramatically fast algorithm. For an array of 100 elements, the binary search will never need to compare more than 7 array elements to the key. A serial search could compare as many as 100 array elements to the key, and on the average will compare about 50 array elements to the key. Moreover, the larger the array is, the more dramatic the savings will be. On an array with 1,000 elements, the binary search will only need to compare about 10 array elements to the key value, as compared to an average of 500 for the serial search algorithm.[1]

iterative version

An iterative version of the method `search` is given in Display 11.9. On some systems, the iterative version will run more efficiently than the recursive version. The algorithm for the iterative version was derived by mirroring the recursive version. In the iterative version, the local variables `first` and `last` mirror the roles of the parameters in the recursive version, which are also named `first` and `last`. As this example

[1]The binary search algorithm has worst-case running time that is logarithmic—that is, $O(\log n)$. The serial search algorithm is linear—that is, $O(n)$. If the terms used in this footnote are not familiar to you, you can safely ignore it.

Display 11.9 **Iterative Version of Binary Search ★**

```
/**
 Searches the array a for key. If key is not in the array segment, then
 -1 is returned. Otherwise returns an index in the segment such that key
 == a[index].
 Precondition: a [lowEnd] <= a[lowEnd + 1]<= ... <= a[highEnd]
*/
public static int search(int[] a, int lowEnd, int highEnd, int key)
{
    int first = lowEnd;
    int last = highEnd;
    int mid;

    boolean found = false; //so far
    int result = 0; //to keep compiler happy

    while ( (first <= last) && !(found) )
    {
        mid = (first + last)/2;

        if (key == a[mid])
        {
            found = true;
            result = mid;
        }
        else if (key < a[mid])
        {
            last = mid - 1;
        }
        else if (key > a[mid])
        {
            first = mid + 1;
        }
    }

    if (first > last)
        result = -1;
    return result;
}
```

extra code on website

illustrates, it often makes sense to derive a recursive algorithm even if you expect to later convert it to an iterative algorithm. You can see the iterative method from Display 11.9 embedded in a full demonstration in the files `IterativeBinarySearch.java` and `IterativeBinarySearchDemo.java` on the accompanying website.

tail recursion

Most modern compilers will convert certain simple recursive method definitions to iterative ones before running the program. A method that uses **tail recursion** has the property that it does nothing after the recursive call except return the method's value. In this case, a tail recursive method can be easily converted to an equivalent iterative solution. This operation may be performed by the compiler or by the JVM.

MyProgrammingLab™

Self-Test Exercise

15. Write a recursive method definition for the following method:

```
/**
 Precondition: n >= 1
 Returns the sum of the squares of the numbers 1 through n.
*/
public static int squares(int n)
```

For example, `squares(3)` returns `14` because $1^2 + 2^2 + 3^2$ is 14.

EXAMPLE: Finding a File

The next program is an example where a recursive solution is much easier to write and understand than an iterative solution. Consider the problem of finding a file buried somewhere in your file system. For example, using the Windows file system, let's say that you have the following file and directory structure on your hard drive:

Display 11.10 Sample File System Structure

```
C:\
   JavaPrograms\
       Recursion\
          FindFile.java
          BinarySearch.java
       Homework\
          Homework1.java
          Homework2.java
       Test.java
    Papers\
       TermPaper.odt
       Workfile.docx
    Letter.txt
```

We would like to find the location of a file given its name. For example, given `TermPaper.odt`, we would like to know that it is located in `C:\Papers`. Given `FindFile.java`, we would like to know that it is located in `C:\JavaPrograms\Recursion`. The general solution is to start at some root directory, such as `C:\`, and to go through all the items in that directory. If an item is a file, check if it matches the target. If an item is a directory, then make a recursive call to restart the search using that directory as the new root directory.

Pseudocode of our recursive solution follows:

```
searchForFile(currentPath, targetFile)
  if currentPath is not a directory
          return error
  for every item i in currentPath
     if i is a directory
          r = searchForFile(i, targetFile)
          if r is a successful match
             return r
  if i is a file
     if i matches targetFile
             return path to file i
return target not found
```

To implement our algorithm, we need a way to determine if a path is a directory or a file, and we need to find a way to get all of the items within a directory. Java's `File` object will do all of this for us. To use it, we must import `java.io.File`. Here is the relevant constructor and methods:

CONSTRUCTORS AND METHODS	DESCRIPTION
`File(String pathname)`	The constructor takes a pathname and creates a `File` object corresponding to the file or directory with that pathname.
`String getAbsolutePath()`	Returns the pathname of the `File` object, e.g., `C:\Papers\TermPaper.odt`.
`String getName()`	Returns the name of the `File` object, e.g., `TermPaper.odt`.
`boolean isDirectory()`	Returns `true` if the `File` object is a directory.
`File[] listFiles()`	If the `File` object is a directory then this returns an array of `File` objects corresponding to all the items within the directory.

Using the `File` object, we can implement the recursive algorithm to find a file. The implementation in Display 11.11 returns an empty string if the target file is not found. If the initial root folder supplied is not a directory, then an error message is returned. The sample results assume the program runs using the directory structure given in Display 11.10.

Display 11.11 **Program to Recursively Find a File**

```
import java.io.File;
public class FindFile
{
  public static String searchForFile(File dir, String target)
  {
    String result = "";
    // If dir is not a directory, return
    if (!dir.isDirectory())
         return "Path is not a directory.";

    // Check each item in the directory
    for (File folderItem : dir.listFiles())
    {
         // Recurse if it's a directory
         if (folderItem.isDirectory())
         {
             result = searchForFile(folderItem,target);
             // Return the result if it is not empty
             if (!result.equals(""))
                  return result;
         }
         // If it's a file, check for a match
         else
         {
             if (folderItem.getName().equals(target))
                  return folderItem.getAbsolutePath();
         }
    }
    // If we got here, nothing was found
    return "";
  }

  public static void main(String[] args)
  {
    // The root folder to search
    File rootFolder = new File("C:\\");
    String result = searchForFile(rootFolder, "FindFile.java");
    if (!result.equals(""))
          System.out.println(result);
    else
          System.out.println("File not found.");
  }
}
```

Sample Dialogue Using Directory Structure of Display 11.10

```
C:\JavaPrograms\Recursion\FindFile.java
```

MyProgrammingLab™

Self-Test Exercises

16. How might you write a nonrecursive version of the program in Display 11.11? You do not have to write actual code, just think of what approach you might use.
17. The program in Display 11.11 could make thousands of recursive calls if you have a lot of subdirectories on your hard drive. Why is it unlikely that you will encounter a stack overflow error?
18. What is the stopping case in Display 11.11?

Chapter Summary

- If a problem can be reduced to smaller instances of the same problem, then a recursive solution is likely to be easy to find and implement.
- A recursive algorithm for a method definition normally contains two kinds of cases: one or more cases that include at least one recursive call and one or more stopping cases in which the problem is solved without any recursive calls.
- When writing a recursive method definition, always check to see that the method will not produce infinite recursion.
- When you define a recursive method, use the three criteria given in the subsection "Recursive Design Techniques" to check that the method is correct.
- When you design a recursive method to solve a task, it is often necessary to solve a more general problem than the given task. This may be required to allow for the proper recursive calls, because the smaller problems may not be exactly the same problem as the given task. For example, in the binary search problem, the task was to search an entire array, but the recursive solution is an algorithm to search any portion of the array (either all of it or a part of it).

Answers to Self-Test Exercises

1. `Hip Hip Hurray`
2.
```
public static void stars(int n)
{
    System.out.print('*');
    if (n > 1)
        stars(n - 1);
}
```

The following answer to Self-Test Exercise 3 is also correct, but is more complicated.

3.
```
public static void stars(int n)
{
    if (n <= 1)
    {
        System.out.print('*');
    }
    else
    {
        stars(n - 1);
        System.out.print('*');
    }
}

public static void backward(int n)
{
    if (n < 10)
    {
        System.out.print(n);
    }
    else
    {
        System.out.print(n%10);//write last digit
        backward(n/10);//write the other digits backward
    }
}
```
4.
```
public static void writeUp(int n)
{
    if (n >= 1)
    {
        writeUp(n - 1);
        System.out.print(n + " "); //write while the
                                   //recursion unwinds
    }
}
```
5.
```
public static void writeDown(int n)
{
    if (n >= 1)
    {
        System.out.print(n + " "); //write while the
                                   //recursion winds
        writeDown(n - 1);
    }
}
```
6. An error message that says *stack overflow* is telling you that the computer has attempted to place more stack frames on the stack than are allowed on your system. A likely cause of this error message is infinite recursion.

7.
```
public static void cheers(int n)
{
    while (n > 1)
    {
        System.out.print("Hip ");
        n--;
    }
    System.out.println("Hurray");
}
```

8.
```
public static void stars(int n)
{
    for (int count = 1; count <= n; count++)
        System.out.print('*');
}
```

9.
```
public static void backward(int n)
{
    while (n >= 10)
    {
        System.out.print(n%10);//write last digit
        n = n/10;//discard the last digit
    }
    System.out.print(n);
}
```

10. The trace for Self-Test Exercise 4: If `n = 3`, the code to be executed is

```
if (3 >= 1)
{
    writeUp(2);
    System.out.print(3 + " ");
}
```

The execution is suspended before the `System.out.println`. On the next recursion, `n = 2`; the code to be executed is

```
if (2 >= 1)
{
    writeUp(1);
    System.out.print(2 + " ");
}
```

The execution is suspended before the `System.out.println`. On the next recursion, `n = 1` and the code to be executed is

```
if (1 >= 1)
{
    writeUp(0);
    System.out.print(1 + " ");
}
```

The execution is suspended before the `System.out.println`. On the final recursion, `n = 0` and the code to be executed is

```
if (0 >= 1) // condition false, body skipped
{
    // skipped
}
```

The suspended computations are completed from the most recent to the least recent. The output is `1 2 3`.

11. The trace for Self-Test Exercise 5: If `n = 3`, the code to be executed is

```
if (3 >= 1)
{
    System.out.print(3 + " ");
    writeDown(2);
}
```

Next recursion, `n = 2`, the code to be executed is

```
if (2 >= 1)
{
    System.out.print(2 + " ");
    writeDown(1)
}
```

Next recursion, `n = 1`, the code to be executed is

```
if (1 >= 1)
{
    System.out.print(1 + " ");
    writeDown(0)
}
```

Final recursion, `n = 0`, and the `if` statement does nothing, ending the recursive calls:

```
if (0 >= 1) // condition false
{
    // this clause is skipped
}
```

The output is `3 2 1`.

12. `6`
13. The output is `24`. The method `rose` is the factorial method, usually written as *n!* and defined as follows:

    n! is equal to $n*(n - 1)*(n - 2)*...*1$

14.
```
public static double power(int x, int n)
{
    if (n < 0 && x == 0)
    {
        System.out.println(
                  "Illegal argument to power.");
        System.exit(0);
    }
    if (n < 0)
        return ( 1/power(x, - n));
    else if (n > 0)
        return ( power(x, n - 1)*x );
    else // n == 0
        return (1.0);
}
```

15.
```
public static int squares(int n)
{
    if (n <= 1)
        return 1;
    else
        return ( squares(n - 1) + n*n );
}
```

16. One approach is to keep a list of all directories that have been encountered. The list could be implemented with an array. Initially, this list would be set to the root directory. While there is at least one directory on the list, repeat the following:
    - Remove a directory from the list.
        - Find all files within the directory. If one of these files matches the target, return the pathname to the file.
        - Find all subdirectories within the directory. Add each subdirectory to the list.

    This approach is a little more complicated than the recursive version because we have to manage the list. In the recursive version, the list is essentially managed for us through the series of recursive calls.

17. A stack overflow in the context of recursion occurs when there is a long chain of recursive calls. In the FindFile program, one link of this chain is created when a subdirectory is in another directory. To create a stack overflow, we would need to have a folder in a folder, which is in a folder, which is in a folder, etc. How many folders must be linked in this way to cause a stack overflow will vary from one system to another, but you can expect hundreds would be necessary, an unlikely scenario in a typical file system. Although there could be thousands of recursive calls when searching for a file, there will likely be many short chains instead of single long chains. This allows recursive calls to exit and prevent a stack overflow.

18. Recursion stops if the file passed in is not a directory, if there are no subdirectories in the directory, or after all subdirectories have been recursively called. If a match is found, then recursion also stops.

MyProgrammingLab™ Programming Projects

Visit www.myprogramminglab.com to complete select exercises online and get instant feedback.

1. A savings account typically accrues savings using compound interest. If you deposit \$1,000 with a 10% interest rate per year, then after one year you have a total of \$1,100. If you leave this money in the account for another year at 10% interest, then after two years the total will be \$1,210. After three years, you would have \$1,331, and so on.

   Write a program that inputs the amount of money to deposit, an interest rate per year, and the number of years the money will accrue compound interest. Write a recursive function that calculates the amount of money that will be in the savings account using the input information.

   To verify your function, the amount should be equal to `P(1 + i)`^{n}, where `P` is the amount initially saved, `i` is the interest rate per year, and `n` is the number of years.

2. There are *n* people in a room, where `n` is an integer greater than or equal to 1. Each person shakes hands once with every other person. What is the total number, *h(n)*, of handshakes? Write a recursive function to solve this problem. To get you started, if there are only one or two people in the room, then

   ```
   handshake(1) = 0
   handshake(2) = 1
   ```

   If a third person enters the room, he or she must shake hands with each of the two people already there. This is two handshakes in addition to the number of handshakes that would be made in a room of two people, or a total of three handshakes.

   If a fourth person enters the room, he or she must shake hands with each of the three people already present. This is three handshakes in addition to the number of handshakes that would be made in a room of three people, or six handshakes.

   If you can generalize this to *n* handshakes, then it should help you write the recursive solution.

VideoNote
Solution to Programming Project 11.3

3. Consider a frame of bowling pins shown below, where each `*` represents a pin:

   ```
       *
      * *
     * * *
    * * * *
   * * * * *
   ```

   There are 5 rows and a total of 15 pins.

   If we had only the top 4 rows, then there would be a total of 10 pins.

   If we had only the top three rows, then there would be a total of six pins.

   If we had only the top two rows, then there would be a total of three pins.

   If we had only the top row, then there would be a total of one pin.

Write a recursive function that takes as input the number of rows *n* and outputs the total number of pins that would exist in a pyramid with *n* rows. Your program should allow for values of *n* that are larger than 5.

4. The game of "Jump It" consists of a board with *n* positive integers in a row except for the first column, which always contains zero. These numbers represent the cost to enter each column. Here is a sample game board where *n* is 6:

0	3	80	6	59	10

The object of the game is to move from the first column to the last column in the lowest total cost. The number in each column represents the cost to enter that column. Always start the game in the first column and have two types of moves. You can either move to the adjacent column or jump over the adjacent column to land two columns over. The cost of a game is the sum of the costs of the visited columns.

In the board shown above, there are several ways to get to the end. Starting in the first column, our cost so far is 0. We could jump to 80, then jump to 57, then move to 10 for a total cost of 80 + 57 + 10 = 147. However, a cheaper path would be to move to 3, jump to 6, then jump to 10, for a total cost of 3 + 6 + 10 = 19.

Write a recursive solution to this problem that computes the cheapest cost of the game and outputs this value for an arbitrarily large game board represented as an array. Your program does not have to output the actual sequence of jumps, only the cheapest cost of this sequence. After making sure that your solution works on small arrays, test your solution on boards of larger and larger values of *n* to get a feel for how efficient and scalable your solution is.

5. Write a recursive method definition for a static method that has one parameter `n` of type `int` and that returns the `n`th Fibonacci number. The Fibonacci numbers are F_0 is 1, F_1 is 1, F_2 is 2, F_3 is 3, F_4 is 5, and in general

$$F_{i+2} = F_i + F_{i+1} \text{ for } i = 0, 1, 2, \ldots$$

Place the method in a class that has a `main` that tests the method.

6. The formula for computing the number of ways of choosing *r* different things from a set of *n* things is the following:

```
C(n, r)= n!/(r!*(n - r)!)
```

The factorial method *n!* is defined by

```
n!= n*(n - 1)*(n - 2)*...*1
```

Discover a recursive version of the formula for *C* (*n*, *r*) and write a recursive method that computes the value of the formula. Place the method in a class that has a `main` that tests the method.

7. *Towers of Hanoi.* There is a story about Buddhist monks who are playing this puzzle with 64 stone disks. The story claims that when the monks finish moving the disks from one post to a second via the third post, time will end.

A stack of n disks of decreasing size (from bottom to top) is placed on one of three posts. The task is to move the disks one at a time from the first post to the second. To do this, any disk can be moved from any post to any other post, subject to the rule that you can never place a larger disk over a smaller disk. The (spare) third post is provided to make the solution possible. Your task is to write a recursive static method that gives instructions for a solution to this problem. We do not want to bother with graphics, so you should output a sequence of instructions that will solve the problem. The number of disks is a parameter to the method.

Hint: If you could move up `n-1` of the disks from the first post to the third post using the second post as a spare, the last disk could be moved from the first post to the second post. Then, by using the same technique (whatever that may be), you can move the `n-1` disks from the third post to the second post, using the first disk as a spare. There! You have the puzzle solved. You have only to decide what the nonrecursive case is, what the recursive case is, and when to output instructions to move the disks.

8. Write a recursive method named `contains` with the following header:

```
public static boolean contains(String haystack, String needle)
```

The method should return `true` if `needle` is contained within `haystack` and `false` if `needle` is not in `haystack`. For example,

`contains("Java programming", "ogr")` should return `true`

`contains("Java programming", "grammy")` should return `false`

You are not allowed to use the `substring` method to find a match.

9. The program to recursively find a file in Display 11.11 stops searching when the first match is found. Modify the program so that if there are multiple files with the same name in different directories, then all matching files are found and output. The simplest way to do this is to output all matches in the recursive method with a print statement. For a more challenging version, modify the method to return an array of Strings containing the pathnames of all matching files. It can return `null` or an empty array if there are no matches. Feel free to create additional helper classes if needed (e.g., to manage the number of items in the array of Strings). In Chapter 14, we will introduce ArrayLists, which make it easier to create an array-like structure with an arbitrary number of entries.

10. Given the definition of a 2D array such as the following,

```
String[][] data = {
    {"A", "B"},
    {"1", "2"},
    {"XX","YY","ZZ"}
};
```

write a recursive program that outputs all combinations of each subarray in order. In the previous example, the desired output (although it does not have to be in this order) is

```
A 1 XX
A 1 YY
A 1 ZZ
A 2 XX
A 2 YY
A 2 ZZ
B 1 XX
B 1 YY
B 1 ZZ
B 2 XX
B 2 YY
B 2 ZZ
```

Your program should work with arbitrarily sized arrays in either dimension. For example, the following data

```
String[][] data = {
    {"A"},
    {"1"},
    {"2"},
    {"XX","YY"}
};
```

should output:

```
A 1 2 YY
A 1 2 YY
```

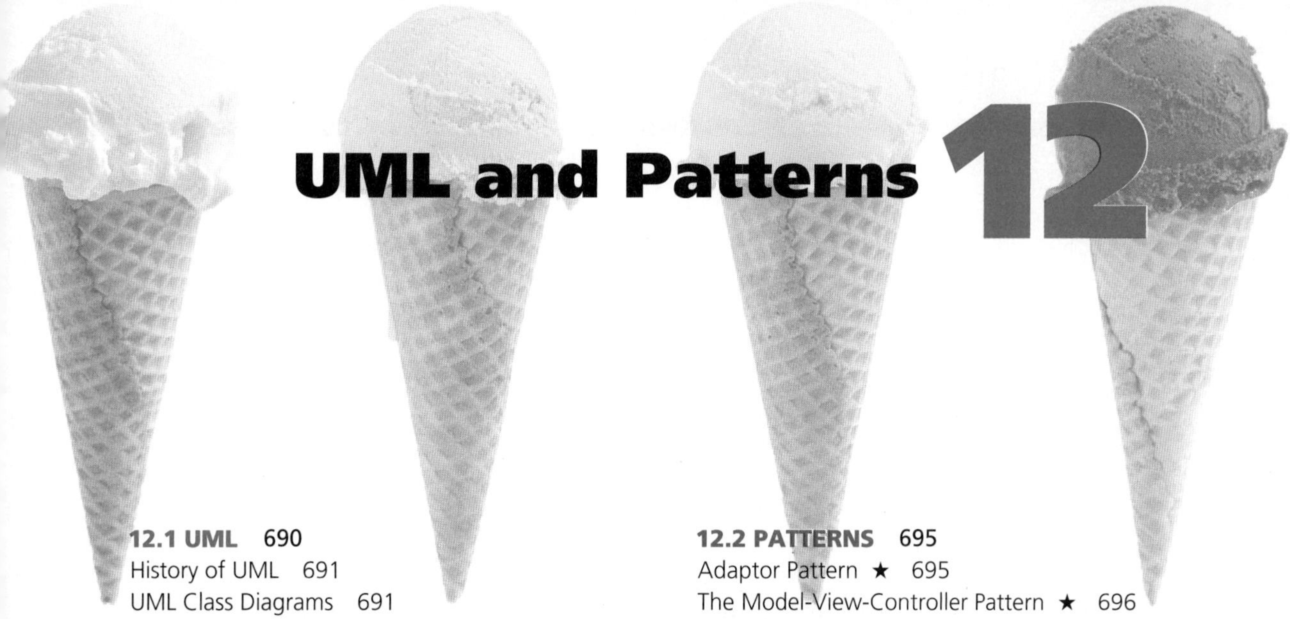

UML and Patterns 12

12 UML and Patterns

Einstein argued that there must be simplified explanations of nature, because God is not capricious or arbitrary. No such faith comforts the software engineer. Much of the complexity that he must master is arbitrary complexity.

F. BROOKS, "No Silver Bullet: Essence and Accidents of Software Engineering," *IEEE Computer*, April 1987

Introduction

UML and patterns are two software design tools that apply no matter what programming language you are using, as long as the language provides for classes and related facilities for object-oriented programming (OOP). This chapter presents a very brief introduction to these two topics. It contains no new details about the Java language.

UML is a graphical language that is used for designing and documenting software created within the OOP framework.

A pattern in programming is very similar to a pattern in any other context. It is a kind of template or outline of a software task that can be realized as different code in different, but similar, applications.

Prerequisites

Section 12.1 on UML and Section 12.2 on patterns can be read in either order. Nothing in the rest of this book requires any of this chapter. Section 12.1 on UML uses material from Chapters 1–5 and Chapter 7 on inheritance. Section 12.2 on patterns uses material from Chapters 1–7 and Chapter 11.

12.1 UML

One picture is worth a thousand words.

Chinese proverb

Most people do not think in Java or in any other programming language. As a result, computer scientists have always sought to produce more human-oriented ways of representing programs. One widely used representation is pseudocode, which is a mixture of a programming language, such as Java, and a natural language, such as English. To think about a programming problem without needing to worry about the syntax details of a language such as Java, you can simply relax the syntax rules and write in pseudocode. Pseudocode has become a standard tool used by programmers, but it is a linear and algebraic representation of programming. Computer scientists have long sought to give software design a graphical representation. To this end, a number of graphical representation systems for program design have been proposed, used, and ultimately found to be wanting. Terms such as *flowchart*, *structure diagram*, and many more names of graphical program representations are today recognized only by those of the older generation. Today's candidate for a graphical representation formalism is the **Unified Modeling Language** (**UML**). UML was designed to reflect and be used with the OOP philosophy. It is too early to say whether or not UML will stand the test of time, but it is off to a good start. A number of companies have adopted the UML formalism to use in their software design projects.

UML

History of UML

UML developed along with OOP. As the OOP philosophy became more and more commonly used, different groups worked out their own graphical or other representations for OOP design. In 1996, Grady Booch, Ivar Jacobson, and James Rumbaugh released an early version of UML. UML was intended to bring together the various different graphical representation methods to produce a standardized graphical representation language for object-oriented design and documentation. Since that time, UML has been developed and revised in response to feedback from the OOP community. Today the UML standard is maintained and certified by the Object Management Group (OMG), a nonprofit organization that promotes the use of object-oriented techniques.

UML Class Diagrams

class diagram

Classes are central to OOP, and the **class diagram** is the easiest of the UML graphical representations to understand and use. Display 12.1 shows the class diagram for a class to represent a square. The diagram consists of a box divided into three sections. (The colors are optional and not standardized.) The top section has the class name, `Square`. The next section has the data specification for the class. In this example, there are three pieces of data (three instance variables), a value of type `double` giving the length of a side, and two more values of type `double` giving the *x* and *y* coordinates of the center of the square. The third section gives the actions (class methods). The notation for method entries is not identical to that of a Java method heading, but it contains the same information. A minus sign indicates a private member. So, for the class `Square`, all data is private. A plus sign indicates a public member. A sharp (#) indicates a protected member. A tilde (~) indicates package access. So, for the class `Square`, the class diagram shows two public methods and one protected method. A class diagram need not give a complete description of the class. When you do not need all the members in a class for the analysis at hand, you do not list all the members in the class diagram. Missing members are indicated with an ellipsis (three dots).

Display 12.1 A UML Class Diagram

Square
– side: double – xCoordinate: double – yCoordinate: double
+ resize(double newSide): void + move(double newX, double newY): void # erase(): void . . .

Class Interactions

Class diagrams by themselves are of little value, because they simply repeat the class interface, possibly with ellipses. To understand a design, you need to indicate how objects of the various classes interact. UML has various ways to indicate class interactions; for example, various sorts of annotated arrows indicate the information flow from one class object to another. UML also has annotations for class groupings into packages, annotations for inheritance, and annotations for other interactions. Moreover, UML is extensible. If what you want and need is not in UML, you can add it. Of course, this all takes place inside a prescribed framework so that different software developers can understand each other's UML. One of the most fundamental of class interactions is inheritance, which is discussed in the next subsection.

Inheritance Diagrams

inheritance diagram

arrows

Display 12.2 shows a possible **inheritance diagram** used in a university's record-keeping software for some of its classes. Note that the class diagrams are incomplete. You normally show only as much of the class diagram as you need for the design task at hand. Note that the arrow heads point up from a derived class to its base class. In UML an unfilled arrowhead is used to indicate an inheritance relationship between two classes.

The arrows also help in locating method definitions. If you are looking for a method definition for some class, the arrows show the path you (or the computer) should follow. If you are looking for the definition of a method used by an object of the class `Undergraduate`, first look in the definition of the class `Undergraduate`; if it is not there, look in the definition of `Student`; if it is not there, look in the definition of the class `Person`.

Display 12.2 A Class Hierarchy in UML Notation

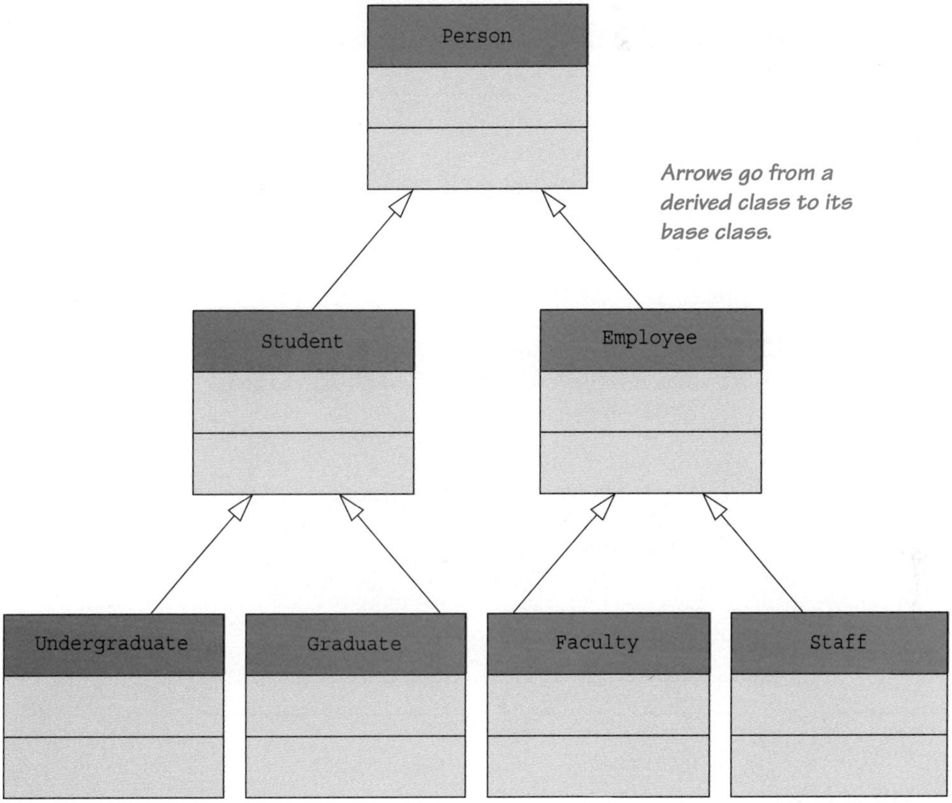

Display 12.3 shows some possible additional details of the inheritance hierarchy for the two classes `Person` and one of its derived classes, `Student`. Suppose `s` is an object of the class `Student`. The diagram in Display 12.3 tells you that you can find the definition of

```
s.toString();
```

and

```
s.set("Joe Student", 4242);
```

in the class `Student`, but the definition of

```
s.setName("Josephine Student");
```

is found in the definition of the class `Person`.

Display 12.3 Some Details of a UML Class Hierarchy

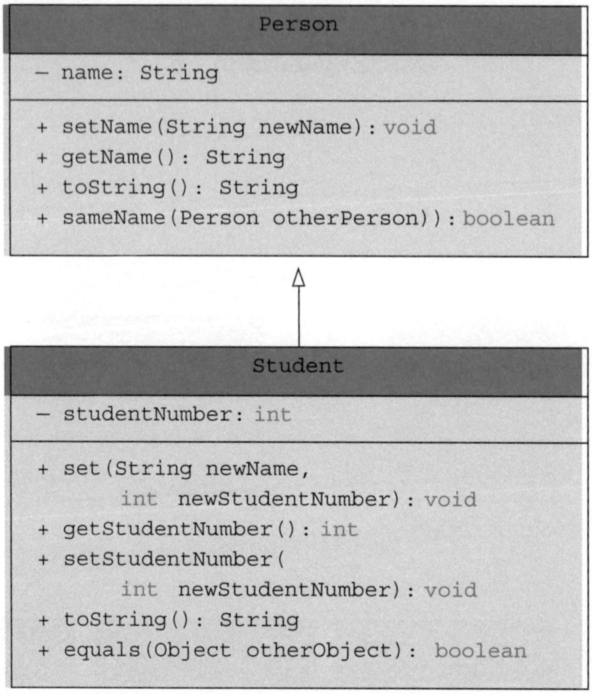

More UML

This is just a hint of what UML is all about. If you are interested in learning more, consult one of the many available references on UML.

MyProgrammingLab™

Self-Test Exercises

1. Draw a class diagram for a class whose objects represent circles. Use Display 12.1 as a model.

2. Suppose `aStudent` is an object of the class `Student`. Based on the inheritance diagram in Display 12.3, where will you find the definition of the method `sameName` used in the following invocation, which compares `aStudent` and another object named `someStudent`? Explain your answer.

```
Student someStudent =
              new Student("Joe Student", 7777);
if (aStudent.sameName(someStudent))
    System.out.println("wow");
```

MyProgrammingLab™

Self-Test Exercises (continued)

3. Suppose aStudent is an object of the class Student. Based on the inheritance diagram in Display 12.3, where will you find the definition of the method used in the following invocation? Explain your answer.

```
aStudent.setNumber(4242);
```

12.2 Patterns ★

I bid him look into the lives of men as though into a mirror, and from others to take an example for himself.

TERENCE (Publius Terentius Afer) 190–159 B.C., *Adelphoe*

pattern

Patterns are design outlines that apply across a variety of software applications. To be useful, the pattern must apply across a variety of situations. To be substantive, the pattern must make some assumptions about the domain of applications to which it applies. For example, one well-known pattern is the **Container-Iterator** pattern. A **container** is a class (or other construct) whose objects hold multiple pieces of data. One example of a container is an array. Other examples, which will be discussed later in this book, are vectors and linked lists. Any class or other construct designed to hold multiple values can be viewed as a container. For example, a String value can be viewed as a container that contains the characters in the string. Any construct that allows you to cycle through all the items in a container is an **iterator**. For example, an array index is an iterator for an array. It can cycle through the array as follows:

Container-Iterator

container

iterator

```
for (int i; i < a.length; i++)
    Do something with a[i]
```

The index variable i is the iterator. The Container-Iterator pattern describes how an iterator is used on a container.

In this brief chapter, we can give you only a taste of what patterns are all about. In this section, we will discuss a few sample patterns to let you see what patterns look like. There are many more known and used patterns and many more yet to be explicated. This is a new and still developing field of software engineering.

Adaptor Pattern ★

Adaptor

The **Adaptor** or **Adapter** pattern transforms one class into a different class without changing the underlying class but merely by adding a new interface. (The new interface replaces the old interface of the underlying class.) For example, in Chapter 11, we mentioned the stack data structure, which is used to, among other things, keep track of recursion. One way to create a stack data structure is to start with an array and add the stack interface. The Adaptor pattern says to start with a container, such as an array, and add an interface, such as the stack interface.

The Model-View-Controller Pattern ★

Model-View-Controller

The **Model-View-Controller** pattern is a way of separating the I/O task of an application from the rest of the application. The Model part of the pattern performs the heart of the application. The View part is the output part; it displays a picture of the Model's state. The Controller is the input part; it relays commands from the user to the Model. Normally, each of the three interacting parts is realized as an object with responsibilities for its own tasks. The Model-View-Controller pattern is an example of a divide-and-conquer strategy. One big task is divided into three smaller tasks with well-defined responsibilities. Display 12.4 gives a diagram of the Model-View-Controller pattern. Note that the arrowheads are open. In UML, an open arrowhead indicates an association where one object has a reference to another object of the type connected by the arrow.

As a very simple example, the Model might be a container class, such as an array. The View might display one element of the array. The Controller gives commands to display the element at a specified index. The Model (the array) notifies the View to display a new element whenever the array contents change or a different index location is given.

Any application can be made to fit the Model-View-Controller pattern, but it is particularly well suited to GUI (Graphical User Interface) design projects where the View can indeed be a visualization of the state of the Model. (A GUI interface is simply a windowing interface of the form you find in most modern software applications, as opposed to the simple text I/O we have used so far in this book.) For example, the Model might be an object to represent your list of computer desktop object names. The View could then be a GUI object that produces a screen display of your desktop icons. The Controller relays commands to the Model (which is a desktop object) to add or delete names. The Model object notifies the View object when the screen needs to be updated.

Display 12.4 Model-View-Controller Pattern

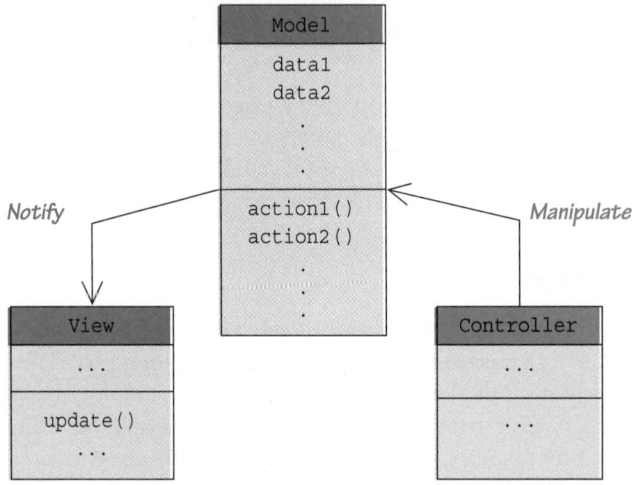

We have presented the Model-View-Controller pattern as if the user is the Controller, primarily to simplify the examples. The Controller need not be under the direct control of the user, but could be some other kind of software or hardware component.

EXAMPLE: A Sorting Pattern

The most efficient sorting algorithms all seem to follow a similar pattern. Expressed recursively, they divide the list of elements to be sorted into two smaller lists, recursively sort the two smaller lists, and then recombine the two sorted lists to obtain the final sorted list. In Display 12.5, this pattern is expressed as pseudocode (in fact, almost correct Java code) for a method to sort an array into increasing order using the < operator.

Our sorting pattern uses a divide-and-conquer strategy. It divides the entire collection of elements to be sorted into two smaller collections, sorts the smaller collections by recursive calls, and then combines the two sorted collections to obtain the final sorted array. The following is the heart of our sorting pattern:

```
int splitPoint = split(a, begin, end);
sort(a, begin, splitPoint);
sort(a, splitPoint + 1, end);
join(a, begin, splitPoint, end);
```

Although the pattern does impose some minimum requirements on the methods `split` and `join`, it does not say exactly how the methods `split` and `join` are defined. Different definitions of `split` and `join` will yield different sorting algorithms.

The method `split` rearranges the elements in the interval `a[begin]` through `a[end]` and divides the rearranged interval at a split point, `splitPoint`. The two smaller intervals `a[begin]` through `a[splitPoint]` and `[splitPoint + 1]` through `a[end]` are then sorted by a recursive call to the method `sort`. Note that the `split` method both rearranges the elements in the array interval `a[begin]` through `a[end]` and returns the index `splitPoint` that divides the interval. After the two smaller intervals are sorted, the method `join` then combines the two sorted intervals to obtain the final sorted version of the entire larger interval.

The pattern says nothing about how the method `split` rearranges and divides the interval `a[begin]` through `a[end]`. In a simple case, `split` might simply choose a value `splitPoint` between `begin` and `end` and divide the interval into the points before `splitPoint` and the points after `splitPoint`, with no rearranging. Display 12.6 realizes the sorting pattern by defining `split` this way. On the other hand, the method `split` could do something more elaborate such as move all the "small" elements to the front of the array and all the "large" elements toward the end of the array. This would be a step on the way to fully sorting the values. We will also see an example in Display 12.8 that realizes the sorting pattern in this second way.

(continued)

Display 12.5 **Divide-and-Conquer Sorting Pattern**

```
/**
 Precondition: Interval a[begin] through a[end] of a have elements.
 Postcondition: The values in the interval have
 been rearranged so that a[begin] <=a[begin+1] <= . . . <= a[end].
*/
public static void sort(Type [] a, int begin, int end)
{
    if ((end - begin) >= 1)
    {
        int splitPoint = split(a, begin, end);
        sort(a, begin, splitPoint);
        sort(a, splitPoint + 1, end);
        join(a, begin, splitPoint, end);
    }//else sorting one (or fewer) elements so do nothing.
}
```

To get a correct Java method definition, `Type` *must be replaced with a suitable type name.*

Different definitions for the methods `split` *and* `join` *will give different realizations of this pattern.*

EXAMPLE: (continued)

The simplest realization of this sorting pattern is the **merge sort** realization given in Display 12.6. In this realization, the array base type, *Type*, is specialized to the type `double`. The merge sort is an example where the definition of `split` is very simple. It just divides the array into two intervals with no rearranging of elements. The `join` method is more complicated. After the two subintervals are sorted, the method `join` merges the two sorted subintervals, copying elements from the array to a temporary array. The merging starts by comparing the smallest elements in each smaller sorted interval. The smaller of these two elements is the smallest of all the elements in either subinterval, so it is moved to the first position in the temporary array. The process is then repeated with the remaining elements in the two smaller sorted intervals to find the next smallest element, and so forth. A demonstration of using the merge sort version of `sort` is given in Display 12.7.

There is a trade-off between the complexity of the methods `split` and `join`. You can make either of them simple at the expense of making the other more complicated. For merge sort, `split` was simple and `join` was complicated. We next give a realization where `split` is complicated and `join` is simple.

Display 12.8 gives the **quick sort** realization of our sorting pattern for the type `double`.

In the quick sort realization, the definition of `split` is quite sophisticated. An arbitrary value in the array is chosen; this value is called the **splitting value**. In our realization, we chose `a[begin]` as the splitting value, but any value will do equally well. The elements in the array are rearranged so that all those elements that are less than or equal to the splitting value are at the front of the array, all the values that are greater

Display 12.6 Merge Sort Realization of Sorting Pattern (part 1 of 2)

```
/**
 Class that realizes the divide-and-conquer sorting pattern and
 uses the merge sort algorithm.
*/
public class MergeSort
{
    /**
     Precondition: Interval a[begin] through a[end] of a have elements.
     Postcondition: The values in the interval have
     been rearranged so that a[begin] < = a[begin+1] < = . . . < =
     a[end].
    */
    public static void sort(double [] a, int begin, int end)
    {
        if ((end - begin) >= 1)
        {
            int splitPoint = split(a, begin, end);
            sort(a, begin, splitPoint);
            sort(a, splitPoint + 1, end);
            join(a, begin, splitPoint, end);
        }//else sorting one (or fewer) elements so do nothing.
    }

    private static int split(double [] a, int begin, int end)
    {
        return ((begin + end)/2);
    }

    private static void join(double [] a, int begin, int splitPoint,
    int end)
    {
        double[] temp;
        int intervalSize = (end - begin + 1);
        temp = new double [intervalSize];
        int nextLeft = begin; //index for first chunk
        int nextRight = splitPoint + 1; //index for second chunk
        int i = 0; //index for temp

        //Merge till one side is exhausted:
        while ((nextLeft <= splitPoint) && (nextRight <= end))
        {
            if (a[nextLeft] < a[nextRight])
            {
                temp[i] = a[nextLeft];
                i++; nextLeft++;
            }
```

The method `sort` is identical to the version in the pattern (Display 12.5) except that `Type` is replaced with `double`.

(continued)

Display 12.6 Merge Sort Realization of Sorting Pattern (part 2 of 2)

```
            else
            {
                temp[i] = a[nextRight];
                i++; nextRight++;
            }
        }
        while (nextLeft <= splitPoint)
        //Copy rest of left chunk, if any.
        {
            temp[i] = a[nextLeft];
            i++; nextLeft++;
        }
        while (nextRight <= end) //Copy rest of right chunk, if any.
        {
            temp[i] = a[nextRight];
            i++; nextRight++;
        }
        for (i = 0; i < intervalSize; i++)
            a[begin + i] = temp[i];
    }
}
```

EXAMPLE: (continued)

than the splitting value are at the other end of the array, and the splitting value is placed so that it divides the entire array into these smaller and larger elements. Note that the smaller elements are not sorted and the larger elements are not sorted, but all the elements before the splitting value are smaller than any of the elements after the splitting value. The smaller elements are sorted by a recursive call, the larger elements are sorted by another recursive call, and then these two sorted segments are combined with the `join` method. In this case, the `join` method is as simple as it could be. It does nothing. Because the sorted smaller elements all precede the sorted larger elements, the entire array is sorted.

A demonstration program for the quick sort method `sort` in Display 12.8 is given in the file `QuickSortDemo.java` on the accompanying website.

(Both the merge sort and the quick sort realizations can be done without the use of a second temporary array, `temp`. However, that detail would only distract from the message of this example. In a real application, you may or may not, depending on details, want to consider the possibility of doing a sort realization without the use of the temporary array.)

Display 12.7 Using the **MergeSort** Class

```
public class MergeSortDemo
{
    public static void main(String[] args)
    {
        double[]b = {7.7, 5.5, 11, 3, 16, 4.4, 20, 14, 13, 42};

        System.out.println("Array contents before sorting:");
        int i;
        for (i = 0; i < b.length; i++)
            System.out.print(b[i] + " ");
        System.out.println();

        MergeSort.sort(b, 0, b.length-1);
        System.out.println("Sorted array values:");
        for (i = 0; i < b.length; i++)
            System.out.print(b[i] + " ");
        System.out.println();
    }
}
```

Sample Dialogue

```
Array contents before sorting:
7.7 5.5 11.0 3.0 16.0 4.4 20.0 14.0 13.0 42.0
Sorted array values:
3.0 4.4 5.5 7.7 11.0 13.0 14.0 16.0 20.0 42.0
```

Display 12.8 **Quick Sort Realization of Sorting Pattern** (part 1 of 3)

```
/**
 Class that realizes the divide-and-conquer sorting pattern and
 uses the quick sort algorithm.
*/
public class QuickSort
{
    /**
     Precondition: Interval a[begin] through a[end] of a have elements.
     Postcondition: The values in the interval have
      been rearranged so that a[begin] <= a[begin+1] <= . . . <=
      a[end].
```

(continued)

Display 12.8 **Quick Sort Realization of Sorting Pattern** (part 2 of 3)

```
    */
public static void sort(double[] a, int begin, int end)
{
    if ((end - begin) >= 1)
    {
        int splitPoint = split(a, begin, end);
        sort(a, begin, splitPoint);
        sort(a, splitPoint + 1, end);
        join(a, begin, splitPoint, end);
    }//else sorting one (or fewer) elements so do nothing.
}
private static int split(double [] a, int begin, int end)
{
    double[] temp;
    int size = (end - begin + 1);
    temp = new double [size];
    double splitValue = a[begin];
    int up = 0;
    int down = size - 1;
    //Note that a[begin] = splitValue is skipped.
    for (int i = begin + 1; i < = end; i++)
    {
        if (a[i] <= splitValue)
        {
            temp[up] = a[i];
            up++;
        }
        else
        {
            temp[down] = a[i];
            down--;
        }
     }
     //0 < = up = down < size
     temp[up] = a[begin]; //Positions the split value
     //temp[i] <= splitValue for i < up
     // temp[up] = splitValue
     // temp[i] > splitValue for i > up
     for (int i = 0; i < size; i++)
```

The method `sort` is identical to the version in the pattern (Display 12.5) except that `Type` is replaced with `double`.

Display 12.8 **Quick Sort Realization of Sorting Pattern** (part 3 of 3)

```
            a[begin + i] = temp[i];
        return (begin + up);
    }

    private static void join(double [] a, int begin,
                                      int splitPoint, int end)
    {
        //Nothing to do.
    }
}
```

Restrictions on the Sorting Pattern

The sorting pattern, like all patterns, has some restrictions on where it applies. As we formulated the sorting pattern, it applies only to types for which the < operator is defined. Also, it applies only to sorting into increasing order; it does not apply to sorting into decreasing order. However, this is a result of our simplifying details to make the presentation clearer. You can make the pattern more general by replacing the < operator with a `boolean` valued method called `compare` that has two arguments of the base type of the array, which returns `true` or `false` depending on whether the first "comes before" the second. Then, the only restriction is that the `compare` method must have a reasonable definition.[1] This sort of generalization is discussed in Chapter 13 in the subsection entitled "The `Comparable` Interface."

Efficiency of the Sorting Pattern ★

Essentially any sorting algorithm can be realized using this sorting pattern. However, the most efficient implementations are those for which the `split` method divides the array into two substantial size chunks, such as half-and-half, or one-fourth and three-fourths. A realization of `split` that divides the array into one or a very few elements and the rest of the array will not be very efficient.

For example, the merge sort realization of `split` divides the array into two roughly equal parts, and merge sort is indeed very efficient. It can be shown (although we will not do so here) that merge sort has a worst-case running time that is the best possible "up to an order of magnitude."

[1]The technical requirement is that the `compare` method be a *total ordering*, a concept discussed in Chapter 13. Essentially, all common orderings that you might want to sort by are total orderings.

The `Comparable` interface has a method `compareTo`, which is slightly different from `compare`. However, the method we described as `compare` can easily be defined using the method `compareTo` as a helping method.

The quick sort realization of `split` divides the array into two portions that might be almost equal or might be very different in size depending on the choice of a splitting value. Since in extremely unfortunate cases the split might be very uneven, the worst-case running time for quick sort is not as fast as that of merge sort. However, in practice, quick sort turns out to be a very good sorting algorithm and usually preferable to merge sort.

Selection sort, which we discussed in Chapter 6, divides the array into two pieces, one with a single element and one with the rest of the array interval. (See Self-Test Exercise 4.) Because of this uneven division, selection sort has a poor running time, although it does have the virtue of simplicity.

TIP: Pragmatics and Patterns

You should not feel compelled to follow all the fine details of a pattern. Patterns are guides, not requirements. For example, we did the quick sort implementation by exactly following the pattern. We did this to have a clean example. In practice, we would have taken some liberties. Notice that, with quick sort, the `join` method does nothing. In practice, we would simply eliminate the calls to `join`. These calls incur overhead and accomplish nothing. Other optimizations can also be done once the general pattern of the algorithm is clear. ■

Pattern Formalism

There is a well-developed body of techniques for using patterns. We will not go into the details here. The UML discussed in Section 12.1 is one formalism used to express patterns. The place within the software design process of patterns and any specific formalisms for patterns is not yet clear. However, it is evident that the basic idea of patterns, as well as certain pattern names, such as *Model-View-Controller*, have become standard and useful tools for software design.

MyProgrammingLab™

Self-Test Exercises

4. Give an implementation of the divide-and-conquer sorting pattern (Display 12.5) that will realize the selection sort algorithm (Display 6.11) for an array with base type `double`.

5. Which of the following would give the fastest run time when an array is sorted using the quick sort algorithm: a fully sorted array, an array of random values, or an array sorted from largest to smallest (that is, sorted backward)? Assume all arrays are of the same size and have the same base type.

Chapter Summary

- The *Unified Modeling Language (UML)* is a graphical representation language for object-oriented software design.
- *Patterns* are design principles that apply across a variety of software applications.
- The patterns discussed in this chapter are the *Container-Iterator*, *Adaptor*, *Model-View-Controller*, and *Divide-and-Conquer Sorting* patterns.
- UML is one formalism that can and is used to express patterns.

Answers to Self-Test Exercises

1. There are many correct answers. The following is one:

```
Circle
--------------------------------------------
– radius: double
– centerX: double
– centerY: double
--------------------------------------------
+ resize(double newRadius): void
+ move(double newX, double newY): void
# erase(): void
. . .
```

2. The method `sameName` is not listed in the class diagram for `Student`. So, you follow the arrow to the class diagram for `Person`. The method `sameName` with a single parameter of type `Person` is in the class diagram for `Person`. Because you know a `Student` is a `Person`, you know that this definition works for the method `sameName` with a single parameter of type `Student`. So, the definition used for the method `sameName` is in the class definition of `Person`.
3. You start at the class diagram for `Student`. The method `setStudentNumber` with a single parameter of type `int` is in the class diagram for `Student`, so you need look no further. The definition used for the method `setStudentNumber` is in the class definition of `Student`.

extra code on website

4. The code for this is also on the website that comes with this book. This code is in the file `SelectionSort.java`. A demonstration program is in the file `SelectionSortDemo.java`.

```
public class SelectionSort
{
    public static void sort(double [] a,
                                       int begin, int end)
    {
        if ((end - begin) >= 1)
        {
            int splitPoint = split(a, begin, end);
            sort(a, begin, splitPoint);
            sort(a, splitPoint + 1, end);
            join(a, begin, splitPoint, end);
        }//else sorting one (or fewer) elements
         //so do nothing.
    }

    private static int split(double [] a,
                             int begin , int end)
    {
        int index = indexOfSmallest(begin, a, end);
        interchange(begin,index, a);

        return begin;
    }

    private static void join(double [] a, int begin,
                             int splitPoint, int end)
    {
      //Nothing to do.
    }

    private static int indexOfSmallest(int startIndex,
                                double [] a, int endIndex)
    {
        double min = a[startIndex];
        int indexOfMin = startIndex;
        int index;
        for (index = startIndex + 1;
                             index < endIndex; index++)
            if (a[index] < min)
            {
                min = a[index];
                indexOfMin = index;
                //min is smallest of a[startIndex]
                //through a[index]
            }
        return indexOfMin;
    }
```

```
    private static void interchange(int i,int j, double [] a)
    {
            double temp;
            temp = a[i];
            a[i] = a[j];
            a[j] = temp; //original value of a[i]
    }
}
```

5. An array of random values would have the fastest run time, because it would divide the array segments into approximately equal subarrays most of the time. The other two cases would give approximately the same running time and would be significantly slower, because the algorithms would always divide an array segment into very unequal size pieces, one piece with only one element and one piece with the rest of the elements. It is ironic but true that our version of the quick sort algorithms has its worst behavior on an already sorted array. There are variations on the quick sort algorithms that perform well on a sorted array. For example, choosing the middle element as the splitting value will give good performance on an already sorted array. But, whatever splitting value you choose, there will always be a few cases with slow running time.

MyProgrammingLab™ Programming Projects

Visit www.myprogramminglab.com to complete select exercises online and get instant feedback.

1. The UML diagram below describes a class named `Movie`. Implement this class in Java and test it from a `main` method that creates several `Movie` objects. The `printDescription()` method should output all member variables for the class.

Movie
– title: String – minutes: int – year: int # price: double
+ Movie(in String title, in int year, in double price) + getTitle( ): String + setTitle(in String newTitle) + printDescription( )

The word "in" means the parameter is used to deliver data to the method.

2. The following UML diagram shows the relationship between a class called `PizzaOrder` and a class called `Pizza`:

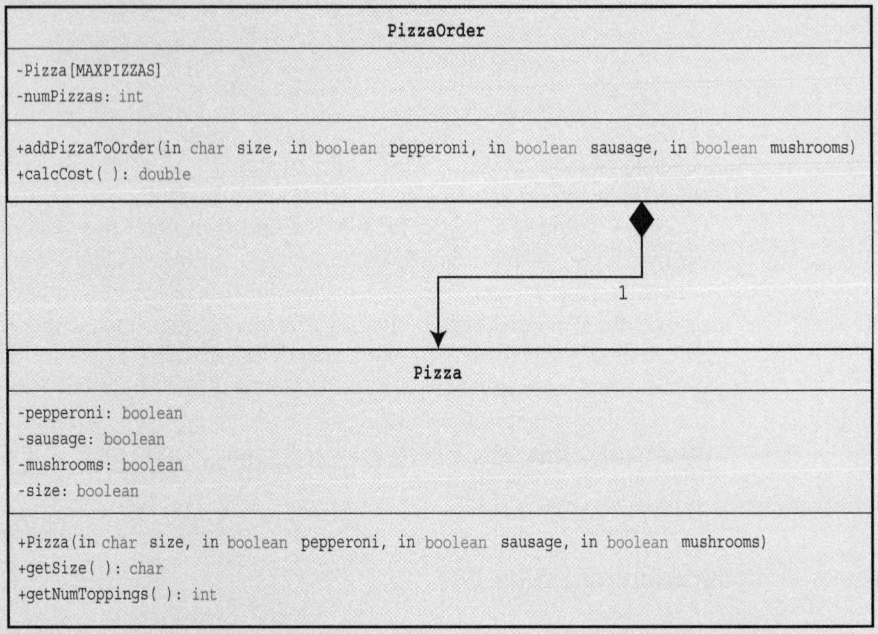

The word "in" means the parameter is used to deliver data to the method.

The `Pizza` class contains information about a specific `pizza`. The variables of pepperoni, sausage, and mushrooms are booleans that indicate whether or not these toppings are present on the pizza. The size variable is a character of value `'s'`, `'m'`, or `'l'` to indicate small, medium, or large. There is also a `Pizza` constructor that initializes all of these values. The `getSize()` method returns the size of the pizza and the `getNumToppings()` method returns a number from 0–3 depending on what toppings are present (e.g., if the pizza has pepperoni and mushrooms, it would be 2).

The `PizzaOrder` class contains an array of `Pizza`'s. There is a method to add a new pizza to the array (which increments `numPizzas`) and also a method to calculate the cost of the entire order. A small pizza costs $8, a medium pizza is $10, and a large pizza costs $12. Each topping adds $1 to the pizza.

The arrow connecting `PizzaOrder` to `Pizza` indicates that the `PizzaOrder` class has a reference to the `Pizza` class, but not vice versa. The solid diamond on the `PizzaOrder` class is a UML construct that indicates that the `PizzaOrder` class has a collection of the `Pizza` class. There may be many (*) `Pizza`'s for a single (one) `PizzaOrder`.

Given this information, write Java code that implements the `Pizza` and `PizzaOrder` classes. Also, write a test main function that creates a pizza order, adds several `pizzas` to it, and outputs the cost of the order.

3. The UML diagram below shows the relationship between four classes. Implement the classes in a test program that creates instances of `CreditCard`, `Cash`, and `Check`. Output the string description of each. Note that the italicized *Payment* class indicates that this is an abstract class. The word "in" means the parameter is used to deliver data to the method.

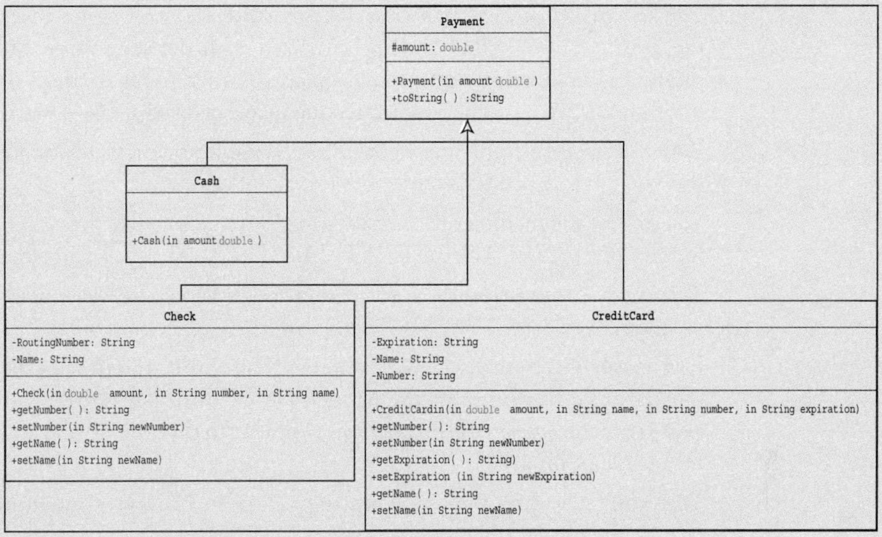

4. Use the Model-View-Controller pattern to implement a simple timer-based counter. The counter should start at a user-specified initial value and increment by one every second until it reaches a user-specified final value. A UML diagram depicting the three classes for the pattern is shown below. The word "in" means the parameter is used to deliver data to the method.

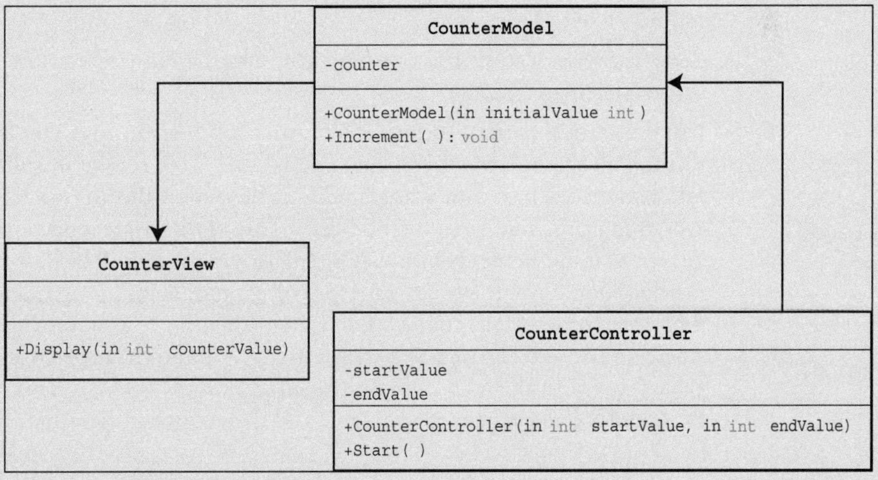

The CounterView class should simply take an input counter value and print it on the console screen.

The CounterModel class should have a variable that represents the counter's value. The Increment method increments the counter by one and calls CounterView's Display method.

The CounterController class takes a start and end value that is specified by the user. CounterModel is then initialized with the start value. When the Start method is invoked, it calls CounterModel's increment method once per second until endValue – startValue seconds have elapsed.

You will need to implement additional variables or methods in addition to those shown above in order to create the linkages between classes.

You can use the method call Thread.sleep(1000) to make the CounterController wait for one second. The call must be placed inside a try/catch block.

Test your program with a main method that counts several different ranges of values.

5. It is possible to purchase "geek" watches that output the time of day in binary. To illustrate the flexibility of the Model-View-Controller pattern, modify the view class (CounterView) of the previous problem so that the display outputs the counter's value in binary.

   Test your new program by counting values in binary. You should not have to change the model or controller classes.

6. Recode the QuickSort class implementation by adding two efficiency improvements to the method sort: (1) Eliminate the calls to join, because it accomplishes nothing. (2) Add code for the special case of an array of exactly two elements and make the general case apply to arrays of three or more elements.

7. Redo the QuickSort class so that it chooses the splitting point as follows: The splitting point is the middle (in size) of the first element, the last element, and an element at approximately the middle of the array. This will make a very uneven split less likely.

8. Redo the QuickSort class to have the modifications given for Programming Projects 12.6 and 12.7.

VideoNote **Solution to Programming Project 12.9**

9. Use the sorting pattern to implement insertion sort. In insertion sort, the split method always returns the value (end – 1). This results in splitting the array into two pieces, one with a single value at the end of the array, and the other with everything else. The join method does more work. A precondition for entry into join is that the elements from a[begin] to a[end-1] will be in sorted order. The method should insert a[end] into the correct spot from a[begin] to a[end] such that sorted order is maintained. For example, if array a contains {2, 4, 6, 8, 5} where begin = 0 and end = 4 then a[end] = 5 and the method should insert the value 5 between the 4 and 6, resulting in {2, 4, 5, 6, 8}. This entails copying the 6 and 8 one element to the right, and then copying the value 5 to index 2.

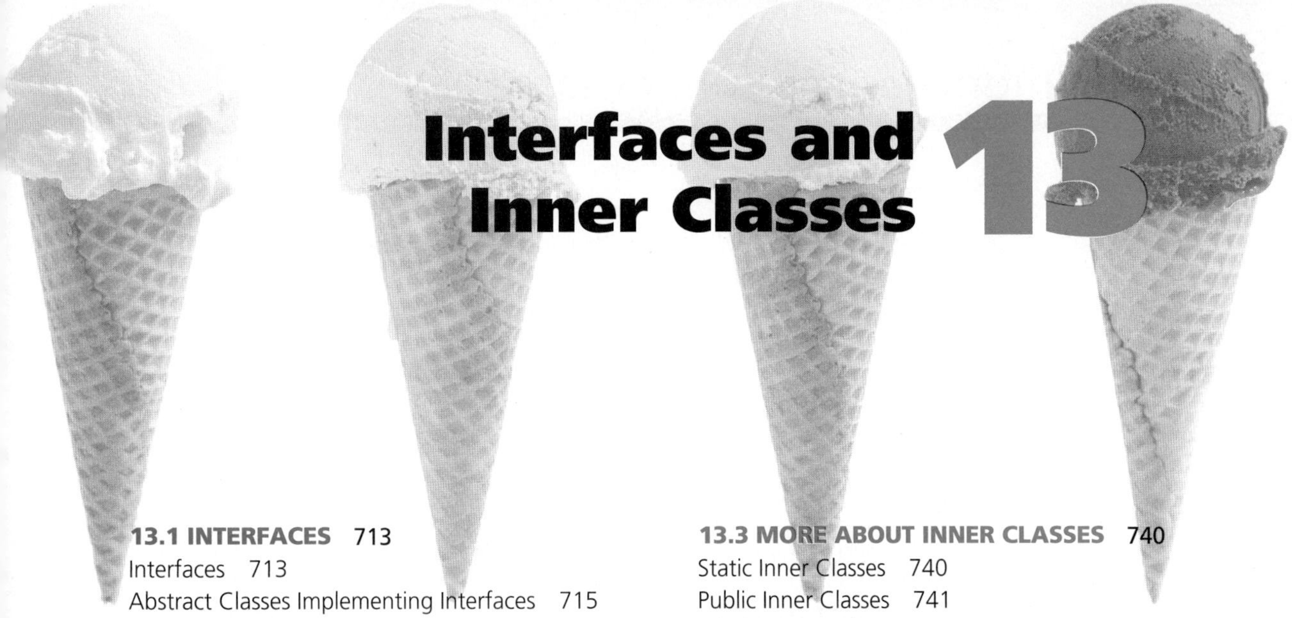

13 Interfaces and Inner Classes

13 Interfaces and Inner Classes

Art, it seems to me, should simplify. That, indeed, is very nearly the whole of the higher artistic process; finding what conventions of form and what details one can do without and yet preserve the spirit of the whole....

WILLA SIBERT CATHER, *On the Art of Fiction*

Introduction

A Java *interface* specifies a set of methods that any class that implements the interface must have. An interface is itself a type, which allows you to define methods with parameters of an interface type and then have the code apply to all classes that implement the interface. One way to view an interface is as an extreme form of an abstract class. However, as you will see, an interface allows you to do more than an abstract class allows you to do. Interfaces are Java's way of approximating multiple inheritance. You cannot have multiple base classes in Java, but interfaces allow you to approximate the power of multiple base classes.

The second major topic of this chapter is *inner classes*. An inner class is simply a class defined within another class. Because inner classes are local to the class that contains them, they can help make a class self-contained by allowing you to make helping classes inner classes.

Prerequisites

Section 13.1 on interfaces and Section 13.2 on simple uses of inner classes are independent of each other and can be covered in any order. Section 13.3 on more subtle details of inner classes requires both Sections 13.1 and 13.2.

Section 13.1 on interfaces requires Chapters 1 through 9. No material from Chapters 10 through 12 is used anywhere in this chapter.

Section 13.2 on simple uses of inner classes requires Chapters 1 through 5. It does not use any material from Chapters 6 through 12.

Section 13.3 on more advanced inner class material requires both Sections 13.1 and 13.2 (and of course their prerequisites). The material in Section 13.3 is not used elsewhere in this book.

13.1 Interfaces

Autonomy of Syntax

A linguistic concept attributed to Noam Chomsky

In this section, we describe *interfaces*. An interface is a type that groups together a number of different classes that all include method definitions for a common set of method headings.

Interfaces

interface

An **interface** is something like the extreme case of an abstract class. *An interface is not a class. It is, however, a type that can be satisfied by any class that implements the interface.* An interface is a property of a class that says what methods it must have.

An interface specifies the headings for methods that must be defined in any class that implements the interface. For example, Display 13.1 shows an interface named `Ordered`. Note that an interface contains only method headings. It contains no instance variables nor any complete method definitions. (Although, as we will see, it can contain defined constants.)

implementing an interface

To **implement an interface**, a concrete class (that is, a class other than an abstract class) must do two things:

1. It must include the phrase

   `implements` *Interface_Name*

   at the start of the class definition. To implement more than one interface, you list all the interface names, separated by commas, as in

   ```
   implements SomeInterface, AnotherInterface
   ```

Display 13.1 The `Ordered` Interface

```
public interface Ordered
{
    public boolean precedes(Object other);

    /**
     For objects of the class o1 and o2,
     o1.follows(o2) == o2.preceded(o1).
    */
    public boolean follows(Object other);
}
```

Do not forget the semicolons at the end of the method headings.

Neither the compiler nor the run-time system will do anything to ensure that this comment is satisfied. It is only advisory to the programmer implementing the interface.

2. The class must implement *all* the method headings listed in the definitions of the interfaces.

For example, to implement the `Ordered` interface, a class definition must contain the phrase `implements Ordered` at the start of the class definition, as shown in the following:

```
public class OrderedHourlyEmployee
        extends HourlyEmployee implements Ordered
{
```

The class must also implement the two methods `precedes` and `follows`. The full definition of `OrderedHourlyEmployee` is given in Display 13.2.

Display 13.2 Implementation of an Interface

```
public class OrderedHourlyEmployee
        extends HourlyEmployee implements Ordered
{
    public boolean precedes(Object other)
    {
        if (other == null)
            return false;
        else if (!(other instanceof OrderedHourlyEmployee))
            return false;
        else
        {
            OrderedHourlyEmployee otherOrderedHourlyEmployee =
                              (OrderedHourlyEmployee)other;
            return (getPay() < otherOrderedHourlyEmployee.getPay());
        }
    }

    public boolean follows(Object other)
    {
        if (other == null)
            return false;
        else if (!(other instanceof OrderedHourlyEmployee))
            return false;
        else
        {
            OrderedHourlyEmployee otherOrderedHourlyEmployee =
                            (OrderedHourlyEmployee)other;
            return (otherOrderedHourlyEmployee.precedes(this));
        }
    }
}
```

Although **getClass** *works better than* **instanceof** *for defining* **equals**, **instanceof** *works better in this case. However, either will do for the points being made here.*

An interface and all of its method headings are normally declared to be public. They cannot be given private, protected, or package access. (The modifier `public` may be omitted, but all the methods will still be treated as if they are public.) When a class implements an interface, it must make all the methods in the interface public.

An interface is a type. This allows you to write a method with a parameter of an interface type, such as a parameter of type `Ordered`, and that parameter will accept as an argument any class you later define that implements the interface.

An interface serves a function similar to a base class, but it is important to note that it is not a base class. (In fact, it is not a class of any kind.) Some programming languages (such as C++) allow one class to be a derived class of two or more different base classes. This is not allowed in Java. In Java, a derived class can have only one base class. However, in addition to any base class that a Java class may have, it can also implement any number of interfaces. This allows Java programs to approximate the power of multiple base classes without the complications that can arise with multiple base classes.

You might want to say the argument to `precedes` in the `Ordered` interface (Display 13.2) is the same as the class doing the implementation (for example, `OrderedHourlyEmployee`). There is no way to say this in Java, so we normally make such parameters of type `Object`. It would be legal to make the argument to `precedes` of type `Ordered`, but that is not normally preferable to using `Object` as the parameter type. If you make the argument of type `Ordered`, you would still have to handle the case of `null` and the case of an argument that (while `Ordered`) is not of type `OrderedHourlyEmployee`.

An interface definition is stored in a `.java` file and compiled just as a class definition is compiled.

Abstract Classes Implementing Interfaces

As you saw in the previous subsection, a concrete class (that is, a regular class) must give definitions for all the method headings given in an interface in order to implement the interface. However, you can define an abstract class that implements an interface but gives only definitions for some of the method headings given in the interface. The method headings given in the interface that are not given definitions are made into abstract methods. A simple example is given in Display 13.3.

Derived Interfaces

extending an interface

You can derive an interface from a base interface. This is often called **extending** the interface. The details are similar to deriving a class. An example is given in Display 13.4.

Display 13.3 An Abstract Class Implementing an Interface ★

```
public abstract class MyAbstractClass implements Ordered
{
    private int number;
    private char grade;

    public boolean precedes(Object other)
    {
        if (other == null)
            return false;
        else if (!(other instanceof HourlyEmployee))
            return false;
        else
        {
            MyAbstractClass otherOfMyAbstractClass =
                                          (MyAbstractClass)other;
            return (this.number < otherOfMyAbstractClass.number);
        }
    }

    public abstract boolean follows(Object other);

}
```

Display 13.4 Extending an Interface

```
public interface ShowablyOrdered extends Ordered
{
    /**
     Outputs an object of the class that precedes the calling object.
    */
    public void showOneWhoPrecedes();
}
```

Neither the compiler nor the run-time system will do anything to ensure that this comment is satisfied.

A (concrete) class that implements the `ShowablyOrdered` *interface must have a definition for the method* `showOneWhoPrecedes` *and also have definitions for the methods* `precedes` *and* `follows` *given in the* `Ordered` *interface.*

> **Interfaces**
>
> An interface is a type that specifies method headings (and, as we will see, possibly defined constants as well). The syntax for defining an interface is similar to the syntax of defining a class, except that the word `interface` is used in place of `class` and the method headings without any method body (but followed by a semicolon) are given only.
>
> Note that an interface has no instance variables and no method definitions.
>
> A class can implement any number of interfaces. To implement an interface, the class must include
>
> `implements` *Interface_Name*
>
> at the end of the class heading and must supply definitions for the method headings given in the interface. If the class does not supply definitions for all the method headings given in the interface, then the class must be an abstract class and the method headings without definitions must be abstract methods.
>
> **EXAMPLE**
>
> See Displays 13.1, 13.2, and 13.3.

MyProgrammingLab™

Self-Test Exercises

1. Can you have a variable of an interface type? Can you have a parameter of an interface type?

2. Can an abstract class ever implement an interface?

3. Can a derived class have two base classes? Can it implement two interfaces?

4. Can an interface implement another interface?

PITFALL: Interface Semantics Are Not Enforced

As far as the Java compiler is concerned, an interface has syntax but no semantics. For example, the definition of the `Ordered` interface (Display 13.1) says the following in a comment:

```
/**
 For objects of the class o1 and o2,
 o1.follows(o2) == o2.preceded(o1).
*/
```

You might have assumed that this is true even if there were no comment in the interface. After all, in the real world, if I precede you, then you follow me. However, that is giving your intuitive interpretation to the word "`precedes`".

(continued)

PITFALL: (continued)

As far as the compiler and run-time systems are concerned, the `Ordered` interface merely says that the methods `precedes` and `follows` each take one argument of type `Object` and return a `boolean` value. The interface does not really require that the `boolean` value be computed in any particular way. For example, the compiler would be satisfied if both `precedes` and `follows` always return `true` or if they always return `false`. It would even allow the methods to use a random number generator to generate a random choice between `true` and `false`.

It would be nice if we could safely give an interface some simple semantics, such as saying that `o1.follows(o2)` means the same as `o2.preceded(o1)`. However, if Java did allow that, there would be problems with having a class implement two interfaces or even with having a class derived from one base class and implementing an interface. Either of these situations could produce two semantic conditions, both of which must be implemented for the same method, and the two semantics may not be consistent. For example, suppose that (contrary to fact) you could require that `o1.follows(o2)` means the same as `o2.preceded(o1)`. You could also define another interface with an inconsistent semantics, such as saying that `precedes` always returns `true` and that `follows` always returns `false`. As long as a class can have two objects, there is no way a class could implement both of these semantics. Interfaces in Java are very well behaved, the price of which is that you cannot count on Java to enforce any semantics in an interface.

If you want to require semantics for an interface, you can add it to the documentation, as illustrated by the comments in Displays 13.1 and 13.4, but always remember that these are just comments; they are not enforced by either the compiler or the run-time system, so you cannot necessarily rely on such semantics being followed. However, we live in an imperfect world, and sometimes you will find that you must specify a semantics for an interface; do so in the interface's documentation. It then becomes the responsibility of the programmers implementing the interface to follow the semantics.

Having made our point about interface semantics not being enforced by the compiler or run-time system, we want to nevertheless urge you to follow the specified semantics for an interface. Software written for classes that implement an interface will assume that any class that implements the interface does satisfy the specified semantics. So, if you define a class that implements an interface but does not satisfy the semantics for the interface, then software written for classes that implement that interface will probably not work correctly for your class. ■

Interface Semantics Are Not Enforced

When you define a class that implements an interface, the compiler and run-time system will let you define the body of an interface method any way you want, provided you keep the method heading as it is given in the interface. However, you should follow the specified semantics for an interface whenever you define a class that implements that interface; otherwise, software written for that interface may not work for your class.

The `Comparable` Interface

This subsection requires material on arrays from Chapter 6. If you have not yet covered Chapter 6, you can skip this section and the following Programming Example without any loss of continuity. But if you have read Chapter 6, you should not consider this section to be optional.

In Chapter 6 (Display 6.11), we introduced a method for sorting a partially filled array of base type `double` into increasing order. It is very easy to transform the code into a method to sort into decreasing order instead of increasing order. (See Self-Test Exercise 20 of Chapter 6 and its answer if this is not clear to you.) It is also easy to modify the code to obtain methods for sorting integers instead of `doubles` or sorting strings into alphabetical order. Although these changes are easy, they seem to be—and in fact are—a useless nuisance. All these sorting methods are essentially the same. The only differences are the types of the values being sorted and the definition of the ordering. It would seem that we should be able to give a single sorting method that covers all these cases. The `Comparable` interface lets us do this.

The `Comparable` interface is in the `java.lang` package and so is automatically available to your program. The `Comparable` interface has only the following method heading that must be implemented for a class to implement the `Comparable` interface:

```
public int compareTo(Object other);
```

The `Comparable` interface has semantics, and it is the programmer's responsibility to follow the semantics when implementing the `Comparable` interface. The semantics says that `compareTo` returns

compareTo

a negative number if the calling object "comes before" the parameter `other`,
a zero if the calling object "equals" the parameter `other`,
and a positive number if the calling object "comes after" the parameter `other`.[1]

Almost any reasonable notions of "comes before" should be acceptable. In particular, all of the standard less-than relations on numbers and lexicographic ordering on strings are suitable ordering for `compareTo`. (The relationship "comes after" is just the reverse of "comes before.") If you need to consider other ordering, the precise rule is that the ordering must be a total ordering, which means the following rules must be satisfied:

(Irreflexive) For no object `o` does `o` come before `o`.
(Trichotomy) For any two objects `o1` and `o2`, one, and only one, of the following holds true: `o1` comes before `o2`, `o1` comes after `o2`, or `o1` equals `o2`.
(Transitivity) If `o1` comes before `o2` and `o2` comes before `o3`, then `o1` comes before `o3`.

The "equals" of the `compareTo` method semantics should coincide with the `equals` methods if possible, but this is not absolutely required by the semantics.

---

[1]Because the parameter to `CompareTo` is of type `Object`, an argument to `CompareTo` might not be an object of the class being defined. If the parameter `other` is not of the same type as the class being defined, then the semantics specifies that a `ClassCastException` should be thrown.

The `Comparable` Interface

The `Comparable` interface is in the `java.lang` package and so is automatically available to your program. The `Comparable` interface has only the following method heading that must be given a definition for a class to implement the `Comparable` interface:

```
public int compareTo(Object other);
```

The method `compareTo` should return

a negative number if the calling object "comes before" the parameter `other`,
a zero if the calling object "equals" the parameter `other`,
and a positive number if the calling object "comes after" the parameter `other`.

The "comes before" ordering that underlies `compareTo` should be a total ordering. Most normal ordering, such as less-than ordering on numbers and lexicographic ordering on strings, is total ordering.

If you define a class that implements the `Comparable` interface but that does not satisfy these conditions, then code written for `Comparable` objects will not work properly. It is the responsibility of you, the programmer, to ensure that the semantics is satisfied. Neither the compiler nor the run-time system enforces any semantics on the `Comparable` interface.

If you have read this subsection, you should also read the following Programming Example.

EXAMPLE: Using the `Comparable` Interface

Display 13.5 shows a class with a method that can sort any partially filled array whose base type implements the `Comparable` interface (including implementing the semantics we discussed in the previous subsection). To obtain the code in Display 13.5, we started with the sorting code in Display 6.11 and mechanically replaced all occurrences of the array type `double[]` with the type `Comparable[]`. We replaced all Boolean expressions of the form

Expression_1 `<` *Expression_2*

with

Expression_1`.compareTo(`*Expression_2*`) < 0`

We also changed the comments a bit to make them consistent with the `compareTo` notation. The changes are highlighted in Display 13.5. Only four small changes to the code were needed.

(continued on page 722)

Display 13.5 Sorting Method for Array of `Comparable` (part 1 of 2)

```
public class GeneralizedSelectionSort
{
    /**
     Precondition: numberUsed <= a.length;
                  The first numberUsed indexed variables have values.
     Action: Sorts a so that a[0], a[1], ... , a[numberUsed - 1] are in
     increasing order by the compareTo method.
    */
    public static void sort(Comparable[] a, int numberUsed)
    {
        int index, indexOfNextSmallest;
        for (index = 0; index < numberUsed - 1; index++)
        {   //Place the correct value in a[index]:
            indexOfNextSmallest = indexOfSmallest(index, a,
                   numberUsed);
            interchange(index,indexOfNextSmallest, a);
            //a[0], a[1],..., a[index] are correctly ordered and
            //these are
            //the smallest of the original array elements. The remaining
            //positions contain the rest of the original array elements.
        }
    }

    /**
     Returns the index of the smallest value among
     a[startIndex], a[startIndex+1], ... a[numberUsed - 1]
    */
    private static int indexOfSmallest(int startIndex,
                                        Comparable [] a, int numberUsed)
    {
        Comparable min = a[startIndex];
        int indexOfMin = startIndex;
        int index;
        for (index = startIndex + 1; index < numberUsed; index++)
          if (a[index].compareTo(min) < 0)//if a[index] is less than min
          {
            min = a[index];
            indexOfMin = index;
            //min is smallest of a[startIndex] through a[index]
          }
        return indexOfMin;
    }
```

(continued)

Display 13.5 Sorting Method for Array of `Comparable` (part 2 of 2)

```
    /**
     Precondition: i and j are legal indices for the array a.
     Postcondition: Values of a[i] and a[j] have been interchanged.
     */
    private static void interchange(int i, int j, Comparable[] a)
    {
        Comparable temp;
        temp = a[i];
        a[i] = a[j];
        a[j] = temp; //original value of a[i]
    }

}
```

EXAMPLE: (continued)

Display 13.6 shows a demonstration of using the sorting method given in Display 13.5. To understand why the demonstration works, you need to be aware of the fact that both of the classes `Double` and `String` implement the `Comparable` interface.

If you were to check the full documentation for the class `Double`, you would see that `Double` implements the `Comparable` interface and so has a `compareTo` method. Moreover, for objects `o1` and `o2` of `Double`,

```
o1.compareTo(o2) < 0 //o1 "comes before" o2
```

means the same thing as

```
o1.doubleValue() < o2.doubleValue()
```

So, the implementation of the `Comparable` interface for the class `Double` is really just the ordinary less-than relationship on the `double` values corresponding to the `Double` objects.

Similarly, if you were to check the full documentation for the class `String`, you would see that `String` implements the `Comparable` interface and so has a `compareTo` method. Moreover, the implementation of the `compareTo` method for the class `String` is really just the ordinary lexicographic relationship on the strings.

This Programming Example uses the standard library classes `Double` and `String` for the base type of the array. You can do the same thing with arrays whose base class is a class you defined, so long as the class implements the `Comparable` interface (including the standard semantics, which we discussed earlier in the Pitfall "Interface Semantics Are Not Enforced").

This Programming Example does point out one restriction on interfaces. They can apply only to classes. A primitive type cannot implement an interface. So, in Display 13.6, we could not sort an array with base type `double` using the sorting method for an array of `Comparable`. We had to settle for sorting an array with base type `Double`. This is a good example of using a wrapper class with its "wrapper class personality."

Display 13.6 Sorting Arrays of `Comparable` (part 1 of 2)

The classes `Double` *and* `String` *do implement the* `Comparable` *interface.*

```
/**
 Demonstrates sorting arrays for classes that
 implement the Comparable interface.
*/
public class ComparableDemo
{
    public static void main(String[] args)
    {
        Double[] d = new Double[10];
        for (int i = 0; i < d.length; i++)
            d[i] = new Double(d.length - i);

        System.out.println("Before sorting:");
        int i;
        for (i = 0; i < d.length; i++)
            System.out.print(d[i].doubleValue() + ", ");
        System.out.println();

        GeneralizedSelectionSort.sort(d, d.length);

        System.out.println("After sorting:");
        for (i = 0; i < d.length; i++)
            system.out.print(d[i].doubleValue() + ", ");
        System.out.println();

        String[] a = new String[10];
        a[0] = "dog";
        a[1] = "cat";
        a[2] = "cornish game hen";
        int numberUsed = 3;

        System.out.println("Before sorting:");
        for (i = 0; i < numberUsed; i++)
            System.out.print(a[i] + ", ");
        System.out.println();

        GeneralizedSelectionSort.sort(a, numberUsed);

        System.out.println("After sorting:");
        for (i = 0; i < numberUsed; i++)
            System.out.print(a[i] + ", ");
        System.out.println();
    }
}
```

(continued)

Display 13.6 Sorting Arrays of **Comparable** (part 2 of 2)

Sample Dialogue

```
Before Sorting
10.0, 9.0, 8.0, 7.0, 6.0, 5.0, 4.0, 3.0, 2.0, 1.0,
After sorting:
1.0, 2.0, 3.0, 4.0, 5.0, 6.0, 7.0, 8.0, 9.0, 10.0,
Before sorting;
dog, cat, cornish game hen,
After sorting:
cat, cornish game hen, dog,
```

MyProgrammingLab™

Self-Test Exercises

These exercises are for the material on the `Comparable` interface.

5. The method `interchange` in Display 13.5 makes no use of the fact that its second argument is an array with base type `Comparable`. Suppose we change the parameter type `Comparable[]` to `Object[]` and change the type of the variable `temp` to `Object`. Would the program in Display 13.6 produce the same dialogue?

6. Is the following a suitable implementation of the `Comparable` interface?

```
public class Double2 implements Comparable
{
    private double value;
    public Double2(double theValue)
    {
        value = theValue;
    }
    public int compareTo(Object other)
    {
        return −1;
    }
    public double doubleValue()
    {
        return value;
    }
}
```

You can think of the underlying "comes before" relationship as saying that for any objects `d1` and `d2`, `d1` comes before `d2`.

MyProgrammingLab™

Self-Test Exercises (continued)

7. Suppose you have a class `Circle` that represents circles which all have centers at the same point. (To make it concrete, you can take the circles to be in the usual *x,y* plain and to all have their centers at the origin.) Suppose there is a `boolean` valued method `inside` of the class `Circle` such that, for circles `c1` and `c2`,

   ```
   c1.inside(c2)
   ```

   returns `true` if `c1` is completely inside of `c2` (and `c2` is not the same as `c1`). Is the following a total ordering?

   `c1` comes before `c2` if `c1` is inside of `c2`
   (that is, if `c1.inside(c2)` returns `true`).

   You could represent objects of the class `Circle` by a single value of type `double` that gives the radius of the circle, but the answer does not depend on such details.

Defined Constants in Interfaces

The designers of Java often used the interface mechanism to take care of a number of miscellaneous details that do not really fit the spirit of what an interface is supposed to be. One example of this is the use of an interface as a way to name a group of defined constants.

An interface can contain defined constants as well as method headings, or instead of method headings. When a method implements the interface, it automatically gets the defined constants. For example, the following interface defines constants for months:

```
public interface MonthNumbers
{
    public static final int JANUARY = 1,
       FEBRUARY = 2, MARCH = 3, APRIL = 4, MAY = 5,
       JUNE = 6, JULY = 7, AUGUST = 8, SEPTEMBER = 9,
       OCTOBER = 10, NOVEMBER = 11, DECEMBER = 12;
}
```

Any class that implements the `MonthNumbers` interface will automatically have the 12 constants defined in the `MonthNumbers` interface. For example, consider the following toy class:

```
public class DemoMonthNumbers implements MonthNumbers
{
    public static void main(String[] args)
    {
        System.out.println(
           "The number for January is " + JANUARY);
    }
}
```

Note that the constant `JANUARY` is used in the class `DemoMonthNumbers` but is not defined there. The class `DemoMonthNumbers` automatically gets the month constants because it implements the `MonthNumbers` interface.

no instance variables

An interface cannot have instance variables, although it can use the syntax for instance variables as a way to define constants. Any variables defined in an interface must be public, static, and final, so Java allows you to omit those modifiers. The following is an equivalent definition of the interface `MonthNumbers`:

```
public interface MonthNumbers
{
    int JANUARY = 1,
       FEBRUARY = 2, MARCH = 3, APRIL = 4, MAY = 5,
       JUNE = 6, JULY = 7, AUGUST = 8, SEPTEMBER = 9,
       OCTOBER = 10, NOVEMBER = 11, DECEMBER = 12;
}
```

Thus, an interface can be used to give a name for a group of defined constants, so that you can easily add the needed constants to any class by implementing the interface. This is really a different use for interfaces than what we have seen before, which was to use interfaces to specify method headings. It is legal to mix these two uses by including both defined constants and method headings in a single interface.

PITFALL: Inconsistent Interfaces

Java allows a class to have only one base class but also allows the class to implement any number of interfaces. The reason that a class can have only one base class is that if Java allowed two base classes, the two base classes could provide different and inconsistent definitions of a single method heading. Because interfaces have no method bodies at all, this problem cannot arise when a class implements two interfaces. The ideal that the designers of Java apparently hoped to realize was that any two interfaces will always be consistent. However, this ideal was not fully realized. Although it is a rare phenomenon, two interfaces can be inconsistent. In fact, there is more than one kind of inconsistency that can be exhibited. If you write a class definition that implements two inconsistent interfaces, that is an error and the class definition is illegal. Let's see how two interfaces can be inconsistent.

inconsistent constants

The most obvious way that two interfaces can be inconsistent is by defining two constants with the same name but with different values. For example,

```
public interface Interface1
{
    int ANSWER = 42;
}

public interface Interface2
{
    int ANSWER = 0;
}
```

PITFALL: (continued)

Suppose a class definition begins with

```
public class MyClass
  implements Interface1, Interface2
{ ...
```

Clearly this has to be, and is, illegal. The defined constant `ANSWER` cannot be simultaneously `42` and `0`.[2]

inconsistent method headings

Even two method headings can be inconsistent. For example, consider the following two interfaces:

```
public interface InterfaceA
{
    public int getStuff();
}
public interface InterfaceB
{
    public String getStuff();
}
```

Suppose a class definition begins with

```
public class YourClass
             implements InterfaceA, InterfaceB
{ ...
```

Clearly this has to be, and is, illegal. The method `getStuff` in the class `YourClass` cannot be simultaneously a method that returns an `int` and a method that returns a value of type `String`. (Remember that you cannot overload a method based on the type returned; so, overloading cannot be used to get around this problem.) ■

MyProgrammingLab™

Self-Test Exercises

8. Will the following program compile? If it does compile, will it run? `Interface1` and `Interface2` were defined in the previous subsection.

```
public class MyClass
             implements Interface1, Interface2
{
    public static void main(String[] args)
    {
        System.out.println(ANSWER);
    }
}
```

(continued)

[2]If the class never uses the constant `ANSWER`, then there is no inconsistency and the class will compile and run with no error messages.

MyProgrammingLab™

Self-Test Exercises (continued)

9. Will the following program compile? If it does compile, will it run? `Interface1` and `Interface2` were defined in the previous subsection.

```
public class MyClass
             implements Interface1, Interface2
{
    public static void main(String[] args)
    {
        System.out.println("Hello");
    }
}
```

10. Will the following program compile? If it does compile, will it run? `InterfaceA` and `InterfaceB` were defined in the previous subsection.

```
public class YourClass
               implements InterfaceA, InterfaceB
{
    public String getStuff()
    {
        return "one";
    }
}
```

11. Will the following two interfaces and the following program class compile? If they compile, will the program run with no error messages?

```
public interface InterfaceA
{
    public int getStuff();
}
public interface InterfaceOtherB
{
    public String getStuff(String someStuff);
}
public class OurClass
            implements InterfaceA, InterfaceOtherB
{
    private int intStuff = 42;

    public static void main(String[] args)
    {
        OurClass object = new OurClass();
        System.out.println(object.getStuff()
                    + object.getStuff("Hello"));
    }
```

MyProgrammingLab™

Self-Test Exercises (continued)

```
        public int getStuff()
        {
            return intStuff;
        }
        public String getStuff(String someStuff)
        {
            return someStuff;
        }
    }
```

The Serializable Interface ★

Serializable

As we have already noted, the designers of Java often used the interface mechanism to take care of miscellaneous details that do not really fit the spirit of what an interface is supposed to be. An extreme example of this is the `Serializable` interface. The `Serializable` interface has no method headings and no defined constants. As a traditional interface, it is pointless. However, Java uses it as a type tag that means the programmer gives permission to the system to implement file I/O in a particular way. If you want to know what that way of implementing file I/O is, see Chapter 10, in which the `Serializable` interface is discussed in detail.

The Cloneable Interface

Cloneable

The `Cloneable` interface is another example where Java uses the interface mechanism for something other than its traditional role. The `Cloneable` interface has no method headings that must be implemented (and has no defined constants). However, it is used to say something about how the method `clone`, which is inherited from the class `Object`, should be used and how it should be redefined.

So, what is the purpose of the `Cloneable` interface? When you define a class to implement the `Cloneable` interface, you are agreeing to redefine the `clone` method (inherited from `Object`) in a particular way. The primary motivation for this appears to be security issues. Cloning can potentially copy private data if not done correctly. Also, some software may depend on your redefining the `clone` method in a certain way. Programmers have strong and differing views on how to handle cloning and the `Cloneable` interface. What follows is the official Java line on how to do it.

The method `Object.clone()` does a bit-by-bit copy of the object's data in storage. If the data is all primitive type data or data of immutable class types (such as `String`), then this works fine and has no unintended side effects. However, if the data in the object includes instance variables whose type is a mutable class, then this would cause what we refer to as *privacy leaks*. (See the Pitfall section entitled "Privacy Leaks" in Chapter 5.) To avoid these privacy leaks when you define the `clone` method in a derived class, you should invoke the `clone` method of the base class `Object` (or whatever the base class is) and then reset the values of any new instance variables whose types are mutable class types. Reset these instance variables to copies of the instance variables in the calling object. There are also issues of exception handling to deal with. An example may be clearer than an abstract discussion.

Let's start with the simple case. Suppose your class has no instance variables of a mutable class type, or to phrase it differently, suppose your class has instance variables all of whose types are either a primitive type or an immutable class type, like `String`. And to make it even simpler, suppose your class has no specified base class, so the base class is `Object`. If you want to implement the `Cloneable` interface, you should define the `clone` method as in Display 13.7.

The `try-catch` blocks are required because the inherited method `clone` can throw the exception `CloneNotSupportedException` if the class does not correctly implement the `Cloneable` interface. Of course, in this case the exception will never be thrown, but the compiler will still insist on the `try-catch` blocks.

Now let's suppose your class has one instance variable of a mutable class type named `DataClass`. Then, the definition of the `clone` method should be as in Display 13.8. First, a bit-by-bit `copy` of the object is made by the invocation of `super.clone()`. The dangerous part of `copy` is the reference to the mutable object in the instance variable

Display 13.7 Implementation of the Method clone (Simple case)

```
public class YourCloneableClass implements Cloneable
{
        .
        .
        .
    public Object clone()
    {
        try
        {
            return super.clone();//Invocation of clone
                                 //in the base class Object
        }
        catch (CloneNotSupportedException e)
        {//This should not happen.
            return null; //To keep the compiler happy.
        }
    }
        .
        .
        .
}
```

Works correctly if each instance variable is of a primitive type or of an immutable type like `String`.

Display 13.8 Implementation of the Method clone (Harder Case)

```
public class YourCloneableClass2  implements Cloneable
{
    private DataClass someVariable;
        .
        .
        .
    public Object clone()
    {
        try
        {
            YourCloneableClass2 copy =
                              (YourCloneableClass2)super.clone();
            copy.someVariable = (DataClass)someVariable.clone();
            return copy;
        }
        catch(CloneNotSupportedException e)
        {//This should not happen.
           return null; //To keep the compiler happy.
        }
    }
        .
        .
        .
}
```

`DataClass` is a mutable class. Any other instance variables are each of a primitive type or of an immutable type like `String`.

If the clone method return type is `DataClass` rather than `Object`, then this type cast is not needed.

The class `DataClass` must also properly implement the `Cloneable` interface including defining the `clone` method as we are describing.

`someVariable`. So, the reference is replaced by a reference to a copy of the object named by `someVariable`. This is done with the following line:[3]

```
copy.someVariable = (DataClass)someVariable.clone();
```

The object named by `copy` is now safe and so can be returned by the `clone` method.

If there are more instance variables that have a mutable class type, then you repeat what we did for `someVariable` for each of the mutable instance variables.

This requires that the class type `DataClass` has a correctly working `clone` method that is marked `public`, but that will be true if the class type `DataClass` implements the `Cloneable` interface in the way we are now describing. That is, `DataClass` should implement the `Cloneable` interface following the model of Displays 13.7 or 13.8,

[3]Depending on how the `clone` method was defined in the class `DataClass`, the type cast may or may not be needed, but causes no harm in any case.

whichever is appropriate; similarly, all classes for instance variables in `DataClass` should follow the model of Displays 13.7 or 13.8, and so forth for classes for instance variables inside of classes all the way down. You want every class in sight and every class used in every class in sight to follow the model of Displays 13.7 or 13.8.

The same basic technique applies if your class is derived from some class other than `Object`, except that, in this case, there normally is no required exception handling. To implement the `Cloneable` interface in a derived class with a base class other than `Object`, the details are as follows: The base class must properly implement the `Cloneable` interface, and the derived class must take care of any mutable class instance variable added in the definition of the derived class. These new mutable class instance variables are handled by the technique shown in Display 13.8 for the instance variable `someVariable`. As long as the base class properly implements the `Cloneable` interface, including defining the `clone` method as we are describing, then the derived class's `clone` method need not worry about any inherited instance variables. Also, usually, you do not need to have `try` and `catch` blocks for `CloneNotSupportedException` because the base class `clone` method, `super.clone()`, normally catches all its `CloneNotSupportedExceptions`, so `super.clone()` will never throw a `CloneNotSupportedException`. (See Self-Test Exercise 15 for an example.)

MyProgrammingLab™

Self-Test Exercises

12. Modify the following class definition so it correctly implements the `Cloneable` interface (all the instance variables are shown):

```
public class StockItem
{
    private int number;
    private String name;
    public void setNumber(int newNumber)
    {
        number = newNumber;
    }
        ...
}
```

13. Modify the following class definition so it correctly implements the `Cloneable` interface (all the new instance variables are shown):

```
public class PricedItem extends StockItem
{
    private double price;

        ...
}
```

MyProgrammingLab™

Self-Test Exercises (continued)

14. Modify the following class definition so it correctly implements the `Cloneable` interface (all the new instance variables are shown):

```
public class PricedItem extends StockItem
{
    private double price;

        . . .
}
```

15. Modify the following class definition so it correctly implements the `Cloneable` interface (all the instance variables are shown):

```
public class Record
{
    private StockItem item1;
    private StockItem item2;
    private String description;

        . . .
}
```

16. Modify the following class definition so it correctly implements the `Cloneable` interface (all the new instance variables are shown):

```
public class BigRecord extends Record
{
    private StockItem item3;

        . . .
}
```

17. Modify the definition of the class `Date` (Display 4.13) so it implements the `Cloneable` interface. Be sure to define the method `clone` in the style of Display 13.7.

18. Modify the definition of the class `Employee` (Display 7.2) so it implements the `Cloneable` interface. Be sure to define the method `clone` in the style of Display 13.8.

19. Modify the definition of the class `HourlyEmployee` (Display 7.3) so it implements the `Cloneable` interface. Be sure to define the method `clone` in the style of Display 13.8.

13.2 Simple Uses of Inner Classes

The ruling ideas of each age have ever been the ideas of its ruling class.

KARL MARX and FRIEDRICH ENGELS, *The Communist Manifesto*

Inner classes are classes defined within other classes. In this section, we will describe one of the most useful applications of inner classes, namely, inner classes used as helping classes.

Helping Classes

inner class

Defining an **inner class** is straightforward; simply include the definition of the inner class within another class, as follows:

```
public class OuterClass
{
    private class InnerClass
    {
        Declarations_of_InnerClass_Instance_Variables
        Definitions_of_InnerClass_Methods
    }
    Declarations_of_OuterClass_Instance_Variables
    Definitions_of_OuterClass_Methods
}
```

outer class

As this outline suggests, the class that includes the inner class is called an **outer class**. The definition of the inner class (or classes) need not be the first item(s) of the outer class, but it is good to place it either first or last so that it is easy to find. The inner class need not be private, but that is the only case we will consider in this section. We will consider other modifiers besides `private` in Section 13.3.

An inner class definition is a member of the outer class in the same way that the instance variables of the outer class and the methods of the outer class are members of the outer class. Thus, an inner class definition is local to the outer class definition. So you may reuse the name of the inner class for something else outside the definition of the outer class. If the inner class is private, as ours will always be in this section, then the inner class cannot be accessed by name outside the definition of the outer class.

There are two big advantages to inner classes. First, because they are defined within a class, they can be used to make the outer class self-contained or more self-contained than it would otherwise be. The second advantage is that the inner and outer classes' methods have access to each other's private methods and private instance variables.

TIP: Inner and Outer Classes Have Access to Each Other's Private Members

Within the definition of a method of an inner class, it is legal to reference a private instance variable of the outer class and to invoke a private method of the outer class. To facilitate this, Java follows this convention: If a method is invoked in an inner class and the inner class has no such method, then it is assumed to be an invocation of the method by that name in the outer class. (If the outer class also has no method by that name, that is, of course, an error.) Similarly, an inner class can use the name of an instance variable of the outer class.

The reverse situation, invoking a method of the inner class from the outer class, is not so simple. To invoke a (nonstatic) method of the inner class from within a method of the outer class, you need an object of the inner class to use as a calling object, as we do in Display 13.9.

As long as you are within the definition of the inner or outer classes, the modifiers `public` and `private` (used within the inner or outer classes) are equivalent.

These sorts of invocations and variable references that cross between inner and outer classes can get confusing. So, it is best to confine such invocations and variable references to cases that are clear and straightforward. It is easy to tie your code in knots if you get carried away with this sort of thing. ■

Access Privileges between Inner and Outer Classes

Inner and outer classes have access to each other's private members.

EXAMPLE: A Bank Account Class

Display 13.9 contains a simplified bank account program with an inner class for amounts of money. The bank account class uses values of type `String` to obtain or return amounts of money, such as the amount of a deposit or the answer to a query for the account balance. However, inside the class it stores amounts of money as values of type `Money`, which is an inner class. Values of type `Money` are not stored as `String`s, which would be difficult to do arithmetic on, nor are they stored as values of type `double`, which would allow round-off errors that would not be acceptable in banking transactions. Instead, the class `Money` stores amounts of money as two integers, one for the dollars and one for the cents. In a real banking program, the class `Money` might have a larger collection of methods, such as methods to do addition, subtraction, and compute percentages, but in this simple example we included only the method for adding an amount of money to the calling object. The outer class `BankAccount` would also have more methods in a real class, but here we included only methods to deposit an amount of money to the account and to obtain the account balance. Display 13.10 contains a simple demonstration program using the class `BankAccount`.

(continued)

EXAMPLE: (continued)

The class `Money` is a private inner class of the class `BankAccount`. So, the class `Money` cannot be used outside of the class `BankAccount`. (Public inner classes are discussed in Section 13.3 and have some subtleties involved in their use.) Because the class `Money` is local to the class `BankAccount`, the name `Money` can be used for the name of another class outside of the class `BankAccount`. (This would be true even if `Money` were a public inner class.)

We have made the instance variables in the class `Money` `private` following our usual conventions for class members. When we discuss public inner classes, this will be important. However, for use within the outer class (and a private inner class cannot be used anyplace else), there is no difference between `public` and `private` or other member modifiers. All instance variables and all methods of the inner class are public to the outer class no matter whether they are marked `public` or `private` or anything else. Notice the method `closeAccount` of the outer class. It uses the private instance variables `dollars` and `cents` of the inner class.

This is still very much a toy example, but we will have occasion to make serious use of private inner classes when we discuss linked lists in Chapter 15 and when we study Swing GUIs starting in Chapter 17.

Display 13.9 **Class with an Inner Class** (part 1 of 2)

```
public class BankAccount
{
    private class Money
    {
        private long dollars;
        private int cents;

        public Money(String stringAmount)
        {
            abortOnNull(stringAmount);
            int length = stringAmount.length();
            dollars = Long.parseLong(
                          stringAmount.substring(0, length - 3));
            cents = Integer.parseInt(
                          stringAmount.substring(length - 2, length));
        }

        public String getAmount()
        {
            if (cents > 9)
```

The modifier `private` *in this line should not be changed to* `public`*. However, the modifiers* `public` *and* `private` *inside the inner class* `Money` *can be changed to anything else and it would have no effect on the class* `BankAccount`*.*

Display 13.9 **Class with an Inner Class** (part 2 of 2)

```
                return (dollars + "." + cents);
            else
                return (dollars + ".0" + cents);
        }

        public void addIn(Money secondAmount)
        {
            abortOnNull(secondAmount);
            int newCents = (cents + secondAmount.cents)%100;
            long carry = (cents + secondAmount.cents)/100;
            cents = newCents;
            dollars = dollars + secondAmount.dollars + carry;
        }
        private void abortOnNull(Object o)
        {
            if (o == null)
            {
                System.out.println("Unexpected null argument.");
                System.exit(0);
            }
        }
    }
    private Money balance;

    public BankAccount()
    {
        balance = new Money("0.00");
    }

    public String getBalance()
    {
        return balance.getAmount();
    }

    public void makeDeposit(String depositAmount)
    {
        balance.addIn(new Money(depositAmount));
    }

    public void closeAccount()
    {
        balance.dollars = 0;
        balance.cents = 0;
    }
}
```

The definition of the inner class ends here, but the definition of the outer class continues in this display.

To invoke a nonstatic method of the inner class outside of the inner class, you need to create an object of the inner class.

This invocation of the inner class method **getAmount()** *would be allowed even if the method* **getAmount()** *were marked as* **private.**

Notice that the outer class has access to the private instance variables of the inner class.

This class would normally have more methods, but we have only included the methods we need to illustrate the points covered here.

Display 13.10 Demonstration Program for the Class `BankAccount`

```
public class BankAccount
{
    public static void main(String[] args)
    {
        System.out.println("Creating a new account.");
        BankAccount account = new BankAccount( );
        System.out.println("Account balance now = $"
                                        + account.getBalance( ));

        System.out.println("Depositing $100.00");
        account.makeDeposit("100.00");
        System.out.println("Account balance now = $"
                                        + account.getBalance( ));
        System.out.println("Depositing $99.99");
        account.makeDeposit("99.99");
        System.out.println("Account balance now = $"
                                        + account.getBalance( ));
        System.out.println("Depositing $0.01");
        account.makeDeposit("0.01");
        System.out.println("Account balance now = $"
                                        + account.getBalance( ));
        System.out.println("Closing account.");
        account.closeAccount( );
        System.out.println("Account balance now = $"
                                        + account.getBalance( ));
    }
}
```

Sample Dialogue

```
Creating a new account.
Account balance now = $0.00
Depositing $100.00
Account balance now = $100.00
Depositing $99.99
Account balance now = $199.99
Depositing $0.01
Account balance now = $200.00
Closing account.
Account balance now = $0.00
```

Helping Inner Classes

You may define a class within another class. The inside class is called an **inner class**. A common and simple use of an inner class is to use it as a helping class for the outer class, in which case the inner class should be marked `private`.

MyProgrammingLab™

Self-Test Exercises

20. Would the following invocation of `getAmount` in the method `getBalance` of the outer class `BankAccount` still be legal if we change the method `getAmount` of the inner class `Money` from `public` to `private`?

```
public String getBalance()
{
    return balance.getAmount();
}
```

21. Because it does not matter if we make the members of a private inner class public or private, can we simply omit the `public` or `private` modifiers from the instance variables and methods of a private inner class?

22. Would it be legal to add the following method to the inner class `Money` in Display 13.9? Remember, the question is would it be legal, not would it be sensible.

```
public void doubleBalance()
{
    balance.addIn(balance);
}
```

23. Would it be legal to add the following method to the inner class `Money` in Display 13.9? Remember, the question is would it be legal, not would it be sensible.

```
public void doubleBalance2()
{
    makeDeposit(balance.getAmount());
}
```

The `.class` File for an Inner Class

When you compile any class in Java, it produces a `.class` file. When you compile a class with an inner class, this compiles both the outer class and the inner class and produces two `.class` files. For example, when you compile the class `BankAccount` in Display 13.9, this produces the following two `.class` files:

`BankAccount.class` and `BankAccount$Money.class`

If `BankAccount` had two inner classes, then three `.class` files would be produced.

PITFALL: Other Uses of Inner Classes

In this section, we have shown you how to use an inner class in only one way, namely to create and use objects of the inner class from within the outer class method definitions. There are other ways to use inner classes, but they can involve subtleties. If you intend to use inner classes in any of these other ways, you should consult Section 13.3. ■

13.3 More about Inner Classes

Something deeply hidden had to be behind things.

ALBERT EINSTEIN, Note quoted in *New York Times Magazine* (August 2, 1964)

In this section, we cover some of the more subtle details about using inner classes. It might be best to treat this section as a reference section and look up the relevant cases as you need them. None of the material in this section is used in the rest of this book.

Static Inner Classes

A normal (nonstatic) inner class, which is the kind of inner class we have discussed so far, has a connection between each of its objects and the object of the outer class that created the inner class object. Among other things, this allows an inner class definition to reference an instance variable or invoke a method of the outer class. If you do not need this connection, you can make your inner class **static** by adding the `static` modifier to your inner class definition, as illustrated by the following sample beginning of a class definition:

static

```
public class OuterClass
{
    private static class InnerClass
    {
```

A static inner class can have nonstatic instance variables and methods, but an object of a static inner class has no connection to an object of the outer class.

You may encounter situations where you need an inner class to be static. For example, if you create an object of the inner class within a static method of the outer class, then the inner class must be static. This follows from the fact that a nonstatic inner class object must arise from an outer class object.

Also, if you want your inner class to itself have static members, then the inner class must be static.

Because a static inner class has no connection to an object of the outer class, you cannot reference an instance variable or invoke a nonstatic method of the outer class within the static inner class.

To invoke a static method of a static inner class within the outer class, simply preface the method name with the name of the inner class and a dot. Similarly, to name a static variable of a static inner class within the outer class, just preface the static variable name with the name of the inner class and a dot.

> **Static Inner Class**
>
> A **static** inner class is one that is not associated with an object of the outer class. It is indicated by including the modifier `static` in its class heading.

MyProgrammingLab™

Self-Test Exercises

24. Can you have a static method in a nonstatic inner class?

25. Can you have a nonstatic method in a static inner class?

Public Inner Classes

`public` inner class

If an inner class is marked with the `public` modifier instead of the `private` modifier, then it can be used in all the ways we discussed so far, but it can also be used outside of the outer class.

The way that you create an object of the inner class outside of the outer class is a bit different for static and nonstatic inner classes. We consider the case of a nonstatic inner class first. When creating an object of a nonstatic inner class, you need to keep in mind that every object of the nonstatic inner class is associated with some object of the outer class. To put it another way, to create an object of the inner class, you must start with an object of the outer class. This has to be true, because an object of the inner class may invoke a method of the outer class or reference an instance variable of the outer class, and you cannot have an instance variable of the outer class unless you have an object of the outer class.

For example, if you change the class `Money` in Display 13.9 from private to public, so that the class definition begins

```
public class BankAccount
{
    public class Money
```

then you can use an object of the nonstatic inner class `Money` outside of the class `BankAccount` as illustrated by the following:

```
BankAccount account = new BankAccount();
BankAccount.Money amount =
             account.new Money("41.99");
System.out.println(amount.getAmount());
```

This code produces the output

```
41.99
```

Note that the object `amount` of the inner class `Money` is created starting with an object, `account`, of the outer class `BankAccount`, as follows:

```
BankAccount.Money amount =
            account.new Money("41.99");
```

Also, note that the syntax of the second line is *not*

```
new account.Money("41.99"); //Incorrect syntax
```

Within the definition of the inner class `Money`, an object of the inner class can invoke a method of the outer class. However, this is not true outside of the inner class. Outside of the inner class, an object of the inner class can only invoke methods of the inner class. So, we could *not* have continued the previous sample code (which is outside the class `BankAccount` and so outside the inner class `Money`) with the following:

```
System.out.println(amount.getBalance()); //Illegal
```

The meaning of `amount.getBalance()` is clear, but it is still not allowed. If you want something equivalent to `amount.getBalance()`, you should use the corresponding object of the class `BankAccount`; in this case, you would use `account.getBalance()`. (Recall that `account` is the `BankAccount` object used to create the inner class object `amount`.)

Now let's consider the case of a static inner class. You can create objects of a public *static* inner class and do so outside of the inner class—in fact, even outside of the outer class. To do so outside of the outer class, the situation is similar to, but not exactly the same as, what we outlined for nonstatic inner classes. Consider the following outline:

```
public class OuterClass
{
    public static class InnerClass
    {
        public void nonstaticMethod()
        { ... }

        public static void staticMethod()
        {...}

        Other_Members_of_InnerClass
    }

    Other_Members_of_OuterClass
}
```

You can create an object of the inner class outside of the outer class as in the following example:

```
OuterClass.InnerClass innerObject =
            new OuterClass.InnerClass();
```

Note that the syntax is *not*

```
OuterClass.new InnerClass();
```

This may seem like an apparent inconsistency with the syntax for creating the object of a nonstatic inner class. It may help to keep in mind that for a static inner class, `OuterClass.InnerClass` is a well-specified class name and all the information for the object is in that class name. To remember the syntax for a nonstatic inner class, remember that for that case, the object of the outer class modifies how the `new` operator works to create an object of the inner class.

Once you have created an object of the inner class, the object can invoke a nonstatic method in the usual way. For example,

```
innerObject.nonstaticMethod();
```

You can also use the object of the inner class to invoke a static method in the same way. For example,

```
innerObject.staticMethod();
```

However, it is more common, and clearer, to use class names when invoking a static method. For example,

```
OuterClass.InnerClass.staticMethod();
```

TIP: Referring to a Method of the Outer Class

As we have already noted, if a method is invoked in an inner class and the inner class has no such method, then it is assumed to be an invocation of the method by that name in the outer class. For example, we could add a method `showBalance` to the inner class `Money` in Display 13.9, as outlined in what follows:

```
public class BankAccount
{
    private class Money
    {
        private long dollars;
        private int cents;

        public void showBalance()
        {
            System.out.println(getBalance());
        }
            ...
    }//End of Money
```

(continued)

TIP: (continued)

```
        public String getBalance()
        {...}
            ...
}    //End of BankAccount
```

This invocation of `getBalance` is within the definition of the inner class `Money`. But the inner class `Money` has no method named `getBalance`, so it is presumed to be the method `getBalance` of the outer class `BankAccount`.

But suppose the inner class did have a method named `getBalance`; then this invocation of `getBalance` would be an invocation of the method `getBalance` defined in the inner class.

If both the inner and outer classes have a method named `getBalance`, then you can specify that you mean the method of the outer class as follows:

```
public void showBalance()
{
    System.out.println(
                  BankAccount.this.getBalance());
}
```

The syntax

Outer_Class_Name.`this`.*Method_Name*

always refers to a method of the outer class. In the example, `BankAccount.this` means the `this` of `BankAccount`, as opposed to the `this` of the inner class `Money`. ■

MyProgrammingLab™

Self-Test Exercises

26. Consider the following class definition:

```
public class OuterClass
{
    public static class InnerClass
    {
        public static void someMethod()
        {
            System.out.println("From inside.");
        }
    }
    Other_Members_of_OuterClass
}
```

Write an invocation of the static method `someMethod` that you could use in some class you define.

MyProgrammingLab™

Self-Test Exercises (continued)

27. Consider the following class definition:

```
public class Outs
{
    private int outerInt = 100;

    public class Ins
    {
        private int innerInt = 25;
        public void specialMethod()
        {
           System.out.println(outerInt);
           System.out.println(innerInt);
        }
    }
    Other_Members_of_OuterClass
}
```

Write an invocation of the method `specialMethod` with an object of the class `Ins`. Part of this exercise is to create the object of the class `Ins`. This should be code that you could use in some class you define.

Nesting Inner Classes

It is legal to nest inner classes within inner classes. The rules are the same as what we have already discussed except that names can get longer. For example, if `A` has a public inner class `B`, and `B` has a public inner class `C`, then the following is valid code:

```
A aObject = new A();
A.B bObject =
              aObject.new B();
A.B.C cObject =
              bObject.new C();
```

Inner Classes and Inheritance

Suppose `OuterClass` has an inner class named `InnerClass`. If you derive `DerivedClass` from `OuterClass`, then `DerivedClass` automatically has `InnerClass` as an inner class just as if it were defined within `DerivedClass`.

Just as with any other kind of class in Java, you can make an inner class a derived class of some other class. You can also make the outer class a derived class of a different (or the same) base class.

It is not possible to override the definition of an inner class when you define a derived class of the outer class.

It is also possible to use an inner class as a base class to derive classes, but we will not go into those details in this book; there are some subtleties to worry about.

Anonymous Classes

If you wish to create an object but have no need to name the object's class, then you can embed the class definition inside the expression with the `new` operator. These sorts of class definitions are called **anonymous classes** because they have no class name. An expression with an anonymous class definition is, like everything in Java, inside of some class definition. Thus, an anonymous class is an inner class. Before we go into the details of the syntax for anonymous classes, let's say a little about where one might use them.

anonymous class

The most straightforward way to create an object is the following:

```
YourClass anObject = new YourClass();
```

If `new YourClass()` is replaced by some expression that defines the class but does not give the class any name, then there is no name `YourClass` to use to declare the variable `anObject`. So, it does not make sense to use an anonymous class in this situation. However, it can make sense in the following scenario:

```
SomeOtherType anObject = new YourClass();
```

Here `SomeOtherType` must be a type such that an object of the class `YourClass` is also an object of `SomeOtherType`. In this case, you can replace `new YourClass()` with an expression including an anonymous class instead of `YourClass`. The type `SomeOtherType` is usually a Java interface.

Here is an example of an anonymous class. Suppose you define the following interface:

```
public interface NumberCarrier
{
    public void setNumber(int value);
    public int getNumber();
}
```

Then the following creates an object using an anonymous class definition:

```
NumberCarrier anObject = new NumberCarrier()
            {
                private int number;
                public void setNumber(int value)
                {
                    number = value;
                }
                public int getNumber()
                {
                    return number;
                }
            };
```

The part in the braces is the same as the part inside the main braces of a class definition. The closing brace is followed by a semicolon, unlike a class definition. (This is because the entire expression will be used as a Java statement.) The beginning part, repeated as follows, may seem strange:

```
new NumberCarrier()
```

The `new` is sensible enough but what is the point of `NumberCarrier()`? It looks like this is an invocation of a constructor for `NumberCarrier`. But, `NumberCarrier` is an interface and has no constructors. The meaning of `new NumberCarrier()` is simply

```
implements NumberCarrier
```

So what is being said is that the anonymous class implements the `NumberCarrier` interface and is defined as shown between the main braces.

Display 13.11 shows a simple demonstration with two anonymous class definitions. For completeness, we have also repeated the definition of the `NumberCarrier` interface in this display.

Display 13.11 **Anonymous Classes** (part 1 of 2)

This is just a toy example to demonstrate the Java syntax for anonymous classes.

```
public class AnonymousClassDemo
{
    public static void main(String[] args)
    {
        NumberCarrier anObject =
                  new NumberCarrier()
                  {
                      private int number;
                      public void setNumber(int value)
                      {
                          number = value;
                      }
                      public int getNumber()
                      {
                          return number;
                      }
                  };

        NumberCarrier anotherObject =
                  new NumberCarrier()
                  {
                      private int number;
                      public void setNumber(int value)
                      {
                          number = 2*value;
                      }
```

(continued)

Display 13.11 **Anonymous Classes** (part 2 of 2)

```
                       public int getNumber()
                       {
                           return number;
                       }
                   };
        anObject.setNumber(42);
        anotherObject.setNumber(42);
        showNumber(anObject);
        showNumber(anotherObject);
        System.out.println("End of program.");
    }

    public static void showNumber(NumberCarrier o)
    {
        System.out.println(o.getNumber());
    }
}
```

This is the file **AnonymousClassDemo.java**.

Sample Dialogue

```
42
84
End of program.
```

This is the file **NumberCarrier.java**.

```
public interface NumberCarrier
{
    public void setNumber(int value);
    public int getNumber();
}
```

TIP: Why Use Inner Classes?

Most simple situations do not need inner classes. However, there are situations for which inner classes are a good solution. For example, suppose you want to have a class with two base classes. This is not allowed in Java. However, you can have an outer class derived from one base class with an inner class derived from the other base class. Because the inner and outer classes have access to each other's instance variables and methods, this can often serve as if it were a class with two base classes.

As another example, if you need only one object of a class and the class definition is very short, many programmers like to use an anonymous class (but I must admit I am not one of them).

When we study *linked lists* in Chapter 15, you will see cases where using an inner class as a helping class makes the linked list class self-contained in a very natural way. We will also use inner classes when defining Graphical User Interfaces (GUIs) starting in Chapter 17. But until you learn what linked lists and GUIs are, these are not likely to be compelling examples. ■

MyProgrammingLab™

Self-Test Exercise

28. Suppose we replace

```
NumberCarrier anObject
```

with

```
Object anObject
```

in Display 13.11. What would be the first statement in the program to cause an error message? Would it be a compiler error message or a run-time error message?

Chapter Summary

- An *interface* is a property of a class that says what methods a class that implements the interface must have.
- An interface is defined the same way as a class is defined except that the keyword `interface` is used in place of the keyword `class` and method bodies are replaced by semicolons.
- An interface may not have any instance variables, with one exception: An interface may have defined constants. If you use the syntax for an instance variable in an inner class, the variable is automatically a constant, not a real instance variable.
- An *inner class* is a class defined within another class.
- One simple use of an inner class is as a helping class to be used in the definition of the outer class methods and/or instance variables.
- A *static* inner class is one that is not associated with an object of the *outer class*. It must include the modifier `static` in its class heading.
- To create an object of a nonstatic inner class outside the definition of the outer class, you must first create an object of the outer class and use it to create an object of the inner class.

Answers to Self-Test Exercises

1. Yes to both. An interface is a type and can be used like any other type.
2. Yes. Any of the interface methods that it does not fully define must be made abstract methods.
3. A derived class can have only one base class, but it can implement any number of interfaces.

4. No, but the way to accomplish the same thing is to have one interface extend the other.

   These exercises are for the material on the `Comparable` interface.

5. Yes, the dialogue would be the same. The change from the parameter type `Comparable[]` to `Object[]` in the method `interchange` is in fact a good idea.
6. No. This will compile without any error messages. However, the less-than ordering does not satisfy the semantics of the `Comparable` interface. For example, the trichotomy law does not hold.
7. Yes. The three required conditions are true for objects of the class `Circle`: (Irreflexive) By definition, no circle is inside itself.

   (Trichotomy) For any two circles `c1` and `c2` with centers at the origin, one, and only one, of the following holds true: `c1` is inside of `c2`, `c2` is inside of `c1`, or `c1` equals `c2`.

   (Transitivity) If `c1` is inside of `c2` and `c2` is inside of `c3`, then `c1` is inside of `c3`.
8. The class will produce a compiler error message saying that there is an inconsistency in the definitions of `ANSWER`.
9. The class will compile and run with no error messages. Because the named constant `ANSWER` is never used, there is no inconsistency.
10. The class will produce a compiler error message saying that you have not implemented the heading for `getStuff` in `InterfaceA`.
11. They will all compile and the program will run. The two definitions of `getStuff` have different numbers of parameters, so this is overloading. There is no inconsistency.
12.
```
public class StockItem implements Cloneable
{
    private int number;
    private String name;
    public void setNumber(int newNumber)
    {
        number = newNumber;
    }
        ...
    public Object clone()
    {
        try
        {
           return super.clone();
        }
        catch (CloneNotSupportedException e)
        {//This should not happen.
           return null; //To keep compiler happy.
        }
    }
}
```

13. Note that you do not catch a `CloneNotSupportedException` because any such thrown exception in `super.clone` is caught inside the base class method `super.clone`.

```
public class PricedItem extends StockItem
                        implements Cloneable
{
    private double price;
       ...
    public Object clone()
    {
       return super.clone();
    }
}
```

14.

```
public class Record implements Cloneable
{
    private StockItem item1;
    private StockItem item2;
    private String description;

       ...
    public Object clone()
    {
        try
        {
            Record copy =
                     (Record)super.clone();
            copy.item1 =
                  (StockItem)item1.clone();
            copy.item2 =
                  (StockItem)item2.clone();
            return copy;
        }
        catch (CloneNotSupportedException e)
        {//This should not happen.
            return null; //To keep compiler happy.
        }
    }
}
```

15. Note that you do not catch a `CloneNotSupportedException` because any such thrown exception in `super.clone` is caught inside the base class method `super.clone`.

```
public class BigRecord extends Record
                       implements Cloneable
{
    private StockItem item3;

        ...
    public Object clone()
    {
        BigRecord copy =
                  (BigRecord)super.clone();
        copy.item3 =
                   (StockItem)item3.clone();
        return copy;
    }
}
```

16. The heading of the class definition changes to what is shown in the following and the method `clone` shown there is added. The version of `Date` for this chapter on the accompanying website includes this definition of `clone`.

extra code on website

```
public class Date implements Cloneable
{
    private String month;
    private int day;
    private int year;

       ...
   public Object clone()
   {
       try
       {
          return super.clone();//Invocation of
                 //clone in the base class Object
       }
       catch(CloneNotSupportedException e)
       {//This should not happen.
          return null; //To keep compiler happy.
       }
     }
}
```

17. The heading of the class definition changes to what is shown in the following and the method `clone` shown there is added. The version of `Employee` for this chapter on the accompanying website includes this definition of `clone`.

extra code on website

```
public class Employee implements Cloneable
{
    private String name;
    private Date hireDate;

      ...
    public Object clone()
    {
        try
        {
        Employee copy =
                (Employee)super.clone();
        copy.hireDate =
             (Date)hireDate.clone();
        return copy;
        }
    catch (CloneNotSupportedException e)
    {//This should not happen.
        return null; //To keep compiler happy.
    }
  }
}
```

18. The heading of the class definition changes to what is shown in the following and the method `clone` shown there is added. Note that you do not catch a `CloneNotSupportedException` because any such thrown exception in `super.clone` is caught inside the base class method `super.clone`. The version of `HourlyEmployee` for this chapter on the accompanying website includes this definition of `clone`.

extra code on website

```
public class HourlyEmployee extends Employee
                            implements Cloneable
{
    private double wageRate;
    private double hours;

      ...
    public Object clone()
    {
        HourlyEmployee copy =
                (HourlyEmployee)super.clone();
        return copy;
    }
}
```

19. It would still be legal. An outer class has access to all the private members of an inner class.

20. Yes, they can be omitted, but the reason is that it indicates package access, and in a private inner class, all privacy modifiers, including package access, are equivalent to public. (Note that the situation for public inner classes will be different.)

21. Yes, it is legal to add the method `doubleBalance` to the inner class `Money` because an inner class has access to the instance variables, such as `balance` of the outer class. To test this out, add the following as a method of the outer class:

```
public void test()
{
    balance.doubleBalance();
}
```

22. It would be legal. The method `makeDeposit` is assumed to be the method `makeDeposit` of the outer class. The calling object `balance` is assumed to be the instance variable of the outer class. These sorts of tricks can lead to confusing code. So, use them sparingly. This is just an exercise.

23. No, a nonstatic inner class cannot have any static methods.

24. Yes, you can have a nonstatic method in a static inner class.

25. `OuterClass.InnerClass.someMethod();`

26.
```
Outs outerObject = new Outs();
Outs.Ins innerObject =
              outerObject.new Ins();
innerObject.specialMethod();
```

27. You would get your first error on the following statement and it would be a complier error:

```
anObject.setNumber(42);
```

With the change described in the exercise, `anObject` is of type `Object` and `Object` has no method named `setNumber`.

MyProgrammingLab™ Programming Projects

Visit www.myprogramminglab.com to complete select exercises online and get instant feedback.

VideoNote
Solution to Programming Project 13.1

1. Modify the recursive implementation of binary search from Chapter 11 so that the search method works on any array of type `Comparable[]`. Test the implementation with arrays of different types to see if it works.

2. Listed next is the skeleton for a class named `InventoryItem`. Each inventory item has a name and a unique ID number:

```
class InventoryItem
{
 private String name;
 private int uniqueItemID;
}
```

Flesh out the class with appropriate accessors, constructors, and mutatators. The `uniqueItemID`'s are assigned by your store and can be set from outside the `InventoryItem` class—your code does not have to ensure that they are unique. Next, modify the class so that it implements the `Comparable` interface. The `compareTo()` method should compare the `uniqueItemID`'s; e.g., the `InventoryItem` with item ID 5 is less than the `InventoryItem` with ID 10. Test your class by creating an array of sample `InventoryItem`'s and sort them using a sorting method that takes as input an array of type `Comparable`.

3. Listed next is a code skeleton for an interface called `Enumeration` and a class called `NameCollection`. `Enumeration` provides an interface to sequentially iterate through some type of collection. In this case, the collection will be the class `NameCollection` that simply stores a collection of names using an array of strings.

```
interface Enumeration
{
 // Returns true if another element in the collection exists
 public boolean hasNext();

 // Returns the next element in the collection as an Object
 public Object getNext();
}

/**
 * NameCollection implements a collection of names using
 * a simple array.
 */
class NameCollection
{
  String[] names;

 /**
  * The list of names is initialized from outside
  * and passed in as an array of strings
  */
 NameCollection(String[] names)
 {
  this.names = names;
 }

 /**
  * getEnumeration should return an instance of a class that
    implements
  * the Enumeration interface where hasNext() and getNext()
  * correspond to data stored within the names array.
  */
 Enumeration getEnumeration ()
 {
  // Complete code here using an inner class
 }
}
```

Complete the method `getEnumeration()` so that it returns an anonymous inner class that corresponds to the `Enumeration` interface for the names array in `NamesCollection`. Then write a `main` method that creates a `NamesCollection` object with a sample array of strings, retrieves the `Enumeration` for this class via `getEnumeration()`, and then iterates through the enumeration outputting each name using the `getNext()` method.

4. In Display 13.5, we described a sorting method to sort an array of type `Comparable[]`. In Display 12.6, we described a sorting method that used the merge sort algorithm to sort an array of type `double[]` into increasing order. Redo the method in Display 12.6 so it applies to an array of type `Comparable[]`. Also, do a suitable test program.
5. In Display 13.5, we described a sorting method to sort an array of type `Comparable[]`. In Display 12.8, we described a sorting method that used the quick sort algorithm to sort an array of type `double[]` into increasing order. Redo the method in Display 12.8 so it applies to an array of type `Comparable[]`. Also, do a suitable test program.
6. Redo the class `Person` in Display 5.19 so that it implements the `Cloneable` interface. This may require that you also redo the class `Date` so it implements the `Cloneable` interface. Also, do a suitable test program.
7. Redo the class `Person` in Display 5.19 so that the class `Date` is a private inner class of the class `Person`. Also, do a suitable test program. (You need not start from the version produced in Programming Project 13.6. You can ignore Programming Project 13.6 when you do this project.)
8. This is a combination of Programming Projects 13.6 and 13.7. Redo the class `Person` in Display 5.19 so that the class `Date` is a private inner class of the class `Person`, and so that the class `Person` implements the `Cloneable` interface. Also, do a suitable test program.
9. Redo the class `Employee` and the class `HourlyEmployee` in Displays 7.2 and 7.3 so that the class `Date` is an inner class of the class `Employee` and an inherited inner class of the class `HourlyEmployee`. Also, do a suitable test program.
10. Define an interface named `Shape` with a single method named `area` that calculates the area of the geometric shape:

    ```
    public double area();
    ```

    Next, define a class named `Circle` that implements `Shape`. The `Circle` class should have an instance variable for the radius, a constructor that sets the radius, accessor/mutator methods for the radius, and an implementation of the `area` method. Also define a class named `Rectangle` that implements `Shape`. The `Rectangle` class should have instance variables for the height and width, a constructor that sets the height and width, accessor and mutator methods for the height and width, and an implementation of the `area` method.

The following test code should then output the area of the `Circle` and `Rectangle` objects:

```
public static void main(String[] args)
{
    Circle c = new Circle(4); // Radius of 4
    Rectangle r = new Rectangle(4,3); // Height = 4, Width = 3
    ShowArea(c);
    ShowArea(r);
}

public static void ShowArea(Shape s)
{
    double area = s.area();
    System.out.println("The area of the shape is " + area);
}
```

VideoNote
Solution to Programming Project 13.11

11. Create a `Student` class that has instance variables for the student's last name and ID number, along with appropriate constructors, accessors, and mutators. Make the `Student` class implement the `Comparable` interface. Define the `compareTo` method to order `Student` objects based on the student ID number. In the `main` method, create an array of at least five `Student` objects, sort them using `Arrays.sort`, and output the students. They should be listed by ascending student number. Next, modify the `compareTo` method so it orders `Student` objects based on the lexicographic ordering of their last name. Without modification to the `main` method, the program should now output the students ordered by name.

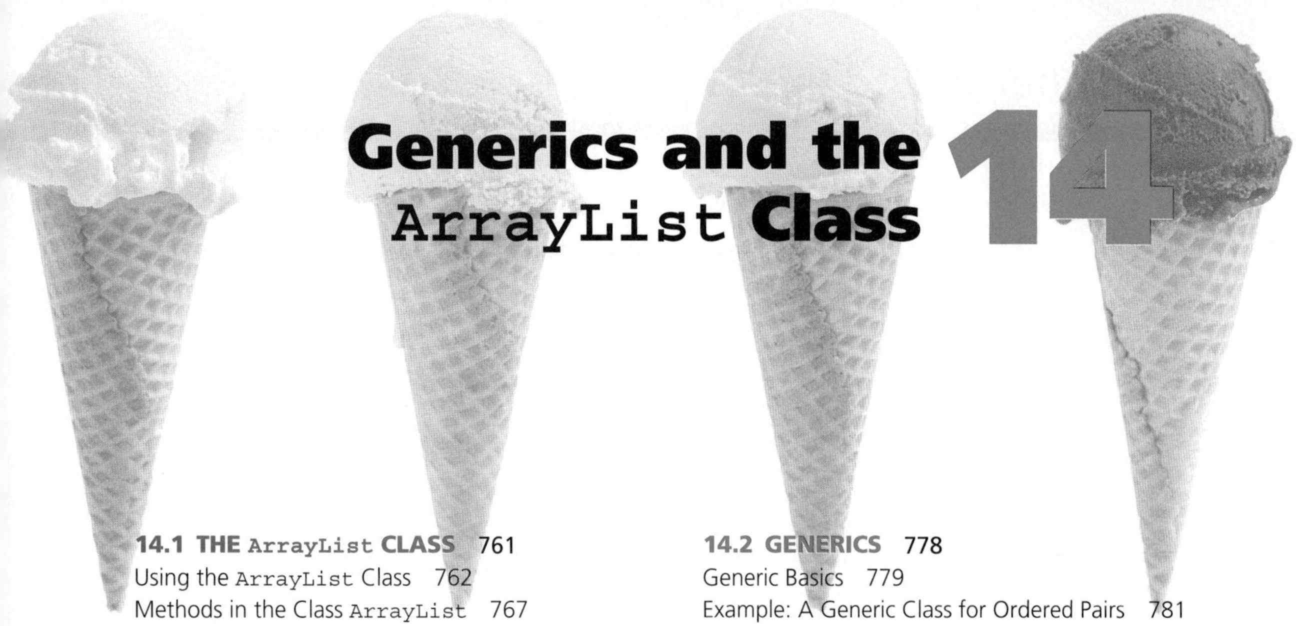

Generics and the ArrayList Class 14

14 Generics and the `ArrayList` Class

Hamlet: Do you see yonder cloud that's almost in shape of a camel?
Polonius: By the mass, and 'tis like a camel, indeed.
Hamlet: Me think it is like a weasel.
Polonius: It is backed like a weasel.
Hamlet: Or like a whale.
Polonius: Very like a whale.

WILLIAM SHAKESPEARE, *Hamlet*

Introduction

generics

Beginning with version 5.0, Java allows class and method definitions that include parameters for types. Such definitions are called **generics**. Generic programming with a type parameter allows you to write code that applies to any class. For example, you can define a class for a list of items of type `T`, where `T` is a type parameter. You can then use this class with the class `String` plugged in for `T` to automatically get a class for a list of `String` objects. Similarly, you can plug in the class `Double` for `T` to obtain a class for a list of `Doubles`, and you can do a comparable thing for any other class. The class `ArrayList` in the standard Java libraries is, in fact, just such a class for a list of items of type `T`, where `T` is a type parameter. We will first show you how to use classes with a type parameter by using the `ArrayList` class as an example. We will then tell you how you can define other classes with a type parameter.

Prerequisites

Section 14.1 covering the `ArrayList` class requires only Chapters 1 through 6 and Chapter 9. It can reasonably be read without first reading Chapter 9 if you ignore all references to "exceptions."

Section 14.2 on generics requires Chapters 1 through 7 and Chapter 9. (There is one very short Tip section entitled "Generic Interfaces" that requires Section 13.1 on interfaces, but that Tip section can easily be skipped if you have not yet read Section 13.1.) You need not read Section 14.1 before Section 14.2, but you are encouraged to do so; Section 14.1 can serve as a motivation for Section 14.2.

14.1 The ArrayList Class

"Well, I'll eat it," said Alice, "and if it makes me grow larger, I can reach the key; and if it makes me grow smaller, I can creep under the door; so either way I'll get into the garden. . . ."

LEWIS CARROLL, *Alice's Adventures In Wonderland*

ArrayList

ArrayList is a class in the standard Java libraries. You can think of an ArrayList object as an array that can grow (and shrink) in length while your program is running. In Java, you can read in the length of an array when the program is running, but once your program creates an array of that length, it cannot change the length of the array. For example, suppose you write a program to record customer orders for a mail-order house, and suppose you store all the orders for one customer in an array of objects of some class called Item. You could ask the user how many items she or he will order, store the number in a variable called numberOfItems, and then create the array item with the following statement:

```
Item[] item = new Item[numberOfItems];
```

But suppose the customer enters numberOfItems and then decides to order another item? There is no way to increase the size of the array item. There are ways around this problem with arrays, but they are all rather complicated. ArrayLists serve the same purpose as arrays, except that an ArrayList can change length while the program is running. So an ArrayList could handle the customer's extra order without any problems.

The class ArrayList is implemented using an array as a private instance variable. When this hidden array is full, a new larger hidden array is created and the data is transferred to this new array. However, you need not concern yourself with this implementation detail. All you need to know is how to use the ArrayList class, and we are about to tell you that.

If ArrayLists are like arrays but have the nice added feature of being able to change length, then why don't we just always use ArrayLists instead of arrays? It often seems that every silver lining has a cloud, and this is true of ArrayLists as well. There are three main disadvantages of ArrayLists: (1) They are less efficient than arrays; (2) they do not have the square bracket notation, and so using an ArrayList is sometimes notationally more awkward than using ordinary arrays; and (3) the base type of an ArrayList must be class type (or other reference type); it cannot be a primitive type, such as int, double, or char. For example, if you want an ArrayList of int values, you must simulate this structure with an ArrayList of Integer values, where Integer is the wrapper class whose objects simulate int values. Automatic boxing and unboxing (as discussed in Chapter 5) make (3) less of a problem, because an ArrayList with base type, for example, Integer can, in effect, store values of type int.

Using the ArrayList Class

import statement

ArrayLists are used in much the same way as arrays, but there are some important differences. First, the definition of the class ArrayList is not provided automatically. The definition is in the package java.util, and any code that uses the class ArrayList must contain the following, normally at the start of the file:

```
import java.util.ArrayList;
```

An ArrayList is created and named in the same way as objects of any class, except that you specify the base type using a new notation. For example,

```
ArrayList<String> list = new ArrayList<String>(20);
```

capacity

This statement makes list the name of an ArrayList that stores objects of the class String and that has an *initial* **capacity** of 20 items. When we say that an ArrayList has a certain capacity, we mean that it has been allocated memory for that many items, but if it needs to hold more items, the system will automatically allocate more memory. By carefully choosing the initial capacity of an ArrayList, you can often make your code more efficient, but this capacity has no effect on how many items the ArrayList can hold. If you choose your capacity to be large enough, then the system will not need to reallocate memory too often, and as a result, your program should run faster. On the other hand, if you make your capacity too large, you will waste storage space. However, no matter what capacity you choose, you can still do anything you want with the ArrayList.

Java 7 supports a slightly shorter but equivalent way to define the ArrayList. In this format, the base type in the call to the constructor is not needed. For example,

```
ArrayList<String> list = new ArrayList<>(20);
```

This feature is called **type inference** and is briefly discussed in Section 14.2.

base type

The type String in the previous ArrayList example is the **base type** of the ArrayList class. An ArrayList—that is, an object of the ArrayList class—stores objects of its base type. You can use any reference type as the base type of an ArrayList class. In particular, you can use any class or interface type. However, you cannot use a primitive type, such as int or double, as the base type of an ArrayList class. This is an example of a type parameter. The ArrayList class is defined as having a type parameter for the type of the elements in the list. Create a concrete class by specifying, in angular brackets, a class type to be substituted for this type parameter. For example, the following code, which we saw earlier in this section, substitutes the type String for the type parameter to create the class ArrayList<String> and an object of this class named list:

```
ArrayList<String> list = new ArrayList<String>(20);
```

ArrayList objects can be used like arrays, but they do not have the array square-bracket notation. If you use

```
a[index] = "Hi Mom!";
```

set

for an array of strings a, then the analogous statement for a suitable ArrayList named list is

```
list.set(index, "Hi Mom!");
```

Creating and Naming an ArrayList Object

An object of the class ArrayList is created and named in the same way as any other object, except that you specify the base type of the ArrayList.

SYNTAX

```
ArrayList<Base_Type> Object_Name = new ArrayList<Base_Type>();
ArrayList<Base_Type> Object_Name =
                      new ArrayList<Base_Type>(Initial_Capacity);
```

The *Base_Type* must be a reference type, usually a class type; it cannot be a primitive type such as int or double. When a number is given as an argument to the constructor, that number determines the initial capacity of the ArrayList.

EXAMPLES

```
ArrayList<String> list = new ArrayList<String>();
ArrayList<Double> list2 = new ArrayList<Double>(30);
```

If you would use

```
String temp = a[index];
```

for an array of strings a, then the analogous statement for a suitable ArrayList named list would be

```
String temp = list.get(index);
```

Accessing at an Index

If list is an ArrayList, its elements can be accessed as follows:

EXAMPLES

```
ArrayList<String> list = new ArrayList<String>();
int index;
    ...

list.set(index, "Here"); //Sets the element
                              //at index to "Here".
String temp = list.get(index); //The expression
                              //list.get(index)
                              //returns the element
                              //at position index.
ArrayList<Integer> list2 = new ArrayList<Integer>();
    ...
list2.set(42, index); //Sets the element at index to
                     //new Integer(42). This example relies on
                     // automatic boxing.
```

(continued)

```
int temp2 = list2.get(index); //The expression
                              //v.get(index) returns the
                              //element at position index.
                              // This example
                              //relies on automatic unboxing.
```

The index must be greater than or equal to 0 and less than the current size of the ArrayList list.

Creating and Using an `ArrayList`

The two methods `set` and `get` give `ArrayList`s approximately the same functionality that square brackets give to arrays. However, you need to be aware of one important point: The method invocation

```
list.set(index, "Hi Mom!");
```

is *not* always completely analogous to

```
a[index] = "Hi Mom!";
```

The method `set` can replace any existing element, but you cannot use `set` to put an element at just any index, as you could with an array. The method `set` is used to change the value of elements, not to set them for the first time. To set an element for the first time, you usually use the method `add`. The basic form of the method `add` adds elements at index position `0`, position `1`, position `2`, and so forth in that order. This means that `ArrayList`s must always be filled in this order. But your code can then go back and change any individual element, just as it can in an array.

`add`

For example, suppose `list` is an `ArrayList` with base type `String`, which has not yet had any elements added to it; that is, `list` is empty. The following statements will add the strings `"One"`, `"Two"`, and `"Three"` to positions `0`, `1`, and `2`:

```
list.add("One");
list.add("Two");
list.add("Three");
```

The method name `add` is overloaded. There is also a two-argument method named `add` that allows you to add an element at any currently used index position or at the first unused position. When inserting into an `ArrayList` with this version of `add`, elements at the specified index and higher (if any) are moved up one position to make room for the new element. For example,

```
list.add(0, "Zero");
```

adds the string `"Zero"` at position `0` and moves elements originally at positions `0`, `1`, `2`, and so forth up one position to positions `1, 2, 3`, and so forth.

Suppose list starts out empty and your code executes our four add invocations, which we repeat below:

```
list.add("One");
list.add("Two");
list.add("Three");
list.add(0, "Zero");
```

After these four invocations of list.add, the list would contain the strings "Zero", "One", "Two", and "Three" in positions 0, 1, 2, and 3, respectively.

Note that the two-argument version of add cannot add an element at just any position. It can only insert an element at some already used position or at the first unused position. The elements in an ArrayList always occupy a contiguous set of positions starting at 0; that is, they are always at positions 0, 1, 2, and so forth up to some last position. This is just like a partially filled array (as discussed in Chapter 6), but unlike a partially filled array, you do not need to do anything to keep track of how many elements are on the list. The method size automatically takes care of this for any ArrayList.

The add Methods

Elements can be added to an ArrayList by using the methods named add. The elements are added to index position 0, then 1, then 2, and so forth so there are no gaps in the indices of elements.

The most straightforward method to use for adding to an ArrayList is the method named add that has only one parameter.

EXAMPLES

```
list.add("Salud");
list.add("Dinero");
list.add("Java");
```

The object list is an ArrayList with base type String.

A second method named add allows you to add an element at any currently used index position or at the first unused position. When inserting into an ArrayList with this version of add, elements at the specified index and higher (if any) are moved up one position to make room for the new element.

```
list.add(1, "Amor");
```

If list starts out empty and all four statements in the two sets of examples are executed, then list would contain the following strings in the order given: "Salud", "Amor", "Dinero", and "Java".

size You can find out how many indices already have elements by using the method size. If list is an ArrayList, list.size() returns the **size** of the ArrayList, which is the number of elements stored in it. The indices of these elements go from 0 to one less than list.size().

> **The size Method**
>
> The method size returns the number of elements in an ArrayList.
>
> **EXAMPLE**
>
> ```
> for (int index = 0; index < list.size(); index++)
>     System.out.println(list.get(index));
> ```
>
> list is an ArrayList object.

TIP: Summary of Adding to an ArrayList

add

To place an element in an ArrayList position (at an ArrayList index) for the first time, you usually use the method add. The simplest method named add has a single parameter for the element to be added and adds elements at index positions 0, 1, 2, and so forth, in that order.

You can add an element at an already occupied list position by using the two-parameter version of add. When inserting into an ArrayList with this version of add, elements at the specified index and higher are moved up one position to make room for the new element. For example, suppose list is an ArrayList object with base type String that has three elements already on its list. Consider the following method invocation:

```
list.add(1, "Amor");
```

Before, there were elements at index positions 0, 1, and 2. When this invocation of add is executed, the element "Amor" is inserted at index 1, and the elements at index positions 1 and 2 are moved to positions 2 and 3.

You can also use the two-argument version of add to add an element at the first unused position. If list has elements at index positions 0, 1, 2, and 3, then the following is legal:

```
list.add(4, "Mucho Amor");
```

Your code can then go back and change any individual element, using set. However, set can reset only the element at an index that already has an element.

The method size can be used to determine how many elements are stored in an ArrayList. ■

MyProgrammingLab™

Self-Test Exercises

1. Suppose list is an object of the class ArrayList<String>. How do you add the string "Hello" to the ArrayList list?
2. Suppose instruction is an object of the class ArrayList<String> that contains the string "Stop" at index position 5. How do you change the string at index position 5 to "Go" (without changing any of the elements at other positions)?
3. Suppose instruction is an object of the class ArrayList<String> that contains strings at index positions 0 through 10. How do you insert the string "Go" at index position 5 so that no strings are removed from the list instruction?

MyProgrammingLab™

Self-Test Exercises (continued)

4. Can you use the method `set` to place an element in an `ArrayList` at any index you want?

5. Can you use the two-argument version of the method `add` to add an element in an `ArrayList` at any index you want?

6. Consider the following two method invocations. Are there values of `index1` that are allowed but that are not allowed for `index2`? Are there values of `index2` that are allowed but that are not allowed for `index1`? `list` is an object of the class `ArrayList<String>`.

```
list.set(index1, "Hello");
list.add(index2, "Hello");
```

7. If you create an `ArrayList` with the following statement, can the `ArrayList` contain more than 20 elements?

```
ArrayList<Double> myList = new ArrayList<Double>(20);
```

Methods in the Class ArrayList

With arrays, the square brackets and the instance variable `length` are the only tools automatically provided for you, the programmer. If you want to use arrays for other things, you must write code to manipulate the arrays. `ArrayLists`, on the other hand, come with a selection of powerful methods that can do many of the things for which you would need to write code in order to do with arrays. For example, the class `ArrayList` has a version of the method `add` that inserts a new element between two elements in the `ArrayList`. Most of these methods are described in Display 14.1.

Display 14.1 Some Methods in the Class **ArrayList** (part 1 of 3)

CONSTRUCTORS

`public ArrayList<`*Base_Type*`>(int initialCapacity)`

Creates an empty `ArrayList` with the specified *Base_Type* and initial capacity.

`public ArrayList<`*Base_Type*`>()`

Creates an empty `ArrayList` with the specified *Base_Type* and an initial capacity of `10`.

ARRAYLIKE METHODS

`public` *Base_Type* `set(int index,` *Base_Type* `newElement)`

Sets the element at the specified `index` to `newElement`. Returns the element previously at that position, but the method is often used as if it were a `void` method. If you draw an analogy between the `ArrayList` and an array a, this statement is analogous to setting `a[index]` to the value `newElement`. The `index` must be a value greater than or equal to `0` and less than the current size of the `ArrayList`. Throws an `IndexOutOfBoundsException` if the `index` is not in this range.

(continued)

Display 14.1 **Some Methods in the Class `ArrayList`** (part 2 of 3)

`public Base_Type get(int index)`

Returns the element at the specified index. This statement is analogous to returning `a[index]` for an array `a`. The `index` must be a value greater than or equal to `0` and less than the current size of the `ArrayList`. Throws `IndexOutOfBoundsException` if the `index` is not in this range.

METHODS TO ADD ELEMENTS

`public boolean add(Base_Type newElement)`

Adds the specified element to the end of the calling `ArrayList` and increases the `ArrayList`'s size by one. The capacity of the `ArrayList` is increased if that is required. Returns `true` if the add is successful. (The return type is `boolean`, but the method is typically used as if it were a `void` method.)

`public void add(int index, Base_Type newElement)`

Inserts `newElement` as an element in the calling `ArrayList` at the specified index. Each element in the `ArrayList` with an index greater or equal to `index` is shifted upward to have an index that is one greater than the value it had previously. The `index` must be a value greater than or equal to `0` and less than or equal to the current size of the `ArrayList`. Throws `IndexOutOfBoundsException` if the index is not in this range. Note that you can use this method to add an element after the last element. The capacity of the `ArrayList` is increased if that is required.

METHODS TO REMOVE ELEMENTS

`public Base_Type remove(int index)`

Deletes and returns the element at the specified index. Each element in the `ArrayList` with an index greater than `index` is decreased to have an index that is one less than the value it had previously. The `index` must be a value greater than or equal to `0` and less than the current size of the `ArrayList`. Throws `IndexOutOfBoundsException` if the `index` is not in this range. Often used as if it were a `void` method.

`protected void removeRange(int fromIndex, int toIndex)`

Deletes all the elements with indices *i* such that `fromIndex` ≤ *i* < `toIndex`. Elements with indices greater than or equal to `toIndex` are decreased appropriately.

`public boolean remove(Object theElement)`

Removes one occurrence of `theElement` from the calling `ArrayList`. If `theElement` is found in the `ArrayList`, then each element in the `ArrayList` with an index greater than the removed element's index is decreased to have an index that is one less than the value it had previously. Returns `true` if `theElement` was found (and removed). Returns `false` if `theElement` was not found in the calling `ArrayList`.

`public void clear()`

Removes all elements from the calling `ArrayList` and sets the `ArrayList`'s size to zero.

SEARCH METHODS

`public boolean contains(Object target)`

Returns `true` if the calling `ArrayList` contains `target`; otherwise, returns `false`. Uses the method `equals` of the object `target` to test for equality with any element in the calling `ArrayList`.

Display 14.1 Some Methods in the Class **ArrayList** (part 3 of 3)

`public int indexOf(Object target)`

Returns the index of the first element that is equal to `target`. Uses the method `equals` of the object `target` to test for equality. Returns `-1` if `target` is not found.

`public int lastIndexOf(Object target)`

Returns the index of the last element that is equal to `target`. Uses the method `equals` of the object `target` to test for equality. Returns `-1` if `target` is not found.

MEMORY MANAGEMENT (SIZE AND CAPACITY)

`public boolean isEmpty()`

Returns `true` if the calling `ArrayList` is empty (that is, has size `0`); otherwise, returns `false`.

`public int size()`

Returns the number of elements in the calling `ArrayList`.

`public void ensureCapacity(int newCapacity)`

Increases the capacity of the calling `ArrayList`, if necessary, in order to ensure that the `ArrayList` can hold at least `newCapacity` elements. Using `ensureCapacity` can sometimes increase efficiency, but its use is not needed for any other reason.

`public void trimToSize()`

Trims the capacity of the calling `ArrayList` to the `ArrayList`'s current size. This method is used to save storage space.

MAKE A COPY

`public Object[] toArray()`

Returns an array containing all the elements on the list. Preserves the order of the elements.

`public` *Type*`[] toArray(` *Type*`[] a)`

Returns an array containing all the elements on the list. Preserves the order of the elements. *Type* can be any class types. If the list will fit in `a`, the elements are copied to `a` and `a` is returned. Any elements of `a` not needed for list elements are set to `null`. If the list will not fit in `a`, a new array is created.

(As we will discuss in Section 14.2, the correct Java syntax for this method heading is

`public <Type> Type[] toArray(Type[] a)`

However, at this point we have not yet explained this kind of type parameter syntax.)

`public Object clone()`

Returns a shallow copy of the calling `ArrayList`. *Warning*: The clone is not an independent copy. Subsequent changes to the clone may affect the calling object and vice versa. (See Chapter 5 for a discussion of shallow copy.)

EQUALITY

`public boolean equals(Object other)`

If `other` is another `ArrayList` (of any base type), then `equals` returns `true` if, and only if, both `ArrayLists` are of the same size and contain the same list of elements in the same order. (In fact, if `other` is any kind of *list*, then `equals` returns `true` if, and only if, both the calling `ArrayList` and `other` are of the same size and contain the same list of elements in the same order. Lists are discussed in Chapter 16.)

Why Are Some Parameters of Type *Base_Type* and Others of Type `Object`?

Look at the table of methods in Display 14.1. In some cases, when a parameter is naturally an object of the base type, the parameter type is the base type, but in other cases, it is the type `Object`.

For example, look at the `add` methods and the second `remove` method in the table. The `add` methods have a parameter of the base type; the `remove` method has a parameter of type `Object`. Why the difference in parameter types? The class `ArrayList` implements a number of interfaces and inherits methods from various ancestor classes. These interfaces and ancestor classes specify that certain parameters have type `Object`.

For example, in Chapter 7, we explained that the parameter for the `equals` method is always of type `Object` because the method heading is inherited from the class `Object`. In other cases, the designers of the `ArrayList` class were free to specify the parameter types for the method.

The "for-each" Loop

In Chapter 16, we will cover a family of classes known as *collections*. The `ArrayList` classes are our first examples of collection classes. Starting with version 5.0, Java has added a new kind of `for` loop that can cycle through all the elements in a collection and can, in particular, cycle through all the elements in an `ArrayList`. This new kind of `for` loop is called a **for-each loop** or **enhanced for loop**. A for-each loop can also be used to cycle through all the elements in an array. The for-each loop was introduced for use with arrays in a starred section of Chapter 6, but you need not go back and read that subsection. The presentation of for-each loops here is complete.

for-each loop

For example, the following code ends with a for-each loop that outputs all the elements in the `ArrayList` named `mylist`:

```
ArrayList<String> myList = new ArrayList<String>(20);
<Some code to fill myList>
for (String element : myList)
    System.out.println(element);
```

You can read the line beginning with `for` as "for each `element` in `myList`, do the following." Note that the variable, `element`, has the same type as the elements in the `ArrayList`. The variable (in this case, `element`), must be declared in the for-each loop as we have done. If you attempt to declare `element` before the for-each loop, you will get a compiler error message.

The general syntax for a for-each loop statement is

```
for (Base_Type Variable : Collection_Object)
     Statement
```

Be sure to notice that you use a colon (not a semicolon) after the *Variable*. You may use any legal variable name for the *Variable*; you do not have to use `element`. The only

Collection_Objects we have seen so far are arrays and `ArrayList` objects. Although it is not required, the *Statement* typically contains the *Variable*. When the for-each loop is executed, the *Statement* is executed once for each element of the *Collection_Object*. More specifically, for each `element` of the *Collection_Object*, the *Variable* is set to the collection element and then the *Statement* is executed.

The program in Display 14.2 includes an example of a for-each loop as well as examples of some of the other `ArrayList` details we have presented.

For-each Loop for `ArrayList` Objects

SYNTAX

`for` *(Array_Base_Type Variable : ArrayList_Object) Statement*

EXAMPLE

```
for (Integer element : numberList)
              element = 42;
```

`numberList` is an `ArrayList` with base type `Integer`. This for-each loop changes the value of each element of `numberList` to `42`. (This example uses automatic boxing. So, `42` really means `new Integer(42)`.)

A good way to read the first line of the example is "For each `element` in `numberList`, do the following."

Display 14.2 A for-each Loop Used with an **`ArrayList`** (part 1 of 2)

```
import java.util.ArrayList;
import java.util.Scanner;

public class ArrayListDemo
{
   public static void main(String[] args)
   {
      ArrayList<String> toDoList = new ArrayList<String>(20);
      System.out.println(
                     "Enter list entries, when prompted.");
      boolean done = false;
      String next = null;
      String answer;
      Scanner keyboard = new Scanner(System.in);

      while (! done)
      {
          System.out.println("Input an entry:");
          next = keyboard.nextLine();
          toDoList.add(next);
```

(continued)

Display 14.2 A for-each Loop Used with an **ArrayList** (part 2 of 2)

```
            System.out.print("More items for the list? ");
            answer = keyboard.nextLine();
            if (!(answer.equalsIgnoreCase("yes")))
                done = true;
        }

        System.out.println("The list contains:");
        for (String entry : toDoList)
            System.out.println(entry);
    }
}
```

Sample Dialogue

```
Enter list entries, when prompted.
Input an entry:
Practice Dancing.
More items for the list? yes
Input an entry:
Buy tickets.
More items for the list? yes
Input an entry:
Pack clothes.
More items for the list? no
The list contains:
Practice Dancing.
Buy tickets.
Pack clothes.
```

MyProgrammingLab™

Self-Test Exercises

8. Suppose `numberList` is an object of the class `ArrayList<Double>`. Give code that will output all the elements in `numberList` to the screen.

9. Write a class for sorting strings into lexicographic order that follows the outline of the class `SelectionSort` in Display 6.11 of Chapter 6. Your definition, however, will use an `ArrayList` of the class `ArrayList<String>`, rather than an array of elements of type `double`. For words, lexicographic order reduces to alphabetic order if all the words are in either all lowercase or all uppercase letters. You can compare two strings to see which is lexicographically first by using the `String` method `compareTo`. For strings `s1` and `s2`, `s1.compareTo(s2)` returns a negative number if `s1` is lexicographically before `s2`, returns `0` if `s1` equals `s2`, and returns a positive number if `s1` is lexicographically after `s2`. Call

MyProgrammingLab™

Self-Test Exercises (continued)

extra code on website

your class StringSelectionSort. A test program you can use to test your class follows. (The program is included with the source code provided on the website that accompanies this book.)

```
Import java.util.ArrayList;

public class StringSelectionSortDemo
{

    public static void main(String[] args)
    {
        ArrayList<String> b = new ArrayList<String>();
        b.add("time");
        b.add("tide");
        b.add("clouds");
        b.add("rain");
        System.out.println("ArrayList values before sorting:");
        for (String e : b)
            System.out.print(e + " ");
        System.out.println();
        StringSelectionSort.sort(b);
        System.out.println("ArrayList values after sorting:");
        for (String e : b)
            System.out.print(e + " ");
        System.out.println();
    }
}
```

EXAMPLE: Golf Scores

The program in Display 14.3 reads in a list of golf scores and then outputs the average of the scores and how much each differs from the average. The scores are read and stored in an ArrayList so that they will be available later in the program to be output along with how much each differs from the average. This is the kind of thing that is well suited to being done with an ordinary array. However, it is much easier and cleaner to use an ArrayList as we did in Display 14.3.

Our program deals with a list of values of type double. But we use an ArrayList with base type Double to store these values. We did not use an ArrayList with base type double because there is no such thing. The base type for an ArrayList must be a class type (or other reference type). However, thanks to Java's automatic boxing, we can program as if an object of type ArrayList<Double> can store values of type double.

The ArrayList automatically keeps track of how many elements are stored in the ArrayList. If we had used an ordinary partially filled array in our program instead of an ArrayList, we would need an extra int variable to keep track of how much of the array is used. When we use an ArrayList, we are spared all the overhead associated

(continued)

EXAMPLE: (continued)

with partially filled arrays. Those details are taken care of for us automatically. The code for those details is in the definition of the `ArrayList` class, but there is no need to look at that code. That code is all implementation detail that we need not worry about when using an `ArrayList`.

Notice the use of for-each loops in our program. The cleanest and easiest way to cycle through all the elements in an `ArrayList` is to use a for-each loop.

It is instructive to compare the program in Display 14.3, which uses an `ArrayList`, with the program in Display 6.4, which does the same thing but uses an ordinary array. The version that uses an `ArrayList` is much cleaner and even much shorter than the one that uses an ordinary array. This is because an `ArrayList` does so many things for you automatically that you would have to explicitly code for if you used an ordinary array. This is a good example of information hiding and code reuse. The programmers who defined the `ArrayList` class did a lot of programming for you so that your programming task is simpler than it would otherwise be.

Display 14.3 **Golf Score Program** (part 1 of 3)

```
import java.util.ArrayList;
import java.util.Scanner;

public class GolfScores
{
    /**
     Shows differences between each of a list of golf scores and their
       average.
    */
    public static void main(String[] args)
    {
        ArrayList<Double> score = new ArrayList<Double> ();

         System.out.println("This program reads golf scores and shows");
         System.out.println("how much each differs from the average.");

         System.out.println("Enter golf scores:");
         fillArrayList(score);
         showDifference(score);
    }

    /**
     Reads values into the array a.
    */
    public static void fillArrayList(ArrayList<Double> a)
```

Parameters of type `ArrayList<Double>()` are handled just like any other class parameter.

Display 14.3 Golf Score Program (part 2 of 3)

```
    {
        System.out.println("Enter a list of nonnegative numbers.");
        System.out.println(
               "Mark the end of the list with a negative number.");
        Scanner keyboard = new Scanner(System.in);

        double next;
        int index = 0;
        next = keyboard.nextDouble();
        while (next >= 0)
        {
            a.add(next);
            next = keyboard.nextDouble();
        }
    }
    /**
     Returns the average of numbers in a.
    */
    public static double computeAverage(ArrayList<Double> a)
    {
        double total = 0;
        for (Double element : a)
            total = total + element;
        int numberOfScores = a.size();
        if (numberOfScores > 0)
        {
            return (total/numberOfScores);
        }
        else
        {
            System.out.println("ERROR: Trying to average 0 numbers.");
            System.out.println("computeAverage returns 0.");
            return 0;
        }
    }

    /**
      Gives screen output showing how much each of the elements
      in a differ from their average.
    */
    public static void showDifference(ArrayList<Double> a)
    {
        double average = computeAverage(a);
        System.out.println("Average of the " + a.size()
                                          + " scores = " + average);
        System.out.println("The scores are:");
        for (Double element : a)
            System.out.println(element + " differs from average by "
                                          + (element - average));
    }
}
```

Because of automatic boxing, we can treat values of type `double` *as if their type were* `Double`*.*

A for-each loop is the nicest way to cycle through all the elements in an `ArrayList`*.*

(continued)

Display 14.3 Golf Score Program (part 3 of 3)

Sample Dialogue

```
This program reads golf scores and shows
how much each differs from the average.
Enter golf scores:
Enter a list of nonnegative numbers.
Mark the end of the list with a negative number.
69  74  68  -1
Average of the 3 scores = 70.3333
The scores are:
69.0 differs from average by -1.33333
74.0 differs from average by 3.66667
68.0 differs from average by -2.33333
```

TIP: Use `trimToSize` to Save Memory

`ArrayList`s automatically increase their capacity when your program needs them to have additional capacity. However, the capacity may increase beyond what your program requires. Also, when your program needs less capacity in an `ArrayList`, the `ArrayList` does not automatically shrink. If your `ArrayList` has a large amount of excess capacity, you can save memory by using the method `trimToSize` to shrink the capacity of an `ArrayList`. If `list` is an `ArrayList`, an invocation of `list.trimToSize()` will shrink the capacity of the `ArrayList list` down to the size of `list`, so that there is no unused capacity in `list`. Normally, you should use `trimToSize` only when you know that the `ArrayList` will not need its extra capacity later. ■

`trimToSize`

PITFALL: The `clone` Method Makes a Shallow Copy ★

There are situations in which you would like to make an independent copy of an `ArrayList` object; that is, you would like to make a deep copy of the `ArrayList` object. (Deep copying and shallow copying were discussed in Chapter 5; you may want to review that material.) For example, if you define a class with a private instance variable of an `ArrayList` type, then you would like an accessor method to return a deep copy of the `ArrayList` stored in the private instance variable. The reason you want a deep copy is the same as the reason that you want a deep copy of an array instance variables. This was discussed in Chapter 6 in the subsection entitled "Privacy Leaks with Array Instance Variables." It would be a good idea to review that subsection before going on with reading this subsection.

As we have often observed, the assignment operator merely copies a reference so that you have another name for the object being copied. So, you do not have an independent

PITFALL: (continued)

copy. You have what is known as a *shallow copy*. For example, assume that Pet is a class with the usual kinds of accessor methods and consider the following code:

```
ArrayList<Pet> petList1 = new ArrayList<Pet>();
<Some code to set the instance variables of elements of petList1.>
ArrayList<Pet> petList2 = petList1;
```

petList2 and petList1 are just two names for the same ArrayList object. Making a change to petList1 or to an element of petList1 will also change petList2 because they are the same list.

If you want an independent copy (deep copy) of petList1, you might think the following would give you your independent copy:

```
ArrayList<Pet> petList2 = petList1.clone();
```

Unfortunately, the clone method also makes a shallow copy. There is no built-in method to give you a deep copy (independent copy) of an ArrayList.

When you need a deep copy of an ArrayList, you will have to resort to some ad hoc tricks. If you have a way to make a deep copy of objects of the base type, then you can create a deep copy of each element in the ArrayList and place them into a new ArrayList object. This is the exact same approach as the one we discussed for making a deep copy of an ordinary array in the subsection of Chapter 6 entitled "Privacy Leaks with Array Instance Variables." The situation with respect to deep copying of an ArrayList is exactly the same as the situation with respect to deep copying of an ordinary array. Although the details of this subsection may seem subtle and difficult, they are not new. You have already faced the exact same problem with ordinary arrays. ■

MyProgrammingLab™

Self-Test Exercises

10. Can you have an ArrayList of ints?

11. The following for-each loop was used in the method showDifference in Display 14.3. Rewrite it as an ordinary for loop. This should help you to see how much cleaner it is to use a for-each loop.

```
for (Double element : a)
  System.out.println(element + " differs from average by "
                                          + (element - average));
```

The Vector Class

Vector

The Java standard libraries have a class named Vector that behaves almost exactly the same as the class ArrayList. In fact, everything we have said about the class ArrayList holds true for the Vector class. Although in almost all situations, you could use either the class ArrayList or the class Vector, a clear preference seems to be developing among programmers for the class ArrayList. There are some differences between the classes Vector and ArrayList, but the differences involve material we have not covered. If you encounter the class Vector in somebody's code, chances are the class Vector could be replaced by the class ArrayList, which would require at most cosmetic changes in the code.[1]

Parameterized Classes and Generics

parameterized class

The class ArrayList is a **parameterized class**. It has a parameter, which we have been denoting *Base_Type*, that can be replaced by any reference type to obtain a class for ArrayLists with the specified base type. ArrayList is just a class that somebody defined (and placed in the standard Java library package java.util), so you should also be able to define these kinds of classes. Starting with version 5.0, Java allows class definitions with parameters for types. These classes that have type parameters are called parameterized class or **generic definitions** or, more simply, **generics**. You already know how to use classes with a type parameter, because we have been using the parameterized class ArrayList. In Section 14.2, we will show you how to write your own parameterized classes.

generics

PITFALL: Nonparameterized ArrayList and Vector Classes

The ArrayList and Vector classes we discussed in this section have a type parameter for the base type. There are also ArrayList and Vector classes with no parameter for the base type. (They have base type Object.) These ArrayList and Vector classes without type parameters are left over from earlier versions of Java. When checking details in the Java documentation, be sure you get the documentation for the ArrayList and Vector classes that have a type parameter. Using notation we introduce in Section 14.2, the versions with type parameters are usually written as ArrayList<E> and Vector<E> or as ArrayList<T> and Vector<T> in the Java documentation. ■

14.2 Generics

You can have this dish prepared with any type of meat or fish.

Entry on a restaurant menu

Starting with version 5.0, Java allows class definitions that contain a parameter (or parameters) for a type (or types). In this section, we teach you how to write class definitions that contain a type parameter.

---

[1] The biggest difference between the Vector and ArrayList classes is that Vectors are *synchronized* whereas ArrayLists are not. However, synchronization is a topic that we do not cover and is not relevant to the kinds of programming we are doing.

Generic Basics

Classes and methods can have a type parameter. The type parameter may then have any reference type, and hence any class type, plugged in for the type parameter. This plugging in produces a specific class type or method. For example, Display 14.4 shows a very simple class definition with a **type parameter** `T`. You may use any nonkeyword identifier for the type parameter; you need not use `T`. However, by convention, type parameters start with an uppercase letter, and there is some tradition of using a single letter for a type parameter. Starting with an uppercase letter makes sense because typically a class type is plugged in for the type parameter. The tradition of using a single letter is not so compelling.

type parameter

A class definition with a type parameter is stored in a file and compiled just like any other class. For example, the parameterized class shown in Display 14.4 would be stored in a file named `Sample.java`. Once the parameterized class is compiled, it can be used like any other class, except that when used in your code, you must specify a class type to be plugged in for the type parameter. For example, the class `Sample` from Display 14.4 could be used as follows:

```
Sample<String> object1 = new Sample<String>();
object1.setData("Hello");
System.out.println(object1.getData());
Sample<Pet> object2 = new Sample<Pet>();
Pet p = new Pet();
<Some code to set the data for the object p>
object2.setData(p);
```

The class `Pet` can be as defined in Chapter 4, but the details do not matter; it could be any class.

A class, such as `Sample<String>`, that you obtain from a generic class by plugging in a type for the type parameter is said to **instantiate** the generic class. So, we would say "`Sample<String>` instantiates the generic class `Sample`."

instantiate

Notice the angular bracket notation for the type parameter and also for the class type that is plugged in for the type parameter.

Display 14.4 A Class Definition with a Type Parameter

```
public class Sample<T>
{
    private T data;

    public void setData(T newData)
    {
        data = newData;
    }

    public T getData()
    {
        return data;
    }
}
```

`T` is a parameter for a type.

Class Definition with a Type Parameter

You can define classes with a parameter for a type. Such a class is called a **generic class** or a **parameterized class**. The type parameter is included in angular brackets after the class name in the class definition heading. You may use any nonkeyword identifier for the type parameter, but by convention, the type parameter starts with an uppercase letter. The type parameter may be used like any other type in the definition of the class. (There are some restrictions on where the type parameter can be used. These are discussed later in the Pitfall section entitled "A Type Parameter Cannot Be Used Everywhere a Type Name Can Be Used.") For an example, see Display 14.4.

A generic class is used like any other class, except that you specify a reference type, typically a class type, to be plugged in for the type parameter. This class type (or other reference type) is given in angular brackets after the name of the generic class, as shown in the following example:

EXAMPLE

```
Sample<String> object1 = new Sample<String>();
object1.setData("Hello");
```

`Sample<String>` is said to **instantiate** the generic class `Sample`.

Type Inference in Java 7

Starting with version 7, Java supports a feature called **type inference**. In type inference, Java is able to infer the base type in the call to the constructor based on the base type used in the variable declaration. That is, the following

```
ClassName<Base_Type> Object_Name = new ClassName<Base_Type>();
```

can equivalently be written in Java 7 as:

```
ClassName<Base_Type> Object_Name = new ClassName<>();
```

The new format saves a little bit of typing and is also somewhat cleaner to read. However, programmers have been using the earlier format for many years, so you are likely to see it in existing code. For greater compatibility, the examples in this book do not use the new syntax supported in JDK 7.

EXAMPLES

```
ArrayList<String> list = new ArrayList<>();
ArrayList<Double> list2 = new ArrayList<>(30);
```

TIP: Compile with the -Xlint Option

There are many pitfalls that you can encounter when using type parameters. If you compile with the -Xlint option, you will receive more informative diagnostics of any problems or potential problems in your code. For example, the class Sample in Display 14.4 should be compiled as follows:

```
javac -Xlint Sample.java
```

If you are using an IDE to compile your programs, check your documentation to see how to set compiler options. (For the TextPad environment, you can set compiler options in the Preferences box under the Configure menu.)

When compiling with the -Xlint option, you will get more warnings than you would otherwise get. A warning is not an error, and if the compiler gives only warnings and no error message, then the class has compiled and can be used. However, in most cases, be sure you understand the warning and feel confident that it does not indicate a problem, or else change your code to eliminate the warning. One warning that you may get on some programs in this text is "no definition of serialVersionUID." Discussion of this warning is beyond the scope of this book, but you can safely ignore the warning. ■

EXAMPLE: A Generic Class for Ordered Pairs

In Display 14.5, we have given a parameterized class for ordered pairs of values.

Notice that the constructor heading does not include the type parameter T. This is counter to many people's intuition, but that is the way it is done. A constructor can use the type parameter, such as T, as the type for a parameter for the constructor, but the constructor heading does not include the type parameter in angular brackets, such as <T>.

By using this parameterized class with the type String plugged in for the type parameter T, as shown next, you get a class whose objects are pairs of String values:

```
Pair<String> secretPair =
             new Pair<String>("Happy", "Day");
```

By using this parameterized class with the type Integer plugged in for the type parameter T, as shown next, you get a class whose objects are pairs of Integer objects:

```
Pair<Integer> rollOfDice =
       new Pair<Integer>(new Integer(2), new Integer(3));
```

If Pet is some class you defined, you can plug in Pet for the type parameter T, as shown next, to get a class whose objects are pairs of objects of type Pet:

```
Pet male = new Pet();
Pet female = new Pet();
<Some code to set the data for the objects male and female.>
Pair<Pet> breedingPair =
             new Pair<Pet>(male, female);
```

Display 14.6 contains a simple example of using our generic class Pair.

Display 14.5 A Generic Ordered Pair Class (part 1 of 2)

```
public class Pair<T>
{
    private T first;
    private T second;

    public Pair()
    {
        first = null;
        second = null;
    }

    public Pair(T firstItem, T secondItem)
    {
        first = firstItem;
        second = secondItem;
    }

    public void setFirst(T newFirst)
    {
        first = newFirst;
    }

    public void setSecond(T newSecond)
    {
        second = newSecond;
    }

    public T getFirst()
    {
        return first;
    }

    public T getSecond()
    {
        return second;
    }

    public String toString()
    {
        return ( "first: " + first.toString() + "\n"
                 + "second: " + second.toString() );
    }

```

Constructor headings do not include the type parameter in angular brackets.

Display 14.5 **A Generic Ordered Pair Class** (part 2 of 2)

```
    public boolean equals(Object otherObject)
    {
        if (otherObject = = null)
            return false;
        else if (getClass() != otherObject.getClass())
            return false;
        else
        {
            Pair<T> otherPair = (Pair<T>)otherObject;
            return (first.equals(otherPair.first)
               && second.equals(otherPair.second));
        }
    }
}
```

Terminology

The terms *generic class* and *parameterized class* mean the same thing, namely a class with one or more type parameters.

Display 14.6 **Using Our Ordered Pair Class** (part 1 of 2)

```
import java.util.Scanner;

public class GenericPairDemo
{
   public static void main(String[] args)
   {
        Pair<String> secretPair =
             new Pair<String>("Happy", "Day");

        Scanner keyboard = new Scanner(System.in);
        System.out.println("Enter two words:");
        String word1 = keyboard.next();
        String word2 = keyboard.next();
        Pair<String> inputPair =
            new Pair<String>(word1, word2);
        if (inputPair.equals(secretPair))
        {
            System.out.println("You guessed the secret words");
            System.out.println("in the correct order!");
```

(continued)

Display 14.6 Using Our Ordered Pair Class (part 2 of 2)

```
            }
            else
            {
                System.out.println("You guessed incorrectly.");
                System.out.println("You guessed");
                System.out.println(inputPair);
                System.out.println("The secret words are");
                System.out.println(secretPair);
            }
        }
    }
```

Sample Dialogue

```
Enter two words:
two words
You guessed incorrectly.
You guessed
first: two
second: words
The secret words are
first: Happy
second: Day
```

PITFALL: A Generic Constructor Name Has No Type Parameter

The class name in a parameterized class definition has a type parameter attached, such as `Pair<T>` in Display 14.5. This can mislead you into thinking you need to use the type parameter in the heading of the constructor definition, but you do not repeat the type parameter specification `<T>` in the heading of the constructor definition. For example, use

```
public Pair()
```

Do not use

```
public Pair<T>()
```

A constructor can use the type parameter, such as `T`, as the type for a parameter for the constructor, as in the following, but the constructor heading does not include the type parameter in angular brackets, such as `<T>`:

```
public Pair(T firstItem, T secondItem)
```

For a complete example, see Display 14.5.

Sometimes it seems that people stay up late at night thinking of ways to make things confusing. As we just noted, in the definition of a parameterized class, a

PITFALL: (continued)

constructor has no type parameter in angular brackets. So, you see the following in Display 14.5:

```
public Pair(T firstItem, T secondItem)
```

But as shown in Display 14.6, when you instantiate a generic class by specifying a type for the type parameter, you do specify the type in angular brackets when writing the constructor name, as in the following from Display 14.6:

```
Pair<String> secretPair =
          new Pair<String>("Happy", "Day");
```

However, this second case is not hard to remember. If you leave out the <String>, Java would not know which Pair class you meant. If you leave out the <String>, the compiler could not tell if you meant Pair<String>, Pair<Double>, or some other Pair class. ■

PITFALL: You Cannot Plug in a Primitive Type for a Type Parameter

The type plugged in for a type parameter must be a reference type. It cannot be a primitive type such as int, double, or char. However, now that Java has automatic boxing, this is not a big restriction in practice. For example, if you want Pair<int>, you cannot have it, but you can have Pair<Integer>, and thanks to automatic boxing, you can use Pair<Integer> with int values. This is illustrated by the program in Display 14.7.

The most typical type to plug in for a type parameter is a class type. However, you can plug in any reference type. So, in particular, you can plug in an array type for a type parameter. ■

PITFALL: A Type Parameter Cannot Be Used Everywhere a Type Name Can Be Used

Within the definition of a parameterized class definition, there are places where an ordinary class name would be allowed but a type parameter is not allowed. In particular, you cannot use the type parameter in simple expressions using new to create a new object. For example, the following are all illegal within the definition of a parameterized class definition with type parameter T:

```
T object = new T(); //The first T is legal,
                    //the second one is illegal.
T[] a = new T[10]; //The first T is legal,
                   //the second one is illegal.
```

This restriction is not as arbitrary as it might at first appear. In the first case, T is not being used as a type name; it is being used as a constructor name. In the second case, T is being used as something like a constructor, although it is not officially a constructor. ■

PITFALL: An Instantiation of a Generic Class Cannot be an Array Base Type

Arrays such as the following are illegal (the generic class `Pair` is the one defined in Display 14.5):

```
Pair<String>[] a = new Pair<String>[10]; //Illegal
```

This is a reasonable thing to want to do, but it is not allowed because of technical details having to do with how Java implements generic classes. The full explanation for this restriction is beyond the scope of this book. ■

Display 14.7 **Using Our Ordered Pair Class and Automatic Boxing** (part 1 of 2)

```
import java.util.Scanner;

public class GenericPairDemo2
{
   public static void main(String[] args)
   {
         Pair<Integer> secretPair =
              new Pair<Integer>(42, 24);

         Scanner keyboard = new Scanner(System.in);
         System.out.println("Enter two numbers:");
         int n1 = keyboard.nextInt();
         int n2 = keyboard.nextInt();
         Pair<Integer> inputPair =
             new Pair<Integer>(n1, n2);
         if (inputPair.equals(secretPair))
         {
             System.out.println("You guessed the secret numbers");
             System.out.println("in the correct order!");
         }
         else
         {
             System.out.println("You guessed incorrectly.");
             System.out.println("You guessed");
             System.out.println(inputPair);
             System.out.println("The secret numbers are");
             System.out.println(secretPair);
         }
   }
}
```

Automatic boxing allows you to use an `int` *argument for an* `Integer` *parameter.*

Display 14.7 Using Our Ordered Pair Class and Automatic Boxing (part 2 of 2)

Sample Dialogue

```
Enter two numbers:
42 24
You guessed the secret numbers
in the correct order!
```

TIP: A Class Definition Can Have More Than One Type Parameter

A generic class definition can have any number of type parameters. The multiple type parameters are listed in angular brackets just as in the single type parameter case, but are separated by commas. For example, in Display 14.8, we have rewritten the class `Pair` so the first and second items of a pair can be of different types. In Display 14.9, we give a simple example of using our generic class with two type parameters. ■

Display 14.8 Multiple Type Parameters (part 1 of 2)

```
public class TwoTypePair<T1, T2>
{
    private T1 first;
    private T2 second;

    public TwoTypePair()
    {
        first = null;
        second = null;
    }

    public TwoTypePair(T1 firstItem, T2 secondItem)
    {
        first = firstItem;
        second = secondItem;
    }

    public void setFirst(T1 newFirst)
    {
        first = newFirst;
    }
    public void setSecond(T2 newSecond)
    {
        second = newSecond;
    }
    public T1 getFirst()
```

(continued)

Display 14.8 **Multiple Type Parameters** (part 2 of 2)

```
    {
        return first;
    }

    public T2 getSecond()
    {
        return second;
    }

    public String toString()
    {
        return ( "first: " + first.toString() + "\n"
                + "second: " + second.toString() );
    }

    public boolean equals(Object otherObject)
    {
        if (otherObject == null)
            return false;
        else if (getClass() != otherObject.getClass())
            return false;
        else
        {
            TwoTypePair<T1, T2> otherPair =
                        (TwoTypePair<T1, T2>)otherObject;
            return (first.equals(otherPair.first)
                && second.equals(otherPair.second));
        }
    }
}
```

The first `equals` *is the* `equals` *of the type* `T1`.
The second `equals` *is the* `equals` *of the type* `T2`.

PITFALL: A Generic Class Cannot Be an Exception Class

If you begin an exception class definition as follows, you will get a compiler error message:

```
public class MyException<T> extends Exception //Illegal
```

It is still illegal if you replace `Exception` with `Error`, `Throwable`, or any descendent class of `Throwable`. You cannot create a generic class whose objects are throwable. ■

Display 14.9 Using a Generic Class with Two Type Parameters

```
import java.util.Scanner;

public class TwoTypePairDemo
{
   public static void main(String[] args)
   {
         TwoTypePair<String, Integer> rating =
             new TwoTypePair<String, Integer>("The Car Guys", 8);

         Scanner keyboard = new Scanner(System.in);
         System.out.println(
                      "Our current rating for " + rating.getFirst());
         System.out.println(" is " + rating.getSecond());

         System.out.println("How would you rate them?");
         int score = keyboard.nextInt();
         rating.setSecond(score);
         System.out.println(
                      "Our new rating for " + rating.getFirst());
         System.out.println(" is " + rating.getSecond());
   }
}
```

Sample Dialogue

```
Our current rating for The Car Guys
is 8
How would you rate them?
10
Our new rating for The Car Guys
is 10
```

Bounds for Type Parameters

Sometimes it does not make sense to plug in just any reference type for the type parameter in a generic class definition. For example, consider the generic class `Pair` defined in Display 14.5. Suppose we want to add a method that returns the maximum of the two elements in an ordered pair. We could add the following method definition to the class `Pair` in Display 14.5:

max

```
public T max()
{
    if (first.compareTo(second) <= 0)
        return first;
    else
        return second;
}
```

compareTo

Recall that the method compareTo is required to be a member of any class that implements the Comparable interface. The Comparable interface is a standard Java interface that was discussed in Chapter 13. Recall that the Comparable interface has only the following method heading that must be implemented:

```
public int compareTo(Object other);
```

When defining a class that implements the Comparable interface, the programmer is expected to define compareTo so that it returns

a negative number if the calling object "comes before" the parameter other,

a zero if the calling object "equals" the parameter other,

and a positive number if the calling object "comes after" the parameter other.

This all works fine, except for one problem: This makes sense only if the type plugged in for the type parameter T satisfies the Comparable interface, but Java allows you to plug in any type for the type parameter T.

You can have Java enforce this restriction on the possible types that can be plugged in for T. To ensure that only classes that implement the Comparable interface are plugged in for T, begin the class definition as follows:

```
public class Pair<T extends Comparable>
```

extends

bound

The part extends Comparable is called a **bound** on the type parameter T. If you attempt to plug in a type for T that does not implement the Comparable interface, you will get a compiler error message. Note that you use the keyword extends, not the keyword implements as you would naturally expect.

Note that the bound extends Comparable is not just an optional little nicety. If you omit it, you will get an error message from the compiler saying it does not know about the method compareTo.

This version of the generic class Pair with the method max is summarized in Display 14.10. On the accompanying website, this version of Pair is in a subdirectory named Bounded Pair.

A bound on a type may be a class name (rather than an interface name) in which case only descendent classes of the bounding class may be plugged in for the type parameters. For example, the following says that only descendent classes of the class Employee may be plugged in for T, where Employee is some class:

```
public class SameGenericClass<T extends Employee>
```

Display 14.10 A Bounded Type Parameter

```
public class Pair<T extends Comparable>
{
    private T first;
    private T second;

    public T max()
    {
        if (first.compareTo(second) <= 0)
            return first;
        else
            return second;
    }

<All the constructors and methods given in Display 14.5
            are also included as part of this generic class definition>

}
```

This explains why the keyword `extends` is used in the bounds expression rather than `implements`.

multiple bounds

You can have multiple interfaces and possibly one class in a bounds expression. Just separate the entries with the ampersand sign, `&`, as in the following example:

```
public class AnotherGenericClass<T extends Employee & Comparable>
```

If you have more than one type parameter, the syntax follows the following example:

```
public class YetAnotherGeneric
    <T1 extends Employee & Comparable, T2 extends Comparable>
```

You can list any number of interfaces in a bounds expression, but you may list only one class in a bounds expression. Moreover, if you do list a class and some interfaces, the class must be first in the list.

Type Parameter Bounds

You can specify that the class plugged in for a type parameter must be a descendent class of a specified class, must implement specified interfaces, or both.

(continued)

SYNTAX (FOR CLASS DEFINITION HEADINGS)

```
public class Class_Name
  <Type extends Ancestor_Class & Interface_1 & Interface_2 & ...
                                                   ...& Last_Interface>
```

If there are multiple type parameters, they are separated by commas. There can be any number of interfaces but only one ancestor class for each type parameter.

EXAMPLES

```
public class Pair<T extends Comparable>
public class MyClass<T extends Employee & Comparable>
public class YourClass <T1 extends Employee & Comparable
                             & Cloneable, T2 extends Comparable>
```

`Employee` is a class. `Comparable` and `Cloneable` are interfaces.

TIP: Generic Interfaces

An interface can have one or more type parameters. The details and notation are the same as they are for classes with type parameters. ■

Generic Methods ★

(This is a starred subsection because it is needed only for Chapter 16, which covers the Java collection classes. If you choose to read Chapter 16, you will need to read this subsection first.)

When you define a generic class, you can use the type parameter in the definitions of the methods for that generic class. You also can define a generic method that has its own type parameter that is not the type parameter of any class. This generic method can be a member of an ordinary (nongeneric) class or a member of some generic class with some other type parameter. For example,

```
public class Utility
{
    ...
    public static <T> T getMidpoint(T[] a)
    {
        return a[a.length/2];
    }
    public static <T> T getFirst(T[] a)
    {
        return a[0];
    }
    ...
}
```

In this case, the class (Utility) has no type parameters, but the methods getMidpoint and getFirst each have a type parameter. Note that the type parameter in angular brackets, <T>, is placed after all the modifiers—in this case, public static—and before the returned type.

When you invoke one of these generic methods, preface the method name with the type to be plugged in, given in angular brackets, as in the following examples:

```
String midString = Utility.<String>getMidpoint(b);

double firstNumber = Utility.<Double>getFirst(c);
```

Note that the dot is before the type in angular brackets; the type is part of the method name, not part of the class name. Also note that the methods getMidpoint and getFirst use different types plugged in for their type parameter. The type parameter is local to the method, not to the class. (The argument b is an array with base type String. The argument c is an array with base type Double.)

You can also define such generic methods inside of generic classes, as in the following example:

```
public class Sample<T>
{
    private T data;

    public Sample(T forData)
    {
        data = forData;
    }
    public <ViewerType> void showTo(ViewerType viewer)
    {
        System.out.println("Hello " + viewer);
        System.out.println("Data is " + data);
    }
     ...
}
```

Note that T and ViewerType are different type parameters. T is a type parameter for the entire class, but ViewerType is a type parameter only for the method showTo. What follows is a sample use of these generic methods:

```
Sample<Integer> object = new Sample<Integer>(42);
object.<String>showTo("Friend");
```

This produces the output

```
Hello Friend
Data is 42
```

Inheritance with Generic Classes ★

You can define a generic class to be a derived class of an ordinary class or a derived class of another generic class. Display 14.11 contains the definition of a generic class called `UnorderedPair`, which is a derived class of the generic class `Pair` (which we gave in Display 14.5). The class `UnorderedPair` overrides the definition of `equals` that it inherits from `Pair`. To a programmer using the class, `UnorderedPair` is just like the class `Pair` with one exception. In `UnorderedPair`, the two components do not have to be in the same order for two pairs to be equal. Less formally, in the `Pair<String>` world, `"beer"` and `"peanuts"` is not the same as `"peanuts"` and `"beer"`. In the `UnorderedPair<String>` world, they are the same. This is illustrated by the demonstration program in Display 14.12.

Just as you would expect, an object of type `UnorderedPair<String>` is also of type `Pair<String>`. As we have seen so far, inheritance with generic classes is straightforward in most cases. However, there are some situations with subtle pitfalls. We discuss those next.

Display 14.11 **A Derived Generic Class** (part 1 of 2)

```
public class UnorderedPair<T> extends Pair<T>
{
    public UnorderedPair()
    {
        setFirst(null);
        setSecond(null);
    }

    public UnorderedPair(T firstItem, T secondItem)
    {
        setFirst(firstItem);
        setSecond(secondItem);
    }

    public boolean equals(Object otherObject)
    {
        if (otherObject = = null)
            return false;
        else if (getClass() != otherObject.getClass())
            return false;
        else
        {
            UnorderedPair<T> otherPair =
                             (UnorderedPair<T>)otherObject;
            return (getFirst().equals(otherPair.getFirst())
               && getSecond().equals(otherPair.getSecond()))
               ||
```

Display 14.11 A Derived Generic Class (part 2 of 2)

```
                    (getFirst().equals(otherPair.getSecond())
                 && getSecond().equals(otherPair.getFirst()));
        }
    }
}
```

Suppose `HourlyEmployee` is a derived class of the class `Employee`. You might think that an object of type `Pair<HourlyEmployee>` is also of type `Pair<Employee>`. You might think that, but you would be wrong. If `G` is a generic class, there is no relationship between `G<A>` and `G<B>`, no matter what the relationship is between the classes `A` and `B`.

Display 14.12 Using **`UnorderedPair`**

```
public class UnorderedPairDemo
{
    public static void main(String[] args)
    {
         UnorderedPair<String> p1 =
              new UnorderedPair<String>("peanuts", "beer");
         UnorderedPair<String> p2 =
              new UnorderedPair<String>("beer", "peanuts");
         if (p1.equals(p2))
         {
             System.out.println(p1.getFirst() + " and " +
                        p1.getSecond() + " is the same as");
             System.out.println(p2.getFirst() + " and "
                               + p2.getSecond());
         }
    }
}
```

Sample Dialogue[2]

```
peanuts and beer is the same as
beer and peanuts
```

[2] A note to the grammar police: I intentionally used "is" instead of "are." If you read and understand the text, you will realize that "peanuts and beer" is a single item. Starting the sentence with a lowercase letter and the absence of a period are also intentional.

MyProgrammingLab™

Self-Test Exercises

12. (This question refers to the starred section "Generic Methods." You should skip this question if you have not yet read that subsection.) Define a generic method named `getMidindex`, which is like `getMidpoint`, but returns the index of the array midpoint as opposed to the element at the midpoint.

13. (This question refers to the starred section "Inheritance with Generic Classes." You should skip this question if you have not yet read that subsection.) Is an array of type `UnorderedPair<String>[]` also of type `Pair<String>[]`?

Chapter Summary

- `ArrayList` is a *parameterized class* that is like an array that can grow (and shrink) while the program is running.
- An `ArrayList` has a number of methods that allow you to use it as a kind of automated partially filled array.
- You can cycle through all the elements in an `ArrayList` using a *for-each loop*.
- You can define classes with one or more type parameters. Such classes are known as *generic classes*.

Answers to Self-Test Exercises

1. `list.add("Hello");`
2. `instruction.set(5, "Go");`
3. `instruction.add(5, "Go");`
4. No. The index for `set` must be greater than or equal to `0` and less than the size of the `ArrayList`. Thus, you can replace any existing element, but you cannot place the element at any higher index. This situation is unlike that of an array. If an array is partially filled to index `10`, you can add an element at index `20`, as long as the array is that large. With an `ArrayList`, you cannot add an element beyond the last-used index.
5. No. The index for add must be greater than or equal to `0` and less than or equal to the size of the `ArrayList`. Thus, you can replace any existing element or add an element to the end of the list, but you cannot place the element at any higher index. This situation is unlike that of an array. If an array is partially filled to index `10`, you can add an element at index `20`, as long as the array is that large. With an `ArrayList`, you cannot add an element beyond one more than the last-used index.

6. The index for `add` (that is, `index2`) is allowed to be one larger than the index for `set` (that is, `index1`). The index for `set` must be strictly less than the size of the `ArrayList`. The index for `add` can also be equal to the size of the `ArrayList`.

7. Yes. The `ArrayList` can contain more than 20 elements. The number `20` used as an argument to the constructor merely gives the initial memory allocation for the `ArrayList`. More memory is automatically allocated when it is needed.

8.
```
for (Double element : numberList)
    System.out.println(element);
```

9.
```
import java.util.ArrayList;
/**
 Class for sorting an ArrayList of Strings lexicographically
 (approximately alphabetically).
*/
public class StringSelectionSort
{
   /**
    Sorts the ArrayList a so that a.get(0), a.get(1),...,
    a.get(a.size() – 1) are in lexicographic order.
   */
   public static void sort(ArrayList<String> a)
   {
      int index, indexOfNextSmallest;
      for (index = 0; index < a.size() 1; index++)
      {//Place the correct value in position index:
           indexOfNextSmallest =
                           indexOfSmallest(index, a);
           interchange(index,indexOfNextSmallest, a);
           //a.get(0), a.get(1),...,a.get(index)
           //are sorted. The rest of the
           //elements are in the remaining positions.
      }
   }
   /**
   Precondition: i and j are legal indices for the ArrayList a.
   Postcondition: The values of a.get(i) and
   a.get(j) have been interchanged.
   */
   private static void interchange(
                          int i, int j, ArrayList<String> a)
```

```
    {
      String temp;
      temp = a.get(i);
      a.set(i, a.get(j));
      a.set(j, temp);
    }
   /**
    Returns the index of the lexicographically first value among
    a.get(startIndex), a.get(startIndex+1),...,a.get(a.size()
    - 1)
   */
   private static int indexOfSmallest(
      int startIndex, ArrayList<String> a)
   {
      String min = a.get(startIndex);
      int indexOfMin = startIndex;
      int index;
      for (index = startIndex + 1; index < a.size(); index++)
      if ((a.get(index)).compareTo(min) < 0)
      {
           min = a.get(index);
           indexOfMin = index;
      }
      return indexOfMin;
   }
}
```

10. No, the base type of an `ArrayList` cannot be a primitive type, such as `int`, `double`, or `char`. You can, however, have an `ArrayList` with base type `Integer` that can be used to store integers.
11. Notice that the following, while correct, is not as easy to understand as the for-each loop.

```
for (int i; i < a.size(); i++)
     System.out.println(a.get(i) + " differs from average by "
                                       + (a.get(i) average));
```

12.
```
public static <T> int getMidindex(T[] a)
{
     return a.length/2;
}
```

13. This is a trick question. As we explained in the text, you cannot have an array of type `UnorderedPair<String>[]` or of type `Pair<String>[]`.

Programming Projects

MyProgrammingLab™

Visit www.myprogramminglab.com to complete select exercises online and get instant feedback.

1. In the sport of diving, seven judges award a score between 0 and 10, where each score may be a floating-point value. The highest and lowest scores are thrown out and the remaining scores are added together. The sum is then multiplied by the degree of difficulty for that dive. The degree of difficulty ranges from 1.2 to 3.8 points. The total is then multiplied by 0.6 to determine the diver's score.

   Write a computer program that inputs a degree of difficulty and seven judges' scores and outputs the overall score for that dive. The program should use an `ArrayList` of type `Double` to store the scores.

2. Write a program that uses an `ArrayList` of parameter type `Contact` to store a database of contacts. The `Contact` class should store the contact's first and last name, phone number, and email address. Add appropriate accessor and mutator methods. Your database program should present a menu that allows the user to add a contact, display all contacts, search for a specific contact and display it, or search for a specific contact and give the user the option to delete it. The searches should find any contact where any instance variable contains a target search string. For example, if "elmore" is the search target, then any contact where the first name, last name, phone number, or email address contains "elmore" should be returned for display or deletion. Use the "for-each" loop to iterate through the `ArrayList`.

3. Many Global Positioning Satellite (GPS) units can record waypoints. The waypoint marks the coordinates of a location on a map along with a timestamp. Consider a GPS unit that stores waypoints in terms of an `(X,Y)` coordinate on a map together with a timestamp `t` that records the number of seconds that have elapsed since the unit was turned on. Write a program that allows the user to enter as many waypoints as desired, storing each waypoint in an `ArrayList`, where each waypoint is represented by a class that you design. Each waypoint represents a successive sample point during a hike along some route. The coordinates should be input as `doubles`, and the timestamp as an integer. Have your program compute the total distance traveled and the average speed in miles per hour. Use the map scaling factor of 1 = 0.1 miles. For example, if the only two waypoints are (X=1,Y=1,T=0) and (X=2,Y=1,T=3600), then the hiker traveled a distance of 0.1 miles in 3,600 seconds, or 0.1 miles per hour.

4. Write a generic class, `MyMathClass`, with a type parameter `T` where `T` is a numeric object type (e.g., `Integer`, `Double`, or any class that extends `java.lang.Number`). Add a method named `standardDeviation` that takes an `ArrayList` of type `T` and returns as a `double` the standard deviation of the values in the `ArrayList`. Use the `doubleValue()` method in the `Number` class to retrieve the value of each number as a double. Refer to Programming Project 6.5 for a definition of computing the standard deviation. Test your method with suitable data. Your program should generate a compile-time error if your standard deviation method is invoked on an `ArrayList` that is defined for nonnumeric elements (e.g., `Strings`).

5. Create a generic class with a type parameter that simulates drawing an item at random out of a box. This class could be used for simulating a random drawing. For example, the box might contain `Strings` representing names written on a slip of paper, or the box might contain `Integers` representing a random drawing for a lottery based on numeric lottery picks. Create an `add` method that allows the user of the class to add an object of the specified type along with an `isEmpty` method that determines whether or not the box is empty. Finally, your class should have a `drawItem` method that randomly selects an object from the box and returns it. If the user attempts to drawn an item out of an empty box, return `null`. Write a `main` method that tests your class.

6. Implement a priority queue capable of holding objects of an arbitrary type, `T`, by defining a `PriorityQueue` class that implements the queue with an `ArrayList`. A priority queue is a type of list where every item added to the queue also has an associated priority. Define priority in your application so that those items with the largest numerical value have the highest priority. Your class should support the following methods:

   - `Add(item, priority)`—Adds a new item to the queue with the associated priority.
   - `Remove()`—Returns the item with the highest priority and removes it from the queue. If the user attempts to remove from an empty queue, return `null`.

   For example, if `q` is a priority queue defined to take `Strings`

```
q.add("X", 10);
q.add("Y", 1);
q.add("Z", 3);

System.out.println(q.remove()); // Returns X
System.out.println(q.remove()); // Returns Z
System.out.println(q.remove()); // Returns Y
```

   Test your queue on data with priorities in various orders (e.g., ascending, descending, mixed). You can implement the priority queue by performing a linear search through the `ArrayList`. In future courses, you may study a data structure called a *heap* that is a more efficient way to implement a priority queue.

VideoNote
Solution to Programming Project 14.7

7. Programming Project 6.13 implemented a simple trivia game using an array of `Trivia` objects. Redo this project but use an `ArrayList` of `Trivia` objects instead of an array. The run-time behavior should remain identical to before.

8. In Programming Project 11.9, you were asked to implement a recursive algorithm to find all files that matched a target file name. Redo this Programming Project where the recursive method returns an `ArrayList` of `String` objects. Each string should store the pathname to the matching file. Return `null` if no matching files are found.

Linked Data Structures 15

15 Linked Data Structures

If somebody there chanced to be
Who loved me in a manner true
My heart would point him out to me
And I would point him out to you.

GILBERT AND SULLIVAN, *Ruddigore*

Introduction

node and link

linked list

head node

A linked data structure consists of capsules of data, known as **nodes**, which are connected via what are known as **links**. These links can be viewed as arrows and thought of as one-way passages from one node to another. The simplest kind of linked data structure consists of a single chain of nodes, each connected to the next by a link; this is known as a **linked list**. A sample linked list can be depicted as shown in Display 15.1. In Display 15.1, the nodes are represented by boxes that can each hold two kinds of data, a string and an integer, as in a shopping list. The links are depicted as arrows, which reflect the fact that your code must traverse the linked list in one direction without backing up. So there is a first node, a second node, and so on up to the last node. The first node is called the **head node**.

That information is all very vague but provides the general picture of what is going on in a linked list. It becomes concrete when you realize a linked list in some programming language. In Java, the nodes are realized as objects of a node class. The data in a node is stored via instance variables. The links are realized as references. Recall that a reference is simply a memory address. A reference is what is stored in a variable of a class type. So the link is realized as an instance variable of the type of the node class itself. In Java, a node in a linked list is connected to the next node by having an instance variable of the node type contain a reference (that is, a memory address) of where in memory the next node is stored.

Java comes with a `LinkedList` library class as part of the `java.util` package. It makes sense to use this library class, because it is well designed and well tested, and will save you a lot of work. However, using the library class will not teach you how to implement linked data structures in Java. To do that, you need to see an implementation of a simple linked data structure, such as a linked list. So to let you see how this sort of thing is done in Java, we will construct our own simplified example of a linked list.

After discussing linked lists, we then go on to discuss more elaborate linked data structures, including sets, hash tables, and trees.

Display 15.1 Nodes and Links in a Linked List

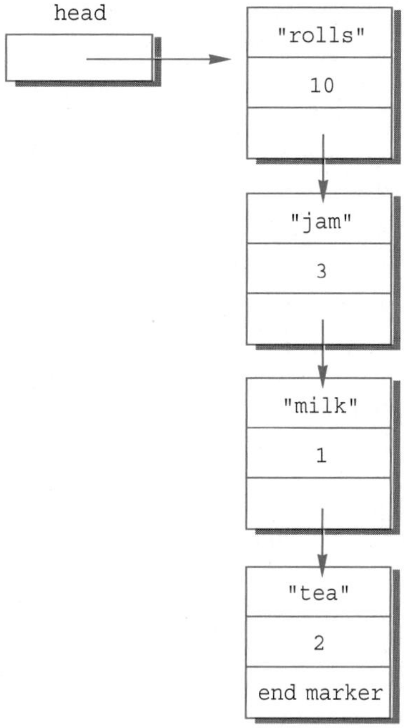

Prerequisites

If you prefer, you may skip this chapter and go directly to Chapter 16 on collection classes or to Chapter 17 to begin your study of windowing interfaces using the Swing library. You have a good deal of flexibility in how you order the later chapters of this book.

This chapter requires material from Chapters 1 through 5, Chapter 14, and simple uses of inner classes (Section 13.2 of Chapter 13). Section 15.7 on trees additionally requires Chapter 11 on recursion.

Sections 15.2 through 15.7 do not depend on each other in any essential way. In particular, you may omit Section 15.2 on cloning and still read the following sections. Sections 15.2 through 15.7 do not depend in any essential way on the material on generic linked lists in subsections of Section 15.1.

15.1 Java Linked Lists

A chain is only as strong as its weakest link.

PROVERB

A linked list is a linked data structure consisting of a single chain of nodes, each connected to the next by a link. This is the simplest kind of linked data structure, but it is nevertheless widely used. In this section, we give examples of linked lists and develop techniques for defining and working with linked lists in Java.

EXAMPLE: A Simple Linked List Class

Display 15.1 is a diagram of a linked list. In the display, the nodes are the boxes. In your Java code, a node is an object of some node class, such as the class `Node1` given in Display 15.2. Each node has a place (or places) for some data and a place to hold a link to another node. The links are shown as arrows that point to the node they "link" to. In Java, the links will be implemented as references to a node stored in an instance variable of the `node` type.

The `Node1` class is defined by specifying, among other things, an instance variable of type `Node1` that is named `link`. This allows each node to store a reference to another node of the same type. There is a kind of circularity in such definitions, but this circularity is allowed in Java. (One way to see that this definition is not logically inconsistent is to note that we can draw pictures, or even build physical models, of our linked nodes.)

The first node, or start node, in a linked list is called the *head node*. If you start at the head node, you can traverse the entire linked list, visiting each node exactly once. As you will see shortly, in Java your code must intuitively "follow the link arrows." In Display 15.1, the box labeled `head` is not itself the head node; it is not even a node. The box labeled `head` is a variable of type `Node1` that contains a reference to the first node in the linked list—that is, a reference to the head node. The function of the variable `head` is that it allows your code to find that first or head node. The variable `head` is declared in the obvious way:

```
Node1 head;
```

In Java, a linked list is an object that in some sense contains all the nodes of the linked list. Display 15.3 contains a definition of a linked list class for a linked list such as the one in Display 15.1. Notice that a linked list object does not directly contain all the nodes in the linked list. It contains only the instance variable `head` that contains a reference to the first or head node. However, every node can be reached from this first or head node. The `link` instance variable of the first and every `Node1` of the linked list contains a reference to the next `Node1` in the linked list. Thus, the arrows shown in the diagram in Display 15.1 are realized as references in Java. Each node object of a linked list contains (in its `link` instance variable) a reference to another object of the class `Node1`, and this other object contains a reference to another object of the class `Node1`, and so on until the end of the linked list. Thus, a linked list object, indirectly at least, contains all the nodes in the linked list.

Display 15.2 A Node Class

```
public class Node1
{
    private String item;
    private int count;
    private Node1 link;

    public Node1( )
    {
        link = null;
        item = null;
        count = 0;
    }
    public Node1(String newItem, int newCount, Node1 linkValue)
    {
        setData(newItem, newCount);
        link = linkValue;
    }

    public void setData(String newItem, int newCount)
    {
        item = newItem;
        count = newCount;
    }
    public void setLink(Node1 newLink)
    {
        link = newLink;
    }

    public String getItem( )
    {
        return item;
    }

    public int getCount( )
    {
        return count;
    }

    public Node1 getLink( )
    {
        return link;
    }
}
```

A node contains a reference to another node. That reference is the link to the next node.

We will define a number of node classes so we numbered the names as in **Node1**.

We will give a better definition of a node class later in this chapter.

Display 15.3 **A Linked List Class** (part 1 of 2)

```
public class LinkedList1
{
    private Node1 head;

    public LinkedList1( )
    {
        head = null;
    }

    /**
     Adds a node at the start of the list with the specified data.
     The added node will be the first node in the list.
    */
    public void addToStart(String itemName, int itemCount)
    {
        head = new Node1(itemName, itemCount, head);
    }

    /**
     Removes the head node and returns true if the list contains at
     least one node. Returns false if the list is empty.
    */
    public boolean deleteHeadNode( )
    {
        if (head != null)
        {
            head = head.getLink( );
            return true;
        }
        else
            return false;
    }

    /**
     Returns the number of nodes in the list.
    */
    public int size( )
    {
        int count = 0;
        Node1 position = head;

```

We will define a letter linked list class later in this chapter.

Display 15.3 **A Linked List Class** (part 2 of 2)

```
        while (position != null)
        {
            count++;
            position = position.getLink( );
        }
        return count;
    }

    public boolean contains(String item)
    {
        return (find(item) != null);
    }

    /**
     Finds the first node containing the target item, and returns a
     reference to that node. If target is not in the list, null is
     returned.
    */
    private Node1 find(String target)
    {
        Node1 position = head;
        String itemAtPosition;
        while (position != null)
        {
            itemAtPosition = position.getItem( );
            if (itemAtPosition.equals(target))
                return position;
            position = position.getLink( );
        }
        return null; //target was not found
    }
    public void outputList( )
    {
        Node1 position = head;
        while (position != null)
        {
            System.out.println(position.getItem( ) + " "
                                        + position.getCount( ));
            position = position.getLink( );
        }
    }
}
```

This last node is indicated by the `link` field being equal to `null`.

This is the way you traverse an entire linked list.

Working with Linked Lists

When dealing with a linked list, your code needs to be able to "get to" that first or head node, and you need some way to detect when the last node is reached. To get your code to the first node, use a variable of type `Node1` that always contains a reference to the first node. In Display 15.3, the variable with a reference to the first node is named `head`. From that first or head node, your code can follow the links through the linked list. But how does your code know when it is at the last node in a linked list?

In Java, indicate the end of a linked list by setting the `link` instance variable of the last node in the linked list to `null`, as shown in Display 15.4. That way your code can test whether or not a node is the last node in a linked list by testing whether its link instance variable contains `null`. Remember that you check for a link being "equal" to `null` by using `==`, and not using any equals method.

empty list

Also use `null` to indicate an empty linked list. The `head` instance variable contains a reference to the first node in the linked list, or it contains `null` if the linked list is empty (that is, if the linked list contains no nodes). The only constructor sets this `head` instance variable to `null`, indicating that a newly created linked list is empty.

Display 15.4 **Traversing a Linked List**

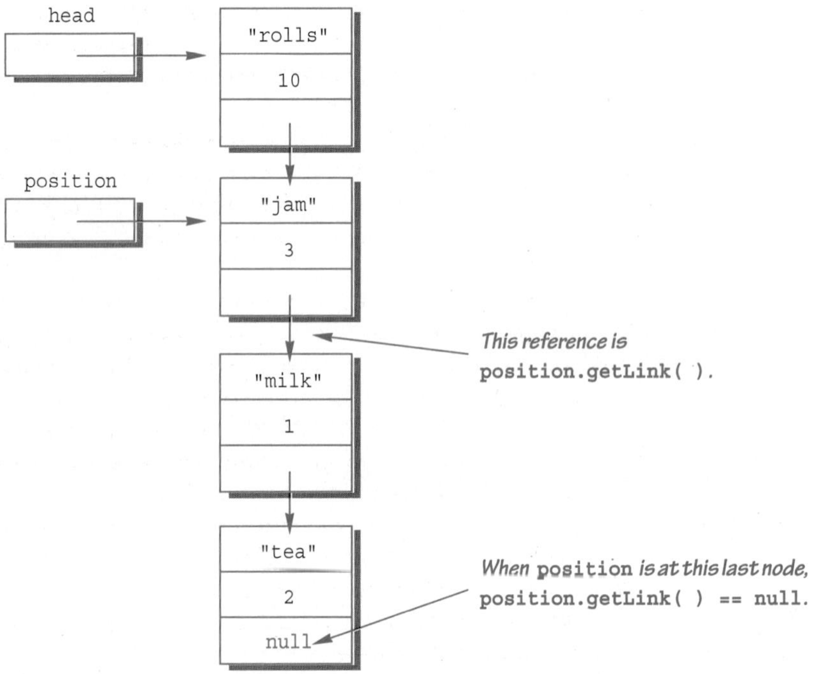

Indicating the End of a Linked List

The last node in a linked list should have its `link` instance variable set to `null`. That way, your code can check whether a node is the last node by checking whether its `link` instance variable is equal to `null`.

An Empty List Is Indicated by `null`

Suppose the variable `head` is supposed to contain a reference to the first node in a linked list. Linked lists usually start out empty. To indicate an empty linked list, give the variable `head` the value `null`. This is traditional and works out nicely for many linked list manipulation algorithms.

traversing a linked list

Before we go on to discuss how nodes are added and removed from a linked list, let us suppose that the linked list already has a few nodes and that you want to write out the contents of all the nodes to the screen. You can do this with the method `outputList` (Display 15.3), whose body is reproduced here:

```
Node1 position = head;
while (position != null)
{
   System.out.println(position.getItem( ) + " "
                            + position.getCount( ));
   position = position.getLink( );
}
```

The method uses a local variable named `position` that contains a reference to one node. The variable `position` starts out with the same reference as the `head` instance variable, so it starts out positioned at the first node. The `position` variable then has its position moved from one node to the next with the assignment

```
position = position.getLink( );
```

This is illustrated in Display 15.4. To see that this assignment "moves" the `position` variable to the next node, note that the `position` variable contains a reference to the node pointed to by the position arrow in Display 15.4. So, `position` is a name for that node, and `position.link` is a name for the link to the next node. The value of `link` is produced with the accessor method `getLink`. Thus, a reference to the next node in the linked list is `position.getLink( )`. You "move" the position variable by giving it the value of `position.getLink( )`.

The method `outputList` continues to move the `position` variable down the linked list and outputs the data in each node as it goes along. When `position` reaches the last node, it outputs the data in that node and then again executes

```
position = position.getLink( );
```

If you study Display 15.4, you will see that when `position` leaves the last node, its value is set to `null`. At this point, we want to stop the loop, so we iterate the loop

```
while (position != null)
```

A similar technique is used to traverse the linked list in the methods `size` and `find`.

adding a node

Next let us consider how the method `addToStart` adds a node to the start of the linked list so that the new node becomes the first node in the list. It does this with the single statement

```
head = new Node1(itemName, itemCount, head);
```

The new node is created with

```
new Node1(itemName, itemCount, head)
```

which returns a reference to this new node. The assignment statement sets the variable `head` equal to a reference to this new node, making the new node the first node in the linked list. To link this new node to the rest of the list, we need only set the `link` instance variable of the new node equal to a reference to the *old first node*. But we have already done that: `head` used to point to the old first node, so if we use the name `head` on *the right-hand side of the assignment operator*, `head` will denote a reference to the old first node. Therefore, the new node produced by

```
new Node1(itemName, itemCount, head)
```

points to the old first node, which is just what we wanted. This is illustrated in Display 15.5.

Later, we will discuss adding nodes at other places in a linked list, but the easiest place to add a node is at the start of the list. Similarly, the easiest place to delete a node is at the start of the linked list.

removing a node

The method `deleteHeadNode` removes the first node from the linked list and leaves the `head` variable pointing to (that is, containing a reference to) the old second node (which is now the first node) in the linked list. This is done with the following assignment:

```
head = head.getLink( );
```

Display 15.5 Adding a Node at the Start

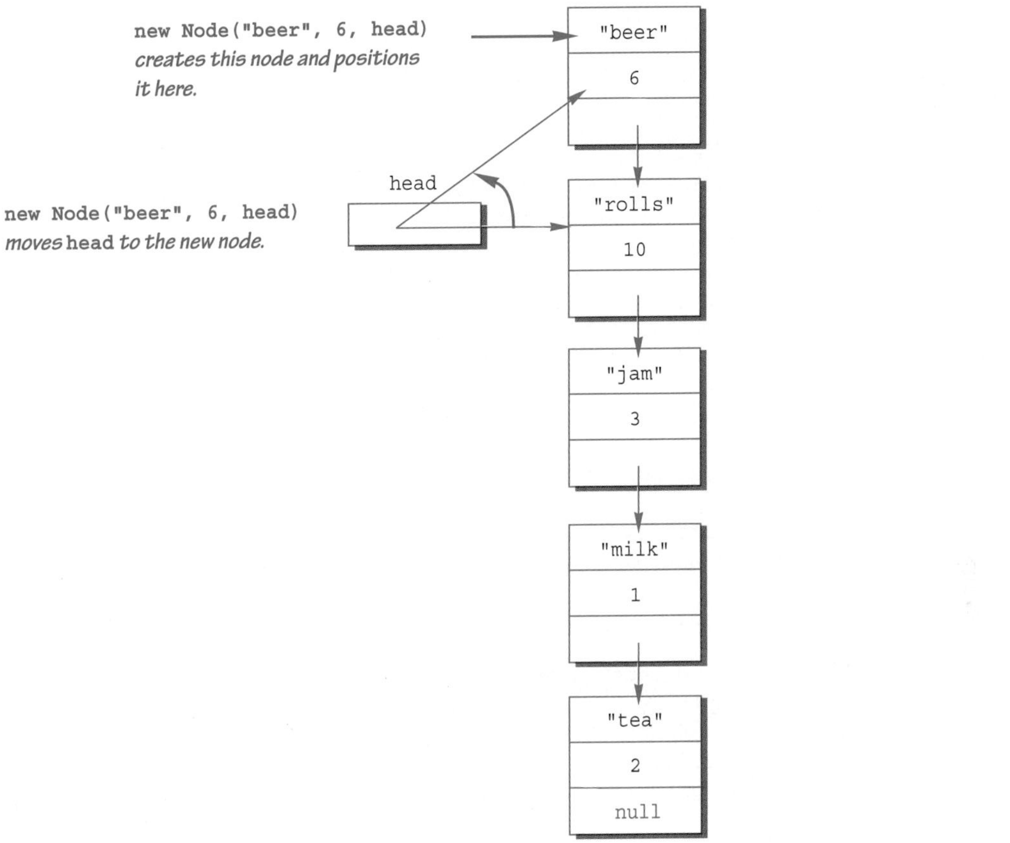

This removes the first node from the linked list and leaves the linked list one node shorter. But what happens to the deleted node? At some point, Java will automatically collect it, along with any other nodes that are no longer accessible, and recycle the memory they occupy. This is known as **automatic garbage collection**.

automatic garbage collection

Display 15.6 contains a simple program that demonstrates how some of the methods in the class `LinkedList1` behave.

Display 15.6 **A Linked List Demonstration**

```
public class LinkedList1Demo
{
    public static void main(String[] args)
    {
        LinkedList1 list = new LinkedList1( );
        list.addToStart("Apples", 1);
        list.addToStart("Bananas", 2);
        list.addToStart("Cantaloupe", 3);
        System.out.println("List has " + list.size( )
                                + " nodes.");
        list.outputList( );
        if (list.contains("Cantaloupe"))
            System.out.println("Cantaloupe is on list.");
        else
            System.out.println("Cantaloupe is NOT on list.");

        list.deleteHeadNode( );

        if (list.contains("Cantaloupe"))
            System.out.println("Cantaloupe is on list.");
        else
            System.out.println("Cantaloupe is NOT on list.");

        while (list.deleteHeadNode( ))
            ; //Empty loop body
        System.out.println("Start of list:");
        list.outputList( );
        System.out.println("End of list.");
    }
}
```

`Cantaloupe` is now in the head node.

Empties the list. There is no loop body because the method `deleteHeadNode` both performs an action on the list and returns a Boolean value.

Sample Dialogue

```
List has 3 entries.
Cantaloupe 3
Bananas 2
Apples 1
Cantaloupe is on list.
Cantaloupe is NOT on list.
Start of list:
End of list.
```

MyProgrammingLab™

Self-Test Exercises

1. What output is produced by the following code?

```
LinkedList1 list = new LinkedList1( );
list.addToStart("apple pie", 1);

list.addToStart("hot dogs", 12);
list.addToStart("mustard", 1);
list.outputList( );
```

2. Define a `boolean` valued method named `is Empty` that can be added to the class `LinkedList1` (Display 15.3). The method returns `true` if the list is empty and `false` if the list has at least one node in it.

3. Define a `void` method named `clear` that can be added to the class `LinkedList1` (Display 15.3). The method has no parameters and it empties the list.

PITFALL: Privacy Leaks

It may help you to understand this section if you first review the Pitfall section of the same name in Chapter 5.

Consider the method `getLink` in the class `Node1` (Display 15.2). It returns a value of type `Node1`. That is, it returns a reference to a `Node1`. In Chapter 5, we said that if a method (such as `getLink`) returns a reference to an instance variable of a (mutable) class type, then the `private` restriction on the instance variable can easily be defeated because getting a reference to an object may allow a programmer to change the private instance variables of the object. There are a number of ways to fix this, the most straightforward of which is to make the class `Node1` a private inner class in the method `Node1`, as discussed in the next subsection.

There is no danger of a privacy leak with the class `Node1` when it is used in the class definition for `LinkedList1`. However, there is no way to guarantee that the class `Node1` will be used only in this way unless you take some precaution, such as making the class `Node1` a private inner class in the class `LinkedList1 Node1`.

An alternate solution is to place both of the classes `Node1` and `LinkedList1` into a package, and change the `private` instance variable restriction to the `package` restriction as discussed in Chapter 7.

Note that this privacy problem can arise in any situation in which a method returns a reference to a private instance variable of a class type. The method `getItem( )` of the class `Node1` comes very close to having this problem. In this case, the method `getItem` causes no privacy leak, but only because the class `String` is not a mutable class (that is, it has no methods that will allow the user to change the value of the string without changing the reference). If instead of storing data of type `String` in our list we had stored data of some mutable class type, then defining an accessor method similarly to `getItem` would produce a privacy leak. ■

Node Inner Classes

You can make a linked list, or any similar data structures, self-contained by making the node class an inner class. In particular, you can make the class `LinkedList1` more self-contained by making `Node1` an inner class, as follows:

```
public class LinkedList1
{
    private class Node1
    {
      <The rest of the definition of Node1 can be
       the same as in Display 15.2.>
    }

    private Node1 head;
   <The constructor and methods in Display 15.3 are inserted here.>
}
```

Note that we have made the class `Node1` a private inner class. If an inner class is not intended to be used elsewhere, it should be made private. Making `Node1` a private inner class hides all objects of the inner class and avoids a privacy leak.

If you are going to make the class `Node1` a private inner class in the definition of `LinkedList1`, then you can safely simplify the definition of `Node1` by eliminating the accessor and mutator methods (the `set` and `get` methods) and just allowing direct access to the instance variables (`item`, `count`, and `link`) from methods of the outer class. In Display 15.7, we have written a class similar to `LinkedList1` in this way. The rewritten version, named `LinkedList2`, is like the class `LinkedList1` in Display 15.3 in that it has the same methods that perform basically the same actions. To keep the discussion simple, `LinkedList2` has only one data field instead of two. We could easily have retained the two data fields, but we wanted a notationally simple example without any distracting details. (See Self-Test Exercise 8 for a version that has the same kind of data in each node as in the nodes of `LinkedList1`.)

Display 15.7 **A Linked List Class with a Node Inner Class** (part 1 of 3)

```
public class LinkedList2
{
    private class Node
    {
        private String item;
        private Node link;

        public Node( )
        {
            item = null;
            link = null;
        }
```

Display 15.7 A Linked List Class with a Node Inner Class (part 2 of 3)

```
        public Node(String newItem, Node linkValue)
        {
            item = newItem;
            link = linkValue;
        }
    }//End of Node inner class

    private Node head;

    public LinkedList2( )
    {
        head = null;
    }
    /**
     Adds a node at the start of the list with the specified data.
     The added node will be the first node in the list.
    */
    public void addToStart(String itemName)
    {
        head = new Node(itemName, head);
    }

    /**
     Removes the head node and returns true if the list contains at
     least one node. Returns false if the list is empty.
    */
    public boolean deleteHeadNode( )
    {
        if (head != null)
        {
            head = head.link;
            return true;
        }
        else
            return false;
    }

    /**
     Returns the number of nodes in the list.
    */
    public int size( )
    {
        int count = 0;
        Node position = head;
        while (position != null)
        {
            count++;
```

(continued)

Display 15.7 **A Linked List Class with a Node Inner Class** (part 3 of 3)

```
            position = position.link;
        }
        return count;
    }

    public boolean contains(String item)
    {
        return (find(item) != null);
    }

    /**
     Finds the first node containing the target item, and returns a
     reference to that node. If target is not in the list, null is
     returned.
    */
    private Node find(String target)
    {
        Node position = head;
        String itemAtPosition;
        while (position != null)
        {
            itemAtPosition = position.item;
            if (itemAtPosition.equals(target))
                return position;
            position = position.link;
        }
        return null; //target was not found
    }
    public void outputList( )
    {
        Node position = head;
        while (position != null)
        {
            System.out.println(position.item );
            position = position.link;
        }
    }

    public boolean isEmpty( )
    {
        return (head == null);
    }

    public void clear( )
    {
        head = null;
    }
}
```

Note that the outer class has direct access to the inner class's instance variables, such as `link`.

MyProgrammingLab™

Self-Test Exercises

4. Would it make any difference if we changed the `Node` inner class in Display 15.7 from a private inner class to a public inner class?

5. Keeping the inner class `Node` in Display 15.7 as `private`, what difference would it make if any of the instance variables or methods in the class `Node` had its access modifiers changed from `private` to `public` or package access?

6. Why does the definition of the inner class `Node` in Display 15.7 not have the accessor and mutator methods `getLink`, `setLink`, or other `get` and `set` methods for the link fields similar to those in the class definition of `Node1` in Display 15.2?

7. Would it be legal to add the following method to the class `LinkedList2` in Display 15.7?

```
public Node startNode( )
{
    return head;

}
```

8. Rewrite the definition of the class `LinkedList2` in Display 15.7 so that it has data of a type named `Entry`, which is a public inner class. Objects of type `Entry` have two instance variables defined as follows:

```
private String item;
private int count;
```

This rewritten version of `LinkedList2` will be equivalent to `LinkedList1` in that it has the same methods doing the same things, and it will hold equivalent data in its nodes.

EXAMPLE: A Generic Linked List

Display 15.8 shows a generic linked list with a type parameter `T` for the type of data stored in a node. This generic linked list has the same methods, coded in basically the same way, as our previous linked list (Display 15.7), but we used a type parameter for the type of data in the nodes.

Display 15.10 contains a demonstration program for our generic linked list. The demonstration program uses the class `Entry`, defined in Display 15.9, as the type plugged in for the type parameter `T`. Note that if you want multiple pieces of data in each node, you simply use a class type that has multiple instance variables and plug in this class for the type parameter `T`.

Display 15.8 **A Generic Linked List Class** (part 1 of 3)

```
public class LinkedList3<T>
{
    private class Node<T>
    {
        private T data;
        private Node<T> link;
        public Node( )
        {
            data = null;
            link = null;

        }

        public Node (T newData, Node<T> linkValue)
        {
            data = newData;
            link = linkValue;
        }
    }//End of Node<T> inner class
    private Node<T> head;

    public LinkedList3( )
    {
        head = null;
    }

    /**
     Adds a node at the start of the list with the specified data.
     The added node will be the first node in the list.
    */
    public void addToStart(T itemData)
    {
        head = new Node<T> (itemData, head);
    }
    /**
     Removes the head node and returns true if the list contains at
     least one node. Returns false if the list is empty.
    */
    public boolean deleteHeadNode( )
    {
        if (head != null)
        {
            head = head.link;
            return true;
        }
        else
            return false;
    }
    /**
```

This linked list holds objects of type `T`*. The type* `T` *should have well-defined* `equals` *and* `toString` *methods.*

Display 15.8 **A Generic Linked List Class** (part 2 of 3)

```
     Returns the number of nodes in the list.
    */
    public int size( )
    {
        int count = 0;
        Node<T> position = head;
        while (position != null)
        {
            count++;
            position = position.link;
        }
        return count;
    }

    public boolean contains(T item)
    {
        return (find(item) != null);
    }
    /**
     Finds the first node containing the target item, and returns a
     reference to that node. If target is not in the list, null is
     returned.
    */
    private Node find(T target)
    {
        Node<T> position = head;
        T itemAtPosition;
        while (position != null)
        {
            itemAtPosition = position.data;
            if (itemAtPosition.equals(target))
                return position;
            position = position.link;
        }
        return null; //target was not found
    }

    /**
     Finds the first node containing the target and returns a reference
     to the data in that node. If target is not in the list, null is
     returned.
    */
    public T findData(T target)
    {
        Node<T> result = find(target);
        if (result == null)
            return null;
        else
            return result.data;
```

Type `T` must have a well-defined `equals` for this method to work.

(continued)

Display 15.8 **A Generic Linked List Class** (part 3 of 3)

Type `T` must have a well-defined `toString` methods for this to work.

```
    }
    public void outputList( )
    {
        Node<T> position = head;
        while (position != null)
        {
            System.out.println(position.data);
            position = position.link;
        }
    }

    public boolean isEmpty( )
    {
        return (head == null);
    }

    public void clear( )
    {
        head = null;
    }
    /*
     For two lists to be equal they must contain the same data items in
     the same order. The equals method of T is used to compare data
     items.
    */
    public boolean equals(Object otherObject)
    {
        if (otherObject == null)
            return false;
        else if (getClass( ) != otherObject.getClass( ))
            return false;
        else
        {
            LinkedList3<T> otherList = (LinkedList3<T>)otherObject;
            if (size( )!= otherList.size( ))
                return false;
            Node<T> position = head;
            Node<T> otherPosition = otherList.head;
            while (position != null)
            {
                if (!(position.data.equals(otherPosition.data)))
                    return false;
                position = position.link;
                otherPosition = otherPosition.link;
            }
            return true; //no mismatch was not found
        }
    }
}
```

Display 15.9 A Sample Class for the Data in a Generic Linked List

```
public class Entry
{
    private String item;
    private int count;

    public Entry(String itemData, int countData)
    {
        item = itemData;
        count = countData;
    }

    public String toString( )
    {
        return (item + " " + count);
    }

    public boolean equals(Object otherObject)
    {
        if (otherObject == null)
            return false;
        else if (getClass( ) != otherObject.getClass( ))
            return false;
        else
        {
            Entry otherEntry = (Entry)otherObject;
            return (item.equals(otherEntry.item)
                       && (count == otherEntry.count));
        }
    }
  <There should be other constructors and methods, including accessor
  and mutator methods, but we do not use them in this demonstration.>
}
```

Display 15.10 A Generic Linked List Demonstration (part 1 of 2)

```
public class GenericLinkedListDemo
{
    public static void main(String[] args)
    {
        LinkedList3<Entry> list = new LinkedList3<Entry>( );

        Entry entry1 = new Entry("Apples", 1);
        list.addToStart(entry1);
        Entry entry2 = new Entry("Bananas", 2);
        list.addToStart(entry2);
        Entry entry3 = new Entry("Cantaloupe", 3);
        list.addToStart(entry3);
        System.out.println("List has " + list.size( )
                            + " nodes.");
```

(continued)

Display 15.10 **A Generic Linked List Demonstration** (part 2 of 2)

```
        list.outputList( );
        System.out.println("End of list.");
    }
}
```

Sample Dialogue

```
List has 3 nodes.
Cantaloupe 3
Bananas 2
Apples 1
End of list.
```

PITFALL: Using Node Instead of Node<T>

This pitfall is explained by example, using the LinkedList3<T> class in Display 15.8. However, the lesson applies to any generic linked structure with a node inner class. The type parameter need not be T and the node class name need not be Node, but for simplicity, we will use T and Node.

When defining the LinkedList3<T> class in Display 15.8, the type for a node is Node<T>; it is not Node. However, it is easy to forget the type specification <T> and write Node instead of Node<T>. If you omit the <T>, you may or may not get a compiler error message, depending on other details of your code. If you do get a compiler error message, it is likely to seem bewilderingly strange. The problem is that Node actually means something. (We do not have time to stop and explain what Node means, but it means something similar to a node with data type Object, rather than data type T.) Your only defense against this pitfall is to be very careful; if you do get a bewildering compiler error message, look for a missing <T>.

Sometimes a compiler warning message can be helpful when you make this mistake. If you get a warning that mentions a type cast from Node to Node<T>, look for an omitted <T>.

Finally, we should note that sometimes your code will compile and even run correctly if you omit the <T> from Node<T>. ■

The equals Method for Linked Lists

The linked lists we presented in Display 15.3 and 15.7 do not have an equals method. We did that to keep the examples simple and not detract from the main message. However, a linked list class should normally have an equals method.

equals

There is more than one approach to defining a reasonable equals method for a linked list. The two most obvious are the following:

1. Two linked lists are equal if they contain the same data entries (possibly ordered differently).

2. Two linked lists are equal if they contain the same data entries in the same order; that is, the data in the first node of the calling object equals the data in the first node of the other linked list, the data in the two second nodes are equal, and so forth.

It is not true that one of these is the correct approach to defining an `equals` method and the other is incorrect. In different situations, you might want different definitions of `equals`. However, the most common way to define `equals` for a linked list is approach 2. A definition of equals that follows approach 2 and that can be added to the class `LinkedList2` in Display 15.7 is given in Display 15.11. The generic linked list in Display 15.8 also contains an `equals` method that follows approach 2.

Note that when we define `equals` for our linked list with type parameter `T`, we trust the programmer who wrote the definition for the type plugged in for `T`. We are assuming the programmer has redefined the `equals` method so that it provides a reasonable test for equality. Situations such as this are the reason it is so important to always include an `equals` method in the classes you define.

Display 15.11 An **equals** Method for the Linked List in Display 15.7

```
/*
 For two lists to be equal they must contain the same data items in
 the same order.
*/
public boolean equals(Object otherObject)
{
    if (otherObject == null)
        return false;
    else if (getClass( ) != otherObject.getClass( ))
        return false;
    else
    {
       LinkedList2 otherList = (LinkedList2)otherObject;
       if (size( ) != otherList.size( ))
           return false;
       Node position = head;
       Node otherPosition = otherList.head;
       while (position != null)
       {
           if ( (!(position.item.equals(otherPosition.item))))
              return false;
           position = position.link;
           otherPosition = otherPosition.link;
       }
       return true; //A mismatch was not found
    }
}
```

15.2 Copy Constructors and the `clone` Method ★

There are three ways to do anything:
The right way,
the wrong way,
and the army way.

Advice reputedly given to new army recruits

The way Java handles cloning, and object copying in general, is complicated and can be both subtle and difficult. Some authorities think that the `clone` method was done so poorly in Java that they prefer to ignore it completely and define their own methods for copying objects. I have some sympathy for that view, but before you dismiss Java's approach to cloning, it might be a good idea to see what the approach entails. Linked data structures, such as linked lists, are an excellent setting for discussing cloning because they are an excellent setting for discussing deep versus shallow copying.

This section first presents a relatively simple way to define copy constructors and the `clone` method, but this approach unfortunately produces only shallow copies. We then go on to present one way to produce a deep copy `clone` method and to do so within the official prescribed rules of the Java documentation.

Readers with very little programming experience may be better off skipping this entire section until they become more comfortable with Java. Other readers may prefer to read only the first subsection and possibly the Pitfall "The `clone` Method Is Protected in `Object` ★"

Simple Copy Constructors and `clone` Methods ★

Display 15.12 contains a copy constructor and `clone` method definitions that could be added to the definition of the generic linked list class in Display 15.8. The real work is done by the private helping method `copyOf`, so our discussion focuses on the method `copyOf`.

The private method `copyOf` takes an argument that is a reference to the head node of a linked list and returns a reference to the head node of a copy of that linked list. The easiest way to do this is to return the argument. This would, however, simply produce another name for the argument list. We do not want another name; we want another list. So, the method goes down the argument list one node at a time (with `position`) and makes a copy of each node. The linked list of the calling object is built up node by node by adding these new nodes to its linked list. However, there is a complication. We cannot simply add the new nodes at the head (start) end of the list being built. If we did, then the nodes would end up in the reverse of the desired order. So, the new nodes are added to the end of the linked list being built. The variable `end` of type `Node<T>` is kept positioned at the last node so that it is possible to add nodes at the end of the linked list being built. In this way, a copy of the list in the calling object is created so that the order of the nodes is preserved.

The copy constructor is defined by using the private helping method `copyOf` to create a copy of the list of nodes. Other details of the copy constructor and the `clone` method are done in the standard way.

Although the copy constructor and the `clone` method each produce a new linked list with all new nodes, the new list is not truly independent because the data objects are not cloned. See the Pitfall "The `clone` Method Is Protected in `Object` ★" for a discussion of this point. One way to fix this shortcoming is discussed later in the Programming Tip entitled "Use a Type Parameter Bound for a Better `clone`."

Exceptions ★

A generic data structure, such as the class `LinkedList` in Display 15.12, is likely to have methods that throw exceptions. Situations such as a `null` argument to the copy constructor might be handled differently in different situations, so it is best to throw a `NullPointerException` if this happens and let the programmer who is using the linked list handle the exception. This is what we did with the copy constructor in Display 15.12. A `NullPointerException` is an unchecked exception, which means that it need not be caught or declared in a `throws` clause. When thrown by a method of a linked list class, it can be treated simply as a run-time error message. The exception can instead be caught in a `catch` block if there is some suitable action that can be taken.

Display 15.12 A Copy Constructor and **`clone`** Method for a Generic Linked List (part 1 of 3)

```
public class LinkedList3<T> implements Cloneable
{
    private class Node<T>
    {
        private T data;
        private Node<T> link;

        public Node( )
        {
            data = null;
            link = null;
        }

        public Node(T newData, Node<T> linkValue)
        {
            data = newData;
            link = linkValue;
        }
    }//End of Node<T> inner class
```

This copy constructor and this `clone` method do not make deep copies. We discuss one way to make a deep copy in the Programming Tip "Use a Type Parameter Bound for a Better `clone`."

(continued)

Display 15.12 **A Copy Constructor and `clone` Method for a Generic Linked List** (part 2 of 3)

```
    private Node<T> head;
    <All the methods from Display 15.8 are in the class definition,
                          but they are not repeated in this display.>

    /**
     Produces a new linked list, but it is not a true deep copy.
     Throws a NullPointerException if other is null.
    */
    public LinkedList3(LinkedList3<T> otherList)
    {
        if (otherList == null)
            throw new NullPointerException( );
        if (otherList.head == null)
            head = null;
        else
            head = copyOf(otherList.head);
    }


    public LinkedList3<T> clone( )
    {
        try
        {
            LinkedList3<T> copy =
                                (LinkedList3<T>)super.clone( );
            if (head == null)
                copy.head = null;
            else
                copy.head = copyOf(head);
            return copy;
        }
        catch(CloneNotSupportedException e)
        {//This should not happen.
            return null; //To keep the compiler happy.
        }
    }

    /*
     Precondition: otherHead ! = null
     Returns a reference to the head of a copy of the list
     headed by otherHead. Does not return a true deep copy.
    */
```

Display 15.12 A Copy Constructor and **clone** Method for a Generic Linked List (part 3 of 3)

```
    private Node<T> copyOf(Node<T> otherHead)
    {
        Node<T> position = otherHead; //moves down other's list.
        Node<T> newHead; //will point to head of the copy list.
        Node<T> end = null; //positioned at end of new growing list.

        //Create first node:
        newHead =
             new Node<T>(position.data, null);
        end = newHead;
        position = position.link;

        while (position != null)
        {//copy node at position to end of new list.
            end.link =
               new Node<T>(position.data, null);
            end = end.link;
            position = position.link;
        }

        return newHead;
    }
}
```

Invoking `clone` *with* `position.data` *would be illegal.*

Invoking `clone` *with* `position.data` *would be illegal.*

PITFALL: The `clone` Method Is Protected in `object` ★

When defining the copy constructor and `clone` method for our generic linked list (Display 15.12), we would have liked to have cloned the data in the list being copied. We would have liked to change the code in the helping method `copyOf` by adding invocations of the `clone` method as follows:

```
newHead =
      new Node((T)(position.data).clone( ), null);
end = newHead;
position = position.link;

while (position != null)
 {//copy node at position to end of new list.
    end.link =
        new Node((T)(position.data).clone( ), null);
    end = end.link;
    position = position.link;
}
```

This code is identical to code in `copyOf` except for the addition of the invocations of `clone` and the type casts. (The type casts are needed because Java thinks `clone` returns a value of type `Object`.)

(continued)

PITFALL: (continued)

If this modified code (with the `clone` method) would compile (and if the type plugged in for `T` has a well-defined `clone` method that makes a deep copy), then this modified code would produce a truly independent linked list with no references in common with the list being copied. Unfortunately, this code will not compile.

If you try to compile this code, you will get an error message saying that the method `clone` is protected in the class `Object`. True, we used the type `T`, not the type `Object`, but any class can be plugged in for `T`. So when the generic linked list is compiled, all Java knows about the type `T` is that it is a descendent class of `Object`. Because the designers of the `Object` class chose to make the method `clone` protected, you simply cannot use the `clone` method in the definition of methods such as `copyOf`.

Why was the `clone` method labeled `protected` in `Object`? Apparently, this was done for security reasons. If a class could use the `clone` method unchanged from `Object`, then that would open the possibility of copying sections of memory unchanged and unchecked and so might give unauthorized memory access. The problem is made more serious by the fact that Java is used to run programs on other machines across the Internet.

The way Java defines the `clone` method in `Object` and the way it specifies how `clone` should be defined in other classes is controversial. Do not be surprised if some future version of Java handles the `clone` method differently. But for now, you are stuck with these `clone` problems.

In many situations, the version of `copyOf` in Display 15.12 (without the use of `clone`) is good enough, but there is a way to get a true deep copy. One way to get a deep copy is to somehow restrict the type `T` to classes that do have a public `clone` method that makes a deep copy. Something such as this can be done and is discussed in the Programming Tip "Use a Type Parameter Bound for a Better `clone`." ■

TIP: Use a Type Parameter Bound for a Better `clone` ★

One way to overcome the problem discussed in the previous Pitfall section is to place a bound on the type parameter `T` (in Display 15.12) so that it must satisfy some suitable interface. There is no standard interface that does the job, but it is very easy to define such an interface. The interface `PubliclyCloneable` given in Display 15.13 is just the interface we need. This short, simple interface guarantees all that we need to define generic linked lists whose clone method returns a deep copy.

Note that any class that implements the `PubliclyCloneable` interface has the following three properties:

1. The class implements the `Cloneable` interface. (This happens automatically because `PubliclyCloneable` extends `Cloneable`.)
2. The class has a public `clone` method.
3. The `clone` method for the class makes a deep copy (in the officially sanctioned way).

Condition 3 is not enforced by the Java compiler or run-time software, but like all interface semantics, it is the responsibility of the programmer defining the class to ensure that condition 3 is satisfied.

TIP: (continued)

It is now easy to define our generic linked list whose `clone` method produces a deep copy. The definition is given in Display 15.14. We have already discussed the main points involved in this definition. The Programming Example subsection, "A Linked List with a Deep Copy clone Method ★," discusses some of the minor, but possibly unclear, details of the definition.[1] ■

Display 15.13 The `PubliclyCloneable` Interface

```
/*
 The programmer who defines a class implementing this interface
 has the responsibility to define clone so it makes a deep copy
  (in the officially sectioned way.)
*/

public interface PubliclyCloneable extends Cloneable
{
    public Object clone( );
}
```

Any class that implements `PubliclyCloneable` must have a public `clone` method.

Any class that implements `PubliclyCloneable` automatically implements `Cloneable`.

Display 15.14 A Generic Linked List with a Deep Copy `clone` Method (part 1 of 3)

```
public class LinkedList<T extends PubliclyCloneable>
                                    implements PubliclyCloneable
{
    private class Node<T>
    {
        private T data;
        private Node<T> link;

        public Node( )
        {
            data = null;
            link = null;
        }
```

(continued)

[1] You might wonder whether we could use a type parameter in the `PubliclyCloneable` interface and so avoid some type casts in the definition `copyOf`. We could do that, but that may be more trouble than it is worth and, at this introductory level of presentation, would be an unnecessary distraction.

Display 15.14 A Generic Linked List with a Deep Copy **clone** Method (part 2 of 3)

```
        public Node(T newData, Node<T> linkValue)
        {
            data = newData;
            link = linkValue;
        }
    }//End of Node<T> inner class

    private Node<T> head;

    public LinkedList( )
    {
        head = null;
    }
    /**
     Produces a new linked list, but it is not a true deep copy.
     Throws a NullPointerException if other is null.
    */
    public LinkedList(LinkedList<T> otherList)
    {
        if (otherList == null)
           throw new NullPointerException( );
        if (otherList.head == null)
           head = null;
        else
           head = copyOf(otherList.head);
    }

    public LinkedList<T> clone( )
    {
        try
        {
           LinkedList<T> copy =
                              (LinkedList<T>)super.clone( );
           if (head == null)
                copy.head = null;
           else
               copy.head = copyOf(head);
           return copy;
        }
        catch(CloneNotSupportedException e)
        {//This should not happen.
            return null; //To keep the compiler happy.
        }
    }

    /*
     Precondition: otherHead != null
     Returns a reference to the head of a copy of the list
     headed by otherHead. Returns a true deep copy.
    */
    private Node<T> copyOf(Node<T> otherHead)
```

Display 15.14 **A Generic Linked List with a Deep Copy `clone` Method** (part 3 of 3)

```
    {
        Node<T> position = otherHead; //moves down other's list.
        Node<T> newHead; //will point to head of the copy list.
        Node<T> end = null; //positioned at end of new growing list.

        //Create first node:
        newHead =
             new Node<T>((T)(position.data).clone( ), null);
             end = newHead;
        position = position.link;
        while (position != null)
        {//copy node at position to end of new list.
            end.link =
               new Node<T>((T)(position.data).clone( ), null);
            end = end.link;
            position = position.link;
        }

        return newHead;
    }

    public boolean equals(Object otherObject)
    {
        if (otherObject == null)
            return false;
        else if (getClass( ) != otherObject.getClass( ))
            return false;
        else
        {
            LinkedList<T> otherList = (LinkedList<T>)otherObject;
```

This definition of `copyOf` gives a deep copy of the linked list.

<The rest of the definition is the same as in Display 15.8. The only difference between this definition of `equals` and the one in Display 15.8 is that we have replaced the class name `LinkedList3<T>` with `LinkedList<T>`.>

```
    }
```

<All the other methods from Display 15.8 are in the class definition, but are not repeated in this display.>

```
    public String toString( )
    {
        Node<T> position = head;
        String theString = "";
        while (position != null)
        {
            theString = theString + position.data + "\n";
            position = position.link;
        }
        return theString;
    }
}
```

We added a `toString` method so `LinkedList<T>` would have all the properties we want `T` to have.

EXAMPLE: A Linked List with a Deep Copy `clone` Method ★

We have already discussed how and why the `clone` method of the generic linked list class in Display 15.14 returns a deep copy. Let us now look at some of the other details and see an example of using this linked list class.

Note the definition of the `clone` method. Why did we not simplify it to the following?

```
public LinkedList<T> clone( )
{
    return new LinkedList<T>(this);
}
```

This simple, alternative definition would still return a deep copy of the linked list and would work fine in most situations. It is likely that you would not notice any difference if you used this definition of `clone` in place of the one given in Display 15.14.

The only reason for all the other detail in the `clone` method definition given in Display 15.14 is to define the `clone` method as specified in the Java documentation. The reason that the Java documentation asks for those details has to do with security issues. (Some might say that there are three ways to define a `clone` method: the right way, the wrong way, and the Java way. This extra detail is the Java way.)

If you look only quickly at Display 15.14, you might think the following at the start of the definition is an unimportant detail:

```
implements PubliclyCloneable
```

However, it ensures that the linked list class implements the `Cloneable` interface. In order for a class to have a Java-approved `clone` method, it must implement the `Cloneable` interface. It also allows you to make linked lists of linked lists and have a deep copy `clone` method in the linked list of linked lists.

A sample class that implements the `PubliclyCloneable` interface is given in Display 15.15. Display 15.16 shows a demonstration program that makes a deep copy `clone` of a linked list of objects of this sample class.

Display 15.15 A **`PubliclyCloneable`** Class (part 1 of 2)

```
public class StockItem implements PubliclyCloneable
{
    private String name;
    private int number;

    public StockItem( )
    {
        name = null;
        number = 0;
    }
```

Display 15.15 A **PubliclyCloneable** Class (part 2 of 2)

```
    public StockItem(String nameData, int numberData)
    {
        name = nameData;
        number = numberData;
    }

    public void setNumber(int newNumber)
    {
        number = newNumber;
    }
    public void setName(String newName)
    {
        name = newName;
    }

    public String toString( )
    {
        return (name + " " + number);
    }

    public Object clone( )
    {
       try
       {
          return super.clone( );
       }
       catch(CloneNotSupportedException e)
       { //This should not happen.
          return null; //To keep compiler happy.
       }
    }


    public boolean equals(Object otherObject)
    {
        if (otherObject == null)
            return false;
        else if (getClass( ) != otherObject.getClass( ))
            return false;
        else
        {
            StockItem otherItem = (StockItem) otherObject;
            return (name.equalsIgnoreCase(otherItem.name)
                       && number == otherItem.number);
        }
    }
}
```

Display 15.16 Demonstration of Deep Copy `clone`

```
public class DeepDemo
{
    public static void main(String[] args)
    {
        LinkedList<StockItem> originalList =
                                new LinkedList<StockItem>( );
        originalList.addToStart(new StockItem("red dress", 1));
        originalList.addToStart(new StockItem("black shoe", 2));

        LinkedList<StockItem> copyList = originalList.clone( );
        if (originalList.equals(copyList))
            System.out.println("OK, Lists are equal.");

        System.out.println("Now we change copyList.");
        StockItem dataEntry =
                  copyList.findData(new StockItem("red dress", 1));
        dataEntry.setName("orange pants");

        System.out.println("originalList:");
        originalList.outputList( );

        System.out.println("copyList:");
        copyList.outputList( );

        System.out.println("Only one list is changed.");
    }
}
```

Sample Dialogue

```
OK, Lists are equal.
Now we change copyList.
originalList:
black shoe 2
red dress 1
copyList:
black shoe 2
orange pants 1
Only one list is changed.
```

TIP: Cloning Is an "All or Nothing" Affair

If you define a `clone` method, then you should do so following the official Java guidelines, as we did in Display 15.14. In particular, you should always have the class implement the `Cloneable` interface. If you define a `clone` method in any other way, you may encounter problems in some situations. If you want to have a method for producing copies of objects but do not want to follow the official guidelines on how to define a `clone` method, then use some other name for your "`clone`-like" method, such as `copier`, or make do with just a copy constructor. ■

MyProgrammingLab™

Self-Test Exercises

9. In the definition of `copyOf` in Display 15.14, can we replace

```
newHead =
          new Node<T>((T)(position.data).clone( ), null);
```

with the following, which uses the copy constructor of `T` instead of the clone method of `T`?

```
newHead =
          new Node<T>(new T(position.data), null);
```

10. The definition of the `clone` method in Display 15.14 returns a value of type `LinkedList<T>`. But the class being defined implements the `PubliclyCloneable` interface, and that interface says the value returned must be of type `Object`. Is something wrong?

15.3 Iterators

Play it again, Sam.

Attributed (incorrectly) to the movie *Casablanca*, which contains similar lines.[2]

iterator

When you have a collection of objects, such as the nodes of a linked list, you often need to step through all the objects in the collection one at a time and perform some action on each object, such as writing it out to the screen or in some way editing the data in each object. An **iterator** is any object that allows you to step through the list in this way.

[2]There is a Woody Allen movie with this title, but it is based on the misquote from *Casablanca*, which was in common use before the movie came out.

Defining an Iterator Class

In Display 15.17, we have rewritten the class `LinkedList2` from Display 15.7 so that it has an inner class for iterators and a method `iterator( )` that returns an iterator for its calling object. We have made the inner class `List2Iterator` public so that we can have variables of type `List2Iterator` outside the class `LinkedList2`, but we do not otherwise plan to use the inner class `List2Iterator` outside of the outer class `LinkedList2`.

Use of iterators for the class `LinkedList2` is illustrated by the program in Display 15.18. Note that, given a linked list named `list`, an iterator for `list` is produced by the method `iterator` as follows:

```
LinkedList2.List2Iterator i = list.iterator( );
```

The iterator `i` produced in this way can only be used with the linked list named `list`. Be sure to notice that outside of the class, the type name for the inner class iterator must include the name of the outer class as well as the inner iterator class. The class name for one of these iterators is

```
LinkedList2.List2Iterator
```

Display 15.17 **A Linked List with an Iterator** (part 1 of 3)

```
import java.util.NoSuchElementException;

public class LinkedList2
{
    private class Node
    {
        private String item;
        private Node link;
```

This is the same as the class in Display 15.7 and 15.11 except that the `List2Iterator` inner class and the `iterator()` method have been added.

<The rest of the definition of the Node inner class is given in Display 15.7.>

```
    }//End of Node inner class

    /**
     If the list is altered any iterators should invoke restart or
     the iterator's behavior may not be as desired.
    */
    public class List2Iterator
    {
        private Node position;
        private Node previous; //previous value of position
        public List2Iterator( )
        {
            position = head; //Instance variable head of outer class.
            previous = null;
        }
```

An inner class for iterators for `LinkedList2`.

Display 15.17 **A Linked List with an Iterator** (part 2 of 3)

```
        public void restart( )
        {
            position = head; //Instance variable head of outer class.
            previous = null;
        }

        public String next( )
        {
            if (!hasNext( ))
                throw new NoSuchElementException( );

            String toReturn = position.item;
            previous = position;
            position = position.link;
            return toReturn;
        }

        public boolean hasNext( )
        {
            return (position != null);
        }
        /**
         Returns the next value to be returned by next( ).
         Throws an IllegalStateExpression if hasNext( ) is false.
        */
        public String peek( )
        {
            if (!hasNext( ))
               throw new IllegalStateException( );
            return position.item;
        }

        /**
         Adds a node before the node at location position.
         previous is placed at the new node. If hasNext( ) is
         false, then the node is added to the end of the list.
         If the list is empty, inserts node as the only node.
        */
        public void addHere(String newData)
        {
            if (position == null && previous != null)
                  // at end of the list, add to end
                  previous.link = new Node(newData, null);
                else if (position == null || previous == null)
                      // list is empty or position is head node
                      LinkedList2.this.addtoStart(newData);
```

(continued)

Display 15.17 **A Linked List with an Iterator** (part 3 of 3)

```
            else
            { // previous and position are consecutive nodes
                Node temp = new Node(newData, position)
                previous.link = temp;
                previous = temp;
            }
        }
        /**
         Changes the String in the node at location position.
         Throws an IllegalStateException if position is not at a node,
        */
        public void changeHere(String newData)
```

< Self-Test Exercise 13 asks you to complete the rest of the method `changeHere`.>

```
        /**
         Deletes the node at location position and
         moves position to the "next" node.
         Throws an IllegalStateException if the list is empty.
        */
        public void delete( )
        {
            if (position == null)
                throw new IllegalStateException( );
            else if (previous == null)
            {   // remove node at head
                head = head.link;
                position = head;
            }
            else // previous and position are consecutive nodes
            {
                previous.link = position.link;
                position = position.link;
            }
        }
    private Node head;

    public List2Iterator iterator( )
    {
        return new List2Iterator( );
    }
```

If **`list`** *is an object of the class* **`LinkedList2`**, *then* **`list.iterator()`** *returns an iterator for list.*

<The other methods and constructors are identical to those in Display 15.7 and 15.11.>

```
}
```

Display 15.18 **Using an Iterator** (part 1 of 2)

```
public class IteratorDemo
{
    public static void main(String[] args)
    {
        LinkedList2 list = new LinkedList2( );
        LinkedList2.List2Iterator i = list.iterator( );

        list.addToStart("shoes");
        list.addToStart("orange juice");
        list.addToStart("coat");

        System.out.println("List contains:");
        i.restart( );
        while(i.hasNext( ))
            System.out.println(i.next( ));
        System.out.println( );

        i.restart( );
        i.next( );
        System.out.println("Will delete the node for " + i.peek( ));
        i.delete( );

        System.out.println("List now contains:");
        i.restart( );
        while(i.hasNext( ))
            System.out.println(i.next( ));
        System.out.println( );

        i.restart( );
        i.next( );
        System.out.println("Will add one node before " + i.peek( ));
        i.addHere("socks");
        System.out.println("List now contains:");
        i.restart( );
        while(i.hasNext( ))
            System.out.println(i.next( ));
        System.out.println( );
        System.out.println("Changing all items to credit card.");
        i.restart( );
        while(i.hasNext( ))
        {
            i.changeHere("credit card");
            i.next( );
        }
        System.out.println( );
        System.out.println("List now contains:");
```

(continued)

Display 15.18 **A Linked List with an Iterator** (part 2 of 2)

```
        i.restart( );
        while(i.hasNext( ))
            System.out.println(i.next( ));
        System.out.println( );
    }
}
```

Sample Dialogue

```
List contains:
coat
orange juice
shoes

Will delete the node for orange juice
List now contains:
coat
shoes

Will add one node before shoes
List now contains:
coat
socks
shoes

Changing all items to credit card.

List now contains:
credit card
credit card
credit card
```

The basic method for cycling through the elements in the linked list using an iterator is illustrated by the following code from the demonstration program:

```
System.out.println("List now contains:");
i.restart( );
while(i.hasNext( ))
    System.out.println(i.next( ));
```

The iterator is named `i` in this code. The iterator `i` is reset to the beginning of the list with the method invocation `i.restart()`, and each execution of `i.next()` produces the next data item in the linked list. After all the data items in all the nodes have been returned by `i.next( )`, the Boolean `i.hasNext( )` becomes `false` and the `while` loop ends.

Internally, the local variable `position` references the current node in the linked list, whereas the local variable `previous` references the node linking to the current node. The purpose of the `previous` variable will be seen when adding and deleting nodes. In the constructor and the `restart( )` method, `position` is set to `head` and `previous` is set to `null`.

To determine if the end of the list has been reached, `hasNext( )` returns whether or not `position` is `null`:

```
return (position != null);
```

To step through the list, the `next( )` method first throws an exception if we have reached the end of the list:

```
if (!hasNext( ))
throw new NoSuchElementException( );
```

Otherwise, the method retrieves the string value of the iterator referenced by `position` in the variable `toReturn`, advances `previous` to reference the current position, advances `position` to the next node in the list, and returns the string:

```
String toReturn = position.item;
previous = position;
position = position.link;
return toReturn;
```

The definition of the method `changeHere` is left to Self-Test Exercise 13. (If necessary, you can look up the definition in the answer to Self-Test Exercise 13.) The techniques for adding and deleting nodes are discussed in the next subsection.

The Java `Iterator` Interface

Java has an interface named `Iterator` that specifies how Java would like an iterator to behave. It is in the package `java.util` (and so requires that you import this package). Our iterators do not quite satisfy this interface, but they are in the same general spirit as that interface and could be easily redefined to satisfy the `Iterator` interface.

The `Iterator` interface is discussed in Chapter 16.

Adding and Deleting Nodes

To add or delete a node in a linked list, you normally use an iterator and add or delete a node at the (approximate) location of the iterator. Because deleting is a little easier than adding a node, we will discuss deleting first.

Display 15.19 shows the technique for deleting a node. The linked list is an object of the class `LinkedList2` (Display 15.17). The variables `position` and `previous` are the instance variables of an iterator for the linked list object. These variables each hold a reference to a node, indicated with an arrow. Each time `next( )` is invoked, `previous` and `position` reference subsequent nodes in the list. As indicated in Display 15.19, the node at location `position` is deleted by the following two lines of code:

```
previous.link = position.link;
position = position.link;
```

In Display 15.19, `next( )` has been invoked twice, so `position` is referencing the node with `"shoes"` and `previous` is referencing the node with `"socks"`.

To delete the node referenced by `position`, the link from the `previous` node is set to `positions` link. As shown in Display 15.19, this removes the linked list's reference to that node. The variable `position` is then set to the next node in the list to remove any references to the deleted node. As far as the linked list is concerned, the old node is no longer on the linked list. But the node is still in the computer's memory. If there are no longer any references to the deleted node, then the storage that it occupies should be made available for other uses. In many programming languages, you, the programmer, must keep track of items such as deleted nodes and must give explicit commands to return their memory for recycling. This is called **garbage collecting** or **explicit memory management**. In Java, this is done for you automatically, or, as it is ordinarily phrased, Java has automatic garbage collection.

garbage collecting

explicit memory management

Note that there are special cases that must be handled for deletion. First, if the list is empty, then nothing can be deleted and the `delete( )` method throws an exception. Second, if the node to delete is the head of the list, then there is no previous node to update. Instead, `head` is set to `head.link` to bypass the first node in the list and set a new head node.

Display 15.20 shows the technique for adding a node. We want to add a new node between the nodes named by `previous` and `position`. In Display 15.20, `previous` and `position` are variables of type `Node`, and each contains a reference to a node indicated with an arrow. Thus, the new node goes between the two nodes referenced by `previous` and `position`. In Display 15.20, the method `next( )` has been invoked twice to advance `previous` to `"orange juice"` and `position` to `"shoes"`.

A constructor for the class `Node` does a lot of the work for us: It creates the new node, adds the data, and sets the link field of the new node to reference the node named by `position`. All this is done with the following:

```
new Node(newData, position)
```

So that we can recognize the node with `newData` in it when we study Display 15.20, let us assume that `newData` holds the string `"socks"`. The following gets us from the first to the second picture:

```
temp = new Node(newData, position);
```

Display 15.19 **Deleting a Node**

1. Existing list with the iterator positioned at "shoes"

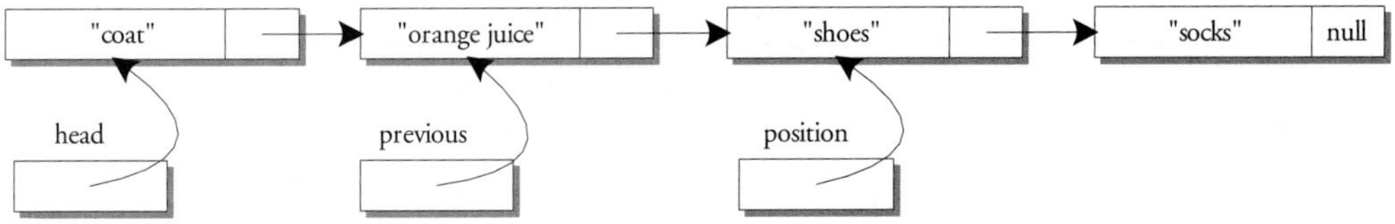

2. Bypass the node at `position` from `previous`

```
previous.link = position.link;
```

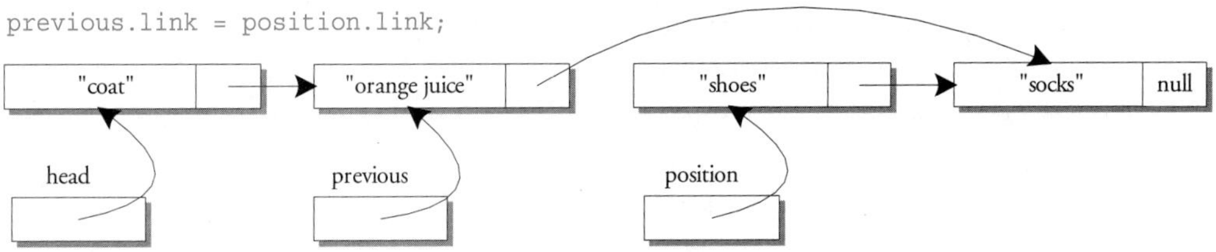

3. Update `position` to reference the next node

```
position = position.link;
```

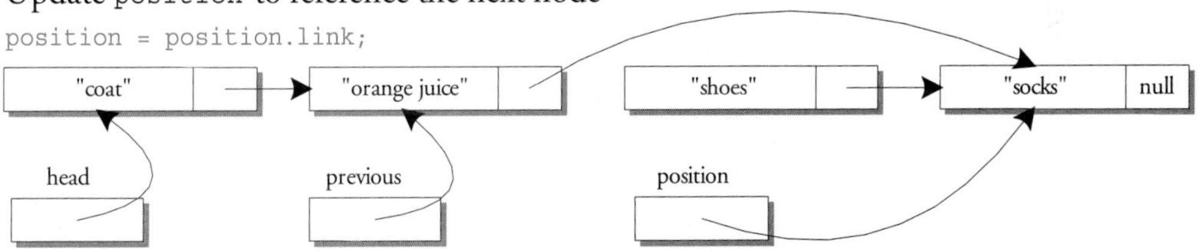

Since no variable references the node "shoes" Java will automatically recycle the memory allocated for it.

4. Same picture with deleted node not shown

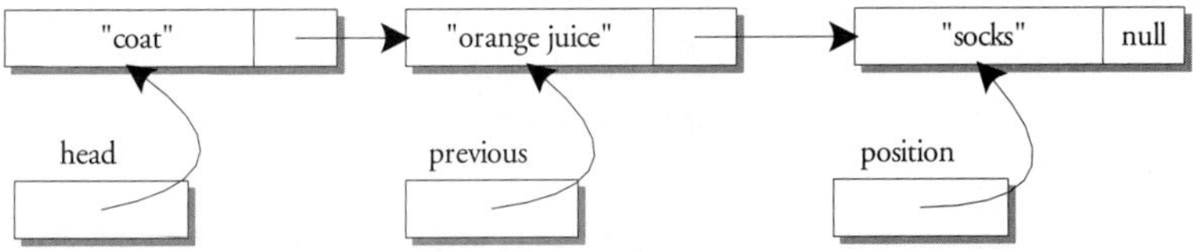

Display 15.20 **Adding a Node between Two Nodes**

1. Existing list with the iterator positioned at "shoes"

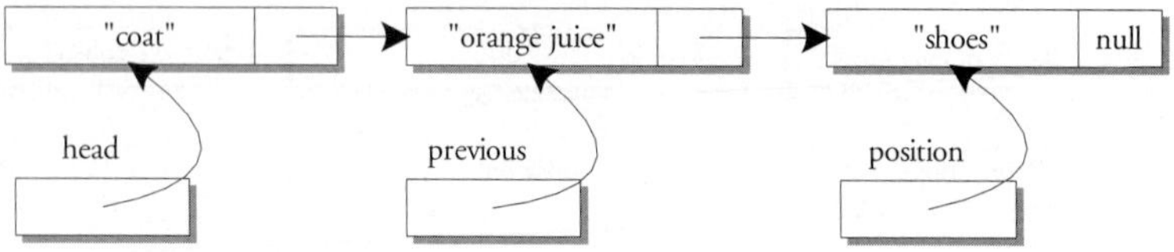

2. Create new Node with "socks" linked to "shoes"

```
temp = new Node(newData, position); // newData is "socks"
```

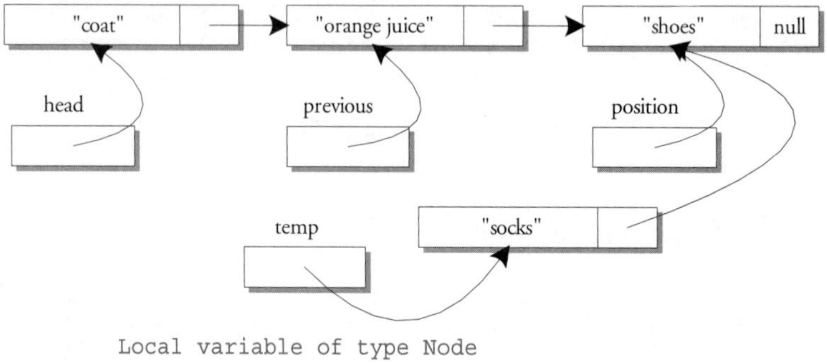

3. Make `previous` link to the Node `temp`

```
previous.link = temp;
```

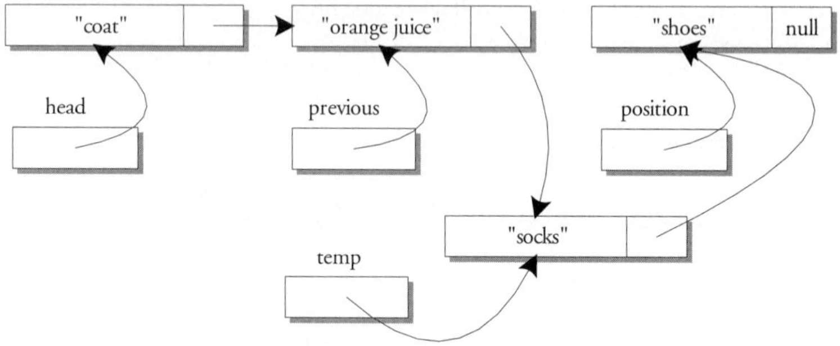

4. Picture redrawn for clarity, but structurally identical to picture 3

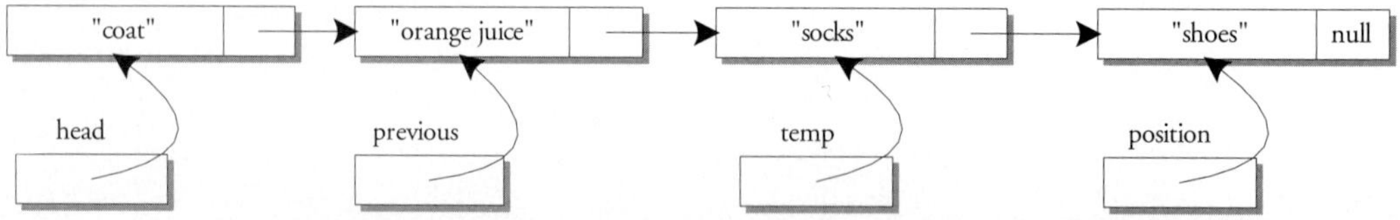

To finish the job, all we need to do is link the previous node to the new node. We want to move the arrow to the node named by `temp`. The following finishes our job:

```
previous.link = temp;
```

The new node is inserted in the desired place, but the picture is not too clear. The fourth picture is the same as the third one; we have simply redrawn it to make it neater.

To summarize, the following two lines insert a new node with `newData` as its data. The new node is inserted between the nodes named by `previous` and `position`.

```
temp = new Node(newData, position);
previous.link = temp;
```

`previous`, `position`, and `temp` are all variables of type `Node`. (When we use this code, `previous` and `position` will be instance variables of an iterator and `temp` will be a local variable.)

Just like deletion, special cases exist for insertion that must be handled. If the list is empty, then addition is done by adding to the front of the list. If the `position` variable is `null`, then the new node should be added to the end of the list.

MyProgrammingLab™

Self-Test Exercises

11. Consider a variant of the class in Display 15.17 with no `previous` local variable. In other words, there is no reference kept to the node that links to the current node position. How could we modify the `delete` method to delete the `position` node and still maintain a correct list? The solution is less efficient than the version that uses `previous`.

12. Consider a variant of the class in Display 15.17 with no `previous` local variable. In other words, there is no reference kept to the node that links to the current node `position`. Write a method `addAfterHere(String newData)` that adds a new node after the node in `position`.

13. Complete the definition of the method `changeHere` in the inner class `List2Iterator` in Display 15.17.

14. Given an iterator pointing somewhere in a linked list, does `i.next( )` return the value that `i` is referencing prior to the invocation of `i.next( )` or does it return the value of the next node in the list?

15.4 Variations on a Linked List

I have called this principle, by which each slight variation, if useful, is preserved, by the term Natural Selection.

CHARLES DARWIN, *The Origin of Species*

In this section, we discuss some variations on linked lists, including the two data structures known as stacks and queues. Stacks and queues need not involve linked lists, but one common way to implement a stack or a queue is to use a linked list.

Doubly Linked List

doubly linked list

An ordinary linked list allows you to move down the list in one direction only (following the links). A **doubly linked list** has one link that has a reference to the next node and one that has a reference to the previous node. In some cases, the link to the previous node can simplify our code. For example, we will no longer need to have a `previous` instance variable to remember the node that links to the current position. Diagrammatically, a doubly linked list looks like the sample list in Display 15.21.

The node class for a doubly linked list can begin as follows:

```
private class TwoWayNode
{
    private String item;
    private TwoWayNode previous;
    private TwoWayNode next;

    ...
```

The constructors and some of the methods in the doubly linked list class will require changes (from the singly linked case) in their definitions to accommodate the extra link. The major changes are to the methods that add and delete nodes. To make our code a little cleaner, we can add a new constructor that sets the previous and next nodes:

```
public TwoWayNode(String newItem, TwoWayNode previousNode,
                                         TwoWayNode nextNode)
  {
      item = newItem;
      next = nextNode;
      previous = previousNode;
  }
```

To add a new `TwoWayNode` to the front of the list requires setting links on two nodes instead of one. The general process is shown in Display 15.22. In the `addToStart` method, we first create a new `TwoWayNode`. Because the new node will go on the front of the list, we set the previous link to `null` and the `next` link to the current head:

```
TwoWayNode newHead = new TwoWayNode(itemName, null, head);
```

Display 15.21 **A Doubly Linked List**

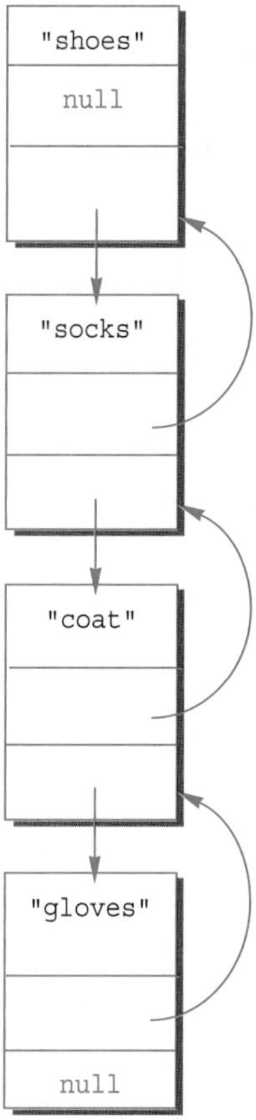

Next, we must set the `previous` link on the old head node to reference the new head. We can do this by setting `head.previous = newHead`, but we must take care to ensure that `head` is not `null` (i.e., the list is not empty). Finally, we can set `head` to `newHead`.

```
if (head != null)
{
      head.previous = newHead;
}
head = newHead;
```

To delete a node from the doubly linked list also requires updating the references on both sides of the node to delete. Thanks to the backward link, there is no need for an instance variable to keep track of the previous node in the list, as was required for the singly linked list. The general process of deleting a node referenced by `position` is shown in Display 15.23. Note that some cases must be handled separately, such as deleting a node from the beginning or the end of the list.

Display 15.22 Adding a Node to the Front of a Doubly Linked List

1. Existing list.

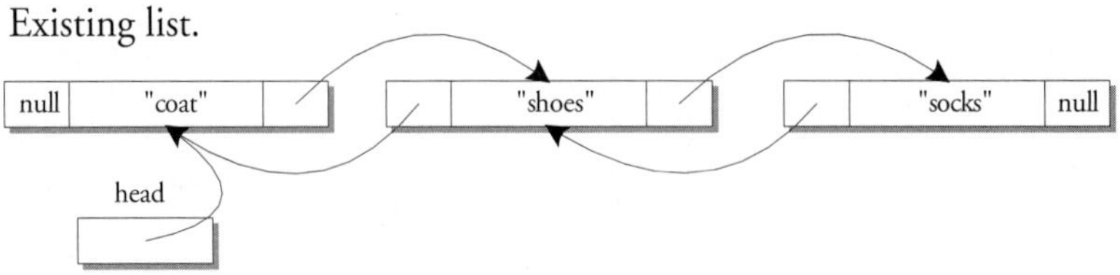

2. Create new TwoWayNode linked to "coat"

```
TwoWayNode newHead = new TwoWayNode(itemName, null, head) // itemName = "shirt"
```

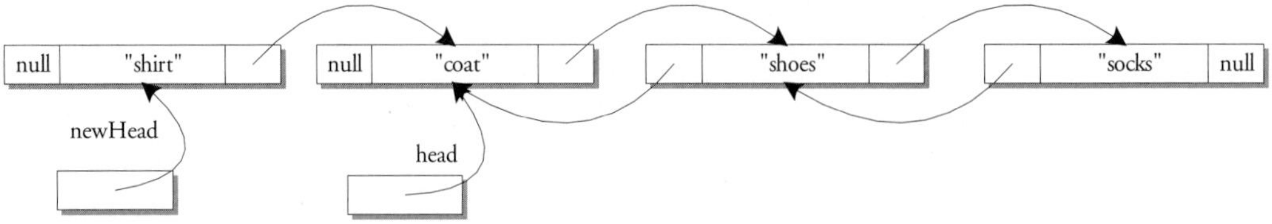

3. Set backward link and set new head

```
head.previous = newHead;
head = newHead;
```

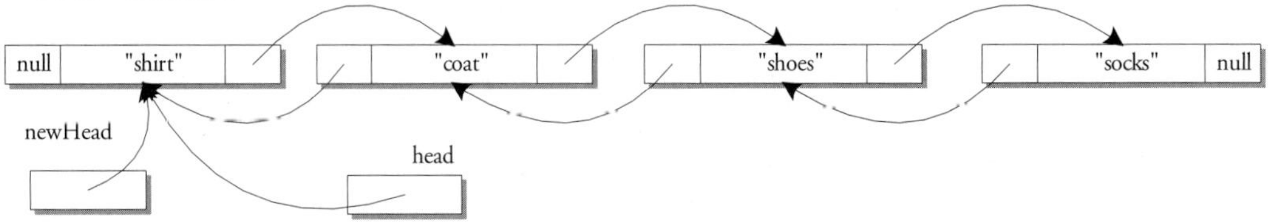

The process of inserting a new node into the doubly linked list is shown in Display 15.24. In this case, we will insert the new node in front of the iterator referenced by `position`. Note that there are also special cases for the insert routine when inserting to the front or adding to the end of the list. Only the general case of inserting between two existing nodes is shown in Display 15.24.

A complete example of a doubly linked list is shown in Display 15.25. The code in Display 15.25 is modified from the code in Display 15.17. Use of the doubly linked list is virtually identical to use of a singly linked list. Display 15.26 demonstrates addition, deletion, and insertion into the doubly linked list.

Display 15.23 **Deleting a Node from a Doubly Linked List**

1. Existing list with an iterator referencing “shoes”

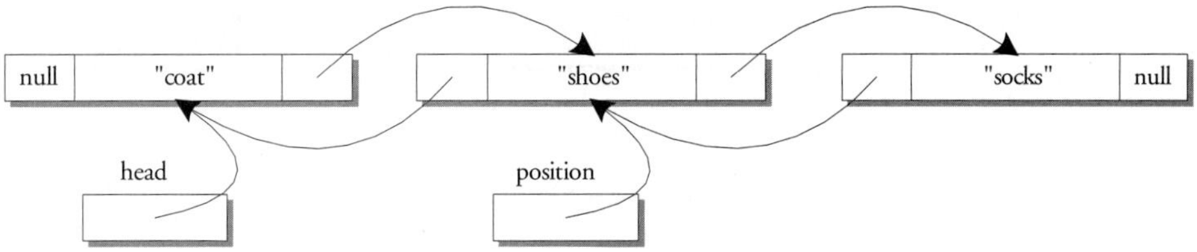

2. Bypass the “shoes” node from the next link of the previous node

```
position.previous.next = position.next;
```

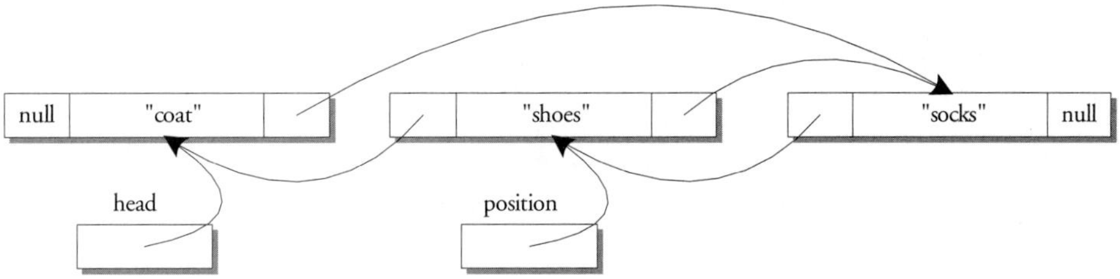

3. Bypass the “shoes” node from the previous link of the next node and move position off the deleted node

```
position.next.previous = position.previous;
position = position.next;
```

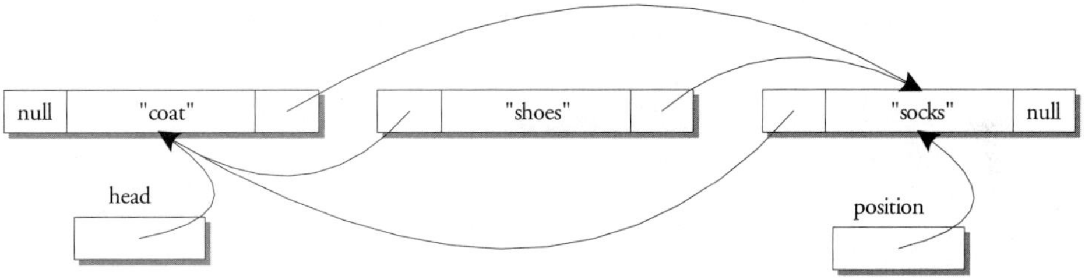

4. Picture redrawn for clarity with the “shoes” node removed since there are no longer references pointing to this node.

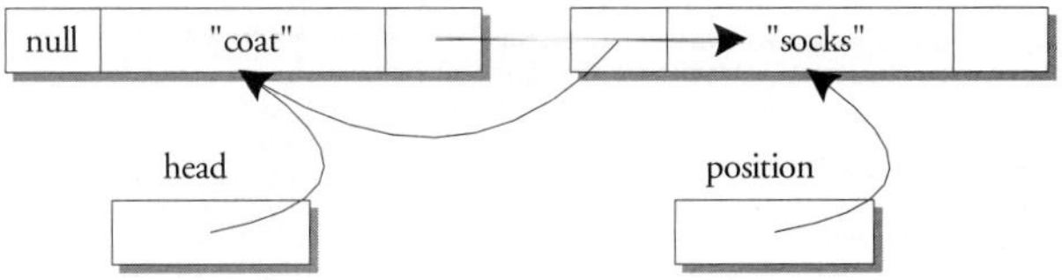

Display 15.24 **Inserting a Node into a Doubly Linked List**

1. Existing list with an iterator referencing "shoes"

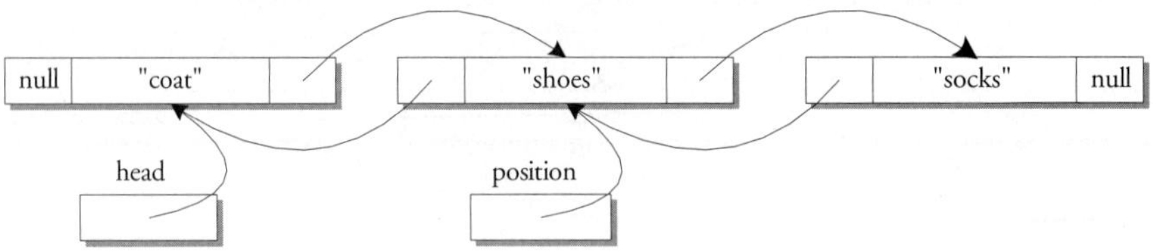

2. Create new TwoWayNode with previous linked to "coat" and next to "shoes"

```
TwoWayNode temp = newTwoWayNode(newData, position.previous, position);
// newData = "shirt"
```

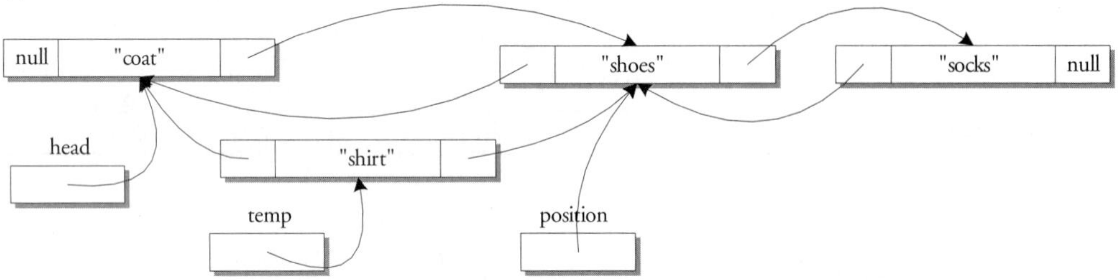

3. Set next link from "coat" to the new node of "shirt"

```
position.previous.next = temp;
```

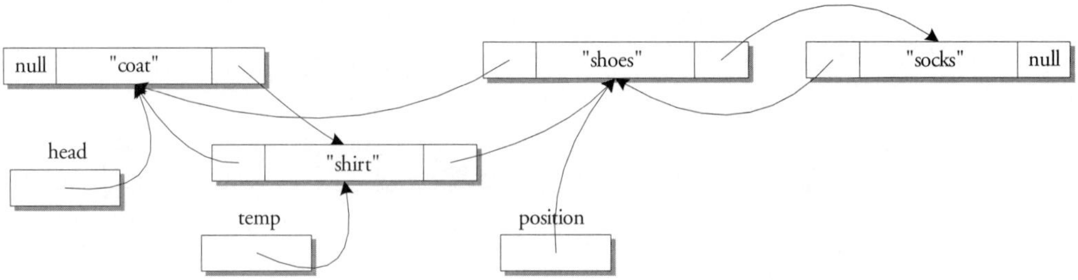

4. Set previous link from "shoes" to the new node of "shirt"

```
position.previous = temp;
```

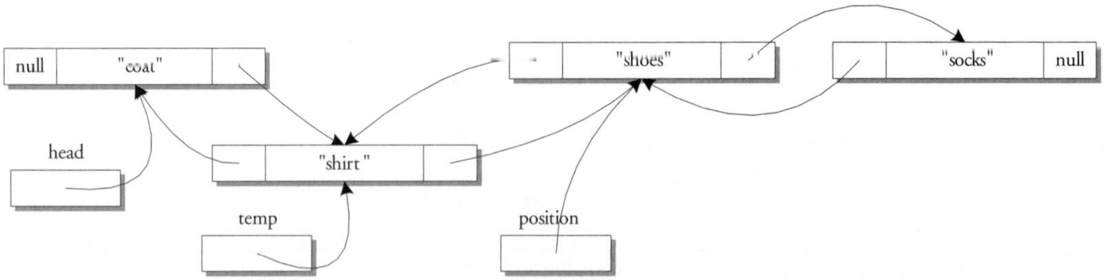

Display 15.25 **A Doubly Linked List with an Iterator** (part 1 of 3)

```java
import java.util.NoSuchElementException;

public class DoublyLinkedList
{
    private class TwoWayNode
    {
        private String item;
        private TwoWayNode previous;
        private TwoWayNode next;

        public TwoWayNode()
        {
             item = null;
             next = null;
             previous = null;
        }
        public TwoWayNode(String newItem, TwoWayNode previousNode,
                                                TwoWayNode nextNode)
        {
            item = newItem;
            next = nextNode;
            previous = previousNode;
        }
    } //End of TwoWayNode inner class

    public class DoublyLinkedIterator
    {
         // We do not need a previous node when using a doubly linked
         // list
          private TwoWayNode position = null;

          public DoublyLinkedIterator( )
          {
               position = head;
          }
           public void restart( )
           {
               position = head;
           }
           public String next( )
           {
               if (!hasNext( ))
                     throw new IllegalStateException( );
               String toReturn = position.item;
               position = position.next;
               return toReturn;
           }
```

(continued)

Display 15.25 **A Doubly Linked List with an Iterator** (part 2 of 3)

```
        public void insertHere(String newData)
        {
            if (position == null && head != null)
            {
                // Add to end. First move a temp
                // pointer to the end of the list
                TwoWayNode temp = head;
                while (temp.next != null)
                    temp = temp.next;
                temp.next = new TwoWayNode(newData, temp, null);
            }
            else if (head == null || position.previous == null)
                // at head of list
                DoublyLinkedList.this.addToStart (newData);
            else
            {
                // Insert before the current position
                TwoWayNode temp = new TwoWayNode(newData,
                    position. previous, position);
                position.previous.next = temp;
                position.previous = temp;
            }
        }

        public void delete( )
        {
            if (position == null)
                throw new IllegalStateException( );
            else if (position.previous == null)
            { // Deleting first node
                head = head.next;
                position = head;
            }
            else if (position.next == null)
            { // Deleting last node
                position.previous.next = null;
                position = null;
            }
            else
            {
                position.previous.next = position.next;
                position.next.previous = position.previous;
                position = position.next;
            }
        }
    }   // DoublyLinkedIterator
```

Display 15.25 **A Doubly Linked List with an Iterator** (part 3 of 3)

```
    private TwoWayNode head;

    public DoublyLinkedIterator iterator( )
    {
        return new DoublyLinkedIterator( );
    }

    public DoublyLinkedList( )
    {
        head = null;
    }

    /**
     The added node will be the first node in the list.
    */
    public void addToStart(String itemName)
    {
        TwoWayNode newHead = new TwoWayNode(itemName, null, head);
        if (head != null)
        {
            head.previous = newHead;
        }
        head = newHead;
    }
  <The methods hasNext, peek, clear, and isEmpty are identical
  to those in Display 15.17. Other methods would also normally
  be defined here, such as deleteHeadNode, size, outputList,
  equals, clone, find, or contains. They have been left off to
  simplify the example.>
}       // DoublyLinkedList
```

Display 15.26 **Using a Doubly Linked List with an Iterator** (part 1 of 2)

```
public class DoublyLinkedListDemo
{
    public static void main(String[] args)
    {
        DoublyLinkedList list = new DoublyLinkedList( );
        DoublyLinkedList.DoublyLinkedIterator i = list.iterator( );

        list.addToStart("shoes");
        list.addToStart("orange juice");
        list.addToStart("coat");
        System.out.println("List contains:");
        i.restart( );
```

(continued)

Display 15.26 **Using a Doubly Linked List with an Iterator** (part 2 of 2)

```
            while (i.hasNext( ))
                System.out.println(i.next( ));
            System.out.println( );

            i.restart( );
            i.next( );
            i.next( );
            System.out.println("Delete " + i.peek( ));
            i.delete( );

            System.out.println("List now contains:");
            i.restart( );
            while (i.hasNext( ))
                System.out.println(i.next( ));
            System.out.println( );

            i.restart( );
            i.next( );
            System.out.println("Inserting socks before " + i.peek( ));
            i.insertHere("socks");

            i.restart( );
            System.out.println("List now contains:");
            while (i.hasNext( ))
                System.out.println(i.next( ));
            System.out.println( );
    }
}
```

Sample Dialogue

```
List contains:
coat
orange juice
shoes

Delete shoes
List now contains:
Coat
Orange juice

Inserting socks before orange juice
List now contains:
coat
socks
orange juice
```

MyProgrammingLab™

Self-Test Exercises

15. What operations are easier to implement with a doubly linked list compared with a singly linked list? What operations are more difficult?

16. If the `addToStart` method from Display 15.25 were removed, how could we still add a new node to the head of the list?

The Stack Data Structure

stack

A **stack** is not necessarily a linked data structure, but it can be implemented as a linked list. A stack is a data structure that removes items in the reverse of the order in which they were inserted. So if you insert "`one`", then "`two`", and then "`three`" into a stack and then remove them, they will come out in the order "`three`", then "`two`", and finally "`one`". Stacks are discussed in more detail in Chapter 11. A linked list that inserts and deletes only at the head of the list (such as those in Displays 15.3 or 15.8) is, in fact, a stack.

push and pop

You can imagine the stack data structure like a stack of trays in a cafeteria. You can **push** a new tray on top of the stack to make a taller stack. Alternately, you can **pop** the topmost tray off the stack until there are no more trays to remove. A definition of a `Stack` class is shown in Display 15.27 that is based on the linked list from Display 15.3. A short demonstration program is shown in Display 15.28. The `addToStart` method has been renamed to `push` to use stack terminology. Similarly, the `deleteHeadNode` method has been renamed to `pop` and returns the `String` from the top of the stack. Although not shown here to keep the definition simple, it would be appropriate to add other methods such as `peek`, `clone`, or `equals` or to convert the class to use a generic data type.

Stacks

A **stack** is a last-in/first-out data structure; that is, the data items are retrieved in the opposite order to which they were placed in the stack.

Display 15.27 A `Stack` Class (part 1 of 2)

```
import java.util.NoSuchElementException;

public class Stack
{
      private class Node
      {
            private String item;
            private Node link;
```

(continued)

Display 15.27 A **Stack** Class (part 2 of 2)

```
        public Node( )
        {
            item = null;
            link = null;
        }
        public Node(String newItem, Node linkValue)
        {
            item = newItem;
            link = linkValue;
        }
    }//End of Node inner class

    private Node head;

    public Stack( )
    {
        head = null;
    }

    /**
        This method replaces addToStart
    */
    public void push(String itemName)
    {
        head = new Node(itemName, head);
    }
    /**
        This method replaces deleteHeadNode and
        also returns the value popped from the list
    */
    public String pop( )
    {
        if (head == null)
            throw new IllegalStateException( );
        else
        {
            String returnItem = head.item;
            head = head.link;
            return returnItem;
        }
    }
    public boolean isEmpty( )
    {
        return (head == null);
    }
}
```

Display 15.28 Stack Demonstration Program

```java
public class StackExample
{
    public static void main(String[] args)
    {
        Stack stack = new Stack( );
        Stack.push("Billy Rubin");
        Stack.push("Lou Pole");
        Stack.push("Polly Ester");

        while (!stack.isEmpty( ))
        {
            String s = stack.pop( );
            System.out.println(s);
        }
    }
}
```

Items come out of the stack in the reverse order that they were added.

Sample Dialogue

```
Polly Ester
Lou Pole
Billy Rubin
```

MyProgrammingLab™

Self-Test Exercise

17. Display 15.27 does not contain a `peek( )` method. Normally this method would return the data on the top of the stack without popping it off. How could a user of the `Stack` class get the same functionally as `peek( )` even though it is not defined?

The Queue Data Structure

queue

A stack is a last-in/first-out data structure. Another common data structure is a **queue**, which handles data in a first-in/first-out fashion. A queue is like a line at the bank. Customers add themselves to the back of the line and are served from the front of the line. A queue can be implemented with a linked list. However, a queue needs a pointer at both the head of the list and at the **tail** (that is, the other end) of the linked list, because action takes place in both locations. It is easier to remove a node from the head of a linked list than from the tail of the linked list. So, a simple implementation will remove nodes from the head of the list (which we will now call the **front** of the list) and we will add nodes to the tail end of the list, which we will now call the **back** of the list (or the back of the queue).

tail

front

back

The definition of a simple `Queue` class that is based on a linked list is given in Display 15.29. A short demonstration program is given in Display 15.30. We have not made our queue a generic queue to keep the definition simple, but it would be routine to replace the data type `String` with a type parameter.

> **Queue**
>
> A **queue** is a first-in/first-out data structure; that is, the data items are removed from the queue in the same order that they were added to the queue.

Display 15.29 A `Queue` Class (part 1 of 2)

```
public class Queue
{
    private class Node
    {
        private String item;
        private Node link;

        public Node( )
        {
            item = null;
            link = null;
        }

        public Node(String newItem, Node linkValue)
        {
            item = newItem;
            link = linkValue;
        }
    } //End of Node inner class

    private Node front;
    private Node back;

    public Queue( )
    {
        front = null;
        back = null;
    }
```

Display 15.29 A `Queue` Class (part 2 of 2)

```
    /**
     Adds a String to the back of the queue.
    */
    public void addToBack(String itemName)
    <The definition of this method is defined in Self-Test Exercise 18.>

    public boolean isEmpty( )
    {
        return (front == null);
    }

    public void clear( )
    {
        front = null;
        back = null;
    }
    /**
     Returns the String in the front of the queue.
     Returns null if queue is empty.
    */
    public String whoIsNext( )
    {
        if (front == null)
            return null;
        else
            return front.item;
    }

    /**
     Removes a String from the front of the queue.
     Returns false if the list is empty.
    */
    public boolean removeFront( )
    {
        if (front != null)
        {
            front = front.link;
            return true;
        }
        else
            return false;
    }
}
```

Display 15.30 Demonstration of the `Queue` Class

```
public class QueueDemo
{
    public static void main(String[] args)
    {
        Queue q = new Queue( );

        q.addToBack("Tom");
        q.addToBack("Dick");
        q.addToBack("Harriet");
        while(!q.isEmpty( ))
        {
            System.out.println(q.whoIsNext( ));
            q.removeFront( );
        }
        System.out.println("The queue is empty.");
    }
}
```

Items come out of the queue in the same order that they went into the queue.

Sample Dialogue

```
Tom
Dick
Harriet
The queue is empty.
```

Items come out of the queue in the same order that they went into the queue.

MyProgrammingLab™

Self-Test Exercise

18. Complete the definition of the method `addToBack` in Display 15.29.

In order to have some terminology to discuss the efficiency of our `Queue` class and linked list algorithms, we first present some background on how the efficiency of algorithms is usually measured.

Running Times and Big-*O* Notation

If you ask a programmer how fast his or her program is, you might expect an answer such as "two seconds." However, the speed of a program cannot be given by a single number. A program will typically take a longer amount of time on larger inputs than it will on smaller inputs. You would expect that a program for sorting numbers would take less time to sort 10 numbers than it would to sort 1,000 numbers. Perhaps it takes 2 seconds to sort 10 numbers, but 10 seconds to sort 1,000 numbers. How, then, should the programmer answer the question "How fast is your program?" The programmer would have to give a table of values showing how long the program took

Display 15.31 Some Values of a Running-Time Function

Input Size	Running Time
10 numbers	2 seconds
100 numbers	2.1 seconds
1,000 numbers	10 seconds
10,000 numbers	2.5 minutes

for different sizes of input. For example, the table might be as shown in Display 15.31. This table does not give a single time, but instead gives different times for a variety of different input sizes.

function

The table is a description of what is called a **function** in mathematics. Just as a (non-`void`) Java method takes an argument and returns a value, so too does this function take an argument, which is an input size, and returns a number, which is the time the program takes on an input of that size. If we call this function T, then $T(10)$ is 2 seconds, $T(100)$ is 2.1 seconds, $T(1{,}000)$ is 10 seconds, and $T(10{,}000)$ is 2.5 minutes. The table is just a sample of some of the values of this function T. The program will take some amount of time on inputs of every size. So although they are not shown in the table, there are also values for $T(1)$, $T(2)$, … , $T(101)$, $T(102)$, and so forth. For any positive integer N, $T(N)$ is the amount of time it takes for the program to sort N numbers. The function T is called the **running time** of the program.

running time

So far we have been assuming that this sorting program will take the same amount of time on any list of N numbers. That need not be true. Perhaps it takes much less time if the list is already sorted or almost sorted. In this case, $T(N)$ is defined to be the time taken by the "hardest" list—that is, the time taken on that list of N numbers that makes the program run the longest. This is called the **worst-case running time**. In this chapter, we will always mean worst-case running time when we give a running time for an algorithm or for some code.

worst-case running time

The time taken by a program or algorithm is often given by a formula, such as $4N + 3$, $5N + 4$, or N^2. If the running time $T(N)$ is $5N + 5$, then on inputs of size N, the program will run for $5N + 5$ time units.

Presented next is some code to search an array `a` with N elements to determine whether a particular value `target` is in the array:

```
int i = 0;
boolean found = false;
while (( i < N) && !(found))
{
    if (a[i] == target)
        found = true;
    else
        i++;
}
```

We want to compute some estimate of how long it will take a computer to execute this code. We would like an estimate that does not depend on which computer we use, either because we do not know which computer we will use or because we might use several different computers to run the program at different times.

One possibility is to count the number of "steps," but it is not easy to decide what a step is. In this situation, the normal thing to do is count the number of **operations**. The term *operations* is almost as vague as the term *step*, but there is at least some agreement in practice about what qualifies as an operation. Let us say that, for this Java code, each application of any of the following will count as an operation: `=`, `<`, `&&`, `!`, `[]`, `==`, and `++`. The computer must do other things besides carry out these operations, but these seem to be the main things that it is doing, and we will assume that they account for the bulk of the time needed to run this code. In fact, our analysis of time will assume that everything else takes no time at all and that the total time for our program to run is equal to the time needed to perform these operations. Although this is an idealization that clearly is not completely true, it turns out that this simplifying assumption works well in practice, and so it is often made when analyzing a program or algorithm.

Even with our simplifying assumption, we still must consider two cases: Either the value `target` is in the array or it is not. Let us first consider the case when `target` is not in the array. The number of operations performed will depend on the number of array elements searched. The operation `=` is performed two times before the loop is executed. Because we are assuming that `target` is not in the array, the loop will be executed N times, one for each element of the array. Each time the loop is executed, the following operations are performed: `<`, `&&`, `!`, `[]`, `==`, and `++`. This adds five operations for each of N loop iterations. Finally, after N iterations, the Boolean expression is again checked and found to be `false`. This adds a final three operations (`<`, `&&`, `!`).[3] If we tally all these operations, we get a total of $6N + 5$ operations when the target is not in the array. We will leave it as an exercise for the reader to confirm that if the target is in the array, then the number of operations will be $6N + 5$ *or less*. Thus, the worst-case running time is $T(N) = 6N + 5$ operations for any array of N elements and any value of `target`.

We just determined that the worst-case running time for our search code is $6N + 5$ operations. But an operation is not a traditional unit of time, such as a nanosecond, second, or minute. If we want to know how long the algorithm will take on some particular computer, we must know how long it takes that computer to perform one operation. If an operation can be performed in one nanosecond, then the time will be $6N + 5$ nanoseconds. If an operation can be performed in one second, the time will be $6N + 5$ seconds. If we use a slow computer that takes 10 seconds to perform an operation, the time will be $60N + 50$ seconds. In general, if it takes the computer c nanoseconds to perform one operation, then the actual running time will be approximately $c(6N + 5)$ nanoseconds. (We said *approximately* because we

[3] Because of short-circuit evaluation, `!(found)` is not evaluated, so we actually get two, not three, operations. However, the important thing is to obtain a good upper bound. If we add in one extra operation, that is not significant.

are making some simplifying assumptions and therefore the result may not be the absolutely exact running time.) This means that our running time of $6N + 5$ is a very crude estimate. To get the running time expressed in nanoseconds, you must multiply by some constant that depends on the particular computer you are using. Our estimate of $6N + 5$ is only accurate to within a constant multiple.

big-O notation

Estimates on running time, such as the one we just went through, are normally expressed in something called **big-O notation**. (The O is the letter "Oh," not the digit zero.) Suppose we estimate the running time to be, say, $6N + 5$ operations, and suppose we know that no matter what the exact running time of each different operation may turn out to be, there will always be some constant factor c such that the real running time is less than or equal to $c\,(6N + 5)$. Under these circumstances, we say that the code (or program or algorithm) runs in time $O(6N + 5)$. This is usually read as "big-O of $6N + 5$." We need not know what the constant c will be. In fact, it will undoubtedly be different for different computers, but we must know that there is one such c for any reasonable computer system. If the computer is very fast, the c might be less than 1—say, 0.001. If the computer is very slow, the c might be very large—say, 1,000. Moreover, because changing the units (say from nanosecond to second) involves only a constant multiple, there is no need to give any units of time.

Be sure to notice that a big-O estimate is an upper-bound estimate. We always approximate by taking numbers on the high side rather than the low side of the true count. Also notice that when performing a big-O estimate, we need not determine an exact count of the number of operations performed. We need only an estimate that is correct up to a constant multiple. If our estimate is twice as large as the true number, that is good enough.

An order-of-magnitude estimate, such as the previous $6N + 5$, contains a parameter for the size of the task solved by the algorithm (or program or piece of code). In our sample case, this parameter N was the number of array elements to be searched. Not surprisingly, it takes longer to search a larger number of array elements than it does to search a smaller number of array elements. Big-O running-time estimates are always expressed as a function of the size of the problem. In this chapter, all our algorithms will involve a range of values in some container. In all cases, N will be the number of elements in that range.

The following is an alternative, pragmatic way to think about big-O estimates:

Only look at the term with the highest exponent and do not pay attention to constant multiples.

For example, all of the following are $O(N^2)$:

$$N^2 + 2N + 1, \quad 3N^2 + 7, \quad 100N^2 + N$$

All of the following are $O(N^3)$:

$$N^3 + 5N^2 + N + 1, \quad 8N^3 + 7, \quad 100N^3 + 4N + 1$$

These big-O running-time estimates are admittedly crude, but they do contain some information. They will not distinguish between a running time of $5N + 5$ and a running time of $100N$, but they do let us distinguish between some running times and so determine that some algorithms are faster than others. Look at the graphs in Display 15.32 and notice that all the graphs for functions that are $O(N)$ eventually fall below the graph for the function $0.5N^2$. The result is inevitable: An $O(N)$ algorithm will always run faster than any $O(N^2)$ algorithm, provided we use large enough values of N. Although an $O(N^2)$ algorithm could be faster than an $O(N)$ algorithm for the problem size you are handling, programmers have found that, in practice, $O(N)$ algorithms perform better than $O(N)$ algorithms for most practical applications that are intuitively "large." Similar remarks apply to any other two different big-O running times.

Display 15.32 **Comparison of Running Times**

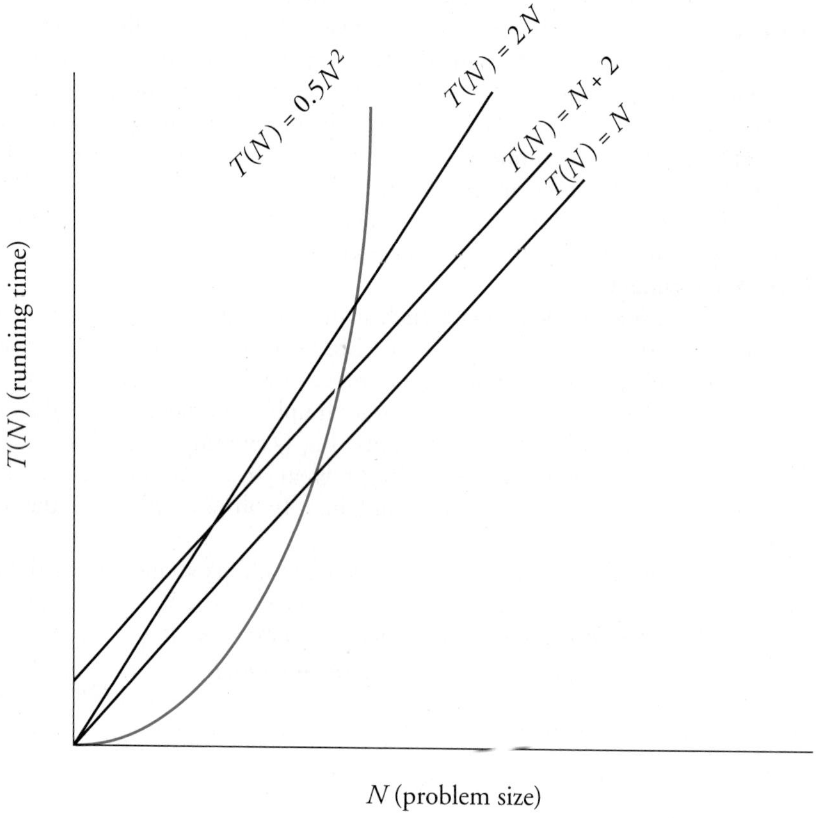

linear running time

quadratic running time

Some terminology will help with our descriptions of generic algorithm running times. **Linear running time** means a running time of $T(N) = aN + b$. A linear running time is always an $O(N)$ running time. **Quadratic running time** means a running time with a highest term of N^2. A quadratic running time is always an $O(N^2)$ running time. We will also occasionally have logarithms in running-time formulas. Those normally are given without any base, because changing the base is just a constant multiple. If you see log N, think log base 2 of N, but it would not be wrong to think log base 10 of N. Logarithms are very slow-growing functions. So, an $O(\log N)$ running time is very fast.

In many cases, our running-time estimates will be better than big-O estimates. In particular, when we specify a linear running time, that is a tight upper bound and you can think of the running time as being exactly $T(N) = cN$, although the c is still not specified.

MyProgrammingLab™

Self-Test Exercises

19. Show that a running time $T(N) = aN + b$ is an $O(N)$ running time. (*Hint:* The only issue is the plus b. Assume N is always at least 1.)

20. Show that for any two bases a and b for logarithms, if a and b are both greater than 1, then there is a constant c such that $\log_a N \leq c\,(\log_b N)$. Thus, there is no need to specify a base in $O(\log N)$. That is, $O(\log_a N)$ and $O(\log_b N)$ mean the same thing.

Efficiency of Linked Lists

Now that we know about big-O notation, we can express the efficiency of various methods for our linked data structures. As an example of analyzing the run-time efficiency of an algorithm, consider the `find` method for the linked list class in Display 15.3. This method starts at the head of the list and sequentially iterates through each node to see whether it matches the target. If the linked list contains many nodes, then we might get lucky if the target is found at the head of the list. In this case, the computer had only to execute one step: Check the head of the list for the target. In the worst case, the computer might have to search through all n nodes before finding (or not finding) the target. In this case, the computer had to execute n steps. The worst case will obviously take longer to execute than the best case. On average, we might expect to search through about half of the list before finding the target. This would require $n/2$ steps. In our big-O notation, the find operation is $O(n)$. However, the `addToStart` method requires linking only a new node to the head of the list. This runs in $O(1)$ steps (that is, a constant upper bound on the running time that is independent of the size of the input).

Next we shall briefly examine more elaborate data structures that are capable of performing find operations in fewer steps. However, a detailed treatment of these more advanced data structures is beyond the scope of this chapter. The goal of this chapter is to teach you the basic techniques for constructing and manipulating data structures based on nodes and links (that is, nodes and references). The linked lists served as good examples for our discussion.

15.5 Hash Tables with Chaining

Seek, and ye shall find.

MATTHEW 7:7

hash table

hash map

A **hash table** or **hash map** is a data structure that efficiently stores and retrieves data from memory. There are many ways to construct a hash table; in this section, we will use an array in combination with singly linked lists. In the previous section, we saw that a linked list generally requires linear, or $O(n)$, steps to determine if a target is in the list. In contrast, a hash table has the potential to execute a fixed number of steps to look up a target, regardless of the size of n. We saw that a constant-time lookup is written $O(1)$. However, the hash table we will present may still require n steps, but such a case is unlikely.

hash function

An object is stored in a hash table by associating it with a *key*. Given the key, we can retrieve the object. Ideally, the key is unique to each object. If the object has no intrinsically unique key, then we can use a **hash function** to compute one. In most cases, the hash function computes a number.

collision

chaining

For example, let us use a hash table to store a dictionary of words. Such a hash table might be useful to make a spell-checker—words missing from the hash table might not be spelled correctly. We will construct the hash table with a fixed array in which each array element references a linked list. The key computed by the hash function will map to the index of the array. The actual data will be stored in a linked list at the hash value's index. Display 15.33 illustrates the idea with a fixed array of 10 entries. Initially, each entry of the array `hashArray` contains a reference to an empty singly linked list. First, we add the word `"cat"`, which has been assigned the key or hash value of 2 (we will show how this was computed shortly). Next, we add `"dog"` and `"bird"`, which are assigned hash values of 4 and 7, respectively. Each of these strings is inserted as the head of the linked list using the hash value as the index in the array. Finally, we add `"turtle"`, which also has a hash of 2. Because `"cat"` is already stored at index 2, we now have a **collision**. Both `"turtle"` and `"cat"` map to the same index in the array. When this occurs in a hash table with **chaining**, we simply insert the new node onto the existing linked list. In our example, there are now two nodes at index 2: `"turtle"` and `"cat"`.

To retrieve a value from the hash table, we first compute the hash value of the target. Next we search the linked list that is stored at `hashArray[hashValue]` for the target, using an iterator to sequentially search the linked list. If the target is not found in this linked list, then the target is not stored in the hash table. If the size of the linked list is small, then the retrieval process will be quick.

Display 15.33 Constructing a Hash Table

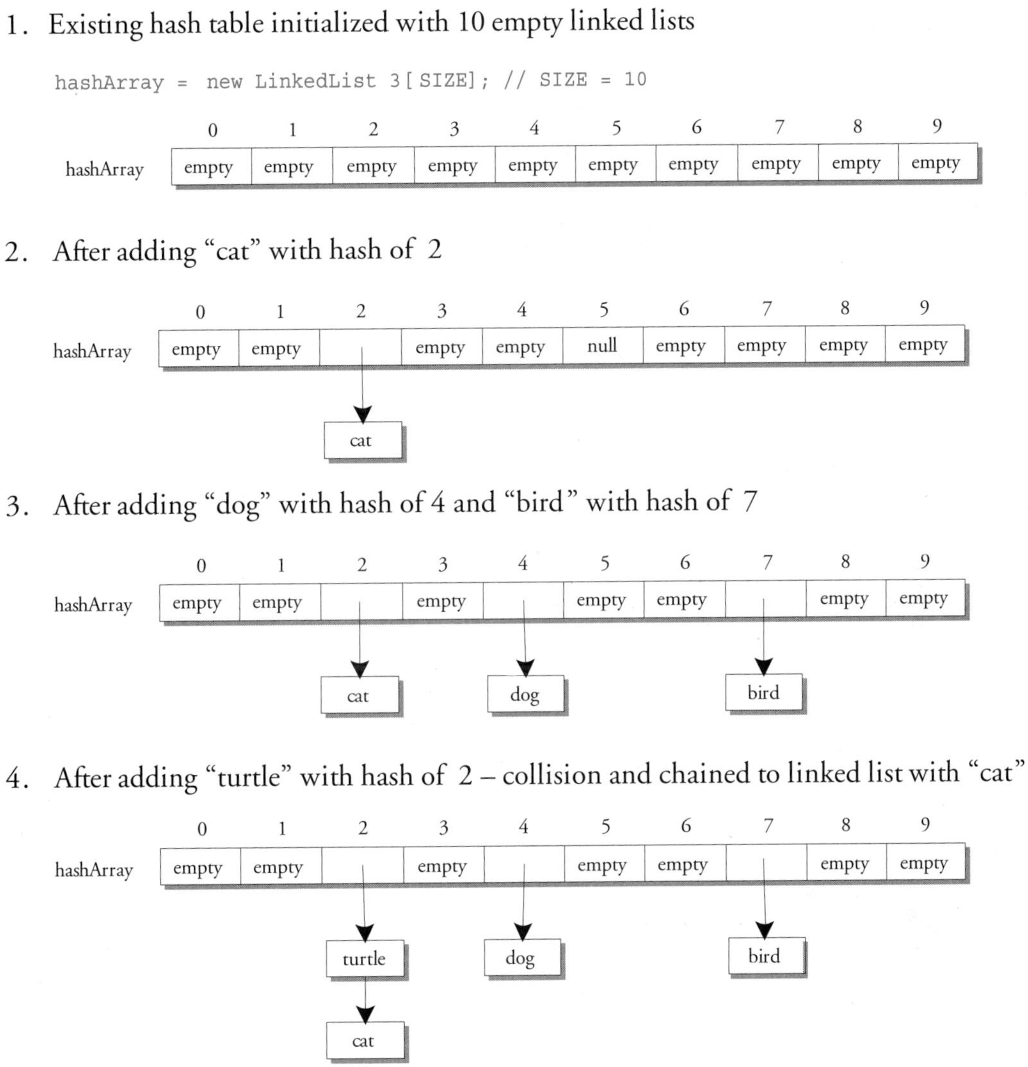

A Hash Function for Strings

A simple way to compute a numeric hash value for a string is to sum the ASCII value of every character in the string and then compute the modulus of the sum using the size of the fixed array. A subset of ASCII codes is given in Appendix 3. Code to compute the hash value is shown next:

```
private int computeHash(String s)
{
   int hash = 0;
```

```
        for (int i = 0; i < s.length(); i++)
        {
            hash += s.charAt(i);
        }
        return hash % SIZE; // SIZE = 10 in example
    }
```

For example, the ASCII codes for the string `"dog"` are as follows:

```
d ->100
o ->111
g ->103
```

The hash function is computed as follows:

```
Sum              = 100 + 111 + 103 = 314
Hash = Sum % 10 = 314 % 10 = 4
```

In this example, we first compute an unbounded value, the sum of the ASCII values in the string. However, the array was defined to only hold a finite number of elements. To scale the sum to the size of the array, we compute the modulus of the sum with respect to the size of the array, which is 10 in the example. In practice, the size of the array is generally a prime number larger than the number of items that will be put into the hash table.[4] The computed hash value of 4 serves like a fingerprint for the string `"dog"`. However, different strings may map to the same value. We can verify that `"cat"` maps to (99 + 97 + 116) % 10 = 2 and also that `"turtle"` maps to (116 + 117 + 114 + 116 + 108 + 101) % 10 = 2.

VideoNote **Walkthrough of the Hash Table Class**

A complete code listing for a hash table class is given in Display 15.34, and a demonstration is provided in Display 15.35. The hash table definition in Display 15.34 uses an array in which each element is a `LinkedList2` class defined in Display 15.7.

Display 15.34 **A Hash Table Class** (part 1 of 2)

```
public class HashTable
{
        // Uses the generic LinkedList2 class from Display 15.7
        private LinkedList2[] hashArray;
        private static final int SIZE = 10;

        public HashTable( )
        {
                hashArray = new LinkedList2[SIZE];
                for (int i=0; i < SIZE; i++)
                     hashArray[i] = new LinkedList2( );
        }
```

[4] A prime number avoids common divisors after modulus that can lead to collisions.

Display 15.34 **A Hash Table Class** (part 2 of 2)

```
    private int computeHash(String s)
    {
        int hash = 0;
        for (int i = 0; i < s.length( ); i++)
        {
            hash += s.charAt(i);
        }
        return hash % SIZE;
    }

    /**
     Returns true if the target is in the hash table,
     false if it is not.
    */
    public boolean containsString(String target)
    {
        int hash = computeHash(target);
        LinkedList2 list = hashArray[hash];
        if (list.contains(target))
            return true;
        return false;
    }
    /**
    Stores or puts string s into the hash table
    */
    public void put(String s)
    {
        int hash = computeHash(s);// Get hash value
        LinkedList2 list = hashArray[hash];
        if (!list.contains(s))
        {
            // Only add the target if it's not already
            // on the list.
            hashArray[hash].addToStart(s);
        }
    }
} // End HashTable class
```

Display 15.35 **Hash Table Demonstration**

```
public class HashTableDemo
{
    public static void main(String[] args)
    {
        HashTable h = new HashTable( );

        System.out.println("Adding dog, cat, turtle, bird");
        h.put("dog");
        h.put("cat");
        h.put("turtle");
        h.put("bird");
        System.out.println("Contains dog? " +
              h.containsString("dog"));
        System.out.println("Contains cat? " +
              h.containsString("cat"));
        System.out.println("Contains turtle? " +
              h.containsString("turtle"));
        System.out.println("Contains bird? " +
              h.containsString("bird"));

        System.out.println("Contains fish? " +
              h.containsString("fish"));
        System.out.println("Contains cow? " +
              h.containsString("cow"));
    }
}
```

Sample Dialogue

```
Adding dog, cat, turtle, bird
Contains dog? true
Contains cat? true
Contains turtle? true
Contains bird? true
Contains fish? false
Contains cow? False
```

Efficiency of Hash Tables

The efficiency of our hash table depends on several factors. First, let us examine some extreme cases. The worst-case run-time performance occurs if every item inserted into the table has the same hash key. Everything will then be stored in a single linked list. With n items, the find operation will require $O(n)$ steps. Fortunately, if the items that we insert are somewhat random, the probability that all of them will hash to the same key is highly unlikely. In contrast, the best-case run-time performance occurs if every item inserted into the table has a different hash key. This means that there will be no collisions, so the find operation will require constant, or $O(1)$, steps because the target will always be the first node in the linked list.

We can decrease the chance of collisions by using a better hash function. For example, the simple hash function that sums each letter of a string ignores the ordering of the letters. The words `"rat"` and `"tar"` would hash to the same value. A better hash function for a string `s` is to multiply each letter by an increasing weight depending upon the position in the word. For example,

```
int hash = 0;
for (int i = 0; i < s.length( ); i++)
{
    hash = 31 * hash + s.charAt(i);
}
```

Another way to decrease the chance of collisions is by making the hash table bigger. For example, if the hash table array stored 10,000 entries but we are only inserting 1,000 items, then the probability of a collision is much smaller than if the hash table array stored only 1,000 entries. However, a drawback to creating an extremely large hash table array is wasted memory. If only 1,000 items are inserted into the 10,000-entry hash table, then at least 9,000 memory locations will go unused. This illustrates the **time-space tradeoff**. It is usually possible to increase run-time performance at the expense of memory space, and vice versa.

time-space tradeoff

MyProgrammingLab™

Self-Test Exercises

21. Suppose that every student in your university is assigned a unique nine-digit ID number. You would like to create a hash table that indexes ID numbers to an object representing a student. The hash table has a size of *N*, where *N* has less than nine digits. Describe a simple hash function that you can use to map from a ID number to a hash index.

22. Write an `outputHashTable( )` method for the `HashTable` class that outputs every item stored in the hash table.

15.6 Sets

There are two classes in good society in England. The equestrian classes and the neurotic classes.

GEORGE BERNARD SHAW, *Heartbreak House*

A set is a collection of elements in which order and multiplicity are ignored. Many problems in computer science can be solved with the aid of a set data structure. A variation on linked lists is a straightforward way to implement a set. In this implementation, the items in each set are stored using a singly linked list. The `data` variable contains a reference to an object we wish to store in the set, whereas the `link` variable refers to the next `Node<T>` in the list (which in turn contains a reference to the next object to store in the set). The node class for a generic set of objects can begin as follows:

```
private class Node<T>
{
    private T data;
    private Node<T> link;

    . . .
```

A complete listing is provided in Display 15.37. The `Node` class is a private inner class, similar to how we constructed the generic `LinkedList3<T>` class in Display 15.8. In fact, the set operations of `add`, `contains`, `output`, `clear`, `size`, and `isEmpty` are virtually identical to those from Display 15.8. The `add` method (which was `addToStart`) has been slightly changed to prevent duplicate items from being added into the set. Display 15.36 illustrates two sample sets stored using this data structure. The set `round` contains `"peas"`, `"ball"`, and `"pie"`, whereas the set `green` contains `"peas"` and `"grass"`. Because the linked list is storing a reference to each object in the set, it is possible to place an item in multiple sets by referencing it from multiple linked lists. In Display 15.36, `"peas"` is in both sets because it is round and green.

Fundamental Set Operations

The fundamental operations that our set class should support are as follows:

- Add Element. Add a new item into a set.
- Contains. Determine if a target item is a member of the set.
- Union. Return a set that is the union of two sets.
- Intersection. Return a set that is the intersection of two sets.

Display 15.36 **Sets Using Linked Lists**

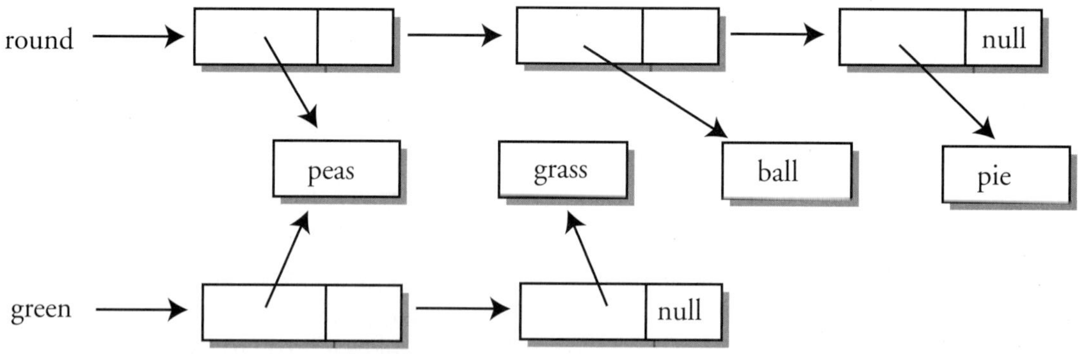

We should also make an iterator so that every element can be retrieved from a set. This is left as a programming project for the reader (Programming Project 15.7). Other useful set operations include methods to retrieve the cardinality of the set and to remove items from the set.

Code to implement sets is provided in Display 15.37. The `add` method is similar to adding a node to the front of a linked list. The `head` variable always references the first node in the list. The `contains` method is identical to the `find` method for a singly linked list. We simply loop through every item in the list looking for the target.

The `union` method combines the elements in the calling object's set with the elements from the set of the input argument, `otherSet`. To union these sets, we first create a new empty `Set<T>` object. Next, we iterate through both the calling object's set and `otherSet`'s set. All elements are added (which creates new references to the items in the set) to the new set. The `add` method enforces uniqueness, so we do not have to check for duplicate elements in the `union` method.

The `intersection` method is similar to the `union` method in that it also creates a new empty `Set<T>` object. In this case, we populate the set with items that are common to both the calling object's set and `otherSet`'s set. This is accomplished by iterating through every item in the calling object's set. For each item, we invoke the `contains` method for `otherSet`. If `contains` returns `true`, then the item is in both sets and can be added to the new set.

A short demonstration program is shown in Display 15.38.

Display 15.37 **`Set<T>`** Class (part 1 of 3)

```
// Uses a linked list as the internal data structure
// to store items in a set.
public class Set<T>
{
    private class Node<T>
    {
        private T data;
        private Node<T> link;
        public Node( )
        {
            data = null;
            link = null;
        }
        public Node(T newData, Node<T> linkValue)
        {
            data = newData;
            link = linkValue;
        }
    }//End of Node<T> inner class
```

(continued)

Display 15.37 **Set<T>** Class (part 2 of 3)

```
    private Node<T> head;

    public Set( )
    {
           head = null;
    }
    /**
     Add a new item to the set. If the item
     is already in the set, false is returned;
     otherwise, true is returned.
    */
    public boolean add(T newItem)
    {
          if (!contains(newItem))
          {
               head = new Node<T>(newItem, head);
               return true;
          }
          return false;
    }

    public boolean contains(T item)
    {
        Node<T> position = head;
        T itemAtPosition;
        while (position != null)
        {
            itemAtPosition = position.data;
            if (itemAtPosition.equals(item))
                return true;
            position = position.link;
        }
        return false; //target was not found
    }

    public void output( )
    {
        Node position = head;
        while (position != null)
        {
            System.out.print(position.data.toString( ) + " ");
            position = position.link;
        }
        System.out.println( );
    }
```

Display 15.37 **Set<T>** Class (part 3 of 3)

```
    /**
     Returns a new set that is the union
     of this set and the input set.
    */
    public Set<T> union(Set<T> otherSet)
    {
        Set<T> unionSet = new Set<T>( );
        // Copy this set to unionSet.
        Node<T> position = head;
        while (position != null)
        {
            unionSet.add(position.data);
            position = position.link;
        }
        // Copy otherSet items to unionSet.
        // The add method eliminates any duplicates.
        position = otherSet.head;
        while (position != null)
        {
            unionSet.add(position.data);
            position = position.link;
        }
        return unionSet;
    }

    /**
     Returns a new set that is the intersection
     of this set and the input set.
    */
    public Set<T> intersection(Set<T> otherSet)
    {
        Set<T> interSet = new Set<T>( );
        // Copy only items in both sets.
        Node<T> position = head;
        while (position != null)
        {
            if (otherSet.contains(position.data))
                interSet.add(position.data);
            position = position.link;
        }
        return interSet;
    }
}
```

The **clear**, **size**, *and* **isEmpty** *methods are identical to those in Display 15.8 for the* **LinkedList3** *class.*

Display 15.38 **Set Class Demo** (part 1 of 2)

```
public class SetDemo
{
    public static void main(String[] args)
    {
        // Round things
        Set round = new Set<String>( );
        // Green things
        Set green = new Set<String>( );

        // Add some data to both sets
        round.add("peas");
        round.add("ball");
        round.add("pie");
        round.add("grapes");

        green.add("peas");
        green.add("grapes");
        green.add("garden hose");
        green.add("grass");

        System.out.println("Contents of set round: ");
        round.output( );
        System.out.println("Contents of set green: ");
        green.output( );
        System.out.println( );

        System.out.println("ball in set round? " +
            round.contains("ball"));
        System.out.println("ball in set green? " +
            green.contains("ball"));
        System.out.println("ball and peas in same set? " +
            ((round.contains("ball") &&
             (round.contains("peas"))) ||
            (green.contains("ball") &&
             (green.contains("peas")))));

        System.out.println("pie and grass in same set? " +
            ((round.contains("pie") &&
             (round.contains("grass"))) ||
            (green.contains("pie") &&
             (green.contains("grass")))));

        System.out.print("Union of green and round: ");
        round.union(green).output( );
```

Display 15.38 **Set Class Demo** (part 2 of 2)

```
            System.out.print("Intersection of green and round: ");
            round.intersection(green).output( );
        }
}
```

Sample Dialogue

```
Contents of set round:
grapes pie ball peas
Contents of set green:
Grass garden hose grapes peas

ball in set round? true
ball in set green? false
ball and peas in same set? true
pie and grass in same set? false
Union of green and round: garden hose grass peas ball pie grapes
Intersection of green and round: peas grapes
```

Efficiency of Sets Using Linked Lists

We can analyze the efficiency of our set data structure in terms of the fundamental set operations. Adding an item to the set always inserts a new node on the front of the list. This requires constant, or $O(1)$, steps. The `contains` method iterates through the entire set looking for the target, which requires $O(n)$ steps. When we invoke the `union` method for sets A and B, it iterates through both sets and adds each item into a new set. If there are n items in set A and m items in set B, then $n + m$ add methods are invoked. However, there is a hidden cost because the `add` method searches through its entire list for any duplicates before a new item is added. Although beyond the scope of this text, the additional cost results in $O(m + n)2$ steps. Finally, the `intersection` method applied to sets A and B invokes the `contains` method of set B for each item in set A. Because the `contains` method requires $O(m)$ steps for each item in set A, then this requires $O(m) \times O(n)$ steps, or $O(mn)$ steps. These are inefficient methods in our implementation of sets. A different approach to represent the set—for example, one that used hash tables instead of a linked list—could result in an `intersection` method that runs in $O(n + m)$ steps. Nevertheless, our linked list implementation would probably be fine for an application that uses small sets or for an application that does not frequently invoke the `intersection` method, and we have the benefit of relatively simple code that is easy to understand.

If we really need the efficiency, then we could maintain the same interface to the `Set<T>` class but replace our linked list implementation with something else. If we used the hash table implementation from Section 15.5, then the `contains` method could run in $O(1)$ steps instead of $O(n)$ steps. It might seem like the `intersection` method will now run in $O(n)$ steps, but by switching to a hash table, it becomes more difficult to iterate through the set of items. Instead of traversing a single linked list to retrieve every item in the set, the hash table version must now iterate through the hash table array and then for each index in the array iterate through the linked list at that index. If the array is size N and the number of items in the hash table is n, then the iteration time becomes $O(N + n)$. In practice, we would expect N to be larger than n. So although we have decreased the number of steps it takes to look up an item, we have increased the number of steps it takes to iterate over every item. If this is troublesome, you could overcome this problem with an implementation of `Set<T>` that uses both a linked list (to facilitate iteration) and a hash table (for fast lookup). However, the complexity of the code is significantly increased using such an approach. You are asked to explore the hash table implementation in Programming Project 15.10.

MyProgrammingLab™

Self-Test Exercises

23. Write a method named `difference` that returns the difference between two sets. The method should return a new set that has items from the first set that are not in the second set. For example, if `setA` contains {1, 2, 3, 4} and `setB` contains {2, 4, 5}, then `setA.difference(setB)` should return the set {1, 3}.

24. What is the run time of the `difference` method for the previous question? Give your answer using big-O notation.

15.7 Trees

I think that I shall never see a data structure as useful as a tree.

ANONYMOUS

The tree data structure is an example of a more complicated data structure made with links. Moreover, trees are a very important and widely used data structure. So, we will briefly outline the general techniques used to construct and manipulate trees. This section is only a very brief introduction to trees to give you the flavor of the subject.

This section uses recursion, which is covered in Chapter 11.

Tree Properties

A tree is a data structure that is structured as shown in Display 15.39. In particular, in a tree you can reach any node from the top (root) node by some path that follows the links. Note that there are no cycles in a tree. If you follow the links, you eventually get to an "end." A definition for a tree class for this sort of tree of `int`s is outlined in Display 15.39. Note that each node has two references to other nodes (two links) coming from it. This sort of tree is called a **binary tree**, because each node has exactly

binary tree

two link instance variables. There are other kinds of trees with different numbers of link instance variables, but the binary tree is the most common case.

Display 15.39 A Binary Tree

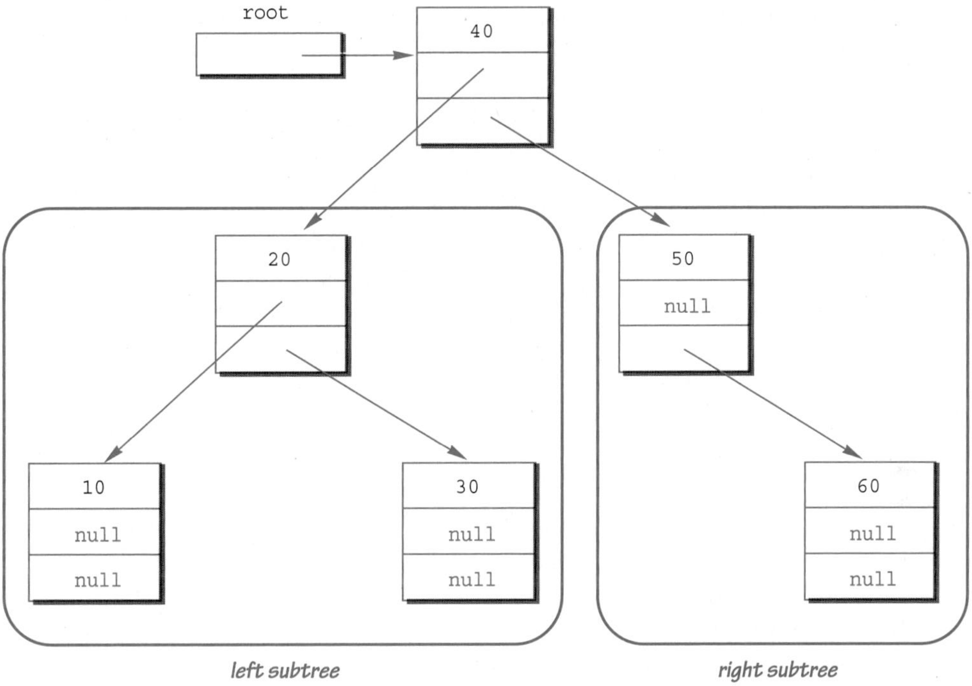


```
public class IntTree
{
    public class IntTreeNode
    {
        private int data;
        private IntTreeNode leftLink;
        private IntTreeNode rightLink;
    } //End of IntTreeNode inner class

    private IntTreeNode root;
  <The methods and other inner classes are not shown.>

}
```

The instance variable named `root` serves a purpose similar to that of the instance variable `head` in a linked list (Display 15.3). The node whose reference is in the root instance variable is called the **root node**. Any node in the tree can be reached from the root node by following the links.

root node

The term *tree* may seem like a misnomer. The root is at the top of the tree, and the branching structure looks more like a root branching structure than a tree branching structure. The secret to the terminology is to turn the picture (Display 15.39) upside down. The picture then does resemble the branching structure of a tree, and the root node is where the tree's root would begin. The nodes at the ends of the branches with both link instance variables set to `null` are known as **leaf nodes**, a terminology that may now make some sense. By analogy to an empty linked list, an **empty tree** is denoted by setting the link variable `root` equal to `null`.

leaf node

empty tree

Note that a tree has a recursive structure. Each tree has, in effect, two subtrees whose root nodes are the nodes pointed to by the `leftLink` and `rightLink` of the root node. These two subtrees are circled in Display 15.39. This natural recursive structure makes trees particularly amenable to recursive algorithms. For example, consider the task of searching the tree in such a way that you visit each node and do something with the data in the node (such as writing it out to the screen). There is a general plan of attack that goes as follows:

Preorder Processing

1. Process the data in the root node.
2. Process the left subtree.
3. Process the right subtree.

Obtain a number of variants on this search process by varying the order of these three steps. Two more versions follow:

inorder

Inorder Processing

1. Process the left subtree.
2. Process the data in the root node.
3. Process the right subtree.

postorder

Postorder Processing

1. Process the left subtree.
2. Process the right subtree.
3. Process the data in the root node.

Binary Search Tree Storage Rule

The tree in Display 15.39 has numbers that were stored in the tree in a special way known as the **Binary Search Tree Storage Rule**. The rule is summarized in the following box.

> **Binary Search Tree Storage Rule**
>
> 1. All the values in the left subtree are less than the value in the root node.
> 2. All the values in the right subtree are greater than or equal to the value in the root node.
> 3. This rule applies recursively to each of the two subtrees.
>
> (The base case for the recursion is an empty tree, which is always considered to satisfy the rule.)

binary search tree

A tree that satisfies the Binary Search Tree Storage Rule is referred to as a **binary search tree**.

Note that if a tree satisfies the Binary Search Tree Storage Rule and you output the values using the Inorder Processing method, then the numbers will be output in order from smallest to largest.

For trees that follow the Binary Search Tree Storage Rule and that are short and fat rather than tall and thin, values can be very quickly retrieved from the tree using a binary search algorithm that is similar in spirit to the binary search algorithm we presented in Display 11.6. The topic of searching and maintaining a binary storage tree to realize this efficiency is a large topic that goes beyond what we have room for here. However, we give one example of a class for trees that satisfy the Binary Search Tree Storage Rule.

EXAMPLE: A Binary Search Tree Class ★

Display 15.40 contains the definition of a class for a binary search tree that satisfies the Binary Search Tree Storage Rule. For simplicity, this tree stores integers, but a routine modification can produce a similar tree class that stores objects of any class that implements the `Comparable` interface. Display 15.41 demonstrates the use of this tree class. Note that no matter in which order the integers are inserted into the tree, the output, which uses inorder traversal, outputs the integers in sorted order.

The methods in this class make extensive use of the recursive nature of binary trees. If `aNode` is a reference to any node in the tree (including possibly the root node), then the entire tree with root `aNode` can be decomposed into three parts:

1. The node `aNode`.
2. The left subtree with root node `aNode.leftLink`.
3. The right subtree with root node `aNode.rightLink`.

The left and right subtrees do themselves satisfy the Binary Search Tree Storage Rule, so it is natural to use recursion to process the entire tree by doing the following:

1. Processing the left subtree with root node `aNode.leftLink`
2. Processing the node `aNode`
3. Processing the right subtree with root node `aNode.rightLink`

Note that we processed the root node after the left subtree (inorder traversal). This guarantees that the numbers in the tree are output in the order smallest to largest. The method `showElementsInSubtree` uses a very straightforward implementation of this technique.

Other methods are a bit more subtle in that only one of the two subtrees needs to be processed. For example, consider the method `isInSubtree`, which returns `true` or `false` depending on whether or not the parameter item is in the tree with root node `subTreeRoot`. To see if the item is anyplace in the tree, set `subTreeRoot` equal

(continued)

EXAMPLE: (continued)

to the root of the entire tree, as we did in the method `contains`. However, to express our recursive algorithm for `isInSubtree`, we need to allow for the possibility of subtrees other than the entire tree.

The algorithm for `isInSubtree` expressed in pseudocode is as follows:

```
if (The root node subTreeRoot is empty.)
    return false;
else if (The node subTreeRoot contains item.)
  return true;
else if (item < subTreeRoot.data)
  return (The result of searching the tree
          with root node subTreeRoot.leftLink);
else
  //item > link.data
  return (The result of searching the tree
          with root node subTreeRoot.rightLink);
```

The reason this algorithm gives the correct result is that the tree satisfies the Binary Search Tree Storage Rule, so we know that if

```
item < subTreeRoot.data
```

then `item` is in the left subtree (if it is anywhere in the tree), and if

```
item > subTreeRoot.data
```

then `item` is in the right subtree (if it is anywhere in the tree).

The method with the following heading uses techniques very much like those used in `isInSubtree`:

```
private IntTreeNode insertInSubtree(
                    int item, IntTreeNode subTreeRoot)
```

However, there is something new here. We want the method `insertInSubtree` to insert a new node with the data item into the tree with root node `subTreeRoot`. But in this case, we want to deal with `subTreeRoot` as a variable and not use it only as the value of the variable `subTreeRoot`. For example, if `subTreeRoot` contains `null`, then we want to change the value of `subTreeRoot` to a reference to a new node containing `item`. However, Java parameters cannot change the value of a variable given as an argument. (Review the discussion of parameters in Chapter 5 if this sounds unfamiliar.) So, we must do something a little different. To change the value of the variable `subTreeRoot`, we return a reference to what we want the new value to be, and we invoke the method `subTreeRoot` as follows:

```
subTreeRoot = insertInSubtree(item, subTreeRoot);
```

That explains why the method `insertInSubtree` returns a reference to a tree node, but we still have to explain why we know it returns a reference to the desired (modified) subtree.

EXAMPLE: (continued)

Note that the method `insertInSubtree` searches the tree just as the method `isInSubtree` does, but it does not stop if it finds `item`; instead, it searches until it reaches a leaf node—that is, a node containing `null`. This `null` is where the item belongs in the tree, so it replaces `null` with a new subtree containing a single node that contains `item`. You may need to think about the method `insertInSubtree` a bit to see that it works correctly; allow yourself some time to study the method `insertInSubtree` and be sure you are convinced that after the addition, like the following,

```
subTreeRoot = insertInSubtree(item, subTreeRoot);
```

the tree with root node `subTreeRoot` still satisfies the Binary Search Tree Storage Rule.

The rest of the definition of the class `IntTree` is routine.

Display 15.40 **A Binary Search Tree for Integers** (part 1 of 2)

```
/**
 Class invariant: The tree satisfies the binary search tree storage rule.
*/
public class IntTree
{
    private static class IntTreeNode
    {
        private int data;
        private IntTreeNode leftLink;
        private IntTreeNode rightLink;

        public IntTreeNode(int newData, IntTreeNode newLeftLink,
                                        IntTreeNode newRightLink)
        {
             data = newData;
             leftLink = newLeftLink;
             rightLink = newRightLink;
        }
    } //End of IntTreeNode inner class

    private IntTreeNode root;

    public IntTree( )
    {
        root = null;
    }

    public void add(int item)
    {
        root = insertInSubtree(item, root);
    }
```

The only reason this inner class is static is that it is used in the `static` methods `insertInSubtree`, `isInSubtree`, and `showElementsInSubtree`.

This class should have more methods. This is just a sample of possible methods.

(continued)

Display 15.40 **A Binary Search Tree for Integers** (part 2 of 2)

```
    public boolean contains(int item)
    {
        return isInSubtree(item, root);
    }

    public void showElements( )
    {
        showElementsInSubtree(root);
    }
    /**
     Returns the root node of a tree that is the tree with root node
     subTreeRoot, but with a new node added that contains item.
    */
    private static IntTreeNode insertInSubtree(int item,
                                               IntTreeNode subTreeRoot)
    {
        if (subTreeRoot == null)
            return new IntTreeNode(item, null, null);
        else if (item < subTreeRoot.data)
        {
            subTreeRoot.leftLink = insertInSubtree(item, subTreeRoot.
                                                          leftLink);
            return subTreeRoot;
        }
        else //item >= subTreeRoot.data
        {
            subTreeRoot.rightLink = insertInSubtree(item, subTreeRoot.
                                                        rightLink);
            return subTreeRoot;
        }
    }

    private static boolean isInSubtree(int item, IntTreeNode
                                                 subTreeRoot)
    {
        if (subTreeRoot == null)
            return false;
        else if (subTreeRoot.data == item)
            return true;
        else if (item < subTreeRoot.data)
            return isInSubtree(item, subTreeRoot.leftLink);
        else //item >= link.data
            return isInSubtree(item, subTreeRoot.rightLink);
    }

    private static void showElementsInSubtree(IntTreeNode subTreeRoot)
    { //Uses inorder traversal.
        if (subTreeRoot != null)
        {
            showElementsInSubtree(subTreeRoot.leftLink);
            System.out.print(subTreeRoot.data + " ");
            showElementsInSubtree(subTreeRoot.rightLink);
        } //else do nothing. Empty tree has nothing to display.
    }
}
```

Display 15.41 Demonstration Program for the Binary Search Tree

```
import java.util.Scanner;

public class BinarySearchTreeDemo
{
    public static void main(String[] args)
    {
        Scanner keyboard = new Scanner(System.in);
        IntTree tree = new IntTree( );

        System.out.println("Enter a list of nonnegative integers.");
        System.out.println("Place a negative integer at the end.");
        int next = keyboard.nextInt( );
        while (next >= 0)
        {
            tree.add(next);
            next = keyboard.nextInt( );
        }

        System.out.println("In sorted order:");
        tree.showElements( );
    }
}
```

Sample Dialogue

```
Enter a list of nonnegative integers.
Place a negative integer at the end.
40
30
20
10
11
22
33
44
-1
In sorted order:
10 11 20 22 30 33 40 44
```

Efficiency of Binary Search Trees ★

When searching a tree that is as short as possible (all paths from root to a leaf differ by at most one node), the search method `isInSubtree`, and hence also the method `contains`, is about as efficient as the binary search on a sorted array (Display 11.6). This should not be a surprise because the two algorithms are in fact very similar. In big-O notation, the worst-case running time is $O(\log n)$, where n is the number of nodes in the tree. This means that searching a short, fat binary tree is very efficient. To obtain this efficiency, the tree does not need to be as short as possible so long as it comes close to being as short as possible. As the tree becomes less short and fat and more tall and thin, the efficiency falls off until, in the extreme case, the efficiency is the same as that of searching a linked list with the same number of nodes.

Maintaining a tree so that it remains short and fat as nodes are added is a topic that is beyond the scope of what we have room for in this book. (The technical term for short and fat is *balanced*.) We will note only that if the numbers that are stored in the tree arrive in random order, then with very high probability the tree will be short and fat enough to realize the efficiency discussed in the previous paragraph.

MyProgrammingLab™

Self-Test Exercises

25. Suppose that the code for the method `showElementsInSubtree` in Display 15.40 were changed so that

```
showElementsInSubtree(subTreeRoot.leftLink);
System.out.print(subTreeRoot.data + " ");
showElementsInSubtree(subTreeRoot.rightLink);
```

were changed to

```
System.out.print(subTreeRoot.data + " ");
showElementsInSubtree(subTreeRoot.leftLink);
showElementsInSubtree(subTreeRoot.rightLink);
```

Will the numbers still be output in ascending order?

26. How can you change the code for the method `showElementsInSubtree` in Display 15.40 so that the numbers are output from largest to smallest instead of from smallest to largest?

Chapter Summary

- A *linked list* is a data structure consisting of objects known as *nodes*, such that each node contains data and also a reference to one other node so that the nodes link together to form a list.
- Setting a link instance variable to `null` indicates the end of a linked list (or other linked data structure). `null` is also used to indicate an empty linked list (or other empty linked data structure).
- You can make a linked list (or other linked data structure) self-contained by making the node class an inner class of the linked list class.
- In many situations, a `clone` method or copy constructor is best defined so that it makes a deep copy.
- You can use an *iterator* to step through the elements of a collection, such as the elements in a linked list.
- Nodes in a *doubly linked list* have two links—one to the previous node in the list and one to the next node. This makes some operations, such as insertion and deletion, slightly easier.
- A *stack* is a data structure in which elements are removed in the reverse of the order they were added to the stack. A *queue* is a data structure in which elements are removed in the same order that they were added to the queue.
- *Big-O notation* specifies an upper bound for how many steps or how long a program will take to run based on the size of the input to the program. This can be used to analyze the efficiency of an algorithm.
- A *hash table* is a data structure that is used to store objects and retrieve them efficiently. A *hash function* is used to map an object to a value that can then be used to index the object.
- Linked lists can be used to implement sets, including common operations such as union, intersection, and set membership.
- A *binary tree* is a branching linked data structure consisting of nodes that each have two link instance variables. A tree has a special node called the *root node*. Every node in the tree can be reached from the root node by following links.
- If values are stored in a binary tree in such a way that the *Binary Search Tree Storage Rule* is followed, then there are efficient algorithms for reaching values stored in the tree.

Answers to Self-Test Exercises

1. ```
   mustard 1
   hot dogs 12
   apple pie 1
   ```
2. This method has been added to the class `LinkedList1` on the accompanying website.

   ```
   public boolean isEmpty( )
   {
       return (head == null);
   }
   ```
3. This method has been added to the class `LinkedList1` on the accompanying website.

   ```
   public void clear( )
   {
       head = null;
   }
   ```

   If you defined your method to remove all nodes using the `deleteHeadNode` method, your method is doing wasted work.
4. Yes. If we make the inner class `Node` a public inner class, it could be used outside the definition of `LinkedList2`, whereas leaving it as private means it cannot be used outside the definition of `LinkedList2`.
5. It would make no difference. Within the definition of an outer class, there is full access to the members of an inner class whatever the inner class member's access modifier is. To put it another way, inside the private inner class `Node`, the modifiers `private` and `package access` are equivalent to `public`.
6. Because the outer class has direct access to the instance variables of the inner class `Node`, no access or mutator methods are needed for `Node`.
7. It would be legal, but it would be pretty much a useless method, because you cannot use the type `Node` outside of the class `LinkedList2`. For example, outside of the class `LinkedList2`, the following is illegal (`listObject` is of type `LinkedList2`),

   ```
   Node v = listObject.startNode( ); //Illegal
   ```

   whereas the following would be legal outside of the class `LinkedList2` (although it is hard to think of anyplace you might use it):

   ```
   Object v = listObject.startNode( );
   ```
8. ```
   public class LinkedList2
   {
       public class Entry
       {
         private String item;
         private int count;

         public Entry( )
   ```

```
        {
            item = null;
            count = 0;
        }

        public Entry(String itemData, int countData)
        {
            item = itemData;
            count = countData;
        }

        public void setItem(String itemData)
        {
            item = itemData;
        }

        public void setCount(int countData)
        {
            count = countData;
        }

        public String getItem( )
        {
            return item;
        }

        public int getCount( )
        {
            return count;
        }
    } // End of Entry inner class

    private class Node
    {
        private Entry item;
        private Node link;

        public Node( )
        {
              item = null;
              link = null;
        }
```

```
        public Node(Entry newItem, Node linkValue)
        {
            item = newItem;
            link = linkValue;
        }
    } //End of Node inner class

        private Node head;

        <Other definitions from LinkedList2 go here>

    } //End of LinkedList2 class
```

The rest of the definition of `LinkedList2` is essentially the same as in Display 15.7, but with the type `String` replaced by `Entry`. A complete definition is given in the subdirectory named "Exercise 8" on the website that accompanies this text.

9. No, `T` is not guaranteed to have a copy constructor. Even if `T` has a copy constructor, it is illegal to use `T` with `new` like this.
10. No, you can use any descendent class of `Object` (which means any class type) as the returned type, because the value returned will still be of type `Object`.
11. The `delete` method must now search through the list to find the previous node and then change the link to bypass the current position. This is less efficient than the code in Display 15.17 because the reference to the previous node is already set.

```
public void delete( )
{
    if (position == null)
    {
        throw new IllegalStateException( );
    }
    else
    {
        Node current = head;
        Node previous = null;
        while (current != null)
        {
          if (current == position)
          {
              // Found the node to delete
              // Check if we're at the head
              if (previous == null)
              {
                  head = head.link;
                  position = head;
              }
```

```
                else // Delete in middle of list
                {
                    previous.link = position.link;
                    position = position.link;
                }
                return;
            }
            previous = current; // Advance references
            current = current.link;
        }
    }
}
```

12. One problem with adding after the iterator's position is that there is no way to add to the front of the list. It would be possible to make a special case in which the new node were added to the front (e.g., if `position` is `null`, add the new data to the head) if desired.

```
public void addAfterHere(String newData)
{
   if (position == null && head != null)
   {
      // At end of list; can't add here
      throw new IllegalStateException( );
   }
   else if (head == null)
      // at head of empty list, add to front
      LinkedList2Iter.this.addToStart(newData);
   else
   {
      // Add after current position
      Node temp = new Node(newData, position.link);
      position.link = temp;
   }
}
```

13.
```
public void changeHere(String newData)
{
    if (position == null)
        throw new IllegalStateException( );
    else
        position.item = newData;
}
```

14. When invoking `i.next( )`, the value of the node that `i` is referencing is copied to a local variable, the iterator moves to the next node in the link, and then the value of the local variable is returned. Therefore, the value that `i` is referencing prior to the invocation is returned.

15. Insertion and deletion is slightly easier with the doubly linked list because we no longer need a separate instance variable to keep track of the previous node due to the previous link. However, all operations require updating more links (e.g., both the next and previous instead of just the previous).

16. Use the iterator:

```
DoublyLinkedList.DoublyLinkedIterator i = list.iterator( );
i.restart( );
i.insertHere("Element At Front");
```

17. Pop the top of the stack and then push it back on:

```
String s = stack.pop( );
Stack.push(s);
// s contains the string on the top of the stack
```

18.
```
public void addToBack(String itemName)
{
     Node newEntry =
           new Node(itemName, null);
     if (front == null) //empty queue
     {
          back = newEntry;
          front = back;
     }
     else
     {
          back.link = newEntry;
          back = back.link;
     }
}
```

19. Just note that $aN + b \leq (a + b)N$, as long as $1 \leq N$.

20. This is mathematics, not Java. So, = will mean *equals*, not assignment.

First note that $\log_a N = (\log_a b)(\log_b N)$.

To see this first identity, just note that if you raise a to the power $\log_a N$, you get N, and if you raise a to the power $(\log_a b)(\log_b N)$, you also get N.

If you set $c = (\log_a b)$, you get $\log_a N = c\ (\log_b N)$.

21. The simplest hash function is to map the ID number to the range of the hash table using the modulus operator:

```
hash - ID % N; // N is the hash table size
```

22.
```
public void outputHashTable( )
{
   for (int i=0; i< SIZE; i++)
   {
      if (hashArray[i].size( ) > 0)
            hashArray[i].outputList( );
   }
}
```

23. This code is similar to `intersection`, but adds elements if they are not in `otherSet`:

```
public Set<T> difference(Set<T> otherSet)
{
   Set<T> diffSet = new Set<T>( );
   // Copy only items in this set but not otherSet
   Node<T> position = head;
   while (position != null)
   {
      if (!otherSet.contains(position.data))
           diffSet.add(position.data);
      position = position.link;
   }
   return diffSet;
}
```

24. As implemented in Answer 23, the complexity is identical to the `intersection` method. For every element in the set, we invoke the `contains` method of `otherSet`. This requires $O(nm)$ steps, where n is the number of items in the calling object's set and m is the number of items in `otherSet`'s set.

25. No.

26. Change

```
showElementsInSubtree(subTreeRoot.leftLink);
System.out.print(subTreeRoot.data + " ");
showElementsInSubtree(subTreeRoot.rightLink);
```

to

```
showElementsInSubtree(subTreeRoot.rightLink);
System.out.print(subTreeRoot.data + " ");
showElementsInSubtree(subTreeRoot.leftLink);
```

Programming Projects

Visit www.myprogramminglab.com to complete select exercises online and get instant feedback.

VideoNote
Solution to Programming Project 15.1

1. In an ancient land, the beautiful princess Eve had many suitors. She decided on the following procedure to determine which suitor she would marry. First, all of the suitors would be lined up one after the other and assigned numbers. The first suitor would be number 1, the second number 2, and so on up to the last suitor, number n. Starting at the suitor in the first position, she would then count three suitors down the line

(because of the three letters in her name), and the third suitor would be eliminated from winning her hand and removed from the line. Eve would then continue, counting three more suitors, and eliminate every third suitor. When she reached the end of the line, she would continue counting from the beginning.

For example, if there were six suitors, the elimination process would proceed as follows:

123456	Initial list of suitors; start counting from 1.
12456	Suitor 3 eliminated; continue counting from 4.
1245	Suitor 6 eliminated; continue counting from 1.
125	Suitor 4 eliminated; continue counting from 5.
15	Suitor 2 eliminated; continue counting from 5.
1	Suitor 5 eliminated; 1 is the lucky winner.

Write a program that creates a circular linked list of nodes to determine which position you should stand in to marry the princess if there are *n* suitors. Your program should simulate the elimination process by deleting the node that corresponds to the suitor that is eliminated for each step in the process.

2. Although the `long` data type can store large integers, it cannot store extremely large values such as an integer with 200 digits. Create a `HugeNumber` class that uses a linked list of digits to represent integers of arbitrary length. The class should have a method to add a new most significant digit to the existing number so that longer and longer numbers can be created. Also add methods to reset the number and to return the value of the huge integer as a `String` along with appropriate constructor or accessor methods. Write code to test your class.

   Note: Use of a doubly linked list will make the next problem easier to implement.

3. Add a copy constructor to the `HugeNumber` class described in the previous problem that makes a deep copy of the input `HugeNumber`. Also create an `add` method that adds an input `HugeNumber` to the instance's `HugeNumber` value and returns a new `HugeNumber` that is set to the sum of the two values. Write code to test the additions to your class.

4. Give the definition of a generic class that uses a doubly linked list of data items. Include a copy constructor, an `equals` method, a `clone` method, a `toString` method, a method to produce an iterator, and any other methods that would normally be expected. Write a suitable test program.

5. Complete the definition of the binary search tree class `IntTree` in Display 15.39 by adding the following: Make `IntTree` implement the `Cloneable` interface, including the definition of a `clone` method; add a copy constructor; add an `equals` method; add a method named `sameContents` as described later in this project; add a `toString` method; and add a method to produce an iterator. Define `equals` so that two trees are equal if (and only if) the two trees have the exact same shape and have the same numbers in corresponding nodes. The `clone` method and the copy constructor should each produce a deep copy that is equal to the original

list according to the `equals` method. The `boolean` valued method `sameContents` has one parameter of type `IntTree` and returns `true` if the calling object and the argument tree contain exactly the same numbers, and returns `false` otherwise. Note that `equals` and `sameContents` are not the same. Also, write a suitable test program.

6. Write an `addSorted` method for the generic linked list from Display 15.8 such that the method adds a new node in the correct location so that the list remains in sorted order. Note that this will require that the type parameter `T` extend the `Comparable` interface. Write a suitable test program.

7. Add a `remove` method and an iterator for the `Set` class in Display 15.37. Write a suitable test program.

8. The hash table from Display 15.34 hashed a string to an integer and stored the same string in the hash table. Modify the program so that instead of storing strings, it stores `Employee` objects as defined in Display 7.2. Use the `name` instance variable as the input to the hash function. The modification will require changes to the linked list, because the `LinkedList2` class created only linked lists of strings. For the most generality, modify the hash table so that it uses the generic `LinkedList3` class defined in Display 15.8. You will also need to add a `get` method that returns the `Employee` object stored in the hash table that corresponds to the input name. Test your program by adding and retrieving several names, including names that hash to the same slot in the hash table.

9. Display 15.34 and 15.35 provide the beginnings of a spell-checker. Refine the program to make it more useful. The modified program should read in a text file, parse each word, see if it is in the hash table, and, if not, output the line number and word of the potentially misspelled word. Discard any punctuation in the original text file. Use the `words.txt` file as the basis for the hash table dictionary. This file can be found on the book's website. The file contains 87,314 words in the English language. Test your spell-checker on a short text document.

10. Change the `Set<T>` class of Display 15.37 so that internally it uses a hash table to store its data instead of a linked list. The headers of the public methods should remain the same so that a program such as the demonstration in Display 15.38 should still work without requiring any changes. Add a constructor that allows the user of the new `Set<T>` class to specify the size of the hash table array.

    For an additional challenge, implement the set using both a hash table and a linked list. Items added to the set should be stored using both data structures. Any operation requiring lookup of an item should use the hash table, and any operation requiring iteration through the items should use the linked list.

11. The following figure is called a *graph*. The circles are called *nodes* and the lines are called *edges*. An edge connects two nodes. You can interpret the graph as a maze of rooms and passages. The nodes can be thought of as rooms, and an edge connects one room to another. Note that each node has at most four edges in the graph that follows.

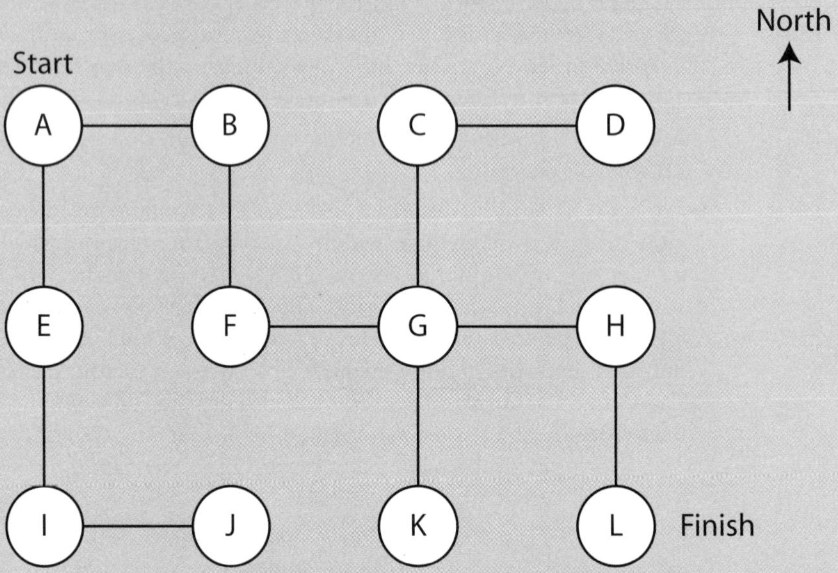

Write a program that implements the previous maze using references to instances of a `Node` class. Each node in the graph will correspond to an instance of `Node`. The edges correspond to links that connect one node to another and can be represented in `Node` as instance variables that reference another `Node` class. Start the user in node A. The user's goal is to reach the finish in node L. The program should output possible moves in the north, south, east, or west direction. Sample execution is shown next.

```
You are in room A of a maze of twisty little passages, all
alike. You can go east or south.
E
You are in room B of a maze of twisty little passages, all
alike. You can go west or south.
S
You are in room F of a maze of twisty little passages, all
alike. You can go north or east.
E
```

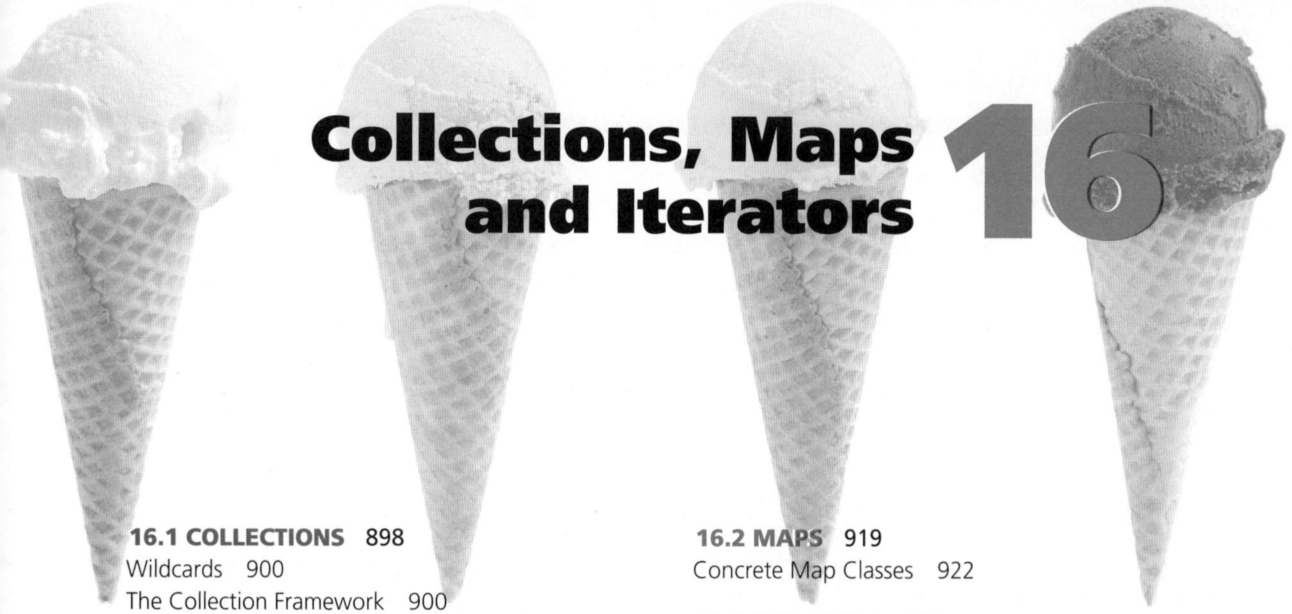

Collections, Maps and Iterators 16

16 Collections, Maps and Iterators

Science is built up with facts, as a house is with stones. But a collection of facts is no more science than a heap of stones is a house.

Jules Henri Poincarè, Quoted by Bertrand Russell in the preface to *Science and Method*

Introduction

collection

iterator

A **collection** is a data structure for holding elements. For example, an `ArrayList<T>` object is a collection. Java has a repertoire of interfaces and classes that give a uniform treatment of collections. An **iterator** is an object that cycles through all the elements in a collection. In this chapter, we discuss collections and iterators.

Prerequisites

Sections 16.1 to 16.3 can be considered one single large topic. These three sections require Chapters 1 through 9, Section 13.1 of Chapter 13, which covers interfaces, Chapter 14 on generics and the `ArrayList<T>` class, and Chapter 15 on linked data structures. The material on inner classes in Chapter 13 (Sections 13.2 and 13.3) is not needed except for a brief reference in the Programming Tip entitled "Defining Your Own Iterator Classes," which requires Section 13.2 (but not 13.3).

None of the material in this chapter is needed to understand Swing and GUIs. So, you may skip this and go directly to Chapter 17 if you prefer to cover Swing GUIs before considering the material of this chapter.

16.1 Collections

Put all your eggs in one basket and
—WATCH THAT BASKET.

MARK TWAIN, Pudd'nhead Wilson

A Java collection is a class that holds objects. This concept is made precise by the `Collection<T>` interface. A Java collection is any class that implements the `Collection<T>` interface. As we shall see, many of these classes can be used as predefined data structures similar to those we defined ourselves in Chapter 15. One example of a Java collection class, which you saw in Chapter 14, is the `ArrayList<T>` class. The `Collection<T>` interface allows you to write code that applies to all Java collections so that you do not have to rewrite the code for each specific collection type. There are other interfaces and abstract classes that are in some sense or another produced from the `Collection<T>` interface. Some of these are shown in Display 16.1. In this section, we give you an introduction to this Java collection framework. The topic is too large to treat exhaustively in this book, so this can only be an introductory treatment.

Display 16.1 The Collection Landscape

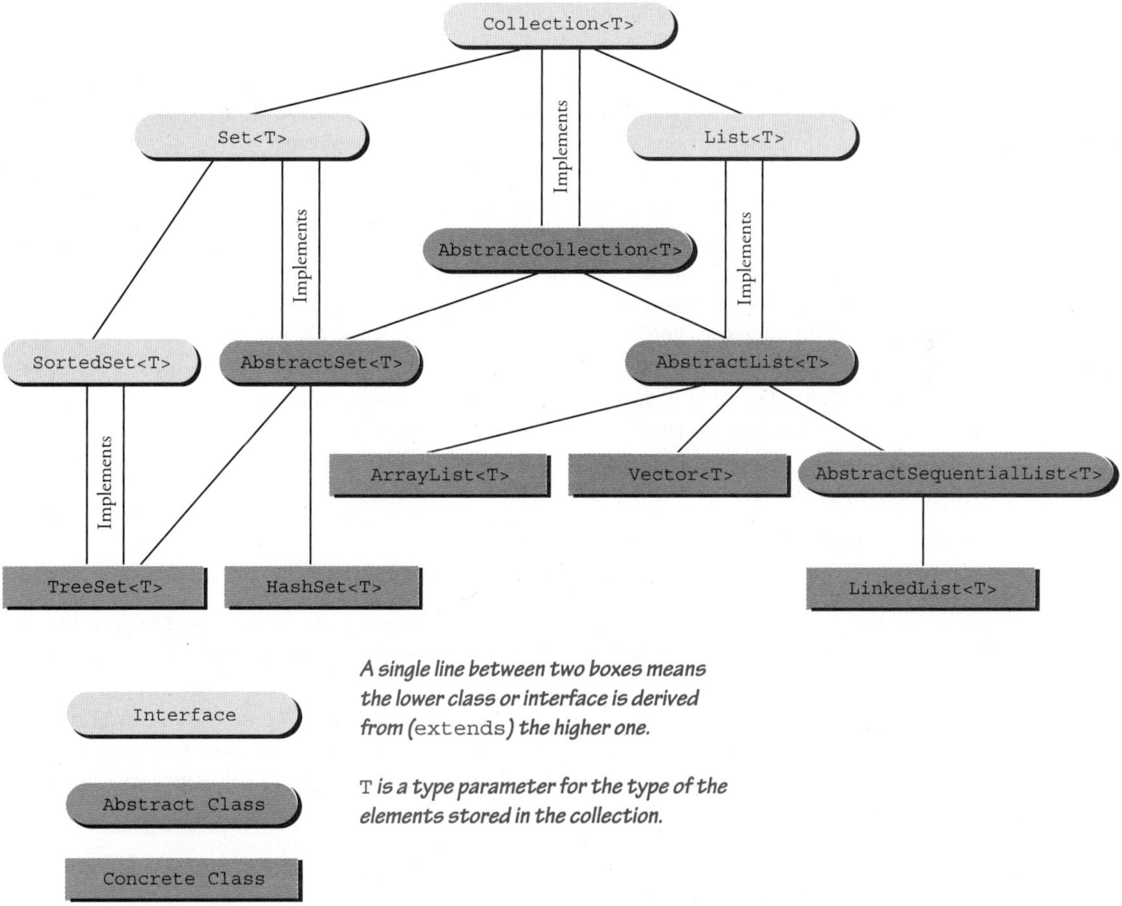

Collections are used along with *iterators*, which are discussed in Section 16.3. Separating collections and iterators into two sections turns out to be a handy way of organizing the material, but the two topics are intimately intertwined. In practice, you normally use them together.

Before we discuss the `Collection<T>` interface, we need a brief detour to learn a bit more about parameter type specifications.

Wildcards

Classes and interfaces in the collection framework use some parameter type specifications that we have not seen before. For example, they allow you to say things such as, "The argument must be a ArrayList<T> but it can have any base type." More generally these new parameter type specifications use generic classes but do not fully specify the type plugged in for the type parameter. Because they specify a wide range of argument types, they are known as **wildcards**.

wildcard<?>

The easiest wildcard to understand is <?>, which says that you can use any type in place of the type parameter. For example,

```
public void sampleMethod(String arg1, ArrayList<?> arg2)
```

is invoked with two arguments. The first argument must be of type String. The second argument can be a ArrayList<T> with any base type.

Note that ArrayList<?> is different from ArrayList<Object>. For example, if the type specification is ArrayList<?>, then you can plug in an argument of type ArrayList<String> (as well as other types); you cannot plug in an argument of type ArrayList<String> if the type specification is ArrayList<Object>.

extends

You can place a bound on a wildcard saying the type used in place of the wildcard must be an ancestor type or a descendent type of some class or interface. For example, <? extends String> says that the argument plugged in can be an object of any descendent class of the class String. The notation, restrictions, and meaning are the same as what we described for type bounds such as <T extends String>, which we discussed in Chapter 14.

For example,

```
public void
     anotherMethod(String arg1, ArrayList<? extends String> arg2)
```

is invoked with two arguments. The first argument must be of type String, but the second argument can be of any ArrayList<T> object provided the base type of the ArrayList<T> is a descendent type of String.

super

To specify that the wildcard type be an ancestor type of some class or interface, use super rather than extends. For example, ArrayList<? super String> specifies an ArrayList<T> whose base type can be any ancestor class of the class String. As it turns out, we will have no occasion to use wildcard types involving super.

The Collection Framework

Collection<T> interface

The Collection<T> interface is the highest level of Java's framework for collection classes. This interface describes the basic operations that all collection classes should implement. A summary of these operations (method headings) for the Collection<T> interface are given in Display 16.2. A more complete description can be found in Appendix 5. Because an interface is a type, you can define methods with a parameter of type Collection<T>. That parameter can be filled in with an argument that is an object of any class in the collection framework (that is, any class that implements the

Collection<T> interface). This turns out to be a very powerful tool. Let us explore the possibilities. So far, we have seen one class that implements the Collection<T> interface, namely the class ArrayList<T>. In addition to the methods given in Chapter 14 for the ArrayList<T> class, the ArrayList<T> class also implements all the methods given in Display 16.2. There are a number of different predefined classes that implement the Collection<T> interface, and you can define your own classes to do this. If you write a method to manipulate a parameter of type Collection<T>, it will work for all of these classes. Also, the methods in the Collection<T> interface ensure that you can intermix the use of different collection classes. For example, consider the method

```
public boolean containsAll(Collection<?> collectionOfTargets)
```

You can use this with two ArrayList<T> objects (the calling object and the argument) to see if one contains all the elements of the other. The two ArrayList<T> objects do not even have to have the same base type. Moreover, you can also use it with an ArrayList<T> object and an object of any other class that implements the Collection<T> interface to compare the elements in these two different kinds of Collection<T> objects.

Display 16.2 **Method Headings in the Collection<T> Interface** (part 1 of 3)

The Collection<T> interface is in the java.util package.

CONSTRUCTORS

Although not officially required by the interface, any class that implements the Collection<T> interface should have at least two constructors: a no-argument constructor that creates an empty Collection<T> object, and a constructor with one parameter of type Collection<? extends T> that creates a Collection<T> object with the same elements as the constructor argument. The interface does not specify whether the copy produced by the one-argument constructor is a shallow copy or a deep copy of its argument.

METHODS

```
boolean isEmpty()
```

Returns true if the calling object is empty; otherwise returns false.

```
public boolean contains(Object target)
```

Returns true if the calling object contains at least one instance of target. Uses target.equals to determine if target is in the calling object.

```
public boolean containsAll(Collection<?> collectionOfTargets)
```

Returns true if the calling object contains all of the elements in collectionOfTargets. For an element in collectionOfTargets, this method uses element.equals to determine if element is in the calling object.

(continued)

Display 16.2 **Method Headings in the `Collection<T>` Interface** (part 2 of 3)

```
public boolean equals(Object other)
```

This is the `equals` of the collection, not the `equals` of the elements in the collection. Overrides the inherited method `equals`. Although there are no official constraints on `equals` for a collection, it should be defined as we have described in Chapter 7 and also to satisfy the intuitive notion of collections being equal.

```
public int size()
```

Returns the number of elements in the calling object. If the calling object contains more than `Integer.MAX_VALUE` elements, returns `Integer.MAX_VALUE`.

```
Iterator<T> iterator()
```

Returns an iterator for the calling object. (Iterators are discussed in Section 16.3.)

```
public Object[ ] toArray()
```

Returns an array containing all of the elements in the calling object. If the calling object makes any guarantees as to what order its elements are returned by its iterator, this method must return the elements in the same order.

The array returned should be a new array so that the calling object has no references to the returned array. (You might also want the elements in the array to be clones of the elements in the collection. However, this is apparently not required by the interface, because library classes, such as `Vector<T>`, return arrays that contain references to the elements in the collection.)

```
public <E> E[ ] toArray(E[ ] a)
```

Note that the type parameter `E` is not the same as `T`. So, `E` can be any reference type; it need not be the type `T` in `Collection<T>`. For example, `E` might be an ancestor type of `T`.

Returns an array containing all of the elements in the calling object. The argument `a` is used primarily to specify the type of the array returned. The exact details are described next.

The type of the returned array is that of `a`. If the elements in the calling object fit in the array `a`, then `a` is used to hold the elements of the returned array; otherwise a new array is created with the same type as `a`.

If `a` has more elements than the calling object, the element in `a` immediately following the end of the copied elements is set to `null`.

If the calling object makes any guarantees as to what order its elements are returned by its iterator, this method must return the elements in the same order. (Iterators are discussed in Section 16.3.)

```
public int hashCode()
```

Returns the hash code value for the calling object. The hash code is a numeric key that is ideally a unique identifier for the calling object. (Hash codes are discussed in Section 15.5.)

Display 16.2 Method Headings in the `Collection<T>` Interface (part 3 of 3)

OPTIONAL METHODS

The following methods are optional, which means they still must be implemented, but the implementation can simply throw an `UnsupportedOperationException` if, for some reason, you do not want to give them a "real" implementation. An `UnsupportedOperationException` is a `RunTimeException` and so is not required to be caught or declared in a `throws` clause.

```
public boolean add(T element) (Optional)
```

Ensures that the calling object contains the specified `element`. Returns `true` if the calling object changes as a result of the call. Returns `false` if the calling object does not permit duplicates and already contains `element`; also returns `false` if the calling object does not change for any other reason.

```
public boolean addAll(Collection<? extends T> collectionToAdd) (Optional)
```

Ensures that the calling object contains all the elements in `collectionToAdd`. Returns `true` if the calling object changes as a result of the call; returns `false` otherwise.

```
public boolean remove(Object element) (Optional)
```

Removes a single instance of the element from the calling object, if it is present. Returns `true` if the calling object contained the element; returns `false` otherwise.

```
public boolean removeAll(Collection<?> collectionToRemove) (Optional)
```

Removes all the calling object's elements that are also contained in `collectionToRemove`. Returns `true` if the calling object is changed; otherwise returns `false`.

```
public void clear() (Optional)
```

Removes all the elements from the calling object.

```
public boolean retainAll(Collection<?> saveElements) (Optional)
```

Retains only the elements in the calling object that are also contained in the collection `saveElements`. In other words, removes from the calling object all of its elements that are not contained in the collection `saveElements`. Returns `true` if the calling object is changed; otherwise returns `false`.

Packages

All the collection classes and interfaces discussed in this chapter are in the `java.util` package.

`Set<T>` and `List<T>` interfaces

The relationships between some of the classes and interfaces that implement or extend the `Collection<T>` interface are given in Display 16.1. There are two main interfaces that extend the `Collection<T>` interface: the `Set<T>` interface and the `List<T>` interface. Classes that implement the `Set<T>` interface do not allow an element in the class to occur more than once. Classes that implement the List<T> interface have their elements ordered on a list, so there is a zeroth element, a first element, a second element, and so forth. A class that implements the List<T> interface allows elements to occur more than once. The ArrayList<T> class implements the List<T> interface.

The Set<T> interface has the same method headings as the Collection<T> interface, but in some cases the semantics (intended meanings) are different. For example, the semantics of adding new elements to the set do not allow duplicates. The add methods are described in Display 16.3. A complete list of the Set<T> interface is given in Appendix 5.

Display 16.3 Adding Elements in the Set<T> Interface

The Set<T> interface is in the java.util package.

The Set<T> interface extends the Collection<T> interface and has all the same method headings given in Display 16.2. However, the semantics of the add methods vary as described below.

public boolean add(T element) *(Optional)*

If element is not already in the calling object, element is added to the calling object and true is returned. If element is in the calling object, the calling object is unchanged and false is returned.

public boolean addAll(Collection<? extends > collectionToAdd) *(Optional)*

Ensures that the calling object contains all the elements in collectionToAdd. Returns true if the calling object changed as a result of the call; returns false otherwise. Thus, if collectionToAdd is a Set<T>, then the calling object is changed to the union of itself with collectionToAdd.

The List<T> interface has more method headings than the Collection<T> interface, and some of the methods inherited from the Collection<T> interface receive somewhat different semantics. For example, the semantics of adding new elements to the set allow duplicates, and rules must be made about which element should be removed when there are duplicates. These methods, along with new method definitions, are described in Display 16.4. A complete list of the List<T> interface is given in Appendix 5.

Display 16.4 Selected Methods in the List<T> Interface (part 1 of 3)

The List<T> interface is in the java.util package.

The List<T> interface extends the Collection<T> interface.

ADDING AND REMOVING ELEMENTS

public boolean add(T element) *(Optional)*

Adds element to the end of the calling object's list. Normally returns true. Returns false if the operation failed, but if the operation failed, something is seriously wrong and you will probably get a run-time error anyway.

Display 16.4 **Selected Methods in the List<T> Interface** (part 2 of 3)

```
public boolean addAll(Collection<? extends T> collectionToAdd) (Optional)
```

Adds all of the elements in collectionToAdd to the end of the calling object's list. The elements are added in the order they are produced by an iterator for collectionToAdd.

```
public boolean remove(Object element) (Optional)
```

Removes the first occurrence of element from the calling object's list, if it is present. Returns true if the calling object contained the element; returns false otherwise.

```
public boolean removeAll(Collection<?> collectionToRemove) (Optional)
```

Removes all the calling object's elements that are also in collectionToRemove. Returns true if the calling object was changed; otherwise returns false.

NEW METHOD HEADINGS

The following methods are in the List<T> interface but were not in the Collection<T> interface. Those that are optional are noted.

```
public void add(int index, T newElement) (Optional)
```

Inserts newElement in the calling object's list at location index. The old elements at location index and higher are moved to higher indices.

```
public boolean addAll(int index,
                      Collection<? extends T> collectionToAdd) (Optional)
```

Inserts all of the elements in collectionToAdd to the calling object's list starting at location index. The old elements at location index and higher are moved to higher indices. The elements are added in the order they are produced by an iterator for collectionToAdd.

```
public T get(int index)
```

Returns the object at position index.

```
public T set(int index, T newElement) (Optional)
```

Sets the element at the specified index to newElement. The element previously at that position is returned.

```
public T remove(int index) (Optional)
```

Removes the element at position index in the calling object. Shifts any subsequent elements to the left (subtracts one from their indices). Returns the element that was removed from the calling object.

```
public int indexOf(Object target)
```

Returns the index of the first element that is equal to target. Uses the method equals of the object target to test for equality. Returns 1 if target is not found.

(continued)

Display 16.4 **Selected Methods in the List<T> Interface** (part 3 of 3)

```
public int lastIndexOf(Object target)
```

Returns the index of the last element that is equal to target. Uses the method equals of the object target to test for equality. Returns 1 if target is not found.

```
public List<T> subList(int fromIndex, int toIndex)
```

Returns a *view* of the elements at locations fromIndex to toIndex of the calling object; the object at fromIndex is included; the object, if any, at toIndex is not included. The *view* uses references into the calling object; so, changing the view can change the calling object. The returned object will be of type List<T> but need not be of the same type as the calling object. Returns an empty List<T> if fromIndex equals toIndex.

```
ListIterator<T> listIterator()
```

Returns a list iterator for the calling object. (Iterators are discussed in Section 16.3.)

```
ListIterator<T> listIterator(int index)
```

Returns a list iterator for the calling object starting at index. The first element to be returned by the iterator is the one at index. (Iterators are discussed in Section 16.3.)

Collection Interfaces

The primary interfaces for collection classes are the Collection<T>, Set<T>, and List<T> interfaces. Both the Set<T> and the List<T> interfaces are derived from the Collection<T> interface. The Set<T> interface is for collections that do not allow repetition of elements and do not impose an order on their elements. The List<T> interface is for collections that do allow repetition of elements and do impose an order on their elements.

For-Each Loops

You can use a for-each loop with any of the collections discussed in this chapter.

PITFALL: Optional Operations

What is the point of an optional method heading in an interface? The whole purpose of an interface is to specify what methods can be used with an object of the interface type so that you can write code for an arbitrary object of the interface type. The reasoning behind these optional methods is that they normally would be implemented, but in unusual situations a programmer may leave them "unsupported." (The alternative would be to have two interfaces, one with and one without the optional operations. Uncharacteristically, Java designers opted for a smaller number of interfaces.) But there is still more to the story.

PITFALL: (continued)

The optional methods are not, strictly speaking, optional. Like the other methods in an interface, the optional methods must have a method body so that the optional method heading is converted to a complete method definition. So, what is optional? The "optional" refers to the semantics of the method. If the method is optional, then you may give it a trivial implementation and you will not have shirked your responsibility to follow the (unenforced) semantics for the interface.

To keep these optional methods from producing unexplained failures, the interface semantics say that if you do not give an optional method a "real" implementation, then you should have the method body throw an `UnsupportedOperationException`. For example, the `add` method of the `Collection<T>` interface is optional and so can be implemented as follows (provided you have good reason for this):

```
public boolean add(T element)
{
    throw new UnsupportedOperationException();
}
```

The `UnsupportedOperationException` class is a derived class of the `RunTimeException` class, so an `UnsupportedOperationException` is an unchecked exception, meaning it need not be caught in a `catch` block or declared in a `throws` clause.

The intention is that the code for a class that implements an interface with optional methods would be written and used in such a way that this `UnsupportedOperation Exception` would only be thrown during debugging. These rules on optional methods are part of the semantics of the interface, and like all other parts of the semantics of an interface, they depend entirely on the good will and responsibility of the programmer defining the class that implements the interface. ■

Optional Methods

When an interface lists a method as "optional," you still need to implement it when defining a class that implements the interface. However, if you do not want to give it a "real" definition, you can simply have the method body throw an `UnsupportedOperationException`.

TIP: Dealing with All Those Exceptions

If you examine the `Collection<T>`, `Set<T>`, and `List<T>` interfaces in Appendix 5, you will see that many of the methods are liberally sprinkled with statements that certain exceptions are thrown. All these exception classes are unchecked exceptions, meaning that they need not be caught in a `catch` block and need not be declared in a `throws` clause. They are there primarily for debugging. If you are using an existing

(continued)

TIP: (continued)

collection class, you can view them as run-time error messages. If you are defining a class as a derived class of some other collection class, then most or all of the exception throwing will be inherited, so you need not worry too much about it. If you are defining a collection class from scratch and want your class to implement one of the collection interfaces, then you do need to throw suitable exceptions as specified for the interface.

With one exception (no pun intended), all the exception classes mentioned in this chapter are in the package `java.lang` and so do not require any import statement. The one exception is the `NoSuchElementException`, which is used with iterators in Section 16.3. The `NoSuchElementException` is in the `java.util` package, which requires an import statement if your code mentions the `NoSuchElementException` class. ■

MyProgrammingLab™

Self-Test Exercises

1. Give the definition of a `boolean` valued static generic method named `inSome`. The method `inSome` has two parameters of type `Collection<T>` and one parameter of type `T`. The method returns `true` if the parameter of type `T` is in either (or both) collections; it returns `false` otherwise.

2. Give the definition of a static generic method named `getFirst` that has one parameter of type `List<T>` and a return type of `T`. The method returns the first element in the list or `null` if the list is empty.

3. Give the definition of a static `boolean` valued method named `noNull`. The method `noNull` has one parameter of type `Set<?>` and removes `null` from the set if `null` is in the set; otherwise it leaves the set unchanged. The method returns `true` if the set is changed and `false` if it is not changed.

Concrete Collection Classes

`Abstract Set<T>`

`Abstract List<T>`

The abstract classes `AbstractSet<T>` and `AbstractList<T>` are there for convenience when implementing the `Set<T>` and `List<T>` interfaces, respectively. They have almost no methods beyond those in the interfaces they implement. Although these two abstract classes have only a few abstract methods, the other (nonabstract) methods have fairly useless implementations that must be overridden. When defining a derived class of either `AbstractSet<T>` or `AbstractList<T>`, you need to define not just the abstract methods but also all the methods you intend to use. It usually makes more sense to simply use (or define derived classes of) the `HashSet<T>`, `ArrayList<T>`, or `Vector<T>` classes, which are derived classes of `AbstractSet<T>` and `AbstractList<T>` and are full implementations of the `Set<T>` and `List<T>` interfaces.

Abstract Collection<T>

The abstract class AbstractCollection<T> is a skeleton class for the Collection<T> interface. Although it is perfectly legal, you seldom, if ever, need to define a derived class of the AbstractCollection<T> class. Instead, you normally define a derived class of one of the descendent classes of the AbstractCollection<T> class.

HashSet<T>

If you want a class that implements the Set<T> interface and do not need any methods beyond those in the Set<T> interface, you can use the concrete class HashSet<T>. So, after all is said and done, if all you need is a collection class that does not allow elements to occur more than once, then you can use the HashSet<T> class and need not worry about all the other classes and interfaces in Display 16.1. The word *Hash* refers to the fact that the HashSet<T> class is implemented using a hash table, which was introduced in Section 15.5. The HashSet<T>, of course, implements all the methods in the Set<T> interface and adds no other methods beyond constructors. A summary of the HashSet<T> constructors and other methods is given in Display 16.5. If you want to define your own class that implements the Set<T> interface, you are probably better off using the HashSet<T> class rather than the AbstractSet<T> class as a base class.

Display 16.5 Methods in the HashSet<T> Class

The HashSet<T> class is in the java.util package.

The HashSet<T> class extends the AbstractSet<T> class and implements the Set<T> interface.

The HashSet<T> class implements all of the methods in the Set<T> interface (Display 16.3). The only other methods in the HashSet<T> class are the constructors. The three constructors that do not involve concepts beyond the scope of this book are given next.

All the exception classes mentioned are the kind that are not required to be caught in a catch block or declared in a throws clause.

All the exception classes mentioned are in the package java.lang and so do not require any import statement.

```
public HashSet()
```

Creates a new, empty set.

```
public HashSet(Collection<? extends T> c)
```

Creates a new set that contains all the elements of c. Throws a NullPointerException if c is null.

```
public HashSet(int initialCapacity)
```

Creates a new, empty set with the specified capacity.

Throws an IllegalArgumentException if initialCapacity is less than zero.

The methods are the same as those described for the Set<T> interface (Display 16.3).

It is important to note that if you intend to use the HashSet<T> class with your own class as the parameterized type T, then your class must override the following methods:

```
public int hashCode();
public boolean equals(Object obj);
```

The hashCode() method should return a numeric key that is ideally a unique identifier for an object in your class. See Section 15.5 for a discussion about hash codes. It is always a good idea to override the equals() method for any class you write, but you must override it in this scenario. Java will use the hash code to index the object and then use the equals() method to check if an object exists in the set. If the hash code for two different objects is identical, the objects will still be indexed correctly as long as equals() indicates they are unique. However, the identical hash codes will cause a collision that will decrease performance.

Display 16.6 shows a sample program that uses the HashSet<T> class. This program is conceptually similar to the program in Display 15.38, in which sets containing strings of round things and green things were manipulated in various

Display 16.6 **HashSet<T>** Class Demo (part 1 of 3)

```
import java.util.HashSet;
import java.util.Iterator;
public class HashSetDemo
{
    private static void outputSet(HashSet<String> set)
    {
        Iterator<String> i = set.iterator();
        while (i.hasNext())
            System.out.print(i.next() + " ");
        System.out.println();
    }

    public static void main(String[] args)
    {
        HashSet<String> round = new HashSet<String>();
        HashSet<String> green = new HashSet<String>();

        // Add some data to each set
        round.add("peas");
        round.add("ball");
        round.add("pie");
        round.add("grapes");

        green.add("peas");
        green.add("grapes");
        green.add("garden hose");
        green.add("grass");
```

*The **outputSet** method uses an iterator to print the contents of a **HashSet<T>** object. Iterators are described in Section 16.3.*

Display 16.6 **HashSet<T>** Class Demo (part 2 of 3)

```
            System.out.println("Contents of set round: ");
            outputSet(round);
            System.out.println("\nContents of set green: ");
            outputSet(green);

            System.out.println("\nball in set 'round'? " +
                  round.contains("ball"));
            System.out.println("ball in set 'green'? " +
                  green.contains("ball"));

            System.out.println("\nball and peas in same set? "+
                  ((round.contains("ball") &&
                   (round.contains("peas"))) ||
                  (green.contains("ball") &&
                   (green.contains("peas”)))));
            System.out.println("pie and grass in same set? "+
                  ((round.contains("pie") &&
                   (round.contains("grass"))) ||
                  (green.contains("pie") &&
                   (green.contains("grass")))));

            // To union two sets we use the addAll method.
            HashSet<String>setUnion = new HashSet<String>(round);
            round.addAll(green);
            System.out.println("\nUnion of green and round:");
            outputSet(setUnion);

            // To intersect two sets we use the removeAll method.
            HashSet<String> setInter = new HashSet<String>(round);
            setInter.removeAll(green);
            System.out.println("\nIntersection of green and round:");
            outputSet(setInter);
            System.out.println();
      }
}
```

Sample Dialogue

```
Contents of set round:
grapes pie ball peas

Contents of set green:
grass garden hose grapes peas
```

(continued)

Display 16.6 **`HashSet<T>`** Class Demo (part 3 of 3)

```
ball in set round? true
ball in set green? false

ball and peas in same set? True
pie and grass in same set? false

Union of green and round:
garden hose grass peas ball pie grapes

Intersection of green and round:
peas grapes
```

ways using our own `Set<T>` class implemented with linked lists. However, the code listing in Display 16.6 uses the `HashSet<T>` class in place of our custom `Set<T>` class. Nevertheless, most of the code is identical because the `Set<T>` class was designed to have an interface similar to the `HashSet<T>` class. Both have `add` and `contains` methods. Functionality similar to our `union` and `intersection` methods can be achieved by using the `HashSet<T>` `addAll` and `removeAll` methods. To output the items in a `HashSet<T>` object, we define an `outputSet` method. This method uses iterators, which are not discussed until Section 16.3, so for now you can ignore the details of how `outputSet` works.

In general, it is recommended that you use the collection classes unless they do not provide the functionality you need for your program. For example, say that you want every item added to the set to have a reference to the set that contains it. This could be useful if you want to determine whether two items are in the same set—you could just follow the reference to the containing set for each item and see whether they are the same. Without such a reference, you would have to invoke the `contains` method for every set to learn whether the items are in the same set. If this were an important feature for your program, you might want to develop your own class instead of using one of the collection classes. If the collection classes were sufficient, the result would be shorter code that is generally easier to develop and maintain. Moreover, the collection classes such as `HashSet<T>` have been designed with efficiency and scalability in mind.

`Vector<T>`

If you want a class that implements the `List<T>` interface and do not need any methods beyond those in this interface, you can use the `ArrayList<T>` or `Vector<T>` class. So, after all is said and done, if all you need is a collection class that allows elements to occur more than once, or you need a collection that orders its elements as on a list (that is, as in an array), or you need a class that has both of these properties, then you can use the `ArrayList<T>` or `Vector<T>` class and need not worry about all the other classes and interfaces in Display 16.1. The `ArrayList<T>` and `Vector<T>` classes implement all the methods in the `List<T>` interface. A table of methods for the `ArrayList<T>` class was given in Chapter 14 and a more complete table is given in

Display 16.7. A table of methods for the Vector<T> class is also given in Display 16.7. A more complete list of the methods in these classes is given in Appendix 5. If you want to define your own class that implements the List<T> interface, you would probably be better off using either the ArrayList<T> or the Vector<T> class rather than the AbstractList<T> class as a base class.

AbstractSequentialList<T>

The abstract class AbstractSequentialList<T> is derived from the AbstractList<T> class. Although it does override some methods inherited from the class AbstractList<T>, it adds no completely new methods. The point of the AbstractSequentialList<T> class is to provide for efficient implementation of sequentially moving through the list at the expense of having inefficient implementation of random access to elements (that is, inefficient implementation of the get method). The LinkedList<T> class is a concrete derived class of the abstract class AbstractSequentialList<T>. (The implementation of the LinkedList<T> class is similar to that of the linked list classes we discussed in Chapter 15.) If you need a List<T> with efficient random access to elements (that is, efficient implementation of

LinkedList<T>

Display 16.7 Methods in the Classes **ArrayList<T>** and **Vector<T>** (part 1 of 4)

The ArrayList<T> and Vector<T> classes and the Iterator<T> and ListIterator<T> interfaces are in the java.util package.

All the exception classes mentioned are unchecked exceptions, which means they are not required to be caught in a catch block or declared in a throws clause. (If you have not yet studied exceptions, you can consider the exceptions to be run-time error messages.)

NoSuchElementException is in the java.util package, which requires an import statement if your code mentions the NoSuchElementException class. All the other exception classes mentioned are in the package java.lang and so do not require any import statement.

CONSTRUCTORS

```
public ArrayList(int initialCapacity)
```

Creates an empty ArrayList<T> with the specified initial capacity. When the ArrayList<T> needs to increase its capacity, the capacity doubles.

```
public ArrayList()
```

Creates an empty ArrayList<T> with an initial capacity of 10. When the ArrayList<T> needs to increase its capacity, the capacity doubles.

```
public ArrayList(Collection<? extends T> c)
```

Creates an ArrayList<T> that contains all the elements of the collection c, in the same order. In other words, the elements have the same index in the ArrayList<T> created as they do in c. This is not quite a true copy constructor because it does not preserve capacity. The capacity of the created list will be c.size(), not c.capacity.

The ArrayList<T> created is only a shallow copy of the collection argument. The ArrayList<T> created contains references to the elements in c (not references to clones of the elements in c).

```
public Vector(int initialCapacity)
```

Creates an empty vector with the specified initial capacity. When the vector needs to increase its capacity, the capacity doubles.

(continued)

Display 16.7 **Methods in the Classes ArrayList<T> and Vector<T>** (part 2 of 4)

```
public Vector()
```

Creates an empty vector with an initial capacity of 10. When the vector needs to increase its capacity, the capacity doubles.

```
public Vector(Collection<? extends T> c)
```

Creates a vector that contains all the elements of the collection c, in the same order. In other words, the elements have the same index in the vector created as they do in c. This is not quite a true copy constructor because it does not preserve capacity. The capacity of the created vector will be c.size(), not c.capacity.

The vector created is only a shallow copy of the collection argument. The vector created contains references to the elements in c (not references to clones of the elements in c).

```
public Vector(int initialCapacity, int capacityIncrement)
```

Constructs an empty vector with the specified initial capacity and capacity increment. When the vector needs to grow, it will add room for capacityIncrement more items.

(ArrayList<T> does not have a corresponding constructor.)

ARRAYLIKE METHODS FOR BOTH ArrayList<T> AND Vector<T>

```
public T set(int index, T newElement)
```

Sets the element at the specified index to newElement. The element previously at that position is returned. If you draw an analogy to an array a, this is analogous to setting a[index] to the value newElement. The index must be a value greater than or equal to zero and strictly less than the current size of the list.

```
public T get(int index)
```

Returns the element at the specified index. This is analogous to returning a[index] for an array a. The index must be a value greater than or equal to 0 and less than the current size of the calling object.

METHODS TO ADD ELEMENTS FOR BOTH ArrayList<T> AND Vector<T>

```
public boolean add(T newElement)
```

Adds newElement to the end of the calling object's list and increases its size by one. The capacity of the calling object is increased if that is required. Returns true if the add was successful. This method is often used as if it were a void method.

```
public void add(int index, T newElement)
```

Inserts newElement as an element in the calling object at the specified index and increases the size of the calling object by one. Each element in the calling object with an index greater than or equal to index is shifted upward to have an index that is one greater than the value it had previously.

The index must be a value greater than or equal to zero and less than or equal to the size of the calling object (before this addition).

Note that you can use this method to add an element after the last current element. The capacity of the calling object is increased if that is required.

Display 16.7 Methods in the Classes ArrayList<T> and Vector<T> (part 3 of 4)

```
public boolean addAll(Collection<? extends T> c)
```

Appends all the elements in c to the end of the elements in the calling object in the order that they are enumerated by a c iterator. The behavior of this method is not guaranteed if the collection c is the calling object or any collection including the calling object either directly or indirectly.

```
public boolean addAll(int index, Collection<? extends T> c)
```

Inserts all the elements in c into the calling object starting at position index. Elements are inserted in the order that they are enumerated by a c iterator. Elements previously at positions index or higher are shifted to higher numbered positions.

METHODS TO REMOVE ELEMENTS FOR BOTH ArrayList<T> AND Vector<T>

```
public T remove(int index)
```

Deletes the element at the specified index and returns the element deleted. The size of the calling object is decreased by one. The capacity of the calling object is not changed. Each element in the calling object with an index greater than or equal to index is decreased to have an index that is one less than the value it had previously.

The index must be a value greater than or equal to zero and less than the size of the calling object (before this removal).

```
public boolean remove(Object theElement)
```

Removes the first occurrence of theElement from the calling object. If theElement is found in the calling object, then each element in the calling object with an index greater than or equal to theElement's index is decreased to have an index that is one less than the value it had previously. Returns true if theElement was found (and removed). Returns false if theElement is not found in the calling object. If the element was removed, the size is decreased by one. The capacity is not changed.

```
protected void removeRange(int fromIndex, int toIndex)
```

Removes all elements with index greater than or equal to fromIndex and strictly less than toIndex. Be sure to note that this method is protected, not public.

```
public void clear()
```

Removes all elements from the calling object and sets its size to zero.

SEARCH METHODS FOR BOTH ArrayList<T> AND Vector<T>

```
public boolean isEmpty()
```

Returns true if the calling object is empty (that is, has size 0); otherwise returns false.

```
public boolean contains(Object target)
```

Returns true if target is an element of the calling object; otherwise returns false. Uses the method equals of the object target to test for equality.

```
public int indexOf(Object target)
```

Returns the index of the first element that is equal to target. Uses the method equals of the object target to test for equality. Returns 1 if target is not found.

```
public int lastIndexOf(Object target)
```

Returns the index of the last element that is equal to target. Uses the method equals of the object target to test for equality. Returns 1 if target is not found.

(continued)

Display 16.7 Methods in the Classes `ArrayList<T>` and `Vector<T>` (part 4 of 4)

ITERATORS FOR BOTH `ArrayList<T>` AND `Vector<T>`

```
public Iterator<T> iterator()
```

Returns an iterator for the calling object. Iterators are discussed in Section 16.3.

```
public ListIterator<T> listIterator()
```

Returns a `ListIterator<T>` for the calling object. `ListIterator<T>` is discussed in Section 16.3.

```
ListIterator<T> listIterator(int index)
```

Returns a list iterator for the calling object starting at `index`. The first element to be returned by the iterator is the one at `index`. (Iterators are discussed in Section 16.3.)

CONVERTING TO AN ARRAY FOR BOTH `ArrayList<T>` AND `Vector<T>`

```
public Object[ ] toArray()
```

Returns an array containing all of the elements in the calling object. The elements of the array are indexed the same as in the calling object.

```
public <E> E[ ] toArray(E[ ] a)
```

Note that the type parameter `E` is not the same as `T`. So, `E` can be any reference type; it need not be the type `T` in `Collection<T>`. For example, `E` might be an ancestor type of `T`.

Returns an array containing all of the elements in the calling object. The elements of the array are indexed the same as in the calling object.

The argument `a` is used primarily to specify the type of the array returned. The exact details are described next.

The type of the returned array is that of `a`. If the collection fits in the array `a`, then `a` is used to hold the elements of the returned array; otherwise a new array is created with the same type as `a`.

If `a` has more elements than the calling object, then the element in `a` immediately following the end of the elements copied from the calling object is set to `null`.

MEMORY MANAGEMENT FOR BOTH `ArrayList<T>` AND `Vector<T>`

```
public int size()
```

Returns the number of elements in the calling object.

```
public int capacity()
```

Returns the current capacity of the calling object.

```
public void ensureCapacity(int newCapacity)
```

Increases the capacity of the calling object to ensure that it can hold at least `newCapacity` elements. Using `ensureCapacity` can sometimes increase efficiency, but it is not needed for any other reason.

```
public void trimToSize()
```

Trims the capacity of the calling object to be the calling object's current size. This is used to save storage.

MAKE A COPY FOR BOTH `ArrayList<T>` AND `Vector<T>`

```
public Object clone()
```

Returns a shallow copy of the calling object.

the `get` method), then use the `ArrayList<T>` or `Vector<T>` class or a class derived from one of these two classes. If you do not need efficient random access but need to efficiently move sequentially through the list, then use the `LinkedList<T>` class or a class derived from the `LinkedList<T>` class.

SortedSet<T>

TreeSet<T>

The interface `SortedSet<T>` and the concrete class `TreeSet<T>` are designed for implementations of the `Set<T>` interface that provide for rapid retrieval of elements (efficient implementation of the `contains` and similar methods). The implementation of the class is similar to the binary tree class discussed in Chapter 15 but with more sophisticated ways to do inserting that keep the tree balanced. We will not discuss the `SortedSet<T>` interface or the `TreeSet<T>` class in this text, but you should be aware of their existence so you know what to look for in the Java documentation should you need them.

MyProgrammingLab™

Self-Test Exercises

4. Can an object that instantiates the `HashSet<T>` class contain multiple copies of some element?

5. Suppose you want to define a class that orders its elements like a `List<T>` but does not allow multiple occurrences of an element like a `Set<T>`. Would it be better to make it a derived class of the `ArrayList<T>` class or a derived class of the `HashSet<T>` class?

6. You would like to use the following class as the type in a `HashSet<T>` collection. What is missing and how would you fix it?

```
public class Customer
{
    private String name;
    private String address;
    public Customer(String newName, String newAddress)
    {
        name = newName;
        address = newAddress;
    }
    public String toString()
    {
        return name + " : " + address;
    }
}
```

Differences between ArrayList<T> and Vector<T>

For most purposes, ArrayList<T> and Vector<T> are equivalent. There are only minor differences between the classes. The methods that are in both classes are given in Display 16.7. The class Vector<T> has more methods than ArrayList<T> does; these methods are not given in Display 16.7. However, most of the extra methods are little more than alternate names for methods that are in both ArrayList<T> and Vector<T>. None of the methods in Vector<T> do anything that cannot easily be done with an ArrayList<T>. The class ArrayList<T> is reputed to be more efficient than Vector<T>. The biggest difference between these two classes is that ArrayList<T> is newer than Vector<T> and was created as part of the Java collection framework, whereas Vector<T> is an older class that was retrofitted with extra method names to make it fit into the collection framework. You are encouraged to use ArrayList<T> rather than Vector<T>. However, a lot of existing code uses Vector<T>, so you should be familiar with it.[1]

Nonparameterized Version of the Collection Framework ★

Before version 5.0, Java did not have type parameters. So, the collection framework consisted of ordinary classes and interfaces, such as Collection, List, ArrayList, and so forth, all of which had no type parameters. Although this older collection framework has been supplanted by the new, generic version, the old version's classes and interfaces, without type parameters, are still in the standard libraries and in a lot of older code. There is no longer any need for the older classes and interfaces that do not have type parameters. They can sometimes be harder to use and are less versatile than the new, generic classes with type parameters. You should not use the older classes and interfaces without type parameters. However, you will often see them used in older code. When reading older code, you will not go too far wrong in thinking of Collection as meaning Collection<Object>, ArrayList as meaning ArrayList<Object>, and so forth. This is not, strictly speaking, correct. For example, the classes ArrayList and ArrayList<Object> are not the same, but they are very similar.

[1]The biggest difference between Vector<T> and ArrayList<T> classes is that Vector<T> objects are *synchronized* while ArrayList<T> objects are not. Synchronization is briefly discussed in Chapter 19.

PITFALL: Omitting the <T>

If you omit `<T>` or a corresponding class name, such as using `ArrayList` instead of `ArrayList<String>`, then you may get a compiler error message. If you do get a compiler error message, it is likely to seem bewilderingly strange. The problem is that `ArrayList` and other class and interface names with `<T>` omitted actually mean something. (We do not have time to stop and explain what they mean, but a hint is given in the starred subsection "Nonparameterized Version of the Collection Framework.") Your only defense against this pitfall is to be very careful; if you do get a bewildering compiler error message, look for a missing `<T>` or a missing `<Class_Name>`.

Sometimes a compiler warning message can be helpful when you make this mistake. If you get a warning that mentions a type case from a class name without a `<T>` to a class name with a `<T>` or with a `<Class_Name>`, look for an omitted `<T>` or an omitted `<Class_Name>`.

Finally, we should note that sometimes your code will compile and even run correctly if you omit the `<T>` from a class name in the collection framework. ■

16.2 Maps

A man has but one mother. But, a mother may have any number of sons.

Saying on a Wall Sampler

map

The Java **map** framework is similar in character to the collection framework, except that it deals with collections of ordered pairs. Objects in the map framework can implement mathematical functions and relations and so can be used to construct database classes. Think of the pair as consisting of a key `K` (to search for) and an associated value `V`. For example, the key might be a student ID number and the value might be an object storing information about the student (such as the name, major, address, or phone number) associated with that ID number. Commonly used interfaces and classes in this framework are shown in Display 16.8. In this chapter, we will focus on the `Map<K,V>` interface, the `AbstractMap<K,V>` class, and the `HashMap<K,V>` class.

`AbstractMap<K,V>`

`HashMap<K,V>`

`Map<K,V>` interface

Because the map interface will map a key to a value, we must now specify two types of parameters instead of one as we did with collections. The `Map<K,V>` interface specifies the basic operations that all map classes should implement. A summary of these operations is given in Display 16.9. A more detailed description is in Appendix 5. Note that there are many similarities to the `Collection<T>` interface.

Display 16.8 The Map Landscape

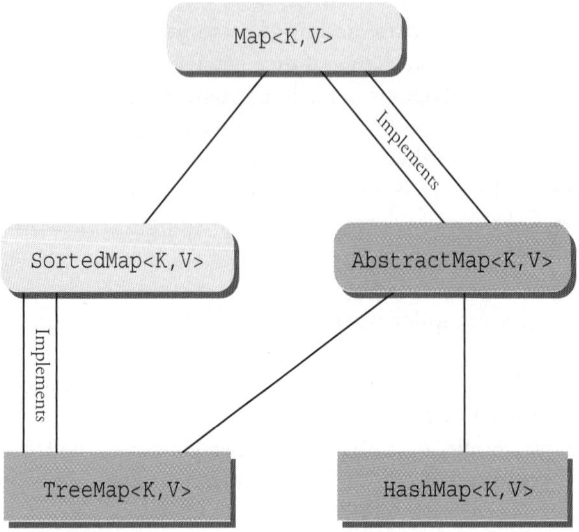

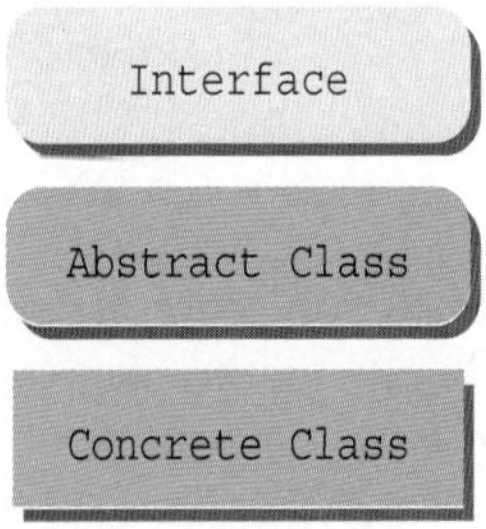

A single line between two boxes means the lower class or interface is derived from (extends) the higher one.

`K` and `V` are type parameters for the type of the keys and elements stored in the map.

Display 16.9 **Method Headings in the `Map<K,V>` Interface** (part 1 of 3)

The `Map<K,V>` interface is in the `java.util` package.

CONSTRUCTORS

Although not officially required by the interface, any class that implements the `Map<K,V>` interface should have at least two constructors: a no argument constructor that creates an empty `Map<K,V>` object, and a constructor with one `Map<K,V>` parameter that creates a `Map<K,V>` object with the same elements as the constructor argument. The interface does not specify whether the copy produced by the one-argument constructor is a shallow copy or a deep copy of its argument.

Display 16.9 Method Headings in the `Map<K,V>` Interface (part 2 of 3)

METHODS
`boolean isEmpty()` Returns `true` if the calling object is empty; otherwise returns `false`.
`public boolean containsValue(Object value)` Returns `true` if the calling object contains at least one or more keys that map to an instance of `value`.
`public boolean containsKey(Object key)` Returns `true` if the calling object contains `key` as one of its keys.
`public boolean equals(Object other)` This is the `equals` of the map, not the `equals` of the elements in the map. Overrides the inherited method `equals`.
`public int size()` Returns the number of (key, value) mappings in the calling object.
`public int hashCode()` Returns the hash code value for the calling object.
`public Set<Map.Entry<K,V>> entrySet()` Returns a set *view* consisting of (key, value) mappings for all entries in the map. Changes to the map are reflected in the set and vice versa.
`public Collection<V> values()` Returns a collection *view* consisting of all values in the map. Changes to the map are reflected in the collection and vice versa.
`public V get(Object key)` Returns the value to which the calling object maps `key`. If `key` is not in the map, then `null` is returned. Note that this does not always mean that the key is not in the map because it is possible to map a key to `null`. The `containsKey` method can be used to distinguish the two cases.
OPTIONAL METHODS
The following methods are optional, which means they still must be implemented, but the implementation can simply throw an `UnsupportedOperationException` if, for some reason, you do not want to give the methods a "real" implementation. An `UnsupportedOperationException` is a `RunTimeException` and so is not required to be caught or declared in a `throws` clause.
`public V put(K key, V value)` *(Optional)* Associates `key` to `value` in the map. If `key` is associated with an existing value, then the old value is overwritten and returned. Otherwise `null` is returned.

(continued)

Display 16.9 Method Headings in the Map<K,V> Interface (part 3 of 3)

```
public void putAll(Map<? extends K,? extends V> mapToAdd) (Optional)
```

Adds all mappings of mapToAdd into the calling object's map.

```
public V remove (Object key) (Optional)
```

Removes the mapping for the specified key. If the key is not found in the map, then null is returned; otherwise the previous value for the key is returned.

Concrete Map Classes

The abstract class AbstractMap<K,V> is convenient for implementing the Map<K,V> interface, just as the AbstractSet<T> class served the same purpose for the Set<T> interface. When defining a derived class of AbstractMap<K,V>, you need to define not just the abstract methods but also all the methods you intend to use. It usually makes more sense to use (or define derived classes of) the HashMap<K,V> or TreeMap<K,V> classes, which are derived classes of AbstractMap<K,V> and are full implementations of the Map<K,V> interfaces. However, if you wish to implement your own map with your own data structures, then it would be appropriate to derive classes from AbstractMap<K,V>.

In this chapter, we will focus only on the HashMap<K,V> class, which is a concrete implementation of the Map<K,V> interface. Internally, the class uses a hash table similar to what we discussed in Chapter 15. Note that this class does not make any guarantee as to the order of elements placed in the map. If you require order, then you should use the TreeMap<K,V> class (which internally uses a tree to store its elements) or the LinkedHashMap<K,V> class, which uses a doubly linked list to maintain order inside a HashMap<K,V> object. The LinkedHashMap<K,V> class is derived from the HashMap<K,V> class.

Knowing how hash tables operate is helpful in optimizing a program that uses a HashMap. When we created a hash table in Chapter 15, we used a fixed-sized array where each array entry referenced a linked list. A hash function mapped an input value, such as a String, to an index in the array. If the size of the array is much smaller than the number of elements added, then there will be lots of collisions and execution performance will be low. On the other hand, if the size of the array is much larger than the number of elements added, then memory will be wasted. A similar trade-off exists with the HashMap<K,V> class. One of the constructors allows us to specify an **initial capacity** and a **load factor**. The initial capacity specifies how many "buckets" exist in the hash table. This would be analogous to the size of the array of the hash table. The load factor is a number between 0 and 1. This variable specifies a percentage such that if the number of elements added to the hash table exceeds the load factor, then the capacity of the hash table will automatically increase. The default load factor is 0.75 and the default initial capacity is 16. This means that the capacity will be increased (by roughly double) once 12 elements are added to the map. This process is called **rehashing**; it can be time consuming if you have a large number of elements in the map. Although the capacity will automatically increase when necessary, your program will run more efficiently if the capacity is initially set to the number of elements you expect will be added to the map.

initial capacity

load factor

rehashing

The `HashMap<K,V>`, of course, implements all the methods in the `Map<K,V>` interface and adds no other methods beyond constructors and an implementation of the `clone()` method. A summary of the `HashMap<K,V>` constructors and `clone()` is given in Display 16.10.

As with the `HashSet<T>` class, if you intend to use your own class as the parameterized type `K` in a `HashMap<K,V>` then your class must override the following methods:

```
public int hashCode();
public boolean equals(Object obj);
```

These methods are required for indexing and checking for uniqueness of the key. See the discussion in Section 16.1 about overriding these methods and Section 15.5 about hash functions.

Display 16.10 Methods in the `HashMap<K,V>` Class

The `HashMap<K,V>` class is in the `java.util` package.

The `HashMap<K,V>` class extends the `AbstractMap<K,V>` class and implements the `Map<K,V>` interface.

The `HashMap<K,V>` class implements all of the methods in the `Map<K,V>` interface (Display 16.9). The only other methods in the `HashMap<K,V>` class are the constructors.

All the exception classes mentioned are the kind that are not required to be caught in a `catch` block or declared in a `throws` clause.

All the exception classes mentioned are in the package `java.lang` and so do not require any import statement.

```
public HashMap()
```

Creates a new, empty map with a default initial capacity of 16 and load factor of 0.75.

```
public HashMap(int initialCapacity)
```

Creates a new, empty map with a default capacity of `initialCapacity` and load factor of 0.75.

Throws an `IllegalArgumentException` if `initialCapacity` is negative.

```
public HashMap(int initialCapacity, float loadFactor)
```

Creates a new, empty map with the specified capacity and load factor.

Throws an `IllegalArgumentException` if `initialCapacity` is negative or `loadFactor` is nonpositive.

```
public HashMap(Map<? extends K,? extends V> m)
```

Creates a new map with the same mappings as `m`. The `initialCapacity` is set to the same size as `m` and the `loadFactor` to 0.75.

Throws a `NullPointerException` if `m` is `null`.

```
public Object clone()
```

Creates a shallow copy of this instance and returns it. The keys and values are not cloned.

The remainder of the methods are the same as those described for the `Map<K,V>` interface (Display 16.9).

A program that demonstrates the `HashMap<K,V>` class is given in Display 16.11. This is a variant of Programming Project 15.8 from Chapter 15. In this example, the program uses the `name` instance variable as the key to map to an `Employee` object as defined in Display 7.2. Several sample `Employee` objects are created and added to the map using the first name as the key. The user is given the opportunity to type in names until enter is pressed on a blank line. Any name that exists in the map is retrieved and its information is output to the screen.

Display 16.11 **`HashMap<K,V>`** Class Demo (part 1 of 2)

```java
// This class uses the Employee class defined in Chapter 7.
import java.util.HashMap;
import java.util.Scanner;
public class HashMapDemo
{
      public static void main(String[] args)
      {
            // First create a hashmap with an initial size of 10 and
            // the default load factor
            HashMap<String,Employee> employees =
                  new HashMap<String,Employee>(10);

            // Add several employees objects to the map using
            // their name as the key
            employees.put("Joe",
                  new Employee("Joe",new Date("September", 15, 1970)));
            employees.put("Andy",
                  new Employee("Andy",new Date("August", 22, 1971)));
            employees.put("Greg",
                  new Employee("Greg",new Date("March", 9, 1972)));
            employees.put("Kiki",
                  new Employee("Kiki",new Date("October", 8, 1970)));
            employees.put("Antoinette",
                  new Employee("Antoinette",new Date("May", 2, 1959)));
            System.out.print("Added Joe, Andy, Greg, Kiki, ");
            System.out.println("and Antoinette to the map.");

            // Ask the user to type a name. If found in the map,
            // print it out.
            Scanner keyboard = new Scanner(System.in);
            String name = "";
            do
            {
                System.out.print("\nEnter a name to look up in the map. ");
                System.out.println("Press enter to quit.");
```

Display 16.11 **HashMap<K,V>** Class Demo (part 2 of 2)

```
                name = keyboard.nextLine();
                if (employees.containsKey(name))
                {
                      Employee e = employees.get(name);
                      System.out.println("Name found: " + e.toString());
                }
                else if (!name.equals(""))
                {
                      System.out.println("Name not found.");
                }
          } while (!name.equals(""));
     }
}
```

Sample Dialogue

```
Added Joe, Andy, Greg, Kiki, and Antoinette to the map.

Enter a name to look up in the map. Press enter to quit.
Joe
Name found: Joe September 15, 1970

Enter a name to look up in the map. Press enter to quit.
Andy
Name found: Andy August 22, 1971

Enter a name to look up in the map. Press enter to quit.
Kiki
Name found: Kiki October 8, 1970

Enter a name to look up in the map. Press enter to quit.
Myla
Name not found.
```

Self-Test Exercises

7. Can an object that instantiates the `HashMap<K,V>` class contain multiple copies of some element as a key? How about multiple copies of some element as a value?

8. Suppose that you want a `HashMap<K,V>` that maps a unique employee ID number to an `Employee` object. Give the definition for a `HashMap<K,V>` variable that defines and allocates the `HashMap`. Expect to have 100 employees in your organization. If the employee ID number is an integer between 0 and 100, is a map a good choice for a data structure to store this information?

16.3 Iterators

The White Rabbit put on his spectacles. "Where shall I begin, please your Majesty?" he asked.
"Begin at the beginning," the King said, very gravely, "And go on till you come to the end: then stop."

LEWIS CARROLL, *Alice in Wonderland*

iterator

An **iterator** is an object that is used with a collection to provide sequential access to the elements in the collection. In this section, we discuss iterators in general, and iterators in the Java collection framework in particular.

The Iterator Concept

In the next subsection, we will discuss the Java Iterator interface, but before that, let us consider the intuitive idea of an iterator. An iterator is something that allows you to examine and possibly modify the elements in a collection in some sequential order. So, an iterator imposes an order on the elements of a collection even if the collection, such as the class HashSet<T>, does not impose any order on the elements it contains.

Something that is not an object—and thus not, strictly speaking, a Java Iterator—but that satisfies the intuitive idea of an iterator is an int variable i used with an array a. This iterator i can be made to start out at the first array as follows:

```
i = 0;
```

The iterator can give you the current element; the current element is simply a[i]. The iterator can go to the next element and give you the next element as follows:

```
i++;
"Gives you a[i]"
```

The concept of an iterator is simple but powerful enough to be used frequently.

The Iterator<T> Interface

Iterator<T> interface

Java formalizes the concept of an iterator with the Iterator<T> generic interface. Any object of any class that satisfies the Iterator<T> interface is an Iterator<T>. So, an array index is not a Java Iterator<T>. However, the index could be an instance variable in an object of an Iterator<T> class.

An Iterator<T> object does not stand on its own. It must be associated with some collection object. How is the association accomplished? In Java, any class that satisfies the Collection<T> interface must have a method, named iterator(), that returns an Iterator<T>. For example, let us say c is an instance of the HashSet<T> collection class with some class plugged in for T. To make things concrete, let us plug in String for T; so c is an instance of the HashSet<String> collection class. You can obtain an iterator for c as follows:

```
Iterator<String> iteratorForC = c.iterator();
```

You may not know what class the `iteratorForC` is an instance of, but you do know it satisfies the `Iterator<String>` interface, so you know it has the methods in the `Iterator<T>` interface. These methods are given in Display 16.12.

Display 16.13 contains a simple demonstration of using an iterator with a `HashSet<T>` object. A `HashSet<T>` object imposes no order on the elements in the `HashSet<T>` object, but the iterator imposes an order on the elements—namely, the order in which they are produced by `next()`. There are no requirements on this ordering. If you run the program in Display 16.13 twice, the order of the elements' output will almost certainly be the same each time. However, it would not be an error if they are output in a different order each time the program runs.

If the collection used with an `Iterator<T>` imposes an order on its elements, such as an `ArrayList<T>` does, then the `Iterator<T>` will output the elements in that order. If you require an order with a `HashSet<T>` object, then you may use the `LinkedHashSet<T>` class, which uses an internal doubly linked list to store the items in the order that they are added.

Display 16.12 Methods in the `Iterator<T>` Interface

The `Iterator<T>` interface is in the `java.util` package.

All the exception classes mentioned are the kind that are not required to be caught in a `catch` block or declared in a `throws` clause.

`NoSuchElementException` is in the `java.util` package, which requires an import statement if your code mentions the `NoSuchElementException` class. All the other exception classes mentioned are in the package `java.lang` and so do not require any import statement.

```
public T next()
```

Returns the next element of the collection that produced the iterator.

Throws a `NoSuchElementException` if there is no next element.

```
public boolean hasNext()
```

Returns `true` if `next()` has not yet returned all the elements in the collection; returns `false` otherwise.

```
public void remove() (Optional)
```

Removes from the collection the last element returned by `next`.

This method can be called only once per call to `next`. If the collection is changed in any way, other than by using `remove`, the behavior of the iterator is not specified (and thus should be considered unpredictable).

Throws `IllegalStateException` if the `next` method has not yet been called, or if the `remove` method has already been called after the last call to the `next` method.

Throws an `UnsupportedOperationException` if the `remove` operation is not supported by this `Iterator<T>`.

Display 16.13 An Iterator

```
import java.util.HashSet;
import java.util.Iterator;

public class HashSetIteratorDemo
{
    public static void main(String[] args)
    {
        HashSet<String> s = new HashSet<String>();

        s.add("health");
        s.add("love");
        s.add("money");

        System.out.println("The set contains:");

        Iterator<String> i = s.iterator();
        while (i.hasNext())
            System.out.println(i.next());

        i.remove();

        System.out.println();
        System.out.println("The set now contains:");

        i = s.iterator();
        while (i.hasNext())
            System.out.println(i.next());

        System.out.println("End of program.");
    }
}
```

You cannot "reset" an iterator "to the beginning." To do a second iteration, you create another iterator.

Sample Dialogue

```
The set contains:
money
love
health

The set now contains:
money
love
End of program.
```

The `HashSet<T>` object does not order the elements it contains, but the iterator imposes an order on the elements.

Iterators

An iterator is something that allows you to examine and possibly modify the elements in a collection in some sequential order. Java formalizes this concept with the two interfaces `Iterator<T>` and `ListIterator<T>`.

TIP: For-Each Loops as Iterators

A for-each loop is not, strictly speaking, an iterator (because, among other things, it is not an object), but a for-each loop serves the same purpose as an iterator: It lets you cycle through the elements in a collection. When dealing with collections, you can often use a for-each loop in place of an iterator, and the for-each loop is usually simpler and easier to use than an iterator. For example, in Display 16.14, we have rewritten the program in Display 16.13 using for-each loops in place of iterators. Note that we needed to do some extra programming with the variable `last` in order to simulate `i.remove()`. Sometimes an iterator works best, and sometimes a for-each loop works best. Many authorities would say that our code would be better if we had not replaced the first iterator loop in Display 16.13 with a for-each loop. ■

Display 16.14 **For-Each Loops as Iterators** (part 1 of 2)

```
import java.util.HashSet;
import java.util.Iterator;

public class ForEachDemo
{
    public static void main(String[] args)
    {
        HashSet<String> s = new HashSet<String>();

        s.add("health");
        s.add("love");
        s.add("money");

        System.out.println("The set contains:");

        String last = null;
        for (String e : s)
        {
            last = e;
            System.out.println(e);
        }
```

(continued)

Display 16.14 **For-Each Loops as Iterators** (part 2 of 2)

```
            s.remove(last);

            System.out.println();
            System.out.println("The set now contains:");

            for (String e : s)
                System.out.println(e);

            System.out.println("End of program.");
        }
}
```

The output is the same as in Display 16.13.

List Iterators

List Iterator<T>

The collection framework has two iterator interfaces: the `Iterator<T>` interface, which you have already seen and which works with any collection class that implements the `Collection<T>` interface; and the `ListIterator<T>` interface, which is designed to work with collections that implement the `List<T>` interface. The `ListIterator<T>` interface extends the `Iterator<T>` interface. A `ListIterator<T>` has all the methods that an `Iterator<T>` has, plus more methods that provide two new abilities: A `ListIterator<T>` can move in either direction along the list of elements in the collection, and a `ListIterator<T>` has methods, such as `set` and `add`, that can be used to change the elements in the collection. The methods for the `ListIterator<T>` interface are given in Display 16.15. See Appendix 5 for a more detailed description that includes all exceptions thrown.

The map framework does not directly support the iterable interface, but you can use the map's `keySet()`, `values()`, or `entrySet()` methods, which return iterable sets containing the keys, values, or (key, value) mappings of the map.

Display 16.15 **Methods in the `ListIterator<T>` Interface** (part 1 of 2)

The `ListIterator<T>` interface is in the `java.util` package.

The *cursor position* is explained in the text and in Display 16.16.

All the exception classes mentioned are the kind that are not required to be caught in a `catch` block or declared in a `throws` clause.

`NoSuchElementException` is in the `java.util` package, which requires an import statement if your code mentions the `NoSuchElementException` class. All the other exception classes mentioned are in the package java.lang and so do not require any import statement.

```
public T next()
```

Returns the next element of the list that produced the iterator. More specifically, returns the element immediately after the cursor position.

Throws a `NoSuchElementException` if there is no next element.

Display 16.15 **Methods in the `ListIterator<T>` Interface** (part 2 of 2)

`public T previous()`

Returns the previous element of the list that produced the iterator. More specifically, returns the element immediately before the cursor position.

Throws a `NoSuchElementException` if there is no previous element.

`public boolean hasNext( )`

Returns `true` if there is a suitable element for `next()` to return; returns `false` otherwise.

`public boolean hasPrevious( )`

Returns `true` if there is a suitable element for `previous()` to return; returns `false` otherwise.

`public int nextIndex( )`

Returns the index of the element that would be returned by a call to `next()`. Returns the list size if the cursor position is at the end of the list.

`public int previousIndex( )`

Returns the index that would be returned by a call to `previous()`. Returns `1` if the cursor position is at the beginning of the list.

`public void add(T newElement)` *(Optional)*

Inserts `newElement` at the location of the iterator cursor (that is, before the value, if any, that would be returned by `next()` and after the value, if any, that would be returned by `previous()`).

Cannot be used if there has been a call to `add` or `remove` since the last call to `next()` or `previous()`.

Throws `IllegalStateException` if neither `next()` nor `previous()` has been called, or if the `add` or `remove` method has already been called after the last call to `next()` or `previous()`.

`public void remove()` *(Optional)*

Removes from the collection the last element returned by `next()` or `previous()`.

This method can be called only once per call to `next()` or `previous()`.

Cannot be used if there has been a call to `add` or `remove` since the last call to `next()` or `previous()`.

Throws `IllegalStateException` if neither `next()` nor `previous()` has been called, or if the `add` or `remove` method has already been called after the last call to `next()` or `previous()`.

`public void set( T newElement)` *(Optional)*

Replaces the last element returned by `next()` or `previous()` with `newElement`.

Cannot be used if there has been a call to `add` or `remove` since the last call to `next()` or `previous()`.

Throws `IllegalStateException` if neither `next()` nor `previous()` has been called, or if the `add` or `remove` method has been called since the last call to `next()` or `previous()`.

The general idea of *next* and *previous* is clear, but we need to make it precise if you are to understand the `next()` and `previous()` methods of the `ListIterator<T>` interface. Every `ListIterator<T>` has a position marker in the list known as the **cursor**. If the list has n elements, they are numbered by indices 0 through $n-1$, but there are $n+1$ cursor positions, as indicated in Display 16.16. When `next()` is invoked, the element immediately following the cursor position is returned and the cursor is moved to the next cursor position. When `previous()` is invoked, the element immediately before the cursor position is returned, and the cursor is moved back to the preceding cursor position.

cursor

> ### The `ListIterator<T>` Interface
>
> The `ListIterator<T>` interface extends the `Iterator<T>` interface. The `ListIterator<T>` interface differs from the `Iterator<T>` interface by adding the following abilities: A `ListIterator<T>` can move in either direction along the list of elements in the collection, and a `ListIterator<T>` has methods, such as `set` and `add`, that can be used to change the elements in the collection.

Display 16.16 `ListIterator<T>` Cursor Positions

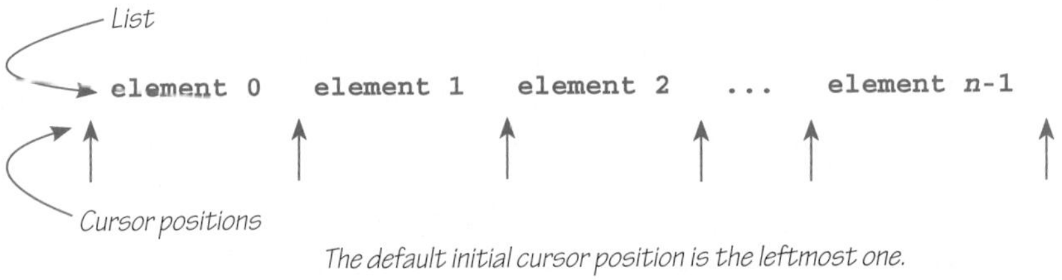

PITFALL: `next` Can Return a Reference

If `i` is an iterator, then `i.next()` returns an element of the collection that created `i`, but there are two meanings of "return an element."

1. The invocation `i.next()` could return a copy of the element in the collection (for example, using a copy constructor or a `clone` method).
2. Alternatively, `i.next()` could return a reference to the element in the collection.

In case (1), modifying `i.next()` *will not* change the element in the collection (provided the copy was a deep copy). In case (2), modifying `i.next()` *will* change the element in the collection. The APIs for both the `Iterator<T>` and `ListIterator<T>` interfaces are vague on whether you should follow policy (1) or (2), but the iterators

PITFALL: (continued)

for the standard predefined collection classes, such as `ArrayList<T>` and `HashSet<T>`, return references. So, you can modify the elements in the collection by using mutator methods on `i.next()`. This is illustrated in Display 16.17. The comments we made about `i.next()` also apply to `i.previous()`.

The fact that `next` and `previous` return references to elements in the collection is not necessarily bad news. It means you must be careful, but it also means you can cycle through all the elements in the collection and perform some processing that might modify the elements. For example, if the elements in the collection are records of some sort, you can use mutator methods to update the records.

If you read the APIs for the `Iterator<T>` and `ListIterator<T>` interfaces, they say that a `ListIterator<T>` can change the collection, but presumably, a plain old `Iterator<T>` cannot. These API comments do not refer to whether or not a reference is returned by `i.next()`. They simply refer to the fact that the `ListIterator<T>` interface has a set method, whereas the `Iterator<T>` interface does not. Do not confuse this with the point discussed in the previous paragraph. ■

Display 16.17 **An Iterator Returns a Reference** (part 1 of 2)

The class `Date` is defined in Display 4.13, but you can easily guess all you need to know about `Date` for this example.

```java
import java.util.ArrayList;
import java.util.Iterator;

public class IteratorReferenceDemo
{
    public static void main(String[] args)
    {
        ArrayList<Date> birthdays = new ArrayList<Date>();

        birthdays.add(new Date(1, 1, 1990));
        birthdays.add(new Date(2, 2, 1990));
        birthdays.add(new Date(3, 3, 1990));

        System.out.println("The list contains:");

        Iterator<Date> i = birthdays.iterator();
        while (i.hasNext())
            System.out.println(i.next());

        i = birthdays.iterator();
        Date d = null; //To keep the compiler happy.
        System.out.println("Changing the references.");
        while (i.hasNext())
        {
            d = i.next();
            d.setDate(4, 1, 1990);
        }
```

(continued)

Display 16.17 **An Iterator Returns a Reference** (part 2 of 2)

```
        System.out.println("The list now contains:");

        i = birthdays.iterator();
        while (i.hasNext())
            System.out.println(i.next());

        System.out.println("April fool!");
    }
}
```

Sample Dialogue

```
The list contains:
January 1, 1990
February 2, 1990
March 3, 1990
Changing the references.
The list now contains:
April 1, 1990
April 1, 1990
April 1, 1990
April fool!
```

TIP: Defining Your Own Iterator Classes

There really is little need to define your own `Iterator<T>` or `ListIterator<T>` classes. The most common and easiest way to define a collection class is to make it a derived class of one of the library collection classes, such as `ArrayList<T>` or `HashSet<T>`. When you do this, you automatically get the method `iterator()`, and if need be, the method `listIterator()`, which takes care of iterators. However, if you should need to define a collection class in some other way, then the best way to define your iterator class or classes is to define them as inner classes of your collection class. ■

MyProgrammingLab™

Self-Test Exercises

9. Does a `HashSet<T>` object have a method to produce a `ListIterator<T>`? Does an `ArrayList<T>` object have a method to produce a `ListIterator<T>`?

10. Suppose `i` is a `ListIterator<T>`. Will an invocation of `i.next()` followed by `i.previous()` return the same element for each of the two invocations or might they return two different elements? What about `i.previous()` followed by `i.next()`?

Chapter Summary

- The main *collection* interfaces are `Collection<T>`, `Set<T>`, and `List<T>`. The `Set<T>` and `List<T>` interfaces extend the `Collection<T>` interface. The library classes that are standard to use and that implement these interfaces are `HashSet<T>`, which implements the `Set<T>` interface, and `ArrayList<T>`, which implements the `List<T>` interface.
- A `Set<T>` does not allow repeated elements and does not order its elements. A `List<T>` allows repeated elements and orders its elements.
- The `Map<K,V>` interface is used to store a mapping between a key `K` and a value `V`. It is commonly used to store databases in memory. The `HashMap<K,V>` class is a standard library class that implements a map.
- An *iterator* is something that allows you to examine and possibly modify the elements in a collection in some sequential order. Java formalizes this concept with the two interfaces `Iterator<T>` and `ListIterator<T>`.
- An `Iterator<T>` (with only the required methods implemented) goes through the elements of the collection in one direction only, from the beginning to the end. A `ListIterator<T>` can move through the collection list in both directions, forward and back. A `ListIterator<T>` has a set method; the `Iterator<T>` interface does not require a set method.

Answers to Self-Test Exercises

1.
```
public static <T> boolean inSome(T target,
                                 Collection<T> c1, Collection<T> c2)
{
        return (c1.contains(target) || c2.contains(target));
}
```

2.
```
public static <T> T getFirst(List<T> aList)
{
    if (aList.isEmpty())
        return null;
    else
        return aList.get(0);
}
```

3.
```
public static boolean noNull(Set<?> s)
{
    return (s.remove(null));
}
```

4. No.

5. It would make more sense to make it a derived class of the `ArrayList<T>` class. Then the elements are ordered. You can ensure against repeated elements by redefining all methods that add elements so that the methods check to see if the element is already in the class before entering it. A derived class of the `HashSet<T>` class would automatically ensure that no element is repeated, but it would seem to take a good deal of work to maintain the elements in order.
6. The `Customer` class must override `hashCode` and `equals`. A simple technique to implement `hashCode` when the class contains strings is to return the string's `hashCode` method. One possible implementation of these methods follows.

```
public int hashCode()
{
   return this.toString().hashCode();
}
public boolean equals(Object obj)
{
   Customer other = (Customer) obj;
   return (other.toString().equals(this.toString()));
}
```

7. Multiple copies of some element are not allowed as a key, but are allowed as values.
8. The variable would be defined as

```
HashMap<Integer,Employee> employeeMap =
new HashMap<Integer,Employee>(100);
```

   If the ID numbers are between 0 and 100, then the map will work, but a simple array or `ArrayList` might be a more appropriate data structure.
9. A `HashSet<T>` does not. An `ArrayList<T>` does.
10. The answer to both questions is the same: They will return the same element.

MyProgrammingLab™ Programming Projects

Visit www.myprogramminglab.com to complete select exercises online and get instant feedback.

1. Redo Programming Project 6.8 in Chapter 6, but this time do it for a vector of strings to be sorted into lexicographic order.
2. The Sieve of Erastothenes is an ancient algorithm that generates prime numbers. Consider the list of numbers from 2 to 10 as follows:

   2 3 4 5 6 7 8 9 10

   The algorithm starts with the first prime number in the list, which is 2, and then iterates through the remainder of the list, removing any number that is a multiple of 2 (in this case, 4, 6, 8, and 10), leaving

   2 3 5 7 9

We then repeat the process with the second prime number in the list, which is 3, and then iterate through the remainder of the list, removing any number that is a multiple of 3 (in this case 9), leaving

2 3 5 7

We then repeat starting with each successive prime number, but no elements are removed because there are no multiples of 5 or 7 (a more efficient implementation of the algorithm would stop without examining 5 or 7). The numbers that remain in the list are all prime numbers.

Implement this algorithm using an `ArrayList` of integers that is initialized to the values from 2 to 100. Your program can iterate numerically through the `ArrayList` from index 0 to index `size()-1` to get the current prime number, but should use an `Iterator` to scan through the remainder of the list to eliminate the multiples. You can use the `listIterator` method to retrieve the iterator starting at a specified index into the `ArrayList`. Output all remaining prime numbers to the console.

VideoNote
Solution to Programming Project 16.3

3. The birthday paradox is that there is a surprisingly high probability that two or more people in the same room happen to share the same birthday. By birthday, we mean the same day of the year (ignoring leap years), but not the exact birthday that includes the birth year or time of day. Write a program that approximates the probability that 2 or more people in the same room have the same birthday, for 2 to 50 people in the room.

   The program should use simulation to approximate the answer. Over many trials (say, 5,000), randomly assign birthdays (i.e., a number from 1–365) to everyone in the room. Use a `HashSet` to store the birthdays. As the birthdays are randomly generated, use the `contains` method of a `HashSet` to see if someone with the same birthday is already in the room. If so, increment a counter that tracks how many times at least two people have the same birthday and then move on to the next trial. After the trials are over, divide the counter by the number of trials to get an estimated probability that two or more people share the same birthday for a given room size.

   Your output should look something like the following. It will not be exactly the same due to the random numbers:

```
For 2 people, the probability of two birthdays is about 0.002
For 3 people, the probability of two birthdays is about 0.0082
For 4 people, the probability of two birthdays is about 0.0163
...
For 49 people, the probability of two birthdays is about 0.9654
For 50 people, the probability of two birthdays is about 0.969
```

4. The text files `boynames.txt` and `girlnames.txt`, which are included in the source code for this book, contain lists of the 1,000 most popular boy and girl names in the United States for the year 2005, as compiled by the Social Security Administration.

   These are blank-delimited files where the most popular name is listed first, the second most popular name is listed second, and so on to the 1,000th most popular name, which is listed last. Each line consists of the first name followed by a blank space followed by the number of registered births in the year using that name. For example, the `girlnames.txt` file begins with

```
Emily 25494
Emma 22532
```

This indicates that Emily is the most popular name with 25,494 registered namings, Emma is the second most popular with 22,532, and so on.

Write a program that determines how many names are on both the boys' and the girls' list. Use the following algorithm:

- Read each girl name as a String, ignoring the number of namings, and add it to a `HashSet` object.
- Read each boy name as a String, ignoring the number of namings, and add it to the same `HashSet` object. If the name is already in the `HashSet`, then the `add` method returns `false`. If you count the number of `false` returns, then this gives you the number of common namings.
- Add each common name to an `ArrayList` and output all of the common names from this list before the program exits.

VideoNote

Solution to Programming Project 16.5

5. Repeat the previous problem except create your own class, `Name`, that is added to a `HashMap` instead of a `HashSet`. The `Name` class should have three private variables, a String to store the name, an integer to store the number of namings for girls, and an integer to store the number of namings for boys. Use the first name as the key to the `HashMap`. The value to store is the `Name` object. Instead of ignoring the number of namings, as in the previous project, store the number in the `Name` class. Make the `ArrayList` a list of `Name` objects; each time you find a common name, add the entire `Name` object to the list. Your program should then iterate through the `ArrayList` and output each common name, along with the number of boy and girl namings.
6. In an ancient land, the beautiful princess Eve had many suitors. She decided on the following procedure to determine which suitor she would marry. First, all of the suitors would be lined up one after the other and assigned numbers. The first suitor would be number 1, the second number 2, and so on up to the last suitor, number *n*. Starting at the first suitor, she would then count three suitors down the line (because of the three letters in her name) and the third suitor would be eliminated from winning her hand and removed from the line. Eve would then continue, counting three more suitors, and eliminating every third suitor. When she reached the end of the line, she would reverse direction and work her way back to the beginning. Similarly, on reaching the first person in line, she would reverse direction and make her way to the end of the line.

   For example, if there were five suitors, then the elimination process would proceed as follows:

12345	Initial list of suitors; start counting from 1.
1245	Suitor 3 eliminated; continue counting from 4 and bounce from end back to 4.

125	Suitor 4 eliminated; continue counting back from 2 and bounce from front back to 2.
15	Suitor 2 eliminated; continue counting forward from 5.
1	Suitor 5 eliminated; 1 is the lucky winner.

Write a program that uses an `ArrayList` or `Vector` to determine which position you should stand in to marry the princess if there are *n* suitors. Your program should use the `ListIterator` interface to traverse the list of suitors and remove a suitor. Be careful that your iterator references the proper object upon reversing direction at the beginning or end of the list. The suitor at the beginning or end of the list should only be counted once when the princess reverses the count.

7. In social networking websites, people link to their friends to form a social network. Write a program that uses `HashMaps` to store the data for such a network. Your program should read from a file that specifies the network connections for different usernames. The file should have the following format to specify a link:

```
source_usernamefriend_username
```

There should be an entry for each link, one per line. Here is a sample file for five usernames:

```
iba          java_guru
iba          crisha
iba          ducky
crisha       java_guru
crisha       iba
ducky        java_guru
ducky        iba
java_guru    iba
java_guru    crisha
java_guru    ducky
wittless     java_guru
```

In this network, everyone links to `java_guru` as a friend. `iba` is friends with `java_guru`, `crisha`, and `ducky`. Note that links are not bidirectional; `wittless` links with `java_guru` but `java_guru` does not link with `wittless`.

First, create a `User` class that has an instance variable to store the user's name and another instance variable that is of type `HashSet<User>`. The `HashSet<User>` variable should contain references to the `User` objects that the current user links to. For example, for the user `iba` there would be three entries, for `java_guru`, `crisha`, and `ducky`. Second, create a `HashMap<String,User>` instance variable in your `main` class that is used to map from a username to the corresponding `User` object. Your program should do the following:

- Upon startup, read the data file and populate the `HashMap` and `HashSet` data structures according to the links specified in the file.

- Allow the user to enter a name.
- If the name exists in the map, then output all usernames that are one link away from the user entered.
- If the name exists in the map, then output all usernames that are two links away from the user entered. To accomplish this in a general way, you might consider writing a recursive subroutine.

Do not forget that your `User` class must override the `hashCode` and `equals` methods.

8. You have collected a file of movie ratings where each movie is rated from 1 (bad) to 5 (excellent). The first line of the file is a number that identifies how many ratings are in the file. Each rating then consists of two lines: the name of the movie followed by the numeric rating from 1 to 5. Here is a sample rating file with four unique movies and seven ratings:

```
7
Harry Potter and the Half-Blood Prince
4
Harry Potter and the Half-Blood Prince
5
Army of the Dead
1
Harry Potter and the Half-Blood Prince
4
Army of the Dead
2
The Uninvited
4
Pandorium
3
```

Write a program that reads a file in this format, calculates the average rating for each movie, and outputs the average along with the number of reviews. Here is the desired output for the sample data:

```
Harry Potter and the Half-Blood Prince: 3 reviews, average of 4.3 / 5
Army of the Dead: 2 reviews, average of 1.5 / 5
The Uninvited: 1 review, average of 4 / 5
Pandorium: 1 review, average of 3 / 5
```

Use a `HashMap` or multiple `HashMaps` to calculate the output. Your map(s) should index from a string representing each movie's name to integers that store the number of reviews for the movie and the sum of the ratings for the movie.

9. The file `words.txt` included on the website contains a list of 87,314 English words. Write a program that uses this word list to implement a simple spell-checker. First, read all of the words into a `HashSet<String>` object. Then, allow the user to enter the name of a text file that contains written English. The program should output all of the words that are not in the set as potentially misspelled words.

Swing I 17

17 Swing I

"It Don't Mean a Thing If It Ain't Got That Swing"

SONG TITLE, *Duke Ellington*

Introduction

Swing

GUI

This is the first of three chapters that present the basic classes in the **Swing** package and teach the basic techniques for using these classes to define *GUIs.* **GUIs** are windowing interfaces that handle user input and output. *GUI* is pronounced "gooey" and stands for **graphical user interface**. Entire books have been written on Swing, so we will not be able to give you a complete description of Swing in just three chapters. However, we will teach you enough to allow you to write a variety of windowing interfaces.

> **GUI**
>
> Windowing systems that interact with the user are often called **GUIs**. *GUI* is pronounced "gooey" and stands for **graphical user interface**.

AWT

The **AWT (Abstract Window Toolkit)** package is an older package designed for doing windowing interfaces. Swing can be viewed as an improved version of the AWT. However, Swing did not completely replace the AWT package. Some AWT classes are replaced by Swing classes, but other AWT classes are needed when using Swing. We will use classes from both Swing and the AWT.

Swing GUIs are designed using a particular form of object-oriented programming that is known as *event-driven programming*. Our first section begins with a brief overview of event-driven programming.

Prerequisites

Before covering this chapter (and the two chapters on applets[1] and more Swing), you need to have read Chapters 1 through 5, Chapter 7 (inheritance), Chapter 13 (interfaces and inner classes), and Section 8.2 of Chapter 8 (abstract classes). (Section 8.2 of Chapter 8 does not require Section 8.1.) Except for one subsection at the end of this chapter, you need not have read any of the other chapters that precede this chapter.

To cover the last subsection of this chapter, entitled "A Swing Calculator," you need to first read Chapter 9, which covers exceptions. If you have not yet read Chapter 9, you can skip that last section.

[1]The chapter on applets is on the website that accompanies this book.

17.1 Event-Driven Programming

My duty is to obey orders.

THOMAS JONATHAN (STONEWALL) JACKSON

event-driven programming

Event-driven programming is a programming style that uses a signal-and-response approach to programming. Signals to objects are things called *events,* a concept we explain in this section.

Events and Listeners

event

listener

firing an event

Swing programs use events and event handlers. An **event** is an object that acts as a signal to another object known as a **listener**. The sending of the event is called **firing the event**. The object that fires the event is often a GUI component, such as a button. The button fires the event in response to being clicked. The listener object performs some action in response to the event. For example, the listener might place a message on the screen in response to a particular button being clicked. A given component may have any number of listeners, from zero to several listeners. Each listener might respond to a different kind of event, or multiple listeners might respond to the same events.

If you have read Chapter 9 on exception handling, then you have already seen one specialized example of event-driven programming.[2] An exception object is an event. The throwing of an exception is an example of firing an event (in this case, firing the exception event). The listener is the `catch` block that catches the event.

event handler

In Swing GUIs, an event often represents some action such as clicking a mouse, dragging the mouse, pressing a key on the keyboard, clicking the close-window button on a window, or any other action that is expected to elicit a response. A listener object has methods that specify what will happen when events of various kinds are received by the listener. These methods that handle events are called **event handlers**. You the programmer will define (or redefine) these event-handler methods. The relationship between an event-firing object, such as a button, and its event-handling listener is shown diagrammatically in Display 17.1.

Event-driven programming is very different from most programming you have seen before now. All our previous programs consisted of a list of statements executed in order. There were loops that repeat statements and branches that choose one of a list of statements to execute next. However, at some level, each run of a program consists of a list of statements performed by one agent (the computer) that executes the statements one after the other in order.

Event-driven programming is a very different game. In event-driven programming, you create objects that can fire events, and you create listener objects to react to the events. For the most part, your program does not determine the order in which things happen. The events determine that order. When an event-driven program is running,

[2] If you have not yet covered Chapter 9 on exceptions, you can safely ignore this paragraph.

Display 17.1 Event Firing and an Event Listener

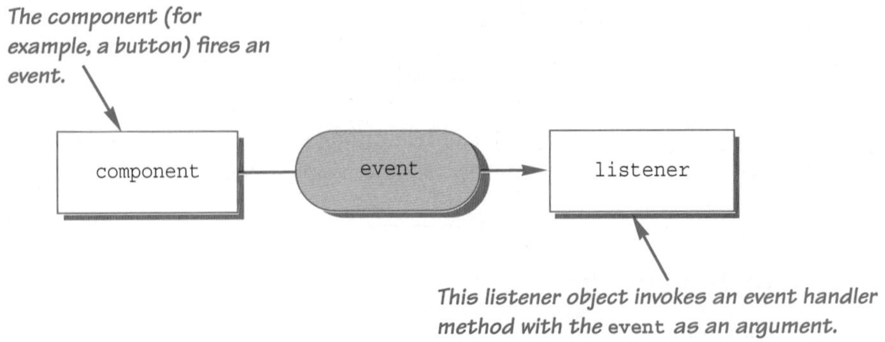
The component (for example, a button) fires an event.
component
event
listener
This listener object invokes an event handler method with the event as an argument.

the next thing that happens depends on the next event. It is as though the listeners are robots that interact with other objects (possibly other robots) in response to events (signals) from these other objects. You program the robots, but the environment and other robots determine what any particular robot will actually end up doing.

If you have never done event-driven programming before, one aspect of it may seem strange to you: *You will be writing definitions for methods that you will never invoke in any program.* This will likely feel a bit strange at first, because a method is of no value unless it is invoked. So, somebody or something other than you, the programmer, must be invoking these methods. That is exactly what does happen. The Swing system automatically invokes certain methods when an event signals that the method needs to be called.

Event-driven programming with the Swing library makes extensive use of inheritance. The classes you define will be derived classes of some basic Swing library classes. These derived classes will inherit methods from their base class. For many of these inherited methods, library software will determine when these methods are invoked, but you will override the definition of the inherited method to determine what will happen when the method is invoked.

17.2 Buttons, Events, and Other Swing Basics

One button click is worth a thousand key strokes.

ANONYMOUS

In this section, we present enough about Swing to allow you to do some simple GUI programs.

EXAMPLE: A Simple Window

Display 17.2 contains a Swing program that produces a simple window. The window contains nothing but a button on which is written `"Click to end program."` If the user follows the instructions and clicks the button with his or her mouse, the program ends.

The `import` statements give the names of the classes used and which package they are in. What we and others call the *Swing library* is the package named `javax.swing`. The *AWT library* is the package `java.awt`. Note that one package name contains an `"x"` and one does not.

This program is a simple class definition with only a `main` method. The first line in the `main` method creates an object of the class `JFrame`. That line is reproduced as follows:

```
JFrame firstWindow = new JFrame();
```

This is an ordinary declaration of a variable named `firstWindow` and an invocation of the no-argument constructor for the class `JFrame`. A `JFrame` object is a basic window that includes a border and the usual three buttons for minimizing the window down to an icon, changing the size of the window, and closing the window. These buttons are shown in the upper-right corner of the window, which is typical, but if your operating system normally places these buttons someplace else, that is where they will likely be located in a `JFrame` on your computer.

The initial size of the `JFrame` window is set using the `JFrame` method `setSize`, as follows:

```
firstWindow.setSize(WIDTH, HEIGHT);
```

In this case, `WIDTH` and `HEIGHT` are defined `int` constants. The units of measure are pixels, so the window produced is 300 pixels by 200 pixels. (The term *pixel* is defined in the box entitled "Pixel.") As with other windows, you can change the size of a `JFrame` by using your mouse to drag a corner of the `JFrame` window.

The buttons for minimizing the window down to an icon and for changing the size of the window behave as they do in any of the other windows you have used. The minimization button shrinks the window down to an icon. (To restore the window, click the icon.) The second button changes the size of the window back and forth from full screen to a smaller size. The close-window button can behave in different ways depending on how it is set by your program.

The behavior of the close-window button is set with the `JFrame` method `setDefaultCloseOperation`. The line of the program that sets the behavior of the close-window button is reproduced next:

```
firstWindow.setDefaultCloseOperation(JFrame.DO_NOTHING_ON_CLOSE);
```

(continued)

EXAMPLE: (continued)

In this case, the argument `JFrame.DO_NOTHING_ON_CLOSE` is a defined constant named `DO_NOTHING_ON_CLOSE`, which is defined in the `JFrame` class. This sets the close-window button so that when it is clicked, nothing happens (unless we programmed something to happen, which we have not done). Other possible arguments are given in Display 17.3.

The method `setDefaultCloseOperation` takes a single `int` argument; each of the constants described in Display 17.3 is an `int` constant. However, do not think of them as `int` values. Think of them as policies for what happens when the user clicks the close-window button. It was convenient to name these policies by `int` values. However, they could just as well have been named by `char` values or `String` values or something else. The fact that they are `int` values is an incidental detail of no real importance.

Descriptions of some of the most important methods in the class `JFrame` are given in Display 17.3. Some of these methods will not be explained until later in this chapter. A more complete list of methods for the class `JFrame` is given in Appendix 5.

A `JFrame` can have components added, such as buttons, menus, and text labels. For example, the following line from Display 17.2 adds the `JButton` object named `endButton` to the `JFrame` named `firstWindow`:

```
firstWindow.add(endButton);
```

The description of how the `JButton` named `endButton` is created and programmed will be given in the two subsections entitled "Buttons" and "Action Listeners and Action Events" a little later in this section.

We end this subsection by jumping ahead to the last line of the program, which is

```
firstWindow.setVisible(true);
```

This makes the `JFrame` window visible on the screen. At first glance, this may seem strange. Why not have windows automatically become visible? Why would you create a window if you did not want it to be visible? The answer is that you may not want it to be visible at all times. You have certainly experienced windows that disappear and reappear. To hide the window, which is not desirable in this example, you would replace the argument `true` with `false`.

JFrame

An object of the class `JFrame` is what you think of as a window. It automatically has a border and some basic buttons for minimizing the window and similar actions. As you will see, a `JFrame` object can have buttons and many other components added to the window and programmed for action.

Display 17.2 **A First Swing Demonstration Program** (part 1 of 2)

```
import javax.swing.JFrame;
import javax.swing.JButton;

public class FirstSwingDemo
{
    public static final int WIDTH = 300;
    public static final int HEIGHT = 200;

    public static void main(String[] args)
    {
        JFrame firstWindow = new JFrame( );
        firstWindow.setSize(WIDTH, HEIGHT);

        firstWindow.setDefaultCloseOperation(
                                   JFrame.DO_NOTHING_ON_CLOSE);

        JButton endButton = new JButton("Click to end program.");
        EndingListener buttonEar = new EndingListener();
        endButton.addActionListener(buttonEar);
        firstWindow.add(endButton);

        firstWindow.setVisible(true);
    }
}
```

This program is not typical of the style we will use in Swing programs.

This is the file `FirstSwingDemo.java`.

```
import java.awt.event.ActionListener;
import java.awt.event.ActionEvent;

public class EndingListener implements ActionListener
{
    public void actionPerformed(ActionEvent e)
    {
        System.exit(0);
    }
}
```

This is the file `EndingListener.java`.

(continued)

Display 17.2 **A First Swing Demonstration Program** (part 2 of 2)

RESULTING GUI

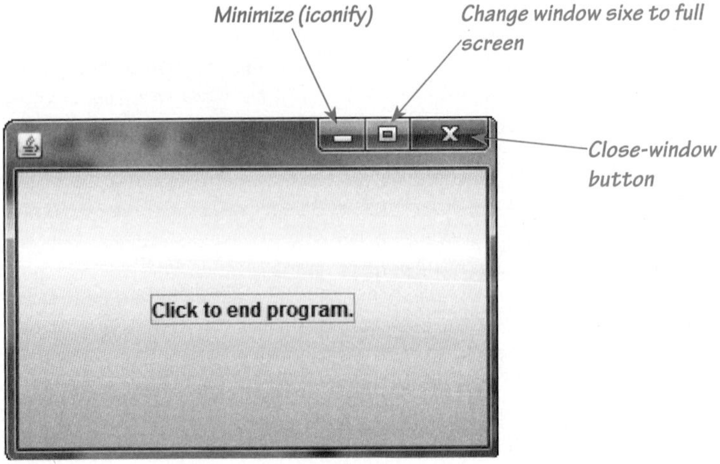

> ### Pixel
>
> A **pixel** is the smallest unit of space on which your screen can write. With Swing, both the size and the position of objects on the screen are measured in pixels. The more pixels you have on a screen, the greater the screen resolution.

pixel

> ### Resolution's Relationship to Object Size
>
> The relationship between resolution and size can seem confusing at first. A high-resolution screen is a screen of better quality than a low-resolution screen, so why does an object look smaller on a high-resolution screen and larger on a low-resolution screen? Consider a very simple case—namely, a one-pixel "dot." For a screen of fixed size, if there are very many pixels (high resolution), then the one-pixel dot will be very small. If there are fewer pixels (low resolution) for the same size screen, then each pixel must be larger because the smaller number of pixels cover the same screen. So, if there are fewer pixels, the one-pixel dot will be larger. Similarly, a two-pixel figure or a figure of any number of pixels will look larger on a low-resolution (fewer pixels) screen.

Display 17.3 **Some Methods in the Class `JFrame`** (part 1 of 2)

The class `JFrame` is in the `javax.swing` package.

```
public JFrame()
```

Constructor that creates an object of the class `JFrame`.

Display 17.3 **Some Methods in the Class JFrame** (part 2 of 2)

```
public JFrame(String title)
```

Constructor that creates an object of the class `JFrame` with the title given as the argument.

```
public void setDefaultCloseOperation(int operation)
```

Sets the action that will happen by default when the user clicks the close-window button. The argument should be one of the following defined constants:

`JFrame.DO_NOTHING_ON_CLOSE`: Do nothing. The `JFrame` does nothing, but if there are any registered window listeners, they are invoked. (Window listeners are explained in Chapter 18.)

`JFrame.HIDE_ON_CLOSE`: Hide the frame after invoking any registered `WindowListener` objects.

`JFrame.DISPOSE_ON_CLOSE`: Hide and *dispose* the frame after invoking any registered window listeners. When a window is **disposed**, it is eliminated but the program does not end. To end the program, use the next constant as an argument to `setDefaultCloseOperation`.

`JFrame.EXIT_ON_CLOSE`: Exit the application using the `System exit` method. (Do not use this for frames in applets. Applets are discussed in Chapter 20 on the website.)

If no action is specified using the method `setDefaultCloseOperation`, then the default action taken is `JFrame.HIDE_ON_CLOSE`.

Throws an `IllegalArgumentException` if the argument is not one of the values listed above[3].

Throws a `SecurityException` if the argument is `JFrame.EXIT_ON_CLOSE` and the Security Manager will not allow the caller to invoke `System.exit`. (You are not likely to encounter this case.)

```
public void setSize(int width, int height)
```

Sets the size of the calling frame so that it has the `width` and `height` specified. Pixels are the units of length used.

```
public void setTitle(String title)
```

Sets the title for this frame to the argument string.

```
public void add(Component componentAdded)
```

Adds a component to the `JFrame`.

```
public void setLayout(LayoutManager manager)
```

Sets the layout manager. `Layout` managers are discussed later in this chapter in Section 17.3.

```
public void setJMenuBar(JMenuBar menubar)
```

Sets the menu bar for the calling frame. (Menus and menu bars are discussed later in this chapter in Section 17.4.)

```
public void dispose()
```

Eliminates the calling frame and all its subcomponents. Any memory they use is released for reuse. If there are items left (items other than the calling frame and its subcomponents), then this does not end the program. (The method `dispose` is discussed in Chapter 19.)

[3] If you have not yet covered Chapter 9 on exceptions, you can safely ignore all references to "throwing exceptions."

The `setVisible` Method

Many classes of Swing objects have a `setVisible` method. The `setVisible` method takes one argument of type `boolean`. If `w` is an object, such as a `JFrame` window, that can be displayed on the screen, then the call

```
w.setVisible(true);
```

will make `w` visible. The call

```
w.setVisible(false);
```

will hide `w`.

SYNTAX

```
Object_For_Screen.setVisible(Boolean_Expression);
```

EXAMPLE (FROM DISPLAY 17.2)

```
public static void main(String[] args)
{
    JFrame firstWindow = new JFrame();
          .
          .
          .
    firstWindow.setVisible(true);
}
```

PITFALL: Forgetting to Program the Close-Window Button

The following lines from Display 17.2 ensure that when the user clicks the close-window button, nothing happens:

```
firstWindow.setDefaultCloseOperation(
                              JFrame.DO_NOTHING_ON_CLOSE);
```

If you forget to program the close-window button, then the default action is as if you had set it the following way:

```
firstWindow.setDefaultCloseOperation(
                              JFrame.HIDE_ON_CLOSE);
```

In the program in Display 17.2, this would mean that if the user clicks the close-window button, the window will hide (become invisible and inaccessible), but the program will not end, which is a pretty bad situation. Because the window would be hidden, there would be no way to click the `"Click to end program."` button. You would need to use some operating system command that forces the program to end. That is an operating system topic, not a Java topic, and the exact command depends on which operating system you are using. ■

MyProgrammingLab™

Self-Test Exercises

1. What Swing class do you normally use to define a window? Any window class that you define would normally be an object of this class.

2. What units of measure are used in the following call to `setSize` that appeared in the `main` method of the program in Display 17.2? In other words, 300 what? Inches? Centimeters? Light years? And similarly, 200 what?

   ```
   firstWindow.setSize(WIDTH, HEIGHT);
   ```

   which is equivalent to

   ```
   firstWindow.setSize(300, 200);
   ```

3. What is the method call to set the close-window button of the `JFrame` `someWindow` so that nothing happens when the user clicks the close-window button in `someWindow`?

4. What is the method call to set the close-window button of the `JFrame` `someWindow` so that the program ends when the user clicks the close-window button in `someWindow`?

5. What happens when you click the minimizing button of the `JFrame` shown in Display 17.2?

6. Suppose `someWindow` is a `JFrame` and `n` is an `int` variable with some value. Give a Java statement that will make `someWindow` visible if `n` is positive and hide `someWindow` otherwise.

Buttons

`JButton`

A button object is created in the same way that any other object is created, but you use the class `JButton`. For example, the following example from Display 17.2 creates a button:

```
JButton endButton = new JButton("Click to end program.");
```

The argument to the construct, in this case, `"Click to end program."`, is a string that will be written on the button when the button is displayed. If you look at the picture of the GUI in Display 17.2, you will see that the button is labeled `"Click to end program."`

adding a button

We have already discussed adding components, such as buttons, to a `JFrame`. The button is added to the `JFrame` by the following line from Display 17.2:

```
firstWindow.add(endButton);
```

In the next subsection, we explain the lines from Display 17.2 involving the method `addActionListener`.

The `JButton` Class

An object of the class `JButton` is displayed in a GUI as a component that looks like a button. Click the button with your mouse to simulate pushing it. When creating an object of the class `JButton` using `new`, you can give a string argument to the constructor and the string will be displayed on the button.

You can add a `JButton` object to a `JFrame` by using the method `add` with the `JFrame` as the calling object and the `JButton` object as the argument. You will later see that you can also add buttons to other GUI objects (known as "containers") in a similar way.

A button's action is programmed by registering a listener with the button using the method `addActionListener`.

EXAMPLE

```
JButton niceButton = new JButton("Click here");
niceButton.addActionListener(new SomeActionListenerClass());
someJFrame.add(niceButton);
```

The Close-Window Button Is Not in the Class `JButton`

The buttons that you add to a GUI are all objects of the class `JButton`. The close-window button and the other two accompanying buttons on a `JFrame` are not objects of the class `JButton`. They are part of the `JFrame` object.

Action Listeners and Action Events

Clicking a button with your mouse (or activating certain other items in a GUI) creates an object known as an event and sends the event object to another object (or objects) known as the listener(s). This is called **firing the event**. The listener then performs some action. When we say that the event is "sent" to the listener object, what we really mean is that some method in the listener object is invoked with the event object as the argument. This invocation happens automatically. Your Swing GUI class definition will not normally contain an invocation of this method. However, your Swing GUI class definition does need to do two things:

registering a listener

- First, for each button, it needs to specify what objects are listeners that will respond to events fired by that button; this is called **registering** the listener.
- Second, it must define the methods that will be invoked when the event is sent to the listener. Note that these methods will be defined by you, but in normal circumstances, you will never write an invocation of these methods. The invocations will take place automatically.

addAction Listener

The following lines from Display 17.2 create an `EndingListener` object named `buttonEar` and register `buttonEar` as a listener to receive events from the button named `endButton`:

```
EndingListener buttonEar = new EndingListener( );
endButton.addActionListener(buttonEar);
```

The second line says that `buttonEar` is registered as a listener to `endButton`, which means `buttonEar` will receive all events fired by `endButton`.

action event

Action Listener

Different kinds of components require different kinds of listener classes to handle the events they fire. A button fires events known as **action events**, which are handled by listeners known as **action listeners**.

An action listener is an object whose class implements the `ActionListener` interface. For example, the class `EndingListener` in Display 17.2 implements the `ActionListener` interface. The `ActionListener` interface has only one method heading that must be implemented, namely the following:

actionPerformed

```
public void actionPerformed(ActionEvent e)
```

In the class `EndingListener` in Display 17.2, the `actionPerformed` method is defined as follows:

```
public void actionPerformed(ActionEvent e)
{
    System.exit(0);
}
```

If the user clicks the button `endButton`, it sends an action event to the action listener for that button. But `buttonEar` is the action listener for the button `endButton`, so the action event goes to `buttonEar`. When an action listener receives an action event, the event is automatically passed as an argument to the method `actionPerformed` and the method `actionPerformed` is invoked. If the event is called `e`, then the following invocation takes place in response to `endButton` firing `e`:

```
buttonEar.actionPerformed(e);
```

In this case, the parameter `e` is ignored by the method `actionPerformed`. The method `actionPerformed` simply invokes `System.exit` and thereby ends the program. So, if the user clicks `endButton` (the one labeled `"Click to end program."`), the net effect is to end the program and so the window goes away.

Note that you never write any code that says

```
buttonEar.actionPerformed(e);
```

This action does happen, but the code for this is embedded in some class definition inside the Swing and/or AWT libraries. Somewhere the code says something like

```
bla.actionPerformed(e);
```

and somehow `buttonEar` gets plugged in for the parameter `bla` and this invocation of `actionPerformed` is executed. But, all this is done for you. All you do is define the method `actionPerformed` and register `buttonEar` as a listener for `endButton`.

Note that the method `actionPerformed` must have a parameter of type `ActionEvent`, even if your definition of `actionPerformed` does not use this parameter. This is because the invocations of `actionPerformed` were already programmed for you and so must allow the possibility of using the `ActionEvent` parameter `e`. As you will see, in other Swing GUIs the method `actionPerformed` does often use the event `e` to determine which button was clicked. This first example is a special, simple case because there is only one button. Later in this chapter, we will say more about defining the `actionPerformed` method in more complicated situations.

PITFALL: Changing the Heading for `actionPerformed`

When you define the method `actionPerformed` in an action listener, you are implementing the method heading for `actionPerformed` that is specified in the `ActionListener` interface. Thus, the header for the method `actionPerformed` is determined for you, and you cannot change the heading. It must have exactly one parameter, and that parameter must be of type `ActionEvent`, as in the following:

```
public void actionPerformed(ActionEvent e)
```

If you change the type of the parameter or if you add (or subtract) a parameter, you will not have given a correct definition of an action listener.[4] The only thing you can change is the name of the parameter `e`, because it is just a placeholder. So the following change is acceptable:

```
public void actionPerformed(ActionEvent theEvent)
```

Of course, if you make this change, then inside the body of the method `actionPerformed`, you will use the identifier `theEvent` in place of the identifier `e`.

You also cannot add a `throws` clause to the method `actionPerformed`.[5] If a checked exception is thrown in the definition of `actionPerformed`, then it must be caught in the method `actionPerformed`. (Recall that a checked exception is one that must be either caught in a `catch` block or declared in a `throws` clause.) ■

TIP: Ending a Swing Program

A GUI program is normally based on a kind of infinite loop. There may not be a Java loop statement in a GUI program, but nonetheless the GUI program need not ever end. The windowing system normally stays on the screen until the user indicates that it should go away (for example, by clicking the `"Click to end program."` button in Display 17.2). If the user never asks the windowing system to go away, it will never go away. When you write a Swing GUI program, you need to use `System.exit` to end the program when the user (or something else) says it is time to do so. Unlike the kinds of programs we saw before this chapter, a Swing program will not end after it has executed all the code in the program. A Swing program does not end until it executes a `System.exit`. (In some cases, the `System.exit` may be in some library code and need not be explicitly given in your code.) ■

`System.exit`

[4]Although it would be rather questionable style, you can overload the method named `actionPerformed` so that you have multiple versions of the method `actionPerformed`, each with a different parameter list. But only the version of `actionPerformed` shown here has anything to do with making a class into an action listener.

[5]If you have not yet covered exception handling (Chapter 9), you can safely ignore this paragraph.

MyProgrammingLab™

Self-Test Exercises

7. What kind of event is fired when you click a `JButton`?
8. What method heading must be implemented in a class that implements the `ActionListener` interface?
9. Change the program in Display 17.2 so that the window displayed has the title `"My First Window"`. *Hint*: Consult the description of constructors in Display 17.3.

EXAMPLE: A Better Version of Our First Swing GUI

Display 17.4 is a rewriting of the demonstration program in Display 17.2 that includes a few added features. This new version produces a window that is similar to the one produced by the program in Display 17.2. However, this new version is done in the style you should follow in writing your own GUIs. Notice that the window is produced by defining a class (`FirstWindow`) whose objects are windows of the kind we want. The window is then displayed by a program (`DemoWindow`) that uses the class `FirstWindow`.

Observe that `FirstWindow` is a derived class of the class `JFrame`. This is the normal way to define a windowing interface. The base class `JFrame` gives some basic window facilities, and then the derived class adds whatever additional features you want in your window interface.

Note that the constructor in Display 17.4 starts by calling the constructor for the parent class `JFrame` with the line

```
super();
```

As we noted in Chapter 7, this ensures that any initialization that is normally done for all objects of type `JFrame` will in fact be done. If the base class constructor you call has no arguments, then it will be called automatically, so we could have omitted the invocation of `super()` in Display 17.4. However, if the base class constructor needs an argument, as it may in some other situations, then you must include a call to the base class constructor, `super`.

Note that almost all the initializing for the window `FirstWindow` in Display 17.4 is placed in the constructor for the class. That is as it should be. The initialization, such as setting the initial window size, should be part of the class definition and not actions performed by objects of the class (as they were in Display 17.2). All the initializing methods, such as `setSize` and `setDefaultCloseOperation`, are inherited from the class `JFrame`. Because they are invoked in the constructor for the window, the window itself is the calling object. In other words, a method invocation such as

```
setSize(WIDTH, HEIGHT);
```

is equivalent to

```
this.setSize(WIDTH, HEIGHT);
```

(continued)

EXAMPLE: (continued)

Similarly, the method invocations

```
setDefaultCloseOperation(
                JFrame.DO_NOTHING_ON_CLOSE);
```

and

```
add(endButton);
```

are equivalent to

```
this.setDefaultCloseOperation(
                JFrame.DO_NOTHING_ON_CLOSE);
```

and

```
this.add(endButton);
```

In the class `FirstWindow` (Display 17.4), we added the title `"First Window Class"` to the window as follows:

```
setTitle("First Window Class");
```

You can see where the title is displayed in a `JFrame` by looking at the picture of the GUI given in Display 17.4.

One thing we did differently in Display 17.4 than in Display 17.2 is to use an anonymous object in the following line:

```
endButton.addActionListener(new EndingListener());
```

The same action was performed by the following lines in Display 17.2:

```
EndingListener buttonEar = new EndingListener();
endButton.addActionListener(buttonEar);
```

In Display 17.2, we were trying to be extra clear and so we used these two steps. However, it makes more sense to use the anonymous object `new EndingListener()` because this listener object is never referenced again and so does not need a name.

The program `DemoWindow` in Display 17.4 simply displays an object of the class `FirstWindow` on the screen.

Almost all of the initialization details for the window in Display 17.4 have been moved to the constructor for the class `FirstWindow`. However, we have placed the invocations of the method `setVisible` in the application program that uses the window class `FirstWindow`. We could have placed an invocation of `setVisible` in the constructor for `FirstWindow` and omitted the invocation of `setVisible` from the application program `DemoWindow` (Display 17.4). If we had done so, we would have produced the same results when we ran the application program. However, in normal situations, the application program knows when the window should be displayed, so it is normal to put the invocation of the method `setVisible` in the application program. The programmer writing the class `FirstWindow` cannot anticipate when a programmer who uses the window will want to make it visible (or hide it).

Display 17.4 The Normal Way to Define a `JFrame`

```
import javax.swing.JFrame;
import javax.swing.JButton;

public class FirstWindow extends JFrame
{
    public static final int WIDTH = 300;
    public static final int HEIGHT = 200;

    public FirstWindow()
    {
       super();
       setSize(WIDTH, HEIGHT);

       setTitle("First Window Class");
       setDefaultCloseOperation(
                                 JFrame.DO_NOTHING_ON_CLOSE);

       JButton endButton = new JButton("Click to end program.");
       endButton.addActionListener(new EndingListener());
       add(endButton);
    }
}
```

The class `EndingListener` *is defined in Display 17.2.*

This is the file `FirstWindow.java`.

This is the file `DemoWindow.java`.

```
public class DemoWindow
{
    public static void main(String[] args)
    {
        FirstWindow w = new FirstWindow();
        w.setVisible(true);
    }
}
```

Resulting GUI

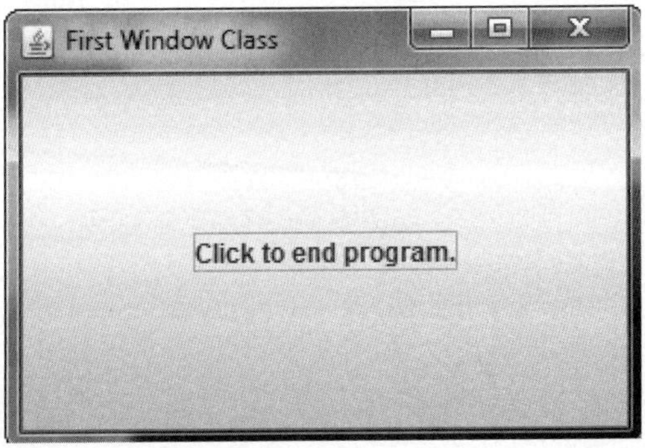

> **`JFrame` Classes**
>
> When we say that a class is a **JFrame class**, we mean the class is a descendent class of the class `JFrame`. For example, the class `FirstWindow` in Display 17.4 is a `JFrame` class. When we say an object is a **JFrame**, we mean that it is an object of some `JFrame` class.

MyProgrammingLab™

Self-Test Exercises

10. Change the program in Display 17.4 so that the title of the `JFrame` is not set by the method `setTitle` but is instead set by the call to the base class constructor. *Hint*: Recall Self-Test Exercise 9.

11. Change the program in Display 17.4 so that there are two ways to end the GUI program: The program can be ended by either clicking the `"Click to end program."` button or clicking the close-window button.

Labels

label

`JLabel`

We have seen how to add a button to a `JFrame`. If you want to add some text to your `JFrame`, use a label instead of a button. A **label** is an object of the class `JLabel`. A label is little more than a line of text. The text for the label is given as an argument to the `JLabel` constructor as follows:

```
JLabel greeting = new JLabel("Hello");
```

The label `greeting` can then be added to a `JFrame` just as a button is added. For example, the following might appear in a constructor for a derived class of `JFrame`:

```
JLabel greeting = new JLabel("Hello");
add(greeting);
```

The next Programming Example, "A GUI with a Label and Color," includes a label in a `JFrame` GUI.

> **The `JLabel` Class**
>
> An object of the class `JLabel` is little more than one line of text that can be added to a `JFrame` (or, as we will see, added to certain other objects).
>
> **EXAMPLE (INSIDE A CONSTRUCTOR FOR A DERIVED CLASS OF `JFRAME`)**
>
> ```
> JLabel myLabel = new JLabel("Hi Mom!");
> add(myLabel);
> ```

Color

You can set the color of a JFrame (or other GUI object). To set the background color of a JFrame, use

getContentPane

set Background

Color.BLUE

```
getContentPane().setBackground(Color);
```

For example, the following will set the color of the JFrame named someFrame to blue:

```
someFrame.getContentPane().setBackground(Color.BLUE);
```

Alternatively, if you set the color in the constructor for the JFrame, the invocation takes the form

```
getContentPane().setBackground(Color.BLUE);
```

which is equivalent to

```
this.getContentPane().setBackground(Color.BLUE);
```

The next Programming Example, "A GUI with a Label and Color," shows a JFrame object (in fact, two of them) with color.

content pane

The method invocation getContentPane() returns something called the **content pane** of the JFrame. So,

```
getContentPane().setBackground(Color.BLUE);
```

actually sets the color of the content pane to blue. The content pane is the "inside" of the JFrame, so coloring the content pane has the effect of coloring the inside of the JFrame. However, you can think of

```
getContentPane().setBackground(Color);
```

as a peculiarly spelled method invocation that sets the color of the JFrame. (In this book, we will not be referring to the content pane of a JFrame except when we want to color the JFrame, so we will explain the content pane no further.)

get Content Pane

Use getContentPane only when you give color to a JFrame. As you will see, to set the color of some component in a JFrame, such as a button, simply use the method setBackground with the button or other component as the calling object. You will see examples of adding color to components in Section 17.3.

color

Color

What kind of thing is a **color** when used in a Java Swing class? Like everything else in Java, a color is an object—in this case, an object that is an instance of the class Color. The class Color is in the java.awt package. (Note that the package name is java.awt, not javax.awt.)

In a later chapter, you will see how you can define your own colors, but for now we will use the colors that are already defined for you, such as Color.BLUE, which is a constant named BLUE that is defined in the class Color. The constant, of course, represents the color blue. If you set the background of a JFrame to Color.BLUE, then the JFrame will have a blue background. The type of the constant Color.BLUE and other such constants is Color. The list of color constants that are defined for you are given in Display 17.5. The next Programming Example, "A GUI with a Label and Color," has an example of a constructor with one parameter of type Color.

Display 17.5 The Color Constants

```
Color.BLACK               Color.MAGENTA
Color.BLUE                Color.ORANGE
Color.CYAN                Color.PINK
Color.DARK_GRAY           Color.RED
Color.GRAY                Color.WHITE
Color.GREEN               Color.YELLOW
Color.LIGHT_GRAY
```

The class `Color` is in the `java.awt` package.

EXAMPLE: A GUI with a Label and Color

Display 17.6 shows a class for GUIs with a label and a background color. We have already discussed the use of color for this window. The label is used to display the text string `"Close-window button works."` The label is created as follows:

```
JLabel aLabel = new JLabel("Close-window button works.");
```

The label is added to the `JFrame` with the method `add` as shown in the following line from Display 17.6:

```
add(aLabel);
```

The GUI class `ColoredWindow` in Display 17.6 programs the close-window button as follows:

```
setDefaultCloseOperation(JFrame.EXIT_ON_CLOSE);
```

This way, when the user clicks the close-window button, the program ends. Note that if the program has more than one window, as it does in Display 17.6, and the user clicks the close-window button in any one window of the class `ColoredWindow`, then the entire program ends and all windows go away.

Note that we set the title of the `JFrame` by making it an argument to `super` rather than an argument to `setTitle`. This is another common way to set the title of a `JFrame`.

If you run the program `DemoColoredWindow` in Display 17.6, then the two windows will be placed one on top of the other. To see both windows, you need to use your mouse to move the top window.

Setting the Title of a `JFrame`

The two most common ways to set the title of a `JFrame` are to use the method `setTitle`, as illustrated in Display 17.4, or to give the title as an argument to the base class constructor `super`, as illustrated in Display 17.6.

MyProgrammingLab™

Self-Test Exercises

12. How would you modify the class definition in Display 17.6 so that the window produced by the no-argument constructor is magenta instead of pink?

13. Rewrite the following two lines from Display 17.6 so that the label does not have the name `aLabel` or any other name. *Hint*: Use an anonymous object.

```
JLabel aLabel = new JLabel("Close-window button works.");
add(aLabel);
```

Display 17.6 A **JFrame** with Color (part 1 of 2)

```
import javax.swing.JFrame;
import javax.swing.JLabel;
import java.awt.Color;

public class ColoredWindow extends JFrame
{
    public static final int WIDTH = 300;
    public static final int HEIGHT = 200;

    public ColoredWindow(Color theColor)
    {

        super("No Charge for Color");
        setSize(WIDTH, HEIGHT);
        setDefaultCloseOperation(JFrame.EXIT_ON_CLOSE);

        getContentPane().setBackground(theColor);

        JLabel aLabel = new JLabel("Close-window button works.");
        add(aLabel);
    }
    public ColoredWindow()
    {
        this(Color.BLUE);
    }
}
```

This is an invocation of the other constructor.

This is the file **ColoredWindow java**.

```
import java.awt.Color;

public class DemoColoredWindow
{
    public static void main(String[] args)
    {
        ColoredWindow w1 = new ColoredWindow();
        w1.setVisible(true);

        ColoredWindow w2 = new ColoredWindow(Color.GRAY);
        w2.setVisible(true);
    }
}
```

This is the file **ColoredWindow java**.

(continued)

Display 17.6 A `JFrame` with Color (part 2 of 2)

RESULTING GUI

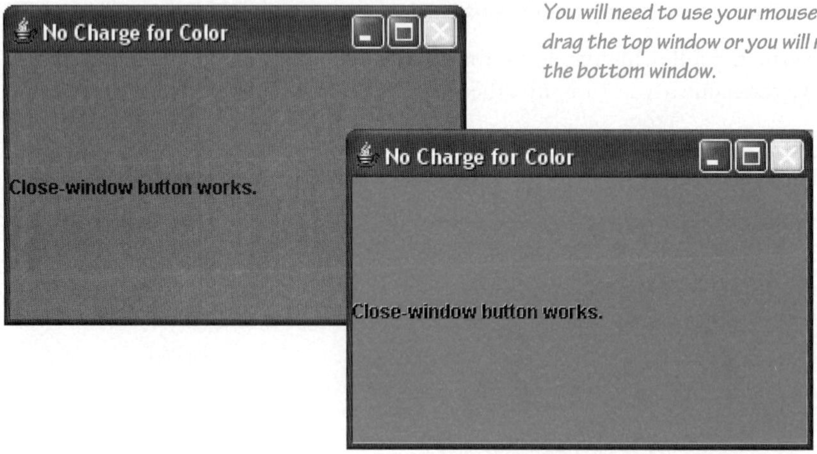

You will need to use your mouse to drag the top window or you will not see the bottom window.

17.3 Containers and Layout Managers

Don't put all your eggs in one basket.

PROVERB

There are two main ways to create new classes from old classes. One way is to use inheritance; this is known as the *Is-A relationship.* For example, an object of the class `ColoredWindow` in Display 17.6 *is a* `JFrame` because `ColoredWindow` is a derived class of the class `JFrame`. The second way to create a new class from an existing class (or classes) is to have instance variables of an already existing class type; this is known as *composition* or the *Has-A relationship.* The Swing library has already set things up so you can easily use composition. The actual code for declaring instance variables is in the Swing library classes, such as the class `JFrame`. Rather than declaring instance variables, add components to a `JFrame` using the `add` method. This does ultimately set some instance variables, but this is done automatically when you use the `add` method. In this section, we discuss adding and arranging components in a GUI or subpart of a GUI.

Thus far, we have only added one component, either a button or a label, to a `JFrame`. You can add more than one component to a `JFrame`. To do so, use the `add` method multiple times, but the `add` method simply tells which components are added to the `JFrame`; it does not say how they are arranged, such as side by side or one above the other. To describe how the components are arranged, you need to use a **layout manager**.

layout manager

In this section, we will see that there are other classes of objects besides `JFrames` that can have components added with the `add` method and arranged by a layout manager. All these classes are known as **container classes**.

container class

Border Layout Managers

If you do not specify a layout, then Java will use a `BorderLayout` by default. Display 17.7 contains an example of a GUI that uses a layout manager to arrange three labels in a `JFrame`. The labels are arranged one below the other on three lines.

A layout manager is added to the `JFrame` class in Display 17.7 with the following line:

`setLayout`

```
setLayout(new BorderLayout());
```

`Border Layout`

`BorderLayout` is a layout manager class, so `new BorderLayout()` produces a new anonymous object of the class `BorderLayout`. This `BorderLayout` object is given the task of arranging components (in this case, labels) that are added to the `JFrame`.

It may help to note that the previous invocation of `setLayout` is equivalent to the following:

```
BorderLayout manager = new BorderLayout();
setLayout(manager);
```

Display 17.7 The **`BorderLayout`** Manager (part 1 of 2)

```
import javax.swing.JFrame;
import javax.swing.JLabel;
import java.awt.BorderLayout;

public class BorderLayoutJFrame extends JFrame
{
    public static final int WIDTH = 500;
    public static final int HEIGHT = 400;

    public BorderLayoutJFrame()
    {
        super("BorderLayout Demonstration");
        setSize(WIDTH, HEIGHT);
        setDefaultCloseOperation(JFrame.EXIT_ON_CLOSE);

        setLayout(new BorderLayout( ));

        JLabel label1 = new JLabel("First label");
        add(label1, BorderLayout.NORTH);

        JLabel label2 = new JLabel("Second label");
        add(label2, BorderLayout.SOUTH);

        JLabel label3 = new JLabel("Third label");
        add(label3, BorderLayout.CENTER);
    }
}
```

This is the file `BorderLayoutJFrame.java`.

(continued)

Display 17.7 The **`BorderLayout`** Manager (part 2 of 2)

This is the file **`BorderLayoutDemo java`**.

```
public class BorderLayoutDemo
{
    public static void main(String[] args)
    {
        BorderLayoutJFrame gui = new BorderLayoutJFrame();
        gui.setVisible(true);
    }
}
```

RESULTING GUI

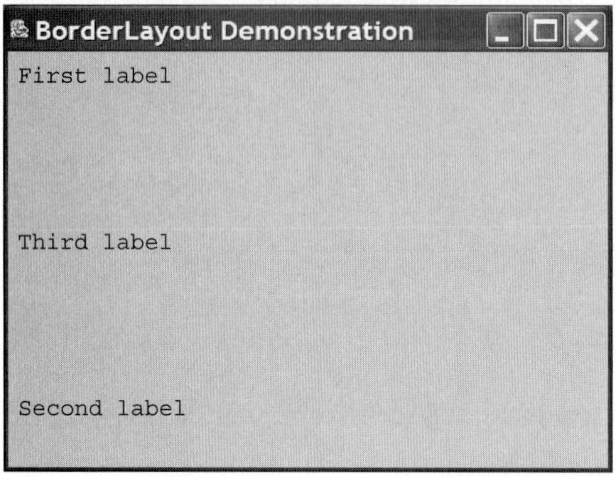

A `BorderLayout` manager places labels (or other components) into the five regions `BorderLayout.NORTH`, `BorderLayout.SOUTH`, `BorderLayout.EAST`, `BorderLayout.WEST`, and `BorderLayout.CENTER`. These five regions are arranged as shown in Display 17.8. The outside box represents the `JFrame` (or other container to which you will add things). None of the lines in the diagram will be visible unless you do something to make them visible. We drew them in to show you where each region is located.

Display 17.8 `BorderLayout` Regions

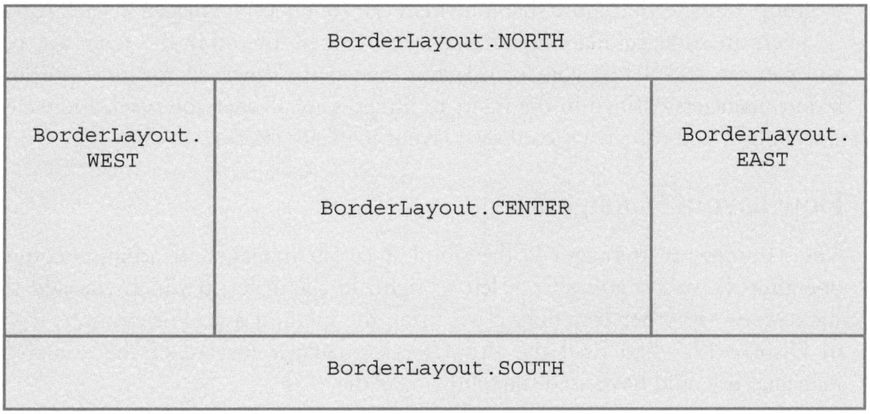

In Display 17.7, we added labels as follows:

```
JLabel label1 = new JLabel("First label");
add(label1, BorderLayout.NORTH);

JLabel label2 = new JLabel("Second label");
add(label2, BorderLayout.SOUTH);

JLabel label3 = new JLabel("Third label");
add(label3, BorderLayout.CENTER);
```

When you use a `BorderLayout` manager, you give the location of the component added as a second argument to the method `add`, as in the following:

```
add(label1, BorderLayout.NORTH);
```

The labels (or other components to be added) need not be added in any particular order, because the second argument completely specifies where the label is placed.

`BorderLayout.NORTH`, `BorderLayout.SOUTH`, `BorderLayout.EAST`, `BorderLayout.WEST`, and `BorderLayout.CENTER` are five string constants defined in the class `BorderLayout`. The values of these constants are `"North"`, `"South"`, `"East"`, `"West"`, and `"Center"`. Although you can use a quoted string such as `"North"` as the second argument to `add`, it is more consistent with our general style rules to use a defined constant such as `BorderLayout.NORTH`.

You need not use all five regions. For example, in Display 17.7 we did not use the regions `BorderLayout.EAST` and `BorderLayout.WEST`. If some regions are not used, any extra space is given to the `BorderLayout.CENTER` region, which is the largest region.

(The space is divided between regions as follows: Regions are allocated space in the order first north and south, second east and west, and last center. So, in particular, if there is nothing in the north region, then the east and west regions will extend to the top of the space.)

From this discussion, it sounds as though you can place only one item in each region, but later in this chapter, when we discuss *panels*, you will see that there is a way to group items so that more than one item can (in effect) be placed in each region.

There are some standard layout managers defined for you in the `java.awt` package, and you can also define your own layout managers. However, for most purposes, the layout managers defined in the standard libraries are all that you need, and we will not discuss how you can create your own layout manager classes.

Flow Layout Managers

The `FlowLayout` **manager** is the simplest layout manager. It arranges components one after the other, going from left to right, in the order in which you add them to the `JFrame` (or other container class) using the method `add`. For example, if the class in Display 17.7 had used the `FlowLayout` manager instead of the `BorderLayout` manager, it would have used the following code:

```
setLayout(new FlowLayout());

JLabel label1 = new JLabel("First label");
add(label1);

JLabel label2 = new JLabel("Second label");
add(label2);

JLabel label3 = new JLabel("Third label");
add(label3);
```

Layout Managers

The components that you add to a container class are arranged by an object known as a **layout manager**. Add a layout manager with the method `setLayout`, which is a method of every container class, such as a `JFrame` or an object of any of the other container classes that we will introduce later in this chapter. If you do not add a layout manager, a default layout manager will be provided for you.

SYNTAX

Container_Object`.setLayout(new` *Layout_Manager_Class*`());`

EXAMPLE (WITHIN A CONSTRUCTOR FOR A CLASS CALLED `BorderLayoutJFrame`)

```
public BorderLayoutJFrame()
{
      . . .
    setLayout(new BorderLayout());

    JLabel label1 = new JLabel("First label");
    add(label1, BorderLayout.NORTH);

    JLabel label2 = new JLabel("Second label");
    add(label2, BorderLayout.SOUTH);
      . . .
}
```

Note that if we had used the `FlowLayout` manager, as in the preceding code, then the `add` method would have only one argument. With a `FlowLayout` manager, the items are displayed in the order they are added, so that the labels above would be displayed all on one line as follows:

```
First label Second label Third label
```

extra code on website

The full program is in the files `FlowLayoutJFrame.java` and `FlowLayoutDemo.java` on the accompanying website. You will see a number of examples of GUIs that use the `FlowLayout` manager class later in this chapter.

Grid Layout Managers

`GridLayout`

A **`GridLayout` manager** arranges components in a two-dimensional grid with some number of rows and columns. With a `GridLayout` manager, each entry is the same size. For example, the following says to use a `GridLayout` manager with `aContainer`, which can be a `JFrame` or other container:

```
aContainer.setLayout(new GridLayout(2, 3));
```

The two numbers given as arguments to the constructor `GridLayout` specify the number of rows and columns. This would produce the following sort of layout:

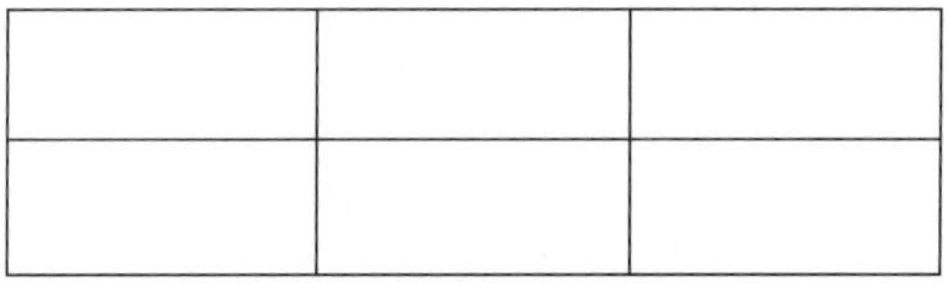

The lines will not be visible unless you do something special to make them so. They are just included here to show you the region boundaries.

When using a `GridLayout` manager, each component is stretched so that it completely fills its grid position.

Although you specify a number of rows and columns, the rules for the number of rows and columns is more complicated than what we have said so far. If the values for the number of rows and the number of columns are both nonzero, then the number of columns will be ignored. For example, if the specification is `new GridLayout(2, 3)`, then some sample sizes are as follows: If you add six items, the grid will be as shown. If you add seven or eight items, a fourth column is automatically added, and so forth. If you add fewer than six components, there will be two rows and a reduced number of columns.

There is another way to specify that the number of columns is to be ignored. You can do this by setting the number of columns to zero, which will allow any number of columns. So a specification of `(2, 0)` is equivalent to `(2, 3)`, and in fact is equivalent to `(2, n)` for any nonnegative value of `n`. Similarly, you can specify that the number of rows is to be ignored by setting the number of rows to zero, which will allow any number of rows.

When using the `GridLayout` class, the method `add` has only one argument. The items are placed in the grid from left to right, first filling the top row, then the second row, and so forth. You are not allowed to skip any grid position (although you will later see that you can add something that does not show and so gives the illusion of skipping a grid position).

A sample use of the `GridLayout` class is given in Display 17.9.

Display 17.9 The `GridLayout` Manager (part 1 of 2)

```
import javax.swing.JFrame;
import javax.swing.JLabel;
import java.awt.GridLayout;

public class GridLayoutJFrame extends JFrame
{
    public static final int WIDTH = 500;
    public static final int HEIGHT = 400;

    public static void main(String[] args)
    {
        GridLayoutJFrame gui = new GridLayoutJFrame(2, 3);
        gui.setVisible(true);
    }

    public GridLayoutJFrame(int rows, int columns )
    {
        super();
        setSize(WIDTH, HEIGHT);
        setTitle("GridLayout Demonstration");
        setDefaultCloseOperation(JFrame.EXIT_ON_CLOSE);
        setLayout(new GridLayout(rows, columns ));

        JLabel label1 = new JLabel("First label");
        add(label1);

        JLabel label2 = new JLabel("Second label");
        add(label2);

        JLabel label3 = new JLabel("Third label");
        add(label3);

        JLabel label4 = new JLabel("Fourth label");
        add(label4);

        JLabel label5 = new JLabel("Fifth label");
        add(label5);
    }
}
```

Display 17.9 The `GridLayout` Manager (part 2 of 2)

Resulting GUI

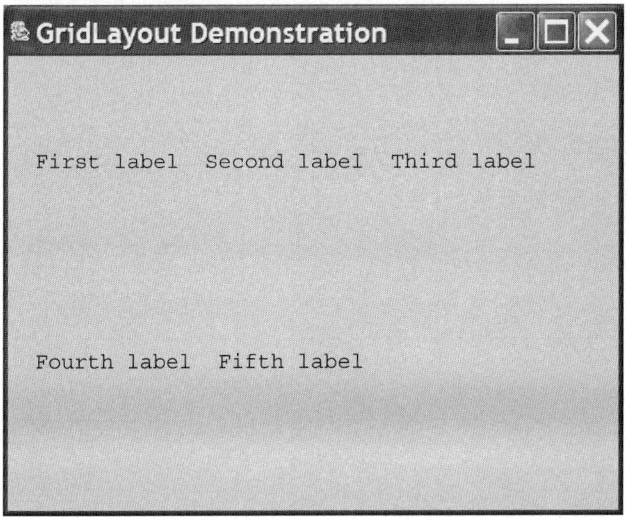

Note that we have placed a demonstration `main` method in the class definition in Display 17.9. This is handy, but is not typical. Normally, a Swing GUI is created and displayed in a `main` method (or other method) in some class other than the class that defines the GUI. However, it is perfectly legal and sometimes convenient to place a `main` method in the GUI class definition so that it is easy to display a sample of the GUI. Note that the `main` method that is given in the class itself is written in the same way as a `main` method that is in some other class. In particular, you need to construct an object of the class, as in the following line from the `main` method in Display 17.9:

```
GridLayoutJFrame gui = new GridLayoutJFrame(2, 3);
```

VideoNote
GUI Layout using an IDE

The three layout managers we have discussed are summarized in Display 17.10.

Next we will discuss *panels,* which will let you realize the full potential of layout managers.

Display 17.10 Some Layout Managers

LAYOUT MANAGER	DESCRIPTION
These layout manager classes are in the `java.awt` package.	
`FlowLayout`	Displays components from left to right in the order in which they are added to the container.
`BorderLayout`	Displays the components in five areas: north, south, east, west, and center. You specify the area a component goes into in a second argument of the `add` method.
`GridLayout`	Lays out components in a grid, with each component stretched to fill its box in the grid.

MyProgrammingLab™

Self-Test Exercises

14. In Display 17.7, would it be legal to replace

```
JLabel label1 = new JLabel("First label");
add(label1, BorderLayout.NORTH);
JLabel label2 = new JLabel("Second label");
add(label2, BorderLayout.SOUTH);
JLabel label3 = new JLabel("Third label");
add(label3, BorderLayout.CENTER);
```

with the following?

```
JLabel aLabel = new JLabel("First label");
add(aLabel, BorderLayout.NORTH);
aLabel = new JLabel("Second label");
add(aLabel, BorderLayout.SOUTH);
aLabel = new JLabel("Third label");
add(aLabel, BorderLayout.CENTER);
```

In other words, can we reuse the variable `aLabel` or must each label have its own variable name?

15. How would you modify the class definition in Display 17.7 so that the three labels are displayed as follows?

```
First label
Second label
Third label
```

(There may be space between each pair of lines.)

MyProgrammingLab™

Self-Test Exercises (continued)

16. How would you modify the class definition in Display 17.7 so that the three labels are displayed as follows?

```
First label
                              Second label

Third label
```

(There may be space between each pair of lines.)

17. Suppose you are defining a windowing GUI class in the usual way, as a derived class of the class `JFrame`, and suppose you want to specify a layout manager for the `JFrame` so as to produce the following sort of layout (that is, a one-row layout, typically having three columns):

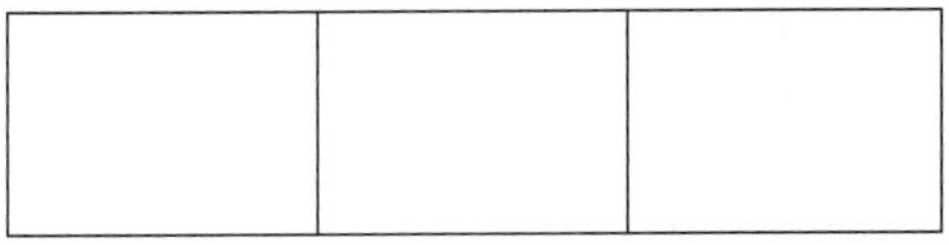

What should the argument to `setLayout` be?

18. Suppose the situation is as described in Self-Test Exercise 17, except that you want the following sort of layout (that is, a one-column layout, typically having three rows):

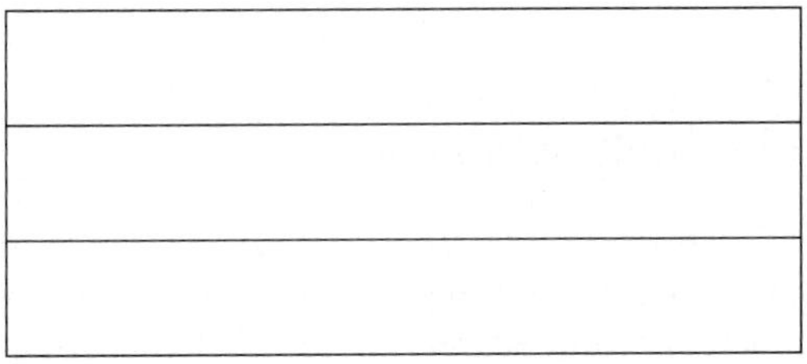

What should the argument to `setLayout` be?

Panels

panel

A GUI is often organized in a hierarchical fashion, with window-like containers, known as *panels*, inside of other window-like containers. A **panel** is an object of the class `JPanel`, which is a very simple container class that does little more than group objects. It is one of the simplest container classes, but an extremely useful one. A `JPanel` object is analogous to the braces used to combine a number of simpler Java statements into a single larger Java statement. It groups smaller objects, such as buttons and labels, into a larger component (the `JPanel`). You can then put the `JPanel` object in a JFrame. Thus, one of the main functions of JPanel objects is to subdivide a JFrame (or other container) into different areas.

For example, when you use a BorderLayout manager, you can place components in each of the five locations BorderLayout.NORTH, BorderLayout.SOUTH, BorderLayout.EAST, BorderLayout.WEST, and BorderLayout.CENTER. But what if you want to put two components at the bottom of the screen in the BorderLayout.SOUTH position? To do this, you would put the two components in a panel and then place the panel in the BorderLayout.SOUTH position.

You can give different layout managers to a JFrame and to each panel in the JFrame. Because you can add panels to other panels and each panel can have its own layout manager, this enables you to produce almost any kind of overall layout of the items in your GUI.

For example, if you want to place two buttons at the bottom of your JFrame GUI, you might add the following to the constructor of your JFrame GUI:

```
setLayout(new BorderLayout());

JPanel buttonPanel = new JPanel();
buttonPanel.setLayout(new FlowLayout());

JButton firstButton = new JButton("One");
buttonPanel.add(firstButton);

JButton secondButton = new JButton("Two");
buttonPanel.add(secondButton);

add(buttonPanel, BorderLayout.SOUTH);
```

The next Programming Example makes use of panels within panels.

EXAMPLE: A Tricolor Built with Panels

When first run, the GUI defined in Display 17.11 looks as shown in the first view. The entire background is light gray, and there are three buttons at the bottom of the GUI labeled "Green", "White", and "Gray". If you click any one of the buttons, a vertical stripe with the color written on the button appears. You can click the buttons in any order. In the last three views in Display 17.11, we show what happens if you click the buttons in left-to-right order.

The green, white, and gray stripes are the JPanes named greenPanel, whitePanel, and grayPanel. At first the panels are not visible because they are all light gray, so no borders are visible. When you click a button, the corresponding panel changes color and so is clearly visible.

Notice how the action listeners are set up. Each button registers the this parameter as a listener, as in the following line:

```
redButton.addActionListener(this);
```

Because this line appears inside of the constructor for the class PanelDemo, the this parameter refers to PanelDemo, which is the entire GUI. Thus, the entire JFrame

(continued)

EXAMPLE: (continued)

(the entire GUI) is the listener, not the `JPanel`. So when you click one of the buttons, it is the `actionPerformed` method in `PanelDemo` that is executed.

When a button is clicked, the `actionPerformed` method is invoked with the action event fired as the argument to `actionPerformed`. The method `actionPerformed` recovers the string written on the button with the following line:

```
String buttonString = e.getActionCommand();
```

The method `actionPerformed` then uses a multiway `if-else` statement to determine if `buttonString` is `"Blue"`, `"White"`, or `"Gray"` and changes the color of the corresponding panel accordingly. It is common for an `actionPerformed` method to be based on such a multiway `if-else` statement, although we will see another approach in the subsection entitled "Listeners as Inner Classes" later in this chapter.

Display 17.11 also introduces one other small but new technique. We gave each button a color. We did this with the method `setBackground`, using basically the same technique that we used in previous examples. You can give a button or almost any other item a color using `setBackground`. Note that you do not use `getContentPane` when adding color to any component other than a `JFrame`.

Display 17.11 Using Panels (part 1 of 4)

```
import javax.swing.JFrame;
import javax.swing.JPanel;
import java.awt.BorderLayout;
import java.awt.GridLayout;
import java.awt.FlowLayout;
import java.awt.Color;
import javax.swing.JButton;
import java.awt.event.ActionListener;
import java.awt.event.ActionEvent;

public class PanelDemo extends JFrame implements ActionListener
{
    public static final int WIDTH = 300;
    public static final int HEIGHT = 200;

    private JPanel bluePanel;
    private JPanel whitePanel;
    private JPanel grayPanel;

    public static void main(String[] args)
    {
        PanelDemo gui = new PanelDemo();
        gui.setVisible(true);
    }
```

In addition to being the GUI class, the class **`PanelDemo`** *is the action listener class. An object of the class* **`PanelDemo`** *is the action listener for the buttons in that object.*

We made these instance variables because we want to refer to them in both the constructor and the method **`actionPerformed`**.

(continued)

Display 17.11 **Using Panels** (part 2 of 4)

```
    public PanelDemo()
    {
        super("Panel Demonstration");
        setSize(WIDTH, HEIGHT);
        setDefaultCloseOperation(JFrame.EXIT_ON_CLOSE);
        setLayout(new BorderLayout());

        JPanel biggerPanel = new JPanel();
        biggerPanel.setLayout(new GridLayout(1, 3));

        bluePanel = new JPanel();
        bluePanel.setBackground(Color.LIGHT_GRAY);
        biggerPanel.add(bluePanel);

        whitePanel = new JPanel();
        whitePanel.setBackground(Color.LIGHT_GRAY);
        biggerPanel.add(whitePanel);
        grayPanel = new JPanel();
        grayPanel.setBackground(Color.LIGHT_GRAY);
        biggerPanel.add(grayPanel);

        add(biggerPanel, BorderLayout.CENTER);

        JPanel buttonPanel = new JPanel();
        buttonPanel.setBackground(Color.LIGHT_GRAY);
        buttonPanel.setLayout(new FlowLayout());

        JButton blueButton = new JButton("Blue");
        blueButton.setBackground(Color.BLUE);
        blueButton.addActionListener(this);
        buttonPanel.add(blueButton);

        JButton whiteButton = new JButton("White");
        whiteButton.setBackground(Color.WHITE);
        whiteButton.addActionListener(this);
        buttonPanel.add(whiteButton);

        JButton grayButton = new JButton("Gray");
        grayButton.setBackground(Color.GRAY);
        grayButton.addActionListener(this);
        buttonPanel.add(grayButton);

        add(buttonPanel, BorderLayout.SOUTH);
    }
    public void actionPerformed(ActionEvent e)
    {
        String buttonString = e.getActionCommand();

        if (buttonString.equals("Blue"))
            bluePanel.setBackground(Color.BLUE);
```

An object of the class `PanelDemo` *is the action listener for the buttons in that object.*

Display 17.11 **Using Panels** (part 3 of 4)

```
        else if (buttonString.equals("White"))
            whitePanel.setBackground(Color.WHITE);
        else if (buttonString.equals("Gray"))
            grayPanel.setBackground(Color.GRAY);
        else
            System.out.println("Unexpected error.");
    }
}
```

RESULTING GUI (When first run)

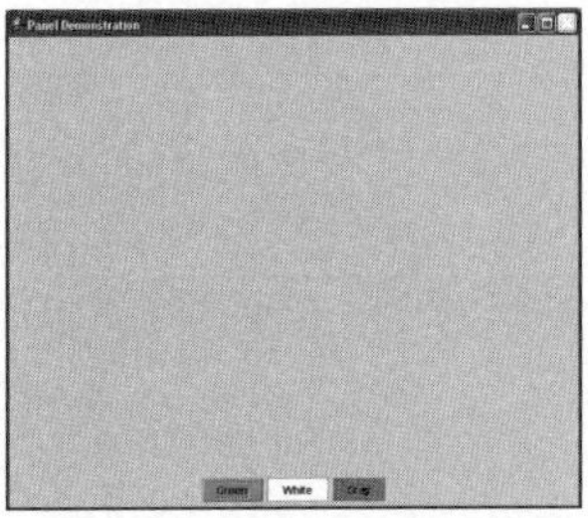

RESULTING GUI (After clicking Blue button)

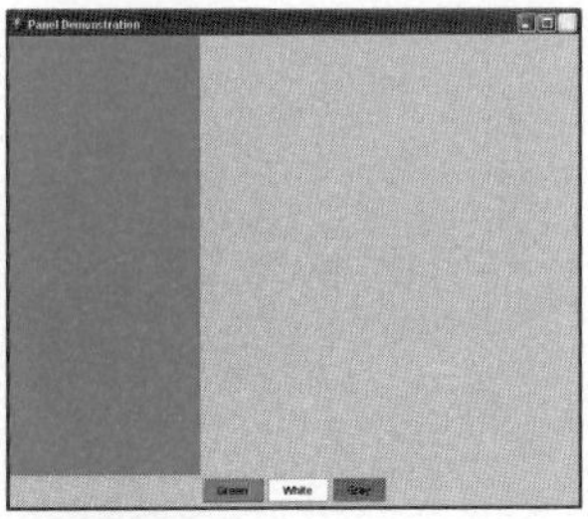

RESULTING GUI (After clicking White button)

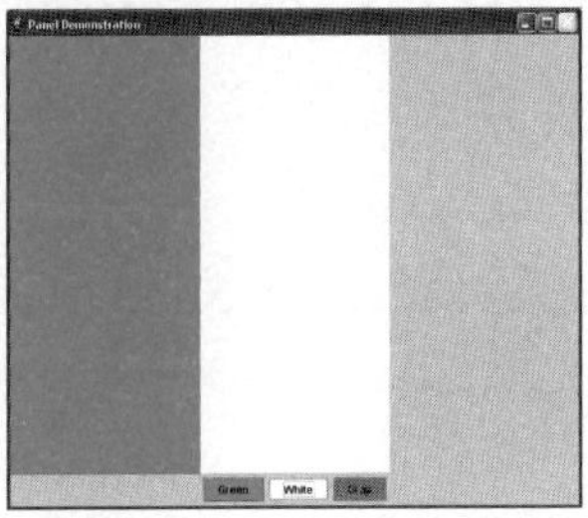

(continued)

Display 17.11 Using Panels (part 4 of 4)

RESULTING GUI (After clicking Gray button)

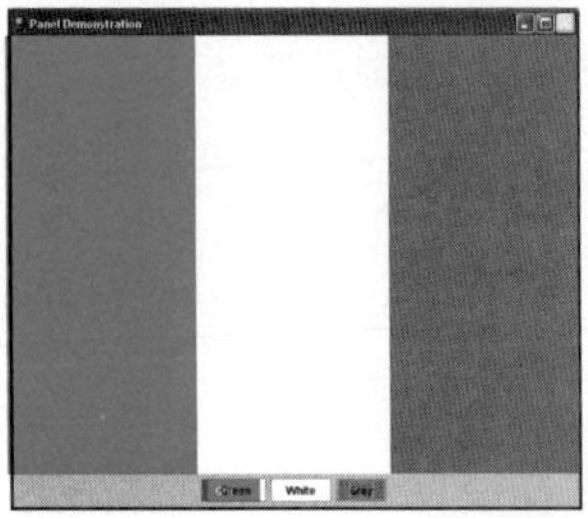

Adding Color

Color a `JFrame` as follows:

JFrame_Object`.getContentPane().setBackground(`*Color*`);`

If this is inside a constructor for the `JFrame`, then the expression simplifies to

`getContentPane().setBackground(`*Color*`);`

or the equivalent

`this.getContentPane().setBackground(`*Color*`);`

Color a button, label, or any other component (which is not a `JFrame`) as follows:

Component_Object`.setBackground(`*Color*`);`

Note that `getContentPane()` is only used with a `JFrame`.

EXAMPLE (INSIDE A CONSTRUCTOR FOR A DERIVED CLASS OF `JFrame`)

```
getContentPane().setBackground(Color.WHITE);
JButton redButton = new JButton("Red");
redButton.setBackground(Color.RED);
```

The `Container` Class

`Container` The class called `Container` is in the `java.awt` package. Any descendent class of the class `Container` can have components added to it (or, more precisely, can have components added to objects of the class). The class `JFrame` is a descendent class of the class `Container`, so any descendent class of the class `JFrame` can serve as a container to hold labels, buttons, panels, or other components.

Similarly, the class `JPanel` is a descendent of the class `Container`, and any object of the class `JPanel` can serve as a container to hold labels, buttons, other panels, or other components. Display 17.12 shows a portion of the hierarchy of Swing and AWT classes. Note that the `Container` class is in the AWT library and not in the Swing library. This is not a major issue, but it does mean that the `import` statement for the `Container` class is

```
import java.awt.Container;
```

container class

component

A **container class** is any descendent class of the class `Container`. The class `JComponent` serves a similar roll for components. Any descendent class of the class `JComponent` is called a `JComponent` or sometimes simply a **component**. You can add any `JComponent` object to any container class object.

The class `JComponent` is derived from the class `Container`, so you can add a `JComponent` to another `JComponent`. Often, this will turn out to be a viable option; occasionally it is something to avoid.[6]

The classes `Component`, `Frame`, and `Window` shown in Display 17.12 are AWT classes that some readers may have heard of. We include them for reference value, but we will have no need for these classes. We will eventually discuss all the other classes shown in Display 17.12.

When you are dealing with a Swing container class, you have three kinds of objects to deal with:

1. The container itself, probably some sort of panel or window-like object
2. The components you add to the container, such as labels, buttons, and panels
3. A layout manager, which positions the components inside the container

You have seen examples of these three kinds of objects in almost every `JFrame` class we have defined. Almost every complete GUI you build, and many subparts of the GUIs you build, will be made up of these three kinds of objects.

MyProgrammingLab™

Self-Test Exercises

19. What standard Java package contains the layout manager classes discussed in this chapter?

20. Is an object of the class `JPanel` a container class? Is it a component class?

21. With a `GridLayout` manager, you cannot leave any grid element empty, but you can do something that will make a grid element look empty to the user. What can you do?

(continued)

[6] In particular, it is legitimate and sometimes useful to add `JComponents` to a `JButton`. We do not have space in this book to develop techniques for doing this effectively, but you may want to give it a try. You have covered enough material to do it.

Display 17.12 Hierarchy of Swing and AWT Classes

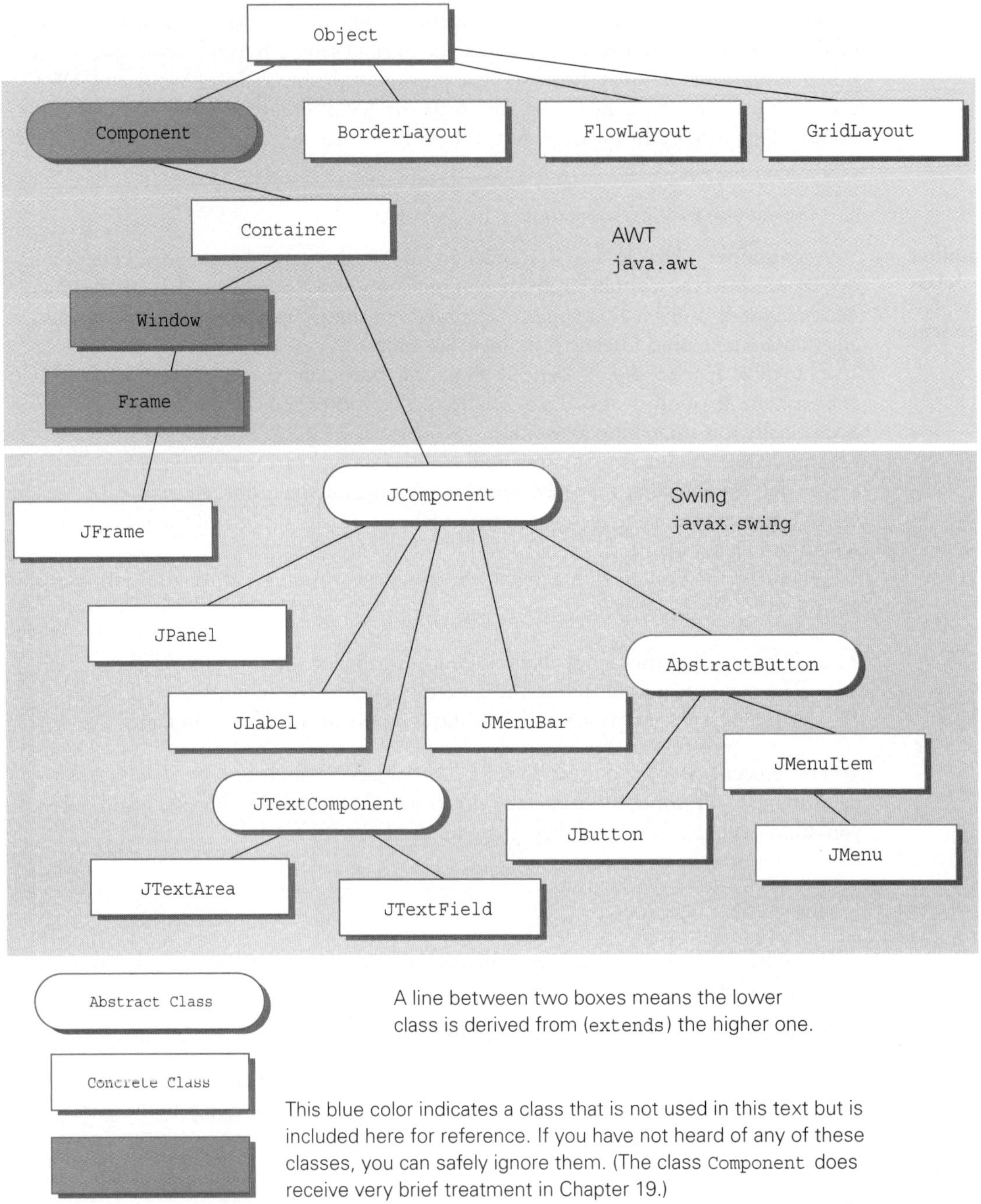

A line between two boxes means the lower class is derived from (extends) the higher one.

This blue color indicates a class that is not used in this text but is included here for reference. If you have not heard of any of these classes, you can safely ignore them. (The class `Component` does receive very brief treatment in Chapter 19.)

MyProgrammingLab™

Self-Test Exercises (continued)

22. You are used to defining derived classes of the Swing class `JFrame`. You can also define derived classes of other Swing classes. Define a derived class of the class `JPanel` that is called `PinkJPanel`. An object of the class `PinkJPanel` can be used just as we used objects of the class `JPanel`, but an object of the class `PinkJPanel` is pink in color (unless you explicitly change its color). The class `PinkJPanel` will have only one constructor—namely, the no-argument constructor. (*Hint*: This is very easy.)

TIP: Code a GUI's Look and Actions Separately

You can divide the task of designing a Swing GUI into two main subtasks: (1) designing and coding the appearance of the GUI on the screen; (2) designing and coding the actions performed in response to button clicks and other user actions. This dividing of one big task into two simpler tasks makes the big task easier and less error prone.

For example, consider the program in Display 17.11. Your first version of this program might use the following definition of the method `actionPerformed`:

```
public void actionPerformed(ActionEvent e)
{}
```

This version of the method `actionPerformed` does nothing, but your program will run and will display a window on the screen, just as shown in Display 17.11. If you click any of the buttons, nothing will happen, but you can use this version of your GUI to adjust details, such as the order and location of buttons.

After you get the GUI to look the way you want it to look, you can define the action parts of the GUI, typically using the method `actionPerformed`.

If you include the phrase `implements ActionListener` at the start of your `JFrame` definition, then you must include some definition of the method `actionPerformed`. A method definition, such as

```
public void actionPerformed(ActionEvent e)
{}
```

stub

which does nothing (or does very little) is called a **stub**. Using stubs is a good programming technique in many contexts, not just in Swing programs.

Alternatively, when writing your first version of a Swing GUI like the one in Display 17.11, you could omit the definition of the method `actionPerformed` completely, *provided you also omit the phrase* `implements ActionListener` *and omit the invocations of* `addActionListener`. ■

The Model-View-Controller Pattern ★

Model-View-Controller

The technique we advocated in the previous Programming Tip is an example of a general technique known as the **Model-View-Controller** pattern. Display 17.13 gives a diagram of this pattern. The Model part of the pattern performs the heart of the application. The View part is the output part; it displays a picture of the Model's state. The Controller is the input part; it relays commands from the user to the Model. Each of the three interacting parts is realized as an object with responsibility for its own tasks. In a simple task such as the `JFrame` in Display 17.11, you can have a single object with different methods to realize each of the roles Model, View, and Controller.

To simplify the discussion, we have presented the Model-View-Controller pattern as if the user interacts directly with the Controller. The Controller need not be under the direct control of the user, but could be controlled by some other software or hardware component. In a Swing GUI, the View and Controller parts might be separate classes or separate methods combined into one larger class that displays a single window for all user interactions.

MyProgrammingLab™

Self-Test Exercises

23. Suppose you omit the method `actionPerformed` from the class in Display 17.11 and make no other changes. Would the class compile? If it compiles, will it run with no error messages?

24. Suppose you omit the method `actionPerformed` and the phrase `implements ActionListener` from the class in Display 17.11 and make no other changes. Would the class compile? If it compiles, will it run with no error messages?

Display 17.13 The Model-View-Controller Pattern

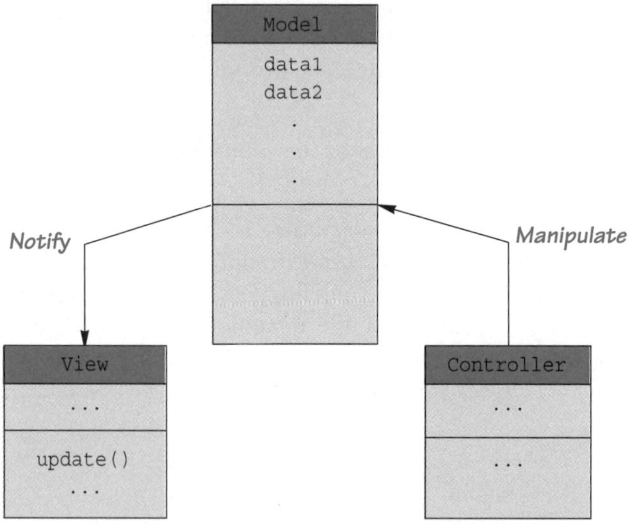

17.4 Menus and Buttons

For hours and location press 1.
For a recorded message describing services press 2.
For instructions on using our website press 3.
To use our automated information system press 4.
To speak to an operator between 8 am and noon Monday through Thursdays press 7.

PHONE ANSWERING MACHINE

In this section, we describe the basics of Swing menus. Swing menu items (menu choices) behave essentially the same as Swing buttons. They generate action events that are handled by action listeners, just as buttons do.

EXAMPLE: A GUI with a Menu

Display 17.14 contains a program that is essentially the same as the GUI in Display 17.11 except that this GUI uses a menu instead of buttons. This GUI has a menu bar at the top of the window. The menu bar lists the names of all the pull-down menus. This GUI has only one pull-down menu, which is named `"Add Colors"`. However, there could be more pull-down menus in the same menu bar.

The user can pull down a menu by clicking its name in the menu bar. Display 17.14 contains three pictures of the GUI. The first is what you see when the GUI originally appears. In that picture, the menu name `"Add Colors"` can be seen in the menu bar, but you cannot see the menu. If you click the words `"Add Colors"` with your mouse, the menu drops down, as shown in the second picture of the GUI. If you click `"Green"`, `"White"`, or `"Gray"` on the menu, then a vertical strip of the named color appears in the GUI.

In the next subsection, we go over the details of the program in Display 17.14.

Menu Bars, Menus, and Menu Items

When adding menus as we did in Display 17.14, use the three Swing classes `JMenuItem`, `JMenu`, and `JMenuBar`. Entries on a menu are objects of the class `JMenuItem`. These `JMenuItem`s are placed in `JMenu`s, and then the `JMenu`s are typically placed in a `JMenuBar`. Let us look at the details.

menu

menu item

A **menu** is an object of the class `JMenu`. A choice on a menu is called a **menu item** and is an object of the class `JMenuItem`. A menu item is identified by the string that labels it, such as `"Blue"`, `"White"`, or `"Gray"` in the menu in Display 17.14. You can add as many `JMenuItem`s as you wish to a menu. The menu lists the items in the order

Display 17.14 A GUI with a Menu (part 1 of 3)

```
import javax.swing.JFrame;
import javax.swing.JPanel;
import java.awt.GridLayout;
Import java.awt.Color;
import javax.swing.JMenu;
import javax.swing.JMenuItem;
import javax.swing.JMenuBar;
import java.awt.event.ActionListener;
import java.awt.event.ActionEvent;

public class MenuDemo extends JFrame implements ActionListener
{
    public static final int WIDTH = 300;
    public static final int HEIGHT = 200;

    private JPanel bluePanel;
    private JPanel whitePanel;
    private JPanel grayPanel;

    public static void main(String[] args)
    {
        MenuDemo gui = new MenuDemo();
        gui.setVisible(true);
    }

    public MenuDemo()
    {
        super ("Menu Demonstration");
        setSize(WIDTH, HEIGHT);
        setDefaultCloseOperation(JFrame.EXIT_ON_CLOSE);
        setLayout(new GridLayout(1, 3));

        bluePanel = new JPanel();
        bluePanel.setBackground(Color.LIGHT_GRAY);
        add(bluePanel);

        whitePanel = new JPanel();
        whitePanel.setBackground(Color.LIGHT_GRAY);
        add(whitePanel);
        grayPanel = new JPanel();
```

Display 17.14 **A GUI with a Menu** (part 2 of 3)

```
        grayPanel.setBackground(Color.LIGHT_GRAY);
        add(grayPanel);

        JMenu colorMenu = new JMenu("Add Colors");

        JMenuItem blueChoice = new JMenuItem("Blue");
        blueChoice.addActionListener(this);
        colorMenu.add(blueChoice);

        JMenuItem whiteChoice = new JMenuItem("White");
        whiteChoice.addActionListener(this);
        colorMenu.add(whiteChoice);

        JMenuItem grayChoice = new JMenuItem("Gray");
        grayChoice.addActionListener(this);
        colorMenu.add(grayChoice);

        JMenuBar bar = new JMenuBar( );
        bar.add(colorMenu);
        setJMenuBar(bar);
    }
```

The definition of `actionPerformed` *is identical to the definition given in Display 17.11 for a similar GUI using buttons instead of menu items.*

```
    public void actionPerformed(ActionEvent e)
    {
        String buttonString = e.getActionCommand( );

        if (buttonString.equals("Blue"))
            bluePanel.setBackground(Color.BLUE);
        else if (buttonString.equals("White"))
            whitePanel.setBackground(Color.WHITE);
        else if (buttonString.equals("Gray"))
            grayPanel.setBackground(Color.GRAY);
        else
            System.out.println("Unexpected error.");
    }
}
```

(continued)

Display 17.14 A GUI with a Menu (part 3 of 3)

RESULTING GUI

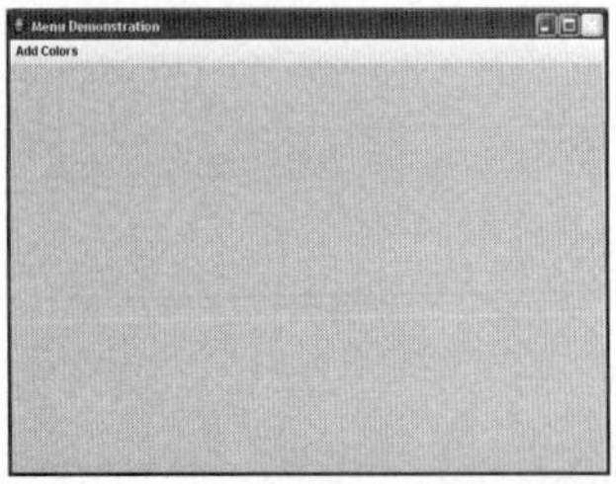

RESULTING GUI (after clicking Add Colors in the menu bar)

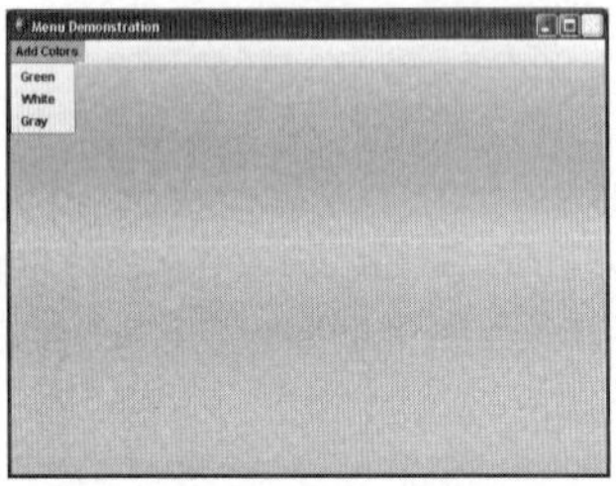

RESULTING GUI (after choosing Blue and White on the menu)

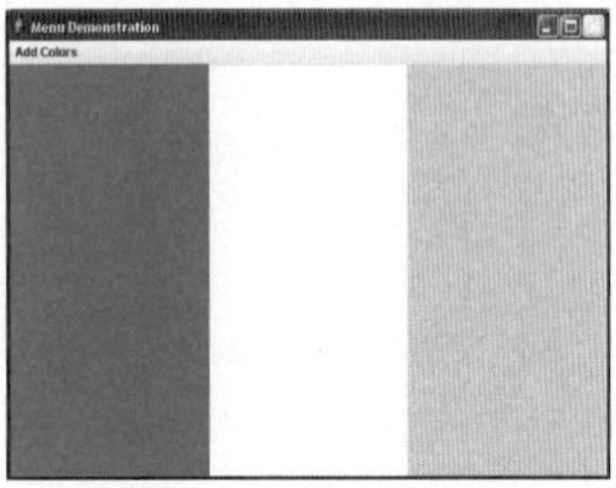

RESULTING GUI (after choosing all the colors on the menu)

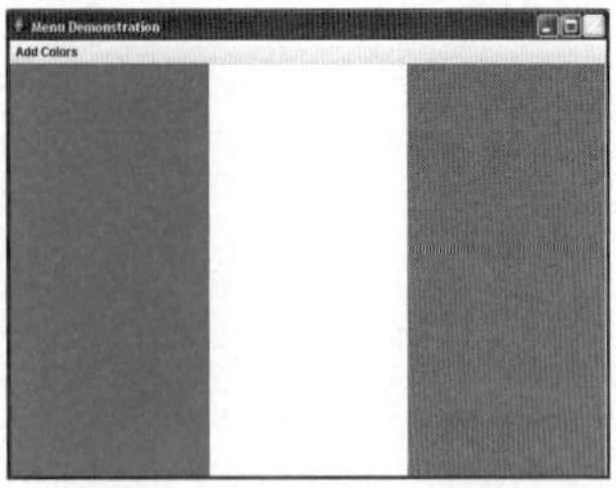

in which they are added. The following code, taken from the constructor in Display 17.14, creates a new `JMenu` object named `colorMenu` and then adds a `JMenuItem` labeled `"Red"`. Other menu items are added in a similar way.

```
JMenu colorMenu = new JMenu("Add Colors");

JMenuItem blueChoice = new JMenuItem("Blue");
blueChoice.addActionListener(this);
colorMenu.add(blueChoice);
```

listeners

Note that, just as we did for buttons in Display 17.11, in Display 17.14 we registered the `this` parameter as an action listener for each menu item. Defining action listeners and registering listeners for menu items are done in the exact same way as for buttons. In fact, the syntax is even the same. If you compare Displays 17.14 and 17.11, you will see that the definition of the method `actionPerformed` is the same in both classes.

Add a `JMenuItem` to an object of the class `JMenu` using the method `add` in exactly the same way that you add a component, such as a button, to a container object. Moreover, if you look at the preceding code, you will see that you specify a string for a `JMenuItem` in the same way that you specify a string to appear on a button.

menu bar

A **menu bar** is a container for menus, typically placed near the top of a windowing interface. Add a menu to a menu bar using the method `add` in the same way that you add menu items to a menu. The following code from the constructor in Display 17.14 creates a new menu bar named `bar` and then adds the menu named `colorMenu` to this menu bar:

```
JMenuBar bar = new JMenuBar();
bar.add(colorMenu);
```

There are two different ways to add a menu bar to a `JFrame`. You can use the method `setJMenuBar`, as shown in the following code from the constructor in Display 17.14:

```
setJMenuBar(bar);
```

This sets an instance variable of type `JMenuBar` so that it names the menu bar named `bar`. Saying it less formally, this adds the menu bar named `bar` to the `JFrame` and places the menu bar at the top of the `JFrame`.

Alternatively, you can use the `add` method to add a menu bar to a `JFrame` (or to any other container). You do so in the same way that you add any other component, such as a label or a button. An example of using `add` to add a `JMenuBar` to a `JFrame` is given in the file `MenuAdd.java` on the accompanying website.

extra code on website

Menus

A **menu** is an object of the class `JMenu`. A choice on a menu is an object of the class `JMenuItem`. Menus are collected together in a **menu bar** (or menu bars). A menu bar is an object of the class `JMenuBar`.

Events and listeners for menu items are handled in exactly the same way as they are for buttons.

Nested Menus ★

As shown in Display 17.12, the class `JMenu` is a descendent of the `JMenuItem` class. So, every `JMenu` object is also a `JMenuItem` object. Thus, a `JMenu` can be a menu item in another menu. This means that you can nest menus. For example, the outer menu might give you a list of menus. You can display one of the menus on that list by clicking the name of the desired menu. You can then choose an item from that menu by using your mouse again. There is nothing new you need to know to create these nested menus. Simply add menus to menus just as you add other menu items. There is an example of nested menus in the file `NestedMenus.java` on the accompanying website.

extra code on website

The `AbstractButton` Class

As shown in Display 17.12, the classes `JButton` and `JMenuItem` are derived classes of the abstract class named `AbstractButton`. All of the basic properties and methods of the classes `JButton` and `JMenuItem` are inherited from the class `AbstractButton`. That is why objects of the class `JButton` and objects of the class `JMenuItem` are so similar. Some of the methods for the class `AbstractButton` are listed in Display 17.15. All these methods are inherited by both the class `JButton` and the class `JMenuItem`. (Some of these methods were inherited by the class `AbstractButton` from the class `JComponent`, so you may sometimes see some of the methods listed as "inherited from `JComponent`.")

Adding Menus to a `JFrame`

In the following, we assume that all code is inside a constructor for a (derived class of a) `JFrame`. To see the following examples put together to produce a complete GUI, see the constructor in Display 17.14.

Creating Menu Items

A menu item is an object of the class `JMenuItem`. Create a new menu item in the usual way, as illustrated by the following example. The string in the argument position is the displayed text for the menu item.

```
JMenuItem redChoice = new JMenuItem("Red");
```

Adding Menu Item Listeners

Events and listeners for menu items are handled in the exact same way as they are for buttons: Menu items fire action events that are received by objects of the class `ActionListener`.

SYNTAX

JMenu_Item_Name`.addActionListener(`*Action_Listener*`);`

EXAMPLE

```
redChoice.addActionListener(this);
```

Creating a Menu

A menu is an object of the class `JMenu`. Create a new menu in the usual way, as illustrated by the following example. The string argument is the displayed text that identifies the menu.

```
JMenu colorMenu = new JMenu("Add Colors");
```

Adding Menu Items to a Menu

Use the method `add` to add menu items to a menu.

SYNTAX

JMenu_Name`.add(`*JMenu_Item*`);`

EXAMPLE(`colorMenu` IS AN OBJECT OF THE CLASS `JMenu`)

```
colorMenu.add(redChoice);
```

Creating a Menu Bar

A menu bar is an object of the class `JMenuBar`. Create a new menu bar in the usual way, as illustrated by the following example:

```
JMenuBar bar = new JMenuBar();
```

Adding a Menu to a Menu Bar

Add a menu to a menu bar using the method `add` as follows:

SYNTAX

JMenu_Bar_Name`.add(`*JMenu_Name*`);`

EXAMPLE (`bar` IS AN OBJECT OF THE CLASS `JMenubar`)

```
bar.add(colorMenu);
```

Adding a Menu Bar to a Frame

There are two different ways to add a menu bar to a `JFrame`. You can use the method `add` to add the menu bar to a `JFrame` (or to any other container). Another common way of adding a menu bar to a `JFrame` is to use the method `setJMenuBar` as follows:

SYNTAX

`setJMenuBar(`*JMenu_Bar_Name*`);`

EXAMPLE

```
setJMenuBar(bar);
```

Display 17.15 Some Methods in the Class `AbstractButton`

The abstract class `AbstractButton` is in the `javax.swing` package.

All of these methods are inherited by both of the classes `JButton` and `JMenuItem`.

```
public void setBackground(Color theColor)
```

Sets the background color of this component.

```
public void addActionListener(ActionListener listener)
```

Adds an `ActionListener`.

```
public void removeActionListener(ActionListener listener)
```

Removes an `ActionListener`.

```
public void setActionCommand(String actionCommand)
```

Sets the action command.

```
public String getActionCommand()
```

Returns the action command for this component.

```
public void setText(String text)
```

Makes text the only text on this component.

```
public String getText()
```

Returns the text written on the component, such as the text on a button or the string for a menu item.

```
public void setPreferredSize(Dimension preferredSize)
```

Sets the preferred size of the button or label. Note that this is only a suggestion to the layout manager. The layout manager is not required to use the preferred size. The following special case will work for most simple situations. The `int` values give the width and height in pixels.

```
public void setPreferredSize(
                     new Dimension(int width, int height))
```

```
public void setMaximumSize(Dimension maximumSize)
```

Sets the maximum size of the button or label. Note that this is only a suggestion to the layout manager. The layout manager is not required to respect this maximum size. The following special case will work for most simple situations. The `int` values give the width and height in pixels.

```
public void setMaximumSize(
                     new Dimension(int width, int height))
```

```
public void setMinimumSize(Dimension minimumSize)
```

Sets the minimum size of the button or label. Note that this is only a suggestion to the layout manager. The layout manager is not required to respect this minimum size.

Although we do not discuss the `Dimension` class, the following special case is intuitively clear and will work for most simple situations. The `int` values give the width and height in pixels.

```
public void setMinimumSize(
                     new Dimension(int width, int height))
```

> **The `Dimension` Class**
>
> Objects of the class `Dimension` are used with buttons, menu items, and other objects to specify a size. The `Dimension` class is in the package `java.awt`. The parameters in the following constructor are pixels.
>
> **CONSTRUCTOR**
>
> `Dimension(int width, int height)`
>
> **EXAMPLE**
>
> `aButton.setPreferredSize(new Dimension(30, 50));`

The `setActionCommand` Method

action command

When the user clicks a button or menu item, it fires an action event that normally goes to one or more action listeners where it becomes an argument to an `actionPerformed` method. This action event includes a `String` instance variable that is known as the **action command** for the button or menu item and that is retrieved with the accessor method `getActionCommand`. The action command in the event is copied from an instance variable in the button or menu item object. If you do nothing to change it, the action command is the string written on the button or the menu item. The method `setActionCommand` given in Display 17.15 for the class `AbstractButton` can be used with any `JButton` or `JMenuItem` to change the action command for that component. Among other things, this will allow you to have different action commands for two buttons, two menu items, or a button and menu item even though they have the same string written on them.

setActionCommand

The method `setActionCommand` takes a `String` argument that becomes the new action command for the calling button or menu item. For example, consider the following code:

```
JButton nextButton = new JButton("Next");
nextButton.setActionCommand("Next Button");
JMenuItem chooseNext = new JMenuItem("Next");
chooseNext.setActionCommand("Next Menu Item");
```

If we had not used `setActionCommand` in the preceding code, then the button `nextButton` and the menu item `chooseNext` would both have the action command `"Next"` and so we would have no way to tell which of the two components `nextButton` and `chooseNext` an action event `"Next"` came from. However, using the method `setActionCommand`, we can give them the different action commands `"Next Button"` and `"Next Menu Item"`.

The action command for a `JButton` or `JMenuItem` is kept as the value of a private instance variable for the `JButton` or `JMenuItem`. The method `setActionCommand` is simply an ordinary mutator method that changes the value of this instance variable.

`setActionCommand` and `getActionCommand`

Every button and every menu item has a string associated with it that is known as the **action command** for that button or menu item. When the button or menu item is clicked, it fires an action event `e`. The following invocation returns the action command for the button or menu item that fired `e`:

```
e.getActionCommand( )
```

The method `actionPerformed` typically uses this action command string to decide which button or menu item was clicked.

The default action command for a button or menu item is the string written on it, but if you want, you can change the action command with an invocation of the method `setActionCommand`. For example, the menu item `chooseNext` created by the following code will display the string `"Next"` when it is a menu choice, but will have the string `"Next Menu Item"` as its action command.

EXAMPLE

```
JMenuItem chooseNext = new JMenuItem("Next");
chooseNext.setActionCommand("Next Menu Item");
```

An alternate approach to defining action listeners is given in the next subsection. That technique is, among other things, another way to deal with multiple buttons or menu items that have the same thing written on them.

Listeners as Inner Classes ★

In all of our previous examples, our GUIs had only one action listener object to deal with all action events from all buttons and menus in the GUI. The opposite extreme also has much to recommend it. You can have a separate `ActionListener` class for each button or menu item, so that each button or menu item has its own unique action listener. There is then no need for a multiway `if-else` statement. The listener knows which button or menu item was clicked because it listens to only one button or menu item.

The approach outlined in the previous paragraph does have one down side: You typically need to give a lot of definitions of `ActionListener` classes. Rather than putting each of these classes in a separate file, it is much cleaner to make them private inner classes. This has the added advantage of allowing the `ActionListener` classes to have access to private instance variables and methods of the outer class.

In Display 17.16, we re-created the GUI in Display 17.14 using the techniques of this subsection.

Display 17.16 **Listeners as Inner Classes** (part 1 of 2)

<Import statements are the same as in Display 17.14.>

```
public class InnerListenersDemo extends JFrame
{
    public static final int WIDTH = 300;
    public static final int HEIGHT = 200;

    private JPanel bluePanel;
    private JPanel whitePanel;
    private JPanel grayPanel;

    private class blueListener implements ActionListener
    {
        public void actionPerformed(ActionEvent e)
        {
            bluePanel.setBackground(Color.BLUE);
        }
    } //End of greenListener inner class

    private class WhiteListener implements ActionListener
    {
        public void actionPerformed(ActionEvent e)
        {
            whitePanel.setBackground(Color.WHITE);
        }
    } //End of WhiteListener inner class
    private class grayListener implements ActionListener
    {
        public void actionPerformed(ActionEvent e)
        {
            grayPanel.setBackground(Color.GRAY);
        }
    } //End of grayListener inner class

    public static void main(String[] args)
    {
        InnerListenersDemo gui = new InnerListenersDemo();
        gui.setVisible(true);
    }

    public InnerListenersDemo()
    {
        super("Menu Demonstration");
        setSize(WIDTH, HEIGHT);
        setDefaultCloseOperation(JFrame.EXIT_ON_CLOSE);
        setLayout(new GridLayout(1, 3));
```

The resulting GUI is the same as in Display 17.14

(continued)

Display 17.16 **Listeners as Inner Classes** (part 2 of 2)

```
        bluePanel = new JPanel();
        greenPanel.setBackground(Color.LIGHT_GRAY);
        add(bluePanel);

        whitePanel = new JPanel();
        whitePanel.setBackground(Color.LIGHT_GRAY);
        add(whitePanel);

        grayPanel = new JPanel();
        grayPanel.setBackground(Color.LIGHT_GRAY);
        add(grayPanel);

        JMenu colorMenu = new JMenu("Add Colors");

        JMenuItem blueChoice = new JMenuItem("Blue");
        blueChoice.addActionListener(new blueListener());
        colorMenu.add(blueChoice);

        JMenuItem whiteChoice = new JMenuItem("White");
        whiteChoice.addActionListener(new WhiteListener());
        colorMenu.add(whiteChoice);
        JMenuItem grayChoice = new JMenuItem("Gray");
        grayChoice.addActionListener(new grayListener());
        colorMenu.add(grayChoice);

        JMenuBar bar = new JMenuBar();
        bar.add(colorMenu);
        setJMenuBar(bar);
    }

}
```

MyProgrammingLab™

Self-Test Exercises

25. What type of event is fired when you click a `JMenuItem`? How does it differ from the type of event fired when you click a `JButton`?

26. Write code to create a `JButton` with `"Hello"` written on it but with `"Bye"` as its action command.

27. Write code to create a `JMenuItem` with `"Hello"` as its displayed text (when it is a choice in a menu) but with `"Bye"` as its action command.

MyProgrammingLab™

Self-Test Exercises (continued)

28. If you want to change the action command for a `JButton`, use the method `setActionCommand`. What method do you use to change the action command for a `JMenuItem`?

29. Is the following legal in Java?

```
JMenu aMenu = new JMenu();
    ...
JMenu aSubMenu = new JMenu();
    ...
aMenu.add(aSubMenu);
```

30. How many `JMenuBar` objects can you have in a `JFrame`?

31. A `JFrame` has a private instance variable of type `JMenuBar`. What is the name of the mutator method to change the value of this instance variable?

32. Write code to create a new menu item named `aChoice` that has the label `"Exit"`.

33. Suppose you are defining a class called `MenuGUI` that is a derived class of the class `JFrame`. Write code to add the menu item `mItem` to the menu `m`. Then add `m` to the menu bar `mBar`, and then add the menu bar to the `JFrame` `MenuGUI`. Assume that this all takes place inside a constructor for `MenuGUI`. Also assume that everything has already been constructed with `new`, and that all necessary listeners are registered. You just need to do the adding.

34. ★How can you modify the program in Display 17.16 so that when the `Blue` menu item is clicked, all three colors are shown? The `Red` and `White` choices remain the same. (Remember the menu items may be clicked in any order, so the `Blue` menu item can be the first or second item clicked.)

35. ★Rewrite the Swing GUI in Display 17.16 so that there is only one action listener inner class. The inner class constructor will have two parameters, one for a panel and one for a color.

17.5 Text Fields and Text Areas

Write your answers in the spaces provided.

COMMON INSTRUCTION FOR AN EXAMINATION

You have undoubtedly interacted with windowing systems that provide spaces for you to enter text information such as your name, address, and credit card number. In this section, we show you how to add these fields for text input and text output to your Swing GUIs.

Text Areas and Text Fields

text field

JTextField

A **text field** is an object of the class `JTextField` and is displayed as a field that allows the user to enter a single line of text. In Display 17.17, the following creates a text field named `name` in which the user will be asked to enter his or her name:

```
private JTextField name;
   ...
name = new JTextField(NUMBER_OF_CHAR);
```

In Display 17.17, the variable `name` is a private instance variable. The creation of the `JTextField` in the last of the previous lines takes place inside the class constructor. The number `NUMBER_OF_CHAR` that is given as an argument to the `JTextField` constructor specifies that the text field will have room for at least `NUMBER_OF_CHAR` characters to be visible. The defined constant `NUMBER_OF_CHAR` is `30`, so the text field is guaranteed to have room for at least `30` characters. You can type any number of characters into a text field but only a limited number will be visible; in this case, you know that at least `30` characters will be visible.

A Swing GUI can read the text in a text field and so receive text input; if this is desired, it can produce output by causing text to appear in the text field. The method `getText` returns the text written in the text field. For example, the following will set a variable named `inputString` to whatever string is in the text field `name` at the time that the `getText` method is invoked:

```
String inputString = name.getText();
```

The method `getText` is an input method, and the method `setText` is an output method. The method `setText` can be used to display a new text string in a text field. For example, the following will cause the text field `name` to change the text it displays to the string `"This is some output"`:

```
name.setText("This is some output");
```

Display 17.17 A Text Field (part 1 of 3)

```
import javax.swing.JFrame;
import javax.swing.JTextField;
import javax.swing.JPanel;
import javax.swing.JLabel;
import javax.swing.JButton;
import java.awt.GridLayout;
import java.awt.BorderLayout;
import java.awt.FlowLayout;
import java.awt.Color;
import java.awt.event.ActionListener;
import java.awt.event.ActionEvent;

public class TextFieldDemo extends JFrame
                          implements ActionListener
{
    public static final int WIDTH = 400;
    public static final int HEIGHT = 200;
```

Display 17.17 **A Text Field** (part 2 of 3)

```
    public static final int NUMBER_OF_CHAR = 30;

    private JTextField name;

    public static void main(String[] args)
    {
        TextFieldDemo gui = new TextFieldDemo();
        gui.setVisible(true);
    }

    public TextFieldDemo()
    {
        super("Text Field Demo");
        setSize(WIDTH, HEIGHT);
        setDefaultCloseOperation(JFrame.EXIT_ON_CLOSE);
        setLayout(new GridLayout(2, 1));

        JPanel namePanel = new JPanel();
        namePanel.setLayout(new BorderLayout());
        namePanel.setBackground(Color.WHITE);

        name = new JTextField(NUMBER_OF_CHAR);
        namePanel.add(name, BorderLayout.SOUTH);
        JLabel nameLabel = new JLabel("Enter your name here:");
        namePanel.add(nameLabel, BorderLayout.CENTER);

        add(namePanel);
        JPanel buttonPanel = new JPanel();
        buttonPanel.setLayout(new FlowLayout());
        buttonPanel.setBackground(Color.BLUE);
        JButton actionButton = new JButton("Click me");
        actionButton.addActionListener(this);
        buttonPanel.add(actionButton);

        JButton clearButton = new JButton("Clear");
        clearButton.addActionListener(this);
        buttonPanel.add(clearButton);

        add(buttonPanel);
    }

    public void actionPerformed(ActionEvent e)
    {
        String actionCommand = e.getActionCommand();

        if (actionCommand.equals("Click me"))
            name.setText("Hello " + name.getText());
        else if (actionCommand.equals("Clear"))
            name.setText("");
        else
            name.setText("Unexpected error.");
    }
}
```

This sets the text field equal to the empty string, which makes it blank.

(continued)

Display 17.17 A Text Field (part 3 of 3)

RESULTING GUI (When program is started and a name entered)

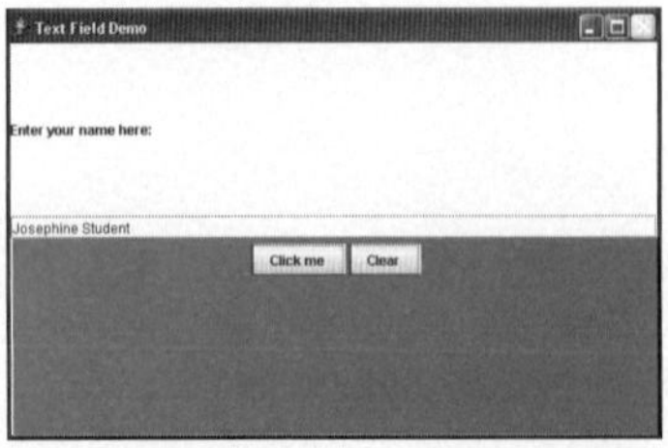

RESULTING GUI (After clicking the "Click me" button)

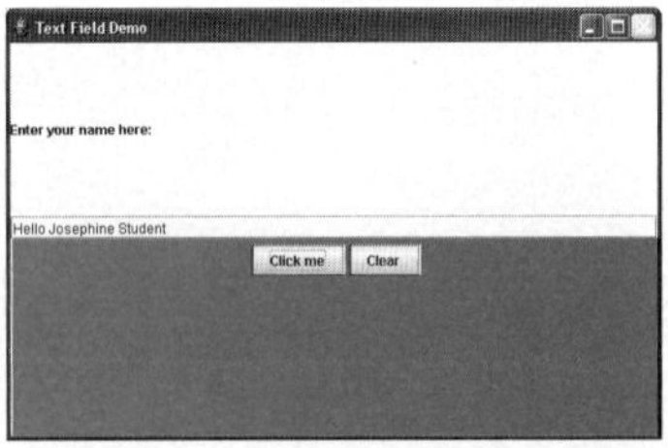

The following line from the method `actionPerformed` in Display 17.17 uses both `getText` and `setText`:

```
name.setText("Hello" + name.getText());
```

This line changes the string in the text field `name` to `"Hello"` followed by the old string value in the text field. The net effect is to insert the string `"Hello"` in front of the string displayed in the text field.

`getText` and `setText`

The classes `JTextField` and `JTextArea` both contain methods called `getText` and `setText`. The method `getText` can be used to retrieve the text written in the text field or text area. The method `setText` can be used to change the text written in the text field or text area.

SYNTAX

Name_of_Text_Component`.getText()` returns the text currently displayed in the text field or text area.

Name_of_Text_Component`.setText(`*New_String_To_Display*`);`

EXAMPLES

```
String inputString = ioComponent.getText();
ioComponent.setText("Hello out there!");
```

`ioComponent` may be an instance of either of the classes `JTextField` or `JTextArea`.

text area

`JTextArea`

A **text area** is an object of the class `JTextArea`. A text area is the same as a text field except that it allows multiple lines. Two parameters to the constructor for `JTextArea` specify the minimum number of lines and the minimum number of characters per line that are guaranteed to be visible. You can enter any amount of text in a text area, but only a limited number of lines and a limited number of characters per line will be visible. For example, the following creates a `JTextArea` named `theText` that will have at least 5 lines and at least 20 characters per line visible:

```
JTextArea theText = new JTextArea(5, 20);
```

There is also a constructor with one additional `String` parameter for the string initially displayed in the text area. For example,

```
JTextArea theText = new JTextArea("Enter\ntext here.", 5, 20);
```

Note that a string value can be multiple lines because it can contain the new-line character `'\n'`.

A `JTextField` has a similar constructor with a `String` parameter, as in the following example:

```
JTextField ioField =
             new JTextField("Enter numbers here.", 30);
```

If you look at Display 17.12, you will see that both `JTextField` and `JTextArea` are derived classes of the abstract class `JTextComponent`. Most of the methods for `JTextField` and `JTextArea` are inherited from `JTextComponent` and so `JTextField` and `JTextArea` have mostly the same methods with the same meanings except for minor redefinitions to account for having just one line or multiple lines. Display 17.18 describes some methods in the class `JTextComponent`. All of these methods are inherited and have the described meaning in both `JTextField` and `JTextArea`.

`setLineWrap`

You can set the line-wrapping policy for a `JTextArea` using the method `setLineWrap`. The method takes one argument of type `boolean`. If the argument is `true`, then at the end of a line, any additional characters for that line will appear on the following line of the text area. If the argument is `false`, the extra characters will be on the same line and will not be visible. For example, the following sets the line wrap policy for the `JTextArea` object named `theText` so that at the end of a line, any additional characters for that line will appear on the following line:

```
theText.setLineWrap(true);
```

output-only

`setEditable`

You can specify that a `JTextField` or `JTextArea` cannot be written in by the user. To do so, use the method `setEditable`, which is a method in both the `JTextField` and JTextArea classes. If theText names an object in either of the classes JTextField or JTextArea, then the following

```
theText.setEditable(false);
```

will set theText so that only your GUI program can change the text in the text component theText; the user cannot change the text. After this invocation of setEditable, if the user clicks the mouse in the text component named theText and then types at the keyboard, the text in the text component will not change.

To reverse things and make theText so that the user can change the text in the text component, use true in place of false, as follows:

```
theText.setEditable(true);
```

If no invocation of setEditable is made, then the default state allows the user to change the text in the text component.

Display 17.18 Some Methods in the Class JTextComponent

All these methods are inherited by the classes JTextField and JTextArea.

The abstract class JTextComponent is in the package javax.swing.text. The classes JTextField and JTextArea are in the package javax.swing.

```
public String getText()
```

Returns the text that is displayed by this text component.

```
public boolean isEditable()
```

Returns true if the user can write in this text component. Returns false if the user is not allowed to write in this text component.

```
public void setBackground(Color theColor)
```

Sets the background color of this text component.

```
public void setEditable(boolean argument)
```

If argument is true, then the user is allowed to write in the text component. If argument is false, then the user is not allowed to write in the text component.

```
public void setText(String text)
```

Sets the text that is displayed by this text component to be the specified text.

The Classes JTextField and JTextArea

The classes JTextField and JTextArea can be used to add areas for changeable text to a GUI. An object of the class JTextField has one line that displays some specified number of characters. An object of the class JTextArea has a size consisting of a specified number of lines and a specified number of characters per line. More text can be typed into a `JTextField` or `JTextArea` than is specified in its size, but the extra text may not be visible.

The number of characters per line and the number of lines are a guaranteed minimum. More lines and especially more characters per line may be visible. (The space per line is actually guaranteed to be *Characters_Per_Line* times the space for one uppercase letter M.)

SYNTAX

```
JTextField Name_of_Text_Field = new JTextField(Characters_Per_Line);
JTextArea Name_of_Text_Area =
            new JTextArea(Number_of_Lines, Characters_Per_Line);
```

EXAMPLES

```
JTextField name = new JTextField(30);
JTextArea someText = new JTextArea(10, 30);
```

There are also constructors that take an additional `String` argument that specifies an initial string to display in the text component.

SYNTAX

```
JTextField Name_of_Text_Field =
             new JTextField(Initial_String, Characters_Per_Line);
JTextArea Name_of_Text_Area =
    new JTextArea(Initial_String, Number_of_Lines, Characters_Per_Line);
```

EXAMPLES

```
JTextField name = new JTextField("Enter name here.", 30);
JTextArea someText =
   new JTextArea("Enter story here.\nClick button.", 10, 30);
```

Number of Characters per Line

The number of characters per line (given as an argument to constructors for `JTextField` or `JTextArea`) is not the number of just any characters. The number gives the number of em spaces in the line. An **em space** is the space needed to hold one uppercase letter M, which is the widest letter in the alphabet. So a line that is specified to hold 20 characters will always be able to hold at least 20 characters and will almost always hold more than 20 characters.

Scroll Bars

Scroll bars for text areas and text fields are discussed in Chapter 18. They are a nice touch, but until you reach Chapter 18, your GUI programs will work fine without them.

TIP: Labeling a Text Field

Sometimes you want to label a text field. For example, suppose the GUI asks for a name and a credit card number and expects the user to enter these in two text fields. In this case, the GUI needs to label the two text fields so that the user knows in which field to type the name and in which field to type the credit card number. You can use an object of the class `JLabel` to label a text field or any other component in a Swing GUI. Simply place the label and text field in a `JPanel` and treat the `JPanel` as a single component. For example, we did this with the text field `name` in Display 17.17. ■

MyProgrammingLab™

Self-Test Exercises

36. What is the difference between an object of the class `JTextArea` and an object of the class `JTextField`?

37. What would happen if when running the GUI in Display 17.17 you were to enter your name and click the `"Click me"` button three times?

38. Rewrite the program in Display 17.17 so that it uses a text area in place of a text field. Change the label `"Enter your name here:"` to `"Enter your story here:"`. When the user clicks the `"Click me"` button, your GUI should change the string displayed in the text area to `"Your story is " + lineCount + "lines long."`. The variable `lineCount` is a variable of type `int` that your program sets equal to the number of lines currently displayed in the text area. Use a `BorderLayout` manager and place your text area in the region `BorderLayout.CENTER` so that there is room for it. You can assume the user enters at least one line before clicking the `"Click me"` button. The last line in the text area will have no `'\n'` so you may need to add one if you are counting the number of occurrences of `'\n'`. Blank lines are counted.

TIP: Inputting and Outputting Numbers

When you want to input numbers using a Swing GUI, your GUI must convert input text to numbers. For example, when you input the number `42` in a `JTextField`, your program will receive the string `"42"`, not the number `42`. Your program must convert the input string value `"42"` to the integer value `42`. When you want to output numbers using a GUI constructed with Swing, you must convert the numbers to a string and then output that string. For example, if you want to output the number `40`, your program would convert the integer value `40` to the string value `"40"`. With Swing, all input typed by the user is string input and all displayed output is string output. The techniques for converting back and forth between strings and numbers were given in Chapter 5 in the subsection titled "Static Methods in Wrapper Classes" and the Programming Example entitled "Another Approach to Keyboard Input." A simple example of a Swing GUI with numeric input and output is given in the next subsection. ■

A Swing Calculator

Designing a realistic Swing calculator is the subject of Programming Project 17.3. In this programming example, we will develop a simplified calculator to get you started on that Programming Project. Display 17.19 contains a GUI for a calculator that keeps a running total of numbers. The user enters a number in the text field and then clicks either the + or − button. The number in the text field is then added into or subtracted from a running total that is kept in the instance variable `result`, and then the new total (the new value of `result`) is given in the text field. If the user clicks the `"Reset"` button, then the running total—that is, the value of `result`—is set to zero. When the GUI is first run, the running total, that is, the value of `result`, is set to zero.

Most of the details are similar to things you have already seen, but one new element is the use of exception handling. If the user enters a number in an incorrect format, such as placing a comma in a number, then one of the methods throws a `NumberFormatException`. If the user enters a number in an incorrect format, such as `2,000` with a comma instead of `2000`, the method `assumingCorrectNumberFormats` invokes the method `stringToDouble` with the alleged number string `"2,000"` as an argument. Then `stringToDouble` calls `Double.parseDouble`, but `Double.parseDouble` throws a `NumberFormatException` because no Java number string can contain a comma. Because the invocation of `Double.parseDouble` takes place within an invocation of the method `stringToDouble`, `stringToDouble` in turn throws a `NumberFormatException`. The invocation of `stringToDouble` takes place inside the invocation of `assumingCorrectNumberFormats`, so `assumingCorrectNumberFormats` throws the `NumberFormatException` that it received from the invocation of `stringToDouble`. However, the invocation of `assumingCorrectNumberFormats` is inside a `try` block. The exception is caught in the following `catch` block. At this point, the `JTextField` (named `ioField`) is set to the error message `"Error: Reenter Number."`.

Notice that if a `NumberFormatException` is thrown, the value of the instance variable `result` is not changed. A `NumberFormatException` can be thrown by an invocation of `stringToDouble` in either of the following lines of code from the method `assumingCorrectNumberFormats`:

```
result = result + stringToDouble(ioField.getText());
```

or

```
result = result - stringToDouble(ioField.getText());
```

If the exception is thrown, execution of the method `stringToDouble` ends immediately and control passes to the `catch` block. Thus, control passes to the `catch` block before the previous addition or subtraction is performed. So `result` is unchanged, and the user can reenter the last number and proceed with the GUI as if that incorrect number were never entered.

Uncaught Exceptions

In a Swing program, throwing an uncaught exception does not end the GUI, but it may leave it in an unpredictable state. It is best to always catch any exception that is thrown even if all that the `catch` block does is output an instruction to redo something, such as reentering some input or just outputting an error message.

Display 17.19 **A Simple Calculator** (part 1 of 4)

```
import javax.swing.JFrame;
import javax.swing.JTextField;
import javax.swing.JPanel;
import javax.swing.JLabel;
import javax.swing.JButton;
import java.awt.BorderLayout;
import java.awt.FlowLayout;
import java.awt.Color;
import java.awt.event.ActionListener;
import java.awt.event.ActionEvent;

/**
 A simplified calculator.
 The only operations are addition and subtraction.
*/
public class Calculator extends JFrame
                              implements ActionListener
{
    public static final int WIDTH = 400;
    public static final int HEIGHT = 200;
    public static final int NUMBER_OF_DIGITS = 30;

    private JTextField ioField;
    private double result = 0.0;

    public static void main(String[] args)
    {
        Calculator aCalculator = new Calculator();
        aCalculator.setVisible(true);
    }

    public Calculator()
    {
        setTitle("Simplified Calculator");
        setDefaultCloseOperation(JFrame.EXIT_ON_CLOSE);
        setSize(WIDTH, HEIGHT);
        setLayout(new BorderLayout());

        JPanel textPanel = new JPanel();
        textPanel.setLayout(new FlowLayout());
        ioField =
             new JTextField("Enter numbers here.",NUMBER_OF_DIGITS);
        ioField.setBackground(Color.WHITE);
        textPanel.add(ioField);
        add(textPanel, BorderLayout.NORTH);
        JPanel buttonPanel = new JPanel();
        buttonPanel.setBackground(Color.BLUE);
        buttonPanel.setLayout(new FlowLayout());
```

Display 17.19 **A Simple Calculator** (part 2 of 4)

```
        JButton addButton = new JButton("+");
        addButton.addActionListener(this);
        buttonPanel.add(addButton);
        JButton subtractButton = new JButton("−");
        subtractButton.addActionListener(this);
        buttonPanel.add(subtractButton);
        JButton resetButton = new JButton("Reset");
        resetButton.addActionListener(this);
        buttonPanel.add(resetButton);

        add(buttonPanel, BorderLayout.CENTER);
    }

    public void actionPerformed(ActionEvent e)
    {
        try
        {
            assumingCorrectNumberFormats(e);
        }
        catch (NumberFormatException e2)
        {
            ioField.setText("Error: Reenter Number.");
        }
    }
```

A `NumberFormatException` *does not need to be declared or caught in a catch block.*

```
    //Throws NumberFormatException.
    public void assumingCorrectNumberFormats(ActionEvent e)
    {
        String actionCommand = e.getActionCommand();

        if (actionCommand.equals("+"))
        {
            result = result + stringToDouble(ioField.getText());
            ioField.setText(Double.toString(result));
        }
        else if (actionCommand.equals("−"))
        {
            result = result - stringToDouble(ioField.getText());
            ioField.setText(Double.toString(result));
        }
        else if (actionCommand.equals("Reset"))
        {
            result = 0.0;
            ioField.setText("0.0");
        }
        else
            ioField.setText("Unexpected error.");
    }
```

(continued)

Display 17.19 **A Simple Calculator** (part 3 of 4)

```
    //Throws NumberFormatException.
    private static double stringToDouble(String stringObject)
    {
        return Double.parseDouble(stringObject.trim());
    }
}
```

Resulting GUI (When started)

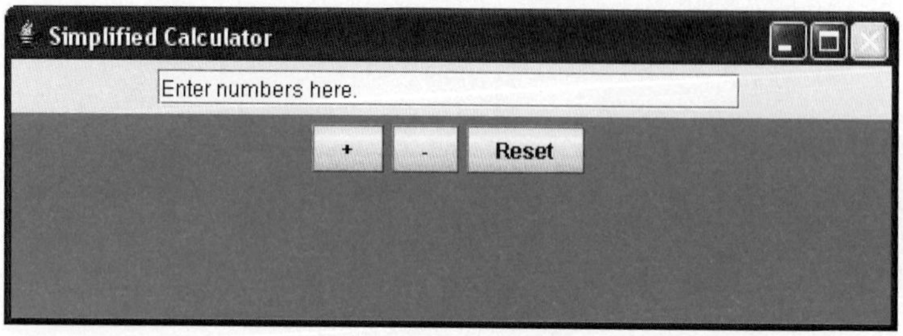

Resulting GUI (After entering 2,000)

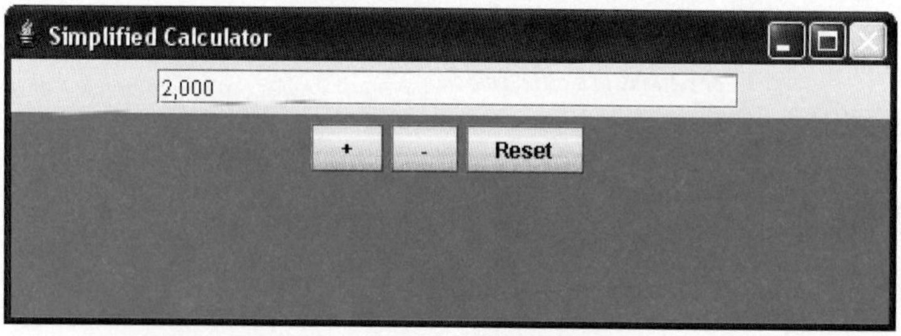

Resulting GUI (After clicking +)

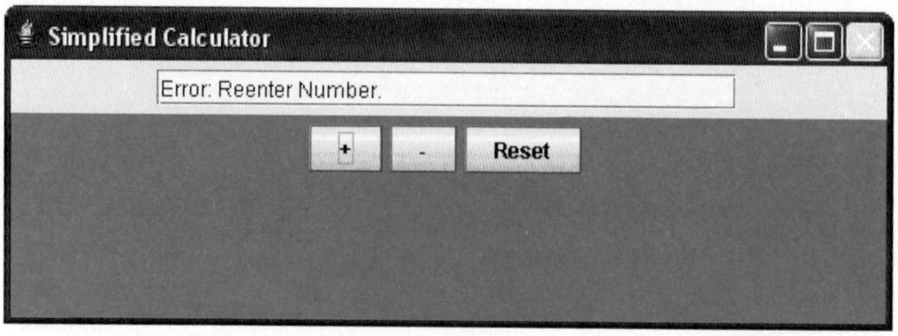

Display 17.19 **A Simple Calculator** (part 4 of 4)

RESULTING GUI (After entering 2000.0 and clicking +)

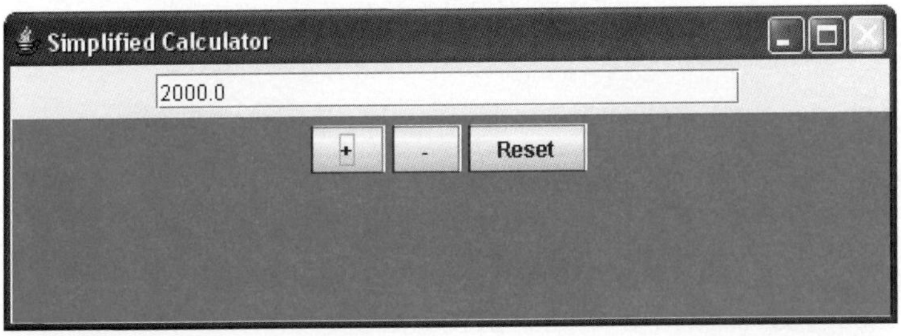

RESULTING GUI (After entering 42)

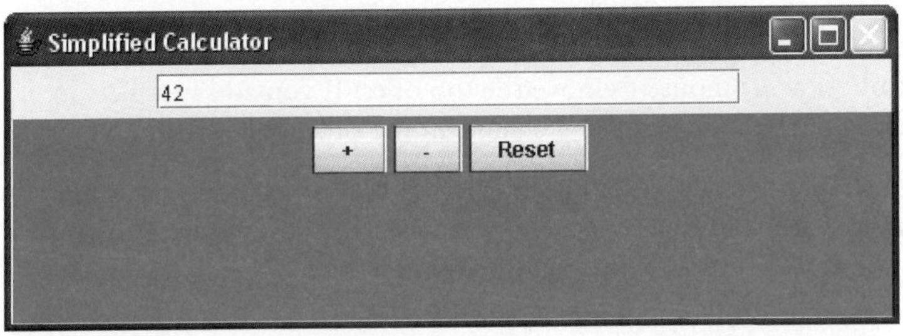

RESULTING GUI (After clicking +)

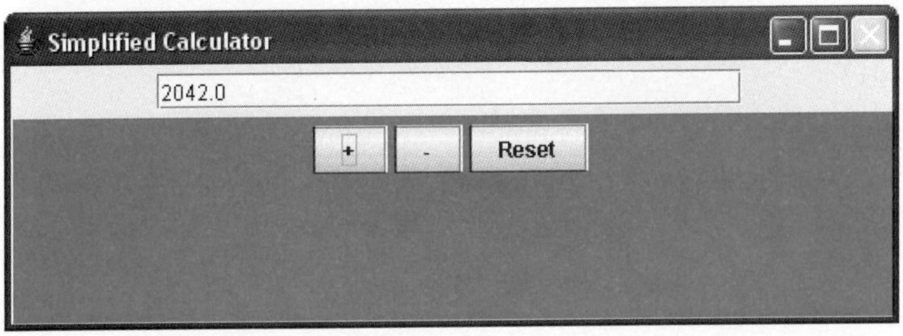

MyProgrammingLab™

Self-Test Exercises

39. In the GUI in Display 17.19, why did we make the text field `ioField` an instance variable but did not make instance variables of any of the buttons `addButton`, `subtractButton`, or `resetButton`?

40. What would happen if the user running the GUI in Display 17.19 were to run the GUI and simply click the addition button without typing anything into the text field?

(continued)

MyProgrammingLab™

Self-Test Exercises (continued)

41. What would happen if the user running the GUI in Display 17.19 were to type the number `10` into the text field and then click the addition button three times? Explain your answer.

42. Suppose you change the `main` method in Display 17.19 to the following:

```
public static void main(String[] args)
{
    Calculator calculator1 = new Calculator();
    calculator1.setVisible(true);
    Calculator calculator2 = new Calculator();
    calculator2.setVisible(true);
}
```

This will cause two calculator windows to be displayed. (If one is on top of the other, you can use your mouse to move the top one.) If you add numbers in one of these calculators, will anything change in the other calculator?

43. Suppose you change the `main` method in Display 17.19 as we described in Self-Test Exercise 42. This will cause two calculator windows to be displayed. If you click the close-window button in one of the windows, will one window go away or will both windows go away?

Chapter Summary

- Swing GUIs (graphical user interfaces) are programmed using event-driven programming. In event-driven programming, a user action, such as a button click, generates an event, which is automatically passed to an event-handling method that performs the appropriate action.
- There are two main techniques for designing a Swing GUI class. You can use inheritance to create a derived class of one of the library classes such as `JFrame` or you can build a GUI by adding components to a container class. You normally use both of these techniques when defining a Swing GUI class.
- A *windowing GUI* is usually defined as a derived class of the class `JFrame`.
- A *button* is an object of the class `JButton`. Clicking a button fires an action event that is handled by an action listener. An *action listener* is any class that implements the `ActionListener` interface.
- A *label* is an object of the class `JLabel`. You can use a label to add text to a GUI.
- When adding components to an object of a container class, such as adding a button to a panel or `JFrame`, use the method `add`. The components in a container are arranged by an object called a *layout manager*.

- A *panel* is a container object that is used to group components inside of a larger container. Panels are objects in the class `JPanel`.
- A *menu item* is a choice on a menu. A menu item is realized in your code as an object of the class `JMenuItem`. A *menu* is an object of the class `JMenu`. A menu item is added to a `JMenu` with the method `add`. A *menu bar* is an object of the class `JMenuBar`. A menu is added to a `JMenuBar` with the method `add`.
- A `JMenuBar` can be added to a `JFrame` with the method `setJMenuBar`. It can also be added using the method `add`, just as any other component can be added.
- Both buttons and menu items fire action events and so normally have one or more action listeners registered with them to respond to the events.

Answers to Self-Test Exercises

1. The `JFrame` class.
2. Sizes in Swing are measured in pixels.
3.
```
someWindow.setDefaultCloseOperation(
                            JFrame.DO_NOTHING_ON_CLOSE);
```
4.
```
someWindow.setDefaultCloseOperation(JFrame.EXIT_ON_CLOSE);
```
5. When you click the minimizing button, the `JFrame` is reduced to an icon, usually at the bottom of your monitor screen.
6.
```
someWindow.setVisible(n > 0);
```
   The following also works but is not good style:
```
if (n > 0)
    someWindow.setVisible(true);
else
    someWindow.setVisible(false);
```
7. An action event.
8.
```
public void actionPerformed(ActionEvent e)
```
9. Change
```
JFrame firstWindow = new JFrame();
```
   to
```
JFrame firstWindow = new JFrame("My First Window");
```
   Alternatively, you can add the following:
```
firstWindow.setTitle("My First Window");
```

10. Delete

```
setTitle("First Window Class");
```

and replace

```
super();
```

with

```
super("First Window Class");
```

11. Change

```
setDefaultCloseOperation(
                JFrame.DO_NOTHING_ON_CLOSE);
```

to

```
setDefaultCloseOperation(
                JFrame.EXIT_ON_CLOSE);
```

12. Change the following line in the no-argument constructor in Display 17.6 from

```
this(Color.PINK);
```

to

```
this(Color.MAGENTA);
```

13. `add(new JLabel("Close-window button works."));`
14. Yes, it is legal. It is OK to reuse a variable name such as `aLabel`.
15. You need to change the `add` statements, as in the following rewritten section of code:

```
JLabel label1 = new JLabel("First label");
add(label1, BorderLayout.NORTH);

JLabel label2 = new JLabel("Second label");
add(label2, BorderLayout.CENTER);

JLabel label3 = new JLabel("Third label");
add(label3, BorderLayout.SOUTH);
```

16. You need to change the `add` statements, as in the following rewritten section of code:

```
JLabel label1 = new JLabel("First label");
add(label1, BorderLayout.NORTH);

JLabel label2 = new JLabel("Second label");
add(label2, BorderLayout.EAST);

JLabel label3 = new JLabel("Third label");
add(label3, BorderLayout.SOUTH);
```

17. The argument should be `new GridLayout(1, 3)`. So, the entire method invocation is

```
setLayout(new GridLayout(1, 3));
```

Alternatively, you could use `new GridLayout(1, 0)`. It is also possible to do something similar with a `BorderLayout` manager or a `FlowLayout` manager, but a `GridLayout` manager will work nicer here.

18. The argument should be `new GridLayout(0,1)`. So, the entire method invocation is

```
setLayout(new GridLayout(0, 1));
```

Alternatively, you could use `new GridLayout(3, 1)`, if you know there will be at most three components added, but if more than three components are added, then a second column will be added. It is also possible to do something similar with a `BorderLayout` manager, but a `GridLayout` manager will work nicer here.

19. `java.awt`

20. An object of the class `JPanel` is both a container class and a component class.

21. To make it look as though you have an empty grid element, add an empty panel to the grid element.

22.
```
import javax.swing.JPanel;
import java.awt.Color;

public class PinkJPanel extends JPanel
{
    public PinkJPanel()
    {
        setBackground(Color.PINK);
    }
}
```

extra code on website

The class `PinkJPanel` is on the website that accompanies this text.

23. It will not compile, but will give a compiler error message saying that `actionPerformed` is not defined (because it claims to implement the `ActionListener` interface).

24. It will not compile, but will give compiler error messages saying that, in effect, the invocations of `addActionListener` such as

```
redButton.addActionListener(this);
```

have arguments of an incorrect type.

25. Clicking a `JMenuItem` fires an action event (that is, an object of the class `ActionEvent`). This is the same as with a `JButton`.

26.
```
JButton b = new JButton("Hello");
b.setActionCommand("Bye");
```

27.
```
JMenuItem m = new JMenuItem("Hello");
m.setActionCommand("Bye");
```

28. To change the action command for a `JMenuItem`, use the method `setActionCommand`, just as you would for a `JButton`.

29. Yes, it is legal.

30. As many as you want. Only one can be added with the method `setJMenuBar`, but any number of others can be added to using the `add` method.

31. `setJMenuBar`

32.
```
JMenuItem aChoice = new
JMenuItem("Exit");
```

33.
```
m.add(mItem);
mBar.add(m);
setJMenuBar(mBar);
```

You could use the following instead of using `setJMenuBar`:

```
add(mBar);
```

This will all take place inside a constructor named `MenuGUI`.

34. Register all three types of listeners with `blueChoice`, as follows:

```
blueChoice.addActionListener(new RedListener());
blueChoice.addActionListener(new WhiteListener());
blueChoice.addActionListener(new BlueListener());
```

35. Replace the three inner classes with the following inner class:

```
private class ColorListener implements ActionListener
{
    private JPanel thePanel;
    private Color theColor;

    public ColorListener(Color c, JPanel p)
    {
        theColor = c;
        thePanel = p;
    }

    public void actionPerformed(ActionEvent e)
    {
        thePanel.setBackground(theColor);
    }
} //End of ColorListener inner class
```

Replace

```
redChoice.addActionListener(new RedListener());
```

with

```
redChoice.addActionListener(
                    new ColorListener(Color.RED, redPanel));
```

Also make similar changes to the menu items `whiteChoice` and `blueChoice`, with the obvious changes to colors and panels.

extra code on website

This is not really preferable to what we did in Display 17.16, but it is a good exercise. The complete program done this way is on the accompanying website in the file named `InnerListenersDemo2.java`.

36. A `JTextField` object displays only a single line. A `JTextArea` object can display more than one line of text.
37. The contents of the text field would change to `"Hello Hello Hello "` followed by your name.
38. This program is on the website that accompanies this text.

extra code on website

```
import javax.swing.JFrame;
import javax.swing.JTextArea;
import javax.swing.JPanel;
import javax.swing.JLabel;
import javax.swing.JButton;
import java.awt.GridLayout;
import java.awt.BorderLayout;
import java.awt.FlowLayout;
import java.awt.Color;
import java.awt.event.ActionListener;
import java.awt.event.ActionEvent;

public class TextAreaDemo extends JFrame
                          implements ActionListener
{
    public static final int WIDTH = 400;
    public static final int HEIGHT = 200;
    public static final int NUMBER_OF_LINES = 10;
    public static final int NUMBER_OF_CHAR = 30;

    private JTextArea story;

    public static void main(String[] args)
    {
        TextAreaDemo gui = new TextAreaDemo();
        gui.setVisible(true);
    }

    public TextAreaDemo()
    {
        setTitle("Text Area Demo");
        setSize(WIDTH, HEIGHT);
        setDefaultCloseOperation(JFrame.EXIT_ON_CLOSE);
        setLayout(new GridLayout(2, 1));
        JPanel storyPanel = new JPanel();
        storyPanel.setLayout(new BorderLayout());
        storyPanel.setBackground(Color.WHITE);

        story = new JTextArea(NUMBER_OF_LINES, NUMBER_OF_CHAR);
```

```
        storyPanel.add(story, BorderLayout.CENTER);
        JLabel storyLabel = new JLabel("Enter your story here:");
        storyPanel.add(storyLabel, BorderLayout.NORTH);

        add(storyPanel);

        JPanel buttonPanel = new JPanel( );
        buttonPanel.setLayout(new FlowLayout( ));
        buttonPanel.setBackground(Color.PINK);
        JButton actionButton = new JButton("Click me");
        actionButton.addActionListener(this);
        buttonPanel.add(actionButton);

        JButton clearButton = new JButton("Clear");
        clearButton.addActionListener(this);
        buttonPanel.add(clearButton);

        add(buttonPanel);
    }

    public void actionPerformed(ActionEvent e)
    {
        String actionCommand = e.getActionCommand( );

      if (actionCommand.equals("Click me"))
      {
            int lineCount = getLineCount();
            story.setText("Your story is "
                                  + lineCount + " lines long.");
      }
      else if (actionCommand.equals("Clear"))
          story.setText("");
      else
          story.setText("Unexpected error.");
    }
    private int getLineCount()
    {
        String storyString = story.getText();
        int count = 0;

        for (int i = 0; i < storyString.length(); i++)
            if (storyString.charAt(i) == '\n')
                count++;

        return count + 1;//The last line has no '\n'.
    }
}
```

39. We made the text field an instance variable because we needed to refer to it in the definition of the method `actionPerformed`. On the other hand, the only direct reference we had to the buttons was in the constructor. So, we need names for the buttons only in the constructor definition.

40. The GUI would try to add the string `"Enter numbers here."` as if it were a string for a number. This will cause a `NumberFormatException` to be thrown and the string `"Error: Reenter Number."` would be displayed in the text field.

41. Every time the user clicks the addition button, the following assignment is executed:

```
result = result + stringToDouble(ioField.getText());
```

So, the number in the text field is added to the total as many times as the user clicks the addition button. But, the value in the text field is the running total, so the running total is added to itself. Thus, the running total is added to the total as many times as the user clicks the addition button.

Let us say that the user starts the GUI, types in `10`, and clicks the addition button. That adds `10` to `result`, so the value of `result` is then `0` plus `10`, which is `10`, and `10` is displayed. Now the user clicks the addition button a second time. That adds `10` to result again, so the value of result is `10` plus `10`, which is `20`, and `20` is displayed. Next the user clicks the addition button a third time. This time, `20` is in the text field, and so it is added to result, which is also `20`. Thus, the value of `result` is now `40`, and `40` is displayed. Note that it is always the number in the text field that is added in.

42. The two calculator windows are completely independent. Each has its own instance variable `result`, which has no effect on the other's instance variable `result`.

43. If you click the close-window button in either calculator window, the entire program ends because that causes an invocation of `System.exit`. There is no invocation of `System.exit` in Display 17.19, but the following ensures that a `System.exit` that is in some library class will be invoked:

```
setDefaultCloseOperation(JFrame.EXIT_ON_CLOSE);
```

MyProgrammingLab™

Programming Projects

Visit www.myprogramminglab.com to complete select exercises online and get instant feedback.

VideoNote **Solution to Programming Project 17.1**

1. Design and code a Swing GUI to translate text that is input in English into Pig Latin. You can assume that the sentence contains no punctuation. The rules for Pig Latin are as follows:

   a. For words that begin with consonants, move the leading consonant to the end of the word and add "ay." Thus, "ball" becomes "allbay"; "button" becomes "uttonbay"; and so forth.

   b. For words that begin with vowels, add "way" to the end of the word. Thus, "all" becomes "allway"; "one" becomes "oneway"; and so forth.

Use a `FlowLayout` with a `JTextArea` for the source text and a separate `JTextArea` for the translated text. Add a `JButton` with an event to perform the translation. A sample application is shown next with the text translated to Pig Latin.

To parse the source text, note that you can use the `Scanner` class on a `String`. For example the following code

```
Scanner scan = new Scanner("foo bar zot");
while (scan.hasNext())
{
  System.out.println(scan.next());
}
```

will output

```
foo
bar
zot
```

2. Design and code a Swing GUI for a two-player tic-tac-toe (noughts and crosses) game on a 3 × 3 game board. The `JFrame` should use a `BorderLayout` with a `JLabel` in the NORTH region to display messages (e.g., who won the game), and a `JPanel` in the CENTER region to display the game board. For the game board in the `JPanel`, use a `GridLayout` manager with a 3 × 3 layout of `JButton`'s in each cell to display the game board. The button labels should initially be blank. When a player clicks on an empty button, an appropriate "X" or "O" should be placed in the label field of the button. If there is a winner (three in a row), then the program should display the winner in the `JLabel` located at the top of the window. If all nine cells have been filled without a winner, the program should indicate that there is a tie.

3. Design and code a Swing GUI calculator. You can use Display 17.19 as a starting point, but your calculator will be more sophisticated. Your calculator will have two text fields that the user cannot change: One labeled `"Result"` will contain the result of performing the operation, and the other labeled `"Operand"` will be for the user to enter a number to be added, subtracted, and so forth from the result. The user enters the number for the `"Operand"` text field by clicking buttons labeled with the digits `0` through `9` and a decimal point, just as in a real calculator. Allow the operations of addition, subtraction, multiplication, and division. Use a `GridLayout` manager to produce a button pad that looks similar to the keyboard on a real calculator.

   When the user clicks a button for an operation, the following occurs: the operation is performed, the `"Result"` text field is updated, and the `"Operand"` text field is cleared. Include a button labeled `"Reset"` that resets the `"Result"` to `0.0`. Also include a button labeled `"Clear"` that resets the `"Operand"` text field so it is blank.

   Hint: Define an exception class named `DivisonByZeroException`. Have your code throw and catch a `DivisonByZeroException` if the user attempts to "divide by zero." Your code will catch the `DivisonByZeroException` and output a suitable message to the `"Operand"` text field. The user may then enter a new substitute number in the `"Operand"` text field. Because values of type `double` are, in effect, approximate values, it makes no sense to test for equality with `0.0`. Consider an operand to be "equal to zero" if it is in the range `-1.0e-10` to `+1.0e-10`.

4. (The Swing part of this project is pretty easy, but to do this programming project you need to know how to convert numbers from one base to another.) Write a program that converts integers from base ten (ordinary decimal) notation to base two notation. Use Swing to perform input and output via a window interface. The user enters a base ten numeral in one text field and clicks a button with `"Convert"` written on it; the equivalent base two numeral then appears in another text field. Be sure to label the two text fields. Include a `"Clear"` button that clears both text fields when clicked. (*Hint:* Include a private method that converts the string for a base ten numeral to the string for the equivalent base two numeral.)
5. Re-do or do for the first time the trivia game described in Programming Projects 6.12 and 6.13, except create a GUI for the game interface. Use a layout of your choice with the appropriate text fields, labels, and buttons to implement your design. The game should ask only one question at a time and output the correct answer if the player answers a question incorrectly. When all questions have been answered, show the final score and exit the program.
6. Write a program that implements a simple text editor. Use a `JTextArea` for the area that the user can enter text. Add a button that allows the user to save the text to a file and a button that allows the user to load the text from a file.

Swing II 18

18 Swing II

Window listeners?
I thought windows were for looking not for listening.

Student answer on an exam

Introduction

This chapter is a continuation of Chapter 17, presenting more details about designing regular Swing GUIs. Chapter 20 on applets is a side issue that may be read after this chapter if you prefer.

Prerequisites

This chapter uses material from Chapter 17 (and its prerequisites).

Section 18.2 on icons and scroll bars is not used in subsequent sections and so may be skipped or postponed.

18.1 Window Listeners

A man may see how this world goes with no eyes.
Look with thine ears. . . .

WILLIAM SHAKESPEARE, *King Lear*

In Chapter 17, we used the method `setDefaultCloseOperation` to program the close-window button in a `JFrame`. This allows for only a limited number of possibilities for what happens when the close-window button is clicked. When the user clicks the close-window button (or either of the two accompanying buttons), the `JFrame` fires an event known as a **window event**. A `JFrame` can use the method `setWindowListener` to register a **window listener** to respond to such window events. A window listener can be programmed to respond to a window event in any way you wish. Window events are objects of the class `WindowEvent`. A window listener is any class that satisfies the `WindowListener` interface.

window event

window listener

`WindowEvent`

`WindowListener`

The method headings in the `WindowListener` interface are given in Display 18.1. If a class implements the `WindowListener` interface, it must have definitions for all seven of these method headings. If you do not need all of these methods, then you can define the ones you do not need to have empty bodies, like this:

```
public void windowDeiconified(WindowEvent e)
{}
```

Display 18.1 Methods in the `WindowListener` Interface

The `WindowListener` interface and the `WindowEvent` class are in the package `java.awt.event`.
`public void windowOpened(WindowEvent e)` Invoked when a window is opened.
`public void windowClosing(WindowEvent e)` Invoked when a window is in the process of being closed. Clicking the close-window button causes an invocation of this method.
`public void windowClosed(WindowEvent e)` Invoked when a window has been closed.
`public void windowIconified(WindowEvent e)` Invoked when a window is iconified. When you click the minimize button in a `JFrame`, it is iconified.
`public void windowDeiconified(WindowEvent e)` Invoked when a window is deiconified. When you activate a minimized window, it is deiconified.
`public void windowActivated(WindowEvent e)` Invoked when a window is activated. When you click in a window, it becomes the activated window. Other actions can also activate a window.
`public void windowDeactivated(WindowEvent e)` Invoked when a window is deactivated. When a window is activated, all other windows are deactivated. Other actions can also deactivate a window.

The `WindowListener` Interface

When the user clicks any of the three standard `JFrame` buttons (for closing the window, minimizing the window, and resizing the window), it generates a window event. Window events are sent to window listeners. In order to be a window listener, a class must implement the `WindowListener` interface. The method headings for the `WindowListener` interface are given in Display 18.1.

EXAMPLE: A Window Listener Inner Class

Display 18.2 gives an example of a `JFrame` class with a window listener class that is an inner class. The window listener inner class is named `CheckOnExit`. A window listener class need not be an inner class, but it is frequently convenient to make a window listener class (or other kind of listener class) an inner class.

The main `JFrame` in Display 18.2 simply displays a message. What is interesting is how the window listener programs the close-window button. You can apply the window listener used in this `JFrame` to any `JFrame`. When the close-window button is clicked, a second, smaller window appears and asks `"Are you sure you want to exit?"` If the user clicks the `"Yes"` button, the entire program ends and so both windows go away. If the user clicks the `"No"` button, only the smaller window disappears; the program and the main window continue. Let us look at the programming details.

When the close-window button in the main window is clicked, this fires a window event. The only registered window listener is the anonymous object that is the argument to `addWindowListener`. Next we repeat the relevant line of code, which is in the constructor for `WindowListenerDemo`:

```
addWindowListener(new CheckOnExit());
```

This anonymous window listener object receives the window event fired when the close-window button is clicked and then invokes the method `windowClosing`. The method `windowClosing` creates and displays a window object of the class `ConfirmWindow`, which contains the message `"Are you sure you want to exit?"` as well as the two buttons labeled `"Yes"` and `"No"`.

If the user clicks the `"Yes"` button, the action event fired by that button goes to the `actionPerformed` method, which ends the program with a call to `System.exit`. If the user clicks the `"No"` button, then the `actionPerformed` method invokes the method `dispose`. The method `dispose`, discussed in the next subsection, makes its calling object go away but does not end the program. The calling object for `dispose` is the smaller window (which is an object of the class `ConfirmWindow`), so this smaller window goes away but the main window remains.

Notice that even though we have registered a window listener, which says what should happen when the close-window button is clicked, we still need to invoke the method `setDefaultCloseOperation`. When the close-window button is clicked, the policy set by `setDefaultCloseOperation` is always carried out in addition to any action by window listeners. If we do not include any invocation of `setDefaultCloseOperation`, then the default action is to make the window go away (but not to end the program). We do not want our main window to go away, so we set the policy as follows:

```
setDefaultCloseOperation(JFrame.DO_NOTHING_ON_CLOSE);
```

This means that clicking the close-window button causes no action other than the actions of any window listeners. If you are using a window listener to set the action of the close-window button, you invariably want an invocation of `setDefaultCloseOperation` with the argument `JFrame.DO_NOTHING_ON_CLOSE`.

Display 18.2 **A Window Listener** (part 1 of 3)

```
import javax.swing.JFrame;
import javax.swing.JPanel;
import java.awt.BorderLayout;
import java.awt.FlowLayout;
import java.awt.Color;
import javax.swing.JLabel;
import javax.swing.JButton;
import java.awt.event.ActionListener;
import java.awt.event.ActionEvent;
import java.awt.event.WindowListener;
import java.awt.event.WindowEvent;

public class WindowListenerDemo extends JFrame
{
    public static final int WIDTH = 300; //for main window
    public static final int HEIGHT = 200; //for main window
    public static final int SMALL_WIDTH = 200; //for confirm window
    public static final int SMALL_HEIGHT = 100; //for confirm window

    private class CheckOnExit implements WindowListener
    {
        public void windowOpened(WindowEvent e)
        {}

        public void windowClosing(WindowEvent e)
        {
            ConfirmWindow checkers = new ConfirmWindow();
            checkers.setVisible(true);
        }

        public void windowClosed(WindowEvent e)
        {}

        public void windowIconified(WindowEvent e)
        {}

        public void windowDeiconified(WindowEvent e)
        {}

        public void windowActivated(WindowEvent e)
        {}

        public void windowDeactivated(WindowEvent e)
        {}
    }//End of inner class CheckOnExit

    private class ConfirmWindow extends JFrame implements
                        ActionListener
    {
        public ConfirmWindow()
        {
            setSize(SMALL_WIDTH, SMALL_HEIGHT);
            getContentPane().setBackground(Color.YELLOW);
```

This `WindowListener` class is an inner class.

A window listener must define all the method headings in the `WindowListener` interface, even if some are trivial implementations.

Another

(continued)

Display 18.2 **A Window Listener** (part 2 of 3)

```
            setLayout(new BorderLayout());
            JLabel confirmLabel = new JLabel(
                           "Are you sure you want to exit?");
            add(confirmLabel, BorderLayout.CENTER);

            JPanel buttonPanel = new JPanel();
            buttonPanel.setBackground(Color.ORANGE);
            buttonPanel.setLayout(new FlowLayout());

            JButton exitButton = new JButton("Yes");
            exitButton.addActionListener(this);
            buttonPanel.add(exitButton);

            JButton cancelButton = new JButton("No");
            cancelButton.addActionListener(this);
            buttonPanel.add(cancelButton);

            add(buttonPanel, BorderLayout.SOUTH);
        }

        public void actionPerformed(ActionEvent e)
        {
            String actionCommand = e.getActionCommand();

            if (actionCommand.equals("Yes"))
                System.exit(0);
            else if (actionCommand.equals("No"))
                dispose(); //Destroys only the ConfirmWindow.
            else
                System.out.println(
                 "Unexpected Error in Confirm Window.");
        }
    } //End of inner class ConfirmWindow

    public static void main(String[] args)
    {
        WindowListenerDemo demoWindow = new WindowListenerDemo();
        demoWindow.setVisible(true);
    }

    public WindowListenerDemo()
    {
        setSize(WIDTH, HEIGHT);
        setTitle("Window Listener Demonstration");

        setDefaultCloseOperation(JFrame.DO_NOTHING_ON_CLOSE);
        addWindowListener(new CheckOnExit());

        getContentPane().setBackground(Color.LIGHT_GRAY);
        JLabel aLabel = new JLabel(
         "I like to be sure you are sincere.");
        add(aLabel);
    }
}
```

Even if you have a window listener, you normally must still invoke **`setDefaultCloseOperation`**.

Display 18.2 A Window Listener (part 3 of 3)

RESULTING GUI

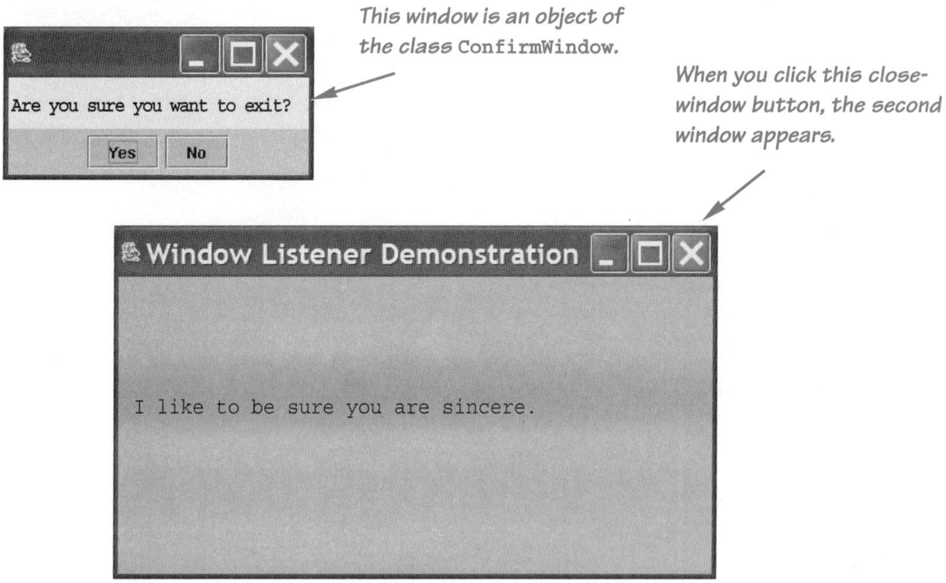
This window is an object of the class ConfirmWindow.
Are you sure you want to exit?
Yes
No
When you click this close-window button, the second window appears.
Window Listener Demonstration
I like to be sure you are sincere.

The `dispose` Method

dispose

The method `dispose` is a method in the class `JFrame` that releases any resources used by the `JFrame` or any of its components. So, a call to `dispose` eliminates the `JFrame` and its components, but if the program has items that are not components of the `JFrame`, then the program does not end. For example, in Display 18.2, the smaller window of the class `ConfirmWindow` invokes `dispose` (if the user clicks the `"No"` button). That causes that smaller window to go away, but the larger window remains.

The `dispose` Method

The class `JFrame` has a method named `dispose` that will eliminate the invoking `JFrame` without ending the program. When `dispose` is invoked, the resources consumed by the `JFrame` and its components are returned for reuse, so the `JFrame` is gone, but the program does not end (unless `dispose` eliminates all elements in the program, as in a one-window program). The method `dispose` is often used in a program with multiple windows to eliminate one window without ending the program.

SYNTAX

JFrame_Object`.dispose();`

The *JFrame_Object* is often an implicit `this`. A complete example of using `dispose` can be seen in Display 18.2.

PITFALL: Forgetting to Invoke `setDefaultCloseOperation`

If you register a window listener to respond to window events from a `JFrame`, you should also include an invocation of the method `setDefaultCloseOperation`, typically in the `JFrame` constructor. This is because the default or other behavior set by `setDefaultCloseOperation` takes place even if there is a window listener. If you do not want any actions other than those provided by the window listener(s), you should include the following in the `JFrame` constructor:

```
setDefaultCloseOperation(JFrame.DO_NOTHING_ON_CLOSE);
```

If you do not include any invocation of `setDefaultCloseOperation`, the default action is the same as if you had included the invocation

```
setDefaultCloseOperation(JFrame.HIDE_ON_CLOSE);
```

which hides the `JFrame` when the close-window button is clicked. (The actions of any registered window listener are also performed.) ■

The `WindowAdapter` Class

In Display 18.2, we gave empty bodies to most of the method headings in the `WindowListener` interface. The abstract class `WindowAdapter` is a way to avoid all those empty method bodies. The class `WindowAdapter` does little more than provide trivial implementations of the method headings in the `WindowListener` interface. So, if you make a window listener a derived class of the class `WindowAdapter`, then you have only to define the method headings in the `WindowListener` interface that you need. The other method headings inherit trivial implementations from `WindowAdapter`. (`WindowAdapter` is unusual in that it is an abstract class with no abstract methods.)

For example, in Display 18.3 we have rewritten the inner class `CheckOnExit` from Display 18.2, but this time we made it a derived class of the `WindowAdapter` class. This definition of `CheckOnExit` is much shorter and cleaner than the one in Display 18.2, but the two implementations of `CheckOnExit` are equivalent. Thus, you can replace the definition of `CheckOnExit` in Display 18.2 with the shorter one in Display 18.3. The file `WindowListenerDemo2` on the accompanying website contains a version of Display 18.2 with this shorter definition of `CheckOnExit`.

extra code on website

The class `WindowAdapter` is in the `java.awt.event` package and so requires an `import` statement such as the following:

```
import java.awt.event.WindowAdapter;
```

You cannot always define your window listeners as derived classes of `Windowdapter`. For example, suppose you want a `JFrame` class to be its own window listener. To accomplish this, the class must be a derived class of `JFrame` and so cannot be a derived class of any other class such as `WindowAdapter`. In such cases, you make the class a derived class of `JFrame` and have it implement the `WindowListener` interface. See Self-Test Exercise 4 for an example.

Display 18.3 Using **`WindowAdapter`**

This requires the following **`import`**

```
        import java.awt.event.WindowAdapter;
        import java.awt.event.WindowEvent;

private class CheckOnExit extends WindowAdapter
{
    public void windowClosing(WindowEvent e)
    {
        ConfirmWindow checkers = new ConfirmWindow();
        checkers.setVisible(true);
    }
} //End of inner class CheckOnExit
```

If the definition of the inner class **`CheckOnExit`** *in Display 18.2 were replaced with this definition of* **`CheckOnExit`**, *there would be no difference in how the outer class or any class behaves.*

MyProgrammingLab™

Self-Test Exercises

1. When you define a class and make it implement the `WindowListener` interface, what methods must you define? What do you do if there is no particular action that you want one of these methods to take?

2. The GUI in Display 18.2 has a main window. When the user clicks the close-window button in the main window, a smaller window appears that says `"Are you sure you want to exit?"` What happens if the user clicks the close-window button in this smaller window? Explain your answer.

3. If you want a Swing program to end completely, you can invoke the method `System.exit`. What if you want a `JFrame` window to go away, but you do not want the program to end? What method can you have the `JFrame` invoke?

4. Rewrite the class in Display 18.2 so that the class is its own window listener. *Hint*: The constructor will contain

```
addWindowListener(this);
```

18.2 Icons and Scroll Bars

I ♥ ICONS.

Bumper sticker

Icons

icon

ImageIcon

`JLabels`, `JButtons`, and `JMenuItems` can have icons. An **icon** is simply a small picture, although it is not required to be small. The label, button, or menu item may have just a string displayed on it, just an icon, or both (or nothing at all). An icon is an instance of the `ImageIcon` class and is based on a digital picture file. The picture file can be in almost any standard format, such as `.gif, .jpg, or .tiff.`

The class `ImageIcon` is used to convert a picture file to a Swing icon. For example, if you have a picture in a file named `duke_waving.gif`, the following will produce an icon named `dukeWavingIcon` for the picture `duke_waving.gif`:

```
ImageIcon dukeIcon = new ImageIcon("duke_waving.gif");
```

The file `duke_waving.gif` should be in the same directory as the class in which this code appears. Alternatively, you can use a complete or relative pathname to specify the picture file. Note that the picture file is given as a value of type `String` that names the picture file. The file `duke_waving.gif` and other picture files we will use in this chapter are all provided on the website that accompanies this text.

setIcon

You can add an icon to a label with the method `setIcon`, as follows:

```
JLabel dukeLabel = new JLabel("Mood check");
dukeLabel.setIcon(dukeIcon);
```

Alternatively, you give the icon as an argument to the `JLabel` constructor, as follows:

```
JLabel dukeLabel = new JLabel(dukeIcon);
```

setText

You can leave the label as created and it will have an icon but no text, or you can add text with the method `setText`, as follows:

```
dukeLabel.setText("Mood check");
```

Icons and text may be added to `JButtons` and `JMenuItems` in the same way as they are added to a `JLabel`. For example, the following is taken from Display 18.4, which is a demonstration of the use of icons:

```
JButton happyButton = new JButton("Happy");
ImageIcon happyIcon = new ImageIcon("smiley.gif");
happyButton.setIcon(happyIcon);
```

Display 18.4 **Using Icons** (part 1 of 2)

```
import javax.swing.JFrame;
import javax.swing.JPanel;
import javax.swing.JTextField;
import javax.swing.ImageIcon;
import java.awt.BorderLayout;
import java.awt.FlowLayout;
import java.awt.Color;
import javax.swing.JLabel;
import javax.swing.JButton;
import java.awt.event.ActionListener;
import java.awt.event.ActionEvent;

public class IconDemo extends JFrame implements ActionListener
{
    public static final int WIDTH = 500;
    public static final int HEIGHT = 200;
    public static final int TEXT_FIELD_SIZE = 30;

    private JTextField message;
    public static void main(String[] args)
    {
        IconDemo iconGui = new IconDemo();
        iconGui.setVisible(true);
    }


    public IconDemo()
    {
        super("Icon Demonstration");
        setSize(WIDTH, HEIGHT);
        setDefaultCloseOperation(JFrame.EXIT_ON_CLOSE);

        setBackground(Color.WHITE);
        setLayout(new BorderLayout());

        JLabel dukeLabel = new JLabel("Mood check");
        ImageIcon dukeIcon = new ImageIcon("duke_waving.gif");
        dukeLabel.setIcon(dukeIcon);
        add(dukeLabel, BorderLayout.NORTH);

        JPanel buttonPanel = new JPanel();
        buttonPanel.setLayout(new FlowLayout());
        JButton happyButton = new JButton("Happy");
        ImageIcon happyIcon = new ImageIcon("smiley.gif");
        happyButton.setIcon(happyIcon);
        happyButton.addActionListener(this);
        buttonPanel.add(happyButton);
        JButton sadButton = new JButton("Sad");
        ImageIcon sadIcon = new ImageIcon("sad.gif");
        sadButton.setIcon(sadIcon);
        sadButton.addActionListener(this);
```

(continued)

Display 18.4 Using Icons (part 2 of 2)

```
        buttonPanel.add(sadButton);
        add(buttonPanel, BorderLayout.SOUTH);

        message = new JTextField(TEXT_FIELD_SIZE);
        add(message, BorderLayout.CENTER);
    }

    public void actionPerformed(ActionEvent e)
    {
       String actionCommand = e.getActionCommand();
       if (actionCommand.equals("Happy"))
           message.setText(
                  "Smile and the world smiles with you!");
       else if (actionCommand.equals("Sad"))
           message.setText(
                  "Cheer up. It can't be that bad.");
       else
           message.setText("Unexpected Error.");
    }
}
```

Resulting GUI[1]

View after clicking the "Sad" button.

button with only an icon

You can produce a button or menu item with (just) an icon on it by giving the `ImageIcon` object as an argument to the `JButton` or `JMenuItem` constructor. For example,

```
ImageIcon happyIcon = new ImageIcon("smiley.gif");
JButton smileButton = new JButton(happyIcon);
JMenuItem happyChoice = new JMenuItem(happyIcon);
```

If you create a button or menu item in this way and do not add text with the method `setText`, you should use `setActionCommand` to explicitly give the button or menu item an action command, because there is no string on the button or menu item.

[1]Java, Duke, and all Java-based trademarks and logos are trademarks or registered trademarks of Oracle, Inc. in the United States and other countries.

All of the classes `JButton`, `JMenuItem`, and `JLabel` have constructors that let you specify text and an icon to appear on the button, menu item, or label. The constructor can specify no text or icon, text only, an icon only, or both text and an icon. When you specify both text and an icon, the text is the first argument and the icon is the second argument; also, the constructor for a `JLabel` requires a third argument, as described in Display 18.5. If you omit either text or an icon (or both) from the constructor, you can add them later with the methods `setText` and `setIcon`. Some of these methods for the classes `JButton`, `JMenuItem`, and `Jlabel` are given in Display 18.5.

Icons and the Class `ImageIcon`

An **icon** is simply a small picture, although it is not really required to be small. The class `ImageIcon` is used to convert a picture file to a Swing icon.

SYNTAX

```
ImageIcon Name_Of_ImageIcon =
        new ImageIcon(Picture_File_Name);
```

The *Picture_File_Name* is a string giving either a relative or absolute path name to the picture file. (So if the picture file is in the same directory as your program, you need give only the name of the picture file.)

EXAMPLE

```
ImageIcon happyIcon =
        new ImageIcon("smiley.gif");
```

Display 18.5 Some Methods in the Classes `JButton`, `JMenuItem`, and `JLabel` (part 1 of 2)

```
public JButton()
public JMenuItem()
public JLabel()
```

Creates a button, menu item, or label with no text or icon on it. (Typically, you will later use `setText` and/or `setIcon` with the button, menu item, or label.)

```
public JButton(String text)
public JMenuItem(String text)
public JLabel(String text)
```

Creates a button, menu item, or label with the text on it.

```
public JButton(ImageIcon picture)
public JMenuItem(ImageIcon picture)
public JLabel(ImageIcon picture)
```

Creates a button, menu item, or label with the icon `picture` on it and no text.

(continued)

Display 18.5 Some Methods in the Classes `JButton`, `JMenuItem`, and `JLabel` (part 2 of 2)

```
public JButton(String text, ImageIcon picture)
public JMenuItem(String text, ImageIcon picture)
public JLabel(
        String text, ImageIcon picture, int horizontalAlignment)
```

Creates a button, menu item, or label with both the `text` and the icon `picture` on it. `horizontalAlignment` is one of the constants `SwingConstants.LEFT`, `SwingConstants.CENTER`, `SwingConstants.RIGHT`, `SwingConstants.LEADING`, or `SwingConstants.TRAILING`.

The interface `SwingConstants` is in the `javax.swing` package.

```
public void setText(String text)
```

Makes `text` the only text on the button, menu item, or label.

```
public void setIcon(ImageIcon picture)
```

Makes `picture` the only icon on the button, menu item, or label.

```
public void setMargin(Insets margin)
```

`JButton` and `JMenuItem` have the method `setMargin`, but `JLabel` does not.

The method `setMargin` sets the size of the margin around the text and icon in the button or menu item. The following special case will work for most simple situations. The `int` values give the number of pixels from the edge of the button or menu item to the text and/or icon.

```
public void setMargin(new Insets(
                int top, int left, int bottom, int right))
```

The class `Insets` is in the `java.awt` package. (We will not be discussing any other uses for the class `Insets`.)

```
public void setVerticalTextPosition(int textPosition)
```

Sets the vertical position of the text relative to the icon. The `textPosition` should be one of the constants `SwingConstants.TOP`, `SwingConstants.CENTER` (the default position), or `SwingConstants.BOTTOM`.

The interface `SwingConstants` is in the `javax.swing` package.

```
public void setHorizontalTextPosition(int textPosition)
```

Sets the horizontal position of the text relative to the icon. The `textPosition` should be one of the constants `SwingConstants.RIGHT`, `SwingConstants.LEFT`, `SwingConstants.CENTER`, `SwingConstants.LEADING`, or `SwingConstants.TRAILING`.

The interface `SwingConstants` is in the `javax.swing` package.

The `Insets` Class

Objects of the class `Insets` are used to specify the size of the margin in a button or menu item. The `Insets` class is in the package `java.awt`. The parameters in the following constructors are in pixels.

CONSTRUCTOR

```
public Insets(int top, int left, int bottom, int right)
```

EXAMPLES

```
aButton.setMargin(new Insets(10, 20, 10, 20));
```

`setIcon` and `setText`

The method `setIcon` can be used to add an icon to a `JButton`, `JMenuItem`, or `JLabel`. The argument to `setIcon` must be an `ImageIcon` object.

SYNTAX

Component.`setIcon`(*ImageIcon_Object*);

The *Component* can be a `JButton`, `JMenuItem`, or `JLabel`.

EXAMPLE

```
JLabel helloLabel = new JLabel("Hello");
ImageIcon dukeIcon = new ImageIcon("duke_waving.gif");
helloLabel.setIcon(dukeIcon);
```

The method `setText` can be used to add text to a `JButton`, `JMenuItem`, or `JLabel`.

SYNTAX

Component.`setText`(*Text_String*);

The *Component* can be a `JButton`, `JMenuItem`, or `JLabel`.

EXAMPLE

```
ImageIcon dukeIcon = new ImageIcon("duke_waving.gif");
JLabel helloLabel = new JLabel(dukeIcon);
helloLabel.setText("Hello");
```

The two examples are equivalent.

MyProgrammingLab™

Self-Test Exercises

5. Write code to create a button that has on it both the text `"Magic Button"` and the picture in the file `wizard.gif`.

6. Write code to add the picture in the file `wizard.gif` to the `JPanel` named `picturePanel`. Assume that `picturePanel` has a `FlowLayout` manager.

7. Suppose you want to create a button that has the picture in the file `wizard.gif` on it and no text. Suppose further that you want the button to have the action command `"Kazam"`. How would you create the button and set up the action command?

Scroll Bars

When you create a text area, you specify the number of lines that are visible and the number of characters per line, as in the following example:

```
JTextArea memoDisplay = new JTextArea(15, 30);
```

The text area `memoDisplay` will have room for 15 lines of text, and each line will have room for at least 30 characters. The user can enter more text, but only a limited amount of text will be visible. It would be better not to have a firm limit on the number of lines or the number of characters per line that the user can see in some convenient way. The way to accomplish this is to add scroll bars to the text area, although, as you will see, the Java code looks more like adding the text area to the scroll bars rather than the other way around.

view port

When using scroll bars, the text is viewed through a **view port** that shows only part of the text at a time. You can view a different part of the text by using the scroll bars that are placed along the side and bottom of the view port. It is as if the text were written on an unbounded sheet of paper, but the paper is covered by another piece of paper with a rectangular cutout that lets you see only a portion of the text. The cutout is the view port. This is illustrated in Display 18.6. You use the scroll bars to move the view port so that different portions of the text can be seen through the cutout view port. (You may prefer to think of the view port as fixed and the text as moving. These two ways of thinking are equivalent.) Swing allows you to add scroll bars to your text areas by using the class `JScrollPane`.

`JScrollPane`

An object of the class `JScrollPane` is essentially a view port with scroll bars. When you create a `JScrollPane`, you give the text area as an argument to the `JScrollPane` constructor. For example, if `memoDisplay` is an object of the class `JTextArea` (as created in the line of code at the start of this subsection), you can place `memoDisplay` in a `JScrollPane` as follows:

```
JScrollPane scrolledText = new JScrollPane(memoDisplay);
```

Display 18.6 View Port for a Text Area

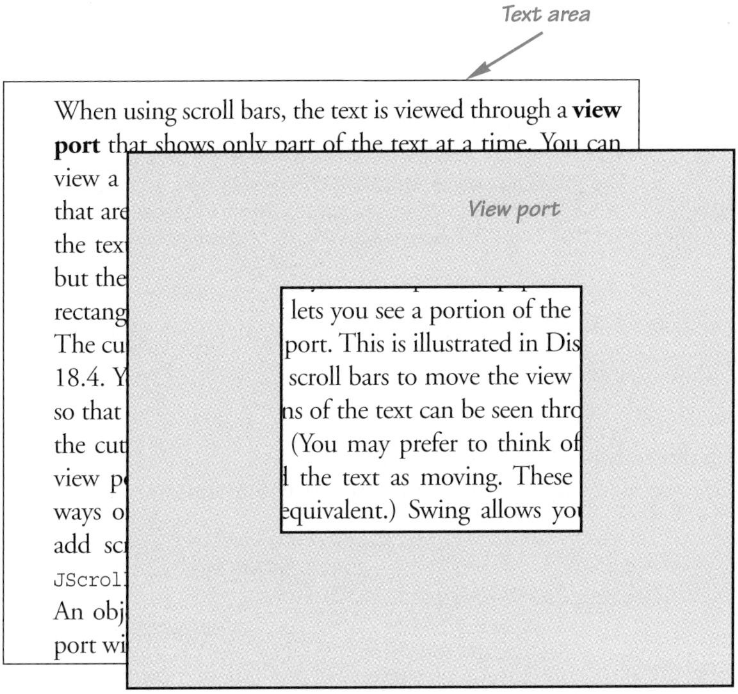

Display 18.7 Some Methods in the Class `JScrollPane` (part 1 of 2)

The `JScrollPane` class is in the `javax.swing` package.

`public JScrollPane(Component objectToBeScrolled)`

Creates a new `JScrollPane` for the `objectToBeScrolled`. Note that the `objectToBeScrolled` need not be a `JTextArea`, although that is the only type of argument considered in this book.

`public void setHorizontalScrollBarPolicy(int policy)`

Sets the policy for showing the horizontal scroll bar. The `policy` should be one of the following:

```
JScrollPane.HORIZONTAL_SCROLLBAR_ALWAYS
JScrollPane.HORIZONTAL_SCROLLBAR_NEVER
JScrollPane.HORIZONTAL_SCROLLBAR_AS_NEEDED
```

The phrase AS_NEEDED means the scroll bar is shown only when it is needed. This is explained more fully in the text. The meanings of the other policy constants are obvious from their names.

(As indicated, these constants are defined in the class `JScrollPane`. You should not need to even be aware of the fact that they have `int` values. Think of them as policies, not as `int` values.)

`public void setVerticalScrollBarPolicy(int policy)`

(continued)

Display 18.7 Some Methods in the Class `JScrollPane` (part 2 of 2)

Sets the policy for showing the vertical scroll bar. The `policy` should be one of the following:

```
JScrollPane.VERTICAL_SCROLLBAR_ALWAYS
JScrollPane.VERTICAL_SCROLLBAR_NEVER
JScrollPane.VERTICAL_SCROLLBAR_AS_NEEDED
```

The phrase AS_NEEDED means the scroll bar is shown only when it is needed. This is explained more fully in the text. The meanings of the other policy constants are obvious from their names. (As indicated, these constants are defined in the class `JScrollPane`. You should not need to even be aware of the fact that they have `int` values. Think of them as policies, not as `int` values.)

The `JScrollPane` can then be added to a container, such as a `JPanel` or `JFrame`, as follows:

```
textPanel.add(scrolledText);
```

This is illustrated by the program in Display 18.8.

Note the following two lines in the constructor definition in Display 18.8:

setting scroll bar policies

```
scrolledText.setHorizontalScrollBarPolicy(
                JScrollPane.HORIZONTAL_SCROLLBAR_ALWAYS);
scrolledText.setVerticalScrollBarPolicy(
                JScrollPane.VERTICAL_SCROLLBAR_ALWAYS);
```

Despite the imposing length of these two method invocations, they perform a very simple task. The first merely specifies that the horizontal scroll bar will always be present. The second specifies that the vertical scroll bar will always be present.

If you omit the invocation of the two methods `setHorizontalScrollBarPolicy` and `setVerticalScrollBarPolicy`, the scroll bars will be visible only when you need them. In other words, if you omit these two method invocations and all the text fits in the view port, then no scroll bars will be visible. When you add enough text to need scroll bars, the needed scroll bars will appear automatically.

Display 18.7 summarizes what we have said about the class `JScrollPane`. We are interested in using `JScrollPane` only with text areas. However, as we note in Display 18.7, `JScrollPane` can be used with almost any sort of component.

Display 18.8 A Text Area with Scroll Bars (part 1 of 3)

```
import javax.swing.JFrame;
import javax.swing.JTextArea;
import javax.swing.JPanel;
import javax.swing.JLabel;
import javax.swing.JButton;
import javax.swing.JScrollPane;
import java.awt.BorderLayout;
import java.awt.FlowLayout;
import java.awt.Color;
import java.awt.event.ActionListener;
import java.awt.event.ActionEvent;
```

Display 18.8 A Text Area with Scroll Bars (part 2 of 3)

```
public class ScrollBarDemo extends JFrame
                           implements ActionListener
{
    public static final int WIDTH = 600;
    public static final int HEIGHT = 400;
    public static final int LINES = 15;
    public static final int CHAR_PER_LINE = 30;

    private JTextArea memoDisplay;
    private String memo1;
    private String memo2;

    public static void main(String[] args)
    {
        ScrollBarDemo gui = new ScrollBarDemo();
        gui.setVisible(true);
    }

    public ScrollBarDemo()
    {
        super("Scroll Bars Demo");
        setSize(WIDTH, HEIGHT);
        setDefaultCloseOperation(JFrame.EXIT_ON_CLOSE);
        JPanel buttonPanel = new JPanel();
        buttonPanel.setBackground(Color.LIGHT_GRAY);
        buttonPanel.setLayout(new FlowLayout());
        JButton memo1Button = new JButton("Save Memo 1");
        memo1Button.addActionListener(this);
        buttonPanel.add(memo1Button);

        JButton memo2Button = new JButton("Save Memo 2");
        memo2Button.addActionListener(this);
        buttonPanel.add(memo2Button);

        JButton clearButton = new JButton("Clear");
        clearButton.addActionListener(this);
        buttonPanel.add(clearButton);

        JButton get1Button = new JButton("Get Memo 1");
        get1Button.addActionListener(this);
        buttonPanel.add(get1Button);

        JButton get2Button = new JButton("Get Memo 2");
        get2Button.addActionListener(this);
        buttonPanel.add(get2Button);

        add(buttonPanel, BorderLayout.SOUTH);

        JPanel textPanel = new JPanel();
        textPanel.setBackground(Color.BLUE);
```

(continued)

Display 18.8 **A Text Area with Scroll Bars** (part 3 of 3)

```
        memoDisplay = new JTextArea(LINES, CHAR_PER_LINE);
        memoDisplay.setBackground(Color.WHITE);

        JScrollPane scrolledText = new JScrollPane(memoDisplay);
        scrolledText.setHorizontalScrollBarPolicy(
                    JScrollPane.HORIZONTAL_SCROLLBAR_ALWAYS);
        scrolledText.setVerticalScrollBarPolicy(
                    JScrollPane.VERTICAL_SCROLLBAR_ALWAYS);

        textPanel.add(scrolledText);

        add(textPanel, BorderLayout.CENTER);
    }
    public void actionPerformed(ActionEvent e)
    {
        String actionCommand = e.getActionCommand();


        if (actionCommand.equals("Save Memo 1"))
            memo1 = memoDisplay.getText();
        else if (actionCommand.equals("Save Memo 2"))
            memo2 = memoDisplay.getText();
        else if (actionCommand.equals("Clear"))
            memoDisplay.setText("");
        else if (actionCommand.equals("Get Memo 1"))
            memoDisplay.setText(memo1);
        else if (actionCommand.equals("Get Memo 2"))
            memoDisplay.setText(memo2);
        else
            memoDisplay.setText("Error in memo interface");
    }
}
```

RESULTING GUI

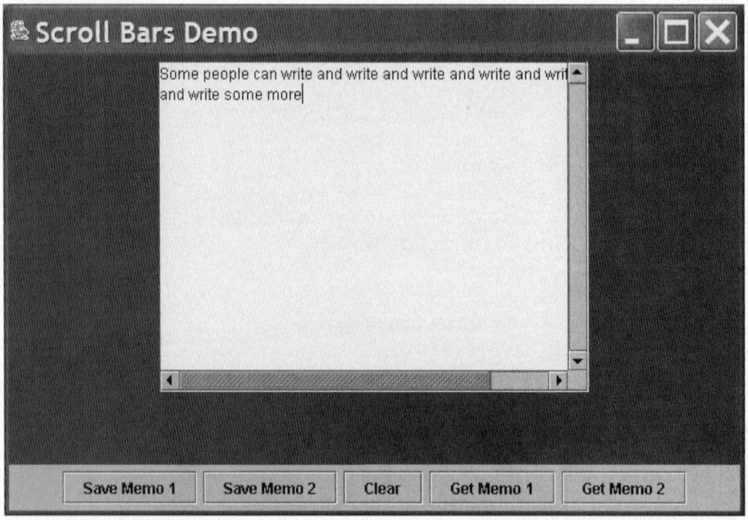

Scroll Bars

The class `JScrollPane` is used to add scroll bars to a `JTextArea` (and certain other components). The `JTextArea` object is given as an argument to the constructor that creates the `JScrollPane`. The `JScrollPane` class is in the `javax.swing` package.

SYNTAX

```
JScrollPane Identifier = new JScrollPane(Text_Area_Object);
```

EXAMPLES

```
JTextArea memoDisplay = new JTextArea(LINES, CHAR_PER_LINE);
JScrollPane scrolledText = new JScrollPane(memoDisplay);
textPanel.add(scrolledText);
```

MyProgrammingLab™

Self-Test Exercises

8. When setting up a `JScrollPane`, do you have to invoke both of the methods `setHorizontalScrollBarPolicy` and `setVerticalScrollBarPolicy`?

9. In Display 18.7, we listed the constructor for `JScrollPane` as follows:

```
public JScrollPane(Component objectToBeScrolled)
```

This indicates that the argument to the constructor must be of type `Component`. But we used the constructor with an argument of type `JTextArea`. Isn't this some sort of type violation?

EXAMPLE: Components with Changing Visibility

The GUI in Display 18.9 has labels that change from visible to invisible and back again. Because the labels contain nothing but an icon each, it appears as if the icons also change roles from visible to invisible and back again. When the GUI is first run, the label with Duke not waving is shown. When the `"Wave"` button is clicked, the label with Duke not waving disappears and the label with Duke waving appears. When the button labeled `"Stop"` is clicked, the label with Duke waving disappears and the label with Duke not waving returns. Note that you can make a component invisible without making the entire GUI invisible.

(continued)

EXAMPLE: (continued)

In this GUI, a label becomes visible or invisible when a button is clicked. For example, the following code from the method `actionPerformed` in Display 18.9 determines what happens when the button with the text `"Wave"` on it is clicked:

```
if (actionCommand.equals("Wave"))
{

    wavingLabel.setVisible(true);
    standingLabel.setVisible(false);
}
```

We used the `setVisible` method on the labels containing the icons rather than directly on the icons because the class `ImageIcon` does not have the `setVisible` method.

The two statements

```
wavingLabel.setVisible(true);
standingLabel.setVisible(false);
```

make `wavingLabel` visible `and` `standingLabel` invisible.

Display 18.9 **Labels with Changing Visibility** (part 1 of 3)

```
import javax.swing.JFrame;
import javax.swing.ImageIcon;
import javax.swing.JPanel;
import javax.swing.JLabel;
import javax.swing.JButton;
import java.awt.BorderLayout;
import java.awt.FlowLayout;
import java.awt.Color;
import java.awt.event.ActionListener;
import java.awt.event.ActionEvent;

public class VisibilityDemo extends JFrame
                            implements ActionListener
{
    public static final int WIDTH = 300;
    public static final int HEIGHT = 200;
    private JLabel wavingLabel;
    private JLabel standingLabel;
```

Display 18.9 **Labels with Changing Visibility** (part 2 of 3)

```
    public static void main(String[] args)
    {
        VisibilityDemo demoGui = new VisibilityDemo();
        demoGui.setVisible(true);
    }

    public VisibilityDemo()
    {
        setSize(WIDTH, HEIGHT);
        setDefaultCloseOperation(JFrame.EXIT_ON_CLOSE);
        setTitle("Visibility Demonstration");

        setLayout(new BorderLayout());

        JPanel picturePanel = new JPanel();
        picturePanel.setBackground(Color.WHITE);
        picturePanel.setLayout(new FlowLayout());

        ImageIcon dukeStandingIcon =
                  new ImageIcon("duke_standing.gif");
        standingLabel = new JLabel(dukeStandingIcon);
        standingLabel.setVisible(true);
        picturePanel.add(standingLabel);

        ImageIcon dukeWavingIcon = new ImageIcon("duke_waving.gif");
        wavingLabel = new JLabel(dukeWavingIcon);
        wavingLabel.setVisible(false);
        picturePanel.add(wavingLabel);

        add(picturePanel, BorderLayout.CENTER);

        JPanel buttonPanel = new JPanel();
        buttonPanel.setBackground(Color.LIGHT_GRAY);
        buttonPanel.setLayout(new FlowLayout());

        JButton waveButton = new JButton("Wave");
        waveButton.addActionListener(this);
        buttonPanel.add(waveButton);

        JButton stopButton = new JButton("Stop");
        stopButton.addActionListener(this);
        buttonPanel.add(stopButton);
        add(buttonPanel, BorderLayout.SOUTH);
    }
    public void actionPerformed(ActionEvent e)
```

(continued)

Display 18.9 **Labels with Changing Visibility** (part 3 of 3)

```
        {
            String actionCommand = e.getActionCommand();
            if (actionCommand.equals("Wave"))
            {
                wavingLabel.setVisible(true);
                standingLabel.setVisible(false);
            }
            else if (actionCommand.equals("Stop"))
            {
                standingLabel.setVisible(true);
                wavingLabel.setVisible(false);
            }
            else
                System.out.println("Unanticipated error.");
        }
    }
```

Resulting GUI (After clicking Stop button)

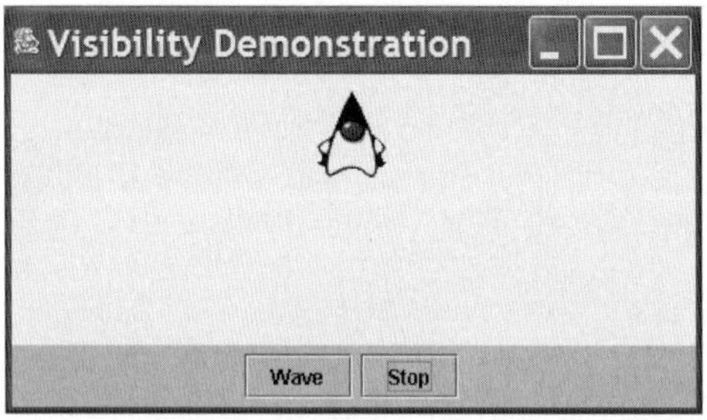

Resulting GUI (After clicking Wave button)

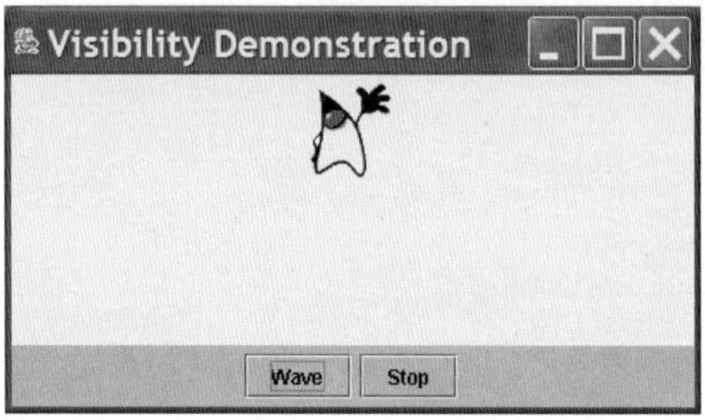

18.3 The `Graphics` Class

Drawing is my life!

THE GRAPHICS CLASS

In this section, we show you how to produce drawing for your GUIs using the `Graphics` class.

Coordinate System for Graphics Objects

When drawing objects on the screen, Java uses the coordinate system shown in Display 18.10. The **origin** point (0, 0) is the upper-left corner of the screen area used for drawing (usually a `JFrame` or `JPanel`). The *x*-coordinate, or horizontal coordinate, is positive and increasing to the right. The *y*-coordinate, or vertical coordinate, is positive and increasing in the downward direction. The point (*x*, *y*) is located *x* pixels in from the left edge of the screen and down *y* pixels from the top of the screen. All coordinates are normally positive. Units as well as sizes of figures are in pixels. When placing a rectangle on the screen, Java often uses a coordinate such as (200, 150) to specify where the rectangle is located.

origin

(*x*, *y*)

Note that, when specifying the location of a rectangle or other figure, the coordinates do not indicate the center of the rectangle, but instead indicate the location of the upper-left corner of the rectangle. In Display 18.10, the X marks the location of the point (200, 150) and the rectangle shown is at location (200, 150).

When placing a figure other than a rectangle on the screen, Java encloses the figure in an imaginary tightly fitting rectangle, sometimes called a **bounding box**, and positions the upper-left corner of the imaginary rectangle. For example, in Display 18.10, the oval displayed is located at point (200, 150).

bounding box

Display 18.10 Screen Coordinate System

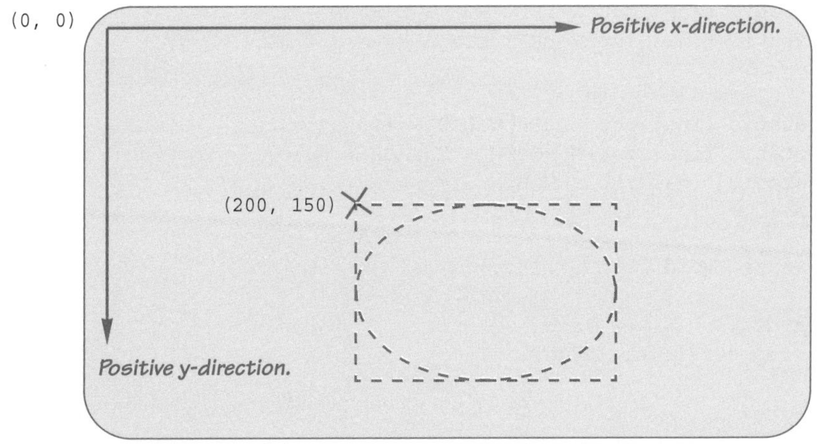

The Method `paint` and the Class `Graphics`

`paint`

Almost all Swing and Swing-related components and containers have a method named `paint`. The method `paint` draws the component or container on the screen. Up until now, we have had no need to redefine this method or to even mention it. It is defined for you and is called automatically when the figure is displayed on the screen. However, to draw geometric figures, such as circles and boxes, you need to redefine the method `paint`. It is this method that draws the figures.

VideoNote **Walkthrough of a Simple Drawing Program**

Display 18.11 shows a GUI program that displays a `JFrame` with a rather primitive face drawn inside of it. The mouth and eyes are just straight line segments. We will soon see how to get round eyes and a smile (and more), but the basic technique can be seen more clearly in this simple figure. The code for drawing the face is given in the method `paint`.

Display 18.11 Drawing a Very Simple Face (part 1 of 2)

```
import javax.swing.JFrame;
import java.awt.Graphics;
import java.awt.Color;
public class Face extends JFrame

{
    public static final int WINDOW_WIDTH = 400;
    public static final int WINDOW_HEIGHT = 400;


    public static final int FACE_DIAMETER = 200;
    public static final int X_FACE = 100;
    public static final int Y_FACE = 100;

    public static final int EYE_WIDTH = 20;
    public static final int X_RIGHT_EYE = X_FACE + 55;
    public static final int Y_RIGHT_EYE = Y_FACE + 60;
    public static final int X_LEFT_EYE = X_FACE + 130;
    public static final int Y_LEFT_EYE = Y_FACE + 60;


    public static final int MOUTH_WIDTH = 100;
    public static final int X_MOUTH = X_FACE + 50;
    public static final int Y_MOUTH = Y_FACE + 150;


    public static void main(String[] args)
    {
        Face drawing = new Face();
        drawing.setVisible(true);
    }
    public Face()
    {
```

Display 18.11 **Drawing a Very Simple Face** (part 2 of 2)

```
        super("First Graphics Demo");
        setSize(WINDOW_WIDTH, WINDOW_HEIGHT);
        setDefaultCloseOperation(JFrame.EXIT_ON_CLOSE);
        getContentPane().setBackground(Color.white);
    }
    public void paint(Graphics g)
    {
        super.paint(g);
        g.drawOval(X_FACE, Y_FACE, FACE_DIAMETER, FACE_DIAMETER);
        //Draw Eyes:
        g.drawLine(X_RIGHT_EYE, Y_RIGHT_EYE,
                             X_RIGHT_EYE + EYE_WIDTH,Y_RIGHT_EYE);
        g.drawLine(X_LEFT_EYE, Y_LEFT_EYE,
                            X_LEFT_EYE + EYE_WIDTH, Y_LEFT_EYE);
        //Draw Mouth:
        g.drawLine(X_MOUTH, Y_MOUTH, X_MOUTH + MOUTH_WIDTH, Y_MOUTH);
    }
}
```

Resulting GUI

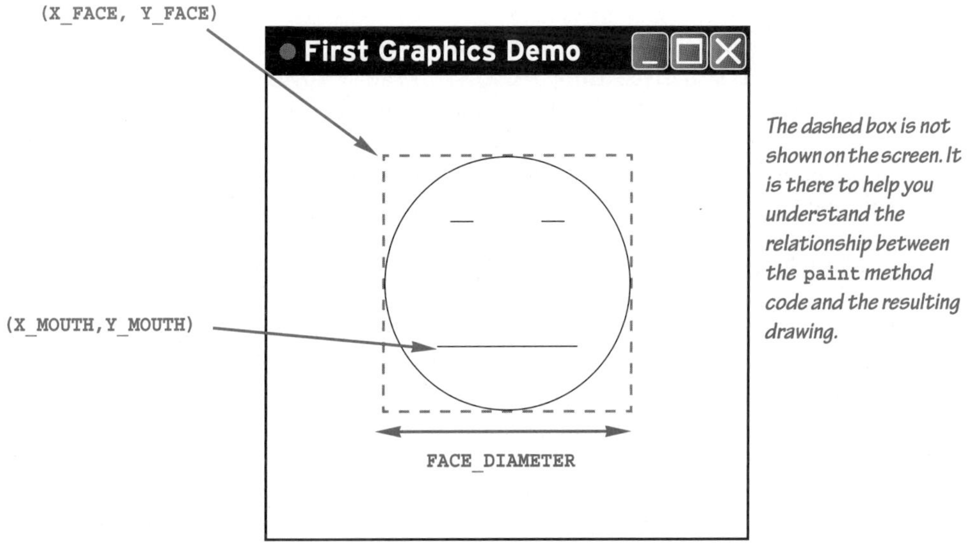

(X_FACE, Y_FACE)
First Graphics Demo
(X_MOUTH,Y_MOUTH)
FACE_DIAMETER
The dashed box is not shown on the screen. It is there to help you understand the relationship between the paint method code and the resulting drawing.

The method `paint` is called automatically, and you normally should not invoke it in your code. If you do not redefine it, the method `paint` for a `JFrame` object simply draws a frame border, title, and other standard features, and then asks the components to all invoke their `paint` methods. If we do not redefine the method `paint`, then the

JFrame would have a border and title but would contain nothing. The code in the redefinition of paint explains how to draw the face. Let us look at the details.

Graphics

Notice that the method paint has a parameter g of type Graphics. Graphics is an abstract class in the java.awt package. Every container and component that can be drawn on the screen has an associated Graphics object. (To be precise, every JComponent has an associated Graphics object.) This associated Graphics object has data specifying what area of the screen the component or container covers. In particular, the Graphics object for a JFrame specifies that the drawing takes place inside the borders of the JFrame object. (Because Graphics is an abstract class, every Graphics object is an instance of some concrete descendent class of the Graphics class, but we usually do not care about which descendent class. All we normally need to know is that it is of type Graphics.)

The Graphics class, and so any Graphics object g, has all the methods that we will use to draw figures, such as circles, lines, and boxes, on the screen. Almost the entire definition of the paint method in Display 18.11 consists of invocations of various drawing methods with the parameter g as the calling object.

When the paint method in Display 18.11 is (automatically) invoked, the parameter g will be replaced by the Graphics object associated with the JFrame, so the figures drawn will be inside the JFrame. Let us look at the code in this method paint.

Notice the first line in the definition of paint in Display 18.11:

```
super.paint(g);
```

Recall that super is a name for the parent class of a derived class. The class in Display 18.11 is derived from the class JFrame, so super.paint is the paint method for the class JFrame. Whenever you redefine the method paint, you should start with this invocation of super.paint. This ensures that your definition of paint will do all the things the standard paint method does, such as draw the title and border for the JFrame. (This lesson applies even if the class is derived from some class other than JFrame.)

drawOval

The following invocation from the method paint draws the circle forming the head:

```
g.drawOval(X_FACE, Y_FACE, FACE_DIAMETER, FACE_DIAMETER);
```

The last two arguments give the width and height of the enclosing rectangle, shown in red. The fact that these two arguments are equal is what makes it a circle instead of a typical oval. The first two arguments give *x*- and *y*-coordinates for the position of the circle. Note that a figure is positioned by giving the position of the upper-left corner of an enclosing rectangle.

drawLine

The only other drawing statements in the method paint are invocations of g.drawLine. The method g.drawLine draws a straight line between two points with *x*- and *y*-coordinates (x_1, y_1) and (x_2, y_2), where the argument positions for the four coordinate numbers are indicated as follows:

```
g.drawLine(x1, y1, x2, y2)
```

For example, the invocation that draws the mouth is as follows:

```
g.drawLine(X_MOUTH, Y_MOUTH, X_MOUTH + MOUTH_WIDTH, Y_MOUTH);
```

Because both *y*-coordinates (`Y_MOUTH`) are the same, the line is horizontal. The line for the mouth begins at coordinates (`X_MOUTH, Y_MOUTH`) and extends to the right for `MOUTH_WIDTH` pixels.

> **The `Graphics` Class**
>
> Every container and component that can be drawn on the screen has an associated `Graphics` object. This associated `Graphics` object has data specifying what area of the screen the component or container covers. In particular, the `Graphics` object for a `JFrame` specifies that the drawing takes place inside the borders of the `JFrame` object.
>
> When an object `g` of the class `Graphics` is used as the calling object for a drawing method, the drawing takes place inside the area of the screen specified by `g`. For example, if `g` is the `Graphics` object for a `JFrame`, the drawing takes place inside the borders of the `JFrame` object.
>
> Some of the commonly used methods of the class `Graphics` are given in Display 18.12.
>
> `Graphics` is an abstract class in the `java.awt` package.

Some of the commonly used methods of the class `Graphics` are given in Display 18.12. Note that most methods come in pairs, one whose name starts with `draw` and one whose name starts with `fill`, such as `drawOval` and `fillOval`. The one that starts with `draw` will draw the outline of the specified figure. The one that starts with `fill` will draw a solid figure obtained by filling the inside of the specified figure. In the next few subsections, we discuss some of these methods.

Display 18.12 Some Methods in the Class **`Graphics`** (part 1 of 3)

`Graphics` is an abstract class in the `java.awt` package.

Although many of these methods are abstract, we always use them with objects of a concrete descendent class of `Graphics`, even though we usually do not know the name of that concrete class.

```
public abstract void drawLine(int x1, int y1, int x2, int y2)
```

Draws a line between points (`x1, y1`) and (`x2, y2`).

```
public abstract void drawRect(int x, int y,
                              int width, int height)
```

Draws the outline of the specified rectangle. (`x, y`) is the location of the upper-left corner of the rectangle.

```
public abstract void fillRect(int x, int y,
                              int width, int height)
```

Fills the specified rectangle. (x, y) is the location of the upper-left corner of the rectangle.

(continued)

Display 18.12 Some Methods in the Class `Graphics` (part 2 of 3)

```
public void draw3DRect(int x, int y, int width,
                                 int height, boolean raised)
```

Draws the outline of the specified rectangle. (`x, y`) is the location of the upper-left corner. The rectangle is highlighted to look like it has thickness. If `raised` is `true`, the highlight makes the rectangle appear to stand out from the background. If `raised` is `false`, the highlight makes the rectangle appear to be sunken into the background.

```
public void fill3DRect(int x, int y, int width,
                                 int height, boolean raised)
```

Fills the rectangle specified by

```
draw3DRec(x, y, width, height, raised)
```

```
public abstract void drawRoundRect (int x, int y,
          int width, int height, int arcWidth, int arcHeight)
```

Draws the outline of the specified round-cornered rectangle. (x, y) is the location of the upper-left corner of the enclosing regular rectangle. `arcWidth` and `arcHeight` specify the shape of the round corners. See the text for details.

```
public abstract void fillRoundRect(int x, int y,
          int width, int height, int arcWidth, int arcHeight)
```

Fills the rounded rectangle specified by

```
drawRoundRec(x, y, width, height, arcWidth, arcHeight)
```

```
public abstract void drawOval(int x, int y,
                                 int width, int height)
```

Draws the outline of the oval with the smallest enclosing rectangle that has the specified width and height. The (imagined) rectangle has its upper-left corner located at (`x, y`).

```
public abstract void fillOval (int x, int y,
                             int width, int height)
```

Fills the oval specified by

```
drawOval(x, y, width, height)
```

```
public abstract void drawArc(int x, int y,
                           int width, int height,
                           int startAngle, int arcSweep)
```

Draws part of an oval that just fits into an invisible rectangle described by the first four arguments. The portion of the oval drawn is given by the last two arguments. See the text for details.

Display 18.12 Some Methods in the Class **Graphics** (part 3 of 3)

```
public abstract void fillArc(int x, int y,
                             int width, int height,
                             int startAngle, int arcSweep)
```

Fills the partial oval specified by

```
drawArc(x, y, width, height, startAngle, arcSweep)
```

Drawing Ovals

An oval is drawn by the method `drawOval`. The arguments specify the location, width, and height of the smallest rectangle that encloses the oval. For example, the following line draws an oval:

drawOval

```
g.drawOval(100, 50, 300, 200);
```

This draws an oval that just fits into an invisible rectangle whose upper-left corner is at coordinates (100, 50) and that has a width of 300 pixels and a height of 200 pixels. Note that the point that is used to place the oval on the screen is not the center of the oval or anything like the center, but is something like the upper-left corner of the oval.

Note that a circle is a special case of an oval in which the width and height of the rectangle are equal. For example, the following line from the definition of `paint` in Display 18.11 draws a circle for the outline of the face:

```
g.drawOval(X_FACE, Y_FACE, FACE_DIAMETER, FACE_DIAMETER);
```

Because the enclosing rectangle has the same width and height, this produces a circle.

Some of the methods you can use to draw simple figures are shown in Display 18.12. A similar table is given in Appendix 5.

Drawing Arcs

Arcs, such as the smile on the happy face in Display 18.13, are described by giving an oval and then specifying what portion of the oval will be used for the arc. For example, the following statement from Display 18.13 draws the smile on the happy face:

drawArc

```
g.drawArc(X_MOUTH, Y_MOUTH, MOUTH_WIDTH, MOUTH_HEIGHT,
                   MOUTH_START_ANGLE, MOUTH_ARC_SWEEP);
```

which is equivalent to

```
g.drawArc(X_MOUTH, Y_MOUTH, MOUTH_WIDTH, MOUTH_HEIGHT, 180, 180);
```

The arguments `MOUTH_WIDTH` and `MOUTH_HEIGHT` determine the size of an invisible rectangle. The arguments `X_MOUTH` and `Y_MOUTH` determine the location of the rectangle. The upper-left corner of the rectangle is located at the point `(X_MOUTH, Y_MOUTH)`. Inside this invisible rectangle, envision an invisible oval that just fits inside the invisible rectangle. The last two arguments specify the portion of this invisible oval that is made visible.

Display 18.14 illustrates how these last two arguments specify an arc of the invisible oval to be made visible. The next-to-last argument specifies a start angle in degrees. The last argument specifies how many degrees of the oval's arc will be made visible. If the last argument is 360 (degrees), then the full oval is made visible.

Display 18.13 **Drawing a Happy Face** (part 1 of 2)

```
import javax.swing.JFrame;
import java.awt.Graphics;
import java.awt.Color;

public class HappyFace extends JFrame
{
    public static final int WINDOW_WIDTH = 400;
    public static final int WINDOW_HEIGHT = 400;


    public static final int FACE_DIAMETER = 200;
    public static final int X_FACE = 100;
    public static final int Y_FACE = 100;

    public static final int EYE_WIDTH = 20;
    public static final int EYE_HEIGHT = 10;
    public static final int X_RIGHT_EYE = X_FACE + 55;
    public static final int Y_RIGHT_EYE = Y_FACE + 60;
    public static final int X_LEFT_EYE = X_FACE + 130;
    public static final int Y_LEFT_EYE = Y_FACE + 60;

    public static final int MOUTH_WIDTH = 100;
    public static final int MOUTH_HEIGHT = 50;
    public static final int X_MOUTH = X_FACE + 50;
    public static final int Y_MOUTH = Y_FACE + 100;
    public static final int MOUTH_START_ANGLE = 180;
    public static final int MOUTH_ARC_SWEEP = 180;
    public static void main(String[] args)
    {
      HappyFace drawing = new HappyFace();
      drawing.setVisible(true);
    }
```

Display 18.13 **Drawing a Happy Face** (part 2 of 2)

```
    public HappyFace()
    {
        super("Graphics Demonstration 2");
        setSize(WINDOW_WIDTH, WINDOW_HEIGHT);
        setDefaultCloseOperation(JFrame.EXIT_ON_CLOSE);
        getContentPane().setBackground(Color.white);
    }
   public void paint(Graphics g)
    {
        super.paint(g);
        g.drawOval(X_FACE, Y_FACE, FACE_DIAMETER, FACE_DIAMETER);
        //Draw Eyes:
        g.fillOval(X_RIGHT_EYE, Y_RIGHT_EYE, EYE_WIDTH, EYE_HEIGHT);
        g.fillOval(X_LEFT_EYE, Y_LEFT_EYE, EYE_WIDTH, EYE_HEIGHT);
        //Draw Mouth:
        g.drawArc(X_MOUTH, Y_MOUTH, MOUTH_WIDTH, MOUTH_HEIGHT,
                    MOUTH_START_ANGLE, MOUTH_ARC_SWEEP);
    }
}
```

Resulting GUI

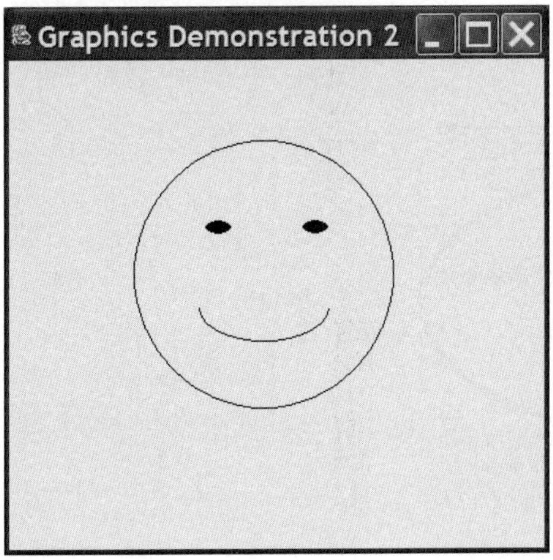

Display 18.14 Specifying an Arc

```
g.drawArc(x, y, width, height, 0, 90);
```

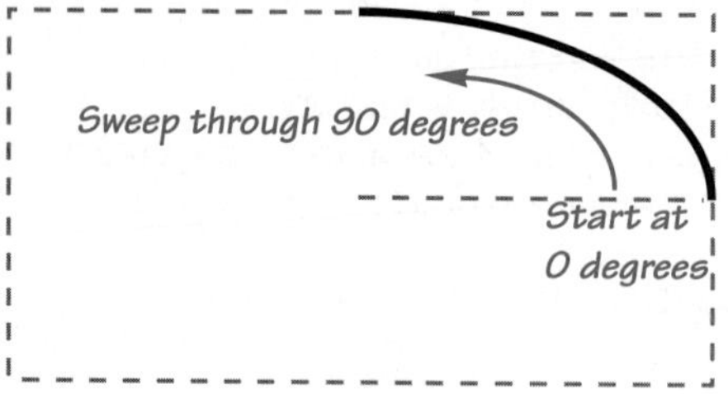


```
g.drawArc(x, y, width, height, 0, -90);
```

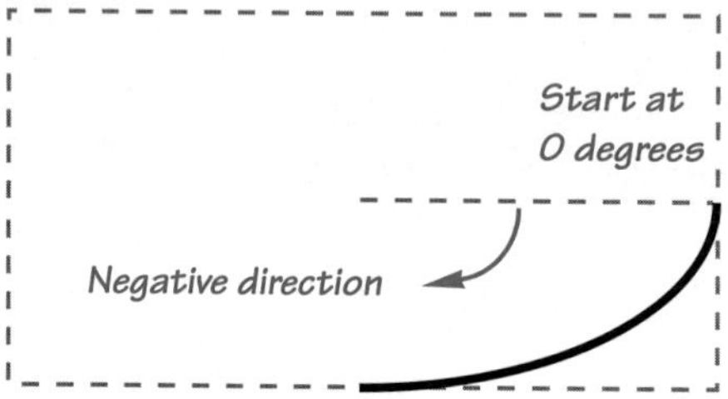


```
g.drawArc(x, y, width, height, 0, 360);
```

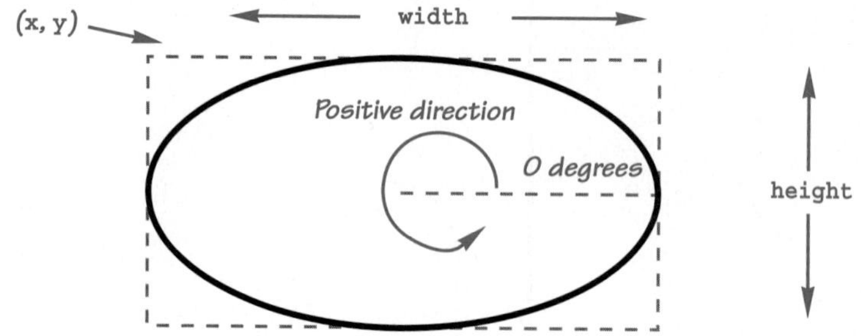


```
g.drawArc(x, y, width, height, 180, 90);
```

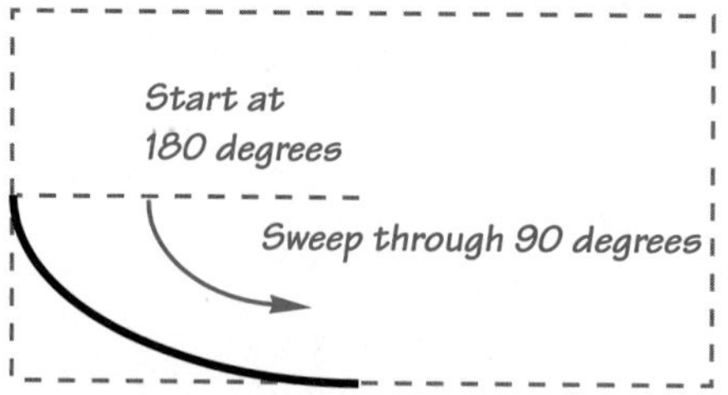

The angles are numbered with zero degrees, as shown in Display 18.14. In the first figure, the start angle is zero degrees. The counterclockwise direction is positive. So a start angle of 90 degrees would start at the top of the oval. A start angle of –90 degrees would start at the bottom of the oval. For example, the smile on the happy face in Display 18.13 has a start angle of 180 degrees, so it starts on the left end of the invisible oval. The last argument is also 180, so the arc is made visible through a counterclockwise direction of 180 degrees, or halfway around the oval in the counterclockwise direction.

MyProgrammingLab™

Self-Test Exercises

10. Give an invocation of a method to draw a horizontal line from point (30, 40) to point (100, 60). The calling object of type `Graphics` is named `g`.

11. Give an invocation of a method to draw a horizontal line of length 100 starting at position (30, 40) and extending to the right. The calling object of type `Graphics` is named `g`.

12. Give an invocation of a method that draws a vertical line of length 100 starting at position (30, 40) and extending downward. Use `graphicsObject` (of type `Graphic`) as the calling object.

13. Give an invocation of a method to draw a solid rectangle of width 100 and height 50 with the upper-left corner at position (20, 30). The calling object of type `Graphics` is named `graphicsObject`.

14. Give an invocation of a method to draw a solid rectangle of width 100 and height 50 with the upper-right corner at position (200, 300). The calling object of type `Graphics` is named `g`.

15. Give an invocation of a method to draw a circle of diameter 100 with the center at position (300, 400). The calling object of type `Graphics` is named `g`.

16. Give an invocation of a method to draw a circle of radius 100 with the center at position (300, 400). The calling object of type `Graphics` is named `g`.

Rounded Rectangles ★

rounded rectangle

A **rounded rectangle** is a rectangle whose corners have been replaced by arcs so that the corners are rounded. For example, suppose `g` is of type `Graphics` and consider what would be drawn by the following:

```
g.drawRoundRect(x, y, width, height, arcWidth, arcHeight)
```

The arguments `x`, `y`, `width`, and `height` determine a regular rectangle in the usual way. The upper-left corner is at the point `(x, y)`. The rectangle has the specified `width` and height. The last two arguments, arcWidth and arcHeight, specify the arcs that will be used for the corners so as to produce a rounded rectangle. Each corner is replaced with a quarter of an oval that is arcWidth pixels wide and arcHeight pixels high. This is illustrated in Display 18.15. To obtain corners that are arcs of circles, just make arcWidth and arcHeight equal.

paintComponent for Panels

You can draw figures on a JPanel and place the JPanel in a JFrame. When defining a JPanel class that contains a graphics drawing, use the method paintComponent instead of the method paint, but otherwise the details are similar to what we have seen for JFrames. JFrames use the method paint. However, JPanels—and in fact all JComponents—use the method paintComponent. A very simple example of using paintComponent with a JPanel is given in Display 18.16.

If you look back at Display 17.12 in Chapter 17, you will see that a JPanel is a JComponent, but a JFrame is not a JComponent. A JFrame is only a Component. This is why they use different methods to paint the screen.

Action Drawings and repaint

The program in Display 18.17 is similar to the program in Display 18.13. It draws a happy face similar to the happy face given in Display 18.13, but with one difference: There is a button at the bottom of the GUI that says Click for a Wink. When you click that button, the left eye winks. (Remember the left eye is on your right.) Let us see the details.

Display 18.15 A Rounded Rectangle

```
g.drawRoundRect(x, y, width, height, arcWidth, arcHeight);
```

produces:

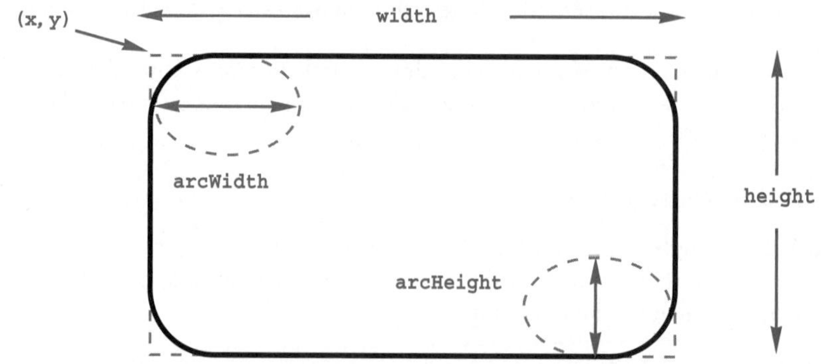

Display 18.16 **paintComponent** Demonstration (part 1 of 2)

```
import javax.swing.JFrame;
import javax.swing.JPanel;
import java.awt.GridLayout;
import java.awt.Graphics;
import java.awt.Color;

public class PaintComponentDemo extends JFrame
{
    public static final int FRAME_WIDTH = 400;
    public static final int FRAME_HEIGHT = 400;

    private class FancyPanel extends JPanel
    {
        public void paintComponent(Graphics g)
        {
            super.paintComponent(g);
            setBackground(Color.YELLOW);
            g.drawOval(FRAME_WIDTH/4, FRAME_HEIGHT/8,
                       FRAME_WIDTH/2, FRAME_HEIGHT/6);
        }
    }

    public static void main(String[] args)
    {
        PaintComponentDemo w = new PaintComponentDemo();
        w.setVisible(true);
    }
    public PaintComponentDemo()
    {
        setSize(FRAME_WIDTH, FRAME_HEIGHT);
        setDefaultCloseOperation(JFrame.EXIT_ON_CLOSE);
        setTitle("The Oval Is in a Panel");
        setLayout(new GridLayout(2, 1));
        FancyPanel p = new FancyPanel();
        add(p);
        JPanel whitePanel = new JPanel();
        whitePanel.setBackground(Color.WHITE);
        add(whitePanel);
    }
}
```

(continued)

Display 18.16 **paintComponent** Demonstration (part 2 of 2)

RESULTING GUI

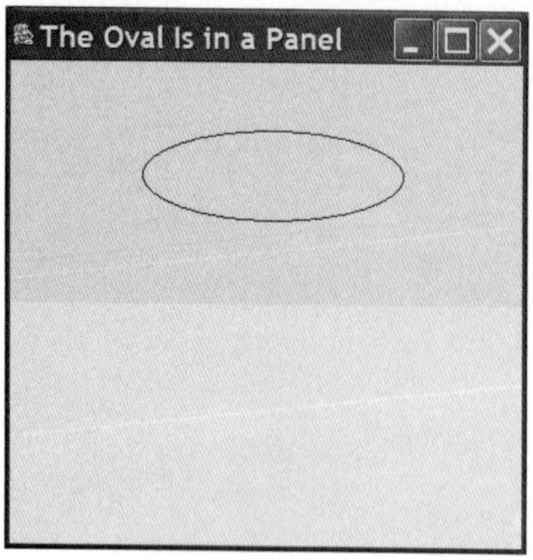

The program in Display 18.17 has a private instance variable `wink` of type `boolean`. When the value of `wink` is `false`, the `paint` method draws an ordinary happy face. When the value of `wink` is `true`, the `paint` method draws the face the same except that the left eye is just a straight line, which looks like the eye is closed. The variable `wink` is initialized to `false`.

When the button labeled `Click for a Wink` is clicked, this sends an action event to the method `actionPerformed`. The method `actionPerformed` then changes the value of the variable `wink` to `true` and invokes the method `repaint`. This use of the method `repaint` is new, so let us discuss it a bit.

repaint

Every `JFrame` (in fact, every `Component` and every `Container`) has a method named `repaint`. The method `repaint` will repaint the screen so that any changes to the graphics being displayed will show on the screen. If you omit the invocation of `repaint` from the method `actionPerformed`, then the variable `wink` will change to `true`, but the screen will not change. Without an invocation of `repaint`, the face will not change, because the method `paint` must be called again with the new value of `wink` before the change takes effect. The method `repaint` does a few standard things and, most importantly, will also invoke the method `paint`, which redraws the screen. Be sure to note that you should invoke `repaint` and not `paint`.

Now we explain why, when `wink` has the value `true`, the method `paint` draws the face with the left eye changed. The relevant part of the code is the following, which draws the left eye:

```
if (wink)
    g.drawLine(X_LEFT_EYE, Y_LEFT_EYE,
                     X_LEFT_EYE + EYE_WIDTH, Y_LEFT_EYE);
else
    g.fillOval(X_LEFT_EYE, Y_LEFT_EYE, EYE_WIDTH, EYE_HEIGHT);
```

Display 18.17 **An Action Drawing** (part 1 of 3)

```
import javax.swing.JFrame;
import javax.swing.JButton;
import java.awt.event.ActionListener;
import java.awt.event.ActionEvent;
import java.awt.BorderLayout;
import java.awt.Graphics;
import java.awt.Color;

public class ActionFace extends JFrame
{
    public static final int WINDOW_WIDTH = 400;
    public static final int WINDOW_HEIGHT = 400;

    public static final int FACE_DIAMETER = 200;
    public static final int X_FACE = 100;
    public static final int Y_FACE = 100;

    public static final int EYE_WIDTH = 20;
    public static final int EYE_HEIGHT = 10;
    public static final int X_RIGHT_EYE = X_FACE + 55;
    public static final int Y_RIGHT_EYE = Y_FACE + 60;
    public static final int X_LEFT_EYE = X_FACE + 130;
    public static final int Y_LEFT_EYE = Y_FACE + 60;

    public static final int MOUTH_WIDTH = 100;
    public static final int MOUTH_HEIGHT = 50;
    public static final int X_MOUTH = X_FACE + 50;
    public static final int Y_MOUTH = Y_FACE + 100;
    public static final int MOUTH_START_ANGLE = 180;
    public static final int MOUTH_ARC_SWEEP = 180;

    private boolean wink;

    private class WinkAction implements ActionListener
    {
        public void actionPerformed(ActionEvent e)
        {
            wink = true;
            repaint();
        }
    } // End of WinkAction inner class
```

(continued)

Display 18.17 **An Action Drawing** (part 2 of 3)

```
    public static void main(String[] args)
    {
        ActionFace drawing = new ActionFace();
        drawing.setVisible(true);
    }

    public ActionFace()
    {
        setSize(WINDOW_WIDTH, WINDOW_HEIGHT);
        setDefaultCloseOperation(JFrame.EXIT_ON_CLOSE);
        setTitle("Hello There!");
        setLayout(new BorderLayout());
        getContentPane().setBackground(Color.white);

        JButton winkButton = new JButton("Click for a Wink.");
        winkButton.addActionListener(new WinkAction());
        add(winkButton, BorderLayout.SOUTH);
        wink = false;
    }

    public void paint(Graphics g)
    {
        super.paint(g);
        g.drawOval(X_FACE, Y_FACE, FACE_DIAMETER, FACE_DIAMETER);
        //Draw Right Eye:
        g.fillOval(X_RIGHT_EYE, Y_RIGHT_EYE, EYE_WIDTH, EYE_HEIGHT);
        //Draw Left Eye:
        if (wink)
            g.drawLine(X_LEFT_EYE, Y_LEFT_EYE,
                       X_LEFT_EYE + EYE_WIDTH, Y_LEFT_EYE);
        else
           g.fillOval(X_LEFT_EYE, Y_LEFT_EYE, EYE_WIDTH, EYE_HEIGHT);
        //Draw Mouth:
        g.drawArc(X_MOUTH, Y_MOUTH, MOUTH_WIDTH, MOUTH_HEIGHT,
                  MOUTH_START_ANGLE, MOUTH_ARC_SWEEP);
    }

}
```

Display 18.17 An Action Drawing (part 3 of 3)

Resulting GUI (When started)

Resulting GUI (After clicking the button)

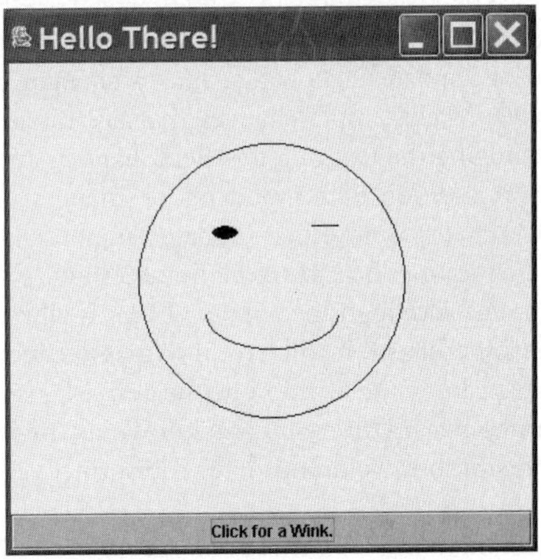

If `wink` has the value `true`, then the eye is drawn as a line, which looks like a closed eye. If `wink` has the value `false`, then the eye is drawn as an oval, which looks like an open eye.

> **The `repaint` and `paint` Methods**
>
> When you change the graphic's contents in a window and want to update the window so that the new contents show on the screen, do not call `paint`; call `repaint`. The `repaint` method takes care of some overhead and then calls the `paint` method. Normally, you do not define `repaint`. As long as you define the `paint` method correctly, the `repaint` method should work correctly. Note that you often define `paint`, but you normally do not call it. On the other hand, normally you do not define `repaint`, but you do sometimes call it.

Some More Details on Updating a GUI ★

Most of the changes to a GUI windowing system that we have seen are updated automatically so that they are visible on the screen. This is done by an object known as the **repaint manager**. The repaint manager works automatically, and you need not even be aware of its presence. However, there are a few updates that the repaint manager will not do for you. You have already learned that you need an invocation of `repaint` when your GUI changes the figure drawn in the `JFrame` as in Display 18.17.

repaint manager

Two other updating methods that you will often see when looking at Swing code are `validate` and `pack`.

`validate`

Every container class has the method `validate`, which has no arguments. An invocation of `validate` causes the container to lay out its components again. An invocation of `validate` is a kind of "update" action that makes changes in the components actually happen on the screen. Many simple changes that are made to a Swing GUI, such as changing color or changing the text in a text field, happen automatically. Other changes, such as some kinds of addition of components or changes in visibility, may require an invocation of `validate` or some other "update" method. Sometimes it is difficult to decide whether an invocation of `validate` is necessary. When in doubt, include an invocation of `validate`. Although invoking `validate` when it is not needed can make your program a little less efficient, it will have no other ill effects on your GUI.

`pack`

The method `pack` causes the window to be resized, usually to a smaller size, but more precisely to an approximation of a size known as the *preferred size*. (Yes, you can change the preferred size, but we do not have room to cover all of the Swing library in these few chapters.)

We do not have enough space in this book to go into all the details of how a GUI is updated on the screen, but these few remarks may make some code you find in more advanced books a little less puzzling.

18.4 Colors

One colored picture is worth a thousand black and white pictures.

VARIATION ON A CHINESE PROVERB

In this section, we tell you how to specify colors for the figures you draw with the graphics methods. We also show you how to define your own colors using the class `Color`.

Specifying a Drawing Color

setColor

When drawing figures with methods such as `drawLine` inside of the definition of the `paint` method, you can think of your drawing as being done with a pen that can change colors. The method `setColor` will change the color of the pen.

extra code on website

For example, consider the happy face that is drawn by the GUI in Display 18.13. If you change the definition of the `paint` method to the version shown in Display 18.18, the eyes will be blue and the mouth will be red. (The file `HappyFaceColor.java` on the accompanying website contains a version of the changed program. It consists of the program in Display 18.13 with the definition of the `paint` method replaced by the one in Display 18.18 and with the class name changed from `HappyFace` to `HappyFaceColor`.)

The `setColor` Method

When you are doing drawings with an object of the class `Graphics`, you can set the color of the drawing with an invocation of `setColor`. The color specified can later be changed with another invocation of `setColor`, so a single drawing can have multiple colors.

SYNTAX

Graphics_Object.`setColor(`*Color_Object*`);`

EXAMPLE

```
g.setColor(Color.BLUE);
```

Display 18.18 **Adding Color**

```
public void paint(Graphics g)
{
    super.paint(g);
    //Default is equivalent to: g.setColor(Color.black);
    g.drawOval(X_FACE, Y_FACE, FACE_DIAMETER, FACE_DIAMETER);
    //Draw Eyes:
    g.setColor(Color.BLUE);
    g.fillOval(X_RIGHT_EYE, Y_RIGHT_EYE, EYE_WIDTH, EYE_HEIGHT);
    g.fillOval(X_LEFT_EYE, Y_LEFT_EYE, EYE_WIDTH, EYE_HEIGHT);
    //Draw Mouth:
    g.setColor(Color.RED);
    g.drawArc(X_MOUTH, Y_MOUTH, MOUTH_WIDTH, MOUTH_HEIGHT,
              MOUTH_START_ANGLE, MOUTH_ARC_SWEEP);
}
```

If you replace the method `paint` *in Display 18.13 with this version of* `paint`, *then the happy face will have blue eyes and red lips.*

Defining Colors

Display 17.5 in Chapter 17 lists the standard colors in the class `Color`, which are defined for you. If that table does not have the colors you want, you can use the class `Color` to define your own colors. To understand how this is done, you need to first know a few basic facts about colors. By mixing red, green, and blue light in varying amounts, the human eye can be given the sensation of viewing any color the eye is capable of seeing. This is what an ordinary television set does to produce all the colors it displays. The television mixes red, green, and blue light and shines these lights on the screen in differing amounts. This is often called the **RGB color system**, for obvious reasons. Because a computer monitor is basically the same thing as a television set, colors for computer monitors can be produced in the same way. The Java `Color` class mixes amounts of red, green, and blue to produce any new color you might want.

RGB color system

`Color` constructors

When specifying the amount of each of the colors red, green, and blue, you can use either integers in the range `0` to `255` (inclusive) or `float` values in the range `0.0` to `1.0` (inclusive). For example, brown is formed by mixing red and green. So, the following defines a color called `brown` that will look like a shade of brown:

```
Color brown = new Color(200, 150, 0);
```

This color `brown` will have a `200.0/255` fraction of the maximum amount of red possible, a `150.0/255` fraction of the maximum amount of green possible, and no blue. If you want to use fractions to express the color, you can. The following is an equivalent way of defining the same color `brown`:

```
Color brown =
new Color((float)(200.0/255), (float)(150.0/255), (float)0.0);
```

You need the type casts `(float)` because the constructors for the class `Color` accept only arguments of type `int` or `float`, and numbers such as `200.0/255` and `0.0` are considered to be of type `double`, not of type `float`.

Some constructors for the class `Color` and some of the commonly used methods for the class `Color` are summarized in Display 18.19.

> **RGB Colors**
>
> The class `Color` uses the RGB method of creating colors. That means that every color is a combination of the three colors red, green, and blue.

Display 18.19 **Some Methods in the Class `Color`** (part 1 of 2)

The class `Color` is in the `java.awt` package.

```
public Color(int r, int g, int b)
```

Constructor that creates a new `Color` with the specified RGB values. The parameters `r`, `g`, and `b` must each be in the range `0` to `255` (inclusive).

Display 18.19 Some Methods in the Class `Color` (part 2 of 2)

```
public Color(float r, float g, float b)
```

Constructor that creates a new `Color` with the specified RGB values. The parameters `r`, `g`, and `b` must each be in the range `0.0` to `1.0` (inclusive).

```
public int getRed()
```

Returns the red component of the calling object. The returned value is in the range `0` to `255` (inclusive).

```
public int getGreen()
```

Returns the green component of the calling object. The returned value is in the range `0` to `255` (inclusive).

```
public int getBlue()
```

Returns the blue component of the calling object. The returned value is in the range `0` to `255` (inclusive).

```
public Color brighter()
```

Returns a brighter version of the calling object color.

```
public Color darker()
```

Returns a darker version of the calling object color.

```
public boolean equals(Object c)
```

Returns `true` if `c` is equal to the calling object color; otherwise, returns `false`.

PITFALL: Using `doubles` to Define a Color

Suppose you want to make a color that is made of half the possible amount of red, half the possible amount of blue, and no green. The following seems reasonable:

```
Color purple = new Color(0.5, 0.0, 0.5);
```

However, this will produce a compiler error. The numbers `0.5` and `0.0` are considered to be of type `double`, and this constructor requires arguments of type `float` (or of type `int`). So, an explicit type cast is required, as follows:

```
Color purple = new Color((float)0.5, (float)0.0, (float)0.5);
```

Java does allow the following method of specifying that a number is of type `float`, which can be simpler than the previous line of code:

```
Color purple = new Color(0.5f, 0.0f, 0.5f);
```

(continued)

PITFALL: (continued)

An even easier way to avoid these problems is to simply use `int` arguments, as in the following:

```
purple = new Color(127, 0, 127);
```

(You may feel that the values of `127` should be replaced by `128`, but that is a minor point. You are not likely to even notice the difference in color between, say, `127` red and `128` red.)

In any final code produced, these `float` numbers should normally be replaced by defined constants, such as

```
public static final float RED_VALUE = (float)0.5;
public static final float GREEN_VALUE = (float)0.0;
public static final float BLUE_VALUE = (float)0.5;
```

Note that even though the defined constants are specified to be of type `float`, you still need a type cast. ■

The `JColorChooser` Dialog Window

The class `JColorChooser` can be used to produce a dialog window that allows you to choose a color by looking at color samples or by choosing RGB values. The static method `showDialog` in the class `JColorChooser` produces a window that allows the user to choose a color. A sample program using this method is given in Display 18.20. The statement that launches the `JColorChooser` dialog window is the following:

```
sampleColor =
   JColorChooser.showDialog(this, "JColorChooser", sampleColor);
```

When this statement is executed, the window shown in the second GUI picture in Display 18.20 is displayed for the user to choose a color. Once the user has chosen a color and clicked the `OK` button, the window goes away and the chosen color is returned as the value of the `JColorChooser.showDialog` method invocation. So, in this example, the `Color` object returned is assigned to the variable `sampleColor`. If the user clicks the `Cancel` button, then the method invocation returns `null` rather than a color.

The method `JColorChooser.showDialog` takes three arguments. The first argument is the parent component, which is the component from which it was launched. In most simple cases, it is likely to be `this`, as it is in our example. The second argument is a title for the color chooser window. The third argument is the initial color for the color chooser window. The window shows the user samples of what the color he or she chooses will look like. The user can choose colors repeatedly, and each will be displayed in turn until the user clicks the `OK` button. The color displayed when the color chooser window first appears is that third argument.

The color chooser window has three tabs at the top labeled `Swatches`, `HSB`, and `RGB`. This gives the user three different ways to choose colors. If the `Swatches` tab is clicked, the window displays color samples for the user to choose from. This is the

Display 18.20 **JColorChooser** Dialog (part 1 of 2)

```
import javax.swing.JFrame;
import javax.swing.JPanel;
import javax.swing.JButton;
import javax.swing.JColorChooser;
import java.awt.event.ActionListener;
import java.awt.event.ActionEvent;
import java.awt.BorderLayout;
import java.awt.FlowLayout;
import java.awt.Color;

public class JColorChooserDemo extends JFrame
                               implements ActionListener
{
    public static final int WIDTH = 400;
    public static final int HEIGHT = 200;

    private Color sampleColor = Color.LIGHT_GRAY;


    public static void main(String[] args)
    {
        JColorChooserDemo gui = new JColorChooserDemo();
        gui.setVisible(true);
    }

    public JColorChooserDemo()
    {
        setDefaultCloseOperation(JFrame.EXIT_ON_CLOSE);
        getContentPane().setBackground(sampleColor);
        setLayout(new BorderLayout());
        setTitle("JColorChooser Demo");
        setSize(WIDTH, HEIGHT);
        JPanel buttonPanel = new JPanel();
        buttonPanel.setBackground(Color.WHITE);
        buttonPanel.setLayout(new FlowLayout());
        JButton chooseButton = new JButton("Choose a Color");
        chooseButton.addActionListener(this);
        buttonPanel.add(chooseButton);
        add(buttonPanel, BorderLayout.SOUTH);
    }
```

(continued)

Display 18.20 `JColorChooser` Dialog (part 2 of 2)

```
    public void actionPerformed(ActionEvent e)
    {
        if (e.getActionCommand().equals("Choose a Color"))
        {
            sampleColor =
               JColorChooser.showDialog(this,
               "JColorChooser", sampleColor);
            if (sampleColor != null)//If a color was chosen
                getContentPane().setBackground(sampleColor);
        }
        else
            System.out.println("Unanticipated Error");
    }
}
```

Resulting GUI (Three views of one GUI)

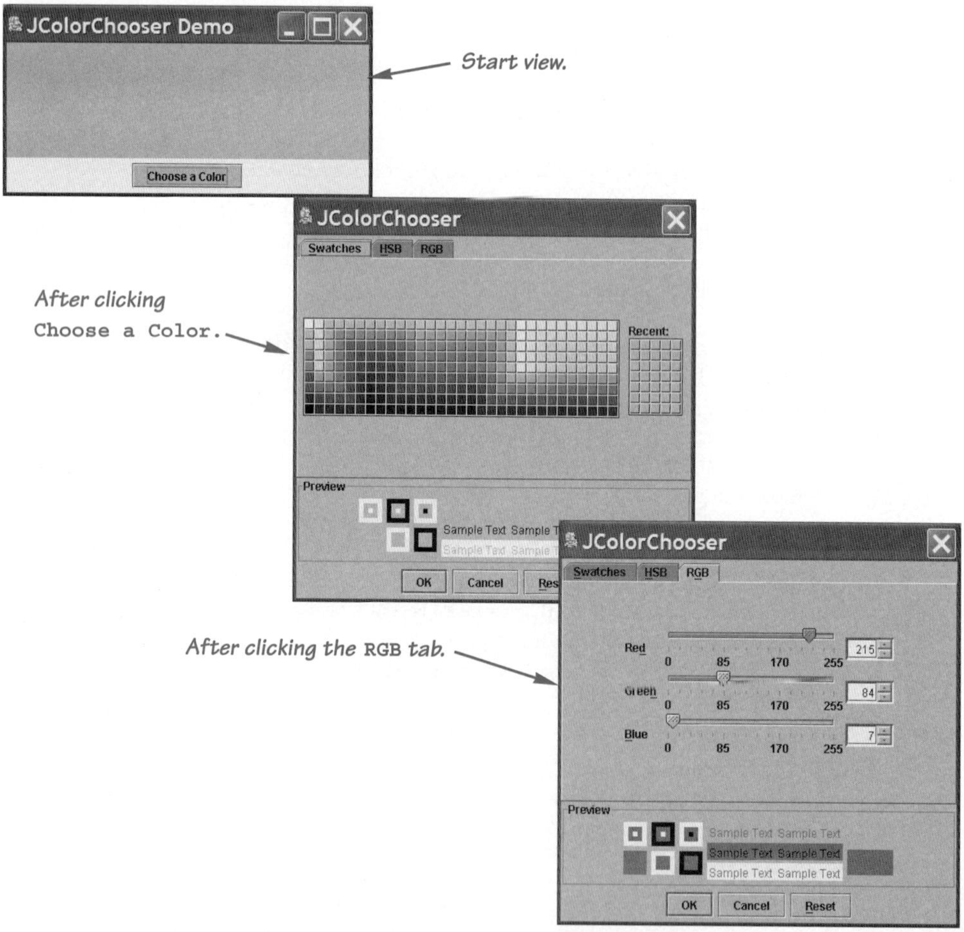

way the window first comes up. So, if the user clicks no tab, it is the same as clicking the `Swatches` tab. The `RGB` tab allows the user to choose a color by specifying the red, green, and blue values. The `HSB` tab gives the user a chance to choose colors in a way we will not discuss. To really understand the `JColorChooser` dialog window, you need to run the program in Display 18.20 to see it in action.

MyProgrammingLab™

Self-Test Exercises

17. How would you change the method `paint` in Display 18.18 so that the happy face has one blue eye (the right eye) and one green eye (the left eye)?
18. How would you change the method `paint` in Display 18.18 so that the happy face not only has blue eyes and a red mouth, but also has brown skin?

18.5 Fonts and the `drawString` Method

It is not of so much consequence what you say,
as how you say it.

ALEXANDER SMITH, *Dreamthorp. On the Writing of Essays*

Java has facilities to add text to drawings and to modify the font of the text. We will show you enough to allow you to do most things you might want to do with text and fonts.

The `drawString` Method

Display 18.21 contains a demonstration program for the method `drawString`. When the program is run, the GUI displays the text `"Push the button."` When the user clicks the button, the string is changed to `"Thank you. I needed that."` The text is written with the method `drawString`.

The method `drawString` is similar to the drawing methods in the class `Graphics`, but it displays text rather than a drawing. For example, the following line from Display 18.21 writes the string stored in the variable `theText` starting at the *x*- and *y*-coordinates `X_START` and `Y_START`:

```
g.drawString(theText, X_START, Y_START);
```

The string is written in the current font. A default font is used if no font is specified. The details about fonts are discussed in the next subsection.

Display 18.21   Using `drawString` (part 1 of 2)

```java
1 import javax.swing.JFrame;
2 import javax.swing.JPanel;
3 import javax.swing.JButton;
4 import java.awt.event.ActionListener;
5 import java.awt.event.ActionEvent;
6 import java.awt.BorderLayout;
7 import java.awt.Graphics;
8 import java.awt.Color;
9 import java.awt.Font;

10 public class DrawStringDemo extends JFrame
11 implements ActionListener
12 {
13 public static final int WIDTH = 350;
14 public static final int HEIGHT = 200;
15 public static final int X_START = 20;
16 public static final int Y_START = 100;
17 public static final int POINT_SIZE = 24;

18 private String theText = "Push the button.";
19 private Color penColor = Color.BLACK;
20 private Font fontObject =
21 new Font("SansSerif", Font.PLAIN, POINT_SIZE);

22 public static void main(String[] args)
23 {
24 DrawStringDemo gui = new DrawStringDemo();
25 gui.setVisible(true);
26 }

27 public DrawStringDemo()
28 {
29 setSize(WIDTH, HEIGHT);
30 setDefaultCloseOperation(JFrame.EXIT_ON_CLOSE);
31 setTitle("drawString Demonstration");

32 getContentPane().setBackground(Color.WHITE);
33 setLayout(new BorderLayout());

34 JPanel buttonPanel = new JPanel();
35 buttonPanel.setBackground(Color.GRAY);
36 buttonPanel.setLayout(new BorderLayout());
37 JButton theButton - new JButton("The Button");
38 theButton.addActionListener(this);

39 buttonPanel.add(theButton, BorderLayout.CENTER);

40 add(buttonPanel, BorderLayout.SOUTH);
```

Display 18.21 Using **drawString** (part 2 of 2)

```
    public void paint(Graphics g)
    {
        super.paint(g);
        g.setFont(fontObject);
        g.setColor(penColor);
        g.drawString(theText, X_START, Y_START);
    }

    public void actionPerformed(ActionEvent e)
    {
        penColor = Color.RED;
        fontObject =
              new Font("Serif", Font.BOLD|Font.ITALIC, POINT_SIZE);
        theText = "Thank you. I needed that.";

        repaint();
    }
}
```

Resulting GUI (Start view)

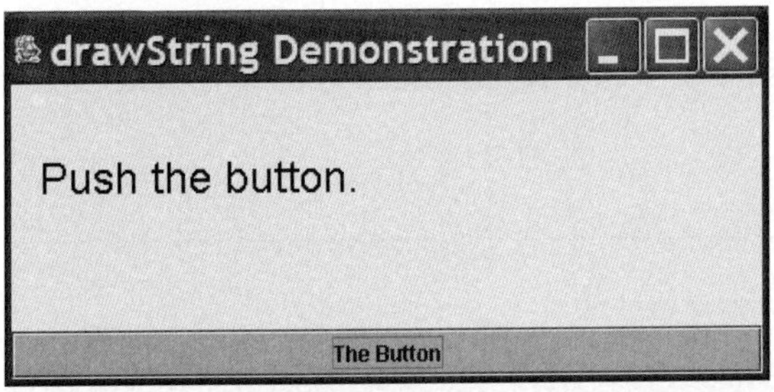

Resulting GUI (After clicking the button)

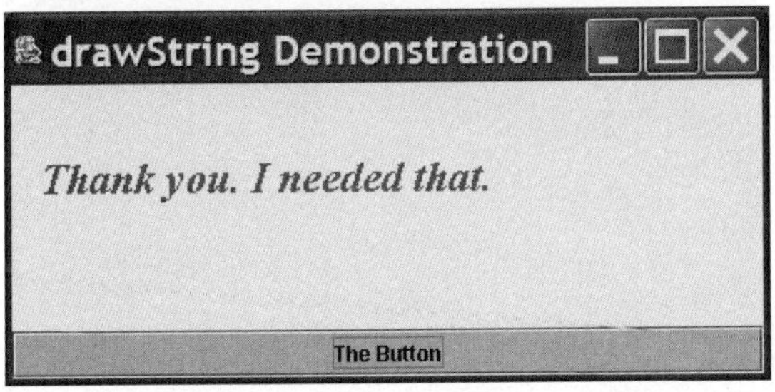

Fonts

The program in Display 18.21 illustrates how the font for the method `drawString` is set. That program sets the font with the following line in the definition of the method `paint`:

`setFont`

```
g.setFont(fontObject);
```

In this program, `fontObject` is a private instance variable of type `Font.Font` is a class in the `java.awt` package. Objects of the class `Font` represent fonts.

In Display 18.21, the variable `fontObject` is set using a constructor for the class `Font`. The initial font is set as part of the instance variable declaration in the following lines taken from Display 18.21:

```
private Font fontObject =
                    new Font("SansSerif", Font.PLAIN, POINT_SIZE);
```

`Font`

The constructor for the class `Font` creates a font in a given style and size. The first argument, in this case `"SansSerif"`, is a string that gives the name of the font (that is, the basic style). Some typical font names are `"Times"`, `"Courier"`, and `"Helvetica"`. You may use any font currently available on your system. Java guarantees that you will have at least the three fonts `"Monospaced"`, `"SansSerif"`, and `"Serif"`. To see what these fonts look like on your system, run the program `FontDisplay.java` on the accompanying website. It will produce the window shown in Display 18.22.

extra code on website

Most font names have no real meaning. The names just sounded right to the creator. However, the terms "Serif," "Sans Serif," and "Monospaced" do mean something,

Display 18.22 **Result of Running `FontDisplay.java`**

Fonts may look somewhat different on your system.

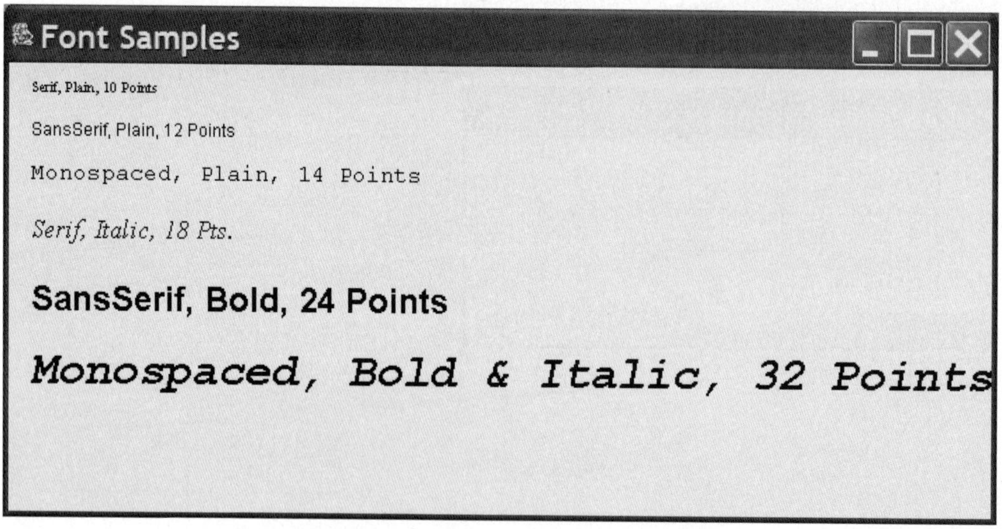

which may help you keep the names of the three guaranteed fonts clear in your mind. **Serifs** are those small lines that sometimes finish off the ends of the lines in letters. For example, **S** has serifs (at the two ends of the curved line), but `S` does not have serifs. The `"Serif"` font will always have these decorative little lines. *Sans* means without, so the `"SansSerif"` font will not have these decorative little lines. As you might guess, `"Monospaced"` means that all the characters have equal width.

Fonts can be given style modifiers, such as bold or italic, and they can come in different sizes. The second and third arguments to the constructor for `Font` specify the style modifications and size for the font, as in the following, which occurs in the `actionPerformed` method in Display 18.21:

```
new Font("Serif", Font.BOLD|Font.ITALIC, POINT_SIZE);
```

The second argument specifies style modifications. Note that you can specify multiple style modifications by connecting them with the symbol | as in `Font.BOLD|Font.ITALIC`.[2] The last argument specifies the size of the letters in the version of the font created.

point size

Character sizes are specified in units known as *points*, so the size of a particular version of a font is called a **point size**. One **point** is 1/72 of an inch, but measurements of font sizes are not as precise as might be ideal; two different fonts of the same point size may be slightly different in size.

The method `setFont` sets the font for the `Graphics` object, which is named `g` in Display 18.21. The font remains in effect until it is changed. If you do not specify any font, then a default font is used.

There is no simple way to change the properties of the current font, such as making it italic. Every change in a font normally requires that you define a new `Font` object and use it as an argument to `setFont`.

Display 18.23 gives some useful details about constructors, methods, and constants that are members of, or are related to, the class `Font`.

The drawString Method

The `drawString` method writes the text given by the *String* at the point (*X*, *Y*) of the *Graphics_Object*. The text is written in the current font, color, and font size.

SYNTAX

Graphics_Object.`drawString(`*String*, *X*, *Y*`);`

EXAMPLE

```
g.drawString("I love you madly.", X_START, Y_START);
```

[2]The symbol | produces a "bitwise or of the numbers," but that detail need not concern you. You need not even know what is meant by a "bitwise or of the numbers." Just think of | as a special way to connect style specifications.

Display 18.23 Some Methods and Constants for the Class `Font`

The class `Font` is in the `java.awt` package.

CONSTRUCTOR FOR THE CLASS `Font`

```
public Font(String fontName, int styleModifications, int size)
```

Constructor that creates a version of the font named by `fontName` with the specified `styleModifications` and `size`.

CONSTANTS IN THE CLASS `Font`

```
Font.BOLD
```

Specifies bold style.

```
Font.ITALIC
```

Specifies italic style.

```
Font.PLAIN
```

Specifies plain style—that is, not bold and not italic.

NAMES OF FONTS (These three are guaranteed by Java. Your system will probably have others as well as these.)

```
"Monospaced"
```

See Display 18.22 for a sample.

```
"SansSerif"
```

See Display 18.22 for a sample.

```
"Serif"
```

See Display 18.22 for a sample.

METHOD THAT USES `Font`

```
public abstract void setFont(Font fontObject)
```

This method is in the class `Graphics`. Sets the current font of the calling `Graphics` object to `fontObject`.

MyProgrammingLab™

Self-Test Exercises

19. Suppose `g` is an object of type `Graphics`. Write a line of code that will set the font for `g` to Sans Serif bold of size 14 points.

20. Suppose `g` is an object of type `Graphics`. Write a line of code that will set the font for `g` to Sans Serif bold and italic of size 14 points.

Chapter Summary

- You can define a *window listener* class by having it implement the `WindowListener` interface.
- An *icon* is an object of the class `ImageIcon` and is created from a digital picture. You can add icons to `JButtons`, `JLabels`, and `JMenuItems`.
- You can use the class `JScrollPane` to add scroll bars to a text area.
- You can draw figures such as lines, ovals, and rectangles using methods in the class `Graphics`.
- You can use the method `setColor` to specify the color of each figure or text drawn with the method of the class `Graphics`.
- You can define your own colors using the class `Color`.
- Colors are defined using the *RGB* (red/green/blue) system.
- You can use the method `drawString` of the class `Graphics` to add text to a `JFrame` or `JPanel`.
- You can use the method `setFont` to set the font, style modifiers, and point size for text written with the `drawString` method of the `Graphics` class.

Answers to Self-Test Exercises

1. All the methods in Display 18.1. If there is no particular action that you want the method to perform, you can give the method an empty body.
2. The smaller window goes away but the larger window stays. This is the default action for the close-window button and we did not change it for the smaller window.
3. `dispose`
4. The import statements are the same as in Display 18.2. The rest of the definition follows. This definition is in the file `WindowListenerDemo3` on the accompanying website.

extra code on website

```
public class WindowListenerDemo3 extends JFrame
                                 implements WindowListener
{
    public static final int WIDTH = 300; //for main window
    public static final int HEIGHT = 200; //for main window
    public static final int SMALL_WIDTH = 200;
                              //for confirm window
    public static final int SMALL_HEIGHT = 100;
                              //for confirm window

    private class ConfirmWindow extends JFrame
                                implements ActionListener
```

```
    {
        public ConfirmWindow()
        {
            setSize(SMALL_WIDTH, SMALL_HEIGHT);
            getContentPane().setBackground(Color.YELLOW);
            setLayout(new BorderLayout());

            JLabel confirmLabel = new JLabel(
                           "Are you sure you want to exit?");
            add(confirmLabel, BorderLayout.CENTER);

            JPanel buttonPanel = new JPanel();
            buttonPanel.setBackground(Color.ORANGE);
            buttonPanel.setLayout(new FlowLayout());

            JButton exitButton = new JButton("Yes");
            exitButton.addActionListener(this);
            buttonPanel.add(exitButton);

            JButton cancelButton = new JButton("No");
            cancelButton.addActionListener(this);
            buttonPanel.add(cancelButton);

            add(buttonPanel, BorderLayout.SOUTH);
        }

        public void actionPerformed(ActionEvent e)
        {
            String actionCommand = e.getActionCommand();

            if (actionCommand.equals("Yes"))
                System.exit(0);
            else if (actionCommand.equals("No"))
                dispose();//Destroys only the ConfirmWindow.
            else
                System.out.println(
                        "Unexpected Error in Confirm Window.");
        }
    } //End of inner class ConfirmWindow

    public static void main(String[] args)
    {
        WindowListenerDemo3 demoWindow =
                             new WindowListenerDemo3();
        demoWindow.setVisible(true);
    }
```

```
    public WindowListenerDemo3()
    {
       setSize(WIDTH, HEIGHT);
       setTitle("Window Listener Demonstration");

       setDefaultCloseOperation(
                    JFrame.DO_NOTHING_ON_CLOSE);
       addWindowListener(this);

       getContentPane().setBackground(Color.LIGHT_GRAY);
       JLabel aLabel =
                new JLabel("I like to be sure you are sincere.");
       add(aLabel);
    }

    //The following are now methods of the class
    WindowListenerDemo3:
    public void windowOpened(WindowEvent e)
    {}

    public void windowClosing(WindowEvent e)
    {
        ConfirmWindow checkers = new ConfirmWindow();
    checkers.setVisible(true);
    }

    public void windowClosed(WindowEvent e)
    {}

    public void windowIconified(WindowEvent e)
    {}

    public void windowDeiconified(WindowEvent e)
    {}

    public void windowActivated(WindowEvent e)
    {}

    public void windowDeactivated(WindowEvent e)
    {}
}
```

5.
```
JButton magicButton = new JButton("Magic Button");
ImageIcon wizardIcon = new ImageIcon("wizard.gif");
magicButton.setIcon(wizardIcon);
```

There are a number of other ways to accomplish the same thing. Here are two of a number of valid alternatives:

```
JButton magicButton = new JButton("Magic Button");
magicButton.setIcon(new ImageIcon("wizard.gif"));

ImageIcon wizardIcon = new ImageIcon("wizard.gif");
JButton magicButton =
              new JButton("Magic Button", wizardIcon);
```

6.
```
ImageIcon wizardIcon = new ImageIcon("wizard.gif");
JLabel wizardPicture = new JLabel(wizardIcon);
picturePanel.add(wizardPicture);
```

There are a number of other ways to accomplish the same thing. Here is one valid alternative:

```
picturePanel.add(new JLabel(
                    new ImageIcon("wizard.gif")));
```

7.
```
ImageIcon wizardIcon = new ImageIcon("wizard.gif");
JButton magicButton = new JButton(wizardIcon);
magicButton.setActionCommand("Kazam");
```

There are a number of other ways to accomplish the same thing. Here is one valid alternative:

```
JButton magicButton =
         new JButton(new ImageIcon("wizard.gif"));
magicButton.setActionCommand("Kazam");
```

8. No. You can invoke none, one, or both methods.
9. No. The class `JTextArea` is a descendent class of the class `Component`. So, every `JTextArea` is also a `Component`.
10. `g.drawLine(30, 40, 100, 60);`
11. `g.drawLine(30, 40, 130, 40);`
12. `graphicsObject.drawLine(30, 40, 30, 140);`
13. `graphicsObject.fillRect(20, 30, 100, 50);`
14. `g.fillRect(200, 300, 100, 50);`
15. `g.drawOval(250, 350, 100, 100);`
16. `g.drawOval(200, 300, 200, 200);`
17. Insert `g.setColor(Color.GREEN)` as indicated next:

```
//Draw Eyes:
g.setColor(Color.BLUE);
g.fillOval(X_RIGHT_EYE, Y_RIGHT_EYE, EYE_WIDTH, EYE_HEIGHT);
g.setColor(Color.GREEN);
g.fillOval(X_LEFT_EYE, Y_LEFT_EYE, EYE_WIDTH, EYE_HEIGHT);
```

18. Replace the following line in the `paint` method

```
g.drawOval(X_FACE, Y_FACE, FACE_DIAMETER, FACE_DIAMETER);
```

with

```
Color brown =
       new Color(200, 150, 0);
g.setColor(brown);
g.fillOval(X_FACE, Y_FACE, FACE_DIAMETER, FACE_DIAMETER);
```

Note that there is no predefined color constant `Color.BROWN`, so you need to define a color for brown. You may prefer some other arguments instead of `(200, 150, 0)` so that you get a shade of brown that is more to your liking.

19. `g.setFont(new Font("SansSerif", Font.BOLD, 14));`

20. `g.setFont(new Font("SansSerif", Font.BOLD|Font.ITALIC, 14));`

MyProgrammingLab™

Programming Projects

Visit www.myprogramminglab.com to complete select exercises online and get instant feedback.

1. A Sierpinski Gasket or Triangle is a type of fractal named after the Polish mathematician Waclaw Sierpinski who described some of its interesting properties in 1916. It is a nice example of how an orderly structure can be created as a result of random, chaotic behavior.

   One way to create the fractal is to start with an equilateral triangle. Let us say that the corners are labeled `X, Y,` and `Z`.

   1. Set `current` equal to point `X`.
   2. Repeat many times (you can try 10000).
      a. Randomly pick `target` as one of the three `X, Y,` or `Z`.
      b. Calculate the point halfway between `current` and `target`.
      c. Set `current` to this halfway point.
      d. Draw a pixel at location `current`. One way to do this is to fill or draw a tiny rectangle at this coordinate.

   Write a program that draws a Sierpinski Gasket. You can pick the coordinates for the corners of the triangle. It may seem like you should get a random mess of dots but instead you get a very orderly picture!

   To draw a single pixel at coordinate (X,Y), use the `drawLine` method where the start and endpoints are both (X,Y).

2. The file named `humphrey-img.txt` contained with the website for this book holds raw image data[3] of a Martian rock called "Humphrey" that was taken by the Mars Exploration Rover Spirit. The format of this text file is as follows:

   First line: single number indicating the height and width of the image (in this case, 461).

   Lines 2–462: A row of 461 numbers each separated by a space. Each number represents a pixel in grayscale and ranges from 0 to 255 where 0 is black and 255 is white.

   For example, the following data describes a 3 × 3 square where every pixel is white except for a black line along the diagonal from the upper-left corner to the bottom-right corner:

```
3
0 255 255
255 0 255
255 255 0
```

   a) Write a program to read in the data from the file and display it in a `JFrame` window. To draw a single pixel at coordinate (X,Y), use the `drawLine` method where the start and endpoints are both (X,Y). For speed, the contents of the file should be read into an array once and the array data used in the `paint()` method to draw the image.

   b) In this particular image, only about 2/3 of the shades of gray are used. For example, if the image consists entirely of shades in the range from 150–160, then the entire image would appear to be almost the same shade of gray. One method to enhance such an image is to scale the shade of each pixel to the entire range from 0 to 255. Pixels that were originally at value 150 would be drawn with the value 0, pixels that were originally 151 would be drawn with the value 25, and so on up to pixels of the shade 160, which would be drawn with the value 255. This technique spaces out the shading so the details are easier to see.

   To compute the new shade for a pixel at coordinate (i, j), do the following:

$$\text{NewShade}(i,j) = \frac{255 \times (\text{OriginalShade}(i,j) - \text{MinOriginalShade})}{(\text{MaxOriginalShade} - \text{MinOriginalShade})}$$

   `MinOriginalShade` is the smallest scale of gray in the original image and `MaxOriginalShade` is the largest scale of gray in the original image.

   Modify your program so that the image is drawn using the scaling technique described above. The brightness and details in the resulting image should be a little bit easier to distinguish.

3. Write a GUI program that uses the methods in the `Graphics` class to draw a smiley face when the window is activated, and a frowny face when the window is deactivated. This will require use of a `WindowListener` to detect the activation or deactivation events.

[3]The original raw image data has been cropped and converted to a textual format for purposes of this project.

4. Write a "skeleton" GUI program that implements the `WindowListener` interface. Write code for each of the methods in Display 18.1 that simply prints out a message identifying which event occurred. Print the message out in a text field. Note that your program will not end when the close-window button is clicked (but will instead simply send a message to the text field saying that the `windowClosing` method has been invoked). Include a button labeled `Exit` that the user can click to end the program.

5. Enhance the face drawing in Display 18.17 in the following ways: Add color so the eyes are blue and the mouth is red. When the face winks, the line that represents a closed eye is black not blue. Add a nose and a brown handlebar mustache. Add buttons labeled `"Smile"` and `"Frown"`. When the `"Frown"` button is clicked, the face shows a frown (upside down smile); when the "Smile" button is clicked, the face shows a smile. When the user clicks the close-window button, a window pops up to ask if the user is sure he or she wants to exit, as in Display 18.2.

6. Write a GUI program to sample different fonts. The user enters a line of text in a text field. The user then selects a font from a font menu. Offer the three guaranteed fonts and at least two other fonts. The user also selects any desired style modifiers (bold and/or italic) from a style menu, and selects point size from a point size menu that offers the following choices: 9, 10, 12, 14, 16, 24, and 32. There is also a `"Display"` button. When the `"Display"` button is clicked, the text is displayed in the font, style, and point size chosen.

VideoNote
Solution to Programming Project 18.7

7. The `MouseListener` interface allows you to retrieve mouse events. A program implements this interface in a manner similar to the `WindowListener` interface. For example, the following program creates a `JFrame` and outputs the X and Y coordinates of any mouse clicks within the `JFrame`. The `MouseListener` interface requires the implementing class to define the `mouseClicked, mouseEntered, mousePressed, mouseReleased,` and `mouseExited` methods. In the example, only the `mouseClicked` method has been completed.

```
import javax.swing.JFrame;
import java.awt.event.MouseListener;
import java.awt.event.MouseEvent;

public class MouseDemo extends JFrame implements MouseListener
{
    public void mouseClicked (MouseEvent e)
    {
        System.out.println(e.getX() + " " + e.getY());
    }
    public void mouseEntered (MouseEvent e) {}
    public void mousePressed (MouseEvent e) {}
    public void mouseReleased (MouseEvent e) {}
    public void mouseExited (MouseEvent e) {}
```

```
    public MouseDemo()
    {
        super();
        setSize(600,400);
        setTitle("Mouse Demo");
        setDefaultCloseOperation(JFrame.EXIT_ON_CLOSE);
        addMouseListener(this); // Add listener for this object
    }

    public static void main(String[] args)
    {
        MouseDemo m = new MouseDemo();
        m.setVisible(true);
    }
}
```

Modify this program to create a simple drawing program. When the mouse button is clicked, a solid circle with a radius of three pixels should be drawn in the `JFrame` centered at the mouse coordinates. Draw the circle in the color of your choice. Make sure that the drawing is correctly redrawn if the `JFrame` is minimized and then displayed again.

8. Write a program that graphically displays a vertical bar chart. The input is an array of integers. Use the index of an array entry as the label on the X axis. The height of the bar should correspond to the value of the array entry. Scale the height proportionally so the bar chart fits on the screen. For example, if the array values are {3000, 4000, 5000}, then the bars should not be drawn 3,000; 4,000; and 5,000 pixels tall. Instead they should fit on the screen but remain in the correct proportion to the original values (e.g., perhaps 300, 400, and 500 pixels tall, but the actual values will depend upon the size of your window).

Java Never Ends 19

19 Java Never Ends

And thick and fast they came at last,
And more, and more, and more—

LEWIS CARROLL, *Through the Looking-Glass*

Introduction

Of course there is only a finite amount of Java, but when you consider all the standard libraries and other accompanying software, the amount of power and the amount to learn seem to be endless. In this chapter, we give you a brief introduction to five topics to give you a flavor of some of the directions you can take in extending your knowledge of Java. The five topics are multithreading, networking with stream sockets, JavaBeans, the interaction of Java with database systems, and Web programming with Java Server Pages.

Prerequisites

You really should cover most of the book before covering this chapter. However, Section 19.1 requires only Chapters 17 and 18 and their prerequisites. Section 19.2 requires Chapters 1 through 5, 9, and 10. Sections 19.3 and 19.4 require only Chapters 1 through 6. Section 19.5 requires an understanding of HTML, which is given in Chapter 20. Chapter 20 is distributed as a file on the website included in this book. Aside from references to Section 19.1 in Section 19.2, all sections are independent of each other and may be read in any order.

19.1 Multithreading

"Can you do two things at once?"
"I have trouble doing one thing at once."

Part of a job interview

thread

A **thread** is a separate computation process. In Java, you can have programs with multiple threads. You can think of the threads as computations that execute in parallel. On a computer with enough processors, the threads might indeed execute in parallel. However, in most normal computing situations, the threads do not really do this. Instead, the computer switches resources between threads so that each thread in turn does a little bit of computing. To the user, this looks like the processes are executing in parallel.

You have already experienced threads. Modern operating systems allow you to run more than one program at the same time. For example, rather than waiting for your virus scanning program to finish its computation, you can go on to, say, read your e-mail while the virus scanning program is still executing. The operating system is using threads to make this happen. There may or may not be some work being done in parallel depending on your computer and operating system. Most likely, the two computation threads are simply sharing computer resources so that they take turns using the computer's resources. When reading your e-mail, you may or may not notice that response is slower because resources are being shared with the virus scanning program. Your e-mail reading program is indeed slowed down, but because humans are so much slower than computers, any apparent slowdown is likely to be unnoticed.

EXAMPLE: A Nonresponsive GUI

Display 19.1 contains a very simple action GUI. When the `"Start"` button is clicked, the GUI draws circles one after the other until a large portion of the window is filled with circles. There is 1/10 of a second pause between the drawing of each circle. So, you can see the circles appear one after the other. If you are interested in Java programming, this can be pretty exciting for the first few circles, but it quickly becomes boring. You are likely to want to end the program early, but if you click the close-window button, nothing will happen until the program is finished drawing all its little circles. We will use threads to fix this problem, but first let us understand this program, which does not really use threads in any essential way, despite the occurrence of the word `Thread` in the program. We explain this Swing program in the next few subsections.

`Thread.sleep`

In Display 19.1, the following method invocation produces a 1/10 of a second pause after drawing each of the circles:

```
doNothing(PAUSE);
```

which is equivalent to

```
doNothing(100);
```

The method `doNothing` is a private helping method that does nothing except call the method `Thread.sleep` and take care of catching any thrown exception. So, the pause is really created by the method invocation

`Thread.sleep`

```
Thread.sleep(100);
```

This is a static method in the class `Thread` that pauses whatever thread includes the invocation. It pauses for the number of milliseconds (thousandths of a second) given as an argument. So, this pauses the computation of the program in Display 19.1 for 100 milliseconds or 1/10 of a second.

"Wait a minute," you may think, "the program in Display 19.1 was not supposed to use threads in any essential way." That is basically true, but every Java program uses threads in some way. If there is only one stream of computation, as in Display 19.1, then that is treated as a single thread by Java. So, threads are always used by Java, but not in an interesting way until more than one thread is used.

You can safely think of the invocation of

```
Thread.sleep(milliseconds);
```

as a pause in the computation that lasts (approximately) the number of milliseconds given as the argument. (If this invocation is in a thread of a multithreaded program, then the pause, like anything else in the thread, applies only to the thread in which it occurs.)

The method `Thread.sleep` can sometimes be handy even if you do not do any multithreaded programming. The class `Thread` is in the package `java.lang` and so requires no import statement.

Display 19.1 **Nonresponsive GUI** (part 1 of 3)

```
import javax.swing.JFrame;
import javax.swing.JPanel;
import javax.swing.JButton;
import java.awt.BorderLayout;
import java.awt.FlowLayout;
import java.awt.Graphics;
import java.awt.event.ActionListener;
import java.awt.event.ActionEvent;

/**
Packs a section of the frame window with circles, one at a time.
*/
public class FillDemo extends JFrame implements ActionListener
{
    public static final int WIDTH = 300;
    public static final int HEIGHT = 200;
    public static final int FILL_WIDTH = 300;
    public static final int FILL_HEIGHT = 100;
    public static final int CIRCLE_SIZE = 10;
    public static final int PAUSE = 100; //milliseconds

    private JPanel box;

    public static void main(String[] args)
    {
        FillDemo gui = new FillDemo();
        gui.setVisible(true);
    }
```

Display 19.1 Nonresponsive GUI (part 2 of 3)

```
    public FillDemo()
    {
        setSize(WIDTH, HEIGHT);
        setTitle("FillDemo");
        setDefaultCloseOperation(JFrame.EXIT_ON_CLOSE);
        setLayout(new BorderLayout());
        box = new JPanel();
        add(box, "Center");

        JPanel buttonPanel = new JPanel();
        buttonPanel.setLayout(new FlowLayout());
        JButton startButton = new JButton("Start");
        startButton.addActionListener(this);
        buttonPanel.add(startButton);
        add(buttonPanel, "South");
    }

    public void actionPerformed(ActionEvent e)
    {
        fill( );
    }

    public void fill()
    {
        Graphics g = box.getGraphics();

        for (int y = 0; y < FILL_HEIGHT; y = y + CIRCLE_SIZE)
            for (int x = 0; x < FILL_WIDTH; x = x + CIRCLE_SIZE)
            {
                g.fillOval(x, y, CIRCLE_SIZE, CIRCLE_SIZE);
                doNothing(PAUSE);
            }
    }

    public void doNothing(int milliseconds)
    {
        try
        {
            Thread.sleep(milliseconds);
        }
        catch(InterruptedException e)
        {
            System.out.println("Unexpected interrupt");
            System.exit(0);
        }
    }
}
```

Nothing else can happen until **actionPerformed** *returns, which does not happen until* **fill** *returns.*

Everything stops for 100 milliseconds (1/10 of a second).

(continued)

Display 19.1 Nonresponsive GUI (part 3 of 3)

RESULTING GUI (When started)

RESULTING GUI (While drawing circles)

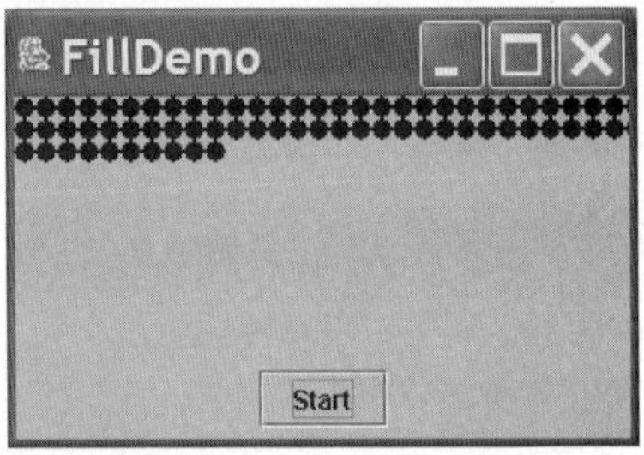

If you click the close-window button while the circles are being drawn, the window will not close until all the circles are drawn.

RESULTING GUI (After all circles are drawn)

The method `Thread.sleep` can throw an `InterruptedException`, which is a checked exception—that is, it must be either caught in a `catch` block or declared in a `throws` clause. We do not discuss `InterruptedException` in this book, leaving it for more advanced books on multithreaded programming, but it has to do with one thread interrupting another thread. We will simply note that an `InterruptedException` may be thrown by `Thread.sleep` and so must be accounted for—in our case, by a simple `catch` block. The class `InterruptedException` is in the `java.lang` package and so requires no import statement.

Thread.sleep

`Thread.sleep` is a static method in the class `Thread` that pauses the thread that includes the invocation. It pauses for the number of milliseconds (thousandths of a second) given as an argument.

The method `Thread.sleep` may throw an `InterruptedException`, which is a checked exception and so must be either caught in a `catch` block or declared in a `throws` clause.

The classes `Thread` and `InterruptedException` are both in the package `java.lang`, so neither requires any import statement.

Note that `Thread.sleep` can be invoked in an ordinary (single thread) program of the kind we have seen before this chapter. It will insert a pause in the single thread of that program.

SYNTAX

`Thread.sleep(`*Number_Of_Milliseconds*`);`

EXAMPLE

```
try
{
    Thread.sleep(100); //Pause of 1/10 of a second
}
catch(InterruptedException e)
{
    System.out.println("Unexpected interrupt");
}
```

The getGraphics Method

The other new method in Display 19.1 is the `getGraphics` method, which is used in the following line from the method `fill`:

getGraphics

```
Graphics g = box.getGraphics();
```

The `getGraphics` method is almost self-explanatory. As we already noted in Chapter 18, almost every item displayed on the screen (more precisely, every `JComponent`) has an associated `Graphics` object. The method `getGraphics` is an accessor method that returns the associated `Graphics` object (of the calling object for `getGraphics`)—in this case, the `Graphics` object associated with the panel box. This gives us a `Graphics` object that can draw circles (or anything else) in the panel box.

We still need to say a bit more about why the program in Display 19.1 makes you wait before it will respond to the close-window button, but otherwise this concludes our explanation of Display 19.1. The rest of the code consists of standard things we have seen before.

getGraphics

Every `JComponent` has an associated `Graphics` object. The method `getGraphics` is an accessor method that returns the associated `Graphics` object of its calling object.

SYNTAX

```
Component.getGraphics( );
```

EXAMPLE (see Display 19.1 for context)

```
Graphics g = box.getGraphics( );
```

Fixing a Nonresponsive Program Using Threads

Now that we have discussed the new items in the program in Display 19.1, we are ready to explain why it is nonresponsive and to show you how to use threads to write a responsive version of that program.

Recall that when you run the program in Display 19.1, it draws circles one after the other to fill a portion of the frame. Although there is only a 1/10 of a second pause between drawing each circle, it can still seem like it takes a long time to finish. So, you are likely to want to abort the program and close the window early. But, if you click the close-window button, the window will not close until the GUI is finished drawing all the circles.

Here is why the close-window button is nonresponsive: The method `fill`, which draws the circles, is invoked in the body of the method `actionPerformed`. So, the method `actionPerformed` does not end until after the method `fill` ends. And, until the method `actionPerformed` ends, the GUI cannot go on to do the next thing, which is probably to respond to the close-window button.

Here is how we fixed the problem: We have the method `actionPerformed` create a new (independent) thread to draw the circles. Once `actionPerformed` does this, the new thread is an independent process that proceeds on its own. The method `actionPerformed` has nothing more to do with this new thread; the work of `actionPerformed` is ended. So, the main thread (the one with `actionPerformed`) is ready to move on to the next thing, which will probably be to respond promptly to a click of the close-window button. At the same time, the new thread draws the circles. So, the circles are drawn, but at the same time a click of the close-window button will end the program. The program that implements this multithreaded solution is given in the next Programming Example.

EXAMPLE: A Multithreaded Program

Display 19.2 contains a program that uses a main thread and a second thread to implement the technique discussed in the previous subsection. The general approach was outlined in the previous subsection, but we need to explain the Java code details. We do that in the next few subsections.

The Class `Thread`

`Thread`

In Java, a thread is an object of the class `Thread`. The normal way to program a thread is to define a class that is a derived class of the class `Thread`. An object of this derived class will be a thread that follows the programming given in the definition of the derived (thread) class.

`run()`

Where do you do the programming of a thread? The class `Thread` has a method named `run`. The definition of the method `run` is the code for the thread. When the thread is executed, the method `run` is executed. Of course, the method defined in the class `Thread` and inherited by any derived class of `Thread` does not do what you want your thread to do. So, when you define a derived class of `Thread`, you override the definition of the method `run` to do what you want the thread to do.

In Display 19.2, the inner class `Packer` is a derived class of the class `Thread`. The method `run` for the class `Packer` is defined to be exactly the same as the method `fill` in our previous, unresponsive GUI (Display 19.1). So, an object of the class `Packer` is a thread that will do what `fill` does, namely draw the circles to fill up a portion of the window.

`start()`

The method `actionPerformed` in Display 19.2 differs from the method `actionPerformed` in our older, nonresponsive program (Display 19.1) in that the invocation of the method `fill` is replaced with the following:

```
Packer packerThread = new Packer( );
packerThread.start( );
```

This creates a new, independent thread named `packerThread` and starts it processing. Whatever `packerThread` does, it does as an independent thread. The main thread can then allow `actionPerformed` to end and the main thread will be ready to respond to any click of the close-window button.

Display 19.2 Threaded Version of **`FillDemo`** (part 1 of 3)

The GUI produced is identical to the GUI produced by Display 19.1 except that in this version the close-window button works even while the circles are being drawn, so you can end the GUI early if you get bored.

```
import javax.swing.JFrame;
import javax.swing.JPanel;
import javax.swing.JButton;
import java.awt.BorderLayout;
import java.awt.FlowLayout;
import java.awt.Graphics;
import java.awt.event.ActionListener;
import java.awt.event.ActionEvent;

public class ThreadedFillDemo extends JFrame implements ActionListener
{
    public static final int WIDTH = 300;
    public static final int HEIGHT = 200;
    public static final int FILL_WIDTH = 300;
    public static final int FILL_HEIGHT = 100;
    public static final int CIRCLE_SIZE = 10;
    public static final int PAUSE = 100; //milliseconds
```

(continued)

Display 19.2 **Threaded Version of `FillDemo`** (part 2 of 3)

```
    private JPanel box;

    public static void main(String[] args)
    {
        ThreadedFillDemo gui = new ThreadedFillDemo();
        gui.setVisible(true);
    }

    public ThreadedFillDemo()
    {
        setSize(WIDTH, HEIGHT);
        setTitle("Threaded Fill Demo");
        setDefaultCloseOperation(JFrame.EXIT_ON_CLOSE);

        setLayout(new BorderLayout());

        box = new JPanel();
        add(box, "Center");

        JPanel buttonPanel = new JPanel();
        buttonPanel.setLayout(new FlowLayout());
        JButton startButton = new JButton("Start");
        startButton.addActionListener(this);
        buttonPanel.add(startButton);
        add(buttonPanel, "South");
    }

    public void actionPerformed(ActionEvent e)
    {
            Packer packerThread = new Packer();
            packerThread.start();
    }

    private class Packer extends Thread
    {
        public void run()
        {
            Graphics g = box.getGraphics();
            for (int y = 0; y < FILL_HEIGHT; y = y + CIRCLE_SIZE)
              for (int x = 0; x < FILL_WIDTH; x = x + CIRCLE_SIZE)
              {
                  g.fillOval(x, y, CIRCLE_SIZE, CIRCLE_SIZE);
                  doNothing(PAUSE);
              }
        }
```

You need a thread object, even if there are no instance variables in the class definition of Packer.

`start` *"starts" the thread and calls* `run`.

`run` *is inherited from* `Thread` *but needs to be overridden. This definition of* `run` *is identical to that of* `fill` *in Display 19.1.*

Display 19.2 **Threaded Version of `FillDemo`** (part 3 of 3)

```
        public void doNothing( int milliseconds)
        {
            try
            {
                Thread.sleep(milliseconds);
            }
            catch(InterruptedException e)
            {
                System.out.println("Unexpected interrupt");
                System.exit(0);
            }
        }
    } //End Packer inner class

}
```

We need only to discuss the method `start` and we will be through with our explanation. The method `start` initiates the computation (process) of the calling thread. It performs some overhead associated with starting a thread and then it invokes the `run` method for the thread. As we have already seen, the `run` method of the class `Packer` in Display 19.2 draws the circles we want, so the invocation

run()

```
packerThread.start( );
```

does this as well, because it calls `run`. Note that you do not invoke `run` directly. Instead, you invoke `start`, which does some other needed things and then invokes `run`.

This ends our explanation of the multithreaded program in Display 19.2, but there is still one, perhaps puzzling, thing about the class `Packer` that we should explain. The definition of the class `Packer` includes no instance variables. So, why do we need to bother with an object of the class `Packer`? Why not simply make all the methods static and call them with the class name `Packer`? The answer is that the only way to get a new thread is to create a new `Thread` object. The things inherited from the class `Thread` are what the object needs to be a thread. Static methods do not a thread make. In fact, not only will static methods not work, the compiler will not even allow you to define `run` to be static. This is because `run` is inherited from `Thread` as a nonstatic method; this cannot be changed to static when overriding a method definition. The compiler will not let you even try to do this without creating an object of the class `Packer`.

The `Thread` Class

A thread is an object of the class `Thread`. The normal way to program a thread is to define a class that is a derived class of the class `Thread`. An object of this derived class will be a thread that follows the programming given in the definition of the derived (thread) class's method named `run`.

Any thread class inherits the method start from the class `Thread`. An invocation of `start` by an object of a thread class will start the thread and invoke the method `run` for that thread.

See Display 19.2 for an example.

The `Runnable` Interface ★

There are times when you would rather not make a thread class a derived class of the class `Thread`. The alternative to making your class a derived class of the class `Thread` is to have your class instead implement the `Runnable` interface. The `Runnable` interface has only one method heading:

```
public void run()
```

A class that implements the `Runnable` interface must still be run from an instance of the class `Thread`. This is usually done by passing the `Runnable` object as an argument to the thread constructor. The following is an outline of one way to do this:

```
public class ClassToRun extends SomeClass implements Runnable
{
     ....
    public void run()
    {
        //Fill this just as you would if ClassToRun
        //were derived from Thread.
    }
     ....
    public void startThread()
    {
        Thread theThread = new Thread(this);
        theThread.run();
    }
     ....
}
```

The previous method `startThread` is not compulsory, but it is one way to produce a thread that will in turn run the `run` method of an object of the class `ClassToRun`. In Display 19.3, we have rewritten the program in Display 19.2 using the `Runnable` interface. The program behaves exactly the same as the one in Display 19.2.

Display 19.3 The **`Runnable`** Interface (part 1 of 2)

```
import javax.swing.JFrame;
import javax.swing.JPanel;
import javax.swing.JButton;
import java.awt.BorderLayout;
import java.awt.FlowLayout;
import java.awt.Graphics;
import java.awt.event.ActionListener;
import java.awt.event.ActionEvent;

public class ThreadedFillDemo2 extends JFrame
                               implements ActionListener, Runnable
{
    public static final int WIDTH = 300;
    public static final int HEIGHT = 200;
    public static final int FILL_WIDTH = 300;
    public static final int FILL_HEIGHT = 100;
    public static final int CIRCLE_SIZE = 10;
    public static final int PAUSE = 100; //milliseconds
    private JPanel box;

    public static void main(String[] args)
    {
        ThreadedFillDemo2 gui = new ThreadedFillDemo2();
        gui.setVisible(true);
    }

    public ThreadedFillDemo2()
    {
        setSize(WIDTH, HEIGHT);
        setTitle("Threaded Fill Demo");
        setDefaultCloseOperation(JFrame.EXIT_ON_CLOSE);

        setLayout(new BorderLayout());

        box = new JPanel();
        add(box, "Center");

        JPanel buttonPanel = new JPanel();
        buttonPanel.setLayout(new FlowLayout());

        JButton startButton = new JButton("Start");
        startButton.addActionListener(this);
        buttonPanel.add(startButton);
        add(buttonPanel, "South");
    }
```

(continued)

Display 19.3 The **`Runnable`** Interface (part 2 of 2)

```
    public void actionPerformed(ActionEvent e)
    {
        startThread();
    }

    public void run()
    {
        Graphics g = box.getGraphics();
        for (int y = 0; y < FILL_HEIGHT; y = y + CIRCLE_SIZE)
          for (int x = 0; x < FILL_WIDTH; x = x + CIRCLE_SIZE)
          {
              g.fillOval(x, y, CIRCLE_SIZE, CIRCLE_SIZE);
              doNothing(PAUSE);
          }
    }

    public void startThread()
    {
        Thread theThread = new Thread(this);
        theThread.start();
    }

    public void doNothing(int milliseconds)
    {
        try
        {
            Thread.sleep(milliseconds);
        }
        catch (InterruptedException e)
        {
            System.out.println("Unexpected interrupt");
            System.exit(0);
        }
    }
}
```

MyProgrammingLab™

Self-Test Exercises

1. Because `sleep` is a static method, how can it possibly know what thread it needs to pause?

2. Where was polymorphism used in the program in Display 19.2? (*Hint*: We are looking for an answer involving the class `Packer`.)

Race Conditions and Thread Synchronization ★

When multiple threads change a shared variable, it is sometimes possible that the variable will end up with the wrong (and often unpredictable) value. This is called a **race condition** because the final value depends on the sequence in which the threads access the shared value.

race condition

For example, consider two threads where each thread runs the following code:

```
int local;
local = sharedVariable;
local++;
sharedVariable = local;
```

The intent is for each thread to increment `sharedVariable` by one so if there are two threads, then `sharedVariable` should be incremented by two. However, consider the case where `sharedVariable` is 0. The first thread runs and executes the first two statements, so its variable `local` is set to 0. Now there is a context switch to the second thread. The second thread executes all four statements, so its variable `local` is set to 0 and incremented, and `sharedVariable` is set to 1. Now we return to the first thread and it continues where it left off, which is the third statement. The variable `local` is 0 so it is incremented to 1 and then the value 1 is copied into `sharedVariable`. The end result after both threads are done is that `sharedVariable` has the value 1, and we lost the value written by thread two!

You might think that this problem could be avoided by replacing our code with a single statement such as

```
sharedVariable++;
```

Unfortunately, this will not solve our problem because the statement is not guaranteed to be an "atomic" action and there could still be a context switch to another thread "in the middle" of executing the statement.

To demonstrate this problem, consider the `Counter` class shown in Display 19.4. This simple class merely stores a variable that increments a counter. It uses the somewhat roundabout way to increment the counter on purpose to increase the likelihood of a race condition.

The way we will demonstrate the race condition is to do the following:

1. Create a single instance of the `Counter` class.
2. Create an array of many threads (30,000 in the example) where each thread references the single instance of the `Counter` class.
3. Each thread runs and invokes the `increment()` method.
4. Wait for each thread to finish and then output the value of the counter. If there are no race conditions, then its value should be 30,000. If there are race conditions, then the value will be less than 30,000.

We create many threads to increase the likelihood that the race condition occurs. With only a few threads, it is not likely that there will be a switch to another thread inside the `increment()` method at the right point to cause a problem.

Display 19.4 The **Counter** Class

```
public class Counter
{
  private int counter;
  public Counter()
  {
          counter = 0;
  }
  public int value()
  {
          return counter;
  }
  public void increment()
  {
          int local;
          local = counter;
          local++;
          counter = local;
  }
}
```

The only new tool that we need for our demonstration program is a way to wait for all the threads to finish. If we do not wait, then our program might output the counter before all the threads have had a chance to increment the value. We can wait by invoking the `join()` method for every thread we create. This method waits for the thread to complete. The `join()` method throws `InterruptedException`. This is a checked exception so we must use the try/catch mechanism.

VideoNote **Walkthrough of a Program with Race Conditions**

The class `RaceConditionTest` in Display 19.5 illustrates the race condition. You may have to run the program several times before you get a value less than 30,000. Problems as a result of race conditions are often rare occurrences. This makes them extremely hard to find and debug!

Display 19.5 The **RaceConditionTest** Class (part 1 of 2)

```
public class RaceConditionTest extends Thread
{
  private Counter countObject;

  public RaceConditionTest(Counter ctr)
  {
       countObject = ctr;
  }
```

Stores a reference to a single `Counter` object.

Display 19.5 The `RaceConditionTest` Class (part 2 of 2)

```
    public void run()
    {
      countObject.increment();
    }

    public static void main(String[] args)
    {
       int i;
      Counter masterCounter = new Counter();
      RaceConditionTest[] threads = new RaceConditionTest[30000];

      System.out.println("The counter is " + masterCounter.value());
      for (i = 0; i < threads.length; i++)
      {
            threads[i] = new RaceConditionTest(masterCounter);
            threads[i].start();
      }

       // Wait for the threads to finish
       for (i = 0; i < threads.length; i++)
       {
            try
            {
              threads[i].join();
            }
            catch (InterruptedException e)
            {
              System.out.println(e.getMessage());
            }
       }
       System.out.println("The counter is " + masterCounter.value());
    }
}
```

Invokes the code in Display 19.4 where the race condition occurs.

The single instance of the `Counter` object.

Array of 30,000 threads.

Give each thread a reference to the single `Counter` object and start each thread.

Waits for the thread to complete.

Sample Dialogue (output will vary)

```
The counter is 0
The counter is 29998
```

So how do we fix this problem? The solution is to make each thread wait so only one thread can run the code in `increment()` at a time. This section of code is called a **critical region**. Java allows you to add the keyword **synchronized** around a critical region to enforce the requirement that only one thread is allowed to execute in this region at a time. All other threads will wait until the thread inside the region is finished.

critical region

synchronized

In this particular case, we can add the keyword `synchronized` to either the method or around the specific code. If we add `synchronized` to the `increment()` method in the `Counter` class, then it looks like this:

```
public synchronized void increment()
{
  int local;
  local = counter;
  local++;
  counter = local;
}
```

If we add `synchronized` inside the code, then we can write

```
public void increment()
{
  int local;
  synchronized (this)
  {
   local = counter;
   local++;
   counter = local;
  }
}
```

Either version will result in a counter whose final value is always 30,000. There are many other issues involved in thread management, concurrency, and synchronization. These concepts are often covered in more detail in an operating systems or parallel programming course.

MyProgrammingLab™

Self-Test Exercises

3. In the `run()` method of Display 19.5, make the thread sleep a random amount of time between one and five milliseconds. You should see an increase in the number of problems caused by race conditions. Can you explain why?

4. Here is some code that synchronizes thread access to a shared variable. How come it is not guaranteed to output 30,000 every time it is run?

```
public class Counter
{
  private int counter;
  public Counter()
  {
       counter = 0;
  }
```

MyProgrammingLab™

Self-Test Exercises (continued)

```
    public int value()
    {
      return counter;
    }
    public synchronized void increment()
    {
      counter++;
    }
}
public class RaceConditionTest extends Thread
{
  private Counter countObject;
  public RaceConditionTest(Counter ctr)
  {
      countObject = ctr;
  }
  public void run()
  {
    countObject.increment();
  }
  public static void main(String[] args)
  {
    int i;
    Counter masterCounter = new Counter();
    RaceConditionTest[] threads = new RaceConditionTest[30000];
    System.out.println("The counter is " + masterCounter.
    value());
    for (i = 0; i < threads.length; i++)
    {
        threads[i] = new RaceConditionTest(masterCounter);
        threads[i].start();
    }
    System.out.println("The counter is " + masterCounter.
    value());
  }
}
```

19.2 Networking with Stream Sockets

Since in order to speak, one must first listen, learn to speak by listening.

MEVLANA RUMI

When computers want to communicate with each other over a network, each computer must speak the same "language." In other words, the computers need to communicate using the same *protocol*. One of the most common protocols today is **TCP**, or the **Transmission Control Protocol**. For example, the HTTP protocol used to transmit Web pages is based on TCP. TCP is a stream-based protocol in which a stream of data is transmitted from the sender to the receiver. TCP is considered a reliable protocol because it guarantees that data from the sender is received in the same order in which it was sent. An analogy to TCP is the telephone system. A connection is made when the phone is dialed and the participants communicate by speaking back and forth. In TCP, the receiver must first be listening for a connection, the sender initiates the connection, and then the sender and receiver can transmit data. The program that is waiting for a connection is called the **server** and the program that initiates the connection is called the **client**.

Transmission Control Protocol (TCP)

server

client

An alternate protocol is **UDP**, or the **User Datagram Protocol**. In UDP, packets of data are transmitted but no guarantee is made regarding the order in which the packets are received. An analogy to UDP is the postal system. Letters that are sent might be received in an unpredictable order, or lost entirely with no notification. Although Java provides support for UDP, we will only introduce TCP in this section.

User Datagram Protocol (UDP)

Sockets

Network programming is implemented in Java using **sockets**. A socket describes one end of the connection between two programs over the network. A socket consists of an address that identifies the remote computer and a **port** for both the local and remote computer. The port is assigned an integer value between 0 and 65,535 that is used to identify which program should handle data received from the network. Two applications may not bind to the same port. Typically, ports 0 to 1,024 are reserved for use by well-known services implemented by your operating system.

sockets

port

The process of client/server communication is shown in Display 19.6. First, the server waits for a connection by listening on a specific port. When a client connects to this port, a new socket is created that identifies the remote computer, the remote port, and the local port. A similar socket is created on the client. Once the sockets are created on both the client and the server, data can be transmitted using streams in a manner very similar to the way we implemented file I/O in Chapter 10.

Display 19.7 shows how to create a simple server that listens on port 7654 for a connection. Once it receives a connection, a new socket is returned by the `accept( )` method. From this socket, we create a `BufferedReader`, just as if we were reading from a text file described in Chapter 10. Data is transmitted to the socket using a `DataOutputStream`, which is similar to a `FileOutputStream`. The `ServerSocket`

Display 19.6 **Client/Server Network Communication through Sockets**

1. The server listens and waits for a connection on port 7654.

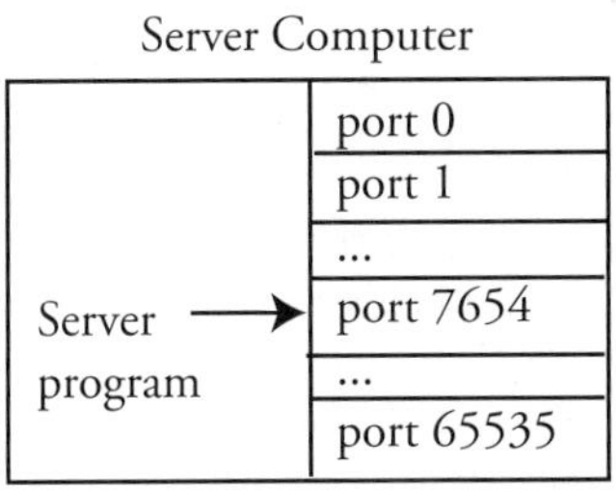

2. The client connects to the server on port 7654. It uses a local port that is assigned automatically, in this case, port 20314.

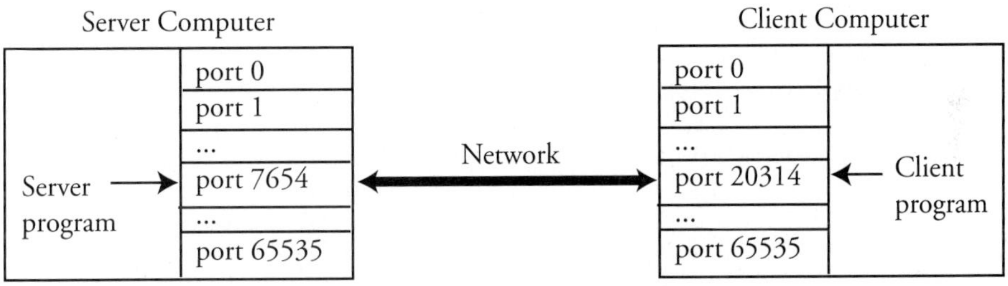

The server program can now communicate over a socket bound locally to port 7654 and remotely to the client's address at port 20314.

The client program can now communicate over a socket bound locally to port 20314 and remotely to the server's address at port 7654.

and `Socket` classes are in the `java.net` package, while the `BufferedReader` and `DataOutputStream` classes are in the `java.io` package. Once the streams are created, the server expects the client to send a name. The server waits for the name with a call to `readLine( )` on the `BufferedReader` object and then sends back the name concatenated with the current date and time. Finally, the server closes the streams and sockets.

`localhost`

Display 19.6 shows how to create a client that connects to our date and time server. First, we create a socket with the name of the computer running the server along with the corresponding port of 7654. If the server program and client program are running on the same computer, then you can use **`localhost`** as the name of the machine. Your computer understands that any attempt to connect across a network to the machine named `localhost` really corresponds to a connection with itself. Otherwise, the hostname should be set to the name of the computer (e.g., my.server.com). After a connection is made, the client creates stream objects, sends its name, waits for a reply, and prints the reply.

Display 19.7 Date and Time Server (part 1 of 2)

```
import java.util.Date;
import java.net.ServerSocket;
import java.net.Socket;
import java.io.DataOutputStream;
import java.io.BufferedReader;
import java.io.InputStreamReader;
import java.io.IOException;

public class DateServer
{
 public static void main(String[] args)
 {
      Date now = new Date();

      try
      {
        System.out.println("Waiting for a connection on port 7654.");
        ServerSocket serverSock = new ServerSocket(7654);
        Socket connectionSock = serverSock.accept();

        BufferedReader clientInput = new BufferedReader(
            new InputStreamReader(connectionSock.getInputStream()));
        DataOutputStream clientOutput = new DataOutputStream(
            connectionSock.getOutputStream());

        System.out.println("Connection made, waiting for client " +
            "to send their name.");
        String clientText = clientInput.readLine();
        String replyText = "Welcome, " + clientText +
            ", Today is " + now.toString() + "\n";
        clientOutput.writeBytes(replyText);
        System.out.println("Sent: " + replyText);

        clientOutput.close();
        clientInput.close();
        connectionSock.close();
        serverSock.close();
      }
      catch (IOException e)
      {
        System.out.println(e.getMessage());
      }
 }
}
```

Display 19.7 Date and Time Server (part 2 of 2)

Sample Dialogue *Output when the client program in Display 19.8 connects to the server program.*

```
Waiting for a connection on port 7654.
Connection made, waiting for client to send their name.
Sent: Welcome, Dusty Rhodes, Today is Sun Nov 20 12:18:21 AKDT 2011
```

Display 19.8 Date and Time Client (part 1 of 2)

```
import java.net.Socket;
import java.io.DataOutputStream;
import java.io.BufferedReader;
import java.io.InputStreamReader;
import java.io.IOException;

public class DateClient
{
  public static void main(String[] args)
  {
      try
      {
        String hostname = "localhost";
        int port = 7654;

        System.out.println("Connecting to server on port " + port);
        Socket connectionSock = new Socket(hostname, port);

        BufferedReader serverInput = new BufferedReader(
            new InputStreamReader(connectionSock.getInputStream()));
        DataOutputStream serverOutput = new DataOutputStream(
            connectionSock.getOutputStream());

        System.out.println("Connection made, sending name.");
        serverOutput.writeBytes("Dusty Rhodes\n");

        System.out.println("Waiting for reply.");
        String serverData = serverInput.readLine();
        System.out.println("Received: " + serverData);

        serverOutput.close();
        serverInput.close();
        connectionSock.close();
      }
```

`localhost` *refers to the same, or local, machine that the client is running on. Change this string to the appropriate hostname (e.g., my.server.com) if the server is running on a remote machine.*

(continued)

Display 19.8 **Date and Time Client** (part 2 of 2)

```
        catch (IOException e)
        {
          System.out.println(e.getMessage());
        }
    }
}
```

Sample Dialogue *Output when client program connects to the server program in Display 19.7.*

```
Connecting to server on port 7654
Connection made, sending name.
Waiting for reply.
Received: Welcome, Dusty Rhodes, Today is Fri Oct 13 03:03:21 AKDT 2011
```

Note that the socket and stream objects throw checked exceptions. This means that their exceptions must be caught or declared in a `throws` block.

Sockets and Threading

blocking

If you run the program in Display 19.7, then you will notice that the server waits, or **blocks**, at the `serverSock.accept( )` call until a client connects to it. Both the client and server also block at the `readLine( )` call if data from the socket is not yet available. In a client with a GUI, you would notice this as a nonresponsive program while it is waiting for data. For the server, this behavior makes it difficult to handle connections with more than one client. After a connection is made with the first client, the server will become nonresponsive to the client's requests while it waits for a second client.

The solution to this problem is to use threads. One thread will listen for new connections while another thread handles an existing connection. Section 19.1 describes how to create threads and make a GUI program responsive. On the server, the `accept( )` call is typically placed in a loop and a new thread is created to handle each client connection:

```
while (true)
{
  Socket connectionSock = serverSock.accept( );
  ClientHandler handler = new ClientHandler(connectionSock);
  Thread theThread = new Thread(handler);
  theThread.start( );
}
```

In this code, `ClientHandler` is a class that implements `Runnable`. The constructor keeps a reference to the socket in an instance variable, and the `run( )` method would handle all communications. A complete implementation of a threaded server is left as Programming Projects 19.7 and 19.8.

MyProgrammingLab™

Self-Test Exercises

5. What is the purpose of a port in the context of a socket?
6. Consider a threaded server that is expected to have up to 100 clients connected to it at one time. Why might this server require a large amount of resources such as memory, disk space, or processor time?

19.3 JavaBeans

Insert tab A into slot B.

Common assembly instruction

JavaBeans

JavaBeans refers to a framework that facilitates software building by connecting software components from diverse sources. Some of the components might be standard existing pieces of software. Some might be designed for the particular application. Typically, the various components were designed and coded by different teams. If the components are all designed within the JavaBeans framework, it simplifies the process of integrating the components and means that the components produced can more easily be reused for future software projects. JavaBeans have been widely used. For example, the AWT and Swing packages were built within the JavaBeans framework.

The Component Model

You are most likely to have heard the word *component* when shopping for a home entertainment system. The individual pieces, such as a receiver/amplifier, DVD player, speakers, and so forth, are called *components*. Connect the components to produce a working system, but do not connect them in just any way. You must connect them following the interface rules for each component. The speaker wire must connect to the correct plug, and there better be a plug for it to connect to. You may think it is obvious that a receiver/amplifier needs to have connections for speakers; it is obvious if the receiver/amplifier design is going to be used to make many identical units for use by many different people. However, if you are only making one receiver/amplifier for one home entertainment system, you might just "open the box" and connect the wire inside. Software systems, unfortunately, are often constructed using the "open the box" approach. The component model says that components should always have well-defined connections for other components—which in our case will be other software components, not speakers—but the idea is the same.

The JavaBeans Model

A component model specifies how components interact with one another. In the case of JavaBeans, the software components (classes) are required to provide at least the following interface services or abilities:

1. **Rules to Ensure Consistency in Writing Interfaces:**
   For example, the rules say, among other things, that the name of an accessor method must begin with `get` and that the name of a mutator method must start with `set`. This same rule has always been a style rule for us in this book, but it was a "should do." In the JavaBeans framework, it becomes a "must do." Of course, there are other rules as well. This is just a sample rule.

event handling

2. **An Event Handling Model:**
   This is essentially the event-handling model we presented for the AWT and Swing. (Remember the AWT and Swing were done within the JavaBeans framework.)

persistence

3. **Persistence:**
   This means that an object has an identity that extends beyond one session. For example, a `JFrame` of the kind we have seen so far may be used; when you are finished using it, it goes away. The next time you use it, it starts out completely new, born again just as it started before. Persistence means the `JFrame` or other component can retain information about its former use; its state is saved, for example, in a database someplace.

introspection

4. **Introspection:**
   This is an enhancement of simple accessor and mutator methods. It includes facilities to find out what access to a component is available as well as providing access.

5. **Builder Support:**
   These are primarily IDEs (Integrated Development Environments) designed to connect JavaBean components to produce a final application. Some examples are the open source NetBeans, the Eclipse Foundation's Eclipse, and JetBrain's IntelliJ IDEA.

What Is a JavaBean?

A **JavaBean** (often called a *JavaBean* component or simply a *Bean*) is a reusable software component (Java class or classes) that satisfies the requirements of the JavaBeans framework and that can be manipulated in an IDE designed for building applications out of Beans.

What Are Enterprise JavaBeans?

The **Enterprise JavaBean** framework extends the `JavaBeans` framework to more readily accommodate business applications.

MyProgrammingLab™

Self-Test Exercises

7. What is meant by *persistence*?
8. What event-handling model is used with JavaBeans?

19.4 Java and Database Connections

It is a capital mistake to theorize before one has data.

Sir Arthur Conan Doyle *(Sherlock Holmes), Scandal in Bohemia*

As an example of how Java has been extended to interact with other software systems, in this section, we will briefly describe how Java interacts with database management systems. This introduction is just enough for you to construct and manipulate databases at a fairly basic level. The intent of this section is to introduce some common database manipulations to let you know what kinds of things are available to you for database programming in Java.

Relational Databases

database management system (DBMS)

A **database** is a structured collection of data, and the software that manages a database is known as a **database management system (DBMS)**. A DBMS is especially useful when dealing with a large amount of data, because it simplifies the data creation, storage, and retrieval from the perspective of an application. Consequently, a database system is almost universally employed with any large-scale application that requires the storage of information. For example, applications that manage financial transactions, employee records, products, or customer data will typically use a database.

relational database

The most common database model used today is the **relational database**, which was defined by Edgar Codd at the IBM Almaden Research Center in 1970. A relational database refers to a collection of relations, which are more commonly referred to as **tables**. A table consists of records that comprise the rows of the table. The fields for each record comprise the columns of the table. Tables may be related to one another through their fields, hence the term *relational database*.

Java DB and JDBC

Java DB

Apache Derby

In this section, we will give examples based on Oracle's relational database management system called **Java DB**. Java DB is a version of the open source database known as **Apache Derby**. It is packaged with version 6 or higher of the Java Software Development Kit (SDK). Depending on what version of the Java SDK that is installed on your system, you may not have the complete Derby package (e.g., one that includes documentation and source code examples) so you may wish to download it from

Oracle's Web page. Alternately, other database systems (such as Oracle, SQL Server, or MySQL) will also work with Java, but they will require appropriate drivers and minor changes to the source code. These changes are primarily in the specification of the connection string.

Installing Derby may require some additional configuration of your system. It will require setting several environment variables in your operating system. The `DERBY_INSTALL` variable should be set to the pathname of the folder that contains the installed Derby files, the `CLASSPATH` variable should include `derby.jar`, which is in the `lib` folder of the main Derby folder, and your `PATH` variable should contain the `bin` folder of the main Derby folder. See the documentation that comes with the Derby software for more detailed instructions.

Derby runs in one of two modes: network server mode or embedded mode. In network server mode, the Derby server program stores and processes the data while a client program connects to the server using sockets. Queries, commands, and results are transmitted between the client and server over sockets. This mode allows the database server to run on one machine, while database clients run on separate machines. In embedded mode, the classes for the Derby engine are embedded in your program and executed in the same thread as your application. In this section, we will only use embedded mode, but only minor changes are required to create a program that runs under server mode.

Application programs typically access databases through several layers of abstraction. The lowest level is the database engine, which handles tasks such as indexing, storing, and retrieving data from the disk drive. In our case, these tasks are performed by the Derby engine. A set of higher-level classes provides a connection to Derby along with a consistent interface so that few code changes are necessary at higher levels if the underlying database provider is changed. **Java Database Connectivity (JDBC)** is a common API used to access databases. JDBC is included in version 5 or higher of the Java SDK. Various Microsoft and Oracle database systems are among the many commercially available database systems that are compatible with JDBC, along with Derby. Typically, you need to download and install a JDBC driver for your database system. Conceptually, JDBC is simple: Establish a connection to a database system (either on your computer or over the Internet) and execute database commands, and do this all within your Java code.

SQL

Finally, applications send commands and queries to JDBC using strings formatted in **SQL**. SQL is a standard for database access that has been adopted by virtually all relational database vendors. The initials *SQL* stand for *Structured Query Language*. Display 19.9 illustrates the relationships among these components for an embedded Derby database.

Display 19.9 Relationships between JDBC, Embedded Derby, and SQL

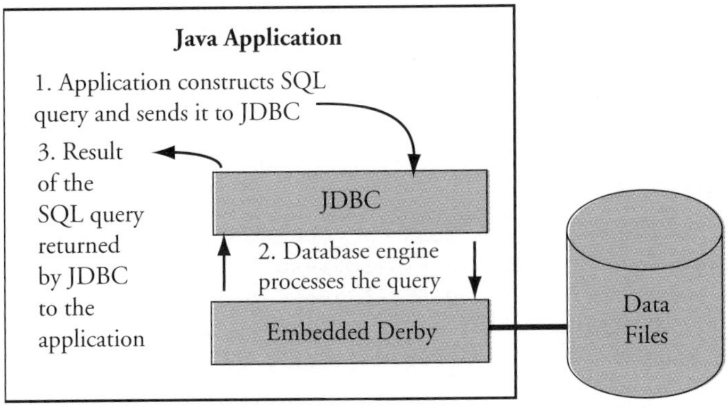

SQL

SQL is pronounced either by saying the letters or by saying the word "sequel." SQL is a language for formulating queries for a relational database. SQL is not part of Java, but JDBC allows you to embed SQL commands in your Java code.

SQL works with relational databases. As an example, suppose we were organizing a catalog of books and authors. A relational database can be thought of as a collection of named tables with rows and columns, such as those shown in Display 19.10. In this case, we have created a table with author information (author name, unique author ID, and URL), a table with book information (title and ISBN), and a table that identifies which author has written which book (unique author ID and ISBN).

In this brief introduction, we will not go into the details of the constraints on tables. However, to see that there are some constraints, note that in the three tables in Display 19.10, no relationship is repeated. If we had one entry for each book with all the information—title, author, ISBN number,[1] and author's URL—then there would be two entries giving Dan Simmons' URL, because he has two books in our database.

To manipulate the database, we issue SQL commands, also known as SQL queries, to the database. The following is a sample SQL command:

```
SELECT Titles.Title, Titles.ISBN, BooksAuthors.Author_ID
FROM Titles, BooksAuthors
WHERE Titles.ISBN = BooksAuthors.ISBN
```

[1]The ISBN number is a unique identification number assigned to (almost) every book published.

Display 19.10 Relational Database Tables

Names

AUTHOR	AUTHOR_ID	URL
Adams, Douglas	1	http:// ...
Simmons, Dan	2	http:// ...
Stephenson, Neal	3	http:// ...

Titles

TITLE	ISBN
Snow Crash	0-553-38095-8
Endymion	0-553-57294-6
The Hitchhikers Guide to the Galaxy	0-671-46149-4
The Rise of Endymion	0-553-57298-9

BooksAuthors

ISBN	AUTHOR_ID
0-553-38095-8	3
0-553-57294-6	2
0-671-46149-4	1
0-553-57298-9	2

Display 19.11 Result of SQL Command in Text

Result

TITLE	ISBN	AUTHOR_ID
Snow Crash	0-553-38095-8	3
Endymion	0-553-57294-6	2
The Hitchhikers Guide to the Galaxy	0-671-46149-4	1
The Rise of Endymion	0-553-57298-9	2

This will produce the table shown in Display 19.11. That table contains all titles with matching ISBN number and author ID. The `ISBN` number is the bridge that connects the tables `Titles` and `BooksAuthors`.

As a more detailed example, let us connect to an embedded Derby database and issue the SQL commands to create a new table, insert a new row (record) into the table, select rows, and modify rows. Note that this is not a comprehensive list of commands but rather a small subset of SQL.

First, our Java program must import the SQL libraries `java.sql.Connection`, `java.sql.DriverManager`, `java.sql.SQLException`, and `java.sql.Statement`. When processing results, we will also need to import `java.sql.ResultSet`. Next we must load the database drivers:

```
String driver = "org.apache.derby.jdbc.EmbeddedDriver";
Class.forName(driver).newInstance( );
```

This code throws three checked exceptions that must be caught: `ClassNotFoundException`, `InstantiationException`, and `IllegalAccessException`. For simplicity, we catch only the superclass `Exception` in the code shown in Display 19.12.

connection string

Once the database drivers are loaded, we can connect to the database. This is done by passing a **connection string** to the `DriverManager.getConnection` method. The connection string specifies the protocol, database name, and other parameters, such as whether or not a new database should be created. For example, to connect to and create a database named `BookDatabase` using Derby, we would use

```
Connection conn = null;
conn = DriverManager.getConnection(
       "jdbc:derby:BookDatabase; create = true");
```

This creates a subdirectory named `BookDatabase` in the active working directory that will contain the database, files. You could specify a pathname in front of `BookDatabase` if you want to create the database somewhere else on the file system. If you ever wish to delete the database, then simply delete the `BookDatabase` directory. Note that if the database already exists, then the attribute `create=true` will not delete the existing database but will instead connect to the existing database.

Additional parameters are specified in the command string by separating them with semicolons. For example, if the database requires a username and password, then the connection string would look like this:

```
conn = DriverManager.getConnection
       ("jdbc:derby:BookDatabase;create=true;user=username;" +
       "password = pass");
```

When we are finished accessing the database, invoke the `close( )` method to close the connection. The `DriverManager.getConnection( )` method requires that `SQLException` be caught, so this code should be placed inside an appropriate try/catch block.

SQL commands or queries can be issued to JDBC once the database connection is established. First, a `Statement` object must be constructed and then invoked by calling the `execute` or `executeQuery` method with a SQL string as its argument. The `execute` method can be used to execute any SQL statement, but it is generally used for SQL commands where return values are not needed or ignored (e.g., creating a new table or deleting a row). It returns `true` if the command results in a set of data and `false` if there is no result or an update count. The `executeQuery` method is used with a SQL query that is expected to return some rows from the database. It returns a `ResultSet` object that contains the data produced by the query. These methods throw `SQLException` if there is a database error. Display 19.12 illustrates how to create a new table and insert three rows using the `CREATE TABLE` and `INSERT` commands. The result is identical to the `names` table in Display 19.10. Note that the program should only be run once. If you attempt to run it a second time, the program will throw an exception when executing the `CREATE TABLE` command, because it is invalid to create a new table that matches an existing name.

Common SQL Statements

SQL Statements are constructed as strings and passed to JDBC. The syntax and examples for the `CREATE TABLE`, `INSERT`, `UPDATE`, and `SELECT` statements follow.

SYNTAX

`CREATE TABLE`	Create a new table named `newtable` with fields `field1`, `field2`, etc. Data types are similar to Java and include: `int`, `bigint`, `float`, `double`, and `var(size)` which is equivalent to a `String` of maximum length `size`.	`CREATE TABLE newtable (field1 datatype, field2 datatype, ...)`
`INSERT`	Insert a new row into the table `tableName` where `field1` has the value `field1Value`, `field2` has the value `field2Value`, etc. The data types for the values must match those for the corresponding fields when the table was created. String values should be enclosed in single quotes.	`INSERT INTO tableName VALUES (field1Value, field2Value, ...)`
`UPDATE`	Change the specified fields to the new values for any rows that match the `WHERE` clause. `Op` is a comparison operator such as =, <> (not equal to), <, >, etc.	`UPDATE tableNameSET field1 = newValue, field2 = newValue, ...WHERE fieldName Op someValue`
`SELECT`	Retrieve the specified fields for the rows that match the `WHERE` clause. The * may be used to retrieve all fields. Omit the `WHERE` clause to retrieve all rows from the table.	`SELECT field1, field2 FROM tableName WHERE fieldname Op someValue`

EXAMPLE

```
CREATE TABLE names(author varchar(50), author_id int, url
       varchar(80))
INSERT INTO names VALUES ('Adams, Douglas', 1, 'http://
       www.douglasadams.com')
UPDATE names SET url = 'http://www.douglasadams.com/dna/bio.html'
       WHERE author_id = 1
SELECT author, author_id, url FROM names
SELECT author, author_id, url FROM names WHERE author_id > 1
```

Display 19.12 **Creating a Derby Embedded Database and Table** (part 1 of 2)

```
import java.sql.Connection;
import java.sql.DriverManager;
import java.sql.SQLException;
import java.sql.Statement;

public class CreateDB
{
     private static final String driver =
       "org.apache.derby.jdbc.EmbeddedDriver";
     private static final String protocol = "jdbc:derby:";
     public static void main(String[] args)
     {
       try

       {
           Class.forName(driver).newInstance();
           System.out.println("Loaded the embedded driver.");
       }
       catch (Exception err)

       {
           System.err.println("Unable to load the embedded driver.");
           err.printStackTrace(System.err);
           System.exit(0);
       }

       String dbName = "BookDatabase";
       Connection conn = null;
       try
       {
           System.out.println(
             "Connecting to and creating the database...");
           conn = DriverManager.getConnection(protocol + dbName +
             ";create=true");
           System.out.println("Database created.");

           Statement s = conn.createStatement();

           s.execute("CREATE TABLE names" +
                "(author varchar(50), author_id " +
                "int, url varchar(80))");
           System.out.println("Created 'names' table.");

           System.out.println("Inserting authors.");
           s.execute("INSERT INTO names " +
             "VALUES ('Adams, Douglas', 1," +
               "'http://www.douglasadams.com')");
```

Load the embedded Derby driver. (points to `try`)

Must catch **ClassNotFoundException, InstantiationException, IllegalAccessException.** (points to `catch (Exception err)`)

Create a statement object to run SQL statements.

Create a table called "names" with three fields, 50 characters for an author and an integer author ID, and 80 characters for a URL, then insert sample data.

(continued)

Display 19.12 **Creating a Derby Embedded Database and Table** (part 2 of 2)

```
            s.execute("INSERT INTO names " +
              "VALUES ('Simmons, Dan', 2, 'http://www.dansimmons.com')");
            s.execute("INSERT INTO names " +
              "VALUES ('Stephenson, Neal', 3, " +
                  "'http://www.nealstephenson.com')");
            System.out.println("Authors inserted.");
             conn.close();
        }
        catch (SQLException err)
        {
             System.err.println("SQL error.");
             err.printStackTrace(System.err);
             System.exit(0);
        }
      }
 }
```

Sample Dialogue

```
Loaded the embedded driver.
Connecting to and creating the database.
Database created.
Created 'names' table.
Inserting authors.
Authors inserted.
```

Display 19.13 shows how to retrieve rows from an existing database and table using the `SELECT` statement. The syntax of the `SELECT` statement is given in the box "Common SQL Statements." The desired fields must be specified or an * placed after the `SELECT` statement to retrieve all fields. After specifying the name of the table, an optional `WHERE` clause may be inserted that contains conditions that must be met, much like the Boolean condition you might place after an if statement. If the `WHERE` clause is left off, then all rows from the table will be retrieved. Otherwise, only those rows that match the conditions of the `WHERE` clause are returned.

A `SELECT` statement can be executed by invoking the `executeQuery( )` method of a `Statement` object. The return value is an object of type `ResultSet`. The `ResultSet` object maintains a cursor to each matching row in the database. Initially, the cursor is positioned before the first row. The `next( )` method is used to advance the cursor to the next row. If there is no next row, then `false` is returned. Otherwise, `true` is returned. Typically, a `while` loop is used to iterate over all rows in the set by looping until the `next( )` method returns `false`. Note that iteration is forward only, similar to reading data from an input stream. Once the cursor is positioned over a row, we can use one of following methods to retrieve data from a specific column in the current row:

```
intVal = resultSet.getInt("name of int field");
lngVal = resultSet.getLong("name of bigint field");
strVal = resultSet.getString("name of varchar field");
dblVal = resultSet.getDouble("name of double field");
fltVal = resultSet.getFloat("name of float field");
```

The program in Display 19.13 can run once the database is created with the program given in Display 19.12. It retrieves and outputs all rows in the table by executing a `SELECT` query with no `WHERE` clause and then retrieves and outputs only those rows with any `author_id` greater than 1. Invoke the `close( )` method to free resources when finished using a `ResultSet` object.

Finally, we can change the contents of an existing row using the SQL `UPDATE` command. In the `UPDATE` command, we specify the table, field(s) to change, new value(s), and a `WHERE` clause to indicate which rows should be changed. If the `WHERE` clause is omitted, then every row in the table is updated. The syntax is described in the box "Common SQL Statements." Display 19.14 shows an example where the `URL` field is changed to a new value entered by the user. The `URL` field is only changed for the row that matches the `author_id` entered by the user.

Display 19.13 **Retrieving Rows with the SELECT Statement** (part 1 of 3)

```
import java.sql.Connection;
import java.sql.DriverManager;
import java.sql.ResultSet;
import java.sql.SQLException;
import java.sql.Statement;

public class ReadDB
{
    private static final String driver =
      "org.apache.derby.jdbc.EmbeddedDriver";
    private static final String protocol = "jdbc:derby:";

    /*
    Outputs the author, ID, and URL of the current
    author in the ResultSet
    */
    public static void displayNameRow(ResultSet rs) throws SQLException

    {
         int id = rs.getInt("author_id");
         String author = rs.getString("author");
         String url = rs.getString("url");
```

The database must be created (Display 19.12) before running the program.

The accessor methods throw the checked exception **`SQLException`**.

(continued)

Display 19.13 **Retrieving Rows with the SELECT Statement** (part 2 of 3)

```
            System.out.println("ID = " + id + ", Author = "
                       + author + ", URL = " + url);
    }

    public static void main(String[] args)
    {
    try
    {
         Class.forName(driver).newInstance();
         System.out.println("Loaded the embedded driver.");
    }
    catch (Exception err)
    {
         System.err.println("Unable to load the embedded driver.");
         err.printStackTrace(System.err);
         System.exit(0);
    }

    String dbName = "BookDatabase";
    Connection conn = null;
    try
    {
         System.out.println("Connecting to the database...");
         conn = DriverManager.getConnection(protocol + dbName);

    System.out.println("Connected.");

    Statement s = conn.createStatement();

    ResultSet rs = null;
    System.out.println("All rows:");
    rs = s.executeQuery("SELECT author, author_id, url FROM names");
    while( rs.next() )
    {
        displayNameRow(rs);
    }
    rs.close();

    System.out.println();
    System.out.println("All rows with an ID > 1:");
    rs = s.executeQuery("SELECT author, author_id, url " +
         "FROM names WHERE author_id > 1");
    while( rs.next() )
    {
        displayNameRow(rs);
    }
```

The text "`create=true;`" has been left off the connection string to connect to an existing database.

Display 19.13 **Retrieving Rows with the SELECT Statement** (part 3 of 3)

```
        rs.close();
        Conn.close();
        }
        catch (SQLException err)
        {
              System.err.println("SQL error.");
              err.printStackTrace(System.err);
              System.exit(0);
              }
        }
    }
```

Sample Dialogue

```
Loaded the embedded driver.
Connecting to the database.
Connected.
All rows:
ID = 1, Author = Adams, Douglas, URL = http://www.douglasadams.com
ID = 2, Author = Simmons, Dan, URL = http://www.dansimmons.com
ID = 3, Author = Stephenson, Neal, URL = http://www.nealstephenson.com

All rows with an ID > 1:
ID = 2, Author = Simmons, Dan, URL = http://www.dansimmons.com
ID = 3, Author = Stephenson, Neal, URL = http://www.nealstephenson.com
```

Display 19.14 **Updating Rows with the UPDATE Statement** (part 1 of 3)

```
import java.sql.Connection;
import java.sql.DriverManager;
import java.sql.ResultSet;
import java.sql.SQLException;
import java.sql.Statement;
import java.util.Scanner;

public class UpdateDB
{
    private static final String driver =
        "org.apache.derby.jdbc.EmbeddedDriver";
    private static final String protocol = "jdbc:derby:";
```

The database must be created (Display 19.12) before running this program. Use the program in Display 19.13 to view the changes made by this program.

(continued)

Display 19.14 **Updating Rows with the `UPDATE` Statement** (part 2 of 3)

```
    public static void main(String[] args)
    {
        try
        {
            Class.forName(driver).newInstance();
            System.out.println("Loaded the embedded driver.");
        }
        catch (Exception err)
        {
            System.err.println("Unable to load the embedded
            driver.");
         err.printStackTrace(System.err);
         System.exit(0);
        }
        String dbName = "BookDatabase";
        Connection conn = null;
        try
        {
           System.out.println("Connecting to the database...");
           conn = DriverManager.getConnection(protocol + dbName);
           System.out.println("Connected.");

           System.out.println(
               "Enter the ID number of the author to change:");
           Scanner scan = new Scanner(System.in);
           int id = scan.nextInt();
           scan.nextLine();
           System.out.println("Enter the new URL for this author.");
           String newURL = scan.nextLine();

           Statement s = conn.createStatement();
           s.execute("UPDATE names " +
                   "SET URL = '" + newURL + "' WHERE author_id = "
                   + id);
           System.out.println("URL changed to " + newURL);
           conn.close();
        }
        catch (SQLException err)
        {
           System.err.println("SQL error.");
           err.printStackTrace(System.err);
           System.exit(0);
        }
    }
}
```

Skips the newline left after `nextInt()`.

Display 19.14 Updating Rows with the `UPDATE` Statement (part 3 of 3)

Sample Dialogue

```
Loaded the embedded driver.
Connecting to the database...
Connected.
Enter the ID number of the author to change:
2
Enter the new URL for this author:
http://www.dansimmons.com/about/bio.htm
URL changed to http://www.dansimmons.com/about/bio.htm
```

There is much more to SQL and JDBC than what we have discussed here. However, this section should give you a good idea about how to integrate SQL into a Java application and provide a starting point to learn more.

MyProgrammingLab™

Self-Test Exercises

9. Give the SQL `SELECT` command to produce a table of book titles with corresponding author and author ID from the table `Result` in Display 19.11 and one of the tables in Display 19.10. Follow the example of the SQL command in the text used to produce the `Result` table.

10. What is a connection string?

11. What is the difference between the `execute( )` and `executeQuery( )` methods of the JDBC `Statement` class?

12. Give the SQL statement to create the `BooksAuthors` table shown in Display 19.10.

13. Give the SQL statement to insert the four entries shown in Display 19.10 into the `BooksAuthors` table.

19.5 Web Programming with Java Server Pages

Everything is connected... no one thing can change by itself.

PAUL HAWKEN

Up to this point, we have used Java to create stand-alone applications. However, Java is also used to create interactive websites. In this section, we briefly introduce ways that Java can be used on the Web with an emphasis on Java Server Pages. This section requires a basic understanding of HTML. An introduction to HTML is given in Chapter 20, which is included on the website with this book. This section is not a complete enough introduction to allow you to immediately start writing Java Web applications. The intent is to introduce the major concepts behind Java Server Pages so you can learn what kinds of things are possible should you wish to learn more with a book or other resource dedicated to the topic.

Applets, Servlets, and Java Server Pages

When you instruct your Web browser to view a page from a Web server on the Internet, your Web browser requests the page from the Web server, the Web server processes the request (which may involve reading the requested page from a file on the hard drive), and then the Web server sends the requested page to your Web browser. Your Web browser formats, or renders, the received data to fit on your computer screen. This interaction is a specific case of the client/server model described in Section 19.2. Your Web browser is the client program, your computer is the client computer, the remote website is the server computer (e.g., http://www.remotesite.com), and the Web server software running on the remote website is the server program.

In the context of a Web application, the client/server model is important because Java code can run in two places: on the client or on the server. There are trade-offs to both approaches. Server-based programs have easy access to information that resides on the server, such as customer orders or inventory data. Because all of the computation is done on the server and results are transmitted to the client as HTML, a client does not need a powerful computer to run a server-based program. On the other hand, a client-based program may require a more powerful client computer, because all computation is performed locally. However, richer interaction is possible, because the client program has access to local resources, such as the graphics display (e.g., perhaps using Swing) or the operating system. Many systems today are constructed using code that runs on both the client and the server to reap the benefit of both approaches.

Java applet

Java servlet

Java Server Pages

Web applications built with Java include **Java applets**, **Java servlets**, and **Java Server Pages (JSP)**. Java applets run on the client computer and are discussed in Chapter 20. JavaScript, which is a different language than Java despite its similar name, also runs on the client computer as part of the Web browser. Java servlets and Java Server Pages run on the server. In this chapter, we focus primarily on Java Server Pages, which are a dynamic version of Java servlets. Servlets must be compiled before they can run, just like a normal Java program. In contrast, JSP code is embedded with

Display 19.15 **Running a Java Applet**

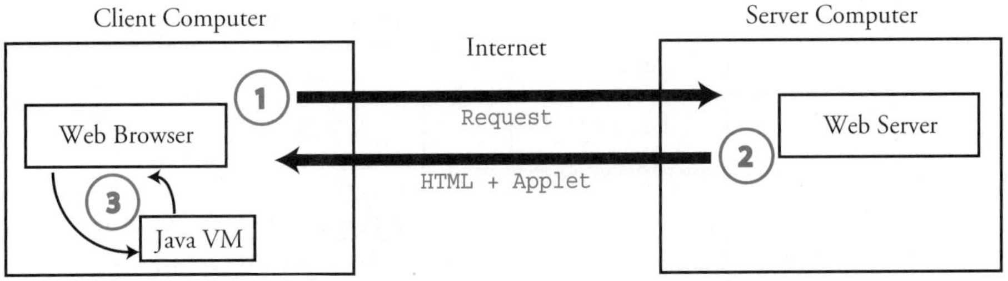

1 The client's Web browser sends a request to the server for a Web page with a Java applet.

2 The server sends the HTML for the Web page and applet class files to the client.

3 The client runs the applet using the Java Virtual Machine and displays its output in the Web browser.

Display 19.16 **Running a Java Servlet**

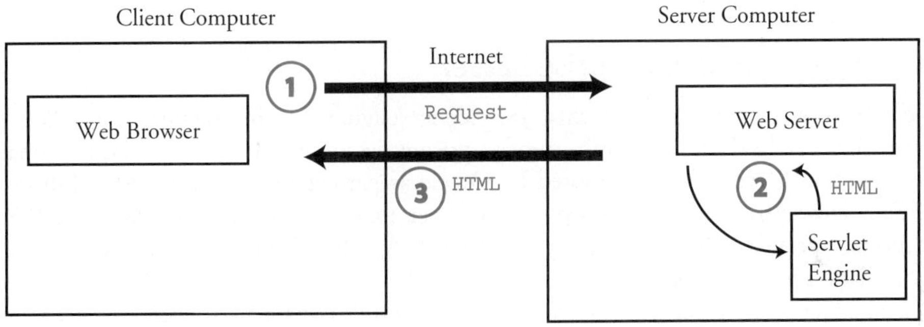

1 The client's Web browser sends a request to the server for a Web page that runs a Java servlet.

2 The Web server instructs the servlet engine to execute the requested servlet, which consists of running precompiled Java code. The servlet outputs HTML that is returned to the Web server.

3 The Web server sends the servlet's HTML to the client's Web browser to be displayed.

the corresponding HTML and is compiled "on the fly" into a servlet when the page is requested. This flexibility can make it easier to develop Web applications using JSP than with Java servlets. Displays 19.15, 19.16, and 19.17 illustrate the differences for a website that runs an applet, servlet, or JSP.

Display 19.17 **Running a Java Server Page (JSP) Program**

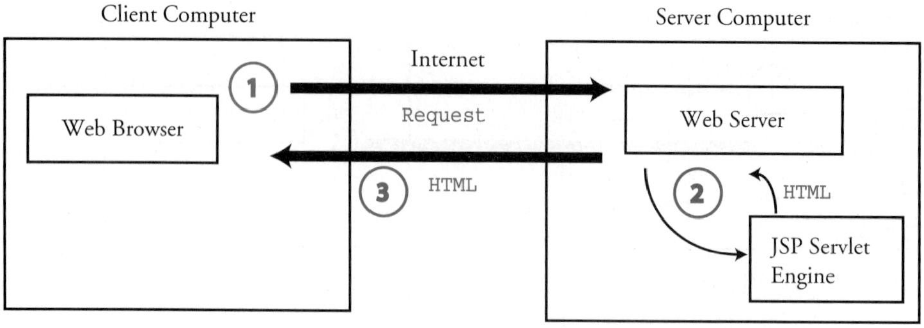

(1) The client's Web browser sends a request to the server for a Web page that contains JSP code.

(2) The JSP servlet engine dynamically compiles the JSP source code into a Java servlet if a current, compiled servlet doesn't exist.
The servlet runs and outputs HTML that is returned to the Web server.

(3) The Web server sends the servlet's HTML to the client's Web browser to be displayed.

Oracle GlassFish Enterprise Server

JSP requires a Web server with a JSP servlet engine. In this section, we will use the Oracle GlassFish Enterprise Server, previously known as the Sun Java System Application Server. It is distributed by Oracle as part of the Java Enterprise Edition SDK. However, you may use any Web server that supports Java servlets and JSP. Another popular choice is the open source Apache Tomcat server. Follow the installation instructions that come with the server that you select.

The GlassFish server will ask you to select an administrator username and password during the installation procedure. It will also ask you for a location on the hard drive to place the server files. We will refer to the pathname you select as <glassfish_home>. On a Windows machine, this may default to C:\Sun\SDK. After the installation is complete, start the GlassFish Web service. If the installation is successful, then you should be able to see the administrator's page by opening http://localhost:4848 in your Web browser. The default URL for accessing applications is http://localhost:8080. Substitute localhost with the name of the machine if you are using a remote server.

At this point, you can test your server by creating or copying an HTML file into <glassfish_home>\domains\domain1\docroot and opening it with your Web browser. For example, if you create an HTML file named test.html in this directory, then you should be able to access it with your Web browser by navigating to http://localhost:8080/test.html. If you cannot read the page, check your configuration settings. To run JSP programs, your Web browser must open the page through the GlassFish Web server and not directly load the page from the HTML file on the disk drive.

HTML Forms—the Common Gateway Interface

HTML Form

The HTML form is a common mechanism for users to input data to Web applications. If you have ever visited a Web page in which you enter data using textboxes and buttons, then you have used an HTML form. In this section, we introduce just a handful of tags that can be used in an HTML form and then show how submitted data can be processed by a JSP program. The information you enter into an HTML form is transmitted to the Web server using a protocol called the **Common Gateway Interface (CGI)**. The server processes the information using a program such as a Java servlet and then returns the results back to the user.

Common Gateway Interface

An HTML form is created with the `<form>`tag. The syntax is as follows:

```
<FORM ACTION="Path_To_CGI_Program" METHOD="GET or POST">
      Form_Elements
</FORM>
```

The `ACTION` string identifies the program that will process the form input. In our case, this will consist of a JSP program. The `METHOD` string specifies how data will be sent to the server and is either `GET` or `POST`. `GET` means that the data will be sent as part of the URL while `POST` means that the data will be sent as part of the data and will not be visible in the URL.

Elements that can be inserted inside the form include selection lists, textboxes, checkboxes, radio buttons, and several other common GUI widgets. In this section, we will only introduce textboxes and submission buttons. A textbox has the following syntax:

```
<INPUT TYPE="TEXT" NAME="Textbox_Name" VALUE="Default_Text"
SIZE="Length_In._Characters"
MAXLENGTH="Maximum_Number_Of_Allowable_Characters">
```

All of the attributes are optional except for the input type. However, the name of the textbox will be required to retrieve the textbox's value from JSP. If you would like a default value to be entered in the textbox, you can put it in the `VALUE` field or leave it blank for no text. The `SIZE` field controls the length of the textbox while `MAXLENGTH` limits the number of characters that may be entered.

The submission button has the following syntax:

```
<INPUT TYPE="SUBMIT" NAME="Name" VALUE="Button_Text">
```

The `NAME` field can be used to identify the submission button in case there are multiple submission buttons and you wish to identify which one was clicked. `VALUE` determines what text is placed in the button's label.

A sample form with two text fields and a submission button is shown in Display 19.18. The form, when opened in a Web browser, is shown in Display 19.19. It asks the user to enter an Author ID and a new URL with the intent of changing the URL to the submitted value for the specified Author ID. Because we have not created a JSP program that processes the form, the Web browser will display an error message if the Submit button is clicked. We will write the JSP program in the next subsection.

Display 19.18 An HTML Form Document

```
<html>
<head>
<title>Change Author's URL</title>
</head>

<body>
<h1>Change Author's URL</h1>
<p>
Enter the ID of the author you would like to change
along with the new URL.
</p>

<form ACTION = "EditURL.jsp" METHOD = POST>

Author ID:
<input TYPE = "TEXT" NAME = "AuthorID"
 VALUE = "" SIZE = "4" MAXLENGTH = "4">

<br/>
New URL:
<input TYPE = "TEXT" NAME = "URL"
 VALUE = "http://" SIZE = "40" MAXLENGTH = "200">

<p>
INPUT TYPE="SUBMIT" VALUE="Submit">

</p>
</form>

</body>
</html>
```

Invokes the JSP program named `EditURL.jsp`*. If this program does not exist, you will see an error message upon clicking the Submit button.* `EditURL.jsp` *is given in the next subsection.*

Creates a textbox named `AuthorID` *that is empty, displays four characters at once, and accepts at most, four characters.*

Creates a textbox named `URL` *that by default contains* `"http://"`*, displays 40 characters at once, and accepts at most 200 characters.*

Creates a Submit button.

Display 19.19 Browser View of Display 19.18

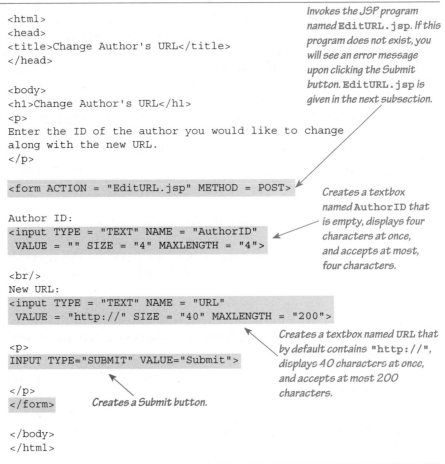

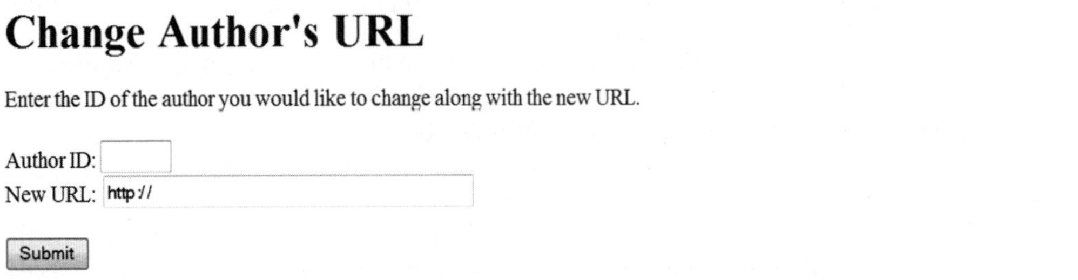
Change Author's URL
Enter the ID of the author you would like to change along with the new URL.
Author ID:
New URL:
http://
Submit

JSP Declarations, Expressions, Scriptlets, and Directives

A JSP Web page is created the same way you make an HTML file, except JSP code is added along with the HTML code. Additionally, instead of naming the file with an extension of `.HTM or .HTML`, the extension is `.JSP`. The file should be placed in the root folder of your Web server so it can be accessed by and processed through the Web server.

JSP elements

The JSP elements we will briefly discuss are **declarations**, **expressions**, **scriptlets**, and **directives**. All of these elements are identified by their own tags. The **declarations** tag allows us to define variables and methods. The variables and methods are accessible from any scriptlets and expressions on the same page. Variable declarations are compiled as instance variables for a class that corresponds to the JSP page. Declarations are defined with the syntax

declaration

```
<%!
   Declarations
%>
```

For example, the following defines an instance variable named `count` and a method named `incrementCount` that increments the `count` variable:

```
<%!
   private int count = 0;

   private void incrementCount()
   {
      count++;
   }
%>
```

expression

We can access variables defined in declarations with **expression**. The syntax to embed an expression is as follows:

```
<%=
   Expression
%>
```

Expressions are embedded directly into the HTML. The Web browser will display the value of the expression in place of the tag. For example, we can output the value of the `count` variable in bold type with the following piece of HTML:

```
The value of count is <b> <%= count %> </b>
```

scriptlet

Blocks of Java code can be embedded in a **scriptlet**. The syntax for a scriptlet is as follows:

```
<%
   Java code
%>
```

If you wish to output HTML within a scriptlet, then this is done using `out.println()`, which is used in the same manner as `System.out.println( )`. The variable `out` is already defined for us and is of type `javax.servlet.jsp.JspWriter`. Also note that

`System.out.println( )` will output to the console, which is useful for debugging purposes, while `out.println( )` will output to the browser. The following scriptlet invokes the `incrementCount( )` method and then outputs the value in `count`:

```
<%
   out.println("The counter's value is " + count + "<br />");
   incrementCount();
%>
```

Display 19.20 is a JSP page with a declaration, expression, and scriptlet that outputs text inside a header tag from levels 1 to 6. The identifier `LASTLEVEL` is declared as the last heading level that is to be displayed. `LASTLEVEL` is modified by `static final`, because it is intended as a constant. A loop inside the scriptlet outputs sample text for each level. The HTML that is generated by the JSP page is shown in Display 19.21, and the browser view is shown in Display 19.22.

Display 19.20 JSP Code to Display Heading Levels

```
<html>
<title>
Displaying Heading Tags with JSP
</title>

<body>
<%!
     private static final int LASTLEVEL = 6;
%>

<p>
This page uses JSP to display Heading Tags from
Level 1 to Level <%= LASTLEVEL %>
</p>

<%
     int i;
     for (i = 1; i <= LASTLEVEL; i++)
     {
          out.println("<H" + i + ">" +
            "This text is in Heading Level " + i +
            "</H" + i + ">");
     }
%>

</body>
</html>
```

JSP declaration.

JSP expression that evaluates to the value 6.

JSP scriptlet that contains a block of Java code.

Display 19.21 HTML Generated by JSP in Display 19.20

```
<html>
<title>
Displaying Heading Tags with JSP
</title>

<body>

<p>
This page uses JSP to display Heading Tags from
Level 1 to Level 6
</p>

<H1>This text is in Heading Level 1</H1>
<H2>This text is in Heading Level 2</H2>
<H3>This text is in Heading Level 3</H3>
<H4>This text is in Heading Level 4</H4>
<H5>This text is in Heading Level 5</H5>
<H6>This text is in Heading Level 6</H6>

</body>
</html>
```

Display 19.22 Browser View of Display 19.21

This page uses JSP to display Heading Tags from Level 1 to Level 6

This text is in Heading Level 1

This text is in Heading Level 2

This text is in Heading Level 3

This text is in Heading Level 4

This text is in Heading Level 5

This text is in Heading Level 6

To make a JSP page more interactive, we can read and process the data entered in an HTML form. One way to read these values is to call the `request.getParameter` method. This method takes a `String` parameter as input that identifies the name of an HTML form element and returns the value entered by the user for that element on the form. For example, if there is a textbox named `AuthorID`, then we can retrieve the value entered in that textbox with the following scriptlet code:

```
String value = request.getParameter("AuthorID");
```

If the user leaves the field blank, then `getParameter` returns an empty string. A simple example is given in Display 19.23. This JSP program echoes back the data entered by the user in Display 19.18. The name of the JSP file must match the value supplied for the `ACTION` tag of the form. In this case, the name is `EditURL.jsp`.

Display 19.23 Echoing Values Submitted by a Browser Viewing Display 19.18

```
<html>
<title>Edit URL: Echo submitted values</title>
<body>
<h2>Edit URL>/h2>

<p>
This version of EditURL.jsp simply echoes back to the
user the values that were entered in the textboxes.
</p>

<%
   String url = request.getParameter("URL");
   String stringID = request.getParameter("AuthorID");
   int author_id = Integer.parseInt(stringID);
   out.println("The submitted author ID is: " + author_id);
   out.println("<br/>");
   out.println("The submitted URL is: " + url);
%>
</body>
</html>
```

This program should be saved as `EditURL.jsp` and must match the value in the `ACTION` field of the HTML form tag.

The `getParameter` method calls return as Strings the values entered by the user in the `URL` and `AuthorID` textboxes from Display 19.18.

Sample Dialogue

Submitted on the Web browser when viewing Display 19.18.

```
Author ID:
2
New URL:
http://www.dansimmons.com/about/bio.htm

Edit URL

This version of EditURL.jsp simply echoes back to the user the
values that were entered in the textboxes.

The submitted author ID is: 2
The submitted URL is:
http://www.dansimmons.com/about/bio.htm
```

Web browser display after clicking Submit.

directive

Finally, let us introduce one more JSP tag, the **directive**. In general terms, directives instruct the compiler how to process a JSP program. Examples include the definition of our own tags, including the source code of other files, and importing packages. The syntax for directives is as follows:

```
<%@
  Directives
%>
```

page import

In this introduction, we will cover only the **page import** directive. The purpose of this directive is the same as the normal Java `import` statement, but the syntax is slightly different. First, we identify the directive and then specify the packages to import inside a string. Multiple packages are separated by a comma, e.g.,

```
<%@
   page import="java.util.*,java.sql.*"
%>
```

A JSP program that uses Derby to create an embedded database is shown in Display 19.24. The page import directive is used to import the necessary SQL packages. The program in Display 19.24 is almost identical to the stand-alone program in Display 19.12, except all of the code has been moved into a scriptlet. If the JSP program is in a file named `CreateDB.jsp`, then it would be invoked by navigating to `http://localhost:8080/CreateDB.jsp`. The database files on a GlassFish server will be created in `<glassfish_home>\domains\domain1\config` if you do not specify a pathname. If you run the program more than once, then it will throw an exception the second time, because the database table `names` already exists and cannot be created again. If you wish to start over with a new database, then you can delete the `BookDatabase` directory in the `<glassfish_home>\domains\domain1\config` directory.

Display 19.24 **JSP Program to Create a Derby Database and Table** (part 1 of 3)

```
<%@ page import="java.sql.*" %>
<html>
<title>Create New Database</title>
<body>
<H2>Create New Database</h2>

<p>
This program creates a new Derby database named 'BookDatabase'
and puts sample data into the 'person' table.
</p>

<%
     String driver = "org.apache.derby.jdbc.EmbeddedDriver";
     String protocol = "jdbc:derby:";
```

Directive to import the Java SQL packages.

Refer to Display 19.12 for an explanation of the database code in this scriptlet.

(continued)

Display 19.24 JSP Program to Create a Derby Database and Table (part 2 of 3)

```
        try
        {
             Class.forName(driver).newInstance();
             out.println("Loaded the embedded driver.<br>");
        }
        catch (Exception err)
        {
             out.println(
               "Unable to load the embedded driver.</body></html>");
            return;
   }
String dbName = "BookDatabase";
Connection conn = null;
try
{
             out.println(
               "Connecting to and creating the database...<br />");
             conn = DriverManager.getConnection(protocol + dbName +
                                                      ";create=true");
             out.println("Connected.<br />");

       Statement s = conn.createStatement();

       s.execute("CREATE TABLE names" +
             "(author varchar(50), author_id int, url varchar(80))");
       out.println("Created 'names' table.<br />");

       out.println("Inserting authors.<br />");
       s.execute("INSERT INTO names " +
            "VALUES ('Adams, Douglas', 1, 'http://www.douglasadams.com')");
       s.execute("INSERT INTO names " +
            "VALUES ('Simmons, Dan', 2, 'http://www.dansimmons.com')");
       s.execute("INSERT INTO names " +
            "VALUES ('Stephenson, Neal', 3," +
            "'http://www.nealstephenson.com')");
       out.println("Authors inserted.<br />");

       conn.close();
      }
      catch (Exception err)
      {
        out.println("SQL error.<br />");
      }
%>
</body>
</html>
```

A `return` statement will terminate the JSP program.

Display 19.24 **JSP Program to Create a Derby Database and Table** (part 3 of 3)

Sample Dialogue

```
Create New Database

This program creates a new Derby database named 'BookDatabase'
and puts sample data into the 'names' table.

Loaded the embedded driver.
Connecting to and creating the database...
Connected.
Created 'names' table.
Inserting authors.
Authors inserted.
```

In this second part, to complete our example, let us modify the `EditURL.jsp` program from Display 19.23 to make it change the contents of the database instead of echoing back values submitted by the HTML form. Our new program will require running the program in Display 19.24 once in order to create and initialize the database. Once this is done, you can open the HTML form in Display 19.18 in a Web browser, which prompts the user to submit a new URL for an author ID, and then the new URL will be updated in the database by the program in Display 19.25. The program in Display 19.25 is a combination of Display 19.14 (updating a Derby database) and Display 19.23 (echoing values submitted by a Web browser). Instead of prompting the user to input an author ID and new URL from the console as in Display 19.14, these values are submitted to the JSP program by the HTML form in Display 19.18. The JSP program then updates the database to the submitted values in the same manner as the program in Display 19.14.

Display 19.25 **JSP Program to Update Database Entries Submitted by a Browser Viewing Display 19.18** (part 1 of 3)

```
<%@ page import="java.sql.*" %>
<html>
<title>Edit URL: Update new URL in a database</title>
<body>
<h2>Edit URL</h2>

<p>
This version of EditURL.jsp updates the URL field
of a Derby database to the submitted value for the
row with a matching Author ID.
</p>

<%
String newURL = request.getParameter("URL");
String stringID = request.getParameter("AuthorID");
int author_id = Integer.parseInt(stringID);
```

This program should be saved as `EditURL.jsp` *and must match the value in the* `ACTION` *field of the HTML form tag.*

The `getParameter` *method calls return as Strings the values entered by the user in the* `URL` *and* `AuthorID` *textboxes from Display 19.18.*

(continued)

Display 19.25 **JSP Program to Update Database Entries Submitted by a Browser Viewing Display 19.18** (part 2 of 3)

```
String driver = "org.apache.derby.jdbc.EmbeddedDriver";
String protocol = "jdbc:derby:";
try
{
  Class.forName(driver).newInstance();
    out.println("Loaded the embedded driver.<br>");
}
catch (Exception err)
{
   out.println("Unable to load the embedded driver.</body></html>");
   return;
}

String dbName = "BookDatabase";
Connection conn = null;
try
{
   out.println("Connecting to and creating the database...<br />");
       conn = DriverManager.getConnection(protocol + dbName +
                                              ";create=true");
   out.println("Connected.<br />");

   Statement s = conn.createStatement();
   s.execute("UPDATE names " +
        "SET URL = '" + newURL + "' WHERE author_id = " + author_id);
   out.println("<br/><b>URL changed to " + newURL +
        "for Author ID = " + author_id + "</b><br />");

   out.println("<br />Displaying all rows:<br />");
   ResultSet rs = null;
   rs = s.executeQuery("SELECT author, author_id, url FROM names");
   out.println("<ol>");
   while( rs.next() )
   {
        int id = rs.getInt("author_id");
        String author = rs.getString("author");
        String url = rs.getString("url");
        out.println("<li>ID = " + id + ", Author = "
        + author + ", URL = " + url + "</li>");
   }
   out.println("</ol>");
   rs.close();

        conn.close();
 }
   catch (Exception err)
   {
        out.println("SQL error.<br />");
   }
```

Refer to Displays 19.13 and 19.14 for an explanation of the database code in this scriptlet.

The URL in the database is changed to the submitted value if the Author IDs match.

This loop outputs all rows in the database inside a numbered list.

Display 19.25 **JSP Program to Update Database Entries Submitted by a Browser Viewing Display 19.18** (part 3 of 3)

```
%>
</body>
</html>
```

Sample Dialogue *Submitted on the Web browser when viewing Display 19.18.*

```
Author ID:
2
New URL:
http://www.dansimmons.com/about/bio.htm
```

Web browser display after clicking Submit.

```
Edit URL

This version of EditURL.jsp updates the URL field of a Derby database to
the submitted value for the row with a matching Author ID.

Loaded the embedded driver.
Connecting to and creating the database...
Connected.

URL changed to http://www.dansimmons.com/about/bio.htm for Author ID = 2

Displaying all rows:

1. ID = 1, Author = Adams, Douglas, URL = http://www.douglasadams.com
2. ID = 2, Author = Simmons, Dan, URL = http://www.dansimmons.com/about/
   bio.htm
3. ID = 3, Author = Stephenson, Neal, URL = http://www.nealstephenson.com
```

Although we have covered enough JSP to write fairly sophisticated programs, there is much more that we have not discussed. For example, beans can be used as a convenient way to encapsulate data submitted from a HTML form. Additionally, we have not covered sessions, tag libraries, security, and numerous other topics that are important in the construction of JSP pages. In particular, the technique of generating SQL read and write queries based on user-entered values is not secure—a malicious user could enter values that potentially run arbitrary SQL Statements. A more secure solution is to use a precompiled SQL statement that is supported by the `java.sql.PreparedStatement` class. Refer to a textbook dedicated to JSP or database programming to learn more.

MyProgrammingLab™

Self-Test Exercises

14. What is a major difference between a website implemented with a Java applet and a website implemented with Java Server Pages?

15. Give the HTML to create a form with two elements: a textbox named `FirstName` that holds a maximum of 50 characters, and a Submit button. The form should submit its data to a JSP program called `ProcessName.jsp` using the `POST` method.

16. Identify the following JSP tags: `<% %>, <%@ %>, <%! %>, <%= %>`

17. Write a JSP scriptlet that handles the form created in Self-Test Exercise 13 and outputs the name in a bold heading font.

Chapter Summary

- A *thread* is a separate computation process. A Java program can have multiple threads.
- Use the class `Thread` to produce multiple threads.
- The static method `Thread.sleep` inserts a pause into the thread in which it is invoked.
- A thread's `join()` method is used to wait for threads to finish. The `synchronized` keyword restricts a critical region of code to a single thread only.
- A *socket* refers to an endpoint that connects two programs over a network.
- *TCP* refers to a reliable, streaming protocol for network communication. It ensures that data is received in the same order it was sent.
- *JavaBeans* refers to a framework for producing Java components that are easy to combine with other JavaBean components to produce new applications.
- A *relational database* organizes data in related tables. Records are stored as rows in a table. The fields for each record are stored as columns in a table.
- *Java DB* or *Derby* is a database that runs in client/server or embedded mode.
- JDBC allows you to insert SQL commands into your Java code to access and manipulate databases.
- The SQL `SELECT, UPDATE, CREATE TABLE`, and `INSERT` commands allow data to be retrieved, modified, created, or inserted into a database.
- *Java Server Pages (JSP)* refers to a framework that allows a programmer to create Web-based Java applications that run on the server. JSP requires a Web server capable of compiling and running Java servlets and JSP.

- HTML forms are a common mechanism to input user-specified data into a JSP application.
- Java code is added to a JSP page through *directive*, *expression*, *declaration*, and *scriptlet* tags.

Answers to Self-Test Exercises

1. The invocation of `Thread.sleep` takes place inside a thread. Every action in Java takes place inside some thread. Any action performed by a method invocation in a specific thread takes place in that thread. Even if it does not know where it is, a method's action takes place where the method invocation is; if you are lost and yell out, you might not know where you are but the yell would still be wherever it is you are.
2. The class `Packer` inherits the method `start` from the base class `Thread` and is not overridden. The method `start` invokes the method `run`, but when `start` is invoked by an object of the class `Packer`, it is the definition of `run` that is given in the class `Packer` that is used, not the definition of `run` given in the definition of `Thread`. That is exactly what is meant by *late binding* or *polymorphism.*
3. In this program, the code that runs in each thread is fairly short. As a result, there is a good chance that each thread runs to completion before the next thread begins. The `sleep` method forces a thread to suspend and another thread to begin. This increases the likelihood that there will be contention for the shared variable and a race condition.
4. The code synchronizes access to the shared variable but the `main` method does not wait for all threads to finish before printing out the value of the shared variable. Thus, it is possible that `main` will output a premature value of `counter` if `main` completes before any one of the threads that it creates. To correct this problem, invoke the `join()` method on each thread before outputting counter as illustrated in Display 19.5.
5. A port is used to identify which program should receive data from the network. One program only may be bound to a specific port.
6. Each client connection may run in its own thread, requiring a large amount of memory, disk space, or processor time.
7. *Persistence* means that a component's state can be saved so that the next time it is used it remembers what state it was in.
8. The same one that is used for Swing and AWT.
9. ```
   SELECT Result.Title, Names.Author, Result.Author_ID
   FROM Result, Names
   WHERE Result.Author_ID = Names.Author_ID
   ```
10. A connection string is used to connect to (and possibly create) a database via JDBC. The protocol, database name, and other parameters (such as the username, password, or flag to create a new database) are specified in the connection string.
11. The `execute` method can be used to execute any SQL statement, but it is generally used for SQL commands where return values are not needed. It returns a Boolean
   ```

value. The executeQuery method returns a ResultSet object that contains the rows matching a query.

12.
```
CREATE TABLE BooksAuthors (ISBN varchar(15), author_id int)
```

13.
```
INSERT INTO BooksAuthors VALUES('0-553-38095-8',3)
INSERT INTO BooksAuthors VALUES('0-553-57294-6',2)
INSERT INTO BooksAuthors VALUES('0-671-46149-4',1)
INSERT INTO BooksAuthors VALUES('0-553-57928-9',2)
```

14. A java applet is downloaded and executed on the client, while a JSP program is written alongside HTML and runs on the server.

15.
```
<html>
<head>
<title>Submit Firstname</title>
</head>

<body>
<form ACTION = "ProcessName.jsp" METHOD = POST>
First Name:
<input TYPE = "TEXT" NAME = "FirstName" VALUE = "" MAXLENGTH = "50">
<input TYPE="SUBMIT" VALUE="Submit">
</form>
</body>
</html>
```

16. <% %> is a scriptlet, <%@ %> is a directive, <%! %> is a declaration, <%= %> is an expression.

17.
```
<%
String firstName = request.getParameter("FirstName");
out.println("<h1><b>" + firstName + "</b></h1>");
%>
```

Programming Projects

Visit www.myprogramminglab.com to complete select exercises online and get instant feedback.

1. Write a GUI program that uses the methods in the Graphics class together with threads to draw a smiley face, wait two seconds, draw a frowny face, wait two seconds, and repeat starting with the smiley face. A separate thread should be started to implement the two-second timer. The application should be responsive and exit immediately if the user decides to close the window.
2. Create a class named TimerAlarm that extends Thread and implements a timer. Do not use the built-in Timer class for this exercise. Your class constructor should take as input an integer named t representing time in milliseconds and an interface object named obj that defines a method named alarmAction( ). You will need to define this interface. Every t milliseconds the class should invoke method obj.alarmAction( ). Add pause( ) and play( ) methods that disable and enable

the invocation of alarmAction( ). Test your class with code that increments and prints out a counter.

VideoNote
Solution to Programming Project 19.3

3. Write a GUI program that animates a four-colored "beach ball" in place by rotating the colors. The beach ball can be drawn as a solid circle with four different colors in each of the four quadrants of the circle. Use a thread to rotate the colors every quarter second.
4. Modify the GUI in Display 19.2 so that the circles are alternately red, white, and blue, and so that they fill the area from bottom to top instead of top to bottom.
5. Produce a GUI similar to the one in Display 19.2 except that instead of filling an area with circles, it launches a ball (which is just a circle) and the ball bounces around inside a rectangle. You can create the illusion of a moving ball by repeatedly erasing the ball and redrawing it at a location a little farther along its path. Look up the method setXORMode in the class Graphics. It will take care of the erasing.
6. This project shows how to create a simple Web server. Create a server program that listens on port 8000. When a client connects to the server, the program should send the following data to the client,

```
"HTTP/1.0 200 OK\n\n" + body
```

where body is the String "<HTML><TITLE>Java Server</TITLE>This web page was sent by our simple <B>Java Server</B></HTML>". If you know HTML, feel free to insert your own content. The header line identifies the message as part of the HTTP protocol that is used to transmit Web pages.

When the server is running, you should be able to start a Web browser and navigate to your machine on port 8000 and view the message. For example, if the server is running on your local machine, you could point your Web browser to http://localhost:8000 and the message in body should be displayed.

7. Modify the server from Programming Project 19.6 so that the content for body is read from a file on the local hard drive instead of hard-coded into the program. This file should contain the HTML string from Programming Project 19.6. In addition, modify the server so that a new thread is created for each connection. Test the server by starting up two or more Web browsers and navigate to your site. Each browser should display the message.
8. Create a threaded chat server and a corresponding chat client. Using the port of your choice, create a server that starts a new thread for every client that connects to it. Every message that the server receives from a client should be broadcast back to all other clients. The chat client should allow the user to type in a string of text and have it sent to the server upon pressing enter. Use threads on the client so messages can be retrieved from the server and displayed even while the user is typing. Test your server by connecting to it with multiple clients and verifying that messages are transmitted back and forth.

9. The program in Display 19.12 creates a database with the `Names` table from Display 19.10. Modify this program so it also creates the `Titles` and `BooksAuthors` tables with identical data entries as shown in Display 19.10. Next, create a separate program that prompts the user to input the name of an author and then outputs all book titles written by that author.

10. Create an HTML form that prompts the user to enter a temperature in Fahrenheit. When the form is submitted, a JSP Web page should run that displays the temperature converted to Celsius. The temperature in Celsius is 5 * (Fahrenheit – 32) / 9.

VideoNote **Solution to Programming Project 19.11**

11. Create an HTML form that serves as a random baby name generator. The form should prompt the user to enter a last name. When the form is submitted, a JSP Web page should run that randomly picks the first name of a boy and the first name of a girl and then outputs the random first names coupled with the entered last name. For example, if the last name entered is "Savitch" and if the JSP program randomly selects "Emma" as the girl name and "Homer" as the boy name, then the output would be

```
If your baby is a boy, consider the name Homer Savitch.
If your baby is a girl, consider the name Emma Savitch.
```

The boy and girl names should be randomly selected from the files `boynames.txt` and `girlnames.txt` that are included in the source code on the website for this book.

These files contain the 1,000 most popular boy and girl names in the United States for the year 2003 as compiled by the Social Security Administration.

12. Recreate Programming Project 19.9 as JSP pages instead of as a stand-alone application. One JSP page should create the database, tables, and populate the tables with data. Create an HTML form that allows the user to enter the name of an author. The form should invoke another JSP page that displays all titles written by the specified author that are stored in the database.

13. This program simulates what might happen if two people who share the same bank account happen to make a simultaneous deposit or withdrawal and the bank does not account for race conditions by recreating the situation described in Displays 19.4 and 19.5 with a simple `BankAccount` class. The `BankAccount` class should store an account balance and have methods to retrieve the balance, make a deposit, and make a withdrawal. Do not worry about negative balances.

Next, create an array of thousands of threads where each thread has a reference to the same `BankAccount` object. In the `run()` method, even numbered threads deposit one dollar and odd numbered threads withdraw one dollar. If you create an even number of threads, then after all threads are done the account balance should be zero. See if you can find a number of threads so that you consistently end up with a balance that is not zero. If you want to increase the likelihood of a race condition, then make each thread sleep a short random number of milliseconds in the `run()` method.

Add the `synchronized` keyword to fix the problem and ensure a balance of zero after all the threads are done.

20 Applets and HTML

This chapter is available on the book's website.

Keywords 1

```
abstract
assert*
boolean
break
byte
case
catch
char
class
const
continue
default
do
double
else
enum
extends
false*
final
finally
float
for
goto
if
implements
import
instanceof
int
interface
long
native
new
null*
package
private
protected
public
return
short
static
strictfp
super
switch
synchronized
this
throw
throws
transient
true*
try
void
volatile
while
```

* These are not listed as keywords in the Oracle documentation. However, some authorities list them as keywords. Preferring to err on the side of more safety, this book treats them as keywords.

Precedence and Associativity Rules 2

PRECEDENCE	ASSOCIATIVITY
From highest at top to lowest at bottom. Operators in the same group have equal precedence.	
Dot operator, array indexing, and method invocation: `.`, `[ ]`, `()`	Left to right
`++` (postfix, as in `x++`), `--` (postfix)	Right to left
The unary operators: `+`, `-`, `++` (prefix, as in `++x`), `--` (prefix), `!`, `~` (bitwise complement)[1]	Right to left
`new` and type casts (*`Type`*)	Right to left
The binary operators `*`, `/`, `%`	Left to right
The binary operators `+`, `-`	Left to right
The binary operators `<<`, `>>`, `>>>` (shift operators)[1]	Left to right
The binary operators `<`, `>`, `<=`, `>=`, `instanceof`	Left to right
The binary operators `==`, `!=`	Left to right
The binary operator `&`	Left to right
The binary operator `^` (exclusive or)[1]	Left to right
The binary operator `|`	Left to right
The binary operator `&&`	Left to right
The binary operator `||`	Left to right
The ternary operator (conditional operator) `?:`	Right to left
The assignment operators `=`, `*=`, `/=`, `%=`, `+=`, `-=`, `&=`, `|=`, `^=`, `<<=`, `>>=`, `>>>=`	Right to left

[1] Not discussed in this book.

ASCII Character Set 3

The characters shown here form the ASCII character set, which is the subset of the Unicode character set that is commonly used by English speakers. The numbering is the same whether the characters are considered to be members of the Unicode character set or of the ASCII character set. Character number 32 is the blank. Printable characters only are shown.

32		56	8	80	P	104	h
33	!	57	9	81	Q	105	i
34	"	58	:	82	R	106	j
35	#	59	;	83	S	107	k
36	$	60	<	84	T	108	l
37	%	61	=	85	U	109	m
38	&	62	>	86	V	110	n
39	'	63	?	87	W	111	o
40	(	64	@	88	X	112	p
41	)	65	A	89	Y	113	q
42	*	66	B	90	Z	114	r
43	+	67	C	91	[	115	s
44	,	68	D	92	\	116	t
45	-	69	E	93	]	117	u
46	.	70	F	94	^	118	v
47	/	71	G	95	_	119	w
48	0	72	H	96	`	120	x
49	1	73	I	97	a	121	y
50	2	74	J	98	b	122	z
51	3	75	K	99	c	123	{
52	4	76	L	100	d	124	|
53	5	77	M	101	e	125	}
54	6	78	N	102	f	126	~
55	7	79	O	103	g		

Format Specifications for `printf` 4

SYNTAX

System.out.printf(*Format_String, Output_1,Output_2, ..., Output_Last*);

Format_String is a string including one format specifier for each *Output* argument. *Format_String* is output with each format specifier replaced by its corresponding *Output* argument in the format given by the *Output* argument's format specifier.

Display A4.1 Format Specifiers for `System.out.printf`

CONVERSION CHARACTER	TYPE OF OUTPUT	EXAMPLES
`d`	Decimal (ordinary) integer.	`%5d` `%d`
`f`	Fixed-point (everyday notation) floating-point.	`%6.2f` `%f`
`e`	E-notation floating point.	`%8.3e` `%e`
`g`	General floating point. (Java decides whether to use E-notation or not.)	`%8.3g` `%g`
`s`	String.	`%12s` `%s`
`c`	Character.	`%2c` `%c`
`b`	Boolean. The corresponding *Output* argument is a Boolean expression. Outputs `true` or `false`.	`%6b` `%b`
`n`	Denotes a line break. This does not correspond to an *Output* argument. It is approximately equivalent to `\n`.	`%n`

A number of the form *N.M* in a format specifier specifies a field width of *N* spaces with *M* digits after the decimal point. If one number *N* is given only, it specifies a field width; if there is a decimal point in the output, then the number of digits after the decimal point is determined by Java.

When the value output does not fill the field width specified, then blanks are added in front of the value output. The output is then said to be *right justified.* If you add a hyphen (-) after the `%`, then any extra blank space is placed after the value output and the output is said to be *left justified.* For example, `%8.2f` is right justified and `%-8.2f` is left justified.

Summary of Classes and Interfaces 5

This appendix summarizes most of the library classes used in this book. This appendix includes some methods, and even some classes, that are not discussed in the text. The lists of class methods and other class members contain the most commonly used members and the members used in this book, but they are not complete lists of methods for the classes given here.

If a class or interface is derived from another class or interface, respectively, then in some cases, the table for the derived class or interface lists only new methods and does not list all the inherited methods.

`Abstract Button`

Package: `javax.swing`
The classes `JButton` and `JMenuItem` are also in this package.
All these methods are inherited by the classes `JButton` and `JMenuItem`.
`AbstractButton` is an abstract class.
Ancestor classes:

```
Object
  |
  +--Component
        |
        +--Container
              |
              +--JComponent
                    |
                    +AbstractButton
                      |          \
                      +--JButton  +--JMenuItem
```

`public void addActionListener(ActionListener listener)`

Adds an `ActionListener`.

`public String getActionCommand()`

Returns the action command for this component.

`public String getText()`

Returns the text written on the component, such as the text on a button or the string for a menu item.

`public void removeActionListener(ActionListener listener)`

Removes an `ActionListener`.

`public void setActionCommand(String actionCommand)`

Sets the action command.

```
public void setBackground(Color theColor)
```

Sets the background color of this component.

```
public void setMaximumSize(Dimension maximumSize)
```

Sets the maximum size of the button or label. Note that this is only a suggestion to the layout manager. The layout manager is not required to respect this maximum size. The following special case will work for most simple situations. The `int` values give the width and height in pixels.

```
public void setMaximumSize(
                        new Dimension(int width, int height))
```

```
public void setMinimumSize(Dimension minimumSize)
```

Sets the minimum size of the button or label. Note that this is only a suggestion to the layout manager. The layout manager is not required to respect this minimum size.
Although we do not discuss the `Dimension` class, the following special case is intuitively clear and will work for most simple situations. The `int` values give the width and height in pixels.

```
public void setMinimumSize(
                       new Dimension(int width, int height))
```

```
public void setPreferredSize(Dimension preferredSize)
```

Sets the preferred size of the button or label. Note that this is only a suggestion to the layout manager. The layout manager is not required to use the preferred size. The following special case will work for most simple situations. The `int` values give the width and height in pixels.

```
public void setPreferredSize(
                      new Dimension(int width, int height))
```

```
public void setText(String text)
```

Makes `text` the only text on this component.

`ArrayList<T>`

Package: `java.util`

Ancestor classes:

```
Object
  |
  +--AbstractCollection<T>
        |
        +--AbstractList<T>
              |
              +--ArrayList<T>
```

All the exception classes mentioned are unchecked exceptions, which means they are not required to be caught in a `catch` block or declared in a `throws` clause.
`NoSuchElementException` is in the `java.util` package, which requires an import statement if your code mentions the `NoSuchElementException` class. All the other exception classes mentioned are in the package `java.lang` and so do not require any import statement.

CONSTRUCTORS

public ArrayList(int initialCapacity)

Creates an empty ArrayList<T> with the specified initial capacity. When the ArrayList<T> needs to increase its capacity, the capacity doubles.
Throws an IllegalArgumentException if initialCapacity is negative.

public ArrayList()

Creates an empty ArrayList<T> with an initial capacity of 10. When the ArrayList<T> needs to increase its capacity, the capacity doubles.

public ArrayList(Collection<? extends <T> c)

Creates an ArrayList<T> that contains all the elements of the collection c in the same order as they have in c. In other words, the elements have the same index in the ArrayList<T> created as they do in c. This is not quite a true copy constructor because it does not preserve capacity. The capacity of the created ArrayList<T> will be c.size(), not c.capacity. The ArrayList<T> created is only a shallow copy of the collection argument. The ArrayList<T> created contains references to the elements in c (not references to clones of the elements in c).

Throws:

NullPointerException if c is null.

ARRAYLIKE METHODS

public T set(int index, T newElement)

Sets the element at the specified index to newElement. The element previously at that position is returned. If you draw an analogy to an array a, this is analogous to setting a[index] to the value newElement. The index must be a value greater than or equal to 0 and strictly less than the current size of the list.

Throws:

IndexOutOfBoundsException if the index is not in this range.

public T get(int index)

Returns the element at the specified index. This is analogous to returning a[index] for an array a. The index must be a value greater than or equal to 0 and less than the current size of the calling object.

Throws:

IndexOutOfBoundsException if the index is not in the required range.

METHODS TO ADD ELEMENTS

```
public boolean add(T newElement)
```

Adds `newElement` to the end of the calling object's list and increases its size by one. The capacity of the calling object is increased if that is required. Returns `true` if the add was successful. This method is often used as if it were a `void` method.

```
public void add(int index, T newElement)
```

Inserts `newElement` as an element in the calling object at the specified index and increases the size of the calling object by one. Each element in the calling object with an index greater than or equal to `index` is shifted upward to have an index that is one greater than it had previously.
The `index` must be a value greater than or equal to `0` and less than *or equal to* the size of the calling object (before this addition).
Note that you can use this method to add an element after the last current element. The capacity of the calling object is increased if that is required.

Throws:

`IndexOutOfBoundsException` if the index is not in the prescribed range.

```
public boolean addAll(Collection<? extends T> c)
```

Appends all the elements in `c` to the end of the elements in the calling object in the order that they are enumerated by a `c` iterator. The behavior of this method is not guaranteed if the collection `c` is the calling object or any collection including the calling object either directly or indirectly.

Throws:

`NullPointerException` if `c` is `null`.

```
public boolean addAll(int index, Collection<? extends T> c)
```

Inserts all the elements in `c` into the calling object starting at position `index`. Elements are inserted in the order that they are enumerated by a `c` iterator. Elements previously at positions `index` or higher are shifted to higher numbered positions.

Throws:

`IndexOutOfBoundsException` if `index` is not both greater than or equal to zero and less than `size()`.
`NullPointerException` if `c` is null.

METHODS TO REMOVE ELEMENTS

```
public T remove(int index)
```

Deletes the element at the specified index and returns the element deleted. The size of the calling object is decreased by one. The capacity of the calling object is not changed. Each element in the calling object with an index greater than or equal to `index` is decreased to have an index that is one less than the value it had previously.
The `index` must be a value greater than or equal to `0` and less than the size of the calling object (before this removal).

Throws:

`IndexOutOfBoundsException` if the `index` is not in the prescribed range.

`public boolean remove(Object theElement)`

Removes the first occurrence of `theElement` from the calling object. If `theElement` is found in the calling object, then each element in the calling object with an index greater than or equal to `theElement`'s index is decreased to have an index that is one less than the value it had previously. Returns `true` if `theElement` was found (and removed). Returns `false` if `theElement` was not found in the calling object. If the element was removed, the size is decreased by one. The capacity is not changed.

`protected void removeRange(int fromIndex, int toIndex)`

Removes all elements with index greater than or equal to `fromIndex` and strictly less than `toIndex`. Be sure to note that this method is `protected`, not `public`.

`public void clear()`

Removes all elements from the calling object and sets its size to zero.

SEARCH METHODS

`public boolean isEmpty()`

Returns `true` if the calling object is empty (that is, has size `0`); otherwise returns `false`.

`public boolean contains(Object target)`

Returns `true` if `target` is an element of the calling object; otherwise returns `false`. Uses the method `equals` of the object `target` to test for equality.

`public int indexOf(Object target)`

Returns the index of the first element that is equal to `target`. Uses the method `equals` of the object `target` to test for equality. Returns `-1` if `target` is not found.

`public int lastIndexOf(Object target)`

Returns the index of the last element that is equal to `target`. Uses the method `equals` of the object `target` to test for equality. Returns `-1` if `target` is not found.

ITERATORS

`public Iterator<T> iterator()`

Returns an iterator for the calling object. Iterators are discussed in Section 16.3.

`public ListIterator<T> listIterator()`

Returns a `ListIterator<T>` for the calling object. `ListIterator<T>` is discussed in Section 16.3.

`ListIterator<T> listIterator(int index)`

Returns a list iterator for the calling object starting at `index`. The first element to be returned by the iterator is the one at `index`. (Iterators are discussed in Section 16.3.)

Throws:

`IndexOutOfBoundsException` if `index` does not satisfy:
`0 <= index <= size()`

CONVERTING TO AN ARRAY

`public Object[] toArray()`

Returns an array containing all of the elements in the calling object. The elements of the array are indexed the same as in the calling object.

`public <E> E[] toArray(E[] a)`

Note that the type parameter `E` is not the same as `T`. So, `E` can be any reference type; it need not be the type `T` in `Collection<T>`. For example, `E` might be an ancestor type of `T`.
Returns an array containing all of the elements in the calling object. The elements of the array are indexed the same as in the calling object.
The argument `a` is used primarily to specify the type of the array returned. The exact details are as follows:
The type of the returned array is that of `a`. If the collection fits in the array `a`, then `a` is used to hold the elements of the returned array; otherwise a new array is created with the same type as `a`.
If `a` has more elements than the calling object, then the element in `a` immediately following the end of the elements copied from the calling object are set to `null`.

Throws:

`ArrayStoreException` if the type of `a` is not an ancestor type of the type of every element in the calling object.
`NullPointerException` if `a` is `null`.

MEMORY MANAGEMENT

`public int size()`

Returns the number of elements in the calling object.

`public int capacity()`

Returns the current capacity of the calling object.

`public void ensureCapacity(int newCapacity)`

Increases the capacity of the calling object to ensure that it can hold at least `newCapacity` elements. Using `ensureCapacity` can sometimes increase efficiency, but its use is not needed for any other reason.

```
public void trimToSize()
```

Trims the capacity of the calling object to be the calling object's current size. This is used to save storage.

MAKE A COPY

```
public Object clone()
```

Returns a shallow copy of the calling object.

Boolean

This is a wrapper class for `boolean`. See Section 5.1 in Chapter 5.

BufferedReader

Package: `java.io`
The `FileReader` class is also in this package.
Ancestor classes:

```
Object
  |
  +--Reader
       |
       +--BufferedReader
```

```
public BufferedReader(Reader readerObject)
```

This is the only constructor you are likely to need. There is no constructor that accepts a file name as an argument. If you want to create a stream using a file name, use

`new BufferedReader(new FileReader(`*File_Name*`))`

When used in this way, the `FileReader` constructor, and thus the `BufferedReader` constructor invocation, can throw a `FileNotFoundException`, which is a kind of `IOException`.
If you want to create a stream using an object of the class `File`, use

`new BufferedReader(new FileReader(`*File_Object*`))`

When used in this way, the `FileReader` constructor, and thus the `BufferedReader` constructor invocation, can throw a `FileNotFoundException`, which is a kind of `IOException`.

```
public void close() throws IOException
```

Closes the stream's connection to a file.

```
public int read() throws IOException
```

Reads a single character from the input stream and returns that character as an `int` value. If the read goes beyond the end of the file, then `-1` is returned. Note that the value is returned as an `int`. To obtain a `char`, you must perform a type cast on the value returned. The end of a file is signaled by returning `-1`. (All of the "real" characters return a positive integer.)

`public String readLine() throws IOException`

Reads a line of input from the input stream and returns that line. If the read goes beyond the end of the file, `null` is returned. (Note that an `EOFException` is not thrown at the end of a file. The end of a file is signaled by returning `null`.)

`public long skip(long n) throws IOException`

Skips `n` characters.

`Byte`

This is a wrapper class for `byte`. See Section 5.1 in Chapter 5.

`Character`

Package: `java.lang`
Ancestor classes:

```
Object
  |
  +--Character
```

Implemented interfaces: `Comparable, Serializable`
The `Character` class is marked `final`, which means it cannot be used as a base class to derive other classes.

`public static boolean isDigit(char argument)`

Returns `true` if its `argument` is a digit; otherwise returns `false`.

EXAMPLES

`Character.isDigit('5')` returns `true`. `Character.isDigit('A')` and `Character.isDigit('%')` both return `false`.

`public static boolean isLetter(char argument)`

Returns `true` if its `argument` is a letter; otherwise returns `false`.

EXAMPLES

`Character.isLetter('A')` returns `true`. `Character.isLetter('%')` and `Character.isLetter('5')` both return `false`.

`public static boolean isLetterOrDigit(char argument)`

Returns `true` if its `argument` is a letter or a digit; otherwise returns `false`.

EXAMPLES

`Character.isLetterOrDigit('A')` and `Character.isLetterOrDigit('5')` both return `true`. `Character.isLetterOrDigit('&')` returns `false`.

`public static boolean isLowerCase(char argument)`

Returns `true` if its `argument` is a lowercase letter; otherwise returns `false`.

EXAMPLES

`Character.isLowerCase('a')` returns `true`. `Character.isLowerCase('A')` and `Character.isLowerCase('%')` both return `false`.

`public static boolean isUpperCase(char argument)`

Returns `true` if its `argument` is an uppercase letter; otherwise returns `false`.

EXAMPLES

`Character.isUpperCase('A')` returns `true`. `Character.isUpperCase('a')` and `Character.isUpperCase('%')` both return `false`.

`public static boolean isWhitespace(char argument)`

Returns `true` if its `argument` is a whitespace character; otherwise returns `false`. Whitespace characters are those that print as whitespace, such as the space character (blank character), the tab character (`'\t'`), and the new-line character (`'\n'`).

EXAMPLES

`Character.isWhitespace(' ')` returns `true`. `Character.isWhitespace('A')` returns `false`.

`public static char toLowerCase(char argument)`

Returns the lowercase version of its `argument`. If the `argument` is not a letter, it is returned unchanged.

EXAMPLE

`Character.toLowerCase('a')` and `Character.toLowerCase('A')` both return `'a'`.

`public static char toUpperCase(char argument)`

Returns the uppercase version of its `argument`. If the `argument` is not a letter, it is returned unchanged.

EXAMPLE

`Character.toUpperCase('a')` and `Character.toUpperCase('A')` both return `'A'`.

Collection<T> Interface

Package: java.util
Ancestor interfaces: none
All the exception classes mentioned are unchecked exceptions, which means they are not required to be caught in a catch block or declared in a throws clause.
All the exception classes mentioned are in the package java.lang and so do not require any import statement.

CONSTRUCTORS

Although not officially required by the interface, any class that implements the Collection<T> interface should have at least two constructors: a no-argument constructor that creates an empty Collection<T> object, and a constructor with one parameter of type Collection<? extends T> that creates a Collection<T> object with the same elements as the constructor argument. The interface does not specify whether the copy produced by the one-argument constructor is a shallow copy or a deep copy of its argument.

```
public boolean contains(Object target)
```

Returns true if the calling object contains at least one instance of target. Uses target.equals to determine if target is in the calling object.

Throws:

ClassCastException if the type of target is incompatible with the calling object (optional).
NullPointerException if target is null and the calling object does not support null elements (optional).

```
public boolean containsAll(Collection<?> collectionOfTargets)
```

Returns true if the calling object contains all of the elements in collectionOfTargets. For element in collectionOfTargets, this method uses element.equals to determine if element is in the calling object.

Throws:

ClassCastException if the types of one or more elements in collectionOfTargets are incompatible with the calling object (optional).
NullPointerException if collectionOfTargets contains one or more null elements and the calling object does not support null elements (optional).
NullPointerException if collectionOfTargets is null.

```
public boolean equals(Object other)
```

This is the equals of the collection, not the equals of the elements in the collection. Overrides the inherited method equals. Although there are no official constraints on equals for a collection, it should be defined as we have described in Chapter 7 and also satisfy the intuitive notion of collections being equal.

```
public int hashCode()
```

Returns the hash code value for the calling object. Neither hash codes nor this method are discussed in this book. This entry is only here to make the definition of the Collection<T> interface complete. You can safely ignore this entry until you go on to study hash codes in a more advanced book. In the meantime, if you need to implement this method, have the method throw an UnsupportedOperationException.

```
public boolean isEmpty()
```

Returns true if the calling object is empty; otherwise returns false.

```
Iterator<T> iterator()
```

Returns an iterator for the calling object. (Iterators are discussed in Section 16.3.)

```
public Object[] toArray()
```

Returns an array containing all of the elements in the calling object. If the calling object makes any guarantees as to what order its elements are returned by its iterator, this method must return the elements in the same order.
The array returned should be a new array so that the calling object has no references to the returned array. (You might also want the elements in the array to be clones of the elements in the collection. However, this is apparently not required by the interface, because library classes, such as Vector<T>, return arrays that contain references to the elements in the collection.)

```
public <E> E[] toArray(E[] a)
```

Note that the type parameter E is not the same as T. So, E can be any reference type; it need not be the type T in Collection<T>. For example, E might be an ancestor type of T.
Returns an array containing all of the elements in the calling object. The argument a is used primarily to specify the type of the array returned. The exact details are as follows:
The type of the returned array is that of a. If the elements in the calling object fit in the array a, then a is used to hold the elements of the returned array; otherwise a new array is created with the same type as a.
If a has more elements than the calling object, the element in a immediately following the end of the copied elements is set to null.
If the calling object makes any guarantees as to what order its elements are returned by its iterator, this method must return the elements in the same order. (Iterators are discussed in Section 16.3.)

Throws:

ArrayStoreException if the type of a is not an ancestor type of the type of every element in the calling object.
NullPointerException if a is null.

```
public int size()
```

Returns the number of elements in the calling object. If the calling object contains more than Integer.MAX_VALUE elements, returns Integer.MAX_VALUE.

OPTIONAL METHODS

The following methods are optional, which means they still must be implemented, but the implementation can simply throw an UnsupportedOperationException if for some reason you do not want to give them a "real" implementation. An UnsupportedOperationException is a RunTimeException and so is not required to be caught or declared in a throws clause.

`public boolean add(T element)` *(Optional)*

Ensures that the calling object contains the specified `element`. Returns `true` if the calling object changed as a result of the call. Returns `false` if the calling object does not permit duplicates and already contains `element`; also returns `false` if the calling object does not change for any other reason.

Throws:

`UnsupportedOperationException` if this method is not supported by the class that implements this interface.
`ClassCastException` if the class of `element` prevents it from being added to the calling object.
`NullPointerException` if element is `null` and the calling object does not support `null` elements. `IllegalArgumentException` if some other aspect of `element` prevents it from being added to the calling object.

`public boolean addAll(Collection<? extends T> collectionToAdd)` *(Optional)*

Ensures that the calling object contains all the elements in `collectionToAdd.` Returns `true` if the calling object changed as a result of the call; returns `false` otherwise. If the calling object changes during this operation, its behavior is unspecified; in particular, it behavior is unspecified if `collectionToAdd` is the calling object.

Throws:

`UnsupportedOperationException` if this method is not supported by the class that implements this interface.
`ClassCastException` if the class of an element of `collectionToAdd` prevents it from being added to the calling object.
`NullPointerException` if `collectionToAdd` contains one or more `null` elements and the calling object does not support `null` elements, or if `collectionToAdd` is `null.`
`IllegalArgumentException` if some aspect of an element of `collectionToAdd` prevents it from being added to the calling object.

`public void clear()` *(Optional)*

Removes all the elements from the calling object.

Throws:

`UnsupportedOperationException` if this method is not supported by the class that implements this interface.

`public boolean remove(Object element)` *(Optional)*

Removes a single instance of `element` from the calling object, if it is present. Returns `true` if the calling object contained `element`; returns `false` otherwise.

Throws:

`UnsupportedOperationException` if this method is not supported by the class that implements this interface.
`ClassCastException` if the type of `element` is incompatible with the calling object (optional).
`NullPointerException` if `element` is `null` and the calling object does not support `null` elements (optional).

`public boolean removeAll(Collection<?> collectionToRemove)` *(Optional)*

Removes all the calling object's elements that are also contained in `collectionToRemove`. Returns `true` if the calling object was changed; otherwise returns `false`.

Throws:

`UnsupportedOperationException` if this method is not supported by the class that implements this interface.
`ClassCastException` if the types of one or more elements in `collectionToRemove` are incompatible with the calling collection (optional).
`NullPointerException` if `collectionToRemove` contains one or more `null` elements and the calling object does not support `null` elements (optional).
`NullPointerException` if `collectionToRemove` is `null`.

`public boolean retainAll(Collection<?> saveElements)` *(Optional)*

Retains only the elements in the calling object that are also contained in the collection `saveElements`. In other words, removes from the calling object all of its elements that are not contained in the collection `saveElements`. Returns `true` if the calling object was changed; otherwise returns `false`.

Throws:

`ClassCastException` if the types of one or more elements in `saveElements` are incompatible with the calling object (optional).
`NullPointerException` if `saveElements` contains one or more `null` elements and the calling object does not support `null` elements (optional).
`NullPointerException` if `saveElements` is `null`.

Color

Package: `java.awt`
Ancestor classes:

```
Object
  |
  +--Color
```

CONSTRUCTORS

`public Color(float r, float g, float b)`

Constructor that creates a new `Color` with the specified RGB values. The parameters `r`, `g`, and `b` must each be in the range `0.0` to `1.0` (inclusive).

`public Color(int r, int g, int b)`

Constructor that creates a new `Color` with the specified RGB values. The parameters `r`, `g`, and `b` must each be in the range 0 to 255 (inclusive).

METHODS

`public Color brighter()`

Returns a brighter version of the calling object color.

`public Color darker()`

Returns a darker version of the calling object color.

`public boolean equals(Object c)`

Returns `true` if `c` is equal to the calling object color; otherwise returns `false`.

`public int getBlue()`

Returns the blue component of the calling object. The returned value is in the range `0` to `255` (inclusive).

`public int getGreen()`

Returns the green component of the calling object. The returned value is in the range `0` to `255` (inclusive).

`public int getRed()`

Returns the red component of the calling object. The returned value is in the range `0` to `255` (inclusive).

CONSTANTS

```
Color.BLACK
Color.BLUE
Color.CYAN
Color.DARK_GRAY
Color.GRAY
Color.GREEN
Color.LIGHT_GRAY
Color.MAGENTA
Color.ORANGE
Color.PINK
Color.RED
Color.WHITE
Color.YELLOW
```

`Comparable` Interface

Package: `java.lang`
Ancestor interfaces: none
The `Comparable` interface has only one method heading that must be implemented.

`public int compareTo(Object other)`

The method `compareTo` should return
a negative number if the calling object "comes before" the parameter `other`,
a zero if the calling object "equals" the parameter `other`,
and a positive number if the calling object "comes after" the parameter `other`.
The "comes before" ordering that underlies `compareTo` should be a total ordering. Most normal ordering, such as less-than on numbers and lexicographic ordering on strings, are total orderings.

Double

This is a wrapper class for `double`. See Section 5.1 in Chapter 5.

File

Package: `java.io`
Ancestor classes:

```
Object
  |
  +--File
```

Many of these methods throw a `SecurityException` if a security manager exists and is unhappy with the method invocation. This is not likely to be a concern for readers of this book, and we have not noted this in the method descriptions.
The class `SecurityException` is an unchecked exception class, which means you need not catch it or declare it in a `throws` clause.

`public File(String fileName)`

Constructor. `fileName` can be either a full or a relative pathname (which includes the case of a simple file name). `fileName` is referred to as the **abstract pathname**.

Throws:

`NullPointerException` if the pathname `fileName` is `null`.

`public boolean canRead()`

Tests whether the program can read from the file. Returns `true` if the file named by the abstract pathname exists and is readable by the program; otherwise returns `false`.

`public boolean canWrite()`

Tests whether the program can write to the file. Returns `true` if the file named by the abstract pathname exists and is writable by the program; otherwise returns `false`.

`public boolean createNewFile()`

Creates a new empty file named by the abstract pathname, provided that a file of that name does not already exist. Returns `true` if successful; returns `false` otherwise.

Throws:

`IOException` if an I/O error occurs.

`public boolean delete( )`

Tries to delete the file or directory named by the abstract pathname. A directory must be empty to be removed. Returns `true` if it was able to delete the file or directory. Returns `false` if it was unable to delete the file or directory.

`public boolean exists()`

Tests whether there is a file with the abstract pathname.

```
public String getName()
```

Returns the last name in the abstract pathname (that is, the simple file name). Returns the empty string if the abstract pathname is the empty string.

```
public String getPath()
```

Returns the abstract pathname as a `String` value.

```
public boolean isDirectory()
```

Returns `true` if a directory (folder) exists that is named by the abstract pathname; otherwise returns `false`.

```
public boolean isFile()
```

Returns `true` if a file exists that is named by the abstract pathname and the file is a normal file; otherwise returns `false`. The meaning of *normal* is system dependent. Any file created by a Java program is guaranteed to be normal.

```
public long length()
```

Returns the length in bytes of the file named by the abstract pathname. If the file does not exist or the abstract pathname names a directory, then the value returned is not specified and may be anything.

```
public boolean mkdir()
```

Makes a directory named by the abstract pathname. Will not create parent directories. See `mkdirs`. Returns `true` if successful; otherwise returns `false`.

```
public boolean mkdirs()
```

Makes a directory named by the abstract pathname. Will create any necessary but nonexistent parent directories. Returns `true` if successful; otherwise returns `false`. Note that if it fails, then some of the parent directories may have been created.

```
public boolean renameTo(File newName)
```

Renames the file represented by the abstract pathname to `newName`. Returns `true` if successful; otherwise returns `false`. `newName` can be a relative or absolute pathname. This may require moving the file. Whether or not the file can be moved is system dependent.

Throws:

`NullPointerException` if parameter `newName` is `null`.

```
public boolean setReadOnly()
```

Sets the file represented by the abstract pathname to be read only. Returns `true` if successful; otherwise returns `false`.

`Float`

This is a wrapper class for `float`. See Section 5.1 in Chapter 5.

`Font`

Package: `java.awt`
Ancestor classes:

```
Object
   |
   +--Font
```

CONSTRUCTOR

```
public Font(String fontName, int styleModifications, int size)
```

Constructor that creates a version of the font named by `fontName` with the specified `styleModifications` and `size`.

CONSTANTS

```
Font.BOLD
```

Specifies bold style.

```
Font.ITALIC
```

Specifies italic style.

```
Font.PLAIN
```

Specifies plain style—that is, not bold and not italic.

NAMES OF Fonts
(These three are guaranteed by Java. Your system will probably have others as well as these.)

```
"Monospaced"
```

See Chapter 18 for a sample.

```
"SansSerif"
```

See Chapter 18 for a sample.

```
"Serif"
```

See Chapter 18 for a sample.

METHOD THAT USES Font

```
public abstract void setFont(Font fontObject)
```

This method is in the class `Graphics`. Sets the current font of the calling `Graphics` object to `fontObject`.

Graphics

Package: java.awt
Ancestor classes:

```
Object
   |
   +--Graphics
```

Graphics is an abstract class.
Although many of these methods are abstract, we always use them with objects of a concrete descendent class of Graphics, even though we usually do not know the name of that concrete class.

```
public abstract void drawRect(int x, int y,
                                      int width, int height)
```

Draws the outline of the specified rectangle. (x, y) is the location of the upper-left corner of the rectangle.

```
public abstract void fillRect(int x, int y,
                                      int width, int height)
```

Fills the specified rectangle. (x, y) is the location of the upper-left corner of the rectangle.

```
public void draw3DRect(int x, int y, int width,
                                     int height, boolean raised)
```

Draws the outline of the specified rectangle. (x, y) is the location of the upper-left corner.The rectangle is highlighted to look like it has thickness. If raised is true, the highlight makes the rectangle appear to stand out from the background. If raised is false, the highlight makes the rectangle appear to be sunken into the background.

```
public void fill3DRect(int x, int y, int width,
                                     int height, boolean raised)
```

Fills the rectangle specified by

```
draw3DRec(x, y,width, height, raised)
```

```
public abstract void drawArc(int x, int y,
                             int width, int height,
                             int startAngle, int arcSweep)
```

Draws part of an oval that just fits into an invisible rectangle described by the first four arguments. The portion of the oval drawn is given by the last two arguments. See Chapter 18 for details.

```
public abstract void drawLine(int x1, int y1, int x2, int y2)
```

Draws a line between points (x1, y1) and (x2, y2).

```
public abstract void drawOval(int x, int y,
                                      int width, int height)
```

Draws the outline of the oval with the smallest enclosing rectangle that has the specified width and height. The (imagined) rectangle has its upper-left corner located at (x, y).

```
public void drawPolygon(int[]x, int[] y, int points)
```

Draws a polygon through the point
`(x[0], y[0]), (x[1], y[1]), ..., (x[points - 1], y[points - 1]).`
Always draws a closed polygon. If the first and last points are not equal, it draws a line from the last to the first point.

```
public void drawPolyline(int[ ] x, int[ ] y, int points)
```

Draws a polygon through the point
`(x[0], y[0]), (x[1], y[1]), ..., (x[points - 1], y[points - 1]).`
If the first and last points are not equal, the polygon will not be closed.

```
public abstract void drawRoundRect(int x, int y,
            int width, int height, int arcWidth, int arcHeight)
```

Draws the outline of the specified round-cornered rectangle. (x, y) is the location of the upper-left corner of the enclosing regular rectangle. `arcWidth` and `arcHeight` specify the shape of the round corners. See Chapter 18 for details.

```
public abstract void drawString(String text, int x, int y)
```

Draws the `text` given by the specified string, using this graphics object's current font and color. The baseline of the leftmost character is at position (x, y) in this graphics object's coordinate system.

```
public abstract void fillArc(int x, int y,
                             int width, int height,
                             int startAngle, int arcSweep)
```

Fills the partial oval specified by

```
drawArc(x, y, width, height, startAngle, arcSweep)
```

```
public abstract void fillOval(int x, int y,
                                     int width, int height)
```

Fills the oval specified by

```
drawOval(x, y, width, height)
```

```
public void fillPolygon(int[] x, int[] y, int points)
```

Fills (with color) the polygon specified by

```
drawPolygon(x,y,points).
```

```
public abstract void fillRoundRect(int x, int y,
            int width, int height, int arcWidth, int arcHeight)
```

Fills the round rectangle specified by

```
drawRoundRec(x, y, width, height,arcWidth, arcHeight)
```

```
public abstract void setFont(Font fontObject)
```

Sets the current font of the calling `Graphics` object to `fontObject`.

`HashMap<K,V>` Class

Package: `java.util`
Ancestor classes:

```
Object
  |
  +--AbstractMap<K,V>
       |
       +--HashMap<K,V>
```

Implements interfaces: `Map<K,V>`, `Cloneable`, `Serializable`
The `HashMap<K,V>` class implements all of the methods in the `Map<K,V>` interface. The only other methods in the `HashMap<K,V>` class are the constructors.
All the exception classes mentioned are the kind that are not required to be caught in a catch block or declared in a throws clause. All the exception classes mentioned are in the package `java.lang` and so do not require any import statement. The class `K` must implement the `equals` and `hashCode` methods.

```
public HashMap()
```

Creates a new, empty map with a default initial capacity of 16 and load factor of 0.75. The capacity is the number of slots in the hash table. The load factor is the percentage of capacity before the size of the table is automatically increased.

```
public HashMap(int initialCapacity)
```

Creates a new, empty map with a default capacity of `initialCapacity` and load factor of 0.75.

Throws:

`IllegalArgumentException` if the initial capacity is negative.

```
public HashMap(int initialCapacity, float loadFactor)
```

Creates a new, empty map with the specified capacity and load factor.

Throws:

`IllegalArgumentException` if the initial capacity or the load factor is negative.

```
public HashMap(Map<? extends K,? extends V> m)
```

Creates a new map with the same mappings as `m`. The `initialCapacity` is set to the same size as `m` and the `loadFactor` to 0.75.

Throws:

`NullPointerException` if `m` is `null`.

```
public Object clone( )
```

Creates a shallow copy of this instance and returns it. The keys and values are not cloned.
The remainder of the methods are the same as those described for the `Map<K,V>` interface.

HashSet<T>

Package: `java.util`
Ancestor classes:

```
Object
   |
   +--AbstractCollection<T>
           |
           +--AbstractSet<T>
                   |
                   +--HashSet<T>
```

Implements interfaces: `Cloneable, Collection<T>, Serializable, Set<T>`
The `HashSet<T>` class implements all of the methods in the `Set<T>` interface. The only other methods in the `HashSet<T>` class are the constructors. The class `T` must implement the `equals` and `hashCode` methods. The two constructors that do not involve concepts beyond the scope of this book are given as follows.
All the exception classes mentioned are the kind that are not required to be caught in a `catch` block or declared in a `throws` clause.
All the exception classes mentioned are in the package `java.lang` and so do not require any import statement.

`public HashSet()`

Creates a new, empty set.

`public HashSet(Collection<? extends T> c )`

Creates a new set that contains all the elements of `c`.

Throws:

`NullPointerException` if `c` is `null`.

`public HashSet(int initialCapacity)`

Creates a new, empty set with the specified capacity.

Throws:

`IllegalArgumentException` if `initialCapacity` is less than zero.

The methods are the same as those described for the `Set<T>` interface.

Integer

This is a wrapper class for `int`. See Section 5.1 in Chapter 5.

Iterator<T> Interface

Package: `java.util`
Ancestor interfaces: none
All the exception classes mentioned are the kind that are not required to be caught in a `catch` block or declared in a `throws` clause.
`NoSuchElementException` is in the `java.util` package, which requires an `import` statement if your code mentions the `NoSuchElementException` class. All the other exception classes mentioned are in the package `java.lang` and so do not require any `import` statements.

`public boolean hasNext()`

Returns `true` if `next()` has not yet returned all the elements in the collection; returns `false` otherwise.

`public T next()`

Returns the next element of the collection that produced the iterator.

Throws:

`NoSuchElementException` if there is no next element.

`public void remove()` *(Optional)*

Removes from the collection the last element returned by `next`.
This method can be called only once per call to `next`.

Throws:

`IllegalStateException` if the `next` method has not yet been called, or the `remove` method has already been called after the last call to the `next` method.
`UnsupportedOperationException` if the `remove` operation is not supported by this `Iterator`.

JButton

See `AbstractButton`.

JFrame

Package: `javax.swing`
Ancestor classes:

```
Object
   |
   +--Component
          |
          +--Container
                 |
                 +--Window
                        |
                        +--Frame
                               |
                               +--JFrame
```

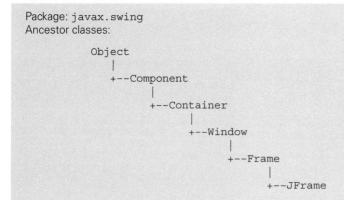

`public JFrame()`

Constructor that creates an object of the class `JFrame`.

`public JFrame(String title)`

Constructor that creates an object of the class `JFrame` with the title given as the argument.

`public Component add(Component componentAdded)`

Adds `componentAdded` to the `JFrame`. Typically used as a `void` method.

`public Container getContentPane()`

Returns the content pane of the calling `JFrame` object. `Container` is a class in the package `java.awt`.

To set the color of a `JFrame`, use

`getContentPane().setBackground(Color c)`

If you use `setBackground` without the `getContentPane()`, you will not get any error messages, but you will probably not see the color.

`public void setDefaultCloseOperation(int operation)`

Sets the action that will happen by default when the user clicks the close-window button. The argument should be one of the following defined constants:

`JFrame.DO_NOTHING_ON_CLOSE`: Do nothing. The `JFrame` does nothing, but if there are any registered window listeners, they are invoked. (Window listeners are explained in Chapter 18.)
`JFrame.HIDE_ON_CLOSE`: Hide the frame after invoking any registered `WindowListener` objects.
`JFrame.DISPOSE_ON_CLOSE`: Hide and *dispose* the frame after invoking any registered window listeners. When a window is **disposed**, it is eliminated but the program does not end. To end the programs, use the next constant as an argument to `setDefaultCloseOperation`.
`JFrame.EXIT_ON_CLOSE`: Exit the application using the `System exit` method. (Do not use this for frames in applets. Applets are discussed on the accompanying CD.)

If no action is specified using the method `setDefaultCloseOperation`, then the default action taken is `JFrame.HIDE_ON_CLOSE`.

Throws:

`IllegalArgumentException` if the argument is not one of the values listed previously.
`SecurityException` if the argument is `JFrame.EXIT_ON_CLOSE` and the Security Manager will not allow the caller to invoke `System.exit`. (You are not likely to encounter this case.)

`public void setLayout(LayoutManager manager)`

Makes `manager` the layout manager for the `JFrame`.

`public void setSize(int width, int height)`

Sets the size of the calling frame so that it has the `width` and `height` specified. Pixels are the units of length used.

`public void setTitle(String title)`

Sets the title for this frame to the argument string.

`public void dispose()`

Eliminates the calling frame and all its subcomponents. Any memory they use is released for reuse. If there are items left (items other than the calling frame and its subcomponents), then this does not end the program. (The method `dispose` is discussed in Chapter 18.)

`public void setJMenuBar(JMenuBar menubar)`

Sets the menu bar for the calling frame.

JMenuItem

See `AbstractButton`.

JPanel

Package: `javax.swing`
Ancestor classes:

```
Object
   |
   +--Component
         |
         +--Container
               |
               +--JComponent
                     |
                     +--JPanel
```

`public JPanel()`

Constructor that creates an object of the class `JPanel`.

`public JPanel(LayoutManager manager)`

Constructor that creates an object of the class `JPanel` with the given layout manager.

`public Component add(Component componentAdded)`

Adds `componentAdded` to the `JPanel`. Typically used as a `void` method.

`public void setBackground(Color c)`

Sets the color of the `JPanel`.

`public void setLayout(LayoutManager manager)`

Makes `manager` the layout manager for the `JPanel`.

JScrollPane

Package: javax.swing
Ancestor classes:

```
Object
   |
   +--Component
         |
         +--Container
               |
               +--JComponent
                     |
                     +--JScrollPane
```

`public JScrollPane(Component objectToBeScrolled)`

Creates a new JScrollPane for the objectToBeScrolled. Note that the objectToBeScrolled need not be a JTextArea, although that is the only type of argument considered in this book.

`public void setHorizontalScrollBarPolicy(int policy)`

Sets the policy for showing the horizontal scroll bar. The policy should be one of
JScrollPane.HORIZONTAL_SCROLLBAR_ALWAYS
JScrollPane.HORIZONTAL_SCROLLBAR_NEVER
JScrollPane.HORIZONTAL_SCROLLBAR_AS_NEEDED
The phrase AS_NEEDED means the scroll bar is shown only when it is needed. This is explained more fully in Chapter 17. The meanings of the other policy constants are obvious from their names.
(As indicated, these constants are defined in the class JScrollPane. You should not need to even be aware of the fact that they have int values. Think of them as policies, not as int values.)

`public void setVerticalScrollBarPolicy(int policy)`

Sets the policy for showing the vertical scroll bar. The policy should be one of
JScrollPane.VERTICAL_SCROLLBAR_ALWAYS
JScrollPane.VERTICAL_SCROLLBAR_NEVER
JScrollPane.VERTICAL_SCROLLBAR_AS_NEEDED
The phrase AS_NEEDED means the scroll bar is shown only when it is needed. This is explained more fully in Chapter 18. The meanings of the other policy constants are obvious from their names.
(As indicated, these constants are defined in the class JScrollPane. You should not need to even be aware of the fact that they have int values. Think of them as policies, not as int values.)

JTextArea

See `JTextComponent`.

JTextComponent

Package: `javax.swing.text`
The classes `JTextField` and `JTextArea` are in the package `javax.swing`.
All these methods are inherited by the classes `JTextField` and `JTextArea`.
Ancestor classes:

```
Object
  |
  +--Component
        |
        +--Container
              |
              +--JComponent
                    |
                    +--JTextComponent
                    |           \
                    +--JTextField  +--JTextArea
```

`public String getText()`

Returns the text that is displayed by this text component.

`public boolean isEditable()`

Returns `true` if the user can write in this text component. Returns `false` if the user is not allowed to write in this text component.

`public void setBackground(Color theColor)`

Sets the background color of this text component.

`public void setEditable(boolean argument)`

If `argument` is `true`, then the user is allowed to write in the text component. If `argument` is `false`, then the user is not allowed to write in the text component.

`public void setText(String text)`

Sets the text that is displayed by this text component to be the specified `text`.

JTextField

See `JTextComponent`.

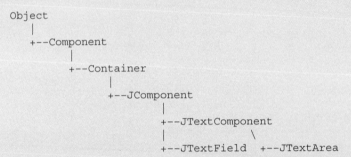

`List<T>` Interface

Package: `java.util`
Ancestor interfaces: `Collection<T>`, `Iterable<T>`
All the exception classes mentioned are the kind that are not required to be caught in a `catch` block or declared in a `throws` clause.
All the exception classes mentioned are in the package `java.lang` and so do not require any `import` statement.

CONSTRUCTORS

Although not officially required by the interface, any class that implements the `List<T>` interface should have at least two constructors: a no-argument constructor that creates an empty `List<T>` object, and a constructor with one parameter of type `Collection<? extends T>` that creates a `List<T>` object with the same elements as the constructor argument. If the argument imposes an ordering on its elements, then the `List<T>` created should preserve this ordering.

```
public boolean contains(Object target)
```

Returns `true` if the calling object contains at least one instance of `target`. Uses `target.equals` to determine if `target` is in the calling object.

Throws:

`ClassCastException` if the type of `target` is incompatible with the calling object (optional).
`NullPointerException` if `target` is `null` and the calling object does not support `null` elements (optional).

```
public boolean containsAll(Collection<?> collectionOfTargets)
```

Returns `true` if the calling object contains all of the elements in `collectionOfTargets`. For `element` in `collectionOfTargets`, uses `element.equals` to determine if `element` is in the calling object. The elements need not be in the same order or have the same multiplicity in `collectionOfTargets` and in the calling object.

```
public boolean equals(Object other)
```

If the argument is a `List`, returns `true` if the calling object and the argument contain exactly the same elements in exactly the same order; otherwise returns `false`. If the argument is not a `List`, `false` is returned.

```
public int hashCode()
```

Returns the hash code value for the calling object. Neither hash codes nor this method is discussed in this book. This entry is only here to make the definition of the `List` interface complete. You can safely ignore this entry until you go on to study hash codes in a more advanced book. In the meantime, if you need to implement this method, have it throw an `UnsupportedOperationException`.

```
boolean isEmpty()
```

Returns `true` if the calling object is empty; otherwise returns `false`.

`Iterator<T> iterator()`

Returns an iterator for the calling object. (Iterators are discussed in Section 16.3.)

`public Object[] toArray()`

Returns an array containing all of the elements in the calling object. The elements in the returned array are in the same order as in the calling object. A new array must be returned so that the calling object has no references to the returned array.

`public <E> E[] toArray(E[] a)`

Note that the type parameter `E` is not the same as `T`. So, `E` can be any reference type; it need not be the type `T` in `Collection<T>`. For example, `E` might be an ancestor type of `T`.
Returns an array containing all of the elements in the calling object. The elements in the returned array are in the same order as in the calling object. The argument `a` is used primarily to specify the type of the array returned. The exact details are described in the table for the `Collection<T>` interface.

Throws:

`ArrayStoreException` if the type of `a` is not an ancestor type of the type of every element in the calling object.
`NullPointerException` if `a` is `null`.

`public int size()`

Returns the number of elements in the calling object. If the calling object contains more than `Integer.MAX_VALUE` elements, returns `Integer.MAX_VALUE`.

OPTIONAL METHODS

As with the `Collection<T>` interface, the following methods are optional, which means they still must be implemented, but the implementation can simply throw an `UnsupportedOperationException` if for some reason you do not want to give them a "real" implementation. An `UnsupportedOperationException` is a `RunTimeException` and so is not required to be caught or declared in a `throws` clause.

`public boolean add(T element)` *(Optional)*

Adds `element` to the end of the calling object's list. Normally returns `true`. Returns `false` if the operation failed, but if the operation failed, something is seriously wrong and you will probably get a run-time error anyway.

Throws:

`UnsupportedOperationException` if the `add` method is not supported by the calling object.
`ClassCastException` if the class of `element` prevents it from being added to the calling object.
`NullPointerException` if `element` is `null` and the calling object does not support `null` elements.
`IllegalArgumentException` if some aspect of `element` prevents it from being added to the calling object.

`public boolean addAll(Collection<? extends T> collectionToAdd)` *(Optional)*

Adds all of the elements in `collectionToAdd` to the end of the calling object's list. The elements are added in the order they are produced by an iterator for `collectionToAdd`.

Throws:

`UnsupportedOperationException` if the `addAll` method is not supported by the calling object.
`ClassCastException` if the class of an element in `collectionToAdd` prevents it from being added to the calling object.
`NullPointerException` if `collectionToAdd` contains one or more `null` elements and the calling object does not support `null` elements, or if `collectionToAdd` is `null`.
`IllegalArgumentException` if some aspect of an element in `collectionToAdd` prevents it from being added to the calling object.

`public void clear()` *(Optional)*

Removes all the elements from the calling object.

Throws:

`UnsupportedOperationException` if the `clear` method is not supported by the calling object.

`public boolean remove(Object element)` *(Optional)*

Removes the first occurrence of `element` from the calling object's list, if it is present. Returns `true` if the calling object contained the `element`; returns `false` otherwise.

Throws:

`ClassCastException` if the type of `element` is incompatible with the calling object *(optional).*
`NullPointerException` if `element` is `null` and the calling object does not support `null` elements (optional).
`UnsupportedOperationException` if the `remove` method is not supported by the calling object.

`public boolean removeAll(Collection<?> collectionToRemove)` *(Optional)*

Removes all the calling object's elements that are also in `collectionToRemove`. Returns `true` if the calling object was changed; otherwise returns `false`.

Throws:

`UnsupportedOperationException` if the `removeAll` method is not supported by the calling object.
`ClassCastException` if the types of one or more elements in the calling object are incompatible with `collectionToRemove` (optional).
`NullPointerException` if the calling object contains one or more `null` elements and `collectionToRemove` does not support `null` elements (optional).
`NullPointerException` if `collectionToRemove` is `null`.

`public boolean retainAll(Collection<?> saveElements)` *(Optional)*

Retains only the elements in the calling object that are also in the collection `saveElements`. In other words, removes from the calling object all of its elements that are not contained in the collection `saveElements`. Returns `true` if the calling object was changed; otherwise returns `false`.

Throws:

`UnsupportedOperationException` if the `retainAll` method is not supported by the calling object.
`ClassCastException` if the types of one or more elements in the calling object are incompatible with `saveElements` (optional).
`NullPointerException` if the calling object contains one or more `null` elements and `saveElements` does not support `null` elements (optional).
`NullPointerException` if the collection `saveElements` is `null`.

NEW METHOD HEADINGS

The following methods are in the `List<T>` interface but were not in the `Collection<T>` interface. Those that are optional are noted.

`public void add(int index, T newElement)` *(Optional)*

Inserts `newElement` in the calling object's list at location `index`. The old elements at location `index` and higher are moved to higher indices.

Throws:

`IndexOutOfBoundsException` if the `index` is not in the range:
`0 <= index <= size()`.
`UnsupportedOperationException` if this `add` method is not supported by the calling object.
`ClassCastException` if the class of `newElement` prevents it from being added to the calling object.
`NullPointerException` if `newElement` is `null` and the calling object does not support `null` elements.
`IllegalArgumentException` if some aspect of `newElement` prevents it from being added to the calling object.

```
public boolean addAll(int index,
                 Collection<? extends T> collectionToAdd)
```
(Optional)

Inserts all of the elements in `collectionToAdd` to the calling object's list starting at location `index`. The old elements at location `index` and higher are moved to higher indices. The elements are added in the order they are produced by an iterator for `collectionToAdd`. Returns `true` if successful; otherwise returns `false`.

Throws:

`IndexOutOfBoundsException` if the `index` is not in the range:
`0 <= index <= size()`.
`UnsupportedOperationException` if the `addAll` method is not supported by the calling object.
`ClassCastException` if the class of one of the elements of `collectionToAdd` prevents it from being added to the calling object.
`NullPointerException` if `collectionToAdd` contains one or more `null` elements and the calling object does not support `null` elements, or if `collectionToAdd` is `null`.
`IllegalArgumentException` if some aspect of one of the elements of `collectionToAdd` prevents it from being added to the calling object.

`public int indexOf(Object target)`

Returns the index of the first element that is equal to `target`. Uses the method `equals` of the object `target` to test for equality. Returns `-1` if `target` is not found.

Throws:

`ClassCastException` if the type of `target` is incompatible with the calling object (optional).
`NullPointerException` if `target` is `null` and the calling object does not support `null` elements (optional).

`public int lastIndexOf(Object target)`

Returns the index of the last element that is equal to `target`. Uses the method `equals` of the object `target` to test for equality. Returns `-1` if `target` is not found.

Throws:

`ClassCastException` if the type of `target` is incompatible with the calling object (optional).
`NullPointerException` if `target` is `null` and the calling object does not support `null` elements (optional).

`public List<T> subList(int fromIndex, int toIndex)`

Returns a *view* of the elements at locations `fromIndex` to `toIndex` of the calling object; the object at `fromIndex` is included; the object, if any, at `toIndex` is not included. The *view* uses references into the calling object; so, changing the *view* can change the calling object. The returned object will be of type `List<T>` but need not be of the same type as the calling object. Returns an empty `List<T>` if `fromIndex` equals `toIndex`.

Throws:

`IndexOutOfBoundsException` if `fromIndex` and `toIndex` do not satisfy:
`0 <= fromIndex <= toIndex <= size()`.

`ListIterator<T> listIterator()`

Returns a list iterator for the calling object. (Iterators are discussed in Section 16.3.)

`ListIterator<T> listIterator(int index)`

Returns a list iterator for the calling object starting at `index`. The first element to be returned by the iterator is the one at `index`. (Iterators are discussed in Section 16.3.)

Throws:

`IndexOutOfBoundsException` if `index` does not satisfy:
`0 <= index <= size()`

`public T get(int index)`

Returns the object at position `index`.
Throws an `IndexOutOfBoundsException` if the `index` is not in the range:
`0 <= index < size()`.

`public T remove(int index)` *(Optional)*

Removes the element at position `index` in the calling object. Shifts any subsequent elements to the left (subtracts one from their indices). Returns the element that was removed from the calling object.

Throws:

`UnsupportedOperationException` if the `remove` method is not supported by the calling object.
`IndexOutOfBoundsException` if `index` does not satisfy:
`0 <= index < size()`

`public T set(int index, T newElement)` *(Optional)*

Sets the element at the specified `index` to `newElement`. The element previously at that position is returned.

Throws:

`IndexOutOfBoundsException` if the `index` is not in the range:
`0 <= index < size()`.
`UnsupportedOperationException` if the `set` method is not supported by the calling object.
`ClassCastException` if the class of `newElement` prevents it from being added to the calling object.
`NullPointerException` if `newElement` is `null` and the calling object does not support `null` elements.
`IllegalArgumentException` if some aspect of `newElement` prevents it from being added to the calling object.

ListIterator<T> Interface

Package: `java.util`
Ancestor interfaces: `Iterator<T>`
The *cursor position* is explained in Chapter 16.
All the exception classes mentioned are the kind that are not required to be caught in a `catch` block or declared in a `throws` clause.
`NoSuchElementException` is in the `java.util` package, which requires an `import` statement if your code mentions the `NoSuchElementException` class. All the other exception classes mentioned are in the package `java.lang` and so do not require any `import` statements.

`public void add(T newElement)` *(Optional)*

Inserts `newElement` at the location of the iterator cursor (that is, before the value, if any, that would be returned by `next()` and after the value, if any, that would be returned by `previous()`). Cannot be used if there has been a call to `add` or `remove` since the last call to `next()` or `previous()`.

Throws:

`IllegalStateException` if neither `next()` nor `previous()` has been called, or the `add` or `remove` method has already been called after the last call to `next()` or `previous()`.
`UnsupportedOperationException` if the `remove` operation is not supported by this `Iterator`.
`ClassCastException` if the class of `newElement` prevents it from being added.
`IllegalArgumentException` if some property other than the class of `newElement` prevents it from being added.

`public boolean hasNext()`

Returns `true` if there is a suitable element for `next()` to return; returns `false` otherwise.

`public boolean hasPrevious()`

Returns `true` if there is a suitable element for `previous()` to return; returns `false` otherwise.

`public int nextIndex()`

Returns the index of the element that would be returned by a call to `next()`. Returns the list size if the cursor position is at the end of the list.

`public T next()`

Returns the next element of the list that produced the iterator. More specifically, returns the element immediately after the cursor position.

Throws:

`NoSuchElementException` if there is no next element.

`public T previous()`

Returns the previous element of the list that produced the iterator. More specifically, returns the element immediately before the cursor position.

Throws:

`NoSuchElementException` if there is no previous element.

`public int previousIndex()`

Returns the index that would be returned by a call to `previous()`. Returns `-1` if the cursor position is at the beginning of the list.

`public void remove()` (*Optional*)

Removes from the collection the last element returned by `next()` or `previous()`.
This method can be called only once per call to `next()` or `previous()`.
Cannot be used if there has been a call to `add` or `remove` since the last call to `next()` or `previous()`.

Throws:

`IllegalStateException` if neither `next()` nor `previous()` has been called, or the `add` or `remove` method has already been called after the last call to `next()` or `previous()`.
`UnsupportedOperationException` if the `remove` operation is not supported by this `Iterator`.

`public void set(T newElement)` *(Optional)*

Replaces the last element returned by `next()` or `previous()` with `newElement`. Cannot be used if there has been a call to `add or remove` since the last call to `next()` or `previous()`.

Throws:

`UnsupportedOperationException` if the set operation is not supported by this `Iterator`.
`IllegalStateException` if neither `next()` nor `previous()` has been called, or the `add` or `remove` method has been called since the last call to `next()` or `previous()`.
`ClassCastException` if the class of `newElement` prevents it from being added.
`IllegalArgumentException` if some property other than the class of `newElement` prevents it from being added.

Long

This is a wrapper class for `long`. See Section 5.1 in Chapter 5.

Math

Package: `java.lang`

```
Object
   |
   +--Math
```

The `Math` class is marked `final`, which means it cannot be used as a base class to derive other classes.

`public static double abs(double argument)`

`public static float abs(float argument)`

`public static long abs(long argument)`

`public static int abs(int argument)`

Returns the absolute value of the `argument`. (The method name `abs` is overloaded to produce four similar methods.)

EXAMPLES

`Math.abs(-6)` and `Math.abs(6)` both return `6.Math.abs(-5.5)` and `Math.abs(5.5)` both return `5.5`.

`public static double ceil(double argument)`

Returns the smallest whole number greater than or equal to the `argument`.

EXAMPLE

`Math.ceil(3.2)` and `Math.ceil(3.9)` both return `4.0`.

`public static double floor(double argument)`

Returns the largest whole number less than or equal to the `argument`.

EXAMPLE

`Math.floor (3.2)` and `Math.floor (3.9)` both return `3.0`.

```
public static double max(double n1, double n2)
public static float max(float n1, float n2)
public static long max(long n1, long n2)
public static int max(int n1, int n2)
```

Returns the maximum of the arguments `n1` and `n2`. (The method name `max` is overloaded to produce four similar methods.)

EXAMPLE

`Math.max(3, 2)` returns 3.

```
public static double min(double n1, double n2)
public static float min(float n1, float n2)
public static long min(long n1, long n2)
public static int min(int n1, int n2)
```

Returns the minimum of the arguments `n1` and `n2`. (The method name `min` is overloaded to produce four similar methods.)

EXAMPLE

`Math.min(3, 2)` returns 2.

```
public static double pow(double base, double exponent)
```

Returns `base` to the power `exponent`.

EXAMPLE

`Math.pow(2.0,3.0)` returns 8.0.

```
public static double random()
```

Returns a random number greater than or equal to 0.0 and less than 1.0.

EXAMPLE

`Math.random()` returns `0.5505562535943004` (example value only; will return a pseudo-random number that is less than 1 and greater than or equal to 0 the next time the statement is executed)

```
public static long round(double argument)
public static int round(float argument)
```

Rounds its `argument`.

EXAMPLES

`Math.round(3.2)` returns `3`. `Math.round(3.6)` returns `4`.

```
public static double sqrt(double argument)
```

Returns the square root of its `argument`.

EXAMPLE

`Math.sqrt(4)` returns `2.0`.

Map<K,V> Interface

Package: java.util
Ancestor interfaces: none
All the exception classes mentioned are unchecked exceptions, which means they are not required to be caught in a catch block or declared in a throws clause. No import statement is required because these exception classes are in the package java.lang.

CONSTRUCTORS

Although not officially required by the interface, any class that implements the Map<K,V> interface should have at least two constructors: a no-argument constructor that creates an empty Map<K,V> object, and a constructor with one Map<K,V> parameter that creates a Map<K,V> object with the same elements as the constructor argument. The interface does not specify whether the copy produced by the one-argument constructor is a shallow copy or a deep copy of its argument.

METHODS

```
public boolean containsKey(Object key)
```

Returns true if the calling object contains key as one of its keys.

Throws:

ClassCastException if the type of key is incompatible with the type for this map (optional).
NullPointerException if the key is null and this map does not permit null keys (optional).

```
public boolean containsValue(Object value)
```

Returns true if the calling object contains one or more keys that map to an instance of value.

Throws:

ClassCastException if the type of value is incompatible with the type for this map (optional).
NullPointerException if the value is null and this map does not permit null values (optional).

```
public Set<Map.Entry<K,V>> entrySet()
```

Returns a set view consisting of (key, value) mappings for all entries in the map. Changes to the map are reflected in the set and vice-versa.

```
public boolean equals(Object other)
```

This is the equals of the map, not the equals of the elements in the map. Overrides the inherited method equals.

```
public V get(Object key)
```

Returns the value onto which the calling object maps key. If key is not in the map, then null is returned. Note that this does not always mean that the key is not in the map, because it is possible to map a key to null. The containsKey method can be used to distinguish the two cases.

Throws:

ClassCastException if the type of key is incompatible with the type for this map (optional).
NullPointerException if the key is null and this map does not permit null keys (optional).

`public int hashCode()`

Returns the hash code value for the calling object. The hash code of a map is defined to be the sum of the `hashCodes` of each entry in the map's `entrySet` view.

`public boolean isEmpty()`

Returns `true` if the calling object is empty; otherwise returns `false`.

`public int size()`

Returns the number of (key, value) mappings in the calling object.

`public Collection<V> values()`

Returns a collection view consisting of all values in the map. Changes to the map are reflected in the collection and vice-versa.

OPTIONAL METHODS

The following methods are optional, which means they still must be implemented, but the implementation can simply throw an `UnsupportedOperationException` if, for some reason, you do not want to give them a "real" implementation. An `UnsupportedOperationException` is a `RunTimeException` and so is not required to be caught or declared in a `throws` clause.

`public V put(K key, V value)` *(Optional)*

Associates `key` to `value` in the map. If `key` was associated with an existing value, then the old value is overwritten and returned. Otherwise `null` is returned.

Throws:

`ClassCastException` if the type of `key` or `value` is incompatible with the type for this map (optional).
`NullPointerException` if the key or value is `null` and this map does not permit `null` keys or values (optional).
`IllegalArgumentException` if some aspect of the key or value prevents it from being stored in this map (optional).
`UnsupportedOperationException` if the `put` operation is not supported by this map (optional).

`public void putAll(Map<? extends K,? extends V> mapToAdd)` *(Optional)*

Adds all mappings of `mapToAdd` into the calling object's map.

Throws:

`ClassCastException` if any type of `key` or `value` of `mapToAdd` is incompatible with the type for this map (optional).
`NullPointerException` if `mapToAdd` is `null` or any key or value of `mapToAdd` is null and this map does not permit null keys or values (optional).
`IllegalArgumentException` if some aspect of the key or value from `mapToAdd` prevents it from being stored in this map (optional).
`UnsupportedOperationException` if the `putAll` operation is not supported by this map (optional).

```
public V remove(Object key) (Optional)
```

Removes the mapping for the specified key. If the key is not found in the map, then `null` is returned, otherwise the previous value for the key is returned.

Throws:

`ClassCastException` if the type of `key` is incompatible with the type for this map (optional).
`NullPointerException` if the key is `null` and this map does not permit `null` keys (optional).
`UnsupportedOperationException` if the remove operation is not supported by this map (optional).

ObjectInputStream

Package: `java.io`
The `FileInputStream` class is also in this package.
Ancestor classes:

```
Object
  |
  +--InputStream
         |
         +--ObjectInputStream
```

```
public ObjectInputStream(InputStream streamObject)
```

There is no constructor that takes a file name as an argument. If you want to create a stream using a file name, use

```
new ObjectInputStream(new FileInputStream(File_Name))
```

Alternatively, you can use an object of the class `File` in place of the *File_Name*, as follows:

```
new ObjectInputStream(new FileInputStream(File_Object))
```

The constructor for `FileInputStream` may throw a `FileNotFoundException`, which is a kind of `IOException`. If the `FileInputStream` constructor succeeds, then the constructor for `ObjectInputStream` may throw a different `IOException`.

```
public void close()throws IOException
```

Closes the stream's connection to a file.

```
public boolean readBoolean()throws IOException
```

Reads a `boolean` value from the input stream and returns that `boolean` value. If `readBoolean` tries to read a value from the file and that value was not written using the method `writeBoolean` of the class `ObjectOutputStream` (or written in some equivalent way), then problems will occur.

If an attempt is made to read beyond the end of the file, an `EOFException` is thrown.

`public char readChar() throws IOException`

Reads a `char` value from the input stream and returns that `char` value. If `readChar` tries to read a value from the file and that value was not written using the method `writeChar` of the class `ObjectOutputStream` (or written in some equivalent way), then problems will occur.

If an attempt is made to read beyond the end of the file, an `EOFException` is thrown.

`public double readDouble() throws IOException`

Reads a `double` value from the input stream and returns that `double` value. If `readDouble` tries to read a value from the file and that value was not written using the method `writeDouble` of the class `ObjectOutputStream` (or written in some equivalent way), then problems will occur.

If an attempt is made to read beyond the end of the file, an `EOFException` is thrown.

`public float readFloat() throws IOException`

Reads a `float` value from the input stream and returns that `float` value. If `readFloat` tries to read a value from the file and that value was not written using the method `writeFloat` of the class `ObjectOutputStream` (or written in some equivalent way), then problems will occur.

If an attempt is made to read beyond the end of the file, an `EOFException` is thrown.

`public int readInt() throws IOException`

Reads an `int` value from the input stream and returns that `int` value. If `readInt` tries to read a value from the file and that value was not written using the method `writeInt` of the class `ObjectOutputStream` (or written in some equivalent way), then problems will occur.

If an attempt is made to read beyond the end of the file, an `EOFException` is thrown.

`public long readLong() throws IOException`

Reads a `long` value from the input stream and returns that `long` value. If `readLong` tries to read a value from the file and that value was not written using the method `writeLong` of the class `ObjectOutputStream` (or written in some equivalent way), then problems will occur.

If an attempt is made to read beyond the end of the file, an `EOFException` is thrown.

`Object readObject() throws ClassNotFoundException, IOException`

Reads an object from the input stream. The object read should have been written using `writeObject` of the class `ObjectOutputStream`.

Throws:

`ClassNotFoundException` if the class of a serialized object cannot be found.
If an attempt is made to read beyond the end of the file, an `EOFException` is thrown.
May throw various other `IOExceptions`.

```
public int readShort()throws IOException
```

Reads a `short` value from the input stream and returns that `short` value. If `readInt` tries to read a value from the file and that value was not written using the method `writeShort` of the class `ObjectOutputStream` (or written in some equivalent way), then problems will occur.

If an attempt is made to read beyond the end of the file, an `EOFException` is thrown.

```
public String readUTF()throws IOException
```

Reads a `String` value from the input stream and returns that `String` value. If `readUTF` tries to read a value from the file and that value was not written using the method `writeUTF` of the class `ObjectOutputStream` (or written in some equivalent way), then problems will occur.

If an attempt is made to read beyond the end of the file, an `EOFException` is thrown.

```
public int skipBytes(int n) throws IOException
```

Skips n bytes.

`ObjectOutputStream`

Package: `java.io`
The `FileOutputStream` class is also in this package.
Ancestor classes:

```
Object
  |
  +--OutputStream
        |
        +--ObjectOutputStream
```

```
public ObjectOutputStream(OutputStream streamObject)
```

There is no constructor that takes a file name as an argument. If you want to create a stream using a file name, use

`new ObjectOutputStream(new FileOutputStream(`*File_Name*`))`

This creates a blank file. If there already is a file named *File_Name*, then the old contents of the file are lost.
If you want to create a stream using an object of the class `File`, use

`new ObjectOutputStream(new FileOutputStream(`*File_Object*`))`

The constructor for `FileOutputStream` may throw a `FileNotFoundException`, which is a kind of `IOException`. If the `FileOutputStream` constructor succeeds, then the constructor for `ObjectOutputStream` may throw a different `IOException`.

```
public void close()throws IOException
```

Closes the stream's connection to a file. This method calls `flush` before closing the file.

```
public void flush()throws IOException
```

Flushes the output stream. This forces an actual physical write to the file of any data that has been buffered and not yet physically written to the file. Normally, you should not need to invoke `flush`.

```
public void writeBoolean(boolean b) throws IOException
```

Writes the `boolean` value `b` to the output stream.

```
public void writeChar(int n) throws IOException
```

Writes the `char` value `n` to the output stream. Note that it expects its argument to be an `int` value. However, if you simply use the `char` value, then Java will automatically type cast it to an `int` value. The following are equivalent:

```
outputStream.writeChar((int)'A');
```

and

```
outputStream.writeChar('A');
```

```
public void writeDouble(double x) throws IOException
```

Writes the `double` value `x` to the output stream.

```
public void writeFloat(float x) throws IOException
```

Writes the `float` value `x` to the output stream.

```
public void writeInt(int n) throws IOException
```

Writes the `int` value `n` to the output stream.

```
public void writeLong(long n) throws IOException
```

Writes the `long` value `n` to the output stream.

```
public void writeObject(Object anObject) throws IOException
```

Writes its argument to the output stream. The object argument should be an object of a serializable class, a concept discussed in Chapter 10.

Throws:

Various `IOExceptions`.

```
public void writeShort(short n) throws IOException
```

Writes the `short` value `n` to the output stream.

```
public void writeUTF(String aString) throws IOException
```

Writes the `String` value `aString` to the output stream. `UTF` refers to a particular method of encoding the string. To read the string back from the file, you should use the method `readUTF` of the class `ObjectInputStream`.

PrintWriter

Package: `java.io`
The `FileOutputStream` class is also in this package.
Ancestor classes:

```
Object
  |
  +--Writer
       |
       +--PrintWriter
```

```
public PrintWriter(OutputStream streamObject)
```

This is the only constructor you are likely to need. There is no constructor that accepts a file name as an argument. If you want to create a stream using a file name, use

`new PrintWriter (new FileOutputStream(`*File_Name*`))`

When the constructor is used in this way, a blank file is created. If there already was a file named *File_Name*, then the old contents of the file are lost. If you want instead to append new text to the end of the old file contents, use

`new PrintWriter(new FileOutputStream (`*File_Name,* `true))`

(For an explanation of the argument `true`, see Chapter 10.)
When used in either of these ways, the `FileOutputStream` constructor, and so the `PrintWriter` constructor invocation, can throw a `FileNotFoundException`, which is a kind of `IOException`.
If you want to create a stream using an object of the class `File`, you can use a `File` object in place of the *File_Name*.

```
public void close()
```

Closes the stream's connection to a file. This method calls `flush` before closing the file.

```
public void flush()
```

Flushes the output stream. This forces an actual physical write to the file of any data that has been buffered and not yet physically written to the file. Normally, you should not need to invoke `flush`.

`public final void print(`*Argument*`)`

Same as `println`, except that this method does not end the line, and so the next output will be on the same line.

`public final void println(`*Argument*`)`

The *Argument* can be a string, character, integer, floating-point number, boolean value, or any combination of these, connected with + signs. The *Argument* can also be any object, although it will not work as desired unless the object has a properly defined `toString()` method. The *Argument* is output to the file connected to the stream. After the *Argument* has been output, the line ends, and so the next output is sent to the next line.

Random

Package: `java.util`
Ancestor classes:

```
Object
   |
   +--Random
```

```
public Random()
```

Creates a new random number generator.

```
public Random(long seed)
```

Creates a new random number generator with the specified seed value.

```
public int nextInt(int n)
```

Returns a pseudo-random, uniformly distributed `int` value between 0 (inclusive) and the value `n` (exclusive).

```
public double nextDouble(double n)
```

Returns a pseudo-random, uniformly distributed `double` value between 0 (inclusive) and 1 (exclusive).

RandomAccessFile

Package: `java.io`

```
Object
   |
   +--RandomAccessFile
```

```
public RandomAccessFile(String fileName, String mode)
```

```
public RandomAccessFile(File fileObject, String mode)
```

Opens the file, does not delete data already in the file, but does position the file pointer at the first (zeroth) location.
The `mode` must be one of the following:
`"r"` Open for reading only.
`"rw"` Open for reading and writing.
`"rws"` Same as `"rw"`, and also requires that every update to the file's content or metadata be written synchronously to the underlying storage device.
`"rwd"` Same as `"rw"`, and also requires that every update to the file's content be written synchronously to the underlying storage device.
`"rws"` and `"rwd"` are not covered in this book text.

```
public void close()throws IOException
```

Closes the stream's connection to a file.

`public void setLength(long newLength) throws IOException`

Sets the length of this file.
If the present length of the file as returned by the `length` method is greater than the `newLength` argument, then the file will be truncated. In this case, if the file pointer location as returned by the `getFilePointer` method is greater than `newLength`, then after this method returns, the file pointer location will be equal to `newLength`.
If the present length of the file as returned by the `length` method is smaller than `newLength`, then the file will be extended. In this case, the contents of the extended portion of the file are not defined.

`public long getFilePointer()throws IOException`

Returns the current location of the file pointer. Locations are numbered starting with `0`.

`public long length()throws IOException`

Returns the length of the file.

`public int read()throws IOException`

Reads a byte of data from the file and returns it as an integer in the range 0 to 255.

`public int read(byte[] a) throws IOException`

Reads up to `a.length` bytes of data from the file into the array of bytes. Returns the total number of bytes read or -1 if the end of the file is reached.

`public final boolean readBoolean()throws IOException`

Reads a `boolean` value from the file and returns that value.

If an attempt is made to read beyond the end of the file, an `EOFException` is thrown.

`public final byte readByte()throws IOException`

Reads a `byte` value from the file and returns that value.

If an attempt is made to read beyond the end of the file, an `EOFException` is thrown.

`public final char readChar()throws IOException`

Reads a `char` value from the file and returns that value.

If an attempt is made to read beyond the end of the file, an `EOFException` is thrown.

`public final double readDouble()throws IOException`

Reads a `double` value from the file and returns that value.

If an attempt is made to read beyond the end of the file, an `EOFException` is thrown.

`public final float readFloat()throws IOException`

Reads a `float` value from the file and returns that value.

If an attempt is made to read beyond the end of the file, an `EOFException` is thrown.

`public final int readInt() throws IOException`

Reads an `int` value from the file and returns that value.

If an attempt is made to read beyond the end of the file, an `EOFException` is thrown.

`public final long readLong() throws IOException`

Reads a `long` value from the file and returns that value.

If an attempt is made to read beyond the end of the file, an `EOFException` is thrown.

`public final short readShort() throws IOException`

Reads a `short` value from the file and returns that value.

If an attempt is made to read beyond the end of the file, an `EOFException` is thrown.

`public final String readUTF() throws IOException`

Reads a `String` value from the file and returns that value.

If an attempt is made to read beyond the end of the file, an `EOFException` is thrown.

`public void seek(long location) throws IOException`

Moves the file pointer to the specified `location`.

`public void write(byte[] a) throws IOException`

Writes `a.length` bytes from the specified byte array to the file.

`public void write(int b) throws IOException`

Writes the specified byte to the file.

`public final void writeBoolean(boolean b ) throws IOException`

Writes the `boolean` `b` to the file.

`public final void writeByte(byte b ) throws IOException`

Writes the `byte b` to the file.

`public final void writeChar(char c ) throws IOException`

Writes the `char c` to the file.

`public final void writeDouble(double d ) throws IOException`

Writes the `double d` to the file.

`public final void writeFloat(float f ) throws IOException`

Writes the `float f` to the file.

`public final void writeInt(int n ) throws IOException`

Writes the `int n` to the file.

```
public final void writeLong(long n ) throws IOException
```

Writes the `long` `n` to the file.

```
public final void writeShort(short n ) throws IOException
```

Writes the `short` `n` to the file.

```
public final void writeUTF(String s ) throws IOException
```

Writes the `String` `s` to the file.

`Scanner`

Package: `java.util`
Ancestor classes:

```
Object
   |
   +--Scanner
```

The `Scanner` class can be used to obtain input from files as well as from the keyboard. Values to be read should be separated by whitespace characters, such as blanks and/or new lines. When reading values, these whitespace characters are skipped. (It is possible to change the separators from whitespace to something else, but whitespace is the default.)

```
public Scanner(InputStream streamObject)
```

There is no constructor that accepts a file name as an argument. If you want to create a stream using a file name, you can use

```
new Scanner(new FileInputStream(File_Name))
```

When used in this way, the `FileInputStream` constructor, and thus the `Scanner` constructor invocation, can throw a `FileNotFoundException`, which is a kind of `IOException`.
To create a stream connected to the keyboard, use

```
new Scanner(System.in)
```

```
public Scanner(File fileObject)
```

If you want to create a stream using a file name, you can use

```
new Scanner(new File(File_Name))
```

```
public int nextInt()
```

Returns the next token as an `int`, provided the next token is a well-formed string representation of an `int`.

Throws:

`NoSuchElementException` if there are no more tokens.
`InputMismatchException` if the next token is not a well-formed string representation of an `int`.
`IllegalStateException` if the `Scanner` stream is closed.

`public boolean hasNextInt()`

Returns `true` if the next token is a well-formed string representation of an `int`; otherwise returns `false`.

Throws:

`IllegalStateException` if the `Scanner` stream is closed.

`public long nextLong()`

Returns the next token as a `long`, provided the next token is a well-formed string representation of a `long`.

Throws:

`NoSuchElementException` if there are no more tokens.
`InputMismatchException` if the next token is not a well-formed string representation of a `long`.
`IllegalStateException` if the `Scanner` stream is closed.

`public boolean hasNextLong()`

Returns `true` if the next token is a well-formed string representation of a `long`; otherwise returns `false`.

Throws:

`IllegalStateException` if the `Scanner` stream is closed.

`public byte nextByte()`

Returns the next token as a `byte`, provided the next token is a well-formed string representation of a `byte`.

Throws:

`NoSuchElementException` if there are no more tokens.
`InputMismatchException` if the next token is not a well-formed string representation of a `byte`.
`IllegalStateException` if the `Scanner` stream is closed.

`public boolean hasNextByte()`

Returns `true` if the next token is a well-formed string representation of a `byte`; otherwise returns `false`.

Throws:

`IllegalStateException` if the `Scanner` stream is closed.

`public short nextShort()`

Returns the next token as a `short`, provided the next token is a well-formed string representation of a `short`.

Throws:

`NoSuchElementException` if there are no more tokens.
`InputMismatchException` if the next token is not a well-formed string representation of a `short`.
`IllegalStateException` if the `Scanner` stream is closed.

`public boolean hasNextShort()`

Returns `true` if the next token is a well-formed string representation of a `short`; otherwise returns `false`.

Throws:

`IllegalStateException` if the `Scanner` stream is closed.

`public double nextDouble()`

Returns the next token as a `double`, provided the next token is a well-formed string representation of a `double`.

Throws:

`NoSuchElementException` if there are no more tokens.
`InputMismatchException` if the next token is not a well-formed string representation of a `double`.
`IllegalStateException` if the `Scanner` stream is closed.

`public boolean hasNextDouble()`

Returns `true` if the next token is a well-formed string representation of a `double`; otherwise returns `false`.

Throws:

`IllegalStateException` if the `Scanner` stream is closed.

`public float nextFloat()`

Returns the next token as a `float`, provided the next token is a well-formed string representation of a `float`.

Throws:

`NoSuchElementException` if there are no more tokens.
`InputMismatchException` if the next token is not a well-formed string representation of a `float`.
`IllegalStateException` if the `Scanner` stream is closed.

`public boolean hasNextFloat()`

Returns `true` if the next token is a well-formed string representation of a `float`; otherwise returns `false`.

Throws:

`IllegalStateException` if the `Scanner` stream is closed.

`public String next()`

Returns the `next token`.

Throws:

`NoSuchElementException` if there are no more tokens.
`IllegalStateException` if the `Scanner` stream is closed.

`public boolean hasNext()`

Returns `true` if there is another token. May wait for a next token to enter the stream.

Throws:

`IllegalStateException` if the `Scanner` stream is closed.

`public boolean nextBoolean()`

Returns the next token as a `boolean` value, provided the next token is a well-formed string representation of a `boolean.`

Throws:

`NoSuchElementException` if there are no more tokens.
`InputMismatchException` if the next token is not a well-formed string representation of a `boolean` value.
`IllegalStateException` if the `Scanner` stream is closed.

`public boolean hasNextBoolean()`

Returns `true` if the next token is a well-formed string representation of a `boolean` value; otherwise returns `false.`

Throws:

`IllegalStateException` if the `Scanner` stream is closed.

`public String nextLine()`

Returns the rest of the current input line. Note that the line terminator `'\n'` is read and discarded; it is not included in the string returned.

Throws:

`NoSuchElementException` if there are no more lines.
`IllegalStateException` if the `Scanner` stream is closed.

`public boolean hasNextLine()`

Returns `true` if there is a next line. May wait for a next line to enter the stream.

Throws:

`IllegalStateException` if the `Scanner` stream is closed.

`public Scanner useDelimiter(String newDelimiter);`

Changes the delimiter for input so that `newDelimiter` will be the only delimiter that separates words or numbers. See the subsection "Other Input Delimiters" in Chapter 2 for the details. (You can use this method to set the delimiters to a more complex pattern than just a single string, but we are not covering that.)

Returns the calling object, but we have always used it as a `void` method.

`Serializable` Interface

See Section 10.4 in Chapter 10.

`Set<T>` Interface

Package: `java.util`
Ancestor interfaces: `Collection <T>`
All the exception classes mentioned are the kind that are not required to be caught in a `catch` block or declared in a `throws` clause.
All the exception classes mentioned are in the package `java.lang` and so do not require any `import` statement.

CONSTRUCTORS

`public boolean contains(Object target)`

Returns `true` if the calling object contains at least one instance of `target`. Uses `target.equals` to determine if `target` is in the calling object.

Throws:

`ClassCastException` if the type of `target` is incompatible with the calling object (optional).
`NullPointerException` if `target` is `null` and the calling object does not support `null` elements (optional).

`public boolean containsAll(Collection<?> collectionOfTargets)`

Returns `true` if the calling object contains all of the elements in `collectionOfTargets`. For `element` in `collectionOfTargets`, this method uses `element.equals` to determine if `element` is in the calling object. If `collectionOfTargets` is itself a `Set <T>`, this is a test to see if `collectionOfTargets` is a subset of the calling object.

Throws:

`ClassCastException` if the types of one or more elements in `collectionOfTargets` are incompatible with the calling object (optional).
`NullPointerException` if `collectionOfTargets` contains one or more `null` elements and the calling object does not support null elements (optional).
`NullPointerException` if `collectionOfTargets` is `null`.

`public boolean equals(Object other)`

If the argument is a `Set <T>`, returns `true` if the calling object and the argument contain exactly the same elements; otherwise returns `false`. If the argument is not a `Set <T>`, `false` is returned.

`public int hashCode()`

Returns the hash code value for the calling object. Neither hash codes nor this method are discussed in this book. This entry is only here to make the definition of the `Set <T>` interface complete. You can safely ignore this entry until you go on to study hash codes in a more advanced book. In the meantime, if you need to implement this method, have it throw an `UnsupportedOperationException`.

`public boolean isEmpty()`

Returns `true` if the calling object is empty; otherwise returns `false`.

`Iterator <T> iterator()`

Returns an iterator for the calling object. (Iterators are discussed in Section 16.3.)

`public Object[] toArray()`

Returns an array containing all of the elements in the calling object. A new array should be returned so that the calling object has no references to the returned array.

`public <E> E[] toArray(E[] a)`

Note that the type parameter `E` is not the same as `T`. So, `E` can be any reference type; it need not be the type `T` in `Collection <T>`. For example, `E` might be an ancestor type of `T`. Returns an array containing all of the elements in the calling object. The argument `a` is used primarily to specify the type of the array returned. The exact details are described in the table for the `Collection <T>` interface.

Throws:

`ArrayStoreException` if the type of `a` is not an ancestor type of the type of every element in the calling object.
`NullPointerException` if `a` is `null`.

`public int size()`

Returns the number of elements in the calling object. If the calling object contains more than `Integer.MAX_VALUE` elements, returns `Integer.MAX_VALUE`.

ADDING AND REMOVING ELEMENTS

Although many are optional, the following methods are almost always implemented for classes that implement the `Set <T>` interface.

`public boolean add(T element)` *(Optional)*

If `element` is not already in the calling object, `element` is added to the calling object and `true` is returned. If `element` is in the calling object, the calling object is unchanged and `false` is returned.

Throws:

`UnsupportedOperationException` if the `add` method is not supported by the set.
`ClassCastException` if the class of `element` prevents it from being added to the set.
`NullPointerException` if `element` is `null` and the set does not support `null` elements.
`IllegalArgumentException` if some other aspect of `element` prevents it from being added to this set.

`public boolean addAll(Collection<? extends T> collectionToAdd)` *(Optional)*

Ensures that the calling object contains all the elements in `collectionToAdd`. Returns `true` if the calling object changed as a result of the call; returns `false` otherwise. Thus, if `collectionToAdd` is a `Set <T>`, then the calling object is changed to the union of itself with `collectionToAdd`.

Throws:

`UnsupportedOperationException` if the `addAll` method is not supported by the set.
`ClassCastException` if the class of some element of `collectionToAdd` prevents it from being added to the calling object.
`NullPointerException` if `collectionToAdd` contains one or more `null` elements and the calling object does not support `null` elements, or if `collectionToAdd` is `null`.
`IllegalArgumentException` if some aspect of some element of `collectionToAdd` prevents it from being added to the calling object.

`public void clear()`

Removes all the elements from the calling object.

Throws:

`UnsupportedOperationException` if the `clear` method is not supported by the calling object.

`public boolean remove(Object element)`

Removes the `element` from the calling object, if it is present. Returns `true` if the calling object contained the `element`; returns `false` otherwise.

Throws:

`ClassCastException` if the type of `element` is incompatible with the calling object (optional).
`NullPointerException` if `element` is `null` and the calling object does not support `null` elements (optional).
`UnsupportedOperationException` if the `remove` method is not supported by the calling object.

`public boolean removeAll(Collection<?> collectionToRemove)` *(Optional)*

Removes all the calling object's elements that are also contained in `collectionToRemove`. Returns `true` if the calling object was changed; otherwise returns `false`.

Throws:

`UnsupportedOperationException` if the `removeAll` method is not supported by the calling object.
`ClassCastException` if the types of one or more elements in `collectionToRemove` are incompatible with the calling object (optional).
`NullPointerException` if the calling object contains a `null` element and `collectionToRemove` does not support `null` elements (optional).
`NullPointerException` if `collectionToRemove` is `null`.

`public boolean retainAll(Collection<?> saveElements)` *(Optional)*

Retains only the elements in the calling object that are also contained in the collection `saveElements`. In other words, removes from the calling object all of its elements that are not contained in the collection `saveElements`. Returns `true` if the calling object was changed; otherwise returns `false`. If the argument is itself a `Set <T>`, this changes the calling object to the intersection of itself with the argument.

Throws:

`UnsupportedOperationException` if the `retainAll` method is not supported by the calling object.
`ClassCastException` if the types of one or more elements in the calling object are incompatible with `saveElements` (optional).
`NullPointerException` if `saveElements` contains a `null` element and the calling object does not support `null` elements (optional).
`NullPointerException` if `saveElements` is `null`.

`Short`

Wrapper class for `short`. See Section 5.1 in Chapter 5.

`String`

Package: `java.lang`
`String` is marked `final` and so you cannot use it as a base class to derive another class.
Implements interfaces: `CharSequence`, `Comparable`, `Serializable`
Ancestor classes:

```
Object
   |
   +--String
```

CONSTRUCTORS

`public String()`

Creates a `String` object that represents an empty character sequence. Note that this is a pretty useless constructor because `String` objects are immutable.

`public String(BufferedString buffer)`

Creates a new `String` object that contains the same sequence of characters that is currently contained in the `BufferedString` argument. This is a deep copy; subsequent modification of the `BufferedString` object does not affect the newly created string.

Throws:

`NullPointerException` if `buffer` is `null`.

`public String(char[] value, int offset, int count)`

Creates a new `String` that contains characters from a subarray of the character array argument. The `offset` argument is the index of the first character of the subarray, and the `count` argument specifies the length of the subarray. The contents of the subarray are copied. This is a deep copy; subsequent modifications of the character array do not affect the newly created string.

Throws:

`IndexOutOfBoundsException` if the elements specified by `offset` and `count` are not all within the bounds of the `value` array.
`NullPointerException` if `value` is `null`.

`public String(String original)`

Creates a new `String` object so that it represents the same sequence of characters as the argument. Unless an explicit copy of `original` is needed, use of this constructor is unnecessary because `String` objects are immutable.

Throws:

`NullPointerException` if `original` is `null`.

METHODS

```
public char charAt(int position)
```

Returns the character in the calling object string at the `position`. Positions are counted 0, 1, 2, etc.

EXAMPLE

After program executes `String greeting = "Hello!";`
`greeting.charAt(0)` returns `'H'`, and
`greeting.charAt(1)` returns `'e'`.

Throws:

`IndexOutOfBoundsException` if `position` is negative or not less than the length of the calling object string.

```
public int compareTo(String aString)
```

Compares the calling object string and the string argument to see which comes first in the lexicographic ordering. Lexicographic order is the same as alphabetical order but with the characters ordered as in Appendix 3. Note that in Appendix 3 all the uppercase letters are in regular alphabetical order and all the lowercase letters are in alphabetical order, but all the uppercase letters precede all the lowercase letters. So, lexicographic ordering is the same as alphabetical ordering when either both strings are all uppercase letters or both strings are all lowercase letters. If the calling string is first, it returns a negative value. If the two strings are equal, it returns zero. If the argument is first, it returns a positive number.

EXAMPLE

After program executes `String entry = "adventure";`
`entry.compareTo("zoo")` returns a negative number,
`entry.compareTo("adventure")` returns `0`, and
`entry.compareTo("above")` returns a positive number.

Throws:

`NullPointerException` if `aString` is `null`.

```
public int compareToIgnoreCase(String aString)
```

Compares the calling object string and the string argument to see which comes first in the lexicographic ordering, treating upper- and lowercase letters as being the same. (To be precise, all uppercase letters are treated as if they were their lowercase versions in doing the comparison.) Thus, if both strings consist entirely of letters, the comparison is for ordinary alphabetical order. If the calling string is first, it returns a negative value. If the two strings are equal, ignoring cases, it returns zero. If the argument is first, it returns a positive number.

EXAMPLE

After program executes `String entry = "adventure";`
`entry.compareToIgnoreCase("Zoo")` returns a negative number,
`entry.compareToIgnoreCase("Adventure")` returns `0`, and
`"Zoo".compareToIgnoreCase(entry)` returns a positive number.

Throws:

`NullPointerException` if `aString` is `null`.

`public boolean contentEquals(StringBuffer stringBufferObject)`

Returns `true` if and only if this `String` represents the same sequence of characters as the `StringBuffer` argument.

Throws:

`NullPointerException` if `stringBufferObject` is `null`.

`public boolean equals(String otherString)`

Returns `true` if the calling object string and the `otherString` are equal. Otherwise returns `false`.

EXAMPLE

After program executes `String greeting = "Hello";`
`greeting.equals("Hello")` returns `true`
`greeting.equals("Good-Bye")` returns `false`
`greeting.equals("hello")` returns `false`
Note that case matters: `"Hello"` and `"hello"` are not equal because one starts with an uppercase letter and the other starts with a lowercase letter.

`public boolean equalsIgnoreCase(String otherString)`

Returns `true` if the calling object string and the `otherString` are equal, considering upper- and lowercase versions of a letter to be the same. Otherwise returns `false`.

EXAMPLE

After program executes `String name = "mary";`
`name.equalsIgnoreCase("Mary")` returns `true`.

`public int indexOf(String aString)`

Returns the index (position) of the first occurrence of the string `aString` in the calling object string. Positions are counted 0, 1, 2, etc. Returns `-1` if `aString` is not found.

EXAMPLE

After program executes `String greeting = "Hi Mary!";`
`greeting.indexOf("Mary")` returns 3, and
`greeting.indexOf("Sally")` returns `-1`.

Throws:

`NullPointerException` if `aString` is `null`.

```
public int indexOf(String aString, int start)
```

Returns the index (position) of the first occurrence of the string `aString` in the calling object string that occurs at or after position `start`. Positions are counted 0, 1, 2, etc. Returns `-1` if `aString` is not found.

EXAMPLE

After program executes `String name = "Mary, Mary quite contrary";`
`name.indexOf("Mary", 1)` returns `6`.
The same value is returned if `1` is replaced by any number up to and including `6`.
`name.indexOf("Mary", 0)` returns `0`.
`name.indexOf("Mary", 8)` returns `-1`.

Throws:

`NullPointerException` if `aString` is `null`.

```
public int lastIndexOf(String aString)
```

Returns the index (position) of the last occurrence of the string `aString` in the calling object string. Positions are counted 0, 1, 2, etc. Returns `-1` if `aString` is not found.

EXAMPLE

After program executes `String name = "Mary, Mary, Mary quite so";`
`greeting.indexOf("Mary")` returns `0`, and
`name.lastIndexOf("Mary")` returns `12`.

Throws:

`NullPointerException` if `aString` is `null`.

```
public int length()
```

Returns the length of the calling object (which is a string) as a value of type `int`.

EXAMPLE

After program executes `String greeting = "Hello!";`
`greeting.length()` returns `6`.

```
public String substring(int start)
```

Returns the substring of the calling object string starting from `start` through to the end of the calling object. Positions are counted 0, 1, 2, etc. Be sure to notice that the character at position `start` is included in the value returned.

EXAMPLE

After program executes `String sample = "AbcdefG";`
`sample.substring(2)` returns `"cdefG"`.

Throws:

`IndexOutOfBoundsException` if `start` is negative or larger than the length of the calling object.

`public String substring(int start, int end)`

Returns the substring of the calling object string starting from position `start` through, but not including, position `end` of the calling object. Positions are counted 0, 1, 2, etc. Be sure to notice that the character at position `start` is included in the value returned, but the character at position `end` is not included.

EXAMPLE

After program executes `String sample = "AbcdefG";`
`sample.substring(2, 5)` returns `"cde"`.

Throws:

`IndexOutOfBoundsException` if the `start` is negative, or `end` is larger than the length of this `String` object, or `start` is larger than `end`.

`public String toLowerCase()`

Returns a string with the same characters as the calling object string, but with all letter characters converted to lowercase.

EXAMPLE

After program executes `String greeting = "Hi Mary!";`
`greeting.toLowerCase()` returns `"hi mary!"`.

`public String toUpperCase()`

Returns a string with the same characters as the calling object string, but with all letter characters converted to uppercase.

EXAMPLE

After program executes `String greeting = "Hi Mary!";`
`greeting.toUpperCase()` returns `"HI MARY!"`.

`public String trim()`

Returns a string with the same characters as the calling object string, but with leading and trailing whitespace removed. Whitespace characters are the characters that print as whitespace on paper, such as the blank (space) character, the tab character, and the new-line character `'\n'`.

EXAMPLE

After program executes `String pause = " Hmm ";`
`pause.trim()` returns `"Hmm"`.

`StringBuffer`

Package: `java.lang`
`StringBuffer` is marked `final` and so you cannot use it as a base class to derive another class.
Ancestor classes:

```
Object
   |
   +--StringBuffer
```

CONSTRUCTORS

`public StringBuffer()`

Creates a `StringBuffer` object with no characters in it and an initial capacity of 16 characters.

`public StringBuffer(int capacity)`

Constructs a `StringBuffer` object with no characters in it and an initial capacity specified by the argument.

Throws:

`NegativeArraySizeException` if `length` is less than 0. `NegativeArraySizeException` is a derived class of `RuntimeException`, and so is an unchecked exception, which means it is not required to be caught or declared in a `throws` clause.

`public StringBuffer(String ordinaryString)`

Constructs a string buffer so that it represents the same sequence of characters as the `ordinaryString` argument; in other words, the initial content of the string buffer is a copy of `ordinaryString`. The initial capacity of the string buffer is 16 plus the length of `ordinaryString`.

Throws:

`NullPointerException` if `ordinaryString` is `null`.

METHODS

`public StringBuffer append(char[] charArray, int offset, int length)`

Appends the string representation of the characters in `charArray` starting at `charArray[offset]` and extending for a total of `length` characters. Note that the calling object is changed and a reference to the changed calling object is returned.

Throws:

`ArrayIndexOutOfBoundsException` if `offset` and `length` are not consistent with the range of `charArray`.

`public StringBuffer append(char c)`

Appends the character argument to the `StringBuffer` calling object and returns this longer string.

`public StringBuffer append(char[] charArray)`

Appends the string representation of the `char` array argument to this string buffer. Note that the calling object is changed and a reference to the changed calling object is returned.

`public StringBuffer append(double d)`

Appends the string representation of the `double` argument to the `StringBuffer` calling object and returns this longer string.

`public StringBuffer append(float d)`

Appends the string representation of the `float` argument to the `StringBuffer` calling object and returns this longer string.

`public StringBuffer append(int n)`

Appends the string representation of the `int` argument to the `StringBuffer` calling object and returns this longer string.

`public StringBuffer append(long n)`

Appends the string representation of the `long` argument to the `StringBuffer` calling object and returns this longer string.

`public StringBuffer append(String ordinaryString)`

Appends the `String` argument to the `StringBuffer` calling object and returns this longer string. If `ordinaryString` is `null`, then the four characters `"null"` are appended to this string buffer. Note that the calling object is hanged and a reference to the changed calling object is returned.

`public StringBuffer append(StringBuffer bufferedString)`

Appends the `StringBuffer` argument to the `StringBuffer` calling object and returns this longer string. If `bufferedString` is `null`, then the four characters `"null"` are appended to this string buffer. Note that the calling object is changed and a reference to the changed calling object is returned.

`public int capacity()`

Returns the current capacity of the calling object. The capacity is the amount of storage currently available for characters. The capacity will automatically be increased if necessary.

`public char charAt(int position)`

Returns the character in the calling object string at `position`. Positions are counted 0, 1, 2, etc.

Throws:

`IndexOutOfBoundsException` if `position` is negative or not less than the length of the calling object.

`contentEquals`

There is no such method for the class `StringBuffer`, but see the method `contentEquals` for the class `String`.

`public StringBuffer delete(int start, int end)`

Removes the characters in a substring of the calling object. The substring to remove begins at the specified start and extends to the character at index `end - 1` or to the end of the calling object if no such character exists. If `start` is equal to `end`, no changes are made. Note that the calling object is changed and a reference to the changed calling object is returned.

Throws:

`StringIndexOutOfBoundsException` if `start` is negative, greater than `length()`, or greater than `end`. `StringIndexOutOfBoundsException` is a derived class of `RuntimeException`, and so is an unchecked exception, which means it is not required to be caught or declared in a `throws` clause.

`public void ensureCapacity(int minimumCapacity)`

Ensures that the capacity of the calling object is at least equal to `minimumCapacity`. If the current capacity of the calling object is less than `minimumCapacity`, then the capacity is increased. The new capacity is the larger of: `minimumCapacity` and twice the old `capacity`, plus `2`. If the `minimumCapacity` is nonpositive, this method takes no action and simply returns.

`Start public boolean equals(Object otherObject)`

Warning: This is the method inherited from `Object`. It is not overridden for the class `StringBuffer` and does not work as you might expect. Normally, it should not be used.

`public int indexOf(String aString)`

Returns the index (position) of the first occurrence of the string `aString` in the calling object. Positions are counted 0, 1, 2, etc. Returns `-1` if `aString` is not found. Note that the argument is of type `String`, not `StringBuffer`.

Throws:

`NullPointerException` if `aString` is `null`.

`public int indexOf(String aString, int start)`

Returns the index (position) of the first occurrence of the string `aString` in the calling object that occurs at or after position `start`. Positions are counted 0, 1, 2, etc. Returns `-1` if `aString` is not found. Note that the argument is of type `String`, not `StringBuffer`.

Throws:

`NullPointerException` if `aString` is `null`.

`public int lastIndexOf(String aString)`

Returns the index (position) of the last occurrence of the string `aString` in the calling object string. Positions are counted 0, 1, 2, etc. Returns `-1` if `aString` is not found. Note that the argument is of type `String`, not `StringBuffer`.

Throws:

`NullPointerException` if `aString` is `null`.

`public int length()`

Returns the length of the calling object as a value of type `int`.

`public StringBuffer replace(int start, int end, String ordinaryString)`

Replaces the characters in a substring of the calling object with characters in the `ordinaryString`. The substring begins at the specified `start` and extends to the character at index `end -1` or to the end of the calling object if no such character exists. First the characters in the substring are removed and then the specified `ordinaryString` is inserted at `start`. (The calling object will be lengthened to accommodate the `ordinaryString` if necessary.) Note that the calling object is changed and a reference to the changed calling object is returned.

Throws:

`StringIndexOutOfBoundsException` if `start` is negative, greater than `length()`, or greater than `end`. `StringIndexOutOfBoundsException` is a derived class of `RuntimeException`, and so is an unchecked exception, which means it is not required to be caught or declared in a `throws` clause.

`public void setLength(int newLength)`

Sets the length of the calling object. The calling object is altered to represent a new character sequence whose length is specified by the argument. For every nonnegative index *k* less than `newLength`, the character at index *k* in the new character sequence is the same as the character at index *k* in the old sequence. If the `newLength` argument is less than the current length of the string buffer, the string buffer is truncated to contain exactly the number of characters given by the `newLength` argument.
If the `newLength` argument is greater than the current length, sufficient null characters `('\u0000')` are appended to the string buffer so that length becomes the `newLength` argument.

Throws:

`IndexOutOfBoundsException` if `newLength` is negative.

`public String substring(int start)`

Returns the substring of the calling object starting from `start` through to the end of the calling object. Positions are counted 0, 1, 2, etc. Be sure to notice that the character at position `start` is included in the value returned. Note that the substring is returned as a value of type `String`, not `StringBuffer`.

Throws:

`StringIndexOutOfBoundsException` if `start` is negative or larger than the length of the calling object. `StringIndexOutOfBoundsException` is a derived class of `RuntimeException`, and so is an unchecked exception, which means it is not required to be caught or declared in a `throws` clause.

`public String substring(int start, int end)`

Returns the substring of the calling object starting from position `start` through, but not including, position `end` of the calling object. Positions are counted 0, 1, 2, etc. Be sure to notice that the character at position `start` is included in the value returned, but the character at position `end` is not included. Also note that the substring is returned as a value of type `String`, not `StringBuffer`.

Throws:

`StringIndexOutOfBoundsException` if `start` is negative, or `end` is larger than the length of this calling object, or `start` is larger than `end`. `StringIndexOutOfBoundsException` is a derived class of `RuntimeException`, and so is an unchecked exception, which means it is not required to be caught or declared in a `throws` clause.

`public String toString()`

Creates a new `String` object that contains the same character sequence calling object and returns that `String` object. Subsequent changes to the calling object do not affect the contents of the `String` returned.

`StringTokenizer`

Package: `java.util`.
Ancestor classes:

```
Object
  |
  +--StringTokenizer
```

```
public StringTokenizer(String theString)
```

Constructor for a tokenizer that will use whitespace characters as separators when finding tokens in `theString`.

```
public StringTokenizer(String theString, String delimiters)
```

Constructor for a tokenizer that will use the characters in the string `delimiters` as separators when finding tokens in `theString`.

```
public StringTokenizer(String theString, String delimiters,
                                 boolean returnDelimiters)
```

Creates a tokenizer similar to `StringTokenizer(String theString, String delimiters)`, but with the following differences: If `returnDelimiters` is `true`, the delimiters are also returned by `nextToken`; each delimiter is returned as a one-character `String`. If `returnDelimiters` is `false`, the deliminters are not returned by `nextToken`. Thus, if `returnDelimiters` is `false`, the tokenizer created is the same as with `StringTokenizer(String theString, String delimiters)`.

```
public int countTokens()
```

Returns the number of tokens remaining to be returned by `nextToken`.

```
public boolean hasMoreElements()
```

Same as `hasMoreTokens`.

```
public boolean hasMoreTokens()
```

Tests whether there are more tokens available from this tokenizer's string. When used in conjunction with `nextToken`, it returns `true` as long as `nextToken` has not yet returned all the tokens in the string; returns `false` otherwise.

```
public String nextToken()
```

Returns the next token from this tokenizer's string.

Throws:

`NoSuchElementException` if there are no more tokens to return. `NoSuchElementException` is one of the exceptions that need not be declared in a `throws` clause or caught in a `catch` block.

Vector<T>

Package: `java.util`
Ancestor classes:

```
Object
   |
   +--AbstractCollection<T>
            |
            +--AbstractList<T>
                     |
                     +--Vector<T>
```

CONSTRUCTORS

```
public Vector()
```

Creates an empty vector with an initial capacity of `10`. When the vector needs to increase its capacity, the capacity doubles.

```
public Vector(Collection<? extends T> c)
```

Creates a vector that contains all the elements of the collection `c` in the same order as they have in `c`. If `c` is a vector, the capacity of the created vector will be `c.size()`, not `c.capacity`.

Throws:

`NullPointerException` if `c` is `null`.

```
public Vector(int initialCapacity)
```

Creates an empty vector with the specified initial capacity. When the vector needs to increase its capacity, the capacity doubles.

```
public Vector(int initialCapacity, int capacityIncrement)
```

Constructs an empty vector with the specified initial capacity and capacity increment. When the vector needs to grow, it will add room for `capacityIncrement` more items.

ARRAYLIKE METHODS

```
public T get(int index)
```

Returns the element at the specified index. This is analogous to returning `a[index]` for an array `a`.

Throws:

`ArrayIndexOutOfBoundsException` if the `index` is not greater than or equal to `0` and less than the current size of the vector.

```
public T set(int index, T newElement)
```

Sets the element at the specified `index` to `newElement`. The element previously at that position is returned. If you draw an analogy between the vector and an array `a`, this is analogous to setting `a[index]` to the value `newElement`.

Throws:

`ArrayIndexOutOfBoundsException` if the `index` is not greater than or equal to `0` and strictly less than the current size of the vector.

METHODS TO ADD ELEMENTS

```
public void add(int index, T newElement)
```

Inserts `newElement` as an element in the calling vector at the specified index. Each element in the vector with an index greater or equal to `index` is shifted upward to have an index that is one greater than the value it had previously.
Note that you can use this method to add an element after the last current element. The capacity of the vector is increased if this is required.

Throws:

`ArrayIndexOutOfBoundsException` if the index is not greater than or equal to `0` and less than *or equal to* the current size of the vector.

`public boolean add(T newElement)`

Adds `newElement` to the end of the calling vector and increases its size by one. The capacity of the vector is increased if this is required. Returns `true` if successful. Normally used as a `void` method.

METHODS TO REMOVE ELEMENTS

`public void clear()`

Removes all elements from the calling vector and sets its size to zero.

`public T remove(int index)`

Deletes the element at the specified index and returns the element deleted. Each element in the vector with an index greater than or equal to `index` is decreased to have an index that is one less than the value it had previously.

Throws:

`ArrayIndexOutOfBoundsException` if the `index` is not greater than or equal to `0` and less than the current size of the vector.

`public boolean remove(Object theElement)`

Removes the first occurrence of `theElement` from the calling vector. If `theElement` is found in the vector, then each element in the vector with an index greater than or equal to `theElement`'s index is decreased to have an index that is 1 less than the value it had previously. Returns `true` if `theElement` was found (and removed). Returns `false` if `theElement` was not found in the calling vector.

SEARCH METHODS

`public boolean contains(Object target)`

Returns `true` if `target` is an element of the calling vector; otherwise returns `false`.

`public int indexOf(Object target)`

Returns the index of the first element that is equal to `target`. Uses the method `equals` of the object `target` to test for equality. Returns `-1` if `target` is not found.

`public int indexOf(Object target, int startIndex)`

Returns the index of the first element that is equal to `target`, but considers only indices that are greater than or equal to `startIndex`. Uses the method `equals` of the object `target` to test for equality. Returns `– 1` if `target` is not found.

`public boolean isEmpty()`

Returns `true` if the calling vector is empty (that is, has size `0`); otherwise returns `false`.

`public int lastIndexOf(Object target)`

Returns the index of the last element that is equal to `target`. Uses the method `equals` of the object `target` to test for equality. Returns `-1` if `target` is not found.

```
public T firstElement()
```

Returns the first element of the calling vector.

Throws:

`NoSuchElementException` if the vector is empty.

```
public T lastElement()
```

Returns the last element of the calling vector.

Throws:

`NoSuchElementException` if the vector is empty.

ITERATORS

```
public Iterator <T> iterator()
```

Returns an iterator for the calling vector. (Iterators are discussed in Chapter 16.)

```
ListIterator <T> listIterator()
```

Returns a list iterator for the calling vector. (Iterators are discussed in Chapter 16.)

```
ListIterator <T> listIterator(int index)
```

Returns a list iterator for the calling vector starting at `index`. The first element to be returned by the iterator is the one at `index`. (Iterators are discussed in Chapter 16.)

CONVERTING TO AN ARRAY

```
public Object[] toArray()
```

Returns an array containing all of the elements in the vector. The elements of the array are indexed the same as in the vector.

```
public <E> E[] toArray(E[] a)
```

Note that the type parameter `E` is not the same as `T`. So, `E` can be any reference type; it need not be the type `T` in `Collection <T>`. For example, `E` might be an ancestor type of `T`. Returns an array containing all of the elements in the calling object. The elements in the returned array are in the same order as in the calling object. The argument `a` is used primarily to specify the type of the array returned. The exact details are described in the table for the `Collection <T>`.

Throws:

`ArrayStoreException` if the base type of `a` is not an ancestor class of all the elements in the vector.
`NullPointerException` if `a` is `null`.

MEMORY MANAGEMENT

```
public int capacity()
```

Returns the current capacity of the calling vector.

`public void ensureCapacity(int newCapacity)`

Increases the capacity of the calling vector to ensure that it can hold at least `newCapacity` elements. Using `ensureCapacity` can sometimes increase efficiency, but its use is not needed for any other reason.

`public void setSize(int newSize)`

Sets the size of the calling vector to `newSize`. If `newSize` is greater than the current size, the new elements receive the value `null`. If `newSize` is less than the current size, all elements at index `newSize` and greater are discarded.

Throws:

`ArrayIndexOutOfBoundsException` if `newSize` is negative.

`public int size()`

Returns the number of elements in the calling vector.

`public void trimToSize()`

Trims the capacity of the calling vector to be the vector's current size. This is used to save storage.

MAKE A COPY

`public Object clone()`

Returns a clone of the calling vector. The clone is an identical copy of the calling vector.

OLDER METHODS

These are methods that are not part of the newer collection framework, but are retained for backward compatibility. You should use the previously described newer methods instead. But, you may find these used in older code.

`public void addElement(T newElement)`

Same as `add`.

`public void insertElementAt(T newElement, int index)`

Same as `add`.

`public T elementAt(int index)`

Same as `get`.

`public void removeAllElements()`

Same as `clear`.

`public boolean removeElement(Object theElement)`

Same as `remove`.

`public void removeElementAt(int index)`

Same as `remove` but does not return the element removed.

`public void setElementAt(T newElement, int index)`

Same as `set` with the arguments reversed but does not return the element replaced.

`WindowListener` Interface

Package: `java.awt.event`
The `WindowEvent` class is also in this package.
Extends the `EventListener` interface.

`public void windowActivated(WindowEvent e)`

Invoked when a window is activated. When you click in a window, it becomes the activated window. Other actions can also activate a window.

`public void windowClosed(WindowEvent e)`

Invoked when a window has been closed.

`public void windowClosing(WindowEvent e)`

Invoked when a window is in the process of being closed. Clicking the close-window button causes an invocation of this method.

`public void windowDeactivated(WindowEvent e)`

Invoked when a window is deactivated. When a window is activated, all other windows are deactivated. Other actions can also deactivate a window.

`public void windowDeiconified(WindowEvent e)`

Invoked when a window is deiconified. When you activate a minimized window, it is deiconified.

`public void windowIconified(WindowEvent e)`

Invoked when a window is iconified. When you click the minimize button in a `JFrame`, it is iconified.

`public void windowOpened(WindowEvent e)`

Invoked when a window has been opened.

Index

J

K

L

M

N

'This warm and engaging cookbook shines a rare light on the fascinating food traditions of Tibet. Yeshi and Julie are brilliant at explaining how dishes such as momo dumplings and sweet ceremonial rice are traditionally eaten on the Tibetan Plateau, yet their recipes are so clear and reassuring they will appeal to readers anywhere. The accompanying photographs offer a glimpse of the captivating beauty of Tibet and an intimate portrait of Tibetan family life.'

Fuchsia Dunlop, bestselling author of *Every Grain of Rice*

'A fascinating exploration of a cuisine steeped in mystique and wonder. The recipes do not just echo the ethos of a people, but are an ode to the most unique of landscapes. I cannot wait to bring a little taste of Tibet to my London kitchen.'

Dr Saliha Mahmood Ahmed, author of *Khazana and Foodology*

'Julie and Yeshi have put together a book that captivates you right from the beginning. The images of the country and the food alongside so many wonderful explanations engross you completely. The recipes I have tried are sublime and I cannot wait to cook literally everything in it. It's comforting, healthy, healing and incredibly full of flavour. Time for Tibet to be on a global culinary map!'

Jouidie Kalla, author of *Palestine on a Plate*

'Fantastic recipes with so much love and passion put into this book! Yeshi and Julie brilliantly captured the essence of what Himalayan food, culture and tradition are all about!'

Norman Musa, author of *Amazing Malaysian*

'One of the most exciting aspects about being in the food and cooking world for over six decades is the discovery of *Taste Tibet*. The book is an insight into a culture and its cuisine that is little known. It brings a once exotic destination into our lives and kitchens. A true culinary delight!'

Ken Hom, OBE, chef, author and broadcaster

'What an extraordinary book this is! At once a love story and recipe manual and a remarkable guide to a way of cooking and living still largely, mistakenly, unknown outside Tibet. If you have never been lucky enough to queue for, then devour *Taste Tibet*'s delicious momos in Oxford's outdoor food market, buy this book immediately to make them for yourself. Those lucky Oxford souls who already love *Taste Tibet*'s dumplings and curries will need no encouragement.'

Sophie Grigson, author of *My Kitchen Table*

Taste Tibet

Taste Tibet

FAMILY RECIPES FROM THE HIMALAYAS

JULIE KLEEMAN
& YESHI JAMPA

murdoch books
Sydney | London

Contents

Khawa Karpo, the sacred Tibetan snow mountain.

Introduction

'The act of bringing food is one of the basic roots of all relationships.'

His Holiness the XIV Dalai Lama, *Freedom in Exile*

Our story

For as long as we have been together, Yeshi and I have dreamed about putting Tibet on the food map.

We met in 2009 in Dharamsala, northern India. Yeshi was a Tibetan studying in the famous hill town, and I was a tourist tagging a week's break onto the end of a work trip to India. We first bumped into each other on a mountain path when we were both taking pictures of the snow monkeys, and later that evening Yeshi invited me back for a meal in the small concrete room he shared with a friend.

And that is where our food journey began. Yeshi had no sink in his house and no kettle. In one corner of the room was his kitchen, which was made up of just two small gas rings fired by a huge gas cylinder. Later I learned that you could only swap your empty cylinder for a full one once a week, when deliveries came into the main square at sunrise. It being a hill town, you had to carry your gas cylinder up and down many steps in the middle of the night and queue for hours, waiting for the truck to arrive. If you were too late and all the new cylinders were already spoken for, that meant no cooking at home for the next week.

This might sound like an improbable set-up for a gastronomic experience, but that simple meal would come to define my understanding of Tibetan food – the whole point is that it can be cooked up anywhere. The first dish that Yeshi ever made for me was *thenthuk*, or hand-pulled noodle soup. This smooth, hearty broth banished the November cold from my bones, and its unique flavours had me sold.

LEFT **Yeshi's village in eastern Tibet.**
ABOVE RIGHT **Yeshi and Julie outside the Taste Tibet restaurant.**

Fast forward several years, and Yeshi and I are now married with two young children, and living in Oxford, in the UK. Together we run Taste Tibet, a restaurant, shop and festival food stall which feeds tens of thousands of people every year. I am not the cook! Yeshi brings most of the food to our family table, and he is Taste Tibet's head chef and chief recipe developer.

My own love affair with Asian flavours predated my first experience of Tibetan food. I first went to Asia in 1992 as a pretty clueless and impressionable seventeen-year-old. My sister had been living in China for a year, teaching English, and she took me on a five-week trip that covered the length and breadth of the country. The closest we got to Tibet was Chengdu, the capital of south-west China's Sichuan province. Historically, much of western Sichuan once belonged to Tibet, but this region was absorbed into mainland China after the annexation of Tibet by the Chinese during the 1950s.

Today, Chengdu is a major hub for Tibetans from across the region, who come to access medical care, to study, and to find work. People say that the Tibetan restaurants here are better than those in Lhasa (Tibet's capital city), but in 1992 the Tibetan quarter was not as well established as it is now. We spotted Tibetan statues and ritual items, and marvelled at monks in their maroon robes, but following them through tea-house doorways felt like a step too far, so we didn't get to try any Tibetan food on this first visit.

I was totally captivated by China, and by the food we ate on our travels, even though much of what was available remained tantalisingly beyond our reach as there were no English menus. My sister spoke limited Chinese, enough to get us the same few plates at almost every meal. This would be punctuated every once in a while by the experience of stumbling into a restaurant where – by chance – we were served something completely novel and sublime. It is not uncommon in China for restaurants to serve just one speciality, and this is how I first encountered Sichuan hotpot: dunking lotus root into the spicy broth was a revelation in terms of both texture and flavour.

I made my next trip to China eighteen months later. This time I stayed for several weeks in some beautiful Tibetan areas that had only just opened up to tourism. I travelled through valleys

surrounded by snow-capped mountains, into virgin forests and past pristine limestone lakes that shimmered with a golden hue. But I ate and drank all the wrong things. The tourist menus, with their extensive range of yak 'burgers', did Tibetan food no favours, and fresh food was hard to come by as effective refrigeration had still not reached these parts. The pièce de résistance was the ubiquitous yak butter tea, which tasted foul as the butter had clearly gone rancid.

My experience of travelling in China during the rather raw, early days of independent tourism in the country took me out of my comfort zone and broadened my horizons. I returned to the UK and embarked on a degree in Chinese – a move not universally understood or supported by

Yaks outside the family's yak-hair tent.

those around me, China not yet having secured economic-powerhouse status. It was a decision borne out of a love for language and an appetite for adventure, and one that inadvertently also helped me to eat a lot better on subsequent visits. By the time I moved to Beijing for work, in 2006, I no longer needed to point to or mime what I wanted to eat.

Over the twenty-odd years that I spent travelling, studying and living in China, I visited the Tibetan region many times. But, as someone with no family connections to the place, I didn't eat well, and if I hadn't met Yeshi I would have come away with a pretty sad impression of Tibetan food.

At home in eastern Tibet, Yeshi learned to cook in a tent on the grasslands of the plateau. Other brothers and sisters went to school in a nearby village, but Yeshi chose to accompany the nomadic herders in his family and their livestock out on the mountains instead. For half of the year they accompanied their animals as they grazed the upland pastures. The herders slept and ate in a tent made from yak hair, where they cooked up warming soups and stews – including the hand-pulled noodles in broth he would later make for me in that simple room in India.

When he was nineteen, Yeshi and his younger brother, Yonten, crossed the Himalayas by foot.

It was a journey that took twenty-four days, at times under cover of darkness. Yeshi had planned to stay away just long enough to help Yonten join their older brother, Nyima, at Gaden Shartse, a Buddhist monastery in Mundgod, southern India, but he ended up enrolling in a charitably-run school in Dharamsala. There he learned to read and write Tibetan for the first time, as well as some basic English.

During this period, the romance of cooking briefly deserted him: it became a means of survival. Having left the rest of his family behind, he had to fend for himself without any of the ingredients and equipment he was familiar with.

After four years at school, Yeshi joined his brothers in Mundgod, where the climate couldn't have been more different, and new worlds of food opened up to him. By then, Nyima was head chef at the monastery, overseeing the meals for some 5,000 monks, three times a day. Yeshi and Nyima come from a long line of keen cooks famed for their expertise in the kitchen – even today, when somebody in their village back home gets married, they call on Yeshi's family to do the lion's share of any catering.

During the five years that Yeshi lived alongside his brothers in the monastery complex at Mundgod, Yeshi did a lot of cooking too. He cared for an elderly relative who was also a monk at Gaden Shartse, and food was arguably the most important part of his duties: keeping his 'grandfather' fed and watered with nourishing meals, made from ingredients that were often new to him, was a daily challenge that Yeshi relished. He drew inspiration from his brother in the monastery kitchens, and the pleasure of cooking returned.

Yeshi's brother, Lhundup, preparing the family's special meatball soup (see recipe on page 133).

By the time Yeshi and I met, in 2009, he had quite a repertoire of dishes at his fingertips; nothing was written down, and he cooked by instinct, using whatever was available. Nyima, now living in New York, had reservations about our relationship, and he saw food as the ultimate barrier to its success: how could a Westerner possibly adapt to the Tibetan diet, and vice versa? But I loved everything that Yeshi cooked, and after we got married, in 2011, Tibetan food quickly became a personal passion.

When our son, Lobsang, was little, Yeshi was shocked by the prevalence of dehydrated and processed baby food on the supermarket shelves. Tibetans perceive the nutritional value of vegetables as starting to decline from the moment they are picked, so you can understand why Yeshi rejected ready-made baby food and insisted on growing and cooking fruit and vegetables from scratch. He spent hours cultivating our allotment while our son slept. Relatives from Tibet sent us packets of seed for varieties of vegetables, such as pak choi, that gardeners on neighbouring plots got very excited about. There is nothing pretty about our allotment ('nomad-style', Yeshi calls it), but it yields on an enviable scale.

In 2014 our daughter, Choenyi, arrived and completed our family. Both children instinctively loved the fresh food we cooked them, even after they discovered fish fingers and baked beans. For me, watching them thrive on home-made Tibetan meals has been fascinating. As for Yeshi, he loves to fill our table with Tibetan tastes and flavours, and it is a relief and joy that they are so warmly welcomed, even when we are so far away from his homeland.

As an added bonus, the kids' familiarity with the food – its textures and tastes, and the Tibetan names for at least some of the dishes – has really

LEFT **First family trip to Tibet, 2016.**
OPPOSITE **Family reunion, 2018.**

helped when we have been lucky enough to visit family in Tibet. The time we have spent there over the years has deepened my interest in Tibetan cuisine: sampling it in its home setting, where eating with the seasons is so engrained, and each mealtime is an occasion for the whole family, has made me re-evaluate my own relationship with food and the role it plays in my life.

One of the most striking things about mealtimes in Tibet is the communal nature of the experience. Food is prepared by several people and shared in large family groups – this was an absolute ice-breaker for me on meeting my in-laws in Tibet for the first time. Lacking a common language, we were still able to work together in the kitchen and savour the fruits of our labour. The enjoyment of food is a shared human experience that breaks down barriers, as we've discovered for ourselves through the running of Taste Tibet.

What is Tibetan food?

Outside Tibet, the idea of Tibetan food as a cuisine in its own right is clearly still evolving. At the restaurant, we are always amazed by the number of people who talk about our food being Nepalese, even though they've been enjoying it under the banner of Taste Tibet for years.

At first glance, Tibetan food looks a lot like Chinese food. Noodles, dumplings and small plates are a big feature of the cuisine. These days many Tibetans use chopsticks, although this is a fairly recent cultural import. Spoons are still the utensil of choice, but hands are best when it comes to eating momos (Tibetan dumplings) and bread – in contrast to China, where food is rarely eaten in this way, and I have often found myself

Food turns out to be a great way to open up conversations about life and family back in Tibet, and to connect the children to Yeshi's culture. It helps to create a sense of his identity beyond that of being a dad; it also sheds light on his values and perspectives, and serves as a primer in Tibetan history.

in awe of the dextrous use of chopsticks to eat chicken legs and even corn on the cob.

In fact, the most iconic flavours in Tibetan cuisine have more in common with the food of Bhutan and Nepal, as well as parts of northern India including Sikkim, Ladakh and Lahaul. The Tibetan kitchen uses liberal amounts of Sichuan peppercorns (known as *yerma* in Tibet), turmeric and cumin, and plenty of aromatics such as ginger, garlic and coriander (cilantro). A distinguishing feature of the Tibetan diet is that much of it is based on barley or wheat – crops which, unlike rice, grow well at high altitude – with bread often being the accompaniment to a main meal. There is also a fair amount of dairy, a food type largely missing from the traditional Chinese diet. Hearty soups, stews and broths are another mainstay – in such a harsh environment, hands and bellies naturally crave a constant supply of warming foods with a high energy content.

Food as medicine

According to the master twelfth-century Tibetan physician Yuthok Yönten Gönpo, 'A wholesome diet aids in sustaining our body and life, but use of any unwholesome diet can cause disease, taking our life.' Tibetan medicine, much like Ayurvedic and traditional Chinese medicine, places the focus on maintaining a healthy diet. It perceives every person to have their own unique constitution and disposition, each with its own needs. As such, keeping our bodies in balance does not mean strictly abiding by a standard diet, nor

Given the geography of Tibet and its relative isolation, Tibetan people have always eaten what is locally available and in season. Over time, they have come to understand the innate properties of the herbs, vegetables and meat that they consume.

does it mean living in the woods in solitary meditation. Each of us knows our own body and mind best, and should adjust the way we live and eat accordingly. But there are some basic principles. Without easy access to hospitals or Western medicine, Tibetans have become expert in the art of healing by identifying the potency of specific food and drinks for treating different ailments. This knowledge has been passed down through time and place, and from generation to generation. So-called 'hot foods' (butter or garlic, for example) generate heat when the body is cold, 'cooling foods' (like yoghurt or spinach) cleanse the body, and 'neutral foods' (such as potatoes or mushrooms) keep the body in balance. All of these foods are usually represented across the different dishes in any shared meal, so that the range of dietary needs can be met. The result is

FAR LEFT Juniper burning on the roof of a neighbour's house – this is a daily offering in Yeshi's village.
LEFT Yeshi's sister, Dolma, picking fresh vegetables.

a diet that doesn't favour one food group to the exclusion of another, or operate according to the protein or carbohydrate content of a meal, but instead offers something for everyone.

You will rarely find any additives in Tibetan food. The flavour-enhancer MSG (monosodium glutamate) has started to make its way in, along with many Chinese imports, but Tibetan people prefer to cook with ingredients that are locally produced. This includes seasonings. The area around Yeshi's village in eastern Tibet is famed for its natural salt flats: shallow ponds where salt water is captured, and the sun and wind evaporate most of the water. Salt production has bolstered the local economy for centuries, and many of Yeshi's friends and family members are involved in the industry in some way. All of them get to avail themselves of the finest salt you can find, purer even than the Himalayan salt now popular in the West (and hailing chiefly from Pakistan), it contains an abundance of minerals and trace elements, and is all the seasoning you need.

If heat is your thing, however, you might like to spice up your bowl with some chilli – *sepen*, or hot chilli dip, is always on hand at the Tibetan table. It takes a variety of forms, and each family has their own winning recipe, but a key ingredient is *yerma* (Sichuan peppercorns), with its unique tongue-tingling taste and woodsy fragrance. We recommend you make a batch of Taste Tibet *sepen* (see page 190) before attempting anything else in this book: it keeps well in the fridge and is a great accompaniment to most dishes, lifting their natural flavours without overpowering them.

Food in Tibetan daily life

Tibet is massive, spanning an area of over a million square miles: it's about the size of Western Europe, or larger than Alaska and California combined. End to end, and peak to peak, the everyday lives and experiences of its people are very varied, and this includes traditions around food and drink.

If you know one thing about Tibet, it's probably that it is home to the highest mountain in the world, Everest, which it shares with Nepal.
The average elevation of the Tibetan plateau is 4,500 metres (almost 15,000 feet), and five of the world's fourteen highest peaks can be found here. For over 8,000 years Tibetan nomads, or *drokpa*, have been herding livestock on vast high-altitude pastures, creating a unique nomadic culture and contributing to a remarkable civilisation – one

In Tibet there are more yaks than people, and they provide all the basic requirements for human life on the plateau.

that, some 1,200 years ago, was the most powerful empire in Asia. Until recently, *drokpa* comprised up to 40 per cent of the Tibetan population. Men and women both play their part, and there is little division of labour. Children have their jobs too, including herding and feeding the livestock. The world of the *drokpa* follows a distinct rhythm, with nomadic lives finely tuned to the growth of grass, the birth of animals and the seasonal movement of their herds. They stay out in the wilderness all day without shelter from wind and rain – and, like many people who live close to nature, they have developed a close connection to the land and the livestock that nurtures them.

The highest grazing lands in the world are found in the Tibetan pastoral area, most of which is above 4,000 metres (just over 13,000 feet), and some nomads maintain permanent camps at altitudes as high as 5,000 metres (about 16,500 feet). Here, snowstorms are common even during summertime. Over thousands of years, wildlife such as the Tibetan antelope, wild yak, wild ass and gazelle, as well as blue sheep, the elusive snow leopard and several species of deer have roamed these high pastures; small mammals like pikas, voles and marmots have exerted their influence on the vegetation too. The resulting grasslands may be limited in terms of species variation and productivity, but the plants that do thrive in these conditions are high in protein, providing nutritious forage.

All *drokpa* raise the same kinds of animals out on the plateau: yaks, yak-cattle hybrids, sheep, goats and horses. These animals, with their proportionately larger lungs, can survive in the thin air at these high altitudes. The *drokpa* move them from place to place, exchanging their produce for grain from agricultural communities at lower elevations. Most of the plateau is too cold and arid to support cultivated agriculture, but barley is the exception and is probably the key crop that has enabled humans to settle here. Today it remains the most important staple of the Tibetan diet. *Tsampa*, or roasted barley flour, is enjoyed by most people every day, and nomads eat it up to three times a day; rolled into dense 'energy balls', it fuels them through long and arduous mountain treks. It is also the first food given to babies – busy parents feed their children a liquid form of *tsampa* at just a few days old (Yeshi was amazed to learn that, in the West, babies are not generally weaned until they reach six months).

The other key to human survival in such an inhospitable environment is the yak. Historically, male yaks were beasts of burden, carrying wool, salt, tea and other goods to India, Nepal and China, as well as bringing cotton, silk, glass and other goods to Tibet. The female yak, or *dhri*, provides valuable dairy products to supplement the diet. *Drokpa* families spend the summer milking their *dhri* and making butter and cheese, some of which they will trade for other local products, but most is kept for use over the winter months. Yak milk has roughly twice the fat content of cow's milk, and a significant percentage of this is in the form of a fatty acid that has been

Our nephew, Jamyang, herding the family goats.

ABOVE LEFT **Baby yak at the family camp.** ABOVE RIGHT **Yeshi's older father, Kelsang, leaving home to feed the animals.**

shown to improve bone mineralisation and also exhibits anti-carcinogenic and anti-diabetic properties. Despite the amount of yak produce consumed by Tibetan nomads, it is unusual to see anybody who is overweight, and instances of cancer and diabetes are mercifully rare.

The situation is a little more nuanced when it comes to yak meat. Traditionally, Tibetan people have lived alongside their livestock, and they consider the suffering experienced by animals to be comparable to that of humans. As Buddhists, they also believe in reincarnation, whereby it is possible for a human to be reborn as another creature, and vice versa; it is therefore conceivable that an animal you slaughter for your dinner table could have been your mother in a previous life.

But while the Buddha and other early leaders of Buddhist practice advocated a suffering-free diet, Buddhist teachings do not explicitly forbid the consumption of meat. For monks, the act of killing is forbidden, so for them to kill an animal for food is taboo – but a monk is permitted to eat meat from an animal killed by someone else, as long as the butcher does not specifically have the monk in mind at the time of its slaughter. The most 'acceptable' way for Tibetans to eat meat is to come upon an animal that has died a natural death. Bypassing smaller animals such as goats, sheep, pigs and chickens – which would feed fewer mouths – the yak emerges as the best option in this context. When a beast reaches the end of its useful life – usually after 20–25 years – it is slaughtered before old age or disease take hold. This is done in the late autumn so that the yak's meat can be preserved. Similar to lean beef or buffalo, but lower in saturated fat, the meat is cured using salt and Sichuan peppercorns. After being hung out to dry in the sunshine for a few days, it is bagged up, ready to be eaten as a raw snack or added to soups and stews during the long winter months.

Everything the yak produces is put to good use. Aside from going into butter tea and *tsampa*, yak butter is also burnt in lamps and used as a skin moisturiser. Yak skin is used to make boots, belts, aprons, saddlebags and the coracles that transport heavy loads along Tibet's many rivers. Yak bones are carved into combs and buttons, and yak dung is used as a fuel in areas where wood is too scarce and precious to burn. Yak tails are used as dusters, and their long, coarse hair is woven into ropes, bags and rainwear, as well as the tents belonging to nomadic families. These keep out the rain and let in the light, yet are strong enough to withstand the fiercest of winter blizzards.

As one yak can provide so much during its lifetime, the sacrifice of this single life seems bearable, especially in comparison to the number of individual lives lost when chicken and fish are consumed. Although fish are abundant in the lakes and rivers of Tibet (more than 150 different species of fish have been found on the plateau), they are rarely seen as a source of food. The double golden fish is one of the Eight Auspicious Symbols of Tibetan Buddhism, a symbol of recovery, eternal life and rebirth. Partly because of this, many consider eating fish to be taboo, and this is compounded by the sometime custom of water burials, in which the deceased is placed on a wooden raft to drift freely down river. Speculating that these bodies will likely be eaten by fish, Tibetan people view the consumption of fish as akin to eating their own kind.

Shifting culinary and cultural landscapes

The day-to-day existence of Yeshi's family is relatively unchanged from that of their ancestors. Some modern conveniences may have made in-roads – electricity, mobile phones – but the food on their plates remains more or less the same. In part, this is due to the relatively low elevation at which they live, which means that there are two growing seasons each year. With such an abundance of fruit and vegetables, much of which grows wild and uncultivated, there is little need to venture far, but the family do trade some of their produce in neighbouring villages and towns. Walnuts and fruit might be exchanged for greens or root vegetables – often for different varieties that grow well elsewhere. Seeds are also swapped, so that everyone can try growing different crops on their own land too. Sometimes cash is involved, which can then be used to buy tea, vegetable oil or rice, but these are uncommon transactions.

Feeding the cows in the backyard.

At higher altitudes, there are no spoils. Hardy greens like mustard and cabbage can be cultivated, as well as some root vegetables such as carrots, mooli (daikon) and potatoes, but historically there has been very little variety. In recent years, however, with more and more Chinese business activity inside Tibet, a wider range of food has begun to make its way in, and Tibetan people are shopping in a way they have never done before. Chinese-made greenhouses also offer the opportunity to grow your own, and in some places a new livelihood has sprung up around this, with local people becoming able to produce and supply fresh produce for themselves and others, sometimes on a commercial scale.

However, one precept of Tibetan medicine holds that in order for vegetables to be potent enough to sustain us and cure us of illness, they must be grown in their natural habitat. For example, vegetables that are warm in nature should be grown in a place that is warm, and those that are cold in nature should be grown in suitably cold conditions. As a result, there has been a lot of resistance to this way of farming and marketing produce, and not all consumers are on board. When a new road was built through Yeshi's village recently, it brought in traders hawking all kinds of temptations, but his family are not buying yet.

And there's another challenge. In some parts of Tibet (although this change hasn't yet reached Yeshi's village), nomads are increasingly being 'resettled' in towns far away from the land and lifestyles that have defined them for so many generations. Some Tibetan monks have started a movement to encourage people in these areas to adopt a vegetarian diet now that they have access to a wider variety of ingredients. These former nomads are coming under pressure to align themselves with a Buddhist approach that is in many ways at odds with their nomadic identity. To complicate things even further, local Chinese authorities have been busy establishing commercial slaughterhouses to meet the demand for yak meat in China. Tibetan people have never slaughtered animals at scale, and the monks worry that such practices will bring bad karma to the region. Increasingly, Tibetans are being pulled in many different directions, and none of it is easy to reconcile.

Finally, as the wider food landscape shifts dramatically, in Tibetan homes and out on the grasslands cooking methods are also changing. Traditional Tibetan stoves are made from mud and stone, and are the focal point of houses and tents alike. Kept alight both day and night, they are a source of constant warmth and a steady supply of yak butter tea, making the kitchen the hub of all activity and the place of greatest comfort. Most of Tibet is above the treeline and

Yeshi's parents circumambulating the village stupa.

In effect, Tibetans are pioneers of what these days is termed 'conscious consumption'. When no part of a slaughtered animal goes unused, and people wear and consume produce that is local, minimally packaged, and often transported by a beast of burden – you have the perfect model right there.

so these stoves usually burn dried yak dung, although at the lower altitudes, where Yeshi's family lives, slow-burning oak logs are used for fuel. Winters are extremely cold in most of Tibet, with temperatures plummeting as low as –15°C (5°F) overnight, and stoves usually serve as the only means of heating a space.

Traditionally, families bed down near their stove and keep warm during the night with the heat from the ash. Today, metal stoves are becoming more popular. A Chinese introduction, these are seen as a desirable, modern alternative, but we have heard that they cannot match the heat given off by the traditional stoves. It will be interesting to see how the dynamic of the home changes if and when the stove ceases to be the principal provider of heat.

At the Tibetan table

In pre-modern Tibet, there was no dining table. Chairs weren't really a thing either. Even today, Tibetan people prefer to sit cross-legged on the ground or on the floor, having grown used to adopting that position when saying prayers and listening to teachings in monasteries.

As for today's tables, these are usually low, coffee-table style pieces holding plentiful teacups. Sometimes just one large pot or steamer takes centre stage. *Thenthuk* (hand-pulled noodle soup) or momos (traditional steamed dumplings) are served in this way. These make for one big, shared meal, but Tibetan people also like to eat from a tableful of shared dishes, all served at once. They will usually eat out of small individual bowls, taking frequent refills.

Traditionally made of wood, these bowls are handcrafted and often hold significant meaning for people. An old Tibetan folk song likens a lover to a wooden bowl, which may not sound very romantic, but Tibetan people originally kept one bowl for life, carrying it with them wherever they went – 'in their bosom', as the song goes. Traditional Tibetan garments are designed to hold all kinds of things, and a Tibetan nomad will produce their bowl, knife, handkerchief or wallet – even a baby – from the folds of their robes without the slightest hint that anything was hidden in there at all.

The bowl might well be the most useful of all. It is made up of two wooden pieces: a big bowl for food, and a smaller bowl that doubles as a lid and teacup, which is used many times a day to hold hot butter tea. Tibetan people claim that butter tea tastes better and stays hotter in a wooden bowl, and they insist that the wood of the bowl adds flavour to *tsampa*. Yeshi says that the best thing about wooden bowls is that they never get too hot to hold. As Tibetan people usually dine at low tables, they tend to bring their bowls close to their mouths to eat, and a wooden bowl makes it possible to savour both boiling broths and hot butter tea without scalding the fingers or burning the lips and tongue.

Because of these many advantages, as well as its durability, the traditional Tibetan wooden bowl hasn't yet been pushed out by cheap Chinese ceramics or other alternatives, and the time-honoured way of making it is still practised. This ancient method involves carving the entire bowl from one solid piece of hard or soft wood, typically taken from the root, trunk or knot of the tree. Yeshi's father and brothers still make bowls for their family, and they are also skilled in the art of polishing the wood to bring out the beauty of its natural grain. When they are on the move, everyone carries their own bowl. Custom dictates that you only take into it as much as you know you can eat. This way there is no waste, and when the meal is finished, all that's needed is a quick lick clean. Yeshi is at pains to point out that not everybody in Tibet uses this technique, but there's no denying its effectiveness and frugality.

Tsampa pot and traditional wooden bowl on the family table.

Good manners, then – and these are definitely highly prized – are a different set of behaviours. For starters, Tibetans believe that food cannot be enjoyed properly if it is not given due attention, so no matter how much you are loving your food, don't shout about it. No whoops, noms or other loud signs of enjoyment. Eating is a quiet affair, and even idle chatter has no place at the dinner table. Yeshi gets very frustrated when our children bring books or toys to the table, or mess about. Tibetan families usually eat together in silence, savouring their food as a gift that nourishes and sustains us.

Restraint and deference also go a long way. You should offer food to others, for example, before filling your own bowl, and make sure that the old and the young are served first. Even if you are ravenous, you should always wait to be offered food in a Tibetan home: asking for something to eat or drink can be considered rude – and even when it is offered, you would do best to decline at least once, and maybe several times before graciously accepting.

Once you are lucky enough to have something delicious land in your bowl, try not to overeat, fill your mouth too full or eat too fast. Ideally, you shouldn't ask for more either, but wait to be offered another helping. At the end of the meal

your bowl should be empty, so fill it little by little, and then you won't end up with more than you can manage.

Finally, remember that food is seen as a gift to be savoured, so you should show due respect by not stepping over any pots or pans, or the food itself. You should also keep your feet off the table, even if there's no food on it, and try to keep your legs crossed – don't stretch them out in front of you. When it comes to the stove, you need to show particular care and reverence. In Tibet, the stove is the residence of the kitchen god. You do not want to offend your kitchen god, and by keeping your stove clean and looking after it, you are protecting your own familial fortunes.

If the kitchen is held to be a sacred place in Tibetan households, outside the home, the pastime of picnicking is taken just as seriously, with food being the talking point and centrepiece. The winters can be long and harsh in Tibet, but the summer, when the sun is bright and the wind is low, is marked by heady months of picnicking. The usual strictures around food are loosened outdoors. Cold salads and fried dishes are brought from home, along with pan-fried bread, cheese, dried meats, nuts and seeds. Butter tea and sweet tea are a constant, fed by a makeshift fire; *chang* (Tibetan barley beer) is also free-flowing. Everything is laid out on hand-woven rugs and is available to snack on during pit stops from music, dancing and games.

LEFT Yeshi's younger father, Tashi, taking butter tea from a traditional bowl.
RIGHT Yeshi's aunt, Dolkar, in prayer.

Mindful eating

Here is a timely reminder: humans eat in order to keep ourselves healthy and alive. In Tibet, this is still an obvious statement of fact. Tibetan people eat the food they need to sustain themselves in the extreme cold, and it so happens that what they need is what is available. Even those who have made a life for themselves in the city will still have deep connections to their roots and the reality of rural life. Hardship and struggle are an inevitable part of the pastoral existence, and everyone is aware of the means by which food reaches the table.

Like the children of many nomadic families, Yeshi began herding livestock out on the mountains from a young age. When he was only eight or nine, he would be away for months at a time, and he suffered from terrible homesickness and, from time to time, extreme hunger and thirst. Daily routines were determined by the seasons, and so there might be days of chopping wood, followed by days of planting, or maybe a week milking the animals followed by a stint collecting river water from the valley below. Occasionally, Yeshi would walk for an entire day to relay a message to the family back home. Some months were busier than others, and one day

might be tougher than the next, but this is definitely not a way of life for the work-shy.

In Tibet every mealtime begins with a simple prayer: an offering to the Buddha, his teachings and the Buddhist monastic order (the so-called

Stopping for a moment to reflect on the work involved in planting, harvesting and transporting what we eat, as well as those who have prepared it, is an act of communion with vast numbers of people in the past, present and future. It is an opportunity to give thanks.

'Three Jewels' in which all Buddhists take refuge). In more religious settings, other prayers serve as a reminder of the generosity of the people whose efforts have ensured that food reaches the table.

And in considering what others have done for us, this is also a chance to reflect on what we are doing for others. Is the food that we are consuming being put to good use in sustaining us? Are we worthy of it as the gift that it is? We must also take care not to succumb to greed; we must remind ourselves that we eat in order to sustain our life and health, so that we may give to and benefit others. Food should not be purely a means of indulging in sensory pleasure (but mindful enjoyment of good food is fine!).

A common Buddhist mealtime prayer translates as follows:

This food is the gift of the whole universe,
each morsel is a sacrifice of life,
may I be worthy to receive it.
May the energy in this food
give me the strength
to transform my unwholesome qualities
into wholesome ones.
I am grateful for this food,
may I realise the Path of Awakening,
for the sake of all beings.
The joys and pains of all beings
are present in the gift of this food.
Let us receive it in love
and gratitude ...
and in mindfulness of our sisters and brothers
among living beings of every kind
who are hungry or homeless,
sick or injured,
or suffering in any way.

Yeshi's older father spinning an old prayer wheel.

Those of us who have the luxury to pick and choose what we eat risk losing sight of the simple fact of food as nutrition. We might eat with the goal of a particular body type in mind (thin/muscular); we might use food as a way of expressing ourselves and what we believe ('I'm an animal lover').

Buddhists say that it is our attachment to things – whether objects, people or beliefs (in this case, those surrounding food) – that causes us suffering. It can also make things difficult for those around us. Their advice would be to accept whatever is offered when you visit a Buddhist home, even if it's not in line with what you normally eat. Consuming something fattening or meaty every once in a while, if necessary, does not compromise your fundamental values or beliefs and will go a long way towards keeping the peace in an otherwise tricky situation. Buddhists believe that our attachments take us out of the present moment, and that in doing so, they limit our enjoyment of that moment. They say that when we focus on accepting food without being fixed in our ideas, we eat without complaint or conceit, and we consume with more moderation. Last but not least, beginning each mealtime with an expression of gratitude and a reminder of the primary purpose of food as sustenance also serves to make it taste better.

In this context, the mindset of the cook is also really important. At Taste Tibet we take care not to allow attachments or greed to enter the kitchen. Our staff understand that our primary goal is to provide nourishment and impart a sense of wellbeing. We strive to be affordable and inclusive, while sourcing the best ingredients possible. Obviously we need to turn a profit, but we know that if this becomes the focus, then we risk losing sight of our motivation, and our food and service will suffer. We truly believe that it is these good kitchen practices that bring us success.

Some recipe notes and tips

The recipes in this book are Yeshi's, or those of his family. We cannot claim to represent Tibetan cuisine as a whole. Those already familiar with Tibetan food may spot some gaps – *guthuk* (traditional Tibetan New Year's Eve soup), for example. Yeshi's family comes from a very rural part of eastern Tibet that has its own traditions and local specialities, and most of the recipes we have chosen are a celebration of the cuisine of this particular corner of the world. They hark back to the days and nights that Yeshi spent huddled around the fire in the family's nomadic tent out on the grasslands, or at home with his mother and auntie during the wintertime. In other dishes, including those for some of the food we serve in the Taste Tibet restaurant and at our festival stall, you can taste the journey Yeshi took through India.

The recipes in the last two chapters are more eclectic, as they reflect the time that Yeshi has spent in Tibet, India and, ultimately, the West, where he has absorbed new influences into his repertoire, coming up with his own ideas for making sweet treats in particular.

But first things first: **the stove**. Having learnt to cook on a traditional Tibetan stove, Yeshi considers electric stoves and induction hobs to be a bit of an anathema, as he finds it frustrating to cook without an actual flame of some kind. But Tibetan people are adaptable, a characteristic that has served them well in their new homes across the world, and the recipes in this book will work equally well on an electric stove, if that is what you have at your disposal. A point to note in this case: an electric ring doesn't usually achieve the same temperatures as a gas burner and, generally speaking, takes longer to heat up, so you may need to adjust the suggested heat settings and increase the cooking times

accordingly. Actually, you might like to do this anyway. Yeshi is comfortable cooking at high temperatures, with flames licking around the wok, but you may need some time to get used to cooking in this way. Don't worry – whether you're using electricity or gas, you'll soon get used to cranking the heat up high!

Otherwise, Tibetan people have very little in the way of kitchen equipment. It is normal for houses to have no water supply inside the home, so there's a lot of to-ing and fro-ing to the outside standpipe using buckets and basins. These basins double up as **mixing bowls**, which are used a lot in Tibetan cooking.

Expect to use **your hands** a lot. Dough features prominently in Tibetan cuisine and it is best

ABOVE LEFT Yeshi's sister, Dolma, with some traditional Tibetan pots.
ABOVE RIGHT Mala prayer beads, made from carved wood.

worked by hand – though you could, of course, use an electric mixer fitted with a dough hook.

A large, ideally wooden **chopping board** is very useful. Big is also the name of the game when it comes to **pots**, **pans** and **woks**. You will need at least one of each of these, and preferably sizeable ones. Don't worry if your wok doesn't come with **a lid**. Our recipes often call for one, but at home we use a lid that's smaller than the wok itself – as long as you have something that will cover whatever's in there, that's the main thing.

Measuring spoons and a **measuring jug** are useful, but remember to use your judgement as well.

(When dealing with dough in particular, you will be the best judge of how much water your flour needs: the stronger the flour, the more water it will absorb. To get the right consistency, make sure you add the suggested amount of water little by little, and be ready to supplement it as necessary.)

You are going to need a **kettle**, and ideally you should always have some boiling water to hand, so do keep it topped up. A **rolling pin** is another essential piece of kit if you want to make momos and noodles. For momos, some sort of **steamer** – bamboo or metal – is useful, but steam-fried momos are just as delicious if you don't have one.

In Tibet, practically nobody uses a **food processor** (electricity has only found its way to remoter regions in recent years), and Yeshi firmly believes that everything tastes better when chopped by hand. But not everybody has the time or the patience, so if you can see a place for a food processor or blender in any of the prep, go for it! The results will not be quite the same, but we're not here to evangelise – and we do sometimes use one ourselves. Finally, Sichuan peppercorns are commonly used in Tibetan cooking, and they often need crushing, so a **pestle and mortar** comes in handy. A **spice or coffee grinder** is also useful if you're planning to make *tsampa*.

As for ingredients, the good news is that you should find them all easy to come by. Yak meat, milk and butter may be off the menu, but **beef**, cow's **milk** and **butter** make great substitutes, and your local Asian supermarkets should have everything else you need to cook some of the more traditional dishes in the book (see page 342 for more detailed information on ingredients). On our visits to Tibet we tend to stock up on the non-perishable goods that go into our favourite dishes, including Sichuan peppercorns, dried mushrooms and Tibetan salt, but a direct line to Tibet is not necessary – it just adds another layer of meaning for us.

It's always best to buy **vegetables** loose if you can. Less packaging is obviously a good thing, but it's also really important to be able to touch, smell and inspect. Asian grocery stores usually sell in this way and their produce tends to be more varied than the average supermarket and is often

cheaper. At farmers' markets you can find organic produce, free of pesticides, hormones, antibiotics and genetic modification – such food is always going to taste better, and will give you an experience closer to that of the Tibetan table.

Make sure you **wash everything well**. In Tibet, people tend not to peel their vegetables, so vegetables such as potatoes and carrots (and aromatics like ginger) are scrubbed in water instead. The best way to clean leafier veg like spinach is to swirl it through a large bowl of water. Once you have washed it well, lift it out of the bowl and onto the chopping board or directly into a pot. If you drain it in a colander, the chances are that some of the gritty residue will travel with it. Some vegetables should really be washed twice – once before you cut them and once after. We note in the recipes where particular care should be taken.

Unless otherwise stated, try to use as much of the vegetable as you can. Broccoli stems, for example, are delicious and should always be added to the pot. The same goes for the green tips of spring onions (scallions). There is little wastage in Tibetan food.

Yeshi is a fast prepper, so he usually chops as he goes, but if you prefer to have everything washed and cut before it needs to go in, we recommend that you **read ahead a little** in the recipe to make sure that you are prepared for each stage.

Finally, I can tell you from experience that Yeshi rarely makes a recipe the same way twice. In Tibet you can never guarantee what will be on hand, so every cook is guided to a large degree by their instinct and knowledge of good ingredient pairings. Putting these recipes together, it has been quite entertaining watching Yeshi get used to working with scales and measuring spoons, as Tibetans tend to cook more intuitively. (Yeshi didn't know that cookbooks existed until he arrived in the UK.) When making dough, some science comes into play, and instructions can be useful. Otherwise, if you are missing a teaspoon of sesame oil here and there, your dish will still taste great without it, so feel free to play with quantities or to substitute one vegetable for another along the way. Learn to **season and taste as you go** – and if you like spice, chuck it in!

Yeshi has so enjoyed creating these recipes, and we are both really excited to be able to share our favourite dishes with you and to get more of you cooking Tibetan food! The dream is complete.

FAR LEFT **Yeshi and Julie at the Taste Tibet stall.**
LEFT **The Taste Tibet festival tent.**

Breakfast

When most of the day is spent outdoors, and it's cold out there, a good, solid, warming breakfast becomes very important. In Tibet, most people start the day with *tsampa*, which is roasted barley flour. Nutty in flavour and higher in fibre and protein than oatmeal, *tsampa* makes for a really nutritious and filling meal – a great way to kick things off.

The most common way to enjoy *tsampa*, and this is how it is usually taken for breakfast, is to mix it by hand in a bowl with butter and boiling water, and then roll or squeeze it into small balls to eat. If you have a sweet tooth, you can add sugar or honey; otherwise, cheese makes a great addition. Add a little more water to make a barley porridge, which can be slurped out of the bowl.

Ideally you will have a bowl of tea to wash down your *tsampa*. Traditionally, Tibetans drink their tea with butter and salt, and sometimes a lump of dried yak cheese for extra flavour – this will be the first thing to touch their lips when they wake up. Some people mix this tea into their *tsampa*. In days gone by, *tsampa* would be squashed down into the bowl to make the tea more nutritious and flavoursome. Once the liquid had been drunk, this dissolved *tsampa*, mixed with butter and salt, would provide a kind of instant bread.

For nomads out on the Tibetan plateau herding yaks and goats, *tsampa* is the most likely breakfast. Being lightweight and portable, it makes a great convenience food. If they are already out and about, *tsampa* can be taken directly from a pouch attached to the belt and eaten as is. The fine powder soon dissolves on the tongue, making the mouth water; the trick is not to get so close as to inhale it, as it can catch in the throat. Those still warm inside their yak-hair tents just need some boiling water to make a substantial breakfast.

In the city, breakfast might be eaten at a tea-house, where noodles or meat pies are a common offering. Tea-houses usually serve sweet tea: once the preserve of well-travelled aristocrats (sweet tea made its way to Tibet via India and Nepal), today a thriving tea-house culture has developed around this highly moreish drink. A tea-house is somewhere to stop by for a quick pick-me-up, a rest area for Buddhist pilgrims and a popular hangout for young and old alike. In Lhasa, Tibet's capital, they are everywhere, and they make a great breakfast option. It's easy to pass time here, and breakfast can all too easily slide into lunch.

In your kitchen at home, with more ingredients to hand, you are more likely to be adventurous with breakfast. There are no rules about what makes a good start to the day, so last night's leftovers (especially noodles) will work fine if that's what you feel like. Or why not tuck into a buckwheat pancake with hot honey and butter dip? As for bread options, you could fry yourself some breakfast bread and enjoy it with eggs – scrambled, boiled or fried – or just dunk your bread in your tea.

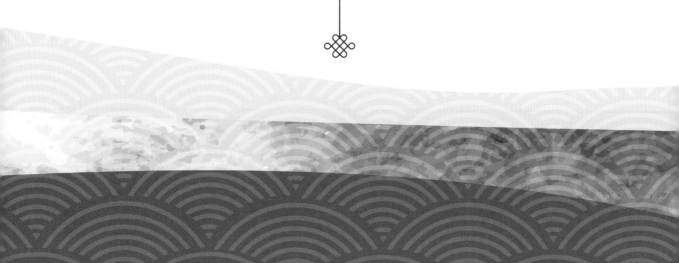

Su-Cha
(Butter Tea) *Serves 2*

Tibetan people drink butter tea in copious quantities throughout the day. More like a broth than tea as we know it, it is deliciously smooth and creamy when it is made using fresh butter. If the butter has become sour, however – as often happens in the more remote areas where refrigeration has not yet reached – it can taste very rancid. Such damage this has done to the reputation of what is actually a very fine drink!

In Tibet, butter tea is made using black tea, crumbled from a large brick (the tea was originally compressed in this way to withstand the rigours of the journey from China). Here we substitute brick tea with English breakfast – tea bags work well – and also add a little milk to match the creaminess of pure yak butter. A blender makes much faster work of the tea than a traditional wooden churn.

1–2 English breakfast tea bags (we like Yorkshire tea), depending how strong you want it
Pinch of salt
25 g (1 oz) unsalted butter
100 ml (3½ fl oz) whole milk

VEGETARIAN

Pour 400 ml (14 fl oz) of water into a saucepan and bring to the boil over a high heat.

When the water is boiling, add the tea bag(s) and boil for a good 3–4 minutes, stirring occasionally, then remove the tea bag(s) from the pan and discard.

Take off the heat and add the salt, butter and milk, then use a hand-held blender to blend the tea until frothy. Gently reheat if needed, but do not bring back to the boil.

Spiced Sweet Tea *Serves 2*

In its simplest form, Tibetan sweet tea can be made with just black tea, milk and a little sugar. Spiced sweet tea is a more complex flavour, similar to Indian chai, but less cloying. We serve this at the Taste Tibet restaurant and stall and it's a real crowd pleaser. In Tibet, it would usually be made with loose-leaf tea, and that's what we use at Taste Tibet, but tea bags are simpler for making small quantities at home.

2 green cardamom pods
2.5 cm (1 inch) cinnamon stick
2.5 cm (1 inch) piece of ginger, washed but not peeled, cut into fine julienne strips
1 tea bag, such as English breakfast – we like Yorkshire Tea
2 teaspoons brown or white (granulated) sugar, to taste
100 ml (3½ fl oz) whole milk

VEGETARIAN

Measure out 300 ml (10½ fl oz) of water and pour it into a saucepan.

Place the cardamom pods on a board. Cupping your non-dominant hand around the pods to keep them from flying around, lightly bash with the end of a rolling pin to break them apart, then use the rolling pin to gently roll over them.

Add the cardamom, cinnamon, ginger, tea bag and sugar to the pan. Bring to the boil, giving it a stir every so often to help dissolve the sugar, then let it bubble for a few minutes. Pour in the milk and, as soon as the tea is simmering again, remove it from the heat and strain into cups through a tea strainer or sieve, or just use a fork to hold back the cardamom, cinnamon, ginger and tea bag.

Vegan Chai *Serves 2*

This recipe deserves its own space as it's not just as simple as substituting one milk for another: the balance between milk and water changes when you're not using dairy. We like to use oat milk, but almond milk works fine as well, or feel free to experiment with your own milk alternative of choice.

1 tea bag – we use English breakfast, and are fans of Yorkshire Tea
3 green cardamom pods
2.5 cm (1 inch) piece of ginger, washed but not peeled, cut into fine julienne strips
2 teaspoons brown or white (granulated) sugar
300 ml (10½ fl oz) unsweetened oat milk – we like Minor Figures

VEGAN

Bring 100 ml (3½ fl oz) of water to the boil in a saucepan and add the tea bag.

Place the cardamom pods on a board. Cupping your non-dominant hand around the pods to keep them from flying around, lightly bash with the end of a rolling pin to break them apart, then use the rolling pin to gently roll over them.

Add the cardamom, ginger and sugar to the pan. Bring back to the boil, giving it a stir every so often to help dissolve the sugar, then let it bubble for a few minutes. Pour in the milk and, as soon as the tea is simmering again, remove it from the heat and strain into cups through a tea strainer or sieve, or just use a fork to hold back the cardamom, ginger and tea bag.

Numtak Balep
(Fried Breakfast Bread) *Makes 6*

Numtak balep is a lovely fluffy, slightly chewy bread that goes down a treat at breakfast time with tea and scrambled eggs, or is just as delicious paired with spicy chickpeas and potatoes (see page 45). Yeshi had his first taste of it when he was about four or five years old. There were eight kids in the family and, from time to time, a couple of them would be sent away to stay with relatives. In his grandmother's hometown, there were shops that promised all kinds of distractions, but the children were not allowed to visit them. Yeshi remembers his uncle doing his best to make something that looked shop-bought, and how much more exciting his home-made bread turned out to be than anything in the windows of the local store.

350 g (2⅓ cups) self-raising flour, plus extra for dusting
2 tablespoons plain yoghurt
300 ml (10½ fl oz) cooking oil

VEGETARIAN

Put the flour, yoghurt and 1 teaspoon of the oil into a mixing bowl. Mix together with your dominant hand, while slowly pouring in 100 ml (3½ fl oz) of warm water with the other. Knead in the bowl until you have a nice soft, fluffy dough – when it's ready, it should no longer stick to your fingers. Cover and set aside for about 10 minutes.

Sprinkle your work surface with a little flour to stop the dough from sticking. Cut or break the dough into six equal pieces. Take the first piece of dough and roll it between your palms into a ball. Using a rolling pin, roll it out from top to bottom and bottom to top several times, turning it over and around as you go. Keep going until you have a circle about 15–20 cm (6–8 inches) in diameter. Then, using the tip of a sharp knife, pierce two slits in it, one to the left of the centre and the other to the right.

Place a frying pan over a medium heat and pour in the rest of the oil. Check the temperature of the oil by tossing in a tiny scrap of dough: if it bubbles vigorously and rises quickly to the surface, you are good to go. Carefully slide the circle of dough into it. As soon as bubbles form on the surface, after about a minute, use tongs to turn it over and give it another minute, or until it is a light golden brown. Turn it again and leave for just a moment, then remove and drain on paper towel.

Turn the heat right down while you quickly roll out your second piece of dough. When it is ready, turn the heat back up to medium and cook as for the first one. Keep going until all six breads are done.

Yeshi says 'It's important to get the temperature of the oil just right – too hot and the bread will darken too quickly, too cool and it will take a long time to cook, which will affect the texture. You are aiming for a nice golden colour, which will build slowly. Go for a good medium heat and adjust the temperature up or down as necessary.'

Potato and Chickpea Breakfast Bomb *Serves 4–6*

This is such a comforting dish, and it makes the best of all hangover cures. The contrast between textures results in a taste explosion – a bomb, you might say. If you want the dish to have a more curry-like consistency, add a little boiling water during the latter stages of cooking.

It's worth cooking a batch of dried chickpeas for this (any leftover will keep for up to four days in the fridge, or a few months in the freezer). They need to be soaked overnight first – but don't worry if you forget, you can always use tinned.

- 2 white potatoes, about 350 g (12 oz), washed but not peeled, diced
- 2 tablespoons cooking oil
- ½ teaspoon cumin seeds
- 1–2 fresh green chillies, thinly sliced, seeds removed
- 1 teaspoon salt
- ½ red onion, finely chopped
- 1 large garlic clove, finely chopped
- 3 tomatoes, diced
- 400 g (14 oz) cooked chickpeas – tinned or cooked from dried
- ¼ teaspoon turmeric
- Chopped coriander (cilantro), to garnish – optional

VEGAN

Put the potatoes into a saucepan of cold water, bring to the boil and cook until tender.

Meanwhile, heat the oil in a wok or frying pan over a medium heat. When it's hot, add the cumin and toss for about 30 seconds, then add the chillies and salt, quickly followed by the onion and garlic. Stir well, then turn the heat up to high and cook until the garlic and onions are visibly softened and golden brown. Now add the tomatoes and stir well. Bring to the boil, then turn the heat down to low-medium and allow to reduce for several minutes, until you have a thick sauce.

Using a slotted spoon, fish the cooked potatoes out of the water and add them to the wok, pushing them down quite hard into the tomatoes, almost mashing them. You're aiming for a consistency that will work well as a dip.

If you are using chickpeas from a tin, drain and rinse them. Add the chickpeas to the wok, along with the turmeric. Stir everything together, then serve – garnished with coriander, if you like.

Yeshi says 'This dish is best served with *Numtak balep* (fried breakfast bread, see page 42). If you are making both at the same time, you can keep the chickpeas simmering over a low heat while you prepare the bread – if the sauce starts to get too thick at any point, just add a little boiling water.'

Buckwheat Pancakes *Serves 4*

This is Yeshi's mother's favourite breakfast. If you pair these pancakes with hot honey and butter dip – and you must! – you'll start to understand why.

Buckwheat is a hardy plant that thrives in difficult conditions. Its seeds are used to make a flour with a distinctive, earthy flavour that can be a bit of an acquired taste. To take the edge off it, replace 50 g (⅓ cup) of the buckwheat flour with plain (all-purpose) white flour.

200 g (1½ cups) buckwheat flour
2 eggs
A little cooking oil, if needed
Hot honey and butter dip (see page 49), to serve

VEGETARIAN

Put the flour into a mixing bowl, break in the eggs and add 500 ml (2 cups) of water. Whisk until you have a smooth batter – it will be pretty runny.

If you have a good non-stick frying pan, there is no need for oil, but if you're at all worried about sticking, then do add a few drops. The pan needs to be hot before you start cooking the pancakes, so let it stand over a high heat for a minute. Now pour in just enough batter to barely cover the base of the pan, tilting the pan this way and that away from the heat to make a very thin pancake.

Turn the heat down to medium and cook the pancake on the first side until any trace of runniness has gone – this could take up to 2 minutes. Carefully flip it over and cook for a further minute on the second side, then turn it again and cook for a few more seconds. Transfer the cooked pancake to a plate and keep warm while you cook the rest.

By the time you are on to your second or third pancake, the pan will be hotter and the cooking time should reduce, so keep a close eye on them.

To eat your pancake like a real Tibetan, shred it in your hands and plunge it into some hot honey and butter dip.

Hot Honey and Butter Dip *Serves 4*

In the spring and summertime, Yeshi's village is a wildflower heaven. Most families keep beehives under the rocks on the mountains above or behind their houses. The bees produce honey in vast quantities, but there is no protective equipment and sometimes people get stung. Yeshi remembers not only the excitement of coming face to face with walls of honeycomb, but also the frisson of danger that accompanied its extraction.

In Tibet, honey has been used for centuries to treat all kinds of diseases and wounds. Yeshi's family keep some types of honey specifically for medicinal use – they say that its potency only builds over time.

At the breakfast table, honey is widely enjoyed with *Tsampa* (roasted barley flour, see page 53), bread and in snacks, but is arguably best when cooked with butter, as here, and enjoyed with Buckwheat pancakes (see page 46).

50 g (1¾ oz) unsalted butter
70 g (2½ oz) runny honey

VEGETARIAN

Put the butter and honey into a saucepan and place over a low-medium heat. Stir gently until melted together, then let it bubble away for 5–10 seconds, before turning the heat off. Be careful not to cook it for too long, or you'll find that the butter and honey separate.

Serve warm. As it cools, it will set a little, which is also delicious, but if you like the runniness you can always put it back onto the heat for round two to melt it again.

Julie and Choeden, Yeshi's mother.

Sweet Balep
(Sweet Flatbread) *Makes 5*

In Lhasa, Tibet's capital, sweet *balep* is widely sold at street stalls. When Yeshi left his village in Tibet, Lhasa was a stopping-off point, and he bought large quantities of it for the arduous journey ahead. As sweet *balep* keeps much better than savoury *balep*, and is delicious just on its own, these flatbreads saw him through those first few difficult days and felt like the gift that kept on giving.

Sweet *balep* is also made in the monasteries, where thousands of monks enjoy it for breakfast every day with tea. Years ago, when I attended a teaching at His Holiness the XIV Dalai Lama's temple in Dharamsala, India, I remember the monks handing out tea and sweet *balep* to us all as we sat cross-legged on the stone floor of the temple. It was everything I needed in that moment.

These flatbreads are delicious spread with jam, honey or butter, and with some Tibetan tea or a cup of good old English Breakfast alongside.

100 g (3½ oz) caster (superfine) sugar
500 g (3⅓ cups) self-raising flour, plus extra for dusting
1 teaspoon baking powder
3 tablespoons cooking oil
2 eggs

VEGETARIAN

Measure out 150 ml (5 fl oz) of warm water in a jug, then add the sugar and stir well until the sugar dissolves completely.

Combine the flour and baking powder in a mixing bowl, then add the oil and break in the eggs. Mix well with your hand, while slowly pouring in the warm sweetened water from the jug. Keep kneading until a dough forms in the bowl. It will feel a bit soggier than you might be comfortable with, but that's the consistency you are after – you don't want the dough to be too hard. Cover and set aside for 10 minutes.

Turn the dough out onto a flour-dusted work surface and knead well – it should feel nice and soft, with a slight gooiness still. Break it into five roughly equal pieces and roll each one between your palms into a ball.

Sprinkle a little more flour onto your work surface. Take the first ball of dough and press it flat with your hand. Using a rolling pin, roll it out from top to bottom and bottom to top several times, turning it over and around as you go. You are aiming for a round flatbread about 15 cm (6 inches) in diameter.

Place a small frying pan over a medium heat – there's no need for any oil. When the pan is hot, carefully lay in your first flatbread. Give it 1–2 minutes on the first side, then 1–2 minutes on the other. To check if the flatbread is done, gently press the edge with your finger: if it springs back, it is cooked; if your finger leaves an impression, you need to cook it for a bit longer.

Repeat with the other flatbreads. Enjoy while they're still warm, or they'll keep well for 4–5 days in an airtight container.

Tsampa
(Roasted Barley Flour) *Makes enough for 4–6 servings*

Once upon a time, the term '*tsampa*-eater' was used to describe all Tibetans, as it was the one unifying custom of a people who spoke many different dialects and whose traditions varied widely. *Tsampa* (roasted barley flour) has travelled across the world with Tibetan people. Outside their homeland, it immediately connects them to their Tibetan identity.

Inside Tibet *tsampa* is enjoying a resurgence in popularity as well. As a whole grain it boasts many health benefits, and at a time when new produce is increasingly making its way into the region, it is a familiar food that people can fall back on when they feel unsure about what else they can trust.

For breakfast it can be made into a porridge; for lunch or dinner it might be eaten with yoghurt or used to thicken a stew. Yeshi even uses it to make some irresistible Chocolate *tsampa* truffles (see page 233). Many Tibetans also carry *tsampa* around with them to enjoy as a snack during the day.

500 g (2½ cups) pearl barley

VEGAN

Place a heavy wok or frying pan over a high heat – cast iron works well. When it is hot, tip in the barley (you are dry-roasting, so there's no need to add any oil) and, after a minute or two, start stirring briskly with a flat wooden spoon. To make sure the barley roasts evenly, turn up the heat as high as possible and keep moving the grains off the bottom of the pan, rotating them from the centre to the outside. Stir backwards and forwards, and from side to side, for about 15 minutes continuously – you need to keep the barley moving so it doesn't get scorched. This is tiring work, but worth it!

When the barley has turned golden brown, transfer it to a saucepan or bowl to cool – it will continue to cook in the residual heat. (Once it has cooled a little, the barley is edible, and our kids love to siphon off a small bowl at this point to snack on like popcorn.)

To grind the roasted barley, a flour mill is best, producing a fine, evenly ground flour, but a coffee or spice grinder works well too – you'll just need a little more patience, as you'll probably need to run it through in batches of about half a cup at a time. To get the most even grind possible, sift the milled flour and regrind any large pieces that remain.

Store the *tsampa* in a sealed container at room temperature.

Breakfast Tsampa *Serves 4*

We've written a lot about the qualities of this superfood already, but not very much about how you should expect it to taste. Whether you prepare your *tsampa* sweet or savoury, porridge-thin or kneaded into hand-pressed pieces, it has a distinct nuttiness to it and a lovely, toasted aroma. When I was little, Ready Brek was the thing: a nutritious and fortifying British porridge made from wholegrain rolled oats. Well, *tsampa* has a similar character, but is more versatile and flavoursome.

This recipe is for *tsampa* in its most solid form, but there's no right or wrong here, so if you end up with something more porridge-like that's great too. As with any flour, just add more water if your mix is too crumbly, or a little more *tsampa* if there's too much water in the bowl.

40 g (1½ oz) cheddar cheese, finely diced
40 g (1½ oz) unsalted butter
150 g (5½ oz) *Tsampa* (roasted barley flour, see page 53)

VEGETARIAN

Put the cheese and butter into a heatproof bowl and pour over 100 ml (3½ fl oz) boiling water. Tip in the *tsampa* and using your hand (if you want to go full Tibetan-style, and you're not afraid of dipping your fingers in hot water!) or a spoon (if you're more faint-hearted, like me), start to stir the *tsampa* into the mix. At first it will feel as if you are not getting very far with melting the cheese or mixing everything through, but after a couple of minutes you should start to see the ingredients come together into a kind of paste.

Once the hot water has been absorbed, the mixture is best worked by hand. If you grab clumps of it and press them together they will begin to form what feels like pieces of play dough, and you might be surprised to find that what felt very sticky and clung stubbornly to your hands or spoon will soon flake off cleanly. If this doesn't happen, add a little more boiling water – but just a tiny amount at a time. Form the mixture into rounded sausage shapes and serve in bowls.

Yeshi says 'This is how we enjoy our *tsampa* at home, but if you like the idea of sweet *tsampa* you can try it with 2 tablespoons of honey or maple syrup, or 1½ tablespoons of sugar instead of the cheese. Butter should always be added. Berries or bananas make a nice addition on the side. You can also try *tsampa* sprinkled over yoghurt. In that case, just dust a little *tsampa* into a bowl of yoghurt to lend it a gorgeous nutty flavour.'

Cold Dishes

During winter, temperatures can drop to minus 40 degrees on the highest reaches of the Tibetan plateau. Even during summertime the nights are cold, with the mercury hovering barely above zero. In such conditions, cold food is not what the doctor orders. Cold dishes are not consumed that often in Tibet – and when they are, they're almost always designed to be served alongside hot food to counterbalance them.

Tibetan doctors say that wherever we live and whatever the season, frequent consumption of salads, smoothies and raw produce (the very things we tend to associate with healthy eating in the West) can have a negative impact on our long-term health, and this is especially the case in cold conditions.

They maintain that the body needs more energy to break down raw and cold food and to digest it, depleting the reserves needed for other vital processes such as healing. Ultimately this can create a situation where circulation is impeded and an acute injury, for example, can become a chronic one.

In the valleys and at lower altitudes, salads and cold side dishes are becoming popular as refreshing accompaniments. However, balance and moderation are key.

In summertime Yeshi's family enjoy foods perceived as having cooling properties. They eat a lot of lettuce and celery – but they don't always eat them cold. Strawberries and pears are also consumed with some gusto as they are considered to have hydrating qualities, and yoghurt is widely enjoyed. Preserved yak meat is eaten year-round as a cold snack, usually with *sepen* (hot chilli dip), and other cold cooked meats are enjoyed with a range of accompanying sauces. And then there is pickled mooli (daikon). Tibetan people usually keep a large barrel of this in the corner of the kitchen for dipping into at any time of day. It tastes great with momos (Tibetan dumplings), meat and barley beer, and is useful to have on hand during winter when fresh vegetables can be hard to find.

Tibetan Yoghurt *Serves 4–6*

In Tibet, food is generally considered to be either white or red, and traditionally people ate white food in summer and red food in winter. Loosely speaking, white food refers to milk and other dairy products, which tend to be more plentiful during the summer, while red food refers to meat, which is more available in wintertime.

Yoghurt has been a staple part of the Tibetan diet for as long as there have been *dhri*, or female yaks. In pre-modern Tibet, nomadic people were heavily reliant on *dhri* milk and its products for their survival – probiotic yoghurt was, quite literally, a life-saver, and an annual festival celebrating yoghurt is among the most important in the Tibetan calendar. The *Shoton* ('yoghurt banquet') festival has been held since the eleventh century and is an opportunity for lay people to offer yoghurt to monks at the end of their hundred-day meditation retreats.

Dhri milk has a higher butterfat content than cow's milk, so this makes for a much creamier yoghurt. But the methods that Yeshi's family use can be replicated outside of Tibet. Whole milk is definitely the best option here – it will give you the thickest consistency – and make sure you use plain, unsweetened yoghurt that contains live cultures. Enjoy your yoghurt with Breakfast *tsampa* (see page 54), mixed with chilli to make *Sho sepen* (see page 200), in salads such as the mooli and yoghurt one on page 63, or in any other way you like.

1 litre (4 cups) whole milk
4 tablespoons natural live yoghurt

VEGETARIAN

Place the milk in a saucepan over a medium-high heat and bring to the boil, stirring frequently. When the milk is properly bubbling, remove from the heat and leave it to cool for about 45 minutes, until it reaches a temperature of about 50°C (122°F). If you don't have a thermometer, wait until you can comfortably dip your finger in the milk, but it still feels pretty hot.

Add the yoghurt to the hot milk and stir it through well, then decant into a steel, glass or ideally earthenware container (not plastic!), cover with a lid, and wrap with 2–3 tea towels or a thick towel. Leave undisturbed for a minimum of 8 hours, or as long as 24 hours – the longer you leave it, the firmer and tangier the yoghurt will become.

Spoon the yoghurt into jars and store in the fridge, where it should keep for up to a week.

Yeshi says 'During winter, when the outside temperature is low, I like to set my yoghurt in the oven overnight. I put the yoghurt into the oven, turn it on to 200°C (400°F) and let it heat up for about 3 minutes, then I turn it off and leave the yoghurt in there all night to set. If your kitchen is a bit cool, you could also just put the yoghurt near a radiator or heater.'

Smacked Cucumber *Serves 2–4*

In Tibet, cucumber is a popular snack for picnicking, when it's usually chopped and dipped in yoghurt. As a dish for the table, it's often prepared in this way. The idea behind smacking the cucumber is that when it's bruised and broken up it's better able to absorb the garlic, oil, vinegar and soy sauce, resulting in a more intense flavour.

1 cucumber
1 small garlic clove, finely chopped
2 teaspoons sesame oil
2 teaspoons Chinkiang black vinegar
2 teaspoons light soy sauce

VEGAN

Peel the cucumber, then use a rolling pin to smack it hard from end to end so that it begins to break apart and bruise. With a knife, slice the cucumber into chunks, smacking it some more as you go if you feel it's not sufficiently broken apart.

Put the cucumber into a mixing bowl and add the garlic, sesame oil, vinegar and soy sauce. Swirl everything around the bowl to mix well, then transfer to a serving dish.

Mooli and Yoghurt Salad *Serves 4–6*

Everybody has a cherished 'mum's recipe', and this one is Yeshi's. His mother is very fond of her mooli and yoghurt salad, which makes a truly refreshing accompaniment to any meal, but especially the warm, meaty dishes that are often the centrepiece of the Tibetan table in wintertime.

Mooli (also known as daikon or white radish) is a fast-growing vegetable that has the look and feel of a large white carrot, and a similar crisp texture. Like the carrot, it is mild and sweet in taste, quite unlike the red summer radishes with which we may be more familiar. The combination of shredded mooli and yoghurt is genius, especially with a hint of Sichuan pepper, and it's incredibly easy to make. Enjoy this alongside your hot dish of choice, or with a few beers – that's how Yeshi likes it!

1 mooli (daikon), about 500 g (1 lb 2 oz)
1 teaspoon salt
5 tablespoons plain yoghurt
¼ teaspoon crushed Sichuan peppercorns (*yerma*)
Pinch of chilli powder or hot chilli flakes
1 small fresh green chilli, finely chopped – optional
Thinly sliced spring onion (scallion), to garnish – optional

VEGETARIAN

Trim off any green leaves from the mooli (don't discard these – they make great additions to soups and stews), then wash but do not peel it.

Using the large holes of a grater – or a food processor, if you have one – shred the mooli and put into a bowl. Add the salt and mix it in well with your hands, gently squashing the mooli with your fingers. As you do this, juices will start to be released from the mooli, and it's important that you drain away as much of these bitter juices as you can, leaving behind just the mild, sweet flesh.

Once you've drained the mooli, add the yoghurt, Sichuan pepper, chilli powder or chilli flakes, and the fresh chilli, if using. Mix everything together, then garnish with spring onion, if you like.

Chilled Chilli Pork *Serves 4*

Pork is not widely eaten in the part of Tibet that Yeshi comes from, so it's a bit of a rare treat. The family do keep pigs, but only about ten of them, and they might slaughter one or two a year. The pigs feed on walnuts and turnips when they are in the fields close to home, and on acorns when they are up in the mountains. This diet produces pork with fat that has a nutritional profile similar to that of olive oil – the Spanish often refer to acorn-fed pigs as 'olive trees on four hooves'.

This chilled chilli pork is Yeshi's dad's favourite dish, and he likes to enjoy it with a whisky on the side. It's simple to make, as long as you remember to marinate the meat in advance.

500 g (1 lb 2 oz) pork belly

For the marinade

1 tablespoon dark soy sauce
1½ teaspoons salt
½ teaspoon turmeric
¼ teaspoon crushed Sichuan peppercorns (*yerma*)
1 small garlic clove, finely chopped
2.5 cm (1 inch) piece of ginger, washed but not peeled, finely chopped

For the sauce

1½ tablespoons light soy sauce
1 tablespoon Chinkiang black vinegar
½ tablespoon white vinegar
½ tablespoon sesame oil
3 spring onions (scallions), washed and cut into 2.5 cm (1 inch) lengths
1 teaspoon Taste Tibet *sepen* (see page 190) or hot chilli flakes

At least a day beforehand, combine the marinade ingredients in a bowl. Cut the pork belly (including the rind, if there is any) into large chunks, then add to the bowl and mix well. Cover and leave to marinate for a day or two in the fridge.

Take the pork out of the marinade and put it into a large saucepan. Pour in about 1.5 litres (6 cups) of boiling water, cover with a lid and boil for 40 minutes over a high heat, checking on it from time to time to ensure it doesn't boil over. Lift the pork out of the water and leave to cool slightly, then put in the fridge to chill.

When you're ready to eat, remove any bones from the pork, then cut the meat into thin slices and place on a serving plate.

To make the sauce, mix together all the ingredients in a small bowl. The sauce can either be mixed with the chilli pork, or served alongside for dipping.

Yeshi says 'This pork can also be enjoyed hot if you prefer: just slice the cooked pork as soon as it is cool enough to handle. You can also keep the broth the pork was cooked in and use it for soup (add spinach, mooli and potatoes) or as a base for noodles. In Tibet, we let it cool and then enjoy it as a kind of savoury jelly, but I realise that this isn't for everyone!'

Yellow Laphing
(Chilled Yellow Jelly Noodles) *Serves 4–6*

This dish of slippery strips of steamed dough, which originated in Tibet, might seem like a bit of a strange concept, but it has been lovingly embraced into Nepalese and Indian street food culture. The dough is made with wheat flour, and the noodles get their beautiful golden colour from turmeric.

Don't be put off by the length of this recipe! At first glance it may look complicated, but it's surprisingly simple and great fun to make. Using a stack of steamer baskets, it's also a bit like a magic trick – you won't believe what you can produce with just a few ingredients cooked in an innovative way.

For the noodles

250 g (1⅔ cups) plain (all-purpose) white flour

½ teaspoon salt

¼ teaspoon turmeric

For the garlic water

3–4 large garlic cloves, peeled

For the sauce – for each serving, you will need

2 teaspoons light soy sauce

1 teaspoon sesame oil

1 teaspoon Chinkiang black vinegar

¼ teaspoon white vinegar

½ teaspoon Taste Tibet *sepen* (see page 190)

Pinch of salt, or to taste

For the garnishes

Soy chunks (a couple of handfuls) – optional

Thinly sliced spring onions (scallions), including green tips

Shredded cucumber – optional

VEGAN

For the noodles, put the flour and salt into a mixing bowl. Slowly drizzle in 130 ml (4½ fl oz) of warm water, while mixing well with your other hand. When all the water is in, use one hand to knead the dough in the bowl until you have a nice smooth ball of dough. Cover and leave to stand for at least 1 hour or until you're ready to make the noodle mixture.

Now pour in 1 litre (4 cups) of warm water and squelch it through the dough, kneading well for 6–7 minutes, until most of the dough has dissolved in the water. (Any stringy, spongy scraps of dough that remain can be boiled in a pan of water for 10 minutes, then drained, cooled and thinly sliced. These boiled dough strips are now ready to be added to the bowls of noodles later. If this all sounds too fiddly, though, they can just be discarded.) Strain the milky-looking noodle mixture through a colander into another bowl and leave to settle in the fridge for 1–2 hours.

Meanwhile, if you're using soy chunks as a garnish, soak them in cold water for 1 hour. Drain, then boil for 4–5 minutes and drain again. Rinse the soy chunks under cold running water to cool them, pressing lightly to squeeze out any excess water, then slice into strips.

For the garlic water, crush the garlic by pressing down on top of it with the flat of a large knife. Place it in a small bowl and add 150 ml (5½ fl oz) of water, then leave in the fridge for 20 minutes to infuse.

Just before you take the noodle mixture out of the fridge, start heating 1.5 litres (6 cups) of water in the base of your steamer (or a wok, if you're using bamboo steamer baskets).

continued >

Now head to the fridge and take out the bowl of noodle mixture – it will have separated into a very watery layer on top and a thick layer of flour sediment at the bottom. Carefully pour away the watery part into the sink. Add the turmeric to the thick milky mixture that remains and stir everything together well.

When the water is at a rolling boil, place a plate in one of the steamer baskets and spoon a little of the noodle mixture onto it, swirling it around to make a thin, even layer – you are aiming for a thickness of 2–3 mm (⅛ inch) or less. If you have a stack of steamer baskets, repeat with more plates in the remaining steamer baskets; if you are working with just one steamer basket, you will need to do this in two or three batches. Steam for 9–10 minutes, then leave the noodles – as they now are, though they will look like wet pancakes for the time being – to cool and set.

Peel the noodle pancakes off the plates (a rice spoon or similar is useful here), then roll them up and slice into very thin strips on a chopping board. If they're not coming away easily, you can just carefully cut them into strips on the plate. Depending on the size of your plates, you will probably need two plates worth of noodles for one bowl of *laphing*.

Decant the noodles into bowls. Add the soy chunks and sliced dough, if using, then pour over a little of the garlic water (don't discard the garlic cloves – they can be reused for other dishes).

Finally, add the soy sauce, sesame oil, both vinegars, *sepen* and salt to each bowl. Garnish with the spring onions – and some shredded cucumber too, if you have it.

White Laphing (Chilled White Jelly Noodles) *Serves 6–8*

Refreshing *laphing* is a summertime favourite in Tibet, especially in the towns and cities. Yeshi didn't come across it until he travelled to the holy Khawa Karpo mountain when he was about twelve, and his abiding memory of this encounter is of his aunt eating as much as she could while the going was good!

These noodles are made from mung bean starch, so they're naturally gluten-free (if this is important, check the label on any soy chunks you use). As the jelly for the noodles can be kept in the fridge for a few days, it's worth making the full amount to enjoy over the course of several meals or snacks. We usually serve bowls of *laphing* with shredded cucumber on top. In traditional Tibetan medicine, both mung beans and cucumber are considered to be cooling foods – but there's plenty of heat in the chilli! Bear in mind that mung bean starch has very little flavour of its own, so don't be tempted to skip the sauce and garnishes. Tibetan people like their *laphing* really fiery, and that would definitely be our recommendation.

For the noodles
100 g (3½ oz) mung bean starch
½ teaspoon salt
For the garlic water
7 large garlic cloves, peeled
For the sauce – for each serving, you will need
3 tablespoons light soy sauce
1 teaspoon sesame oil
2 teaspoons Chinkiang black vinegar
¼ teaspoon white vinegar
½ teaspoon Taste Tibet *sepen* (see page 190) or more to taste
Pinch of salt, or to taste
For the garnishes
Shredded cucumber
Thinly sliced spring onions (scallions), including green tips
Soy chunks (a couple of handfuls) – optional
Boiled dough strips (see page 67) – optional

VEGAN

To make the noodles, put the mung bean starch and salt in a mixing bowl, then add 500 ml (2 cups) of cold water and whisk briskly for a couple of minutes. In a saucepan, bring 600 ml (21 fl oz) of water to the boil over a high heat. When the water is just boiling, turn the heat down to medium and pour in the mung bean starch mixture, whisking briskly and continuously as it thickens. After about 5 minutes the mixture will start to turn translucent and become very gloopy, with the texture of a cake batter. At this point, turn off the heat and pour the mixture into a small square or rectangular baking dish. Set aside to cool for at least 1½ hours or until set.

Meanwhile, if you're using soy chunks as a garnish, soak them in cold water for 1 hour. Drain, then boil for 4–5 minutes and drain again. Rinse the soy chunks under cold running water to cool them, pressing lightly to squeeze out any excess water, then slice into strips.

For the garlic water, crush the garlic by pressing down on top of it with the flat of a large knife. Place it in a small bowl and add 300 ml (10½ fl oz) of water, then leave in the fridge for 20 minutes to infuse.

When the noodle mixture has set, turn the dish upside down and empty the jelly out onto a chopping board, then cut into thin strips.

Place a handful of noodles in each bowl and pour over a little of the garlic water (don't discard the garlic cloves – they can be reused for other dishes).

For the sauce, add soy sauce, sesame oil, both vinegars, *sepen* and salt to each bowl and mix well. Garnish with shredded cucumber and sliced spring onion for colour and texture. Other great additions include soy chunks and, if you're ok with gluten, boiled dough strips.

Chilled Sesame Noodles *Serves 4–6*

This take on the popular Tibetan snack of White *laphing* (see page 71) is just a bit easier and quicker to make. We can eat vast quantities of these noodles, but then we are addicts! With all the raw garlic, spring onions and Sichuan pepper, this dish packs quite a punch and so is probably better served as a side rather than a main. It makes perfect summertime party food, mixed and matched with some other chilled dishes and a nice cold beer.

180 g (6 oz) glass noodles
1 cucumber
2 large garlic cloves, finely chopped or crushed
5 spring onions (scallions), washed and thinly sliced, including green tips
1 tablespoon sesame oil
2 tablespoons light soy sauce
1 tablespoon Chinkiang black vinegar
1 teaspoon Taste Tibet *sepen* (see page 190) or hot chilli flakes
1 teaspoon crushed Sichuan peppercorns (*yerma*) or Sichuan pepper oil – optional

VEGAN

Soak the noodles in a bowl of hot – but not boiling – water for about half an hour, to hydrate them and make them more pliable.

Bring a large saucepan of water to the boil over a high heat. Lift the noodles out of their soaking water and into the pan, stir them gently through the water, then leave to cook for about 2 minutes. Taste one to make sure they are done before draining them in a colander. Transfer the noodles to a bowl and run cold water over them to cool them, then leave to sit in the cold water while you prepare the cucumber.

Peel the cucumber and slice it thinly on the diagonal, then carefully turn it slightly on its side and cut into thin strips – you should end up with thin, fairly uniform slivers of cucumber. Put the cucumber into a bowl and add the garlic, spring onions, sesame oil, soy sauce and vinegar.

Drain the noodles well, then place on a chopping board. Cut them roughly into lengths, then add to the bowl, along with the *sepen* or chilli flakes – and the Sichuan peppercorns or oil, if you have them. Mix everything well using chopsticks or a fork and serve.

Son Labu
(Tibetan Pickled Mooli) *Makes about 2.5 kg (5 lb 8 oz)*

Tibetan people love pickling, and it's a great way to preserve vegetables until the next growing season. In the late autumn, Yeshi's family make two or three massive jars of pickled mooli that last them until spring. Spicy, sour and salty, this can be snacked on at any time during the day, but it's also brought out at mealtimes to enjoy alongside other dishes. Pickled mooli can be added to stir-fried meat dishes as well for a bit of pungency, or in place of fresh veg over the barren winter months. Feel free to adjust the quantities if you're not after as big a jar as resides in our fridge!

Traditionally, pickling brine is not usually thrown out. Instead, the leftover brine is topped up with salted water and the jar is filled up again with more mooli. The only important point to note is that you must make sure no oil gets into the bowl or jar, or it will contaminate and spoil the pickles.

3 mooli (daikon), about 1.5 kg (3 lb 5 oz) in total, washed but not peeled
2 tablespoons sea salt flakes
5–6 dried red chillies, about 50 g (2 oz)
2 tablespoons crushed Sichuan peppercorns (*yerma*)
200 g (7 oz) garlic cloves, about 5 bulbs, peeled but left whole
2 tablespoons whole garam masala spices – optional

VEGAN

Pictured on page 111.

Chop the mooli into circular chunks about 1 cm (½ inch) thick. Place in a large bowl, add the salt and mix it through very well. Crush the chillies slightly between your fingers, just enough to release some of their heat, then add to the bowl, along with the Sichuan peppercorns, garlic and garam masala.

Mix everything together, then transfer directly into an airtight container, preferably earthenware, ceramic or glass, but if all you have is plastic, that's fine too. The most important thing is that your container has a lid that seals well.

Press the mooli down into the container, then add 1.25 litres (5 cups) of cold water to the bowl. Give it a swirl to rinse out any remnants, then pour over the mooli. Seal the container and leave in a cold place (ideally the fridge) for about 3 weeks before using. The pickled mooli should then keep well for at least 6 months.

Yeshi says 'You can pickle almost any vegetable in this way as long as it's nice and fresh. Mooli is my favourite, but I also enjoy Chinese (napa) cabbage.'

Cold Beef Salad *Serves 4*

This is a great way of using up the leftovers from your Sunday roast – in which case, you can skip the first step. Chicken or pork would work well too, ideally chicken breast or pork belly.

If you're making a tableful of dishes to share, then this one sits happily alongside hot food as well as cold. It is perfect party food.

450 g (1 lb) beef top rump
Salt and black pepper
2 tablespoons light soy sauce
2 teaspoons Chinkiang black vinegar
1 tablespoon sesame oil
1–2 teaspoons Taste Tibet *sepen* (see page 190) or hot chilli flakes
½ teaspoon crushed Sichuan peppercorns (*yerma*) or 1 teaspoon Sichuan pepper oil – optional
2–3 spring onions (scallions), washed

Preheat the oven to 220°C (425°F). Place the beef in a roasting tin, season with salt and pepper and roast for 20 minutes, then turn the oven down to 180°C (350°F) and roast for a further 20 minutes. Remove and leave to cool, then chill in the fridge – ideally the meat should be served fridge-cold.

Slice the meat very thinly into bite-sized pieces no more than 5 mm (¼ inch) thick. Place in a bowl and add the soy sauce, vinegar, sesame oil, *sepen* and the Sichuan pepper or Sichuan pepper oil, if using. Mix everything together well.

Using chopsticks (or tongs), carefully place the meat on a plate, piece by piece. Cut the spring onions into 5 cm (2 inch) lengths. Arrange on top of the meat, then serve.

Rice and Stir-Fries

The recipes in this chapter are a celebration of all the vegetables and other ingredients that Yeshi learned to cook with as a child. In the valleys of eastern Tibet, where he grew up, there was always a good deal of variety. This section showcases some of the dishes he enjoyed from a young age, plus a few others he has picked up along the way.

Historically, rice was an expensive commodity in Tibet. It was carried in on the backs of porters and yaks over frozen peaks, on journeys that could take up to four months. Imported alongside tea, sugar, spices and dried fruit from neighbouring countries such as India, China and Nepal, rice was once a byword for riches. The name of one of Tibet's three leading monasteries, the Drepung, literally translates as 'rice heap' – a nod to its spiritual, rather than material or culinary, wealth.

Such luxury foods have always made their way into Tibet somehow, and the Tibetan diet has always been evolving. Tibetan people, with their extraordinary culinary flair and imagination, have long enjoyed exploring new flavours and ingredients and experimenting with new cooking techniques. But today the pace of culinary change is accelerating. Rice and warm-season vegetables are becoming easy to procure. Transport links into and across Tibet are constantly being upgraded, bringing in new produce all the time. Yeshi's parents talk about how the younger generation is becoming fussy and developing a taste for fast food. The Tibetan diet is gradually being diluted.

Fill your table with as many of these dishes as you feel like cooking. This kind of food is designed to be mixed and matched. Everything keeps well in the fridge overnight and many dishes can be thrown together in one pot for round two. Generally speaking, you can just add a little boiling water to the pan the next day, and enjoyment will be yours again in just a few minutes. Note that while stir-fries can be eaten with rice, the more traditional accompaniment is bread – either *Tingmo* (steamed bread, see page 169) or flatbreads cooked on the stovetop, such as *Balep* (Tibetan flatbread, see page 173).

Dad's Rice *Serves 4–6*

Yeshi has two fathers (you can read more about the Tibetan tradition of brides taking more than one husband on page 133), and his older father makes this dish for lunch every Tibetan New Year. In Tibet, partying – and eating! – is an important part of the celebrations, but the new year is also marked with a number of religious observances, including *bsang*, a purification practice.

People in Yeshi's village make a big bonfire on the hill, and they then place ritual offerings of *tsampa* (roasted barley flour), butter, tea and *chang* (barley beer) on juniper leaves in the middle of the fire. These release highly fragrant smoke that is said to create a pathway or channel to the Buddha. While the rest of the family head out to make their offerings, Yeshi's older father busies himself making this special rice dish, which is waiting for them on their return.

Rice was scarce in pre-modern Tibet, which made it a food for special occasions such as New Year. If you'd like to 'purify' this dish by removing the meat, wild mushrooms make a great substitute. If you have a rice cooker, you can of course use that to cook the rice; leftover rice is also ideal for this dish – you'll need 600 g (3¼ cups) of cooked rice. Note that there's no spice or kick to this, so do serve this with some Taste Tibet *sepen* (see page 190) if you want that feeling of fire.

300 g (1½ cups) basmati rice
1 red onion, thinly sliced
300 g (10½ oz) minced (ground) beef or pork
1 teaspoon salt
150 g (1 cup) peas (frozen is fine)
80 g (2¾ oz) butter
3 spring onions (scallions), washed and thinly sliced, including green tips

In a saucepan with a tight-fitting lid, rinse the rice well, then drain. Pour in 400 ml (14 fl oz) of water, put the lid on the pan and place over a medium-high heat. When the water starts to boil turn the heat down to medium, and then, when there is no water visible on the surface of the rice, reduce the heat to as low as it will go and leave for 5–6 minutes or until the rice is cooked.

Place a wok or large frying pan over a high heat. When it's hot, add the onion, beef and salt – there's no need to add any oil – and stir-fry until the meat is browned and cooked through. When the meat juices start to run, turn the heat down to low, and if it looks as if the meat is starting to burn, add a little boiling water.

Once the beef is cooked, stir in the peas (from frozen if that's how they come) and cook over a low heat for 1–2 minutes, then add the spring onions and cook for a further minute.

Meanwhile, melt the butter in a separate saucepan. Tibetan people say that you know when butter has fully melted by the chirping sounds it makes in the pan – listen out for it!

Once the butter bird has sung, remove from the heat and add the melted butter to the wok or frying pan. Give everything a stir, then tip in the rice and stir through the meat. If you are using cold leftover rice, you will need to leave this for a few minutes over the heat; otherwise just turn the heat off completely, mix everything together and serve.

Perfect Basmati Rice *Serves 4*

There are so many different varieties of rice, but for Yeshi basmati has the best fragrance and is the easiest to cook. A rice cooker can of course do the job for you, and makes a great investment, but getting it right every time on the stove is not as tricky as you might think.

350 g (1¾ cups) basmati rice
Olive oil – optional

VEGAN

Put the rice into a saucepan and rinse it several times – this releases any excess starch and helps to make the cooked rice tender and fluffy. Drain off the rinsing water and place the pan on the stove, then add 500 ml (2 cups) of cold water and turn the heat to high. If you like, you can also add a drop of olive oil – this isn't strictly necessary, but it gives a nice fragrance to the rice. Cover the pan with a tight-fitting lid.

When the water has come to the boil, lower the heat to medium and let the rice cook for 8–10 minutes. You will need to keep an eye on the pan to make sure it doesn't boil over: if it starts to look as if it will, set the lid at an angle to allow more steam to escape. When there is no water visible above the rice, turn the heat down to low and leave to simmer until the water has been completely absorbed, then serve.

Reheating rice

If you have any leftover rice, leave it to cool before putting it in the fridge, and don't keep it for longer than a day or two. When you want to reheat it, here is a simple trick that will change your life. Just add a little boiling water to the pan (if reheating on the stove) or bowl (if using a microwave) and make sure to cover it tightly. This way the rice will steam a little as it reheats, retaining the fluffiness of the just-cooked grains. Depending on the amount you are reheating, it will take about 3–5 minutes on the stove, slightly less in the microwave.

Yeshi says 'If you want to scale the quantities of rice up or down, as a general rule you should use just enough water to cover the rice by the depth of the first joint of your middle finger.'

Simple Vegetable Stir-Fried Rice *Serves 4–6*

Fried rice is the perfect way to use up your leftovers, and there are many different possible variations here. The vegetables we have suggested are just ideas for what can be used, so try replacing them with seasonal veg from the market, or your garden or weekly box – anything with a good flavour and some crunch is ideal. Enjoy with Egg and tomato soup (see page 134) or a nice fresh salad.

3 tablespoons cooking oil
2 large garlic cloves, thinly sliced
1 red onion, thinly sliced
1 teaspoon salt
200 g (7 oz) green beans, topped and tailed, chopped small
200 g (7 oz) Tenderstem broccoli (broccolini)
2 teaspoons soy sauce
1 teaspoon sesame oil
600 g (1 lb 5 oz) chilled cooked rice, brown or white

VEGAN

Place a wok over a high heat and add the oil. When it is starting to smoke, add the garlic followed by the onion and stir-fry for a couple of minutes, or until the onion has softened. Add the salt and stir briskly for a couple of minutes, then turn the heat down slightly and add the beans. Let them cook for 4–5 minutes, stirring often.

Meanwhile, wash the broccoli, then cut the florets into pieces slightly larger than the green beans. The long, thin stems are really juicy and shouldn't be discarded. Remove their hard outer skin and slice them thinly. Add the florets and stems to the wok and cook, stirring occasionally, for a further 4–5 minutes. Then stir in the soy sauce and sesame oil.

When the broccoli is still a little bit crunchy, add the rice and a splash of boiling water to the wok and turn the heat down to low. Don't stir too much at this stage, as this will cause the rice grains to break. Instead, cover the wok with a lid (or foil) and let everything heat through for about 2 minutes before you start moving things around.

Now, with a spatula, lightly press down on the rice in the wok – it will still feel a little hard. Mix gently for a couple of minutes by pressing and then lifting sections of the rice up and over, rather than digging your spatula into it. Cover the wok again and let everything cook for another 2 minutes, stirring midway through. If the rice looks dry, add a drop more water, but just a splash – you don't want to make it soggy.

Dresil
(Ceremonial Rice) *Serves 4*

In Tibet the colour white is highly valued as a symbol of purity and good fortune. Tibetans present each other with white *khata* (scarves) on meeting or bidding farewell – these symbolise the pure heart of the giver. This goes some way to explain why *dresil*, a sweet, white-coloured rice dish, is the first food to be made and offered on Tibetan New Year's Day, usually alongside *Su-cha* (butter tea, see page 38). The idea is to bring in the new year in the most auspicious way possible.

Tibetan New Year, or *Losar*, is the most important event in the Tibetan calendar: a fifteen-day celebration, with much feasting and dancing, it is also marked by many different ceremonial and religious offerings. The kitchen, which is considered to be the most important part of the home, gets a thorough spring clean in the run-up to the festivities, and is a hive of activity during the holiday.

In Tibet *dresil* is usually made with *droma*, a small, highly nutritious root vegetable that tastes a bit like sweet potato, but sweeter. You can't find *droma* outside of Tibet, but everything else in the dish is easily come by. Add other nuts – pecans or pine nuts – if you fancy.

250 g (1¼ cups) basmati rice
70 g (2½ oz) unsalted butter
70 g (2½ oz) honey
60 g (2¼ oz) raw, unsalted cashews
100 g (3½ oz) golden raisins

VEGETARIAN

Place the rice in a bowl and rinse it thoroughly with cold water, then drain and empty into a medium-sized saucepan. Place the pan over a high heat, add 400 ml (14 fl oz) of cold water and cover with a lid. When the water starts to boil, turn the heat down to medium, and then, when there is no water visible on the surface of the rice, reduce the heat to as low as it will go and leave for 5–6 minutes or until the rice is cooked.

Meanwhile, melt the butter in a small saucepan, then take off the heat and set aside.

Once the rice is cooked, add the honey, followed by the melted butter, cashews and raisins. Stir well over a low heat, then replace the lid for just a minute to give the cashews a little time to soften. Spoon into small bowls and serve.

Stir-Fried Sweetheart Cabbage *Serves 2–4*

In many parts of Tibet, few vegetables flourish even at the best of times, but the hardy cabbage can be grown in industrial quantities, harvested in the autumn and made to last right through the barren wintertime. Yeshi's family cut the roots off the cabbages and then store them in caves they've dug out from the mountainside. This keeps the vegetables from perishing in the frost – Chinese (napa) cabbage, mooli (daikon), potatoes and turnips are all stored in this way too. The cave entrance is sealed with soil so it is completely airtight, but the stored vegetables can be accessed at any time as long as the caves are properly re-sealed on exit.

Serve this simple stir-fry with basmati rice or *Balep* (Tibetan flatbread, see page 173).

- 1 large sweetheart (pointed) cabbage, about 750 g (1 lb 10 oz), or the same weight of any other green cabbage
- 3 tablespoons cooking oil
- 2 dried red chillies
- ½ teaspoon crushed Sichuan peppercorns (*yerma*)
- 2 large garlic cloves, roughly chopped
- 2.5 cm (1 inch) piece of ginger, washed but not peeled, thinly sliced
- ½ teaspoon salt
- 1½ tablespoons Chinkiang black vinegar
- 2 teaspoons light soy sauce
- 1 teaspoon sugar

VEGAN

Wash the cabbage and, layer by layer, shred each leaf into bite-sized pieces. Discard the hard stem.

Put the oil into a wok and place over a high heat until it is starting to smoke. Throw the dried chillies and Sichuan pepper into the wok, then swirl around until they brown. Quickly add the garlic and ginger and stir-fry for about a minute. Now add the cabbage and keep stirring and cooking for 2 minutes.

Mix together the salt, vinegar, soy sauce and sugar in a small bowl, then add to the wok and cook for a further 2 minutes.

Tofu with Pak Choi *Serves 4*

In Tibetan Buddhist monasteries and nunneries inside Tibet and in India there are a large number of Tibetans who follow an entirely vegan or vegetarian diet. Here tofu and pak choi, both non-native foods to Tibet, have been lovingly embraced, and they have also become standard fare in households throughout the region. In Yeshi's hometown area, villagers grow so many different varieties of pak choi, each with its own unique flavour or texture, that they have run out of names for them. Outside Tibet, we take what we can find – and if you can't get your hands on pak choi at all, you can substitute with green beans or even spinach and this dish will taste just as delicious. For the tofu, make sure you buy firm or extra firm; this dish will not work with Japanese-style silken or soft tofu, which crumbles very easily. Enjoy with Giant fluffy sharing bread (see page 177) or basmati rice.

300 g (10½ oz) firm tofu
3 bunches of pak choi, about 300 g (10½ oz) in total
2 tablespoons cooking oil
1 small dried red chilli – optional
2–3 large garlic cloves, thinly sliced
2 teaspoons light soy sauce
2 teaspoons sesame oil
1 teaspoon Chinkiang black vinegar
Pinch of salt – optional

VEGAN

Drain the tofu and slice it into finger-sized strips. Cut the pak choi in half crossways on the diagonal, then rinse thoroughly and set aside in a bowl of cold water.

Heat the oil in a wok over a high heat for 1–2 minutes. If you want some chilli in this dish, now is the time to add it: throw the chilli in whole and let it brown (watch it closely, as it can quickly burn), then add the garlic. If it starts to spit, turn the heat down a little. When the garlic has browned, add the tofu and leave it to cook for a couple of minutes – you want to let it brown slightly before moving it. Move the tofu carefully, so that it doesn't break apart, and let it brown on the other side for another few minutes. Keep gently stirring the tofu until it is golden on both sides – this will take at least 5 minutes.

Lift the pak choi out of the water and into the wok. Any water on its leaves will help to steam the pak choi and add juices to the dish. Stir in the soy sauce, sesame oil and Chinkiang vinegar. You might want to add a pinch of salt to taste. Turn the heat down to medium-high and stir gently for 2 minutes or until the pak choi is tender.

Tofu with Broccoli and Tomato *Serves 4*

According to the principles of traditional Tibetan medicine, it's important not only that we eat a broad range of foods, but also that every meal includes different-coloured foods, since each brings different health benefits. This is a dish that will please the doctors, as it's relatively complete in itself. Make sure you use fresh broccoli – it should never be bendy – and the juiciest tomatoes you can find. Serve with basmati rice. Yeshi's dal (see page 206) is great on the side.

400 g (14 oz) firm tofu
150 g (5½ oz) broccoli, about half a head
2 tomatoes
500 ml (2 cups) cooking oil
2 dried red chillies
2.5 cm (1 inch) piece of ginger, washed but not peeled, cut into fine julienne strips
2 large garlic cloves, thinly sliced
1 tablespoon light soy sauce
1 tablespoon sesame oil
Salt

VEGAN

Drain the tofu and slice it into finger-sized strips. Wash the broccoli and cut it into bite-sized pieces. The stalks are delicious too – they keep their crunch and have a lovely sweetness. Just remove their hard outer skin, slice thinly and use them as well. Cut the tomatoes in half and then into wedges.

In a wok, heat the oil over a high heat. After 3–4 minutes, test the heat of the oil by dipping or dropping a piece of tofu into the wok. If it sizzles straight away, you can add the rest of the tofu; if it doesn't, heat the oil for a little longer and test again. Gently stir the tofu through the oil every couple of minutes and let it fry until it turns pale brown in colour, about 10 minutes. Using a slotted spoon, remove the tofu and set aside on paper towel to drain. Carefully pour all except about 2 tablespoons of the oil out of the wok. (The deep-frying oil can be strained and reused – leave it to cool before decanting it into a container.)

Return the wok to a high heat and, when the oil is hot, add the chillies, followed by the ginger and then the garlic. Swirl them around in the wok until everything starts to brown. Now add the broccoli, along with the soy sauce and sesame oil, and cook for 4–5 minutes, stirring occasionally. If the wok looks dry, or the broccoli is struggling to cook, add a little boiling water.

When the broccoli has softened but still has a good bite to it, return the tofu to the wok and let it cook for a minute, then add the tomatoes and cook for a final minute. Season with salt to taste.

Beef Shaptak (Beef Stir-Fry) *Serves 4–6*

Shaptak means fried meat, and this dish is all about the meat. Traditionally, yak meat would be used, but beef makes a good substitute – and since we're substituting already, do go for chicken if you prefer. *Shaptak* is widely enjoyed all over Tibet and there are many variations, so feel free to play around with the veg: we've gone for Chinese (napa) cabbage, but peppers (capsicums) make a great pairing too, and are more colourful. If you like celery, that has a good texture and flavour to work with as well.

Rice goes well with *shaptak*, but *Tingmo* (steamed bread, see page 169) is the traditional accompaniment. This steamed bread absorbs all the juices, which should hopefully be very flavoursome, whichever meat or vegetables you have chosen. You can also enjoy *shaptak* with couscous or bulghur wheat, which do a good job of lapping up the sauce too.

- 1 Chinese (napa) cabbage, about 500 g (1 lb 2oz)
- 2 dried red chillies
- 3 tablespoons cooking oil
- 2 fresh green chillies, thinly sliced
- 2 large garlic cloves, thinly sliced
- 4 cm (1½ inch) piece of ginger, washed but not peeled, thinly sliced
- 1 red onion, thinly sliced
- 500 g (1 lb 2 oz) rump or sirloin steak or topside of beef, sliced into long, thin strips
- 1½ teaspoons salt
- ½ teaspoon crushed Sichuan peppercorns (*yerma*)
- 1 tablespoon sesame oil
- 1 tablespoon light soy sauce
- 2 spring onions (scallions), washed and thinly sliced, including green tips

Wash the Chinese cabbage and cut it in half lengthways. Thinly slice each half at an angle and decant into a bowl.

Place the dried chillies on a chopping board and press down on them, just to break them apart a little, then thinly slice them.

Heat the oil in a large wok over a medium-high heat. When it is hot, add both dried and fresh chillies and stir briskly until they darken, then add the garlic and ginger. After a minute, when the garlic and ginger have started to brown, add the onion and keep stir-frying for several minutes, until the onion is golden brown.

Now add the beef, salt and Sichuan pepper. Stir-fry for 6–7 minutes to seal the meat. If you find that the juices are not being released from the meat (which can happen with coarser cuts), cover the wok for a minute or so to help things along. When the juices have run and been reabsorbed, add the Chinese cabbage, followed by the sesame oil and soy sauce. Stir everything well, then turn up the heat to high and stir-fry for about 5 minutes, taking care not to overcook the veg.

Garnish with the spring onions and serve.

Tomato and Egg Stir-Fry

Serves 2 as a main or 4 as part of a shared meal

Tibetans do not usually consume chicken meat, but they do keep chickens. Yeshi says that they make great alarm clocks and are wonderful companions around the home. Although eggs are not eaten in many parts of Tibet, in Yeshi's village they are widely used in the cuisine.

This is a lovely comforting dish, and is delicious with rice and some green vegetables on the side. Yeshi recommends Stir-fried sweetheart cabbage (see page 86) or Pak choi with black cloud fungus (see page 101). *Tingmo* (steamed bread, see page 169), *Balep* (Tibetan flatbread, see page 173) or our Giant fluffy sharing bread (see page 177) are also good accompaniments.

6 eggs
½ teaspoon salt
2 tablespoons cooking oil
4 tomatoes, diced
Black pepper
1 teaspoon light soy sauce
1 teaspoon Chinkiang black vinegar
Sliced spring onion (scallion) greens, to garnish

VEGETARIAN

Break the eggs into a bowl, add the salt and beat well. Place a wok over a high heat and add the oil. When it is starting to smoke, carefully pour in the beaten eggs and cook on one side until just set, moving the cooked parts aside with a spatula to let the runny egg flow beneath, as if you were making an omelette. Turn over using a spatula and cook on the other side until lightly golden. Transfer the cooked eggs to a plate and set aside.

Add the tomatoes to the wok, season with a little black pepper and stir well, then leave to cook for a few minutes, until the tomatoes have softened slightly.

Return the eggs to the wok and use your spatula to break them apart and mix into the tomatoes. When the eggs are heated through, add the soy sauce and vinegar and stir well. Garnish with a little spring onion to serve.

Stir-Fried Baby Aubergines with Chilli *Serves 4*

The summer before he left Tibet, Yeshi spent several months picking oranges and watermelons at his uncle's farm. A wide variety of produce was grown on the farm that Yeshi had never seen before, including aubergine, a vegetable he got to know well during this time. His cousin used to make this particular dish, which became a firm favourite. Baby aubergines are best for this because their skin is softer, so they don't take as long to cook; you may need to increase the cooking time slightly if you can only come by the larger variety.

Serve with basmati rice or a bread, such as *Numtak balep* (fried breakfast bread, see page 42) or *Balep* (Tibetan flatbread, see page 173).

- 500 g (1 lb 2 oz) baby aubergines (eggplants), about 5–6, or fewer if you are using a larger variety
- 2 tablespoons cooking oil
- 1 large garlic clove, thinly sliced
- 2.5 cm (1 inch) piece of ginger, washed but not peeled, cut into fine julienne strips
- 2–3 fresh green chillies, thinly sliced, including seeds
- 1½ teaspoons salt

VEGAN

Wash the aubergines, then cut at a slight angle into thin slices.

Place a wok over a high heat and add the oil. When it is starting to smoke, add the garlic and ginger and stir-fry briefly before adding the chillies and cooking for another minute or so.

Now turn the heat down to medium, add the aubergines to the wok and stir well, then add the salt and let them cook for 8–10 minutes, turning occasionally. Covering the wok with a lid (or foil) will help to speed up the cooking time by a couple of minutes, but check every so often to make sure that nothing is sticking or burning.

When the aubergines start to wilt, turn the heat down to low and cook for a further 3–5 minutes. The aubergines will darken a little and should be very soft and yielding – not chewy – when they're done.

Stir-Fried Garlic Shoots *Serves 4*

Yeshi's family grow garlic in the fields near their house. When it first emerges from the ground, they cut off the long, thin flowering shoots of the plant, to allow the bulbs to grow bigger. These tender young shoots are edible and add a delicate garlic flavour to salads, soups and sauces – you can use them just as you would use chives.

For a vibrant taste of early spring, they can also be stir-fried. If you like, you can throw in some meat as well, adding it to the wok just before the garlic shoots go in. Bacon – smoked or unsmoked – makes a great addition, lending a delicious extra layer of texture and flavour to the dish.

2 tablespoons cooking oil
400 g (14 oz) garlic shoots
½ tablespoon light soy sauce

VEGAN

Wash the garlic shoots and cut them into 2.5 cm (1 inch) lengths.

Heat the oil in a wok over a high heat, and when it is steaming add the garlic shoots and stir-fry for a few minutes. Add the soy sauce and mix everything well. Turn down the heat to medium and cook for a further 2 minutes, or until the garlic shoots are tender, then serve.

Yeshi says 'Garlic shoots make a delicious substitute for beans, asparagus, etc. in all kinds of dishes. You will soon be hooked. In late spring and early summer, you sometimes see them at farmers' markets, or they are easy to come by in your local Chinese supermarket, where they may also be known as garlic scapes – just ask.'

Pak Choi with Black Cloud Fungus *Serves 2–4*

Black cloud fungus is a prized ingredient in Yeshi's corner of Tibet. This edible mushroom grows on trees and is picked during the first rainy season around June time. It's dried on bamboo trays for about a week in the sunshine and can then be kept for years – if not forever.

Tibetans love black cloud fungus for its smooth, crunchy and gelatinous texture; it's also said to be good for the digestion. It is great in stews and salads, as well as in stir-fries like this one, with pak choi. You can find it in most Asian supermarkets – it comes dried, in packets, and needs to be soaked before use.

20 g (¾ oz) dried black cloud fungus
3 bunches of pak choi, about 300 g (10½ oz) in total
2 tablespoons cooking oil
1–2 dried red chillies
3 large garlic cloves, thinly sliced
1 teaspoon salt
1 tablespoon light soy sauce
½ teaspoon Sichuan pepper oil or ¼ teaspoon crushed Sichuan peppercorns (*yerma*)
Coriander (cilantro) leaves, to garnish

VEGAN

Soak the black cloud fungus in a bowl of warm water for at least half an hour, or until it has softened. Then rub each piece between your fingers in the water and tear it into smaller pieces, transferring them to a colander as you go. Rinse well under cold running water.

Slice the pak choi in half, then cut into thin strips crossways on the diagonal, starting at the base. Place in a colander and wash well.

Heat the oil in a wok over a high heat. When it's hot, add the chillies and let them sizzle until they are brown – keep a close eye on them as they can easily burn. Add the garlic and stir-fry for about a minute.

Add the black cloud fungus to the wok and stir briefly, then add the salt and stir-fry for 3–4 minutes. Finally, add the pak choi, soy sauce and Sichuan pepper oil or pepper, turn the heat down to medium-high and stir well for about 5 minutes.

Garnish with coriander and serve.

Stir-Fried Beef with Courgettes *Serves 4*

The courgette is not a vegetable that Yeshi was familiar with growing up, and in Tibet he would probably cook this dish with potato or mooli (daikon), but courgettes work really well visually and texturally, releasing lots of tasty juices as they cook. Play around and find your own favourite vegetables to stir-fry in this way. Serve with basmati rice, *Tingmo* (steamed bread, see page 169) or Giant fluffy sharing bread (see page 177) to soak up the sauce.

500 g (1 lb 2 oz) rump steak
2 courgettes (zucchini) – about 500 g (1 lb 2 oz) in total
2 tablespoons cooking oil
4 cm (1½ inch) piece of ginger, washed but not peeled, cut into fine julienne strips
2 large garlic cloves, thinly sliced
2 large fresh green chillies, thinly sliced, seeds removed
1 teaspoon white vinegar
Sliced spring onions (scallions), to garnish

For the marinade

2 large garlic cloves, finely chopped
1 teaspoon dark soy sauce
½ teaspoon salt
Dash of black pepper

Combine the marinade ingredients in a bowl. Cut the steak into strips about 4 cm (1½ inches) in length, then add to the bowl and mix well. Cover and leave to marinate at room temperature for 15–20 minutes.

Slice the courgettes crossways on the diagonal, then turn the slices slightly on their side and cut again into thin strips. Set aside.

Heat the oil in a wok over a high heat. When it's hot, add the ginger, garlic and chillies. When they have browned a little, add the marinated steak and stir briskly for 3–4 minutes.

Add the courgettes to the wok, followed by the vinegar, and keep stirring for 2–3 minutes. If the wok looks dry, add a splash of boiling water to make sure the dish has some juices.

Garnish with spring onions and serve.

Yeshi says 'The soy sauce is not essential here – it just lends a nice dark colour to the marinade. So if you need to avoid gluten, you can use a gluten-free soy sauce or leave it out altogether (if you do leave it out, you might like to add a little more ginger and a pinch more salt for flavour).'

Stir-Fried Shredded Potatoes *Serves 4–6*

When Yeshi first arrived in the UK he was surprised to learn that potatoes were seen as a staple food, just like noodles, rice or bread. Although potatoes are frequently used in Tibetan cooking, they aren't really treated as a stand-alone dish or a substantial side. This dish is usually served with rice and other sharing plates such as stir-fried pak choi or cabbage. At home, we call it 'Tibetan chips' – but as we still have rice alongside, the kids are not entirely fooled.

3–5 white or red potatoes, about 800 g (1 lb 12 oz) in total
3 tablespoons cooking oil
3 dried red chillies
2 large garlic cloves, cut into fine julienne strips
2.5 cm (1 inch) piece of ginger, washed but not peeled, cut into fine julienne strips
1 teaspoon Chinkiang black vinegar
1 tablespoon light soy sauce
1 teaspoon salt
1 tablespoon sesame oil
Sliced spring onions (scallions), to garnish

VEGAN

Wash the potatoes and leave the skin on or peel them as you choose. Using a sharp knife, slice each potato into strips just a bit thicker than a matchstick. Alternatively, coarsely shred the potatoes using the largest holes of a grater, or a food processor. Decant into a large bowl, fill with cold water and rinse the potatoes through the water.

Measure out about 1.5 litres (6 cups) of boiling water into a large saucepan and place over a high heat. When the water returns to the boil, use your hands to transfer the potatoes from the bowl to the saucepan, then blanch for about 3 minutes or until they have lost their rawness but still have some bite to them.

Meanwhile, heat the oil in a wok over a high heat. When it's hot, add the chillies and toss until they turn a shade darker. Add the garlic and ginger and stir-fry until they are golden brown. (If the potatoes are still going, remove the wok from the heat so nothing burns.)

When the potatoes are ready, drain in a colander and add to the wok, making sure it's hot. Stir briskly over a high heat, then add the vinegar and soy sauce and stir these through. Now add the salt and sesame oil and cook for 3–4 minutes, stirring every so often, then taste a little of the potatoes – if they are still a little undercooked, give them another minute.

Transfer to a serving plate and garnish with sliced spring onions.

Stir-Fried Broccoli *Serves 4*

We include this one because it's something of a revelation. When Yeshi first came to the UK, he was very troubled by the way most of us cook vegetables, boiling them into submission – especially as he had not come across boiling as a method of cooking veg before.

Maybe this is one reason why broccoli doesn't have a great name for itself here. Broccoli that has been boiled (and often over-boiled) loses its natural juices and crunch, but stir-frying it with garlic and soy sauce, and maybe some chilli if you want, transforms it into a gastronomic experience. This method can be used for all kinds of green vegetables, and we urge you to try it with green beans, pak choi and so on, bearing in mind that the cooking time may need to be adjusted to suit the tenderness or robustness of each vegetable.

We serve this at Taste Tibet, and we take considerable pleasure in winning people over to a much-maligned vegetable that brings colour and joy alongside momos and more.

400 g (14 oz) broccoli
2–3 dried red chillies
2 tablespoons cooking oil
3 garlic cloves, thinly sliced
1 tablespoon light soy sauce

VEGAN

Cut the broccoli into small florets, some with long tails. Make sure you use the stems as well (just remove the hard outer skin and slice thinly) – they are deliciously sweet. Wash all the broccoli thoroughly.

On a chopping board, lightly crush the chillies, just to break them apart slightly. Heat the oil in a wok over a medium heat until it is starting to smoke, then add the chillies and toss for 20–30 seconds before you add the garlic. Let the chilli and garlic brown a little in the oil, tilting the wok to one side a little so they get the best of the oil and don't burn.

Now add the broccoli and stir briskly, then add the soy sauce. If the wok looks dry, add 3–4 tablespoons of water to get some more juices going. Stir well for a few minutes before turning the heat down a little and covering the wok with a lid (or foil) for 2 minutes so the broccoli steams as it fries. The total cooking time for the broccoli should be about 5–6 minutes, but if it still has too much bite for you, then leave it a minute or two longer.

There's no need to remove the chillies on serving – just be careful you don't eat them!

Noodles, Soups and Stews

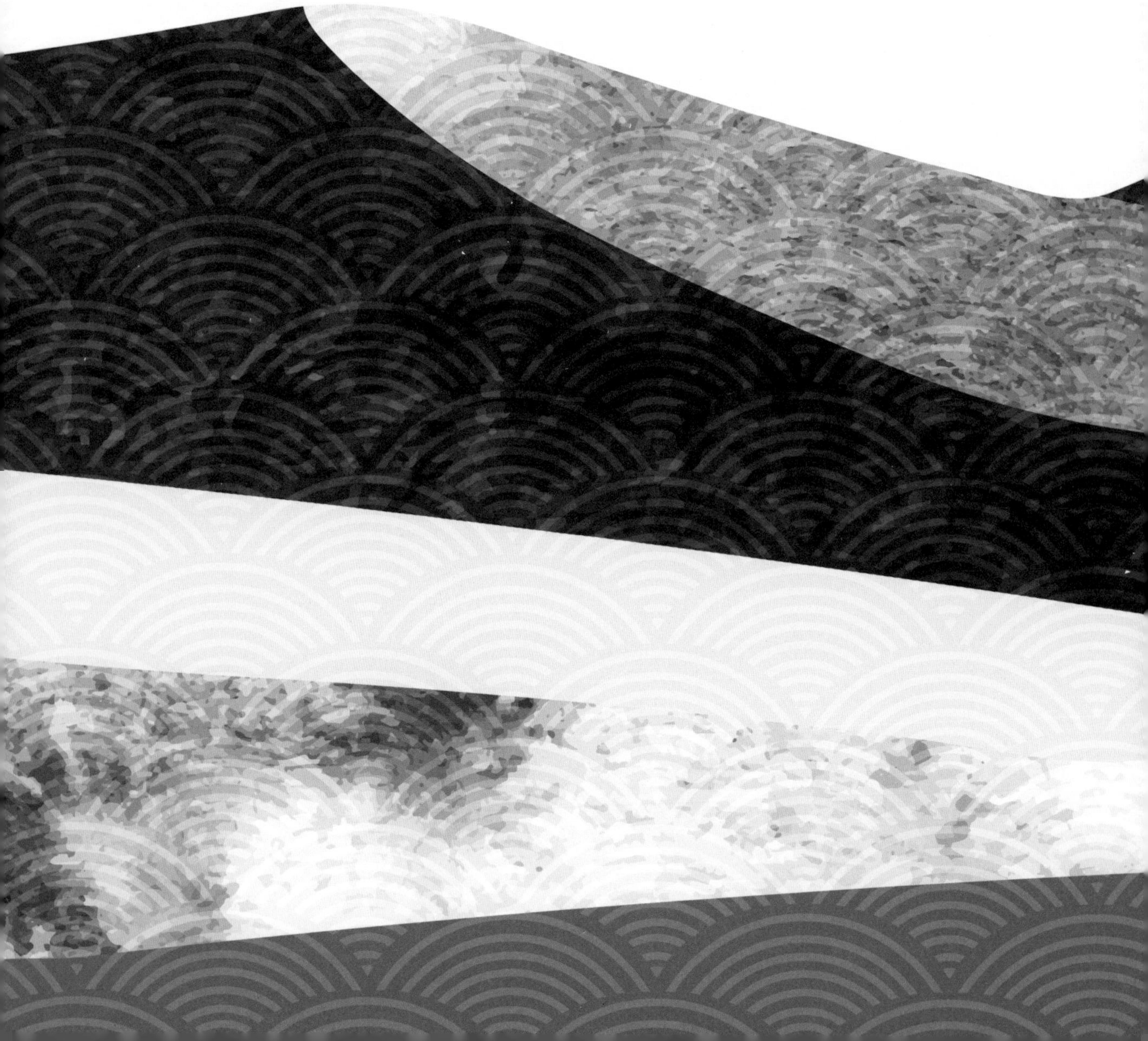

This chapter is really the heart of our book. Noodles, soups and stews are everyday meals in Tibet. For centuries Tibetans have relied on these dishes to fuel them in cold weather – noodles in particular. The most popular noodle dish is *thenthuk*, a hand-pulled noodle soup that is usually served at dinnertime. Soups and stews are also generally eaten during the evening as they are perceived to be light but warming. Tibetans really excel at this kind of comfort food.

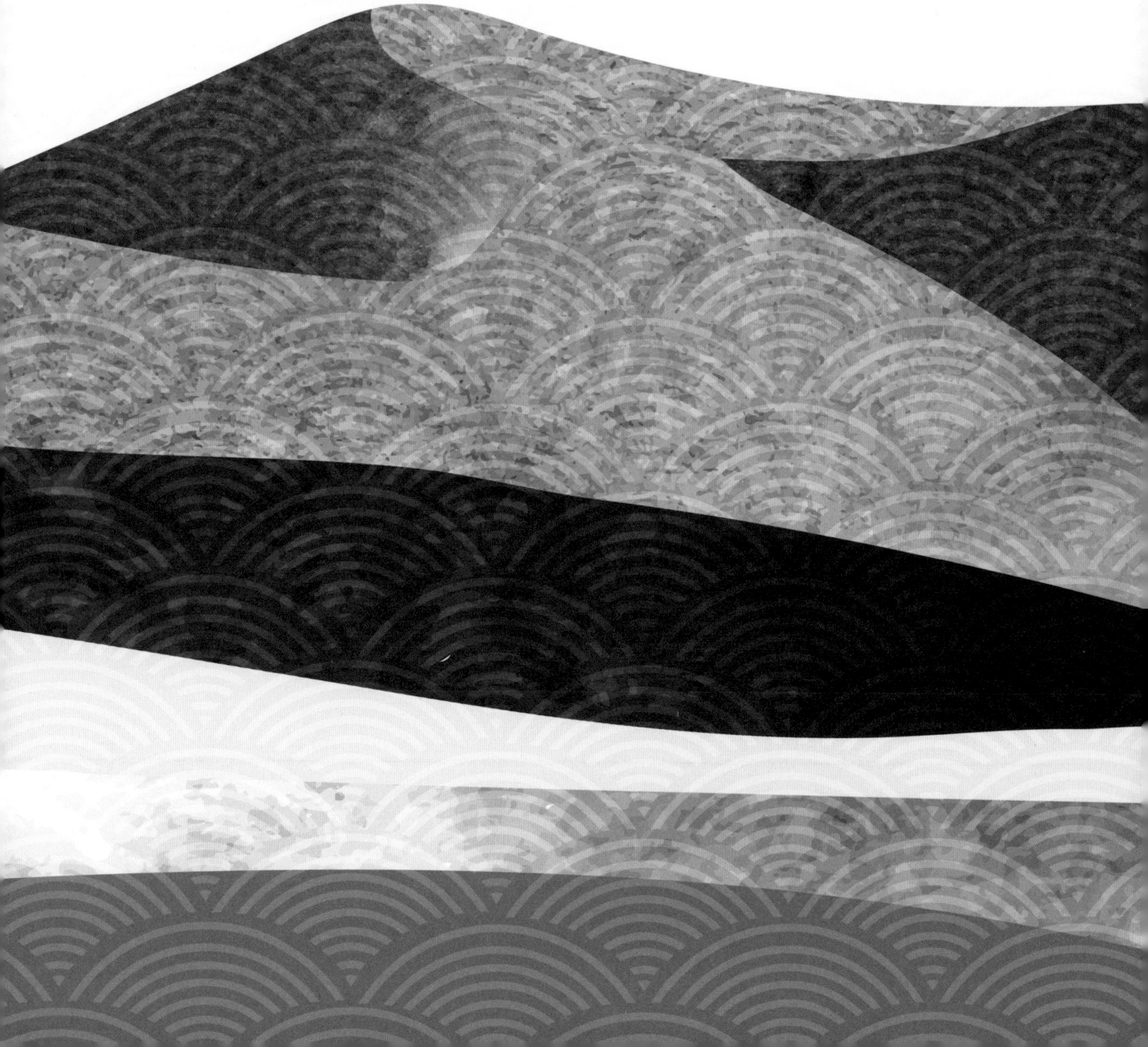

We highly recommend having a go at making your own noodles, even if this is your first time. Don't let the length of some of the recipes put you off! Each noodle dish is made slightly differently in Tibet, and we wanted to share the various tricks and techniques with you – but if you find a way that works well for you, feel free to use this method every time. Cut yourself some slack (nothing has to be perfect) and allow plenty of time. Rolling out noodle dough does take a bit of practice, but it's totally achievable and hand-made always gives the best results.

When we moved into our house in Oxford, one of the first things Yeshi did was to saw off a slab of the wooden kitchen benchtop to accommodate the fridge of his dreams. In the process, he inadvertently landed himself the world's biggest wooden chopping board. This is handy. In an ideal world, we'd all have a board this big – but don't worry, you can still make noodles without chopping up your kitchen bench. Just divide the dough into batches, and roll it out directly on your work surface if necessary.

It's important to use strong white bread flour with a high gluten content for making noodle dough – the gluten adds elasticity to the dough and helps to give the noodles their lovely chewy texture. On a side note, we haven't used a pasta machine to roll out the dough for any of these recipes as Yeshi has never really had one, and there's also a pleasing purity that comes with doing everything by hand. But by all means use your pasta machine, if you like.

For broths, feel free to play around with ingredients, as the Tibetans do. Generally speaking, root vegetables are delicious in stews and soups, and it's always nice to be able to chuck in some fresh greens towards the end of the cooking time. Pak choi, water spinach, mustard greens and Chinese broccoli, plus good old spinach, all work well in this way, so have a go with whatever takes your fancy and keep condiments on hand (Chinkiang black vinegar, light soy sauce, chilli, etc.) to be added at the table.

Finally, remember that leftovers can be the starting point for simple soups – especially water that has been used to boil noodles, or to steam bread or momos. Tibetan people love to make use of this water for its nutritional value as much as its flavour. If you have some unused momo filling to hand or a small amount of yesterday's stir-fry, these ingredients can often be quickly thrown together to make flavoursome soups that both aid digestion and warm the cockles. In Tibet, such soups are often served as a side to accompany drier dishes, such as momos, fried rice or fried noodles.

Vegetable Thukpa (Vegetable Soup Noodles) *Serves 4–6*

Yeshi describes this as 'simple fast food', so we hope you will also find it easy to recreate. It can form the basis of a more deeply flavoured soup depending on how far you want to take it, and how much extra soy and vinegar you want to add. Chilli too, of course. There's lots of scope for other additions as well. Slivers of carrot are good, and we often cook a little omelette in a small frying pan, cutting it into strips before adding a little to the top of each bowl on serving.

Salt
2 tablespoons cooking oil
2 large garlic cloves, thinly sliced
400 g (14 oz) pak choi, washed and roughly chopped
1 tablespoon sesame oil
1 tablespoon light soy sauce, plus extra to serve
1 tablespoon Chinkiang black vinegar, plus extra to serve
½ teaspoon crushed Sichuan peppercorns (*yerma*)
3 spring onions (scallions), washed and thinly sliced
Taste Tibet *sepen* (see page 190) and *Son labu* (Tibetan pickled mooli, see page 73), to serve – optional

For the noodles

500 g (3½ cups) strong white bread flour, plus extra for dusting
3 large free-range eggs

VEGETARIAN

For the noodles, put the flour into a mixing bowl and crack in the eggs. Mix the eggs through the flour with your dominant hand, while slowly pouring in about 100 ml (3½ fl oz) of warm water with the other – depending on the flour you are using, you may need to add slightly more water. Work the dough into a ball in the bowl, then cover and set aside for about 15 minutes.

Take out the dough and knead it for a minute or so until smooth, then divide it into four roughly equal pieces. Return three of the pieces to the mixing bowl and cover again.

Using a rolling pin, roll out the first piece of dough on a flour-dusted work surface. Press down hard, turning it around and around and over and over until you have a large, roughly circular sheet of dough about 2–3 mm (⅛ inch) thick. Finally, sprinkle a little more flour onto the dough and, starting from one side, roll the sheet of dough up and over the rolling pin, wrapping it around several times until you reach the other side.

Now slide out the rolling pin to leave behind a hollow cylinder of dough. Using a sharp knife, cut the cylinder into slices on the diagonal. The width of the slices will determine the thickness of your noodles – it's good to aim for a chopstick's width.

When you are done, sprinkle a little more flour over the noodles. Using both hands, lift them and dance them about in the flour until all of them are coated and you can prise them apart. Place in a mixing bowl and repeat with the remaining balls of dough.

continued >

To cook the noodles, bring 2.5 litres (10 cups) of water to the boil in a large saucepan. When the water is boiling, add a teaspoon of salt and half the noodles. Stir the noodles very gently, ideally using chopsticks, then add the rest of the noodles and give them a very gentle stir too – you don't want to break them in the process. Leave them to boil for about 5 minutes, then taste one to see if they are cooked. When the noodles are done, turn off the heat, but do not drain them.

Meanwhile, heat a wok over a high heat. Add the oil, and when it's hot, turn the heat down to low-medium and add the garlic. It should take less than a minute for this to turn golden brown, at which point add the pak choi and stir-fry briskly for about a minute. Now add the sesame oil, soy sauce, vinegar and a teaspoon of salt and keep stirring for a further 1–2 minutes, or until the vegetables have softened and reduced, releasing their juices in the pan.

Carefully tip the contents of the wok into the pan of noodles, rinsing out the last of the veg in the wok using some of the water from the noodles. Gently stir everything together, then serve in large bowls and garnish with the spring onions. Add some *sepen* if you want a chilli kick, and a dash of extra soy sauce or vinegar to taste.

Serve with a small bowl of pickled mooli on the side, if you have some in the fridge.

Beef and Bacon Noodle Soup *Serves 4–6*

We eat a lot of this super-warming and flavoursome soup at home. In Tibet, it would be made with yak meat and dried pork; Yeshi finds that beef and bacon are the closest he can get outside the region. Smoked ham also makes a good substitute for the dried pork. Although the pork isn't intentionally smoked in Tibet, it's hung to dry near the fire, where it naturally absorbs the flavour, becoming blackened from the smoke and needing to be washed before use.

- 2 tablespoons cooking oil
- 2 large garlic cloves, thinly sliced
- 2.5 cm (1 inch) piece of ginger, washed but not peeled, cut into fine julienne strips
- 1 small red onion, thinly sliced
- 200 g (7 oz) smoked bacon, about 10 rashers – back or streaky, chopped small
- 200 g (7 oz) rump steak (dry-aged is best) or topside of beef, diced
- 1 teaspoon salt
- ¼ teaspoon crushed Sichuan peppercorns (*yerma*)
- 6 spring onions (scallions), washed and thinly sliced, including green tips
- Taste Tibet *sepen* (see page 190), Chinkiang black vinegar and soy sauce, to serve

For the noodles

- 500 g (3⅓ cups) strong white bread flour, plus extra for dusting
- 2 eggs
- 2 teaspoons olive oil

For the noodles, put the flour into a mixing bowl and break in the eggs. Mix the eggs through the flour with your dominant hand, while slowly pouring in 200 ml (7 fl oz) of warm water with your other hand. Don't pour in all the water at once in case it's too much for your dough – little by little is best. Work the dough into a ball in the bowl, then cover and set aside for 15–20 minutes.

Meanwhile, put the cooking oil into a wok and place over a high heat. When it is hot, add the garlic and ginger and stir-fry briefly, then add the onion and stir-fry until golden brown. Now add the bacon to the wok and, after a couple of minutes, stir in the beef, salt and Sichuan pepper and cook for about 5 minutes. Cover and leave to cook for 2 minutes, then check to make sure the meat is not catching – the meat juices will have been reabsorbed and you don't want anything to burn. Add about 500 ml (2 cups) of boiling water and turn the heat down to low. Cover the wok and let everything simmer for about 15 minutes or until the beef is cooked to your liking. (If the noodles are not ready by the time the soup is done, just take it off the heat and leave to stand.)

Take the dough out of the bowl, then measure out the olive oil into the empty bowl. Knead the dough well on a flour-dusted work surface until smooth. Cut the dough into three equal pieces. If the dough feels sticky at all, dip your fingers into the oil in the bowl and then roll each piece of dough into a ball.

Using a rolling pin, roll out a ball of dough, turning it over and around as you go, until it is about ½ cm (¼ inch) thick. If it starts to stick, sprinkle a little flour onto the work surface. Repeat with the remaining two balls of dough.

continued >

Bring a large saucepan of water to the boil, then turn down to a simmer.

Using a sharp knife, slice the sheets of dough from top to bottom to create long noodles about 1 cm (¾ inch) wide. Now grease your fingers with a little oil from the bowl and stretch each noodle by pulling it gently between your hands until it is very long and thin. Then place the noodle in the pan of simmering water. Keep going with the rest of the noodles.

When all the noodles are in the pan, turn the heat up high and stir well, then let them boil for 3 minutes or so to make sure they're cooked through.

Meanwhile, put the wok back over a medium heat, add the spring onion and cook for about a minute, then turn off the heat.

Take the noodles off the heat, but don't drain them. Rather, using a pair of tongs, lift them out into the bowls, then ladle the soup from the wok over the noodles. Add some *sepen* directly to each bowl or have it on the side, along with black vinegar and soy sauce to taste.

Yeshi says 'Don't worry about some of the noodles cooking for longer than others. You'll be surprised to find that, unlike dried pasta, nothing overcooks, so relax and take your time over them.'

Beef Thenthuk
(Beef Hand-Pulled Noodles) *Serves 4*

This is the first dish Yeshi ever made me, and it tastes as good now as it did in his freezing concrete room up in the foothills of the Himalayas. It doesn't take a genius to work out why this traditional noodle soup is loved and devoured so much across the entire region. It soothes hands and bellies, and its soft textures explode with the deep flavours of meat and garlic. There's nothing more comforting or wholesome on a cold winter's night.

In Tibetan, *then* means 'pull' and *thuk* means 'noodles': these noodles are torn or 'pulled' from long strips of wheat-flour dough and dropped straight into the broth during the final stages of cooking. You can substitute the vegetables in this dish for others that take your fancy. As a general rule, root vegetables will need to cook for longer, while greens should be thrown in towards the end. Swap the mooli for carrot if that's easier to come by, or pak choi for the spinach.

2 tablespoons cooking oil
2 large garlic cloves, thinly sliced
1 red onion, thinly sliced
2 teaspoons salt
2 tomatoes, diced
300 g (10½ oz) topside of beef, diced
½ mooli (daikon), about 250 g (9 oz), washed but not peeled, thinly sliced
Black pepper
100 g (3½ oz) spinach, washed and roughly chopped
2 teaspoons white vinegar – optional
1 teaspoon Chinkiang black vinegar – optional
2 teaspoons light soy sauce – optional
1 teaspoon sesame oil – optional
Chopped chives, spring onion (scallion) or coriander (cilantro), to garnish

For the noodles

300 g (2 cups) strong white bread flour, plus extra for dusting
1 egg

For the noodles, put the flour into a mixing bowl and crack in the egg. Mix the egg through the flour with your dominant hand, while slowly pouring in about 100 ml (3½ fl oz) of warm water with the other. Make sure you don't drown the flour – you are aiming for quite a firm dough. Once you have a nice tight ball of dough in the bowl, cover and set aside for 15–20 minutes.

Meanwhile, heat the oil in a large saucepan or wok over a high heat. When it's hot, add the garlic, onion and salt. Stir-fry for 2 minutes, then add the tomatoes and cook for a few more minutes before adding the meat. Stir well and cook for 3–4 minutes, then add the mooli and a grind of pepper and stir-fry over a high heat for about 3–4 minutes. Pour in about 1.5 litres (6 cups) of boiling water, then cover and leave the broth to simmer for 10 minutes.

Take the noodle dough out of the bowl and divide it in half. Put one piece back under cover in the bowl, then roll the other piece into a ball, pinching a slight depression into the middle with your fingers.

Sprinkle some flour onto your work surface. Using a rolling pin, roll out the ball of dough, then turn over and roll it out again. Keep turning and rolling out the dough until it is about 2–3 mm (⅛ inch) thick. Now you need to slice the dough into wide strips: using your rolling pin as a measure, cut all the way across with a sharp knife, moving the rolling pin along by one width – about 3 cm (1¼ inches) – each time.

Repeat the rolling and cutting with the other half of the dough.

continued >

> Beef Thenthuk *continued*

Just before you pull the dough into the broth, add the spinach. Now drape one strip of dough over the wrist of your non-dominant hand, pinching the tip between your thumb and forefinger. Use your other hand to pull 2.5–5 cm (1–2 inches) lengths of dough, pinching them off and chucking them into the broth. We deliberately say to chuck the noodles in, as you need to keep your hands at a slight distance from the hot broth – if you get too close, the steam will make the dough go sticky. Give everything a stir and then repeat with the remaining strips of dough. This will take a while and may be something of a thumb work out! When all the noodles are in the broth, leave them to cook for another minute.

Test one of the noodles to check they are cooked through, then stir in the white vinegar, if using. The *thenthuk* is delicious as it is, but feel free to add Chinkiang vinegar, soy sauce and sesame oil to taste, if you like. Stir well and serve in large bowls, garnished with chives, spring onion or coriander.

Thenthuk Fry (Tibetan Pasta) with Side Soup *Serves 4*

When Yeshi first settled in India he lived alongside Tibetans from across the region. They spoke very different dialects and cooked all kinds of different foods. He loved watching his friends at work in the kitchen and picking up new dishes along the way. *Thenthuk* fry is very popular in north-eastern Tibet, and this is Yeshi's take on it. The cherry tomatoes are definitely a Western touch, and you can add more vegetables (baby corn works well) or meat if you'd like to fill it out.

Alongside what is otherwise a fairly dry dish, the side soup is designed to whet the palate. If you're coming to this recipe from elsewhere, this simple broth can also be made using just boiled water instead of the pasta-cooking water. If so, you should add a couple of tablespoons of rolled (porridge) oats to the pan to achieve a similar cloudy effect.

½ red onion
2 tablespoons cooking oil
2 large garlic cloves, thinly sliced
½ teaspoon salt
200 g (7 oz) chestnut mushrooms, wiped clean and thinly sliced
2 bunches of pak choi, about 200 g (7 oz) in total
1 teaspoon Chinkiang black vinegar
1 teaspoon light soy sauce
1 teaspoon sesame oil
½ teaspoon crushed black peppercorns
½ teaspoon chilli powder – optional
1 spring onion (scallion), washed and thinly sliced, including green tips
10–12 cherry tomatoes, halved – optional
Parmesan cheese, to serve

For the pasta

2 large eggs
½ teaspoon salt
300 g (2 cups) strong white bread flour, plus extra for dusting

For the pasta, break the eggs into a mixing bowl, then add the salt and 100 ml (3½ fl oz) of warm water. Beat well using a fork. Add the flour and use your hand to mix everything and bring it together, then knead well in the bowl for a couple of minutes until you have a smooth dough. Roll it into a ball, cover and leave to rest for 15–20 minutes.

Turn the pasta dough out onto a work surface and sprinkle with a little flour if it needs it. Flatten the dough into a thick, roughly circular shape with your hands. Using a sharp knife, cut the dough into long strips about 1 cm (½ inch) wide. Sprinkle a little flour over them and jiggle them about a bit so each strip gets a light dusting. One by one, hang them over the lip of the mixing bowl.

Take one of the strips and put it on the chopping board, dusting it with a little more flour if necessary. Using a rolling pin, roll the strip out quickly from bottom to top, holding (but not pulling) the bottom end in your other hand. Turn the strip around and do the same again. It should now be quite long and about 2.5 cm (1 inch) wide. Sprinkle with a little flour, then quickly slice the strip of dough at about 1 cm (½ inch) intervals. You will end up with small, thin, flat pieces of pasta. Place these in the mixing bowl, then take another of the strips hanging around the side and repeat the process. Check the pieces of pasta in the bowl every so often and if they are starting to stick together, sprinkle a little flour into the bowl and jiggle the pieces around to loosen them.

continued >

For the side soup
½ teaspoon salt
70 g (1½ cups) baby spinach leaves
1 egg

VEGETARIAN

Once all the pasta is made, bring a large saucepan of water to the boil over a high heat. When the water is really bubbling, empty the pasta into the pan and stir gently using a pasta strainer or slotted spoon. Try to separate any pieces of pasta that may have stuck together. Bring back to the boil – this should take about 3 minutes – then place a colander inside your mixing bowl and drain the pasta into the colander.

Take the bowl of pasta-cooking water and pour half of it back into the saucepan – this will be used to make the side soup later.

Rinse the pasta gently under the cold tap, then sit the colander in a bowl of cold water – this stops the pasta from going soggy and helps it to retain a nice bite.

Cut the pak choi in half, then thinly slice each half on the diagonal. Rinse thoroughly and set aside in a bowl of cold water. Cut the onion in half. Take each half and thinly slice, then cut through the middle of each half. Put the oil into a wok and place over a medium-high heat. When it's hot, add the garlic and stir until it starts to brown, then add the onion and stir well. Once the onion has softened, add the salt and mushrooms and stir-fry until the mushrooms have wilted. Now lift the pak choi out of the water and into the wok. Stir everything together well, then add the vinegar and soy sauce. At this point it will look a bit watery, so let it bubble and reduce for 3–4 minutes.

Drain the pasta thoroughly and add it to the wok, along with the sesame oil, black pepper, chilli powder (if using) and spring onion. Mix thoroughly for a good 3–4 minutes, then check to make sure the pasta is hot before serving.

Meanwhile, for the side soup, add the salt to the pasta-cooking water in the saucepan. Bring to the boil, then add the spinach and break in the egg. Stir well and bring to the boil, then ladle into small bowls.

Serve the pasta in large bowls, adding some halved cherry tomatoes, if you like, and grating over a little parmesan cheese. Serve the soup on the side.

Vegetable Thenthuk (Vegetable Hand-Pulled Noodles) *Serves 6*

Veggie *thenthuk* is made just as often as meat *thenthuk* in Tibet, and is widely enjoyed by those who exclude meat from their diet. The use of eggs to make the noodle dough means this dish is not vegan, but you could of course substitute dairy-free noodles and leave out the feta if you wanted to make a vegan version. The soup will still give you all the happiness and warmth offered by this dish, and it will be just as moreish.

½ mooli (daikon), about 400 g (14 oz)
2 tablespoons cooking oil
3 large garlic cloves, thinly sliced
1 red onion, thinly sliced
2 tomatoes, finely chopped
1 tablespoon salt
2 small potatoes, about 350 g (12 oz), washed but not peeled, diced
150 g (5½ oz) baby spinach (leek or pak choi also work well), washed and roughly chopped
200 g (7 oz) feta cheese, crumbled – optional
1½ tablespoons Chinkiang black vinegar
½ tablespoon sesame oil
1 tablespoon light soy sauce
3 spring onions (scallions), washed and thinly sliced, including green tips
Finely chopped coriander (cilantro), to garnish

For the noodles

500 g (3⅓ cups) strong white bread flour
2 eggs
2 teaspoons olive oil

VEGETARIAN

For the noodles, put the flour into a mixing bowl and crack in the eggs. Mix the eggs through the flour with your dominant hand, while slowly pouring in about 160 ml (5¼ fl oz) of warm water with the other. Make sure you don't drown the flour – you are aiming for quite a firm dough. Once you have a nice tight ball of dough in the bowl, cover and set aside for 15–20 minutes.

Meanwhile, cut the mooli in half lengthways, then cut each half lengthways again. Now thinly slice it crossways to give you quarter-circles. Put the oil into a large saucepan over a medium heat. When it is hot, add the garlic and onion and cook for a minute before adding the tomatoes. Next add the mooli to the pan, along with the salt. Stir well, then leave to cook for about 5 minutes, stirring occasionally. Add the potatoes, pour in 600 ml (21 fl oz) of boiling water and mix everything well. Cover and leave to cook for 8–10 minutes, stirring occasionally. When the potatoes are done (taste to check), add the spinach and stir for a minute, just until the spinach has wilted, then take off the heat.

To cook the noodles, pour about 2.5 litres (10 cups) of boiling water into a large wok or saucepan over a low heat.

Take the noodle dough out of the bowl and divide it into about ten pieces. Roll each piece between your hands to make a sausage shape, pulling slightly to lengthen it, then hang each one over the edge of the bowl. Put the olive oil into the bowl – you will need to dab your fingers into this to stop the dough from sticking to your hands. Starting at the centre of one of the strips of dough, hold the dough between the thumb and forefinger of both hands and press it flat between them, working first in a downward direction and then up again. Finally, stretch it out between your hands so it's very long and very flat – it should be about 2.5–5 cm (1–2 inches) wide.

When the water returns to a simmer, drape the strip of dough over the wrist of your non-dominant hand, pinching the tip between your thumb and forefinger. Use your other hand to pull 2.5–5 cm (1–2 inches) lengths of dough, pinching them off and chucking them into the broth. We deliberately say to chuck the noodles in, as you need to keep your hands at a slight distance from the hot water – if you get too close, the steam will make the dough go sticky. Give everything a stir and then repeat with each piece of dough. This will take a while and will be a bit of a test for your thumbs!

When all the noodles are in, turn the heat up to high for a couple of minutes, then test one of the noodles to check it is cooked through.

Feta cheese makes the broth lovely and creamy. If you want to use it, add it now, turn the heat down a little and leave for about a minute. Tip in the contents of the vegetable pan and stir well, making sure that everything is hot. Finally, add the vinegar, sesame oil, soy sauce and spring onions, then ladle into bowls and garnish with coriander.

Lamb Soup Noodles *Serves 4–6*

'Food tastes better when mother serves it,' as the Tibetan saying goes. Yeshi's mother used to cook some form of these noodles almost daily, and usually for at least twelve people at a time. This is a very traditional local recipe that involves chilling the noodles in iced water. If you follow Yeshi's instructions here, you can be sure that you will be serving them just as his mum does back home ... But will you be carrying your ice from the river in the valley? Yeshi remembers his sister-in-law lugging massive hunks of ice up the hill in the depths of winter.

2 tablespoons cooking oil
2 large garlic cloves, thinly sliced
1 red onion, finely chopped
500 g (1 lb 2 oz) lamb rump, diced
1 teaspoon salt
½ teaspoon crushed Sichuan peppercorns (*yerma*)
2–3 spring onion (scallions), washed and thinly sliced, including green tips
Chopped coriander (cilantro), to garnish

For the noodles

450 g (3 cups) strong white bread flour, plus extra for dusting
3 large eggs
Ice cubes – optional

For the noodles, put the flour into a mixing bowl and crack in the eggs. Mix the eggs through the flour with your dominant hand, while slowly pouring in 90 ml (3 fl oz) of warm water with the other. Keep kneading until you have a firm ball of dough in the bowl, then cover and set aside for 15–20 minutes.

Meanwhile, put the oil into a wok (or a large saucepan) over a medium-high heat. When it is hot, add the garlic and stir-fry until golden brown, then add the onion. Mix well and cook, stirring, until the onion is browned too.

Add the lamb, salt and Sichuan pepper and give everything a stir. The aim is to seal the lamb first, and then for it to fry in its own juices. Cover with a lid (or foil), but check on it frequently, giving everything a good stir, to make sure nothing sticks or burns. After 7–8 minutes, the juices should have been absorbed. At this point, turn the heat right down and let it cook, still covered, for another 5 minutes, stirring occasionally. The meat should be fully cooked by now. Add 850 ml (29 fl oz) of boiling water, replace the lid, and leave the soup to simmer over a low heat until the noodles are ready.

Take out the dough and knead it for a minute or so until smooth, then divide it into four roughly equal pieces. Return three of the pieces to the mixing bowl and cover again.

Using a rolling pin, roll out the first piece of dough on a flour-dusted work surface. Press down hard, turning it around and around and over and over until you have a large, roughly circular sheet of dough about 2–3 mm (⅛ inch) thick. Finally, sprinkle a little more flour onto the dough and, starting from one side, roll the sheet of dough up and over the rolling pin, wrapping it around several times until you reach the other side. Now slide out the rolling pin to leave behind a hollow cylinder of dough. Using a sharp knife, cut the cylinder into slices on the diagonal. The width of the slices will determine the thickness of your noodles – it's good to aim for a chopstick's width.

When you are done, sprinkle a little more flour over the noodles. Using both hands, lift them and dance them about in the flour until all of them are coated and you can prise them apart. Place in a mixing bowl and repeat with the remaining balls of dough.

Bring a large saucepan of water to the boil. You'll need to cook the noodles in a couple of batches. Lift half of them into the boiling water and stir them very gently. Let the noodles cook for about 3 minutes, or until they have risen to the top and the water is bubbling and foaming – this is a sign that they are ready, but you can taste to make sure.

Drain in a colander set over a bowl, so you can keep the cooking water for your second batch. Rinse the noodles under the cold tap, then decant them into another bowl of cold water to chill. Add some ice cubes to the bowl, if you can – the iced water stops the noodles from getting soggy and helps them to retain a really nice bite.

Repeat with the second batch of noodles, adding those to the chilled water as well.

When all the noodles are cooked, increase the heat under the soup to high and add the spring onions. For each serving, pinch out some noodles from the chilled water and place them in an individual bowl. Spoon out enough broth from the wok to cover the noodles before draining the broth back into the wok, then repeat – this process blasts the cold noodles with the heat of the broth and warms them through, as they will taste stodgy if they are cold. The third time you go into the wok, spoon out some meat as well as enough broth to cover the noodles. They are now ready to eat! Garnish with coriander and serve.

Yeshi says 'If you find that you are running low on broth by the time you have served out a few bowls, add some boiling water to the wok and a little more salt to taste. This will help to make the broth go a bit further. Traditionally we don't use soy sauce or vinegar in this dish, but if you like the idea, you can add light soy sauce and Chinkiang black vinegar at the table. If you fancy a blast of heat, throw in some Taste Tibet *sepen* too (see page 190).'

Stir-Fried Veggie Noodles *Serves 4*

Elderly Tibetans rely on soup noodles for their warming qualities, but fried noodles are more popular among young Tibetans and in restaurants.

If you like chow mein, you will surely love these stir-fried noodles. If you want to make them meaty, just add some pieces of lamb, beef, chicken or pork to the pot once the onions have browned and before the vegetables go in. You can also add strips of omelette if you fancy: cook the omelette separately in a small frying pan, then slice it up and add it to the wok or individual bowls just before serving.

400 g (14 oz) dried egg noodles (egg-free noodles are also fine)
1 small sweetheart (pointed) cabbage, about 350 g (12 oz), or the same weight of any other green cabbage
3 bunches of pak choi, about 300 g (10½ oz) in total
4 tablespoons cooking oil
2–3 large fresh green chillies, thinly sliced, including seeds
3 large garlic cloves, thinly sliced
1 red onion, thinly sliced
2 teaspoons salt
1 teaspoon chilli powder, or to taste – optional
2 teaspoons dark soy sauce
1 tablespoon light soy sauce
1 tablespoon sesame oil
2 teaspoons white vinegar
Chopped spring onions (scallions) and/or chives, to garnish

VEGETARIAN

Place a large saucepan of boiling water over a high heat. When the water is bubbling away, add the noodles and gently move them around in the water using chopsticks. Cook for 6–7 minutes or according to the instructions on the packet.

Drain the noodles in a colander, then place the colander inside a bowl and run cold water through the noodles – the cold water will fill the bowl and cool the noodles. Once they are completely cold, remove the colander from the bowl and leave the noodles to drain in the colander while you prepare the vegetables.

Wash the cabbage and remove its hard core, then cut in half and shred very finely. Cut each head of pak choi in half lengthways, then cut in half crossways on the diagonal. Rinse thoroughly and set aside in a bowl of cold water.

Put the oil into a wok over a high heat. When it's hot, add the chillies and garlic and stir-fry until browned, then add the onion and salt. Keep cooking and stirring until the onion has browned, then add the cabbage and cook for 2–3 minutes. Lift the pak choi out of the water and into the wok. Cook for 3–4 minutes, stirring often. If you like your noodles spicy, you can add some chilli powder at this point too.

Now add the noodles to the wok, along with both soy sauces, the sesame oil and the vinegar. Using tongs or chopsticks, toss together well for 3–4 minutes, then garnish with spring onions and/or chives.

Yeshi says 'Have some Taste Tibet *sepen* (see page 190) ready on the side if you want more of a kick out of this dish. Sriracha sauce also works well.'

Phing Tsel
(Veggie Glass Noodle Stew) *Serves 4–6*

This is a super-traditional dish that showcases some of the more unusual ingredients in Tibetan cuisine: *phing* (glass noodles, also known as mung bean vermicelli) and black cloud fungus (sometimes called wood ear fungus). The noodles are not the main attraction here, offering just an extra layer of texture.

Phing tsel should ideally be served with some other dishes alongside. We recommend Yeshi's dal (see page 206) and some simple stir-fried greens, such as pak choi or garlic shoots. You could also try it with *Tingmo* (steamed bread, see page 169), Giant fluffy sharing bread (see page 177) or basmati rice.

100 g (3½ oz) glass noodles
40 g (1½ oz) black cloud fungus
2 tablespoons cooking oil
3 large garlic cloves, thinly sliced
1 teaspoon Bassar curry masala (or hot chilli powder)
½ red onion, thinly sliced
2 tomatoes, diced
2 white potatoes, about 300 g (10½ oz), washed but not peeled, cut into fine julienne strips
2 teaspoons salt
4–5 spring onions (scallions), washed and thinly sliced, including green tips

VEGAN

Put the glass noodles and the black cloud fungus into a mixing bowl, cover with warm water and set aside for about half an hour.

Heat the oil in a large wok over a high heat. When it is hot, add the garlic, curry masala and onion and stir-fry for a couple of minutes. Add the tomatoes and stir well, then leave to cook for about 5 minutes.

Meanwhile, drain the glass noodles and black cloud fungus, rubbing the fungus between your fingers a little to check it's clean – give it another rinse if you find any gritty bits. Using scissors, cut the noodles into lengths and the fungus into smaller pieces.

Now add the potatoes and salt to the wok and pour in 500 ml (2 cups) of boiling water. Give everything a good stir, then add the glass noodles and black cloud fungus. Leave to cook for about 10 minutes, or until the potatoes are done – covering the wok will speed things up a bit.

Finally, add the spring onions and cook for a further 1–2 minutes, then serve.

Sabtuk
(Nettle Soup) *Serves 4*

Everybody in Tibet knows the story of Milarepa, the twelfth-century holy man who transformed himself from a murderous sorcerer into one of Tibet's most renowned yogis. It is said that during the years when he lived alone in his meditation cave near Mount Everest, he lived off nothing but nettles, and that over time his skin turned green.

Tibetan people love eating nettles. With a similar taste and texture to spinach, they are an amazing source of iron and calcium, and are packed full of vitamins. Nettles are best gathered in early springtime, when the leaves are tender, before they flower and the stalks and leaves toughen, but they can be enjoyed throughout the summer and even into early autumn. They can also be dried for use later in the year. The toxin that causes nettle stings is destroyed during cooking, but make sure you wear gloves when picking (and washing) them to avoid getting stung, and gather just the tops with the juiciest leaves.

In this recipe we use a mix of nettles and leeks for the combination of flavours and shades of green. Feel free to play with the ratio of nettle to leek, or to omit the leeks altogether if you are after a purer, earthier flavour. Serve the soup with *Balep* (Tibetan flatbread, see page 173) or Giant fluffy sharing bread (see page 177) for dunking.

2½ tablespoons cooking oil
3 large garlic cloves, thinly sliced
2 teaspoons salt
1 red onion, thinly sliced
2 leeks, washed and diced
150 g (5½ oz) nettle tops (discard any thick stalks), washed
Black pepper, to taste
Chives and/or plain yoghurt or cream, to garnish – optional

VEGETARIAN/VEGAN

Heat the oil in a wok or large saucepan over a high heat (Milarepa used an earthenware pot, and so do Yeshi's family, when they are making *sabtuk* at home). When it's hot, add the garlic and fry for a minute or two until it's lightly browned. Add the salt and onion and fry gently for a further minute, then add the leeks and stir-fry for a couple of minutes over a medium-high heat until starting to soften.

Meanwhile, cook the nettles in a separate pan of boiling water for 1 minute until softened, then drain and add to the wok.

Pour 1.5 litres (6 cups) of boiling water into the wok. Let the soup simmer for 10 minutes, then turn the heat down to low and mash everything using a wooden spoon or puree with a hand-held blender.

Serve in warm bowls, seasoned with pepper to taste and garnished with some chopped chives and a swirl of yoghurt or cream, if you like.

Yeshi says 'In Tibet, dried salted lamb fat is used to give a nice smoky flavour to this soup – you could throw in some chorizo for a similar effect. This can be fried separately and added just before serving, or cooked alongside the vegetables and blended into the soup.'

Tibetan Meatball Soup *Serves 4*

In Tibet, the practice of brides taking several husbands from the same family has been commonplace since ancient times. Yeshi's mother married two brothers, and Yeshi and his brothers and sisters know them simply as 'older father' and 'younger father'. Officially this system is now forbidden under Chinese law, but in rural areas it remains normal practice. Given the specific challenges of Tibet's topography, it has advantages: with little arable land available, and much labour needed to tend it, the marriage of a family's sons to one bride ensures that the land stays within the family, and that there are sufficient hands to both work in the fields and guarantee a male presence in the home. The practice also tends to reduce the number of heirs, and hence the number of mouths the land must feed.

Although Yeshi's younger father is now vegetarian, he used to enjoy meatballs way back when. Yeshi remembers that this dish would be his contribution to weddings and other major events taking place in the village. Weddings typically last two or three days and have up to 400 guests, so you can imagine how many meatballs would be needed!

- 350 g (12 oz) minced (ground) beef, ideally 15–20% fat content
- 1 free-range egg
- ½ small red onion, finely chopped
- 1 large garlic clove, finely chopped
- ½ teaspoon crushed Sichuan peppercorns (*yerma*)
- 1½ teaspoons ground coriander
- 1 teaspoon salt
- Plain (all-purpose) white flour, for dusting
- 125 g (4½ oz) baby spinach leaves, washed
- Coriander (cilantro) leaves, to garnish

Place the minced beef in a mixing bowl and crack in the egg. Mix together very well using your hand or a fork, then add the onion, garlic, Sichuan pepper, coriander and ½ teaspoon of salt and mix everything together thoroughly.

Sprinkle a little flour onto a chopping board. Pinch off a 2.5 cm (1 inch) piece of the meat mixture and roll it between your palms to make a ball, then roll it through the flour on the board. Don't douse it in flour – you are aiming for a light coating. Pick up the meatball and roll it between your hands again, then give it another roll in the flour before setting aside. Repeat with the rest of the meat mixture, adding a little more flour to the board as needed. You should end up with about 30 meatballs all told.

Measure out 1 litre (4 cups) of boiling water into a large wok and place over a medium heat. When the water returns to the boil, add the meatballs and stir them around gently, adding a little more water if the meatballs are not fully covered. Add the remaining ½ teaspoon of salt, turn the heat up as far as it will go and simmer the meatballs for 4–5 minutes, stirring occasionally. In the final minute of cooking, add the spinach to the soup.

Just before you take the wok off the heat, check that the meatballs are cooked by fishing one out and cutting it open: it should be brown all the way through, not pink.

Serve the meatball soup in bowls, garnished with coriander.

Egg and Tomato Soup *Serves 2–4*

We enjoy this as a light, refreshing lunch, with some *Balep* (Tibetan flatbread, see page 173) or toast. In Tibet it's usually eaten with *Tsampa* (roasted barley flour, see page 53), and it also makes a nice accompaniment to drier meat dishes. Use the best free-range eggs you can find, and the ripest tomatoes. The spinach is optional, but it adds more texture and colour to the dish.

- 4 eggs
- 2 tablespoons plain (all-purpose) flour
- 2 tomatoes, halved and then thinly sliced
- 1 teaspoon salt
- 2 spring onions (scallions), washed and thinly sliced, including green tips
- 60 g (2¼ oz) spinach, washed and chopped – optional

VEGETARIAN

Measure out 1 litre (4 cups) of water into a saucepan and bring to the boil.

Meanwhile, break the eggs into a bowl, sprinkle the flour on top and mix well with a fork. Once the water is boiling, add the egg mixture to the pan, rinsing the last of it out of the bowl with some water from the pan. Stir well, then add the tomatoes and salt and leave to cook for 2–3 minutes.

Add the spring onions and the spinach, if using, and give everything a good stir. When the soup comes back to the boil again, it's ready to serve.

Leek and Potato Congee *Serves 4*

Congee is a cure-all of miraculous frugality. All you need is a little rice, some water and salt and you can make a recuperative broth that will see you through another day. Many countries have a version of this rice porridge: South Asians have *khichri*, a rice and dal dish, and the Chinese have *xiaomizhou*, a millet congee. In Tibet, if you are unwell, chances are someone will serve you a bowl of congee.

Congee isn't just the preserve of the sick, though. We enjoy it when we have overindulged in all kinds of ways! If you don't need your congee to be vegan, chorizo is a good addition to spice things up a little, or try it with chicken thigh fillets for a more subtle flavour. Sweet potato makes for another good variation. We also recommend some *Balep* (Tibetan flatbread, see page 173) or Giant fluffy sharing bread (see page 177) on the side.

130 g (⅔ cup) basmati rice
1 leek, about 250 g (9 oz)
1 white potato, about 125 g (4½ oz)
1 teaspoon salt

VEGAN

Wash and drain the rice, then put it into a large saucepan. Add about 1.5 litres (6 cups) of cold water to the pan and place over a medium-high heat.

Wash the leek well. Cut it in half lengthways, then cut both white and green parts across into thin slices. Wash but don't peel the potato, then cut it into dice.

Add the leek and potato to the pan, then turn the heat down to medium. Cover and cook, stirring occasionally, for 20–25 minutes, or until everything is done.

Now add the salt and another 250 ml (1 cup) of boiling water, or slightly more if you want the congee to be soupier. Bring back to the boil, then serve.

Labu Shaku
(Tibetan Lamb Stew) *Serves 4–6*

This dish spells autumn for Yeshi. At the end of the summer season, when he had spent months away from the village tending the animals, his homecoming celebration would feature this flavoursome stew, made with meat from the family flock. No part of the sheep would be wasted: sheep's intestine, stuffed with fat, blood and flour, then lightly boiled, is considered a delicacy in Tibet (Yeshi's older father makes an absolutely delicious take on this); and dried salted lamb fat makes its way into momos, soups and stews. The sheep's skin is used to make winter jackets, while its horns are fashioned into bells.

Labu shaku is delicious with rice or Giant fluffy sharing bread (see page 177), which is so often made in Yeshi's home.

1 tablespoon cooking oil
1 dried red chilli
3 garlic cloves, thinly sliced
1 red onion, thinly sliced
2 tomatoes, diced
1 kg (2 lb 4 oz) bone-in lamb – ribs or flank are best, but leg is fine too
2 teaspoons salt
½ teaspoon crushed Sichuan peppercorns (*yerma*)
½ teaspoon ground coriander
200 g (7 oz) mooli (daikon), washed but not peeled, diced
200 g (7 oz) potatoes, washed but not peeled, diced
Chopped spring onions (scallions) or coriander (cilantro), to garnish

Put the oil into a large saucepan and place over a high heat. Crush the chilli lightly, just to break it apart a little, and when the oil is hot, throw it in. Let it sizzle until it browns, then add the garlic and onion, stir well and cook them until golden brown before adding the tomatoes.

Cut the lamb into pieces that will fit in your saucepan, removing some but not all of the meat from the bone – you can ask your butcher to do this, if you like. Add the lamb to the pan, stirring it well so that it begins to seal on all sides, then add the salt, Sichuan pepper and ground coriander and let it cook for 15–20 minutes, or until the meat is browned. Keep an eye on it and give it a stir occasionally to make sure nothing sticks.

Now add 1 litre (4 cups) of boiling water, cover and cook for 15 minutes, stirring every so often. Add the mooli and potatoes and stir everything well, then cover and leave to cook for a further 10–15 minutes, checking to make sure that the vegetables are tender before serving.

Ladle the stew into bowls and garnish with spring onions or coriander.

Sha Tsöma (Classic Tibetan Boiled Beef) *Serves 6–8*

In Tibet this dish would usually be made with yak meat, which is a bit leaner than beef. Tibetans like some bite to their meat – hence the widespread custom of chewing cured yak meat as a snack outside of mealtimes. The cooking time below reflects this. If you'd like the meat to be more fall-apart tender, by all means cook it for longer.

One reason that Tibetan people like their meat to be more robust is so that it can stand up to a good dunking in some chilli dip. Bear this in mind as you tuck into this dish – fingers should probably be used and *sepen* or hot chilli flakes should definitely be on hand, even if you decide to do without the dipping sauce below. For a truly Tibetan culinary experience, serve this with *Tingmo* (steamed bread, see page 169), sit back and imagine you're eating in a nomadic tent: you have a fire to warm your toes, and this meat, broth and chilli are going to do their job as well.

4 large garlic cloves, thinly sliced
7.5–10 cm (3–4 inch) piece of ginger, washed but not peeled, thinly sliced
1 teaspoon salt
½ teaspoon crushed Sichuan peppercorns (*yerma*)
1 kg (2 lb 4 oz) beef rib or rump, on the bone, or about 800 g (1 lb 12 oz) topside of beef
4–5 large potatoes
1 mooli (daikon)
5 baby parsnips
5 baby carrots
100 g (1½ cups) chopped baby spinach or 50 g (1 cup) chopped coriander (cilantro)

For the dipping sauce

2 tablespoons light soy sauce
½ tablespoon Chinkiang black vinegar
1 tablespoon sesame oil
1–2 teaspoons Taste Tibet *sepen* (see page 190) or hot chilli flakes
½ teaspoon crushed Sichuan peppercorns (*yerma*) or 1 teaspoon Sichuan pepper oil – optional

Pour 1.5 litres (6 cups) of boiling water into a stockpot or large saucepan, and place over a high heat. Add the garlic, ginger, salt and Sichuan pepper.

Cut the beef between the bones, or if the meat you're using is not on the bone, cut it into chunks that will fit in the pot. Add the meat to the pot and bring to the boil, then cover with a lid and turn down to a simmer. Let it cook for 30–40 minutes – or longer, depending on how lean the beef is and how tender you like your meat.

Meanwhile, wash the potatoes, mooli, parsnips and carrots well, but do not peel them. Cut the potatoes into large chunks, and the mooli into similar-sized pieces, leaving on any green tips.

After about 35 minutes, or when you're happy with the cooking of the beef, add the potatoes, mooli, parsnips and carrots to the pot, cover and cook for 10 minutes or until the vegetables are done. (If your beef is quite lean, you may want to remove it at this point so that it doesn't dry out, then return it to the pot afterwards; otherwise just leave it in with the vegetables.)

For the dipping sauce, just mix all the ingredients together in a small bowl.

To serve, lift out the vegetables and meat from the pot and place on a chopping board. Stir the spinach or coriander through the broth for a bit of greenery, then ladle into individual bowls. Cut the meat to size and share out with the vegetables. Place the dipping sauce in the middle of the table for dunking.

Dumplings, Pasties and Bread

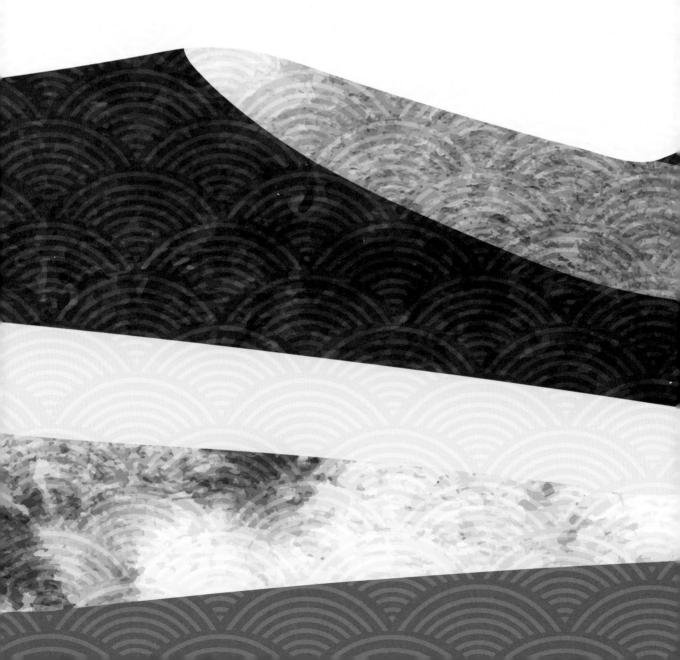

It's time to talk about momos (Tibetan dumplings). These steaming parcels of comfort are the hamburgers of the Himalayas. Momos have come to be associated with Nepalese cuisine, but in fact their origins lie in Tibet. Traditionally made with yak meat, but equally succulent when made with beef or vegetables, this is the Tibetan food that has travelled furthest and received most acclaim.

This chapter includes recipes for a variety of momos. Steamed rather than boiled, and made using a wheat-flour dough, they're not as delicate as Chinese dumplings. Momos have a skin that is firm enough to be handled without breaking, which makes them great finger food. Tibetan people always eat momos with their hands – all the better for squidging into some hot sauce on the side.

These are simple recipes that do not require the dough to be rested for hours, and beautiful shapes or pleats are not necessary – they're just fun to play around with. The dough we use is easy to handle and doesn't break, which is the secret of successful momo-making. For tips and tricks on momos, take a look at pages 146–9. You'll find all the instructions you need there, plus a guide on how best to eat momos. You may think you know how, but there's a uniquely Tibetan way.

Most of the dishes in this chapter are eaten with the hands in Tibet. Bread is meant to be dipped into sauce or used to scoop up other dishes. Usually, Yeshi doesn't use a plate when he's eating *tingmo* (steamed bread) or *balep* (flatbread), even when they're accompanied by the runniest of dishes – it's as if the bread becomes an extension of his body. A *sha balep* (Tibetan pasty) is also best eaten with the hands; after all, who really gets maximum enjoyment from eating a pasty with a knife and fork?

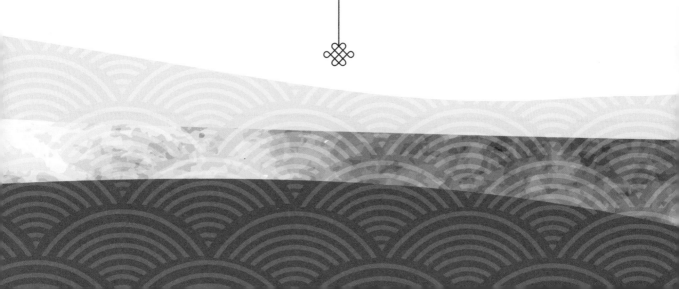

Making and eating momos

Momos are the unofficial national dish of Tibet. Even if you have never knowingly eaten Tibetan food before, you may well be familiar with momos. Tibetan people brought them to Nepal, where they take pride of place on many a Nepalese menu, and they have also popularised them in India, where local people have rolled out huge chains of momo shops across the country. The momo has become big business.

Essentially, momos are dumplings. In Tibet these are usually steamed or steam-fried. Made with a wheat-flour dough, they are chewier than Chinese dumplings or Japanese gyoza, and they can hold more filling. They are the ultimate comfort food. Served straight out of the steamer, momos burst with all their cooking juices. Steam-fried in a little oil, they crunch in the mouth like pot-stickers. It's always worth making a big batch, so you can enjoy them both ways – steamed for round one, then pan-fried when reheated for round two.

Yeshi makes thousands of momos a week for our shop, restaurant and food stall, but back in Tibet momo-making is usually reserved for special occasions. When friends and relatives get together everybody helps out, and this makes light work of what can otherwise be a time-consuming job, especially when there are lots of mouths to feed.

If you want to have a go but are daunted by the process of making dough, ready-made dumpling wrappers are available to buy at all good Chinese supermarkets. You'll usually find them in the frozen-food section and they'll need to be defrosted overnight before use. But it goes without saying that the best dumplings are made with fresh, hand-made dough, and momo dough is relatively simple to make and work with, so hopefully you will be surprised by how easy the process is.

Wrapping

Yeshi has been making momos since he was little, and it's a learned and fine art! But your momos will taste delicious no matter how you fold them, so try not to get too caught up with producing something beautiful, especially if this gets in the way of the fun.

To start with, place a wrapper on your chopping board and spoon about a tablespoon of filling into the centre. Less is more when you are just starting out; you can add more filling as your confidence builds. Gently fold one side of the circle over the filling to meet the other side and, starting in the middle, use your fingertips to press the edges together into the board. (If you are using shop-bought wrappers, you'll need to wet the edges before sealing.) If the momo is not completely sealed, the juices will escape during steaming, so try to ensure there are no gaps.

Place the completed momos on a wooden chopping board or lined baking tray, leaving at least 1 cm (½ inch) between them, and covering them with a tea towel to prevent drying out. Repeat until all the filling or dough is used up. Leftover momo filling has myriad uses, depending on what filling it is – use it in soups or salads as appropriate. Any leftover dough can be rolled up and cut to make *Tingmo* (steamed bread, see page 169), a delicious accompaniment to lots of different Tibetan dishes.

If you're feeling adventurous, here's how the most common momo shapes are made.

Half-moon

Place the wrapper in your left hand (or reverse these instructions if you are left-handed). Spoon a tablespoon of filling into the centre and pinch together two sides of the wrapper to meet and seal in the middle. Stabilise this with the thumb and forefinger of your left hand, and then use the thumb and forefinger of your right to seal the right side of the wrapper. To do this, make little pleats with your index finger in towards the join you have made at the centre, pressing the other side of the wrapper with your thumb to meet it; your thumb also does the job of pushing in the filling as you go. Repeat with the left side of the wrapper.

Round

This shape can be a little trickier. Have a look at the step-by-step instructions on pages 150–51. We use it for our vegan momos, but there are no rules!

Place the wrapper in your left hand (or reverse these instructions if you are left-handed). Using your right hand, spoon a tablespoon of filling into the centre, then pinch a small fold in the dough to make a pleat. Keep pinching and pleating, little by little, rotating the momo slightly as you work your way around. Your thumb shouldn't move: as your index finger keeps pinching in a circular motion, each new fold should meet the first fold held by your thumb. Use the thumb of your left hand to gently push in the filling as needed. Eventually you should end up back where you started. Seal the momo with a final pinch.

Tsi-tsi ('mouse')

Tibetans traditionally fold dumplings this way for *Mothuk* (Momos in soup, see page 165), where they are boiled in broth rather than being steamed.

Place the wrapper in your left hand (or reverse these instructions if you are left-handed). Using your right hand, spoon a tablespoon of filling into the centre and pinch together the top and bottom of the wrapper at the right-hand end. Then, pushing the filling inside the wrapper with your left thumb, press together the sides of the wrapper first with the index finger of your right hand, then with the thumb, all the way along. Seal the momo with a final pinch.

Steaming

This is the traditional Tibetan way. You can use a metal or bamboo steamer. If you're using a metal one, lightly brush each steamer basket with oil or line with greaseproof paper. If you're using a bamboo steamer, line the steamer baskets with greaseproof paper. The momos will need to steam for about 15 minutes, but check each recipe for more specific timings. The water in the base of the steamer or in the wok should be boiling at the point at which the steamer baskets go on and you start counting down the cooking time. Generally speaking, a gas ring will get hotter, and therefore cook faster than an electric one – if you know that your stovetop doesn't achieve a very high heat, you may need to add a couple of minutes to the stated cooking times.

One way of testing whether your momos are ready is to press them gently. If the dough doesn't stick to your finger, then they are done. (The water that the momos have steamed over can be made into a simple side soup: just add a little salt and serve as is, or you could add some chopped spinach as well.)

Steam-frying

If you don't own a steamer, this is a great option. Basically you fry your momos until they are crisp and golden underneath, then cover the pan so they steam and cook through. To do this, place a large non-stick frying pan (not a wok) over a high heat and drizzle in 2 tablespoons of cooking oil, making sure the oil completely covers the base of the pan. Gently place the momos in the pan, fitting as many as possible, while leaving a little gap between each momo. Tilt the pan if the oil seems to be favouring one side of it. Let the momos fry for 1–2 minutes, then gently pour in about 100 ml (3½ fl oz) of boiling water and place a lid on the pan or cover with foil. Leave to cook for 8–9 minutes, turning the heat down low once the water has evaporated – this will take a couple of minutes. You may need to check in on the momos towards the end of the cooking time, just to make sure they are not starting to stick to one another – if so, carefully separate them using a spatula. When the momos are done, gently prise them out of the pan with your spatula.

Momo dips and sauces

Finally, some kind of dip or sauce on the side is essential! We recommend Tomato *sepen* (see page 193) – you can omit the chilli if you don't want it spicy. Otherwise the Taste Tibet momo sauce (see page 194), containing just a few ingredients, is light and super-simple, while Yeshi's super salsa (see page 200) makes a great partner for steam-fried momos. Of course, Taste Tibet *sepen* (see page 190) should always be on hand as well.

Eating

A word of caution! Momos straight out of the steamer or pan contain seriously hot juices. This is handy in one way, as they will hold their heat well if you are cooking them in batches – but if you want to tuck in straight away, we suggest doing as the Tibetans do and biting off just a small corner of the momo to let in a little cooling air and sucking out the juices before they burst out all over. You can then shovel your dip of choice inside the hole you've made, or squidge your momo into your chosen sauce.

Reheating

However you've cooked your momos, when it comes to reheating those leftovers, you're in for a treat, especially if they were steamed first time around.

Microwaving or re-steaming are of course options – these help the momos to retain their juices – but pan-frying in a flat-bottomed pan (not a wok) is best. If you have a really good non-stick frying pan there is no need for any oil, but if you are worried the momos will stick, or you just like a bit of oil, add a drizzle to the pan before you put in the momos. Place your pan over a low-medium heat, add the momos and cover with a lid or foil. Leave them to brown slightly for 3–4 minutes one side, then turn them over and let them brown for 3–4 minutes on the other side, checking them occasionally to make sure they don't burn.

The reheated momos will be slightly drier than when they were fresh out of the steamer, but they will have a crunch to them that is totally moreish.

STEP 1: when you're ready to fill, wrap and fold your momos, roll out one wrapper at a time, turning it little by little as you go

STEP 4: pinch a small fold in the dough to make a pleat, using your thumb to gently push in the filling as needed

STEP 5: keep pinching and pleating, rotating the momo slightly as you work your way around

STEP 2: hold the wrapper in your non-dominant hand

STEP 3: spoon a tablespoon of filling into the centre

STEP 6: when you get back to where you started, seal the momo with a final pinch

STEP 7: repeat with the remaining wrappers and filling

Heavenly Vegan Momos

Makes about 40 momos

These may be the dish for which Taste Tibet is most famous – we shift huge quantities of these momos at our restaurant and stall. They are almost as healthy as they sound, and many confirmed meat-eaters actually prefer them. Serve with Taste Tibet *sepen* (see page 190), Taste Tibet momo sauce (see page 194) or Walnut and chilli dip (see page 199).

For the dough

500 g (3⅓ cups) self-raising flour, plus extra for dusting

For the filling

1 sweetheart (pointed) cabbage, about 500 g (1 lb 2 oz), or the same weight of any other green cabbage
200 g (7 oz) spinach
200 g (7 oz) Chinese chives
2 teaspoons salt
2 tablespoons cooking oil

VEGAN

For the dough, put the flour into a mixing bowl. Slowly pour in about 250 ml (1 cup) of warm water – a hot handwash temperature is good – into the flour with one hand, while mixing with the other. Add just enough water to make a dough – you don't want it to get too sticky. Knead until the dough forms a ball in the bowl, then cover and set aside for 15–20 minutes.

Meanwhile, make the filling. Wash the cabbage and chop it very finely, then put it into a large mixing bowl. Wash the spinach thoroughly and chop it finely, then add it to the bowl. Add the salt and oil and squish it through the vegetables with your hand – this will help to draw out excess moisture – then set aside for 5 minutes.

Tip the vegetables into a colander and press down firmly with your hands to extract as much liquid as possible. Return the vegetables to the bowl. Chop the chives very finely and stir through the filling.

Take the dough out of the bowl and knead it for a couple of minutes, then divide it into four equal pieces and return to the bowl. Sprinkle a little flour onto your work surface – but don't overdo it, as too much flour can stiffen the dough, making the momos harder to wrap later.

Take the first piece of dough, keeping the rest covered in the bowl to stop them from drying out. Roll out the dough into a sausage shape about 25 cm (10 inches) long, then cut into ten equal slices, lightly flattening each one with your hand.

Using a rolling pin, and making one wrapper at a time, push and pull the flattened piece of dough up and down quickly and firmly, holding it with your spare hand and turning it little by little as you go. The middle should end up a bit thicker than the outer edges, and it should fill the palm of your hand; it doesn't need to be a perfect circle.

When you're ready to fill, wrap and fold your momos, follow the instructions on page 146–8 (the process is also shown on pages 150–51), shaping them however you like.

For best results, steam these momos (see page 148) over a high heat for 13–16 minutes, cooking them in batches according to the size of your steamer.

Beef Momos *Makes about 40 momos*

In Tibet these momos are usually made with yak meat, but beef is a great substitute. When I first met Yeshi in India, he would mince the meat for these from a slab of rump steak. In a country where meat is not consumed in large amounts – particularly beef, as Hindus consider cows to be sacred – all the neighbourhood cats would come running, hoping to share in this forbidden pleasure. The momos were the most delicious I'd tasted, containing all the natural fats of a good cut of beef. Serve these with Yeshi's super salsa (see page 200), Tomato *sepen* (see page 193) or Taste Tibet momo sauce (see page 194).

For the dough

500 g (3⅓ cups) self-raising flour, plus extra for dusting

For the filling

1 red onion, finely chopped

2 large garlic cloves, finely chopped

500 g (1 lb 2 oz) minced (ground) beef, ideally 15–20% fat content

50 g (1¾ oz) spinach or sweetheart (pointed) cabbage, washed and finely chopped

2 teaspoons cooking oil

2 teaspoons salt

For the dough, put the flour into a mixing bowl. Slowly pour in about 250 ml (1 cup) of warm water – a hot handwash temperature is good – into the flour with one hand, while mixing with the other. Add just enough water to make a dough – you don't want it to get too sticky. Knead until the dough forms a ball in the bowl, then cover and set aside for 15–20 minutes.

Meanwhile, put all the filling ingredients into a bowl, add 100 ml (3½ fl oz) of cold water and mix together well, ideally using your hands.

Take the dough out of the bowl and knead it for a couple of minutes, then divide it into four equal pieces and return to the bowl. Sprinkle a little flour onto your work surface – but don't overdo it, as too much flour can stiffen the dough, making the momos harder to wrap later.

Take the first piece of dough, keeping the rest covered in the bowl to stop them from drying out. Roll out the dough into a sausage shape about 25 cm (10 inches) long, then cut into ten equal slices, flattening each one slightly with your hand.

Using a rolling pin, and making one wrapper at a time, push and pull the flattened piece of dough up and down quickly and firmly, holding it with your spare hand and turning it little by little as you go. The middle should end up a bit thicker than the outer edges, and it should fill the palm of your hand; it doesn't need to be a perfect circle.

When you're ready to fill, wrap and fold your momos, follow the instructions on pages 146–8, shaping them however you like.

These momos are delicious either steamed or steam-fried (see page 148). If you steam them, they will need 15–16 minutes over a high heat. If you steam-fry them, allow about 12 minutes in total. Cook them in batches, according to the size of your steamer or frying pan.

Yeshi says 'The best beef momos hold a good deal of juice, and this surges out on first bite. Take care – momo splatter is real!'

Cheesy Momos

Makes about 40 momos

Yeshi's mum loves making these momos. Tibetan cheese is complex in flavour: sharp/sweet and with herbal hints, it makes for delicious dumplings. Feta is a good substitute here. It has all the sour creaminess of Tibetan cheeses and its crumbly texture means that the filling is quick to prepare. Yeshi's mother likes to pair the cheese with pak choi, picking it while it's still very young and tender, so have a go with pak choi if you can find it. Otherwise, spinach makes the momos very juicy – and the stems give a nice crunch, so don't discard these as you chop. Serve your cheesy momos with Tomato *sepen* (see page 193) or Walnut and chilli dip (see page 199).

For the dough

500 g (3⅓ cups) self-raising flour, plus extra for dusting

For the filling

3 bunches of whole leaf spinach, about 500 g (1 lb 2 oz) in total

1 teaspoon salt

2 tablespoons cooking oil

200 g (7 oz) feta cheese, finely diced

VEGETARIAN

For the dough, put the flour into a mixing bowl. Slowly pour in about 250 ml (1 cup) of warm water – a hot handwash temperature is good – into the flour with one hand, while mixing with the other. Add just enough water to make a dough – you don't want it to get too sticky. Knead until the dough forms a ball in the bowl, then cover and set aside for 15–20 minutes.

Meanwhile, make the filling. Finely chop the spinach – ideally the pieces should be as small as 5 mm (¼ inch). Put it into a large mixing bowl, then fill the bowl with water and wash the spinach by swirling it with your hand. Leave it to stand for 2 minutes, then swirl again. Transfer the spinach to a colander in the sink and leave to drain for a minute or two. Rinse out the mixing bowl and tip the spinach back into it. Add the salt and oil and mix well by hand, then leave to stand for about 5 minutes.

Put the feta into another mixing bowl. Now transfer the spinach into the feta bowl, batch by batch. Squeeze the spinach between your hands as you lift it out, so that any excess liquid drains back into the original bowl before you add it to the feta for the filling (otherwise, the momos will be soggy and hard to wrap). Mix the spinach and feta together well.

Take the dough out of the bowl and knead it for a couple of minutes, then divide it into four equal pieces and return to the bowl. Sprinkle a little flour onto your work surface – but don't overdo it, as too much flour can stiffen the dough, making the momos harder to wrap later.

Take the first piece of dough, keeping the rest covered in the bowl to stop them from drying out. Roll out the dough into a sausage shape about 25 cm (10 inches) long, then cut into ten equal slices, lightly flattening each one with your hand.

continued >

Using a rolling pin, and making one wrapper at a time, push and pull the flattened piece of dough up and down quickly and firmly, holding it with your spare hand and turning it little by little as you go. The middle should end up a bit thicker than the outer edges, and it should fill the palm of your hand; it doesn't need to be a perfect circle.

When you're ready to fill, wrap and fold your momos, follow the instructions on pages 146–8, shaping them however you like.

For best results, steam these momos (see page 148) over a high heat for about 13–16 minutes, cooking them in batches according to the size of your steamer.

Yeshi says 'If you have any filling left over, it goes really well in a salad – just add some sliced red onion or avocado, for example, and off you go.'

Tofu, Chinese Cabbage and Mushroom Momos *Makes about 40 momos*

If you like mushrooms, this is the filling for you. By nature, tofu and Chinese (napa) cabbage are great at absorbing the flavour of other vegetables they are cooked with, so mushroom is the dominant taste here, but there's plenty of texture. Feel free to use other vegetables as you prefer – sweetheart (pointed) cabbage is a good substitute for Chinese cabbage, for example. Serve with Taste Tibet *sepen* (see page 190), Tomato *sepen* (see page 193) or Taste Tibet momo sauce (see page 194).

For the dough
500 g (3⅓ cups) self-raising flour, plus extra for dusting

For the filling
250 g (9 oz) chestnut mushrooms
200 g (7 oz) pak choi
½ Chinese (napa) cabbage, about 225 g (8 oz)
4 spring onions (scallions), washed and thinly sliced
2 teaspoons salt
2 tablespoons cooking oil
1 teaspoon coriander seeds
225 g (8 oz) firm tofu

VEGAN

For the dough, put the flour into a mixing bowl. Slowly pour in about 250 ml (1 cup) of warm water – a hot handwash temperature is good – into the flour with one hand, while mixing with the other. Add just enough water to make a dough – you don't want it to get too sticky. Knead until the dough forms a ball in the bowl, then cover and set aside for 15–20 minutes.

Meanwhile, make the filling. Wipe the mushrooms clean, then chop them very finely. Put them into a large mixing bowl. Cut each pak choi in half lengthways. Now thinly slice each half lengthways from the base upwards, then thinly slice again, going crossways this time, so you end up with very finely chopped pak choi. Add to the mushrooms in the bowl. Slice the Chinese cabbage in the same way and add to the bowl, along with the spring onions, salt and oil.

Mix everything well, ideally by hand – the juices will start to run. Now empty the mixture into a colander in the sink to let the excess liquid drain away. Leave to stand for 5 minutes, then gently press down on the vegetables with your hands to squeeze out as much liquid as possible. (If the filling is too wet, the momos will be difficult to wrap as the dough will get a dousing.) Return the filling to the bowl, add the coriander seeds and crumble in the tofu, then mix everything together thoroughly.

Take the dough out of the bowl and knead it for a couple of minutes, then divide it into four equal pieces and return to the bowl. Sprinkle a little flour onto your work surface – but don't overdo it, as too much flour can stiffen the dough, making the momos harder to wrap later.

Take the first piece of dough, keeping the rest covered in the bowl to stop them from drying out. Roll out the dough into a sausage shape about 25 cm (10 inches) long, then cut into ten equal slices, lightly flattening each one with your hand.

continued >

Using a rolling pin, and making one wrapper at a time, push and pull the flattened piece of dough up and down quickly and firmly, holding it with your spare hand and turning it little by little as you go. The middle should end up a bit thicker than the outer edges, and it should fill the palm of your hand; it doesn't need to be a perfect circle.

When you're ready to fill, wrap and fold your momos, follow the instructions on pages 146–8, shaping them however you like.

These momos are delicious steamed or steam-fried (see page 148): either steam over a high heat for 13–16 minutes, or steam-fry for about 12 minutes. Cook them in batches, according to the size of your steamer or frying pan.

Yeshi says 'If you have some Chinese chives knocking about, these make a delicious addition to the filling and add some nice colour to the momos. One bunch, about 60 g (2¼ oz), is a good amount.'

Shogo Momos
(Spiced Potato Momos) *Makes about 30–35 momos*

This is another of Yeshi's mum's favourites. She likes to add dried lamb or pork fat, which obviously gives the dumplings a whole other dimension, but this version is vegan!

There is something so completely comforting about potato momos – they are very redolent of childhood. The ground cumin in the filling of these ones gives them warmth, but really the trick is to get the right dip for them. Tomato *sepen* (see page 193) is a great choice, but if you're after something sharper, rather than hot, then we recommend Yeshi's super salsa (see page 200).

For the dough

500 g (3⅓ cups) self-raising flour, plus extra for dusting

For the filling

700 g (1 lb 9 oz) potatoes (white, red or a mix), washed but not peeled

1 tablespoon salt

2 tablespoons cooking oil

1 tablespoon ground cumin

125 g (4½ oz) baby spinach, or 2–3 spring onions (scallions), washed and finely chopped

VEGAN

For the dough, put the flour into a mixing bowl. Slowly pour in about 250 ml (1 cup) of warm water – a hot handwash temperature is good – into the flour with one hand, while mixing with the other. Add just enough water to make a dough – you don't want it to get too sticky. Knead until the dough forms a ball in the bowl, then cover and set aside for 15–20 minutes.

Meanwhile, make the filling. Wash the potatoes and shred them using the large holes of a grater. Put them into a mixing bowl, along with the salt, oil and cumin, and mix well by hand. Stir through the spinach or spring onions, then leave to stand for 5 minutes. Now use your hands to transfer the mixture to a colander in the sink to let the excess liquid drain away. Gently press down on the mixture with your hand to squeeze out as much liquid as possible (otherwise, the momos will be soggy and hard to wrap), then tip the filling back into the bowl.

Take the dough out of the bowl and knead it for a couple of minutes, then divide it into four equal pieces and return to the bowl. Sprinkle a little flour onto your work surface – but don't overdo it, as too much flour can stiffen the dough, making the momos harder to wrap later.

Take the first piece of dough, keeping the rest covered in the bowl to stop them from drying out. Roll out the dough into a sausage shape about 25 cm (10 inches) long, then cut into eight equal slices, lightly flattening each one with your hand. (Note that these momos will turn out slightly larger than some of the others in the book – the traditional way is to make these ones a bit bulkier.)

continued >

Using a rolling pin, and making one wrapper at a time, push and pull the flattened piece of dough up and down quickly and firmly, holding it with your spare hand and turning it little by little as you go. The middle should end up a bit thicker than the outer edges, and it should fill the palm of your hand; it doesn't need to be a perfect circle.

When you're ready to fill, wrap and fold your momos, follow the instructions on pages 146–8, shaping them however you like.

For best results, steam these momos (see page 148) over a high heat for about 13–16 minutes, cooking them in batches according to the size of your steamer.

Mothuk (Momos in Soup)

Serves 4–6 (makes about 40–45 momos)

Soups and broths are a very important part of the Tibetan cuisine. As well as helping to keep hands and stomachs warm in Tibet's extreme cold, they also serve to aid digestion. Getting the right balance between dry and wet foods is an important principle of healthy eating, according to traditional Tibetan medicine. Momos are usually accompanied by a soup made from the water over which they have steamed, but *mothuk* gives you everything in one bowl. Serve with Yeshi's super salsa (see page 200) on the side, or throw in some Taste Tibet *sepen* (see page 190). You might like to add some Sichuan pepper oil too.

For the dough

350 g (2⅓ cups) plain (all-purpose) flour, plus extra for dusting

For the filling

350 g (12 oz) minced (ground) beef, ideally 15–20% fat content
1 large garlic clove, finely chopped
½ red onion, finely chopped
¾ teaspoon salt
2 teaspoons cooking oil
Small handful of finely chopped cabbage – optional
Black pepper, to taste

For the broth

1 tablespoon cooking oil
2 large garlic cloves, thinly sliced
1 small red onion, thinly sliced
150 g (5½ oz) spinach, Chinese mustard greens or other seasonal greens
1 tablespoon light soy sauce
½ tablespoon Chinkiang black vinegar
½ tablespoon sesame oil
1 teaspoon salt
Chopped spring onions (scallions) or coriander (cilantro), to garnish
Sichuan pepper oil – optional

To make the dough for the momo wrappers, put the flour into a mixing bowl. Slowly pour in about 160 ml (5¼ fl oz) of warm water – a hot handwash temperature is good – into the flour with one hand, while mixing with the other. Add just enough water to make a dough – you don't want it to get too sticky. Knead until the dough forms a ball in the bowl, then cover and set aside for 15–20 minutes.

Meanwhile, for the filling, put all the ingredients into a bowl with 50 ml (2½ tablespoons) of water and mix everything together well, ideally using your hands.

Take the dough out of the bowl and knead it for a couple of minutes, then divide it into three equal pieces and return to the bowl. Sprinkle a little flour onto your work surface – but don't overdo it, as too much flour can stiffen the dough, making the momos harder to wrap later.

Take the first piece of dough, keeping the rest covered in the bowl to stop them from drying out. Roll out the dough into a sausage shape about 25 cm (10 inches) long, then cut into 14–15 slices, each weighing about 15 g (½ oz) – *mothuk* dumplings are made smaller than other momos. Press each one lightly to flatten.

Using a rolling pin, and making one wrapper at a time, push and pull the flattened piece of dough up and down quickly and firmly, holding it with your spare hand and turning it little by little as you go. The middle should end up a bit thicker than the outer edges, and it should fill the palm of your hand; it doesn't need to be a perfect circle.

When you're ready to fill, wrap and fold your momos, follow the instructions on pages 146–8. For *mothuk*, Tibetans usually fold these dumplings into the *tsi-tsi* ('mouse') shape, but you can do something simpler if you like, as long the dumplings are well sealed.

continued >

For the broth, heat the oil in a large saucepan or wok over a medium-high heat. When the oil is starting to smoke, add the garlic and onion and cook until browned, then carefully – it may spit – pour in 1 litre (4 cups) of boiling water.

Wash the spinach, chop it roughly and rinse again. When the water in the pan is at a rolling boil, add the spinach or greens and the dumplings, then stir gently. (If you have any leftover dumpling dough, you can roll it into a sausage, flatten it a little and then pull small pieces off it into the broth.) Now add the soy sauce, vinegar, sesame oil and salt. Bring back to the boil, then turn the heat down to medium and leave to simmer for 6–7 minutes, or until the momos are cooked right through.

Garnish with spring onions or coriander. If you're using spring onions, give them a couple of minutes in the broth before ladling the dumplings and soup into bowls and serving.

Tingmo (Steamed Bread) *Serves 4–6*

This is a beautifully light accompaniment to all kinds of Tibetan dishes – it just loves to soak up both meat and vegetable juices. In Yeshi's village, *tingmo* is a staple, and he learned to make it out on the mountains when he was still a child.

It's also a very healthy bread – omit the sugar if you want, as it only serves to add a little softness to the texture. Likewise the eggs, if you want a vegan version. The *tingmos* will come out super-fluffy either way. You can serve *tingmo* with all kinds of dishes, and they are great with melted butter and honey for breakfast. If you have any leftover, *tingmos* are also delicious at room temperature, or they can be reheated like momos: a few minutes on each side in a dry frying pan gives them a bit of a crunch.

450 g (3 cups) self-raising flour, plus extra for dusting
1¼ teaspoons dried yeast
2 teaspoons olive oil, plus extra for drizzling
1¼ teaspoons caster (superfine) sugar – optional
2 eggs – optional

VEGETARIAN/VEGAN

Measure out the flour into a mixing bowl and add the yeast, olive oil and sugar (if using). Break in the eggs – or, if you're not using them, just add 100 ml (3½ fl oz) of warm water instead – and, while mixing with your dominant hand, gradually pour in 150 ml (5½ fl oz) of warm water with the other hand. Knead the dough in the bowl until it forms a smooth ball. Cover and set aside for 20 minutes, lightly kneading the dough in the bowl halfway through.

When the dough is ready, turn it out onto a work surface and knead with both hands until smooth, then roll into a ball. Divide the dough into three equal pieces, returning two of them to the bowl and keeping them covered.

Using a rolling pin, roll out the other piece on a flour-dusted work surface, turning it one way and then the other. You want it to be about 2 mm (1/16 inch) thick and 30–40 cm (12–16 inches) across.

Drizzle 1 teaspoon of olive oil over the centre of the dough and gently flap the edges into and then out of the centre several times, so that all parts of the dough make contact with the oil. Starting from one side, roll up the dough – you should end up with what looks like a large rolled-up pancake. Using a sharp knife, cut the roll of dough on the diagonal into 5 cm (2 inch) slices. This shape is shown on page 171.

The *tingmo* pieces can be placed directly into the steamer in this form, but if you would like to shape them decoratively, now is the time to do it. Use a chopstick to press firmly into the centre of each *tingmo*, fanning its layers up on either side, then gently twist the *tingmo* and pull the chopstick out, giving the *tingmo* a flower-like shape.

continued >

Repeat the rolling, cutting and shaping process with the two remaining pieces of dough.

If you are using a bamboo steamer, line each basket with baking paper. If you are using a metal steamer, drizzle a little oil onto your hands and lightly oil the inside of the steamer basket. Place the *tingmos* in the steamer baskets, leaving a 2.5 cm (1 inch) gap between each one. (If you are working with just one steamer basket, you will need to steam them in several batches.)

Pour about 1.5 litres (6 cups) of water into the base of your steamer (or a wok, if using bamboo steamer baskets) and bring to the boil; the *tingmos* can stand in the steamer while it heats up. When the water starts to boil, steam the *tingmos* for 10–12 minutes, then carefully remove and serve hot.

Balep (Tibetan Flatbread) *Makes 6*

Balep is very easy and quick to make. It has all the best qualities of yeasted breads – crispy on the outside, fluffy on the inside – without using yeast, or even an oven. With just flour, water and a stovetop, you can have fresh, aromatic bread in the space of half an hour. This version includes eggs and milk to make it extra-fluffy, but flour and water alone make for a delicious Vegan *balep* (see page 174).

Enjoy this versatile bread for breakfast with butter or dipped in warm honey, as the Tibetans do, or with soups, stews or stir-fries. I've also found that it tastes great with hummus or peanut butter, does a good job of mopping up salad dressings, and works really well with curries too.

500 g (3⅓ cups) self-raising flour, plus extra for dusting
2 eggs
100 ml (3½ fl oz) whole milk

VEGETARIAN

Put the flour into a mixing bowl. Break the eggs into the bowl, and mix through the flour using one hand, while you slowly add the milk, followed by 50 ml (2½ tablespoons) of warm water. As the dough comes together, knead it well for a few minutes until it forms a nice ball in the bowl, then cover and set aside for 10 minutes.

Take the dough out of the bowl and knead it for 2–3 minutes – just a bit more muscle! – before dividing it into six equal-sized pieces and rolling each one between your palms into a ball.

Sprinkle some flour onto your work surface and lightly flatten one of the dough balls with your hand. Use a rolling pin to roll it up and down, turning it over frequently and sprinkling your work surface with a little more flour if needed. Mould the flatbread by shuffling it between your hands – you're aiming for a circle about 12 cm (4½ inches) in diameter and with a thickness of about 1 cm (½ inch), perhaps a little thicker in the middle.

Put a frying pan over a medium heat – there's no need for any oil. When the pan is hot, carefully lay in your first flatbread. Let it cook for about 1 minute, or until it bubbles a little and starts to rise, then turn it over and leave to cook for another minute. (If you have a lid for your pan, you can put it on at this point to help the bread to steam and cook through.)

Turn down the heat to low and continue to cook the bread for a further 2–3 minutes, turning occasionally. When it's ready, the bread should be flecked with brown spots and will feel springy when you press it with your finger; if your finger leaves an impression, it needs a bit longer.

Repeat with the remaining five pieces of dough.

Vegan Balep
(Vegan Flatbread) *Makes 4*

This is the simplest of all foods: all you need is flour and water. Yeshi's family make this basic bread all the time, cooking it over the fire in a kind of wok. It's super-light and fluffy and can be enjoyed at any time of day – with something sweet, or as an accompaniment to savoury dishes. If you make more than you need, it can be kept in an airtight container for a day or so and reheated in the toaster (slice it in half first) on a very short setting.

400 g (14 oz) self-raising flour, plus extra for dusting

Put the flour into a mixing bowl and start pinching it with your dominant hand, while you slowly pour in 200 ml (7 fl oz) of warm water with your other hand. Add just enough water to make a dough – you don't want it to get too sticky. Work the dough with some muscle until you have a ball of firm dough in the bowl, then cover and set aside for 10 minutes.

Take the dough out of the bowl and divide it into four equal-sized pieces, rolling each one between your palms into a ball.

Sprinkle some flour onto your work surface and lightly flatten one of the dough balls with your hand. Use a rolling pin to roll it up and down, turning it over frequently and sprinkling your work surface with a little more flour if needed. Mould the flatbread by shuffling it between your hands – you're aiming for a circle about 12 cm (4½ inches) in diameter and with a thickness of about 1 cm (½ inch), perhaps a little thicker in the middle.

Put a frying pan over a high heat – there's no need for any oil. When the pan is very hot, reduce the heat to medium and carefully lay in your first flatbread. Let it cook for a couple of minutes while you roll out the other pieces of dough.

After 3–4 minutes the flatbread should rise slightly in the pan, with small bubbles forming. Turn it over and leave to cook on the second side for a further 2–3 minutes. If large bubbles form in the bread, press down gently on them using a wooden spoon or spatula – this will cause bubbles to rise elsewhere. Press these down as well.

When it's ready, the bread should be flecked with brown spots and will feel springy when you press it with your finger; if your finger leaves an impression, it needs a bit longer.

Repeat with the remaining flatbreads.

Our daughter, Choenyi, inside a monastery complex in eastern Tibet.

Giant Fluffy Sharing Bread *Serves 2–4*

This is a staple food in Yeshi's corner of Tibet. Yeshi learned to make it as a child of nine or ten, when he was already spending months of the year away from home out on the mountains. After a long day outdoors with the animals he'd go looking for a large, thick, flat stone to bake the bread on, placing it over the fire inside the family tent. It's surprisingly easy to replicate this traditional method on the stovetop at home, and Yeshi says that every time he does so, it takes him back to his days as a nomad. This bread might look massive, but it disappears fast – it's delicious with stir-fries, soups and stews.

500 g (3⅓ cups) self-raising flour, plus extra for dusting
¼ teaspoon salt
60 ml (¼ cup) whole milk
2 tablespoons plain yoghurt
1 tablespoon cooking oil – optional

VEGETARIAN

Put the flour into a mixing bowl and add the salt, milk and yoghurt. While mixing everything together with one hand, slowly pour in 150 ml (5 fl oz) of warm water with the other. As the dough comes together, keep kneading until you have a nice ball of dough in the bowl. Cover and set aside for 15–20 minutes.

Take the dough out of the bowl and knead it well, working the dough into a rough circle. Using a rolling pin, roll out the dough to a thickness of about 1 cm (½ inch) and 30 cm (12 inches) in diameter. If the dough starts to stick, sprinkle a little flour onto your work surface.

Place a large frying pan over a high heat and add the oil, if using, making sure it completely covers the base of the pan. (Oil isn't essential here, but it will help to make the bread slightly crisp on the outside, which is delicious.) When it is hot, gently lay the bread in the pan and let it cook for 1–2 minutes, or until the dough starts to bubble slightly. Turn the bread over and cover with a lid or foil, then leave to cook for 4–5 minutes. Turn the bread back over, reduce the heat to low and cover again, then leave to cook for a final 4–5 minutes. When it's done, it should spring back when you press it with your finger; if your finger leaves an impression, it needs a little longer.

Bhatsa Marku (Tibetan Gnocchi with Meat) *Serves 4–6*

Yeshi calls this sort of dish 'nomad food': wholesome and filling, it's everything the nomad needs, and is often made on the first day at a new camp. Every month or so, relatives from his village come to help family members move the tent and animals to the next grazing spot, and at the end of a very hard day's work, sometimes in dire weather, someone will cook this up and all will be well.

- 450 g (3 cups) plain wholemeal flour, plus extra for dusting
- Salt
- 500 g (1 lb 2 oz) lean beef steak, diced
- 300 g (10½ oz) chestnut mushrooms, wiped clean and roughly chopped
- 100 g (3½ oz) butter
- 2 spring onions (scallions), washed and thinly sliced, including green tips
- 70 g (1½ cups) baby spinach leaves – optional

Measure out the flour into a mixing bowl. Put ½ teaspoon of salt into a measuring jug with 175 ml (⅔ cup) of cold water and stir until the salt has fully dissolved. Slowly start pouring the water into the flour, while gently kneading the mixture in the bowl with your dominant hand. You are aiming for a firm dough, so add just enough water to bring the dough together – you may not need it all. Remember that the dough should tend towards hard rather than the soft. Once you have a nice ball of dough, cover and set aside for 10–15 minutes. When it is ready, the dough will be firm to the touch.

Put the beef into a heavy-based wok or saucepan over a medium heat and add a teaspoon of salt (no oil is needed, as the meat will cook in its own juices). Stir well, then cover and cook for about 20–25 minutes, until the meat is cooked through. (You may need to turn off the heat if it turns out that rolling and cutting the dough takes you longer than this, so you don't overcook the meat.)

Meanwhile, take the dough out of the bowl and divide into two balls. Using a rolling pin, roll out each one into a circle about 1 cm (¾ inch) thick, then cut each circle in half and slice the semicircles into thin strips, so they look a bit like French fries. Sprinkle a little flour over the dough pieces and dance them about in the flour so that it catches. Line up the dough pieces and cut them again to make small squares, then return to the mixing bowl and jig them about a bit to ensure that each piece is separated from the next.

Bring a large saucepan of water to the boil. Tip in the dough pieces, stir and bring back to the boil – this will take about 4–5 minutes. Give them another stir, then drain in a colander, reserving the cooking water.

Meanwhile, add the mushrooms to the wok and stir over a high heat for a couple of minutes. Melt the butter in a small saucepan until all traces of the white milk solids that will bubble to the surface have sunk to the bottom of the pan.

continued >

Spoon the melted butter over the meat and mushrooms, then add the dough pieces and the spring onion. Turn the heat right down and stir until everything is heated through.

Meanwhile, if you want to make a simple side soup, pour about half of the reserved cooking water back into the saucepan and add ½ teaspoon of salt. Bring to the boil, then add the spinach and return to the boil.

Spoon the gnocchi into bowls and serve the soup separately alongside.

Yeshi says '*Bhatsa marku* is a complete meal in itself, but Tibetans hate to throw away a potful of boiled water and say that soups aid digestion. Don't expect a taste explosion – the soup serves the function of a warm drink here.'

Bhatsa Marku
(Tibetan Gnocchi with Mushrooms) *Serves 4*

Bhatsa marku is not always meaty. Nomads will take what they can get, and during summertime the meadows are filled with wild mushrooms – their fibrous texture and full-bodied taste make them a really delicious alternative. Yeshi is great at identifying what mushrooms can and cannot be consumed. We've suggested oyster mushrooms for this recipe, but do go for something wilder if you can come by it safely.

450 g (3 cups) plain wholemeal flour
Salt
100 g (3½ oz) butter
300 g (10½ oz) oyster mushrooms
2 spring onions (scallions), washed and thinly sliced, including green tips
Parmesan or feta cheese
Thinly sliced cucumber – optional

VEGETARIAN

To make the *bhatsa marku* dough, follow the instructions on page 178. Once you have a nice ball of dough, cover and set aside for 10–15 minutes. When it is ready, the dough will be firm to the touch.

Take the dough out of the bowl and divide into two balls. Using a rolling pin, roll out each one into a circle about 1 cm (¾ inch) thick, then cut each circle in half and slice the semicircles into thin strips, so they look a bit like French fries. Sprinkle a little flour over the dough pieces and dance them about in the flour so that it catches. Line up the dough pieces and cut them again to make small squares, then return to the mixing bowl and jig them about a bit to ensure that each piece is separated from the next.

Bring a large saucepan of water to the boil. Tip in the dough pieces, stir and bring back to the boil – this will take about 4–5 minutes. Give them another stir, then drain in a colander.

Meanwhile, melt the butter in a small saucepan until all traces of the white milk solids that will bubble to the surface have sunk to the bottom of the pan. Clean the mushrooms and tear them into long thin strips by hand. Place a heavy-based frying pan over a high heat, and when it's hot, add a couple of spoonfuls of the melted butter, followed by the mushrooms and ½ teaspoon of salt. Stir well, then leave for a few minutes until cooked. Add the spring onions to the pan and let them sizzle for a minute.

When the gnocchi are ready, stir them through the mushrooms. Turn off the heat and grate in a generous amount of parmesan or feta cheese. Mix everything together and serve in bowls, garnishing with cucumber, if using. You can drizzle a little more melted butter into each bowl if you fancy a more buttery finish.

Yeshi says 'Feel free to add peppers (capsicums) or other veg to the mushroom mix, and don't drain away the gnocchi cooking water – add some spinach and feta or other sharp cheese to it, maybe a few tomatoes as well, to make a lovely, light side soup that really complements the *bhatsa marku*.'

Sha Balep
(Tibetan Pasties) *Makes 10*

Sha balep (literally, 'meat breads') are widely and wildly loved by Tibetans. Vegans, do not look away now! You can make a vegan version using the tofu, Chinese cabbage and mushroom filling on page 161. Potatoes are another good fit, but have a go with any veggies you enjoy and have to hand.

There's a saying in Tibetan, 'If you mess up, I'll give you a *sha balep*', which means that if you step out of line, you'll get a slap. The Tibetan rapper Shapaley has produced a wonderful ode to *sha balep* that references this expression. It's a very catchy tune to listen to – YouTube is your friend – while you make these delicious pasties.

In central Tibet many people eat them for breakfast, but they are more typically served for lunch or dinner, usually with a soup side. We like to serve them with Yeshi's super salsa (see page 200): the trick is to take a bite out of the *sha balep* and then spoon in some of the fresh-tasting salsa for a wonderfully refreshing contrast.

Cooking oil, for deep-frying

For the dough

450 g (3 cups) self-raising flour, plus extra for dusting

1 tablespoon cooking oil

For the filling

500 g (1 lb 2 oz) minced (ground) beef, ideally 15–20% fat content

1 teaspoon fine sea salt

2 tablespoons cooking oil

½ teaspoon crushed Sichuan peppercorns (*yerma*)

½ teaspoon ground coriander

1 small red onion, finely chopped

1 large garlic clove, finely chopped

50 g (1¾ oz) spinach, washed and finely chopped

For the dough, place the flour and oil in a mixing bowl. Using your dominant hand, start pinching together the oil and the flour, while slowly pouring in 200 ml (7 fl oz) of warm water with the other. Mix and then knead, adding just enough water to make a dough. As the dough comes together, keep kneading until you have a nice ball of dough in the bowl. Cover and set aside for 15 minutes.

Meanwhile, for the filling, put the beef, salt and 1 tablespoon of the oil into a bowl and mix together, either with a fork or by hand. Add the Sichuan pepper and coriander and stir well, followed by the onion, garlic and spinach. Mix thoroughly. Heat the other tablespoon of oil in a frying pan, and when it's hot, stir the meat mixture through it for 4–5 minutes until the beef browns. Set aside and allow to cool.

Sprinkle a little flour onto your work surface. Take the dough out of the bowl and loosely roll it into a sausage shape. Divide it evenly into eight pieces, then roll each piece between your palms into a ball.

Working with one ball of dough at a time, lightly flatten it with your hands and then roll it out with a rolling pin, pushing and pulling the dough up and down quickly and firmly. Use your other hand to hold the dough and turn it little by little as you go. You are aiming for a circle about 10–12 cm (4–4½ inches) in diameter, with the middle a bit thicker than the edges.

Spoon a generous amount (about 2–3 tablespoons) of the cooled filling into the centre, then gently fold one side of the circle over the filling to meet the other side.

continued >

Dolkar, Yeshi's auntie, playing with the kids.

> Sha Balep *continued*

Starting in the middle, use your fingertips to press the edges together into the board, trying not to trap any pockets of air inside. Just before you completely seal the pasty, gently press down on it to release any trapped air and then close. Lift the joined edge up bit by bit, pressing it back into the pasty to seal it again. When you are confident it is well sealed, you can crimp the edge with as much flair as you dare – and if you are not satisfied with the design, you can always use a fork. Set aside while you make the rest of the pasties.

When you're ready to cook your *sha balep*, pour a 7.5 cm (3 inch) depth of cooking oil into a large, stable wok and place over a high heat. (Alternatively, you could use a frying pan to shallow-fry the *sha balep*, turning them over once halfway through, in which case you will only need a 2 cm (¾ inch) depth of oil.) Check the temperature of the oil by tossing in a tiny scrap of dough: if it bubbles vigorously and rises quickly to the surface, you are good to go. Turn the heat down to low and slide in as many *sha balep* as will fit into the pan – probably no more than four at a time. Once they are in the oil, you can use tongs to move them around and turn them over from time to time, so they cook evenly.

Let the *sha balep* cook for 4–5 minutes, or until they are golden brown, then drain on paper towel before serving.

Yeshi says 'If you make your *sha balep* nice and plump, you shouldn't end up with any leftover filling, but if you do it can be boiled for a few minutes in some water to make a nice side soup – add a little coriander (cilantro) for greenery and extra flavour. If by any chance you have any dough left over, roll it out flat and use it to make some *Numtak balep* (fried breakfast bread, see page 42) or *Balep* (Tibetan flatbread, see page 173).'

Sauces and Dips

Tibetan food is not usually spicy, unless you slap on the hot chilli. Spices do feature in some dishes, but the ultimate level of heat tends to be determined by how much *sepen* (hot chilli dip) you add to them. A super-fiery blend of dried chilli, garlic, ginger and Sichuan peppercorns (*yerma*), *sepen* has a wonderfully tongue-numbing effect, and is a singular Tibetan culinary experience. In this chapter, we've also included other dips that are the perfect pairing for momos (Tibetan dumplings), *sha balep* (Tibetan pasties), and more.

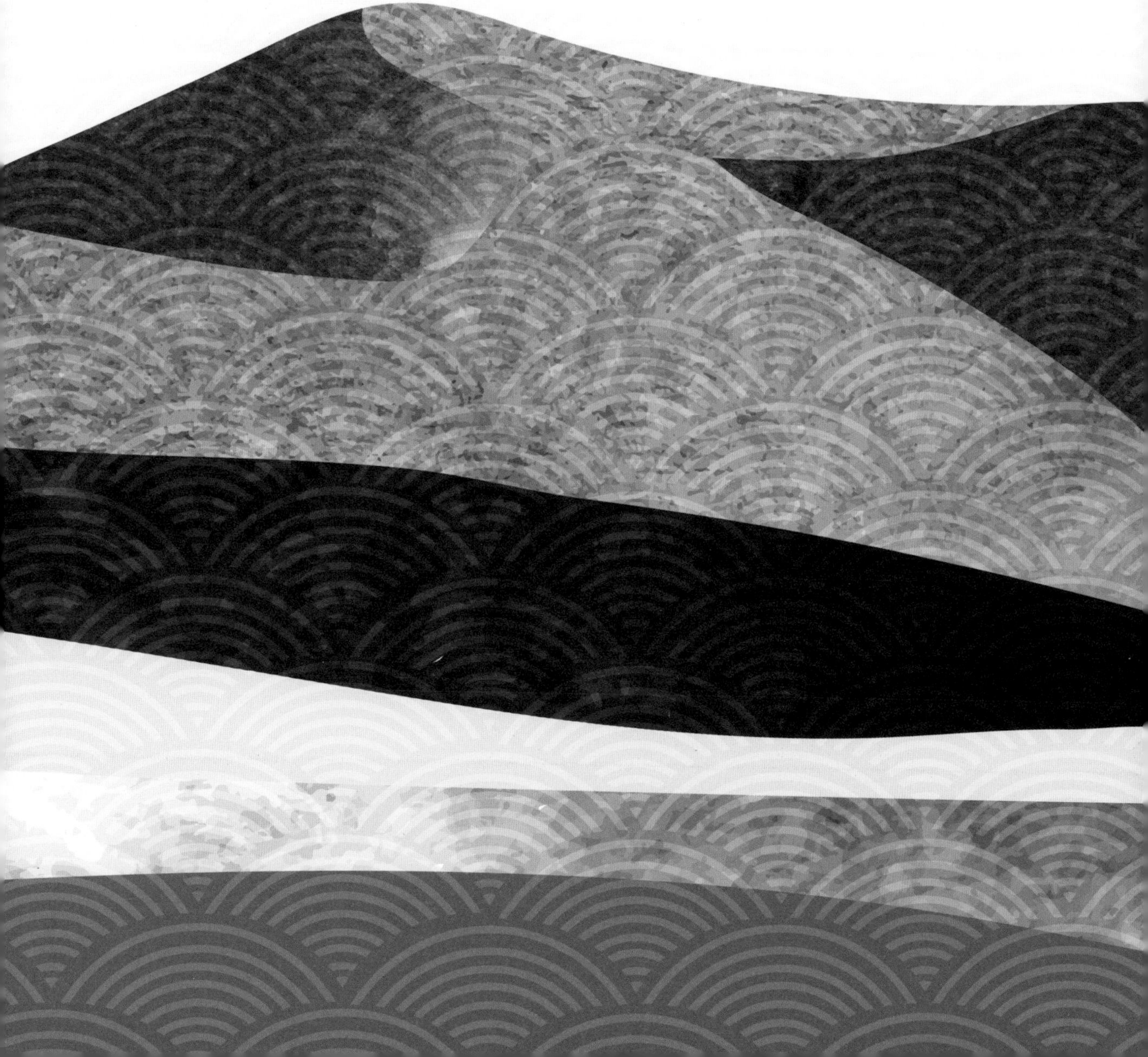

When I make a nice shepherd's pie, only to watch Yeshi pile on the *sepen*, I have to remind myself that he's not doing it because the food tastes bland – this is just the way Tibetan people eat.

Sepen, in one form or another, is sprinkled on just about everything, including at breakfast. This hot chilli condiment is a permanent fixture on every Tibetan table, and every family and region has their own special recipe, just as we do at Taste Tibet. Most Tibetan dishes, and especially soups, stews and noodles, rely on it to bring out their full flavour. You can bring heat to your dishes in other ways, of course, but we think that once you've mastered the art of making your own *sepen* you will be reluctant to accept any substitutes!

We are also excited to introduce you to the joys of chilli with cheese, chilli with yoghurt, chilli with walnuts – and so on. Yeshi loves experimenting with new combinations and making sure that a sauce or dip is always close to hand, whatever else he's dishing up.

Finally, not every sauce must be spicy, so you'll find dips in this chapter that don't contain any chilli at all. Momos love a condiment or two, and we've included the recipe for the simple sauce we always serve with ours at the Taste Tibet restaurant and stall. We've also indicated where chilli is optional in a recipe so you can choose to omit it if you like, or if the kids would rather have milder flavours.

Taste Tibet Sepen
(Hot Chilli Dip) *Makes about 100 g (3½ oz)*

This unique and fiery dip can be used as the basis of many different chilli sauces, and is the perfect accompaniment to most Tibetan dishes. We hope that it will become your go-to condiment. The principal ingredient is chilli, but as it is slow-cooked with Sichuan pepper and other spices, there is a gentle release of heat in the mouth and it's a complex and intriguing set of flavours, rather than a sudden chilli hit.

The good news is that *sepen* is the gift that keeps on giving: because it's a fairly dry mix you can store it in the fridge for many months, taking a bit out at a time, and maybe adding a little light soy sauce or Chinkiang black vinegar, depending on what you are enjoying it with and how you fancy it on the day.

3 large garlic cloves
6 cm (2½ inch) piece of ginger, washed but not peeled, roughly chopped
1 teaspoon salt
½ teaspoon Sichuan peppercorns (*yerma*)
1 teaspoon coriander seeds (or ½ teaspoon ground coriander)
½ teaspoon cumin seeds
170 ml (⅔ cup) cooking oil
50 g (1¾ oz) hot chilli flakes
1 tablespoon sesame oil

VEGAN

In a blender or small food processor, blend together the garlic, ginger, salt, Sichuan peppercorns, coriander and cumin seeds to a rough paste, adding a tablespoon of water to help everything move a bit more easily. (If you don't have a blender, you can chop or grind everything by hand – just make sure that everything is as finely chopped or crushed as you can get it.)

Put 1 tablespoon of oil into a frying pan over a medium heat. When it is hot, add the blended ingredients to the pan and cook for 4–5 minutes, stirring constantly to make sure nothing burns. You can add a drop of water if necessary, but definitely don't add too much. When you have a nice, dry paste, add the chilli and mix everything through, then turn off the heat and set aside to let the flavours mellow a little in the pan.

Meanwhile, in a saucepan, heat 150 ml (5½ fl oz) of oil until it is very hot (you can test it by dropping in a tiny amount of your chilli mix – if it's hot enough, you should get a good sizzle). Put the frying pan back over a low heat and carefully pour the hot oil into the pan – it should really sing as it hits the chilli. Stir briskly for 4–5 minutes. Keep a very close eye on it, and take it off the heat immediately if it looks like it's starting to burn. As soon as the chilli darkens to a rich reddish-brown, it is ready.

Quickly decant the *sepen* into a serving bowl and keep stirring for a further minute, then add the sesame oil and stir it through. Allow it to cool a little before serving.

Yeshi says 'A jam jar is a good vessel to store *sepen* in, but whatever you use, make sure the *sepen* is cool before you put it away. It will keep in the fridge for months, but can disappear surprisingly fast once addiction takes hold … '

Tomato Sepen (Tomato and Chilli Dip) *Serves 2–4*

This isn't a very spicy dip, but it bursts with the flavours of garlic and ginger, and has a real zing to it. It's the perfect mate for a freshly cooked momo. If you want extra heat you can always add more chilli powder, or you might like to serve something more fiery alongside – Taste Tibet *sepen* (see page 190) is a great option here. Of course, the chilli can be omitted altogether if you are looking for a delicious companion for your momos that isn't going to overpower them. Either way, this dip is highly moreish.

1 tablespoon cooking oil
2 cm (¾ inch) piece of ginger, washed but not peeled, finely chopped
2 large garlic cloves, finely chopped
1 red onion, finely diced
¼ teaspoon crushed Sichuan peppercorns (*yerma*) or black pepper
3 tomatoes, finely chopped
½ teaspoon chilli powder
½ teaspoon salt
Juice of ½ lemon

VEGAN

In a frying pan, heat the oil over a high heat. When it's hot, add the ginger, garlic and onion and cook, stirring well, until browned. Add the Sichuan or black pepper, followed by the tomatoes, and keep cooking and stirring for 2–3 minutes.

Now add the chilli powder and salt, lower the heat to medium and keep stirring, adding a little water each time anything starts to stick. You are aiming to reduce everything to a paste, and this will take about 8–10 minutes.

To speed the process up, or if you are after a very smooth consistency, you can put everything into a blender after it has finished cooking. Otherwise, just mash the paste in the pan with a spoon or hand-held masher for a more rustic finish.

When it's ready, decant into a bowl and squeeze in the lemon juice just before serving. Any leftovers will keep for 2–3 days in the fridge.

Taste Tibet Momo Sauce *Serves 4*

When Yeshi was little his father used to bring home packets of something that, to Yeshi's nomadic eye at least, resembled dried blood. Later he learned that this thick, hard, black stuff was actually soy sauce, which at the time travelled from China in solid form. It isn't sold in this way anymore, but then the roads are better now, so the journey is less bumpy!

Yeshi's dad would add water to this concentrated soy brick, producing a sauce as thick or thin as he liked. Soy sauce can be pretty potent, but watered down you have a condiment that allows the natural flavours of a dish to shine, with just a hint of saltiness and umami. You can always add some Taste Tibet *sepen* (see page 190) to the sauce if you want the best of both worlds.

2 tablespoons light soy sauce
1 teaspoon Chinkiang black vinegar
Sliced chives, to serve

VEGAN

Measure out the soy sauce and vinegar into a bowl, then stir in 2½ tablespoons of cold water – this dilutes the sauce so it doesn't taste too strong. Sprinkle with the chives, just to provide a bit of colour and bite.

Aubergine and Chilli Dip *Serves 4*

This is Yeshi's invention made from two of his great loves – think of it as a Tibetan take on baba ganoush, but spicier. It can be enjoyed warm or fridge-cold, with *Balep* (Tibetan flatbread, see page 173), Giant fluffy sharing bread (see page 177) or just toast.

- 1–2 fresh green chillies
- 3 baby aubergines (eggplants), about 175 g (6 oz) in total, or the same weight of regular aubergines
- 1 tablespoon cooking oil
- 2–3 large garlic cloves, thinly sliced
- 2.5 cm (1 inch) piece of ginger, washed but not peeled, thinly sliced
- ½ teaspoon salt
- ¼ teaspoon cumin seeds
- Juice of ½ lime
- 1–2 teaspoons extra virgin olive oil

VEGAN

If you use a gas stove, place the chillies directly onto a high flame, where they will singe. Using tongs, turn them after about a minute. Once they start to blacken, remove them from the gas. (If you have an electric stove, just omit this step – it adds flavour to the chillies but isn't a deal-breaker.)

Thinly slice the chillies, removing or keeping the seeds as you prefer. Cut the aubergines into 2.5 cm (1 inch) dice.

Put the cooking oil into a frying pan over a low heat. When it's hot, add the chillies and cook, stirring occasionally, for 1–2 minutes. Add the aubergines to the pan, along with the garlic, ginger, salt and cumin seeds. Stir well, then leave to cook for 10–12 minutes, stirring occasionally.

Now transfer the contents of the frying pan to a blender, add 100 ml (3½ fl oz) of boiling water and whizz until smooth.

Decant into a bowl, then squeeze over the lime juice and drizzle with the olive oil.

Cheesy Chilli Dip *Serves 4*

Tibetans were among the first Asians to make use of dairy products, and their cheeses are quite unique. There is some soft curd, made from buttermilk, which resembles cottage cheese, but most Tibetan cheeses are hard. The hardest type is made using solidified yoghurt, and other hard cheeses are made using the curds produced by boiling buttermilk. However, as none of them are made commercially, they are hard to come by outside the region.

Cheese is a staple of the Tibetan diet, and Tibetans love to make a variety of cheesy chilli dips – this is the simplest of all cheesy chillies. If you like the idea of getting more adventurous, add some vegetables: potatoes, green beans or mushrooms are a good place to start. If you eat meat, strips of beef or pork would work well. However you make it, cheesy chilli is great with chips, baked potato or flatbread, depending on your mood, need or whim.

1 tablespoon cooking oil
¼ teaspoon cumin seeds
1 fresh green chilli, finely chopped, including seeds
2 large garlic cloves, finely chopped
½ red onion, finely chopped
½ teaspoon salt
150 g (5½ oz) brie or similar cheese

VEGETARIAN

In a small frying pan, heat the oil over a medium heat. When it's hot, add the cumin seeds and let them sizzle for abut 30 seconds. Next, add the chilli and garlic and stir-fry until golden brown. Add the onion, turn the heat down to low and stir everything well for a minute or two, or until the garlic and onion have softened, then pour in 100 ml (3½ fl oz) of water. Now add the salt.

Cut the cheese into 1–2 cm (½–¾ inch) slices and add to the pan, stirring it in gently so it melts – you may need to turn the heat up a little to encourage it. When all the cheese has melted, transfer the dip to a serving bowl.

Walnut and Chilli Dip *Serves 4*

In eastern Tibet there is no shortage of walnut trees. They grow all over the mountains and valleys, and some of them are more than a thousand years old. Yeshi's village is filled with them. Years ago we brought back some walnuts from Tibet and planted a tree near our home in East Oxford. Yeshi loves to throw together snacks and dips made from these rich, earthy nuts, and our hope is that, in a few years' time, we will be able to pick Tibetan walnuts from our very own tree.

Enjoy this tasty dip warm or cold with *Balep* (Tibetan flatbread, see page 173) or *Tsampa* (roasted barley flour, see page 53). This dip also goes well with crunchy veg – take your pick from chicory (witlof) leaves, carrots, cucumber and so on.

1 dried red chilli, seeds removed
100 g (3½ oz) walnuts
¼ teaspoon ground cumin
¼ teaspoon ground coriander
¼ teaspoon salt
Juice of 1 lime
1 tablespoon extra virgin olive oil

VEGAN

Pictured on page 152.

Put the dried red chilli into a small saucepan over a medium-high heat and toast in the dry pan for 2–3 minutes or until it turns a shade darker, then add the walnuts, cumin and coriander. Toast the walnuts and spices for another 2–3 minutes, jiggling everything around in the pan to make sure nothing burns.

Now transfer to a blender and add the salt and 100 ml (3½ fl oz) of boiling water. Blend until smooth, then decant into a bowl. Stir in the lime juice and drizzle with the olive oil.

Yeshi's Super Salsa *Serves 2–4*

This really refreshing sauce (in the white bowl in the photo) makes a great partner for momos – and especially for anything deep-fried, as it is sharp and super-light. It can also be used as a salad dressing. Freshness is key here. Make sure that all your raw ingredients are in good condition, and use it fast! It will only keep for a day in the fridge.

- 40 g (1½ oz) coriander (cilantro), about half a large bunch – the freshest you can find
- 2 spring onions (scallions)
- 2 tomatoes
- Juice of 2 limes
- ½ teaspoon salt
- ½ teaspoon hot chilli powder

Chop the coriander as finely as you can, stems and all. Wash and finely chop the spring onions, green tips included, and the tomatoes too. (A blender makes quick work of all this chopping, if you have one.)

Tip the coriander, spring onions and tomatoes into a bowl, then squeeze in the lime juice. Add the salt and chilli powder and mix everything together very well, then serve.

VEGAN

Sho Sepen (Chilli with Yoghurt) *Serves 2–4*

For Yeshi's family, this is a go-to recipe. Sometimes there might be no meat or vegetables close at hand, but yoghurt and chilli are almost always available, and they make a great combination. This is a wondrous quick fix if eaten together with *Tsampa* (roasted barley flour, see page 53), *Tingmo* (steamed bread, see page 169) or *Balep* (Tibetan flatbread, see page 173). *Sho sepen* (in the pink bowl in the photo) is best enjoyed warm, but it's also delicious chilled: refrigerate any leftovers and enjoy with some crunchy veg when you come back for round two.

- 150 g (5½ oz) plain yoghurt
- 1 tablespoon olive oil
- ¼ teaspoon salt
- ¼ teaspoon cumin seeds
- ½ teaspoon hot chilli flakes
- Sprig of coriander (cilantro), to garnish – optional

Place the yoghurt in a bowl.

Heat the oil in a small frying pan over a medium heat and add the salt, cumin seeds and chillies. As soon as the chilli starts to brown, drizzle the mixture over the yoghurt, garnish with a sprig of coriander, if using, and serve.

VEGETARIAN

Street Food Favourites

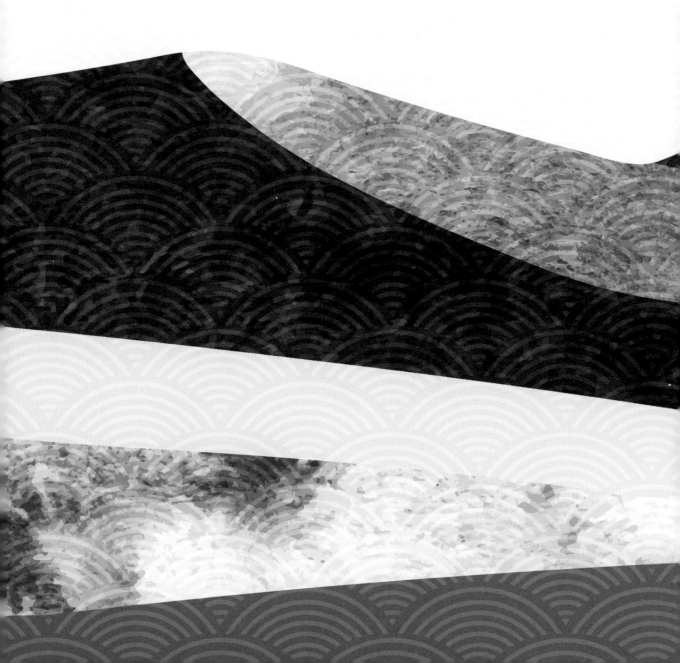

This chapter is especially for all the people who have supported Taste Tibet over the years. Here, at last, we reveal the secrets behind your favourite Himalayan dishes, including Yeshi's legendary dal and our much-loved chicken curry, the festivalgoer's cure-all, and now – officially – the Taste Tibet Famous Chicken Curry.

These dishes came into being a few months into the life of Taste Tibet. When we first started our stall in 2014, selling only momos, Yeshi was a one-man band. We had a four-month-old and a two-year-old in the house, and my hands were too full for me to be any help in the kitchen. Poor Yeshi would stay up late into the night making dough and wrapping momos.

After word of his dumplings got out and the momo-making hours became even more punishing in order to meet demand, we briefly took them off the menu altogether. During this time, Yeshi dished up a range of curries to replace them. We called these Himalayan curries, as they boasted the tastes and aromas of the region as a whole: a little bit of India, a little bit of Nepal, but unmistakably Tibetan by twists and turns.

Tibetan people have been leaving their homeland for India and Nepal for over sixty years now. Their spiritual leader, His Holiness the XIV Dalai Lama, fled Lhasa for India when the Chinese took control of Tibet in 1959, and there has been a steady exodus ever since. Nobody knows how many Tibetans are now living outside of Tibet – but, like Yeshi, the majority of those who reach the West spend time in India or Nepal first.

For many years, Yeshi lived in India, where he was inspired by all kinds of new ingredients and flavours. He tells me that his family wouldn't recognise many of the dishes in this chapter, as they are his own creations, influenced by his years of travel, life and gastronomic experiences in other parts of the Himalayas. Walk into any Tibetan restaurant outside Tibet and you'll encounter the same story. Each chef has made a unique journey out of Tibet, picking up new recipes and ideas along the way.

Do not miss these delicious dishes! They are a wonderful fusion of flavours, and the curry dishes are light and nutritious. Try to cook at least a couple of them at a time if you can – any leftovers will taste even better the following day.

Yeshi's Dal *Serves 4–6*

Some dals are hugely labour intensive and take an age to make. This one is a Taste Tibet crowd favourite, and it's incredibly easy to reproduce at home. In India, where Yeshi learned to cook this dish, everybody has their favourite dal, and mung dal is his. It is light, cooks fast and is easy to digest. It also has many health benefits. According to Ayurvedic medicine, it has a calming and grounding effect on both mind and body. From a Western perspective, it is rich in vitamin C, and if cooked with basmati rice provides a meal that is complete in terms of protein and essential amino acids.

You should be able to find mung dal in any good Indian corner shop or larger supermarket. Just make sure you get yellow split mung beans and not the whole beans – these have a green skin and take a lot longer to cook. If you can't find mung dal, yellow split peas or even red lentils make a great dal too. The same instructions apply, but note that the cooking time will be a little longer for yellow split peas.

300 g (1⅓ cups) mung dal
2 tablespoons cooking oil
1 teaspoon cumin seeds
2 large garlic cloves, thinly sliced
½ red onion, thinly sliced
2 tomatoes, diced
½ teaspoon turmeric
2 tablespoons salt
½ teaspoon Bassar curry masala (or hot chilli powder)
70 g (1½ cups) baby spinach leaves

VEGAN

Put the mung dal into a mixing bowl and wash it thoroughly, then drain well.

Heat the oil in a large saucepan over a medium-high heat and add the cumin seeds. When they start popping, add the garlic and stir for about a minute, then throw in the onion and cook for a further minute. Stir in the tomatoes, turmeric, salt and curry masala and keep cooking until the onions and tomatoes have softened, about 3–4 minutes.

Now add the dal to the pan, using a little boiling water to rinse out any grains stuck inside the bowl. Stir the dal through the mixture for 3–4 minutes, then pour in 1 litre (4 cups) of boiling water and turn the heat down to medium. Cover and cook for 30–35 minutes, stirring occasionally.

When the dal is cooked, add the baby spinach and stir it through. If you like your dal runny, you might like to add some more boiling water at this point too – about 200 ml (7 fl oz) should do it. When the spinach has wilted, ladle the dal into a serving bowl.

Spinach and Chickpea Curry

Serves 4

Yeshi learned to cook this dish in India, and it has become Taste Tibet's most popular vegan curry. It is easy to make, light on the stomach and seriously wholesome. Serve it with Yeshi's dal (see page 206) and basmati rice, as we do at our festival stall.

- 200 g (1 cup) dried chickpeas or 2 x 400 g (14 oz) tins of chickpeas
- 2 tablespoons cooking oil
- 2 large garlic cloves, finely chopped
- 6 cm (2½ inch) piece of ginger, washed but not peeled, finely chopped
- 1 red onion, finely chopped
- 2 tomatoes, diced
- ½ teaspoon turmeric
- 2 teaspoons Madras curry powder
- 1 teaspoon salt
- 1 x 400 ml (14 fl oz) tin of coconut milk
- 200 g (7 oz) baby spinach leaves, including stems
- 100 g (3½ oz) frozen spinach – optional
- Coriander (cilantro) sprigs, to garnish

VEGAN

If you're using dried chickpeas – and we recommend it – soak them in 800 ml (28 fl oz) of water overnight, or from morning to evening at least. Boil the soaked chickpeas for about 1½ hours in their soaking water; they need to cook in 1 litre (4 cups) of water, so top it up with more water to this level. If you're using tinned chickpeas, drain off all the liquid and rinse them well.

Place a large saucepan over a high heat and add the oil. When it is hot, add the garlic and ginger and cook, stirring, for a couple of minutes, or until lightly golden. Add the onion and cook until golden brown, then stir in the tomatoes, turmeric, curry powder and salt. Keep cooking until the tomatoes have completely softened, about 3–4 minutes, then pour in the coconut milk and stir it through.

Turn the heat down to low-medium and leave to simmer for 25–30 minutes, stirring frequently. You are aiming to reduce this sauce to a very soft paste, so you don't want any bite left in the onions or garlic, but be careful not to let anything stick or burn.

Meanwhile, roughly chop the spinach into 2.5–5 cm (1–2 inch) pieces. Wash it thoroughly in cold water, then set aside in a bowl of fresh cold water.

When the sauce is ready, add the chickpeas and the frozen spinach, if using. Stir everything together for 4–5 minutes, then lift the fresh spinach out of the water and into the pan (this way you leave behind any gritty residue at the bottom of the bowl). Stir well until the spinach has wilted. If you'd like the curry to be a bit runnier, you can add about 100 ml (3½ fl oz) of boiling water to the pan, but remember that the spinach will radically reduce, so give it a chance to come together and thicken first.

Garnish the curry with coriander sprigs and serve.

Taste Tibet Famous Chicken Curry *Serves 4–6*

If you take momos out of the equation, then Taste Tibet's famous chicken curry is definitely our biggest seller. Its name did not come about without the wild appreciation for all the joy it provides to starving festivalgoers across the land and to the fine, curry-loving people of Oxford. So here we are – the great reveal. We've kept nothing back, and we hope you'll enjoy making it as much as we enjoy serving it. For the full Taste Tibet experience, pair it with basmati rice or *Balep* (Tibetan flatbread, see page 173) and Yeshi's dal (see page 206).

2 tablespoons cooking oil
2 large garlic cloves, thinly sliced
2.5 cm (1 inch) piece of ginger, washed but not peeled, thinly sliced
1 small red onion, thinly sliced
2 large tomatoes, thinly sliced
¼ teaspoon turmeric
1 teaspoon Bassar curry masala (or hot chilli powder)
1½ teaspoons Madras curry powder
2 tablespoons coconut milk powder
6–8 fresh curry leaves, or 10–12 dried
1 x 400 ml (14 fl oz) tin of coconut milk
600 g (1 lb 5 oz) chicken breast fillets, cut into bite-sized pieces
1 teaspoon salt
Chopped coriander (cilantro), to garnish – optional

Place a heavy-bottomed saucepan over a medium-high heat and add the oil. When it's hot, add the garlic and ginger and let it brown for a couple of minutes, then add the onion and stir for a further 2 minutes. Now add the tomatoes, turmeric, curry masala and curry powder. Mix together and cook for 10–15 minutes, turning the heat down a little and adding about 50 ml (2½ tablespoons) of water if anything starts to catch, then add the coconut milk powder, curry leaves and coconut milk and mix thoroughly. Take your time here: you are making a curry paste, and it needs to be cooked through completely before you can add the chicken.

Now add the chicken and salt. Turn the heat back up to high, stir the chicken through the sauce and cook for 8–10 minutes, adding a little boiling water – but only a little – if anything sticks. The pan should be quite dry to begin with, before the juices from the chicken start to be released, so wait a while before adding any water.

After the chicken has been in for 8 minutes, check to make sure it is fully cooked. To do this, take a piece out and cut it through the middle – it should be white all the way through. If the sauce looks too thick, add a little more boiling water and stir briskly for 2 minutes. Garnish with coriander, if you like, then serve.

Sesame Chicken *Serves 4*

Yeshi came up with this one here in the UK, and it has become a real crowd favourite at our restaurant and food stall. The name has stuck as it has a lovely ring to it, but the sesame element is in fact a bit incidental. There's very little heat to this dish – the kids love it. Serve with basmati rice and Yeshi's dal (see page 206).

600 g (1 lb 5 oz) chicken breast fillets
3 tablespoons cornflour (cornstarch)
600 ml (21 fl oz) cooking oil
1 large garlic clove, thinly sliced
2–3 fresh green chillies, thinly sliced on the diagonal
1 small red onion, thinly sliced
1 green pepper (capsicum), diced
1 red pepper (capsicum), diced
1 tomato, diced
1 teaspoon sesame oil
Pinch of salt
Coriander (cilantro) sprigs, to garnish – optional

For the marinade

2–3 large garlic cloves, finely chopped
6 cm (2½ inch) piece of ginger, washed but not peeled, finely chopped
1 teaspoon salt
½ teaspoon cumin seeds
1 teaspoon Bassar curry masala (or hot chilli powder)
2 teaspoons dark soy sauce
1 teaspoon sesame oil

Combine the marinade ingredients in a bowl. Cut the chicken breast fillets on the diagonal to make bite-sized strips. Add the chicken to the marinade and mix well using a fork or your hands, then cover and leave in the fridge for 1 hour.

Take the marinated chicken out of the fridge. Tip the cornflour into the bowl and use your hands to massage it through the chicken so that it is mixed through completely.

Pour the oil into a large wok and place over a high heat. To check if the oil is hot enough, toss in just a little bit of chicken first: if it bubbles furiously, you're good to go. Using a slotted spoon, lift the chicken out of the bowl and carefully lower it into the hot oil. Stir gently, then let it cook for 7–8 minutes or until golden brown and cooked through, then remove and set aside.

You now need to carefully pour off all but 2 tablespoons of oil from the wok. (We pour ours into a heatproof jug and leave it to cool, then it can be strained and re-used.)

Return the wok, with its remaining 2 tablespoons of oil, to a medium heat. Add the garlic and chillies and stir-fry for about a minute, then add the onion and cook for a further 2 minutes – the onion won't look cooked at this point, but this is fine as it only needs to be lightly stir-fried. Add the green and red peppers and stir-fry for just a few minutes, then return the chicken to the wok. Stir everything together for 3–4 minutes.

Just before you serve up, add the tomato to the wok and mix it in well, then stir in the sesame oil and salt. Garnish with coriander, if you like, but the dish is plenty colourful without.

Potato and Pea Curry *Serves 4*

Spicy potatoes are a favourite at Tibetan picnics and parties. They can be served hot or cold, as a main or a side. There are many variations, and here Yeshi has added peas and increased the amount of sauce to make more of a curry. This is the version we serve at our Taste Tibet festival stall. It is made with fresh green chilli and packs a bit more punch than some of our other festival dishes; if you have a beer in your hand, it really hits the spot. To make a meal of it, serve with *Numtak balep* (fried breakfast bread, see page 42) or basmati rice and Yeshi's dal (see page 206).

3 tablespoons cooking oil
4 large garlic cloves, thinly sliced
½ teaspoon cumin seeds
6 cm (2½ inch) piece of ginger, washed but not peeled, thinly sliced
1 small red onion, thinly sliced
1 fresh green chilli, finely chopped
1 teaspoon Bassar curry masala (or hot chilli powder)
½ teaspoon turmeric
1 teaspoon salt
4 tomatoes, about 400 g (14 oz) in total, diced
500 g (1 lb 2 oz) potatoes, washed but not peeled, diced
100 g (⅔ cup) peas (frozen is fine)
Chopped coriander (cilantro) or chives, to garnish

VEGAN

Heat the oil in a large wok or saucepan over a medium-high heat. When it's hot, add the garlic and cumin seeds and stir-fry for a minute. Now add the ginger, onion and chilli (you could, of course, omit this if you prefer the curry to be less spicy) and stir for another minute, then add the Bassar curry masala, turmeric and salt and leave to cook for 2–3 minutes.

Now add the tomatoes to the pan and stir everything well, then cover with a lid (or foil) and turn the heat right down. Allow to simmer for about 5 minutes, checking every minute or so and giving the tomatoes a little squash.

When the tomatoes and onions are very soft and the sauce has reduced to a paste, you can put the potatoes in. Mix well, and if the pan looks a bit dry, add a little boiling water. Cover again and leave to cook for about 15 minutes or until the potatoes are tender (taste one to check). Add the peas and stir well, then leave to cook for a final 2–3 minutes.

Garnish with coriander or chives and serve.

Tibetan Keema
(Minced Beef with Green Peppers) *Serves 4–6*

I've often thought of this as dish as a kind of Asian chilli con carne. Yeshi used to cook it for me a lot in India and it is incredibly moreish. These days we often serve it at our restaurant and stall. *Keema* tastes great with green peppers, but you could also use peas (frozen is fine) or okra, which is super delicious. Serve with basmati rice and Yeshi's dal (see page 206) alongside.

2 tablespoons cooking oil
4 cm (1½ inch) piece of ginger, washed but not peeled, finely chopped
3 large garlic cloves, thinly sliced
1 red onion, diced
1 tomato, diced
1 teaspoon salt
500 g (1 lb 2 oz) minced (ground) beef
1 teaspoon Bassar curry masala (or hot chilli powder)
1 large or 2 small green peppers (capsicums), cut into 2.5 cm (1 inch) pieces
1 tablespoon sesame oil

Pictured on page 204.

Heat the oil in a large wok or frying pan over a medium-high heat. When it's hot, add the ginger and garlic and stir-fry until they are golden brown. Stir in the onion, tomato and salt and keep cooking until the onion and tomato have softened, about 5 minutes.

Now add the beef and curry masala and stir everything together for 7–8 minutes, pressing down on the meat every once in a while to help release its juices. Once these have become reabsorbed, turn the heat down and stir well to stop everything sticking.

Finally, add the green peppers and sesame oil and stir-fry for a further 6–7 minutes, depending on how soft you like your peppers. If it looks a bit dry, just add a little boiling water.

Mixed Vegetable Creamy Coconut Curry

Serves 4–6

In Tibet – and in India, where he lived for many years – Yeshi found it impossible to get vegetables that were out of season. When he first arrived in the UK, he found it fascinating that the markets and shops stocked the same fruit and veg all year round, regardless of the season. However, he soon grew weary of the sameness of fruit and vegetable shopping here on this small island and has since found it one of the hardest things to get used to.

Happily, as the years have gone by, and through the contacts we've made with wholesalers for our restaurant and festival stall, we've found ways of accessing fresh, local and seasonal produce, and we always try to cook with it when we can. If you'd like to do the same, feel free to substitute the courgette with squash (pumpkin) in autumn, or the cauliflower with peppers (capsicums) in summer, and so on. Serve the curry with basmati rice.

- 4 cm (1½ inch) piece of ginger, washed but not peeled
- 4 large garlic cloves
- 1 red onion
- 2 large tomatoes
- 2 tablespoons cooking oil
- ¼ teaspoon turmeric
- 1 teaspoon Bassar curry masala (or hot chilli powder)
- 2 teaspoons Madras curry powder
- 1 x 400 ml (14 fl oz) coconut milk
- 9 baby potatoes, about 400 g (14 oz)
- 2 carrots, about 250 g (9 oz)
- ½ cauliflower, about 350 g (12 oz)
- 1 courgette (zucchini), about 250 g (9 oz)
- 2 teaspoons salt
- 3 tablespoons coconut milk powder – optional
- Chopped coriander (cilantro), including stems, to garnish – optional

VEGAN

Finely chop the ginger, garlic, onion and tomatoes – make sure everything is very small, as this will form the basis of your curry paste.

Put the oil into a large wok and place over a medium-high heat. When it is hot, add the ginger and garlic and stir-fry until golden, then add the onion and stir-fry for about 2 minutes. Stir in the tomatoes, turmeric, curry masala and curry powder and mix thoroughly into the paste. Now turn the heat up as high as it will go and add the coconut milk. Stir well, then cook for 15 minutes, stirring occasionally.

Meanwhile, cut the rest of the vegetables into bite-sized pieces: the cauliflower pieces can be a little larger than the others. Put the potatoes and carrots into one bowl, as these will go in first, and the cauliflower and courgette in the other.

Add the salt, potatoes and carrots to the wok, along with the coconut milk powder, if using. Pour in 100 ml (3½ fl oz) of boiling water and stir well, then turn the heat down to low-medium, cover and leave to simmer for about 10 minutes, stirring occasionally. At this point you can add the cauliflower and courgette. If the wok looks a bit dry, add another splash of boiling water. Cook, stirring every so often, for a further 7–8 minutes, or until all the vegetables are tender.

Garnish with coriander, if you like, and serve.

Quick Lamb Biryani *Serves 4*

Yeshi's older brother Nyima spent many years living as a monk in the Gaden Shartse Monastery at Mundgod, in southern India's Karnataka state. The life of a Tibetan monk is not spent purely in meditation or prayer, but is actually very active, involving many hours of philosophical debate and practical work. During his time at the monastery, Nyima held the role of head chef. He was well known to all the vegetable sellers around town, and became famous for the wide variety of meals he and his team cooked for the monastery's thousands of monks. Nyima is now head chef at an Indian restaurant in New York. Yeshi's biryani recipe is mostly borrowed from Nyima, who he says makes the best of any he has tasted. This version is quick to make, unlike many traditional Indian biryanis. Tomato *sepen* (see page 193) is good to have alongside, as is a spinach and egg side soup (see page 119).

2 tablespoons cooking oil
2 large garlic cloves, thinly sliced
2 star anise
2–3 bay leaves
3–4 fresh curry leaves, or 7–8 dried
1 red onion, thinly sliced
2 tomatoes, finely diced
600 g (1 lb 5 oz) lamb shoulder, on the bone, cut into bite-sized pieces – save the bone to add to the pan
2 teaspoons salt
1 teaspoon Bassar curry masala (or hot chilli powder), or more to taste
2 teaspoons Madras curry powder, or more to taste
½ teaspoon turmeric
2 carrots, about 300 g (10½ oz), washed but not peeled, finely diced
1 potato, about 150–200 g (5½–7 oz), washed but not peeled, finely diced
300 g (1½ cups) basmati rice, washed
Juice of ½ lime
Coriander (cilantro) leaves, to garnish – optional

Heat the oil in a large saucepan over a medium-high heat. When it's hot, add the garlic. After half a minute or so, add the star anise, bay leaves and curry leaves and give everything a good stir for a further minute. Now add the onion, quickly followed by the tomatoes, and stir well for 4–5 minutes.

Add the lamb to the pan, popping the bone in as well. Stir in the salt, curry masala, curry powder (add more of both of these if you like your food hot) and turmeric and cook for 10–15 minutes. The pan will seem quite dry, but you are aiming to seal the meat, so this is right – just keep stirring to make sure it doesn't stick. Turn the heat down to medium and add the carrot and potato. Stir everything well, then cover with a lid and cook for 2–3 minutes.

Now add the rice, along with 700 ml (24 fl oz) of cold water. Stir well and make sure that everything in the pan is submerged, then replace the lid, turn the heat up to high and bring to the boil. When the water has been absorbed by the rice, reduce the heat to low and let it simmer for 10 minutes, checking every so often to make sure that nothing is sticking. You will know that the biryani is ready when the rice at the top of the pan has softened. At this point, turn the heat off and let it stand for 5 minutes to allow the rice to absorb all the juices.

Just before serving, squeeze over a little lime juice and garnish with some coriander leaves, if you like.

Yeshi says 'You can try this dish with other types of meat, but lamb is a good one because it has a high fat content, which makes it super-juicy. You definitely don't want anything too lean.'

Mooli and Spinach Stew *Serves 4–6*

If you ever find mooli being sold with their green tips still attached, snap them up! These freshly harvested mooli have a softer flavour, and their greens can be used in a wide range of cooked dishes. Easy to grow, mooli thrives throughout the Tibetan winter and can also be stored for long periods, making it a staple food. That said, it rarely takes centre stage, but here it's the main attraction. Enjoy this wholesome stew with basmati rice or *Tingmo* (steamed bread, see page 169).

- 2 tablespoons cooking oil
- 2 fresh green chillies, thinly sliced, including seeds
- 2 large cloves garlic, thinly sliced
- 1 red onion, halved and thinly sliced
- 2 tomatoes, halved and thinly sliced
- ½ teaspoon ground cumin
- 1½ teaspoons salt
- ½ teaspoon black pepper or crushed Sichuan peppercorns (*yerma*)
- 2 mooli (daikon), about 500 g (1 lb 2 oz) in total, washed but not peeled
- 1 bunch of whole leaf spinach, about 175 g (6 oz)
- 1 teaspoon sesame oil
- Chopped coriander (cilantro) or spring onions (scallions), to serve

VEGAN

Heat the oil in a wok or large saucepan over a medium-high heat. When it's hot, add the chillies and garlic and stir-fry for a minute, then add the onion. After another minute, add the tomatoes, cumin, salt and black pepper or Sichuan pepper.

Cut the mooli into thick slices on the diagonal, and then into thin strips like French fries. Add to the pan and cook for 6–7 minutes, stirring often.

Meanwhile, roughly chop the spinach into 2.5–5 cm (1–2 inch) pieces, including the stems. Wash it well in cold water, then set aside in a bowl of cold water.

When the mooli is done, lift the spinach out of the water and into the wok (this way you leave behind any gritty residue at the bottom of the bowl). Stir well for 2–3 minutes, then add about 400 ml (14 fl oz) of cold water and bring to the boil. When the spinach has just wilted, add the sesame oil and cook for a further minute.

Garnish with coriander or spring onions and serve.

Yeshi's Special Fried Pork *Serves 4–6*

In the book *My Spiritual Journey*, His Holiness the XIV Dalai Lama reflects on his father's love of pork. As a young boy, the Dalai Lama was moved to the Potala Palace in Lhasa, where the kitchens traditionally held no place for pork, eggs or fish, and he remembers how he would beg like a dog for pork morsels on his visits home. 'It was a little illegal!' he laughs.

Yeshi loves pork, but I get the sense it's something he feels a little guilty about too. He doesn't cook with it very often, and when he does he always uses a marinade, as if to disguise the meat's origins. He says that otherwise it somehow lacks flavour, and perhaps it does if you're more used to eating cured meat.

Serve this special pork dish with basmati rice, *Tingmo* (steamed bread, see page 169) or Giant fluffy sharing bread (see page 177).

500 g (1 lb 2 oz) pork belly
2 tablespoons cooking oil
2 large garlic cloves, thinly sliced
6 cm (2½ inch) piece of ginger, washed but not peeled, thinly sliced
4 fresh green chillies, thinly sliced
1 teaspoon salt
1 teaspoon granulated sugar
1 red onion, roughly chopped
1 green pepper (capsicum), roughly chopped
1 yellow or orange pepper (capsicum), roughly chopped
2 tomatoes, roughly chopped
1 tablespoon light soy sauce
2 teaspoons Chinkiang black vinegar
2 teaspoons sesame oil

For the marinade

1 tablespoon dark soy sauce
1½ teaspoons salt
½ teaspoon turmeric
¼ teaspoon crushed Sichuan peppercorns (*yerma*)
1 small garlic clove, chopped
2.5–4 cm (1–1½ inch) piece of ginger, washed but not peeled, chopped

Combine the marinade ingredients in a bowl. Cut the pork belly into large chunks, then add to the bowl and mix well. Cover and leave in the fridge to marinate overnight, or for a good full day.

Take the pork out of the marinade and put it into a large saucepan. Pour in about 1.5 litres (6 cups) of boiling water, cover with a lid and boil for 40 minutes over a high heat, checking on it from time to time to ensure it doesn't boil over. Lift the pork out of the water and leave it to cool slightly, then remove any bones from the meat and cut it into dice.

Heat the oil in a wok over a high heat. When it is hot, add the garlic, ginger and chillies and stir-fry briefly, then turn down the heat slightly. Add the salt and sugar and mix this through. Next add the onion and cook, stirring, until the onion has softened but not browned, then add the peppers and stir-fry for a couple of minutes.

Now add the pork and tomatoes, turn the heat back up to high and stir well. Add the light soy sauce, vinegar and sesame oil and keep cooking, stirring gently every so often, for about 5 minutes, or until the peppers have softened a little, then serve.

Sweet Tooth

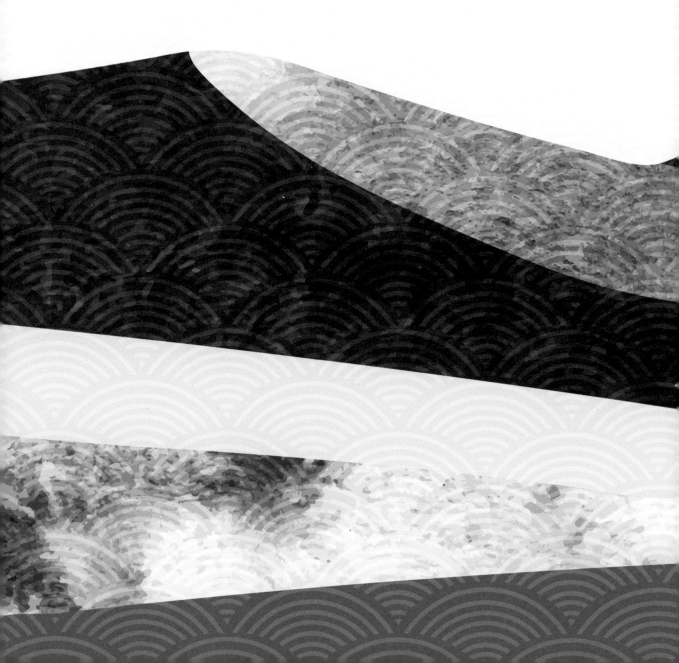

Dessert isn't really a thing in Tibet, but in Yeshi's village, where there are two harvests in a year, all kinds of fruit trees thrive and provide an abundance of pleasure for those with a sweet tooth. Honey is also widely collected and used in snacks and with bread.

A hallmark of sweet Tibetan food is that it is usually combined with savoury ingredients to form dishes that non-Asian people may find surprising. The sweetest treats, for example, are typically made with cheese. In some parts of Tibet one popular sweet snack is a hand-made pasta-based dish cooked with sugar, butter and grated cheese – essentially a sweet mac 'n' cheese. Elsewhere, *thue* is a sweet dish made of cheese, walnuts, brown sugar and butter.

During *Losar* (Tibetan New Year), *dresil*, a sweet dish made with rice, butter, raisins, dates and nuts (see page 85), is traditionally the first bowl of food offered on the day. An assortment of other nut- and seed-based snacks are made and enjoyed during this time of year, but these are essentially designed to keep the mouth busy while other dishes are being prepared. The clue is in the name: *khabsey*, the most widely consumed of all *Losar* treats, literally translates as 'mouth, eat'.

There is, however, no real culture of desserts or sweet treats. When we gave Yeshi's parents their first taste of chocolate, they thought it was disgusting. Perhaps it's about texture. The family is clearly familiar with sugar: our kids' abiding memory of our most recent trip to Tibet is that of Yeshi's aunt picking up one of the sachets of sugar we'd brought from the plane and tipping the lot into her mouth without so much as a backward glance.

Yeshi may not have eaten many sweet snacks when he was growing up in Tibet, but he's certainly making up for things now! Our kids call him the 'secret chocolate eater' as, despite protestations that he finds many desserts 'too sweet', cakes, chocolates and Halloween hauls do seem to mysteriously disappear after they have gone to bed.

Yeshi has enjoyed learning to bake since moving to the UK – cupcakes, crumbles and cakes of all kinds – but he's still getting to know and understand the foibles of our oven. With the exception of the *tsampa* boules, all of the recipes in this chapter are made on top of the stove – with a steamer, a frying pan or a wok.

Khabsey
(Ceremonial Biscuits) *Makes 30–40 biscuits*

Biscuits and cakes are not everyday fare in Tibet, but during the New Year (*Losar*) celebrations Tibetans go to town with *khabsey*. As these simple biscuits are made into all kinds of beautiful shapes, this is the ultimate opportunity to get the creative and artistic juices flowing.

A symbolic scorpion-shaped cookie is made first. This is an offering to ward off bad luck, including any mishaps in the kitchen, and it will be hung near the stove for the duration of *Losar*. Other large *khabsey* are stacked one on top of the other in a criss-cross formation to make an altar display that represents the Eight Auspicious Symbols of Tibetan Buddhism. Less ornate *khabsey* are enjoyed as a snack, or are offered to visitors, and there will be literally sackloads of these around the kitchen during the New Year period. Instructions for shaping the most commonly made style are given below, but you might prefer to make *hrug-hrug* ('small pieces'), which are basically just small rectangles or triangles.

150 g (⅔ cup) caster (superfine) sugar
500 g (3⅓ cups) self-raising flour, plus extra for dusting
1 litre (4 cups) cooking oil, for deep-frying, plus 2 tablespoons extra
Icing (confectioners') sugar, for sprinkling

VEGAN

Put the sugar into a bowl and pour 170 ml (⅔ cup) of boiling water over it. Stir well until the sugar is fully dissolved, then leave to cool for 5–10 minutes.

Put the flour into a mixing bowl and add the extra 2 tablespoons of oil. While mixing the oil through the flour with your dominant hand, slowly drizzle in the sweetened water with the other. Knead well until the mixture forms a dough in the bowl, then cover and set aside for 15–20 minutes.

Take the dough out of the bowl and knead it for about a minute, then divide it into four pieces of roughly equal size. Take the first piece of dough, keeping the rest covered in the bowl to stop them from drying out, and roll it into a ball. Flatten it slightly with your hand, then use a rolling pin to roll it out, turning it around and over as you go, until you have one large, roughly circular sheet of dough about 2 mm (1⁄16 inch) thick. Sprinkle a little flour onto your work surface if the dough starts to stick.

You can now make your *khabsey* into any shape you fancy, using biscuit cutters if you like.

The traditional *kong-chen* shape is made as follows. Using a sharp knife, slice the sheet of dough in half, then slice your semi-circle into triangles with two sides longer than the other one – ideally your triangles should be about 6–8 cm (2½–3¼ inches) long. Cut a slit down the centre of each triangle, then feed the pointed end all the way through the slit, so you can pull it through and down the other side.

continued >

> Khabsey *continued*

However you've made your biscuits (the shape will not affect the taste!), transfer them to a bowl and set aside while you roll and shape the rest of the dough.

Pour the deep-frying oil into a large frying pan or stable wok and heat over a medium-high heat. To check the temperature of the oil, toss in a tiny scrap of dough: if it immediately sizzles, you are good to go. Working in batches, carefully lower each *khabsey* into the oil individually so the oil doesn't splatter, then use tongs or long chopsticks to gently move them around in the oil – they will only take a few minutes to cook. When they are golden brown on one side, turn them over so that they can brown on the other. Once they are done, lift them out and drain on paper towel. Keep going until all the *khabsey* are cooked.

Sprinkle a little icing sugar over the *khabsey* and serve. Any leftovers can be stored in an airtight container for up to a week.

Yeshi says 'For best results, make sure the dough is rolled out thinly, and always make sure the oil is piping-hot before the *khabsey* go in. Note that the first batch of *khabsey* is likely to be a little lighter in colour than those that follow. Either way, they should taste deliciously crunchy if you've cooked them right. The cooking oil can be strained and reused – don't throw it away.'

Honey Nut Granola Bars *Serves 6–8*

In Tibet, these are made for weddings and other special occasions. Walnuts are always used, as they are plentiful and grown locally. Grains such as roasted barley and wheat are usually included, and hemp seeds often make their way in too, so do feel free to add some if you have them. Recent analysis of ancient pollen suggests that cannabis may have evolved on the Tibetan Plateau, and it has certainly been cultivated and used there for centuries. Yeshi tells me that he often came across it in Tibet, but until he left he had no idea of its uses beyond food and manufacturing.

300 g (10½ oz) walnuts
150 g (5½ oz) cashews
150 g (5½ oz) almonds
50 g (⅓ cup) sesame seeds
Coconut powder (see page 243) or *Tsampa* (roasted barley flour, see page 53), for sprinkling
200 g (7 oz) caster (superfine) sugar
100 g (3½ oz) runny honey

VEGETARIAN

Using a pestle and mortar, crush the walnuts, cashews and almonds in batches, transferring them to a bowl as you go. (You could also put the nuts inside a zip-lock food bag and roll over them with a rolling pin, if you prefer.) Add the sesame seeds to the bowl and mix well.

Line a baking tray with baking paper and sprinkle over some coconut powder or *tsampa* – just enough to cover the base.

Place a large saucepan over a low heat and add the sugar and honey. Stir well with a wooden spoon for several minutes until the mixture starts to bubble. Now add all the nuts and stir everything through gently but thoroughly for a couple of minutes.

Empty the mixture onto the baking tray and press it down gently with the wooden spoon, getting into all the corners and making it as even as possible in the tray.

Cover with a sheet of baking paper and use your hands to press it down onto the surface. Leave to cool and set for about an hour, then cut into small pieces to serve.

Chocolate Tsampa Truffles *Makes 15–20 truffles*

This one is Yeshi's invention. He created it for a formal dinner he catered at a seventeenth-century mansion just outside Oxford. He was tasked with coming up with something to go with coffee, and this was the result. I love these truffles, and so do the punters at Taste Tibet. They have all the nuttiness of *tsampa* wrapped up in the warmest of chocolate embraces. They are equally delicious whether you cook them with sugar or honey, but honey makes them a bit more melt-in-the-mouth.

100 g (3½ oz) chocolate, 70% cocoa
100 g (3½ oz) runny honey or caster (superfine) sugar
100 g (3½ oz) butter
100 g (3½ oz) *Tsampa* (roasted barley flour, see page 53)

VEGETARIAN

Break up the chocolate and put it into a non-stick saucepan, along with the honey or sugar and the butter. Place over a low heat and stir gently using a wooden spoon. When the mixture has melted, take the pan off the heat and add the *tsampa*. Mix everything together, then leave to cool for a minute or two, but no longer – the mixture should still be hot to the touch.

Now reach into the pan and scoop out truffle-sized amounts, each about 15 g (½ oz). Squeeze them between your palms and roll into small balls. Let the truffles cool slightly before serving.

Yeshi says 'These quantities will work well if your *tsampa* is ground very finely. If you've used a spice/coffee grinder (rather than a flour mill) it is likely to be coarser and therefore less absorbent, so if the mixture doesn't quite come together, just add more *tsampa* to make it mouldable in your hands.'

Tibetan Sesame Snaps *Serves 6–8*

This snack is often made during the Tibetan New Year. Sesame seeds are not native to Tibet, but they are used in Chinese cookery and are now widely available on the plateau. Yeshi says that he often had his eye on the sesame snacks that you could buy in convenience stores in town, but his family didn't trust anything ready-made and insisted on preparing their own. They are simple to make.

500 g (1 lb 2 oz) sesame seeds
150 g (⅔ cup) caster (superfine) sugar
150 g (5½ oz) runny honey

VEGETARIAN

Line a baking tray with greaseproof paper.

Put the sesame seeds into a wok and toast them over a medium heat, stirring frequently to make sure the heat reaches all the seeds, until they are golden brown and smell nutty. This will take about 7–8 minutes.

Meanwhile, put the sugar and honey into a heavy-based saucepan and cook over a low heat, stirring frequently, until golden brown – this should also take about 7–8 minutes.

When the sugar and honey start to bubble but are still very runny (you don't want the mixture to harden), tip the sesame seeds into the pan and mix well over the heat.

Empty the sweet sesame mix onto the baking tray, pressing it down evenly with a lightly oiled spatula or palette knife.

Leave to cool and set for a few minutes before cutting into snack-sized pieces.

Chocolate Momos *Makes about 20 momos*

This one is just a bit of fun. Our relatives in Tibet have no taste for chocolate, so they would probably be horrified with what Yeshi has come up with here! But the kids have a lot of fun making chocolate momos, and this unique dessert is certainly a crowd-pleaser.

Plain yoghurt, to serve

For the dough

90 g (3¼ oz) chocolate, 70% cocoa
50 g (1¾ oz) unsalted butter
300 g (2 cups) self-raising flour, plus extra for dusting
1 large egg

For the filling

90 g (3¼ oz) chocolate, 70% cocoa
70 g (2½ oz) unsalted butter
70 g (2½ oz) caster (superfine) sugar
100 g (3½ oz) plain digestive biscuits, about 7
60 g (2¼ oz) *Tsampa* (roasted barley flour, see page 53) – optional

VEGETARIAN

For the dough, fill a medium-sized saucepan about a quarter full of boiling water and place over a low heat. Sit a heatproof bowl on top, making sure that its base isn't touching the water. Break up the chocolate into small pieces and add to the bowl, along with the butter. Stir gently for 2–3 minutes, until everything has melted, then take off the heat and leave to cool for a minute or two.

Meanwhile, put the flour into a mixing bowl, break in the egg and use your dominant hand to roughly combine. Add the slightly cooled chocolate mixture and, while mixing with your hand, slowly pour in 60 ml (¼ cup) of warm water. Keep mixing and kneading until you have a ball of dough, then cover and set aside for 15–20 minutes.

Meanwhile, for the filling, break the chocolate into a saucepan and add the butter and sugar, then place over a low heat. In a bowl, crush the biscuits to crumbs using the end of a rolling pin. (You could also do this in a blender and then transfer the crumbs to a bowl). Add 100 ml (3½ fl oz) of boiling water – and the *tsampa*, if using – and mix well. When the chocolate mixture has completely melted, work it into the biscuit mixture using a spatula.

Knead the dough for a couple of minutes, then divide it in half. Sprinkle a little flour onto your work surface – but don't overdo it, as too much can stiffen the dough, making the momos harder to wrap later. Take the first piece of dough, keeping the other covered in the bowl. Roll it out into a sausage shape about 25 cm (10 inches) long, then cut into ten equal slices, lightly flattening each one with your hand. Using a rolling pin, and making one wrapper at a time, push and pull the flattened piece of dough up and down quickly and firmly, holding it with your spare hand and turning it little by little as you go. The middle should end up a bit thicker than the outer edges, and it should fill the palm of your hand; it doesn't need to be a perfect circle.

When you're ready to fill, wrap and fold your momos, follow the instructions on pages 146–8, shaping them however you like.

As these chocolate momos have a nice buttery skin, there's no need to grease or line your steamer baskets. Steam them (see page 148) over a high heat for about 14–16 minutes, then serve with yoghurt.

Apple and Pear Momos *Makes about 20*

When we went to Tibet to meet with Yeshi's family for the first time since he had left, seventeen years earlier, his parents brought with them some apples from a tree he had planted shortly beforehand. The symbolism of Yeshi's tree continuing to thrive in his absence was powerful – and the apples tasted amazing. We often remember this gesture when we eat these momos at home. We usually make them at the end of summer using apples from the allotment and pears from a tree in our garden. They go down a treat with a bit of custard or yoghurt (or vegan versions of these) on the side.

For the dough

250 g (1⅔ cups) self-raising flour, plus extra for dusting

For the filling

2 apples, about 200 g (7 oz) in total, peeled and finely chopped

1 ripe conference pear, about 200 g (7 oz), peeled and finely chopped

1 teaspoon ground cinnamon

2 tablespoons caster (superfine) sugar

2 tablespoons cooking oil

VEGAN

For the dough, put the flour into a mixing bowl. Slowly pour in about 125 ml (½ cup) of warm water – a hot handwash temperature is good – into the flour with one hand, while mixing with the other. Add just enough water to make a dough – you don't want it to get too sticky. Knead until the dough forms a ball in the bowl, then cover and set aside for 15–20 minutes.

Meanwhile, put all the filling ingredients into a mixing bowl and stir everything together well.

Take the dough out of the bowl and knead it for a couple of minutes, then divide it in half and return to the bowl. Sprinkle a little flour onto your work surface – but don't overdo it, as too much flour can stiffen the dough, making the momos harder to wrap later.

Take the first piece of dough, keeping the other one covered in the bowl to stop it from drying out. Roll out the dough into a sausage shape about 25 cm (10 inches) long, then cut into ten equal slices, lightly flattening each one with your hand.

Using a rolling pin, and making one wrapper at a time, push and pull the flattened piece of dough up and down quickly and firmly, holding it with your spare hand and turning it little by little as you go. The middle of the wrapper should end up a bit thicker than the outer edges, and it should fill the palm of your hand; it doesn't need to be a perfect circle.

Repeat the process with the rest of the dough.

When you're ready to fill, wrap and fold your momos, follow the instructions on pages 146–8, shaping them however you like.

For best results, steam these momos (see page 148) over a high heat for about 16–19 minutes, cooking them in batches according to the size of your steamer.

Tsampa Boules *Makes about 15 boules*

Tsampa is great to play around with in the kitchen. When mixed with boiling water to the right consistency it's every bit as good as play dough – if not better, as it has more elasticity. Yeshi loves coming up with new ways of getting the kids involved with *tsampa*. He's made all kinds of sweet treats over the years, and these boules are the best.

Note that the stated quantity of *tsampa* assumes your *tsampa* has been ground very finely. If you've used a spice or coffee grinder, it is likely to be coarser and less absorbent, which means that you may need to add a little more of it to achieve a mouldable consistency.

125 g (4½ oz) unsalted butter
2 tablespoons runny honey
200 g (7 oz) *Tsampa* (roasted barley flour, see page 53)
50 g (1¾ oz) caster (superfine) sugar
Sesame seeds, for sprinkling

VEGETARIAN

Preheat the oven to 170°C (325°F). Line a baking tray with greaseproof paper.

Melt the butter and honey in a saucepan over a low heat, stirring occasionally. Meanwhile, combine the *tsampa* and sugar in a bowl.

When the butter and honey have melted, take the saucepan off the heat and add the *tsampa* and sugar, using a spatula to mix well.

Using your hands, roll the *tsampa* mixture into balls about 4 cm (1½ inches) in diameter, then flatten them slightly, moulding them between the crook of your thumb and forefinger and making a slight depression in the centre of each one.

Place on the baking tray – you should end up with fifteen or so. Sprinkle some sesame seeds on top of each one, then bake in the oven for 8 minutes. Leave to cool before you tuck in.

Store any leftover boules in an airtight container for 2–3 days.

Ingredients

Tibetan cooks almost never use pre-prepared sauces or pastes. At Taste Tibet and at home, we always make everything ourselves, starting with raw ingredients. And the good news is that there is very little investment involved. You can make a lot of delicious Tibetan food using just a few simple staples, some of which you may already have – and if you don't, you should be able to find most of the store cupboard ingredients you need in your local Chinese (C) or Indian (I) grocery store. It's best to buy them here as they are likely to be cheaper and more authentic than anything you'll find in the supermarket. If your local shops can't oblige, then everything is available online.

Bay leaves: This delicate, aromatic leaf tends to play second fiddle to other, more prominent flavours, but like a sprinkling of black pepper it has its part to play. Unlike many other herbs and spices, bay leaves retain a good flavour when dried, and in this form they will keep well for a good few months.

(I) ***Bassar curry masala:*** This is probably Yeshi's biggest secret weapon when it comes to curries. You can use generic hot chilli powder if you don't have it, but this one is really worth digging out if you're after great flavour. Bassar is used mainly in Pakistan and India and contains not only chilli powder but also an amazing blend of coriander, turmeric, cumin, fenugreek, bay leaves, mustard seeds, cardamom, cinnamon, black pepper and nutmeg.

(C) ***Black cloud fungus:*** Also known as wood ear mushroom, the various descriptions are a nod to its shape. Yeshi says that the best black fungi is found on oak trees, but it grows on all kinds of damp wood. Usually sold dried, in packets, it should be soaked in hot water for at least half an hour before use.

Buckwheat flour: Although treated as a grain, buckwheat is actually the seed of a flowering fruit closely related to wild rhubarb, which means it's completely gluten-free. Buckwheat flour makes a great substitute for wheat flour and is super-easy to work with. It can be used for bread, scones, pancakes and more, and you can find it in all the big supermarkets, as well as in health food stores.

(I) ***Cardamom:*** A spice in the ginger family, cardamom has been used for centuries to jazz up tea, coffee, rice dishes and pastries. It has an intense aroma and a wonderful spicy-sweet flavour that complements both sweet and savoury dishes. Cardamom thrives at high altitude, but is not widely used in Tibetan food; we do like to add it to our chai, though.

(C) ***Chinese (napa) cabbage:*** This large oblong-shaped pale green cabbage is mild and juicy and picks up other flavours from the food it's cooked with. It's easy to grow and great at resisting the cold, making it a firm favourite in the Tibetan kitchen. It works really well in stir-fries, noodles, soups and even salads.

(C) ***Chinese chives:*** Sometimes referred to as garlic chives, these have a strong, garlicky taste and aroma. We use them in momos, but they are sometimes added to stir-fries too. If you can't find them, substitute the thinly sliced green parts of spring onions (scallions).

(C) ***Chinkiang black vinegar:*** Also known as Zhenjiang black vinegar, this has a wonderfully complex, smoky flavour that is milder and less acidic than some vinegars, with a subtle sweetness, and its naturally dark colour comes from scorched rice grains. Black vinegar is widely used in Tibetan cooking and is particularly good in noodles and soups.

(I) ***Cinnamon:*** Harvested from the inner bark of a tropical evergreen tree, cinnamon has a sweet, woodsy note. We sometimes use it in our chai, and it's also delicious in desserts.

Coconut milk: At Taste Tibet we use a lot of this in our curries. Coconut milk is the thick, milky-white liquid extracted from the grated pulp of the coconut. Widely available in tinned form, it is vegan and lactose-free and brings a little luxury to everything you cook with it.

(I) ***Coconut milk powder:*** This is a dehydrated form of coconut milk. It is made by spray-drying the coconut flesh until it becomes a powder, which you then reconstitute by adding water to make as little or as much coconut milk as you need. We use coconut milk powder to add a subtle, sweet coconut flavour and a creamy mouth feel to our curries. It is usually sold in packets.

(I) ***Coconut powder:*** Not to be confused with coconut milk powder, this is a powder made from desiccated (dried) coconut that is used in desserts and can be added to curries. Regular supermarkets will often only have coconut milk powder, rather than powdered coconut, so your best bet is to head for an Indian grocery shop; otherwise, you can find it online.

Cooking oil

Yeshi's family usually cook with cow or yak butter. They also use a lot of walnut oil. They press their own from the fruits of the many walnut trees that grow in and around the village. It is roasted, then crushed, then boiled, and the oil that rises to the top is then extracted.

In India, Yeshi started cooking with vegetable, sunflower and rapeseed oil, and in the UK he has added olive oil to this repertoire. Unless otherwise indicated, we usually cook with rapeseed or vegetable oil, but feel free to use your preferred cooking oil, as long as it's something fairly neutral in flavour, with a high smoke point.

Some dishes call for a litre (4 cups) or more of oil for deep-frying – this oil can be reused. Let it cool before straining it into a bottle or other container, then store in a cool, dry place.

(I) ***Coriander:*** Also called cilantro, this is a very divisive herb. If you hate it, feel free to omit it, but if you love it you will be pleased to know that fresh coriander is used often in Tibetan cookery.

(I) ***Coriander seeds:*** In Tibet, fresh coriander (cilantro) isn't available year-round, so Yeshi's family also use the plant's crushed seeds during the off-season. Definitely get some seeds or powder in, as well as the fresh stuff – if coriander is to your taste, you will find yourself using these quite a lot.

(I) ***Cumin:*** Otherwise known as *jeera*, cumin is a lovely warm spice that perks up all kinds of dishes and makes the kitchen smell great. Ground and whole seeds are both useful to have on hand.

(I) ***Curry leaves:*** Fresh curry leaves look a bit like small, shiny lemon leaves, and you should be able to find them in Indian grocery stores. Dried curry leaves are more widely found, but they have less aroma and flavour. If you can't find any at all, just leave them out. If you do use them, don't remove them on serving – they can be eaten! Note that curry powder and curry leaves are not the same thing and cannot be substituted for one another.

(C) ***Dark soy sauce:*** This is much thicker and darker than light soy sauce, and has a sweeter taste. Don't be tempted to use it in place of light soy sauce. Light soy sauce can be used to substitute for dark soy sauce, however – you just won't achieve the same rich colour.

(C) (I) ***Dried red chillies:*** We like to use whole dried chillies and are fans of the TRS brand. These are medium-hot to taste, and large enough that you can pick them out on serving, as ideally they shouldn't be eaten. They usually go into the wok first thing to flavour the oil. If you chop or crush them, releasing the seeds – or use dried chillies that are already broken up when you buy them – you'll get more heat. Dried chillies keep for a long time in the cupboard. (*See also* Hot chilli flakes.)

(I) ***Garam masala:*** Literally 'hot flavour powder', this is a fragrant blend of ground spices that usually includes cloves, cinnamon and cardamom. This makes it a stronger, more pungent mix than curry powder.

(C) ***Garlic shoots:*** The thin, green, curly stalks of the garlic bulb are delicious to eat in their own right. They can be harvested during late spring and early summer and are mild in flavour, with the texture of asparagus.

(C) ***Glass noodles:*** Known in Tibetan as *phing* (pronounced, very satisfyingly, as 'ping'), and also sometimes called cellophane or thread noodles, these transparent, very fine noodles are made from mung bean starch or potato starch. Either type is good for Tibetan cooking. *Phing* tend to be added to stews, are delicious cooked with black cloud fungus, and are widely enjoyed as a cold snack during summertime.

(I) ***Hot chilli flakes:*** These are often sold as 'crushed chillies'. We use the TRS brand, but they come in all forms in Indian supermarkets. A little goes a long way! We use hot chilli flakes to fire up our Taste Tibet *sepen*. You can also use them in place of the *sepen* itself to add heat to sauces and dips, noodles and stir-fries.

(I) ***Jeera:*** *see* Cumin.

(C) ***Light soy sauce:*** We use a lot of this fine-grade soy. It's versatile and lends a salty, savoury flavour to stir-fries. It's usually added towards the end of cooking or at the table in dips. We use Lee Kum Kee Premium Light Soy Sauce, but the Pearl River brand is also good.

(I) ***Madras curry powder:*** Also known as Kashmiri bassar, this contains many of the same ingredients as standard curry powder, but added cayenne pepper makes it spicier and gives it more heat and fragrance.

(I) ***Mooli:*** Also known as daikon, this is a white root vegetable with a crisp texture and mild, slightly sweet taste that is widely used in Tibetan cookery, notably for pickling and in soups and stir-fries. It is fast-growing and thrives in cold climates.

(C) ***Mung bean starch:*** Also known as green bean starch, this gluten-free starch is used to make glass noodles or white *laphing*, the street-food snack of chilled noodles that is wildly popular in Tibet during the summertime. Potato starch or cornflour (cornstarch) will work in its place if you can't find it.

(I) ***Mung dal:*** There's a lot of confusion about lentils, beans and dals – pulses, in other words. Pulses can be bought whole, split with their skins on, or split with their skins removed. Split pulses are also known as dal. Mung dal is a split mung bean, and it is yellow in colour. Make sure you don't accidentally buy whole mung beans, which have a green skin and take a lot longer to cook.

(I) ***Mustard greens:*** These are the leaves of the mustard plant. Try to choose bunches that are rich green in colour, free from any yellowing or brown spots. Mustard greens have a sharp, peppery flavour when raw; cooked, they taste a bit like spinach, but with more body. If you can't find them you can substitute with kale or another hearty, bitter leaf.

Olive oil: Light olive oil is usually best for Tibetan cooking, as it keeps longer and has a higher smoke point than other varieties. Note that the term 'light' refers to the oil's relatively light colour and neutral flavour, rather than its calorie content.

(C) ***Pak choi:*** Also known as bok choy, this is widely available in supermarkets. We usually use pak choi in stir-fries or soups. There are many different varieties, and any will work well.

Red onions: These grow in Yeshi's village and he prefers them to white, which he finds too sweet. Red onions have a thicker skin and flesh to white onions, making them meatier and therefore a better choice for sauces, curry pastes and soups.

Salt

We like to use the rock salt that comes from the salt pans near Yeshi's village in Tibet, rather than refined table salt, which contains additives to stop it from clumping. Sea salt is usually coarser, and can have a different mouth feel, depending on when it's added to a dish. Himalayan pink salt may be visually appealing, but there's no need to rush out and buy it unless it speaks to you – and note that most of it actually comes from Pakistan, rather than Tibet. Note also that table salt is altogether much saltier than unrefined salt, so do reduce the suggested quantities if that's what you're using.

(C) ***Sesame oil:*** This is a lovely, seductively flavoured oil, and we tend to drizzle some in towards the end of the cooking process, or add it at the table to taste. We use Lee Kum Kee Pure Sesame Oil, but any pure sesame oil is better than a blended alternative.

(C) ***Sichuan peppercorns:*** The Sichuanese have claimed these rusty-red berries of the prickly ash plant as their own, but some of the best *yerma*, as it's called in Tibet, actually grows inside the Tibet Autonomous Region. According to studies, sanshool – the active ingredient of Sichuan peppercorns – causes a vibration on the lips measured at 50 hertz. It has a uniquely numbing and tingling taste and a clean, floral scent. *Yerma* is widely used in Tibetan cookery, especially in soups and stews. Most of the recipes in this book call for it in its crushed form. Although you can buy a powdered form of Sichuan pepper in Asian grocery stores, the flavour can be quite compromised, so it's better to buy it whole and grind or crush your own. A pestle and mortar is the best way to do this – but don't do too much at a time as, once ground, its aroma and tongue-numbing effect decrease over time. You can keep freshly ground *yerma* in an airtight container for up to two weeks, but the fresher the better.

(C) ***Sichuan pepper oil:*** Also known as prickly oil, this can be used as a substitute for Sichuan peppercorns, especially as a final seasoning for noodles or stir-fries.

(C) ***Soy chunks:*** A by-product of the extraction of soy-bean oil, these chunks of dehydrated soy bean have a rough texture, but this changes to soft and spongy once they have been soaked. Soy beans absorb the juices of other ingredients they are cooked with, making them super-versatile and a great substitute for meat.

Spring onions: These are also known as scallions or green onions. We usually add them at the end of the cooking process for fragrance and colour. Make sure to use all parts of the onion: the green tips are especially good in garnishes as they have a more subtle flavour.

Sweetheart cabbage: This pointy-shaped green cabbage is also known as hearted or hispi cabbage. It is more tender than other varieties, and so takes less time to cook. Sweetheart cabbage tastes great in stir-fries, and we use it in our vegan momos for its sweetness and crunch. It's often available in supermarkets and farmers' markets, but feel free to use another variety of green cabbage if you can't find it.

(C) ***Tofu:*** Also known as bean curd, tofu is a vegan-friendly food derived from soy beans. Tibetan cooking primarily uses firm tofu, which is tofu that has been pressed to extract most of its water. Its texture is similar to that of mozzarella, and it can be deep-fried, stir-fried or added to soups.

(I) ***Turmeric:*** A member of the ginger family, dried and ground turmeric is commonly used as a spice, and for its beautiful colour. It is widely used in Tibetan cookery.

(C) ***Yerma:*** *see* Sichuan peppercorns.

Pronunciation Guide

It's really hard to convey the sounds of spoken Tibetan in written form. Although a system for transliterating the Tibetan alphabet does exist, it is not intended to help with pronunciation and is rarely used outside academia.

What you'll find instead is a very flexible approach to romanising the Tibetan language, which varies considerably from one end of Tibet to the other, reflecting the many different dialects spoken.

For me, this only came to light when our son, Lobsang, was born and we needed to register his birth. Yeshi told me that he was unsure how to spell the baby's Tibetan name in English. I was a dictionary editor at the time: much investigation ensued.

In addition to the issue of regional variation, I discovered that many Tibetan sounds just don't have an equivalent in any Western language. For example, a common sound in Tibetan is midway between the pronunciation of a 'k' and a 'g'. Similarly, there is no way to convey the sound that lies between a 'd' and a 't', or a 'p' and a 'b'. Thus the kids write 'bala' for dad, but it is read as 'pala' in many of their Tibetan children's books.

What follows is an expression of how the Tibetan language is spoken in Yeshi's home. Bear in mind that Yeshi grew up in a very rural area of eastern Tibet, some distance from the capital city of Lhasa, and so this transliteration will have its quirks. However, given that most of the recipes we've supplied Tibetan names for are regional specialities, or are made in a distinctively local way, there shouldn't be too much argument about how they are pronounced.

Note that we've only included those sounds that require further explanation. Good luck, or *tashi delek* (pronunciation: 'tashi delay')!

a is pronounced like the 'u' in 'hut'

e is pronounced like the 'e' in 'let' unless it's at the end of a word, in which case it's pronounced like the 'ay' in 'hay'

i is pronounced somewhere between the 'i' in 'sing' and the 'e' in 'see'

o is pronounced like the 'o' in 'low' unless it's followed by a 'd', 'n', 'l' or 's', in which case see 'ö'

ö is pronounced like the 'eu' in the French word 'feu'

u is pronounced like the 'oo' in 'moon' unless it's followed by a 'd', 'n', 'l' or 's', in which case see 'ü'

ü is pronounced with pursed lips like the French 'u'

ny is pronounced like the 'ni' in 'onion' or like the Spanish 'ñ'

g is pronounced like the 'g' in 'goat' unless it's at the end of a word, in which case it's almost silent, e.g. 'yag' (meaning yak: do not pronounce the 'g') or 'chig' (meaning the number one: the 'g' is basically swallowed here too)

r is a rolled 'r' sound (but not exaggerated like the Italian or French 'r') unless it comes at the end of a word, in which case it's like the 'r' in 'better'

ng is used at the end of a word and is almost silent

b is pronounced somewhere between a 'b' and a 'p' unless it's in the middle of a word, in which case it's almost silent, e.g. in our son Lobsang's name (pronunciation is closer to 'Lo-sun')

k is used at the end of a word and is almost silent

h used after a consonant (except after a 'c') is a breathy consonant. Thus:
- 'ph' is not read as the 'ph' in 'photo' but as a breathy 'p'
- 'th' is not read as 'th' in 'three' or but as a breathy 't'
- 'dhr' should be pronounced like the 'dr' in 'drum'

Generally speaking, the emphasis of a word falls on its final syllable, but there are of course exceptions. One important example is 'mòmo' (grandmother), who may hold a different – but no less special – place in your heart to 'momò' (the dumpling).

Acknowledgements

When Yeshi and I first started the Taste Tibet food stall he didn't yet have a UK driving license, and getting to and from markets and festivals was obviously a challenge. Instead, every Thursday night inquisitive strangers would come to our house for takeaway and the side-line spectacle that was our daughter bum-shuffling down the hallway to greet them. We sent out a weekly newsletter and menu, and some of our earliest supporters encouraged us to develop the stories from Tibet that we shared in our emails. Thank you in particular to Larissa Wakefield, Julie Norris and Caroline Krantz for first planting the idea of working these into a book: you gave us the confidence to see ourselves as writers as well as momo-makers.

In 2019 I won the Yan-Kit So Memorial Award for Food Writers on Asia. This was a life-changing event, and I am hugely grateful to the team of eminent judges including David Thompson, Fuchsia Dunlop, Carol Michaelson, Paul Bloomfield and Donald Sloan, who backed me. Massive thanks also to Freya Aitken-Turff and Betty Yao, who administered the award. We met our agent, Heather Holden-Brown, as a direct result of this incredible win. Thanks, Heather, for taking a punt on us and for making the introduction to Murdoch Books who have been so fantastic to work with. Our publisher, Corinne Roberts, instinctively understood what we wanted the book to become, and the design team of Kristy Allen and Vivien Valk had a vision that effortlessly chimed. Justin Wolfers and Alison Cowan made invaluable editorial inputs with great sensitivity. Thank you, Murdoch, for bringing our story to life. We have enjoyed every minute of working with you.

Photography has also had a vital part to play. Keiko Wong took the extraordinary photos of our family in Tibet that really make the book. Thank you, Keiko, and thanks to all the friends and family in Yeshi's village who took Keiko in and ferried her about during her stay. Ola Smit and Anna Wilkins happened to be doing the food shots during the same week, and it was joyous and very moving to be able to watch the book's beautiful photography come together in real time. Thank you Ola and Anna for your stunning pictures.

Deborah Duke was chief recipe tester. Her enthusiasm for Yeshi's nomad fare knew no bounds, and we are deeply grateful. Thanks to everyone else who also gave their time and energy to this important part of the process: Anne Cori, Lydia Hodgins, Fflur Jones, Anna Nicholl, Russell Hitchings, Stefan Ramsden, Chloe Maunsell, Isabel Paz, Poppy Toland, Bridget Rooth, Jenny Kleeman, Nicole Kleeman, Susanna Kleeman, Lara Scott Bosley and Jo Stockdale. These friends and family members have all been a huge support in many other ways over the years – thank you.

Thanks also to the Taste Tibet team: amazing Amanda Knight, who is really the face of Taste Tibet, and who took our picture for this book, Livio Dos Santos, chief momo-maker, and all the Tibetan people and others in Oxford who have helped out over the years.

Tim and Susanna – what would Taste Tibet be without your guidance, support and input? Alicia Constable – thank you for believing in us before anyone else did, and thank you so much for your friendship. Thanks also to Nyima Tsering for convincing Yeshi to stay in India, where we met, and for steering him in the kitchen. And thank you to my parents, David and Manou, who gave me the opportunity and freedom to travel the world from a very young age. This changed the way I look at everything and opened all the doors for me. It also changed the way I eat.

Finally, thank you to our children, Leo (Lobsang) and Uma (Choenyi), who have kept themselves busy at the back of the stall since the age of zero, and who somehow understood how massive this book is for us and gave us all the time we needed to bring it together, even while Covid had the schools closed. You are amazing. May this book inspire you to continue cooking Pala's food for your children. This is why we do what we do.

Index

W

Y

Z